HIPPOLYTUS
AND THE ROMAN CHURCH
IN THE THIRD CENTURY

SUPPLEMENTS TO

VIGILIAE CHRISTIANAE

Formerly Philosophia Patrum

TEXTS AND STUDIES OF EARLY CHRISTIAN LIFE AND LANGUAGE

EDITORS

J. DEN BOEFT — R. VAN DEN BROEK — A.F.J. KLIJN
G. QUISPEL — J.C.M. VAN WINDEN

VOLUME XXXI

HIPPOLYTUS
AND THE ROMAN CHURCH
IN THE THIRD CENTURY

COMMUNITIES IN TENSION BEFORE THE EMERGENCE
OF A MONARCH-BISHOP

BY

ALLEN BRENT

E.J. BRILL
LEIDEN · NEW YORK · KÖLN
1995

The paper in this book meets the guidelines for permanence and durability of the Committee on Production Guidelines for Book Longevity of the Council on Library Resources.

ISSN   0920-623X
ISBN   90 0410245 0

CONTENTS

ABBREVIATIONS

AAWG	Abhandlungen der Akamedie der Wissenschaften in Göttingen
ABAW	Abhandlungen der Bayerischen Akademie der Wissenschaften
ABenRev	American Benedictine Review
AHAW	Abhandlungen der Heidelberger Akademie der Wissenschaften
AKWG	Abhandlungen der Königlichen Gesellschaft der Wissenschaften zu Göttingen
ArLiW	Archiv für Liturgiewissenschaft
AmJArch	American Journal of Archaeology
AmJPhil	American Journal of Philology
AnBoll	Analecta Bollandiana
AnLov	Analecta Lovanensia biblica et orientalia
ANRW	Aufstieg und Niedergang der Römischen Welt: Geschichte und Kultur Roms im Spiegel der neueren Forschung, Ed. H. Temporini and W. Haase (Berlin and New York: De Gruyter)
Antiqu.	*Antiquitas:* Beiträge zur Historia-Augusta Forschung, Ed. J. Straub und A. Alfoldi (Bonn: R. Habelt Verlag 1963—)
ArcCl	Archeologia Classica
ArFil	Archivio di Filosophia
Ath.	Athenaeum
AThR	Anglican Theological Review
ATNT	Abhandlungen zur Theologie des Alten und Neuen Testaments
Aug	Augustinianum
BArC	Bulletino di archeologia cristiana
BeitrHistTh	Beiträge zur Historischen Theologie
BiLit	Bibel und Liturgie
BLitE	Bulletin de littérature ecclésiastique
BR	Biblical Research
BRev	Biblical Review
BSGT	Bibliotheca Scriptorum Graecorum et Romanorum Teubnerianae (Akademie der Wissenschaften der DDR Zentralinstitut für alte Geschichte und Archäologie), (Leipzig: Teubner 1984).
BThAM	Bulletin de Théologie Ancienne et Médiévale
Byz	Byzantion: Revue Internationale des Études Byzantines
ByzZ	Byzantinische Zeitschrift
BZHT	Beiträge zur Historischen Theologie
CCa	Civiltà Cattlica
ChH	Church History
CIG	Corpus Inscriptionum Graecarum, Ed. A Boeck and J. Franz (Berlin: Reimer 1828—)
CIL	Corpus Inscriptionum Latinarum (Berlin : Reimer 1866-)
Class Rev	Classical Review
ClPl	Classical Philology

CSCO	Corpus Scriptorum Christianorum Orientalium (Louvain: Secrétariat du Corpus SCO: 1975).
CSLE	Corpus Scriptorum Latinorum Ecclesiasticorum (Vienna: Gerold 1866-)
DACL	*Dictionnaire d' Archéologie Chrétienne et de Liturgie*, (Ed.) F. Cabrol and H. Leclercq (Paris: Libraire Letouzey et Ané 1924)
DomSt	Dominican Studies
DR	Downside Review
EglTheo	Église et Theologie
EphL	Ephemerides Liturgicae
EThL	Ephemerides Theologicae Lovanienses
FRLANT	Forschungen zur Religion und Literatur des Alten und Neuen Testaments
FZPhTh	Freiburger Zeitschrift für Philosophie und Theologie
GCS	Die Griechischen Christlichen Schriftsteller der ersten beiden Jahrhunderte (Hinrich: Leipzig 1897).
Greg	Gregorianum
Gym	Gymnasium
HA	Handbuch der Altertumswissenschaft
Herm	Hermes
Hermath	Hermathena
Hesp	Hesperia
HeyJn	Heythrop Journal
HThR	Harvard Theological Review
ILCV	Inscriptiones Latinae Christianae Veteres, Ed. E. Diehl, Vols 1-3 (Berlin: Weidmann 1924, 1927).
ICUR	Inscriptiones christianae urbis Roma septimo saeculo antiquiores, Ed. De Rossi G.B. and Silvagni A., Nova series (Rome 1921-)
IG	Inscriptiones Graecae, Ed. Kirschner J. (Berlin: Rheimarus 1913—; De Gruyter 1924—)
JbAC	Jahrbuch für Antike und Christentum
JBL	Journal of Biblical Literature
JEgArch	Journal of Egyptian Archeology
JEH	Journal of Ecclesiastical History
JES	Journal of Ecumenical Studies
JLiW	Jahrbuch für Liturgiewissenschaft
JRH	Journal of Religious History
JRomS	Journal of Roman Studies
JSNT.S	Journal for the Study of the New Testament: Supplementary Series
JThS	Journal of Theological Studies
LeDiv	Lectio Divina
MD	La Maison-Dieu
MGH	Monumenta Germaniae Historica
MSR	Mélanges de Science Religieuse
MuThZ	Münchener Theologische Zeitschrift
NA	Neutestamentliche Abhandlungen
NT	Novum Testamentum
NTS	New Testament Studies
OECT	Oxford Early Christian Texts, H. Chadwick (Ed.), (Oxford: Clarendon Press)

OrChr	Oriens Christianus
OrChrA	Orientalia Christiana Analecta
OrSyr	Oriens Syriens
OstkiSt	Ostkirchliche Studien
PL	P.G. Migne, Patrologia Latina (Paris 1857-)
Phil	Philologus, Zeitschrift für Klassische Altertum
PO	Patrologia Orientalis, Ed. R. Graffin and F. Nau, (Paris 1903-)
PG	P.G. Migne, Patrologia Graeca-Latina (Paris 1857-)
PWK	A. Paulys-Wissowa, *Real-encyclopädia der classischen Altertumswissenschaft* (Metzler: Stuttgart 1899)
QLP	Questions Liturgiques et Paroissiales
RAC	Reallexikon für Antike und Christentum
RBen	Revue Benedictine
Rbib	Revue Biblique
RDroitCan	Revue de Droit Canonique
RevHisRel	Revue de l'histoire des religions
RecSciRel	Recherches de Science Religieuse
RelStudRev	Religious Studies Review
RendPontAcc	Rendiconti della Pontificia Accademia Romana di Archeologia
RevBelg	Revue belge de philologie de d'histoire
RevEtByz	Revue des Études Byzantines
RevHE	Revue d'histoire ecclésiastique
RevHPhR	Revue d'histoire et de philosophie religieuse
RevScPhTh	Revue des sciences philosophiques et théologiques
RevSR	Revue des Sciences Religieuses
RGG	Religion in Geschichte und Gegenwart
RivAC	Rivista Archeologia Cristiana
RPARA	Rendiconti della P. Accademia Romana di Archeologia
RThAM	Recherches de théologie ancienne et médiévale
SBAW	Sitzungsberichte der Bayrische Akademie der Wissenschaften
SbMn	Sitzungberichte der Bayerischen Akademie der Wissenschaften, Philos-philol.-hist. Klasse (München)
SC	Sources Chrétiennes (Paris: Les Éditions du Cerf 1944-)
SciEspirit	Science et Espirit
ScuCat	La Scuola Cattolica
SecCent	The Second Century
Set	Studi e Testi
SGK	Schriften der Königsberger Gelehrten Gesellschaft
SHAW	Sitzungsberichte der Heidelberger Akademie der Wissenschaften
SPAW	Sitzungsberichte der preussischen Akademie der Wissenschaften: Philosophische historische Klasse
StEphAug.	Studia Ephemeridis «Augustinianum» (Institutum Patristicum «Augustinianum», Rome)
StPB	Studia Post-Biblica
StTh	Studia Theologica
StudPatr	Studia Patristica
StuPat	Studia Patavina
TheolStKrit	Theologische Studien und Kritiken
Theoph	Beiträge zur Religions- und Kirchengeschichte des Altertums
TheoRev	Theologische Revue

ThG	Theologie und Glaube
ThQ	Theologische Quartalschrift
ThR	Theologische Rundschau
ThS	Theological Studies
ThZ	Theologische Zeitschrift
TU	Texte und Untersuchungen der Altchristlichen Literatur
TWNT	Theologisches Wörterbuch zum Neuen Testament
VC	Verbum Caro
VCh	Vigiliae Christianae
WMANT	Wissenschaftliche Monographien zum Alten und Neuen Testament
WUNT	Wissenschaftliche Untersuchungen zum Neuen Testament (Mohr: Tübingen)
ZKG	Zeitschrift für Kirchengeschichte
ZKTh	Zeitschrift für Katholische Theologie
ZNW	Zeitschrift für Neutestamentliche Wissenschaft und Kunde der älteren Kirche
ZRGG	Zeitschrift für Religion und Geistgeschichte
ZThK	Zeitschrift für Theologie und Kirche
ZWTh	Zeitschrift für Wissenschaftliche Theologie

PREFACE

Firstly my heartfelt thanks to Dr Caroline Bammel, distinguished Origen scholar, who undertook to read the manuscript for Brill but who has been a constant source of encouragement and inspiration in my task, as has my former teacher at Cambridge, Dr Ernst Bammel.

Next I would thank Professor Christopher Stead in 1989 and to Dr Lionel Wickham in 1994 who gave me the opportunity to air many points of my thesis before the critical audience of the Faculty of Divinity's Patristics Seminar which they chaired.

A further debt must not go unacknowledged to Dr Amanda Claridge, former Deputy Director of the British School of Archaeology at Rome, but now of Oxford University, where I spent many January months working, and receiving her invaluable help. During such visits to Rome critical assistance was also generously afforded to me by Praeses P. Professore Vittorino Grossi, and Vice Praeses P. Dottore R. Dodaro, at the Institutum Augustinianum, Rome, which has, under their leadership and that of their predecessors, become such a power house of Patristic scholarship.

I would like to give special thanks to Dr James Carleton Paget, Fellow of Peterhouse, for reading my manuscript and making so many helpful, incisive and critical suggestions about both the form and substance of my text. It has proved invaluable to have the guidance of a young scholar of great promise, at the cutting edge of so many problems of the second century for the development of Jewish Christianity, and our discussions over the years that have proved so informative of my present argument. Finally I would thank Dr Philip Burton who read and corrected the manuscript so painstakingly, and whose impressive knowledge of the tradition of Latin *ms.* was of great assistance to my treatment of the *Apostolic Tradition*.

The University of North Queensland gave me the generous support of a sabbatical in Cambridge, in order to take up my Visiting Fellowship at Clare Hall, for which I am also thankful.

I hereby acknowledge the kind permission of the following to reproduce photographic plates:

(i)   Pontificio Istituto di Archeologia Cristiana, Rome (Plates 1, 3, 12, 13, 15-21, and 23-24).

(ii) Istituto Poligrafico e Zecca dello Stato P.V., Rome (Plates 2, 4, and 5).

(iii) The British Library, London (Plates 8, 9, 10 and 11).

    (iv)   Bibliotheca Nazionale di Vittorio Emmanuel III, Naples (Plates 6 and 7).

    (v)   Musée du Louvre, Paris (Plate 14).

I also acknowledge with thanks the permission of the Syndics of Cambridge University Library to use their reproductions of item (i) and Plates 13, 22, and 23. The Laser Symbol SuperGreek Font used in this work are available from Linguist's Software Inc., P.O. Box 580, Edmonds WA 98020-0580.

ALLEN BRENT   CLARE HALL
1st December 1994   CAMBRIDGE

PLATES

Plate 1.   Statue of Hippolytus (Vatican Library): Front view

Plate 2.   Statue of Hippolytus: Side view

Plate 3.   Left side of the Chair: Easter Tables

Plate 4.   Right Side of the Chair: Paschal Calendar

Plate 5.   Plinth: Inscription of List of Literary Works

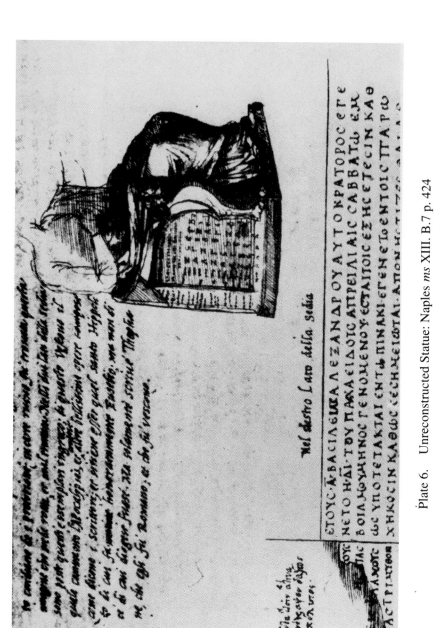

Plate 6.   Unreconstructed Statue: Naples *ms* XIII. B.7 p. 424

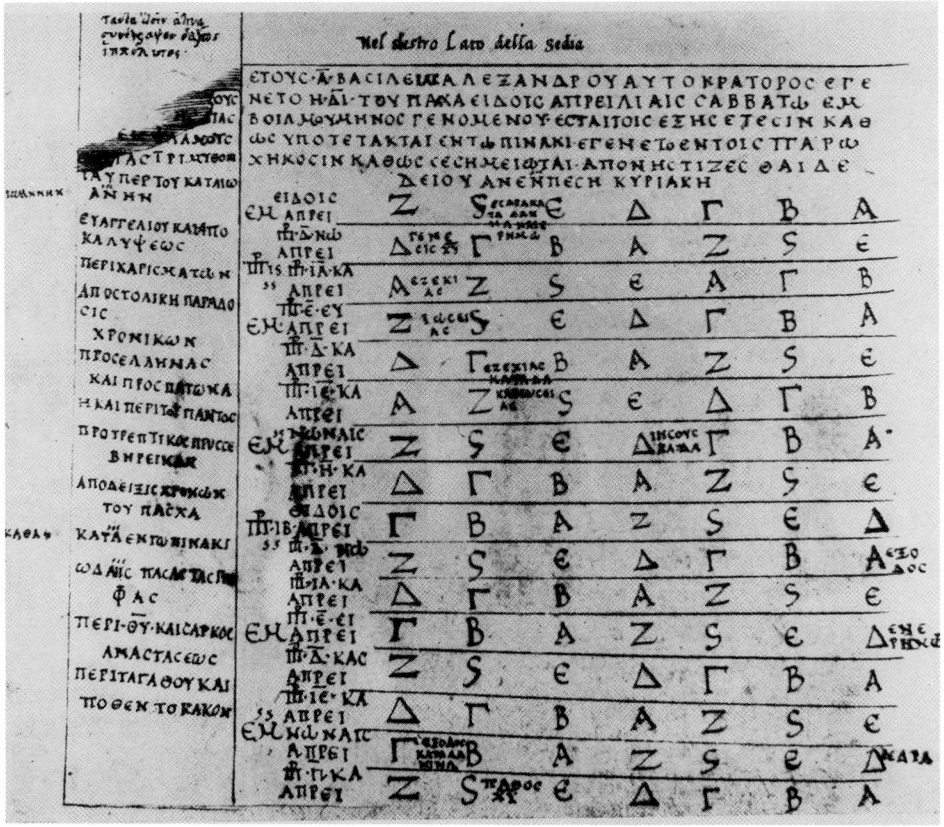

Plate 7. Ligorio's transcription of the Easter and Paschal Tables

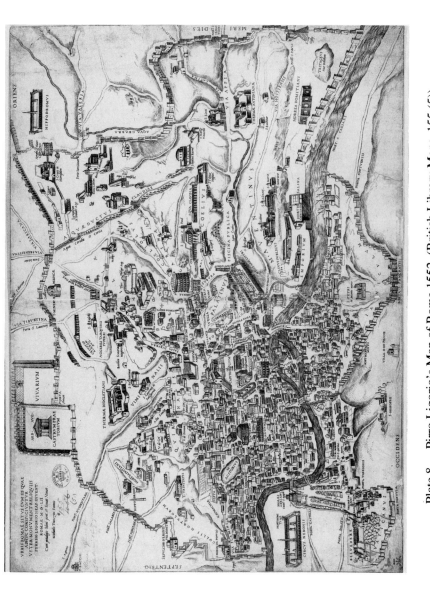

Plate 8.   Pirro Ligorio's Map of Rome 1552. (British Library Maps 155 (5))

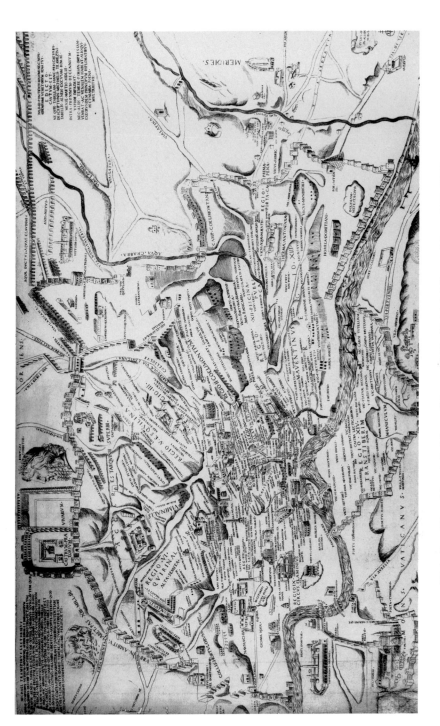

Plate 9. Pirro Ligorio's Map of Rome 1553. (British Library Maps 155 (35))

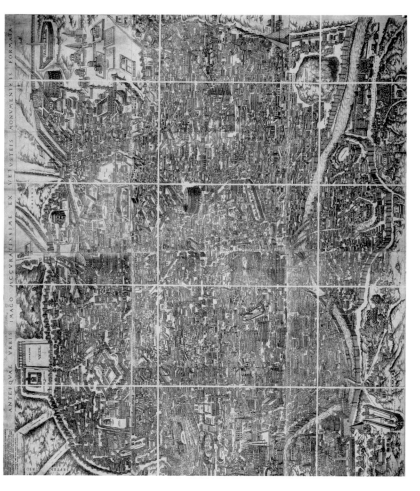

Plate 10. Ligorio: Map of Rome 1561. (British Library Maps C.25.d.9(i))

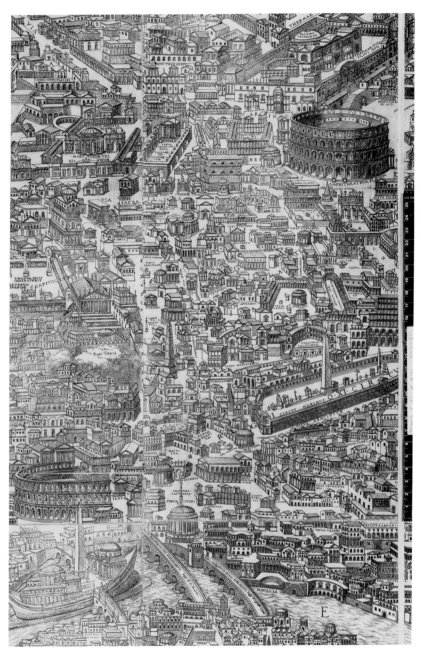

Plate 11. Detail: Ligorio Map of Rome 1561

Plate 12. Drawing in Fulvius Ursinus *ms*. 3439

Plate 13. Female Statue of Christ-Serapis: Museo di Roma

Plate 14. Statuette of Euripides with list of Plays: Louvre MA 343

Plate 15. Cemetery of Praetextatus: Man and girl with scrolls: *ICUR* V, 15058

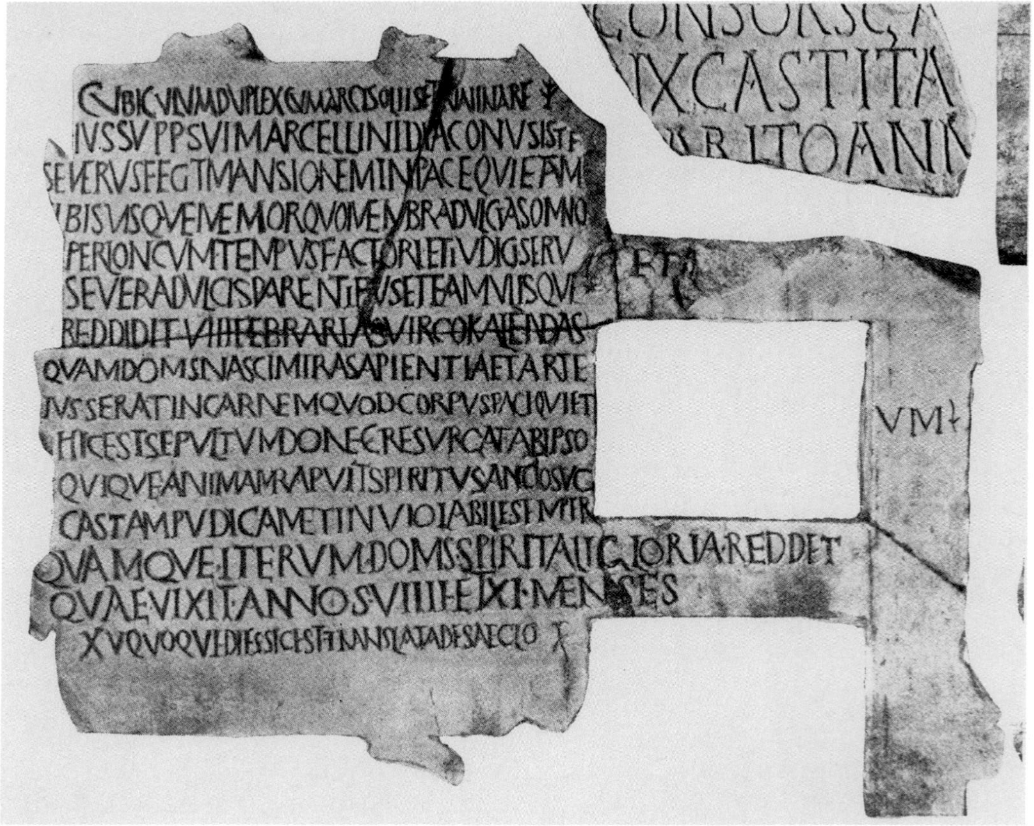

Plate 16. Cemetery of Callistus: Deacon Severus: *ICUR* IV 10183

Plate 17. Idem: OYΡBANOC: *ICUR* IV,10664

Plate 18. Idem: ΕΥΤΥΚΙΑΝΟC ΕΠΙC: *ICUR* IV,10616

Plate 19. Idem: ΦABIANOC . ΕΠΙC . M͞P: *ICUR* IV,10694

Plate 20. Idem: CORNELIUS MARTYR EP: *ICUR* IV,9367

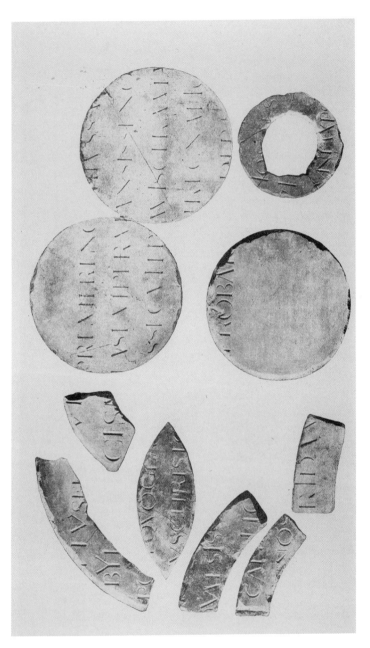

Plate 21. Damasian Fragments, *Hippolytus fertur.* Lateran Pavement

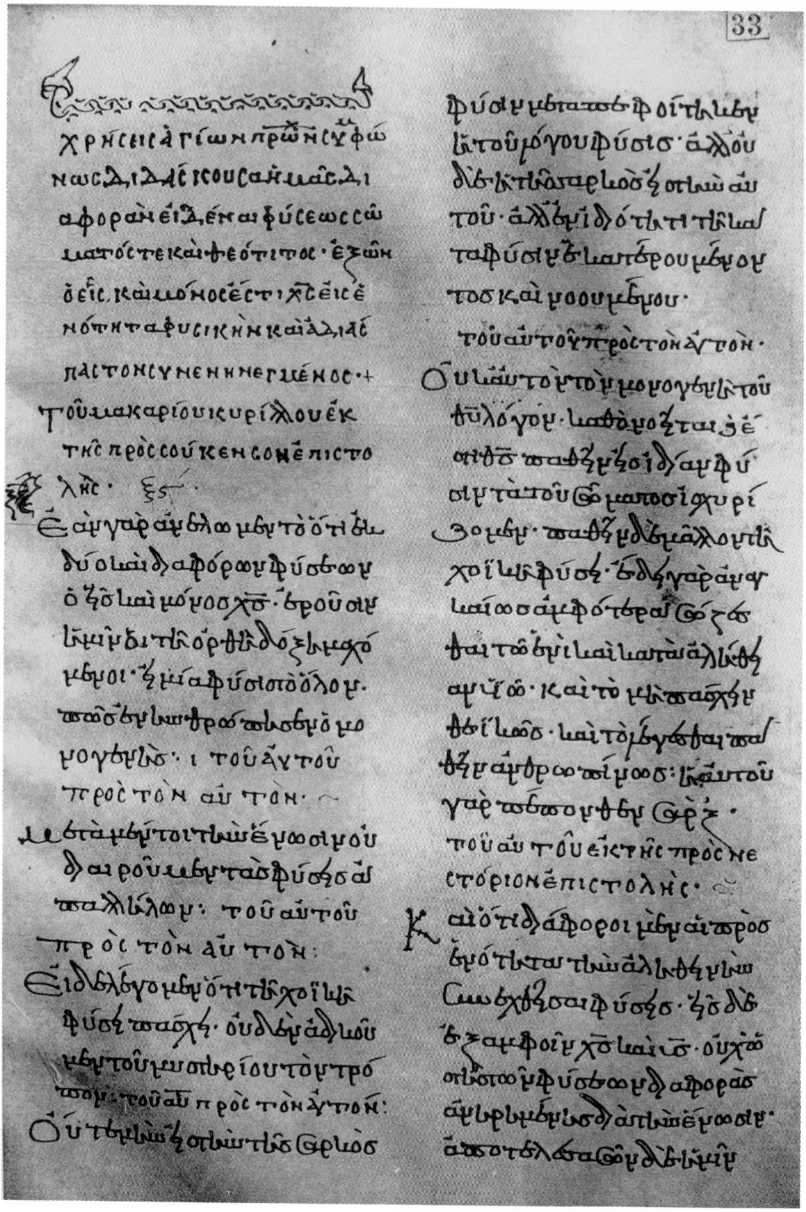

Plate 22. *Ms. Vaticanus Graecus* 1431: Scribal Change

Plate 23. Sarcophagus: S. Maria Antiqua: Christian Catechesis

Plate 24. Catechista: Cemetry of Praetextatus

INTRODUCTION

This work is concerned with the literary works attributed to Hippolytus, the last Roman Christian writer to write in Greek. It seeks to elucidate what these works reflect of the kind of community or communities that existed in Rome in the late second and early third century, the kind of Church Order that had at this time reached a stage of dynamic development, and the social and theological tensions that characterised the organizational and theological melting pot of the Roman community at that time.

Hippolytan studies are marked by continued controversy over a number of positions. Scholars still fiercely dispute over whether there was one or two authors in the literary *corpus* that has come down to us, what was the character of the original Statue reconstructed by Pirro Ligorio in the sixteenth century as the seated father of the Church, and standing at the entrance staircase of the Vatican Library today, the relationship between the latter and the cult-centre on the Via Tiburtina excavated by De Rossi in the last century, whether Hippolytus was the first anti-pope, etc. Related to such problems is the apparently interminable and hoary controversy over whether Tertullian's *Pontifex Maximus* with his indulgence edict was in fact Callistus of Rome, and whether the self-same Callistus, accused of Monarchianism, was indeed Tertullian's opponent Praxeas.

My book has been written in the conviction that these problems are now resolvable in terms of the new reconstruction of second century church history pioneered in the work of E.A. Judge and P. Lampe. It is now possible in the light of that reconstruction to see more clearly the social context in which the disputes to which *Elenchos* Books IX and X, as well as Hippolytus' *Contra Noetum,* bear witness. We can see now in these events a factionalised community of house Churches in the throes of a revolution, not yet complete, which was to lead to a single Monarch Bishop to be marked by the real dates of reigns that are apparent in the succession lists only after Hippolytus' martyrdom with bishop Pontian in 235 A.D.

Whether there is one author of the *corpus* or two, and whether the other is to be named Gaius, or Josephus, or is simply a second person named Hippolytus, has been variously debated, principally by, amongst others, M. Richard and P. Nautin from 1947 until 1955 when it had seemed that everything possible had been said, and both sides remained far and often acrimoniously apart. But the debate was not simply revived but other Hippolytan studies were moved significantly forward by the outstanding contributions made by all connected with the two symposia held at the Lateran University at Rome under the aegis of the Pontificium Institutum Augustinianum in 1977 and 1989 respectively. Here I believe that, despite the later highly articulate and incisive critique of J. Frickel, the thesis of at least two authors in the *corpus* was decisively established by M. Simonetti, with original corroboration on particular points by some other symposiasts.

One particular further and critical contribution to those symposia was of course the work of the distinguished archaeologist, M. Guarducci. Her work has proven fundamental to my discussion, since I accept her view of the originally allegorical character of the iconography of the seated figure. However, I have sought to refute her current argument that dissociates the original location of the Statue from the cult-centre on the Via Tiburtina. I have furthermore reinterpreted the character of the Statue quite different from that of a personal monument to an individual that she still presupposes. Instead I propose to interpret the Statue as a community artefact and icon, indicative of social currents and tensions that arise from the corporate life of one particular Christian community.

Indeed, as I show, the name of Hippolytus itself, in the *Apostolic Constitutions* and elsewhere, came increasingly to stand, just like Clement's name both in that and in the Clementine literature, as the cipher not of an individual but of the tradition of a community whose historical origins had been obscured and submerged by later developments in the direction of uniform and monarchical Church Order. It is possible in the light of this discovery to apply to the literary problem of at least two authors in the *corpus* the methodology known to New Testament scholars as redaction criticism. In the light of such a methodology, the currents and tensions within a community moving to a Monarch Bishop, and later Trinitarian orthodoxy can be traced and assessed. The relations in such a dynamic state of flux between conflicting communities within Callistus' Rome, and similar communities in Tertullian's North Africa can in conclusion be reassessed.

CHAPTER ONE

THE STATUE OF HIPPOLYTUS: DISCOVERY

Ligorio's discovery, its location, provenance and genuineness

The discovery of a mutilated Statue of a figure seated upon a chair and bereft of arms and head, found putatively in a ruined church between the via Tiburtina and the via Nomentana, was claimed by the famous renaissance antiquarian, Pirro Ligorio (1500-1583). (Plates 6 and 12) He subsequently reconstructed what he had found as the Statue of St. Hippolytus, the last Father of the late second-century Roman Church to write in Greek, and which stands at the entrance to the Vatican Library today (Plate 1). His associate, Martin Smetius, was, as we shall see, to date that discovery in 1551. The mutilated figure, without originally any identification of author by inscription, was found, Ligorio claimed, between the via Nomentana and the via Tiburtina, at the Ager Veranus near the Castro Pretorio. If this claim is true—and we shall discuss in this chapter on what grounds it has been questioned—the Statue would have been found in the vicinity of the excavations of the 19th and 20th century of Hippolytus' cult-centre.[1]

The Statue retains its original inscription, palaeographically dated to the first half of the third century. On the right hand plinth of the curved back of the chair is a list of literary works (Plate 5), the left hand lacking any inscription. The flat side of the chair on the seated figure's right is inscribed with a Paschal Calendar calculating the Passover from AD. 222 until AD. 333 in seven cycles of sixteen years. Passover day will always be the day of the full-moon in the month nearest to the spring equinox, which in the Jewish Calender is 14 Nisan (Plate 4). The left side is inscribed with a table calculating the corresponding dates for Easter which, on the Western but not the Eastern, Quartodeciman practice, will always be on the Sunday follow-

---

[1] G.B. De Rossi, Il cimitero di S. Ippolito presso la via Tiburtina e la sua principale cripta storica ora dissepolta, in *BArC* 7 (1882) ser.4 anno 1 p. 9-76; —, Notizie: Continuazione delle scoperte nella cripta storica e nelle adiacenti gallerie del cimitero di s. Ippolito, in *BArC*, (1882-1883), p. 176-177; F. Gori, *Della Porta e Basilica di S. Lorenzo*, (Rome: 1862); O. Maruchi, *Le Catacombe Romane secondo gli ultimi studi e le più recenti scoperte*, (Roma: Desclée Lefebure 1903), p. 185-191; F. Fornari, Giornale di Scavo, in Archives of *Pontificia Commissione di archeologia cristiana*, (Rome 1925-1960), Vol 4 p. 37; P. Styger, *Die Römischen Martyrgrüfte*, Vol. I, (Berlin: Verlag für Kunstwissenschaft 1935), p. 185-218; G. Bertonière, The Cult Centre of the Martyr Hippolytus on the Via Tiburtina, in *B.A.R. International Series* 260, (Oxford 1985); For the list of works on the plinth, see G. Morin, La liste épigraphique des travaux de Saint Hippolyte au Musée du Lateran, in *RBen* 17 (1900), p. 246-251.

ing Nisan 14 (Plate 3). We shall be examining the significance of this fact later in this chapter.

Both tables begin with the name of the Emperor, Alexander Severus and the year of his reign (for the Paschal ἔτους α΄ βασιλείας Ἀλεξάνδρου αὐτοκράτορος, for the Easter Calendar ἔτει Ἀλεξάνδρου καίσαρος τῷ α΄ ἀρχή). The information from the Hebraic lunar calendar is poorly and inaccurately adapted to the Roman solar one. The Easter Cycle would have become more and more unworkable through the course of over a century. Salmon pointed out that in the probable year of Hippolytus' death (236) full moon ought to have fallen on April 5th but in fact it fell on April 9th. Since the Cycle would have only been functional during the earlier years of the Table, this fact corroborates the palaeographical judgement of an early third-century date for the inscription.[2]

As we shall see in Chapters 3, the Statue stands at the centre of a web of an hypothesized set of literary relations that have been used to attempt to chart and determine the Hippolytan *corpus*, whether that *corpus* has one or two or more distinct authors. We shall argue that the centrality of the Statue for such hypothesized literary relations has been largely ignored. It has been treated too often as only a single item in a series of evidential propositions each of which can nevertheless stand in their own right. Once we question, with Guarducci (Chapter 2), the reliability of Ligorio's reconstruction as an actual figure of Hippolytus, then the argumentative bonds for the unity of the *corpus* whether in one or even two authors dissolve, and some interesting unexplored consequences then follow (Chapters 3-5).

But as important as the question of authorship is that relating to the characterization of the Hippolytan events themselves as they emerge in the dispute with Callistus described in *El.* IX. In Chapter 6 we shall ask: was indeed Hippolytus a presbyter or a schismatical bishop? In either case, what was the character of the community over which he presided, and how did it fit with the situation in the Church of Rome in the late second to early third century, and indeed how did it relate, if at all, to Tertullian's relationship with the church in North Africa at the same time (Chapter 7)? If it is, as we shall argue, as anachronistic to use words like 'schism' of Hippolytus' community as it was for Damasus to describe him as a presbyter of the Novatian schism, what precise testimony do the Hippolytan events bear to the kind of Church Order that preceded monarchical episcopacy at Rome?

The period 195-250 is critical for the emergence of monarchical episcopacy at Rome, and for the development of the λόγος theology and the doctrine of the Trinity. What role did Hippolytus and his community play in the development of both Church Order and Trinitarian theology? These are some of the questions for which we must seek answers in Chapter 7.

---

[2] G. Salmon, The Chronology of Hippolytus, in *Hermath* 1 (1873), p. 82-128.

For the moment, in our first two chapters, we shall consider the questions raised by the Statue itself, central as its witness is for all subsequent questions regarding the literary identity of the Hippolytan *corpus* and the kind of community which read and treasured that *corpus*. What particular value or significance was originally given by such a community to the artefact that was reconstructed by Ligorio as Hippolytus' Statue? The true character of this statue and its inscriptions are of central importance for the various sets of Hippolytan problems and the solutions that have been advocated up to now.

Since the true character of the Statue has been considerably debated, and since, I believe, its wider sociological and literary implications have not been fully understood, it will repay us to begin this first chapter with a consideration firstly of Ligorio's circle and the validity of his statement with regard to the provenance of the Statue (Part 1A). We shall consider secondly Guarducci's attack on his reliability (Part 1B). In our second chapter we shall then be in a position to consider critically Guarducci's identification of the original Statue with Themista of Lampsacus (2A) and her location of the Statue in the Patheon Library (2B).

PART A. LIGORIO'S REPUTATION AND THE STATUE

In our first section (1A 1) we survey Mandowsky's defence of Ligorio's general reliability on the grounds of a general and principled method of historical reconstruction. In the second section (1A 2) we shall survey in general terms the case for the discovery of the Statue in the location claimed by Ligorio. Thus the ground will be prepared for a consideration of Guarducci's attack on Ligorio's reliability (Part B) and our own more detailed defence of Ligorio worked out in response to Guarducci's claims.

1A 1. *Naples ms XIII. B.7 and Turin J.A. II 10; III.11*

Pirro Ligorio was responsible for the reconstruction of the Statue, and the manuscripts of his notes and drawings survive in *ms*. XIII. B.7 of the National Library of Naples, and in J.A. II 10 and III 11 of the Turin State Archives. Ligorio arrived at Rome c. 1534, originally from Naples, at the age of about twenty. He acquired his interest in the restoration of antiquity some ten years later from his acquaintance with Agustin (1517-1586). Agustin, later Archbishop of Tarragona, gathered around himself a circle of fellow-humanist antiquaries who transformed "the study of ancient monuments from virtually a medieval relic-cult into a modern literary and historical Hilfswissenschaft."[3]

However the charge was made that his manuscripts in Cardinal Farnese's library were "all cooked up (*a tutto pasto*)."[4] Nevertheless Agustin was to commend Ligorio's drawings of coins and buildings, and Orsini was to use drawings of monuments in his *Imagines Illustrium*. Ligorio relied on others for translating Greek inscriptions into Latin, and this was true of what was inscribed on the Statue that he reconstructed as Hippolytus. As we shall see, the transcription of the catalogue of works on the plinth of the chair of the Statue along with the Paschal and Easter Calendars on the sides was probably executed by the Dutch scholar, Smetius.

The argument within Agustin's circle further illustrate some diffidence felt regarding Ligorio's judgement. Over the debate on fragments of the consular *fasti* discovered in 1546, he hinted that Ligorio had added the words of the *fasti* to the base of a statue in Palestrina in order to identify it with a statue there mentioned by Suetonius. Agustin repeated this accusation to Panvinio and advised him to avoid Ligorio's version of an inscription, since *qualche volta scrive sua interpretatione* ("many times he introduces his own interpretation"). It was ironic that evidence came to light after two hundred years, in 1770, proving that the hemicyle was not on the site of the forum mentioned by Suetonius. Ligorio was shown to be right, but not for the evidence on which he believed that he was right, which he had thus manufactured.

Such considerations must make us cautious about a too *prima facie* acceptance of his reconstruction of the Statue, and the Latin inscription with Hippolytus' title that he engraved upon it. But we must also be wary about generalising over all of Ligorio's work doubts generated by such particular instances. We shall have to consider further the general reliability of Ligorio's reconstructions and inscriptions (1B 2.4) in view of the doubts that Guarducci casts upon him in the light of such an incident (1B 1.2).

For the moment, let us record that Ligorio's notes raise a number of problems. Although in one *ms.*, Naples XIII B 7, p. 424, he describes the mutilated statue as found *in certe ruine*, in the other, Turin J.A. II 10, and III.11, he mentions the discovery in the vicinity *a Roma oltre al Castro Pretorio un'altra Chiesa dall' Heretici rovinata*, and it has proven difficult to determine the identity of this "church ruined by (*dall'*) heretics."[5] (Plate

---

[3] E. Mandowsky and C. Mitchell, *Pirro Ligorio's Roman Antiquities. The Drawings in ms. XIII. B.7 in the National Library in Naples.* (London: Warburg Institute 1963), p. 30.

[4] Ibid. p. 32.

[5] The full text of the Turin *ms.* is: santo Hippolito... hebbe a Roma oltre al Castro pretorio un'altra Chiesa dall'Heretici rovinata dove fu trovata guasta la sua statua... la quale statua essendo malamente trattata io Pyrro Ligorio havvendo la cura di fabbricare et curare l'atrio palatino apostolico sotto il santissimo pontificato di papa Pio quarto, l'ho fatta restaurare. (J.A.

6) One possible candidate would be the church associated with the grave of Novatian (6A 2.1), but it would be difficult to argue that schismatics ruined a church when they were using it as a place of worship. Consequently Testini came to the conclusion that Ligorio was referring to some legend now lost of events surrounding Alaric's (AD. 410) or Geneseric's (AD. 455) sack of Rome, or the siege of Vitigius (AD. 536-7). There is an inscription of pope Vigilius (537-555) about works of restoration conducted by the presbyter Andrea and found at the cult-centre on the via Tiburtina, which evokes in its poetry images of destruction.[6] But this inscription before the 19th century excavations of the crypt was unavailable to Ligorio. It is better therefore to understand Ligorio's description against the background of his grand, renaissance design of restoring Classical Rome from the barbarian ravages (1B 2.4).

Although Ligorio was part of Agustin's circle which sought to develop a properly scientific analysis of archaeological remains, he himself was suspected by that circle of over-imaginative reconstructions. In the area of textual criticism he was influenced by Lambinus' reconstruction of Lucretius' *De Rerum Natura,* in which manuscript readings were collated and compared but then amended speculatively on the assumption that what appeared literary and philologically unpleasant were scribal mutilations of a text whose original perfections could be recovered intuitively.

Ligorio's archaeological restorations can be seen partly in relation to the somewhat analogical tendency of contemporary textual criticism. This lead to an inevitable syncretism in his reconstruction of monuments. He belonged to a school of renaissance mythography which drew upon literary texts from different ages without any considerations of chronology, from Herodotus and Plato through Virgil, Porphyry and Augustine to Suidas, discerning what appeared to him as the timeless forms of deities whose syncretistic features he built into his reconstructed Ulna Lucifer, Diana Lucifer, Juno-Dolichena and others. Mandowsky and Mitchell, whose general account we shall largely follow and apply specifically to the problem of the Statue, have convincingly argued, as we shall see in 1B 2.4 below, that Ligorio's reconstructions always follow a principled plan, however fanciful such a plan may appear to us. It is the very absence of such a plan into which a

---

III, 11, f. 52v), quoted P. Testini, Vetera et nova su Ippolito, in *StEphAug* 30 (1989) p. 11 cf.
—, Di alcune testimonianze relative a Ippolito, in *StEphAug* 13 (1977), p. 47.
    [6] *ICUR* 7, 19937; Styger (1935) p. 189:
"Devastata iterum summota plebe precantum,
Priscum perdiderant antra sacrata decus,
Nec tua iam martyr poterant venerande sepulcra,
Huic mundo lucem mittere qua fueris...
Frustra barbaricis fremuerunt ausibus hostes,
Foedaruntque sacrum tela cruenta locum...
Praesule Vigilio sumpserunt antra decorem,
Praesbyteri Andreae cura peregit opus."

Christian statue would have fitted that will be part of our case for relying on Ligorio's account of the place of its discovery.

His reconstruction of the mutilated statue as 'Hippolytus' reflects his syncretistic method. The type of figure represented in the restoration recalls that of St. Peter in the marble statue in the Grottos, which itself was a re-used classical statue, or the bronze St. Peter in the Vatican basilica itself. Guarducci has argued that Ligorio's style was further influenced in this case by the intended location of the statue in the Belvedere Theatre of the Medici Pope, Pius IV. It was to stand parallel to the statue of Aelius Aristeides, the second century orator and author of the *Encomium* of Rome. She observes perceptively that the feminine form of the original figure was easily adapted to the idealised form of a medieval prelate as a counterpoise to the starkly masculine Aristeides. Certainly Ligorio's own commentary suggests such a symmetrical relationship between Aristeides who *scrisse le lode di Roma* and Hippolytus whose statue Ligorio restored because "he had written on the sides of his chair such beautiful things as the festivals of the Hebrews (*per essenti scritto nei lati della sua sedia alcune cose belle, come le feste delli Hebrei*)."[7]

But in this instance he was true to the tradition of Agustin and his circle, whose concern was to identify archaeological monuments by literary sources in order to licence the details of their reconstruction, however tenuously. As with the dispute over the location of the statue mentioned in Suetonius, so it was with the mutilated statue claimed to be from the Ager Veranus. The archaeological statue was to be identified by literary references that suggested the reconstruction. The original Latin inscription, now lost, on the marble base of the Statue in the Belvedere theatre was, like that of the consular *fasti*, made by Ligorio himself, and read: *Statua Hippolyti Portuensis episcopi/ qui vixit Alexandro Pio im./ ex urbis ruinis effossa/ a Pio IV Medice pont. maximo/ restituta.*[8]

Although Ligorio's patron bore the name of Hippolytus as Cardinal Ippolito d'Este, it was undoubtedly what was inscribed on the back and arms of the chair of the mutilated statue that lead him to reconstruct the seated figure as that of Hippolytus. Some titles on the list corresponded to those attributed by Eusebius to Hippolytus. We shall show grounds for considering that, though both the reconstructed Statue as Hippolytus and the title of his See are false, the forgery is not dishonest. As such Ligorio will not be able to be convicted of a deliberate lie regarding the location of the discovery of the Statue.

---

[7] Guarducci (1977) p. 24.
[8] *Cod. Barb. lat.* 2733, f. 462r cited in M. Guarducci, La Statua di «Sant'Ippolito», in *StEphAug* 13 (1977), p. 23 cf. ——, La Statua di «Sant'Ippolito» e la sua provenienza, in *StEphAug* 30 (1989), p. 61-74.

1A 2. *Ligorio's account of the Statue's discovery*

Originally both Guarducci and Testini agreed that Ligorio had been truthful in his account of the location of the discovery of the Statue. Ligorio did not know in the middle of the sixteenth century that De Rossi would discover the cult-centre on the via Tiburtina, excavated via Msg Gori's vineyard, and that he would also establish its original separation from the underground catacomb complex which was finally to connect it with the crypt of San Lorenzo.[9] It was only in 1829 that digging began for the excavations of this site where, between 1842-1851, De Rossi and Marchi carried out their work. They found remains of the via Tiburtina itself at a deep level in the cemetery of Cyriaca.[10] This later find therefore originally seemed to confirm the veracity of Ligorio's claim, as indeed did the *Depositio Martyrum* of the Liberian Catalogue, unknown to Ligorio and his contemporaries, which recorded the deposit of Hippolytus' remains *in Tiburtina* and not *in Callisto* as in the case of Pontian.[11]

Furthermore, its veracity seems to be confirmed by Ligorio's contemporary, the Netherlands epigraphist Martin de Smet. In his work published in 1565, he shows himself to have knowledge of the Statue where he publishes its inscriptions and adds *reperta non procul ab aede Divi Laurentii extra muros, ut vocant, anno MDLI.*[12] Ligorio's own description of the location is quite different. In the earlier (1553) Naples manuscript he writes:

> Tra la via Nomentana et quella di Tivoli [ie. via Tiburtina] fuor delle mura di Roma, e poco discosto dal Castro, over Allogiamento coridiano [sc. cottidiano] de i [sc. dei] pretoriani; in certe ruine fù trovata questa imagine che siede rotta et mal trattata. Nelli dui lati del[l]a sedia sono poste questi essemplari in greco; di questo Vescovo il quale commentò l'Apocalypsis, et compose altre bellissime opere come dicono i scrittori; et si tiene esser quel santo Hippolito di cui fà mentione honorammente Eusebio; mà non dice di cui diogese fusse.

---

[9] G.B. De Rossi (1882) ser.4 anno 1 p. 9-76.

[10] Ibid. p. 49-50.

[11] Th. Mommsen, Über den Chronographien vom Jahre 354, in *Abhandlungen der philologische-historische Classe der Königlichen Sächs. Gesellschaft der Wissenschaften* I (1850), p. 549 ff. See also 1B 2.3.1.4 and 1B 2.3.3.5.

[12] Smetius, *Inscriptionum antiquarum quae passim per Europam, liber. Accessit Auctarium a I. Lipsio.* (Ex officina Plantiniana, apud Franciscum Raphelengium: Lugduni Batavorum 1588), ff. 37 v and 38: "Tabulae inveniendi Paschatis, descriptae è sede statuae sedentis (ut videtur) Hippolyti Episcopi cuius meminit Divus Hieronymus in Catalogo Scriptorum ecclesiasticorum reperta non procul ab aede Divi Laurentii extra muros, ut vocant, anno eo MDLI," (referred to in Guarducci (1989) p. 64 mistakenly as "27 v and 38."). Testini (1989) p. 12 also cites *Vat. Lat.* 5324 f. 89 where an inscription for the Statue is recorded "non procul a S.to Laurentio extra muros." The author of the *ms.* is Aldo Manuzio around 1588.

Mà solamente scrive Thephane,[13] che egli fù Romano; et che fù vescovo.

Naples XIII B.7 p. 424[14]

Neither in the Naples, nor in the Turin *ms.* which we quoted previously, do we find Smetius' *non procul ab aede Divi Laurentii extra muros* but rather the *Castro Pretorio*, the *via Nomentana*, and the *via Tiburtina*.[15] We shall argue that Smetius' location could not have been derived from the association of Hippolytus the martyr and soldier converted by St. Laurence and one of the figures venerated at the latter's shrine.

It is important however to note that geographical area marked by the "Castro Pretorio," "via Nomentana," and "via Tiburtina" of Ligorio's description was associated in the consciousness of Ligorio's contempories with the shrine of Hippolytus the soldier-martyr. Yet the identification of the Hippolytus of the Statue is not with the soldier-martyr but with Hippolytus the bishop (*di questo Vescovo*) and writer who wrote a commentary on the *Apocalypse* (*il quale commentò l'Apocalypsis*) and whom Eusebius mentions honourably (*di cui fà mentione honorammente Eusebio*). That identification was the direct result of Smetius' decipherment and translation of the Greek inscriptions of which Ligorio himself was linguistically ignorant (Plate 7). In consequence we shall argue, in view of the fact that there are several shrines to Hippolytus throughout Rome, that the identification of the Statue as that of Hippolytus the writer with no mention of any connection with Hippolytus the soldier-martyr would have excluded a forged connection with San Lorenzo and its associated cult if it had not actually be found there.

Smetius saw the Statue with his colleague Stephan Winnants Pighe, who was in Rome from 1547 until 1555. Smetius himself had been there from 1545 and left in 1551, the year to which he and not Ligorio attributes the discovery of the Statue when he writes in 1565. The only discordant voice is that of Baronius in 1586, who claims in his *Martyrologium Romanum* that

---

[13] The reference appears to be to Theophanes Abbot (760-818) and confessor (from the viewpoint of Rome on the iconoclast controversy). His *Chronography*, as the title states, is, translated from Greek into Latin, A *Diocletiano ad Michaelem et Theophylactum eius Filium Imperatores* (ΧΡΟΝΟΓΡΑΦΙΑ ΑΠΟ ΔΙΟΚΛΗΤΙΑΝΟΥ ΕΩΣ ΜΙΧΑΗΛ ΚΑΙ ΘΕΟΦΥΛΑΚΤΟΥ ΤΟΥ ΥΙΟΥ ΑΥΤΟΥ ΒΑΣΙΛΕΩΣ), *P.G.* CVIII, 63-1186. However, Theophanes continued the work of his friend George Syncellus, and in the Latin translation available to Ligorio, clearly the two works combined appeared under Theophanes' name. The actual reference is Georgius Syncellus, *Ecloga Chronographia*, 674: Ἱππόλυτος ἱερὸς φιλόσοφος ἐπίσκοπος Πόρτου κατὰ τὴν Ῥώμην....ἄλλας παντοίας παλαιὰς καὶ νέας γραφάς. For fuller quotation see 3C 7 footnote 185.

[14] "Between the via Nomentana and that of Tivoli outside the walls of Rome and a little distant from the Camp, that is to say the daily place of lodging for the pretorians; this statue, which was broken and badly handled, was found in certain ruins. On the two sides of the chair these copied letters have been placed in Greek; of that bishop who made a commentary on the Apocalypse, and composed other very beautiful works, as the writers say; and it is thought that he is that Saint Hippolytus of whom Eusebius made honourable mention; but he does not say of which diocese he was. But only Theophanes writes that he was a Roman; and that he was a bishop."

[15] Cited in Mandowsky and Mitchell (1963) no. 101 p. 105.

the Statue was dug out of the ruins of Portus where it was taken directly to the Vatican Library. But in the second edition of that work he agrees with Ligorio and Smetius that the Statue was *ex agro Verano, e Memoriae Hippolyti antiquae ruderibus effossum.*[16] We shall argue later in this chapter that Baronius' correction does not give the support that Guarducci thinks to her more recent thesis of a forged location for the discovery, which she wrongly believes to be on Ligorio's word alone, and in the light of which Baronius is claimed to have made his correction.

Let us now examine the details of Guarducci's more recent thesis, in the course of examining and criticizing which we shall develop our more detailed defence of the position that we have just outlined.

PART B. GUARDUCCI'S ATTACK ON LIGORIO'S RELIABILITY

In her more recent work Guarducci claims that Ligorio has been deceitful in this passage. Her argument may be summarised as follows:

1B 1. *A summary of Guarducci's argument*

1. Central to her case is the evidence of *Vaticanus Latinus* 3965, folio 24, which is a catalogue of items delivered between 1548-1555 to the Vatican Library. On 16th April 1551 payment was authorized for "the transport of the stone inscribed with the Greek Calendar from the Loggia of the Pope to the Library (*far portare dalla Loggia del Papa alla libraria il sasso dove è inscritto il Calendario greco*)."[17]

2. The discovery, allegedly in the Ager Veranus, took place in 1551. Smetius, who deciphered the inscriptions on the Statue for Ligorio who did not read Greek, left Rome some time in 1551. There would not have been time for the Statue to be deciphered first in the Ager Veranus and then brought to Loggia where it was situated on 16th April. Thus the transcription of the inscriptions by Smetius and Pighius would have taken place in the Loggia of the Pope.[18]

3. Ligorio invented the discovery of the Statue in the Ager Veranus. The invention was suggested by the Mons Hippolytus that existed in the vicinity, and by certain passages in the Medieval Itineraries.[19] In consequence, Smetius, Pighius and Baronius are dependent solely on Ligorio's testimony

---

16 C. Baronius, *Martyrologium Romanum,* 2nd Ed., (Romae 1602), p. 468 cf. 1st Ed. (1586) p. 379 and C. Baronius, *Annales ecclesiastici* (Romae 1590), p. 323, referred to Guarducci (1989) p. 65.

17 Guarducci (1989) p. 65-66 reads "trasportare" for the true reading of *Vat. Lat.* 3965, which I confirm to be "portare." See also Simonetti (1989) p. 118-119.

18 Ibid. p. 66

19 Ibid. p. 65-66, cf. p. 68-69.

that the Statue was found somewhere in the Ager Veranus. They had no independent corroboration, and had never seen it there themselves first hand.[20]
4. Ligorio's evidence alone is not to be trusted. Since he forged very many
epigraphs, his description of where those epigraphs were found must also be
fraudulent. His mysterious phraseology, *in certe ruine* or *una altra chiesa
dall'eretici ruinata* show that his location of the Statue is an imaginative invention.

The catalogue entry showing the cost of moving "the stone inscribed with
the Greek Calendar (*il sasso dove è inscritto il Calendario greco*)" from the
Loggia to the Library is not inconsistent, as she is well aware, with an original discovery in the Ager Veranus (1). These separate objections do not
therefore stand alone but are mutually dependent on each other. Guarducci
needs therefore to stress both the inadequacy of the time-sequence, and the
dependence of Smetius on Ligorio's own account (2). But even this would
not be enough for the argument to be conclusive. She must show (3) that
Ligorio's word on which she claims that Smetius thus relied was in this instance not to be trusted. We are finally brought (4) to the need to examine
the credentials of Ligorio as a witness far more thoroughly than Guarducci
has attempted. We must now therefore turn to a detailed examination of
these further steps in Guarducci's argument, on which the validity of that argument clearly depends.

Let us now turn to a detailed examination of these objections, and an
analysis of their assumptions.

1B 2. *Guarducci's four fundamental assumptions*

We shall examine each of the assumptions that underlie Guarducci's objections to the veracity of Ligorio's account of his discovery in the four separate sub-sections which follow. Initially the most convincing part of her argument must be the citation from *Vat. Lat.* 3965. I do not however believe
that Guarducci's case is as conclusive as some have maintained.[21] We shall
begin therefore with a consideration of this document.

1B 2.1. Ms. Vat. Lat. *3965: The Statue and the Loggia*

The entry (folio 24) in the account-book that is *Vat. Lat.* 3965 gives us no
indication about how long the Statue had been in what was presumably the
Loggia of Raphaelo. The evidence of Ligorio himself, leaving aside for the

---

[20] Ibid. p. 64-65.
[21] E. dal Covolo, I Severi e il cristianesimo, in *Biblioteca di Scienze Religiose* 87 (Las:
Roma 1989), p. 17: "Resta diffusa invece la convinzione che l'effigie si trovasse nella zona di
Castro Pretorio... Ulteriori indagini della Guarducci... rivelano del tutto infondata questa
opinione, e assegnano piuttosto il luogo della statua alla zona del Pantheon," and Simonetti
(1989) p. 119 : "La recente nuova precisazione della Guarducci elimina ogni residua possibilità
di collegare la statua con questa località."

moment whether or not Smetius' evidence was truly independent, would, other things being equal, normally suggest that its placement there, from the Ager Veranus, had been short. Let us look briefly at what kind of location the Loggia was in the sixteenth century.

Today in the *Galleria delle Statue* we find some mutilated Statues which are now housed there.[22] But we must remember the situation of the Loggia in Ligorio's own time. There were in 1551 then two Loggias, one around the Court of St. Damasus, and one directly North of where Bernini was latter to construct the Scala Regia. Both constituted the access ways to the rooms of the papal palace before the building of the present side road behind and adjacent to the Square. Guarducci identifies the *Loggia del Papa* of *Vat. Lat.* 3965 fol. 24 with the *Loggia di Raphaelo*[23], and thus with the Loggia north of what is now the Scala Regia. This was decorated for Julius II by Raphael, who died in 1520, eleven years before the Statue made its appearance there. The process of painting the 48 Old Testament sciences and 4 from the Gospels themselves would have excluded the presence of a Statue. The scenes themselves were an introduction to the triumphalism of the decorations of the apartments into which the Loggia lead.[24]

The Statue, according to the Turin *ms.*(Cod.a.III. II J.9, p.52v) was *essendo malamente trattata*, and according to that of Naples it was *rotta e mal trattata*.[25] It would not be unreasonable to ask what role a Statue so described could possibly have played as a permanent fixture brought there some time in the past from a place unknown. It could not have stood there during execution of the decorative work of Raphael. And after that work it would not have fitted in with Raphael's original ambience. The Statue was if not clearly in view of Ligorio's contrary evidence at least arguably placed there in transit, at what was the entrance Loggia to the Vatican Library which adjoined the Loggia as did the Belvedere theatre for which Ligorio originally intended it.

It is plausible therefore that the Statue stood in the position identified by *Vat. Lat.* 3965 as a temporary resting-place, whilst the Belvedere theatre was in process of completion. Its form, mutilated until the restoration of 1564 for the Belvedere Theatre, would hardly make it suitable for the Loggia of

---

22 W. Amelung, *Die Sculpturen des Vaticanischen Museums*, (Berlin: Reimer 1908), Band II Tafeln, e.g. Taf. 45 (Amore), Taf. 46 (Triton without legs) or Taf. 67 in the Sala of Busts showing a torso without head, arms, or feet.

23 Guarducci (1989) p. 66.

24 J. Barrington Bayley, Letarouilly on Renaissance Rome, in *The Classical America Series in Art and Architecture*, (New York: Architectural Book Publishing Co. 1984), plate 1 p. 111, plate 6 p. 154, and p. 147-148

25 Mandowsky and Mitchell (1963) p. 128: "... la qual statua essendo malamente trattata, io pyrrho ligorio, havendo la cura di fabricare, et curare l' Atrio palatino Apostolico sotto 'l santissimo Ponteficato di Papa Pio quarto, l' ho fatta ristaurare, et finalmente, è posta nella libreria Apostolica, et tolta all' Hemyciclo dove era posta nella parte dell' Atrio sudetto verso Belvedere."

Raffael. Its list of works would have commended it in preference to the
Vatican Library. It would have been quickly grasped that a far better temporary resting-place was the Library in view of its list of works on the plinth. If
the Loggia was intended to be its permanent place before Ligorio's plans for
the Belvedere Theatre, then indeed no need would have been felt for a temporary resting-place in the more suitable Vatican Library.

Guarducci further claims that the inscriptions in Greek would already
have had to have been deciphered and translated for Ligorio, who was ignorant of that language, because of the time-sequence, in Ligorio's workshop
or in the Loggia itself, and not in the Ager Veranus.[26] A Ligorio who knew
no Greek but for whom Smetius had already deciphered the inscriptions
would have sent the Statue directly to his workshop with eventual transfer-
ence to the Library in mind. That the Statue resided even temporarily in the
Loggia would have meant that Ligorio was as yet unaware of its true character and identity.

But if Ligorio had not yet identified the Statue as that of Hippolytus, as
Guarducci claims, where were the raw materials for his alleged fiction about
its discovery in the Ager Veranus? He would not even have had as yet
Hippolytus' name to associate with the left side of the via Tiburtina, even
granted that there were other literary grounds available to him at this time
for associating Hippolytus—and Hippolytus the writer at that—with this particular location. He would have thought that he had uncovered a pagan
statue, with leonine feet etc.—and such indeed, though reworked by a
Christian community, the statue originally was (Chapter 2). We shall
demonstrate later that at all events the main focus of his activity at this time
was in Tivoli, in the reconstruction of the Villa Hadriana, where his pre-oc-
cupation was with pagan statues, and where a Christian Statue hardly fitted
into his activities and schemes at this time (1B 2.4.2). Are we to assume that
Ligorio pointed out a Statue to Smetius in the Loggia or in his workshop,
said nothing about its character or origin, and only when he heard how it had
been deciphered proceeded to devise a fiction about the location of its discovery? Prior to this event, he could not have invented the discovery in the
Ager Veranus since the Statue would have been completely incomprehensible to him. But why should we be so certain that Smetius and Pighius could
not have visited the Ager Veranus but could only have seen the Statue in the
Loggia or Ligorio's workshop?

Guarducci claims that there would not have been time for such activity
before Smetius left Rome in 1551. Thus he was dependent upon Ligorio's
report and had never therefore witnessed the Statue in the Ager Veranus but
only in the Loggia. But if Smetius had worked on the decipherment only at

---

[26] Guarducci (1989) p. 68: "Non è improbabile che proprio nella Loggia della Papa sia
avvenuta la decifrazione dello Smetius e del Pighius."

this time, the consequence of that fact, as we have indicated, would be quite the reverse of what Guarducci wishes to conclude, unless Ligorio had behaved very oddly about an incomprehensible artefact. But was the time span of such significance? We now turn to a consideration of this claim for the location of the decipherment.

1B 2.2. *The time-sequence for Smetius' decipherment*
The inference that the transcription of the inscriptions took place in the Loggia, and not in Ligorio' workshop where it would have no point before the decipherment which established what it was, does not of itself lead to the conclusion that the Statue had not come from the Ager Veranus. It would simply mean that Smetius' witness is no more independent of Ligorio's than was Baronius' final conviction on this matter. But was Smetius so dependent and was his work executed in the Loggia?

Guarducci argues that Smetius gives the date of discovery as 1551, and concludes that the time was too short therefore between 1st January and 16th April, the date of its deposit in the Vatican Library, for it to be transcribed in the Ager Veranus, transferred to the Loggia, and then to the Library. But this requires from us some subjective assumptions about quantities of time and motion for such work, and indeed the quickness with which Smetius was able to operate. As Guarducci states, Smetius left Rome in 1551. If his departure was planned, he may well have transcribed in haste, being anxious not to lose such an opportunity.

Furthermore, it should be noted that the date for the discovery of the Statue in 1551 comes not from Ligorio but from Smetius himself. The objection based therefore on this date and hence on availability of time for deciphering rests heavily therefore on the accuracy of Smetius' memory. He cites this date in the *Inscriptionum antiquarum* in 1588[27] as the occasion on which, according to Guarducci, he heard from Ligorio alone the place of its alleged discovery, but curiously gave his own description of the location in quite different language from Ligorio's. Indeed, this would not have been the first occasion that Smetius misdated a discovery of which he is a witness, whether independent or not, alongside Ligorio.

Both, for example, describe in different terms the large altar showing a subjected province between its two shoulders, with a corresponding inscription.[28] Ligorio in the Naples *ms.* dates the find in 1547, as do Metellus and Smetius in Naples *ms.* 117. But later, in his *Inscriptionum antiquarum* (1588) he gives the date as the 1st March, 1548.[29] Ligorio located this altar in the church of San Adriano near the place where it was excavated, but in

---

27 See footnote 12 above.
28 Mandowsky and Mitchell (1963) Cat. no. 36 p. 72. For the inscription see *CIL* VI, 197.
29 Smetius (1588) 50,3: "Ara marm. grandis, undique confracta, effossa in foro Rom. ante aedem sanctae Mattinae, Anno 1548."

ms. 117 Smetius locates it at the vineyard of Cardinal Carpensis (*haec basis nunc ad vineam Card. Carpensis transportata est*). Smetius described a single bird in the branches of the laurel whilst Ligorio's version depicts two.[30] The error here in dating, if not in description, it should be noted, is on the side of Smetius, who in the earlier *ms.* 117 agrees with Ligorio, but in his published work gives a date of a year later.

It is therefore equally possible that Smetius poorly recalled the date of the discovery of the statue fourteen years later, in 1564, and confused an earlier date of discovery with 1551 and his departure from Rome. Guarducci's objection regarding the time sequence would fall to the ground were the discovery of the Statue to have taken place a year or more before in the Castro Pretorio, before transportation first to the Loggia and then to the Vatican Library. Her case perhaps places too great a weight on Smetius' memory.

But Guarducci claims also that it was in the Loggia that Smetius heard from Ligorio his lie of the discovery in the Ager Veranus. We have already partly answered this with the objection that unless Smetius deciphered it first, Ligorio would not have known what to lie about. Yet when he deciphered it, he must have had grounds for thinking that its presence there was recent otherwise there would not have been any need for an explanation. Let us now turn to the substance of this objection.

1B 2.3. *Smetius' dependence on an alleged Ligorian fiction*
The entry in Smetius' own work does not *prima facie* appear to be dependent on Ligorio's description and designation of the place of the Statue's discovery. His description of the location of the discovery is quite different from Ligorio's namely *reperta non procul ab aede Laurentii... anno MDLI*. It should be noted that if Smetius is simply dependent upon Ligorio, he does not mention any of Ligorio's points of location such as the Castro Pretorio, the Ager Veranus, via Nomentana etc. Rather he mentions the proximity to San Lorenzo which would suggest an independent recollection. Furthermore, Ligorio identifies the Statue with reference to Eusebius' list, whilst Smetius appeals to Jerome (*Episcopi cuius meminit Divus Hieronymus in Catalogo Scriptorum ecclesiasticorum*), which is again indicative of a certain independence in examination.[31]

Guarducci's claim rests, moreover, on her supposition that when Smetius speaks of having seen and deciphered the inscriptions on the Statue, this cannot have been in the Ager Veranus but must have been in Ligorio's workshop situated in the Vatican. But this is simply another supposition. One factor that would mitigate against such an assumption is Smetius' own notes in the *Inscriptionum Antiquarum*. Smetius writes in fol. 38: *Egomet vidi et unà cum Pighio legi atque exscripsi*. Guarducci assumed that this

---

[30] Mandowsky and Mitchell (1963) p. 73.
[31] See footnote 12.

meant that he claims to have seen it with Pighius in Ligorio's workshop. Yet the straightforward meaning of such a note would surely be to indicate that he saw it with Pighius *non procul ab aede Laurentii extra muros.*

It should be noted that at other points in his work Smetius makes it clear when he is relying on Ligorio's or Pighius' testimony alone. For example under ff. 18,10 and 20,1 he writes: *Hoc à Pyrrho Logorio accepi, reliqua egomet vidi.* Under fol. 26,4 he writes: *Reperta fuerunt haec duo in agro Tusculano, et postmodum in calcem redacta; sed Pyrrhus Ligorius Neapolitanus prius exscripserat, è cuius archetypo ego posteà descripsi.* Though no comparable alteration had taken place to the Statue at Ligorio's hands before the decipherment, I would suggest that this last note makes it clear that nevertheless any intervention of a second party between Smetius and his direct viewing of the evidence would have been noted. Had matters been as Guarducci supposed, I would suggest that Smetius would have written something like: *statua reperta à Pyrrho Ligorio, cuius inscriptiones egomet vidi.*

The entry in Smetius' description *reperta non procul ab aede Laurentii... anno MDLI.* suggest a location near but distinct from the basilica of S. Lorenzo. As Ligorio does not mention S. Lorenzo, this too suggests that the location of his discovery, whether pretended or real, was seen by him to be quite separate from that church and its associated cult. It is necessary for Guarducci therefore to find contemporary references to a cult separate from San Lorenzo and free-standing in the Ager Veranus, Castro Pretorio, via Tiburtina, and via Nomentana where Ligorio located his find. Only thus can she show that what she claims was Ligorio's forgery and deception of Smetius was suggested by the literary remains that they had read rather than first-hand experience.

One strong argument in favour of Ligorio's reliability about the location of his discovery was that the location corresponded with the cult-centre, discovered in the 19th century, in Msg. Gori's vineyard, in the very locality suggested by his description of whose existence on this spot Ligorio would earlier have been in ignorance. Guarducci, as we shall see, rests her hypothesis on the availability of certain written sources in Ligorio's time that were able to suggest to him the fictitious site on the Ager Veranus.

Only some written testimony available today was current in the sixteenth century. Moreover, that he did in fact use what could have been available to him is, as we shall now argue, pure hypothesis, since the sources in question are cited neither by him nor his contemporaries. Let us list this written testimony and establish what might have been, and what could not have been available to him, in order to assess further the strength of Guarducci's case[32]:

1B 2.3.1. *Literary sources: the crypt of St. Hippolytus*
The sources may set out as follows:

1B 2.3.1.1. *Act of Rent for 30th January 1110 A.D.*
Posita extra porta sancti Laurenti in montem sancti Ypoliti: fines eius duobus partibus possident monasteria beati Laurentii, a tertio Iohannes Bonelle, a quarto est cripta sancti Ypoliti.[33]

1B 2.3.1.2. Liber Pontificalis Vita Hadriani *(A.D. 772-795)*
Simul et cymiterium beati Yppoliti martyris iuxta sanctum Laurentium, quae a priscis marcuerant temporibus, noviter restauravit. Pari modo et ecclesiam beati Christi martyris Stephani, sitam iuxta praedictum cymiterium sancti Yppoliti, similiter restauravit.[34]

1B 2.3.1.3. Passio Polychronis *(5th-6th Cent.)*
Eadem hora dimiserant corpora in campo, iuxta nimpham, ad latus agri Verani. Idibus augusti.[35]

1B 2.3.1.4. *Liberian* Depositio
Idus Aug.   Ypoliti in Tiburtina et Pontiani in Calisti.[36]

---

[32] R. Valentini and G. Zucchetti, *Codice topografico della città di Roma*, Vol. 2, (Rome: Istituto Storico Italiano 1942), and Vol. 3 (1946). Various references also in G.-B. De Rossi, *La Roma Sotteranea Cristiana*, (Rome: Croma 1864-1867), Vol. I p. 187-189 and J.B. Lightfoot, *The Apostolic Fathers*. (London: MacMillan 1890) Part I S. Clement of Rome vol. II, p. 352-354. O. Maruchi, *Le Catacombe Romane Secondo gli ultimi studi e le più recenti scoperte*, (Roma: Desclée Lefebure 1903), p. 298-320 gives 1 B 2.3.1.5-7 and adds 1 B 2.3.1.8-9 whilst giving the *Eisiedeln Itinerary (Topographia)* (1 B 2.3.1.9) its more usual name, and 1 B 2.3.1.11 on p. 320. See also Bertonière (1985) p. 75.

[33] Quoted by Bertonière (1985) p. 75 from *Archivio della Società Romana di Storia Patria* (Rome 1878 ff.) 24 (1901) n. XXXV (p. 163-164). The expression "foris portam sancti Laurentii in monte sancti Ypoliti" is also used in Acts of Sale for (i) 1st February 1063 *ASRSP* 23 (1900), n. XX (p. 219), (ii) 19th November 1063 *Ibid.* XXI (p. 221), (iii) 1st September 1070- 30th August 1071 Ibid. XXIII (p. 224). There are also other Acts of Rent for (i) 6th August 1184 in *ASRSP* 26 (1903) n. CXXII (p. 69), (ii) 21st January 1198 Ibid. CLVII (p. 116-117). The Bull of Innocent IV of 5th May 1244 (to the Abbott of the Monastery of S. Lorenzo fuori le mura, mentioned by Bertonière (p. 474), and given in *ASRSP* (1903) n. I (p. 398) came originally from De Rossi's misreading of "eiusdem montis" as the "mons Yppoliti" whereas it refers to the Esquiline near S. Maria Maggiore, see Testini (1977) p. 48 n. 13.
English translation:
Located outside the gate of St. Laurence towards the mountain of St. Hippolytus: it is bordered on two sides by the monastery of St. Laurence, on the third [by the property of] Iohannes Bonelle, on the fourth by the crypt of St. Hippolytus.

[34] Liber Pontificalis Duchesne I, p. 151; Lightfoot (1890) 1, II p. 341.
English translation:
Also the cemetery of St. Hippolytus the martyr next to St. Laurence, both of which had experienced decay from ancient times, [Hadrian] restored as new. Equally also the church of the blessed martyr of Christ Stephen, likewise he restored.

[35] Bertonière (1985) p. 45.
English translation:
At the same hour they left the bodies in the plain next to the brook, beside the Campus Veranus. 13th August.

[36] Lightfoot (1890) 1,II p. 328.
English translation:
13th August. [remains of] Hippolytus in Tiburtina and of Pontian in Calistus.

1B 2.3.1.5. Passio Sancti Sixti, Laurentii, Hippolyti

Dum autem eum traherent, reddidit spiritum. Tunc corpus eius rapuerunt Christiani et posuerunt in crypta quae est iuxta agrum praetorianum die id. aug.[37]

1B 2.3.1.6. Notitia ecclesiarum urbis Romae (Itinerarium Codicis Salisburgensis) (A.D. 625-638)

Postea illam viam demittis et pervenies ad sanctum Ypolitum martirem, qui requiescit sub terra in cubiculo, et Concordia mulier eius martir ante fores, altero cubiculo sancta Triphonia regina et martir... et Cyrilla... et Genisius... Postea pervenies ad ecclesiam Sancti Laurentii; ibi sunt magnae basilicae duae in quarum speciosiore et pausat; et est parvum cubiculum extra ecclesiam in occidente. Ibi pausat sanctus Abundius et Herenius martyr via Tiburtina...[38]

1B 2.3.1.7. De locis sanctis. Martyrum quae sunt foris civitatis Romae (625-650)

Iuxta viam Tiburtinam... ecclesia est sancti Agapiti... Et prope eandem viam ecclesia est sancti Laurenti maior, in qua corpus eius primum fuerat humatum, et ibi basilica nova mirae pulchritudinis, ubi ipse modo requiescit; ibi quoque sub eodem altare Abundus est depositus, et foris in portico lapis est, qui aliquando in collo eiusdem Abundi pendebat, in puteum missi; ibi Hereneus, Julianus, Primitivus, Tacteus, Nemeseus, Eugenius, Justinus, Crescentianus, Romanus sunt sepulti, et sancta. Cyriaca, sancta. Simferosa, et Justina cum multis martyribus sunt sepulti. Inde in boream, sursum in monte, basilica sancti Hyppoliti est, ubi ipse cum familia sua tota xviiii martyres iacet; carcer ibi est in quo fuit Laurentius; ibi est Triphonia uxor Decii Caesaris et Cyrilla filia eius; inter utrasque Concordia et sanctus. Geneseus, et multi martyres ibi sunt.[39]

---

[37] P. Lagarde, *Hippolyti Romani, quae feruntur omnia graece et recognitione*. (London: Williams & Norgate 1858) p. xiii; Lightfoot (1890) 1, II p. 364; H. Delahaye, *Recherches sur le légenier romain*, in *AnBoll* 51 1933 p. 95, cf the description παρὰ τὸν πραιτωριανὸν ἀγρὸν in the *Passio Sancti Laurenti* of *Vat. Graec.* 1671 fol. 130, see G. Bovini, *Sant' Ippolito dottore e martire del III secolo*, in *Pontificio Studio di Archeologia Cristiana* 18 (Rome 1943), p. 45.
English translation:
While [the horses] were dragging him, he gave up the ghost. Then the Christians seized his body and placed it in [the] crypt, which is next to the pretorian field [Castrum pretorianum] on the 13th August.
[38] Valentini-Zucchetti (1942) II, 79-80; Lightfoot (1890) 1,II p. 353; Maruchi (1903) p. 298; Bertonière (1985) p.45; Delahaye (1933) p. 95.
English translation:
Afterwards you leave that road and come to St. Hippolytus the martyr, who reposes under the earth in a cubicle, and the martyr Concordia his wife at the entrance, in the other cubicle St. Triphonia queen and martyr... and Cyrilla... and Genisius... Afterwards you come to the church of St. Laurence; there are there two great churches in the more handsome of which he rests and there is a small cubicle outside that church where they lie dead. There rests Abundius and Herenius the martyr, on the via Tibertina...
[39] Valentini-Zucchetti (1942) II, 114-115, where the title is given as *De locis sanctis martyrum quae sunt foris civitatis Romae* (p. 101). Title *De locis sanctis* etc taken from Valentini-Zucchetti (1942) II p. 17. Lightfoot (1890) 1,II p. 353-354 entitles this *Epitome de locis ss. Martyrum* etc.
English translation:
Next to the via Tiburtina... is the church of St. Agapitus... And near the same road is the church of St. Laurence the great, in which his body had been first buried, and there a new church of marvellous beauty, where he himself reposes. There even under the same altar Abundus has been laid and outside in a porch there is the stone which once hung around the neck of the same Abundus when thrown in the well; there Hereneus, Julian, Primitivus, Tacteus, Nemeseus,

1B 2.3.1.8. Notitia Portarum viarum Ecclesiarum *(A. D. 648-682) (Itinerary of William of Malmesbury (1120-1140))*
Sexta porta et via Tiburtina, quae modo dicitur porta sancti Laurentii. Iuxta hanc viam iacet sanctus Laurentius in sua ecclesia et Abundius martyr. Et ibi prope in altera ecclesia pausant hi martyres: Ciriaca, Romanus, Iustinus, Crescentianus. Et ibi non longe basilica Sancti Ipoliti, ubi ipse cum familia sua pausat, id est decem et octo...[40]

1B 2.3.1.9. Topographia Einsiedlensis *(after A.D. 750)*
In via Tiburtina foris murum. In sinistra Sancti Ypoliti. In dextera Sancti Laurentii.[41]

1B 2.3.1.10. De mirabilibus Urbis Romae
Templum etiam Palladis opus quondam insigne fuit... Ibi magna congeries est fractarum effigierum. Ibi etiam armata ymago Palladis, adhuc super altissimam testudinem exstans, amisso capite, truncum mirandum intuentibus exhibet... Ad hoc ydolum vel simulacrum Ypolitus cum familia sua adductus, quod illud neglexit, equis distractus martirium subit.[42]

1B 2.3.1.11. *Redaction of* De Mirabilibus Urbis Romae, *c. 6*
... cimiterium Ursi Pilati ad Sanctam Bivianam [Bibianam]; cimiterium in agrum Veranum ad sanctum Laurentium; cimiterium Priscillae ad pontem Salarium...[43]

1B 2.3.1.12. Graphia Aurea Urbis
Cimiterium... inter Duas Lauros ad sanctam Helenam; ad Ursum Pileatum ad sanctam Bibianum; in agrum [Veranum] ad sanctum Laurentium...[44]

Eugenius, Justinus, Crescentanus, Romanus are buried, and St. Cyriaca, St. Sympherusa, and Justina are buried with many martyrs.
[40] Valentini-Zucchetti (1942) II, 145; Lightfoot (1890) 1,II p.354; Maruchi (1903) p. 298-299.
English translation:
The sixth gate and the via Tiburtina which sometimes is called [the gate of] St. Laurence, by this road lies St. Laurence in his own church and the martyr Habundius. And there in the other church rest these martyrs, Ciriaca, Romanus, Justinus, Crescentianus, and not far further the church of St. Hippolytus, where he and his family rests, that is 18 persons...
[41] Valentini-Zucchetti (1942) II,189; Lightfoot (1890) 1,II p. 354; Maruchi (1903) p. 298.
English translation:
On the via Tiburtina outside the wall. On the left [the church of] St. Hippolytus. On the right that of St. Laurence.
[42] Valentini- Zucchetti (1946) III, p.155-157, 16-18.
English translation:
The temple of Pallas was once a famous work... There is a great mass of broken images. There the image of Pallas armed, still standing atop a most lofty arch, her head removed, she shows her marvellous trunc to those who gaze on her... To this idol or statue Hippolytus was lead with his family, upon whom it looked with suspicion, [Hippolytus] who was torn apart between the horses and submitted to martyrdom.
[43] Valentini-Zucchetti (1946) III p.27: 7.
English translation:
... Cemetery of Ursus Pilatus at St. Viviane; cemetery in the Ager Veranus at St. Laurence; cemetery of Priscilla at the Salarian bridge.
[44] Ibid. 85: 2-4-86:5.
English translation:
Cemetery... between the Two Laurels at St. Helena; at Ursus Pileatus at St. Vivienne; in the [Ager] Veranus at St Laurence.

1B 2.3.1.13. *Magistri Gregorii*, De Mirabilibus Urbis Romae
Cimiterium in agro Verano prope Sanctum Laurentium foris muros.[45]

Let us now examine the precise significance of these sources for Guarducci's claim that Ligorio's place of discovery was an invention foisted upon Smetius and his contemporaries.

1B 2.3.2. *Commentary on the crypt of St. Hippolytus*
Guarducci's thesis that Ligorio's location for the discovery of the Statue was his own invention rests on the claim that he would have been able to trade on the association with a cult-centre of St. Hippolytus, separate from San Lorenzo, in the sixteenth century. The justification of the claim requires two stages in the establishment of supporting evidence. The first stage is the establishment of actual contemporary, 16th century documentary testimony that there was such a separate shrine, and the second is to show that Ligorio and his associates were actually aware of and had read such testimony.

Guarducci would accept that the literary evidence available today was not available to Ligorio and his contemporaries. Yet at least some of such evidence, connecting the writer to the cult-centre, needed to have been available to him if her thesis is to stand. But the *Liber Pontificalis* (1B 1.3.1.2) was available and read, and there we read of the *cymiterium beati Yppoliti martyris iuxta sanctum Laurentium*. It would not however have been immediately obvious to Ligorio and his contemporaries that "next to San. Lorenzo (*iuxta sanctum Laurentium*)" could indicate the separate basilica (*basilica sancti Hyppoliti*) mentioned in the *De locis sanctis* (1B 1.3.1.7) as located *in boream, sursum in monte*, in other words, in the "church of St. Hippolytus not farther on (*ibi non longe basilica sancti Ipoliti*)" from San Lorenzo, of the *Notitia Portarum* (1B1.3.1.8). Such words would, furthermore, not of themselves suggest that a cemetery (*cimiterium*) "next to (*iuxta*)" was equivalent to a separate basilica on the left hand side (*in sinistra sancti Ypoliti*) of the via Tiburtina (*in via Tiburtina*) opposite San Lorenzo on the right (*in dextera sancti Laurentii*), of which the *Topographia* (1B 1.3.1.9) speaks, as does also the *Notitia Ecclesiarum* (1B 1.3.1.6) (*pervenies ad sanctum Ypolitum martirem,... Postea pervenies ad ecclesiam Sancti Laurentii*).

Since Guarducci denies the availability of these texts to Ligorio, she is left with the testimony of the acts of rent (1B 1.3.1.1). The *Liber Pontificalis* (1B 1.3.1.2) describes neither a separate cult-centre nor mentions a *mons Hippoliti*. Nor can she claim that Ligorio himself had read these acts, but only that they noted a *mons Hippoliti* in the vicinity of Hippolytus' shrine as a witness to an ongoing recognition of the association of Hippolytus' name

---

[45] Valentini-Zuccetti (1946) 188: 4-5.
English translation:
Cemetery in the Ager Veranus near St. Laurence Without -the Walls.

with the fourth part of the region at the foot of a mountain (*porta sancti Laurenti in montem sancti Ypoliti*) which had also his crypt (*a quarto est cripta sancti Ypoliti*) separate from San Lorenzo (*fines eius duobus partibus possident monasterio beati Laurentii*). Guarducci therefore can only conjecture that Ligorio and his contemporaries would therefore have recognised a mountain bearing Hippolytus' name some four hundred years later (1110-1551), and from this mountain derived the fictitious location of the discovery of the Statue.

Guarducci is nevertheless aware of Testini's objection that the name of the *mons Ippolyti* had slipped out of medieval maps by Ligorio' time. Those maps show that the location of Hippolytus' remains were believed to be at his basilica in Portus, where Baronius originally located the discovery of the Statue, and the name of which See, as we observed, Ligorio inserted in the base of the Statue restored by him for the Belvedere Theatre.[46] If such were the case, then the claim must be highly tendentious that Ligorio and his contemporaries were acquainted with a *mons Ippoliti* in the light of which his fiction was made credible. Guarducci concedes Testini's point that the documents in question date from the 10th to the 13th century, but nevertheless expresses the opinion that it is "exceedingly probable (*oltremodo probabile*)" that this place name still existed in the time of Ligorio.[47]

In this connection, however, Guarducci's assumption that some of 1B 1.3.1.2-1.12 were available to Ligorio requires closer examination. It is not simply the earliest publication dates of the manuscripts to which we must look, but rather the availability of the manuscripts themselves to Ligorio and his contemporaries. We will take first the sources on our list to which there were no manuscripts available to Ligorio prior to published editions, and then secondly those that might have been.

The *depositio martyrum,* as opposed to the information contained in the *catalogus episcoporum* of the Liberian List (1B 1.3.1.4), otherwise known as the *Chronograph for 354* and the work of Damasus' epigrapher, Furius Dionysius Philocalus, was not reproduced in the *Liber Pontificalis* (Duchesne I p. 511). The first published edition was that of Boucher in the seventeenth century.[48] Surviving manuscripts, found in the Vienna Library (no. 3416 (cc. 46r, 44rr)), Brussells (nn. 7524-7555 (cc. 186, 185), and Amiens (n. 467) were hardly likely to have been available to Ligorio.

Similarly the *Notitia Ecclesiarum* (1B 2.3.1.6), found in an 8th century *ms.* (Salzburg n. 140), now in the National Library of Vienna (n. 795), represents an autograph written under Honorius I (625-638) or Theodore I (642-649). But this

---

[46] Of the Ligorian location he says: "... il luogo non trovava rispondenza con le indicazioni delle fonti allora note, neppure con la toponomastica; si era infatti ormai perduta la denominazione di mons Ippolyti data nelle carte medievali alla collina posta a sinistra della via Tiburtina." (Testini (1989) p. 13 and photograph, cf. Testini (1977) p. 48 and note 13.

[47] Guarducci (1989) p. 69 note 15: "I documenti appartengono ai secoli X- XIII, ma è oltremodo probabile che ai tempi di Pirro Ligorio il toponimo sussistesse ancora."

[48] G. Boucher, *De doctrina temporum. Commentarius in Victorium Aquitanum,* (Antwerp 1634 and 1664), p. 267-269. Later published texts were edited by Ianninck (1717), Eckhart (1723), Mommsen (1850), and Duchesne (1884), see Valentini-Zucchetti (1942) II p.10.

manuscript was only rediscovered by Frobenius (Forster), abbot of the monastery of St. Emmeramus in the 18th century.[49] The *De locis sanctis* (1B 2.3.1.7), is found first in a 9th or 10th century *ms.* (Vienna, National Library n. 1008 (formerly Salzburg n. 178) of an autograph contemporaneous with 1B 1 2.3.1.6, which seems to predate translations of remains of martyrs from the cemeteries to the cities. It is found in the 15th century *ms.* of Würzburg University (theol. fol. n. 49). Moreover it is found in the same Vienna *ms.* as 1B 2.3.1.6. These *mss.* were also then unavailable to Ligorio, and Eckhart's first printed edition of 1B 2.3.1.6 only appeared in 1729.[50]

Regarding the *Notitia Portarum* (1B 2.3.1.8), the *mss.* are all of English provenance, since this originally 7th century itinerary is found as an appendix to William of Malmesbury's *Gesta Regum Anglorum*.[51] Editions of this latter work containing the former were published by Commelin (1587) and Savile (1596) only after Ligorio's death.[52] The *Topographia Einsiedlensis* (1B 1.3.1.9) was likewise unavailable to Ligorio in *ms.* form. The 14th century codex (*Fabariense* n. 326) which was found in the monastery in Einsiedeln, Switzerland, included it in the work whose title appears on the cover, namely *Gesta Salvatoris: Evangelium Nicodemi*. The apocryphal Gospel of Nicodemus nevertheless was clearly an unlikely place to look for information regarding itineraries for martyrs' shrines. Editions were furthermore only published in the late seventeenth and early eighteenth centuries. Mabillon's editions (1685 and 1723), significantly, both omitted mention of both Hippolytus and Laurence for the entry *in via Tiburtina*.[53]

If, however, we now turn to 1B 1.3.1.10-1.13 we find material which, though not published in printed editions, could have been available to Ligorio in *ms.* form, since the provenance of the *ms.* tradition is Roman and Florentine. The texts are clearly related to one another in terms of a literary chain of successive editions. The *De mirabilibus Urbis Romae* (1B 1.3.1.10) was composed in its present recension by Nicholas Russell (1314-1362), and survives in the 14th century Vatican *Codex Ottoboniensis Latinus* 3082, amongst others. Even though this may not therefore have been published before that of Urlichs in 1869, it is possible that either Ligorio or Ligorio's contemporaries had access to this Vatican codex.[54]

---

[49] Published in the appendix of Frobenius, *Beati Flacci Albini seu Alcuini Abbatis, Caroli Magni Regis ac Imperatoris, Magistri, Opera Omnia*, (Ratisbone: S. Emmeramus 1777) t. II Part 2 Appendix 3, p. 597-600, and republished in Migne *P.L.* CI col. 1395-1363), see Valentini-Zucchetti (1942) II p. 71.

[50] The Würzburg codex was first edited by Eckhart, *Commentari de rebus Franciae orientalis*, (Wurceburgi 1729) t. I, p. 831-833. It was followed by Froben (1777) t. II part II appendix p. 598-600; Migne *P.L.* CI col. 1363-1365; De Rossi (1864-1867), Vol. I p. 141-143, 175; and L' Urlichs, *Codice urbis Romae* top. p. 82-85

[51] *Mss.* of this work found in England are British Museum *Arundel* 35 (A.D. 1130); British Museum *Addit.* 23147 (A.D. 1130); Cambridge *Trinity College R. 7.* 10 (A.A. 1170); Oxford Bodleian Library *Laud misc.* 548 (12-13 century); Oxford All Souls College 35 (140) etc.

[52] J. Commelin, *Rerum Britannicarum id est Angliae, Scotiae, vicinarumque insularum ac regionum; scriptores vetustiores ac praecipui*, (Heidelberg 1587); H. Savile, *Rerum Anglicarum Scriptores Post Bedam, praecipui, ex vetustissimis codicibus, manuscriptis nunc primum in lucem editi,*, (Frankfurt: Wechelianis apud Claudium 1601), where a *Notitia Portarum* is found in Lib. IV, p. 134-136. See also Valentini-Zucchetti (1942) II p. 136-137.

[53] It was published defectively in J. Mabillon, *Veterum Analectorum: Complectens Iter Germanicum Domini Johannis Mabillon et Domini Michaelis Germain è Congregatione Sancti Mauri, cum monumentis in eo repertis*, (Luteciae Parisiorum 1685), IV, p. 506-516 and more correctly in the *Nova Editio* (1723), p. 364-367. See p. 509 and p. 365 respectively for the omissions. See also Valentini-Zucchetti (1942) II p. 162.

[54] Valentini-Zucchetti (1946) III p. 180. See also C.L. Urlichs, *Codex Urbis Romae Topographicus*, (Wirceburgi: Ex Aedibus Steahelianis 1871), p. 126-133.

The Redaction of *De mirabilibus* is earlier and descended from the Einsiedeln Itinerary, and its autograph comes from the same period as the *Liber Politicus* of Benedict, canon of St. Peter's, and written in Santa Maria in Trastevere (A.D. 1140-1143).[55] Before the publication of this document in 1820,[56] therefore, its information was available in Vatican circles and is found in a series of Vatican *mss.* from the 12th to the 15th century.[57] Of the *Graphia* (1B 1.3.1.12) itself, which appears to be dependent on a recension of the *De Mirabilibus* of 1154, one 14th century *ms.* remains, the *codex Florentinus Plut.* LXXXIX, inf. 41 (once *Gaddianus* 267).[58]; Of Magister Gregorius, *De Mirabilibus Urbis Romae* (1B 1.3.1.13), there exists moreover a popular Italian version, *Le miracole de Roma*, found in a 13th century *ms. Gaddianus* 148 in the Laurentian Library at Florence.[59]

That however 1B 1.3.1.10-1.13 could have been available to Ligorio and was certainly known to his contemporaries points to the complete opposite of Guarducci's claim. Although descended ultimately from the Einsiedeln Itinerary, which was unknown to Ligorio's contemporaries, the various versions of *De Mirabilibus* do not identify a shrine separate from San Lorenzo as that of Hippolytus as did that Itinerary (*In sinistra sancti Ypoliti. In dextera sancti Laurentii*). Each of the lists of cemeteries given in 1B 1.3.1.10-1.13 record an *unnamed* cemetery in the Ager Veranus (*cimiterium in agrum Veranum/ in agro Verano*) by or near San Lorenzo (*prope/ ad sanctum Laurentium*). Such is the case even with the popularized *Le Miracole*.[60] The designation of a cemetery to the left of the via Tiburtina with Hippolytus' name has slipped out of the tradition.

As such the tradition of the *mss.* of 1B 1.3.1.10- 1.13 fully accords with the dropping of the older designation of the *mons Hippolyti* from later medieval maps, to which Testini had drawn attention and which Guarducci contested. Had the name of the mountain been known popularly in Ligorio's time and associated with a shrine that stood at its foot on the Ager Veranus, then we should have expected that in one of the many versions of the *De Mirabilibus* the omission of the designation would have been corrected, in particular in the popularised *Le Miracole*, as is usual in such cases. Certainly, as Testini points out, Panvinius (1529-68) in Chapter 12 of *De coemeteriis urbis Romae* gives a list of 43 cemeteries on the basis of literary sources and omits that of Hippolytus.[61]

---

[55] Ibid. p. 5-6.

[56] A. Nibby, *Effemeridi letterarie di Roma*, t. I (Roma 1820), p. 62-82, 147-164, 378-392, see Valentini-Zucchetti (1946) III p. 15.

[57] Cambrai *ms.* 554 (512) of the 12th century, including a letter of Ivo of Chartres and the *Politicus* of Benedict; Rome, *Codex Vallicelliana* folio 73 (15th century); *Vat. Lat.* 5348 (15th century); *Vat. Lat.* 636 (12-13th century), amongst others, see Valentini-Zuccetti (1946) III, p. 11-16.

[58] Ibid. p. 113-114.

[59] Valentini-Zucchetti (1946) III, p. 73

[60] Ibid. p. 135- 136.

[61] Testini (1989) p. 13.

We see therefore that the existence of a known, separate shrine on the left hand side of the via Tiburtina is unacknowledged by any evidence available in Ligorio's time. The sole source for the identification of the Statue with the Ager Veranus could only have been, if this were fictitious, the association of that site with San Lorenzo, and the cult of Hippolytus the soldier celebrated there. But if Smetius' description (which Ligorio does not echo) of the find (*non procul ab aede Laurentii*) was suggested by the cult of the soldier-martyr associated with the cult of St. Laurence, it is surprising, if Guarducci were correct, that Ligorio makes no mention of that cult with which the Itineraries (1B 1.3.1.6-1.8) abound, with their references to his family, the eighteen other martyrs, etc. (*cum familia sua pausat, id est xviii...ipse cum familia sua tota xviiii martyres iacet*). On this cult Ligorio is completely silent. Instead he makes his identification between the Statue and Hippolytus the writer mentioned by Eusebius, and not the soldier-martyr commemorated in the shrine mentioned by these texts.

In the Naples *ms.* XIII B 7 p. 424 Ligorio made it quite clear that it was the list of Eusebius, which included a Paschal Table, that enabled Ligorio to identify the mutilated figure. Any further evidence for this identification, in the material fabric of the mutilated Statue, we shall see to be denied by Guarducci's archaeological examination. The works inscribed were, Ligorio said: *di questo Vescovo il quale commentò l'Apocalypsis, et ...quel santo Hippolito di cui fà mentione honorammente Eusebio; mà non dice di cui diogese fusse.*[62] We see, therefore, that it was the list of works attributed by Eusebius to Hippolytus, whose See the latter claimed not to know (*H.E.* VI,20,2), that led Ligorio to conclude that he must reconstruct the mutilated figure as St. Hippolytus. His justification (Turin J.A. II 10, p.12) was also Eusebius' mention of the Paschal Table, as we discover from his justification for its place in the Belvedere theatre (*per essenti nei lati della sua sedia alcune cose belle, come le feste delli Hebrei*).[63] Had it been the influence of the cult at San Lorenzo, then he would have surely mentioned Hippolytus as the soldier who guarded St. Laurence, his family of eighteen, and other features from the accompanying legendary cycles.

Guarducci's citing of the existence of the *mons Hippoliti* as the reason for Ligorio's invention of a fictitious place of discovery is therefore speculative and unconvincing. Adrian I (772-795) is credited with restoring the church of St. Agnes on the via Nomentana as well as the cemetery of St. Hippolytus the martyr next to San Lorenzo (*simul et cymiterium beati Hippolyti martyris iuxta Sanctum Laurentium*). But no where does Ligorio mention the *mons Hippolyti* which would have given veracity to his forgery, nor the cemetery, nor San Lorenzo, nor the fact that Hippolytus was a martyr. The

---

[62] Mandowsky and Mitchell (1963) Catalogue no. 101 p. 105.
[63] Footnote 121.

mention of all these places would have furthered his forgery if he had read the via Nomentana from this document.

Furthermore, we have seen that, had he read this document in terms of the conceptual register of his contemporaries, he would have understood a shrine adjoining San Lorenzo, even if his maps had contained the further denomination of the *mons Hippoliti* also to be read there which we have shown that it could not. But, as we have seen, his identification of the mutilated Statue with Hippolytus is purely on the basis of the name of an early Christian writer, and not a martyr. The *mons Hippolyti* was not a location available to him from his sources any more than was a separate shrine, which, though mentioned in the Itineraries of which we have seen Ligorio to have been ignorant, was never in any event associated with Eusebius' writer.

The argument that arises from the limited extent of Ligorio's knowledge of these texts is further reinforced when we examine, as we shall now do, the reaction to, and misunderstanding of, the site of Ligorio's claimed discovery on the part of his contemporaries. Indeed, as we shall now see, those contemporaries, by their insistence upon associating Ligorio's discovery with San Lorenzo, and by their lack of comprehension regarding his references to an independent shrine, in fact demonstrate the absence of any motive other than the truth for what he claims.

1B 2.3.3. *San Lorenzo and Ligorio's contemporaries*
The fact of the non existence of evidence contemporary with Ligorio regarding the *mons Hippolyti* and the separate shrine is corroborated moreover by the events of the century after Ligorio's death. Panvinio (1529-1568), his younger contemporary, in chapter XII of his *De coemeteriis urbis Romae*, omits the cemetery of Hippolytus from his catalogue derived from available literary sources.[64] Bosio, some sixty years after Ligorio, read the famous inscription in the vineyard of the Caetanni, later to be that of Msg. Gori, on the left hand side of the via Tiburtina: REFRIGERI TIBI DOMNUS IPOLITUS.[65] Bosio could not enter the basilica which was yet to be excavated, but in the course of his own exploration which began sometime after 1597, simply read this inscription from above.[66] Yet he persisted in identifying this, not with a separate shrine, but with the cemetery of Cyriaca attached to San Lorenzo. He described this cemetery in the vineyard of the fathers of San Lorenzo on the right side of the via Tiburtina, and believed that what he saw protruding from the ground on the left side was part of the same cemetery.[67]

---

[64] Panvinius, *De coemeteriis urbis Romae*, (Maternum Cholinum: Coloniae 1568)
[65] A. Bosio, *Roma Sotteranea, opera postuma compiuta, disposta et accresciuta dal M. R.P. Giovanni Severani*, (Roma: Faciotti 1632), Vol. III p. 41.
[66] Bertonière (1985) p. 5.
[67] Ibid. p. 409 cf. G.-B. De Rossi, Principale cripta storica ora dissepolta, in *BArC* IV anno 1 (1882) p. 44. Of Bosio on p. 45 the latter says: "Imperocchè, dopo descritto il cimitero di

Only from the time of Boldetti, after Bosio's death, was Hippolytus' name associated with a separate cemetery, but even then still as a continuation of San Lorenzo. Whatever may have been the reason for this new association, whether it was Ligorio's testimony itself being at last understood in connection with inscriptions continuing to be found there, or whether some other reason, it will be clear that I cannot accept, in view of the literary evidence that I have established to the contrary, that the reason was any lingering memory of a *mons Hippolyti* amongst inhabitants of the region.[68] Although Mabillon discovered the Einsiedeln Itinerary, the phrases *in via Tiburtina.... in sinistra sancti Ypoliti* did not lead him to identify here the shrine with the eponymous martyr mentioned by Prudentius. Ruggeri still placed the inscriptions unearthed there in the category of unknown commemorative epitaphs.[69] The inscription, found on this site in 1646 and which reads AT EPOLITV (*Ad Hippolytum*), is described as having come *nell'arenaria presso il cimetero di Callisto sull' Appia*.

These writers therefore demonstrate clearly that there was no association of the locality to the left of the via Tiburtina or any mountain in its vicinity with the name of Hippolytus, in separation from one of the figures in the cult of San Lorenzo, at the time of Ligorio and his contemporaries. If moreover such a mountain had been known, its association would have been, in view of the proximity of San Lorenzo, with Hippolytus the soldier and not the writer and Novatian schismatic. If Smetius therefore had identified a Statue whose only originally known location had been in the *Loggia di Raphaelo* as that of Hippolytus who was Eusebius' writer, Ligorio could not on that account have identified him with Hippolytus the soldier and on that ground invented a place for a pretended discovery. Yet Guarducci's claim that his discovery was fictitious requires such an identification on Ligorio's part otherwise he could never have even thought of a site near San Lorenzo, a church which, incidentally, is never named by him in this context. In fact we shall see (1B 2.4.3) that when fragments of an ancient church were discovered some time before 1552 in the Castro Pretorio dedicated to a Saint but without a name, Ligorio was not predisposed to name it after Hippolytus with any forged inscription. Indeed the church in question could have been Ligorio's *altra chiesa dalli eretici rovinata*.

Ciriaca nella vigna dei padri di s. Lorenzo, alla destra della via, narra d'essere disceso in un'altra parte, come credette, del medesimo cimitero, poco più oltre verso Tivoli, a mano manca."

[68] I believe that De Rossi misled others in this respect when he wrote: "Forse il vocabolo di quella e delle contigue vigne nel monte di s. Ippolito, registrato in pubblico instrumento dell' anno 1071, durava nella bocca dei campagnoli all' età del Boldetti e suggerì il vero nome della sotterranea necropoli." (De Rossi (1882) p. 45).

[69] As De Rossi claims: "Nel rimanente del passato secolo niuno, per quanto ricordo, fa espressa menzione di scavi nel cimitero di che ragiono. Non era mutata l'opinione, che le due contigue necropoli di Ciriaca e di Ippolito fossero una sola." (Ibid. p. 46)

Ligorio's claim therefore to have discovered the Statue of Hippolytus in *certe ruine* or *in un' altra chiesa dall' eretici rovinata* described an unexpected find in an area where there were no indications still available in his time that it ought to have been. The inevitability of his description of heretical destruction (*un' altra chiesa*) is simply a reflection of the spirit of his renaissance labours—at this time at the Villa Hadriana at Tivoli—restoring the grandeur of ancient Rome from the barbarian ravages. Barbarians destroy classical works, and heretics churches. We know of course from De Rossi's excavations that there was a separate cult-centre there, and we have earlier documentary evidence in the Medieval Itineraries, confirming Prudentius' description, that it had been known to be there.

But we have also seen that in the documentary evidence available to Ligorio and his contemporaries the martyr shrine had become anonymous, in the same way that the designation of the *mons Hippolyti* had fallen out of copies of medieval maps. Indeed, the very action of Bosio and Boldetti in consistently regarding further finds as part of the San Lorenzo complex demonstrates how alien a separate shrine was in view of the aetiology of St. Laurence's soldier-companion in his martyrdom.

Ligorio's successors clearly interpreted his 'Hippolytus' in the context of that complex. But Ligorio never did. The Statue found near his *chiesa dall' eretici rovinata* was subsequently deciphered by Smetius and Pighius for a Ligorio who knew no Greek, as Hippolytus the writer, and before that identification, there was nothing either in San Lorenzo itself, or in the ruins quite separate from San Lorenzo that would have suggested the name of that writer. Even a mountain of this name, if so identified, would not have been identified with the writer but the soldier.

This point applies moreover *a fortiori* had the Statue come from a location unknown to the Loggia of Raphael and been deciphered there. There was nothing in the original inscriptions on the Statue, attributed by Smetius to Eusebius' writer (*H.E.* VI,20,2), to identify it in any way with the environs of San Lorenzo *extra muros* or the Ager Veranus. What Guarducci, as we shall see in Chapter 2, was to identify from Ligorio's drawings as the feminine form of that Statue would certainly not have suggested a male figure without Smetius' decipherment. In any forgery based upon the locality, therefore, the *motif* of Hippolytus the soldier would have had to have been added to that of Hippolytus the writer, and the former's nearness to San Lorenzo would have had to have been emphasized by Ligorio, which, unlike his contemporaries, he never did.

Baronius, like Bosio and Boldetti, continued to reinterpret Ligorio's words as applying to San Lorenzo. References to the via Nomentana, via Tiburtina, Ager Veranus, Castro Pretorio etc. are all assumed by Baronius in his note on the Roman Martyrology under 13th August to indicate a site of a church of Hippolytus near San Lorenzo where *antiqua vestigia inter vineta adhuc exstare dicuntur.* [70] But he too regarded the *vineta* as part of the monastery of San Lorenzo.[71] It was only as late as the years immediately following 1829 that De Rossi established the independence of the shrine on the left hand side of the via Tiburtina, to which the Itineraries and Prudentius had born witness.[72] De Rossi in fact took over the excavations in 1841-1842 along with Marchi, where remains of the via Tiburtina were found at a deep level of the cemetery of Ciriaca, and thus the separation established between the cult of Cirilla, Trifonia etc that was part of Ciriaca on the right, and that of the separate cult-centre on the left of that road. Thus De Rossi was able to distinguish what Bosio had confused.[73]

We thus see that the witness of Ligorio's contemporaries confirm the testimony of the written sources available to him that there was no reason for him to have invented a separate shrine of Hippolytus on the left-hand side of the via Tiburtina. He did not share with them the language that indicates that they associated his discovery with San Lorenzo and the martyr-soldier Hippolytus venerated there. Had he done so, he would have used language similar to theirs to describe the shrine's location, and this he has not done.

Furthermore, had he conformed to what his contemporaries would have expected, given the information of the locality available to them, he would have identified Hippolytus not as Eusebius' writer but as the soldier and companion of St. Laurence. Moreover, he needed Smetius' knowledge of Greek and his skills as a transcriber to reach the conclusion that a headless statue, feminine in form, was that of an early Christian writer. If Smetius' work had taken place in the *Loggia di Raphaelo* or some workshop nearby, then there would have been nothing in his identification of Hippolytus the writer to lead Ligorio to place the allegedly fictitious discovery of the Statue near San Lorenzo. In fact Ligorio does not include San Lorenzo in his description, unlike Baronius, and Bosio. Consequently and *a fortiori* there was no reason for him to associate, before De Rossi, the headless Statue with any Hippolytus, even a soldier-martyr and not a writer, *in una chiesa rovinata* on the Ager Veranus apart from San Lorenzo.

But Guarducci, in seeking to dissociate the true location of the discovery of the Statue from the cult-centre on the via Tiburtina, appeals at one point

---

[70] De Rossi (1882) p.43.

[71] C. Baronius, *Memorie delle sette Chiese*, I p. 647 where of the church of St. Hippolytus he says: "si vedono ancora i vestigi in una vigna del monastero di S. Lorenzo vicino alla detta basilica."

[72] De Rossi (1882) p. 49: "...nel' 1829 e negli anni seguenti i nostri fossori tornarono al cimitero d'Ippolito." See also F.X. Kraus, *Roma Sotterranea. Die römischen Katakomben. Eine Darstellung der älteren und neueren Forschungen, besonders derjenigen De Rossi's,* (Freiburg im Bresgau: Herder 1879).——, Hippolytus, *Real-Encyklopaedia der christlichen Altertümer.* Band 1 (Freiburg 1882), p. 660-664.

[73] Bosio (1632) III p. 398-399 cf G.-B. De Rossi, Elogio Damasiano del celebre Ippolito martire sepolto presso la via Tiburtina, in *BArC* IV, 6 (1881) p. 29.

to the work of Cecchelli,[74] who raises objections similar to, but not identical with, her own. As Cecchelli's arguments would lead to a quite different interpretation of the absence of references amongst Ligorio's contemporaries to Hippolytus the schismatical writer, it will be well for us to examine her case in some greater detail.

1B 2.3.3.1. The epigrams of Damasus and the cult-centre
Cecchelli seeks to dissociate the cult of Hippolytus the martyr of the via Tiburtina from the cult of the Novatian presbyter, later to be associated, she claims, with the basilica at Porto.[75] In order to do so she has to dissociate the two Philocalian epigrams of Damasus that mention Hippolytus' name, and give them reference to two different martyrs.[76]

It is impossible to dissociate *ICUR* 7,19936 from the cult-centre, since it is dated 366-384 and was discovered during the excavations of 1882-1883 near the bottom of the stairs of the present day entrance *via* the Vicolo dei Canneti.[77] The inscription clearly was not found in its original position, but it marks extensive reconstruction whether of the underground crypt or the above-ground basilica.[78] But the inscription makes no mention of the ecclesiastical status of the martyr as a presbyter, nor does it refer to the method or place of his execution. A further inscription, not marble but impressed into limestone wall, is too fragmentary to be admitted as evidence, though Ferrua infers *supplex*, and therefore some martyrological information, from the traces of a double PP, and *fratres* from FRA.[79]

---

[74] Guarducci (1989) p. 67.
[75] M. Cecchelli, Note storico-topografiche: ancora su Ippolito, in *Archeologia Classica*, 34 (1982), p. 210-217, see p.211-213, and 215.
[76] *ICUR* 7 Nos. 19932 and 19936 and A. Ferrua, *Epigrammata Damasiana.* (Rome: Pontificio Istituto di Archeologia Cristiana, Città del Vaticano 1943), no. 35 (*ICUR* 7, 19932) p. 169-173 which I cite in footnote 86. No. 35[1] (*ICUR* 7, 19936) reads:
LAETA DEO PLEBS SANCTA CANAT QV[OD] MOENIA CRESCVNT ET RENOVATA
DOMVS MARTYR[IS] [IPP]OLITI
ORNAMENTA OPERIS SVRGV[NT AVCTORE DAM]ASO
NATVS QVI ANTISTES SEDIS A[POSTOLICAE]
INCLITA PACIFICIS FACTA ES[T HAEC AVLA TRIVMPHIS]
SERVATVRA DECVS PERPET[VAMQUE FIDEM]
HAEC OMNIA NOVA QVAEQUE VIDIS LE[O PRESBY]TER HORNAT
English translation:
Let the holy people sing to God rejoicing that the walls spring up,
and the restored martyr's house of Hippolytus
distinguished signs of the work they rise, that Damasus commissioned,
who was born a bishop of the apostolic See,
for deeds done directed at offerings of peace
an everlasting glory is to be stored up
all these new works that you see Leo the presbyter decorates.
[77] G.-B. De Rossi, Notizie: Continuazione delle scoperte nella cripta storica e nelle adiacenti gallerie del cimitero di s. Ippolito, in *BArC*, (1882-1883), p. 176-177. Cf. W.N. Schuhmacher, Prudentius an der Via Tiburtina, in, *Spanische Forschungen der Görresgesellschaft*, 1 Reihe (Gesammelte Aufsätze zur Kulturgeschichte Spaniens 16 Band) (Münster: 1960) p. 1-15.
[78] Bertonnière (1985) p. 29-30.
[79] Ferrua (1943) no. 36 p. 174-175.

We might rule out *ab initio* any further discussion by claiming that Damasus knew the cult-centre on the via Tiburtina as the grave of Hippolytus because it was his association of that grave with that of Novatian that was in the vicinity that lead to his claim that Hippolytus was a Novatian martyr. But such a conclusion might at very most be considered probable only in the light of our later discussion of the archaeological evidence for the genuineness of Novatian's tomb as that of the third century schismatic (6A 2.1). For the moment we shall ignore that probability, and consider Cecchelli's case without the support of that discussion which we believe to be questionable even so.

Regarding *ICUR* 7, 19932, Cecchelli points out in what is the strongest point of her case that this inscription that gives an account of Hippolytus as a Novatian presbyter was only located originally at the cult-centre on the via Tiburtina by De Rossi's conjecture.[80] Martin V in 1425 issued the Brief for the reconstruction of the Lateran pavement from materials to be taken from ruined churches. As a result, De Rossi hypothesized that the *titulus* of the buried crypt of Hippolytus was ripped away, and lost forever, but the accompanying epigraph became part of the Lateran pavement until Marucchi (1912) and Josi (1934) and (1938) recovered them. Cecchelli wishes therefore to argue that De Rossi's conjecture was wrong. The epigram on the Novatian presbyter buried in the Lateran pavement in fragments derive from another place apparently unknown.

But De Rossi's identification of the original site cannot be abstracted from the pattern of his general argument as Cecchelli has done. We shall argue that Cecchelli dismisses too readily the evidence of the collection of epigraphs in the *Codex Corbiensis*. Let us trace in detail the process of De Rossi's argument that Cecchelli rightly characterizes as "only an opinion not accompanied unfortunately by certain proofs *(solamente una opinione non corredata purtroppo da certe prove)*."[81] But deductive truth is a rare possibility in historical argument, and De Rossi's argument nevertheless possesses an inductive probability which cannot be characterized as pure conjecture.[82]

1B 2.3.3.2. *De Rossi's use of the Codex Corbeiensis*
De Rossi began his study with the examination of the *Codex Corbeiensis*, which had found its way in the course of the political upheavals of the 18th Century from the library of St. Germaine in Paris to the Tsarist imperial museum in Petrograd. It originally came from the monastery of St. Peter in Corbei in France. The manuscript contains mainly the hymns of Venantius

---

[80] G.B. De Rossi, Elogio Damasiano del celebre Ippolito martire sepolto presso la via Tiburtina, in *BArC.* IV, 6 (1881) p. 26-55, and Cecchelli (1982) p. 212. For the full text of *ICUR* 7,19932 see footnote 86.
[81] Cecchelli (1982) p. 212.
[82] Thus Cecchelli's overbearing conclusion: "Nessuna prova poi abbiamo e bisogna sottolinearlo, che questa epigrafa provenga dal cimitero della via Tiburtina." Ibid. p. 212.

Fortunatus, but also an anthology of Christian poets of the sixth, seventh, and eighth centuries. Folios 122-133 contained epigraphic poems of considerable archaeological significance, amongst which were copies of the epigrams of Pope Damasus.[83]

Among these, in a section of the manuscript specifically devoted to the martyrs of the via Tiburtina, was a text of an epigram headed IN SCO HYPOLITO MARTYRAE (folio 24—"on the grave of Hippolitus martyr").[84] De Rossi argued that this represented the lost *titulus* of the shrine on the via Tiburtina under which the epigram was inscribed whose text was given in the *Codex Corbeiensis,* three fragments of which were located in the Lateran pavement.

Three fragments of a marble disc were originally discovered with fragmentary inscriptions in the distinguished hand of Furius Dionysius Philocalus, which were clearly original parts of the epigram recorded in *Codex Corbeiensis.*[85] Josi added his four fragments to these three, which in the meantime had been dug out of the pavement and acquired by Marucchi for the Lateran Museum (1912).[86] Both sets of fragments came from the

---

[83] G.B. De Rossi, La silloge epigrafica d'un codice già corbeiense ora nella Biblioteca imperiale di Pietroburgo, in *BArC* 6 1881 ser.3, p. 5-7, 26-27.

[84] The full text reads:
Praesbyter ornavit renovans vicenius ultro (*)
Hypolitus fertur p̲m̲erent cum iussa tyranni (1)
Pr̲b̲s̲t̲ in scisma sem̲p̲ mansisse novati (2)
Tempore quo gladius secuit pia viscera matris (3)
Devotus X̲p̲o̲ peteret cum regna piorum (4)
Quaesisset populus ubinam procedere possit (5)
Catholicam dixisset fidem sequerentur ut omnes (6)
Sic n̲t̲ meruit confessus martyr ut e̲e̲t̲ (7)
                              as
Haec audita refert damasus probat omnia X̲p̲s̲ (8)
See De Rossi (1881) op. cit. 26-27.

[85] The two discs exhibit the phrases PREMERE̲N̲T̲ Cu̲M IUSSA T̲y̲rani, SECVIT P̲i̲A VISCERA MA̲tris, REGNA PIO̲rum, and DAM̲asus. De Rossi op. cit. p. 38-39; Lightfoot (1890) 1,II p. 328-329.

[86] *ICUR* 7, 19932:
i) *tempor*E QUO GLA*dius*
*devo*TVS CHRISTO (verses 3-4)
(ii) *catho*LIC*am* (verse 6).
(iii) CATH*olicam* (verse 6) and *s*IC NOSt*er* (verse 7)
(iv) *po*SSE*t* (verse 5), *u*T *o*MnES (verse 6), VT E*sset* (verse 7), and *o*MNIA X̲P̲S̲.(verse 8)
See E. Josi, Quatro nuovi frammenti del carme di Damaso in onore di S. Ippolito, in *RivAC* 13 1936, p. 233-235, and
(i) fertYR (verse 1), sCISma (verse 2)
(ii) *Hippo*LYTUS FE*rtur*.(verse 1), *pres*BYTe*r* (verse 2), and *tem*PORe (verse 4)
(iii) PrOBAt Omnia (verse 8)
See E. Josi, Altre tre frammenti, in *RivAC* 16 1939, p. 320-321. Subsequently it was rendered by A. Ferrua, Epigrammata Damasiana, in *Sussidi allo Studio delle Antichità Cristiane* 2 (1942), p. 169 no. 35 (*ICUR* 7, 19932):
Hippol YTVS FErtVR PREMERENT CuM IVSSA tyranni (1)
PresBYTer in sCISMA SEMPER MANSISSE NOvati (2)
TemPOrE QUO GLAdius SECVIT PIA VISCERA MAtris (3)
dEvoTVS CHRISTO peteret cuM REGNA PIOrum (4)
QUAESISSet populus ubinam proceDERe pOSSEt (5)
CATHoLICam dixisse fidem sequerentur VT OMNES (6)

excavated pavement of the Lateran Basilica, but this had not been their original home. As De Rossi pointed out, the Brief of Martin V (1st July 1425) had authorized the use of materials from "churches, chapels, and church grounds (*quibuscumque ecclesiis, capellis et locis ecclesiasticis campestribus*), whether they exist within or without the city (*tam intra quam extra Urbem existentibus*).[87] The ruined and buried cemetery on the via Tiburtina represented well "ecclesiastical grounds (*locis ecclesiasticis campestribus*)... outside the city (*extra Urbem*)." (Plate 21)

1B 2.3.3.3. *What Prudentius did not hypothesize*
We should now note that the *titulus* IN SCO HYPOLITO MARTYRAE, clearly connected with the epigram, was not therefore purely hypothetically associated with the cult-centre on the via Tiburtina. Nor moreover was it located there on the evidence of the Chronographer of 354 (*Liberian Catalogus*) alone, a thesis which Cecchelli wishes to deny. De Rossi also established the connection of the Damasian inscription specifically with the cult-centre with reference to the epigram of the deacon Florentius (in *Corbeiensis* folio 131), which mentions his unnamed bishop identified with a martyred bishop Leo. He had discovered in the Ager Veranus fragments of that epigram, written in Philokalian letters, with the words *sancte sacerdos, iam sorte secunda, hoc superante, spiritus orae, iste seni, morte beatus, quod patris.*[88] In consequence he had uncovered a connection not only between such Philokalian inscriptions and the text of the *Codex Corbeiensis* but also between them both and the cult-centre on the Ager Veranus that underlined the conclusion that here was found the site seen by Prudentius. Cecchelli has clearly not taken adequate notice of this link in the chain of De Rossi's evidence.

Furthermore, Prudentius in *Peristephanon* XI claimed to have *seen* the *titulus* on the entrance to the cult-centre on the via Tiburtina. Prudentius had spoken of:

> *Plurima litterulis signata sepulcra loquuntur*
> *Martyris aut nomen aut epigramma aliquod.* (v. 7-8)[89]

And he could then proceed to read Hippolytus' name and epigram:

> *Haec dum lustro oculis, et sicubi forte latentes*
> *Rerum apices veterum per monumenta sequor;*

SiC NOSter meruit confessus martyr UT EsseT(7)
Haec audita refeRT DAMasusPROBAT OMNIA XPS (8)

[87] De Rossi (1881) op. cit. p. 39-40. For the text of Martin's decree: "...cum Lateranensis ecclesia... solo deformata permaneat, pavimento minime refulgens... concedimus ut a quibuscumque ecclesiis, capellis, et locis ecclesiasticis campestribus... et.c." see A. Ferrua, *Epigrammata Damasiana.* (Rome: Pontificio Instituto di Archeologia Cristiana, Città del Vaticano 1943) no. 35 p. 171.
[88] De Rossi (1881) p. 36-38 ff.
[89] "Very many graves inscribed with tiny letters tell the name or some epigram of a martyr."

Invenio Hippolytum.... (v.17-19a)

The lines which follow bear a close resemblance to Damasus' inscription. To Damasus':

> *Tempore quo gladius secuit pia viscera matris*
> *Devotus Christo peteret cum regna piorum* (v. 3-4)

corresponds Prudentius':

> *Cum iam vesano victor raperetur ab hoste*
> *Exultante anima carnis ad exitium* (v. 25-26)

For Damasus':

> *Quaesisset populus ubinam procedere posset*
> *Catholicam dixisse fidem sequerentur ut omnes* (v. 5-6)

Prudentius versifies:

> *Plebis amore suae multis comitantibus ibat*
> *Consultus quaenam secta foret melior*
> *Respondit: fugite o miseri execranda Novati*
> *Schismata, catholicis reddite vos populis* (v. 27-30)

We thus have evidence, in addition to that of the Philocalian epigram to the martyr Leo (*Corbeiensis* fol. 131), that the inscription was located at the cult-centre on the Ager Veranus on the opposite side of the via Tiburtina from San Lorenzo. Prudentius, like the author of the *Codex Corbeiensis*, associated the epigram of Damasus on the Novatian presbyter with the cult-centre on the via Tiburtina, of whose remains known to us from the excavations he gives a fair descriptions, because that was where he had read it.[90]

1B 2.3.3.4. *Hippolytus, Nonnus and the martyrs of Portus*

In order to deny this claim, Cecchelli must now establish that Prudentius has confused the shrine of Hippolytus the martyr of the via Tiburtina with that of Hippolytus the writer and Roman presbyter. She argues that the Novatian presbyter and writer was associated with Portus, and that the martyr of the via Tiburtina always was the companion of St. Laurence and the group of martyrs surrounding him. Prudentius' claim about seeing the *titulus* was therefore accurate, but his association of it with the resting place of the Novatian presbyter, and Damasus' epigram, was a complete confusion. Moreover, the author of the *Codex Corbeiensis* shared in Prudentius' confusion, and thus Cecchelli claims that is valueless as evidence.

But it is difficult to see what confusion there was on the part of the former for the latter to share in. The very plausible and highly probable thesis of De Rossi is that Prudentius saw both the *titulus* and the epigram that fol-

---

[90] De Rossi (1881) *op. cit.* p. 43.

lowed it, and that the *Codex Corbeiensis* corroborates this juxtaposition. The thesis is not that Prudentius saw the *titulus* alone, and then proceeded to associate with it recollections in his mind about a Damasian epigram on the Novatian presbyter. He *saw* Hippolytus' name inscribed on the *titulus* on the via Tiburtina and then versified the Damasan inscription that followed and which he was reading.

In the *Depositio Martyrum* of the Chronographer of 354 we find mentioned for Nones (5th) September: *Aconti in Porto et Nonni et Herculani et Taurini*. In the *Martyrologium Hieronymianum* in spaces between 22nd and 23rd August (11th and 10th Kalends of September) August we read: *In portu urbis Romae natalis sancti Hippolyti qui dicitur Nunnus cum sociis suis*.[91] Cecchelli wishes to conclude that Nonnus is a description of age rather than a name, and therefore identified with the *presbyter* of Damasus' epigram who therefore becomes a martyr of Portus rather than the via Tiburtina. Subsequently he is called *senior* in the *passiones portuenses* in the sense of presbyter rather than old man.[92]

We now reach at this point the fundamental premise of Cecchelli's argument, namely that the Chronographer of 354 has produced a composite work, and that the presbyter who accompanied Pontian to Sardinia in the *Catalogus Episcoporum* was not the martyr of the *Depositio* laid to rest *in Tiburtina*. Unless she can establish this distinction between the two names, then Hippolytus the presbyter is bound irrevocably to the cemetery on the via Tiburtina. But even if the *Catalogus* and the *Depositio* were two distinct documents combined by the Chronographer of 354, the fact that Pontian and Hippolytus are mentioned conjointly in both entries is indicative that it is the same person in both cases.

From such a dubious premise that there are two different people of the same name mentioned by the Chronographer, Cecchelli now has recourse to her own conjecture which is itself *solamente una opinione non corredata purtroppo da certe prove*. She infers that Hippolytus the presbyter survived the Sardinian experience, only to be later martyred at Portus.[93] The date which she accordingly gives for the martyrdom, in the Valerian persecution, is 258—the date of the martyrdom of St. Laurence.

1B 2.3.3.5. *The evidence of the Chronographer of 354*
For her conjecture to have any support, as we have argued, it would require the establishment of two different Hippolyti in the *Catalogus* and the *Depositio* given to us by the Chronographer of 354. But even were we to

---

[91] Lightfoot (1890) 1,II p. 355 cf. Cecchelli (1982) p. 215.
[92] Ibid. p. 215.
[93] Cecchelli (1982) p. 215: "Al limite si potrebbe pure, con un buon margine di credibilità, sostenere che una volta rimandato a Roma, dopo aver scontato la pena, egli sia come di norma sbarcato a Porto, ove abbia continuato la sua missione sino alla morte, coronata dal martirio." For further criticisms of this thesis see Testini (1989) p. 11.

grant this dubious premise, the inference from the words of the former document that Hippolytus the presbyter survived is equally dubious. The entry
in the *Catalogus* reads:

> PONTIANUS, ann. v, m. ii, d. vii. Fuit temporibus Alexandri, a cons.
> Pompeiani et Peligniani. Eo tempore Pontianus episcopus et Yppolitus pres-
> byter exoles sunt deportati in Sardinia, in insula nociva, Severo et Quintiano
> cons. In eadem insula discinctus est iiii Kl. Octobr., et loco eius ordinatus est
> Antheros xi Kl. Dec. cons. ss.[94]

Thus in A.D. 235 (*Severo et Quintiano cons.*), during the reign of Maximus
and in that persecution, Pontian died in Sardinia. But it is by no means exceptional that a bishop exiled to the Sardinian salt mines should die there as
a result of his treatment. It must therefore be asked why it was necessary to
draw attention to the unhealthy character of the island (*in insula nociva*).
The likely explanation is that Hippolytus died as a result of the treatment he
had received there but not on the island itself, as had Pontian. Furthermore,
as Bovini originally pointed out, the *Digest* makes it quite clear that no return was intended from such and exile.[95]

The closeness of their death to each other is indicated by the common
date of the *Depositio*, however symbolic in other ways the coincidence of
both their names may be for the history of the Roman community at that
time. We shall return to a consideration of that signifance in 4B 2.2.3-2.2.4
and 6A 2.2. That symbolism, of what would later be regarded as a schism
healed, would lose its point if the episcopal and presbyteral leaders of both
parties had not shared a common fate in near proximity in time. At all
events, as I have said, it is highly dubious that two different Hippolyti could
have been associated in life and death with the one Pontian.

Furthermore, in order to dissociate Damasus' presbyter from the martyr
commemorated on the via Tiburtina, Cecchelli has been forced to break one
of accepted canons of criticism in this area. Not only does she wish to dissociate the martyr of the 13th August from the Sardinian exile of the same
name without in consequence being able to assign any date to the latter, but
she wishes to identify a martyr of a different name (Nonnus) with a different
date with one and the same person. When martyrologies assign different

---

[94] Lightfoot (1890) 1,I p. 255.
English translation:
Pontian [reigned as bishop] five years two months and seven days. It was during the time of
[Emperor Severus] Alexander, from the time when Pompeian and Pelignian were consuls. At
that time bishop Pontian and presbyter Hippolytus were deported as exiles to Sardinia, an unhealthy island, when Severus and Quintianus were consuls. On the same island he died on 25th
September and in his place Antheros was ordained on 18th November.
[95] G. Bovini, Saint'Ippolito, dottore e martire del III secolo, in *Coll. amici delle catacombe*
15 (Città del Vaticano: Pontificio Instituto di Archeologia cristiana 1943), p. 25-26, where he
points to Modestinus in Justinian *Dig.* XLVIII, 22,17: "Deportatis vero hae solent insulae assig-
nari quae sunt asperrimae, quaeque sunt paulo minus summo supplicio comparandae."

dates to a name this is usually held to indicate different persons. Nonnus is mentioned in the Liberian *Depositio* on the Nones (5th) September. It is therefore according to such a canon quite impossible that the Hippolytus of the Ides (13th) August should be identical with him even if the Hippolytus of the *Depositio* who companioned Pontian was different from the Hippolytus of the same companion in the *Catalogus*.

Thus the association of *Ypoliti in Tiburtina* on the *Idus Aug.* (13th August) with *in Porto* on *Non. Sept.* or *Hippolytus qui dicitur Nunnus in portu urbis Romae* on x Kal. Sept. (23rd August) of the *Martyrologium Hieronymianum* would normally be held to be indicative also of the conflation into one of two different martyrs on different occasions. But where the same *Martyrologium Hieronymianum* mentions two other Hippolyti, one for the *xiii Kal. Sept.* (18th August) and one for the *x Kal Sept.* (20th August) both from Portus, and qualifies one *with qui dicitur Nunnus*,[96] it is more plausible to infer that two aetiological legends, one of Hippolytus and one of Nonnus are being combined rather than a reference being made to a cult with any historical core.

1B 2.3.3.6. *Aetiology of the Hippolytus-Nonnus conflation*

Cecchelli needs such an historical identification of Nonnus with Hippolytus, or else she cannot establish the connection of Damasus' presbyter with Portus rather than the via Tiburtina. She needs also to insist that Nonnus is a description of age rather than a cognomen. While this is linguistically possible, the *Acta SS. Cyriaci, Hippolyti, Aureae* etc. suggest differently. In the Greek version of these *Acts* we have the story of the martyr Chryse drowned at sea with a large stone hung around her neck. Her body is recovered and buried on his own property outside the walls of Ostia by ὁ μακαριώτατος Νόνος ὁ καὶ μετονομασθεὶς ῾Ιππόλυτος.

The sense of μετονομασθείς clarifies the meaning of *qui dicitur* in the *Martyrologium Hieronymianum*. The Greek word does not simply mean "called" but "given a new name," so that the phrase is to be translated "the most blessed Nonus who was also renamed Hippolytus." It is only after having combined the account of the martyrdom of Nonnus with Hippolytus' name that the writer can now go on to refer to him as ὁ μακαριώτατος ῾Ιππόλυτος ὁ πρεσβύτερος who now proceeds to make his confession and is sunk into a pit of the harbour of Portus.[97] Thus the martyr of Portus only be-

---

96 Lightfoot (1890) 2,I p. 356.

97 For text and commentary see Lagarde (1858) p. v; Lightfoot (1890) 1,II p. 364-365, 474-476. For the original Latin version see *Bibliotheca Hagiografica Latina* (Brussells: 1898-1901), 1722. See also H. Quentin and H. Delehaye, *Martyrologium Hieronymianum*, in Acta SS. Novembris II,2, p. 460; Lagarde (1858) p. v; E. Follieri, Giovani Mauropode metropolita di Eucaita, Otto canoni paracletici a N.S. Gesù Cristo, in *Archivio italiano per la storia della pietà* 5 (1968), p. 17-18; —, S. Ippolita nell' Agriofia e Liturgia Bizantina, in *StEphAug* 13 (1977), p. 38-39; V. Palachkovsky, La Tradition hagiographique sur S. Hippolyte, in *StudPatr* 3*TU* 78 (Berlin: 1961), p. 97-107.

comes a *senex* by association with Nonnus and not with the ecclesiastical presbyter and writer of the via Tiburtina.

These *Acts* themselves are moreover preserved in a relatively late manuscript, *Taurinus Graecus* 116 of 15th- 16th Century. Follieri has argued that the *Passio* of Cyriaca, Hippolytus, and her companions was originally a Latin work of the 6th century that itself arbitrarily combined together martyrs of Ostia and Portus. He claims that these Greek words reveal that the it was the Greek translator of the Latin *Acts* who first associated Nonnus with Hippolytus the presbyter, and that the name of the former alone stood in the original. At this point the appeal to the *Martyrologium Hieronymianum* with its claim that it was rather Hippolytus who was renamed Nonnus (*Yppoliti qui dicitur Nonnus*) rather than vice versa will not help. These words occur alongside different dates in the Berne (22nd August) and the Wissemb. *mss.* The name alone is found in Eptern. *ms.* The ambiguity of the manuscript tradition is indicative of aetiological manipulation and precludes any historical core.

Saxer's conclusion that Hippolytus of Portus is a creation of the end of the fourth century is thus consistent with the archaeological evidence of the basilica at Portus whose earliest remains only extend to that time as we shall see later (6A 2.5-6).[98] It is also consistent with an analysis of both the aetiology of the legends and indeed their manuscript tradition. The cult-centre on the via Tiburtina existed before 354, and therefore well before there was any such centre at Portus whose earliest remains date from 385.

1B 2.3.3.7. *Summary*

In these sections I have drawn attention to:

(i) The distinction between San Lorenzo and the cult-centre established by De Rossi's excavations, corroborated implicitly and unintentionally by both Smetius, Pighius and Baronius.

(ii) Ligorio's description of the location of his discovery in contrast with the assumptions of his aforementioned contemporaries.

The close association to the point of near identity of the cult-centre with San Lorenzo took place, as we have shown, after the sale of rents were forgotten and in later editions of the *Notitae* etc., published as the *De Mirabilibus* etc. Furthermore, Prudentius cannot be held unequivocally responsible for Ligorio's identification of the Statue with a locality apart from San Lorenzo since the latter never mentions him but only Eusebius, who has no Damasan references. He does not identify the figure on the Chair with

---

[98] V. Saxer, Note di agiografia critica: Porto, l'Isola Sacra e Ippolito. A proposito di studi recenti, in *Miscellanea Amato Pietro Frutaz*, (Roma 1978): "L'Ippolito di Porto è una creazione della fine del IV secolo, progressivamente sviluppata a partire dall'omonimo romano. Il centro primitivo dello sviluppo fu una basilica paleocristiana circa dal 385..." See also E. Follieri, Sant' Ippolito nell' agiografia Bizantina: Ricerche recenti, in *StEphAug* 30 (1989) p. 131-135.

any presbyter, let alone Damasus' Novatian presbyter. Obviously Ligorio had never read the *Codex Corbeiensis* .

The text of the epigraph in that codex is clearly headed IN S(EPUL)C(R)O HYPOLITO MARTYRAE, and this obviously was the *titulus* now lost from the fragments reintegrated from the Lateran pavement. Though there may be no need to locate the epigraph located originally on cult-centre at the via Tiburtina from the codex as it stands, Prudentius' *carmen* shows that its author *read* these words together with the epigram on the Novatian presbyter at the entrance of the small basilica and crypt that De Rossi excavated on the via Tiburtina. Prudentius therefore saw and not merely imagined their juxtaposition.

Having therefore given strong grounds for rejecting Guarducci's claim that the place of discovery was Ligorio's fiction (1B 2), let us now consider the fourth and final objection (1B 4) founded upon his general reliability. In pursuing our case, our argument will inevitably now be more circumstantial. It will nevertheless help us generally to provide an account with some degree of probability regarding the personal circumstances in which Ligorio made his discovery.

1B 2.4. *Ligorio's general reliability*

We argued in 1B 2.3 that we are not entitled to share Guarducci's certainty that Ligorio is the sole witness to the location of the discovery. Smetius uses different words to describe the location (*reperta non procul ab aede Laurentii... anno MDLI*), which could, as I have suggested, be a puzzled correction of Ligorio's language in order to associate his unknown *chiesa rovinata* with the known cult and shrine of San Lorenzo. If the cult-centre was thus unknown to himself and his contemporaries, he would have had no reason other than the truth to locate the Statue there.

Alternatively, these words could indicate Smetius' direct experience of seeing the Statue on the actual site and noting the nearness of San Lorenzo across the via Tiburtina, as opposed to visiting the site on Ligorio's say-so, as did Baronius when he described the vineyard of the monks of St. Laurence. But let us assume for the moment that Ligorio is the only witness, and that the Statue was first seen by Smetius in or after its placement in the Loggia which (in section 1B 2.3) we gave grounds for doubting. What reliability can we ascribe to Ligorio's testimony in that case, given some otherwise extraordinary forgeries in other instances? Can his reliability be assailed regarding this particular work simply because in other instances either his temperament or his methodology has failed us?

As we have seen, Ligorio was responsible for some misleading reconstructions and accompanying inscriptions. Agustin claimed that he had added the words from the consular *fasti* of 1546 to the base of the hemicycle in Palestrina. There are also the famous *epigrafi ligoriane*.[99] But these were not the acts of a dishonest forger as opposed to an over-imaginative disciple of Agustin's lacking the fully critical approach of modern archaeology, but at least transcending the phantasies of the earlier pilgrim guides. His philological method, applied to sculpture, lead him to look for universal forms in particular statues, and to restore in them a putative symmetry and perfection that they may originally never have had. Likewise in his manuscripts he pieces together biographies from a variety of sources. The editors of Lucretius were doing no less in perfecting his style and grammar on the grounds that such perfection must have been what was there originally.

There was moreover a movement in the development of Ligorio's thought in this respect between making 'typical' restorations and 'syncretic' ones. A comparison between his 1553 plan of Rome with that of 1561 exemplifies the movements of his highly imaginative mind in this respect (Plates 8-11). As Mandowsky and Mitchell say:

> His earlier 1553 plan of the ancient city was a 'typical' reconstruction based on the ancient regionaries and the actual surviving ruins. The 1561 plan is a 'syncretic' creation, rising on the wings of Ligorio's learned imagination above the particular world of specific archaeological remains into an ideal exemplary sphere where all is made perfect. It was Ligorio's vision of a *Roma Triumphans*.[100]

In the light of such a cast of mind we can, I believe, understand Ligorio' use of such cryptic phrases as *in certe ruine* or *una chiesa dall'eretici ruinata*. They may be descriptions *ex post facto* of the discovery, since they record the emergence of what he subsequently believed was a seated doctor of the Church out of the rubble of a Rome desecrated by the heretics in the general and universal battle between truth and falsehood, perfection and its loss of literary or sculptured artistic form. But there is no need to dispute the basic fact of the discovery there, to which everything otherwise seems to point and which is itself the stimulus to Ligorio's fervid imagination. It is simply not true to say that his identification of the place of discovery has the vagueness of the deceitful. *Tra la via Nomentana e la via Tiburtina presso il Castro Pretorio* are pretty clear locations for the site of what was latter Msg. Gori's vineyard. The *heretici* may be *misteriosi* and part of the Ligorian fantasy, but not the location.[101]

It must be emphasised firstly that the phrase *in certe ruine* is not as mysterious as Guarducci thinks, nor necessarily to be equated with the phraseol-

---

[99] *CIL* VI 5 p. 19-213 nn. 101-1093 referred to by Guarducci (1989) p. 68 where she draws particular attention to n. 236, 43, 2315.

[100] Mandowsky and Mitchell (1963) p. 43.

[101] "si sia espresso in termino quanto mai vaghi... corrisponde ad una zona un po' troppo vasta." Guarducci (1989) p. 67.

ogy of inscriptions that have been held to be forged, such as *CIL* VI,5 p. 19*-213* nn. 101*-3093; V nn. 43* 2315* etc.[102] The phrase occurs also in *Parisinus* 1129, in connection with the discovery of a mirror, which is also recorded in a letter to Orsinus and which speaks instead of *dentro certi muri* (*Vat. Lat.* 4105 ff. 254-255). Far from recording some vague location, the phrase *in certe ruine* are used in connection with a clearly specified locality, namely the vineyard of the painter Giovanni Bellino on the Esquiline around the Baths of Trajan.[103]

Secondly, as we have seen, the reputation of Ligorio as a forger has been considerably questioned in the twentieth century as a result of the work of Mandowsky and Mitchell. We have seen that Ligorio's fabrications are of a limited kind in that they are subject to his plan of seeing or inferring the form of classical Rome in the ruins of renaissance Rome. As Mandowsky in an earlier work said:

> In his recreation of a mythical figure, it became his practice to use not just a single reference, but to endow it in his design with an accumulation of attributes derived from a variety of sources, often monumental and literary combined. The majority of Ligorio's critics have abused him as an irresponsible forger, who deliberately falsified his presentation of classical works... It is essential, however, to emphasise that Ligorio's method was by no means arbitrary but based on a definite plan; it was not his intention to invent the formal appearance of a mythical figure, but rather to revive it, by consulting as much ancient material, statuary as well as literary, as was available... it became a kind of idealised form of a personification which bodied forth the great variety of qualities that had been ascribed to it in ancient times throughout its cult.[104]

Though Ligorio was mainly concerned with mythological figures, as this quotation makes clear, we can nevertheless apply the method here to what he did regarding the discovery of an ecclesiastical Statue that we shall shortly argue was completely unsought by him. Smetius provided him with the "literary material" from Eusebius for the identification of the original Statue, which he proceeded to endow "in his design with an accumulation of attributes derived from a variety of sources, often monumental." Thus he reconstructed the ruined *sasso* on the analogy of statues of St. Peter, and of the slightly effeminate form of a typical renaissance cleric. But it is to be noted that his method is one of fabrication limited to a certain kind of inference. In completing statues generally, as in completing the Statue of

---

[102] Cited Guarducci (1989) p. 68 note 13.

[103] P. De Nolhac, Notes sur Pirro Ligorio, in *Mélanges Léon Renier*, in *Bibliothèque de l'École des Hautes Études* 73 (Paris: Vieweg 1887), p. 324-325 compares "Nell' Esquilie circa le Terme di Traiano, nella vigna di Giouan Bellino pittore, ove dentro di un muro in una fenestra murata fù trovato un specchio molto grasso," (*Parisinus* 1129) with "... dentro certi muri... fù prima trovato da Giouan Bellino pittore nella sua vigna nell' Esquilie." (*Vat. Lat.* 4105 ff. 254-255)

[104] E. Mandowsky, Some Observations on Pyrrho Ligorio's drawings of Roman Monuments, in Cod. B XIII 7 at Naples, in *RendPontAcc* XXVII (1952-1954), p. 340-341.

Hippolytus, he scrupulously respected the surviving features of the original fragments. This is precisely what we find in the case of the Statue where the joins that separate original from reconstruction are left bare for all to see where the one begins and the other leaves off.[105]

Ligorio made epigraphs to go with his reconstructed herm portraits. Some of these Guarducci cited, as we saw, in justification of her suspicion of Ligorio as a compulsive forger. It must however be asked, in the light of Mandowsky and Mitchell's convincingly argued rehabilitation, whether simply because an epigraph has been forged to locate a herm within his "syncretic creation" of an idealized *Roma triumphans* that it necessarily follows that his description of the original location has also been forged. The truncated and barely recognisable fragments could have come from where he says they were found, however much their significance has been interpreted in the light of a fanciful inscription to go with an equally fanciful reconstruction. As Mandowsky and Mitchell say:

> This is not to deny, however, that there was not sometimes perhaps an element of inference and conjecture in Ligorio's locations, just as there was in his restorations. Thus... his assertion that the socle (No. 29)—which was seen by Smetius and others in the Conservatori Palace with a statue of Hercules on it— actually came from the Forum Boarium may be an inference from Sabinus' location of the statue of Hercules in that forum. On the other hand it could equally well—and more probably—be the result of his independent inquiries... On the evidence of our manuscript, then, we can say this. *In no instance can a location of Ligorio's be proved definitely false.* In some cases his word is clearly corroborated by other witnesses; and *in many cases his statements are so circumstantial that they deserve credit.* In short, even where Ligorio is the sole authority for the provenance or even the existence of monuments his word—*prima facie*—deserves respect.[106]

There was a motive in the refashioning of a figure connected with his imaginative, syncretistic reconstruction, and hence with the epigraph labelling that reconstruction, quite apart from the epigraphy itself which may also betray the forgery. But we need to assign a similar motive for the invention of the place of discovery itself if we wish to include this in the forgery.

We have in the case of the Statue shown that the motive that Guarducci tries to give for the alleged forgery regarding the location simply does not exist. There was no documentary evidence still available in Ligorio's time that would have led Ligorio to assign the discovery to a ruined church on the left side of the via Tiburtina apart from San Lorenzo. There had never been any evidence at any time for the association of any such shrine with

---

[105] Mandowsky and Mitchell (1963) p. 43: "Like Smetius he devised a system of diacritical signs ("sic", etc.) to show the actual condition of the inscriptions in the originals, and while he had no such regular system to indicate the state of figured sculptures or to show where the originals stopped and his own restorations began, he nevertheless did occasionally show fractures in the stones (e.g., 36 and 111)..."

[106] Ibid. p. 43-44, my italics.

Hippolytus the writer with whom the Statue is associated. We have shown grounds furthermore that though Ligorio's own word is to be trusted outside a context in which such specific motives apply, in this case "his word is clearly corroborated by other witnesses," when we compare the quite different description of the place of discovery given by Smetius. Furthermore it must be noted that the date of the Naples *ms.* is 1553, the year, as we saw from Mandowsky and Mitchell, which was during the period of 'typical' reconstruction based on "actual surviving ruins," and not his later, imaginative 'syncretic' creation, as can be seen from a comparison between his maps of 1553 and 1561 (Plates 8-10).

We must further point out that in this case we do have a forged inscription by Ligorio assigning the Statue to a known frame of reference, even though in this case that frame of reference he holds in common with his contemporaries and it is not his own syncretic creation. His inscription on the base of the reconstructed Statue is: *Statua Hippolyti Portuensis episcopi... ex urbis ruinis effossa.* The inscription makes Hippolytus the bishop of Portus, his traditional See in the West from the time of the *Chronicon Paschale* (A.D. 630) and Anastasius Apocrisarius (A.D. 665).[107] It was the title of this See by which Ligorio was now to refer to Hippolytus, as in the Turin *ms.* (J.A. II 10, p.12).

It was indeed this inscription that perhaps led Baronius to infer that the Statue had been unearthed originally at Portus, later corrected by him, particularly in view of the remains visible there of the great sanctuary of Hippolytus recorded by Eneas Silvius Piccolominius on his visit to Isola Sacra in 1492.[108] Clearly if Ligorio had been inventing a place of discovery to match a forged inscription in this case he would have located the unearthing of the Statue at Portus. In consequence, the false identification with Portus in this inscription becomes another instance of the general lack of association of Hippolytus, whether writer or martyr, in separation from the cult of St. Laurence, with the Ager Veranus.

We see, therefore, that quite apart from issues of Ligorio's general reliability, a specific case can be made for the reliability of his location of the Statue. There was no motive for inventing the location that he gives in the literature, and the false inscription that he gives regarding Hippolytus' See conforms to popular expectations of the main location of his cult but is at

---

107 Lightfoot (1890) 1,III p. 344-345 and p. 428-430.
108 Baronius, *Martyrologium Romanum*, (Romae: Dominicus Basa 1586) p. 379: "Viget adhuc in Portu Romano memoria sancti Hippolyti...His adijcimus, eiusdem Romani Portus ruderibus effossum esse eiusdem Hippolyti antiquum marmoreum simulachrum solio insidens, in quo circumcirca Graecis litteris inscripti sunt cycli Paschales annorum sexdecim: quod inde Romam delatum, positum est in Vaticana bibliotecha." This description and location was repeated by him in *Annales ecclesiastici*, II (Romae: Ex typographia Vaticana 1590), p. 323: He corrected this latter editions of both works as "in agro Verano" and "Ex agro Verano, e Memoriae Hippolyti antiquae ruderibus effossum." See Testini (1989) p. 13.

variance with his description of the location on the Ager Veranus. We shall argue that the general events in Ligorio's own biography that surround the discovery of the Statue fit well with Ligorio's own record of that discovery.

1B 2.4.1. *Ligorio's biography and the discovery of the Statue*
We can indeed now seek to reconstruct the situation of the discovery in Ligorio's own biography around the year 1551, in the light of Mandowsky and Mitchell's most perceptive analysis. Guarducci located Ligorio at this time in a workshop near the Vatican Library where she alleged that he and Smetius worked on a Statue that they found in the Loggia originally transported there from a place unknown. But where is the evidence for Ligorio's activity in such a workshop at this time? Rather at this time, since 1549, Ligorio was in the service of his patron, Cardinal Ippolito II d' Este (1509-1572) who was the governor of Tivoli (1550-1555). Ligorio resided with him at Tivoli, some eighteen miles along the road to Tivoli, the self-same via Tiburtina itself, off which he claimed the Statue to have been discovered.

1B 2.4.2. *Ligorio and the Villa Hadriana*
Ligorio's major preoccupation at this time was the reconstruction of Hadrian's Villa at Tivoli, of which he was the architect. The work was inter-rupted (1552-1559) by Ippolito d'Este's fall from favour and his decision to join the French in Siena during the war between Charles V of Spain and France. Indeed, we have three records of payment for materials for the fabric of the villa in Tivoli and for various objects dated the 24th March, 1551, which name him as architect.[109] Ligorio resumed his work on the villa in 1559, which was completed before D' Este's death in 1571.

Thus Ligorio was active in Tivoli, authorizing documents for payment, on the 24th March, some twenty-three days before the 15th April 1551, when *Vat. Lat.* 3965 fol. 24, as we have seen, mentions the removal of the Statue from the Loggia to the Vatican Library. At this location, along the via Tiburtina outside the walls of Rome, he was preoccupied with the recovery of herms for the decoration of that and other villas. Leo X, on the 27th August 1515, had issued his Brief on the reconstruction of St. Peter's, and instructed Raphael to purchase on his behalf any suitable stones found within a ten-mile radius of Rome, and had appointed him Prefect in charge. The Brief furthermore prohibited stone-cutters from destroying any inscribed stones without Raphael's permission.[110]

The excavations at the Villa Hadriana therefore were conducted in the context of a commonly-assumed ground-plan for renaissance reconstruction.

---

[109] F.S. Seni, La Villa d' Este in Tivoli, in *Memorie Storiche tratte da documenti inediti*, (Roma: Tata Giovanni 1902), p. 53-56.
[110] Ibid. p. 15-16.

Raphael viewed the Gothic domination of Rome as destroying the classical style which he regarded as true art. Ligorio shared this common assumption as he sought ruined statues for classical reconstruction for Hadrian's Villa. It would not be surprising therefore in the course of collecting such statues over a wide area if there were drawn to his attention a putative classical statue with leonine feet in the Ager Veranus.

First of all he would regard this as requiring classical reconstruction, but then Smetius would be able to inform him that it was an ecclesiastical artefact. He then hypothesizes that under the spot from which it has been dug there must be, not a classical villa ruined by the Goths but, as an ecclesiastical counterpart, *un'altra chiesa dall'eretici rovinata*. It should be noted, moreover, that Fulvio Orsini bears testimony to the fact that the Villa Hadriana was not the only destination for ruined statues being actively recovered and reconstructed during this period.[111] There was thus a quite general transportation to and from that locatility and from a wide range of locations of unidentifiable headless and mutilated statues (*licet nonnullis literae tantum, deiectis vetustate capitibus*) on that side of Rome. If such statues were being actively recovered and brought to Rome from Tivoli itself, then there is no reason to doubt that a similar process was true of locations in the vicinity of the via Tiburtina far nearer to Rome.

We know that the site excavated by De Rossi had attracted attention in the century before Ligorio. Any hope that the shrine whose name, as we have seen, had slipped out of later editions of the *De Mirabilibus* (1 B 2.3.1.10-13) might be re-identified had lapsed when Martin V in 1425 issued the Brief for the reconstruction of the Lateran pavement, as we have already mentioned, as a result of which the *titulus* was removed from the entrance. We see therefore once again that the site was thus quite unidentifiable by Ligorio's time. But it was worked for stones, so that it was quite plausible that it should have been one of the localities whose ruins attracted Ligorio's notice for his particular concerns which were classical and not ecclesiastical.

Furthermore, we have direct evidence that some time prior to 1553 Ligorio observed the ruins of an unnamed church in the area of the Castro Pretorio, and to this we now turn.

1B 2.4.3. *The ruined church in the Castro Pretorio*
Ligorio published in 1553 his *Libro delle Antichità di Roma* under the patronage of Julius III. Here we have described the location of the Castro Pretorio described in words that mirror that of the *un'altra chiesa dall' eretici rovinata* (1 B 2.3.3). *Il castro pretorio* is located *tra la via*

---

111 Fulvius Ursinus, *Imagines et Elogia Virorum Illustrium, etc.*, (Lafrery-Formeis: Rome 1570), p. 6: "Ex iis autem quos impressimus, Hermis (sic enim statuas illas quadratas sine manibus, et pedibus nominandas esse existimamus) multi sunt superioribus annis ex Hadriani villa Tiburtina eruti, et Romam inde translati: licet nonnullis literae tantum, deiectis vetustate capitibus, supersint.."

Nomentana e Tiburtina... overo alloggiamento della guardia de gli Imperatori. He then continues:

> The Castrum was made of the most beautiful walls of brick, and of opus
> reticulatum, with painted appartments, with a most beautiful porch of columns
> made of cement, stuccoed over with supreme care, just as one sees in some
> fragments found beneath the ruins, other than those which are from modern
> church buildings after whose time everything noble has been subjected to our
> saints and to our Redeemer, Jesus Christ. In a place where there was such a
> church building there had been a church dedicated to one of our saints (but at
> what time did he live?) now the ancient and the modern church was
> devastated, and the entire site overgrown with vines and flattened.[112]

This ruined ancient church, the fragments of whose remains were distinguished by Ligorio from those of the Castro Pretorio itself and a more modern church, could or could not have been that mentioned by Ligorio in Naples XIII *ms.* B.7 p. 424 (1A 3) and subsequently discoverd in Msg. Gori's vineyard. But at very least this passage shows a real interest at the time of the construction of the Villa Hadriana of pre-critical renaissance excavations on Ligorio's part. If however he is recording the first discovery of the *altra chiesa dall' eretici rovinata*, then his inability to name it reveals no prejudiced disposition on his part to associate Hippolytus with that locality and so to devise on such a basis a fiction about the original location of the Statue.

1B 2.4.4. *Ligorio's interest in classical herms*

What Ligorio had been searching for at this time, over a wide area, for the Villa Hadriana and the Villa Julia and other places where classical civilization was to be reconstructed from the rubble, were herms, and other Statues, with Greek inscriptions, which, as we have seen, were in such short supply.[113] The number of herms with Greek inscriptions was small. There was for example the herm of Theophrastus in the Palazzo Maximus at S.

---

112 Pirro Ligorio, *Libro delle Antichità di Roma*, (Venetia 1553), p. 24: "Il Castro fu di
bellissimi muri fatti di mattoni, e d'opera reticolata, con le stanze dipinte, con un bellissimo
portico di colonne fatte di cimento, stuccate de sopra con somma diligentia, secondo che si vede
per alcuni pezzi trovati sotto le rovine, oltre quelli che sono ne tempii moderni, poi che ogni
cosa de gentile fù sottoposta alli nostri santi, e al nostro Redentore Giesu Christo. Nel luogo,
dove era quel tempio, fu fatta una chiesa dedicata à uno di nostri santi (ma secondo che'l tempo
è solito di fare) hora è annullata l'antica, e la moderna chiesa; e tutto'l sito è occupato di vigne,
e fatto piano." See also Ligorio as an authority on the site of the Castro Pretorio in Andrea
Fulvio, *L'Antichità di Roma*, (Francini: Venetia 1588), p. 200: "Ma Pirro Ligorio Napolitano,
che à tempi nostri fu buon Pittore, e eccellente disegnatore, antiquario, e architetto, nella
Chorografia, ò disegno di Roma antica ch'egli produsse, la quale fino hoggi in molti luoghi si
vede, locò i Castri Pretorii dentro le mura di Roma."
113 Ch. Hülsen, Die Hermeninschriften Berühmter Griechen und die ikonographischen
Sammlungen des XVI Jahrhunderts, in *Mitteilungen des k. D. Archeologischen Instituts Rom*
(Roma: Lincei 1901) Bd. XVI p. 123-208 and plates VII and VII.

Pantaleus. There was also a statue of Philemon with an inscription mentioned by Piero Valeriano, who is a reliable witness.[114]

Pighius, a well-known associate of Smetius and Ligorio during his period in Rome, which corresponds to the period under discussion (1547-1555), saw stone figures at the *latebrae* at Tivoli (= S. Maria in Pisone) which he encouraged Julius III to use for the building of his new villa in front of the Porta del Popolo. Indeed, Pighius had assisted Smetius in the decipherment of the tables on the Statue.[115] These figures were truncated herms with names such as Themistocles, Miltiades, Isocrates, Heraclitius, Aristogiton etc. They were transported to Julius III's house "on the Flaminian way on this side of the Milvian Bridge (*ad flaminiam viam citra pontem Mulvium*)" from where Hadrian had originally located them in his villa at Tivoli.[116] Thus Pighius, a transcriber of the inscriptions on the Statue along with Smetius substantiates his and Ligorio's interest at that time in Greek statues, and in herms in particular. That interest was moreover focused on Tivoli itself, some twenty miles out along the via Tiburtina.

To be sure, in 1901 Hülsen mistrusted Pighius' account because it had possibly come from Ligorio himself, on the grounds of the latter's notoriety at that time as the forger of inscriptions and statues. He claimed rather that the herms had come from the Villa Julia.[117] But Hüslen wrote before the rehabilitation of Ligorio's general reliability, outside of the special contexts that we have described, attested by the work of Mitchell and Mandowsky that we have been following. Guarducci cannot simply resurrect the pre-Mandowskyan scepticism about Ligorio simply to sustain her preconceived position.

Ligorio clearly therefore had a known and much publicized interest in the recovery of herms and other kinds of statues that was vigorously achieving results around 1551, as we have seen. It is by no means implausible that his attention should be drawn to a mutilated Statue in ruins from which stones had already been taken earlier for the pavement of the Lateran basilica and which was clearly already in use as a quarry for stones for such purposes, on the road to Tivoli where he was at this time engaged on the restoration of Hadrian's Villa. There is no reason why, as we have seen, that he should have invented such a location for an ecclesiastical artefact in which he had otherwise no interest, in view of his aims to restore the artefacts of classical

---

114 Ibid. p. 125.
115 Smetius (1588) ff. 27 and 38 cited by Guarducci (1989) p. 65.
116 "Colligi ex fragmentis, quae nuper ibidem vidi cum titulis adhuc suis, utpote Themistoclis, Cimonis, Alcibiadis, Isocratis, Aeschinis, Aristotelis, Carneadis, Aristogitonis, et Aristophanis... plurimas eius generis statuas a Graecis in villam suam Tiburtinam transtulisse Hadrianum imperatorem colligo ex fragmentis." Pighius, *Imagines*, quoted Hülsen (1901) p. 127.
117 Pighius *Imagines* p. 34-42: "Pyrrhus Ligorius Neapolitanus a quo multa accepimus quae ad huius libri institutum pertinent." cf Hülsen (1901) p. 141.

civilisation. While it is true that Pighius did not include this Statue in his drawings of the herms found at Tivoli, this may be accounted for by the absence of classical relevance.

1B 2.4.5. *Ligorio and the Leonine Statues in* Vat. Lat. *3439*

Where a drawing of the Statue does occur is in *Vat. Lat.* 3439 of Fulvius Orsinus. Now this manuscript is clearly related to Ligorio's Naples manuscript.[118] Dated somewhere between 1564 and 1570, it incorporates many items of the Naples manuscript completed in 1553.[119] Guarducci has identified the Statue as originally female in form, correctly, as we shall argue shortly. The Statue also is characterized by lions' heads on the two arms, and lions' paws at each of their feet. Now the one ecclesiastical Statue sticks out like a sore thumb in both the manuscript of Orsinus (*Vat. Lat.* 3439) and Ligorio amongst the general classical examples. Its presence in Orsinus can only be there, set in reverse for printing, because of the features that it shares in common with pagan statues, namely the leonine features of the chair and the feminine figure seated there.[120]

Both Ligorio and Orsinus were thus clearly interested in statues of this kind as well as herms at this time. The Naples *ms.* (Mandowsky (1963) cat. 17 p. 63) shows mutilated drawings of a seated female dedicated to *Deae Syriae* with two lions seated at the foot of her chair, which is replicated in *Vat. Lat.* 3439 fol. 120.[121] Furthermore Folio 92 of the latter shows a drawing of two female figures with the right bust exposed, each of whom are wearing boots with leonine figures around their tops. In *fol.* 99, above the inscription: βίος·τὸ ζῆν γλυκὺ·τὸ θανεῖν ὑποψία, we can see a female reclining on a *chaise-longue* with right breast almost bare. There is furthermore a table with three leonine legs. On the bends in the legs lions' heads are drawn and the feet of the legs are lions' paws, just like the feet and sides of the chair of the Statue. Such a *motif* is also continued in folios 100,

---

[118] P. de Nolhac, Notes sur Pirro Ligorio, in Mélanges Léon Renier, in *Bibliothèque de l'École des Hautes Études* 73 (Paris: Vieweg 1887), p. 263: "Ligorio avait exécuté pour lui un grand nombre de dessins à la plume d' après l' antique... Ils ont été réunis dans un recueil célèbre, où Borghesi a reconnu le premier la main de Ligorio, et qui a été plusies fois depuis utilisé par la science; j' ai nommé le 3429."

[119] Mandowsky and Mitchell (1963) catalogue no. 62 must have been included before the death of Julius III (1555) as it refers to "nostro signore Giulio tertio."

[120] P. de Nolhac, La Bibliothèque de Fulvio Orsini, in *Bibliothèque de l'École de Hautes Études* 64 (Paris: Bouillon and Vieweg 1887), p. 23: "Un archéologue... le trop fameux Pirro Ligorio, avait entretenu avec Orsini des rapports assez suivis, et exécuté pour lui un grand nombre de dessins à la plume d'après l'antique. Ces œuvres, presque toutes assez soignées, représentent des bas-reliefs, statues, cippes, utensiles, meubles, etc., et comprennent des restitutions et plans d'édifices, des croquois de monuments, des inscriptions et les fragments du plan de Rome au Capitole. Ils ont été réunis dans un recueil célèbre, où Borghesi a reconnu le premier la main de Ligorio... j'ai nommé le 3439..."

[121] A similar *motif* is found in cat. no. 5 Juppiter Dolchenus, where there is a bull rather than a lion on either side of a chair. Mandowsky and Mitchell (1963) p. 17.

107-110, and 114. The herm depicted in folio 124v ΣΑΠΦΩ ΕΡΕΣΙΑ, was also mentioned in the Naples *ms.* as destined for the Belvedere Theatre.[122]

Ligorio's interest in finding and unearthing, not simply ruined herms, but ruined female statues with leonine features—an interest which Orsinus shares and extends—is clearly witnessed therefore in the Naples *ms.* and *Vat. Lat.* 3439. Sappho Eresia was intended for the Belvedere Theatre, like the Statue itself according to the Turin *ms.*[123] As such the Statue is of a piece with the unearthing of other such finds, sought by Ligorio for similar purposes, whilst working from 1549-1553 on the Villa Hadriana.[124] As Mandowsky and Mitchell remind us: "Most of the items in Naples XIII B.7 came from Rome or from the route between Naples and Rome where Ligorio was on home ground."[125] Though the feminine features of the Statue and the leonine feet would have commended it to Ligorio, the ecclesiastical character, revealed by Smetius' decipherment and translation of the Greek inscriptions, would have left him somewhat at a loss where to place it in his grand classical scheme.

The position of the Statue in the Belvedere Theatre would therefore have been an afterthought rather than a premeditated spot for a Statue whose location had been forged. Even then Ligorio still had to find a relevance for it with reference to the classical ambience of Aelius Aristeides. If such classical *motifs* as the leonine feet and the half-bare breasted female were well known as the interests of the circle of Ligorio and Orsinus, it is highly probable that such an artefact as the Statue would have been brought to Ligorio's notice from a site on left hand side the via Tiburtina which was the road to Tivoli and therefore to the scene of Ligorio's reconstruction of the Villa Hadriana for his patron Ippolito d' Este. That the Statue would have been brought to Ligorio's notice rather than sought out by him is more probable in view of the fact that his interests were always classical and never patristic.

We have thus submitted Guarducci's claims regarding the allegedly fictitious location of Ligorio's discovery to such searching analysis because the location is vital to our interpretation of the character and significance of the

---

[122] Mandowsky and Mitchell (1963) p. 140 Appendix III.

[123] J.A. II 10, p.12: "Costui [sc. Elio Aristide] scrisse le lodi di Roma... et per premio i Romani li posero la statua in Capitoglio, che per haventura potrebbe esser' la sudetta che si trova nel palazzo Apostolico, presso la imagine di Hippolito vescovo portuense, restaurata dal medesimo pontefice Maximo per essenti scritto nei lati della sua sedia alcune cose belle, come le feste delli Hebrei." Quoted by Guarducci (1977) p. 18-19. See also Mandowski (1963) p. 123-124.

[124] In Mandowsky and Mitchell's (1963) catalogue we have the following herms from Tivoli and its environs: no. 79 Heracleitus. ("Fù anche nella villa Caiana o Germania Tiburtina," Ligorio Turin 23 p. 42), which Pighius drew independently and located there also; no. 81 Aristogiton; no. 83 Thales (Esquiline Turin 23 p. 100 Ursinus Tivoli); no. 86 Euripides (headless). (Villa Hadriana Turin 23 p. 78); no. 87 Hesiod (Villa Hadriana Turin 23 p.142); no. 143 Theophrastus (Tivoli naples Naples *ms.* XIII. B.7. p.405).

[125] Ibid. p. 42.

Statue in its original setting. Guarducci's current argument that the Statue was originally feminine in form and destined originally as a monument for the Pantheon Library dedicated to Severus Alexander rests heavily, as we shall now further argue, on her success in disentangling the Statue from Ligorio's original setting in the cult-centre on the via Tiburtina. We have argued that this attempt has failed. But let us nevertheless turn to her further analysis, which we shall argue notwithstanding will have positive merits in revealing the true character of the Statue, and of the early third century Roman, Christian community whose icon it was.

CHAPTER TWO

THE STATUE AND THEMISTA OF LAMPSACUS

The role of the Statue in the Hippolytan Community

Guarducci changed her originally favourable opinion regarding Ligorio's reliability as a witness to the original location of the Statue. She has however been consistent in her claim that the Statue was originally feminine and of the *grande dame* of Epicurean philosophy, Themista of Lampsacus. In Part A of this chapter we will be exploring her more convincing case for this identification, and drawing conclusions of our own for the character of Hippolytus' community which treasured such an artefact. We shall argue that, in reality, the dispute about the location of the Statue that we considered in Chapter 1 is a dispute about the kind of artefact that the Statue represents, and about the precise significance it had in the life of the Roman community. The original location of the Statue is important in so far as it relates to its original function and the significance that it bore.

Guarducci now wishes to argue that the Statue's original significance was that of a monumental tribute to the inclusive religious policy of the Severans, as witnessed by an account of Severus Alexander's private chapel (*lararium*), and the purported interest of Julia Mamaea's court in Christianity. This is undoubtedly why she has accepted the burden, so difficult as we have shown, of demonstrating that its original location was in fact unknown, and not the cult centre on the via Tiburtina (1B 2). In that event she can divorce the Statue from any role in the discourse of meaning of a Christian community at whose centre, on the via Tiburtina, we shall argue that it originally stood, as the original house-church which the martyr shrine was to replace in course of time.

In other words, she must set the Statue free from its usually accepted place of discovery if it is to bear the significance of being a monument to the emperor Severus Alexander, outside the community of faith, and not one with a significance internal to that community. In Part B we shall therefore be examining in detail the case in principle for the location in the Pantheon Library as part of the Severan cultural ambience of an alleged *filo-cristianesimo,* as opposed to a weaker syncretistic tolerance. We shall explore in this part of our chapter the critical references to our literary sources which might be held to establish such a strong *filo-cristianesimo*— as opposed to a weaker tolerance—in the pagan context of which Guarducci would explain the significance of the Statue, external to the Hippolytan community, and outside the church.

PART A. TRANSFORMATION OF THEMISTA OF LAMPSACUS

Guarducci examined Ligorio's two sets of notes and drawings preserved in the Naples and Turin libraries, to which we have already drawn attention (1A). In consequence she came to the conclusion that the figure, albeit mutilated, was originally feminine in form, as the drawings indicated (Naples *ms.* XIII B 7, p. 424).[1] In one respect she thus followed Bovini's earlier comparison of the figure on the Statue with the female depiction of the Catechista in the catacomb of Praetextatus, who had also claimed that an ealier statue of a philosopher had been remodelled as a personal monument to Hippolytus (Plates 15 and 24).[2] But Guarducci was the first to regard the figure itself as allegorical, and not a personal depiction of a Father of the church of the early third century. As her account of Ligorio's restoration has been directly challenged, we begin with a discussion of that challenge.

2A 1. *The identification of the original with Themista*

It must be emphasized that the primary evidence for the Statue as originally feminine rests primarily upon Ligorio's notes and drawings, and what can be inferred from them regarding the Statue whose original condition had been *guasta* and *malamente trattata* (1A 1 footnote 5). As Guarducci has more recently made clear, Ligorio's restoration involved the use of two different Statues with feminine features, both of which replaced whatever figure was originally depicted on the Chair.[3] But D'Onofrio's account had threatened to cut the link between those drawings and the mutilated Statue by claiming that what was described in *Vat. Lat.* 3965, folio 24 (1B 1 and 1B 2.1) as *il sasso dove è iscritto il Calendario greco* was in fact simply a

---

[1] M. Guarducci, La Statua di sant'Ippolito, in *Epigrafia Greca* IV (Istituto Poligrafico dello Stato: Roma 1978), p. 535-545; ——, La statua di «sant' Ippolito» in Vaticano, in *RPARA* (1974-5), p. 166-170; ——, La Statua di «sant'Ippolito», in *StEphAug* 13 (1977), p. 17-30; ——, La «Statua di sant' Ippolito» e la sua provenienza, in *StEphAug* 30 (1989), p. 61-74.

[2] For the picture of the Catechista, see G. Bovini, Sant'Ippolito, dottore e martire del III secolo, in *Coll. amici delle catacombe* 15 (Città del Vaticano: Pontificio Istituto di Archeologia cristiana 1943), p. 79, and for its reconstruction p. 80-81. See also Plate 24.

[3] M. Guarducci, *San Pietro e Sant'Ippolito: Storia di statue famose in Vaticano*, (Istituto Poligrafico dello Stato: Roma 1991), p. 115: "Costui infatti pensò di utilizzare per la creazione di un «Sant'Ippolito» due mutile statue antiche assai diverse l'una dall'altra... and p. 118: "due mutile statue antiche, ambedue femminili, e una parte aggiunta, o fatta aggiungere, dall'ingegnoso Pirro Ligorio." See also p. 121. But cf. E. Mandowsky and C. Mitchell, *Pirro Ligorio's Roman Antiquities. The Drawings in ms. XIII. B.7 in the National Library in Naples.* (London: Warburg Institute 1963) p. 105 (no 101. p. 424) where it is claimed: "The head, shoulders, and hands are restored." For a photograph of the drawing see ibid. plate 60 a. The authority cited is B. Nogara, *Guida ai Musei del Laterano*, (Vatican: Rome 1948) p. 37. See also Plate 6.

chair, or rather a rock-like object (=*il sasso*), deprived of any identifiably seated figure except for a section of groin (*bacino*). Indeed he argues that *sasso= saxum* has precisely this connotation.[4] The usual meaning of *sasso* in Italian is "rock" and the ruined chair would have thus resembled originally a piece of rock.[5]

Guarducci accepts that there existed lower and upper parts of two originally quite different statues used to reconstruct what was in the original, surviving chair itself.[6] In this respect she and Ferrua are in agreement, despite their disagreement over the original forms and location of the Statue.[7] Ligorio's drawings and notes thus become critical as evidence for what was seated on the Chair, information which an archeological analyis of the artefact in itself can, subsequent to its 'restoration,' no longer give us. If those drawings and notes show that the two female statues used in the restoration were true to the feminine figure originally seated there, then Guarducci's further argument about the true character of the original feminine figure can proceed. If the original figure was in such a state of ruin that only the groin was visible, then the feminine reconstruction has no bearing on the original form of the seated figure. Why Ligorio placed a female rather than a male figure there could only then be explained, as D'Onofrio does, tenuously and speculatively, with reference to the effeminate stereotype of a renaissance cleric perhaps typified in the attire of St. Laurence in one contemporary statue who also holds a book in his hand.[8]

Guarducci correctly, I believe, maintains that the drawings and notebooks do not depict what Ligorio envisaged as a reconstruction, but what he saw in the ruined Statue that stood before him. What he saw and described, by contrast with what was entered roughly in an account book to register a payment (*Vat. Lat.* 3965, folio 24), was an **imagine** *che siede rotta et mal trattata* (1A 2). The drawing in the Naples *ms.* accompanying his description shows a female torso and shoulders, apparently with one breast bare,

---

[4] C. D'Onofrio, *Un Popolo di Statue Racconta: storie, fatti, leggende della città di Roma antica, medievale, moderna*, (Romana Società: Rome 1990), p. 94: "Sicché, in definitiva, ne concludi che soltanto quel settore del bacino (che è anche di marmo diverso dagli altri due) assieme al seggio), è la parte veramente originaria e originale di una figura che stava seduta... una figura seduta cui mancava tutta intera la parte superiore, del bacino..."

[5] Ibid. p. 96: "Di antico, in tal modo, restava soltanto il bacino ed il seggio con la lunga scritta in greco... conciata in questo stato, la statua non appariva più come una statua, ma soltanto un sasso..."

[6] See footnote 2 with which cf. D'Onofrio (1990) p. 94: "Ridotta in tali condizioni, perché ritornasse «statua» ora aveva bisogno di un rifacimento totale sia della parte superiore, sia di quelle due parti che in precedenza abbiamo riconosciuto (il che è sotto gli occhi di tutti) come aggiunte «moderne.»"

[7] A. Ferrua, Recensione [on Dal Covolo, *I Severi ed il cristianesimo*] in *CCa* 141 (1990), on *ICUR* VII, 19933-935, says, p. 409: "... l'analisi moderna fattane dai Musei Vaticani ha dimostrato che è un raccozzamento di pezzi diversi incoerenti sicché non si può dedurne quale fosse primieramente." Therefore he feels safe in concluding: "È certo però che i cristiani del sec. III stimarono la statua, che allora era completa, come effigie del dottore cristiano sepolto nella catacomba di S. Ippolito, come dimostrano le tre epigrafi."

[8] Ibid. p. 98 and p. 100 fig. 56.

which itself is dressed as a female person. Clearly the reconstruction of the head and the shoulders as a feminine form was suggested by a whole torso, and not simply a groin, which itself was feminine. Clearly this original design, actually executed as described in the Turin *ms.* J.A. II,10 and III 11, fol. 52v as the male St. Hippolytus in 1563, was by this time changed. But the Naples *ms.* XIII B7, fol. 424s, written some ten years before, in 1553, had clearly shown not what was planned some ten years later, but what was seen to warrant the upper torso of a female person, which accordingly was sketched roughly (Plate 6). As we have already mentioned, that sketch was also found in Fulvio Orsini's *ms.* Vat. Lat. 3439, fol. 124a (1B 2.4.5).[9] Bertonière noted that Ligorio's sketch in the Naples *ms.* shows that the truncated seated figure already existed and was added to, so that the lower portion never was an amorphous marble block.[10]

It had always been absurd, in terms of the history of Christian representative art, to believe that, in the first half of the third century, there could have been constructed a marble Statue of a Father of the Church seated on a throne with leonine feet. Early Christian art self-consciously refused the pagan, classical models in which statuary or portraiture represented the individual personality that it depicted. Characteristically the early Christians constructed symbolic, and even cryptographic, art such as that exhibited by the anchor, Jonah and the Whale, loaves and fishes, etc. which contained their own hidden meaning regarding Christ's salvation and his spiritual gifts.[11]

If Toynbee and Perkins were correct in their interpretation of the iconography of the two rows of mausolea that stood on the Vatican hillside before Constantine's basilica of St. Peter, then there were pagan counterparts to such symbolic and cryptographic art. The floor mosaic depicting the Rape of Persephone, for example, in the Tomb (I) of the Quadriga, contains the telltale figure of Hermes Psychopompus which converts the whole scene into an allegory of the soul's escape from death. The Lunette of Tomb G in which is depicted the Teacher or Steward likewise has an allegorical and eschatological significance. Furthermore, the famous mosaic of Christ/Apollo riding his chariot from the sun in the Tomb (M) of the Julii, surrounded by vine leaves which were no longer Bacchanalic but Eucharistic symbols,

---

[9] Cf. also Guarducci (1991) p. 119.
[10] G. Bertonière, The Cult Center of the Martyr Hippolytus on the Via Tiburtina, in *BAR International Series*, 260 (1985), p. 5: "However, much of the original lower portion of the seated figure has been preserved today despite the reworking of some of this area by Ligorio. Furthermore, the sketch made by Ligorio before his work of restoration shows that he found this lower frontal area largely intact. Thus the Christian "adaptation" did not remove this frontal portion of the seated figure."
[11] W. Lowrie, *Art in the Early Church*, (New York: Pantheon 1947), p. 24-28, 63-80 ff. See also 2A 3.2.

demonstrates graphically the syncretistic ability of early Christian art to transform its pagan models in its own symbolic terms.[12]

But if that was the likely character of the particular example of Christian art that Ligorio remodelled as the Statue of Hippolytus, we must ask who or what was represented by the original Statue, and what was the precise nature of the symbol into which it was transformed by an early Christian community? Guarducci regards the leonine features of the protruding feet of the chair as typical of statuary depicting Epicurus and his philosophic disciples. The lion was characteristic of Samian art and of art in South-West Asia Minor, and Samos was Epicurus' birthplace. Such Statues were found exposed in the Epicurean κῆπος, the characteristic meeting place of an Epicurean school. It is attractive, given the feminine features of the drawings of the unreconstructed Statue, and indeed the shape and folds of its robe as it stands today, particularly at the hem around the feet, to connect the original with a female Epicurean philosopher.[13]

The "representative" figure of the lady philosopher, in a philosophical school that accepted women and men equally, was, as can be ascertained from the literature, the figure of Themista of Lampsacus, wife of Leontius, whose correspondence with Epicurus is quoted in Diogenes Laertius, and to whom the former dedicated a book. Cicero and Seneca mention her as a famous Epicurean philosopher, and so her fame spread to the Roman as well as Greek world. Guarducci concludes that this particular copy of her Statue could have been executed at Rome, to judge from the stylistic characteristics of the leonine throne, at the beginning of the second-century in the age of Trajan or, latest, Hadrian (117-138). It was Themista, therefore, whom the Statue originally depicted.

It must be noted that the general existence of statues of Themista is a matter of conjecture. It will be well therefore for us to look more carefully at the stages in her argument that produce this conjectural conclusion. Having thus shown the original character of the Statue (2A 1) we shall at a later point be then in a position to discuss into what arguably such a Statue underwent a process of symbolic transformation in the immagination of Hippolytus' community (2A 2).

2A 1.1. *The archaeology of the identification with Themista*
Guarducci does not produce any examples of photographs of any figure of Themista herself.[14] Rather she produces photographs of Epicurus' statue at Athens, itself naturally a male figure, seated on a chair with lions heads and feet decorating its arms and legs (fig. 9 p. 175). Furthermore all the surviv-

---

12 J. Toynbee and J. Ward Perkins, *The Shrine of St. Peter and the Vatican Excavations*, (London: Longmans Green 1956), p. 75-96, 109-117.
13 Guarducci (1974-5) p. 180-182; Guarducci (1977) p. 19-20, 30; Guarduci (1978) p. 536; Guarducci (1989) p. 62-63.
14 Guarducci (1974-5) p. 175-178 cf. (1991) p. 118-119, figs. 45-46.

ing statues are male. The 'Epicurus' from Athens has by its side an unnamed male philosopher (fig. 10 p. 175) also on a chair with leonine features. Further examples of Epicurus are found in the Archaeological Museum of Florence (fig. 11-12 p. 177) and of an unnamed male philosopher from the Capitol Museum at Rome (fig. 13 p. 177). The National Museum of Naples furnishes us with a statue of Metrodorus of Lampsacus, and the museum at Ostia a statue of Ermacus of Mytilene (figs 14 and 15 p. 178). Both have chairs with leonine features, and both were known members of Epicurus' school, the latter succeeding to the headship. Other examples have been found at Ince Blundell Hall in Lancashire, and in the American Embassy in Rome which today stands on the site of the Villa Margherita.[15]

Thus the association with Epicurus and his disciples of seated leonine statues is proven. The problem with this particular Statue is that it is feminine in form. The folds of the robes and the hemline are almost stereotypes of female clothing in Roman statuary (fig. 7 p. 169). Moreover, the "supple line of the neck" observed by Mariani in the drawings, traces of an abdomen with remains of an umbilical cord covered with a light layer of material a part of which is still visible, etc. point conclusively in this direction (Plate 1).[16] One conclusion is that the Statue was originally that of a goddess. We have already made reference to *Deae Syriae* which Ligorio's Naples' *ms.* shares in common with that of Orsinus (1B 2.4.4). There is, for example, a statue of Athena on a throne with leonine feet discovered in the theatre of Dionysius at Athens.[17] But according to the drawing, and corresponding to the reconstructed Statue, this female figure holds a volume between her hands so that a goddess cannot be implied.[18]

The veneration of Epicurus' school was for their master and his associates rather than for the gods who were present but with a highly reduced significance in his atomic universe.[19] Cicero makes the Epicurean Pomponius mention that he could not forget his master though dead because of the pictures of him that his disciples possessed along with likenesses on drinking cups and rings.[20] Pliny, in lamenting the decline of living

---

[15] Ibid. p. 176. See also G.M.A. Richter, *The Portraits of the Greeks*, (London: Phaidon 1965), figs 1212-1213, 1216-1217, upon which latter an alien head has been reconstructed as in Ligorio's case.

[16] Guarducci (1977) p. 21: "Le braccia infatti si addicono più ad una donna che ad un uomo; decisamente femminile poi (osserva giustamente il Mariani) è la linea flessuosa del collo,". and p. 29: "... l' addome con indicazione dell'ombelico era.. ricoperto di stoffa leggera (una zona di esso è ancora visibile nell'originale... la femminiltà risulta anche dalla ricostruzione a disegno delle braccia, dei seni, del collo." See also Guarducci (1974-75) p. 167-169.

[17] A. Giuliano *et. al.*, *Villa Adriana*, (Roma: Silvana 1988), p. 52.

[18] Guarducci (1991) p. 120-121.

[19] A.J. Festiguère, *Epicurus and his Gods*, (Oxford: B. Blackwell, 1955) and C. Bailey, *The Greek Atomists and Epicurus*, (Oxford: Clarendon Press 1928), p. 438-481.

[20] Cicero, *De Fin.*, V, 1, 3: "...nec tamen Epicuri licet oblivisci, si cupiam, cuius imaginem non modo in tabulis nostri familiares sed etiam in poculis et in anulis habent."

portraiture, also mentions representations (*Epicuri voltus*) of Epicurus displayed in bedrooms and carried around on their persons, though the reference here is clearly to medallions rather than statues.[21] Guarducci thus seeks a female equivalent of Epicurus, as a venerated teacher of his school, as the person depicted on the original Statue.

The one name that fulfilled such a feminine role was Themista of Lampsacus, whose significance is, however, identified in literary rather than archaeological remains. We shall now examine the relevant literary references.

2A 1.2. *The literary identification with Themista*

Cicero, in the dialogue already mentioned, rebukes the Epicurean Torquatus for following the principle of pleasure, which has never produced examples of the self-denying heroism of Lycurgus, Solon and others. One should talk of such men as these rather than of great volumes about Themista (*quam tantis voluminibus de Themista*). Cicero is referring here neither to volumes "dedicated to Themista" in the sense of their authors mentioning their composition in her honour, despite what Rackham's translation might otherwise suggest, nor is the reference to books about her teaching as a philosopher.[22] There was one teacher in the Epicurean school, Epicurus. Themista is introduced rather as a symbolic figure—almost as the Greek counterpart of effeminate pleasure to the masculinity of Stoic philosophy in Roman hands.[23] It would be difficult therefore from this passage alone to infer that Themista was the kind of person with whom to identify hypothetically an originally headless statue.

Cicero also seems to make similar symbolic use of Themista in his attack on Piso. The latter ought not to reproach those who desired the laurel crown because their military successes were small any more than despise his own great accomplishments in this field won by himself with little dangers. He indeed does not despise these granted that he is "wiser than Themista (*sis licet Themista sapientior*)." Once again the contrast is between Themista as the representative of Epicurean pleasure on the one hand, and the self-sacrifice leading to great Roman military achievements on the other.[24] Once

---

21 Pliny, *H.N.*, XXXV, 2,5: "Itaque nullius effigie vivente imagines pecuniae, non suas reliquunt. Iidem palaestrae athletarum imaginibus et ceromata sua exornant, Epicuri voltus per cubicula gestant et circumferunt secum."

22 Cicero *De Fin.* II, 21,68: "Would it not be better to talk of these *rather than devote those bulky volumes to Themista.*" (My italics)

23 Ibid. II, 21,67-68: "Numqam audivi in Epicuri schola Lycurgum, Solonem, Miltiadem, Themistoclem, Epaminondam nominari, qui in ore sunt ceterorum philosophorum omnium. Nunc vero, quoniam haec nos etiam tractare coepimus, suppeditabit nobis Atticus noster e thesauris suis quos et quantos viros! Nonne melius est de his aliquid quam tantis voluminibus de Themista loqui? Sint ista Graecorum; quamquam ab iis philosophiam et omnes ingenuas disciplinas habemus; sed tamen est aliquid quod nobis non liceat, liceat illis."

24 Cicero, *In Pis.*, 26,63: Quos si reprehendis quod cupidi coronae laureae fuerint, cum bella aut parva aut nulla gessissent, tu, tantis nationibus subactis, tantis rebus gestis minime fructum laborum tuorum, praemia periculorum, virtutis insignia contemnere debuisti. Neque

again Themista is used not by an adherent of Epicurus himself as a great ex-
ponent of his philosophy, but by a critic to emphasize the femininity of the
Greek school in contrast with masculine Roman virtues.

However, we do have a reference to Themista in Diogenes Laertius, in-
dicative of her importance, from what must originally have come from an
Epicurean source. We have mention, immediately following the record of
Epicurus' death from paralysis, of "Leonteus of Lampsacus, and his wife
Themista, to whom Epicurus wrote letters."[25] A book was dedicated to her
with the title Νεοκλῆς πρὸς Θεμίσταν, who was another disciple of
Epicurus.[26] We will have occasion to treat in greater detail (7B 5.2) the
significance of letter writing in Diogenes' work which itself parallels the
letter writing of the διαδοχαί of James and Peter in the *Clementines*.[27] Both
Leonteus and Themista are described as ἐλλόγιμοι, as are the successors of
the apostles (Clement *Cor.*, 44,4), and the usual formula applies throughout
the list that they head (διαδεξάμενος... ὃν διεδέξατο).[28] As clearly one who is
ἐλλόγιμος and included in the διαδοχή, Themista could therefore, as
Guarducci suggests, have been, on Diogenes' evidence, the subject of an
Epicurean statue with leonine feet which Ligorio was to reconstruct. But
what of Christian writers themselves?

2A 2. *Early Christianity and Themista of Lampsacus*

Despite the general antagonism of the Church Fathers against Epicurus and
his school, Themista is mentioned by Clement of Alexandria favourably.
Such a favourable mention helps to explain why an Epicurean statue could
be taken over by Hippolytus' Christian community. Affective acknowledgment can sometimes accompany cognitive rejection, and we shall argue
that such affective affinity could exist between the school of Jesus,
represented for example by the Johannine community, and the school of
Epicurus. Clement reflects his conviction that philosophy was the school-
master bringing the Greek to Christ as the Law had the Jews when he gives
a list of names of distinguished women, beginning with Judith, Esther, and
Susanna, in the middle of which come Greek heroines too. His purpose is to

---

vero contempsisti, sis licet Themista sapientior, sed os tuum ferreum senatus convicio verberari
noluisti."
    [25] Diogenes Laertius, *Succ.*, 10, 25: ἐτελεύτα δὲ παραλύσει, γενόμενος ἱκανὸς ἀνήρ.
Λεοντεύς τε Λαμψακηνὸς ὁμοίως καὶ ἡ τούτου γυνὴ Θεμίστα, πρὸς ἣν καὶ γέγραφεν ὁ
Ἐπίκουρος. For the letter to Themista see X,5.
    [26] Ibid. 10, 28; Guarducci (1974--5) p. 181.
    [27] See also A. Brent, Diogenes Laertius and the Apostolic Succession, in *JEH* 44,3 (1993),
p. 375-380.
    [28] Ibid. 10,25: καὶ οὗτοι μὲν ἐλλόγιμοι, ὧν ἦν καὶ Πολύστρατος ὁ διαδεξάμενος
Ἕρμαρχον ὃν διεδέξατο Διονύσιος· ὃν Βασιλείδης...

show that "it is possible for a man as well a woman to participate in this perfection."[29]

We can thus see that there is substance to Guarducci's conjecture that the Statue was originally a female counterpart to a statue of Epicurus in the κῆπος, and that the female figure in question was that of Themista. The references in Cicero would not themselves have suggested the existence of such a statue. But those of Diogenes Laertius and Clement of Alexandria make its hypothetical existence plausible, even though no actual statues have as yet been discovered apart from the one reconstructed by Ligorio as Hippolytus. It would also explain Cicero's references to Themista as the corporate embodiment of the Epicurean school, and as such meriting iconographic expression evocative of affective response.

Moreover, if the Statue originally had been that of a lady philosopher and not a goddess, this would make it clearer as to how a Christian community at Rome in the early third century could have taken over the Statue and inscribed it with paschal and easter calendars and a list of titles of works. Such a statue, in view of the assumptions of early Christian art, could only be given an allegorical meaning, but indeed the figure itself, as Cicero's allusions make clear, would already have symbolised the spirit and ethos of a philosophical school rather than representing the personality of an individual. The iconographic and allegorical assumptions were already there in the pagan artefact which eased the way for its Christian re-interpretation. But as *prima facie* an Epicurean statue of a human lady representing the spirit of Epicurus' school might not appear any more acceptable to a Christian community than one of a goddess, we must now examine more closely the possible grounds for its acceptance and use by Hippolytus' community.

2A 2.1. *Christianity and the school of Epicurus*
One solution to the problem is that Ligorio's was not the first reconstruction. There are examples of heads of Marcus Aurelius placed upon female figures. Pliny criticises the decline of the custom of transmitting exact likenesses in portraiture. Not only is there very little difference between the figures shown in silver designs on bronze monuments commemorating a particular individual, but "heads of statues are exchanged for others (*statuarum capita permutantur*)."[30] It is possible therefore that, for example, a statue of Athena seated on a leonine throne, of which we have seen there are exam-

---

[29] Clement, *Stromat.* 4,19: ταύτης τοι τῆς τελειότητος ἔξεστιν ἐπ' ἴσης μὲν ἀνδρὶ ἐπ' ἴσης δὲ καὶ γυναικὶ μεταλαβεῖν... Ναὶ μὴν καὶ Θεμιστὼ ἡ Ζωΐλου, ἡ Λαμπακηνὴ, ἡ Λεοντέως γυνὴ τοῦ Λαμψακηνοῦ, τὰ' Ἐπικούρεια ἐφιλοσόφει...

[30] Pliny *H.N.* XXXV, 2,4: "Imaginum quidem pictura, qua maxime similes in aevum propagabantur figurae, in totum exolevit. aerei ponuntur clipei argentea facie, surdo figurarum discrimine; statuarum capita permutantur, volgatis iam pridem salibus etiam carminum. adeo materiam conspici malunt omnes quam se nosci..."

ples, could have been decapitated and reused by the Hippolytan community, or indeed a statue of Themista such as Guarducci hypothesizes—soundly, as I believe—to have existed.

There are however good grounds for rejecting a pre-Ligorian reconstruction of the original. Notwithstanding examples of reused statues from the time of Caligula and Nero, in the age of Alexander Severus marble was abundant. There was therefore no need to re-use older monuments and to re-model them.[31] Furthermore, the existence of the head of a church leader of the early third century on an earlier statue is quite incongruous with what we know about early Christian iconography which was symbolic and allegorical and not representative, as we have seen (2A 1). If however it is difficult to believe that a Christian group could have taken over the statue of a goddess, is it any easier to believe that they felt at home with an Epicurean statue of a lady philosopher?

Guarducci at this point has made too much of the implacable Christian opposition to atomistic and ethical Epicureanism, and so concluded that it was only with extreme difficulty that they could ever have taken over and made into their own artefact such a such a statue. Guarducci may be substantively correct in so far as, at the level of formally articulated doctrines, the Christian faith was incompatible with Epicureanism and according condemned by Fathers such as Tertullian.[32] But as we have seen, Clement of Alexandria at least was able, contemporaneously with Hippolytus, to disengage his admiration for Themista as a person, whom he includes with Esther, Judith, and Susanna as a seeker after the pre-existent λόγος in their use of reason, from the epistemological and ethical assumptions made by their philosophy.

Moreover, recent work has pointed out that at the level of community ethos and organisation there are formal comparisons to be made uniquely between the school of Epicurus and Christian schools of the late first and second centuries. Simpson notes that though "there were fundamental antitheses between Epicurean mechanistic materialism and Christian providential theism... temperamentally... they were not dissimilar." Indeed he argued that both Octavius, and Minucius in the *Octavius,* are converted Epicureans and not Stoics as is commonly believed.[33] Seen from the

---

[31] Guarducci (1977) p. 20.

[32] Tertullian, *De Anima* 46,2: "Vana in totum somnia Epicurus iudicavit liberans a negotiis divinitatem et dissolvens ordinem rerum et in passivitate omnia spargens, ut eventui exposita et fortuita."

[33] A.D. Simpson, Epicureans, Christians and Atheists in the Second Century, in *Transactions of the American Philological Association* LXXII (1941), p. 372-381. The full quote is :"There were fundamental antitheses between Epicurean mechanistic materialism and Christian providential theism, between Epicuran tranquility in accepting annihilation at death and Christian confidence in joyous immortality... Temperamentally however they were not dissimilar, for both showed themselves impatient with sham, certain of their own convictions,

external pagan standpoint, both Epicurean and Christian schools seemed similar both in ethos and in particular charges brought against them. Both vigorously rebutted the accusations of atheism, and both asserted free-will as the foundation for ethics against Stoicism.[34]

But more specifically, there is a connection between the ethos of the Epicurean school and the community represented by the Johannine literature in the New Testament.

2A 2.2. *Epicurus and the Johannine School*

Culpepper has argued that "Epicurus' garden was probably the first philosophical school intentionally established by its founder."[35] Around both the discourses and personality of Epicurus there arose a devotion by his followers unmatched by those of Plato, Aristotle, or Chrysippus. He wrote epitomes of his work and required his students to commit them to memory, and Cicero mentions the κυρίαι δόξαι or "authoritative doctrines". (*De Fin.* 2, 20)[36] A pertinent example of this devotion is Lucretius, who describes Epicurus as a semi-divine figure who has personally redeemed his followers from the fear of death by means of the atomic theory that establishes that death is disintegration and the after-life an illusion.

As Culpepper further notes, τέκνα and φίλοι were the characteristic descriptions of members of the sect/school—φίλοι in relation to each other, τέκνα in relation to Epicurus who is called πατήρ (Lucretius *Rer. Nat.* 3,9)—who gathered for a common banquet. The ethos of calm friendship at a common meal, is characteristic of the community of the Fourth Gospel as found in the Farewell discourses (*Jn.* 14-16). φίλος is used specifically of members of the community of Jesus in *Jn.* 11, 11; 15, 13-15, and 3 *Jn.* 15. τέκνα is similarly used in Jn. 1, 12; 11, 52 and throughout the Johannine epistles.[37] Epicurus in his Will mentions a common meal on the twentieth of each month in honour of himself and Metrodorus and also the celebration of his birthday once a year (Diogenes Laertius, *Succ.* X, 18,22). Such sentiments of personal thanksgiving to Epicurus were therefore orchestrated and developed generally by members of his school.

---

willing to challenge commonly accepted ideas, and believers in the practical value of community living." p. 379.

[34] Ibid. p. 373-375. Simpson compares Lucian, *Juppiter Tragoedus*, 4: καὶ ὁ μὲν Δᾶμις [ὁ Ἐπικούρειος] οὔτ᾽ εἶναι θεοὺς ἔφασκεν οὔτε ὅλως τὰ γιγνόμενα ἐπισκοπεῖν ἢ διατάττειν and Minucius Felix, *Octavius*, 19,8: "Etiam Epicurus ille, qui deos aut otiosos fingit aut nullos, naturam tamen superponit" with Justin *Apol.* I, 13,1: ἄθεοι μὲν οὖν ὡς οὐκ ἐσμεν, τὸν δημιουργὸν τοῦδε τοῦ παντὸς σεβόμενοι or I, 6,1· ἔνθεν δὲ καὶ ἄθεοι κεκλήμεθα· καὶ ὁμολογοῦμεν τῶν τοιούτων νομισμένων θεῶν ἄθεοι εἶναι... and Athenagoras *Legatio* 4: οὐκ ἐσμὲν ἄθεοι.

[35] R.A. Culpepper, The Johannine School: An evaluation of the Johannine-School hypothesis based on an investigation of the nature of ancient schools, in *Society for Biblical Literature* DS 26, (Missoula Montana: Scholars Press 1975), p. 101.

[36] Ibid. p. 108.

[37] 1 *Jn* 3, 1-2, 10; 5, 2; 2 *Jn.* 1, 4, 13; 3 *Jn.* 4, cf. Culpepper (1975) p. 272-273.

So far our discussion would connect the ethos of the Johannine community with that of Epicureanism and therefore with the feelings and emotions associated with Themista's Statue. But there would appear to be some more specific links with Hippolytus' community in itself, and not through its links, albeit complex, with the Johannine community, and to these links we now turn.

2A 2.3. *Epicurean ethos and the Hippolytan community*

As προεστώς of his school, Epicurus seems to have received "first fruits (ἀπαρχαί) for the care of his sacred body, both for himself and his children (εἰς τὴν τοῦ ἱεροῦ σώματος θεραπείαν, ὑπέρ τε αὐτοῦ καὶ τέκνων),"[38] and this practice seems to be reflected in the injunctions regarding what is to be given to bishops in *Ap. Trad.* 31, as we shall discuss in greater detail later (6 C 4). Culpepper considers that "the words "sect" or "cult" describe some aspects of the Garden better than "school"."[39] We shall argue later in greater detail (7 B 5.1) that the Hippolytan sacerdotal image of the bishop as high-priest are his or his community's imposition on the original, Irenaean teaching model. Furthermore, DeWitt has argued that the Epicurean school was organised hierarchically, with Epicurus as ὁ σόφος, but beneath him Metrodorus, Hermarchus, and Plyaenus as φιλόσοφοι or καθηγεμόνες, with καθηγηταί as next in rank. These taught two groups of pupils, the συνηθεῖς and the κατασκευαζόμενοι.[40] The latter is of course the Greek equivalent of the Latin word *catechumeni*. Given, as we shall see in chapter 6, the external appearance of second century Christian communities at Rome to a collection of rival philosophical schools, we do well to note the common ethos of such schools bears comparison to that of Epicurus. But we see here in the hierarchical organisation which places a catechumen at the lowest rung of learner and catechist at the lowest rung of teacher a specific parallel with what the *Ap. Trad.* 15, 17 and 18 reveals to us in particular about the Hippolytan community.[41]

Such are the direct links between the school-ethos of the Epicurean Statue and the Hippolytan community. The indirect links through the Johannine community are, as I mentioned, more complex and now require more detailed consideration.

---

[38] H. Usener, *Epicurea,* (Leipzig: B.J. Teubneri 1887) fr. 130, p. 141,9; Plutarch *Adv. Col.* 1117E.

[39] Culpepper (1975) p. 106.

[40] N.W. DeWitt, Organisation and Procedure in Epicurean groups, in *ClPl* 31 (1936), p. 208-211.

[41] *Ap. Trad.* 15: "Qui autem adducuntur noviter ad audiendum verbum, adducuntur primum coram doctores priusquam omnis populus intret...," *Ap. Trad.* 17 (*Ap. Con.* 32, 16 (*Ep.*): Catechumeni per tres annos audiant verbum (ὁ μέλλων κατηχεῖσθαι τρία ἔτη κατη-χείσθω)..." and *Ap. Trad.* 18 (*Ap. Con.* 32,17 *Ep.*): "Quando (ὅταν) doctor cessavit instructionem dare (κατηχεῖσθαι), catechumeni orent seorsum..."

2A 2.4. *The paschal chronologies of Hippolytus and St. John*

Although φίλοι and τέκνα are not characteristic descriptions used by the Hippolytan community of its members, ἀδελφοί is. We find this word used rhetorically and frequently in *Contra Noetum*.[42] but also in the *Elenchos*, specifically of the Christian community that suffered from Callistus' fraud, and that watched him bringing under his spell the allegedly simple Zephyrinus. In connection with Callistus' teaching activity, the words φιλία and κατασκευάζων are used. [43] In the post-resurrection accounts of the fourth gospel, this word describes the community (*Jn.* 20,17 and 21,23). Moreover, throughout 1 *Jn.* 3-5 and 3 *Jn.* ἀδελφοί is used in the context of the mutual moral obligations that members of the community have towards each other. The constant and continuous use of this term as a characteristic description of the community is found elsewhere in the New Testament only in *Acts* (e.g. 1,14-16; 9,30; 15,1 etc.).

Similarly this is also the case with the term ἀγαπητοί. It is used occasionally as a parainetic expression.[44] But in 1 and 3 *John* it occurs nine times in the three chapters of the former and the fifteen verses of the latter.[45] The characteristic Johannine expression ἀγαπητοί is used also in *El.* V, 26,5; IX, 11,4. The use of the two characteristic Johannine terms, ἀγαπητοί and ἀδελφοί is suggestive of a Johannine ethos of the Hippolytan community in which the evocative associations of Epicureanism at an effective level makes plausible the claim that Themista's Statue would not have been alien on such a level.

We should further note the acceptance by the Hippolytan community of the Johannine dating for the last supper. The ἀπόδειξις χρόνων τοῦ πάσχα, inscribed upon the right side of the Statue, dates the crucifixion on the 25th March (14th Nisan), 29 A.D. and we have apparent citations of this work in the *Chronicon Paschale* by an anonymous Byzantine writer of the 7th century. He refers to a work that he attributes to Hippolytus martyr and bishop of Portus in the phrase ἐν τῷ πρώτῳ λόγῳ τοῦ περὶ τοῦ ἁγίου πάσχα συγγράμματος. Here we find an attempt to argue for the date of the Crucifixion on Friday 14 Nisan, the day of the Passover, and against the synoptic chronology, so that the Last Supper could not have been a Passover

---

42 *C.N* . 3,2; 4,8; 8,3; 9,1; 14,1; 15,3; 16,1 or μακάριοι ἄδελφοι 17,2. Butterworth saw the rhetorical character as part of the features of a diatribe into which *genre* he sought to place this work, see R. Butterworth, Hippolytus of Rome, Contra Noetum: Text introduced, edited, translated, in *Heythrop Monographs* 2 (1977), chapter 4.

43 In *El.* IX, 11,1 [of Callistus' influence over Zephyrinus]: ἔπειθεν αἰεὶ στάσεις ἐμβάλλειν ἀνὰ μέσον τῶν ἀδελφῶν, αὐτὸς τὰ ἀμφότερα μέρη ὕστερον κερκώπων λόγοις πρὸς ἑαυτοῦ φιλίαν κατασκευάζων. In 12,1 of Callistus' fraud: ᾧ οὐκ ὀλίγαι παραθῆκαι τῷ χρόνῳ ἐπιστεύθησαν ὑπὸ χηρῶν καὶ ἀδελφῶν προσχήματι τοῦ Καρποφόρου. In 12,5, of the intercession of the church to Carpophorus on Callistus' behalf: προσελθόντες ἄδελφοὶ παρεκάλουν τὸν Καρποφόρον.

44 Excluding the later 2 *Peter* and *Jude*, in *Rom.* 12,19; 1 *Cor.* 10,14; 15,58; 2 *Cor.* 7,1; 12,19; *Philip.* 2,12; 4,1; 1 *Thess.* 2,8; 1 *Tim.* 6,2; *Heb.* 6,9; *Jam.* 1,16,19; 2,1

45 1 *Jn.* 2,7; 3,21; 4,1,7,11; 3 *Jn.* 2,5,11.

meal. Thus the contrary synoptic text of *Luke* 22,15-16 is reinterpreted so as to favour the Johannine date.[46]

We must remember that such chronological arguments in the second and third centuries did not service objective academic inquiries into Christian origins. Rather chronological positions of this kind tended to constitute symbols of particular group identity, and thus serviced and conserved cultural differentiation in what Judge and Lampe have argued to be the fractionalized Roman community of the late second and early third century.[47] We shall return to a more detailed consideration of his thesis (5A 2.4.2). Here we should briefly note that the first examples of schism or potential schism was the Quartodeciman practice, whose representative at Rome appears to have been Blastus, to whom Irenaeus addressed a letter περὶ σχίσματος.

Eusebius' account associates Blastus for no other reason apparently than the contingency of archival material about all three of them, with the Valentinian Florinus and with the Montanists.[48] But as Pseudo-Tertullian

---

[46] C. Martin, Un περὶ τοῦ πάσχα de s. Hippolyte retrouvé? in *RecSciRel* 16 1926, p. 148-65; V. Loi, Il 25 Marzo data pasquale e la cronologia giovannea della Passione in età patristica, in *EphLit* 85,1 (1971), p. 48-69; ——, L'identità letteraria di Ippolito di Roma, in *StEphAug* 13 1977, p. 67-71; ——, L' omelia «In sanctum Pascha» di Ippolito di Roma, in *Aug* 17 (1977) p. 461-484; R. Cantalamessa, L' omelia «In S. Pascha» dello Pseudo-Ippolito di Roma, in *Scienze Filologiche e Letteratura,* (Milan: Società Editriche vita e pensiero 1967). H. von Campenhausen, Ostertermin oder Osterfasten? Zum Verständnis des Irenäusbriefs an Viktor (Euseb. Hist. Eccl. 5,24,12-17, in *VCh* 28 (1974) p. 119: "Es geht, sagt er, nicht nur um die Frage, wann die Fasten zu beenden und das Passa zu feiern sei, sondern es bestehen auch erhebliche Unterschiede in der Dauer der Fasten selbst. Die Osterfasten waren damals zwar schon in der ganzen Kirche üblich, wurden aber in den einzelnen Gemeinden oder Kirchengebieten verschieden lang gehalten und in verschiedener Weise berechnet."

[47] E.A. Judge, *The Social Pattern of the Christian Groups in the First Century,* (London: Tyndale 1960); ——, The Early Christians as a Scholastic Community II, in *JRH* 2 (1961), p. 125-137; ——, The Early Christians as a Scholastic Community I, in *JRH* 1 (1960), p. 4-15; ——, The Social Identity of the First Christians. A question of Method in Religious History, in *JRH* 11 (1980) p. 210-217; ——, Christliche Gruppen in nicht christlicher Gesellschaft, in *Neue Studienreihe* 4 (Wuppertal 1964); P. Lampe, Die stadtrömischen Christen in den ersten beiden Jahrhunderten, in *WUNT* 2,18 (1989), p. 302-334. See also J.S. Jeffers, *Conflict at Rome: Social Order and Hierarchy in Early Christianity,* (Minneapolis: Augsburg Fortress 1991).

[48] Eusebius' reflections on Blastus are, to say the least, confused, particularly when he insists on associating him with the gnostic Florinus. associated with Florinus. In V, 15,1 his language suggests that they were associated in his eyes alone: "Florinus was expelled from the presbyterate of the church (Φλωρῖνος, πρεσβυτερίου τῆς ἐκκλησίας ἀποπεσών) and Blastos with him (Βλάστος τε σὺν τούτῳ)" implies at first sight membership of the same group, but the "fall" (πτώματι) with which he is described as "afflicted" (κατεσχημένος) is only "similar" (παραπλησίῳ) "These drew away more from the church (οἳ καὶ πλείους τῆς ἐκκλησίας περιέλκοντες) and introduced them to their own opinion (ἐπὶ τὸ σφῶν ὑπῆγον βούλημα), each attempting to innovate regarding the truth in their *own way* (θάτερος ἰδίως περὶ τὴν ἀλήθειαν νεωτερίζειν πειρώμενος). The words italicized suggest they led separate groups. *H.E.* V, 20,1 mentions a letter of Irenaeus περὶ σχίσματος, addressed to Blastus, just before he sets out the former's letter to the Valentinian Florinus and it may simply have been the justaposition of the two letters in the archives of Aelia Capitolina that lead Eusebius to associate the two. Certainly Blastus is not associated with Florinus in the extract from Irenaeus' letter itself. The distinction between schism and heresy is worth pointing to here although it cannot be stressed with the tightness of later definition in the Fathers of the second century. As Lampe (1989) p. 326-333 ff. points out that the general charge against second century heretics

makes clear, Blastus' claim was that "the Passover ought to be observed according to the law of Moses on the 14th day."[49] Thus Blastus' schism was Quartodeciman in its claims and represented at Rome that which, as Polycrates of Ephesus' letter to Victor of Rome makes clear, was the Asiatic cultural practice associated with the historical traditions of those groups. The Quartodeciman practice of holding the Easter celebrations on 14th Nisan, irrespective of the day of the week on which it fell, was an inviolable part of a culture and considered on the same level as ancestral graves (*HE* III, 31,2; V, 24-25).

The Johannine date of the crucifixion was central to the Quartodeciman claims, as Polycrates reveals when he claims that it was κατὰ τὸ εὐαγγέλιον, namely St. John's.[50] But as the letter of Irenaeus makes clear, the cultural practice was not principally about the date of a festival in itself, but also the length of the associated fast.[51] It is of course important in this connection not to antedate the recognition of Good Friday as distinct from Easter Day itself, celebrated in the West on the Sunday after the 14th Nisan, as opposed to the 14th Nisan itself in the East. As the homily of Melito of Sardis (A.D. 160-180) makes clear, the 14th Nisan was the day of celebration of the cross *and* resurrection for the Quartodeciman East. The fast extended from the 14th Nisan to near dawn on the 15th, with baptisms administered between an agape-meal and a Eucharist at cockcrow. Death and new life, the sacrifice of the paschal lamb and deliverance, crucifixion and resurrection were thus celebrated as a continuous event.[52]

If we compare this situation with what is proposed on the Statue, we find some interesting differences between the observation of a community which wished both to acknowledge the Johannine date of the Crucifixion, but wished to accommodate nevertheless to the Western, Roman practice.

2A 2.5. *The Statue, the* Elenchos *and the Quartodecimans*
The Easter Calendar inscribed on the left side of the Statue proposes that the day of the resurrection be transferred to Sunday in accordance with the

---

at Rome is that they left the church themselves rather than being expelled, as was the case with Marcion and Valentinus.

[49] Pseudo Tertullian, *Adv. Haer.* 8,1: "Est praeterea his omnibus [sc. haereticis] etiam Blastus accedens, qui latenter Iudaismum vult introducere. Pascha enim dicit non aliter custodiendum esse, nisi secundum legem Moysi XIIII mens. Quis autem nesciat, quoniam evangelica gratia evacuatur, si ad legem Christum redigis?" Cf. W.H.C. Frend, *The Rise of Christianity*, (London: Darton Longman and Todd 1984), p.341-342.

[50] *H.E.* V, 24,2-6: Ἡμεῖς οὖν ἀραδιούργητον ἄγομεν τὴν ἡμέραν, μήτε προστιθέντες μήτε ἀφαιρούμενοι. καὶ γὰρ κατὰ τὴν Ἀσίαν μεγάλα στοιχεῖα κεκοίμηται.... ἔτι καὶ Ἰωάννης ὁ ἐπὶ τὸ στῆθος τοῦ κυρίου ἀναπεσών... οὗτοι πάντες ἐτήρησαν τὴν ἡμέραν τῆς τεσσαρεσκαιδεκάτης τοῦ πάσχα κατὰ τὸ εὐαγγέλιον...

[51] *H.E.* V, 24,12: οὐδὲ γὰρ μόνον περὶ τῆς ἡμέρας ἐστὶν ἡ ἀμφισβήτησις, ἀλλὰ καὶ περὶ τοῦ εἴδους αὐτοῦ τῆς νηστείας. οἱ μὲν γὰρ οἴονται μίαν ἡμέραν δεῖν αὐτοὺς νηστεύειν, οἱ δὲ δύο, οἱ δὲ καὶ πλείονας.

[52] O. Perler, Melito de Sardis sur la Pâque et fragments, in *SC* 123 (Paris 1966), p. 53; S.G. Hall (Ed.), Melito of Sardis: On Pascha and Fragments, in *OECT* (Oxford: University Press 1972). See also Frend (1984) p. 240-241.

Western practice regarding the "day of the sun" celebrated in Justin Martyr *Apol.* I, 67. I say "proposes" that it be "transferred" rather than "records that it is the case" because both the Johannine dating of the crucifixion and the paschal table on the right hand side emphasize the importance of 14th Nisan and would otherwise support the Quartodeciman practice. It is in the light of a group that shares the ethos of the Johannine and Asiatic tradition that we can understand the less than censorious description of the Quartodecimans in *El.* VIII, 18,1.

Although the Quartodecimans are here described as "loving discord (φιλόνεικοι)," their practice is considered their one divergence from the apostolic tradition.[53] Moreover, the particular accusations of the Quarto-decimans as following Jewish custom here parallels pseudo-Tertullian's description of Blastus,[54] and so confirms our identification of him as the Quartodeciman representative in Rome, despite Eusebius garbled account. This kind of criticism is precisely what we should expect from a community that has developed a compromise but is impatient with the failure of exponents of an extreme version of their own position to follow them in this regard.

Irenaeus revealed that the issue was as much about the length and character of the fast as it simply was an academic dispute about the correct date of Easter. The different disciplines of fasting in the fractionalized Roman community of the late second and early third century would have provided a powerful mechanism for sustaining and promulgating those cultural differences. We can thus see here, in the programme for Easter celebrations on the sides of the Statue, a sociological means of both distinguishing the Hippolytan group from the Quartodecimans under Blastus excommunicated by Victor with their agreement, and their own divergence from the Western tradition of Callistus with whom they were later to cease communion.[55]

The Table on the Statue makes it clear that if the Sunday following the 14th Nisan is to be observed as the Easter festival, the Sunday itself cannot be included as a fast day. If Sunday fell on the 14th Nisan in a Quartodeciman community, it would have had to be held as a fast, as Melito of Sardis shows that any 14th Nisan was for such a community. Prominently, after stating in the heading of the table that in Severus Alexander's first year full moon occurred on Saturday 13th April, and recording that it will take place in the following years as in years past as stated, we read that: "the fast must be broken off on the Sunday

---

[53] *El.* VIII, 18,2: ἐν δὲ τοῖς ἑτέροις οὗτοι συμφωνοῦσι πρὸς πάντα τὰ τῇ ἐκκλησίᾳ ὑπὸ τῶν ἀποστόλων παραδεδομένα.

[54] Ibid. 18,1: ὑφορώμενοι τὸ γεγραμμένον ἐν τῷ νόμῳ... οὐ προσέχουσι δὲ ὅτι Ἰουδαίοις ἐνομοθετεῖτο, τοῖς μέλλουσι τὸ ἀληθινὸν πάσχα ἀναιρεῖν τὸ εἰς ἔθνη χωρῆσαν καὶ πίστει νοούμενον, οὐ γράμματι συντηρούμενον. Cf. *Adv. Haer.* 8,1 cited footnote 49.

[55] For a discussion of excommunication in early third century Rome , see Chapters 6 and 7.

(ἀπονηστίζεσθαι δὲ δεῖ οὗ ἂν ἐνεπέσῃ κυριακή)."⁵⁶ In other words, Sunday was abrogated expressly as a fast day.

Furthermore, the Table is insistent on two principles, namely that the fast associated with the 14th Nisan must be kept on the one hand, but on the other hand the Sunday directly dissociated with it. The principle lead to an obvious problem, namely what to do if the Sunday itself was 14 Nisan. When this happens, or indeed if Sunday immediately follows a Saturday that is Nisan 14th, the Easter feast is deferred from both Nisan 14 and Nisan 15 and transferred to the immediately following Sunday. Thus in A.D. 222 the 14th Nisan falls on the Ides April (13th) which is a Saturday and marked with the letter Z accordingly on the Paschal Table.

Accordingly on the corresponding Easter Table, Easter Sunday (marked there by ΚΥ) is eight days latter, on 11 Kalends May (21st May). In 283 for example, Hippolytus proposes that Easter would follow seven days after 14th Nisan or 15 Kalends April (18th March) on Sunday (marked Σ) which is 8 Kalends April, namely 25th March. Thus the inscribed instruction was directed against either the 14th Nisan itself or the Sunday after 14th Nisan if that Sunday happened to follow immediately on a Saturday.

An instruction such as this is not given where there is no grounds for its not being observed. It is therefore to be read here in the context of a community that otherwise would have fasted on a Sunday if it had been part of an original 14th Nisan Easter celebration. It is a community that would, moreover, have continued its fast on the 14th Nisan for as many days as separated that day from the following Sunday which would now be a period of variable length, and those variable lengths will be expressed by the Table in which full moon will fall on different days of the week for eight years when it returns to its original day.⁵⁷ Thus there would have been a difference between the cultural practice of Hippolytus' community both with the Quartodecimans and Western Roman communities on the length and nature

---

⁵⁶ *ICUR* 7, 19933 and Guarducci (1978), p. 539. The full inscription reads:
ἔτους α´ βασιλείας Ἀλεξάνδρου αὐτοκράτορος ἐγέ–
νετο ἡ δι᾿ τοῦ πάσχα εἰδοῖς Ἀπρειλίαις σαββάτῳ ἐμ–
βολίμου μηνὸς γενομένου, ἔσται τοῖς ἐξῆς ἔτεσιν καθ–
ὼς ὑποτέτακται ἐν τῷ πίνακι. ἐγένετο δὲ ἐν τοῖς παρω–
χηκόσιν καθὼς σεσημείωται. ἀπονηστίζεσθαι δὲ
δεῖ οὗ ἂν ἐνεπέσῃ κυριακή.
For a full transcription of the Table see Migne P.G. tom. 10, p.874-885; H. Leclercq, "Hippolyte (Statue et Cimitière de Saint)," in *DACL* 6 Pt. 1 cols 2419-2483.
English Translation:
Salmon (1873) p. 83:
"In the first year of the reign of Caesar Alexander, the fourteenth day of the Paschal moon occurred on Saturday April 13, after the intercalary month. It will fall in the following years as set out in the table, and it has fallen in past years as indicated. The fast must always be broken off on Sunday. "
⁵⁷ Salmon (1873) p. 84. For a general description of the problem of calendars in the early church see W.K. Lowther Clarke and C. Harris, *Liturgy and Worship: A Companion to the Prayer books of the Anglican Communion*, (London: S.P.C.K. 1936), p. 202-210.

of the Easter fast arising out of their commitment to the Johannine dating of the crucifixion.

The practice of the Easter fast was notoriously divergent in the pre-Nicene church, and it is important not to read the Lenten fast of forty days back to this early period. Guarducci has misinterpreted the significance in this regard of the instruction of the Statue to break the fast, and in consequence failed to interpret it in the context of the essentially fractionalized character of the second-century Roman community to which Lampe has drawn attention. There is no evidence that there existed a fast "of some weeks (*di alcune settimane*)" which was then interrupted when a Sunday occurred, nor that the fractionalized Roman community revealed in *El.* IX and elsewhere possessed a uniform practice in this regard, as Guarducci asserts (*Ippolito e la sua cerchia... e probabilimente anche gli altri cristiani di Roma*).[58] We shall return to a consideration of this matter in 3A 2.

For the moment, let us therefore note the quite complex relation that appears to hold between the Hippolytan community and both that of Victor on the one hand and the Quartodecimans on the other. We are witnessing, in the community for which the Statue was a clearly central artefact, how the calendar had to be changed by a group that otherwise had espoused the Quartodeciman practice, but now was modifying that practice in quest for a *modus vivendi* with Western congregations at Rome. The fast became extended for as many days as lay between 14th Nisan and that Sunday. To claim that the crucifixion took place on Passover Day, 14th Nisan is not of course to maintain that the 14th Nisan should be observed always as Easter Day, the day of the crucifixion and resurrection being rolled into one, as appears to have been the Quartodeciman practice from the homily of Melito of Sardis. Hippolytus' community was therefore adopting one mediating position between the Eastern and Western practice for celebrating Easter. His contemporary Julius Africanus, followed by Anatolius of Laodicaea, was the first to propose what later became the universal practice of dating the crucifixion on Friday 23rd March, and the day of the resurrection on Sunday 25th March.[59]

I submit that the Statue, therefore, had clearly a function of importance to the inner-life of the Christian community that preserved it. But that function must of course have been a symbolic one. However much the image may, at an affective level, have evoked positive community response, at the

---

[58] Guarducci (1977) p. 28 claims following E. Vancandard, "Carême," in *DACL* 2 (1910) 2141 that "Se ne deduce che a quei tempi Ippolito e la sua cerchia, e probablmente anche gli altri cristiani di Roma, osservano prima della Pasqua un digiuno di alcune settimane, che però interrompevano ad ogni domenica."

[59] Our knowledge comes from later citations in *Chronicon Paschale* and the *Chronographia* of George Syncellus, see V. Grumel, *Traité d' Études Byzantines*, vol. 1: La Chronologie, (Paris: 1958) p. 23, 28, 92 cited by Loi (1971) p. 60-61

cognitive level of that community there was no sympathy with an Epicurean world-view. 'Themista' must have therefore assumed an allegorical or symbolic significance quite removed in Christian eyes from a pagan and atheistic lady philosopher. A robed female figure might represent Science, or a particular discipline, probably in this case the figure of Astronomy or Arithmetic in view of the requirement of such disciplines for the computation of the Paschal Calendar. We must therefore now ask precisely how and for what purpose the statue of Themista underwent allegorical and symbolic transformation in the life of the Hippolytan community.

2A 3. *The significance of the symbolism of the Statue*

The Statue was thus an artefact expressing, through its Paschal Calendar, a distinct cultural identity, the desire to maintain which was significantly heightened by the liberalism of Callistus. Already that community had changed part of its practice, considered apostolic, regarding the date of the Passover, in response to the demands of Victor. In consequence, Guarducci is wrong to infer from the fact that an Epicurean lady philosopher, reinterpreted allegorically, originally stood there that the Statue could not be an ecclesiastical artefact but was intended for the pagan library of the Pantheon.

The immediate impact made by the Statue upon the observer is not the catalogue of works on the plinth but rather the Paschal and Easter Tables on the sides of the chair (Plate 2). This would be particularly the case if, as is almost certain, the Statue stood originally at a tangent to a wall to which it was attached. Roman statuary was not normally free-standing but structurally attached in this way. Testini was to regard it as a funeral monument situated in such a position.

Whatever the original character of the Statue, however, and whether its significance was within the community or in its external relations with the pagan world, it must be accepted that the female figure that sat on the Chair was interpreted allegorically by a Christian community. As we saw in 2A 1, early Christian art was allegorical and symbolic, and self-consciously eschewed pagan representational portraiture. Indeed, we also saw from out reference to Pliny (*H.N.* 35,2) that pagan representational portraiture during this period was also in decline. (*Imaginum quidem pictura, qua maxime similes in aevum propagabantur figurae, in totum exolevit.*) This had lead to an "absurd incoherence of shape (*surdo figurarum discrimine*)," when "the heads of statues were altered (*statuarum capita permutantur*)."

As such, it may have been the case that people desired to identify themselves with allegorical or symbolic forms rather than transmit their actual likeness, and certainly, as we have mentioned, Toynbee and Perkins seem to have interpreted the funerary sculpture of the Vatican excavations along such lines (2A 1). Of course, conservative critics of art forms like Pliny invariably attribute innovations to a desire for empty display (*adeo materiam conspici malunt omnes quam se nosci*) rather than take seriously the reasons for their production.

When however a Christian community in the second century took over such a Statue, it would have been to give the Statue a wholly symbolic form rather than to associate general valued attributes to a new head that would replace an old one, given the Judaeo-Christian aversion to graven images. We have argued that, at an effective level, there were associations between such a Christian community and the spirit of a philosophical school, to which the Johannine community and the Easter and Paschal Calendars, as well as the existence of catechists also point. Such a Statue, reinterpreted allegorically, would well stand for the collective personality of the community of Hippolytus.

More particularly, the particular iconographic function of the transformed imagery of the Statue would be doctrinal, and express therefore a doctrine characteristic of the party position of the school/church. Externally, as Bardy, La Piana and Barnard originally pointed out in papers that we shall be discussing in Chapter 4,[60] the Church of Rome of the second century resembled a group of conflicting philosophical schools, however much internally both Irenaeus and the *Elenchos* may use the terms διδασκαλεῖον pejoratively. Just as the dating of Easter on the Tables inscribed on the sides of the chair enabled us to locate a party position within that conflict, so too the iconography of the Statue itself may enable us to do likewise. Was the figure of Themista allegorised as Astronomy or Mathematics in view of the astronomical knowledge presupposed by those tables? Or was the figure more generally that of Σοφία or Wisdom?[61]

2A 3.1. Σοφία, Contra Noetum, *Tatian and Athenagoras*

Certainly the Statue re-interpreted as σοφία would have fitted a community whose λόγος-Christology set it at variance with Callistus' group. There has been a tendency to regard the literary profile of the author of *C.N.* as that of a conservative biblical exegete untouched by contemporary philosophical and religious currents. We shall demonstrate, in 5A 8.4 and 5B 3.1.1-2, that this is a quite facile assessment. We shall show there how his exegesis of the New Testament passages on Christ as the Second Adam contain shadows of the Naasene psalm reconstructed by Frickel from the *El.* The school of

---

[60] G. Bardy, Les écoles romaines du second siècle, in *RevHE* 28 1932, p. 501-532.; L.W. Barnard, The Church of Rome in the first two centuries, in *NTS* 10 1963-4 p. 251-260; G. La Piana, *Il Problema della Chiesa Latina in Roma*. (Roma: 1922); ——, *La Successione episcopale in Roma e gli albori del Primato*, (Roma: 1922); ——, La primitiva communità cristiana di Roma e l' epistola ai Romani, in *Richerche religiose* 1 (1925), p. 210-226, 305-326; ——, The Roman Church at the end of the second century, in *HThR* 18 (1925), p. 201-277. See also footnote 47.

[61] The two alternatives given by Guarducci (1977) p. 20.

Hippolytus was far more daring in the use of categories derived from a Gnostic *milieu* that it sought ostensibly to reject than such a conservative portrait of the author of *C.N.* suggests.

For the moment it is well for us to note how unblushingly the author of *C.N.* is prepared to associate his λόγος Christology, when speculating on creation as opposed to incarnation, with both νοῦς and σοφία, both of which terms are avoided by previous second century Fathers because of their Gnostic and aeonistic associations.[62] His use of such terms constitutes a far greater concession to emanation theory in connection with the relation of the pre-existent Christ to the Father than ever Justin, Irenaeus, or any other of the Fathers of the second century had been prepared to concede, in the process of refuting the Monarchian positions of Zephyrinus and Callistus.

Indeed, the detailed examination of Monarchian proof-texts from the Fourth Gospel and their reinterpretation in the *C.N.* shows that gospel to be central to the Monarchian case, and with considerable justification. The λόγος doctrine of that Gospel neither identified λόγος with νοῦς nor admitted of any thesis of emanation. It is the Son and not the λόγος who is begotten according to the Fourth Gospel. One strong *ms.* reading, μονογενής θεός in *Jn.* 1,18, implies that the indwelling in the Father (ὁ ὢν εἰς τὸν κόλπον τοῦ πατρὸς) is post-incarnational.[63] The λόγος is not begotten as such in the sense of an eternal, pre-existent begetting. All other references to the unity of the Son and the Father before the incarnation supports the Monarchian contention.[64] In *El.* IX, 12,17-18 moreover it was *Jn.* 14,10 that was used by Callistus against the author in support of his charge that the latter was a ditheist.[65]

---

62 *C.N.* 10,2-4: αὐτὸς δὲ μόνος ὢν πολὺς ἦν. οὔτε γὰρ ἄλογος οὔτε ἄσοφος ... ὅτε πλάσσει, σοφίζεται. πάντα γὰρ τὰ γενόμενα διὰ λόγου καὶ σοφίας τεχνάζεται, λόγῳ μὲν κτίζων, σοφίᾳ δὲ κοσμῶν... ἐγέννα λόγον... ὃν λόγον...φῶς ἐκ φωτὸς γεννῶν, προῆκεν τῇ κτίσει κύριον τὸν ἴδιον νοῦν... ,
and,
Ibid. 11,4:
οὗτος ὁ νοῦς, ὃς προβὰς ἐν κόσμῳ ἐδείκνυτο παῖς θεοῦ. (11,4)
English Translation:
"He himself alone was manifold. For neither was he without reason or wisdom... when he creates, his wisdom is at work, for all things that exist are crafted through his reason and wisdom, establishing by reason and ordering through wisdom... He begat the Word... which word...begetting as light from light, he attached to the creation as its Lord, his own mind,"
and,
"This mind which proceeded in the world was revealed as son of God."
63 𝔭66 ℵ* B C* L head the impressive list cited supporting the reading in K. Aland (and others), *The Greek New Testament*, United Bible Societies, (Stuttgart: Biblia Druck GmbH 1983). The reference μόνογενὴς θεὸς ὁ ὢν εἰς τὸν κόλπον τοῦ πατρὸς is clearly not to the pre-existent Christ since ἐκ τοῦ πληρώματος αὐτοῦ ἡμεῖς ἐλάβομεν (1,17) takes place after ὁ λόγος σὰρξ ἐγένετο (1.14). It is the incarnate Son who declares (ἐκεῖνος ἐξηγήσατο) the pre-existent God who in such a form cannot been seen (θεὸν οὐδεὶς ἑώρακεν πώποτε).
64 For a full list of such Johannine citations, see Butterworth (1977) p. 148.
65 *El.* IX, 12,17-18: καὶ τοῦτο εἶναι τὸ εἰρημένον «οὐ πιστεύεις ὅτι ἐγὼ ἐν τῷ πατρὶ καὶ ὁ πατὴρ ἐν ἐμοί;» τὸ μὲν γὰρ βλεπόμενον ὅπερ ἐστὶν ἄνθρωπος, τοῦτο εἶναι τὸν υἱόν, τὸ δὲ ἐν τῷ υἱῷ χωρηθὲν πνεῦμα, τοῦτο εἶναι τὸν πατέρα. οὐ γάρ, φησίν, ἐρῶ δύο θεούς, πατέρα καὶ υἱόν, ἀλλ᾽ ἕνα.

Therefore in order to rescue the Fourth Gospel from the Monarchians the author of *C.N.* had to make a very radical and daring move indeed. He had to apply the action of God in begetting directly onto the pre-existent λόγος when he claimed: ἐγέννα λόγον... ὃν λόγον... προῆκεν τῇ κτίσει κύριον τὸν ἴδιον νοῦν... (*C.N.* 10,3-4). Indeed, as he proceeds with his argument, he admits the strangeness to his hearers of calling the Son "Word."[66] He uses moreover the concept νοῦς to suggest the idea of emanation, but describes it as "proceeding (προβὰς)" rather than "emanating (προβαλλόμενος or παραβαλλόμενος)," as he knows that the Valentinians and others would have done (*C.N.* 11,2-3). This attempt to veil the origin of his conception was not however able to deceive those who later produced, as we shall see (5B 3.1.2), the legend of Hippolytus as a Valentinian presbyter and condemned as such by Callistus. Thus he imposed the concepts of generation and procession (οὗτος ὁ νοῦς, ὃς προβὰς ἐν κόσμῳ... (11,4)) on a Johannine theology that radically excluded such a notion.

Only Athenagoras and Tatian before him had approached to this level of metaphysical speculation. But Athenagoras was careful not to describe the νοῦς ἀίδιος as being anywhere other than in the Father. The παῖς is a γέννημα only in the sense of Hippolytus' ἴδιον νοῦν being made visible in creation and thus being a product (οὐκ ὡς γενόμενον... ἀλλ' ὡς τῶν ὑλικῶν ξυμπάντων... ἐπ' αὐτοῖς ἰδέα καὶ ἐνέργεια εἶναι, προελθών), but νοῦς as such cannot be described by Athenagoras as προβὰς.[67] Only the Holy Spirit is described as ἀπόρροια ὡς φῶς ἀπὸ πυρὸς τὸ πνεῦμα, and thus allowed to process.[68]

Only in Tatian do we find such expressions as "the λόγος sprang forth (προσπηδᾷ) as the firstborn work of the Father (ἔργον πρωτότοκον τοῦ πατρὸς)" but with the following qualification:

> But that took place by division (γέγονεν δὲ κατὰ μερισμὸν), not by severation, (οὐ κατὰ ἀποκοπὴν) for that which is severed is separated from its origin (τὸ γὰρ ἀποτμηθὲν τοῦ πρώτου κεχώρισται), but what is divided took on a distinctive function (τὸ δὲ μερισθὲν οἰκονομίας τὴν διαίρεσιν προσλαβὸν), and does not diminish the source from which it is taken (οὐκ ἐνδεᾶ τὸν ὅθεν εἴληπται πεποίηκεν).
>
> *Orat. ad Graec.* 5

---

[66] *C.N.* 15,1: ἀλλ' ἐρεῖ μοί τις, Ξένον μοι φέρεις λόγον λέγων υἱόν. Ἰωάννης μὲν γὰρ λέγει λόγον, ἀλλ' ἄλλως ἀλληγορεῖ.

[67] Athenagoras, *Legatio*, 10,3: ... ὁ παῖς... πρῶτον γέννημα εἶναι τῷ πατρὶ, οὐχ ὡς γενόμενον (ἐξ ἀρχῆς γὰρ ὁ θεός, νοῦς ἀίδιος ὤν, εἶχεν αὐτὸς ἐν ἑαυτῷ τὸν λόγον, ἀιδίως λογικὸς ὤν) ἀλλ' ὡς τῶν ὑλικῶν ξυμπάντων... ἐπ' αὐτοῖς ἰδέα καὶ ἐνέργεια εἶναι, προελθών.

[68] Ibid. 24,1: ... νοῦς, λόγος, σοφία ὁ υἱὸς τοῦ πατρὸς καὶ ἀπόρροια τοῦ θεοῦ ὡς φῶς ἀπὸ πυρὸς τὸ πνεῦμα. Cf. also 10,4: καίτοι καὶ αὐτὸ τὸ ἐνεργοῦν τοῖς ἐκφωνοῦσι προφητικῶς ἅγιον πνεῦμα ἀπόρροιαν εἶναί φαμεν, τοῦ θεοῦ, ἀπορρέον καὶ ἐπαναφερόμενον ὡς ἀκτῖνα ἡλίου.

But Tatian does not use νοῦς as equivalent to λόγος even though he will use the expression προβαλλόμενος in connection both with φωνή and ὕλη (Ibid. 5), and the passage just quoted seems to service emanationist notions that could lead to the accusation of ditheism. Moreover, in *El.* VIII, 16,1 and X, 18,1 Tatian is accused of teaching παραπλήσιως τῷ Οὐαλεντίνῳ καὶ τοῖς ἑτέροις... αἰῶνας τινας ἀοράτους. That Hippolytus is prepared in *C.N.* to go farther than Tatian whom his predecessor condemned in *El.* speaks eloquently of the way in which he is prepared to take quite radical, hellenistic concepts and use them in what he believes to be a defence of orthodoxy (5B 3.1-3.2).

We may wonder in consequence of his need to adapt radically the λόγος doctrine why he did not simply reject the Gospel and *Apocalypse* of John. Gaius certainly is alleged to have done so and this in consequence excludes him from being the author of *El.* We shall argue later that the position of the historical Gaius is problematic (3B and C). Gaius undoubtedly attacked Montanism (Eusebius, *H.E.* II, 25,6). The author of *El.* VIII, 19,1-2 accuses Montanus along with Prisca and Maximilla of being "more heretical (αὐτοὶ αἱρετικώτεροι)" than the Quartodecimans. They are, however, charged with adding uncritically to the law, prophets and gospels rather than positive error.[69] His other accusation is the invention of new fasts and festivals.[70] Nevertheless he links some Montanists with Noetus,[71] and thus with the Monarchians who rested their case upon the Fourth Gospel, as we have seen.

The reasons for this acceptance of the authority of the Fourth Gospel may be several. The Statue, we have argued, shows the unique cultural identity of Hippolytus' group in the fractionalized Roman community of the late second century. We have argued that the individual *rapprochement* between the Western and the Quartodeciman computation of Easter indicated by the Paschal and Easter Tables represented a distinct group with its own cultic practice distinct from both of these alternatives. The Fourth Gospel may therefore have been accepted, in the radically re-interpreted form of proposed by the *C.N.,* because it was the essential authority for the group's distinctive use of the Johannine date for the Crucifixion.

---

[69] *El.* VIII, 19,1-2: ... μήτε τὰ ὑπ᾽ αὐτῶν λελαλημένα λόγῳ κρίνοντες, μήτε τοῖς κρῖναι δυναμένοις προσέχοντες, ἀλλ᾽ ἀκρίτως τῇ πρὸς αὐτοὺς πίστει προσφέρονται, πλεῖόν τι δι᾽ αὐτῶν φάσκοντες ὡς μεμαθηκέναι ἢ ἐκ τοῦ νόμου καὶ προφητῶν.

[70] Ibid. 19,2: ...ὁμολογοῦσι καὶ ὅσα τὸ εὐαγγέλιον περὶ τοῦ Χριστοῦ μαρτυρεῖ, καινίζουσι δὲ νηστείας καὶ ἑορτὰς καὶ ξηροφαγίας καὶ ῥαφανοφαγίας, φάσκοντες ὑπὸ τῶν γυναίων δεδιδάχθαι.

[71] Ibid. 19,3: τινὲς δὲ αὐτῶν τῇ τῶν Νοητιανῶν αἱρέσει συντιθέμενοι, τὸν πατέρα αὐτὸν εἶναι καὶ τὸν υἱὸν λέγουσι, καὶ τοῦτον ὑπὸ γένεσιν καὶ πάθος καὶ θάνατον ἐληλυθέναι. Cf also *El.* X, 25,1 and 26,1 and 7 C 2.2 below, where the relationship between Tertullian's Montanist work, *Adv. Prax.,* and the Hippolytan school is discussed, since this work seems to reject the connexion between Monarchianism and Montanism.

Perhaps also the connection between Irenaeus, quoted extensively without acknowledgment in *El.*, and Hippolytus's group meant that they would have felt it also necessary to defend the authenticity of the Fourth Gospel against Gaius. The acknowledgment of the Fourth Gospel, therefore, was an essential condition of the group's self-identity, even though the price of that acknowledgment was a daring use of the idea of emanation which must have appeared to Callistus as dangerously close to Gnosticism.

It was thus this daring use of Gnostic concepts in an orthodox cause that helps to explain why the figure of λόγος was associated with σοφία in several places in the *C.N.* and could remain feminine whilst retaining such Christological associations. λόγος and σοφία are presented initially as passive principles (οὔτε γὰρ ἄλογος οὔτε ἄσοφος), but the verbal form of the latter σοφίζεται is used to associate both as active principles in creation (ὅτε πλάσσει, σοφίζεται. πάντα γὰρ τὰ γενόμενα διὰ λόγου καὶ σοφίας τεχνάζεται) (*C.N.* 10,3). 'Themista' was taken over by an orthodox community to express its σοφία–λόγος Christology, in self-conscious opposition to what they believed to be heretical Monarchianism of Zephyrinus and Callistus. We shall now find the evidence for this in a common tradition of early Christian iconographic art.

2A 3.2. *Serapis-*Σοφία *and the transformation of Themista*
Irenaeus mentions one sect of the followers of Carpocrates (*alii vero ex ipsis signant*), who were at all events renowned as licentious rather than aesthetic Gnostics, as lead by one Marcellina, who came to Rome during the time of Anicetus. They possessed images, some painted and others made from different materials (*imagines quasdam quidem depictas, quasdam autem et de reliqua materia fabricatas*), which they venerated by different kinds of ceremonies including crowning with a garland (*has coronant*). Amongst these images were images of Christ made by Pilate (*formam Christi factam a Pilato*). The sect associated this image with those of Pythagoras, Plato and Aristotle, and thus emphasized their self-understanding of their community as a philosophical school (*proponunt eas cum imaginibus mundi philosophorum*).[72]

---

[72] Irenaeus, *Adv. Haer.* I, 25,6: "Alii vero ex ipsis signant, cauteriantes suos discipulos in posterioribus partibus exstantiae dextrae auris. Unde et Marcellina, quae Romam sub Aniceto venit, cum esset huius doctrinae, multos exterminavit. Gnosticos se autem vocant: et imagines quasdam quidem depictas, quasdam autem et de reliqua materia fabricatas habent, dicentes formam Christi factam a Pilato, illo in tempore quo fuit Jesus cum hominibus. Et has coronant et proponunt eas cum imaginibus mundi philosophorum, videlicet cum imagine Pythagorae et Platonis et Aristotelis et reliquorum: et reliquam observationem circa eas, similiter ut gentes faciunt." Cf. W. Elliger, Die Stellung der alten Christen zu den Bilden in den ersten 4 Jahrhunderte, nach den Angaben der zeitgenössischen kirchlichen Schriftstellerei, in *Studien über christlichen Denkmäler*, N.F. 20 (Leipzig: Dieter 1930), p. 24-26.

One of these images of the Carpocratian Gnostics, reflecting the feminine qualities of σοφία, appears to have been produced by taking over a statue of Serapis and making it an icon of Christ as Σοφία. Though Σοφία is not mentioned particularly regarding their beliefs, Irenaeus does say that they believed the world to have been made through angelic creators, and that the man Jesus was adopted by a power in order to rescue him with the rest of mankind from the dominion of the angelic creators.[73] We may infer that such a power could be conceived as the aeon Σοφία.

What appears to have been one of their statues stands today in the Museo Nazionale di Roma, still beardless with feminine breasts, but reconstructed with a scroll in one hand to represent the Gospel, and the other raised in the gesture of a teacher (Plate 13). Jesus thus sits, like the Carpocratian Statue, amongst the philosophers (*cum imaginibus mundi philosophorum*), having become Christ by the endowment with σοφία.[74] He/she wears a female form because souls transmigrate and should have experience of every kind of life and every kind of action (*Adv. Haer.* I, 25,4).

Gnostics, like Catholics, practiced unambiguous allegorical and icono-graphic and not representative art, and both were clearly prepared to develop symbolically and allegorically transformed images of paganism. There is the transformation of the sea-dragon, particularly associated with the myth of Perseus and Andromache, into Jonah and the Whale as an icon of Christ's death and resurrection, on sarcophagi from Copenhagen and from S. Maria Antiqua. There is also on a coin of Apamea an inscription of Noah arising from a chest like ark as a transformation of the myth of Danäe and Perseus set adrift on the sea, or Deucalion and Pyrrha as the Greek counterpart of the story of the Flood.[75]

In the context of examples of such transformations, neither the allegoriza-tion of Serapis as Σοφία in Gnostic circles, nor that of Themista by the more orthodox, is that surprising. The use of the sedate figure of Themista, whose breasts hardly appear as luxuriant as those of the transformed Serapis/Σοφία, must have appeared a very tame orthodox counterpart as an icon of an embryonic Trinity. At this time embryonic persons in a relationship of procession from each other were described by *C.N.* 10,4 (ἐγέννα λόγον... ὃν λόγον... προῆκεν τῇ κτίσει), as we have seen.

But if the Statue was thus able in a reinterpreted form to speak of the col-lective life of a community expressed through its distinctive Christology,

---

[73] *Adv. Haer.* I, 25,1-2: "Carpocrates autem, et qui ab eo mundum quidem et ea quae in eo sunt, ab angelis multo inferioribus ingenito patre factum esse dicunt. Jesus autem ex Joseph natum... missam esse ei virtutem uti mundi fabricatores effugere posset..."

[74] Lowrie (1947) p. 32 and Plate 101a. See also P. Ducati, *L'arte in Roma dalle origini al secolo VIII*, in *Storia di Roma* 26, (Bologna: Istituto di Studi Romani 1939), p. 337-338 (Tav. CCXXX). cf. C. Cecchelli, *I Monumenti cristiano-eretici di Roma*, (Rome: Fratelli Palombi 1944).

[75] Ibid. p. 83-84 and Plates 22b and 23c, and 33b.

then indeed such an expression would be more suitably made in the midst of
a worshipping community and not as an apology in a pagan library to those
outside its common life. Guarducci was quite wrong to have excluded the
possibility of its presence in a place of Christian worship because its original
form was Epicurean, and thus to have denied its original place in the cult-
centre on the via Tiburtina (1B 2.3.3.7). At all events, it would simply not
follow that in the sixteenth century such an Epicurean reference would still
have been detected so as *ipso facto* to exclude its presence in a place of
Christian worship, albeit to experience heretical desecration.[76]

That a monument functions for a community as an icon of its collective
life does not of course preclude it from having more specific associations,
namely with the death of its leader as a funerary monument, or indeed as a
monument to its leader forming part of a tribute to the multiculturalism of
the wider community of which it forms part. Though the significance of the
Paschal and Easter Calendars weigh heavily, in my opinion, particularly
against the latter, it remains part of Guarducci's present conclusion
regarding the character of the Statue. It is to a consideration of a funerary or
multicultural (as opposed to ecclesiastical) setting for the Statue that we
must therefore now turn in our second part.

PART B. LOCATION OF THE STATUE: CEMETERY OR LIBRARY?

Both Guarducci and Testini emphasize at the beginning of both of their discussions that they have to explain a unique artefact in the history of early
Christianity. I would not wish to deny the uniqueness of the Statue as one of
several quite unique and puzzling artefacts (like the Σοφία/Christ of the
Museo delle Terme) but would suggest that uniqueness to be a function of
the fragmentary nature of surviving remains. Our discussion so far has emphasized that although the Statue is such a unique survival, it is by no means
inexplicable given what we can reasonably conclude about the cultural and
artistic assumptions of the late second century. Whilst regarding the Statue
and its various features as a *hapax inspiegabile*, Testini nevertheless argued
that its character was ultimately that of a funeral monument, and to an
examination of his case we first turn.[77]

---

[76] Guarducci (1989) p. 67: "A parte i misteriosi «heretici» che sarebbero stati gli autori di
quelle rovine, non è ammissibile– a me pare– la presenza di una statua di donna, e per giunta
epicurea, in una chiesa o comunque in un ambiente cristiano dove i fedeli praticassero il culto."
[77] P. Testini, Di alcune testimonianze relative a Ippolito, in *StEphAug*, 13 (1977), p.46-52,
where he says: "... in quanto significa soppressione di un *hapax* inspiegabile nel quadro della
primitiva arte cristiana."

2B 1. *Testini and the Statue as a funerary monument*

While pointing out that the Statue itself is unique and unexampled not only in the third century, but throughout classical antiquity, Testini nevertheless claimed that the salient features of the Statue paralleled significantly those of inscriptions and decorated marble slabs which closed *loculi* in mausolea, and thus showed the Statue to be a personal funeral monument.[78] He pointed to those features of pagan art to which we have already referred, namely the received ideas on life and death such as the Persephone Mosaic or the Bacchic sarcophagi, to which he claimed commemoration of office such as that of a reader or catechist was the Christian counterpart.[79]

But Testini cannot agree that a statue as such could at this time have formed part of Christian art.[80] In section 2A 3.1 and 2 above, I have tried to show that indeed it could, and that the unique character of the Statue is an illusion created by the fragmentary character of surviving artefacts. But let us for the moment follow Testini in what he argues.

2 B 1.1. *Testini: the Statue originally a marble block?*

From the premise of there being no early Christian statuary of this kind, Testini concluded that what Ligorio found was an earlier statue reduced to a marble block which was fixed tangentially into a wall or some other structure such as a pilaster. The marble block contained both the catalogue of works, presumably the Paschal and Easter Tables, and also a picture carved into the flat marble of a catechist or teacher like that of the deacon Severus in the cemetery of Callistus (Plate 16).[81] What presumably those Tables did

---

[78] Ibid. p. 46-47: "La «statua» infatti era finora un unicum come prodotto della scultura cristiana, talchè nella disperata ricerca di trovarle riscontri si son dovute segnalare iscrizioni o lastre marmoree di chiusura di loculi, sulle quali s'incisero immagini relative alla vita intellettuale del defunto..."

[79] Ibid. p. 47: "... immagini però communi al repertorio pagano e cristiano, anche se per un pagano si connettevano con le idee ricevute sulla vita, la morte, l'aldilà, mentre per un cristiano, più che all'ufficio di lettore o catechista, alludevano al possesso della dottrina e dunque alla fedeltà alle leggi del Signore."

[80] Ibid. p. 47 where he refers to "un'altra singolarità non meno imbarazzante, quella d' una immagine monumentale di personaggio" with reference to "il peso dell' atteggiamento negativo degli scrittori cristiani verso le immagini." Ducati (1939) pointed to the surprising character of what he believed to be a funerary representation of Hippolytus, and compared this with the feminine statue of Christ, p. 337: "Più che sculture a tutto tondo, si hanno sculture a rilievo, quasi totalmente sarcofagi. Adattamenti di statue profane ad un nuovo significato cristiano sono le due statue, quella di Sant'Ippolito... ove la testa, insieme a varie parti del corpo, è moderna, e quella di San Pietro del Vaticano." Lowrie (1947) p. 28-30; Elliger (1930), p. 7-24; H. Koch, *Die altchristliche bilderfrage nach den literarischen Quellen*, in *FRLANT* N.F. 10 (Göttingen 1917), p. 3-14.

[81] Ibid. p. 50: "In altri termini io vedrei nel III secolo l'immagine ridotta a un masso marmoreo (per accidente ma non escludendo necessariamente l'intenzione di ridurla in tale condizione) per utilizzare il blocco ad altro fine, come si fece per la transenna su cui s' incise l' iscrizione del diacono Severo nel cimitero di Callisto, benchè la transenna sia di dimensioni e peso differenti dal marmo della «statua.»" The inscription is found in *ICUR* 4, 10183 (Tab. vol. IV 10 a 5) and also in P. Testini, *Le catecombe e gli antichi cimiteri cristiani in Roma*, (Bologna: Cappelli 1966), Vol. II p. 201. For similar sepulchral *motifs* see also P. Testini, *Vetera et nova su Ippolito*, in *StEphAug* 30 (1989), p. 10, citing *ICUR* 5, 15058 (Tab. vol. V, 24 a 4) where a man is seated holding an open scroll and a girl stands holding the same volume,

was act as an extension to the catalogue of books which in turn acted as an extension to the figure of the representation itself. They reinforced the message regarding the character and office of the deceased.

In Testini's original discussion, the hypothesized existence of a iconographic representation of a teacher set in the marble block could hardly have suggested to Ligorio by itself the construction of a Statue of Hippolytus. Testini therefore believed that Ligorio discovered the identity of the teacher from both the neighbouring *mons Ypoliti*, the crypt of St. Hippolytus, and the catalogue of works identifiable as Eusebius' writer. We have already given detailed grounds against the former claim that the Statue could have been identified with Hippolytus the writer, partly for reasons that Testini himself later gave.[82] We have also refuted a similar and more recent thesis about the Statue as originally simply a *sasso*, as argued by D' Onofrio (2 A 1). The grounds for the identification with whatever form the original ruined Statue had, whether Testini's block or Guarducci's 'Themista,' must therefore have been both the catalogue of works and whatever Ligorio saw also protruding from the ruins that stood in what was later Msg. Gori's vinyard.

But Testini did well to insist nevertheless on the Statue's uniqueness, despite his argument for the identification with a funery monument, since it does not easily fit into the features of such monuments.

2 B 1.2. *The Statue and other sepulchral monuments*
It is not without significance in this regard that Testini has to hypothesize, without further evidence, that Ligorio's Statue was in fact a marble block on which there was a pictorial representation. We have for example a pagan and classical monument that would fit part of Testini's hypothesis in the sepulchral Stele from Aquileia of the 3rd century B.C. It is dedicated "to the actress Bassilla (μειμάδι Βασσίλλη)" by one Heirakleides on behalf of her fellow actors (οἱ σύσκηνοί σου).

Following an elaborate panegyric in which she is addressed as "the tenth Muse (τῇ δεκάτῃ Μούσῃ)", the more sombre and tragic epitaphal style is followed with the words: "Be of good cheer, Basilla (εὐψύχει, Βάσιλλα), no-one is immortal (οὐδεὶς ἀθάνατος)."[83] Here we have a pagan counterpart to the Statue if it depicted a catechist, which instead depicts an actress and commemorates her. But even if the original form of the Statue was as Testini claims it to be, there are no corresponding words of ironic consolation or expressions of κοίμησις ἐν εἰρήνῃ. A commemoration in terms of a

---

and 15197 (Tab.vol. V 32 c 4) which depicts a catechist. For a discussion of this picture in comparison with the Statue see also G. Bovini, La Statua di S. Ippolito del Museo Lateranense, in *Bollettino della commissione archeologica del governo di Roma*, (1941) p. 109 ff.; ——, (1943) p. 72-81. See also G. Wilpert, *I sarcofagi cristiani antichi*, (Rome 1929) Vol. 1, p. 193 fig. 115 table XXIV a 4.
[82] Testini (1989) p. 12-13 cf 1 B 2.3.2.
[83] Guarducci (1978) p. 187-189 and fig. 75; *IG* 14, 2342 and p. 704.

list of works, and Paschal and Easter Tables in which the deceased is not even named, would be quite unprecedented.

A similar objection would also apply even if the original had been a Statue unreduced to a marble block. There is the female seated figure of Ampharete the grandmother, who holds an image of her grandchild in her arms and commemorates also her daughter in the verses inscribed. But there is no analogy between the Statue and this sepulchral monument either with respect to the naming of the persons commemorated or the accompanying tragic epigram.[84]

Testini's inability to locate a full-blown statue within Christian art of the early third century is however related to his insistence on regarding the original of the Statue as a personal, sepulchral monument.[85] Once he has made that assumption, then the Statue is indeed reinforced in his mind as an *hapax inspiegabile*. Furthermore, any parallel with a community artefact is thus ruled out of consideration. The baptistery and the area dedicated to worship uncovered by the excavations of the house Church at Dura Europas is thus excluded *ex hypothesi* because such artefacts are more community than individual artefacts. Such community artefacts clearly did not evoke the horror of graven images that private and personal artefacts would cause.[86] But we have already argued that the significance of the Statue was that of a community artefact, and we shall argue further (Chapters 6-7) for its location at the centre of a house/school/church in what Lampe has characterised as the fractionalized Roman community of the late second and early third century.

2B 1.3. *Testini's sepulchral thesis: in conclusion.*

For the moment let us record our conclusion that (i) the hypothesis of the Statue reduced to a block arises solely because Testini assumes that it is a monument to a person. In consequence he argues (ii) because the Dura baptistry and wall paintings are not individual but group artefacts, these cannot be true parallels and therefore the Statue could not have existed as a statue. But I have shown that it need not be, and indeed was not the individual monument that Testini assumes, but the icon of a community's self-identity.

---

[84] Ibid. p. 183-184 and fig. 73; *IG*, II/III² 10650.

[85] In this respect he followed the earlier work, e.g. Bovini (1943), p. 69-72, in which the fundamental assumption was that of a personal monumument with a list of works by a single author.

[86] Testini (1977) p. 47: "si rivaluta in un certo senso il peso dell' atteggiamento negativo degli scrittori cristiani verso le immagini; atteggiamento ritenuto da taluni di assoluto rigore e come tale poi smentito dai monumenti, dovendosi in realtà distinguere tra battistero e aula di culto (es. di Dura Europos) come tra manufatto privato o ad uso personale e manufatto per la comunità..." Thus the judgement of Elliger (1930) needs qualifying by this distinction (p. 33: "So war es möglich, dass Irenäus und Tertullian unbeschadet ihrer persönlichen Abneigung gegen die Bilder Gedanken vortragen konnten, die von anderen zur gleichen Zeit bildlich veranschaulicht wurden, und dass die selbst so durch die Betonung des gleichen Inhaltes unbewusst und unbeabsichtigt eine Entwicklung begüngstigen, die sie im Grunde ablehnten."

The case for a sepulchral monument in terms of an original block or *sasso* is in consequence superfluous (2 A 1). There are no funerary parallels to a list of works expressing the office of the person who is buried there, but which do not include the usual funerary inscriptions. So the funerary hypothesis will not be saved simply by additionally hypothesizing a marble pictorial representation but not in statue form, which would, by reason of its size as well as artistic form, have not fitted into a funeral situation.

But if Testini's sepulchral interpretation of the Statue is open to serious objection, what of Guarducci's more recent claim that the Statue was intended for, and in fact stood in, the Pantheon library as a tribute to the religious and cultural syncretism of the Severans. We shall see here too that Guarducci's most recent thesis is still distorted by the fixation on the Statue as basically a monument to an individual writer named Hippolytus, which leads to the disregarding of its true character as a community artefact.

2B 2. *The Pantheon Library: general cultural ambience*

Guarducci originally conceded herself the possibility that 'Themista's' Statue, in its allegorized form as Wisdom or Astronomy, had sepulchral parallels, whilst indeed preferring its location in a library situation.[87] As such she compared it with the sepulchral stone of the cemetry of Praetextatus early in the third century.[88] We have argued that, with the depersonalizing and allegorizing of the Statue, unless other features suggest a sepulchral context, the need to see what originally bore no personal name as a personal monument of any kind is considerably reduced. More recently Guarducci divorced even further the Statue from such a sepulchral context whilst still maintaining its essentially individualistic character.

Guarducci thus continues to regard it as nevertheless a personalization, in allegorical form, as a memorial to an individual whose collected works are shown on the Statue. In her more recent opinion, she clearly considers the Statue, as dedicated to the reigning emperor, Severus Alexander, by Hippolytus or his associates, as a memorial of his personal contribution to the life of the Roman Empire, by analogy with Julius Africanus' contemporary dedication of his Κήστοι to the same emperor.

Assailing Ligorio's veracity regarding the location of the discovery of the Statue, instead of the via Tiburtina (Chapter 1), she now prefers the Pantheon Library as the Statue's original location. Indeed, she needed to divorce the Statue from any location in an original cult-centre to remove any

---

[87] Guarducci (1977) p. 20: "La statua arricchita dalle iscrizioni non dovette essere oggetto di dedica... E' invece possibile, anzi logico pensare ad una statua collocata in un ambiente di cultura e in particolare in una biblioteca."

[88] Ibid. p. 20: "Una figura femminile seduta, con un rotolo spiegato fra le mani, da intendersi certamente come figura allegorica, è rappresentata, ad esempio, in una lapide sepolcrale della catacomba di Pretestato databile al III secolo."

grounds whether for a sepulchral or for an intra-communal interpretation of its significance. But nevertheless, according to her, the Statue must still stand there as a personal monument, like the Κήστοι written by the architect of that library, Julius Africanus. It must represent symbolically the representatives of the great movements of thought that the Severans sought to unite into the expression of the unity-in-diversity of the empire. The ghost of Ligorio's personal reconstruction and interpretation still retains a certain force that outlives its earthly decomposition.[89]

There are two requirements for the success of Guarducci's argument for an original location in the Pantheon Library. She needs first to construct the Severan *Zeitgeist* in a way that will provide a unique cultural and social context in terms of which the location of a unique monument to a Christian writer in a pagan library could make sense. Thus she will focus on the relations between Origen and Julius Africanus within the circle of Julia Mamaea.[90] The second requirement of her argument is consequently to show that the Statue as an artefact would fit into the architecture of what we know of ancient libraries.[91] We will now turn to the consideration of these two requirements and in this order.

2 B 2.1. *The religious policy of the Severans*

With the possible exception of Septimius Severus (193-211), the founder of the Severan dynasty, there does not appear to be a deliberate policy of persecution of Christianity on the part of the Roman government. It is only after the fall of the dynasty on the murder of Severus Alexander, and his mother Julia Mamaea, in the campaign against the Persians (235), and the succession of Maximinus the Thracian, that church leaders such as Pontian and Hippolytus suffer martyrdom (Eusebius, *H.E.* VI 28).[92]

It remains however a much discussed question as to whether there was any general persecution during the reign of Septimius Severus, or whether indeed Tertullian's *Apology* was addressed to a specifically North African situation, and one involving a law against converts.[93] Regarding Maximinus, Eusebius mentions that the persecution involved "the leaders of the Church

---

[89] With Guarducci (1977) p. 26 cf. Guarducci (1989) p. 72-73. See also Testini (1977) p.46-51; Testini (1989) p. 9-12; V. Saxer, La questione di Ippolito Romano, in *StEphAug* 30 (1989), p. 4.

[90] Guarducci (1977) p. 25: "La corte di Severo Alessandro, dominata dal potente influsso della madre, la siriana Guilia Mamaea... donna intelligente ed ambiziosa, ci teneva a brillare nella vita della cultura e s'interessava perciò alle correnti spirituali del suo tempo, fra cui non poteva esser trascurata la corrente cristiana."

[91] Ibid. p. 73-74.

[92] W.H.C. Frend, Open Questions concerning Christians and the Roman Empire in the Age of the Severi, in *JThS* n.s. 25 (1974), p. 333-351; T.D. Barnes, The Family and Career of Septimius Severus, in *Historia* 16 (1967) p. 87-107; H. Grégoire, Les Persécutions dans l'empire romain, in *Mémoires de l'Academie royale de Belgique* 46,1 (1951) p. 108-109.

[93] E. dal Covolo, I Severi e il cristianesimo: Ricerche sull'ambiente storico-istituzionale delle origini cristiane tra il secondo e il terzo secolo, in *Biblioteca di Scienze Religiose*, 87 (Libreria Ateneo Salesiano: Rome 1989), p. 29-33.

alone (τῶν ἐκκλησιῶν ἄρχοντας μόνους),” and that they were the victims of
“spite (κατὰ κότον)” due to the good favour they had enjoyed with Severus,
of whose “house the majority were believers (’Αλεξάνδρου οἶκον, ἐκ
πλειόνων πιστῶν συνεστῶτα).”[94] Though the word “majority (ἐκ πλειόνων)”
would appear to be an exaggeration, there is some evidence from the inscriptions to support a more moderate version of Eusebius’ claim,[95]
although he does not make it clear why the household itself should not have
been persecuted rather than the church leaders.

2B 2.1.1. *Eusebius on Origen, and Julia Mamaea*
There is a well known problem with Eusebius’ historiography, in that he is
always determined to regard “good” emperors as friends of the Church.[96] He
clearly regards Severus Alexander as friendly towards Christianity, and
records that the emperor’s mother, Julia Mamaea, sent an armed escort for
Origen (μετὰ στατιωτικῆς δορυφορίας αὐτὸν ἀνακαλεῖται) whilst she was
at Antioch.[97] Julia was “a most religious woman (θεοσεβεστάτη γυνή).”[98]
Clearly it was Mamaea’s idea, if Eusebius’ account is true, to summon
Origen, and not one of the putative ἐκ πλειόνων πιστῶν of her son’s
household. As Eusebius does not claim her specifically as a Christian, her
receptiveness to Origen’s fame implies someone who was interested in
religious and philosophical ideas generally.[99] The fact that Philostratus attributed his writing the *Life of Apollonius of Tyanna* to the instigation of her

---

[94] *H.E.* VI, 28: ... ὃς δὴ κατὰ κότον τὸν πρὸς τὸν ’Αλεξάνδρου οἶκον, ἐκ πλειόνων
πιστῶν συνεστῶτα, διωγμὸν ἐγείρας, τοὺς τῶν ἐκκλησιῶν ἄρχοντας μόνους ὡς
αἰτίους τῆς κατὰ τὸ εὐαγγέλιον διδασκαλίας ἀναιρεῖσθαι προστάττει.
[95] Aurelius Prosthenes *CIL* VI², 8498. Cf. G.W. Clarke, Two Christians in the *Familia
Caesaris*, in *HTR* 64 (1971), p. 121-124.
[96] M. Gödecke, Geschichte als Mythos: Eusebs „Kirchengeschichte”, in *Europäische
Hochschulschriften*, 23, (Frankfurt am Main: Peter Lang 1987), p. 307 ff.
[97] *H.E.* VI, 21,3: τοῦ δ’ αὐτοκράτορος μήτηρ, Μαμαία τοὔνομα, εἰ καί τις ἄλλη
θεοσεβεστάτη γυνή, τῆς ’Ωριγένους πανταχόσε βοωμένης φήμης, ὡς καὶ μέχρι τῶν
αὐτῆς ἐλθεῖν ἀκοῶν, περὶ πολλοῦ ποιεῖται τῆς τοῦ ἀνδρὸς θέας ἀξιωθῆναι καὶ τῆς
ὑπὸ πάντων θαυμαζομένης περὶ τὰ θεῖα συνέσεως αὐτοῦ πεῖραν λαβεῖν. ἐπ’
’Αντιοχείας δῆτα διατρίβουσα, μετὰ στατιωτικῆς δορυφορίας αὐτὸν ἀνακαλεῖται·
παρ’ ᾗ χρόνον διατρίψας πλεῖστα τε ὅσα εἰς τὴν τοῦ κυρίου δόξαν καὶ τῆς τοῦ θείου
διδασκαλείου ἀρετῆς ἐπιδειξάμενος, ἐπὶ τὰς συνήθεις ἔσπευδεν διατριβάς.
[98] W.H.C. Frend, *The Rise of Christianity*, (London: Darton Longman and Todd 1984), p.
273 attributes this description without explanation to Origen himself, but Eusebius’ words εἰ
καί τις ἄλλη θεοσεβεστάτη γυνή (“a religious woman if there ever was one”) are clearly his
own reflection. Cf Lampridius SHA *Alex. Sev.* 14,7: “mulier sancta.” See also W.H.C. Frend,
Martyrdom and Persecution in the Early Church, (Oxford: Blackwell 1965), p. 329-330 where
he cites Eusebius *H.E.* V, 28,14. I. Mundle, Dea caelestis in der religionspolitik des Septimius
Severus und der Julia Domna, in *Historia* 10 (1961), p. 228-237 presents an argument for the
political divination of Julia is articulated which accords ill with her allegedly Christian
sympathies, M. Gilmore Williams, Empress Julia Domna, in *Am. J. Arch.* 6 (1902), p. 259-305;
A. Jardé, *Études critiques sur la vie et le règne de Sévère Alexandre* (Paris: Boccard 1925),
chap. 2; R. MacMullen, *Enemies of the Roman Order*, (Cambridge Mass.: Harvard U.P. 1967),
p. 114-127.
[99] Frend (1965) p. 330 attributes too great significance to Eusebius’ account at its face
value when he says: “It implied recognition, albeit through the personality and teaching of
Origen, of Christianity as one of the accepted religions of the Roman world... The Severan
dynasty marks the turn of the tide in the history of the Church.”

aunt, Julia Domna, is perhaps indicative of an interest in religion on the part of the Severan dynasty which was characterised by an eclectic syncretism.[100]

The hypothesis, for such it clearly is, of a Severan interest in religious syncretism is nevertheless given additional plausibility, beyond Eusebian apologetic, by three further considerations.

2B 2.1.2. *The imperial cult and the* Constitutio Antoniana

The *Constitutio Antoniana* was the achievement of Severus Alexander's predecessor, Caracalla, as a result of which citizenship was extended to inhabitants of towns and villages beyond the cities.[101] It is possible to see this, with Millar,[102] as merely a method of extending taxation, or, with Rostovtzeff, as an attack upon the senatorial aristocracy,[103] but its justification was sincerely religious and involved more wider and altruistic concerns despite such political and economic bonuses.[104] One inscription makes it clear that the primary motivation was religious, and that it was an extension of the imperial cult.[105] The emperor and his consort were to possess the religious function of effecting sacramentally the unity of the empire for which the extension of citizenship contained the hope. Caracalla her son appears on coins as the Lord of the world and the reflection of the divine light of the sun, permeating all things and creating universal order.

Images of Septimius Severus previously had appeared with that of Julia Domna his wife and aunt of Julia Mamaea on the arch at Leptis Magna (erected 203), where they represent Serapis and Isis. Julia Domna was there described as *mater castrorum,* like Fausta the wife of Marcus Aurelius before her, but with the addition *et senatus et patriae.* She is also portrayed

---

[100] Philostratus, *Life of Apollonius,* 1,3: καὶ προσήκων τις τῷ Δάμιδι τὰς δέλτους τῶν ὑπομνημάτων τούτων οὔπω γιγνωσκομένας ἐς γνῶσιν ἤγαγεν Ἰουλίᾳ τῇ βασιλίδι. μετέχοντι δέ μοι τοῦ περὶ αὐτὴν κύκλου– καὶ γὰρ τοὺς ῥητορικοὺς πάντας λόγους ἐπῄνει καὶ ἠσπάζετο– μεταγράψαι τε προσέταξε τὰς διατριβὰς ταύτας καὶ τῆς ἀπαγγελίας αὐτῶν ἐπιμεληθῆναι... R. Syme, *Historia Augusta* Papers, (Oxford: Clarendon 1983), whilst conceding that Philostratus, Life of Apollonius of Tyana, *Ep.* LXIII (addressed to Julia Domna) is generally regarded as genuine, nevertheless concludes "doubt is legitimate." (p. 7)

[101] Ulpian, *Digest* 1,5,17: "Idem (sc. Ulpianus) libro vicensimo secundo ad edictum. In orbe Romano qui sunt ex constitutione imperatoris Antonini cives Romani effecti sunt." Cf. P. Giessen, p.40; S.N. Miller, Caracalla, in *CAH* xii, p. 45-47.

[102] F. Millar, The date of the *Constitutio Antoniana,* in *JEgArch* 48 (1962) p. 124-131.

[103] Cf. M. Rostovtzeff, *Social and Economic History of the Roman Empire,* (Oxford: Clarendon 1957) p. 418-428.

[104] A.H.M. Jones, Another Interpretation of the Constitutio Antoniana, in *JRomS,* 26,2 (1936) p. 223-225.

[105] J. Stroux, Die Constitutio Antoniana, in *Phil* 88 (42) (1933) p. 272-295, inscription cited p. 294: τοιγαροῦν νομίζω οὕτω με [γαλοπρεπῶς καὶ θεοσεβ]ῶς δύνασθαι τῇ μεγαλειότητι αὐτῶν τὸ ἱκανὸν ποιεῖν εἰ τοσάκις μυρίους ὁσάκις ἐὰν ὑπεισέλθωσιν εἰς τοὺς ἐμοὺς ἀνθρώπους [συνθύοντας] εἰς τὰ ἱερὰ τῶν θεῶν συνεισενέγκοιμι, cited also in Frend (1965) p. 338. See also F. Ghedini, Giulia Domna tra Oriente ed Occidente: Le fonti archeologiche, in *La Fenice, Collana di Scienze dell' Antichità* 5, (Roma: «L'Erma» di Bretschneider 1984), p. 57-90, 122-160.

on coins as the *mater deorum*.[106] Elagabalus was the priest of the Syrian Baal of Emesa, who succeeded Caracalla, the immediate predecessor of Severus Alexander who in turn succeeded him in A.D. 222. Like the later policy of Aurelian (270-275), the Sun God of Emesa, as part of the ideology of the imperial cult, was worshipped too by his successor Probus (276-282) whose coins exult his person as *soli invicto comiti*.[107]

The Severan developments in extended citizenship accompanied by a development of the ideology of the imperial cult in the direction of greater religious syncretism and universality could have had punitive effects upon Christianity as the reign of Decius (249-251) was to show. But in fact it was not until after the death of Severus Alexander that the *Constitutio Antoniana* was to produce the general persecution that it made possible.[108] The Severan policy was generally one of persuasion and comprehension, despite Septimius' prohibition of conversions, and isolated local judicial processes, as was exemplified in Julia Mamaea's interest both in the Apollonius of Tyana of Philostratus' Life, and the Christ of Origen. But it will be important for us to distinguish between an interest in Christianity, or at least some of its philosophical representative or representatives, and a positive *filo-cristianesimo*.

Let us see how such a policy of syncretism as such is reflected generally in the response of the Christian community itself both in literature and in art, whilst distinguishing a culture of syncretism from a more positive *filo-cristianesimo*.

2B 2.1.3.1. *Literature: Dedications to Julia Mamaea*

Although Eusebius *H.E.* VI, 21,3 might record Origen as the focus of Julia Mamaea's interest, it is in works attributed to Hippolytus that we find the main recognition of her kindly disposition towards Christianity. Jerome (*De vir. ill.* 61) lists a work *De Resurrectione*, mentioned also on the Statue as περὶ θ[εο]ῦ καὶ σαρκὸς ἀναστάσεως.[109] This work would also appear to be identical with the that entitled περὶ ἀναστάσεως καὶ ἀφθαρσίας λόγου in Anastasius Sinaita, *Hodegus* 23 (680). One Syriac extract connects the title with a dedication in the heading "Of Hippolytus Bishop and Martyr: On the Resurrection to the Empress Mamaea; for she was the mother of Alexander who was at that time emperor of the Romans."[110]

---

[106] SHA *Caracalla*, 9,10; H. Mattingly, *Coins of the Roman Empire in the British Museum*, (London 1950) cxxxiii and *CAH* xii 356-357; Abd el Mohsen el Khachab, ὁ καράκαλλος κοσμοκράτωρ, in *JJEgArch*, 47 (1961), p. 119-133; F. Cumont and L. Canet, Mithra ou Serapis ΚΟΣΜΟΚΡΑΤΩΡ, in *Comptes rendus de l' Académie des Inscriptions*, (Paris 1857-), cited in Frend (1965) p. 327 and p. 344. See also J. Réville, *La réligion à Rome sous les Sévères*, (Paris: Leroux 1886), p. 30-35, 210-283.
[107] Frend (1984) p. 440.
[108] Frend (1965) p. 407.
[109] Lightfoot (1890) p. 325 l. 23-24; Guarducci (1978) IV, p. 543, l. 23-24.
[110] P. Lagarde, *Analecta Syriaca*, (Lipsius 1858), p. 87. See also Lightfoot (1890) p. 397 and J. Quasten, *Patrology*, (Westminster, Maryland: Christian Classics 1986) II p. 196-197. For

The Statue furthermore is sole witness to a work entitled προτρεπτικὸς πρὸς Σεβηρεῖναν, and a reasonable hypothesis would be that the "exhortation (προτρεπτικὸς)" is addressed to a princess, and thus equivalent to the work quoted by Theodoret on two occasions as πρὸς βασιλίδα τινὰ ἐπιστολὴ of the Severan dynasty.[111] Lightfoot rejected the attempts both of Le Moyne to identify the person addressed with Severa wife of Philippus, and Döllinger with Julia Aquilia Severa the second wife of Elagabalus. Severina as the βασιλίς of Theodoret is better identified with Julia Mamaea herself.[112] That two works in the *corpus Hippolytanum* are thus attributed to her is an indication of the high regard in which the Hippolytan community held her as the sympathetic face of the Severan dynasty.

But if Guarducci's thesis is correct, it is strange that the name of Julia Mamaea herself is not inscribed upon the Statue at the beginning of the Paschal and Easter Tables instead of Severus Alexander. That thesis rests on the significance of the presence of the emperor's name as indicative of the Statue's character as a dedication to him as a positive Christian sympathizer. Furthermore, if he was seen in such a light, it is strange in turn that no volumes of Hippolytus are dedicated to him instead of his mother.[113]

Hippolytus was furthermore associated with Origen by Jerome in the same passage. The final work on the list, the προσομιλία *de Laude Domini Salvatoris*, was a sermon in which the writer "claimed to have preached in church (*se loqui in ecclesia significat*) when Origen was present (*praesente Origene*)." Thus the two men, both possessing, as we shall later argue (Chapters 6 and 7), a mutual aversion to the developing monarchical episcopate, and the consequent loss of status for the presbyterate, might well have shared a similar view that the imperial court would lend a sympathetic ear to their presentation of the claims of Christianity. But whether the general culture of syncretism had lead them too far in this respect to expect something more positive in terms of recognition than that which in fact was on offer is something that we shall have to consider further.

2B 2.1.3.2. *Literature: Julius Africanus and Hippolytus*
In Oxyrinchus Papyrus III (412) we have preserved a fragment from the Κήστοι, the encyclopaedia of Julius Africanus dealing with the alleged edition of Homer by Peisistratus. The fragment ends with the title and author of

texts see H. Achelis, *GCS* 1,2 (1897) p. 249-253 cf H. Achelis, *Hippolytstudien*, in *TU* 16,4 (1891), p. 189-193.
[111] Ibid. p. 542 l. 16-17; J.B. Lightfoot, *The Apostolic Fathers*. (London: MacMillan 1890) Part I S. Clement of Rome vol. II, p. 325 cf. Theodoret, *Dialog.* ii and iii.
[112] Lightfoot (1890) p. 397.
[113] Guarducci (1989) p.72-73: "in quella biblioteca (sc. the Pantheon) la statua abbia avuto la sua prima sede. A questa opinione contribuiscono... il ricordo dell'imperatore Severo Alessandro che compare nelle due fiancate del trono iscritto... Severo Alessandro è dunque, quasi eponimo del Computo, eseguito da Ippolito con meritoria fatica e probabilmente a lui dedicato."

the work (Ἰούλιους Ἀφρικανοῦ κῆστος) and the number of the entry (ιη= 18). In the final fourteen lines of the entry he records that the thirteenth verse of the passage of Homer under discussion was read "in Rome at the baths of Alexander in the beautiful library in the Pantheon which I myself designed for the Augustus."[114] Africanus dedicated this work to Severus Alexander, according to Syncellus.[115]

Thus Julius Africanus clearly cultivated the patronage of Severus Alexander, as later Hippolytus, and perhaps Origen, was to cultivate the patrongage of Julia Mamaea. We can moreover establish similar contacts between the work of Africanus and the Hippolytan community as we observed in the case of Origen. Caspar defended against Bauer the Hippolytan authorship of the first part of the Liberian *Catalogus*.[116] The insertion of the undated episcopal succession lists into regnal, consular, and other dated lists *via* Chronographies that first placed them in columns side-by-side, and then assimilated them into a common chronological scheme, was the concern both of Africanus and Hippolytus, both of whom were authors of chronographies.

Eusebius (*H.E.* VI, 31, 1-3) mentions not only Africanus' authorship of the Κῆστοι, but also associates him with Origen in an exchange of letters on the authencity of the story of Susanna in *Daniel*, and mentions his five books of *Chronographies*, in which Africanus recorded his visit to Alexandria to meet with bishop Heraclas.[117] In Hippolytus' case we have the Χρονικῶν mentioned on the Statue and in *El.* X, 30,2, a Latin text of which survives as the *Liber Generationis*.[118] Julius Africanus' letter to Aristides, preserved in Eusebius *H.E.* I, 7, reconciles the genealogies of *Matthew* and *Luke* on the basis of the combined royal and sacerdotal blood-lines of the Maccabaean dynasty, which reflected his general interest in Chronology. Both were therefore influenced in the construction of their episcopal lists, as Ehrhardt showed, by eschatological considerations with particular regard to the prophecies of *Daniel* and the regnal/sacerdotal lists of the Maccabaean kings, which in turn produced what was in reality the

---

[114] B.P. Grenfell and A.S. Hunt Oxyrinchus Papirus III (412) (London: Egyptian Exploration Fund 1903): μέχρι δὲ τοῦ τρισκαιδεκάτου ἐν ᾽Ρώμη πρὸς ταῖς ᾽Αλεξάνδρου θερμαῖς ἐν τῇ ἐν Πανθείῳ βιβλιοθήκη τῇ καλῇ ἣν αὐτὸς ἠρχιτεκτόνησα τῷ Σεβαστῷ. F. Granger, Julius Africanus and the Library of the Pantheon, in *JThS*, 34 (1933), p. 157-161. See also *CIG* 3, 9 and J.-R. Viellefond, *Les «Cestes» de Julius Africanus: Étude sur l'ensemble des fragments avec édition, traduction, et commentaires*, (Firenze: Sansoni/ Paris: Didier 1970), p. 284-291.
[115] Georgius Syncellus, *Ecloga Chronographia*, 676: ᾽Αφρικανὸς τὴν ἐννεάβιβλον τῶν Κεστῶν ἐπιγεγραμμένην πραγματείαν ἰατρικῶν καὶ γεωργικῶν καὶ χυμευτικῶν περιέχουσαν δυνάμεις ᾽Αλεξάνδρῳ τούτῳ προσφωνεῖ.
[116] E. Caspar, Die älteste römische Bischofsliste, in *Schriften der Königberger Gelehrten Gesellschaft*, Geisteswissenschaftliche Klasse, 2,4, (Berlin: 1926), p. 386-392.
[117] Eusebius, *H.E.* VI, 31,2: τοῦ δ᾽ αὐτοῦ ᾽Αφρικανοῦ καὶ ἄλλα τὸν ἀριθμὸν πέντε Χρονογραφιῶν ἦλθεν εἰς ἡμᾶς ἐπ᾽ ἀκριβὲς πεπονημένα σπουδάσματα· ἐν οἷς φησιν ἑαυτὸν πορείαν στείλασθαι ἐπὶ τὴν ᾽Αλεξάνδρειαν διὰ πολλὴν τοῦ ᾽Ηρακλᾶ φήμην.
[118] A. Bauer and R. Helm, Chronicon, in *GCS* 46(36), (1955).

novel sacerdotal iconography in one strand of the liturgy for episcopal consecration (in *Ap. Trad.* 3).[119]

We shall later (7B 2) be arguing, against Ehrhardt, in favour of the novel character, in the late second-century, of such sacerdotal images of the episcopal succession. But let us note here that the relations between the kinds of communities and concerns represented by Origen, Hippolytus, and Africanus were nevertheless more complex than Guarducci's account would initially suggest. Certainly the character of the works dedicated to Mamaea, and indeed to Severus, goes beyond that of the earlier apologists. The latter address reasonably and assume the goodwill of emperors who are nevertheless hostile to their claims for legal recognition. Yet it must be remembered that the eschatology of both, involved as it was with the exegesis of *Daniel* and its application to contemporary circumstances, did not sit well with any final *rapprochement* with the pagan imperial power, and certainly did not go as far as Origen and his Alexandrian associates in reducing apocalypticism in favour of the gradual evolution of history transformed by the divine λόγος.

Lactantius claimed that Ulpian around 215 began codifying various laws against Christianity.[120] He cites in this connection Book 7 of the lost *De Officio Proconsulis*, and Frend and Honoré amongst others accept Lactantius' claim at its face value.[121] We possess however extracts from this work in the *Digest* of Justinian, particularly in Book 48,16,14, but Christians as such are never mentioned.[122] It may therefore be that Lactantius is simply referring to general laws codified by Ulpian that were used against the Christians, rather than specific laws against Christianity itself. Indeed his language seems more applicable to Book 8 rather than 7, from which *Digest* 48,18,1 quotes extensively Ulpian on torture (*de quaestionibus*). Thus Ulpian's lack of specificity in laws that might be but were not necessarily used against Christians argues once again for a background of tolerant syncretism rather than a positive support for Christianity as such.

It must moreover be noted that, even in the light of the general persecution of converts, instigated by Septimius Severus, neither the Emperor himself nor the Empire was identified with Antichrist by either Hippolytus or

---

119 A. Ehrhardt, *The Apostolic Tradition in the First Two Centuries of the Church*, (London: Lutterworth Press 1953), p. 40-61. Cf. A. Brent, Diogenes Laertius and the Apostolic Succession, in *JEH* 44,3 (1993), p. 367-389, and see also 7 B 2.

120 Lactantius, *Institutes* V,11,19: "Domitius [sc. Ulpianus], de officio proconsulis libro septimo, rescripta principum nefaria collegit ut doceret quibus poenis affici oporteret eos qui se cultores dei confiterentur."

121 Frend (1965) p. 327; T. Honoré, *Ulpian*, (Oxford: Clarendon 1982), p. 32.

122 See the most telling observation of P. Monat, Lactance, Institutions Divines, in *SC* 205 (1973), Livre V, tome II Commentaire et Index, p. 109: "Parmi les rescrits sur les châtiments cités par Ulpien et relevés par le Digeste.... la plus grande partie se trouve rapportée aux livres 7-9 de cet ouvrage, mais il n'y est pas explicitement question des chrétiens."

Tertullian, in the writings that bear the former's name.[123] Hippolytus, as Dunbar is the most recent writer to show, used his mystical interpretation of *Daniel* and the *Apocalypse* to show that the *parousia* was *not* imminent, despite the expectations of the Montanists and the suffering by some convert groups in the persecution of Septimius Severus (in 202) and subsequently.

Like Julius Africanus and Theophilus of Antioch before him, world history consists of six one-thousand-year days, with the millennium occurring as the seventh day.[124] Africanus, whom Hippolytus now follows, had gone further and established that the incarnation took place 5500 years after Adam. Since two hundred years had elapsed after the incarnation the date of which he had thus established, the second coming would have to be three hundred years still in the future. The events of the reign of the Severans were thus neatly detached from any apocalyptic context, and relations between Church and State could proceed to develop according to their own momentum.[125]

Thus around the time of the construction of the Statue, before the first year of Severus Alexander, whose name and date it bears, we can detect a literary and cultural ambience of mutual toleration and measured respect between his dynasty (and in particular his mother Julia Mamaea) and the Christian church. As such the appearance of the Christology of the *Contra Noetum* with its theory of the λόγος as procession—which despite the staid and orthodox appearance of that work and works associated with it represents a quite radical *rapprochement* with its pagan cultural ambience (5 B 3.1)— and the Statue of Themista re-interpreted as λόγος/σοφία reveals a cultural confluence with the Severan *Zeitgeist*. As such the Statue could stand as the symbol of a Christian community reflecting within itself and in its own terms the general cultural ambience in which it was found and by which to some extent it was formed.

But Guarducci's account requires more than our ability to reconstruct a general pagan culture of tolerant syncretism. She now claims that the Statue was specifically a monument presented by a Christian community, or constructed by a pagan sculptor under Christian influence, in honour of Severus Alexander and accepted by him as an honour to such an extent that it was placed in the Pantheon Library. She has to extend not merely the interested tolerance shown by Mamaea to her son himself, and to convert that restricted tolerance for Christianity in philosophical guise into her emperor-son's positive recognition. She has moreover to do so despite Ulpian's

---

[123] Tertullian, *Adv. Marc.* 3,24; *De Cult. Fem.* II,13,6; *Apol.* 1,1.
[124] Theophilus, *Ad Autol.* 3,28; H. Gelzer, *Sextus Julius Africanus und die Byzantinische Chronologie*, 1 (Leipzig: Teubner 1880) p. 24-26. Cf. Hippolytus, *Dan.* 4,22-24 cf. *Rev.* 17,10.
[125] D.G. Dunbar, The Delay of the Parousia in Hippolytus, in *VCh* 37 1983, p. 313-17. For an earlier version of the thesis which Dunbar here espouses see K.J. Neumann, *Hippolyt von Rom in seiner Stellung zu Staat und Welt: Neufunde und Forschungen zur Geschichte von Staat und Kirche in der römischen Kaiserzeit*, (Leipzig: Veit 1902), p. 75-94.

contemporary legal opposition, and the specific importance of the imperial cult in the Severan claim to political legitimacy.

Guarducci even suggests that the presence of the Statue in the Pantheon library was perhaps due to the influence of its Christian architect, Julius Africanus. But it is one thing to employ an architect to construct a library whose particular religious background might be neither known nor relevant, and another to support positively the exhibition of a Statue the particular religious beliefs to which that architect is committed. We have shown grounds so far against regarding the general background of religious syncretism as necessarily favouring the positive recognition of Christianity that such a positive dedication to Africanus would imply. It is to an examination of this stronger claim that we must now turn.

2B 2.2. A Statue of λόγος/σοφία in the Pantheon Library?

In order to make this further and stronger claim Guarducci has to appeal to three further pieces of evidence in support of a mutual Severan and a Christian interest in such artefacts as the Statue, and in the beliefs of the community that it represents. These respectively are (i) the conversion of Abgar and the Edessan portrait of Christ (2B 2.2.1), (ii) representations of Christ in the Dura Frescos (2B 2.2.2) and (iii) the account of Severus Alexander's *lararium* in SHA, *Alex. Sev.* 51, 6-8 (2B 2.2.3). We must now consider whether these three pieces of evidence can assist us in locating the λόγος/σοφία Statue more precisely in a pagan library as a dedicatory monument to an emperor or his dynasty.

2B 2.2.1. Julius Africanus and Severus Alexander

Guarducci seeks to unite the alleged *filo-cristianesimo* of Alexander Severus, shown in his commissioning of Africanus as the Pantheon architect, and Africanus' earlier connection with Edessa and Abgar. However, we should, *prima facie*, be on our guard against moving too quickly from the congruence of cultural ambience, witnessed in the interest of Julia Mamaea in philosophical defences of Christianity as propounded by Origen and Hippolytus, and a positive like of Christianity by her son Severus Alexander himself.

We should remember that it was to Julia Mamaea. that περὶ θ[εο]ῦ καὶ σαρκὸς ἀναστάσεως, and perhaps the προτρεπτικὸς πρὸς Σεβηρεῖναν were dedicated and not to Alexander himself. Were it not for the questionable evidence of pseudo Lampridius (SHA, *Alex. Sev.* 51, 6-8) that we consider in the next section, there would be no direct connection between the emperor himself and reverence for Christ. Indeed, the dedication to Mamaea. herself may be no more than an encouraging compliment to her fascination for occult philosophy when this happened to be Christian, particularly in the form espoused by Origen which she may not have associated with that of the illegal cult. Furthermore, the choice of Africanus may have been because of his technical competence as an architect without any particular regard for his religious persuasion.

Nevertheless, let us pursue the link between Africanus and Abgar as providing an Edessan connection for Severan syncretism, specifically in the form of an artistic tradition of portraiture.

2B 2.2.1.1. *Abgar IX and the Edessan portrait of Christ*
Before he was at Rome, Julius Africanus was at Edessa in Mesopotamia, and a friend of Abgar IX (A.D. 179-214). Abgar IX (179-214) converted from astral worship to Christianity.[126] Consequently it was during his reign that the famous letter from Christ to his predecessor Abgar V made, she claims, its appearance.[127] But Guarducci will claim that this is not all. An earlier tradition whose first recorded instance is in 544 claims for Edessa the most ancient portrait of Christ.[128] Thus she claims that the ambience of Edessa is represented at Rome by Africanus and embraced by Severus Alexander's alleged *filo-cristianesimo*.[129] Thus she is able to connect this with the statue of Christ that allegedly stood in the *lararium* of Severus Alexander, with which we have yet to deal.

But even if the conversion of Abgar was that certain and sincere, the antiquity of the tradition regarding the portrait of Christ is highly questionable. Segal pointed out that the tradition arose in a sectarian context, and in self-conscious opposition to the group that held the letter as their own. The letter was prized by the Jacobite community who, in the 5th and 6th century objected to portraits, whilst the Melkites, who did not, treasured their portrait but not the Jacobite letter. The latter together with the portrait, is mentioned for the first time in the Syriac *Doctrine of Addai* which was composed in its present form in the late fourth century. Hannan writes the *Acts* on a first visit, and then, on a second, receives Jesus' reply to a letter

---

[126] Guarducci (1977) p. 27: "Ora, i legami che intercorsero fra Severo Alessandro e Giulio Africano e fra Giulio Africano e l'ambiente di Edessa assumono una certa importanza." Cf. H.J.W. Drijvers, Edessa und das Jüdische Christentum, in *VCh* 24 (1970), p. 4-33, however, who emphasises the hostility of Edessa to Rome and the absence of such *legami* (p. 6-7: "Diese wenigen Bemerkungen mögen deutlich machen: (a) eine grosse Abneigung in Edessa gegen die Römer; eigentlich eine grosse Abneigung gegen jede Zentralgewalt im Westen; (b) politische Verbindungen mit der Adiabene, dem jüdischen Fürstentum östlich des Tigris.") Such a state of affairs is hardly conducive to Julius Africanus, bringing an alleged cultural ambience to Rome to form part of a cultural syncretism when that ambience was clearly constructed against such a syncretism. See also E. von Dobschütz, Christbilder. Untersuchungen zur christlichen Legende, in *TU* 18, (1899).
[127] Eusebius mentions this letter in *H.E.* I, 13,3-22. The Syriac text of this letter says that its contents were spoken by Christ to Ananias who then wrote it down. For a full discussion of the legend see J.B. Segal, *Edessa "the Blessed City,"* (Oxford: Clarendon 1970), p. 62-81.
[128] At least Guarducci is convinced that it is an earlier tradition ("una tradizione il cui primo ricordo è del 544"), ibid. p. 27.
[129] Ibid. p. 27: "Tutto ciò induce a ritenere che Giulio Africano abbia avuto qualche parte nel filocristianesimo di Severo Alessandro e di Giulia Mamaea.."

which Abgar had sent with him. Hannan, as royal painter, then painted the portrait. In subsequent accounts Jesus paints the picture himself.

Unfortunately for Guarducci's case we can show that the picture and its significance was subsequent to even the edition of the letter which Eusebius publishes. It was only subsequent to this edition that the words were added: "Your city shall be blessed and no enemy shall ever be master of it." This led to the claim, on which Procopius in the sixth century was to comment sarcastically, that the city would never be captured. In consequence the letter assumed the character of a talisman the possession of which would keep the city secure. The Melkite portrait became the counterpart of the Jacobite letter. But since the words of protection were added to the letter only at the end of the fourth century and subsequent to the Eusebian citation, then the legend of the portrait must date subsequent to that time too.[130] If this is the case, there is no tradition of portraiture at Edessa such as to connect its cultural ambience on that ground with Africanus, and in turn with a statue of Christ allegedly in the *lararium* of Severus Alexander.

However, there are the eastern examples of the Dura frescoes where the earlier, Roman iconographic tradition of symbol and allegory is replaced for the first time in the history of early Christian art with representations of the historical Christ. Guarducci and Testini both see the possibility of a cultural ambience here that might be held to support the historical accuracy for the time of Severus Alexander of allusions to a Statue of Christ in the work of the otherwise historically questionable *Scriptores Historiae Augustae*.

2B 2.2.1.2. *The Dura Frescoes and Africanus' Syrian ambience*
As we have seen, early Christian art was symbolic and allegorical, and was not concerned, as was its pagan counterpart, with representations of the individual personality. Indeed this was part of Guarducci's case that originally the Statue could not have represented Hippolytus in person. In this respect her most powerful case regarding the feminine form of the Statue's allegorical original belies the historical credibility of a Statue of Christ in Severus Alexander's *lararium*. If the Statue stood as a monument to the *filo-cristianesimo* of the Severans in the Pantheon Library, then why was it not an actual statue of Christ similar to that claimed for the *lararium*?

The very fact that the Statue was an allegorical symbol in which the figure of Themista was transformed into Christ as *Logos/Sophia* belies any tradition of Christian representative art at this time. In consequence, the connection between Julius Africanus as the architect of the Pantheon Library, and his alleged contact with an alleged Edessan tradition of portraiture cannot be used to support the historical character of the statue of Christ recorded in SHA. That account cannot, except at the cost of *petitio principii*,

---

[130] Segal (1970) p. 73-78.

then be used to document a cultural background for the Statue as a Christian monument in a pagan library when that cultural background, as the Statue itself testifies, is to a symbolic rather than representational tradition in art. It will not do, moreover, to point to the Carpocratian statue of Christ mentioned by Irenaeus according to which Christ's bust was depicted *more philosophorum*. If the allegorical figure whether of Themista or of *Logos/Sophia* was a monument to the *filo-cristianesimo* centred on the figures of Hippolytus and Africanus and their group, then a Carpocratian realistic representation clearly would not have formed part of Severus Alexander's complimentary repertoire.

A closer analysis of the art of the house-church at Dura Europos will not however give the clear artistic tradition of portraiture appearing for the first time there in the mid-third century that the thesis of the historicity of the statue of Christ in the *lararium* requires.[131] The original focus for the iconography of the house church was the large painting of the Good Shepherd, where the shepherd is depicted beardless with the flock curiously facing away from him as he is almost dwarfed by the huge sheep that he carries. This was the central picture placed on the wall at the end of a long narrow room, and set in a vaulted baldachin which surmounted the basin of the baptistery by analogy with the position of the cult-god of a pagan shrine. The painting of Adam and Eve with trees and a serpent is a latter addition to the scene. Here therefore the central scene for the iconography of worship was still Christ under the guise of the allegorical symbol of the Good Shepherd of the parable, and not in terms of a literal representation of the historical Jesus as recounted in the gospels.

However, the remaining walls were decorated with three scenes. One scene takes up part of the east and north walls and involved originally five women, whose feet with hemmed robes have been preserved. Around the corner of the room, beyond a half-open door, the second episode of the scene was recounted where the present spaces for five persons, four of whom have been preserved, are moving towards a large, white sarcophagus. The natural interpretation as a resurrection scene seemed initially obviated

---

[131] I am indebted for these paragraphs to A. Perkins, *The Art of Dura-Europos*, (Oxford: Clarendon 1973), p. 52-55. For the remains of the pictures themsleves see Plates 17 and 18. See also J.P. Kirsch, Die Entdeckung eines christlichen Gotteshauses und einer jüdischen Synagoge mit Malereien aus der ersten Hälfte des 3. Jahrhunderts in Dura-Europos in Mesopotamien, in *OrChr*, ser. 3, vol. 8 (1933), p. 202-204; P.V.C. Baur, The Christian Chapel at Dura, in *AmJArch* 37 (1933), p. 377-380. See also E. Dinkler, Dura-Europas III, Bedeutung für die christliche Kunst, in *RGG* 2 (1958), cols. 290-292; C. Hopkins, (B. Goldman (Ed.)), *The Discovery of Dura Europos*, (Newhaven: Yale U.P. 1979); ——, The Christian Chapel at Dura-Europos, in *Atti del III congresso internazionale di archeologia cristiana*, (Rome 1934), p. 483-492; C. Watzinger, Die Christen Duras, in *Theologische Blätter* 18 (1938), p. 117-119.

by the facts that (i) a resurrection scene involving five women is based on no gospel account and (ii) there are no figures of angels present.[132]

Villette has resolved the second difficulty (ii) by pointing to the two bright stars that shine over the sarcophagus, and the association particularly in the Eastern tradition, of stars with angelic beings.[133] Regarding (i) the scene has been held to represent the resurrection according to the composite account of Tatian's *Diatessaron,* a parchment fragment of which, dated around 222, was found on the site and which records the visitors to the Tomb.[134] Villette, less plausibly in view of the evidence of this fragment, regards the presence of five women as including two angels along with Mariam, Salome and Arsenia, according to a Manichean text.[135]

For our purpose it must be noted that no figure of the risen Christ is here preserved, although we are now clearly in the area of depiction of Gospel narratives and not of symbolism and allegory. Nevertheless, there is no interest still in portraiture as such. The scenes of the Good Shepherd and the Tomb by night on Easter Eve, along with those that we are about to consider where the figure of Christ does appear, namely with Peter on the water and at the side of the paralytic, form part of the symbolism of baptism with which the baptistery is clearly thus iconographically associated.

These two miracles are depicted in their surviving remains on the remainder of the North Wall. But although we may note a clear change in early Christian allegorical art, we are still far short of any example of portraiture. Indeed the gospel scenes now are made part of the allegorical imagery of baptism. The Jesus depicted with outstretched arms is the Christ of faith whose significance is the spiritual power that he embodies in these scenes. It

---

132 Consequently they are held to represent the parable of the Wise and Foolish Virgins in O. Casel, Älteste christliche Kunst und Christusmysterium, *JLiW* 12 (1934) p. 74, and J. Pijoan, The parable of the Virgins from Dura-Europos, in *The Art Bulletin*, 1937, p. 592-595 (figs. 1-5). Such an explanation would avoid the need to posit, according to Perkins (1973) p. 54: "an episodic treatment of narrative with repetition of figures to indicate different 'scenes' which 'has a long history in Near Eastern art and leads to the 'continuous method' common in the decoration of narrative scrolls." See also C. Kraeling *et. al.,* Narration in Ancient Art: A Symposium, in *AmJArch* 56 (1957), p. 44-91. An alternative proposal, of H. Grégoire, Les Baptistères de Cuicul et de Doura, in *Byz* (1938), p. 589-593, is that the scene is of a festival of lights symbolizing the illumination of baptism, p. 593: "Je n'entends pas nier que la procession de Doura puisse évoquer aussi la parabole des Vierges sages et des Vierges folles, surtout si l'on admet que la scène commence sur le mur ouest. Mais il ne peut s'agir d'une illustration littérale. La procession symbolise avant tout l'illumination du baptême," which is given some credence by the fragments that appear to be of torches born by the women. See also W. Seston, L'Église et le baptistère de Doura-Europos, in *Annales de l'école des hautes études de Grand,* (1937), p. 161-177.

133 J. Villette, Que représente la grande fresque de la maison chrétienne de Dura? in *Rbib* 60 (1953), p. 398-413 where he argues p. 399: "... deux étoiles, anormales par leur taille immense, ne brillaient sur le sarcophage comme deux acrotères célestes," and p. 400: "... pour les Sémites surtout, un astre n'est pas seulement une créature magnifique... c'est un être animé, d'une essence supérieure..."

134 Perkins (1973) p. 34 cf. C.H. Kraeling, A Greek Fragment of Tatian's Diatessaron from Dura, in K. and S. Lake (eds) *Studies and Documents* (ed. K. and S. Lake) 3 (London: Christophers 1935), p. 3-7.

135 Ibid. p. 409-410, footnote 2.

is not without significance, I submit, that the very scene that would admit of
the interest in personal characteristics presupposed by portraiture, namely
that of the Samaritan woman at the Well depicted below the doorway in the
south wall, lacks any space for an original figure of Jesus as part of that
scene.[136]

There is nothing resembling the quite elaborate pagan statuary found
elsewhere at Dura, which would tend to show the persistence in the
Christian artistic tradition here to the self-denying ordinance of Rome that
we have noted in this respect. Even though therefore many features of the
art may reflect distinctively Syrian characteristics, nevertheless there is little
here to support a statuary representation of Christ at this period, the feeling
for which Africanus could somehow have taken with him to Rome and influenced the alleged contents of Severus Alexander's *lararium*.[137]

We may thus conclude that Guarducci's alleged connection between
Abgar and Africanus fails because (i) the latter does not acknowledge
unambiguously the Christianity of the former, and, (ii) the cultural ambience
in terms of a statuary representing Christ cannot be substantiated before the
end of the fourth century. We have already made part of our case in any
event against the *filo-cristianesimo* of Severus Alexander as opposed to a
general cultural ambience witnessed by the interests of his mother Julia
Mamaea. But let us now consider the question of the purported statue in the
lararium.

2B 2.2.2. *The* lararium *in SHA Alex. Sev. 29, 2; 31, 4-5*
According to this passage Severus Alexander possessed a private chapel
where the *lares et penates*, the gods of hearth and home, were venerated and
which is accordingly called a *lararium*. The chapel contained, according to a
putative writer of his own time (*quantum scriptor suorum temporum dicit*),
"portraits" or "images (*effigies*)" of "divine leaders (*divos principes*)" and
the "chosen best (*optimos electos*)" were objects of divine worship (*rem
divinam faciebat*).[138] It is important however to note that 31,4-5 makes it
clear that he possessed two *lararia*, the second of which was for poets and
heroes (*Vergilium... eius imaginem cum Ciceronis simulacro in secundo
larario habuit*), reserving the first and greater for Alexander the great

---

[136] Perkins (1973) p. 54.
[137] Kirsch (1933) p. 204 notes: "Die Komposition, die Auffassung der Gegenstände wie die
Art der künstlerischen Ausführung weisen auf lokale syrische Kunstrichtung hin; die Szenen,
die Parallelen in der römischen zömeterialen Malerei des 3. und 4. Jahrhunderts haben,
unterscheiden sich in der Komposition und der künstlerischen Art von den Denkmälern Roms."
[138] SHA *Alex. Sev.* 29,2-3: "Usus vivendi eidem hic fuit: primum [ut], si facultas esset, id
est si non cum uxore cubuisset, matutinis horis in lar<ar>io suo, in quo et divos principes sed
optimos electos et animas sanctiores, in quis Apollonium et, quantum scriptor suorum temporum dicit, Christum, Abraham et Orfeum et huius<modi> ceteros habebat ac maiorum effigies,
rem divinam faciebat. Si id non poterat, pro loci qualitate vel vectabatur vel piscabatur vel
deambulabat vel venabatur."

amongst the *optimos et divos*.[139] Can we therefore find in this description either the support for the existence of a statue of Christ in either the *lararium secundum* or the *lararium maiorem* though it is clearly the former where such a statue would be located? Can we further find here support for a *filo-cristianesimo* and a cultural ambience that would give credibility to the notion of a Statue contributed by a Christian community to the Pantheon Library in acknowledgment of the friendship of Severus Alexander?[140] This we shall now see to be questionable.

2B 2.2.2.1. *The* SHA *is an anachronistic forgery*

The first point that must be made is that the *SHA* by its own claim emanates from the time of Diocletian and Constantine and purports to be written by six courtiers of their reigns. (*Elagab.* 34-35) But this ostensible claim has long been recognised as a forgery. The style and vocabulary of the six writers points to a single hand which is quite prepared to invent some thirty-five fictitious writers in order to support his fraud.[141] If however the six writers are a forger's literary device, so also is likely to be the chronological location in the last years of Diocletian and the first of Constantine. Both are given to create a fictional setting in past history so as to make a contemporary point in an age after them.

What then was the point being made by the literary and historical fiction, and at what point of time? Baynes originally argued, supported recently by Syme, that the *SHA* emanated from the period of Julian, or of the circle of Symmachus that survived him and with whom Ambrose did battle.[142] In

---

139 Ibid. 31,4-5: "Vergilium autem Platonem poetarum vocabat eiusque imaginem cum Ciceronis simulacro in secundo larario habuit, ubi et Achillis et magnorum virorum. Alexandrum vero Magnum inter optimos et divos in larario maiore consecravit."

140 Such as is suggested in S. Settis, Severo Alessandro e i suoi Lari. (SHA, 29, 2-3) in *Ath.* 60 1972, p. 237-251, and in Dal Covolo (1989) p. 19-22, 81-90, who defends the account inSHA as within limits reliable evidence.

141 First established by H. Dessau, Über Zeit und Persönlichkeit der Scriptores Historiae Augustae, in *Herm 24* (1889), p. 337-392, and defended by various writers up until Syme (1983), in which, for full bibliography, see p. 224-229. The argument of A. von Domaszewski, Die Personennamen bei den Scriptores Historiae Augustae, in *SHAW.*, Phil.-hist. Kl. (1918) was particularly cogent. See also E. Hohl, Über den Ursprung der Historia Augusta, in *Herm* 55 (1920) p. 296-310.

142 N.H. Baynes, The date and composition of the Historia Augusta, in *ClassRev*, 38 (1924) p. 165-169; ——, The Historia Augusta, *Its Date and Purpose*, (Oxford: Clarendon 1926) p. 57-63 and chp. 3; Syme (1983) p. 220-221. Syme (1983) could well have been directed at Settis (1972) when he says: "The beliefs of the Syrian prince do not fail to seduce adepts of religious syncretism." (p. 214). See also Hohl (1920) p. 309: "Dass der Verfasser der Historia Augusta ein Grammatiker der theodosianischen Zeit ist, dünkt mir in hohem Grad wahrscheinlich geworden zu sein; ist es allzu kün die Möglichkeit zu erwägen, ob er nicht den Anschluss an die Symmachi tatsächlich erreicht hat?" K. Bihlmeyer, *Die Syrischen Kaiser zu Rom (211-235) und das Christentum*, (Rothenburg: Bader 1916), p. 75-77; ——, Die syrischen Kaiser Karacalla, Elagabal, Severus Alexander, und das Christentum, in *ThQu* 97 (1915) p. 71-91; J. Straub, Heidenische Geschichtsapologetik in der Spätantike. Untersuchungen über Zeit und Tendenz in der *Historia Augusta*, in *Antiqu.* 4,1 (1963) p. 40-44; 109-110; p. 180-181; cf. J. Béranger, Julien l'Apostat e l'hérédité du pouvoir impérial, in *Antiqu.* 4,10 (1972) p. 75-93 who concludes: "Or l'une d'elles serait la critique et la condamnation de l'hérédité du pouvoir impérial, justement au précepte et à l'exemple de Julien qui, en réaction contre ses

such a context, Constantine, whilst he was still a worshipper of the *sol invictus*, combined with Diocletian, the inveterate supporter of paganism, would have both proven attractive icons of the universal syncretism of the sun's disk which Aurelian had espoused and which Julian sought to revive as part of the pagan reaction. The primary motive therefore for producing an account of an apparent religious syncretism amongst the emperors was not to advocate a comprehensivist approach to Constantine as the first Christian Emperor. Rather it was to assist Julian or the pagan sympathisers who survived him, in their attempt to produce a rival universal syncretism with which to replace the narrowness of dogmatic Christian universalism. Furthermore, the veneration of statues accompanied by miraculous tales played a prominent role in Julian's response to Christian monotheism.[143] Indeed, part of that response was to divorce the Jesus of history from the Church, and to admire him as a Hellenistic divine teacher such as those who appeared in the *lararium secundum*.

2B 2.2.2.2. *Julian is idealized as Severus Alexander*

Significantly for our purpose it was in such a context that Baynes understood in particular many of the features of the description of the life of Severus Alexander to which Settis appeals and which Guarducci cites as of fundamental importance to her case.[144] A comparison between the character of Julian as described by contemporary writers and that of the Severus Alexander of the *SHA* show significant parallels. Ammianus stresses the chastity of Julian.[145] Likewise Alexander is described as *castus* (7,6), or *usus veneris moderatus* (39,2).

It is important to note in connection with the former reference that it occurs in the speech attributed to the Senate where divine or priestly honours are associated with the use of the name of Antoninus who was also called Pius (7,2). As an Antoninus he is thus to dedicate the temples of the Antonines (*Antoninorum templa Antoninus dedicat* (7,5), the *divos principes* whose statues are later located in the *lararium* in 39,1. He receives the sacred name as one who has himself been made sacred (*sacrum nomen sacratus accipiat* (7,6).Thus his chastity here is seen in the context of his pagan high-priesthood. In the following chapter it is the name of Augustus and the office of *pontifex maximus* that begin his thanks to the Senate (*Augusti nomine addito et de pontificatu maximo et de tribunicia potestate et*

---

prédécesseurs au trône, réalise le régime idéal où, enfin, l'empire revient au mérite, et non plus au privilège de la naissance. Une des thèmes favoris de l'Histoire Auguste..." (p. 92) A.D. Nock, Orphism or popular philosophy? in *HThR*, 33 (1940), p. 301-315.

[143] T. Pekáry, Statuen in der Historia Augusta, in *Antiqu.* 4,7 (1970) p. 151-172, and his conclusion "Wie ersichtlich, zeigt der Verfasser der HA ein reges Interesse für Statuen im allgemeinen und für Statuenwunder im besonderen, beides typisch für die Zeit um 400n. Chr."

[144] Settis (1972); cf. Guarducci (1977) p. 26 note 15 and (1989) p.72.

[145] Ammianus Marcellinus, *Res Gestae*, XXV,4,2: Et primum ita inviolata castitate enituit, ut post amissam coniugem nihil umquam venereum attigisse eum constaret.

proconsulari imperio (8,1). The name of the Antonines are associated with their divinity (*Antoninorum nomen vel iam numen potius quantum fuerit* (9,1).

2B 2.2.2.3. *The character of Alexander's priesthood*

Settis was wrong in consequence to point to the direct influence of Judaic notions of sexual cleanness before participating in religious ritual in explication of *Sev. Alex.* 29, 2-3. When it is said of Alexander that he celebrated as a priest religious rites (*rem divinam faciebat*) on condition that he had abstained from sexual intercourse (*si non cum uxore cubuisset*), it is with reference to his imperial office of pagan *pontifex maximus* over the syncretistic universal pagan religion that Julian attempted to establish rather than anything directly levitical.[146] The quite fictitious Severus Alexander of the author of the *SHA* is therefore the idealized model for an emperor like Julian who presides over the pagan cult of the sun's disk which unites the Graeco-Roman pantheon into a syncretism which comprehends Judaism as well as Christianity.[147] The scene, attributed to a nameless writer introduced in order to support the fiction (*quantum scriptor suorum temporum dicit*), and describing him as standing in the midst of the statues of the *divi principes, optimi electi et animae sanctiores*, is likewise an icon of the universalist pagan cult of Julian, rather than a chapel that had any actual, historical existence during the reign of Severus Alexander.[148]

2B 2.2.2.4. *Jews and Christians under Julian*

It is in this context that we should therefore locate also the Judaeo-Christian practices attributed to Severus Alexander. Julian is recorded as wishing to rebuild the temple at Jerusalem but was prevented because of volcanic activity that impeded the workmen.[149] In SHA *Sev. Alex.* 22,4, it is for the Jews that Alexander is described as "preserving from extinction" (= the sense of *reservare* here) privileges (*Iudaeis privilegia reservavit*) whilst the Christians he merely allows to exist (*Christianos esse passus est*). Here Julian stands mirrored in the fictitious Severus Alexander, since the rebuilding of the Jewish temple represented a calculated granting of privilege to the Jews at the same time as privileges were being withdrawn from the Christians whom he merely "allowed (*passus*)."

---

[146] Settis (1972) p. 238-240; Bihlmeyer (1916) p. 121.
[147] Frend (1984) p. 596-598.
[148] For an account of Julian's designs, see G.W. Bowersock, *Julian the Apostate*, (London: Duckworth 1978), p. 85-93, and W. Koch, Comment l'empereur Julien tâcha de fonder une église païenne, in *Revue belge de philologie de d'histoire* 6 (1927), p. 123-146; ——, 7 (1928) p. 49-82; ——, 7 (1928) p. 511-550; ——, 7 (1928) p. 1363-1385.
[149] Ammianus, *Res Gestae*, XXIII, 1,2: "... imperiique sui memoriam, magnitudine operum gestiens propagare, ambitiosum quondam apud Hierosolymam templum... instaurare sumptibus cogitabat immodicis, negotiumque maturandum Alypio dederat..."

Nevertheless, in the sentence immediately following, his deference to the
council of pontiffs and augurs must immediately be mentioned.[150]
Alexander is called by the title of *archisynagogus*, but only, it should be
noted, in derision as by the Alexandrians[151] and there conjoined with the
title *archiereus*, which refers to him as *pontifex maximus* rather than the
leader of a synagogue.[152] Julian as the founder of the pagan reaction is thus
lampooned for his syncretistic combination of Jewish and pagan images in
his proposed universalistic cult.

Julian's suppression of catholic Christianity as inconsistent with a
Christianity comprehended in his universalist cult is not belied by the description *Christianos esse passus est*. According to the writer, Alexander
had wished to build a temple to Christ so that he should have his place
amongst the other gods whose shrines he was frequenting. However, the
augurs foresaw that everyone would become Christians and the temples be
abandoned so that he did not.[153] Nowhere would this appear clearer than in
this instance, the origin of which is obviously an historically fictitious story
in the events of Julian's pagan reaction. Furthermore at one point Julian did
order Bishop Eleusis of Cyzicus to rebuild a Novatian church.[154]

His action in sacking Christian classics professors was never understood
by Julian as an act of persecution, but rather the establishment of academic
integrity since Christians could not be expected to learn and to teach the literature of a religion and civilization in which they did not themselves believe.[155] Otherwise it could be said of Julian *Christianos esse passus est*,
even though general toleration could be cynically regarded as serving to stir
up internal Christian strife.[156] In his letter to the Bostrans, written from
Antioch on 1st August 362, he was to admonish "those who are zealous for

---

[150] SHA, *Sev. Alex* 22,5: "pontificibus tantum detulit et quindecimviris atque auguribus, ut
quasdam causas sacrorum a se finitas iterari et aliter distingui pateretur."
[151] Ibid. 28,7: "Volebat videri originem de Romanorum gente trahere, quia eum pudebat
Syrum dici, maxime quod quodam tempore festo, ut solent, Antiochenses, Aegyptii,
Alexandrini lacessiverant conviciolis, et Syrum archisynagogum eum vocantes et archiereum."
It is difficult to accept the historicity of a text which treats *archisynagogus* as the equivalent of
archiereus, which hardly establishes a claim to precise knowledge of Jewish practices. The
historicity of the title was defended by A. Momigliano, Severo Alessandro Archisynagogus.
Una conferma alla Historia Augusta, in *Athen.* n.s. 12 (1934), p. 151-153, with which cf. Syme
(1983) p. 123, 186-188 and bibliography. Baynes (1926) p. 141-142 explained the writer's
desire to detach his fictitious Alexander from the criticisms levelled at the Syrians by Julian,
Misopogon 348, where the Greek qualities of adherence to ancient virtues are claimed for
Syrians also: εἰ δὲ ἐκεῖνοι διασώζουσιν εἰκόνα τῆς παλαίας ἐν τοῖς ἤθεσιν ἀρετῆς,
εἰκὸς δήπουθεν τὸ αὐτὸ ὑπάρχειν καὶ Σύροις...
[152] Settis (1972) p. 239 fails to detect the subtlety of the forger here.
[153] SHA, *Sev. Alex*. 43,5-7: "... templa frequentavit. Christo templum facere voluit eumque
inter deos recipere... sed prohibitus est ab iis qui consulentes sacra reppererant omnes
Christianos futuros, si id fecisset, et templa reliqua deserenda."
[154] Socrates, *H.E.* III,11; Frend (1984) p. 602.
[155] Ammianus, *Res Gestae*, XXV,4,20 and Frend (1984) p. 604-605.
[156] Ibid. XXII,5,4 and Frend (1984) p. 601-602.

the true religion not to injure the communities of the Galileans or to attack or insult them."[157]

2B 2.2.2.5. *Julian's organization of paganism and ordination*

The success of the Church, organized episcopally and exercising discipline through patriarchs or archbishops, impressed Julian sufficiently to try to set up a similarly organised pagan priesthood with provincial high priests. There were to be Platonic guardians set over this pagan state-church which would include Basil, bishop of Caesarea and thus comprehend a modified Christianity once again within its syncretism.[158] The older urban aris-tocracies invariably held such priestly offices along with their secular and civic ones. Pseudo-Lampridius again shows these arrangements reflected in the deeds of his Alexander. He informs us that governors of provinces, procurators and other officials were appointed (*ordinare*) by means of the names of the candidates being publicly announced and charges invited against the unworthy. This moreover was done by direct analogy with a Jewish or Christian ordination (*in praedicandis sacerdotibus, qui ordinandi sunt*).[159] Once again Julian's pagan cult mirrors the organisation of the Christian Church and is idealized historically in Severus Alexander, the imperial and sacerdotal model of the president or *pontifex maximus* of that cult.[160]

2B 2.3. *The case against Severan Philo-Christianity*

We have thus seen in this major section (2B 2) that Guarducci's argument fails to establish a general cultural and religious ambience for the presence of a Christian statue in a public building such as a library commemorating the Severan dynasty in general, and Severus Alexander in particular. The historiography of Eusebius in making good emperors favourable towards Christianity (2B 2.1) should not make us transform an interest on the part of Julia Mamaea in some philosophical forms of Christianity (2B 2.1.1) into a more positive disposition belied by the development of the imperial cult as the focus of religious syncretism (2B 2.1.2). Literary dedications to Julia Mamaea could be no more than the apologetic response of Hippolytus,

---

[157] Julian, *Ep.* 41, 438B: αὖθις δὲ καὶ πολλάκις παραινῶ τοῖς ἐπὶ τὴν ἀληθῆ θεοσέβειαν ὁρμωμένοις μηδὲν ἀδικεῖν τῶν Γαλιλαίων τὰ πλήθη, μηδὲ ἐπιτίθεσθαι μηδὲ ὑβρίζειν εἰς αὐτούς.

[158] Julian, *Ep.* 15 and 26, and cf. Philostorgius *HE* III,15.

[159] SHA, *Sev. Alex.* 45, 6-7: "... ubi aliquos voluisset vel rectores provinciis dare vel praepositos facere vel procuratores, id est rationales, ordinare, nomina eorum proponebat, hortans populum, ut si quis quid haberet criminis, probaret manifestis rebus, si non probasset, subiret poenam capitis. dicebatque grave esse, cum id Christiani et Iudaei facerent in praedi-candis sacerdotibus, qui ordinandi sunt, non fieri in provinciarum rectoribus, quibus et fortunae hominum committerentur et capita."

[160] Ibid. 51, 6-8 portrays Alexander as quoting the golden rule (*quod tibi fieri non vis, alteri ne feceris*) which thus appears in its negative, talmudic form *a quibusdam sive Iudaeis sive Christianis audierat et tenebat*. See Julian's use of Scripture in references in Baynes (1926) 143-144. For additional comparisons between Julian and the SHA see idem p. 118-144.

Origen and their communities to expressions of interest rather than commitment. If, moreover, the Statue's inscription mentioning Severus Alexander's first year are in some way a dedication to him, it is surprising that no book either of Origen or Hippolytus is dedicated to him as opposed to his mother, or indeed that Mamaea's name did not occur there in place of her son's (2B 2.3.1).

The appeal furthermore to Africanus in support of a positive thesis of Severan support for Christianity such as would establish the Statue's pagan provenance proved problematic. Africanus shared with Hippolytus an interest in apocalyptic concerns that might have reduced the fear of the Roman Empire as directly the representative of Antichrist, but yet would hardly have countenanced a more positive acceptance as was later attempted by the Eusebian ideology. Though the Statue interpreted as λόγος/σοφία might, when compared with the Christology of the *Contra Noetum*, be regarded as culturally confluent with the Severan *Zeitgeist*, it would be a monument to a community's understanding of itself rather than a dedicatory statue to a Roman emperor (2B 1.3.2).

Guarducci's thesis at this point required further strengthening by demonstrating a connection between Julius Africanus and a tradition of Christian portraiture at Edessa. This connection was required not by the need to explain λόγος/σοφία, which was not at all events a portrait, but because of the statue of Christ in Severus Alexander's *lararium*, whose historicity would confirm irrefutably his *filo-cristianesimo*, and thus the existence of an ambience for the Statue as a dedicatory work to him (2B 2.2-2.2.1). The alleged personal portrait of Christ as indicative of an artistic tradition with which Africanus could have come into contact was shown to be based upon an anachronistic legend (2B 2.2.1.1). Moreover the Dura frescoes themselves, on examination, failed to corroborate the tradition of personal portraiture (2B 2.2.1.2).

In the final analysis we were left with the *SHA,* standing by itself, and a close examination demonstrated that it had no real connection with the history of Severus Alexander. The *lararium* was a fiction which read back into the past the proposals of Julian for a form of pagan religious universalism (2B 2.2.3-2B 2.2.3.5). In consequence, the positive syncretistic, pagan cultural ambience in which to locate the Statue in the time of Severus Alexander was proved to be at that time non-existent.

We must now turn from Guarducci's case for the general cultural ambience to her specific proposals for where and how the Statue could have fitted into the physical dimensions of a pagan library such as the Pantheon. To a consideration of the physical as opposed to cultural space in which the Statue was originally located we must now turn.

2B 3. *The position of the Statue in the Pantheon Library?*

We come therefore to the final part of Guarducci's argument for the location of the Statue in the Pantheon Library. We have presented serious objections to her analysis of the general Severan cultural ambience, assisted by the alleged Syrian influence upon Julius Africanus, into which she claimed the Statue fitted. But she also sought to argue that the material artefact represented by the Statue actually fitted the architecture and arrangement of an ancient library such as presumably the Pantheon Library must have been. As such she was supported by Leclerq's earlier statement who, it must nevertheless be remembered, was writing before Guarducci had established the undoubted fact that the Statue was originally feminine.

Leclerq attributed the production of the Statue to a pagan workshop, and regarded Hippolytus as depicted in the pose of a philosopher. Yet the library for which it was constructed was, he believed, a Christian library. Clearly he shared the conviction of implausibility that the Paschal and Easter Tables could have conveyed any meaning in the context of a pagan Library such as the Pantheon.[161] Likewise also Wendel also believed that the Statue evidenced a Roman community that possessed a library adjoining the house where it gathered for the Eucharist and for fellowship, by analogy with pagan libraries that adjoined temples.[162]

It was Frickel who originally suggested to Guarducci that the Statue had stood originally in the Pantheon Library, though he persisted in believing that it was a statue of Hippolytus himself, as a monument to an alleged *filocristianesimo*.[163] Africanus took a statue of a male or female philosopher originally not Hippolytus but attributed to him when his list of works were

---

161 H. LeClerq in *DACL* 6,2 p. 2420: "La statue... a pu être exécutée dans un atelier païen où l'on fabriquait en série les rhéteurs et les philosophes, comme on peut supposer qu' Hippolyte aura posé pur la ressemblance du visage... Était-ce pour orner une bibliothèque chrétienne que fut sculptée la statue?"

162 C. Wendel, art Bibliothek, in *RAC*, Bd. II p. 247: "Glaubensstandpunkte wurden noch dringender zZt. der innerkirchlichen dogmatischen Kämpfe. So entstand in den grosstädtischen Gemeinden neben der für den Gottesdienst und das Gemeindeleben unentbehrlichen Bücher- und Archivalien-Sammlung zwangläufig eine theologische Bibliothek. Eine solche muss zu Beginn des 3 Jh. die römische Gemeinde besessen haben, wenn ihr Presbyter Hippolytos dort seine vielseitige Schriftstellerei ausüben konnte." Likewise the connection is drawn between such pagan models and later libraries attached to Churches, see K. Dziatzko, art. Bibliotheken, in *PWK* Bd. 3, p. 421: "Noch wesentlicher ist für die antiken Bibliotheken ihre stete Verbindung mit einem Heiligtum, besw. einer geweihten Stätte, mag der Schutzgott in einem inneren Zusammenhang stehen mit der Bibliothek..." See also B. Götze, Antike Bibliotheken, in *JDAI* 203 (1937), p. 225-247; E.A. Parsons, *The Alexandrian Library: Glory of the Hellenic World*, (London: Elsevier 1952).

163 J. Frickel, *Das Dunkel um Hippolyt von Rom: Ein Lösungsversuch: die Schriften Elenchos und Contra Nöetum.* (Grazer Theologische Studien: Bauer 1988), p. 81: "... Julius Africanus die Hippolytstatue für die Bibliothek des Kaiser neu anfertigen liess," cf. Guarducci (1989) p. 71-72. Frickel found the suggestion in C. Wendel, Versuch einer Deutung der Hippolyt-Statue, in *TheolStKrit*, 26 (1937-1938), p. 362-369. This location is rejected in C.P. Bammel, The State of Play with regard to Hippolytus and the *Contra Noetum*, in *HeyJn* 31 (1990), p. 196.

placed upon the plinth.[164] Africanus then added the Paschal and Easter
Tables, since their inscriptions "spill over on both sides of the lower edge of
the Chair."[165] But I find it frankly incredible, and for reasons that I have already given, that those Tables could have had any significance outside the
community which needed them to calculate the date of its celebration of
Easter.[166] (2A 2.4).

Like Guarducci, Frickel had to rely not simply on a *Synkretismus* in the
time of Severus Alexander, but also to an alleged *Christenfreundlichkeit* that
we have challenged.[167] Frickel nevertheless believed that the Statue had
been removed during the next reign under the persecutor Maximinus the
Thracian to the place where Ligorio claimed to have found it on the via
Tiburtina.[168]

Guarducci, as we saw in 1 B, endeavoured to undermine Ligorio's
reliability, and so believed that the Statue had always stood in the Patheon
Library. But she now went further and tried to specify precisely how the
Statue would have fitted into the internal architecture of such a Library. The
roughness of the back of the Statue, and the catalogue of works on the plinth
indicates to her that the Statue was set into a wall alongside of which was a
capsa (which she translates *armadio* or "cupboard")[169] which was set into
the wall itself and which contained the scrolls.[170] Thus one could read on the
plinth the catalogue of the works that the adjoining *capsa* contained. It is to
these claims regarding the original physical and architectural location of the
Statue that we must now turn.

2B 3.1. *Archaeological examples of Library artefacts*
If the Statue thus stood as an ordinary artefact alongside of other ordinary
artefacts, one has only to look at the inadequacy of any parallel advanced to
support any particular category for it. Guarducci's location, whether in the

---

[164] Frickel (1988) 81-82: "Denn die "Hippolyt-Statue hat mit grosser Wahrscheinlichkeit
ursprünglich nicht Hippolyt dargestellt, sondern war das Standbild eines Philosophen oder einer
Philosophin der epikuräischen Schule, das erst nachträglich durch Anbringung der Inschriften
dem christlichen Lehrer Hippolyt gewidmet wurde."
[165] Ibid. p. 82 note 255: "Die Eingravierung der Ostertafeln war bei der ursprünglichen
Konzeption der Statue nicht eingeplant, denn sie überborden auf beiden Seiten den unteren
Rand der Kathedra, sind also sichtlich zu einem späteren Zeitpunkt eingemeisselt worden."
[166] Ibid. p. 82-83: "Wohl aber könnte Julius Africanus auf einer ihm verfügbaren älteren
Statue die damals noch bestaunten Ostertabellen und ein auch für heidenische Betrachter
verständliches kurzes Schriftenverzeichnis haben anbringen lassen, um die so umgewidmete
Statue dann in der öffentlichen Bibliothek des Alexander Severus neben anderen Statuen
aufzustellen."
[167] Ibid. p.84-87.
[168] Ibid. p. 86-88.
[169] Guarducci (1989) p. 73: "... la nostra statua venisse collocata presso un armadio o una
capsa in cui le opere dell'elenco fossero custodite e che, per comodità dei frequentatori, l'elenco
stesso fosse riportato sul montante del trono."
[170] Ibid. p. 73: "... i rotoli di papiro contenenti i vari testi erano depositi sui palchetti degli
armadi che si aprivano nelle pareti, oppure erano infilati nelle *capsae librariae*."

library of the villa of the via Tiburtina or that of the Pantheon, presents great problems.

One principal problem is our lack of knowledge of how the Pantheon library itself was arranged. Indeed its actual site is difficult to place, since Africanus' location ἐν ῾Ρώμῃ πρὸς ταῖς᾽ Ἀλεξάνδρου θερμαῖς rules out any identification with the excavations of a possible site at the Thermae Agrippae. Rather the site of the library must therefore have been the Thermae Neronianae rebuilt by Severus Alexander. But this site has no clear remains with which to identify the Pantheon Library to which literary references are made.[171] We are therefore thrown back on what we can recover about the furniture and arrangement of ancient libraries in general.

I am sure that in a Roman library of the third century the papyrus rolls were deposited in cupboards set in the walls or inserted into *capsae librariae*. But that the Statue was positioned alongside such a cupboard or *capsa* is pure conjecture. We have inscriptions of lists of books on library pillars, such as that of the Ptolemaeon at Athens or the gymnasium at Rhodes both dated around late 2nd to early 1st Century B.C., though they are few and far between since catalogues were normally on papyrus and not on stone. They list books given by the *Epheboi*. The former (Ptolemaion) consists of a list on the corner of a marble pillar, inscribed with a list of authors and works such as tragedies of Menander and philosophical dialogues of Plato's disciple Eukleides, with the names of two Attic demes.[172] The latter (Rhodes) is a marble block only complete on the left side consisting of an alphabetical list of authors in two columns, together with their works.[173] But nowhere have we found a Statue in a library with a catalogue of books inscribed on its side.

The Statue in the Pantheon library would not stand as any the less an unusual artefact, therefore, even without a *capsa* or cupboard with papyri scrolls adjoining. We have references to Statues of philosophers in the libraries of the schools and held and handed down in common possession, such as those mentioned in Theophrastus' Will.[174] But we have no references to any list of books of Aristotle or of anyone else actually inscribed on the base of such Statues.[175] Indeed, we have an inscription from Aphrodisias

---

171 S.B. Platner and T. Ashby, *A Topograpical dictionary of Ancient Rome*, (Oxford: University Press 1929), p. 382-386; p. 518-520; p. 531-532.

172 *IG* II/III².2 2363 Cf. Guarducci M., Epigrafi di Biblioteche, in *Epigrafia Greca* II (Istituto Poligrafico dello Stato: Roma 1978), p. 574-575. See also *I.G.* II/III¹.² 1041 for a reference to βιβλία ἀνέθηκαν..εἰς τὴν ἐν Πτολεμαίῳ βυβλιοθήκην from a decree of the Athenian Boule between 47-43 B.C,.

173 Guarducci II (1978) p. 576-577.

174 Diogenes Laertius, *Succ.* V, 51-52. For an exhaustive collection of primary sources for ancient libraries, see J. Platthy, *Sources of Earliest Greek Libraries*, (Amsterdam: Hakkert 1968).

175 The description of the library built by Hadrian next to the temple of Hera and Zeus Pallenios is described in Pausanias, *Graeciae Descriptio* I, 18,9 as ...οἰκήματα ἐνταῦθά ἐστι... ἀγάλμασι κεκοσμημένα καὶ γραφαῖς· κατάκειται δὲ ἐς αὐτὰ βιβλία. καὶ

recording the decree granting Gaius Julius Longianus citizenship. He is to be honoured with bronze likenesses in prominent places of the city, in particular the precinct of the Muses and the gymnasium of the *Epheboi*. But his books themselves are to be shelved in the public libraries. There is no attempt to associate the list of works with the bronze likenesses.[176]

Not only therefore was a Statue as opposed to a pillar not the location of a list of works of the author, but, as we shall now see, there was a general physical separation between the location of lists (πίνακες) and such likenesses in the form of statues or herms.

2B 3.2. *Statues and bookshelves/cases in ancient libraries*
Dio Chrysostom makes reference to the likeness made of him set up by a friend in his library, in order to encourage the youth to follow his profession.[177] Pliny mentions libraries decorated with the busts of departed authors and a statue of Trajan placed in a library.[178] But the archaeological evidence tends to point to such statues not resting beside or even in the same rooms as bookshelves or cases. Furthermore, the evidence that we have of pictures, medallions, or statues associated with book stacks are far smaller than the life-size Statue of Themista/σοφία.

2B 3.2.1. *Temple Libraries at Pergamon and the Pallantine*
There was a base for a statue, probably that of Athena, at the entrance of the library that adjoined the north wall of the colonnade of the court of the

---

γυμνάσιόν ἐστιν ἐπώνυμον Ἀδριανοῦ. γραφαῖς should be translated "paintings" and not "writings." See also Plutarch, *Vitae decem Oratorum*, 841: εἰσήνεγκε δὲ καὶ νόμους (sc. Lycurgus) τὸν δε, ὡς χαλκὰς εἰκόνας ἀναθεῖναι τῶν ποιητῶν, Αἰσχύλου, Σοφοκλέους, Εὐριπίδου, καὶ τὰς τραγωδίας αὐτῶν ἐν κοινῷ γραψαμένους φυλάττειν. Cf. A.E. Raubitsche, Greek inscriptions, in *Hesp.* 35 (1966), p. 241-251, Panataïnos Herm 8 (plate 66) p. 247, which describes two joining fragments of a herm of Pentelic marble, broken on all sides but preserving at the top part of the herm the Athenian archon and founder of the library. 115/116 A.D. See also J.A. Notopoulos, Studies in the Chronology of Athens, in *Hesp.* 18 (1949, p. 26-27.

[176] P. Le Bas and W.H. Waddington, *Inscriptions greques et latines recueilles en Grèce et en Asie Mineure*, (Paris: Librairie Firmin Didot Frères: 1870), III,1 no. 1618.a.127 p:.. ταῖς τε ἄλλαις πολιτείαις καὶ τειμαῖς τετειμῆσθαι ταῖς ἐκ τῶν νόμων μεγίσταις καὶ εἰκόσιν χαλκαῖς, ἅς ἐν τε τοῖς ἄλλοις ἀνασταθῆναι τοῖς ἐπισημοτάτοις τῆς πόλεως χωρίοις καὶ ἐν τῷ τῶν Μουσῶν τεμένει καὶ ἐν τῷ γυμνασίῳ τῶν ἐφήβων παρὰ τὸν παλαιὸν Ἡρόδοτον· ἐψηφίσθαι δὲ καὶ τοῖς βυβλίοις αὐτοῦ δημοσίαν ἀνάθεσιν ἔν τε βυβλιοθήκαις ταῖς παρ' ἥμειν...

[177] Dio Chysostom, *Orations* 37,8 (ΚΟΡΙΝΘΙΑΚΟΣ) : ... ἀλλά γε τὴν εἰκὼ τοῦ σώματος ἐποιήσασθε καὶ ταύτην φέροντες ἀνεθήκατε εἰς τὰ βιβλία (sc. εἰς τὴν βιβλιοθήκην), εἰς προεδρίαν οὗ μάλιστ' ἂν ᾤεσθε τοὺς νέους προκαλέσασθαι τῶν αὐτῶν ἡμῖν ἐπιτηδευμάτων ἔχεσθαι.

[178] Pliny Minor, *Ep.* X, 81,7: "Ipse in re praesenti fui et vidi tuam (sc. Traiani) quoque statuam in bibliotheca positam, id autem, in quo dicuntur sepulti filius et uxor Dionis, in area collocatum, quae porticibus includitur." Thus Wendel *R.A.C.* II p. 265-266: "Alle bibliotheken, von denen wir Nähres wissen, waren mit den Statuen, Büsten, oder gemalten Bildnissen bedeutender Autoren geschmückt. Wir können diese Sitte verfolgen von der Bibliothek der Attaliden, aus der sich die Basen der Statuen von Alkaios, Herodot, und Demosthenes gefunden haben, über die Privat-Besitze des Herennius, dem Plinius die erforderlichen Porträtbilder verschaften wollte..."

Temple of Athena at Pergamon. But this stood in an entrance set apart.[179] The remaining statues that the library housed were found in the easternmost section of the remains, which showed evidence of a half-partition separating the area from the rest. Dziatzko's view, supported by Callmer, was that this was a vestible where such statues and medallions were located, whilst the books were stored in the separate adjoining rooms.[180] Certainly fragments, bearing the names of Herodotus, Alcaeus, Timotheus of Miletus, and Homer, were considered to be the remains of herms or portrait medallions.[181] It is small wonder if this were the general plan for such libraries that there was such a reluctance to list the works of authors at the base of herms or full-length statues. Their position away from the bookshelves themselves would have rendered such lists pointless.[182]

Similarly in the remains of the Temple and area of Apollo on the Palatine Hill, begun by Augustus in B.C. 36 and dedicated B.C. 28, we find two libraries, one of Greek and the other of Latin books. Between them originally stood a vestibule or reading room in which there was a large statue of Apollo, accompanied by statues of celebrated writers in the same bronze material, and portrait reliefs in the form of medallions on walls.[183] A further example would also be the Greek and Latin Libraries which stood in the Forum of Trajan to the right and left of the column, which shows in its plan a striking similarity with that of Pergamon.[184] The Pergamon Library was therefore no idiosyncratic artefact but reflected the generally assumed architecture of ancient libraries that housed statues in different rooms from bookcases. Indeed, there is a logic to placing such statues were the books will be read as opposed to where they are stored. Fehrle has pointed out that these Roman libraries followed the Greek model in that their purpose was seen

179 C. Callmer, Antike Bibliotheken, in *Opuscula Archaeologica* III (1944), p. 148-151 and Abb. 1 and 2 p. 149-150.
180 K. Dziatzko, Die Bibliotheksanlage von Pergamon, in *Beiträge zur Kenntnisse des Schrift, Buch, und Bibliothekswesens,* (Leipzig: Spirgatis 1896) 3, 10, p. 38-47, cited in J.W. Clark, *The Care of Books: An Essay on the Development of Libraries and their Fittings, from the earliest times to the end of the XVIII century,* (Cambridge: U.P. 1902), p.11. Cf. Callmer (1944) p. 152 ff.: "Dziatkos Vorschlag ist somit zweifellos der richtige." Wendel, *R.A.C.* II, p. 231-274; V.M. Strocka, Römische Bibliotheken, *Gymnasium* 88 (1981), p. 302-304. See also Th. Mommsen, Inschriften Büsten, in *Archeologische Zeitung* 38 (1880), p. 32-36; E. Bethe, *Buch und Bild in Altertum,* E. Kirsten (Ed.), (Leipzig and Vienna: Harrassowitz 1945). F.G. Kenyon, *Books and their Readers in Ancient Greece and Rome,* (Oxford: Clarendon 1932).
181 Clark (1902) p. 11; Dziatzko (1896) p. 40-41.
182 Dziatzko (1899), cited in Clark (1902), previous footnote, registers a hesitant "vielleicht" to this well substantiated conclusion: "... im grossen aber in der Gruppierung der Schriftsteller, vermutlich nach den im Altertum geläufigen Arten der Schriftstellerei, und in der Aufstellung entsprechender Verzeichnisse (πίνακες) *innerhalb der Benützungs- und vielleicht auch der Lagerräume.*" (my italics)
183 Clark (1902) p. 14-15. The original library was destroyed by fire and rebuilt under Domitian, see also R. Fehrle, *Das Bibliothekswesen im alten Rom,* (Wiesbaden: Ludwig Reichert 1986), p. 62-65; Strocka (1981) p. 307-308.
184 Ibid. p. 15 fig. 4 and p. 16; Fehrle (1986) p. 67-68 abb. 2; Strocka (1981) p. 309-311. Wendel, *R.A.C.* II, p. 245: "Alle stadtrömischen Bibliotheken bestanden aus zwei getrennten Abteilungen, einer bibliotheca Graeca und einer bibliotheca Latina."

primarily for the gathering of academics for their work rather than for the
preservation of books themselves.[185] But if the Library of the Pantheon, the
plan of whose original architecture is no longer available to us, followed this
general pattern, then indeed the idea that the Statue of Themista/σοφία could
have stood originally *collocata presso un armadio o una capsa in cui le
opere dell'elenco fossero custodite* become very difficult to sustain.

We have however more specific evidence of the arrangement of books
and statuary in private libraries to which we now turn.

2B 3.2.2. *Lanciani's discovery of a private library in 1883*

The real character of figures adorning private libraries and their relation to
bookshelves was illuminated by the discovery of a library by Lanciani in
1883 in the ruins of a private house excavated near the church of San
Martino on the Esquiline.[186] The walls uncovered were found to have been
bare up to a certain height but then, above the stucco-work, beautifully decorated. Each compartment consisted of a medallion between pilasters with an
author's name, e.g. POLONIUS THYAN (= Apollonius of Tyana). The
height of the blank wall below the stucco-work was 3 feet 6 inches, where
the bookshelves stood. There was simply no room by the stacks themselves
for a Statue of this size and having the function of providing a catalogue of
works stored in an adjoining cupboard. Even the niches for certain kinds of
statues would not support a statue of this size and kind involving a seated
figure on a chair set tangentially into a wall.

In view therefore of the size and position of the bookshelves themselves,
it is difficult to find space for an artefact of the size of the Statue of
Themsta/σοφία. It was thus the wall spaces above the book-cases that were
decorated with the likenesses of celebrated authors,[187] but, as Clark said,
"we are not told of how these portraits were commonly treated—whether
they were busts standing clear of the wall; or forming part of its decoration
in plaster work or distemper."[188] It was the innovation of the construction of
the library of the Temple of Apollo under Augustus in which the bookcases
were sunk into niches that for the first time created the spaces above which

---

[185] Fehrle (1986) p. 69: "Die Ausschmückung öffentlicher Bibliotheken mit Bildnissen
verstorbener oder auch lebender Schrifsteller war überhaupt gebräuchlich, doch folgte man hier
griechischen Vorbildern. Neue am Typus öffentlicher Bibliotheken in Rom war dagegen die
Art der Präsentation der Bestände. Während wir es in der Zeit davor mit Magazinbibliotheken
zu tun haben, deren Hauptraum nicht der Aufbewahrung der Buchrollen, sondern, wie in
Pergamon, für Versamlungszwecke im Zusammenhang mit dem akademischen Betrieb diente,
vollzieht die öffentliche römische Bibliothek den Übergang zur direkten Zugänglichkeit der
Bestände für den Benutzer."

[186] R. Lanciani, *Ancient Rome in the Light of Recent Discoveries*, (London: MacMillan
1888), p. 193-197.

[187] Pliny, *Nat. Hist.*, VII, 30,115: "M. Varronis in bibliotheca, quae prima in orbe ab Asinio
Pollione ex manubiis publicata Romae est, unius viventis posita imago est..." and cf. 35,2;
Martial, *Epigram 9*.

[188] Clark (1909) p. 37.

could thus be decoratively filled.[189] Thus the size of the statues, portraits or other representations, once they were taken from the entrance or adjoining lecture rooms and introduced amongst the stacks themselves, would have been determined by the smallness of those spaces thus created which would have been insufficient to contain a life-sized Themista/σοφία.

2B 3.2.3. *General literary evidence of library arrangement*
At all events, as we have mentioned, the *imago* of Epicurus already mentioned by Cicero (*De Fin.* V, 1,3) was *in poculis et in anulis*, and as such could be carried around as an *effigies* described by Pliny (*N.H.*, XXXV, 2,5). When such statues were associated with the stacks themselves, as opposed to the anteroom where lectures took place, they must therefore have been of a corresponding smaller size. Seneca accordingly associates such small pictures with what immediately adorns the *tecto tenus exstructa loculamenta* with the description of *cum imaginibus suis descripta sacrorum opera ingeniorum in speciem et cultum parietum* (*De Tranqu.* 9, 7). It is thus small pictures or images that are clearly associated with the stacks, and the room in which these are found.

Thus the racks on which the scrolls were stored, called by such terms as *armaria, foruli, loculi,* and *loculamenta,*[190] reached to the ceiling. The ends of the rolls has fixed to them tickets on which their titles (*index, titulus*) were given.[191] Sometimes the rolls were numbered and catalogued, and the catalogues inscribed in stone.[192] Yet we have no examples of statues of authors inscribed with catalogues of their works, nor indeed of an allegorical figure standing for the ethos and character of a collection of certain kinds of books. Such statues, even those representing the spirit of their authors, were located separately from the bookshelves themselves.[193]

---

[189] Seneca, *De Tranqu.* 9,7: "Apud desidiosissimos ergo videbis quicquid orationum historiarumque est, tecto tenus exstructa loculamenta..." Wendel *R.A.C.* II p. 262: "Ein wichtiger Verbesserung technischer Art hat Augustus mit der Bibliotheke des Apollo-Tempels auf dem Palatin eingeführt, indem er die Rollenschränke nicht mehr frei vor die Wände des Saals stellte, sondern in Nischen versenkte, die aus den Mauern ausgespart waren." See also *Digest* XXX, 41,9; XXXII, 52,7; Pliny, *Ep.* II, 17,8. Cf. Strocka (1981) p. 301 who cites a bookcase depicted on a sarcophagus-relief set into a wall.
[190] Apollonius Sidonius, *Ep.* II, 9,4; Martial, *Epig.* 1, 117; 7, 17; Cicero, *Ad Atticum*, IV,4,5,8. See also Dziatzko (1899) p. 421.
[191] Seneca, *De Tranqu.* 9, 6: "Quid habes, cur ignoscas homini armaria e citro atque ebore captanti, corpora conquirenti aut ignotorum auctorum aut improbatorum et inter tot milia librorum oscitanti, cui voluminum suorum frontes maxime placent titulique?" Cf. Cicero, *Ad Atticum*, 4,89.
[192] F. Schmidt, Die Pinakes des Kallimachos, in *Klassischen-Philologischen Studien* 1, (Berlin 1922); F.J. Witty, The Pinakes of Callimachus, in *Library Quarterly* 28 (1958), p. 132-136. See also Pliny, *N.H.* VII, 58.
[193] Pliny, *N.H.* XXXV, 2,9: "Non est praetereundum et novicum inventum, siquidem non ex auro argentove, at certe ex aere in bibliothecis dicantur illis, quorum immortales animae in locis iisdem loquuntur, quin immo etiam quae non sunt finguntur, pariuntque desideria non traditos vultus, sicut in Homero evenit."

2B 3.2.4. *The Statuette of Euripides and his works*

Indeed the most striking evidence for the kind of artefact that Guarducci assumed the Statue of Themista/σοφία to have been, as yet unnoticed by anyone in this discussion, is the marble statuette of Euripides (Plate 14). Euripides is seated on a chair on whose plinth his name (Εὐρι[πίδης]) appears. On the marble panel, which forms the backcloth, a list of the works of Euripides is found. But this statue, found in 1704 at Rome in the gardens of the canons regular of St. Anthony, and transferred initially to the villa of Cardinal Albani and then to the Louvre in Paris, is better described as a statuette since it is all of 55 cm in height.[194] Thus precisely the kind of artefact with which Guarducci identifies the Statue is shown to deny by its very size the possibility of that identification. A life-size Statue could not have existed adjacent to a book-case with the purpose of giving a catalogue of the volumes which it contained.

2B 3.2.5. *False parallels at Ravenna and Apollo Palatinus*

Furthermore, it is inappropriate, I believe, to regard as a parallel with an early third century pagan library the example from the Mausoleum of Gallia Placida at Ravenna of the *capsa* in which the gospels were housed where there is depicted a figure of a teacher, and the title of the gospels is shown on the doors.[195] The true parallel for such an artefact, I submit, is not a pagan library but a pagan temple, since we are describing the iconography surrounding holy writ, which was hardly the case with the catalogue of Hippolytus' works on the Statue of Themista/σοφία. The pagan parallel of books attached directly to a statue associated with their contents would therefore be the copies of the Sibylline oracles deposited under the base of the statue of Apollo at the temple of the Palatine set up by Augustus.[196]

Let us now discuss where our discussion has lead us, and the positive conclusions that we can draw about the Statue and its relation to the community of Hippolytus.

---

[194] *CIG* 3, 6047: "In tabula anaglypho ornata, in quo repraesentatur Euripides in sella sedens, reperta circa a 1704 Romae in hortis canonum regularium S. Antonii, in villam Albani translata, indeque Parisios in museum Louvre. Tituli in sella poetae utrinque incisi sunt; pars titulorum ad sinstram prospectanti incisorum in fine mutila est." See also Le Cte de M. Clarac, *Desription du Musée Royal Des Antiques du Louvre*, (Paris: Vinchon 1830), Salle des saisons 65, p. 32: "La table de marbre adossée au siège sur lequel le poète est assis, augemente le prix de ce monument. On y a gravé le catalogue de ses pièces. Trouvé en 1704 sur le mont Esquilin, dans le jardins de etc..."; W. Froehner, *Les Inscriptions Greques*, (Paris: Musée National du Louvre 1864); J.J. Bernoulli, *Griechische Ikonographie mit Ausschluss Alexanders und der Diadochen*, Erster Teil, (München: Bruckmann 1901) p. 152 no. 17; G.M.A. Richter, The Portraits of the Greeks, Vol. 1, (London: Phaidon 1965), p. 137 and figs 760-761; A. Nauck, *Euripidis Tragoediae*, (Lipsae: Teubner 1885), 3rd Edit. Vol. 1, p. xxv.

[195] Wendel *R.A.C.* II p. 270 abb. 4.

[196] Suetonius, *Augustus* 31: "Libros Sibyllinos condidit duobus forulis auratis sub Palatini Apollonis basi."

PART C: CONCLUSION: HIPPOLYTUS' HOUSE

We have seen therefore that the thesis that the Statue stood in the pagan Pantheon Library is highly questionable. What can be established regarding the architecture and arrangement of ancient libraries belies the notion that a life-size statue could have existed in relation to a *capsa* or book-cupboard such as to exhibit a catalogue of the scrolls stored there. Furthermore, we have carefully scrutinized both the cultural and artistic ambience in terms of which a Christian Statue in a pagan library could have been made credible and intelligible, and found this not to have existed.

We have found both the alleged artistic tradition of Edessa with which Africanus had contact, and the alleged Severan *filo-cristianesimo,* as opposed to a weaker eclectic syncretism, unsustainable on such a Julianic hypothesis. The evidence of the Severan *lararium* of the SHA fell to the ground when examined in its real and contemporary Julian, context. Without such evidence Eusebian apologetic exaggeration of the importance of Julia Mamaea's eclectic interest in philosophical versions of occult religions offered us too weak a support for the hypothesis as the legend of a real picture of Christ in the Edessan tradition. Such a legend was never current as early as the beginning of the third century.

Without such support, we are thus thrown back on our earlier argument that the claimed position of the Statue in the Pantheon Library is belied by the Paschal and Easter Tables that are by far the most prominent features of this artefact. Such tables, even under the symbolic figure of Wisdom, into which Themista had been depersonalized, would have meant nothing to the pagans who saw such an artefact. Rather its purpose and function is in-house or in-church. The artefact is the centre of a Christian community with the Johannine date for the Crucifixion and a consequent eastern date for Easter ascertainable from the Calendar.[197] We cited examples of such differences of practice as a means of establishing the distinctive social identity and ethos of such communities. We drew out the Epicurean ethos at an affective level that would have been denied at the cognitive, by both the Johannine school and that of Hippolytus. The φιλοί and the ἀγαπητοί, the *catech-umenoi* and the καθηγετής etc., as shared expressions of the Johannine literature, the *Ap. Trad.* and the Epicurean fragments, all told this story well (2A 2.2).

The true significance of the Statue within the Church was its position at the centre of a community which had a doctrine of the generation of the λόγος that set it apart from the Monarchianism of the wider community. Their λόγος Christology was also a σοφία Christology whose ethos was well represented by the figure of Wisdom. We shall argue (Chapters 4 and 5) that

---

197 Simonetti (1989) p.119-120: "...l'ipotesi celebrativa non è affatto l'unica possibile..."

this was a Christology of a sectarian group that was to win the theological controversy, even though it was to submit to a monarch bishop who arose from an opposing group. One of their writers, Hippolytus, was to be commemorated, in 235 during Maximinus' persecution, along with bishop Pontian as a presbyter, even though he was hardly the only presbyter, with whom he had shared exile in Sardinia, in a community now reunited. The author of the *Elenchos*, and another writer of a work on the Statue, the περὶ τοῦ παντός, was the uncommemorated bishop of the earlier division.

The picture that thus begins to emerge bears striking resemblance to that drawn by Lampe in his recent seminal work which characterises in terms of fractionalization the Christian, Roman community at the end of the second century. We shall see later, in our detailed analysis of the relationship between the community of Hippolytus and that of Callistus revealed in *El.* and *Ap. Trad.* how that relationship fits in with our picture of a fractionalized group before the final emergence of the monarchical episcopate in Rome in its final and definitive form. In view of the organization of the church of Rome in the second century, if not in house-churches, then in what we shall argue in Chapter 6 to have been house-schools, we can also associate the Statue with such a house.

One of Damasus' inscriptions commemorating the rebuilding of the cult centre describes it after all as a *domus*. Guarducci herself, in her earlier work, considered that the Statue was located in a Roman Villa, perhaps in a private library after Hippolytus' death, where around such a personal memorial the later cemetery could develop.[198] It was precisely because she now wished to locate the Statue in the Pantheon Library, designed by Julius Africanus, as a Christian contribution to the religious multi-culturalism of Severus Alexander and Julia Mamaea, that she now finds the case against this original and natural location untenable. It will be well for us therefore, as part of our conclusion, to point to Damasus' *domus* as one piece of evidence for the emergence of the cult-centre on the via Tiburtina, which we established in Chapter 1 was rightly the original location of the Statue.

The *carmen* of Damasus celebrates the renovation of the shrine of the martyr Hippolytus that Cecchelli sought, as we saw in Chapter 1, unsuccessfully to distinguish as the companion of St. Laurence from the martyr bishop and writer of Portus.[199] Indeed ironically Guarducci's establishment of the symbolic character of the Statue considerably alleviates a problem felt by earlier scholars in connection with this epigram. If the Statue stood on

---

[198] Guarducci (1977) p. 26-28 where she says, e.g.: "Le iscrizioni del Computo pasquale e dell'elenco delle opere rivelano...la stessa mano. Ciò conferma la convinzione che uno solo sia l'autore di tutti quegli scritti." (p. 28). See also Guarducci (1989) p. 73: "Si è generalmente ritenuto, ed io stessa ho condiviso quest'opinione, che tutte quelle opere fossero da attribuirsi ad Ippolito." With her opinion regarding authorship concurs V. Saxer, La questione di Ippolito Romano, in *StEphAug* 30 (1989), p. 47-49;

[199] 1B 2.3.3.1 footnote 75.

the via Tiburtina in the *domus* of Hippolytus here described, why was no mention of it made by Damasus, Jerome or Prudentius?[200] One answer might be that, because it was an allegorical figure, like so many contemprary statues, and not the actual figure of Hippolytus, it failed for this reason to stand out. In the light of my later discussion in Chapter 6, I would wish to argue that the Statue was ignored by Eusebius and hence by Damasus because of the role that it played in the inner life of a community that they could only regard as suspect and schismatic, from their ana-chronistic conceptualisation of schism.

De Rossi argued against the thesis that historically the cult-centre could have existed on the site of Hippolytus' own villa, which was the meeting place of his own house or school church. He claimed rather that it was the imposition of the cult of Hippolytus the soldier that lead to the invention that the cult centre was his own house.[201] But Da Bra insisted to the contrary that *domus* is not used by Damasus as a house of repose but of paradise.[202] Whenever *domus* is used of a martyr's tomb in inscriptions it is usually qualified in some way, for example by *alma*.[203] Thus a reference to Hippolytus' house as opposed to his grave appears to be implied by Damasus as already existing in the tradition before the cult of the soldier was superimposed upon it, and before that word by itself could mean a tomb.

But nevertheless if we accept, as we have argued that we should, the testimony of the Liberian *Catalogus* and *Depositio*, then indeed Hippolytus' remains would have been deposited in his house. Does this mean that in this case the *domus* would have been used as a burial place before Hippolytus was laid to rest there? This fact is a problem in view of the way in which pagan mausolea may have existed alongside other houses and temples as did the rows along the Vatican hillside, but they were never dual purpose.

---

[200] G. da Bra, *Studio su s. Ippolito Dottore*, (Roma: Scuola Typografia Pio X 1944), p. 11.

[201] G.-B. De Rossi, Il cimitero di S. Ippolito presso la via Tiburtina e la sua principale cripta storica ora dissepolta, in *BArC* 7 (1882) ser. 4 anno 1, p. 15: "Ciò significa che l'Ippolito, martire eponimo del luogo [coemeterium Hippolyti in Tiburtina], fu assai probabilmente o l'istitutore del cimitero od il proprietario del terreno quivi destinato alla sepoltura dei fedeli."

[202] G. de Bra, *I Filosofumeni sono di Ippolito?*, (Roma: Scuola Typografia Pio X 1942), p. 36. Felicissimus and Agapetus are described as "ministri rectoris sancti meritamque fidem se-cuti, aetherias petere domos regnaque piorum." (Ferrua (1942) 25, p. 154 lines 3-5; Felix and Philippus are "Cultores domini Felix pariterque Philippus, hinc virtute pares, contempto principe mundi, aeternam petere domum regnaque piorum." (Ibid. 39 p. 179 lines 6-9); and of the 62 martyrs, "... confessi Christum, superato principe mundi, aetheriam petere domum reg-naque piorum." (Ibid. 43 p. 185 lines 4-5).

[203] E.g. *ILCV* 1765,4 where we have a reference to the "*sacrae*...domus" of Pope Leo to which Amnia Demetrias has contributed "extrema suorum." In idem 1830,2 the memoria of the martyr Emeritus (hic memoria beati martiris dei consulti [E]mer[iti]) is called Christ's house (hic domus *dei nostri Christi*). Alternatively, as in 1835 the shrine is called "domus *orationis*." In 2184 Flavia Ursacia is deposited "in domo *dei*" and not in her own house-shrine. In 2422 the references is to "*aecle[si]ae* domus." In 3482,3 "domus" is qualified by "alma," where Cinegius rests "in aula sancta... [illum nu]nc Felicis habet domus alma beati." See also *ILCV* 1783, 1791, 1800, 1812, 1833-, 1842-1844, 1900, 1902C, 2138A, 2184, 2435A, 2464.

Furthermore, burial grounds could only be legally located outside the *pomerium* or boundary of the city of Rome itself.

The answer to this conundrum lies, I believe, in the fact that this particular area on the via Tiburtina outside the Porta Tiburtina witnessed a mixture of building development with the outward extension of the *pomerium* during this period.[204] A house that stood within the city walls in this period could therefore have found itself outside the city walls with the boundary change and thus eligible for use as a burial place. The association of relics and their veneration was established in 258 at the shrine of Peter and Paul *A d Catacombas*, excavated under St. Sebastino on the via Appia Antica. The excavations there reveal a room with a kitchen used undoubtedly for *refrigeria* by a schismatical and populist group in self-conscious opposition to the *Aedicula* on the Vatican Hillside. But the nagging question is whether indeed a private house stood originally as the nucleus of a later burial complex, or whether the later tradition of the private residence of Peter and Paul is completely legendary.[205]

The tradition of a private house might be the genuine core that gave credence to the undoubted legend of both apostles living there. Clearly the presbyter Hippolytus alone of the martyred presbyters of Rome was considered worthy of being named with bishop Pontianus. When the latter was laid in the tomb of the popes *in Callisto*, would it not have been appropriate that Hippolytus was laid to rest in his *domus*?

But not laid there, I would suggest, out of the sentimentality and hagiographic enjoyment of later martyrologies obsessed with the desire for personal details of the martyr. In Chapter 6 we shall develop more fully the significance of the almost cryptographic allusions that we find in the Liberian *Catalogus* and *Depositio*. Hippolytus was clearly a very special presbyter to be mentioned alone alongside his bishop. Furthermore the date of the commemoration for both Hippolytus and Pontianus on the 13th August we shall also see to have been the festival of Diana commemorating the incorporation of the Italian allied cities into the Roman Federation. There is, we shall argue, a hidden message about unity and concord after strife which had implications for the ecclesiastical division between *Pontianus episcopus* and *Yppolytus presbyter*, the real nature of which will require further discussion in 6A 2.1.

The very hidden character of the message was critical to both sides in such a division remembered but healed. Hippolytus' house or villa, where

---

[204] Platner (1929) p. 392-396.
[205] Toynbee and Ward Perkins (1956) p. 168-182; M. Guarducci, Die Ausgrabungen unter St. Peter, in *Das frühere Christentum im Römischen Staat*, (Ed.) R. Klein) (Darmstadt: Wissenschaftliche Buchgesellschaft 1971), p. 406-414; H. Chadwick, St. Peter and St. Paul in Rome: The problem of the Memoria Apostolorum ad Catacumbas, in *JThS*, n.s. 8,1 (1957), p. 45-52; Lampe (1989) p. 114-116.

his community met, could well have become the place of deposit for his relics before the expansion of the *pomerium* at this time, which would have made the burial within the walls of Rome and therefore illegal. That community may have possessed a collection of the works of him and his associates, and pagan works too if the considerable sources of the *Elenchos* were not copied by its author from public libraries. Guarducci originally believed that the Statue had stood originally in a private villa in this locality to which a library might have been attached.[206] In this villa stood the Statue, either attached tangentially to the external walls of its gardens, or indeed in the walls of its *aula*, though not directly with the book-stacks themselves. Indeed, it would not have been unknown in pagan history for people to have been buried in the vicinity of their villa and private library.[207]

But the Statue itself, as a unique artefact, was unusual in any place. It stood there as part of the hidden message of a community that wished to remember but not advertise its earlier stances on controversial issues, particularly in respect of the prominent Paschal Tables that could no longer give accurately the date of Easter, but paid silent tribute to a group that accepted the Johannine date of the Passover and wished to compromise with the Quartodeciman practice that it qualified in the way that we have suggested (2A 2.3). It was moreover the same group that held Montanism at a respectable distance in the *Elenchos*, but nevertheless succeeded, in the *Contra Noetum*, in detaching the Fourth Gospel from its use in providing proof texts for the Monarchians. (2A 2.4).

The figure depicted of Themista/σοφία also paid silent and unobtrusive witness to a λόγος-Christology that admitted procession against the Monarchian indivisibility of the Godhead, as did the *Contra Noetum* itself. The *Elenchos*, moreover, told the story of the group under Zephyrinus and Callistus whose theology had been thus vanquished, however much Callistus' name adorned the agreed succession list now compiled with real dates of actual episcopal successions and deaths. The community of *presbyter* Hippolytus may have lost the argument for their leader to appear in the nascent idea of *personal,* monepiscopal succession (see further Chapter 6), but they had won the Christological argument.

And thus we come to the real reason why neither the *Elenchos* nor the *Contra Noetum* were mentioned in the list on the plinth of the Chair. Frickel, whom Guarducci followed (2B 3), claimed that their names were omitted since they would have had no significance in the pagan, Pantheon Library.

---

206 Guarducci (1977) p. 28: "Forse in questa località esisteva una villa d'Ippolito o di uno dei suoi amici... Nemmeno sarebbe strano, che in quella villa una esedra o una sala o, meglio ancora, una biblioteca avesse ospitato, ancora prima della morte d'Ippolito, la statua iscritta."

207 Pliny Minor, *Ep.* X, 81,2 and 7: "Ipse in re praesenti fui et vidi tuam (sc. Traiani) quoque statuam in bibliotheca positam, id autem, in quo dicuntur sepulti filius et uxor Dionis, in area collocatum quae porticis includitur."

Instead the catalogue on the plinth emphasizes the philosophical writings of more interest to the pagan world.[208] But we have already argued that the main feature of the Statue, namely the Paschal and Easter Tables, could have had no such significance.

Philosophical writings such as πρὸς "Ελληνας and πρὸς Πλάτωνα ἢ καὶ περὶ τοῦ παντός occur after ἀποστολικὴ παράδοσις and Χρονικῶν which have a significance only within the community, and certainly it could not be said that they *gerade auch dem heidnischen, verständlich waren.* Likewise though ᾠδαὶ εἰς πάσας τὰς γραφάς might be *allgemein auf die im strengen Sinn biblische-exegetischen Schriften,* nevertheless titles like τὰ ὑπὲρ τοῦ κατὰ 'Ιωάννην εὐαγγελίου καὶ ἀποκαλύψεως can hardly be regarded as *popularwissenschaftliche Titel.* If the latter work is a defence of the authenticity of the latter work against Gaius, then most certainly it has its real significance within the community and would mean less to paganism than the *Contra Noetum* and the *Elenchos,* particularly in view of the controversial and diatribic style of the former.

The real reason for the omission of the *Contra Noetum* and the *Elenchos* was part of the message which the community now united in a monarchical church Order wished to leave implicit and unvoiced. Their Christological victory was expressed too blatantly by those works. Better to let sleeping dogs lie and express their victory more subtly by means of the icon of Themista/σοφία, which expressed symbolically and implicitly the procession of the λόγος from the Father against the Monarchian negation of that doctrine (2A 3.1-2).

We have now exhaustively discussed the character of the Statue and adumbrated our argument regarding the kind of Christian community of the early third century within whose pale it found its significance. The time has now come for us to examine the question of the integrity of the Hippolytan *corpus*, its authorship and indeed its recovery and reconstruction since Ligorio's time from several diverse sources. We shall not however lose sight of the conclusions of these first two chapters. The Statue and its catalogue of works has proven critical in the recovery and reconstruction of the *corpus* of works, as we shall see, and the re-interpretation of its significance in these opening chapters will have important implications for the literary question too.

---

[208] Frickel (1988) p. 84: "... die Schriftenliste der Statue eher popularwissenschaftliche Titel bietet, also Schriften über Fragen aufzählt, die jedem Bibliotheksbesucher, gerade auch dem heidnischen, verständlich waren, dagegen nur ganz allgemein auf die im strengen Sinn biblische-exegetischen Schriften des durch die Statue Geehrten hinweist."

CHAPTER THREE

THE STATUE AND THE HIPPOLYTAN *CORPUS*

The Statue and the reconstruction of the Hippolytan corpus

The catalogue of works on the plinth of the chair of the Statue has played a critical role in reconstructing the Hippolytan *corpus*. In this chapter we shall seek to demonstrate how, in a manner as yet not fully worked out by Hippolytan scholars, Guarducci's re-interpretation of the Statue as Themista-σοφία has critical implications for the edifice of that *corpus* reconstructed over the five hundred years that separate us from Ligorio's work. The Statue, up until the work of Nautin and Simonetti, formed the lynch pin of that re-construction by means of which the various different titles, sometimes shared, sometimes different, mentioned by Eusebius, Jerome, Theodoret, Photius, and others have been brought together as the work of a single author. Since the work of Nautin and Simonetti, it has acted as the means of identifying one group of writings of one of the two putative authors who are held to be jointly responsible for the *corpus* of works that bear Hippolytus' name.

We shall be arguing that, once one accepts that the figure seated on the Chair was not the actual representation of an individual Father of the Church but an allegorical figure (2B), then the notion that each of the works listed in the catalogue must be the works of a single author, whether of the whole or some half of the *corpus*, becomes questionable. We shall see that the bonds of a single author, corresponding to the single figure that bind the *corpus* as a whole, or one block of writings within the *corpus*, become considerably slackened. In consequence those works could represent the writings of a school, rather than of one or two individuals, particularly in the light of what we have argued in the last chapter regarding the Statue as an artefact that gives a distinctive cultural identity to one of the cultural groups of the frac-tionalized Roman community of the late second century.

In this chapter we shall review the process of recovery and reconstruction of the *corpus Hippolytanum* that has taken place since Ligorio's day principally in terms of external evidence. In Chapters 4-5 we shall analyse principally the internal arguments for two distinct writers who were allegedly responsible for the *corpus* that we now have. In both chapters we shall be drawing attention to the centrality of the Statue both for the reconstruction of *corpus* and questions of authorship, and how indeed the position that we have outlined and defended in Chapters 1-2 critically alter the conclusions that must now be drawn.

PART A. THE REDISCOVERY OF THE *CONTRA NOETUM*

We argued in Chapter 1 (1A 2) that Ligorio originally identified the Statue, *rotta e mal trattata*, with reference to some items on the list of works on the plinth. The bishop mentioned by Eusebius had written a commentary on the *Apocalypse* (*questo Vescovo il quale commentò l'Apocalypsis*) and composed other beautiful works (*et compose altre bellissime opere*). But his authorities, apart from Eusebius, were purely unspecified literary allusions (*come dicono i scrittori*), and Theophanes (Naples XIII B.7 p. 424). Indeed Eusebius (*H.E.* VI, 22), to whom Ligorio refers, does not mention the work *De Apocalypsi*, as opposed to Jerome (*De Vir. Ill.* 61) who does.

It may be, however, that since no *ms.* of *De Apocalypsi* survives, that Ligorio is here referring to *De Christo et Antichristo*, since 36-48 of that work contains protracted extracts from the *Apocalypse*. *De Antichristo* was known in the sixteenth century under the name of Hippolytus, along with some fragmentary works.

The major literary rediscovery of the *Contra Noetum* was to occur after Ligorio's death, and to this we now turn.

3A 1. *The rediscovery of the fragmentary Contra Noetum*

The *C.N* was first published in 1604 in Latin translation executed by Torres and printed by Vossius. The Greek text itself survives in a single *ms.*, *Vat. Graec.* 1431, which is a later copy of a *florilegium* compiled by the Monophysite Bishop of Alexandria, Timothy Aelurus, during his exile (A.D. 458-474), in which the writings of Cyril against Nestorius predictably prefigure (fol. 24ʳ-165ᵛ etc.). At the very close of this work, having cited from various works of Athanasius and the two Gregories amongst others (fol. 258ᵛ-340ᵛ), he finally reaches Zeno's Edict (fol. 341ʳ), Ἡδικτὸν Ζήνωνος).

Timothy then appends pope Leo's letter to Flavian (*Ep.* 28), the Chalcedonian Canon, and Leo's letter (*Ep.* 65) to the emperor Leo (fol. 342ᵛ-353ʳ). Finally comes the text of *C.N.* (fol. 360ʳ, ὁμιλία Ἱππολύτου ἀρχι-επισκόπου Ῥώμης καὶ μάρτυρος εἰς τὴν αἵρεσιν Νοητοῦ τινος) and *Against the Jews* (fol. 367ʳ, πρὸς Ἰουδαίους ἀποδεικτική). This appendage clearly consists of works of which the anti-Chalcedonian Monophysite does not approve, and believes to be heretical (τῆς ἐν αὐτοῖς κακοπιστίας), as he makes clear in the heading to fol. 342ᵛ: ἀναγκαῖον δὲ ἡγησάμην καὶ ταῦτα προσθεῖναι τῷ βιβλίῳ πρὸς εἴδησιν τῆς ἐν αὐτοῖς κακοπιστίας.[1]

Vat. Graec. 1431 was not available to Ligorio and his contemporaries. It was copied apparently at the Rossano Abbey in Calabria in southern Italy at its foundation in the twelfth or thirteenth century, the founder of which visited Constantinople in order to collect Greek manuscripts.[2] It was not however lodged in the Vatican Library before Pius IV had ordered the making of an inventory of manuscripts in religious establishments in Sicily (26th May 1563). This attracted the attention of Francois Accidas, a Sicilian prelate who gave several volumes to Cardinal Sirleto in July 1583, including *Vat. Graec.* 1431. On 26th February 1585, Sirleto was to present this together with a number of other works to the Vatican Library.[3]

But the Latin translation of 1604 under the title *Contra Noetum* was clearly not without difficulties. There was no work of this title by Hippolytus recorded by any ancient author. Was there therefore a work of which it may have formed part prior to its extraction as a fragment for Aelurus' *florilegium*?

3A 2 *The* Contra Noetum *and Photius'* σύνταγμα

From the work of Tillemont[4] onwards however the thesis that has carried greatest conviction, though not without problems, has argued that *C.N.* is in fact part of a lost work (σύνταγμα) "against 32 heresies beginning with the Dositheans up until the time of Noetus and the Noetians," mentioned by Photius.[5] The title found in *Vat. Graec.* 1431 fol. 360ʳ could not in any event have been authentic. The description of Hippolytus' rank was late and reflected the post-Chalcedonian insistence on the equality of eastern patriarchal Sees with that of Rome ('Ιππολύτου **ἀρχιεπισκόπου** 'Ρώμης). To have

---

[1] E. Schwartz, Codex Vaticanus Graecus 1431: Eine antichalkedonische Sammlung aus der Zeit Kaiser Zenos, in *ABAW*, Phil. und hist. Kl., 32, 6 (1927), p. 5-9; R. Devreesse, Les premières années du monophysime: une collection antichalcédonienne, in *RevScPhTh* 19 (1930), p. 251-253 ff.; P. Nautin, Notes sur le catalogue des oeuvres d'Hippolyte, in *RecSciRel* 34 (1947), p. 351-353; R. Butterworth, Hippolytus of Rome, Contra Noetum: Text introduced, edited, translated, in *Heythrop Monographs* 2 (1977), p. 1-2, 4-6. I have used Schwartz's ennumeration here. Butterworth (1977) p. 3; P. Batiffol, *L'abbaye de Rossano: Contribution à l'histoire de la Vaticana,* (Variorum Reprint) (Paris: 1859), cf. R. Devreesse, Les manuscrits grecs de l'Italie méridionale, in *Studi e Testi* 183, (Città dal Vaticano: 1955), p. 20-22; R. Draguet, Le florilège antichalcédonien du *Vatic. Graec.* 1431, in *RevHE* 24 (1928), p. 51-62; W. Holtzmann, Die ältesten Urkunden des Klosters S. Maria del Patir, in *ByzZ* 26 (1926), p. 328-351.
[3] Devreesse (1955), p. 18.
[4] L.S. de Tillemont Le Nain, *Mémoires pour servir à l'histoire ecclésiastique des six premiers siècles justifiez par les citations des auteurs originaux,* III (Paris: 1695). Butterworth (1977) p. 7-14 thus sees him as beginning what he regards as a false trail.
[5] Photius, *Bibliotheca,* 121: ἦν δὲ τὸ σύνταγμα κατὰ αἱρεσέων λβ ἀρχὴν ποιούμενον Δοσιθεανοὺς καὶ μέχρι Νοητοῦ καὶ Νοητιανῶν διαλαμβάνον.

continued to regard *C.N.* as a self-standing ὁμιλία, as Schwartz sought to do,[6] would also have flown in the face of Gelasius' letter *De Duabus Naturis* in which, under the heading of *Hippoliti episcopi et martyris Arabum metropolis in memoria haeresium*, he quotes apparently sometimes in free-form from *C.N.* 16,5-18,7.[7] Clearly a volume entitled *memoria **haeresium*** would have contained more than one heresy, and therefore would not have been concerned with Noetus alone.

Moreover, *C.N.* 8,4 appears to acknowledge the broader concern dealt with in its larger original when it claim to have "now *also* refuted Noetus (ἤδη καὶ ὁ Νοητὸς ἀνατέτραπται)," and to be passing on to a positive statement of truth in order to silence "all such heresies (πᾶσαι τοσαῦται αἱρέσεις)."[8] It seems reasonable to conclude that we have here the title of this work and its original wider intention, which would thus connect the *memoria* with the πρὸς ἀπάσας τὰς αἱρέσεις/ *adversus omnes hereses* of the Eusebius/Jerome lists.[9]

Furthermore, this precise title is associated with the term σύνταγμα in *Chronicon Paschale* 8: ῾Ιππόλυτος... ἐν τῷ πρὸς ἀπάσας τὰς αἱρέσεις συντάγματι. As we saw there (2A 2.5), the cited passage was in support of the Johannine date of the Crucifixion, which was also that of the Quartodecimans, from which the Hippolytan community distanced itself. Indeed, there was a reference there to the "love of contention" (ὁρῶ μὲν οὖν ὅτι φιλονεικίας τὸ ἔργον) of which the Quartodecimans were expressly accused (*El.* VIII *praesc.* 5 (φιλονεικοῦντες); 8,1 (φιλόνεικοι τὴν φύσιν)). Thus the Quartodecimans were clearly listed in the σύνταγμα. Despite this clear and tight association of titles in the literature, problems have nevertheless been raised with the identification of *C.N* with the σύνταγμα.

3A 3. *Theodoret of Cyrus and the* ἑρμηνεία τοῦ β′ ψαλμοῦ

One problem is that Theodoret of Cyrus (*Eranistes* II)[10] has a Greek text corresponding precisely with Gelasius' Latin translation which he attributes to a work on *Psalm 2* (τοῦ αὐτοῦ ἐκ τῆς ἑρμηνείας τοῦ β′ ψαλμοῦ).[11] We shall see in Chapter 4 how this citation was to be used by Richard in his attack

---

[6] E. Schwartz, Zwei Predigten Hippolyts, in *SBAW*, Philos.-hist. Abt. 3, (1936) cf. C. Martin, Le Contra Noetum de saint Hippolite, fragment d'Homélie ou finale du Syntagma, in *RevHE*, 37 (1941), p. 5-23; P. Nautin, *Hippolyte, Contra les hérésies, fragment. Étude et édition critique*, (Paris: Les Éditions du Cerf 1949), p. 59 notes 1-2.

[7] Martin (1941) p. 8-11; P. Nautin, *Le dossier d'Hippolyte et de Méliton dans les florilèges dogmatiques et chez les historiens modernes*, (Paris: Les Éditions du Cerf 1953), p. 17-18.

[8] *C.N.* 8,4: ἐπειδὴ οὖν ἤδη καὶ ὁ Νοητὸς ἀνατέτραπται ἔλθωμεν ἐπὶ τὴν τῆς ἀληθείας ἀπόδειξιν, ἵνα συστήσωμεν τὴν ἀλήθειαν καθ᾽ ἧς πᾶσαι τοσαῦται αἱρέσεις γεγένηνται μηδὲν δυνάμεναι εἰπεῖν. Cf. also Martin (1941) p. 12-15.

[9] *H.E.* 6, 22; *De Vir. Ill.* 61. Cf. also Nautin (1947) p. 99-107, 347-359.

[10] G.H. Ettlinger, *Theodoret of Cyrus: Eranistes: Critical Text and Prolegomena.* (Oxford: Clarendon Press 1975).

[11] Nautin (1953), p. 17.

upon the authenticity of *C.N.,* at least in its present form (4 A 1.3). It was this reference in Theodoret that lead Schwartz to propound the thesis that *C.N.* had originally been a self-standing homily on Psalm 2.[12] But it is difficult to accept that this "interpretation" (ἑρμηνεία) refers to a Scripture commentary with a title, since the content of the passage is clearly homiletic, and only distantly related to *Psalm* 2,7, with which the content can be only generally connected.[13] Other titles given by Theodoret to his extracts do not inspire confidence that he has accurately here identified the work in question. For example, the extracts (ἐκ τοῦ λόγου τοῦ) cited as εἰς τὸ Κύριος ποιμαίνει με, εἰς τὴν τῶν ταλάντων διανομήν, and εἰς τοὺς δύο λῃστάς are hardly titles but descriptions of contents of the passage concerned.[14]

The further question inevitably raised by the Theodoret/ Gelasius recension is whether that version is more authentic than the text of *Vat. Graec.* 1431 or *vice versa.* Nautin gave careful attention to this question and after an exhaustive comparison came to the conclusion that the priority lay with the latter.[15] The substitution for example of θεὸς καὶ ἄνθρωπος for θεὸς ἐνσώματος, as did also the positive omissions of the former, reflected the anti-docetism of *C.N.* which was transformed into the anti-monophysitism of the latter.[16] We shall see in Chapter 4 how it was necessary for him to establish the relative uncontamination of the single *ms. Vat. Graec.* 1431 in support of the two-authors thesis against Richard.

If however we go from a consideration simply of titles to an actual identification of textual sources, we can find such a source in Epiphanius' *Panarion.*

3A 4. *The* σύνταγμα *as the source of Epiphanius'* Pan. *57*

Epiphanius description of Noetus' early career and his condemnation by the blessed presbyters is clearly derived from *C.N.* 1.[17] Furthermore he also expressly mentions Hippolytus with Clement and Irenaeus, amongst many others whose work he has both read and assembled (τοῖς ὑπὸ τῶν τῆς ἀληθείας

---

12 See footnote 6.

13 οὗτος ὁ προελθὼν εἰς τὸν κόσμον θεὸς καὶ ἄνθρωπος ἐφανερώθη (Thedoret)/ Hic procedens in mundum deus et homo apparuit (Gelasius)/ οὗτος προελθὼν εἰς τὸν κόσμον θεὸς ἐνσώματος ἐφανερώθη τέλειος ἄνθρωπος (*C.N.* 17,5)/ Κύριος εἶπεν πρὸς μέ υἱός μου εἶ συ, ἐγὼ σήμερον γεγέννηκά σε (*Ps.* 2,7 LXX).

14 Nautin (1949) p. 59-60: "Il suffit d'ailleurs d'examiner les intitulés que Théodoret a donnés aux autres citations d'Hippolyte, pour mieux voir que son autorité ne peut aucunement prévaloir sur le témoignage très clair du texte du fragment." See also P. Nautin, Le texte des deux derniers chapitres de livre d'Hippolyte contre les hérésies, in *RevSR* 25 (1951), p. 76-83.

15 Nautin (1949) p. 49-54.

16 Ibid. p. 55: "L'orientation différente des deux textes confirme cette conclusion. Le texte du fragment est tourné contre le docétisme... Le texte de la citation de Théodoret, au contraire, ne cherche plus directement à combattre le docétisme, mais à établir une distinction stricte entre l'humanité et la divinité du Christ."

17 For a further discussion establishing this relationship, see J. Frickel, *Das Dunkel um Hippolyt von Rom: Ein Lösungsversuch: die Schriften Elenchos und Contra Nöetum,* (Grazer Theologische Studien: Bauer 1988), p. 175-204.

συγγραφέων τούτων λεχθεῖσί τε καὶ συνταχθεῖσιν) over and above his small additions (ἡμεῖς δὲ ἀρκεσθέντες τοῖς τε παρ᾽ ἡμῶν λεχθεῖσιν ὀλίγοις). Clearly therefore Hippolytus' written work was one of his sources, who is given credit as one of those who have "made a refutation (τὴν... πεποίηνται ἀνατροπήν)".[18]

Now Epiphanius also has a list of heresies which go back to Dositheus and beyond, in fact right back to sects of the Samaritans (Gortheni, Sebuaei, and the Essenes)—of which Dositheus is the last—and then to those of Hellenism (Platonists, Pythagoreans, Stoics, and Epicureans) and finally Barbarism and Scythism. We can detect, as Nautin says, "dans ces notices du *Panarion* l'image d'ensemble la plus fidèle des notices correspondantes du *Syntagma*."[19] From the Dositheans onwards in Epiphanius' text, each heresy is systematically handled first by means of an exposition (ἐπίδειξις) and then a refutation (ἀνατροπήν), which focuses upon an examination of the Scripture references used by the heretics in question. ἀνατροπή is moreover used in this sense in *C.N.* 4,1.

The list of some 32 heresies is not however found in Epiphanius alone, but also in Pseudo-Tertullian's *Adversus Omnes Haereses* which occurs as an appendix to the genuine *Praescriptio Haereticorum*.[20] Here the list ends with Praxeas and Victorinus rather than Noetus, but the *Contra Praxeam* makes it clear that Noetus is intended by this name (7C 2).[21] Furthermore, Philaster of Brescia in his *Liber De Heresibus,* shares also a closely similar list for the block Dositheans-Noetians. But the entries for each heresy are highly abbreviated in contrast with those of Epiphanius. In consequence Volkmar sought to identify the work of pseudo-Tertullian with the σύνταγμα of Photius, and to claim it as a first draft in Greek of the Latin translation.[22]

---

[18] *Pan.* 31,33,3: ἡμεῖς δὲ ἀρκεσθέντες τοῖς τε παρ᾽ ἡμῶν λεχθεῖσιν ὀλίγοις καὶ τοῖς ὑπὸ τῶν τῆς ἀληθείας συγγραφέων τούτων λεχθεῖσίν τε καὶ συνταχθεῖσιν, καὶ ὁρῶντες ὅτι ἄλλοι πεπονήκασι, φημί δὲ Κλήμης καὶ Εἰρηναῖος καὶ ῾Ιππόλυτος καὶ ἄλλοι πλείους, οἳ καὶ θαυμαστῶς τὴν κατ᾽ αὐτῶν πεποίηνται ἀνατροπήν...

[19] Ibid. p. 69.

[20] Printed as chapters 45-53 of *De Praescriptione* in Migne *P.L.* II p. 60-74 but seperately in A. Kroyman (Ed.), Pseudo-Tertullian: Adversus Omnes Haereses, in *C.S.E.L., Tertulliani Opera*, Pars III, (Vienna 1906). It appears as an appendix in Part II of A. Gerlo's *Tertulliani Opera* in *CCSL*, p. 1401-1410. For the source of Epiphanius *Panarion* 48 see also E. Rolffs, Urkunden aus dem antimontanistischen Kampfe des Abendlandes, in *TU* 12,4, (1895), p. 127-167.

[21] *Adv. Omn. Haer.* 8,4: "Sed post hos omnes etiam Praxeas quidam haeresim introduxit, quam Victorinus corroborare curavit. Hic deum patrem omnipotentem Iesum Christum esse dicit; hunc crucifixum passumque contendit et mortuum: praeterea se ipsum sibi sedere ad dextram suam, cum prophana et sacrilega temeritate proponit."

[22] G. Volkmar, Die Zeit der ältesten Haeresis und die Quellen ihrer Geschichte mit besonderer Beziehung auf Lipsius' neue Untersuchung, in *Jener Literaturzeitung*, No. 531 (1875), reprinted separately (Jena: H. Dufft 1875), was to refine his thesis in the light of Harnack's criticism by which he was clearly challenged, cf. G. Volkmar, *Die Quellen der Ketzergeschichte bis zum Nicäum*. I, Hippolytus und die römischen Zeitgenossen. (Zürich: 1855).

3A 5. *The* σύνταγμα *and the* Adv. Omnes Haereses

Following Döllinger[23], and accepting the Hippolytan authorship of the (in 1853) newly discovered *Elenchos*, Volkmar associated the *Adv. Omnes Haereses*, as had Döllinger, with the earlier 'summary' (ἀδρομερῶς) mentioned in *El.*[24] But Volkmar failed to explain the lack of correspondence between the list of Pseudo-Tertullian and that of *El.*[25] Furthermore, such an argument could only hold if in fact Hippolytus, the author, attested by Photius of the σύνταγμα, was in fact one and the same as the author of *El.* We shall be examining later the strong argument for their difference.

Lipsius was to introduce the work of Philaster into the picture by claiming that the similarities between Epiphanius, Pseudo-Tertullian, and the *Liber De Heresibus*, were due to the use of a common document, the *Grundschrift* (G).[26] It was accordingly G that was the σύνταγμα of Photius. Harnack initially followed Lipsius regarding *G*'s existence, but disagreed with him regarding its contents.[27] He focused on the word βιβλιδάριον in Photius' account, and came to the conclusion that *C.N.* was far too long to have formed part of that document. Rather it was part of a lost work against the Monarchians, who would have been considered sufficiently a plurality to warrant the description πᾶσαι τοσαῦται αἱ αἱρέσεις. Thus Harnack was lead to support Volkmar's thesis of the σύνταγμα as the summary work, mentioned by *El.*, but different from *C.N.*, without himself being able to explain any better the lack of correspondence between the list of *G* and the order of the heresies of *El.*

Harnack was finally to accept the argument of Kunze who proposed dispensing with the former's distinction between the σύνταγμα and *C.N.*[28] Pseudo-Tertullian and Epiphanius had both used the σύνταγμα directly, but Philaster's lack of consistency was due to his tendency sometimes to follow Epiphanius where he added to or diverged from it. Harnack then refined the theory by arguing that Philaster and pseudo-Tertullian had not used the σύνταγμα directly but an *epitome* of it, which would explain why they cite it so

---

23 I von Döllinger, *Hippolytus und Kallistus oder die römische Kirche in der ersten Hälfte des dritten Jahunderts, mit Rücksicht auf die Schriften und Abhandlungen der Herren Bunsen, Wordsworth, Baur und Gieseler,* (Regensburg: Joseph Manz 1853), p. 11-24.

24 *El.* proem. 1: ὧν καὶ πάλαι μετρίως τὰ δόγματα ἐξεθέμεθα, οὐ κατὰ λεπτὸν ἐπιδείξαντες, ἀλλὰ ἀδρομερῶς ἐλέγξαντες... Cf. Döllinger (1853) p. 19-23.

25 Nautin (1949) p. 19-22.

26 R.A. Lipsius, *Die Quellen des ältesten Ketzergeschichte. Neu untersucht.* (Leipzig: Barth 1875), p. 91-125 ff.; ——, *Zur Quellenkritik des H. Epiphanios.* (Vienna: Braumüller 1865), p. 16-32 ff.; Nautin (1949) p. 22-24.

27 A. von Harnack, *Zur Quellenkritik der Geschichte des Gnostizismus,* (Leipzig: Bidder 1873), p. 57-76; ——, Zur Quellenkritik der Geschichte des Gnosticizmus: Über das verlorengegangene Syntagma Hippolyt's, die Zeit seiner Abfassung und die Quellen, die ihm zu grunde liegen, in *Zeitschrift für die historische Theologie* 44, 2 (1874), p. 141-226.

28 J. Kunze, *De historiae gnosticismi fontibus novae questiones criticae,* (Leipzig 1894), p. 45-76.

summarily, whereas Epiphanius' account was more detailed.[29] Epiphanius had used the σύνταγμα directly, and the fuller notices to it in Philaster had come not directly but *via* Epiphanius.

Indeed the shortness of Pseudo-Tertullian and the length of both *C.N.* and Epiphanius continued to prove a problem in the discussion, as we shall now see.

3A 6. Against Artemon *and the* Little Labyrinth

Caspari continued to support Harnack's earlier position.[30] Moreover Bardenhewer, like Harnack originally, focused on the length of the *C.N.* and its absence in a last and final place in the string of short notices of Pseudo-Tertullian.[31] Accordingly he claimed that the anonymous work against Artemon (σπούδασμα κατὰ τῆς 'Αρτέμωνος αἱρέσεως), cited in Eusebius, was one part of an anti-Monarchian work which contained the *C.N.*[32] In Theodoret, *Haereticae Fabulae* 2, 5 we are informed that Artemon was an associate of Theodotus of Byzantium ("the cobbler"), who was excommunicated in Victor's time and was a well-known Monarchian. This clearly anti-Monarchian polemic Bardenhewer associated in turn with the *Little Labyrinth* mentioned by Theodoret.[33]

Here, as with the arguments of Bunsen[34], Döllinger, and Volkmar previously, Bardenhewer assumed that *El.* and *C.N.* were by the same author. If he had not made that assumption, then he could not have connected the ὁ σμικρός λαβύρινθος of Theodoret with the τὸν λαβύρινθον τῶν αἱρέσεων of *El.*,[35] and thus hypothesized that both titles were referring to *El.*, the author

---

[29] A. Harnack, *Geschichte der altchristlichen Litteratur bis Eusebius*, 2/II: Die Chronologie der Litteratur von Irenäus bis Eusebius, (Leipzig: Hinrich 1904), p. 220-232.

[30] C.P. Caspari, Ungedruckte, unbeachtete und wenig beachtete Quellen zur Geschichte des Taufsymbols und der Glaubensregel, III *Christiania* (Oslo: Malling 1875).

[31] O. Bardenhewer, *Geschichte der altkirchlichen Literatur*, (Freiburg im Breigau: : Herder 1902), Vol. 1, p. 525-527.

[32] Eusebius *H.E.* V, 28, 1: τούτων ἕν τινος σπουδάσματι κατὰ τῆς 'Αρτέμωνος αἱρέσεως πεπονημένῳ, ἣν αὖθις ὁ ἐκ Σαμοσάτων Παῦλος καθ' ἡμᾶς ἀνανεώσασθαι πεπείραται...

[33] Theodoret, *Haer. Fab.*, 2, 5: καὶ Θεόδοτος δὲ ὁ Βυζάντιος ὁ σκυτεὺς ταὐτὰ τούτῳ [τῷ 'Αρτέμωνι] πεφρονηκὼς ἑτέρας ἡγήσατο φρατρίας. τοῦτον δὲ ὁ τρισμακάριος Βίκτωρ ὁ τῆς 'Ρώμης ἐπίσκοπος ἀπεκήρυξεν, ὡς παραχαράξαι πειραθέντα τῆς ἐκκλησίας τὰ δόγματα. κατὰ τῆς τούτων αἱρέσεως ὁ σμικρὸς συνεγράφη λαβύρινθος, ὅν τινες 'Ωριγένους ὑπολαμβάνουσι ποίημα, ἀλλ' ὁ χαρακτὴρ ἐλέγχει τοὺς λέγοντας.

[34] C.C.J. Bunsen, *Hippolytus and his Age; or the Doctrine and Practice of the Church of Rome under Commodus and Alexander Severus and Ancient and Modern Christianity and Divinity Compared.* (London: Longman, Brown, Green, and Longmans 1852), I, p. 15, 21-120 regarded *El.* as the πρὸς ἁπάσας τὰς αἱρέσεις, for which he was criticised by V. Baur, Die Hippolytus-Hypothese des Herrn Ritter Bunsen, in *Theologisches Jahrbuch* (Tübingen: L.F. Fues) XII,3 (1853), p. 435-442, who concludes, p. 437: "Diess ist sosehr die Haupttendenz der Schrift [sc. *El.*], dass sie immer wieder auf das Philosophische zurückkommt, und hierin besonders Wiederholungen sich erlaubt, wie sie Photius in seiner Schrift nicht gefunden haben kann."

[35] *El.* X, 5,1: τὸν λαβύρινθον τῶν αἱρέσεων οὐ βίᾳ διαρρήξαντες, ἀλλὰ μόνῳ ἐλέγχῳ καὶ ἀληθείας δυνάμει διαλύσαντες, πρόσιμεν ἐπὶ τὴν τῆς ἀληθείας ἀπόδειξιν.

of which they believed to be Hippolytus. But Lightfoot had earlier argued that it was *El.* itself that constituted the *Labyrinth*, and it was the earlier summary (ἁδρομερῶς) that would have therefore have merited the title the *Little Labyrinth*, of which *C.N.* would have formed part.[36] But this smaller and earlier work was anonymous, and could only be attributed to Hippolytus if he were the author of the later work too. At this point the correspondence between the list of heretics and the order in which they were dwelt between *El.* and the reconstruction from Epiphanius of the work of which *C.N.* originally stood part became critical. It was a correspondence that, as we shall see, it was to prove impossible to establish convincingly and thus connect *El. and* its associated λαβύρινθος and σμικρός λαβύρινθος with the fragment of *C.N.* and the works with which it formed originally part.

At this point the σμικρός λαβύρινθος not only began to assume the diminutive size of Pseudo-Tertullian, but to fail to deal with the heresies that *El.* itself dealt with, and thus failed to be either in content or in extent that which Bardenhewer's thesis required. It was in the light of what he saw as an inconsequential discussion that Butterworth was to reject any attempt to locate the original text of the *C.N.* within any larger work.

3A 7. *Butterworth and* C.N. *as a self-standing work*

More recently, however, Butterworth has attempted to dismiss the quest for the work in which *C.N.* was originally imbedded, and to argue that it was originally a self-standing work.[37] Only part of Butterworth's argument, however, covers the ground originally charted by Schwartz and countered by Martin.[38] Butterworth's contribution is extremely valuable in terms of his new literary analysis, as well as a careful rechecking of the text as restored by Nautin.

Butterworth has carefully drawn out the style and method of argument represented as derived from that of a Cynic diatribe, such as identification of audience with speaker by means of such terms as ἀδελφοί, (*C.N.* 3,2; 4,8; 8,3; 9,1; 14,1; 15,3; 16,1; 17,2), the first person plural etc. (7,3; 9,1; 12,5; 17,6), the use of alliteration and pun particularly to vilify the Noetians as ἀνόητοι etc. (8:3: Νοητὸς μὴ νοῶν τὴν ἀλήθειαν).[39] Furthermore, he has shown that the plan of the argument as it unfolds is careful and structured. However

---

[36] J.B. Lightfoot, *The Apostolic Fathers,* (London: MacMillan 1890), Part I: S. Clement of Rome vol. II, p. 378-381 ff.
[37] Butterworth (1977) p. 7-33, 118-141, cf. P. Wendland, Philo und die kynisch-storische Diatribe, in *Beiträge zur Geschichte der griechischen Philosophie und Religion,* (Ed.) P. Wendland und O. Kern, (Berlin: 1895); R. Hirzel, *Der Dialog, ein literar- historischer Vesuch,* (Leipzig: Hirzel 1895); A. Oltramre, *Les origines de la diatribe romaine,* (Université de Genève, Faculté des Lettres Thesè no 47), (Geneva: 1926).
[38] See 3A 2.1-2.
[39] Butterworth (1977) p. 122-131.

none of his analysis is inconsistent with *C.N.* having been originally one section of a longer work.

Critical in this regard is the opening sentence: ἕτεροι τινες ἑτέραν δι-δασκαλίαν παρεισάγουσιν γενόμενοι τινος Νοητοῦ μαθηταί. (1,1) The ἕτεροι τινες ἑτέραν διδασκαλίαν suggest that other heresies have already been dealt with, and now there is a change of track in the narrative from what has already gone before. Butterworth argues that this is simply another example of alliteration from the diatribe of the ἕτεροι– ἑτέραν type such as are found also in 5,1 and 11,1.[40] But the latter two passages involve an Old Testament quotation (*Baruch* 3,36) where there is no diatribic context.

The translation "strangers have brought in a heterodox doctrine" seems moreover strained in the light of the use of similar phrases in *El.* where it is frequently used to introduce a discussion of yet another heresy in a series. The Elkasites are introduced in the ἐπιτομὴ πασῶν τῶν αἱρέσεων of Book X after a summary consideration of Callistus and then Hermogenes with an introductory phraseology almost identical.[41] The Quartodecimans and the Montanists too are introduced by means of this phraseology.[42]

Similarly too in *El.* X, 23,1, following a consideration of the teaching of Theodotus who is introduced with the description εἰσηγήσατο αἵρεσιν τοιάνδε, paralleling the ἑτέραν διδασκαλίαν παρεισάγουσιν of *C.N.* 1,1, the phrase ἕτεροι δὲ ἐξ᾽ αὐτῶν is used to introduce the putative subdivisions of his heresy in the form of Montanism and Noetianism (*El.* X, 24,1 and 26,1). Indeed it was this use of ἕτεροι... ἑτέραν that suggested to Bardenhewer that *C.N.* was originally part of a longer, anti-Monarchian work identified with the *Little Labyrinth* of Theodoret, of which *Contra Artemon* had also formed part (3A 6). We have yet to discuss this suggestion, but suffice it to record here that the most natural reading of *C.N.* 1,1 is in the context of a discussion of other heresies that originally preceded.

The introduction 1,1 is moreover not the only indication that the work was originally larger and containing other heresies. In *C.N.* 8,4, as we have seen, the τὴν τῆς ἀληθείας ἀπόδειξιν is introduced in conclusion to the work as a refutation of a number of heresies, and not simply that of Noetus (καθ᾽ ἧς πᾶσαι τοσαῦται αἱρέσεις γεγένηνται μηδὲν δυνάμεναι εἰπεῖν). Butterworth clearly pushes his argument from diatribic style too far when he wishes to dispose of the clear meaning of the phrase πᾶσαι τοσαῦται αἱρέσεις in this context by appealing to the "derogatory hissing effect it has in repetition."[43] We have already drawn attention to the evidence of Epiphanius for a text of

---

[40] Ibid. 132.
[41] *El.* X, 29,1: ἕτεροι δέ τινες, ὡς καινόν τι παρεισάγοντες, ἐκ πασῶν αἱρέσεων μύθους ἐρανισάμενοι, ξένην βίβλον ἐσκευάσαντο...
[42] The Quartodecimans in VIII, 18,1: ἕτεροι δέ τινες, φιλόνεικοι τὴν φύσιν... and the Montanists in 19,1: ἕτεροι δὲ, καὶ αὐτοὶ αἱρετικώτεροι τὴν φύσιν, Φρύγες τὸ γένος...
[43] Ibid. p. 133.

Hippolytus underlying the *Panarion* which was longer than *C.N.* but of which the latter formed part.

Given then that the *C.N.* was part of a larger work, was that larger work the σμικρὸς λαβύρινθος of Theodoret or the πρὸς ἁπάσας τὰς αἱρέσεις/ *adversus omnes hereses* of the Eusebian/ Jerome lists? Was it, in other words, part of the latter document whose author was named, or of the former which was anonymous, even though other works were clearly identified by Theodoret and cited under the name of Hippolytus? It is to this question that we must now turn.

3A 8. *The* σύνταγμα *and Photius'* βιβλιδάριον

It must first be asked why Volkmar, initially Harnack, and then Bardenhewer made what must be an extraordinary series of moves in order to solve the problem of *C.N.* as part of the likely σύνταγμα κατὰ αἱρεσέων λβ. The σμικρὸς λαβύρινθος, the attribution of which to Origen Theodoret (*Haer. Fab.* 2,5) records but prefers some other unknown writer, is to be attributed to Hippolytus even though it does not appear in the Eusebius/Jerome catalogue. This work is now connected to the λαβύρινθος mentioned by Photius as the work of Gaius, as the longer version of the σμικρὸς λαβύρινθος.[44] The σπούδασμα κατὰ τῆς Ἀρτέμωνος αἱρέσεως, recorded by Eusebius *H.E.* V, 28, 1 as the work of an anonymous author, can now be also made part of the reconstructed work. But it must be asked, *prima facie*, why such an identification of different or anonymous authors should be so made, since both Eusebius, Theodoret, and Photius know of works that they attribute to Hippolytus?

There are two reasons equally questionable. The first is the desire to assert the Hippolytan authorship of *El.* from the time of Jacobi, Bunsen and Döllinger onwards. If Hippolytus, as the author of *C.N.*, is identical with the author of *El.*, then indeed he who claims to have "broken through (δια–ρρήξαντες) ...the labyrinth of heresies (τὸν λαβύρινθον τῶν αἱρέσεων)" (*El.* X, 5,1) can be claimed as both the author of the λαβύρινθος and the σμικρός λαβύρινθος. That identification of authorship we must shortly question.

The second reason is the diminutive description of the σύνταγμα as a βιβλιδάριον.[45] The σύνταγμα, as described by Photius, was considered too short to have included a section as long as *C.N.* along with 31 other heresies. If the Eusebius/Jerome title πρὸς ἁπάσας τὰς αἱρέσεις/ *adversus omnes*

---

44 Photius *Bibliotheca* 48: εὗρον δὲ ἐν παραγραφαῖς ὅτι οὐκ ἔστιν ὁ λόγος Ἰωσήπου, ἀλλὰ Γαΐου τινὸς πρεσβυτέρου ἐν Ῥώμῃ διατρίβοντος ὅν φασι συντάξαι καὶ τὸν λαβύρινθον...
45 Ibid. 121: ἦν δὲ τὸ σύνταγμα κατὰ αἱρέσεων λβ´ ἀρχὴν ποιούμενον Δοσιθεανούς καὶ μέχρι Νοητοῦ καὶ Νοητιανῶν διαλαμβάνον. ταύτας δὲ φησιν ἐλέγχοις ὑποβληθῆναι ὁμιλοῦντος Εἰρηναίου, ὧν καὶ σύνοψιν ὁ Ἱππόλυτος ποιούμενος τόδε τὸ βιβλίον φησὶ συντετάχεναι.

hereses corresponds with the σύνταγμα, then *C.N.* must belong possibly with the *Contra Artemon* in a larger, hypothesized work, since the σύνταγμα would have been too small to contain it.

But firstly it must be pointed out that the terms βιβλιδάριον and βιβλίον contrasts with σύνοψις in Photius *Bibliotheca* 121. The σύνοψις as lecture notes (ὧν καὶ σύνοψιν ὁ ʿΙππόλυτος ποιούμενος) from hearing Irenaeus (ὁμιλοῦντος Εἰρηναίου) is quite distinct from the βιβλιδάριον–βιβλίον. The description of Hippolytus' lecture attendance may be simply a legendary gloss on the resemblance between Irenaeus' work and the βιβλιδάριον. But the legendary σύνοψις is the summary and the βιβλιδάριον clearly the longer and finished product, for Photius does not claim that the βιβλιδάριον–βιβ – λίον was transcribed from Irenaeus' lectures but simply the σύνοψις on which it was based. First Hippolytus makes the σύνοψις, and then composes the βιβλίον (τόδε τὸ βιβλίον φησὶ συντετάχεναι).

Secondly, as Rolffs pointed out, *C.N.* consists of 4300 words. In *Bibliotheca* 126 Photius describes as a βιβλιδάριον a manuscript which included both letters of Clement and that of Polycarp comprising 99 chapters and 15700 words. The same term is also used to describe Theodore's περὶ τῆς ἐν Πέρσιδι μαγικῆς which comprises three discourses or λόγοι (*Bibliotheca* 81), Dionysius' Δικτυακῶν , with 100 chapters (κεφάλαια) (*Bibliotheca* 185), amongst others.[46] It would at all events be a mistake to conclude that every section on each of the 32 heresies must have been of the same length as the account and refutation of the Noetians.

Noetus in *C.N.* plays a similar role in the πρὸς ἁπάσας τὰς αἱρέσεις that Callistus does in *El.* IX, 11-12. The last and greatest of the heretics can be given the largest space, though it should be remembered that *C.N.* 10,1-18 is a refutation (ἀπόδειξις τῆς ἀληθείας) of all such heresies (πᾶσαι τοσαῦται αἱρέσεις) and not simply that of Noetus alone (*C.N.* 1-8). The section given to Noetus specifically was therefore not large. Once again we see that there is not the problem of size that would prevent *C.N.* being part of a work against 32 heresies which is the πρὸς ἁπάσας τὰς αἱρέσεις/ *adversus omnes hereses* of the Eusebius/Jerome list and clearly appearing under the name of Hippolytus.

As we have already mentioned, (i) the σύνταγμα is already linked with that title independently of Photius in *Chronicon Paschale* 8 (ʿΙππόλυτος... ἐν τῷ πρὸς ἁπάσας τὰς αἱρέσεις συντάγματι, and (ii) in Gelasius *De Duabus Naturis* where under the title *Memoria haeresium*, he gives a free quotation from *C.N.* 16,5-18,7. The account of the condemnation of Noetus in *C.N.* 1 is moreover reproduced in Ephiphanius *Pan.* 57, 1, as we have already mentioned. If *C.N.* formed part of a work against Monarchians alone, including Artemon, then Epiphanius would have mentioned Artemon with an

---

[46] Rolffs (1895) p. 156-157.

account of his heresy, yet he does not.[47] The conclusion is inescapable that Epiphanius found *C.N* in a work of Hippolytus against 32 heresies that began with the Dosistheans and ended with Noetus, and that is also witnessed to, as we have mentioned, by Philaster and Pseudo-Tertullian.

Indeed, the pressure to assign Hippolytan authorship to the λαβύρινθος and the σμικρὸς λαβύρινθος, in the face of the fact that both Theodoret and Photius regarded them as anonymous and apart from the works of Hippolytus that they both clearly knew and identified, must be understood to arise from the desire to locate *El.*, on its rediscovery, within the Hippolytan *corpus*. If clearly the *C.N.*, which could be definitely assigned to Hippolytus, could be linked with these works and the apparent reference to them in *El.* X, 5,1, then indeed firm bonds were forged between *El.* and Hippolytus' authorship. Similar bonds would also link works mentioned in *El.* and works appearing on the plinth of the Statue, and Hippolytan authorship would be supported on this second flank too, so long as the questionable thesis is maintained that the Statue commemorated a single person whose works as those of a single author were clearly listed there. It is therefore time for us now to consider the rediscovery of *El.* and its identification as a work of Hippolytus or of someone else.

PART B. THE REDISCOVERY OF ἔλεγχος κατὰ πασῶν αἱρέσεων

In 1840 Minoides Mynas, was sent to the Levant by Villemain, Louis Philippe's Minister of Public Instruction, to collect manuscripts for the Bibliothèque Royale, supportive of the former's lecture course in ancient Greek literature in the University of Paris.[48] On the 25th February 1842 he reported to Faugère, Villemain's secretary, to whom he was responsible, the acquisition of thirty-five manuscripts or in some cases copies of them. Amongst them was an anonymous refutation in six discourses (*El.* IV-X), which he was to attribute to Origen on the grounds that the form of argument resembled *Contra Celsum.*[49]

The 14th Century manuscript was deposited in the Bibliothèque Royal as Parisinus *suppl. gr.* 464. Miller recognised that the first and one of the missing parts of this manuscript *El.* I—books II-III remaining lost—was already

---

[47] Ibid. p. 126.

[48] H. Omont, Minoïde Mynas et ses missions en Orient (1840-1856), in *Mémoires de l'Académie des Inscriptions et Belles-Lettres* XL, (Paris: 1916), p. 337-419; P. Nautin, Hippolyte et Josipe: Contribution à l'histoire de la littérature chrétienne du troisième siècle, in *Etudes et Textes pour l'histoire du dogme de la Trinité*, 1 (Paris: Les Éditions du Cerf 1947), p. 20-22.

[49] Ibid. 370: "Réfutation, en dix discours, par Origène des hérésies des anciens et de celles de son temps; les trois premiers et une partie du quatrième manquent. Le nom de l'auteur n'y est pas, mais d'après ce qu'il dit vers la fin du dixième, où il expose sa profession de foi, l'ouvrage parait être à lui... Le style de l'ouvrage, la manière d'argumentation ressemble à celui de l'ouvrage de l'Origène contre Celse."

known from five manuscripts,[50] editions of which had been published under the title of *Origenis Philosophumena*.[51] Indeed, the text itself of *Taurinensis B VI 25* commenced: Ὠριγένους πάντιμα τοῦ σοφωτάτου, whilst the margins of *Laurentianus IX,32*, *Barberinianus 496* and *362*, and *Ottobonianus 194* note: Ὠριγένους φιλοσοφουμένων. The latter is also headed: Ὠριγένους κατὰ πασῶν αἱρέσεων ἔλεγχοι.[52] Marcovich has shown that the loss of *Taurinensis* was not in the fire in the National Library of Turin in 1904, but earlier due to theft in 1749, in consequence of which Wolf's edition (1713) is the source of all subsequent citations from this *ms.*[53]

Thus Miller's text of *ms. Parisinus suppl. gr. 464 (El. IV-X)*, combined with the five manuscripts of *El.* I already known, was to bear the name of Origen as author. The authorship was seemingly confirmed by the marginal note in red before *El.* X, 32,1: Ὠριγένης καὶ Ὠριγένους δόξα.[54] Clearly the second corrector of the 14th century scribe of *ms. Parisinus*, the monk Michael, had also believed that the ἀπόδειξις τῆς ἀληθείας with which *El.* ends so resembled the creed of Origen that he must be the author. Yet the claim for Origen as author was to be soon challenged on grounds of the office in the church claimed by the author of *El.*

3B 1. *The episcopal authorship of the* ἔλεγχος

Origen had been a presbyter but never claimed to be a bishop. Yet in *El.* I *prooem.* 6 the claim to be a bishop in the apostolic succession seemed inescapable.[55] In almost Irenaean terms he speaks of the teaching office against heresy being given by the Holy Spirit only to a certain person (ταῦτα δὲ ἕτερος οὐκ ἐλέγξει ἢ τὸ ἐν ἐκκλησίᾳ παραδοθὲν ἅγιον πνεῦμα) who stands in the apostolic succession (οὗ τυχόντες πρότεροι οἱ ἀπόστολοι μετέδοσαν τοῖς

[50] M. Marcovich, Hippolyts Refutatio Omnium Haeresium, in *Patristische Texte und Studien*, 25, (Berlin: De Gruyter 1986), p. 1-5.

[51] Nautin (1947) p. 22 draws attention to Delarue, *Origenis opera omnia*, tom. I, Paris 1733 p. 872-909, Lommatzsch, *Origenis opera omnia*, tom. 25, Berlin 1848, p. 279-338, and Migne, *P.G.* XVI,3 3009-3458. See also Marcovich (1986) p. XIV.

[52] Ibid. p. 1, 8-9.

[53] J.C. Wolf, *Compendium historiae philosophae antiquae, h.e. Pseudorigenis Philosophumena, ex ipso M.S. Mediceo denuo collato et alio Taurinensi repetita vice emendata*, (Hamburgi: Christ. Liebzeit 1713) cf. M. Marcovich, Note on Hippolytus' Refutatio, in *JThS* n.s. 15 (1964), p. 73-74.

[54] Marcovich (1986) p. 9 and 408 footnote c. 32:1.

[55] So Bunsen (1852) I p.12: "Interpreting these words in the sense of writers of the first three centuries, I am quite sure Hippolytus did not attach to the title of high-priesthood any Pagan or Jewish sense, but simply the office of a Christian bishop," and C.C.J. Bunsen, *Hippolytus and his Age; or the beginnings and prospects for Christianity. Christianity and Mankind.* Vols I: Hippolytus and the Teachers of the Apostolical Age.(London: Longman, Brown, Green, and Longmans 1854), p. 268-270; Döllinger (1853) p. 1: "Origen hat es nicht geschrieben: dies ist so klar, und ist bereits so bündig nachgewiesen, dass wir uns dabei nicht lange aufhalten wollen; schon der eine Umstand, dass der Verfasser sich die kirchliche Würde der ἀρχιερατεία beilegt, ist gegen den Alexandriner entscheidend."; C. Wordsworth, *St. Hippolytus and the Roman Church in the Earlier Part of the Third Century, from the Newly Discovered Philosophumena*, (London: Rivington 1853), p. 21-26. But cf. C. Curti, Osservazioni su un passo dell'Ellenchos (I, praef. 1), in *StEphAug* 13 (1977), p. 89-95.

ὀρθῶς πεπιστευκόσιν). He claims to be such a person (ὧν ἡμεῖς διάδοχοι τυγχάνοντες, τῆς τε αὐτῆς χάριτος μετέχοντες ἀρχιερατείας τε καὶ διδασκαλίας). Jacobi (1851 and 1853),[56] followed by Bunsen (1852 and 1854),[57] Döllinger (1853),[58] Wordsworth (1853),[59] Fessler (1852),[60] Baur (1853),[61] Gieseler (1853),[62] Volkmar (1855),[63] and Lightfoot (1890)[64] were to concur with the identification of an author other than Origen, and almost unanimously as Hippolytus, for various reasons that have become commonplace.

Nautin was undoubtedly correct to draw attention to how the discovery of *El.* was used in inter-denominational polemic in the course of the nineteenth century.[65] Wordsworth was to draw Anglican attention to how he whom he regarded as the orthodox Hippolytus clearly mocked papal pretensions as represented by Callistus.[66] Bunsen tried to use the picture of the divided Church of the early third century as a critical mirror regarding the destructiveness of dogmatic as opposed to scientific religion.[67]

Döllinger, who, in the light of his later stand regarding the definition of papal Infallibility, cannot be charged with an overtly dogmatic approach, nevertheless defended the "papacy of Callistus" against the attacks of the alleged Hippolytus. He claimed *inter alia* that the criticism of Callistus in *El.* IX, 12,24 reveals the later to be in favour of evangelical equality in Christ against the class divisions of contemporary secular society.[68] Furthermore, because he believed that the author of *El.* was Hippolytus and had also writ-ten *C.N.* 10, Döllinger was able to convict the author of heresy in asserting that Christ's sonship was only realised and completed in the incarnation, so

---

56 D. Jacobi, Besprechung von E. Miller's Erstausgabe der Refutatio (Elenchos), in *Deutsche Zeitschrift für christliches Leben und christliche Wissenschaft* (Berlin: Wiegandt und Grieben) no. 26 June-July (1851), p. 203-206, cf. L. Duncker, Besprechung von E. Miller's Erstausgabe der Refutatio (Elenchos), in *Göttingische gelehrte Anzeigen,* (1851) Band 3, p. 1530-1550.

57 Bunsen (1852) and (1854) op. cit. footnote 56.

58 Döllinger (1853) op. cit. footnote 56.

59 Wordsworth (1853).

60 J. Fessler, Über den wahren Verfasser des unter dem Titel: Philosophoumena Origenis, jüngste erschienenen Werkes, in *(Tübinger) Theologischen Quartalschrift,* (1852), p. 299-309.

61 V. Baur, Über die Philosophoumena Origenis, inbesondere ihren Verfasser, in *Theologisches Jahrbuch* (Tübingen: L.F. Fues) XII,1 (1853) p. 152-161 and Die Hippolytus-Hypothese des Herrn Ritter Bunsen, in idem XII,3 p. 428.

62 J.C.L. Gieseler, Über Hippolytus, die ersten Monarchianer und die römische Kirche in der ersten Hälfte des dritten Jahrhunderts, in *Theologische Studien und Kritiken,* (Hamburg: F. Perthes) IV (1853), p. 759-789.

63 Volkmar (1855) op. cit. footnotes 22 and 27.

64 J.B.Lightfoot, *The Apostolic Fathers.* Part I Vol. 2 S. Clement of Rome: A Revised Text with Introductions, Notes, Dissertations, and Translations, (London: MacMillan 1890).

65 Nautin (1947) p. 23-32.

66 Wordsworth (1853) p. 210-211: "... two bishops of Rome in succession, Zephyrinus and Callistus, fell into the opposite heresy—that of Noetus... Hence it is apparent, that the Bishops of Rome may err, and have erred... in matters of Faith."

67 Bunsen (1852) II, p 75-117; III, p. 179-367; IV, 3-115.

68 Döllinger (1853) Chapter 3.

that he could not be begotten by the Father in a personal sense "before all worlds."[69]

Yet despite Döllinger's lack of dogmatism, it is impossible not to detect some disquiet on the part of some nineteenth century Catholic scholars, in the historical context of the events leading up to the definition of Papal Infallibility at the first Vatican Council (1870), that Callistus who appears on the succession lists as the legitimate bishop of Rome could have been convicted of heresy by a Church Father such as Hippolytus who later, as *Vat. Graec.* 1431 shows amongst others, was regarded as central to the orthodox case. Far better stick with the Father of Origenism![70] Newman in particular proved sensitive to this confessional dimension to the discussion at that point of time.[71]

In part the argument for Hippolytan authorship rested on a process of elimination. It would however be a mistake to follow Nautin in regarding such arguments on the basis of *El.* I prooem. 6 to rest simply and wholely on an argument by elimination.[72] As we shall later see, Nautin believed that the name which could not be eliminated was that of Josephus (5B 1.1). Simonetti, who believed that the latter could equally be eliminated, proposed that these anonymous works were by a different Hippolytus of the same name, and that this would account for the confusion over titles (5B 1.2). Let us however take the argument by elimination first, and then examine other more direct ways support has been claimed for Hippolytan authorship.

---

[69] Ibid. p. 217: "...er leugnete die hypostatische Präexistentz des Sohnes; sein Logos ist nicht gezeugt, sondern war von Anfang an unpersönlich in Gott, ging aber durch eine Ausdehnung der bisher ungetheilten Monas zum Behuf schöpferische Thätigkeit oder eigentlich als diese Thätigkeit (als λόγος ἐνεργός) oder als schöpferischer mit Weisheit gepaarte Allmacht aus Gott hervor, ohne jedoch dadurch zu einer besondern Person zu werden." See further 5B 3.

[70] Hence e.g. Jallabert, Examen du Livre des Philosophoumena, (Paris 1853); P. Cruice,. *Études sur de nouveaux documents historiques empruntés à l'ouvrage récemment découvert des Philosophumena.* (Paris: 1855); ———, Observations Nouvelles sur la première partie des Philosophumena, in *Journal Général de l'Instruction Publique,* (Paris: Dupont 1859); ———, *Philosophoumena sive Haeresium Omnium Confutatio; Opus Origeni adscriptum,* (Paris: Imperial Press 1860), p. xiii-xl, particularly p. 24; T. Armellini, *De prisca refutatione haereseon Originis nomine ac philosophumenon titulo recens vulgata commentarius.* (Romae: Societas Jesu 1862).

[71] J.H. Newman, *Tracts, Theological and Ecclesiastical,* (London: Pickering 1874), p. 219: "That a name so singularly honoured—a name which a breath of ecclesiastical censure has never even dimmed— should belong, as so many men think just now, to the author of that malignant libel on his contemporary Popes which is appended to the lately discovered *Elenchus,* is to my mind simply incredible..." Quoted in I. von Döllinger, *Hippolytus and Callistus, or The Church of Rome in the First Half of the Third Century, with Special Reference to the writings of Bunsen, etc.* (Trans.) A. Plummer (Edinburgh: T. & T. Clarke 1876), Appendix B p. 343.

[72] Nautin (1947) p. 22: "L'Allemand Jacobi... procédait par élimination. L'ouvrage ne peut pas être d'Origène... L'*Elenchos* ne peut pas être davantage du prêtre romain Caïus..." and p. 29: "Doellinger admettait: cependent que l'*Elenchos*... était l'oeuvre d'Hippolyte. Pour le prouver, le savant professeur reprenait la méthode par élimination qu'avait employée Jacobi..."

3B 2. *The elimination of Origen and Gaius*

It might be argued that to rule out Origen alone because of his un-ambiguously presbyteral status would be dubious. Certainly Jacobi originally ruled out Origen on quite different grounds, namely that he enters a genuine dialogue with Greek philosophy, whereas the author of *El.* simply believes that a heresy is sufficiently refuted if its premises can be derived from such philosophy.[73] We shall argue in Chapters 6-7 that, though the threefold Order was fixed in something like its form later and universally recognised in the age of Cyprian and Origen, the clear articulation and adoption of such a form of church government was by no means unambiguous in the fractionalized Roman community of the early third century of which the events of *El..* IX, 11-13 form part.

Certainly Irenaeus had also claimed πρεσβύτεροι as well as ἐπισκόποι as standing in the apostolic succession, and the author's use of the first person plural rather than singular may not therefore be purely stylistic. It was how-ever the assumption that the author must be a bishop in the Cyprianic sense of a generation later that led to the problems of how as the first anti-pope he obtained his episcopal consecrators, by what council was he or Callistus de-posed, etc. To these questions we must return in greater detail in Chapter 6. For the moment let us look at the claim of Gaius.

Photius reports the attribution to Gaius of the λαβύρινθος, which we have seen to bear at least some relationship to the anonymous σμικρός λαβύρ-ινθος, mentioned by Theodoret *Haer. Fab.* 2, 5, and which prefigured in our discussion of the work of which *C.N.* originally formed part (3 A 8). Though we denied any connection with *C.N.*, we nevertheless identified the λαβύρ-ινθος with *El.* on the grounds of the specific citation of its title in X, 5,1 (τὸν λαβύρινθον τῶν αἱρέσεων... διαρρήξαντες). Certainly the Hippolytan events, set in the time of Zephyrinus and Callistus, rule out Origen who was a generation later.

But Gaius, according to Photius *Bibliotheca* 48, not only was the contem-porary of these two pontiffs (τῆς κατὰ ῾Ρώμην ἐκκλησίας ἐπὶ Οὐίκτορος καὶ Ζεφυρίνου τῶν ἀρχιερέων) but also was as a presbyter ordained by them "bishop of the nations" (τοῦτον τὸν Γάϊον πρεσβύτερόν... χειροτονηθῆναι δὲ αὐτὸν καὶ ἐθνῶν ἐπίσκοπον). Photius would have known that the succession lists contained Callistus and not Gaius as the successor of Zephyrinus.[74] In

---

[73] Jacobi (1851) No. 25 p. 204: "Denn wenn Origenes, dieser Nachricht zufolge, darin die christlichen Lehren in ihrer Verwandtschaft mit der griechischen Philosophie darstellte, so war das eine seinen Gesichtspunkten sehr angemessene Aufgabe; das vorliegende Buch aber stellt sich grade die entgegengesetzte, indem es die Verwertlichkeit der Häresien aus ihrer philosophischen Abkunft erweist."

[74] Nautin (1947) originally dismissed the claims of Gaius to be the author of *El.* on the grounds that Eusebius does not know of, and therefore cannot associate him with, the latter so that the equivalence rested purely on the coincidence of his presence at Rome during the pon-tificates of Victor and Zephyrinus, (p. 102-103: "... tous les critiques accordent que son

consequence, he could have concluded from the *Demonstratio Veritatis* at the close of this work, where a whole collection of named nationalities are addressed (*El.* X,34,1 ff.), that the writer was "bishop of the pagans." Furthermore, at the end of *El.* or the λαβύρινθος, the author cites another work as his own, περὶ τῆς τοῦ παντὸς οὐσίας.[75] Undoubtably Photius cannot be relied upon in this identification, since he himself is not recording his own opinion but recording what he read ἐν παραγραφαῖς. Photius records Gaius merely as hearsay (τοῦτον τὸν Γάϊον πρεσβύτερόν **φασι** γεγενῆσθαι), and reads conflicting titles on various manuscripts attributing the work to Josephus, Justin Martyr, Irenaeus, and Origen.[76]

Photius is clearly hesitant himself about what credibility can be given to such hearsay (εἰ δὲ ἕτερος καὶ οὐχ οὗτός ἐστιν, οὔπω μοι γέγονεν εὔδηλον). Furthermore, the information that he gives us does not go beyond the text of *El.* itself, which is clearly the λαβύρινθος of which he speaks, not simply in view of *El.* X, 5,1, but also of both the dating (κατὰ ῾Ρώμην ἐκκλησίας ἐπὶ Οὐίκτορος καὶ Ζεφυρίνου cf. *El.* IX, 12, 13-14), and the description ἐθνῶν ἐπίσκοπον which might seem to be a gloss on *El.* X, 34,1-2. Photius' description is clearly anachronistic.

The presbyterate seems to have been a life office at Rome, and progression, whether at the of Callistus or of Damasus later, appears to have been directly from the diaconate. Yet Gaius as a presbyter is described as ordained a bishop (τοῦτον τὸν Γάϊον πρεσβύτερόν... χειροτονηθῆναι... ἐπίσκοπον). Whatever the author's true office was, which we will consider in a later chapter, he would not have seen at this point Victor and Zephyrinus as having an ἀρχιερατεία (ἐπὶ Οὐίκτορος καὶ Ζεφυρίνου τῶν **ἀρχιερέων**) which he did not possess himself (μετέχοντες ἀρχιερατείας). (*El.* I *prooem.* 6) The conjecture about Gaius is supported therefore by no further information than

témoignage, lorsqu'il attribue l'*Elenchos* à Caïus, est de nulle valeur, parce qu'il repose seulement sur un rapprochement tout superficiel entre ce qu'Eusèbe dit de Caïus et ce que révèle la lecture de l'*Elenchos*..."). I make it clear that the case does not rest on "un rapprochement tout superficiel" since his ordination as bishop ἐθνῶν ἐπίσκοπον is a unique title and implied also by *El.* X, 34,1. The real grounds for suspicion of later interpretation is of course the notion that πρεσβύτερος and ἐπίσκοπος were distinct offices, and that also one could nevertheless progress from one to the other in Zephyrinus' time. But even a latter interpretation may preserve some indication of the facts that it represents misleadingly, and what remained of the memory of Hippolytus' position in later times was sufficiently perplexing to require explanation, as we shall see in Chapter 6.

[75] Photius *Bibliotheca* 48: εὗρον δὲ ἐν παραγραφαῖς ὅτι οὐκ ἔστιν ὁ λόγος ᾽Ιωσήπου, ἀλλὰ Γαΐου τινὸς πρεσβυτέρου ἐν ῾Ρώμῃ διατρίβοντος ὅν φασι συντάξαι καὶ τὸν λαβύρινθον... ἐπεὶ Γαΐου ἐστὶ πόνημα τῇ ἀληθείᾳ τοῦ συντεταχότος τὸν Λαβύρινθον, ὡς καὶ αὐτὸς ἐν τῷ τέλει τοῦ Λαβυρίνθου διεμαρτύρατο ἑαυτοῦ εἶναι τὸν περὶ τῆς τοῦ παντὸς οὐσίας λόγον. τοῦτον τὸν Γαΐον πρεσβύτερόν φασι γεγενῆσθαι τῆς κατὰ ῾Ρώμην ἐκκλησίας ἐπὶ Οὐίκτορος καὶ Ζεφυρίνου τῶν ἀρχιερέων, χειροτονηθῆναι δε αὐτὸν καὶ ἐθνῶν ἐπίσκοπον

[76] Ibid. 48: ἀνεγνώσθη ᾽Ιωσήπου περὶ τοῦ παντός... ἀνεπιγράφου δὲ καταλειφθέντος τοῦ λόγου φασὶ τοὺς μὲν ᾽Ιωσήπου ἐπιγράψαι, τοὺς δὲ ᾽Ιουστίνου τοῦ μάρτυρος, ἄλλους δὲ Εἰρηναίου, ὥσπερ καὶ τὸν Λαβύρινθόν τινες ἐπέγραψαν ᾽Ωριγένους. Cf. Jacobi (1851) p. 205: "Ist nun aber der historische Wert dieser Aussage sehr unsicher, so ist der Schluss auf die Abkunft der Philosophoumena von Gaius hier nicht sicherer."

what can be derived from the text of *El.*, now identified clearly with the λαβύρινθος itself.

In Eusebius *H.E.* VI, 20,3 there is one work attributed to Gaius, and that is the anti-Montanist work διάλογος πρὸς Πρόκλον. His writing is located ἐπὶ ʿΡώμης κατὰ Ζεφυρῖνον. Photius mentions this work too, adding that Gaius rejected the Pauline authorship of *Hebrews*.[77] Photius here adds the κατὰ τῆς ᾿Αρτέμωνος αἱρέσεως, which Eusebius *H.E.* V, 28, 1 cites as the σπουδάσμα κατὰ τῆς᾿Αρτέμωνος αἱρέσεως, and as the work of an anonymous writer. But it is unlikely that Photius in the ninth century can know more than Eusebius in the fourth, so that it is likely that the giving of Gaius' name to an anonymous work was done quite arbitrarily.

Photius may have been too impressed by the fact that the work against Artemon that he read about in Eusebius was called a σπουδάσμα. Hence he concluded that it was the work of Gaius who had composed such a **σπουδαίαν** διάλεξιν against (**κατὰ**) Πρόκλου δὲ **σπουδαστοῦ** Μοντανοῦ The attempt to take Photius or his contemporaries seriously, and thus find in this work part of a lost anti-Monarchian work with which *C.N.* formed part, we have already rejected on other grounds (3A 5).

Any attempt, however, to associate Gaius with the *El.* and the περὶ τῆς τοῦ παντὸς οὐσίας has frequently been ruled out on the grounds that Gaius believed the Gospel and Apocalypse of St. John to be the work of the heretic Cerinthus, whereas *El.* clearly accepts this work as canonical.[78] As I believe that the evidence for Gaius' position is highly problematic, and in the final analysis rests on statements of Ebed-Jesu and Dionysius Barsalîbî that are too late to be very convincing, we must examine this particular evidence further at this point.

3B 2.1. *Gaius and the Johannine Literature*
If we did not have these late statements, but had only the early evidence alone, our conclusions might well be very different. Eusebius *H.E.* VI, 20,3, like Jerome, knows only one work of Gaius, the διάλογος πρὸς Πρόκλον, as does Theodoret in *Haer. Fab.*3, 3. In Eusebius we read that :

> Cerinthus has lied and introduced us to wonders (τερατολογίας) shown to him by angels, by means of revelations (δι᾿ ἀποκαλύψεων) purportedly written by a great apostle (ὡς ὑπὸ ἀποστόλου μεγάλου γεγραμμένων), claiming that after the

---

77 Photius *Bibliotheca* 48:.. Γαΐου ... οὗ καὶ διάλογος φέρεται πρὸς Πρόκλον τινὰ ὑπέρμαχον τῆς τῶν Μοντανιστῶν αἱρέσεως... συντάξαι δὲ καὶ ἕτερον λόγον ἰδίως κατὰ τῆς ᾿Αρτέμωνος αἱρέσεως, καὶ κατὰ Πρόκλου δὲ σπουδαστοῦ Μοντανοῦ σπουδαίαν διάλεξιν συντετάχεναι, ἐν ᾗ τρισκαίδεκα μόνας ἐπιστολὰς ἀριθμεῖται Παύλου, οὐκ ἐγκρίνων τὴν πρὸς᾿Εβραίους.
78 *El.* VII, 36,3: πολλῆς δὲ αὐτοῖς συστάσεως κακῶν αἴτιος γεγένηται Νικόλαος, εἷς τῶν ἑπτὰ εἰς διακονίαν ὑπὸ τῶν ἀποστόλων κατασταθείς. ὃς ἀποστὰς τῆς κατ᾿ εὐθεῖαν διδασκαλίας ἐδίδασκεν ἀδιαφορίαν βίου τε καὶ βρώσεως· οὗ τοὺς μαθητὰς ἐνυβρίζοντας τὸ ἅγιον πνεῦμα διὰ τῆς ᾿Αποκαλύψεως ᾿Ιωάννης ἤλεγξεν ὡς πορνεύοντας καὶ εἰδωλόθυτα ἐσθίοντας. Cf. *Apoc.* 2, 14-15; 2,6.

resurrection there will be an earthly kingdom of Christ and again that our flesh dwelling in Jerusalem will be slave to its lusts and pleasures. As he was at enmity with God's Scriptures, he said in his desire to deceive that the marriage feast (ἐν γάμῳ ἑορτῆς) would take place for one thousand years (ἀριθμὸν χιλιονταετίας).[79]

At first sight the revelations seem to be other than the text of the *Apocalypse*. ἐν γάμῳ ἑορτῆς seems to have little connection with τὸ δεῖπνον τοῦ γάμου τοῦ ἀρνίου (*Apoc*. 19,9) either philologically or in terms of the idea expressed, since the latter is in the context of martyrdom rather than a millennium-feast. Furthermore, though τερατολογίας ἡμῖν ὡς δι᾽ ἀγγέλων αὐτῷ δεδειγμένας may seem characteristic of what various angelic beings reveal to the writer of *Apoc*. 5,2; 7,1 etc., ἀριθμὸν χιλιονταετίας seems to be a very free allusion, if that is what it is, to phrases such as ἄχρι τελεσθῇ τὰ χίλια ἔτη or βασιλεύσουσιν μετ᾽ αὐτοῦ χίλια ἔτη. (*Apoc*. 20,3,4,6,7) Moreover, although Cerinthus regarded himself as a great apostle (ὡς ὑπὸ ἀποστόλου μεγάλου γεγραμμένων), the writer of the *Apocalypse* neither claims apostolic authorship nor especial prominence in the community.

Eusebius does however mention immediately following this passage the second book of Dionysius, bishop of Alexandria, on the *Apocalypse* (ἐν δευτέρῳ τῶν ἐπαγγελιῶν περὶ τῆς Ἰωάννου Ἀποκαλύψεως). Dionysius declares that someone else had passed on the information (εἰπών τινα ὡς) that Cerinthus had wished, by his own fabrication, to attach the name of the author of the *Apocalypse* to himself (ἀξιόπιστον ἐπιφημίσαι θελήσαντα τῷ ἑαυτοῦ πλάσματι ὄνομα). He then proceeds to set out his anonymous informant's account of Cerinthus' teaching (τοῦτο γάρ εἶναι τῆς διδασκαλίας αὐτοῦ τὸ δόγμα) in the following terms:

> There would be the kingdom of Christ on earth (ἐπίγειον ἔσεσθαι τὴν τοῦ Χρίστοῦ βασιλείαν), and he [Cerinthus] dreamed that this would consist (ἐν τούτοις ὀνειροπολεῖν ἔσεσθαι) in those things for which he himself yearned (ὧν αὐτὸς ὠρέγετο), since he was a lover of the body (φιλοσώματος ὤν) and entirely carnal (καὶ πάνυ σαρκικὸς), in satisfactions of the stomach and of the parts below the stomach (γαστρὸς καὶ τῶν ὑπὸ γαστέρα πλησμοναῖς), that is to say (τοῦτ᾽ ἐστὶ) in nourishment and in drink (σιτίοις καὶ πότοις) and by those means by which he thought to make them more presentable (καὶ δι᾽ ὧν εὐφημότερον ταῦτα ᾤήθη πορεῖσθαι), in festivals and sacrifices and sacrifice of sacred victims (ἑορταῖς καὶ θυσίαις καὶ ἱερείων σφαγαῖς).
>
> Eusebius *H.E.* III, 28,5

---

[79] *H.E.* III, 28,2: ἀλλὰ καὶ Κήρινθος ὁ δι᾽ ἀποκαλύψεων ὡς ὑπὸ ἀποστόλου μεγάλου γεγραμμένων τερατολογίας ἡμῖν ὡς δι᾽ ἀγγέλων αὐτῷ δεδειγμένας ψευδόμενος ἐπεισάγει, λέγων μετὰ τὴν ἀνάστασιν ἐπίγειον εἶναι τὸ βασίλειον τοῦ Χριστοῦ καὶ πάλιν ἐπιθυμίαις καὶ ἡδοναῖς ἐν Ἱερουσαλὴμ τὴν σάρκα πολιτευομένην δουλεύειν. καὶ ἐχθρὸς ὑπάρχων ταῖς γραφαῖς τοῦ θεοῦ, ἀριθμὸν χιλιονταετίας ἐν γάμῳ ἑορτῆς, θέλων πλανᾶν, λέγει γίνεσθαι.

Undoubtably Dionysius believed that Cerinthus has claimed to have been the author of the *Apocalypse* (ἀξιόπιστον ἐπιφημίσαι θελήσαντα τῷ ἑαυτοῦ πλάσματι ὄνομα). This claim is further made clearer in Eusebius *H.E.* VII, 25,1-5 where the same passage is quoted more extensively. But it does not follow, on the evidence of *H.E.* III, 28,2 alone, that Gaius joined him in this direct attribution of the *Apocalypse* to Cerinthus as part of his anti-Montanist polemic.

It cannot be doubted that in Dionysius' lost work he attributed to Cerinthus the claim to have written the *Apocalypse* that it was his intention to refute. But does the evidence of Eusebius suggest that Gaius accepted Cerinthus' claim? Dionysius makes two quite distinct statements, namely that (i) Cerinthus taught a carnal millenarianism and (ii) he claimed authorship of the *Apocalypse*. Dionysius clearly did not believe that Cerinthus' teaching as set out (τοῦτο... τῆς διδασκαλίας αὐτοῦ τὸ δόγμα) was equivalent to what is found in the *Apocalypse*. Indeed to have admitted that equivalence would have meant accepting Cerinthus' claim that he wishes to deny.

But in any event, we have argued that such a claim would be very tenuous indeed. There would have to be far more of the actual text of the *Apocalypse* in the statement to make Cerinthus vision (ὀνειροπολεῖν) of the carnal millenium equivalent to the text itself. No doubt Cerinthus appealed to the text of the *Apocalypse*, which he claimed to have also written, to support his own vision, and used it as a model for constructing that quite separate statement of his belief.[80] But the two were not equivalent.

If the two were not equivalent, then it does not follow in Gaius' case that because he cites (i) Cerinthus' own prophecy, he must also know and accept (ii) his claim to the authorship of the *Apocalypse*. All that Gaius claims in his words quoted by Eusebius is that Cerinthus modelled his prophecy of a carnal millennium on the literary model of the *Apocalypse* (ὁ δι᾽ ἀποκαλύψεων ὡς ὑπὸ ἀποστόλου μεγάλου γεγραμμένων τερατολογίας ἡμῖν ὡς δι᾽ ἀγγέλων αὐτῷ δεδειγμένας). Theodoret clearly interpreted these words as the claim by Cerinthus to distinct revelations quite apart from his claim to authorship of the *Apocalypse*. In *Haer. Fab.* 2, 3 he deals with Cerinthus in a passage which owes much to Dionysius as Eusebius quotes him.[81] But

---

80 V. Baur originally argued as much against Jacobi (1851) when he concluded, following Lücke, in Über die Philosophoumena Origenis, inbesondere ihren Verfasser, in *Theologisches Jahrbuch* , 12,1 (1853) p. 158: "... Gaius demnach nicht die Apocalypse dem Cerinth zuschrieb, sondern nur sagen wollte, Cerinth habe, indem er sich den Ton und das Ansehen eines Apostels gab, und wie Johannes in der Apocalypse Engel erscheinen liess, Offenbarungen, wie von einem grossen Apostel geschrieben, solche, welche den johanneischen in der Apocalypse ihrer äussern Form nach ganz ähnlich waren, erdichtet und im Widerspruch mit der Schrift vorgegeben, die Zahl der tausend Jahre werde in den sinnlichsten Vergnügungen sich vollenden." In reply see D. Jacobi, Der Verfasser der Philosophoumena und ihr Zeugnis vom Evangelium Johannes, in *Deutsche Zeitschrift für christliches Leben und christliche Wissenschaft*, (Berlin: Wiegandt und Grieben) no. 24 (1853), p. 194, and no, 25 p. 195-201.

81 Theodoret *Haer. Fab.* 2,3 mirrors Eusebius' diction: τοῦ Κυρίου τὴν βασιλείαν ἔφησεν ἐπίγειον (ἐπίγειον εἶναι τὸ βασίλειον τοῦ Χριστοῦ) ἔσεσθαὶ καὶ βρῶσιν καὶ

Theodoret here claims that Cerinthus had visions of his own (οὗτος καὶ ἀποκαλύψεις τινὰς ὡς αὐτὸς τεθεαμένος ἐπλάσατο).[82]

It has often been claimed that the mention of Dionysius directly after Gaius by Eusebius in *H.E.* III, 28,3 is of itself sufficient to establish that Eusebius identified the former's views completely with the latter's.[83] But on the evidence of this quotation, even if this were so, he has not demonstrated that so complete an identification was well founded. If his quotation from Dionysius appears immediately after that of Gaius, it *may* mean that the written accounts of both before him were identical, and that Gaius was one of those whom Dionysius attacked for the belief that the *Apocalypse* was written by Cerinthus. But on the other hand it may be that Eusebius has combined sources dealing with similar millenarian themes and come to the conclusion that the similarity in some respects is equivalent to an identity in all.

Moreover, Eusebius is well aware that there were many writers on millenarian themes at the time, not all of whom attributed the *Apocalypse* to Cerinthus. For example Eusebius mentions in *H.E.* VII, 24,1-2 Nepos, bishop of the Egyptians (ἐπίσκοπος τῶν κατ' Αἴγυπτον), who was the subject of Dionysius' first book of τὰ περὶ τῶν ἐπαγγελιῶν. He too taught a carnal millenium (διδάσκων καί τινα χιλιάδα ἐτῶν τρυφῆς σωματικῆς ἐπὶ τῆς ξηρᾶς ταύτης ἔσεσθαι). But there is no attempt to connect Nepos with the Montanists, even though he supported his opinion, as we have argued that Gaius said that Cerinthus did, without necessarily claiming that Cerinthus was the author of the *Apocalypse* himself (δόξας γοῦν οὗτος ἐκ τῆς Ἀποκαλύψεως Ἰωάννου τὴν ἰδίαν κρατύνειν ὑπόληψιν). Nepos did not produce Montanist-like visions of his own, but rather a measured treatise opposing the predominant Alexandrian exegesis represented by Dionysius in his work ἔλεγχος ἀλληγοριστῶν.

If therefore Gaius did not exclude the *Apocalypse*, on the early evidence, as the work of Cerinthus, he cannot on that evidence alone be eliminated as the author of *El.* and possibly other anonymous works mentioned by Eusebius, Theodoret, and Photius. What Gaius says, as opposed to what Dionysius says, points to a Cerinthus who mimics the visions of the *Apocalypse*, and whose mimicked version is rejected by Gaius rather than the

---

πόσιν ὠνειροπόλησε (ἐν τούτοις ὀνειροπολεῖν). Furthermore he connects Gaius and Dionysius as attacking Cerinthus' doctrine in general, without mentioning the question of Cerinthian authorship of the *Apocalypse*: κατὰ τούτου δὲ οὐ μόνον οἱ προρρηθέντες συνέγραψαν, ἀλλὰ σὺν ἐκείνοις καὶ Γάιος, καὶ Διονύσιος ὁ τῆς Ἀλεξανδρέων ἐπίσκοπος.

[82] Lightfoot (1890) 1,II p. 386-387 cf. Wordsworth (1853) p. 37 footnote 2; Döllinger (1853) p. 2; Jacobi (1853) no. 25 p. 195: "Ausserdem liefern die Gegner der Apocalypse, welche Dionysius von Alexandria in der gleich folgenden Stelle erwähnt, und welche das Buch ganz ausdrücklich von Cerinth herleiten, ein Beispiel so nahe verwandter Polemik dass um so weniger ein Grund vorhanden ist, von der unmittelbar sich ergebenden Deutung die von Eusebius... offenbar beabsichtigt ist, abzugehen" But what is only circumstantial evidence is, as I show, not so overwhelming as Jacobi supposes.

[83] A view mentioned but dissented to by Lightfoot (1890) 1,II p. 386-387.

work itself. Thus on the early evidence the affirmation of the *Apocalypse* by *El.* does not rule out Gaius, author of διάλογος πρὸς Πρόκλον, as the author of the latter, who could also, in terms of such evidence alone, have also accepted the former work.[84]

It must also be noted that Dionysius is credited by Eusebius with a book on the subject of the *Apocalypse* alone (ἐν δευτέρῳ τῶν ἐπαγγελιῶν περὶ τῆς Ἰωάννου Ἀποκαλύψεως). It is purely hypothetical to suggest that a defence of the Gospel and Epistles of St. John must be read in the context of a defence of these writings against extreme Montanists. Yet this is precisely what we are required to assume if we read the title τὰ ὑπὲρ τοῦ κατὰ Ἰωάννην εὐαγγελίου καὶ ἀποκαλύψεως as directed against Gaius, because his attack on Montanism *ipso facto* implied an attack on the Johannine writings, and therefore as precluding Gaius as the author of any works associated with the Hippolytan *corpus*.

Indeed, the protracted fragment of Dionysius' work in Eusebius *H.E.* VII, 25 reveal that his work was concerned with showing the canonical validity of the *Apocalypse* rather than defending that of the Gospel and Epistles. Dionysius did not believe that the author of the *Apocalypse* was identical with the author of the Gospel and Epistles. But the latter, interpreted allegorically, was as acceptable as the former. As he defends the latter rather than the former, he shows in consequence that the opponents of Montanism did not necessarily include the Gospel and Epistle as Montanist works to be attacked.[85] Furthermore, the date of his writings was far later than the threat of Montanism at its peak to the great Church, so that his concerns with the Johannine literature at all events cannot have been specifically anti-Montanist ones. Opposition to the Johannine Literature as a whole was not therefore necessarily characteristic of the opponents of Montanism, and it would be difficult to follow Gieseler's oversimplistic schema.

According to Gieseler the Monarchians opposed the Johannine Literature because they also opposed Montanism, whereas the school of Hippolytus

---

84 It is significant that, on the earlier evidence alone, other commentators also came to the conclusion that Gaius had not attacked the canonical *Apocalypse* and only reluctantly concluded that he had on the later evidence of Barsalîbî and Ebed-Jesu, which we have yet to discuss, see P. Ladeuze, Caius de Rome, le seul Aloge connu, in *Mélanges Godefroid Kurth*, Vol. 2 (Honoré Champion/Vaillant-Carmanne: Paris/Liége 1908), p. 50: "On a voulu jadis entendre ce texte d'une Apocalypse apocryphe. Mais le doute n'est pas possible depuis la publication de cinq passages de Denys bar Salibi... émpruntés par Denys à l'ouvrage perdu Κεφάλαια κατὰ Γαίου que mentionne Ebedjesu."

85 One should note in this respect the careful and precise scholarship exhibited by J.N. Sanders, *The Fourth Gospel in the Early Church: Its Origin and Influence on Christian Theology up to Irenaeus*, (Cambidge: U.P. 1943), when he says judiciously on p. 37: "Gaius attacked the Apocalypse as the work of Cerinthus... and, as he was also hostile to Montanism, *he may be* one of those persons mentioned by Epiphanius who rejected the Gospel as well as the Apocalypse, since the Gospel, from its emphasis on the promise of the coming of the Holy Spirit, *may have been thought* to favour Montanism." (my italics) The words that I have italicized show clearly that Sanders was aware that both propositions thereby introduced rested upon an indirect inference and not on any express evidence.

supported the rigorism of the one and opposed the enthusiasm of the other.[86] If this is the case, we ought not to draw too close a connection between the position of Dionysius of Alexandria, defending the orthodoxy of the Johannine Literature as a whole against its general and not necessarily anti-Montanist detractors, and the work mentioned on the Statue as τὰ ὑπὲρ τοῦ κατὰ Ἰωάννην εὐαγγελίου καὶ ἀποκαλύψεως. Such an apologetic work, clearly indicated by the ὑπὲρ, could have been of far wider scope than merely an attack on the detractors of Montanism, and directed against more than one group. Once again, the author of works on the Statue is not precluded from being Gaius on account of the fact that Gaius attacks whereas this work defends the *Apocalypse* since as we have argued the visions that Gaius attributes to Cerinthus are not necessarily to be identified with those of the *Apocalypse*.

We tend in the light of modern exegesis to regard the Fourth Gospel with its promise of the Paraclete and an apparent absence of hierarchy as supporting Montanism. But undoubtedly late second and early third century interpretation read *Jn.* 20 as limiting the charisma of the Spirit within the ordered, presbyteral/episcopal succession. The consequence of such an exegesis was that there was no need to attack the Fourth Gospel as opposed to simply reclaiming it from the Montanists who had allegedly distorted it. Schwartz held that Irenaeus had in mind the rejection of the Fourth Gospel by the anti-Montanists in his celebrated criticism of them.[87] But he perhaps went too far.[88]

Irenaeus does not say that those whom he criticizes formally rejected the Fourth Gospel. Rather he accuses them in the position that they hold presumably against Montanism (*ut donum spiritus frustrentur, quod in noviss-*

---

[86] Only when the enthusiasm was a past phase could Hippolytus, allegedly having survived Sardinia, have become influential in Novatianism. See Gieseler (1853) p. 769: "Diesen Antimontanisten und Monarchianern gegenüber wurden die montanistisch Gesinnten in Rom wohl immer unbedeutender. Dagegen trat ihnen eine andere Partei entgegen, welche die antimontanistischen, wie die montanistischen Auswüchse in gleicher Weise verwarf, aber Veranlassung fand, vorzugsweise die ersteren zu bekämpfen, und welche ihnen gegenüber inbesondere die göttliche Person Christi als von dem Vater verschieden betrachtet und die alte Kirchendisciplin festgehalten wissen wollte. Diese Partei hatte in dem Presbyterium ihre Vertreter (die ἡμεῖς im Elenchus), und zu denselben gehörte auch Hippolytus. " For Gieseler (p. 514) the author of *El.* was an unknown Novatian before Novatian made of it a fully fleged schism. His views were partly accepted in that they were used in support of Novatian himself, before his later schism, as the author of *El.*, by H. Grisar, Bedarf die Hippolytus-Frage einer Revision? in *ZKTh* 2 (1878), p. 505-533.

[87] Irenaeus, *Adv. Haer.*, III, 11,9: Alii vero, ut donum spiritus frustrentur, quod in novissimis temporibus secundum placitum patris effusum est in humanum genus, illam speciem non admittunt quod est secundum Ioannis euangelium, in qua paraclitum se missurum dominus promisit, sed simul et euangelium et propheticum repellunt spiritum. Infelices vere qui pseudoprophetas quidem esse volunt, propheticam vero gratiam repellunt ab ecclesia, similia patientes his qui propter eos qui in hypocrisi veniunt etiam a fratrum communicatione se abstinent.

[88] E.Schwartz, Über den Tod der Söhne Zebedaei. Ein Beitrag zur Geschichte des Johannesevangeliums, in *AKWG* Phil.-Hist. Kl. N.F. Band 7,5, (1904) p. 29-30: "Irenaeus [3,11⁹] spricht von Leuten welche in der Polemik gegen die montanistischen Propheten... dass sie das Johannesevangelium verwarfen."

imis temporibus secundum placitum patris effusum est) of rejecting the image of the Spirit as Paraclete that is found in the Fourth Gospel (*illam
speciem non admittunt quod est secundum Ioannis euangelium, in qua paraclitum se missurum dominus promisit*). Irenaeus does not therefore claim directly that they reject the Fourth Gospel itself but only that in rejecting the
Spirit as Paraclete they are indirectly rejecting that Gospel which they might
indeed have formally accepted whilst being oblivious to the contradictions in
such a position.

If indeed Irenaeus had associated the rejection of the Fourth Gospel with
its alleged Montanist association with the Paraclete, it is curious that the
great church did not find need to give any full apology for its association of
the Paraclete with episcopal order and succession. None of the defences of
the Fourth Gospel recorded in Dionysius or in Epiphanius show any
preoccupation with Montanist use of the Paraclete passages. Gieseler
mistakenly directly associated the defence of the Johannine Literature
mentioned on the Statue with the περὶ χαρισμάτων ἀποστολικὴ παράδοσις
also found there.[89] We shall see shortly that the latter work, at least as
allegedly restored by Connolly and Schwartz, is not self-consciously an
attack specifically on Montanist ecstasy, however much the ordination rites
found there might be regarded as a response to it.

Furthermore, we argued in 2A 3 that the *C.N.* reveals that the Fourth
Gospel furnished the Monarchian Noetians with their proof-texts. As far
therefore as concerns the Gospel and Epistles of John, the position of the
Hippolytan school is one that rescues that work from the Monarchians who
were their opponents rather than the Montanists. We argued there, as we
shall shortly argue further, that the λόγος doctrine, shorn of any account of
emanation, served the cause of Monarchianism from which the kind of
radical and emanationist Christology of the *C.N.* rescued it in a quite daring
fashion.[90]

In support of our argument for a broader concern of a work defending the
Johannine literature, which does not necessarily have Gaius as its focus, we

---

[89] Ibid. p. 769: "Zu seiner schriftstellerischen Thätigkeit gegen die Antimontanisten gehören
namentlich die Schriften: Ἀπολογία ὑπὲρ τοῦ κατὰ Ἰωάννην εὐαγγελίου καὶ
ἀποκαλύψεως und περὶ χαρισμάτων ἀποστολικὴ παράδοσις, da bekanntlich die
entscheidensten Antimontanisten die Echtheit jener biblischen Bücher, wie die Fortdauer der
Charismen leugneten."

[90] I cannot therefore accept that it was from Zephyrinus and his circle that opposition to the
Fourth Gospel would have come. It was not the λόγος doctrine *per se* to which the Monarchians
objected, but to the granting of the status of a person by procession or emanation. *C.N.* reveals
the Fourth Gospel to contain the essentially Monarchian proof text that the λόγος doctrine of
C.N. expressly transforms. Thus I cannot accept the claim of E. Prinzivalli, Gaio e gli Alogi, in
Studi storico-religiosi, 5 (Japadre Editore L'Aquila: Rome 1981), p. 63: "Non bisogna poi
dimenticare che con Zephyrino si era sviluppato un indirizzo cristologico marcamente
monarchiano, avverso alla teologia del Logos, la quale aveva il suo punto di appoggio nel prologo
del IV evangelo."

can find some support from an examination of Epiphanius' account of the
Ἄλογοι, to which we will now give attention.

3B 2.2. *Epiphanius* Pan. *51 on the* Ἄλογοι

Epiphanius nowhere mentions Gaius' διάλογος πρὸς Πρόκλον. He does,
however, mention the claim of the Ἄλογοι that Cerinthus was the author at
least of the Fourth Gospel and Epistles, though we can hypothesize, if we
wish, that Epiphanius intended to represent them as claiming his authorship
for the *Apocalypse* too on the ground that he believes in common Johannine
authorship. Epiphanius' claim is that Cerinthus' authorship would be
inconsistent with the contents of the work.[91] But it is not on the grounds of
Cerinthus' millennarianism that Epiphanius rejects his authorship, but on the
grounds that his adoptionism is inconsistent with the λόγος–doctrine.[92]

Epiphanius, moreover, makes it clear that he is constructing a heresy. The
Ἄλογοι clearly are not a group of people who define themselves in this
way.[93] He makes it clear that this is a title that he is giving to any who reject
the "books of John."[94] Clearly he is therefore grouping under this one term
disparate groups of people not necessarily doctrinally united, such as the
Montanists alone.[95] But if this is the case, there cannot be one single writer
behind such disparate material.[96] As he continues:

---

[91] Epiphanius, *Pan.* 51, 4,1: καὶ ἀπ' αὐτῆς τῆς ἐπιβολῆς εὐθὺς ἐλέγχονται, μήτε ἃ
λέγουσι νοοῦντες μήτε περὶ τίνων διαβεβαιοῦνται. πῶς γὰρ ἔσται Κηρίνθου τὰ κατὰ
Κηρίνθου λέγοντα. Cf. 51,3,6· λέγουσι γὰρ μὴ εἶναι αὐτὰ Ἰωάννου ἀλλὰ Κηρίνθου καὶ
οὐκ ἄξια αὐτά φασιν εἶναι ἐν ἐκκλησίᾳ.

[92] Ibid. 51, 4,2: Κήρινθος γὰρ πρόσφατον καὶ ψιλὸν τὸν Χριστὸν λέγει ἄνθρωπον, ὁ
δὲ Ἰωάννης ἀεὶ ὄντα αὐτὸν Λόγον κεκήρυκε καὶ ἄνωθεν ἥκοντα καὶ σαρκωθέντα.

[93] *Pan.* 51, 3,1: φάσκουσι τοίνυν οἱ Ἄλογοι– ταύτην γὰρ αὐτοῖς ἐπιτίθημι τὴν
ἐπωνυμίαν· ἀπὸ γὰρ τῆς δεῦρο οὕτως κληθήσονται καὶ οὕτως ἀγαπητοί, ἐπιθῶμεν
αὐτοῖς ὄνομα, τουτέστιν Ἀλόγων.

[94] Ibid. 51, 3,2: εἶχον μὲν γὰρ τὴν αἵρησιν καλουμένην, ἀποβάλλουσαν Ἰωάννου
τὰς βίβλους.

[95] I find it difficult to accept, for the reasons that I give here, that there is a single writer as
the source of Epiphanius' attack on the *Alogi*. The phrase τί με φασίν occurs only in 51,32 to
introduce an objection and not generally. Cf. Schwartz (1904) p. 33: "Sei dem wie ihm wolle, in
den Bruchstücken die Epiphanius erhalten hat, redet kein Irrlehrer, Gnostiker, Markioniter usw.,
sondern ein scharfsinniger, nüchterner Mann, der mit seiner Kritik der Kirche einen Dienst
erweisen will; vor allem, es redet ein einzelnes Individuum, keine Schule, keine Secte, und keine
Gemeinde... so konnte darum auch keine Gemeinschaft entstehen, die sich von der Grosskirche
durch nichts unterschied als dadurch dass sie ein Evangelium verwarf, und mit ihr harmonierte
in der Verurteilung der montanischen Prophetie." That there is *ein einzelnes Individuum keine
Schule, keine Secte, und keine Gemeinde* is only suggested by Epiphanius' construction of a
heresy from disparate criticisms of the Johannine Literature, which he always introduces with a
plural and not a singular subject. The rejection of the Fourth Gospel ("sie ein Evangelium
verwarf") is not bound up with an attack upon Montanism ("und mit ihr harmonierte in der
Verurteilung der montanischen Prophetie") which is never associated by Epiphanius with the
Alogi.

[96] Prinzivalli (1981) p. 67, whilst adhering finally to the postion of Schwartz and Ladeuze,
nevertheless conceded that this position was at variance with what the text of Epiphanius, taken
by itself, appears to imply ("Con ciò non si vuol escludere che Epifanio avessa la possibilità di
attingere in qualche modo anche a materiale ippolitano. L'impressione però che si ricava dalla
lettura della notizia di Epifano è che egli abbia raccolto una serie di materiali di varia
provenienza, che egli forse non riferiva nemmeno ad una determinata situazione storica... e dei
quali... in vari luoghi e periodi... Epifano su questa base ha cercato di personalizzare il discorso,

Alien in every way to the preaching of the truth (ἀλλότριοι τοίνυν παντάπασιν ὑπάρχοντες τοῦ κηρύγματος τῆς ἀληθείας), they deny the purity of the preaching (ἀρνοῦνται τὸ καθαρὸν τοῦ κηρύγματος), and neither receive the Gospel of John nor his *Apocalypse* (καὶ οὔτε τὸ τοῦ ᾿Ιωάννου εὐαγγέλιον δέχονται οὔτε τὴν αὐτοῦ᾿Αποκάλυψιν). If however they accepted the gospel on one hand (καὶ εἰ μὲν ἐδέχοντο τὸ εὐαγγέλιον), and on the other they rejected the *Apocalypse* (τὴν δὲ ᾿Αποκάλυψιν ἀπεβάλλοντο), we would say (ἐλέγομεν ἂν) that they do not do so on accurate grounds (μή πη ἄρα κατὰ ἀκριβολογίαν τοῦτο ποιοῦνται) because they do not accept a hidden work (ἀπόκρυφον μὴ δεχόμενοι) on the grounds that sayings in the *Apocalypse* are deep and darkly veiled (διὰ τὰ ἐν τῇ ᾿Αποκαλύψει βαθέως καὶ σκοτεινῶς εἰρημένα).

Epiphanius *Pan.* 51, 3,3

Clearly we have to do with at least two groups here, namely one group that accepts neither the Gospel nor the *Apocalypse* (οὔτε τὸ τοῦ ᾿Ιωάννου εὐ-αγγέλιον δέχονται οὔτε τὴν αὐτοῦ᾿Αποκάλυψιν), and a second that accepts the Gospel but rejects the *Apocalypse* (καὶ εἰ μὲν ἐδέχοντο τὸ εὐαγγέλιον τὴν δὲ ᾿Αποκάλυψιν ἀπεβάλλοντο). Since the advocates of opinions of such groups are always referred to in the plural, it is difficult to follow Schwartz in maintaining the document of an individual author containing all the criticisms that he attributes to the ῎Αλογοι.[97]

Furthermore, the reasons that Epiphanius gives in support of Johannine authorship of the New Testament Johannine *corpus* have nothing to do with Montanism. Gaius' name is not only absent but also the grounds on which he would attribute the *Apocalypse* alone to Cerinthus. It is not because the visions of the *Apocalypse* provide the model of the Montanist prophet in pneumatic ecstasy speaking with inspired utterances on which Epiphanius' opponents grounds their attack but because it is an ἀπόκρυφον whose words are βαθέως καὶ σκοτεινῶς. There is no discussion of the carnal millennium (Eusebius *H.E.* VI, 20,3) to which Gaius took such a clear exception.

---

creando la setta degli Alogi." Thus he admits, p. 65, the difficulty of regarding Epiphanius' source as a dialogue of Hippolytus, whom, as he says on p. 66 is not mentioned by name. I submit that the "serie di materiali di varia provinenza" reveal that Gaius is not claimed as the author of the opinions of the ῎Αλογοι because Epiphanius had not read any work of Hippolytus concerning Gaius. This being the case, later developments of such texts in the form of a dialogue between the two individuals, Hippolytus and Gaius are plainly pseudonymous. Cf also the assumption of A. von Harnack, *Lehrbuch der Dogmengeschichte,* I (J.C.B. Mohr (Paul Siebeck): Tübingen 1909), p. 619 and footnote 1-2.

[97] Schwartz was followed in this respect by Ladeuze (1908) who argued, examining "toutes les sources relatives au problème,": "Nous arrivons à cette conclusion générale qu'on ne connaît, au second siècle, d'autre Aloge que Caius de Rome." (p. 50). But if "they" are in fact only one, "they" cannot be the "alii" referred to in Irenaeus, *Adv. Haer.,* III, 11,9, see footnote 88 and accompanying discussion. Consequently Ladeuze had rather inanely to argue that "le seul raison que l'on ait de penser ici à une secte ou à un groupe, c'est le pluriel employé par Irénée, et à sa suite, par Épiphane et par Philastre... il nous arrive facilement, en rapportant l'avis d'un homme que nous ne voulons pas nommer, de recourir au pluriel de catégorie: «Il y en a qui disent...» On sait même que, chez les Grecs, l'expression οἱ περί τινα ne signifie pas toujours l'entourage d'une personne, mais parfois cette personne seule." (p. 57) I would suggest that a better explanation is that, through the medium of Epiphanius, what are clearly the diverse views of several different groups have been focused on one, and that one set of such views have been attributed much later to a single individual.

There are two kinds of objection raised by Epiphanius' amorphous opponents. One kind is exemplified in the passage about the seven angels and seven trumpets (*Apoc.* 8,2), raised by "people of this kind (οἱ τοιοῦτοι)," who mock (χλευάζοντες) the obscurity (τὰ ἐκεῖσε σκοτεινὰ) of these words. Epiphanius' reply is that the passage be interpreted spiritually (εἰς πνευματικά) or allegorically.[98] The second objection of another part of the amorphous group is that the author writes to the church of Thyateira in *Apoc.* 2,18, but that there is no church in Thyateira.[99]

This second objection is rebutted with reference to the Montanist heresy, but in a passage in which no claim is recorded that they considered the *Apocalypse* to be their own. Their apostasy at Thyateira is made responsible for there being no church there, but this is incidental to the attack of the Ἄλογοι who are not recorded themselves as directing their apologetic against the *Apocalypse* specifically against the Montanists. As Epiphanius says:

> For since those who dwell there are also Cataphrygians (ἐνοικησάντων γὰρ τούτων ἐκεῖσε καὶ τῶν κατὰ Φρύγας), who like wolves have snatched away the intelligences of those of simple faith (καὶ δίκην λύκων ἁρπαξάντων τὰς διανοίας τῶν ἀκεραίων πιστῶν), they have converted the whole city to their heresy (μετήνεγκαν τὴν πᾶσαν πόλιν εἰς τὴν αὐτῶν αἵρεσιν), and they, in denying the *Apocalypse* on account of this passage (οἵ τε ἀρνούμενοι τὴν Ἀποκάλυψιν κατὰ τοῦ λογοῦ τούτου), are campaigning in support of the change at that time (εἰς ἀνατροπὴν κατ᾽ ἐκεῖνο καιροῦ ἐστρατεύοντο).
>
> *Pan.* 51, 33,3

Epiphanius is far from clear in this passage regarding with whom the Ἄλογοι agree who deny, on the basis of *Apoc.* 2,18, the authenticity of the *Apocalypse*. It seems that he intends to claim that the Montanists themselves deny the authority of the text that he regards as foretelling and condemning their heresy in the description of the church of Thyateira. The οἵ τε ἀρνού–μενοι τὴν Ἀποκάλυψιν reads grammatically as the subject of μετήνεγκαν τὴν πᾶσαν πόλιν εἰς τὴν αὐτῶν αἵρεσιν, and thus apparently refers to the Montanists themselves.[100]

Thus the Montanists are not seen as adopting the *Apocalypse* on the grounds that the Church of Thyateira is in fact their church, the only church there to be addressed. Rather they reject it and are numbered amongst the Ἄλογοι themselves. Schwartz found this passage particularly embarrassing to

---

[98] Ibid. 32. See also 34, 3-8 on the four angels seated on the Euphrates (*Apoc.* 9,4).

[99] Ibid. 33,1: εἴτά τινες ἐξ αὐτῶν πάλιν ἐπιλαμβάνονται τούτου τοῦ ῥητοῦ... ἀντιλέγοντες ὅτι εἶπεν πάλιν· γράψον τῷ ἀγγέλῳ τῆς ἐκκλησίας τῆς ἐν Θυατείροις, καὶ οὐκ ἔνι ἐκεῖ ἐκκλησία Χριστιανῶν ἐν Θυατείροις. πῶς οὖν ἔγραψε τῇ μὴ οὔσῃ.

[100] Migne *PG.* XLI p. 947 translates: "Cum enim illic tam haeretici illi, quam Phryges habitaverint, et eorum fidelium, qui simpliciores sunt, animas luporum more diripuerint, oppidum universum ad suam haeresin traduxerunt. *Qui cum Apocalypsin, atque omnem illam doctrinam respuerent,* ad evertendam religionem vires suas, ac velut exercitus compararunt." Note too that Stephanus, in the *Thesaurus* vol. VII col. 1910, regards τε as a copulative and equivalent to "atque."

his case that in fact Epiphanius was using Hippolytus' lost ἀπολογία, which he believed to have been directed specifically against Gaius' anti-Montanism. We might claim in consequence that Epiphanius has garbled the evidence and that what he was recording was the Montanists rejection of a Catholic interpretation of the *Apocalypse* as prophetic of their own ruin. But in the light of what the early literary evidence licenses us to believe so far he might be excused for his confusion.

In the light therefore of both my general discussion of Epiphanius, and this passage in particular, it would be wrong to see a Montanist focus in *Pan.* 51, 35,1-3. Such phrases as μὴ δεξάμενοι πνεῦμα ἅγιον ἀνακρίνονται μὲν πνευματικῶς οr οὐκ εἰδότες τὰ ἐν τῇ ἁγίᾳ ἐκκλησίᾳ χαρίσματα, or οἵ τε ἅγιοι προφῆται καὶ οἱ ἅγιοι ἀπόστολοι· ἐν οἷς καὶ ὁ ἅγιος Ἰωάννης διά τε τοῦ εὐαγγελίου καὶ τῶν ἐπιστολῶν καὶ τῆς Ἀποκαλυψεως ἐκ τοῦ αὐτοῦ χαρίσματος τοῦ ἁγίου μεταδέδωκε τῇ ἁγίᾳ ἐκκλησίᾳ refer both to John's claim to both the prophetic and apostolic office, and to the right of the church generally claimed from Irenaeus onwards against heresy in general.

Turning to Epiphanius' defence of the Fourth Gospel itself, the absence of a specific anti-Montanist polemic on the part of the ῎Αλογοι is likewise evident. There is no discussion of the Paraclete passages nor of *Jn.* 21, and the relationship between charisma and Order. Instead the argument for the authenticity of the Fourth Gospel proceeds by Epiphanius reconciling the synoptic chronology with the Johannine over the date of the Passover,[101] justifying the omission of synoptic incidents whilst showing that there is chronological space to allow for what is omitted to have happened, etc.[102] Moreover, the association of these kinds of chronological objections to the Fourth Gospel with a group denying the gifts of the Spirit is peculiar to Epiphanius, and not paralleled in Irenaeus or Philaster of Brescia, which further evidences our claim that he is constructing a quite composite heresy.[103] He does not name any of the ῎Αλογοι, with the exception of Porphyry, Celsus, and Philosabbatius, who are rightly described as τινες ἄλλοι ἐξ῾ Ἑλλήνων φιλοσόφων who criticised all the Gospels.[104] Clearly some

---

101 *Pan.* 51, 26-27,1-3.
102 Ibid. 16-18.
103 See also Ladeuze (1908) p. 50: "Dans l'exposé de S. Épiphane (H. 51) au contraire, il y a deux parties à distinguer, l'une également générale comprenant le commencement (n. 3-4 n.) et la fin (n. 5) du chapitre, et l'autre dans laquelle sont énoncées et réfutées une à une des objections contre des textes particuliers d'abord de l'Évangele, puis de l'Apocalypse." But clearly these objections to particular texts are also to be distinguished on the grounds that one is directed against serious chronological problems but the other directed against the rational absurdity of the *Apocalypse*. We have only evidence of the latter as being represented in the contributions of Barsalîbî's "Gaius" and not the former. In the light of Epiphanius' clear construction from a variety of sources, it thus becomes questionable on grounds of his composition to believe that there is testimony here to the work of a single author in which both kinds of specific reply were to be found.
104 *Pan.* 8,1: ὅθεν καί τινες ἄλλοι ἐξ ῾Ελλήνων φιλοσόφων, φημὶ δὲ Πορφύριος καὶ Κέλσος καὶ Φιλοσαββάτιος... εἰς τὴν κατὰ τῆς εὐαγγελικῆς πραγματείας διεξιόντες ἀνατροπὴν τῶν ἁγίων εὐαγγελιστῶν κατηγοροῦσιν...

of these chronological objections must come from these sources, and not Schwartz's single ecclesiastical writer.

We would thus conclude, on the early evidence, that Gaius' attack on Cerinthus is to be distinguished from an attack on the *Apocalypse*—and further the Johannine Literature—itself. On the grounds therefore of the negation of that distinction alone the Gaius mentioned by Eusebius cannot be eliminated as the author of *El.* and associated works, however much our confidence might be shaken by Photius' lack of certainty shown in citing this one name amongst many from *ms.* headings and margins. But there are two pieces of late evidence that would challenge this reading of the earlier witness of Eusebius, with which we have argued that Epiphanius is consistent, and that we have seen both Lightfoot and Baur wished to support.

These pieces of late evidence are Barsalîbî's *Commentary* on the *Apocalypse*, and the citations from a Hippolytus/Gaius dialogue that it contains, and the apparent description of those citations in the Catalogue of Ebed-Jesu as the κεφάλαια κατὰ Γαΐου. One of these citations claims Hippolytus as the assailant of a Gaius attacking both the *Apocalypse* and Gospel of John , as the work of Cerinthus. Moreover, in the remainder he is clearly attacking someone other than himself who at least does not like the *Apocalypse*. Were this late evidence to be valid, then Gaius and Hippolytus could not be identical persons. To the account of this third important alleged rediscovery since Ligorio's time, of the lost κεφάλαια, we shall now turn.

PART C. κεφάλαια κατὰ Γαΐου AND THE ἀπολογία OF THE STATUE

The publication and translation by Gwynn of the Syriac text of Dionysius Barsalîbî's commentary on the *Apocalypse* was to challenge the analysis of the early material that we have given (3B 2.1 and 2.2).[105] It was further to furnish an important objection to the denial of Hippolytan authorship to the works listed on the Statue. If the author of the κεφάλαια is Hippolytus, and if that work is to be identified with the τὰ ὑπὲρ τοῦ κατὰ Ἰωάννην εὐαγγελίου καὶ ἀποκαλύψεως (the so-called ἀπολογία) of the Statue, then indeed at least one work in the catalogue on the plinth is to be attributed to Hippolytus. In that event, that catalogue cannot be a list of a *corpus* of works of a different author. A careful analysis of the force of Barsalîbî's evidence is therefore vital to our discussion for both reasons.

Barsalîbî's *Commentary* cites statements under the name of Hippolytus in defence of the *Apocalypse* against statements under that of Gaius. Essentially the discovery was thus to lead to the thesis that, despite the difficulties and ambiguities of the early sources which I have set out, Hippolytus did

---

[105] J. Gwynn, Hippolytus and his 'Heads against Gaius,' in *Hermath.* 6 (1888), p. 397-418; ——, Hippolytus on St. Matthew xxiv.15, in idem 7 (1890), p. 137-150.

nevertheless refute specifically the anti-Montanist Gaius, whose dialogue was addressed to Proclus. In the light of this evidence it is thus argued that appearances have been highly deceptive. Thus Gaius' description in *H.E.* III, 28,2 of a carnal millennium does in fact apply to the text of the *Apocalypse* itself which he claims that Cerinthus wrote, and that text is the substance of the vision mentioned by Theodoret *Haer. Fab.* 2, 3. It was thus further argued by Schwartz that the anonymous objections to the *Apocalypse* in Epiphanius *Pan.* 51 were taken from Hippolytus' lost work, which was thus the unacknowledged source of a single writer.[106]

Let us look more carefully at the fragmentary commentary of Dionysius Barsalîbî, and his quotations under the names of Gaius and Hippolytus.

3C 1. *Barsalîbî and the Hippolytus/Gaius dialogue*

Schwartz's solution was too neat in that he lost sight of Gwynn's original contention that "in none of these objections do we find any trace of doubt cast by Gaius on the Johannine authorship of the Fourth Gospel."[107] Gwynn's contention was not quite exact, since in the preface such a connection is made, though one which does not square with the citations themselves. At one point Hippolytus is described as citing against Gaius *Jn.* 1,10 and 12,35-36, and thus indirectly acknowledges that his opponent will recognise the Gospel as an authority.[108] The one fragment that would directly attribute to Gaius the kind of chronological objection to the Fourth Gospel that Epiphanius records of the ῎Αλογοὶ is poorly attested in the *ms.* tradition. There is clear evidence that in the *mss. Bodleian Fell* 6 and 7, which was a Latin translation made by Dudley Loftus from a *ms.* in Trinity College, Dublin, the mention of the name translated by Loftus as *Gaius haereticus* was based on a scribal correction of for a nameless heretic. In the *ms. British Museum Add.* 7184 the nameless heretic is given Gaius' name, while in *ms. Add.* 12,143 he remains nameless.[109]

Thus is still ruled out any equivalence, required by Schwartz's thesis, between the disparate groups called by Epiphanius the ῎Αλογοι, Gaius and the anti-Montanist attack upon the *Apocalypse*, and those against whom

---

106 Schwartz (1904) p. 38-44.
107 Gwynn (1888) p. 406.
108 Barsalîbî *Apoc.* cap. 8, cf. Gwynn (1888) p. 406.
109 "A certain heretic [amended "Gaius"] censured John because he did not agree with his companions when he says that afer the baptism he went into Galilee and performed the miracle of the wine at Cana." J. Rendel Harris, *Hermas in Arcadia and other Essays*, (Cambridge: University Press 1896), p. 48-49, who nevertheless insists that "the name is rightly added by way of identification," since "Sanctus Hippolytus e contrario" "immediately recalls the title "Heads against Gaius." However it does not recall the name that Ebed-Jesu apparently gave to Barsalîbî's work, nor the latter's characteristic title "Hippolytus Romanus." Cf. also Ladeuze (1908) p. 55. I find it once again impossible therefore to accede to the claim of Prinzivalli (1981) p. 55: "Questo passo presenta un problema filologico: è necessario reintegrare il nome Gaio perché i mss. dicono «un certo eretico dice,» and that the argument of Rendel Harris "si può considerare certa."

Dionysius of Alexandria defended both the Gospel, Epistles, and *Apocalypse* of John whilst acknowledging different authors. Furthermore, no reference is given in Gaius' actual quotations to the authorship of Cerinthus nor of any passage representing a carnal millennium.

Barsalîbî does, as I have said, accuse Gaius in the preface to his commentary of denying both the Gospel and *Apocalypse*, and attributing both to Cerinthus.[110] But we must remember that he is, as the Syrian Monophysite who became metropolitan of Amida in 1161 and died on 2nd November 1171, a late writer.[111] He refers directly to Eusebius on Dionysius of Alexandria, though strangely not to Gaius himself in his summary of past authors. It is a reasonable conjecture that he does not do so because he had already assumed that the Gaius of *H.E.* III, 28,2 is attacking an identical foe to the Dionysius of Alexandria of *H.E.* VII, 25,1-5, and that the *Apocalypse* itself had been at issue in the former as clearly it was in the latter.

We have already seen that for the latter the authencity of the Johannine Gospel and Epistles were not at issue, nor did he see any need to argue their case as opposed to that of the *Apocalypse* whom he claimed to be not by the same author but nevertheless canonical. It is only by Epiphanius' time that the Gospel and Epistles are included with the *Apocalypse* as also the work of Cerinthus, according to his artificially constructed heresy of the Ἄλογοι built out of quite disparate elements. Barsalîbî, by the second millennium, has arguably become heir to a line of legendary literary development for which he is principally dependent upon Epiphanius.

As such he may be regarded as the first of a long line of critics in the secondary literature whose conclusions we have already argued from the primary sources not to add up. There is no reference in any actual quotation under the name of Gaius either to an attack on the assailants of the Fourth Gospel itself, or to Cerinthus' authorship, or to the carnal millennium.[112] Indeed, there is no evidence from primary citations in Barsalîbî's extant works on the Gospels of any attack on the authenticity of the Fourth Gospel by Gaius. The secondary comment in the prologue of his *Commentary on the Apocalypse* is therefore all the evidence that we have.

It is important however not to conclude from the fact that the apostolic authorship of the *Apocalypse* was uncontested come the second millennium, that there would have been no reason to construct a pseudonymous defence if

---

[110] Ibid. *proem.*: Hippolytus Romanus dixit: Apparuit vir, nomine Gaius, qui asserebat Evangelium non esse Iohannis, nec Apocalypsim, sed Cerinthi haeretici ea esse. Et contra hunc Gaium surrexit beatus Hippolytus et demonstravit aliam esse doctrinam Iohannis in Evangelio et in Apocalypsi, et aliam Cerinthi.

[111] J.-B. Chabot et. al., Scriptores Syri, *in CSCO* Latin Translation, H. Babourt, (Paris and Leipzig: Poussielgue and Harrassowitz 1903), Series Secunda, Tom XCIII, p. 1-2 gives a list of his extensive works on the Old and New Testament, on the Fathers and Theology, and on baptism and the liturgy, amongst which are includes polemical tracts against the Arabs, Jews, Nestorians, Chalcedonians, and Armenians.

[112] Gwynn (1888) p. 405.

that defence was not genuine. Barsalîbî is not moved by contemporary attacks on the apostolic authorship but on the literary problem posed by Eusebius' evidence that there were authoritative denials in antiquity. Thus Barsalîbî *Apoc.* praescr. begins his commentary with Eusebius' mention of the claim of Dionysius of Alexandria that it was John the presbyter and not the apostle who was author of the *Apocalypse*. Thus Barsalîbî is dealing with a literary and historical problem which as such is real to him.

In this circumstance we are therefore justified in claiming that Barsalîbî has in his preface gone beyond what the text before him will actually justify and entered the realm of reconstructive speculation encouraged by the Eusebian fragments. Furthermore, as we shall now see, simply because two names appear as those of rival characters in a literary dialogue, it does not necessarily follow that either of them is the dialogue's actual author. We shall now examine both the chronological problem posed by the Eusebian references, and the problems of literary form in terms of an alleged dialogue of which Hippolytus is both author and one of the participating characters.

3C 2. *Eusebius's chronology and Gaius' claims*

It must be emphasized that the fragments record a dialogue in which Gaius and Hippolytus are the names of the participants. From this fact it could but does not necessarily follow that Hippolytus was the actual author. Certainly, as Schwartz frankly and honestly admitted, there is both this literary and, in addition, a chronological problem regarding the form of the citations from Gaius and Hippolytus as they now stand.

Schwartz argued that these citations are from a document constituting an actual dialogue which was that which Eusebius (*H.E.* II, 25,6; VI, 20,3) dated in the time of Zephyrinus at Rome (κατὰ Ζεφυρὶνον), and read as the διάλογος πρὸς Πρόκλον. But if this were the case, then it seems strange that Eusebius should have called him an ἐκκλησίαστικὸς ἀνήρ, or his dialogue that of a λογιωτάτου ἀνδρός by contrast with Πρόκλον τῆς κατὰ Φρύγας αἱρέσεως ὑπερμαχοῦντα. Gaius is clearly of the Church and its divine λόγος, and not of a heresy like that of the Cataphrygians. That Gaius in Barsalîbî's fragments should have become described as αἵρετικός is clearly an indication that the fragments are secondary and late.

But Schwartz can hardly be correct in his claim that Eusebius has located Gaius anachronistically as a contemporary of Hippolytus, because he had read a fictitious dialogue between the two of them fragments of which are found in Barsalîbî's commentary. The original Gaius had lived before the tradition of the late old age of John of Ephesus was recorded in the letter of Polycrates of Ephesus (*H.E.* III, 31,3-4) and accepted by Irenaeus.[113] Thus

---

[113] Schwartz (1904) p. 41 related Gaius' famous claim against the Montanists that the Roman Church possessed τὰ τρόπαια τῶν ἀποστόλων... ἐπὶ τὸν Βασικανὸν ἢ ἐπὶ τὴν

Schwartz believed that Gaius could only have been ranked as an
ἐκκλησιαστικὸς ἀνήρ before 165 A.D, when he would have been reckoned
as a heretic following Polycrates' successful claim for the catholicity of the
Fourth Gospel. His introduction as a figure in the dialogue by Hippolytus
was therefore a fiction born of an historical anachronism. But to have
described Gaius as αἱρετικός was not the anachronism of a half-century but
of a millennium. We have already seen the tendency of writers exemplified
by the alteration in *ms. Add.* 7184 to change what was originally αἱρετικός
τις to Γάιος αἱρετικός.[114]

Schwartz's assumption here, which I have rejected, is that Gaius, in his
πρὸς Πρόκλον, had ever attacked the Gospel of John as part of his anti-
Montanist case. The only evidence was, as we saw, Barsalîbî's interpretation
of the secondary literature recorded by Eusebius which we argued to be as
mistaken as more modern inferences to the same effect. His actual citations
from the Gaius of the dialogue gave no support to the secondary contention
of the preface. It must be admitted against my case that those citations, if
they are from the author of πρὸς Πρόκλον, show that he did attack the
Apocalypse in Eusebius *H.E.* III, 28,2 despite my argument to the contrary.
But even if this is the case, then, in view of the lateness of the reception of
the *Apocalypse* into the New Testament canon, there is no problem with
Eusebius' dating of Gaius during the time of Zephyrinus. Gaius can still attack the Montanists, regard the *Apocalypse* as their own fabricated text, and
be a λογιωτάτος or ἐκκλησιαστικὸς ἀνήρ and not a heretic.

However, the problem of this dialogue I believe to reside not in the historical character of the participants, such as the chronological difficulty assumes, but in its literary form, and to this we now turn.

3C 3. *The literary form of Barsalîbî's dialogue*

Simply because someone is given in a dialogue the fictitious name of Gaius,
which was a very common *praenomen* in Roman antiquity, it does not follow
that he must be the same Gaius as the author of the πρὸς Πρόκλον, nor
modelled on anything that Gaius said in that work. Schwartz was to conclude
that Gaius' contributions to the dialogue were the fictions of the author and
not a verbatim report on account of a chronological divergence, the basis for

---

ὁδὸν τὴν ᾿Ωστίαν (Eusebius *H.E.* II, 25,7) to a defence of Petrine and Pauline primacy before
the Asiatic claims for John had been made: "... der montanistische Kleinasiat Proklos gegen die
römischen „Siegeszeichen" des Petrus und Paulus zwar das Grab des Philippus und seiner
Töchter ausspielt, aber über den ephesischen Johannes schweigt... Es sieht wenigstens so aus als
habe Gaius nur mit der älteren Anschauung gerechnet, welche von dem ephesischen Johannes
nichts wusste."

[114] Footnote 110. Cf. Ladeuze (1908) p. 58, having accepted Gaius' heretical status
throughout and compared him with Valentinus simply concludes without further elaboration:
"Caius, en effet, n'était pas hérétique: c'était d'après Eusèbe ἐκκλησιαστικὸς ἀνήρ..." See
also Prinzivalli (1981) p. 53 who does concede the problem ("grande stima per Gaio
sottolineandone... l'ortodossia (ἐκκλησιαστικός) e la cultura (λογιώτατος)."

which is clearly questionable (3C 2). But there are other grounds for claiming that the name of Gaius is a fiction in the Barsalîbî citations.

"The passages as they stand in Barsalîbî's *Commentary*," as Gwynn pointed out, "... have the air rather of brief summaries of the arguments on either side: those of Gaius being stated in the barest possible form, whilst those of Hippolytus are given in more detail, yet highly compressed."[115]. Certainly the claims of the preface regarding the rejection of the Gospel as well as the *Apocalypse* by the Gaius mentioned by Eusebius we have argued to be fictional. Furthermore, we do well to add here that the prefix *Hippolytus Romanus dixit* does not at all events accord with the character of the dialogue being identical with the author. Hippolytus, writing between the time of Zephyrinus and Pontianus, would have had no cause to call himself Hippolytus *Romanus*.

It is important furthermore to note that Barsalîbî does not identify *Hippolytus Romanus* with the Hippolytus mentioned in Eusebius, since in reviewing Eusebius' testimony he calls in support not simply Dionysius of Alexandria but also *Irenaeus episcopus et Hippolytus Bosrae*. It is Hippolytus of Rome and not of Bostra who is cited, and who is thus dissociated from the Eusebian evidence. Eusebius' catalogue of Hippolytus' works in *H.E.* VI,22 would have been attributed by him to the bishop of the unknown See identified by Rufinus (A.D. 410) in *H.E.* VI, 16 as *episcopus... apud Bostram Arabiae urbem maximam* as well as by Gelasius (492-496).[116] *Hippolytus Romanus* was not therefore identified by Barsalîbî as author of these works.

If these fragments are summaries of a position on the *Apocalypse*, any reason for assigning them specifically to the πρὸς Πρόκλον mentioned by Eusebius is as tenuous as the supposition that that dialogue was still available in the 11th Century. It could of course be argued that the summary was that of Hippolytus himself, but there is no evidence before Epiphanius that an opponent of the *Apocalypse* deserved the description of Γαῖος ὁ αἱρετικός rather than—and as late as Eusebius—λογιωτάτος or ἐκκλησιαστικὸς ἀνήρ. This is the first reason why, I believe, the authentic Hippolytan authorship of a dialogue with Gaius preserved in Barsalîbî is to be seriously questioned.

The second is that Barsalîbî's dialogue does not fit into the usual literary form of a dialogue in relation to its author. We can regard neither Justin's dialogue with Trypho nor Origen's *Contra Celsum* as true parallels, though in both the main character is the author. In both of these works Justin as well as Origen reply to Trypho and Celsus in the first person. The author of the

---

115 Gwynn (1888) p. 404-405.
116 Gelasius, *Bibl. Patr.*, VIII, p. 704 and Lagarde p. 90: HIPPOLYTI EPISCOPI ET MARTYRIS ARABUM METROPOLIS IN MEMORIA HAERESIUM. See also Jerome, *Chronicon* II, Ann. Abr. 2244, Alexandr. 6: "Geminus presbyter Antiochenus et Hippolytus et Beryllus episcopus Arabiae Bostrenus clari scriptores habentur."

document before Barsalîbî, if there is one, reports the conversation in the third person.

The *Octavius* of Minucius Felix could be cited where he who is the author, according to Lactantius *Div. Inst.* 5,1,21, appears as a minor character, facilitating the major dialogue between the Christian Octavius and the pagan Caecilius. But here there is a careful drawing of character and stylizing of argument as part of a literary *genre* that is not present in Barsalîbî's citations. Furthermore, Minucius is writing to honour Octavius his departed friend, and it is this which accounts for the author's inclusion of himself as a minor actor in the dialogue. Such considerations clearly do not apply to Barsalîbî's citations, where the alleged author is also the major character of the dialogue.

Let us now turn to a detailed comparison of Barsalîbî's citations under the name of 'Gaius' and the possible sources of those citations. We shall then be in a position to compare our findings with the claims in Epiphanius made by the Ἄλογοι χλευάζοντες, and to offer grounds for rejection of Schwartz's thesis that the anonymous citations from these people were in fact citations from the κεφάλαια where they were refuted.

3C 4. *Hippolytan* Fragments *in Barsalîbî's Commentary*

Prigent sought to confirm the Hippolytan character of Barsalîbî's citations first by locating other passages from Hippolytus' known works, *Dan.* and *Ant.* He would then be able to delineate these, and thus be able to establish the probability that remaining parts of Barsalîbî's commentary were in fact from Hippolytus and not his own.[117] But in view of Gwynn's earlier judgement that Barsalîbî's quotations bear the stamp of highly compressed summaries, it is well to inquire whether in fact his commentary is not based upon a *florilegium* rather than his own collection of passages from Hippolytus. Were the latter to have been the case, then the quotations would have been given in their full form and not abbreviated and condensed.

Prigent considered the possibility that Barsalîbî had derived his citations of the κεφάλαια from such a *florilegium*, only to reject it.[118] To some extent that rejection was surprising in view of the fact that he readily argued that the citations from the *De Apocalypsi* were not from any such genuine work of that name but from a *florilegium* constructed out of other works of

---

117 P. Prigent, Hippolyte, commentateur de l'Apocalypse, in *ThZ* 28,6 (1972), p. 392: "De nombreux passages du commentaire sont en réalité des extraits d'œuvres hippolytiennes bien que rien ne vienne signaler leur origine. De plus certaines interprétations sont indéniablement marquées au coin de l'exégèse hippolytienne." See also ——, Les fragments du De Apocalypsi d'Hippolyte, in *ThZ* 29,5 (1973), p. 313-333.

118 Prigent (1972) considered this possibility (p. 411: "Il a... composé son commentaire à partir d'un florilège regroupant des exégèses de l'Apocalypse éparses dans plusieurs œuvres d'Hippolyte.") only to reject such a move as not economical ("... un florilège hippolytien sur l'Apocalypse n'aurait pu faire l'économie."). It is the patently contrived character of the dialogue and its compressed citations that require a hypothesis and makes the difference that requires the distinction.

Hippolytus known under other titles such as *Dan.* and *Ant.* It will be interesting now to consider precisely why he held the *De Apocalypsi* to be a spurious construction, and yet held that the κεφάλαια were genuine even if they came down to us themselves *via* such a *florilegium*.

3C 4.1. *Citations from an alleged* De Apocalypsi

Prigent argued that the publication of fragments by Achelis and others as the *De Apocalypsi* were a figment. He wished to claim that Jerome's citation of (*De Vir Ill.* 61), followed by Sophronius, Nicephorus Callistus, and George Syncellus, were in fact references to the κεφάλαια that he held to be genuine. He therefore considered the sources of the alleged *De Apocalypsi* as follows:

3C 4.1.1 Ms. Bodleian Syr. *140*

Quotations from Hippolytus in *ms. Bodleian Syr.* 140 were adopted by Achelis from Payne-Smith's translation under the title of *De Apocalypsi.*[119] But Prigent argued that in fact a close examination shows these to be in fact from a *florilegium* composed from sections of the *Ant.* and, as he claimed, the κεφάλαια.[120] *Fragment* I (folios 277 and 278) on *Ap.* 12,1-15 was from *Ant.* 61 and also represented in Barsalîbî's *Ap.* 12,1, and *frag.* II (folio 279) on *Ap.* 13,11-12.15.17 from *Ant.* 49.[121] Both fragments respectively exhibit a high degree of correspondence with the Arabic text published by Achelis, which we shall now consider.

3C 4.1.2 Ms. Parisinus arab. *67*

It was from this manuscript, in conjunction with a citation from *De Antichristo in Benedictione Dan.* by the Monophysite bishop James of Edessa (*frag.* XIX) and from an Old Slavic witness (*frag.* XXII), that Achelis derived his twenty two passages in attempted reconstruction of the *De Apocalypsi.*[122] But once again these passages show derivation from other works where their citations are sufficiently precise to be identifiable.

Let us discuss in detail these passages, distinguishing those which stand alone from those which are either dependent or derived from other works. If we can show that at least some of these works purporting to be from a lost *De Apocalypsi* are from other known works of Hippolytus, then we shall be in a position to question whether the others which appear not to come from any known source are in fact from such a work. In turn we shall be then in a

---

119 H. Achelis, Hippolytus's Werke, Band 1,2 Hippolyt's Kleinere Exegetische und Homiletische Schriften, in *GCS* (1897), p. 236-237. Accordingly they inserted into Lagarde's original numeration the addition of *frag.* XIX (*Apoc.* 17,4-7) from James of Edessa. Although Prigent (1972) and (1973) follows the Lagarde enumeration, we have preferred that of Achelis.
120 P. Prigent and R. Stehly, Citations d'Hippolyte trouvées dans le ms. Bodl. Syr. 140, in *ThZ* 30,2 (1974) p. 84-85: "... c'est sans doute que la source en question n'est ni un commentaire sur l'Apocalypse, ni même le corpus hippolytien, mais bien plutôt une littérature exégétique présentée sous forme de chaîne." P. Prigent, Les fragments du De Apocalypsi d'Hippolyte, in *ThZ* 29,5 (1973), p. 313-333.
121 Achelis (1897) p. 231-232, cf. Prigent (1974) p. 83-85.
122 Ibid. (1897) p. 231-238, cf. Prigent (1973) p. 318-332.

position to ask whether the same phenomenon of pseudepigraphic composition might not also apply to Barsalîbî's alleged κεφάλαια, rather than to assume, as we shall argue that Prigent does, on inadequate grounds, that the latter could have constituted in turn and instead the genuine *De Apocalypsi* under a different title.

Let us begin with passages where the often garbled derivation from existing works can be reasonably demonstrated.

3C 4.1.2.1. *Fragments derived from* Dan.

Frag. VI (*Apoc.* 12, 3-4) associates the great dragon with seven heads with the seven heads and ten horns of *Dan.* 7,2-12, as does Hippolytus, *Dan.* IV, 5-6. Clearly this fragment represents a summary of this passage rather than a statement from a separate work.[123] Furthermore the summary is not true to the position taken historically by Hippolytus who never identified the Roman Empire with the Antichrist as this fragment clumsily claims that he did (*das römische Reich, und das Reich des Antichrists*) in what is clearly a misreading. *Dan.* IV, 5,4 (... ἡμᾶς δεῖ... δέεσθαι ἵνα μὴ εἰς τοιούτους χρόνους ἐμπέσωμεν) expressly denies that the contemporary Roman empire even when persecuting is Antichrist itself, contrary to contemporary Montanism. The end for Hippolytus, as we have seen, is under another kingdom some centuries after his time (2 B 2.1.3.2 and Chapter 2, footnote 110). It would be difficult, therefore, to read this summary as genuine Hippolytus from another lost work such as *De Apocalypsi*.

Frag. XIII (*Apoc.* 13,11) attributes to Hippolytus the interpretation of the "two horns like those of a lamb" as the law and the prophets, worn by the dragon who is Antichrist as the perverse reflection of Christ, (*das sanfte Erscheinen dieses Tieres, das doch inwendig ein reissender Wolf*).[124] This is a theme of *Ant.* in general, and parallels here *Ant.* 6, where the Antichrist appears as a lamb like Christ but within is a wolf.[125] The two horns moreover are interpreted as Antichrist and the false prophet in *Ant.* 49 specifically in

---

[123] *Dan.* IV, 5,3: ὥσπερ γὰρ ἐπὶ τῆς παραδάλεως προεῖπεν ὁ προφήτης, ὅτι «τέσσαρες κεφαλαὶ τῷ θηρίῳ» καὶ ἐγένετο καὶ ἐμερίσθη ἡ βασιλεία Ἀλεξάνδρου εἰς τέσσαρας ἀρχάς... ἕως ἀναβήσεται δέκα κέρατα ἐξ αὐτῆς ταύτης, ὅταν ὁ χρόνος τοῦ θηρίου πληρωθῇ καὶ τὸ σμικρὸν κέρας, ὅπερ ἐστὶν ὁ ἀντίχριστος... Cf. Achelis (1897) p. 232,14-18: "... erklärt er [Hippolytus]: "Die sieben Köpfe sind sieben Könige, nämlich folgende: Nebukadnezar der Chaldäer, Kores der Meder, Darius der Perser, Alexander der Grieche, und die vier Diener Alexanders zählen als ein Reich, das römische Reich, und das Reich des Antichrists." Cf. Prigent (1973) p. 323-324.

[124] Achelis (1897) p. 234,23-28: "... das Bild der zwei Hörner bereits vorgekommen in der Vision Daniels... wo die beiden Hörner als zwei Königreiche gedeutet werden, das medische und das persische. Hippolytus aber deutet die beiden als das Gesetz und die Propheten, und sagt, sie seien ein Hinweis auf das sanfte Erscheinen dieses Tieres, das doch inwendig ein reissender Wolf sei."

[125] *Ant.* 6: Βασιλεὺς ὁ Χριστὸς, καὶ βασιλεὺς ἐπίγειος ὁ ἀντίχριστος. ἐδείχθη ὁ σωτὴρ ὡς ἀρνίον, καὶ αὐτὸς ὁμοίως φανήσεται ὡς ἀρνίον, ἔνδοθεν λύκος ὤν.

relation to *Apoc.* 13,11.[126] But in the vision of *Dan.* IV, 57,2 the two men standing on the bank of the Euphrates are the law and the prophets.

It would of course be possible to consider the indirectness of such parallels, either because they are summaries (*frag.* VI) or compilations from different passages (*frag.* XIII), as compatible with a later work of Hippolytus himself in which he uses his earlier writings. This as we have seen would be difficult to maintain in the case of *frag.* VI on grounds of identification of the Roman Empire with Antichrist which was certainly not Hippolytan. But in the case of *frag.* XIII we have the first of a number of parallels with Andreas of Caesarea, who cites Hippolytus in some instances but not in this case. Rather Andreas gives this interpretation as that of Irenaeus,[127] and thus clearly give evidence for these citations as part of a common apocalyptic tradition, incorporated in *florilegia* or a *florilegium*, in which the names of the original contributors have been confused or suppressed altogether.

Finally in *frag.* XXI[128] (*Apoc.* 17,10) we find an Hippolytan quotation once again with parallels with *Dan.* The five kings which are fallen are Nebuchadnezar, Kores, Darius, Alexander, and they have five successors in a partitioned Hellenistic empire. Thus *frag.* XXI parallels *Dan.* IV, 5,4, as does *frag.* VI. The present kingdom, however, is the Roman empire, but the kingdom which is "not yet" is Antichrist.[129]

In contrast with *frag.* VI, therefore, this citation far more accurately reflects Hippolytus' view of eschatology. But rather than being a real candidate for a fragment of a lost *De Apocalypsi*, it bears all the marks of being yet again a very approximate summary of Hippolytus' original words. Certainly a quite different exegesis of *Apoc.* 17,10 is given in *Dan.* IV, 23,6, in which it is the millennium rather than the Antichrist that is yet to come. Furthermore, Andreas of Caesarea attributes this interpretation of the passage expressly to Hippolytus, but mentions nothing of any other interpretation in terms of the Antichrist. He surely he would have so mentioned if he had in

---

126 *Ant.* 49: τὸ μὲν οὖν «θηρίον τὸ ἀναβαῖνον ἐκ τῆς γῆς» τὴν βασιλείαν τὴν τοῦ ἀντιχρίστου ἐσομένην λέγει, τὰ δὲ δύο κέρατα αὐτὸν καὶ τὸν μετ᾽ αὐτοῦ ψευδοπροφήτην.

127 Andreas of Caesarea, *Comm. in Apoc.*, (ed.) J. Schmid, Studien zur Geschichte des griechischen Apocalypse-Textes, 1. Der Apocalypse-Kommentar des Andreas von Kaisareia, in *Münchener Theologische Studien* (Karl Zink: München 1955) p. 140-141: τὸ θηρίον τοῦτο οἱ μὲν τὸν ἀντίχριστόν φασιν, ἑτέροις δὲ ἔδοξε τὰ δύο αὐτοῦ κέρατα τὸν ἀντίχριστον καὶ τὸν ψευδοπροφήτην αἰνίττεσθαι... οὐκ ἄτοπον ἡγούμεθα τὸν μὲν δράκοντα εἰς τὸν σατανᾶν, τὸ δὲ θηρίον τὸ ἐκ τῆς θαλάσσης ἀναβαῖνον εἰς τὸν ἀντίχριστον, τὸ δὲ παρόν, κατὰ τὸ δοκοῦν τῷ μακαρίῳ Εἰρηναίῳ, εἰς τὸν ψευδοπροφήτην ἐκλαμβανέσθαι ἐκ τῆς γῆς μὲν ἀνερχόμενον... ἔχον δὲ κέρατα ὅμοια ἀρνίῳ...

128 I have retained Achelis' enumeration XXI rather than XX (Prigent (1974) p. 331) even though I concede that the inclusion of the fragment from James of Edessa as XIX was an unwarranted intrusion into a separate discussion of *ms. Parisinus arab.* 67.

129 Achelis (1897) p. 237,7-18: "Was Hippolytus anbelangt, so meint er, dieses Tier bedeute den Götzendienst, und seine „fünf Köpfe, die abgefallen sind," seien fünf Könige... Diese Königreiche nun sind untergegangen. Und das, „welches existiert," ist das römische... Und was „das andere" betrifft, das „noch nicht gekommen ist," so ist dies nach allgemeiner Annahme der Antichrist."

addition a the putative *De Apocalypsi* before him.[130] The clear implication is that some parts of this exegesis accrues to Hippolytus' name from latter developments of a general apocalyptic exegesis.[131]

Let us now look at parallels with *Ant.*

3C 4.1.2.2. *Fragments as garbled derivations from* Ant.

In *frag.* XI (*Ap.* 13,13) p. 234,8-10 there is discussion of the beast from the sea to whom the dragon (Satan) has given his throne, one of whose heads is healed from a mortal wound. Hippolytus' alleged interpretation is that the beast is Antichrist, whom some despise when he begins to reign, but who are convinced by the miraculous healing.[132] But the citation in reality is a conflation of two quite different interpretations. In the middle of this literalist prediction about an individual, there is the assertion that in fact the beast represents a kingdom, and that the wound represents weakness and laxity found therein.[133]

It is clearly difficult to place very much credence on the integrity and genuineness of a citation so obviously constructed in this way. Andreas preserves both an individual and a collective and symbolic interpretation but neither are remotely Hippolytan nor related to *frag.* XI.[134] However, there does appear to be a genuinely Hippolytan source (*Ant.* 49) for this fragment to which this fragement could count as a garbled reference. Here *Apoc.* 13,3 is interpreted so as to make the beast a symbol of the Roman Empire only in the future to be injured by dissolution into ten kingdoms, from one of which

---

[130] Schmid (1955) p. 188: ὁ μακάριος Ἱππόλυτος αἰῶνας τούτους ἐξέλαβεν, ὧν τοὺς μὲν πέντε παρῳχηκέναι, τὸν δὲ ἕκατον ἑστάναι, ἐν ᾧ ταῦτα ἑώρα ὁ ἀπόστολος, τὸν δὲ ἕβδομον, τὸν μετὰ τὰ ἑξακισχίλια ἔτη μήπω μὲν ἐληλυθέναι... Cf. Prigent (1973) p. 315-316.

[131] *Dan.* IV, 23,6: ἐπεὶ οὖν ἐν ἓξ ἡμέραις ἐποίησεν ὁ θεὸς τὰ πάντα, δεῖ τὰ ἑξασχίλια ἔτη πληρωθῆναι· οὐδέπω γὰρ πεπλήρωνται, ὡς Ἰωάννης λέγει· "οἱ πέντε ἔπεσον, ὁ δὲ εἷς ἔστιν," τοῦτ' ἔστιν ὁ ἕκτος, "ὁ ἄλλος οὔπω ἦλθεν," τὸν ἄλλον δὲ λέγων τὸν ἕβδομον διηγεῖται, ἐν ᾧ ἔσται ἡ κατάπαυσις.

[132] Achelis (1897) p. 234,7-18: "Er erklärt nämlich die Wunde so, dass viele den Antichrist verachten und beschimpfen bei den Anfängen seines Kommens... Und ihr Geheiltwerden erklärt er so: dass sie sich dem Gehorsam gegen ihn zuwenden, wenn Zeichen geschehen, die davon (von der Zuversicht) abirren machen, dass der Zustand der Toten sowohl als das Sprechen der Götzen sich in ihre Gegenteile verwandeln werden."

[133] Ibid p. 234,8-10 where inserted in what I omitted ("...") from the quotation in footnote 132 we find: "und das Haupt erklärt er als sein Reich. Und diese ihm bewiesene Verachtung und die Verweigerung des Gehorsams ist Schwäche und Schlaffheit darin, und das ist wie eine Wunde."

[134] Schmid (1955) p. 137: κεφαλὴν ὡς ἐσφαγμένην εἴτε τινὰ τῶν ἀρχόντων αὐτοῦ τεθανατῶσθαι καὶ ὑπ' αὐτοῦ διὰ γοητείας ἀπατηλῶς ἀνίστασθαι φαινόμενόν φησιν, ὡς Σίμων ὁ μάγος πεποιηκὼς ὑπὸ τοῦ κορυφαιοτάτου τῶν ἀποστόλων ἠλέγχετο, ἢ τὴν Ῥωμαίων βασιλείαν τῇ διαιρέσει σφαγὴν τρόπον τινὰ ὑπομένουσαν τῇ μοναρχίᾳ τεθεραπεῦσθαι δοκοῦσαν κατὰ τὴν εἰκόνα Αὐγούστου καίσαρος. Neither the specific examples of Simon Magus in defence of the individualist interpretation, nor of the civil war before August on the corporate view are mentioned in Hippolytus or attributions to him. Cf. Prigent (1973) p. 236-237. See also Bodenmann R., Naissance d' une Exégèse Daniel dans l' Église ancienne des trois premiers siècles, in *Beiträge zur Geschichte der Biblischen Exegese* 28 (Tübingen: Mohr 1986).

Antichrist will come.[135] Here we find the clear symbolic/literal distinction preserved in Hippolytus' hermeneutic that the fragment has clearly garbled.

In *frag.* XIV (*Ap.* 13,16) we find attributed to Hippolytus an interpretation which apparently identifies the mark of the beast both on hand and on forehead with the wearing of garlands in the cult of Dionysius. Here the reference to *Ant.* 49 is clearly highly derivative since the compiler, either of the fragment or the *florilegium* on which it is based, has changed the reference of the mark on the forehead from the practice of Antiochus Epiphanes. He has also changed the reference of the mark on the hand from buying and selling and applied it to a mark of adoration.[136]

In *frag.* XV (*Ap.* 13,18) Hippolytus is cited as the authority for the names of Antichrist, "Titan, Euanthos, Latinos and Dantialos," derived from the letters that are the equivalent of 666.[137] Moreover, Andreas of Caesarea directly cites Hippolytus in this regard, and shares in common with this fragment Teitan and Lateinos, and, according to *ms. Athos Dionysu* 163, Euanthas.[138] But his mention of Benedictus and Lampetis in their number show that his citation is highly anachronistic as genuine Hippolytus, since the latter was a heretic of the 6th century and the former seems to refer to pope Benedict XI.[139]

The parallel here is with *Ant.* 50, but clearly taken up and developed by the general tradition of apocalyptic hermeneutic.[140] It further shows that this fragment itself is the product of a such a long tradition of re-adaptation and re-interpretation and cannot refer to any genuine lost Hippolytan work. Indeed, when Hippolytus is accurately cited on *Apoc.* 13,18 as in *ms Bodleian Syr.* 140 in fragment II (folio 279) on *Ap.* 13,11-12 from *Ant.* 50,

---

135 *Ant.* 49: .«.. τὸ θηρίον τὸ πρῶτον, οὗ ἐθεραπεύθη ἡ πληγὴ τοῦ θανάτου αὐτοῦ» τοῦτο σημαίνει, ὅτι κατὰ τὸν Αὐγούστου νόμον, ἀφ᾽ οὗ καὶ ἡ βασιλεία ᾽Ρωμαίων συνέστη, οὕτω καὶ αὐτὸς κελεύσει καὶ διατάξει... διὰ τούτου δόξαν ἑαυτῷ πλείονα περιποιούμενος. τοῦτο γὰρ ἐστι τὸ θηρίον τὸ τέταρτον, οὗ ἐπλήγη ἡ κεφαλὴ καὶ πάλιν ἐθεραπεύθη διὰ τὸ καταλυθῆναι αὐτὴν καὶ ἀτιμασθῆναι καὶ εἰς δέκα διαδήματα ἀναλυθῆναι, ὥστε πανοῦργος ὢν ὡς περιθεραπεύσειν αὐτὴν καὶ ἀνανεώσειν.

136 Achelis (1895) p. 235,2-4: "Hippolytus erklärt es so, dass „das Stigma an der Hand" das sich Niederwerfen bedeute, und das Stigma „an der Stirn" das bedeute, dass jeder Einzelne es auf seine Stirn erhebe wie einen Kranz." cf. Ant. 49: ...κελεύει πάντας... ἵνα μή τις δύνηται τῶν ἁγίων μήτε ἀγοράσαι μήτε πωλῆσαι ἐὰν μὴ πρῶτον ἐπιθύσῃ. τοῦτο γὰρ ἐστι «τὸ χάραγμα τὸ ἐπὶ τῆς χειρὸς τῆς δεξιᾶς» διδόμενον. τὸ δὲ «ἐπὶ τὸ μέτωπον» εἰπεῖν, ἵνα πάντες ὦσιν ἐστεφανωμένοι, πύρινον καὶ οὐ ζωῆς ἀλλὰ θανάτου στέφανον μεθ᾽ ἑαυτῶν περιφέροντες. οὕτω γὰρ ἐτεχνάσατο κατὰ τῶν ᾽Ιουδαίων καὶ ᾽Αντίοχος ὁ ᾽Επιφανής...

137 Achelis (1897) p. 235,6-8: "Hippolytus, der römische Bischof, hat vier Namen herausgetüfelt, deren Buchstabenzahl die erwähnte Zahl ausmacht,— aber das ist zweifelhaft..."

138 Schmid (1955) p. 145: πολλὰ ἐστιν εὑρεῖν κατὰ τὸν μακάριον ᾽Ιππόλυτον καὶ ἐτέρους ὀνόματα τὸν ἀριθμὸν τοῦτον περιέχοντα, προσηγορικά τε καὶ κύρια. κύρια μέν, οἷον Λαμπέτις, Τειτὰν διὰ τῆς διφθόγγου ἐκ τοῦ τενῶ μέλλοντος, καθ᾽ ᾽Ιππόλυτον, Λατεῖνος ὁμοίως, Βενέδικτος, ὅπερ ἑρμηνεύεται εὐλογημένος ἢ εὐλογητὸς κατὰ μίμησιν... For Euanthas see Prigent (1973) p. 315.

139 Prigent (1973) p. 315 footnote 11, where he also points to the dependence of Andreas on Oecumenius' commentary there.

140 For this passage in comparison with Barsalîbî's commentary see ibid. footnote 152 (v).

we find a far more accurate summary of the argument of the connection between power, *Lateinos*, and the *Latini*.[141] But in exhibiting the practice of commentaries to summarize and not quote directly, we are given additional support for our decision not to read other less accurate, secondary, summaries as though they were witnesses to lost primary works.[142]

If, however, we have clearly shown that where we know of parallels with Hippolytus' surviving writings in the fragments, such parallels have been garbled and distorted, we have no real basis for feeling secure about the genuineness of those which stand alone. If, furthermore, as we have also seen, such fragments are not simply distortions of existing works, but also confuse Hippolytus with the interpretations of others, as in the case of *fragments* XIII, XIV, and XV, then these fragments themselves may quite well be the work of others. Let us look therefore at the most salient of those fragments discussed by Prigent under the category of standing alone.

3C 4.1.2.3. *Fragments which stand alone*

Frag. VII (*Ap.* 12,10) attributes to Hippolytus the claim that the source of the voice is from the angels.[143] But Oecumenius and Andreas use this interpretation without attributing it to Hippolytus, even though the latter cites him on four other occasions. The suspicion is therefore aroused that, either different writers cited in a *florilegium* are being confused with one another, or indeed that the combined direct use of various commentators have lead to them being confused with one another.[144]

Similarly in *frag.* XVI (*Ap.* 14,18) no known text of Hippolytus refers to the identification of "the Lord of All" with the angel sitting upon the cloud (*Ap.* 14,14). But Andreas does mention this as a possible interpretation, which is also found in Oecumenius, without ascribing it to Hippolytus.[145] Once again the suspicion is raised that Hippolytus has been identified with, and in consequence absorbed by, a general apocalyptic tradition, in a way evidenced by the *De Consummatione Mundi* amongst his *Spuria*.

---

[141] Achelis (1897) p. 236,23- 237,3 inserts this into the fragments from *ms. Parisinus arab. christ.* 67 as frag. XIX and reads: "... Dieses Reich, erklärte der den Heiligen innewohnende Geist, ist die Machtstellung derer, die *Latini* genannt werden; und so hat es denn auch der Geist ausgelegt, der durch den heiligen Bischof und Zeugen Hippolytus gesprochen hat, indem er jene Offenbarung auslegte, die dem Theologen Johannes geworden."

[142] Prigent (1973) p. 332 places *frag.* XX (*Ap.* 17,8), which he numbers XIX in this category, but it is too sparse a reference to merit real consideration.

[143] Achelis (1897) p. 233,3-4: "Woher aber „der Schall" kommt, erklärt Hippolytus durch die Annahme, er kommt von den Engeln."

[144] Prigent (1973) p. 324. Schmid (1955) p. 10: τῶν μακαρίων Γρηγορίου τοῦ θεολόγου καὶ Κυρίλλου, προσέτι δὲ καὶ τῶν ἀρχαιοτέρων Παππίου, Εἰρηναίου, Μεθοδίου καὶ Ἱππολύτου ταύτῃ προσμαρτυρούντων τὸ ἀξιόπιστον.

[145] Schmid (1955) p. 155: ...δι' ὧν λογιζόμεθα Χριστὸν εἶναι τὸν ἐπὶ τῆς νεφέλης ὀπτανθέντα υἱῷ ἀνθρώπου ὅμοιον [=*Ap.* 14,14], idem p. 156 εἰ καὶ ὁ Χριστὸς ὀνομάζεται μεγάλης βουλῆς τῆς πατρικῆς ἄγγελος [=14, 17-18]. Cf. Prigent (1973) p. 329 and Achelis (1897) p. 235: "Wenn jener der Herr ist, der „auf den Wolken sitz," wie Hippolytus in seiner Erklärung annimmt, so ist es nicht nötig anzunehmen, dass mit diesen Engel auf den Herr des Alls hingewiesen werde."

In *frag*. XVII (*Ap*. 16,12) Hippolytus is claimed for the interpretation that the eastern kings come to submit to and not to fight against the Antichrist.[146]. Once again Andreas reflects this interpretation, but does not attribute it to Hippolytus whom he cites by name on four occasions in his Commentary.[147]

Prigent's final inclusion in the category of "no certain conclusion" is *frag*. XVIII (*Ap*. 16,16). The authority of Hippolytus is claimed for locating Armageddon in the valley of Josaphat on the grounds of its name meaning in Hebrew "trodden down."[148] Once again there is a parallel with Andreas and Oecumenius who likewise reproduce this interpretation with no Hippolytan attribution.[149]

In each of these cases therefore we find what is attributed to Hippolytus to come from a general hermeneutic tradition represented by Andreas and Oecumenius. Neither writer identifies any of them with Hippolytus whose works they both know and otherwise cite by name. Indeed, in *frag*. I (*Apoc*. 7,4-8) we have reproduced under Hippolytus' name an interpretation of Oecumenius to which Andreas appears to prefer another interpretation.[150] Here Hippolytus is invoked in order to support the interpretation of the 144, 000 as referring to Jewish Christians dispersed by the Romans.[151] Would Andreas have expressed such a preference in the face of a genuine statement of Hippolytus to the contrary? In view of this fact, the balance of probability would be against accepting Prigent's open verdict on the genuineness of these fragments.

---

146 Ibid. p. 235,14-16-236,6: "... handelt es sich bei diesen Königen des Ostens... Gehören sie zum Anhang und zu Vertretern des Antichrists?... Hippolytus nun, soweit er darüber Auskunft giebt, meint bezüglich... sie gehören zum Anhang und zu den Vertretern des Antichrists..."

147 Schmid (1955) p. 173-174: εἰκὸς δὲ καὶ τὸν ἀντίχριστον ἐκ τῶν ἀνατολικῶν μερῶν τῆς Περσικῆς γῆς, ἔνθα ἡ φυλὴ τοῦ Δὰν ἐκ ῥίζης Ἑβραίων ἐξερχόμενον, ἅμα ἑτέροις βασιλεῦσιν ἢ μεγιστᾶσι βασιλικὸν κληρουμένοις ὄνομα...

148 Achelis (1897) p. 236,12-14: "„Der im hebräischen Dialekt Harmagedon genannte Ort" bedeutet „der weiche (oder: getretene) Ort"; und bezüglich seiner speziellen Bedeutung sagt Hippolytus, er sei Wâdî Josaphat."

149 Schmid (1955) p. 175: τὸ δὲ Ἀρμαγεδὼν «διακοπὴ» ἢ «διακοπτομένη » ἑρμηνεύεται. Prigent added in a category of works definitely not by Hippolytus (i) *Frag*. X (*Ap*. 12,17) which challenges Hippolytus' putative claim that the "seed of the woman" were weak because of their riches and concern for possessions." (Achelis (1897) p. 233,24-26: "Wären sie aber gewichen wegen ihres Reichtums und wegen ihrer Sorge um ihren Besitz, wie Hippolytus sagt, warum sind sie dann standhaft geblieben bei diesen Drangsalen?"). I can however see no real parallel with *Dan*. II,21 as Prigent tentatively claims (Prigent (1973) p. 325-326: "Une pareille distinction est-elle pensable chez Hippolyte? Un développement comme celui qu'on peut lire dans le Commentaire sur Daniel (II,21) l'exclut formellement."). (ii) *Frag*. XII (*Ap*.13,11) contradicts the alleged opinion of Hippolytus that the beast from the land came before, instead of after the Antichrist, *frag*. VIII (*Ap*. 12,10), also being doubtful.

150 Schmid (1955) p. 78-80 where Andreas comments : ἡ δὲ ἀκρίβεια τῆς ἐξ ἑκάστης φυλῆς ἰσότητος ἐμφαίνειν μοι δοκεῖ τὸν πολυπλασιασμὸν τοῦ ἀποστολικοῦ σπόρου... ἁρμόδιος δὲ τούτοις ὁ λεχθεὶς ἀριθμός, ὡς εἴρηται, διά τε τοὺς πάλαι Ἑβραίων δώδεκα φυλάρχους, διά τε τοὺς ἀντ' αὐτῶν καταστάντας ἄρχοντας... θεσπεσίους ἀποστόλους.

151 Achelis (1897) p. 231,15-16 where Schulthess translates: "Hippolytus nun, der römische Bischof, vertritt in seiner Auslegung dieses Punktes der Vision diese Ansicht, und diese ist die richtige."

We must remember that, come the thirteenth century in which this *ms.* was produced (c. 1275), Hippolytan *Spuria* abounded. One such example is witnessed by *ms Monacensus arab.* 235, dated by Achelis *c.* 1550, in which some commentaries on passages from the Pentateuch, in a style and perspective utterly dissimilar to Hippolytus' known works, are attributed to "Hippolytus, the commentator on the Targum."[152] A second would be those Arabic fragments, one from Renaudot and the others from *ms. Vat. arab.* 121 Bl. 7-10v, and Bl. 65 (16th century). Here statements of Julius I, bishop of Rome, to Dionysius, Prosdocius and others on the theology of the two natures are attributed to *S. Hippolytus Romanus Episcopus* (Renaudot) or *Bulidus* (=Hippolytus) *Patrarcha Romae.*[153]

Thus we find a certain tendency in Arabic *mss.* of this period to use Hippolytus' name pseudepigraphically. Furthermore, as we shall shortly see, what appears to be a possible separate work can prove to be a loose quotation, or indeed the development of what was originally genuine Hippolytan into near *pseudepigrapha* by the free-ranging tradition of apocalyptic hermeneutic. We must now examine the two fragments from this particular *ms.* which Prigent claims to come from the κεφάλαια, which he believes to equate with the *De Apocalypsi* of Jerome, Sophronius, Nicephorus Callistus, and George Syncellus.

3C 4.1.2.4. *Fragments derived from the* κεφάλαια

Frag. II, if on *Apoc.* 10,2-4 which is far from certain, attributes to Hippolytus the claim that the prophecy of the book open and then sealed referred to the general resurrection and not to the Maccabees.[154] It may, however, be read as a commentary on *Apoc.* 7, 9-17.[155]   The parallel with Barsalîbî's *Commentary* is however as remote as fragments such as *frag.* XV with *Ant.* Barsalîbî simply reports the denial of Hippolytus that *Mt.* 24,21 applies to Vespasian. We could interpret this as betraying a common Hippolytan hermeneutic form and claim that both are therefore genuine. But in that case the genuineness of *frag.* II would depend upon the genuineness of the κεφάλαια, and that is an assumption with which I am seeking to take issue. At all events, it would be problematic, in view of what we have seen to be the summary and haphazard character of these citations generally, to propose to add by way of re-construction this fragment to Barsalîbî's extracts.

Even if it is claimed that Barsalîbî has added to an original κεφάλαια from a separate (genuine) Commentary on *Mt.*, 24,7 nevertheless the latter might

---

[152] Achelis (1897) p. 85-119.
[153] Ibid. p. 281-286.
[154] Ibid. p. 231,26-28: "Hippolytus, der römische Bischof, tritt der Ansicht bei, dass die erwähnte Weissagung auf diejenigen Toten, die auferstehen, gehe, und nicht auf die Makkabäer."
[155] Hence Prigent (1973) p. 321: "... la foule en vêtements blancs où André reconnaît les martyrs?"

be held if genuine to support the formal identification of the hermeneutic of *frag.* II with what was originally found in the κεφάλαια at this point. But this passage also concerns a citation from Epiphanius on the Ἄλογοι claimed to be from the κεφάλαια. We shall argue later (3C 5.8) that the thesis of the separate derivation by Barsalîbî at this point has problems of its own.

In *frag.* IX two interpretations are given of the stream of water which the serpent ejected from his mouth after the woman in *Ap.* 12,16. One of these is attributed to Hippolytus, namely that the waters represent armies who stray from their objective.[156] I find Prigent's parallels in Barsalîbî particularly weak at this point. The references to his commentary on *Apoc.* 8,8 on the plagues, or 8, 11 on the miracle at Mara, or 8,12 on the Flood as types of the last things are too common to apocalyptic hermeneutic in general to yield any specific parallel.[157] Thus we must conclude that, on the basis of these two fragments allegedly from the κεφάλαια in *Parisinus arab.* 67, we can hardly conclude the existence of a genuine work behind the *De Apocalypsi* constructed from a *florilegium.*

Let us now look at the citations in Barsalîbî in order to now assess directly whether they differ significantly from the kind of citations that we have so examined and found simply garbled versions of some of his genuinely surviving works.

3C 4.2. *Barsalîbî's citations and an alleged De Apocalypsi*

In many of these citations, as Prigent has pointed out in meticulous detail, we find not merely parallels with *Ant.* and *Dan.* but almost direct references.[158]

---

156 Achelis (1897) p. 233,11-13: "... „sie verschlang dieselben" so viel ist als: sie (die Heere) irrten auf ihr umher und kamen von ihrem Marschziel ab. Diese (letztere) hat Hippolytus."

157 Prigent (1973) p. 325: "Sur Ap. 8,8: les paies d'Egypte, types des prodiges eschatologiques; sur Ap. 8,11: le miracle de Mara, type des événements finaux; sur Ap. 8,12: le déluge comme prophétie partielle de l'eschaton. Cf. encore sur Ap. 9, 2-3; 9, 14-15."

158 Prigent (1972) p. 392-393. I set out his citations with the text of *Ant.* and in parenthesis text and references from Sedlacek's Latin translation of Dionysius Barsalîbî, *In Apocalypsim Iohannis,* from J.-B.Chabot et. al., Scriptores Syri, 2a CI *in Corpus Scriptorum Christianorum Orientalium,* (Latin Translation I Sedlacek), (Rome, Paris and Leipzig: De Luigi, Poussielgue and Harrassowitz 1910). (i) *Ant.* 36 : λέγε μοι, ὦ μακάριε Ἰωάννη, ἀπόστολε καὶ μαθητὰ τοῦ κυρίου, τί εἶδες καὶ τί ἤκουσας περὶ Βαβυλῶνος (XVII: "quae venient super Babyonem in fine"). γρηγόρησον καὶ εἰπέ· καὶ γὰρ αὐτή σε ἐξώρισεν (XVI: "...de Babylone quae eum pepulit in exilium.") (ii) *Ant.* 60: περὶ μὲν οὖν τοῦ διωγμοῦ καὶ τῆς θλίψεως τῆς γινομένης ἐπὶ τὴν ἐκκλησίαν ὑπὸ τοῦ ἀντικειμένου (XII,1-2: "ille hic indicat persecutiones et vexationes quas patietur ecclesia ab Antichristo"). (iii) *Ant.* 61: σαφέστατα τὴν ἐκκλησίαν ἐδήλωσεν, ἐνδεδυμένην τὸν λόγον τὸν πατρῷον ὑπὲρ ἥλιον λάμποντα (XII,2: ""Mulierem" enim ecclesiam vocat; "amictam sole" quia amicta est verbo paterno quod splendet magis quam sol.") «σελήνην» δὲ λέγων «ὑποκάτω τῶν ποδῶν αὐτῆς» δόξῃ ἐπουρανίῳ ὡς σελήνην κεκοσμημένην (""Et luna sub pedibus eius;" h.e. pulcritudine caelesti sicut lunam ornatam") τὸ δὲ λέγειν «ἐπάνω τῆς κεφαλῆς αὐτῆς στέφανος ἀστέρων δώδεκα» δηλοῖ τοὺς δώδεκα ἀποστόλους, δι' ὧν καθίδρυται ἡ ἐκκλησία... (""Et super caput eius duodecim stellae;" h.e. duodecim apostoli quorum est firmitas ecclesiae.")... «καὶ ἔτεκεν,» φησίν, «υἱὸν ἄρσενα, ὃς μέλλει ποιμαίνειν πάντα τὰ ἔθνη» τὸν ἄρσενα καὶ τέλειον Χριστόν, παῖδα θεοῦ, θεὸν καὶ ἄνθρωπον, ὃν κατήγγειλαν οἱ προφῆται, ὃν ἀεὶ τίκτουσα ἡ ἐκκλησία διδάσκει πάντα τὰ ἔθνη. (XII,5: ""Et peperit filium masculum, qui pasturus est omnes gentes;" h.e. "masculum Christum nominabat qui est Deus et ipsemet homo, quem parit ecclesia continuo et docet omnes

But for many citations we arguably find a similar kind of parallelism with the fragments that we have so far been considering. Prigent himself chronicles the kind of garbled derivations exhibited in *Parisinus arab.* 67 which were

---

gentes.")... «ὁ δράκων καὶ ἐδιώξε τὴν γυναῖκα... ὅπου τρέφεται ἐκεῖ καιρὸν καὶ καιροὺς καὶ ἥμισυ καιροῦ»... αὗται εἰσιν αἱ «χίλιαι διακόσιαι ἑξηκοντα ἡμέραι τὸ ἥμισυ τῆς ἑβδομάδος,» (ΧΙΙ,13: "tempus et cetera sunt illi mille ducenti et sexaginta dies seu dimidium hebdomadis) ἃς κρατήσει ὁ τύραννος διώκων τὴν ἐκκλησίαν φεύγουσαν «ἀπὸ πόλεως εἰς πόλιν» καὶ ἐν ἐρημίᾳ κρυβομένην καὶ ἐν τοῖς ὄρεσιν, (quando occupabit pseudochristus et persequetur ecclesiam, quae fugiet e loco in locum et se occultabit in montibus et in deserto) "ἔχουσαν μεθ᾿ ἑαυτῆς οὐδὲν ἕτερον εἰ μὴ τὰς «δύο πτέρυγας τοῦ ἀετοῦ τοῦ μεγάλου,» τουτέστι τὴν εἰς Χριστὸν Ἰησοῦν πίστιν, ὃς ἐκτείνας τὰς ἁγίας χεῖρας ἐπὶ τῷ ξύλῳ (h.e fideles in Christum qui cum expandit manus suas in ligno) ἥπλωσε, δυὸ πτέρυγας δεξιὰν καὶ εὐώνυμον, προσκαλούμενος πάντας τοὺς εἰς αὐτὸν πιστεύοντας ("h.e. dextram et sinistram suam; et vocabit fideles) καὶ σκεπάζων «ὡς ὄρνις νεοσσούς» ("et congregabit eos uti gallina pullos suos") διὰ Μαλαχίου φησίν «καὶ ὑμῖν τοῖς φοβουμένοις τὸ ὄνομα μοῦ ἀνατελεῖ ἥλιος δικαιοσύνης, καὶ ἴασις ἐν ταῖς πτέρυξιν αὐτοῦ» ("et per Malachiam dixit: "Vobis timentibus nomen meum, oriri faciam Solem iustitiae: et sanationem in alis eius."") (iv) *Ant.* 49: τὸ μὲν οὖν «θηρίον τὸ ἀναβαῖνον ἐκ τῆς γῆς» τὴν βασιλείαν τὴν τοῦ ἀντιχρίστου ἐσομένην λέγει, (ΧΙΙΙ,11: "h.e. animal quod adscendit e terra, regnum futurum Antichristi edicit") τὰ δὲ δύο κέρατα αὐτὸν καὶ τὸν μετ᾿ αὐτοῦ ψευδοπροφήτην ("duo autem cornua: ipsum et pseudoprophetam qui cum eo est") τὸ δὲ εἰπεῖν «τὰ δύο κέρατα αὐτοῦ ὅμοια ἀρνίῳ» ὅτι ἐξομοιοῦσθαι θέλει τῷ υἱῷ τοῦ θεοῦ, καὶ αὐτὸς ἑαυτὸν βασιλέα ἐπιδεικνύων, ("i.e cupit similis fieri Filio Dei et se regem praestabit")... τὸ δὲ «καὶ τὴν ἐξουσίαν... ἡ πληγὴ τοῦ θανάτου αὐτοῦ» τοῦτο σημαίνει, ὅτι κατὰ τὸν Αὐγούστου νόμον, ἀφ᾿ οὖ καὶ ἡ βασιλεία᾿ Ῥωμαίων συνέστη, οὕτω καὶ αὐτὸς κελεύσει καὶ διατάξει, κυρῶν ἅπαντα, διὰ τούτου δόξαν ἑαυτῷ πλείονα περιποιούμενος. (ΧΙΙΙ,12: "h.e. illud significat: ad instar legis Augusti, a quo imperium romanum ordinatum est, ita etiam hic ordinavit et posuit legem de omnibus, cum fortis esset, et per illud sibi magnam laudem comparavit.") τοῦτο γὰρ ἐστι τὸ θηρίον τὸ τέταρτον, ("Hoc autem erat "animal quartum,"") οὗ ἐπλήγη ἡ κεφαλὴ καὶ πάλιν ἐθεραπεύθη ("cuius caput vulneratum est et iterum sanatum,") διὰ τὸ καταλυθῆναι αὐτὴν καὶ ἀτιμασθῆναι (nam dissolutum et contumelia affectum est") καὶ εἰς δέκα διαδήματα ἀναλυθῆναι, ὥστε πανοῦργος ὢν ὡς περιθεραπεύσειν αὐτὴν καὶ ἀνανεώσειν ("et obtigit decem diademata," quod cum studeret malitiae erat simile illi, qui curavit et renovavit ipsum"). τοῦτο γὰρ ἐστι τὸ εἰρημένον ὑπὸ τοῦ προφήτου, ("Hoc est quod dictum est a propheta") ὅτι, «δώσει πνεῦμα τῇ εἰκόνι καὶ λαλήσει ἡ εἰκὼν τοῦ θηρίου·» ἐνεργήσει γὰρ καὶ ἰσχύσει πάλιν διὰ τῶν ὑπ᾿ αὐτοῦ ὁριζομένων νόμων, (ΧΙΙ,15: "h.e. faciet ut roborarentur per legem ii qui ab ipso definiti sunt) καὶ ποιήσει ὅσοι ἂν μὴ προσκυνήσωσιν τῇ εἰκόνι τοῦ θηρίου ἀποκτανθῶσιν». δολίος γὰρ ὢν καὶ ἐπαιρόμενος κατὰ τῶν δούλων τοῦ θεοῦ, βουλόμενος ἐκθλίβειν καὶ ἐκδιώκειν αὐτοὺς ἐκ τοῦ κόσμου διὰ τὸ μὴ διδόναι αὐτοὺς αὐτῷ δόξαν (ΧΙΙΙ,16: "h.e. astutus enim est et exaltari super servos Dei studet. Et vult vexare et expellere eos e mundo quia non dant ipsi laudem")... τὸ δὲ «ἐπὶ τὸ μέτωπον» εἰπεῖν, ("Illud autem dicit imponi "super sedem oculorum" seu frontem") ἵνα πάντες ὦσιν ἐστεφανωμένοι, πύρινον καὶ οὐ ζωῆς ἀλλὰ θανάτου στέφανον ("quia omnes coronabunt corona peregrina, non vitae sed mortis") μεθ᾿ ἑαυτῶν περιφέροντες ("quos secum circumducent). οὕτω γὰρ ἐτεχνάσατο κατὰ τῶν Ἰουδαίων καὶ Ἀντίοχος ὁ᾿ Ἐπιφανὴς ὁ τῆς Συρίας γενόμενος βασιλεύς, ὢν ἐκ γένους Ἀλεξάνδρου τοῦ Μακεδόνος ("Ita fecit Antiochus Epiphanes, Antiochenus, et familia Alexandri"). καὶ γὰρ αὐτὸς τοῖς τότε καιροῖς ἐπαρθεὶς τῇ καρδίᾳ ("cum enim gloriaretur in corde suo"), ἔγραψε ψήφισμα βωμοὺς ("praecepit ut extruantur altaria") πρὸ τῶν θυρῶν τιθέντας ἅπαντας ἐπιθύειν, καὶ κισσοὺς ἐστεφανωμένους πομπεύειν τῷ Διονύσῳ ("et quidem ut coronati omnes in ligneto festum Dionysi agerent"), τοὺς δὲ μὴ βουλομένους ὑποτάσσεσθαι, τούτους μετὰ σπλαγχνισμῶν καὶ ἐτασμῶν καὶ βασάνων ἀναιρεῖσθαι ("eos vero, qui non sacrificarunt, occiderunt"). (v) *Ant.* 50: πλὴν ὅσον νοοῦμεν ἀμφιβάλλοντες λέγωμεν (ΧΙΙΙ,18: "h.e. de nomine eius non licet adaequate definire"). πολλὰ γὰρ εὑρίσκομεν ὀνόματα τούτῳ τῷ ἀριθμῷ ἰσόψηφα περιεχόμενα, ("multa enim nomina videmus attingere calculum hunc") οἷον ὡς φέρε εἰπεῖν τὸ Τειτάν ἐστιν, ἀρχαῖον καὶ ἔνδοξον ὄνομα, ἢ τὸ Εὐάθας ("verbi gratia Titin aut Auntos, et alia huiusmodi")... φανερὸν δὲ πᾶσίν ἐστιν ὅτι οἱ κρατοῦντες ἔτι νῦν εἰσι Λατεῖνοι, ("manifestio est eorum qui nunc dominantur") εἰς ἑνὸς οὖν ἀνθρώπου ὄνομα μεταγόμενον γίνεται Λατεῖνος ("Romani antequam haberent hoc nomen Latini vocabantur et unus eorum appellatur Latinus").

clearly also available to Barsalîbî in the form of a similar *florilegium* incorporating similarly what had become a quite amorphous and anonymous tradition of apocalyptic hermeneutic.[159] He could therefore use Hippolytus in some cases directly, but in others from the garbled hermeneutic represented by such *florilegia*.

Prigent was therefore correct in his claim that Barsalîbî is quoting sometimes from *Ant.* and *Dan.*, and sometimes from their garbled versions in a *florilegium*. He admitted that this process has produced a fictitious work (the *De Apocalypsi*) in the minds of some medieval as well as modern writers, from some exact, and some garbled citations from a *florilegium* whose heading indicated its subject matter ("citations *De Apocalypsi*"). But Prigent insisted nevertheless that the κεφάλαια is genuine and not itself the product of a similar process of literary transmission. We need to ask whether in that case Prigent may be wrong in concluding that sometimes Barsalîbî is quoting from these two works as part of his own commentary, but in other parts, those directed at Gaius, from the κεφάλαια as a genuine work. The κεφάλαια may well be the product of such secondary material whose garbled character has produced, as in the case of the putative *De Apocalypsi*, the illusion of being citations from a genuine lost work. In the case of *ms. Parisinus arab.* 67 we agreed largely with Prigent that the presence of such parallels, however garbled, spelled the death of the notion that the fragments witnessed to a genuine, lost *De Apocalypsi*.

We now need to examine whether such parallels in the case of the κεφάλαια too are not explicable as from a *florilegium* composed mainly from *Dan.* and *Ant.*, with the appearance of citations from a distinct lost work but which in fact is an illusion created by an identical process of transmission. Prinzivalli, though accepting the common view that the citations of Barsalîbî were genuine, neverthertheless accepted the possibility that he had derived his text from a *florilegium*.[160] As we are helped in our quest by some very similar citations much earlier in Epiphanius of Salamis where the nameless Ἄλογοι voice similar views to Barsalîbî's Gaius, it will be well to explore whether we can substantiate a case for these as witnesses to the κεφάλαια as a genuine work of Hippolytus, or whether these too represent a general apocalyptic hermeneutic in which the views of different commentators have simply been garbled, as we noted was the case with *Parisinus arab.* 67.

---

[159] Prigent (1972) p. 395-403 Barsalîbî *Apoc.* XI,2b (*Ant.* 47); XI,3-4 (*Ant.* 43); XI,7-8 (*Ant.* 25); I,13a (*Dan.* IV, 11,5); I,13b (*Cant.* frag. III (Achelis (1897) p. 344-345); *Ant.* 59; *Dan.* IV, 37,2); I,15b (*Dan.* I,17); II,7 (*Dan.* I,17); IV,5-6 (*Ezek.* frag. I (Achelis (1897) p. 183); V,1 (*Dan.* IV, 33,5; 34,1); V,9 (*Dan.* IV, 34,3); IX, 17b (*Ben. Mos.* Deut. 23,22); XI,1b (*Ant.* 6).

[160] Prinzivalli (1981) p. 59: "Si può tuttavia avanzare il dubbio se egli effettivamente leggesse l'opera completa di Ippolito, oppure non si basasse su una silloge di passi scelti." But if that were the case, it becomes far easier to concede the stronger possibility that the passages from such a *florilegium* were themselves garbled forms of existing works and not an hitherto completely unknown one.

3C 5. *Barsalîbî's Commentary and Epiphanius' citations*

Schwartz claimed a definite connection between the Barsalîbî citations and Epiphanius' account of the Ἄλογοι which led him to conclude that they both shared a common source, namely the dialogue allegedly written by Hippolytus in which the author included himself, dubiously as we have argued, as the major spokesperson. It will be relevant, therefore, to our consideration to examine closely Epiphanius and Barsalîbî's citations and their putative relation, using Schwartz's own reconstruction of the Greek *Vorlage* of the Syriac.

3C 5.1. Pan. *51, 34, 2-7 and Barsalîbî Apoc. IX,15*
These references allow the closest comparison that might be made between Epiphanius and Barsalîbî. But even here there are no sufficiently close correspondences for which a straight quotation or even an approximate one might account. There are similarities in the interpretation but the actual wording of the description is very dissimilar. The fundamental similarity is the acceptance by the writers of both texts of the fundamental hermeneutical principle that angelic beings in apocalyptic writings represent the corporate personalities of nations. The justification is taken from *Deut.* 32, 7-9.[161] But even here the precise point is differently expressed. It is, according to Epiphanius, because the nations are subject to angels that the angels must be released if they are to proceed to command those nations to war.[162]

According to Barsalîbî, on the other hand, it is not so much a case of being "subject" (τεταγμένα) as in Epiphanius, but rather the nations are "delivered over into the allotted angelic boundaries" (ἀγγέλοις τῶν ἐθνῶν παραδοθέντων καὶ ἑκάστου ἑνὶ ἔθνους ἀγγέλῳ λαχόντος).[163] Furthermore, the angels are described as "ordered" or "arranged" over the nations (ὅτε γὰρ οἱ ἄγγελοι οἱ ἐπὶ τῶν ἐθνῶν τεταγμένοι) rather than the nations "subjected" under them as in Epiphanius.

They are not ordered to move those allotted to them (οὐ κελεύονται κινῆσαι τοὺς ὑπ' αὐτούς) because of the restraining bond (δεσμός τις... τοῦ ἐπέχοντος αὐτούς), the power of the word (ἡ τοῦ λόγου δύναμις), until the Last day and the Almighty's command (μέχρι τοῦ ἐλθεῖν τὴν ἡμέραν καὶ προστάξαι τὸν παντοκράτορα).[164] In Epiphanius it is clearly the desire of the

---

[161] *Pan.* 51, 34,5-6: τὰ γὰρ ἔθνη ὑπὸ ἀγγέλους τεταγμένα εἰσίν, ὡς ἐπιμαρτυρεῖ μοι Μωυσῆς ὁ ἅγιος τοῦ θεοῦ θεράπων...
[162] Ibid. 34,6-7: εἰ οὖν τὰ ἔθνη ὑπὸ ἀγγέλους εἰσὶ τεταγμένα, δικαίως εἶπε· λῦσον τοὺς τέσσαρας ἀγγέλους τοὺς ἐπὶ τοῦ Εὐφράτου, ἐφισταμένους δηλόντι καὶ ἐπεχομένους ἐπιτρέπειν τοῖς ἔθνεσιν εἰς πόλεμον...
[163] Barsalîbî *Apoc.* IX translated by Schwartz (1904) p. 36-37: τὸ δὲ τέσσαρας ἀγγέλους οὐκ ἀλλότριον τῆς γραφῆς Μωσέως λέγοντος [*Deut.* 32,8] ὅτε διέσπειρεν υἱοὺς Ἀδάμ, ἔστησεν ὅρια ἐθνῶν κατὰ ἀριθμὸν ἀγγέλων θεοῦ. ἀγγέλοις οὖν τῶν ἐθνῶν παραδοθέντων καὶ ἑκάστου ἑνὶ ἔθνους ἀγγέλῳ λαχόντος δικαίως ὁ Ἰωάννης λέγει διὰ τῆς Ἀποκαλύψεως [9,14] ὅτι λῦσον τοὺς τέσσαρας ἀγγέλους, οἵ εἰσιν Πέρσαι καὶ Μῆδοι καὶ Βαβυλώνιοι καὶ Ἀσσύριοι.
[164] Ibid. IX,15, Schwartz (1904) p. 37.

angelic beings themselves to stir up the nations subject to them. The concept of "loosing" the four angels is clearly separate in both cases and indicative of two commentators, with distinct perspectives, but nevertheless operating within the common hermeneutical framework set by *Deut.* 32,8.

In Epiphanius *Pan.* 51, 34, the four angels are mentioned on the Euphrates (λῦσον τοὺς τέσσαρας ἀγγέλους τοὺς ἐπὶ τοῦ Εὐφράτου) in order to indicate the difference between the nations there (ἵνα δείξῃ τὰς διαφορὰς τῶν ἐκεῖσε ἐθνῶν καθεζομένων ἐπὶ τὸν Εὐφράτην), as Daniel's four kingdoms, the Assyrians, Babylonians, Medes, and Persians, which succeed one another (αὗται γὰρ αἱ τέσσαρες βασιλεῖαι κατὰ διαδοχὴν). But there is no mention of this difference and succession in Barsalîbî. As we have seen, the emphasis is on the angels ranked over those nations being restrained within their allotted boundaries until δεσμός τις ἡ τοῦ λόγου δύναμις... τοῦ ἐπέχοντος is removed and ταῦτα δὲ συμβήσεται ὅταν ἔλθῃ ὁ ἀντίχριστος. There is no mention of Antichrist in Epiphanius *Pan.* 51, 34.

There is mention in Epiphanius of the constraint of these angels who are "commanded and restrained by the Spirit" (κρατοῦνται γὰρ οἱ ἐπιτεταγμένοι ἄγγελοι ὑπὸ τοῦ πνεύματος), but this is related to the historical succession (κατὰ διαδοχὴν) of their kingdoms. The reason for their not yet being released (διὰ τὸ μηδέπω λύειν αὐτοὺς) is to prevent the rest of the nations also being released (τὴν δίκην τοῦ τὰ λοιπὰ ἔθνη λύεσθαι), and exercising violence towards the saints (ἕνεκεν τῆς εἰς τοὺς ἁγίους ὕβρεως). When they are moved, they will move their nations to an impulse to vengeance (καὶ γὰρ κινούμενοι οἱ ἄγγελοι κινοῦσι τὰ ἔθνη εἰς ὁρμὴν ἐκδικίας). Their movement is thus a movement of historical succession in time, not the movement of geographically allotted, spatial boundaries as in Barsalîbî. It is difficult to explain these differences simply in terms of Epiphanius freely translating a common source that he shares with Barsalîbî. A comparison of this passage with Barsalîbî does not suggest the use a free translation of a common source but of two authors taking a common hermeneutic tradition and applying it quite differently.

Once we proceed from the commonality of the hermeneutic base to the conclusions drawn, we find increasingly more radical divergences. Further comparisons between other details of the expositions found in Epiphanius and Barsalîbî reveal a quite different interrogatory context. In Epiphanius it is the thought of the four angels sitting on the Euphrates that excites the ridicule of the Ἄλογοι χλευάζοντες. In Barsalîbî, however, the 'Gaius' of the dialogue is not moved by the humorous aspects of angels sitting on a river. His objection is that it is contrary to Scripture to assert that angels will make war or that a third part of the human race would perish. *Mat.* 24,7 had stated that ἐγερθήσεται ἔθνος ἐπ᾽ ἔθνος, not that angel would rise against angel, nor that any proportion would perish. It was four nations and not four angels that would arise from the Euphrates region and ravage the earth.[165] 'Hippolytus' then replies, as we have, seen with the standard apocalyptic hermeneutic that equates a nation with its guardian angel.

If we now turn to the other arguments attributed to Gaius by Barsalîbî, we can compare their formal structure with what we find in Epiphanius, even though the substantive content is not found there. The remainder of Barsalîbî's citations attributed to 'Gaius' are partly similar in form to the objection attributed by Epiphanius to the Ἄλογοι. The logical form of the argument that constitutes the objection and the response is quite literal in Barsalîbî, and allegorical features only appear in connection with the response in Epiphanius' version. In this respect, they resemble the garbling of *frag.* XI that we witnessed in *Parisinus arab.* 67 in which a mystical and allegorical exegesis is confused by being made literal (3C 4.1.2.2). Epiphanius does however have a brief argument of the Ἄλογοὶ which has no parallel in Barsalîbî, but which will admit of some comparison with the form of the latter and to this we turn first.

3C 5.2. Pan. *51,32,2*

Epiphanius has a brief argument of the Ἄλογοι χλευάζοντες ridiculing seven angels with seven trumpets.[166] There is no parallel with this passage in Barsalîbî which on the face of it is an objection of a plurality of individuals and not one author alone (φάσκουσι). Initially there is a significant difference in the kind of reply given by Epiphanius and in Barsalîbî. Epiphanius' reply here initially allegorises the criticised passage, claiming that ἡ βίβλος πνευματικῶς ἡμῖν ἀπεκαλύφθη, that πνευματική ἐστιν ἡ πᾶσα τοῦ θεοῦ πραγματεία, and that πνευματικῶς νοήσωμεν ἀπ᾽ οὐρανοῦ εἶναι τῆς ἐκκλησίας τὸ κήρυγμα. (51, 32,7-8)

But the second part of Epiphanius' criticism does however resemble in kind the citations of Gaius in Barsalîbî. Here the method of refutation is not allegorical but simply the literal demonstration from other parts of Scripture that the statements of the *Apocalypse* are in accord with them. Those that mock the angelic trumpeters are also mocking the statement of Paul the Apostle too in 1 *Thess.* 4,16.[167] Thus we have a parallel to the methodology of the citations.

---

[165] Ibid. IX,15 and Schwartz (1904) p. 36: Γάιος· οὐ γέγραπται ὅτι ἄγγελοι πολεμοῦσιν οὐδὲ ὅτι ἀπολεῖται τὸ τρίτον τῶν ἀνθρώπων [*Apoc.* 9,14 ff.], ἀλλ᾽ ὅτι ἐγερθήσεται ἔθνος ἐπ᾽ ἔθνος [*Mt.* 24,7] καὶ ᾽Ἱππόλυτος κατ᾽ αὐτοῦ· οὐ λέγει τοὺς ἀγγέλους εἰς πόλεμον ἔρχεσθαι, ἀλλὰ τὰ τέσσαρα ἔθνη ἀναστήσεσθαι ἐκ τοῦ κλίματος τοῦ ἐπὶ τῷ Εὐφράτῃ καὶ ἐπιδραμεῖσθαι τὴν γῆν καὶ πολεμήσειν τῇ ἀνθρωπότητι.

[166] *Pan.* 51,32,2: φάσκουσι δὲ κατὰ τῆς ᾽Αποκαλύψεως τάδε χλευάζοντες οὕτως· τί με φησίν, ὠφελεῖ ἡ᾽Αποκάλυψις ᾽Ιωάννου, λέγουσά μοι περὶ ἑπτὰ ἀγγέλων καὶ ἑπτὰ σαλπίγγων.

[167] Ibid. 51, 32,10-11: εἰ δὲ χλευάζονται παρ᾽ ὑμῖν, ὦ οὗτοι, αἱ τῶν ἀγγέλων σάλπιγγες διὰ τὸ ἐν τῇ ᾽Αποκαλύψει γεγράφθαι, χλευάζεται ἄρα καὶ ἡ παρὰ τῷ ἁγίῳ ἀποστόλῳ σάλπιγξ εἰρημένη· καταβήσεται γάρ φησιν, κύριος ἀπ᾽ οὐρανοῦ ἐν τῇ ἐσχάτῃ σάλπιγγι καὶ οἱ νεκροὶ ἀναστήσονται ἐν τῇ ἐσχάτῃ ἡμέρᾳ ἐν φωνῇ

So much therefore for the one additional citation of an objection to the *Apocalypse* that Epiphanius does not share with Barsalîbî. If we now look at the additional citations that would, on Schwartz's hypothesis, have had to come from a document that Epiphanius and Barsalîbî read in common, we find the tradition of a hermeneutic that is literal and that seeks coherence between the *Apocalypse* and other parts of Scripture without resorting to allegory to soften the otherwise ridiculous imagery.

Indeed, it is only Epiphanius' Ἄλογοι χλευάζοντες who introduce ridicule into their argument that requires allegory to replace ridicule with spiritual profundity. The 'Gaius' in this dialogue takes the claims of the *Apocalypse* utterly seriously, but regards them as inconsistent with other parts of Scripture. Even the objection recorded by Epiphanius regarding the absence of a church in Thyateira (*Pan.* 51, 33,1) that we discussed earlier (3 B 2.2) had an element of ridicule about it, though no allegorization was involved there in the refutation. Let us now look at the citations found in Barsalîbî alone, comparing their argumentative form, literalist and Scriptural, by contrast with that of Epiphanius revealed here.

3.C 5.3. *Barsalîbî* Apoc. *VIII, 8*

Here 'Gaius' objects that if the coming of the Lord is "as a thief coming in the night," as stated in 1 *Thess.* 5,2, then the futuristic program of the *Apocalypse* is inconsistent with that Scripture, with the prophecy that one third of the sea will become blood at the opening of the vial by the second angel, etc.[168]

The 'Hippolytus' of the dialogue replies that the plagues are the general antitype to the particular type of those of the Egyptians in *Exodus*. The plagues of the *Apocalypse* were not those of the Day of the Lord, but of the prior events leading up to them. *Matt.* 24,21, *Joel* 2, 30-31, and *Amos* 5, 18-19 are then quoted to demonstrate the consistency of the *Apocalypse* with the rest of Scripture. Finally it is explained that the "night" in which the Lord comes is only so for unbelievers, and this interpretation is justified with reference to *Jn.* 11,10 and 12, 35-36, which may show that the author of the dialogue assumed Gaius not to have questioned the authority of the Fourth Gospel itself, and thus the title on the Statue could not have been directed against him. Thus we have typology and otherwise literal comparison with other Scriptural texts but no attempt to soften the literalism of the *Apocalypse* with reference to an allegorical interpretation.

ἀρχαγγέλου. [1 *Thess.* 4,16] συνᾴδοντος τοίνυν τοῦ Παύλου τῷ ἁγίῳ ἀποστόλῳ Ἰωάννῃ ἐν τῇ Ἀποκαλύψει, ποία τις ὑπολείπεται ἀντιλογία;

[168] Schwartz (1904) p. 36: Γάιος ὁ αἱρετικὸς ἐναντιοῦται τῇ Ἀποκαλύψει λέγων ὅτι ταῦτα οὐχ οἷόν τε γενέσθαι· «ὡς γὰρ κλέπτης ἐν νυκτὶ ἐρχόμενος» [1 *Thess.* 5,2] ἔσται ἡ παρουσία τοῦ κυρίου.

3C 5.4. Barsalîbî Apoc. VIII,12

'Gaius' objects that the smiting by the fourth angel of a third part of sun, moon and stars, and their darkening, is contrary to *Mt.* 24,37 and 1 *Thess.* 5,3.[169] In the days of Noah the elements were suddenly destroyed all at once and together when they were submerged, and not lifted away.

The character 'Hippolytus' replies quite literally once more, and without dint of allegory. The flood of Noah was simply partial and the deluge could come suddenly. But when heaven and earth pass away, it is necessary that such an event proceed by degrees, such as those that the *Apoc.* 8,12, in congruence with *Luke* 21,25 and *Joel* 2,10.

3C 5.5. Barsalîbî Apoc. IX,2

'Gaius' objects that the punishment of the locusts upon the lawless is contrary to 2 *Tim.* 3,12-13 in which it is stated that it is the believers who will be persecuted.[170]

'Hippolytus' argues to the contrary that according to the *Exodus* typology the Hebrews are sealed and delivered, whilst the Egyptians suffer the plagues, and this is found antitypically in the last things. *Luke* 21,28 and 2 *Tim.* 3,8-9, 12-13 are cited in support of the contention that indeed the faithful will suffer persecution in the eschatological events.

3C 5.6. Barsalîbî Apoc. XX, 2

'Gaius' here objects that the future binding of Satan for one thousand years is contrary to *Mt.* 2,29, where Christ has already bound Satan.[171]

'Hippolytus' replies that in that case why is Satan described in the Gospels as coming to Jesus at other times after the binding of Satan, and why are the daemonic powers still real to Paul. He cites Scripture once again, including the Fourth Gospel which Barsalîbî has concluded in his preface that Gaius rejected, but once again in the citations themselves indicates that he would have found them authoritative otherwise there would have been no point in citing them against him. (*Jn.* 14,30; *Mt.* 6,13; 12,29,30; 13,19; *Lk.* 22,31; *Eph.* 6,12) Furthermore, in the course of his argument here, he cites 2 *Pet.* 3,8, and defends the thousand years as equivalent to Scriptural expectations regarding the "Day of God." That the 'Hippolytus' here cited is anywhere

---

[169] Ibid. p. 36: Γάιος λέγει ὅτι ὡς ἐν τῷ κατακλυσμῷ οὐκ ἤρθη τὰ στοιχεῖα καὶ ἀθρόως κατεκλύσθησαν οὕτως καὶ ἐν τῷ τέλει γενήσεται κατὰ τὸ γεγραμμένον «ὥσπερ αἱ ἡμέραι τοῦ Νωε, οὕτως ἔσται ἡ παρουσία τοῦ υἱοῦ τοῦ ἀνθρώπου» [*Mt.* 24,37] καὶ τὸ Παύλου [1 *Thess.* 5,3] «ὅταν λέγωσιν εἰρήνη καὶ ἀσφάλεια, τότε ἐπιστήσεται αὐτοῖς ὄλεθρος.»

[170] Ibid. p. 36: ἐνταῦθα ἀντιλέγει Γάιος πῶς κολάζονται οἱ ἄνομοι ὑπὸ τῶν ἀκρίδων [*Apoc.* 9,3 ff.] τῆς γραφῆς λεγούσης ὅτι οἱ ἁμαρτωλοὶ εὐθηνοῦσι καὶ οἱ δίκαιοι διωκόμενοι ἐν τῷ κόσμῳ καὶ τοῦ Παύλου ὅτι «οἱ πιστεύοντες διωχθήσονται καὶ οἱ πονηροὶ προκόψουσιν πλανῶντες καὶ πλανώμενοι.» [2 *Tim.* 3,12-13]

[171] Ibid. p. 37: Γάιος ὁ αἱρετικός ἀντιλέγει ὅτι ὁ Σατανᾶς ἐδέθη ὧδε [*Apoc.* 20,2] διότι γέγραπται ὅτι εἰσῆλθεν ὁ Χριστὸς «εἰς τὴν οἰκίαν τοῦ ἰσχυροῦ καὶ ἔδησεν αὐτὸν καὶ ἡμᾶς τὰ σκεύη αὐτοῦ ἥρπασεν.» [*Mt.* 2,29]

close to any historical bearer of his name in the early third century should excite our suspicion in view of the use of 2 *Peter* thus attributed to him.

There are however two further citations from 'Hippolytus' alone, without any corresponding objection from 'Gaius.' Let us now consider these.

3C 5.7. *Hippolytus alone on* Apoc. *I,4*

Barsalîbî records that Hippolytus had claimed that John in the *Apocalypse* wrote his thirteen epistles to seven churches. Thus he concluded that he did not consider *Hebrews* to be Paul's but instead Clement's.[172]

The form of this argument, though unaccompanied by an objection of Gaius, is similar to the other citations from their alleged dialogue. The authenticity of the *Apocalypse* is demonstrated by showing that it is coherent with other parts of Scripture and, as Paul wrote to seven Churches, so John in so doing follows scriptural practice. One of Lightfoot's arguments that Gaius and Hippolytus had been one and the same person was that both rejected *Hebrews* as well as both conforming to Eusebius' description in *H.E.* VI, 20,2. We have no citation from *Hebrews* in any extant work associated with Hippolytus' name. The particular substantive argument could nevertheless have been read in the Muratorian canon, which has been argued by some to be the work of Hippolytus himself,[173] where Paul is described as following his predecessor John in writing to seven churches.[174]

It could be concluded from this argument that this citation was part of a written dialogue against Gaius, but that Gaius's particularly objection at this point had been omitted. On the other hand it could equally be argued, as matters stand, that the other citations make sense as general observations on the *Apocalypse* and general difficulties that it raised, and that their dramatisation in the mouth of 'Gaius' could have been an afterthought on the part of the author or indeed added for dramatic effect by Barsalîbî himself. Indeed Epiphanius, as we have seen, raised general objections attributed to the amorphous Ἄλογοὶ, without using the name of a specific person called 'Gaius.'

Let us now examine the second and more protracted comment attributed to 'Hippolytus' alone apparently with no instigating objection of 'Gaius.'

3C 5.8. *Hippolytus alone on* Apoc. *XI,2*

Schwartz agreed with Gwynn that this fragment, originally published by Gwynn, did not come from the dialogue with Gaius, but from a lost com-

---

172 Barsalîbî *Apoc.* I,4: "Hippolytus dicit: Scribens septem ecclesiis scripsit, sicut Paulus epistulas suas tredecim septem ecclesiis scripsit. Illam ad Hebraeos non existimat esse Pauli, sed fortasse Clementis."

173 Lightfoot (1890) 1,II p. 411-412, but see my comments on the identification with the Statue's ᾠδαὶ εἰς πάσας τὰς γραφάς in 5A 9 below.

174 Ibid. p. 412: "...de quibus singulis non necesse est disputari, cum ipse beatus apostolus Paulus, sequens predecessoris sui Iohannis ordinem non nisi nominatim septem ecclesiis scribat ordine tali..."; Schwartz (1904) p. 29.

mentary on *Matthew*.[175] It is rather odd, if this is the case, that this commentary of Hippolytus is not cited in Barsalîbî's extant commentary on the synoptic gospels. I have endeavoured to show that the evidence for the existence of that dialogue is by no means unambiguous, dependent as was Schwartz's case on a common document shared with Epiphanius and corroborated by Eusebius on a doubtful interpretation of Gaius as the assailant of the *Apocalypse* itself, and not on Cerinthus' visions that were based on distortions of it (3B 2.1).

Barsalîbî here produces his own interpretation before that of Hippolytus, conceding that Hippolytus' interpretation of the text at this point is other than his own.[176] The instruction to measure only within the temple and not its outer court given over to the gentiles is interpreted as applying to the expulsion of those who, though believers now, are to be numbered with sinful nations because they have nevertheless "not conducted themselves according to the measure of grace."[177] The treading down of the holy city for forty-two months is connected with *Dan.* 9,27, and the holy city is equated with the Church and the cutting off of sacrifice to the ceasing of the prayers of the just.

Barsalîbî's own exposition at this point is clearly allegorical in that for him the holy city is the church. 'Hippolytus,' in interpreting this passage otherwise (*aliter applicans*), is on Barsalîbî's own admission, not speaking allegorically. The *pollutio desecrationis* is indeed spoken *non de Iudaeis nec de vastione Ierusalem ... sed de fine et Antichristo*. But the end and Antichrist are regarded as quite literal. The just are literally the Christians of that generation, and thus the allusion to the flight on the Sabbath (*Mt.* 24,20) has to be taken figuratively as not preoccupied with worldly affairs (*operibus mundanis*), when the *pollutio* takes place, since they are Christians and not Jews. Though he does not define the location of the *pollutio*, the allusion is nevertheless to what will happen literally in some temple, even if what is described cannot have happened during Vespasian's siege. There were no general terrors of the end, but only what was usual in sieges.[178] The idol

---

[175] Schwartz (1904) p. 37 note 1: "Das Hermathena 7,147 ff. veröffentlichte Fragment Hippolyts enthält nichts von Gaius und braucht nicht aus den Κεφάλαια κατὰ Γαίου entnommen zu sein." cf. Gwynn (1890) p. 137 who agrees that the passage is "given by Hippolytus, apparently in some other of his writings which has not reached us."
[176] Barsalîbî *Apoc.*11,2: "Scribit Hippolytus aliter applicans quod dictum est in evangelio [Mat. 24,15]... Dicit enim non de Iudaeis nec de vastatione Ierusalem illa dicta esse, sed de fine et Antichristo."
[177] Ibid. 11,2: "hoc adduxit, quia multi qui nunc existimantur interiores esse, quia crediderunt, tunc repellentur, cum gentibus peccatricibus computandi, quia non secundum mensuram gratiae se gesserunt..."
[178] Ibid. 11,2: "Hoc [*Mat.* 24,21] non evenisse in obsidione Vespasiani, non enim accidit quidquam novi in mundo in diebus eius, praeter ea, quae iam antea evenerant."

named Kore was moreover erected there by someone else, Traianus Quintus.[179]

In consequence, we must say that it is somewhat gratuitous to argue that this passage comes from a lost commentary on *Matthew* not cited by Barsalîbî elsewhere in his extant work on the gospels. The passage is of a similar literary form as the other replies of 'Hippolytus' to 'Gaius,' even though an objection of Gaius was not mentioned in this instance. There is an absence of allegorization the presence of which we noted at some points in Epiphanius, and a quite literalist approach to the prophecy of the end, which is quite foreign to Hippolytus' hermeneutic, but characteristic of garbled versions such as we saw witnessed to in *Parisinus arab.* 67, in particular in connection with *frag.* XI (3C 4.1.2.2).

We have therefore from a detailed comparison of the relevant texts seen that the hermeneutical treatment of the *Apocalypse* by the 'Gaius' of Barsalîbî differs significantly from that of Epiphanius' Ἄλογοι χλευάζ–οντες, despite the exposition of two texts in common. Thus there was no common document shared by Barsalîbî with Epiphanius as opposed to a common hermeneutic tradition. We cannot therefore regard Epiphanius as an early witness to the dialogue between Hippolytus and Gaius in Barsalîbî. A further corroboration of this fact is that, in addition to Epiphanius not naming Gaius as the author of the opinions of the Ἄλογοι χλευάζοντες, neither does Anastasius Sinaitae, Patriarch of Antioch (died 599). The latter quotes from Epiphanius by name (Ἐπιφανίου ἐκ τῶν Παναρίων) in *Quaestiones* LVII (*Pan.* 51,34,5: ἑκάστῳ ἔθνει ἄγγελον ἐφεστάναι... κινοῦσι τὰ ἔθνη εἰς ὁρμὴν ἐκδικήσεως) and thus attributes to Epiphanius a quote that in fact would have to be from Hippolytus if he had been Epiphanius' original source. It would be strange if such a dialogue were in circulation that Anastasius fails to identify its true author as Hippolytus.

We have already mentioned the chronological problem that would preclude the record of an actual dialogue between the two, and the problem of clear and unambiguous literary attestation that would make this particular Gaius identical with the author of the διάλογος πρὸς Πρόκλον (3C 2). We have furthermore already had occasion to point out that it is not clear that Gaius in this dialogue, as Eusebius reports it, denies the authenticity of the *Apocalypse*, as clearly does the 'Gaius' of Barsalîbî (3B 2.1). Furthermore we must not lose sight of the fact already established that Barsalîbî himself distinguishes the *Hippolytus Romanus* of the dialogue from the Hippolytus, bishop of Bostra, mentioned by Eusebius-Jerome and therefore from the author of the works mentioned in their respective catalogues. However, there is one piece of counter evidence that we must briefly consider now.

---

179 Ibid. 11,2: "Et Vespasianus non erexit idola in templo, sed illa legio quam collocavit Traianus Quintus, vir nobilis Romanorum, erexit ibi idolum quod vocatur Kore."

3.C 6 *Barsalîbî and Ebed-Jesu's Catalogue*

Ebed-Jesu (1300) has a catalogue of works of "Lord Hippolytus martyr and bishop" in which is mentioned a work entitled ἀπολογία ὑπὲρ τῆς ἀποκαλύψεως καὶ τοῦ εὐαγγελίου Ἰωάννου.[180] Now this title has been identified with the work mentioned on the Statue under the title usually transcribed: ὑπὲρ τοῦ κατὰ Ἰωάννην εὐαγγελίου καὶ ἀποκαλύψεως. At this point the quest for the author of the works on the Statue would apparently cease to be simply a process of elimination, as Nautin claimed, and become instead a direct identification.[181] In consequence at least one of the works on the Statue would have to be held to have been composed by Hippolytus, and, on the generally accepted thesis that I have opposed, would therefore have had to be author of the other titles on the list since the Statue, on that questionable thesis, represents a monument to a single person.

Consequently the reference to a work listed on the Statue by Ebed-Jesu under the name of Hippolytus was potentially fatal to Nautin's thesis that all the works on the Statue were not by Hippolytus, nor indeed by Gaius, but rather by the other name mentioned by Photius, namely Josephus. But at this point we must note that, on the fairest reading of Ebed-Jesu's list, the work entitled κεφάλαια κατὰ Γαίου is not the same work as the ἀπολογία. If the one title that precedes the other was indeed intended to be a subtitle or alternative title, the conjunction would not be καὶ but ἢ as in the title also on the Statue: πρὸς Ἕλληνας καὶ πρὸς Πλάτωνα ἢ καὶ περὶ τοῦ παντός, where the former is clearly the subtitle, or alternative title, of the latter.

Nautin is clearly correct therefore to question the plausibility of the existence of two works of Hippolytus on approximately the same theme, namely the κεφάλαια and the ἀπολογία .[182] If Ebed-Jesu had in fact before him Barsalîbî's text, then from that alone rather than an actual document in his possession he could have been lead to conclude the existence of the ἀπολογία from Barsalîbî *Apoc.* praescr. alone. Richard, in supporting Nautin in this respect, is forced to the contrived conclusion that the one work contained two parts corresponding to, presumably, the ἀπολογία and the κεφάλαια, even

---

[180] Ebed-Jesu, *Catalogus* 7: Κύριος Ἱππόλυτος μάρτυς καὶ ἐπίσκοπος ἔγραψε βιβλίον περὶ οἰκονομίας καὶ ἑρμηνείαν Δανιὴλ τοῦ μικροῦ καὶ Σουσάννας καὶ κεφάλαια κατὰ Γαίου καὶ ἀπολογίαν ὑπὲρ τῆς ἀποκαλύψεως καὶ τοῦ εὐαγγελίου Ἰωάννου τοῦ ἀποστόλου καὶ εὐαγγελιστοῦ. Translation into Greek from Syriac in Lightfoot (1890) Part I vol. II p. 350.

[181] See footnote 72.

[182] On the subject of the *Capita* and the *Apologia* he says: .. "l'hypothèse tout à fait invraisemblable qu'on possédait sous le nom d'Hippolyte deux traités pareils sur le même sujet, on doit admettre que les deux indications fournies par Ebed-Jesu se rapportent l'une et l'autre à l'ouvrage lu par Denys." (Nautin (1953) p. 146) cf. V. Loi, L'identità letteraria di Ippolito di Roma, in *St.Eph.Aug.* 13 (1977), p. 72-73, who accepts this work as that of Hippolytus, but considers the *corpus* to be the product of two different authors of the same name.

though there is no evidence for the former as it is claimed only the latter is quoted from by Barsalîbî.[183]

Nautin and Richard are, however, I believe, mistaken is in maintaining that the κεφάλαια can be an alternative title. It is arguably a legendary, literary gloss upon the dialogue between Hippolytus and Gaius in Barsalîbî. We have already drawn attention to the dependence of Barsalîbî on Eusebius, and the way in which he appears to create an alternative Hippolytus *Romanus* to the Hippolytus *Bosrae* that he read there. It is arguable that the κεφάλαια, a work mentioned by no other writer, is in fact a title produced by a kind of legendary creation of literary products that we have generally observed to have been the case.

I have already mentioned that Barsalîbî cannot have made reference to a work on the *Apocalypse* that included a defence of the Fourth Gospel since he has no citations of Gaius on the Gospel itself. Barsalîbî concluded that such a refutation must also have been made by Hippolytus probably due to Epiphanius' account of the Ἄλογοὶ which we have argued assembles material from different sources in order to construct a heresy. At all events Barsalîbî has moved too easily from (i) a written document that simply records a dialogue between the two character of Hippolytus and Gaius (*Apparuit vir, nomine Gaius, qui asserebat... Et contra hunc Gaium surrexit beatus Hippolytus*) to (ii) the claim that Hippolytus the character must have written the account of the dialogue in which his name appears (Hippolytus Romanus dixit: *Apparuit vir...etc.*).

Ebed-Jesus has therefore followed the secondary sources, including Barsalîbî's *Commentary*, and hypothesized from the citations of Hippolytus against Gaius the existence of a book written, according to Barsalîbî's hypothesis too, by Hippolytus who is also one of the characters. He has in ad-

---

183 M. Richard, Les difficultés d'une édition des oeuvres de s. Hippolyte, in *Studia Patristica* XII Part 1 (*Texte und Untersuchungen*115) (Berlin 1975), p. 68-69: "Il a constaté que les emprunts de Denys à Hippolyte étaient beaucoup plus nombreux que ne l'avait pensé Gwynn, que, d'autre part, ni ces emprunts, ni les allusions d'André de Césarée, ni les fragments de la chaîne arabe, ne permettaient de conclure à l'existence d'un commentaire d'Hippolyte sur l'Apocalypse distinct de son Apologie de l'Apocalypse et de l'Evangile de S. Jean, écrite contre Gaius. A la suite de M. P. Nautin, il explique la distinction faite par Ebed Jesus entre cette Apologie et les chapitres contre Gaius par une interprétation erronée du commentaire de Denys. On pourrait aussi penser que l'Apologie était divisée en deux livres, dont le premier était plus directement dirigé contre Gaius." But the quotations from Hippolytus cited by Andreas of Caesarea (C. A.D. 500) *In Apocalypsem* are (i) *Apoc.* 13, 1 where it is recorded simply amongst others Hippolytus equates the beast with the Antichrist (τοῖς δὲ ἁγίοις, Μεθοδίῳ καὶ Ἱππολύτῳ καὶ ἑτέροις, εἰς αὐτὸν τὸν Ἀντίχριστον τὸ παρὸν θηρίον ἐξείληπται); (ii) 13,18 which simply gives the name of the beast as Lateinos (καθ᾽ Ἱππόλυτον· Λατεῖνος); and (iii) 17, 10 which interprets the seven kings as seven ages (τοὺς δὲ ἀπὸ τῶν ἑπτὰ βασιλέων πεσόντας πέντε βασιλεῖς, ὁ μακάριος Ἱππόλυτος αἰῶνας τούτους ἐξέλαβεν· ὧν τοὺς μὲν πέντε, παρῳχηκέναι, τὸν δὲ ἕκτον, ἑστάναι· ἐν ᾧ ἑώρακεν ὁ Ἀπόστολος· τὸν δὲ ἕβδομον, τὸν μετὰ τὰ ς᾽ ἔτη, μήπω μὲν ἐληλυθέναι, ἐρχόμενον δὲ, ὀλίγον δεῖ μεῖναι). In none of these quotations is there any allusion to an ἀπολογία for apostlic authorship so that testimony to the Part II of the work allegedly cited by Barsalîbî remains elusive. At all events the attribution of (i) to Hippolytus specifically is problematic because he does not directly equate the beast with Antichrist, see 3C 8.1.

dition purely hypothesized a second treatise which defended the authorship of both *Apocalypse* and gospel, which he saw to be different from the citations. Cerinthus is not mentioned by Barsalîbî nor his opinions, yet in this putative other work Hippolytus *demonstravit aliam esse doctrinam Iohannis in Evangelio et in Apocalypsi, et aliam Cerinthi.* There is no such point-by-point doctrinal comparison in the Hippolytus/ Gaius citations.

It is important to recall that the title τὰ ὑπὲρ τοῦ κατα' Ἰωάννην εὐαγγελίου καὶ ἀποκαλύψεως occurs only on the Statue, and it would be idle to claim that Ebed-Jesu, a Syrian, could have read this title on its plinth at the cult-centre on the via Tiburtina by the thirteenth century surely already *rovinata dall' eretici.* The Statue itself could not in such a condition in Rome have been the source for the title of the work in the East. But it is also unlikely that a work of this title was available in the 14th century, when in no catalogue is it ever mentioned besides in that on the plinth of the third century Statue.

Furthermore, Ebed-Jesu's title does not correspond precisely with that on the Statue. Although the ancient convention was not to fix titles accurately and cite works variously, nevertheless there is I believe a sufficient difference of meaning between Ebed-Jesu's title and that of the Statue to give grounds for doubting their equivalence. If Ebed-Jesu had read this title on the Statue, or learned of it from the fourteenth century pilgrims who were his contemporaries, then his interpretation of the word ὑπέρ in the title by the addition of the word ἀπολογία would not have been entirely accurate. Though Lightfoot, for example, on the basis of De Rossi's original transcription of the title as beginning ὑπέρ had regarded one meaning of this preposition as corroborating Ebed-Jesu's version of the title, Guarducci has detected a [τ]ά before the ὑπὲρ that means that ἀπολογία was not part of the original title.[184] Furthermore [τ]ὰ ὑπὲρ τοῦ κατα' Ἰωάννην εὐαγγελίου... κ.τ.λ. is of wider scope than the more definite ἀπολογία and means rather "matters concerning the Gospel according to John... etc." We have seen for example that the Johannine dating of the Crucifixion on Passover Day to have been critical for the community that owned the Statue (2A 2.4).

We have already seen that the Hippolytan community, as witnessed by *C.N.*, was involved in depriving the Monarchians of their Johannine proof texts with the aid of the imposition of an emanation doctrine upon the λόγος-Christology. There were wider problems for the acceptance of the Fourth Gospel than simply its Montanist associations, shared with the *Apocalypse,* and a dispute about authorship (2A 2.5). Ebed-Jesus calls the work an ἀπολογία not because he had read it, but because he hypothesized the existence of such a work from the introduction to Barsalîbî's *Commentary,* which he saw was at variance with the cited Hippolytus/Gaius dialogue. That

---

[184] Lightfoot (1890) 1,II p. 394.

dialogue, which contained no reference to objections to the Fourth Gospel nor to Cerinthus, he called the κεφάλαια κατὰ Γαΐου. The hypothesized other document to which Barsalîbî allegedly referred he called the ἀπολογία.

There is, moreover, another reason why it would not have been the title read on the plinth of the Statue but Barsalîbî's *Commentary* itself which was responsible for an hypothesised title appearing in Ebed-Jesu's Catalogue. Ebed-Jesu begins with the *Apocalypse* itself (ἀπολογία   ὑπὲρ τῆς ἀποκαλύψεως... κ.τ.λ.) and then adds the Gospel (καὶ τοῦ εὐαγγελίου Ἰωάννου) but the Statue mentions the Gospel first ([τ]ὰ ὑπὲρ τοῦ κατὰ Ἰωάννην εὐαγγελίου καὶ ἀποκαλύψεως). If it had been the title on the Statue that had occasioned the addition of ἀπολογία, despite the τά before ὑπέρ, then the one would have preceded the other. Ebed-Jesu puts the *Apocalypse* first because he has not seen the title on the Statue but has read Barsalîbî's *Commentary* where the defence of the *Apocalypse* is given alone.

Thus Ebed-Jesu is heir to the tradition of Epiphanius that succeeded in uniting a disparate group of objectors and objections into a composite heresy called the Ἄλογοι. That tradition was later to combine Gaius' objections to Cerinthus' visions recorded in Eusebius with those of other groups who attacked both the *Apocalypse* and the Gospel more directly, and whom Dionysius of Alexandria originally addressed. Thus the ascription of the work by Ebed-Jesus to Hippolytus was not on the basis of any manuscripts in his possession, but the result of a conjectural naming of an anonymous work in the case of Barsalîbî's citations themselves, which record the names of characters in a dialogue and not necessarily the name of the author of the dialogue itself. Both titles, which we have argued to be intended to be different works, were found in no other catalogue before that of Ebed-Jesu.

Thus Nautin's problem on this count that (i) the κεφάλαια were the ἀπολογία, and were also a work of Hippolytus, and that therefore (ii) Hippolytus was associated with one and therefore probably all of works listed on the Statue is thereby dissipated. Ebed-Jesu has simply assumed that one character in the Hippolytus/Gaius dialogue recorded by Barsalîbî is the author himself, and from the introduction to his *Commentary* simply extrapolated the existence of a further work which he hypothesised as an ἀπολογία for the *Apocalypse* which included the Gospel in addition. He may have been reinforced in his belief in the existence of such a work, in addition to Barsalîbî's introduction, to Epiphanius' account of the Ἄλογοι which had already harmonized and synthesized different criticisms of the Johannine Literature into a composite, manufactured heresy.

Granted however that the ἀπολογία and κεφάλαια were different works, and granted that he hypothesized the former from Barsalîbî alone, could not the latter have survived over one thousand years and be equivalent to the title frequently cited as *De Apocalypsi* that first appears on Jerome's list? This, as we have seen, was Prigent's position when he rejected the Arabic and Syriac citations as testifying to a separate work *De Apocalypsi*, but tried instead to find a testimony to the κεφάλαια in those fragments instead (3C 4-4.5). If this could be done, then indeed the dissipated hermeneutic attested by Epiphanius could be given a definite Hippolytan attribution *via* this work. Thus my case for a legendary composition of items from that hermeneutic first into the heresy of the Ἄλογοὶ and then by Barsalîbî or his predecessors into a specifically Hippolytan composition could be undermined. Let us look at one further putative citation of the κεφάλαια as *De Apocalypsi* during the alleged one thousand years' gap in the *Chronographia* of Georgius Syncellus.

3C 7. κεφάλαια *as the* De Apocalypsi *of George Syncellus*

Jerome mentions *De Apocalypsi* along with *De Daniele* and *De Antichristo* in *De Vir. Ill.* 61. We cannot therefore equate *De Apocalypsi* with *Ant.* because of the large number of quotations from the former in the latter. When therefore Georgius Syncellus (A.D. 792) refers to a work εἰς τὴν ἐν Πάτμῳ τοῦ θεολόγου ἀποκάλυψιν in his *Chronographia*,[185] he cannot without further evidence be simply held to refer to *Ant.* simply because he does not mention this work. Cannot therefore the one thousand year gap between Barsalîbî and the origins of the *corpus Hippolytanum* be closed by postulating the identity between the *De Apocalypsi* of Jerome (4th century) with the εἰς τὴν ἐν Πάτμῳ... κ.τ.λ. of Syncellus (8th century) and the κεφάλαια of Barsalîbî (12th century) and Ebed-Jesus (14th century)? The κεφάλαια could then be held to be cited on the Statue, if not as τὰ ὑπὲρ... κ.τ.λ. for the reasons that I gave (3C 6), then under the comprehensive ᾠδαὶ εἰς πάσας τὰς γραφάς.

If the assertion of Cerinthian authorship and the attack on the Fourth Gospel was Barsalîbî's dubious inference, and the Hippolytus/Gaius citations were the product of two characters in a dialogue imposed on a text that was originally quite general, could not that text have been Hippolytus' *De Apocalypsi*? His opponents in that text would have been quite general ones like those of Epiphanius' Ἄλογοι, although we have already argued that the actual text of Barsalîbî's citations are not reflected in Epiphanius beyond a shared, general hermeneutic tradition so that Epiphanius is not himself a direct witness to the *De Apocalypsi*.

---

[185] Georgius Syncellus, *Ecloga Chronographia*, 674: Ἱππόλυτος ἱερὸς φιλόσοφος ἐπίσκοπος Πόρτου τοῦ κατὰ τὴν Ῥώμην σφόδρα διαπρεπῶς ἤνθει ἐν τῇ κατὰ Χριστὸν φιλοσοφίᾳ, πλεῖστα ψυχωφελῆ συντάττων ὑπομνήματα. εἰς τε γὰρ τὴν ἐξαήμερον καὶ εἰς τὰ μετὰ τὴν ἐξαήμερον, εἰς πολλά τε τῶν προφητῶν, μάλιστα Ἰεζεκιὴλ καὶ Δανιὴλ τῶν μεγάλων, ἔτι μὴν εἰς τὰ ᾄσματα καὶ εἰς ἄλλας παντοίας παλαιὰς καὶ νέας γραφάς, ἐν οἷς καὶ εἰς τὴν ἐν Πάτμῳ τοῦ θεολόγου ἀποκάλυψιν, πρὸς Μαρκίωνα καὶ τὰς λοιπὰς αἱρέσεις, καὶ τὸν ἑξκαιδεκαετηρικὸν τοῦ πάσχα κανόνα ἐξέθετο περιγράψας εἰς τὸ α΄ ἔτος Ἀλεξάνδρου τοῦ Μαμμαίας τούτου...

But in order to discover the true character of the work to which Syncellus made reference we need to go to Georgius Hamartolus (c. A.D. 810) where he cites a treatise of ὁ θεῖος ᾿Ιππόλυτος ῾Ρώμης περὶ τοῦ κηρύγματος καὶ τῆς τελείωσις τῶν ἀποστόλων. Syncellus' title εἰς τὴν ἐν Πάτμῳ τοῦ θεολόγου ἀποκάλυψιν is reflected in the phrase: ᾿Ιωάννης... ἐξωρίσθη ἐν Πάτμῳ in Hamartolus.[186] But it is clear from Hamartolus' passage that the reference is to pseudo Hippolytus, *De Duodecim Apostolis*.[187] It may therefore be that Syncellus derived the existence of *De Apocalypsi* from Jerome's reference combined with the description of John in the latter work. Nicephorus Callistus may owe the περὶ ἀποκαλύψεως of his own list to such a source.[188] And at this point our discussion makes contact with the undisputed fact of the popularity of Hippolytus' name in connection with the pseudepigrapha of the Eastern Church from at least the seventh century onwards.

Were we to accept the genuineness of the Hippolytus/Gaius dialogue (Ebed-Jesu's κεφάλαια) in Barsalîbî's *Commentary*, we would have also to accept that this work, neither identical with the [τ]ὰ ὑπὲρ τοῦ κατὰ ᾿Ιωάννην εὐαγγελίου καὶ ἀποκαλύψεως of the Statue nor with the *De Apocalypsi* of Syncellus and later writers, had survived unmentioned until the twelfth century. We gave grounds against the view that Epiphanius had in fact cited from that work. In the light of these grounds, we are justified in allowing the earlier analysis of the text of Eusebius to stand, in the light of which Gaius directly attributed neither the *Apocalypse* nor the Fourth Gospel to Cerinthus. We have with justification refused to be impeded by the evidence of a late literary myth whose development we have traced from Epiphanius onwards, which was so contrary to the whole texture of the analysis of the earlier evidence and that would require the distortion of such evidence.

Let us now ask finally whether the pseudepigraphic dialogue between Hippolytus and Gaius that Barsalîbî used was before him in written form already created by his predecessors, or whether Barsalîbî himself had simply created a pseudonymous dialogue. His introduction would suggest that he already had before him the names of 'Hippolytus' and 'Gaius' in dialogue in the text before him. In consequence we can now develop in finer detail our

---

186 Georgius Hamartolus, *Chronicon* 3, 134: οὐ μὴν δὲ ἀλλὰ καὶ ὁ θεῖος ᾿Ιππόλυτος ῾Ρώμης περὶ τοῦ κηρύγματος καὶ τῆς τελείωσεως τῶν ἀποστόλων διεξιὼν ἔφη· ᾿Ιωάννης [δὲ] ὁ ἀδελφὸς ᾿Ιακώβου κηρύσσων ἐν τῇ ᾿Ασίᾳ τὸν λόγον τοῦ εὐαγγελίου ἐξωρίσθη ἐν Πάτμῳ τῇ νήσῳ ὑπὸ Δομετιανοῦ βασιλέως ῾Ρώμης, κἀκεῖθεν πάλιν εἰς ῎Εφεσον ἐκ τῆς ἐξορίας ἀνακληθεὶς ὑπὸ Νερβᾶ καὶ τὸ κατ᾿ αὐτὸν εὐαγγέλιον συγγραψάμενος, ἔνθα καὶ τὴν ἀποκάλυψιν θεασάμενος ἐτελεύτησε, οὗ τὸ λείψανον ζητηθὲν οὐχ εὑρέθη. (Lightfoot (1890) 1, II p. 347; Migne *P.G.* CX p. 521).
187 Hippolytus, *De Duodecim Apostolis*: ᾿Ιωάννης δὲ ἐν ᾿Ασίᾳ ὑπὸ Δομετιανοῦ τοῦ βασιλέως ἐξορισθεὶς ἐν Πάτμῳ τῇ νήσῳ, ἐν ᾗ καὶ τὸ Εὐαγγέλιον συνεγράψατο καὶ τὴν ἀποκάλυψιν ἐθεάσατο, ἐπὶ Τραϊανοῦ ἐκοιμήθη ἐν ᾿Εφέσῳ· οὗ τὸ λείψανον ζητηθὲν οὐχ εὑρέθη. (*P.G.* X, 951-954; Achelis (1987)
188 Nicephorus Callistus, *H.E.* 4,31 mentions περὶ ἀποκαλύψεως with εἰς τὸν Δανιήλ and περὶ τῆς παρουσίας τοῦ ἀντιχρίστου but no κεφάλαια.

case against the authenticity of that dialogue, whose authorship Barsalîbî confused with one of its characters.

3C 8. *Barsalîbî and Pseudo-Hippolytan constructions*

That Hippolytus was the author of the dialogue in which he was a character we have seen to have been at least questionable (3C 3). Barsalîbî undoubtedly wished to make Hippolytus the author, which is why he introduces his quotation with *Hippolytus Romanus dixit*, even though he makes Hippolytus thereby refer to himself quite unnaturally when he goes on to say *contra hunc Caium surrexit beatus Hippolytus*. Caesar as author of the *Bellum Gallicum* may have referred to himself in the third person, but even he had not the arrogance to claim sainthood for himself as we must suppose *beatus* Hippolytus to have done were he the author as well as the leading character.

Barsalîbî, as we have seen, did not associate Hippolytus of [sic] *Bosrae* (Bostra), whom he mentions in the context of the works on the Johannine *corpus* cited from him and others (Irenaeus, Dionysius of Alexandria etc.) by Eusebius and others. By contrast he quotes Hippolytus *Romanus* apparently quoting himself in saintly proportions. Undoubtedly the Gaius of his first quotation, *qui asserebat Evangelium non esse Iohannis, nec Apocalypsim, sed Cerinthi haeretici ea esse*, was the Gaius of Eusebius who, though not accused of attributing the *Apocalypse* itself to Cerinthus, was associated in the literary tradition by Barsalîbî with those who did, in particular the ῎Αλογοι to whom as a group Epiphanius contrives to assign such a composite opinion. But Barsalîbî emerges at the end of the production of such a literary legend in which the diversity of attacks on the Johannine Literature, some of which only contained the association with Cerinthus are first reduced by Epiphanius to the views of a particular group, the Αλογοι, for whom he constructs a heresy, and then the amorphous group is finally by Barsalîbî given a leader, namely Gaius who in Eusebius attacked Cerinthus' personal visions, and not the *Apocalypse* itself as did the nameless opponents of Dionysius of Alexandria.

We have furthermore argued, however, following Gwynn, that Barsalîbî's literary legend in his preface does not correspond with the citations from Gaius in the dialogue since neither Cerinthus nor the Fourth Gospel are mentioned there. I therefore propose to treat the Hippolytus/Gaius citations that follow in the text quite differently from the literary legend of the preface. I would in the case of these citations wish to follow Lightfoot's modification of his original thesis to suggest that 'Gaius' could have been a fictitious name in a dialogue for a speaker that could have represented the views of the historic Gaius, or could simply have been a title for 'everyman' in view of its common use as a Roman *praenomen*, and its counterpart here to the fictitious Hippolytus *Romanus* as opposed to the historical Hippolytus *Bosrae*.[189]

3C 8.1. *Barsalîbî's 'Gaius' as a reference to 'everyman'*

The understanding of 'Gaius' as 'everyman' is consistent with the objections to the specific passages of the *Apocalypse* as quoted, which are naive often in the extreme. Indeed it was this feature of them that lead Gwynn to conclude that:

> The passages as they stand in Barsalîbî's *Commentary* are, probably, not actual excerpts from the '*Heads*'; they have the air rather of brief summaries of the arguments on either side: those of Gaius (whom it will be observed Barsalîbî brands as a 'heretic') being stated in the barest possible form, whilst those of Hippolytus are given in more detail, yet highly compressed.[190]

Thus even Gwynn, who accepted the authenticity of all the citations except the one that occurs in Barsalîbî's preface, nevertheless did not believe that those citations were direct quotations but rather summaries "stated in the barest possible form" or otherwise "highly compressed."

In this belief, Gwynn was undoubtedly strengthened by Ebed-Jesus's title for this summary work, the κεφάλαια κατὰ Γαίου. But we have argued that this title was an inference from Barsalîbî's *Commentary* itself, and not an independent attestation for the existence of such a document. Furthermore, our analysis of the Hippolytus/Gaius citations has revealed that what Gwynn alleged to be a summary or compression was in fact comparable with a general tradition of hermeneutic on the *Apocalypse*, which Epiphanius puts into the mouths of his amorphous Ἄλογοι, even though substantive points of that hermeneutic do not sufficiently coincide between Barsalîbî and Epiphanius as to arouse confidence that they come from a single author whom only Barsalîbî names as 'Gaius.'

It is not therefore a summary by Barsalîbî or someone else with which we are dealing here but a general hermeneutic tradition on the *Apocalypse*. It is with that general hermeneutic tradition, therefore, that we should compare

---

[189] Lightfoot (1890) Part 1 Vol. II, p. 377-388. Lightfoot, originally embarrassed by the phenomenon mentioned above of works whose author was in some cases unknown, and in others ascribed to Gaius (or even Josephus), and wishing to include such works in the Hippolytan *corpus*, proposed that Hippolytus' *praenomen* had in fact been "Gaius" and the separation of authorship had arisen as it were through the separation of the two names. See also J.B. Lightfoot, Gaius or Hippolytus? in *Journal of Philology*, 1 (1868), p. 98-112. Schwartz emphasised unfairly, I believe, this embarrassment in view of the problems that I have shown above, in Schwartz (1904) p. 43-44: "Es zwar seiner Zeit Lightfoot nicht zu verärgern wenn er auch den Dialog Hippolyt zuschrieb und Gaius für einen fingirten Namen erklärte: diese einfache Lösung des Räthsels ist durch die Bruchstücke der Κεφάλαια κατὰ Γαίου unmöglich gemacht. Aber dass der Gaius des Dialogs und der von Hippolyt bekämpfte 'Aloger' Gaius bald identisch, bald verschieden zu sein scheinen, hängt in irgend einer, nicht mehr völlig aufzuklärenden Weise mit der Uebertragung eines Teils der hippolyteischen Schriften auf Gaius zusammen."

[190] Gwynn (1888) p. 404-405.

the citations placed in the mouth of 'Hippolytus' or 'Gaius' in Barsalîbî's dialogue. Barsalîbî is arguably dramatizing that tradition in terms of a dialogue between his characters, 'Hippolytus' on the one hand, and 'Gaius' or 'everyman' on the other. Even if the character of Gaius as 'everyman' takes on in Barsalîbî's mind a modicum of historical colouring for that dramatic presentation, that colouring is hardly very accurate. It is as large a misreading of Eusebius (*H.E.* II, 25,6-7; VI, 19, 3) as making the historical Gaius αἱρετικός as it is to accuse him of equating Cerinthus' vision (*H.E.* III, 28,1-2) with the *Apocalypse* itself, for reasons that we have seen. Such a pseudepigraphic use of the name of Hippolytus in the East is quite well documented, as we shall now see.

3C 8.2. *Hippolytan Eastern pseudepigrapha*

That Hippolytus was used as a character in such a dialogue in the East by Barsalîbî should not strike us as surprising. Hippolytus' name was used there to create a number of pseudonymous works, amongst which were κατὰ Βήρωνος καὶ Ἥλικος and περὶ τῆς συντελείας τοῦ κόσμου and the *In Sancta Theophania*.[191] The former represents a rough parallel with Barsalîbî's dialogue since it consists of a number of extracts allegedly from Hippolytus directed against a heresy. Κατὰ Βήρωνος is found as part of a *florilegium* entitled *Doctrina Patrum*, whose original dates from *c.* A.D. 650, and is preserved in a Latin translation of Anastasius Bibliothecarius.

Simonetti has argued that the original collection, anti-Monothelite in character, was made by Theodosius of Gangra. This collection contained a letter of Anastasius Apocrisarius, with which he enclosed "eight testimonies of St. Hippolytus, bishop of Portus of Rome and martyr of God Christ," and which forms a separate section of the collection. These eight testimonies are therefore the Κατὰ Βήρωνος, but which Simonetti has convincingly demonstrated that the Apocrisarius composed himself.[192] Thus a series of extracts composed with a polemical purpose were pseudepigraphically assigned to Hippolytus.

A second example of such Hippolytan pseudepigrapha is to be found in the edition of the Arabic Pentateuch with commentaries by the Fathers found in *ms.* Hutling 84 and *ms. Bodleian NE* c.33 and printed in Fabricus' edition of Hippolytus' works.[193] Here citations are given introduced by *dixit*

---

[191] *PG.* X col. 829-852 and 903-952 and Achelis (1897) p. 255-263. For the identification of the author of the latter as Leontius of Constantinople (6th cent.) see S.J. Voicu, Pseudoippolito in Sancta Theophania e Leonzio di Constantinopoli, in *StEphAug* 30 (1989), p. 137-146.

[192] M. Simonetti, Un falso Ippolito nella polemica monotelita, in *Vetera Christianorum* 24, (1987), p. 113-146, esp. p. 114-121.

[193] J.A.S. Fabricius, *Hippolyti Opera non antea collecta,* (Hamburg: Christian Liebezeit 1716). ——, *Hippolyti, Episcopi et Martyris, quae superant opera. et fragmenta,* (Hamburg: Christian Liebezeit 1716); Migne *P.G.* X, 701-712; Achelis (1897) p. 86-119. See also H. Coxe, *Catalogi codicum manuscriptorum bibliothecae Bodleianae, pars prima,* (Oxford: U. P. 1853) col. 369-372.

Hippolytus expositor Targumista (*Sect.* II-III), or *dixit Hippolytus expositor Syrus Targum* (*Sect.* IV) or *dixit Hippolytus, expositor Targum et Dominus meus Jacobus Rohaviensis* (*Sect.* V). As Lumper originally pointed out, it is strange that Hippolytus is not called *episcopus* or *martyr* when Athanasius is introduced as *patriarcha Alexandrinus*, Basil is *episcopus Caesareae*, or Epiphanius as *episcopus Cypri* etc.[194] His explanation was that this was the means by which the writer sought, albeit by some very crude interpretations, to honour the true Hippolytus whose genuine works made him renowned as a Biblical commentator.[195] At all events we have a parallel in *dixit Hippolytus expositor Syrus* with *dixit Hippolytus Romanus* by contrast with *Hippolytus Bosrae* in Barsalîbî's preface.

It could nevertheless be argued that each of these pseudonymous works have good internal grounds for denying Hippolytan authorship which go beyond mere external suspicion. Let us now therefore look at certain critical features of the internal content of the Hippolytus/Gaius dialogue with commentaries extant under the name of Hippolytus such as *Dan.* or *Ant.*

3C 9. *The Hippolytus/Gaius dialogue: The internal evidence*

We will find that there are two critical differences, namely (i) a lack of substantive exegetical agreement on the interpretation of the prophecy of the Antichrist and (ii) a Christological concern in such commentaries not to be found in the Barsalîbî citations. The alleged Hippolytus-citations of Barsalîbî, though wearing the general literary form of a common hermeneutic, lack the specific features of *Dan.* or *Ant.* This is the first internal feature that suggests that Barsalîbî has no individual author for what he places into the mouth of the Hippolytus-figure in his dialogue.

3C 9.1. Apoc. *11,2 and* Ant. *28 and 47*

The citation of *Apoc.* 11,2 (3C 5.8) claimed that Hippolytus connected the *pollutio desolationis* (*Mt.* 24,15) in *Dan.* with the Antichrist (*de fine et Antichristo*), whereas Barsalîbî's own interpretation is that it is the "little horn" of *Dan.* 7, 8; 20-21 that is to be identified with Antichrist. As such Barsalîbî is following the author of *Ant.* 28 and 47 and expressing his views as his own.[196] It may be plausibly suggested, therefore, that Barsalîbî regards himself as following *Hippolytus Bosrae*, whose works the catalogues of Eusebius and Jerome were believed by him to record, rather than the

---

[194] G. Lumper, De Vita et Scriptis Sancti Hippolyti, in *P.G.* X, 345-346.

[195] Ibid. 345, para III: "Accedit Hippolyti huius Targumistae interpretationes sapere plerumque rabbinorum ineptias, indignas plane tanto Patre, quantus fuisse perhibetur in sacris litteris potissimum explanandis verus Hippolytus."

[196] Hippolytus *Ant.* 28: ... τὰ δέκα κέρατα, τὰ μέλλοντα ἔσεσθαι· κέρας ἕτερον μικρὸν ἀναφυόμενον, ὁ ἐν αὐτοῖς Ἀντιχρίστος... Idem. 47: τὸ θηρίον τὸ ἀναβαῖνον ἐκ τῆς ἀβύσσου ποιήσει μετ᾽ αὐτῶν πόλεμον, καὶ νικήσει αὐτοὺς, καὶ ἀποκτενεῖ αὐτοὺς διὰ τὸ μὴ θέλειν αὐτοὺς δόξαν δοῦναι τῷ Ἀντιχρίστῳ. τουτέστι, τὸ ἀναφυὲν μικρὸν κέρας.

Hippolytus Romanus that is the figure in his dialogue, which would indicate that they were separate figures in his eyes. As we have already noted, Andreas of Caesarea at one point (on *Apoc.* 13,1) attributes the view to Hippolytus that the beast is to be equated with Antichrist, but he may have confused Hippolytus with the other writers that he mentions with him as being collectively of this opinion (τοῖς δὲ ἁγίοις, Μεθοδίῳ καὶ ᾽Ιππολύτῳ καὶ ἑτέροις).[197]

3C 9.2. *Hippolytan* corpus: *Christology and eschatology*

Prescinding from our discussion in Chapter 4 on the internal arguments for the integrity or otherwise of the Hippolytan *corpus*, we may agree with Simonetti that whether of identical authorship or not, a distinctive feature of both the *Ant.* and the *Dan.* is the use of apocalyptic exegesis to make Christological points.[198]

As Simonetti points out, the λόγος-Christology of *C.N.* 15 was fundamentally different from that of Justin and Irenaeus. In the case of the latter two authors, the λόγος was God's son before the incarnation in a kind of Philonic, analogical sense. But Hippolytus insists to the contrary that the λόγος cannot be God's Son apart from the incarnation.[199] Thus he was able to distinguish between the λόγος as second God of the Monarchian critique, and the λόγος as merely a phased projection of the Father as they held. The λόγος becomes God's Son therefore prospectively, in view of the incarnation, but not perfectly.

It was certain Old Testament, exegetical *cruces* that led Hippolytus to this conclusion, combined with the Christology of the λόγος ἄσαρκος on which that exegesis was premised. The preface to the *Ant.* speaks of the μακάριοι προφῆται... προορῶντες διὰ πίστεως τὰ τοῦ λόγου μυστήρια. The description which follows regards the λόγος as a personal force actively revealing in mystery the things to come. The λόγος is the plectrum which moves them like strings to a lyre to announce the future.[200]

Although the λόγος can be called "of old" (πάλαι) the "servant of God" (ὁ τοῦ θεοῦ παῖς), he does not, before the incarnation, join us together as the "perfect man" (εἰς ἕνα τέλειον ἄνθρωπον) that we desire to be.[201] But the

---

[197] See footnote 144 .

[198] M. Simonetti, Prospettive Escatologiche della Cristologia di Ippolito, in *La Cristologia nei Padri della Chiesa* (Accademia Cardinale Bessaronis: Rome 1979), p. 85-101.

[199] Simonetti (1979) p. 87: "... l'interesse d'Ippolito è rivolto in modo tutto particolare all' economia dell'incarnazione e della redenzione: a differenza di Giustino e d'Ireneo, che avevano definito come Figlio di Dio il Logos, in quanto tale, anche prima dell'incarnazione, in *Noet.* 15 Ippolito chiarisce che il Logos è definito Figlio da *Rom.* 8, 3-4 in vista della futura incarnazione, in quanto privo di carne e in se stesso il Logos non era figlio perfetto di Dio e si è manifestato tale soltanto quando ha rivestito la carne umana."

[200] *Ant.* 2: ... ἔχοντες ἐν ἑαυτοῖς ἀεὶ τὸν λόγον ὡς πλῆκτρον, δι᾽ οὗ κινούμενοι ἀπήγγελλον ταῦτα...

[201] Ibid. 3: ὅπως ἃ πάλαι τοῖς μακαρίοις προφήταις ἀπεκάλυψεν ὁ τοῦ θεοῦ λόγος, νῦν αὐτὸς πάλιν ὁ τοῦ θεοῦ παῖς, ὁ πάλαι μὲν λόγος ὤν, νυνὶ δὲ καὶ ἄνθρωπος δι᾽ ἡμᾶς ἐν κόσμῳ φανερωθείς... εἰς γὰρ ὁ τοῦ θεοῦ παῖς, δι᾽ οὗ καὶ ἡμεῖς τυχόντες τὴν διὰ τοῦ

selfsame λόγος–παῖς that moves as with a plectrum the vocal cords of the prophets, weaves as the λόγος–ἄσαρκος the robe of his flesh in the Virgin's womb so as to "blend the corruptible with incorruption (μίξας τῷ ἀφθάρτῳ τὸ φθαρτὸν)... and save our lost humanity (σώσῃ τὸν ἀπολλύμενον ἄνθρωπον)."[202] There is thus a clear relation in the author's mind between the τὰ τοῦ μυστήρια of Daniel (as re-expressed also in the Johannine *Apocalypse*) regarding the future, and the μυστήρια οἰκονομίας of the pre-existent λόγος–παῖς–ἄσαρκος and his prospective incarnation. Indeed, as Simonetti perceptively pointed out, it is only within such a Christological perspective that the anti-Christology becomes possible in terms of which the full-blown description of a personal future Antichrist can be delineated.[203]

Similarly the vision in *Dan.* 10,2-21 of the angel Gabriel is interpreted as referring to an ἀποκάλυψιν μυστηρίου concerning the λόγος and τὸ μέλλον ἀποβῆναι δι' αὐτοῦ. The appearance beside the Tigris, παρὰ τὸν ποταμὸν τὸν μέγαν is interpreted as prefiguring the appearance beside the Jordan, for the λόγος–παῖς must appear "where he was destined to forgive sins."[204] The Opaz with which he is girded represents, when the word is translated into Greek, pure gold. This in turn represents the perfect body which the λόγος joined to himself. The Tharsis of which Gabriel's body was composed indicated the difficulty of understanding mystically the prophet's word about the future incarnation.[205] Thus for the *Dan.* as the *Ant.* the interpretation of the apocalyptic mystery was inseparable from the interpretation of the Christological mystery of the incarnation.

The absence of any such Christological dimension to the mystery of apocalyptic interpretation in the Hippolytus/Gaius dialogue is extremely suspicious, and constitutes as significant a discrepancy as the interpretation of the Antichrist passages discussed in 3C 8.2. We have seen that, following Simonetti, this figure for the genuine Hippolytus of *Ant.* was produced by a

ἁγίου πνεύματος ἀναγέννησιν, εἰς ἕνα τέλειον καὶ ἐπουράνιον ἄνθρωπον οἱ πάντες καταντῆσαι ἐπιθυμοῦμεν.

[202] Ibid. 4: ἐπειδὴ γὰρ ὁ λόγος τοῦ θεοῦ ἄσαρκος ὢν ἐνεδύσατο τὴν ἁγίαν σάρκα ἐκ τῆς ἁγίας παρθένου, ὡς νυμφίος ἱμάτιον ἐξυφήνας ἑαυτῷ ἐν τῷ σταυρικῷ πάθει, ὅπως συνκεράσας τὸ θνητὸν ἡμῶν σῶμα τῇ ἑαυτοῦ δυνάμει, καὶ μίξας τὸ φθαρτὸν τῷ ἀφθάρτῳ καὶ τὸ ἀσθενὲς τῷ ἰσχυρῷ, σώσῃ τὸν ἀπολλύμενον ἄνθρωπον

[203] Especially *Ant.* 6 cf. Simonetti (1978) p. 99: "Non è perciò esagerato affermare che l'Anticristo è stato concepito da Ippolito come la proiezione negativa ma fedelissima di Cristo; e proprio la complementarietà dei due personaggi caratterizza in senso fondamentalmente cristologico anche questo punto dell'escatologia del nostro autore."

[204] *Dan.* IV, 36,3: ... εὐχόμενος τῷ θεῷ τῷ ζῶντι, ἀπαιτῶν παρ' αὐτοῦ ἀποκάλυψιν μυστηρίων. καὶ δὴ εἰσακούσας ὁ πατὴρ ἀπέστειλεν λόγον ἴδιον, ἐνδεικνύμενος τὸ μέλλον ἀποβῆναι δι' αὐτοῦ· καὶ δὴ ἐγένετο παρὰ τὸν ποταμὸν τὸν μέγαν· ἔδει γὰρ ἐκεῖ τὸν παῖδα δείκνυσθαι, ὅπου καὶ ἁμαρτίας ἀφίεναι ἔμελλεν.

[205] Ibid. IV, 37, 1-3: τὸ δὲ ὠφὰζ καθαρὸν σημαίνει, ἐκ τῆς 'εβραΐδος εἰς τὴν 'ελληνίδα μετατιθέμενον· καθαράν οὖν περιεζωσμένος περὶ τὴν ὀσφὺν ζώνην· πάντας γὰρ ἡμᾶς ἤμελλεν ὁ λόγος, περὶ τὸ ἑαυτοῦ σῶμα τῇ ἰδίᾳ ἀγάπῃ. ὡς ζώνην σφίγξας, βαστάζειν· τὸ γὰρ σῶμα τέλειον αὐτοῦ ἦν... Θαρσεῖς δὲ ἑρμηνεύεται Αἰθίοπες· τὸ γὰρ δυσεπίγνωστον αὐτοῦ ἤδη ὁ προφήτης προκατήγγειλεν, ὡς μελλήσει ὁ λόγος ἔνσαρκος ἐν κόσμῳ φανεὶς δύσγνωστος ἔσεσθαι πολλοῖς.

kind of anti-Christological exegesis that mirrored his Christological exegesis of apocalyptic material. Apocalyptic was a personal confrontation with the λόγος–ἄσαρκικος, not as completely (τέλειος) personal, but sufficiently personal as to be called παῖς. This λόγος Christology would have been even more serviceable as linking the defence of the Johannine authorship of the *Apocalypse* with the Fourth Gospel, if the statement in Barsalîbî's preface was any more than the literary legend that we have argued it to have been.

We have thus shown both that (i) Barsalîbî distinguished between *Hippolytus Bosrae*, identified by a direct reference to Eusebius, from the *Hippolytus Romanus* of the dialogue (3C 7), (ii) 'Hippolytus' was a much-used pseudonym in the East for various works (3C 7.2), and (iii) an internal comparison between the *Dan.* and *Ant.* with the Hippolytus/Gaius dialogue show essential divergences (3C 8; 8.1 and 8.2). Moreover, 'Gaius' in the tradition had become a reference to 'everyman,' even though Barsalîbî had sought to give this some historical colouring from his somewhat confused reading of Eusebius/Rufinus (3C 7.1). He was however clear that the particular 'Hippolytus' to whom he referred on this occasion, the Hippolytus *Romanus,* was different from the author mentioned by Eusebius/Rufinus *H.E.* VI, 16 as Hippolytus *Bosrae.* Thus the connection between what Ebed-Jesus called the κεφάλαια and the Hippolytan *corpus* is very tenuous indeed. The description 'pseudonymous' may not here even be appropriate since the contributor to the dialogue was not regarded by Barsalîbî as the same author as the Hippolytan *corpus* which he believed to have been written by a different, eastern Hippolytus.

That Barsalîbî should have used *Hippolytus Romanus* as the general cipher for an orthodox position against the stereotyped Γάϊος αἵρετικος should not strike us as surprising, in view of both (i) the use of his name as part of a distant and pristine apostolic age by certain Fathers, both Eastern and Western, and (ii) by the occurrence of his name alongside that of Clement in some manuscripts of the apostolic Church Order literature, which mirrors the use of Clement's name as such a cipher in the *Homilies* and *Recognitions.* (ii) will be better dealt with as part of our discussion of the rediscovery and authenticity of the ἀποστολικὴ παράδοσις in 3 D, and its relevance to the discussion at that point. In conclusion to our account of *Hippolytus Romanus* in Barsalîbî's *Commentary*, we will deal with (i) here.

3C 10. *'Hippolytus' as a cipher for the apostolic age*

There was a clearly documented attempt to locate Hippolytus in the apostolic age, and to make him a sign of apostolic witness, regardless of true historical chronology. It is arguably to that tradition that Barsalîbî's Hippolytus/Gaius dialogue belongs. Let us now list these testimonies:

1. Theodoret (c. A.D. 446) *Ep.* 145 speaks of: οἱ τούτων πρεσβύτεροι Ἰγνάτιος καὶ Πολύκαρπος καὶ Εἰρηναῖος καὶ Ἰουστῖνος καὶ Ἱππόλυτος, who are both "bishops (ἀρχιερέων)" and "martyrs (μαρτύρων)."

2. Palladius (c. A.D. 421) *Hist. Lausiac.*, 148 introduces us to the "story (διήγημα τοιοῦτον) as found in another book (ἐν ἄλλῳ βιβλιδαρίῳ) entiitled (ἐπιγεγραμμένῳ) "Of Hippolytus the close companion of the apostles (Ἱππολύτου τοῦ γνωρίμου τῶν ἀποστόλων)."

3. Andreas of Caesarea (c. A.D. 500), *In Apoc.* 13,1 associates him with Papias of the early second century with whom he is grouped alongside Irenaeus and Methodius as οἱ ἐκκλησιαστικοὶ πατέρες.

4. Cyrillus of Scythopolis (c. A.D. 555), in *Vita S. Euthymii*, p. 82 quotes chronographic information also given ὑπὸ τῶν ἁγίων πατέρων Ἱππολύτου τοῦ παλαιοῦ καὶ γνωρίμου τῶν ἀποστόλων.

5. Leontius of Byzantium (c. A.D. 620), in *De Sectis* 3,1, mentions him in company with Clement as "bishops of Rome (Κλήμης καὶ Ἱππόλυτος ἐπίσκοποι Ῥώμης)," in a list which also contains the names of Ignatius, Irenaeus, and Justin.

6. Pseudo-Chrysostom, *De Pseudo-prophetis*, (ποῦ Ἰγνάτιος τὸ τοῦ θεοῦ οἰκητήριον; που ὁ Διονύσιος τὸ πετεινὸν τοῦ οὐρανοῦ; ποῦ Ἱππόλυτος ὁ γλύκυτατος καὶ εὐνούστατος) again brackets Hippolytus with both Ignatius and Pseudo-Dionysius (the Areopagite) and the apostolic age.

How are we to understand this process of literary development? Clearly Hippolytus has been removed from any historical context in the early third century and made "an acquaintance (γνωρίμου)" of the apostles. Indeed, we shall later argue that there is here a parallel instance of legend construction by these Eastern writers to that of Damasus in what we was his creation of the legend of the Novatian presbyter (6 A). Regardless of the documentary evidence, Damasus chose to set his epigram in the "never never" time of when *Tempore quo gladius secuit pia viscera matris ecclesiae.* Likewise too Palladius (2) and Cyrillus (4) set Hippolytus in the age the apostles by making him their companion (γνωρίμος). Hippolytus according to Theodoret, is an Irenaean elder–one of the πρεσβύτεροι—like Ignatius and Polycarp (1), and, according to Andreas to be mentioned in the same breath as Papias (3). He is one of "the holy fathers (ἁγίων πατέρων)," or "one of the ecclesiastical fathers (οἱ ἐκκλησιαστικοὶ πατέρες)" (3 and 4). In Pseudo-Chrysostom Hippolytus ranks with pseudo-Dionysius as well as Ignatius (6).

Barsalîbî has thus selected the *Hippolytus Romanus* as distinct from the historical *Hippolytus Bosrae* from the apostolic never-never land of figures once historical but who now inhabit that distant and ideal time. As such the figure has been disassociated from any historical connections that it might once have had, and become the orthodox 'everyman' as a counterpart to Gaius, the heterodox 'everyman', even though the historical orthodoxy and heterodoxy of both was by no means clear in their original historical location.

We can therefore conclude Part 3C of this chapter.

3C 11. *In conclusion: The Statue and the* κεφάλαια

If the authenticity of the Hippolytus/Gaius dialogue in Barsalîbî can be denied, then the elimination of Gaius as the author of all the works on the
Statue, and *El* with which those works are linked, can also be denied (Part
3B). Our discussion however has not offered any prospect of that line of inquiry being at all fruitful regarding the identity of the author of certain
anonymous works otherwise linked with Hippolytus by one group of recent
scholars (Part 3 A). Though as a positive means of identification that dialogue, called by Ebed-Jesus the κεφάλαια, can be denied as equivalent to the
[τ]ὰ ὑπὲρ τοῦ κατα᾽ Ἰωάννην κ.τ.λ..., nevertheless both external and internal
considerations preclude it from being anything else than a general exegetical
tradition dressed up pseudepigraphically under the cipher-names of
'Hippolytus' and 'Gaius'.

   The connection with the anonymous part of the *corpus* is as tenuous as
with that clearly assigned to Hippolytus. At all events, my discussion in the
first two chapters has revealed my own position to be indifferent as regards
the debate between one or two authors in so far as it centres on the Statue.
My interpretation of the significance of the Statue is that it is a community
artefact with a corporate significance. As such, all the inscribed works do not
have to be by the same author. If anyone wishes therefore still to assert
against my argument in Part 3C that the κεφάλαια was mentioned on the
Statue and was composed by Hippolytus, on my quite separate argument in
Chapter 2 it would not follow that necessarily all works were by Hippolytus
simply because one of them was.

   There is however one other work whose rediscovery could be held to provide a definite Hippolytan link with the Statue, and that is the Egyptian
Church Order, identified by Connolly and Schwartz as the ἀποστολικὴ παράδοσις, in the argument for which the Statue clearly prefigured. As we fore-
shadowed in the closing paragraph of 3C 8, the general use of 'Hippolytus'
as a cipher for orthodoxy is also bound up with the question of the
rediscovery and authenticity of the ἀποστολικὴ παράδοσις, as it is with
Damasus' legend of the Novatian presbyter, with which we shall be dealing
more fully in Chapter 6. To the former of these two questions we must now
turn.

PART D. REDISCOVERY OF THE ἀποστολικὴ παράδοσις

The text published today under the title *Apostolic Tradition* is one of a series
of similar documents the order of whose priority was established to the
general satisfaction of contemporary scholars by Schwartz and Connolly in

1910 and 1916 respectively.[206] The first and original document in the chain of dependence was shown to be the *Egyptian Church Order,* preserved in the *Synodicon* of the Church of Alexandria, composed originally in Greek but which survives in four translations, Sahidic, Bohairic, Arabic, and Ethiopic, of which the Verona palimpsest preserves fragments in Latin.[207]

It is important to note, however, that they are not independent witnesses to a common text. The Sahidic is very much the stock from which the text of the Arabic version was translated, which in turn was the version used by the Bohairic translator.[208] The Arabic and the Verona Latin are therefore the better witnesses for restoring the true readings of the text of the *Synodicon* in its four versions, together with the following documents which, on the thesis of Schwartz and Connolly, derive from it:

(i) *Apostolic Constitutions* VIII (Greek),
(ii) (Hippolytus) *Epitome* of the *Apostolic Constitutions* (Greek),
(iii) *Testamentum Domini* (Syriac), and
(iv) *Canones* of St. Hippolytus (Arabic).

The *Egyptian Church Order* was therefore claimed as the parent document of a series, two items of which are connected directly with Hippolytus' name. Both the *Canones* and the *Epitome* carried the name of Hippolytus.[209] The Arabic version of the *Canones* is headed: "These are the canons of the Church, the commandments which Hippolytus wrote," and the Ethiopic, after "Canons of the apostles which number CXXVII," add "Canons of Hippolytus, doctor, pope of Rome, XXXVIII canons." In consequence, the title *Canones Hippolyti* as such was given in 1870 in Haneburg's edition.[210]

---

[206] A. Vööbus, The Synodicon in the West Syrian Tradition, in *CSCO*, 367 (1975), Scriptores Syri Tom. 161. See also R.H. Connolly, New Attributions to Hippolytus, in *JThS* 46 1945, p. 192-200; ——, The so-called Egyptian Church Order and derived documents, in *Texts and Studies* 8,4, (Cambridge: U.P. 1916); E. Schwartz, Über die pseudapostolischen Kirchenordnungen, in *Schriften wissensch. Gesellschaft im Strassburg*, 6, (Strasbourg: 1910); Bunsen (1852) II, p. 413 appealed to the title of *Ap. Con.* VIII in Oxford (Barrocci, and Vienna) *mss.* διδασκαλία [πάντων] τῶν ἁγίων ᾽Αποστόλων περὶ Χαρισμάτων. See Oxford Bodleian Lib. *ms. Codex Barrocciani* 26, 14 (fol. 146 b.) and *Vindoboniensis hist. graec.* 7 1ʳ-4ᵛ. But he did not, as did Connolly and Schwartz, associate the work as a result with the *Egyptian Church Order* but with the *Ordinances* or *Canons of Hippolytus*, which he considered more ancient because more direct and succinct (p. 247-248, 271-359). These reflections were to provide the basis for Bunsen's quite fanciful and composite reconstruction of what he described as "The Church- and House- Book of the Ancient Christians" and the "Law Book of the Ante-Nicene Church." (III, vii, Part 1 p. 1-176), a historical source book in support of which was given in IV, 237-447. See also R. Lorentz, *De Egyptische Kerkordening en Hippolytus van Rom*, (Leiden: E.J. Brill 1929); A.F. Walls,The Latin Version of Hippolytus' Apostolic Tradition, in *StudPatr* 3 (1961), p. 155-162.

[207] B. Botte, La Tradition apostolique de saint Hippolyte. Essai de reconstitution, in *Liturgiewissenschaftliche Quellen und Forschungen*, 39 (1963) (Aschendorffsche Verlagsbuchhandlung: Munster: 1988), p. XI-XII.

[208] Botte (1989) p. XXIII-XXIV.

[209] Ibid p. XIII: "... l'*Epitomé* et les *Canons d'Hippolyte* portent le nom d'Hippolyte, l'*Epitomé* dans le titre de la section qui réspond précisement au début de la *Constitution de l'Eglise égyptienne*, les *Canons* dans le titre général."

[210] Migne *P.G.* Tom. 1, p. 526. F.X. Funk, *Didascalia et Constitutiones Apostolorum*, Vol II, (Turin: Bottega d'Erasmo 1979), p. XXV: "Canones Hippolyti secundum editionem

The *Canones Sancti Hippolyti* were therefore originally entitled in Greek: ὅροι τῶν ἁγίων ἀποστόλων περὶ χειροτονιῶν διὰ ʿΙππολύτου.

Now Botte, following the Schwartz-Connolly thesis, was to argue that not only does the *Egyptian Church Order* closely resemble *Apostolic Constitutions* VIII, but also the *Epitome* of those Constitutions prefixes book VIII with a title which in Greek would have read διατάξις διὰ ʿΙππολύτου. That thesis had argued correctly that the *Egyptian Church Order* was the original document, or as we should prefer, group of documents in the chain of dependence that they successfully established. But they wished to go further. Not only did they wish to attribute this now anonymous document to Hippolytus as the author, but to claim that its original title was the ἀποστο–λικὴ παραδόσις. Since this was a title listed on the Statue, the Statue could thus prove that 'Hippolytus' had been no pseudonym for this work like the others which derive from it, but that in fact he was its real author. Let us begin, therefore, by asking the question whether the original title of the *Egyptian Church Order* was in fact the ἀποστολικὴ παραδόσις.

3D 1. *The original title of the* Egyptian Church Order

The so-called *Epitome*, on which *Ap. Const.* had, despite its title, in fact been originally dependent, had, as its original title, διατάξεις τῶν ἀποστόλων διὰ ʿΙππολύτου. This title would have been read originally at the beginning of the *Egyptian Church Order*, and not ἀποστολικὴ παράδοσις, if in fact it had any title at all. *Epitome* I is headed: διδασκαλία τῶν ἁγίων ἀποστόλων περὶ χαρισμάτων, and II: διατάξεις τῶν ἀποστόλων διὰ ʿΙππολύτου. The title: ἐπιτομή τοῦ βιβλίου η΄ τῶν διαταγῶν τῶν ἀποστόλων clearly adds the word διαταγαί to the title because the scribe who wrote it believed that it was, what it was not, a precis of the longer διαταγαί by which title he knew the *Ap. Con.* διατάξεις clearly therefore separated originally the *Epitome* from the διαταγαί of the *Ap. Con.* Thus διατάξεις as a title was arguably added by a scribe who connected it to the *Ap. Con.* subsequent to its incorporation into that later work.

But as Richard pointed out, the *florilegium* represented by the *ms. Ochrid* 86 of the National Museum of Yugoslavia used διατάξεις of the *Egyptian Church Order*. In chapter 23 of this collection, the extract devoted to the Eucharist was prefixed by the title ἐκ τῶν διατάξεων τῶν ἁγίων ἀποστόλων. This fragment corresponded to Chapter 32 of the Verona Latin and Chapter 58 of the Coptic version. Like the Verona Latin *ms.* 55, this fragment

---

Hanebergianam designantur, pluribus etiam versus editionis Achelisianae adnotantur." See D.B. von Haneberg, *Canones S. Hippolyti arabice*, e *codicibus Romanis cum versione Latina et prolegomena*, (Munich 1870) followed by H. Achelis, Die ältesten Quellen des orientalischen Kirchenrechtes. I. Die Canones Hippoliti, in *TU* 6,4 (1891). For an English translation see P.F. Bradshaw (Ed.), The Canons of Hippolytus (trans. C. Bebawi), in Alcuin/Grove Liturgical Study 2, (Nottingham: Grove 1987).

followed a citation from the *Didascalia Apostolorum*, though in the case of the former the *Canons of the Apostles* came in between, which, in the original Greek, would have been entitled ὅροι τῶν ἀποστόλων.

As neither the *Didascalia* nor the *Canones* were generally[211] called διατάξεις but διαταγαί and ὅροι respectively, then *ms. Ochrid* 86 is testimony to the *Egyptian Church Order* having been called διατάξεις τῶν ἁγίων ἀποστόλων, and possibly even, following the title which precedes the prayer of episcopal consecration in *Epitome* III: διατάξεις τῶν ἁγίων ἀποστόλων **περὶ χειροτονίων διὰ 'Ιππολύτου**. The title τῶν ἁγίων ἀποστόλων... **παράδοσις** only occurs later and as a gloss on this title (ἐπιτομὴ ὅρων... κ.τ.λ) of the *Epitome* in a later *ms.* which mark its inclusion in composite Church Orders.[212]

Thus we have no title recorded in the *ms.* tradition which corresponds precisely to what Botte has restored under the title of ἀποστολικὴ παράδοσις. The words of the prologue *ad verticem traditionis,* found in Old Latin Verona Palimpsest (L) and confirmed by the Ethiopian version (E), translate as the reading ἐπὶ τὸ κορυφαιότατον τῆς ἐκκλησιαστικῆς διατυπώσεως of *Ap. Con.* VIII, 3,1-2 and not as ἀποστολικὴ παράδοσις.[213] How then was Botte to sustain his case that the latter was the original title and thus corresponds with the title on the Statue?

---

211 A single *ms. Vaticanus* 839, p. XXIV gives as the title before *Ap. Con.* I,1: αἱ τῶν ἁγίων ἀποστόλων διατάξεις, with a note in the upper margin: ἀρχὴ σὺν θεῷ τῶν ἀποστολικῶν διατάξεων, διαταγαὶ τῶν ἀποστόλων συγγραφεῖσαι περὶ Κλήμεντος πάππα ʽΡώμης καὶ μαθητοῦ Πέτρου. Moreover, *ms. Hierosolymitanus* III, omitting Book VIII, 1-15, has as the title of VIII, 16: διαταγαὶ περὶ χειροτονίας πρεσβυτέρων, διακόνων, ὑποδιακόνων, ἀναγνώστων, διακονισσῶν, βιβλίον ἡ. There is no mention of ἐπισκόπων since this *ms.* lacks VIII, 15. See Funk (1979) p. 3 and 460.

212 *Ms. Cod. Paris. graec.* A (s. XIV), on which *ms. Cod. Ottob. graec.* 408 (s. XIV) is dependent, gives: ἐπιτομὴ ὅρων τῶν ἁγίων ἀποστόλων καθολικῆς **παραδόσεως**, cited in T. Schermann, Eine neue Handschrift zur Apostolischen Kirchenordnung, in *OrChr* 2 (1902), p. 399-402; ————, Eine Elfapostelmoral oder die X-Recension der „beiden Wege," in *Veröffentlichungen aus dem Kirchenhistorischen Seminar München,* 2,2 (Lentner: München 1903), p. 16. See also J. Magne, La prétendue Tradition Apostolique d' Hippolyte de Rome s' appellait-elle ΑΙ ΔΙΑΤΑΞΕΙΣ ΤΩΝ ΑΠΟΣΤΟΛΩΝ- Les statuts des saints apôtres? in *OstkiSt* 14 (1965), p. 63-66. See also M. Cotone, The Apostolic Tradition of Hippolytus of Rome, in *ABenR* 19 (1968), p. 495-501; J.A. Jungman, Beobachtungen zum Fortleben von Hippolyts „Apostolische Überlieferung," in *ZKTh* 53 (1929), p. 579-585.

213 M. Richard, Le Florilège Eucharistique du Codex Ochrid, Musée National 86, in Quelques nouveaux fragments des Pères Anténicéens et Nicéens, in *Symbolae Osloenses,* 38 (1963), p. 76-83, reprinted in ————, *Opera Minora,* (Turnhout/Leuven: Brepols/U.P.) 1,6. On p. 52 he says: "Nous devons en effet admettre simplement que l'ouvrage communement appelé ʼΑποστολικὴ παράδοσις a circulé sous le titre διατάξεις τῶν ἁγίων ἀποστόλων. Ceci ne doit pas trop nous surprendre. On sait que, dans l'Épitomé des Constitutions apostoliques, la prière pour le sacre des évêques, qui provient de la «Tradition apostolique» est introduite par le titre διατάξεις τῶν ἁγίων ἀποστόλων περὶ χειροτονίων διὰ ʽΙππολύτου et ceci nous assure que le titre attesté par notre florilège remonte au moins au IVe siècle." A. Faivre, La documentation canonico-liturgique de l'Église ancienne, in *RevSR* 54 (1980), p. 285-286, cf. A.-G. Martimort , Nouvel examen de la «Tradition Apostolique» in *BLitE* 88 (1987) p. 7-11. Cf. also Magne (1965) p. 35-67.

3D 1.1. *Botte's restoration of the title* ἀποστολικὴ παράδοσις

Botte has to rely on showing that the *Egyptian Church Order* had this title through its connection with the title of *Ap. Con.* VIII. The phrase however with which the latter begins is also found in the title of the *Epitome*, namely περὶ χαρισμάτων, and it is this which corresponds with the title of the work that immediately precedes ἀποστολικὴ παράδοσις on the Statue.[214] But even here there is a problem regarding whether the title περὶ χαρισμάτων did in fact come from the Constitutionalist's source. The so-called *Epitome*, which was in fact prior, begins as we have said διδασκαλία τῶν ἁγίων ἀποστόλων περὶ χαρισμάτων. It is *Ap. Con.* VIII which rephrases this, bringing the last phrase to the beginning as: περὶ χαρισμάτων καὶ χειροτονίων καὶ κανόνων ἐκκλησιαστικῶν. It seems likely therefore that the title: διδασκαλία τῶν ἁγίων ἀποστόλων was the original title of the whole of the *Epitome*, and that the scribe simply added περὶ χαρισμάτων to indicate the contents of the particular section. The Constitutionalist then simply took his last phrase and made it the first words of his title for Chapter VIII, which was not therefore part of the original title of the *Epitome* let alone the *Egyptian Church Order*.

The connection with that Church Order and the περὶ χαρισμάτων of the Statue is therefore even to begin with tenuous. But he must now pursue the further connection and show that this work that he tenuously named περὶ χαρισμάτων was in fact part of the same work as the ἀποστολικὴ παράδοσις which immediately follows it on the list on the plinth. The opening words of the prologue in L read: *Ea quidem quae verba fuerunt digne posuimus de donationibus*, and with the latter phrase E agrees. Botte therefore can claim that the author refers to his preceding discourse *de donationibus* (περὶ χαρισμάτων). Thus Botte believed that the title on the Statue περὶ χαρισμάτων, joined in a single discourse with the ἀποστολικὴ παράδοσις, was confirmed as being a work of Hippolytus.

But we should note that, in order to make this connection, he has to assume that the title περὶ χαρισμάτων that precedes ἀποστολικὴ παράδοσις are two parts of one and the same work. Yet if it is, one would have expected an ἤ between them by analogy with πρὸς Ἕλληνας καὶ πρὸς Πλάτωνα ἤ καὶ περὶ τοῦ παντός (which we shall discuss in 3E 1). Without this connection, all that the Verona Latin permits us to conclude from the text is that originally it may have been entitled περὶ χαρισμάτων. Botte may claim further that the Statue additionally corroborates the ascription of Hippolytus' name to the *Apostolic Tradition*, but the Statue does this if and only if

---

[214] A position characteristically stated in B. Botte, Les plus anciennes collections canoniques, in *OrSyr* 5 (1960), p. 333: "Cette diversité de titres est une cause de confusion pour beaucoup, et il est important de la signaler. Mais il est évident que le titre authentique est bien «Tradition apostolique» quel que soit l'auteur. La préface du texte latin (omise dans les versions coptes et arabes) dit très clairement qu'après avoir traité des charismes, l'auteur se tournait vers la tradition apostolique." My remarks in this paragraph show that nothing here is either "évident" or "très clairement."

Ligorio's reconstruction of the seated figure genuinely represents what was there in the second quarter of the third century.[215]

However, if we follow Botte, we are faced with a situation in which an anonymous first document in an interdependent series is identified with an actual historical author only because other works in the series are attributed to him clearly pseudonymously. The tendency moreover to apply Hippolytus' name as fictitiously as that of Clement may be seen in the Syriac *ms. Vaticanus* 107 that claims instead that the *Apostolic Constitutions* are "through Hippolytus" and not "through Clement," though the latter is their usual title. The ascription of Hippolytus' name to this document at least need not imply anything historical about the original author of what quite clearly is, in its present form, a post-Nicene text. Furthermore, in the West Syrian tradition, the *Testamentum Domini* is attributed to Clement of Rome, the disciple of Peter."[216] We shall need to return to this literary rivalry between these two names in the *ms.* tradition. Let us consider further for the moment the role in Botte's argument of the second work whose title allegedly originally contained Hippolytus' name, namely the *Epitome*.

3D 1.2. Epitome *and the* Egyptian Church Order

The full title, διατάξεις τῶν ἁγίων ἀποστόλων περὶ χειροτονιῶν διὰ Ἱππολύτου, does not precisely occur where the Egyptian Church Order (*Apostolic Tradition*) begins, in any manuscript of the *Epitome*. It is an exaggeration for Botte to claim that this title occurs *précisément au début de la Constitution de l'Eglise égyptienne*.[217] The *Epitome* after this title begins

---

215 Botte (1988): p. XIII: "L'authenticité de ce prologue est confirmée par les Constitutions apostoliques et partiellement par la version éthiopienne. Or sur le socle de la statue romaine, le titre Ἀποστολικὴ παράδοσις est précédé immédiatement de Περὶ χαρισμάτων."

216 Vööbus (1975) p. 27: "The Testament, or words which our Lord, when he rose from the dead, spoke to the holy apostles, and which were written in eight books by Clement of Rome, the disciple of Peter."

217 Botte (1963) p. XI. Previously Botte had claimed that the dispute was simply about whether the *Epitome* was, as its name falsely suggested, dependent upon the *Ap. Con.* or was indeed its source. The question was clearly whether the *Epitome* had derived this title from the *Egyptian Church Order* and was faithfully recording it as the title of its original author where it in fact began. H. Engberding, Das angebliche Dokument römischer Liturgie aus dem Beginn des dritten Jahrhunderts, in *Miscellana Liturgica in honorem L.C. Mohlberg*. Band 1 (Rom: 1948), p. 47-71 made the mistake of treating these separate issues as one. Cf. B. Botte, L' authenticité de la *Tradition apostolique* de saint Hippolyte, in *RThAM* 16 (1949), p. 178: "Quelle est la valeur de cette indication? Elle est nulle, répond dom E., puisque l'*Épitomé* n'est qu'un résumé des *Constitutions* et que celles-ci ne contiennent aucune mention semblable." It should be noted how in ensuing versions of his argument Botte consistently wrote "*Tradition*" instead of "Egyptian Church Order" and thus assumed what he had yet to prove, see e.g. Botte (1960) p. 335: "Il aut noter que, dans les manuscrits, le nom d'Hippolyte ne figure pas au début du recueil, mais à la seconde section qui coïncide avec le début de la *Tradition*: Ordonnances des saints apôtres par Hippolyte." B. Botte, Le traité des charismes dans les «Contitutions apostoliques,» in *StudPatr* 12 (Berlin 1975) *TU* 93, p. 85 modified his previous insistence: "Cependent, il a bien dû s'apercevoir que, même ainsi transformé, ce traité ne répondait pas exactement à ce qui est dit dans le prologue de la *Tradition*." Even Magne (1965) p. 62 denied that the name and title were present in the original of the *Egyptian Church Order*, but added, in view of the confusion with the correspondence of beginnings (in comparison with the Epitome) the hypothesis of a marginal note by someone who knew the truth ("Il faut donc plutôt penser à l'indication

with an address of "we the twelve apostles of the Lord (ἡμεῖς οἱ δώδεκα τοῦ κυρίου ἀπόστολοι)," and mentions the presence of "Paul our fellow apostle and James the bishop, with the rest of the presbyters and along with the seven deacons." Peter as the first orders the ordination rite for a bishop with which they all agree (III (IV), 1-2). It is only at this point that the *Epitome* converges with the *Apostolic Tradition/Egyptian Church Order*. The Verona Latin's *Episcopus ordinetur electus ab omni populo, quique cum nominatus fuerit et placuerit omnibus (Ap. Trad.* 2) corresponds to οὗ ὀνομασθέντος καὶ ἀρεσθέντος συνελθών... etc. (*Epitome* III(IV), 3) The Prologue (*Ap. Trad.* 1) is thus not represented in the *Epitome*.

In consequence, Pirro Ligorio's reconstruction of the Statue as Hippolytus becomes once again critical for arguments for the integrity of the Hippolytan *corpus*. Indeed the retitling of the *Egyptian Church Order* as ἀποστολικὴ παράδοσις comes from the fact that there is a work of that name on the back of the Statue. Since the *Epitome* (but not the *Egyptian Church Order* itself) introduces *Ap. Trad.* 2 with a title containing Hippolytus' name (διὰ Ἱππολύτου), it is therefore concluded that Hippolytus' name also occurred in the initial and original document in the chain of authorship, namely the *Egyptian Church Order*. That otherwise tenuous deduction is licensed by the fact that in that Church Order (*Ap. Trad.* 1) there is mention of a previous discourse *de donatibus* in a Latin text whose original Greek can be fairly reconstructed as: τὰ μὲν οὖν πρῶτα τοῦ λόγου ἐξέμεθα περὶ τῶν χαρισ–μάτων.[218] But we have already argued in 3D 1.1 that the περὶ τῶν χαρισ–μάτων on a fair reading of the list of works on the plinth was not part of the same work as ἀποστολικὴ παράδοσις as this thesis requires.

The mention of a work περὶ χαρισμάτων immediately before ἀποστολικὴ παράδοσις does not lead us therefore conclude with Connolly and Schwartz that the *Egyptian Church Order* and *Epitome* III (IV)- and *Epitome* I-II are both parts of a single work, and that they were written by Hippolytus. We have in such an argument, however, a prime example of what I argued in Chapter 1 was the extent to which the identification of the figure on the Statue as Hippolytus was necessary to secure the single authorship of the list of works found there. Once lose that identity, as it is lost as a result of Guarducci's identification of its original as a Themista of Lampsacus understood as an allegorical figure, and the certainty of a single author for the works, and their mutual identification on such a basis becomes less certain.

---

marginale d'un lecteur érudit: Ἱππολύτου ἐκ τῆς περὶ χαρισμάτων ἀποστολικῆς παραδόσεως. Cette référence a été ignorée, semble-t-il, par les uns, bien comprise par les autres qu'elle a pu aider à éliminer l'interpolation, mal par d'autres qui l'ont prise pour le titre.") See also E. Hennecke, Hippolyt's Schrift „Apostolische Überlieferung," in *Harnack Ehrung*, (Leipzig 1921), p. 159-162; ——, Der Prolog zur „Apostolische Überlieferung," in *ZNW* 22 (1923), p. 144-146.

[218] Ibid. p. 2 footnote. See also Connolly (1916) p. 136-138.

If it were not for the conditioning of Pirro Ligorio's reconstruction, we should certainly not necessarily identify the περὶ χαρισμάτων was part of the same work mentioned on the Statue before ἀποστολικὴ παράδοσις on the literary evidence before us. Without the Statue, we should simply conclude that only *Epitome* (III(IV)-) might be the work of Hippolytus, since it was here that the identifying sentence was placed, and not before *Epitome* I-II (= περὶ χαρισμάτων).[219]

Without evidence of the catalogue on the Statue, the mention of Hippolytus' name in the title of one section of the *Epitome* could not, without considerable argument, enable another document, namely the *Egyptian Church Order*, to be ascribed to the authorship of that name, simply because some passages appeared in common. Without being able to strengthen this particular link in the chain of evidence, therefore, the former work that it mentions (*de donatibus*= περὶ χαρισμάτων) could not be identified with Hippolytan authorship either.[220]

At first sight, the description of one section of the *Epitome* as διὰ ʿΙππολύτου does not assert Hippolytan authorship at all. It claims that the real authors were the apostles who transmitted these instructions (διατάξεις) "through Hippolytus." We can in support of Hippolytan authorship argue that this shows that the real invention was the apostles, and that no one would have invented a reference to Hippolytus if he were not in fact the author. But unfortunately for such an argument there is considerable evidence that Hippolytus' name, like that of Clement, was used to create pseudonymous works. We have already drawn attention to such a tradition of using Hippolytus like Clement as a cipher in 3C 9 above. Let us now turn to such evidence specifically in relation to the Church Order literature.[221]

---

219 H. Elfers, Neue Untersuchungen über die Kirchenordnung Hippolyts von Rom, in *Abhandlungen über Theologie und Kirche., Fest. Karl Adam*, (Ed.) M. Reding, (Düsseldorf: 1952), p. 201-203, and Loi (1977) p. 78 both argue for a single document combining the two titles on the grounds that the true charismata are given through ordination. But cf. Martimort (1987) p. 19: "... mais cette explication n'est pas pleinement satisfaisante, puisque dans le Prologue l'auteur distingue expressément les charismes, dont il a parlé, et ce *vertex traditionis* qu'il va traiter maintenant. De sorte que, finalement, il vaut mal venu, au moins d'un point de vue pratique, à récuser le nom de *Tradition apostolique* à l'ouvrage que nous avons l'habitude d'appeler ainsi et dont le contenu correspond bien à un tel titre." See also V. Saxer, La questione di Ippolito Romano, in *StEphAug*. 30 (1989) p. 57-58: "mi sembra potersi trarre da questi fatti una doppia conclusione. 1. I tratti sono due, 2. Tutti e due sono d'Ippolito romano."

220 See the comments of M. Simonetti, Aggiornamento su Ippolito, in *StEphAug*. 30 (1989) p. 123, 127-128, note 160 where he limits himself "a chiosare che la presenza sporadica del nome di Ippolito nei documenti che sono serviti alla ricostruzione di questo antico testo, se non è da riportare alla straordinaria fortuna di cui questo nome cominciò a godere da un certo momento del IV secolo..."

221 We should note how pronounced this tendency became in Botte (1960) p. 341: "Deux documents indépendents l'un de l'autre, l'*Epitomé* des *Constitutions apostoliques* et les *Canons d'Hippolyte*, dont les auteurs ont eu accès au texte original, nomment tous les deux Hippolyte comme auteur, le second comme archevêque de Rome. Ce sont deux apocryphes. Mais il n'est pas vraisemblable qu'il ait là pure coïncidence. Pourquoi avoir choisi ce nom d'un personnage assez secondaire, sinon parce qu'ils l'avaient trouvé dans le recueil qui leur a servi de base?" Furthermore in 3C 10 I showed quite clearly that Hippolytus' name became increasingly a

3D 2. διὰ Ἱππολύτου *and* διὰ Κλήμεντος *in the* ms. *tradition*

It must in the first place be mentioned that Clement was given as the author in the title of the *Apostolic Constitutions* in the Syriac version, whose original Greek form would have been διαταγαὶ τῶν ἁγίων ἀποστόλων διὰ Κλήμεντος. Turrinianus in his first printed edition (1578) entitled the work: διαταγαὶ τῶν ἁγίων ἀποστόλων διὰ Κλήμεντος τοῦ Ῥωμαιων ἐπισκοπου τε καὶ πολίτου καθολικὴ διδασκαλία διὰ βιβλίων ὀκτώ. He claimed to base his text on three manuscripts, the first from Calabria (*ms. Vaticanus* 2088), the second from Sicily (*ms. Vaticanus* 1056 and 2089), and the third from Crete (*ms. Vaticanus* 838).[222] It was this title, supported by these late manuscripts from the abbey of St. Mary Hodigitria, famous for such documents, that inspired the correction of De Magistris which was to divide the authorship of the *Constitutions*, attributing the διαταγαί to Clement, but the καθολικὴ διδασκαλία to Hippolytus (by amending πολίτου to Ἱππολύτου).[223]

But as we have seen, the absence of this fuller title in the Syriac version would not support the originality of such a subscription of *part* of the *Apostolic Constitutions*, namely the *Didascalia*, to Hippolytus. We have seen that one Syriac ms. does attribute the whole of that work to Hippolytus and not to Clement. Furthermore, there has been no attempt to claim for Hippolytus the restored *Didascalia Apostolorum*, embedded in the text of the *Apostolic Constitutions*, and distinguishable from it with the aid of a Syriac fragment and the Verona Latin. But this example shows that there was no reticence in certain ms. traditions to claim, not Hippolytan authorship, but transmission διὰ Ἱππολύτου on the same basis as διὰ Κλήμεντος, and with as little claim to historical veracity.

The Syriac version, moreover, that attributes the *Apostolic Constitutions* to St. Hippolytus is joined by some other mss. in an interest in Hippolytan authorship of such Clementine documents. *Ms. Petropolitanus* 254 (transcribed in A.D. 1111) is a collection of documents containing the *Constitutiones*, but also including *Epitomae* of Basil and Theodore Stydetes, and the *Capitula* of Timothy of Alexandria. We find that this concludes with a document attributed to "Hippolytus bishop of Rome (Ἱππολύτου ἐπισκόπου Ῥώμης) and Dorotheus bishop of Tyre and holy martyr (καὶ δωροθέου ἐπισκόπου τύρου ἱερομάρτυρος). On the disciples of the Lord and where each of them preached the gospel of Christ and were martyred (ἐτελειώθη)." In this *ms.* once again (in fol. 138b-139a) *Ap. Con* VIII,47 is singled out as a

---

cipher for the apostolic age from the fourth fifth century onwards, and in 3D 2 that the *ms.* tradition as well supported the reading of his name as a cipher for a tradition, like Clement. In those circumstances clearly Hippolytus was not "un personnage assez secondaire." See also A.F. Walls, A Note on the Apostolic Claim in the Church Order Literature, in *StudPatr* 2,2 (1957), p. 83-92.
[222] Funk (1979) I, p. XX-XXI and XXXVIII-XL.
[223] Migne *P.G.* T. 1 p. 523-525.

separate document by ὅρος κανονικὸς τῶν ἁγίων ἀποστόλων, though not attributed here to Clement. We note that this document, therefore, which is concerned with Hippolytan authorship, is also concerned with *Ap. Con.*, whether or not attributed to Clement.

At all events, *Ap. Con* VIII,47, is clearly an addition to which Clement's name was added in another *ms. Vaticanus* 827 (11-12 cent.) where there is inserted, after *Ap. Con.* VIII,46, 13: κανόνες ἐκκλησιαστικοὶ τῶν ἁγίων ἀποστόλων ἀποσταλέντες διὰ Κλήμεντος. We may ask why this emphasis was given to what is already claimed regarding authorship in the body of the text itself, where Clement and James speak in the first person (46, 13)? Granted that the *Epitome* is falsely named and was probable prior to the *Ap. Con.*, and granted the former was read and used by the latter, the author of the latter would have read the attribution of one section of the *Epitome* to Hippolytus. Was it this fact that lead him to emphasise the longer list of διατάξεις in VIII, 47, introduced by 46, 13, where διὰ Κλήμεντος stands almost in rivalry with the διὰ ῾Ιππολύτου which heads section B of the *Epitome*?

There is indeed a strong manuscript tradition for claiming for Clement the section of the *Epitome* (XXII) following that for which Hippolytan transmission is claimed (III-XXI). Before the title: Παύλου τοῦ ἁγίου ἀποστόλου διατάξεις etc. is prefaced ἐκ τῆς βίβλου τῶν διαταγῶν διὰ Κλήμεντος γραφέντων in *ms. Vaticanus* 1980 (12th Cent.) with XIX-XXI removed from the second (διὰ ῾Ιππολύτου) to the end of the fifth part. Certainly something of this kind is also the concern of the tradition embodied in *ms. Vindobonensis hist. gr.* 7 where a section of Hippolytus' second part (III (IV)) is itself claimed for Clement. Chapter XIX of the *Epitome* begins τοῦ αὐτοῦ κανόνες ἐκκλησιαστικοί. In the original text the αὐτοῦ clearly refers to Simon the Cananite who has just given instructions on the canonical number of bishops needed to consecrate another. But in this *ms.*, before this heading, is inserted: αἱ διαταγαὶ αἱ διὰ Κλήμεντος καὶ κανόνες ἐκκλησιαστικοὶ τῶν ἁγίων ἀποστόλων.[224] Simon's remaining canons are transmitted according to the author of this insertion, not διὰ ῾Ιππολύτου, as the section is headed, but διὰ Κλήμεντος. Clearly there are associations of rivalry between these two names.

I believe that, in Connolly and Schwartz's claim for Hippolytan authorship of the *Egyptian Church Order*, the significance of this posthumous literary rivalry was not sufficiently noted. No one would claim that the concealed message of διὰ Κλήμεντος was anything more than that of the Clementine literature itself, whose message has become superimposed on the *Apostolic Constitutions*. Neither Clement, nor James, nor the association claimed between them and the thirteen apostles (including Paul), is present in the

---

[224] Funk (1979) II p. IX and XVII.

demonstrably prior document, the *Didascalia*, which the Syriac combined with the Verona Latin enables us to restore over against the *Constitutions* into which it has been incorporated.[225] All such names, whether apostolic or sub-apostolic, were added pseudepigraphically to an originally anonymous document, which professed to be, as its pseudepigraphic title claimed, *Didascalia Apostolorum*.

Having argued successfully that the *Egyptian Church Order*, as a collection of rites, was the prior document in the chain which lead to the later *Synodicon*, Connolly then made a further and more dubious step. Because there was a connection between the *ms.* ascriptions to Clement and the pseudonymous Clementine literature, Connolly assumed that the ascription διὰ Κλήμεντος was the fictitious attribution, and by a process of elimination διὰ ῾Ιππολύτου could thus be allowed to stand as the real one.[226] But in so doing he ignored the use of Hippolytus' name as a cipher and thus similarly to that of Clement.

In the *Homilies*, Clement has become first after Peter and not third, as in Irenaeus' succession list, to enable Clement to be commanded by Peter to write to James, after his death, in order to record his ordination as bishop (*Ep. Clementis ad Iacob.* 2 ff.). Thus the encoded message is the convergence of Jewish and Gentile Christianity, with the catholic church legitimized by Peter's recognition of the Roman Clement and the former's convergence with James. So too in *Ap. Const.* VII,46 Peter informs us of the Jacobean succession up to Theophilus in third place (2), of Evodius consecrated at Antioch by himself, and of Ignatius by Paul, and at Rome Linus first by Paul, and after his death Clement in second place (6). Thus the Constitutionalist can reconcile Irenaeus list with the *Clementines*. Finally he is to claim that Clement's two letters, and the eight books of the *Constitutions*, belong in the Canon of Holy Scripture (VIII,47, 85).

It is against such a background of the assertion of the message, encoded in the *Clementines*, and now applied to the Didascalian material by the Constitutionalist, that we should understand the assertion of the transmission of a tradition about Church Order διὰ Κλήμεντος. A proponent of Hippolytan authorship—not for the *Epitome* as a whole, but for Funk's section B of that work which does bear his name as transmitter—will argue that the διὰ ῾Ιππολύτου is simply the way that the author of the *Epitome* as a whole registers his knowledge of the authorship of his source, the *Egyptian Church Order*, even though this does not bear Hippolytus' name.[227] Such an

---

[225] R. H. Connolly, *Didascalia Apostolorum: The Syriac Version Translated and accompanied by the Verona Latin Fragments*, (Oxford: Clarendon Press 1929).

[226] Connolly (1916) p. 138-141.

[227] Thus Connolly (1916) p. 140: "As then... Hippolytus' name could not have stood in any title of A.C. [*Apostolic Constitutions*]... the Epitomist *must* have got it from elsewhere. It is my conviction that he took the name from the same source from which he took his text of the bish-

explanation is, however, a-historical in that it is unrelated to anything we know and can exemplify of how ancient writers actually worked. It is almost pre-critical in that it is largely coloured by how we in the twentieth century might use and record such sources. There are no good grounds for making only Clement's name a cipher in these texts, and for excluding Hippolytus' from that category in a quest for a putatively "real" author, as we shall now see.

3D 3. *Literary* genre *of the so-called* ἀποστολικὴ παράδοσις

Indeed Faivre, I believe, was right in questioning the basis for the existence of an original archetype for the ἀποστολικὴ παράδοσις such as would constitute a distinct document with a 'real' author.[228] Hippolytus' name may well stand for an ecclesiastical tradition in the Church Order literature added later to an anonymous and amorphous series of documents.[229] Both Hanssens and Botte[230] have admitted their inability to establish satisfactorily a definite text behind the variant readings. Instead they have rested content with setting the various versions, the Verona Latin, the Sahidic, Arabic, Aethiopic, together with *Epitome* and *Apostolic Constitutions* side by side or with the various versions underneath one another.

Thus the study of the text of the *Apostolic Tradition* resembles a study of the synoptic gospels by means of Huck's parallels rather than the reading of a classical text reconstructed by means of clear canons of textual criticism that can distinguish the readings of the archetype from later corruptions.[231] It is arguable therefore that the assumption of an autograph named ἀποστολικὴ παράδοσις which once existed as the work of a single, "real" author is chimerical. Far from regarding the various parallel versions as corrupt representatives of the single autograph text of the *Ap. Trad.* (*Egyptian Church Order*), we should perhaps better regard them as a *genre* on their own in

---

op's ordination prayer and his passage on the reader, that is direct from Eg. C.O. [*Egyptian Church Order*]."
[228] Faivre (1980) p. 273-297.
[229] Ibid. p. 279: "On a tellement écrit sur ce texte, que l'on est parfois tenté de se demander s'il ne constitue pas plus une certaine façon de poser les problèmes qu'un document ayant eu un jour une réelle existence. Ce document, en effet, n'est plus en possession de l'historien. Quant à la plupart des commentaires liturgiques ou théologiques, c'est à partir de *rétroversions* qu'ils sont habituellement réalisés." Cf. B. Botte, Le texte de la Tradition apostolique, in *RThAM* 22 (1955), p. 161-172, and ——, A propos de la Tradition Apostolique, in *RThAM* 33 (1966), p. 177-186. See also J. Blanc, Lexique comparé des versions de la Tradition apostolique de saint Hippolyte, *Rechthéolancmédiév* 22 (1955), p. 173-192.
[230] Botte (1989) and J.-M. Hanssens, La liturgie d'Hippolyte: ses documents, son titulaire, ses origines et son caractère, in *OrChrA* 155, (Rome: 1959).
[231] Faivre (1980) p. 281-282: "Les documents canonico-liturgiques apparentés à la «Tradition Apostolique» sont, en effet, à mi-chemin entre les documents évangéliques (pour l'étude desquels une synopse est indispensible) et l'édition d'un texte littéraire classique (que l'on peut éditer après étude des différents manuscrits et de leurs variantes)." See also H. Dünsig, Der aethiopische Texte der Kirchenordnung des Hippolyt, nach 8 Handschriften herausgegeben und übersetzt, in *AAWG* Phil.-hist. Kl. 3,32 (1946); A. Gelston, A Note on the Text of the Apostolic Tradition of Hippolytus, in *JThS* 39 (1988), p. 112-117.

which liturgical rites, directions etc. remained somewhat fluid as incorporating the ongoing tradition of a living community.

That tradition as such had no one individual, "real" author and may never have been directly defined as such in an original single text. Our analysis of the Hippolytan community (Chapter 6), reflected in the ἀποστολικὴ παράδοσις, will indeed give substance to that view. We shall find community tension and development in conflicting images between different ordination rites in that group of parallel documents to which Botte and others have given this title.

Thus the use of Hippolytus' name in connection with such an amorphous set of liturgical traditions and practices could well be understood by analogy with the additions to the *Didascalia Apostolorum*. That document, originally an anonymous text, of corporate and community rather than individual authorship, was furnished by the *Apostolic Constitutions* with a host of apostolic and sub-apostolic names. Such a set of community practices, changing and developing quite fluidly, could then have been associated with the name of Hippolytus as a cipher standing for a community and not identifying an individual, 'real' author.

3D 4. *In conclusion: Names as ciphers in the Church Orders*

We must therefore relate the purpose of the Epitomist to the clear example that we already have of how the Constitutionalist actually behaved about the *Didascalia*. First he attributed that document to the thirteen apostles as well as Clement and James, and then asserted transmission διὰ Κλήμεντος. Here the Epitomist is also parcelling out the *Egyptian Church Order* between the twelve apostles, along with James, Paul, and the seven deacons (III, 1). Peter directs episcopal ordinations (III, 2), the Beloved Disciple (ὁ φιλούμενος) presbyteral (V, 1) and Philip diaconal ones (VII, 1), and so on with an apostle for each section. But he is claiming this διὰ ῾Ιππολύτου and not διὰ Κλήμεντος. It was presumably after this claim that a corresponding claim for Paul's section, or even Simon the Canaanite's canons, appearing originally in Hippolytus' own section, are claimed to have been transmitted διὰ Κλήμεντος. The Epitomist, unlike the Constitutionalist, never includes in his text itself Clement along with James as an apostolic associate.

Thus the assertion of διὰ Κλήμεντος is added historically after the assertion διὰ῾Ιππολύτου and not before. But before we regard this as evidence for a genuine Hippolytan in contrast to a fictitious Clementine authorship, we should note that the process of adding the names of either Clement or Hippolytus comes only after the work of assigning the various canons or διατάξεις to apostles or apostolic associates. The assignment of the designation διὰ῾Ιππολύτου just as much as διὰ Κλήμεντος is not an expression of the view of the scribe about the identity of the actual, historical author, but is rather an integral part of his strategy in creating a pseudonymous literature out of a pre-existing, anonymous one.

Just as therefore the assertion of the role of Clement in both the *Clementines*, and in the work of the Constitutionalist on the *Didascalia* contains an encoded message about mutual recognition of conflicting church traditions in the writers' own times, so indeed we shall argue in Chapter 5 does the assertion of transmission under the name of Hippolytus. We are fortunate in the case of Clement to have the *Homilies* and the *Recognitions* as well as the *Ap. Con.*, and to have recovered the *Didascalia* incorporated into the latter. As a result we can deduce clearly and in far greater detail the encoded message behind διὰ Κλήμεντος than we can that behind διὰ Ἱππολύτου. But the method of encoding the literary and ecclesiological messages in the pseudonymous form of the one will give us adequate grounds for regarding the encoding process as the same in the case of the other, however much we may lack be lacking in specific details about the encoded message in this latter case.

But for the moment, let us summarize where this chapter has taken us.

PART E. THE STATUE AND THE *CORPUS HIPPOLYTANUM*

Throughout this chapter we have noted the critical though often discrete role that the Statue has played in the reconstruction of the Hippolytan *corpus*. In Part A we saw how certain works whose author or authors were unknown to Theodoret, Photius, and others, or known under a variety of conflicting names such as Gaius, Origen, or Josephus were identified with Hippolytus' authorship by means of the Statue. *El.* was identified with the Statue through the identification of works claimed by the author with those listed on the plinth such as περὶ τοῦ παντός or the σμικρὸς λαβύρινθος *etc.* Let us now consider what we would have to conclude about the authorship of such works without the Statue.

3E 1. *Works otherwise anonymous without the Statue*

We find the philosophical titles on the Statue referred to by authors other than Eusebius and Jerome. Here we find Theodoret, Photius, and John Damascene attributing such works to someone other than Hippolytus, and if we wish to claim that such attributions are erroneous, we need the Statue as our crown witness. Here Ligorio's reconstruction is not confirmed by such works which rather deny that reconstruction, and in their case we need the reconstructed Statue itself, independently corroborated, in order to correct their alleged error.

If there had been no Ligorian reconstruction of the Statue, we should have clearly reconstructed the Hippolytan *corpus* very differently. On the evidence

of John Damascene and Photius that we have discussed, we should have certainly distinguished the Hippolytus (who wrote *Dan. Ant.* and a βιβλιδάριον
or a σύνταγμα against thirty-two heresies) and either a Josephus, or Gaius, or
Origen who wrote περὶ τοῦ παντός and the *Labyrinth.* which we identified
with *El.* (3A 5- 3 A 8 and 3B 2). We would have in consequence associated
the former work mentioned, in *Proem.* 1 as a "limited (μετρίως)," "undetailed
(οὐ κατὰ λεπτὸν)," and "summary (ἀδρομερῶς)" exposition, neither with
Photius' βιβλιδάριον or σύνταγμα, which he expressly says that Hippolytus
wrote, but rather with the *Little Labyrinth* (σμικρὸς λαβύρινθος) mentioned
by Theodoret (*Haer. Fab.* 2,5) as an anonymous work. Both Theodoret and
Photius knew, could and did identify Hippolytus' genuine works, as we have
shown (3A 8).

When we came to the events of *El.* IX,6-13, we should have readily
identified Photius' Gaius with his description of him as "a presbyter of the
Church of Rome in the time of Victor and Zephyrinus the high priests, and
who was ordained bishop of the pagans (ἐθνῶν ἐπίσκοπον)" (*Biblioth.* 48),
with the writer who describes his dispute with Callistus. The writer of the
Elenchos clearly claims to be a bishop (*Proem.* 6), and to address the pagans
in the *Demonstratio Veritatis* as we have pointed out in 3B 2. In view of the
association by the writer of Callistus and Zephyrinus with the
Monarchianism of Sabellius and Noetus, we should find an additional
corroboration that the author of the σμικρὸς λαβύρινθος, whose name
Theodoret does not know, was the Gaius mentioned by Photius as the author
of κατὰ τῆς Ἀρτέμωνος αἱρέσεως. If, however, the arguments denying
Gaius' authorship—notwithstanding my refutation of them in 3C 1-5—be
allowed to stand, nevertheless the case for separate authorship whether
anonymous or under some other name (such as Josephus) would be made for
the λαβύρινθος (*El.*), the σμικρὸς λαβύρινθος, and the κατὰ τῆς Ἀρτέμωνος
αἱρέσεως if that work is not identical with the latter.

But without the Statue our argument would not allow us as yet to add any
further works to the three. On Photius' evidence we are allowed to add the
title περὶ τῆς τοῦ παντὸς οὐσίας to the *corpus* of two or three works thus
established in order to make a third or fourth. *Bibliotheca* 48 attributes the
work, not to Hippolytus whom he does not mention in connection with this
work, but perhaps to Josephus. But with the latter's authorship Photius believes the work to be inconsistent, on grounds of its non-Jewish anthropology
(ἀναξίως τῆς τε τῶν Ἰουδαίων περὶ ἀνθρώπου φυσιολογίας ταῦτα εἰπὼν) and
the absence of a common phraseology with his other works (οὐδὲν δὲ τὸ τῆς
φράσεως αὐτῷ πρὸς τὰ ὑπόλοιπα τοῦ ἀνδρὸς ἀποδεῖ). So he conceded here
that this work was also attributed ἐν παραγραφαῖς to Gaius, author of the
λαβύρινθος, as well as the πρὸς Πρόκλον (3B 2). Furthermore, in the *Sacra
Parallela* attributed to John Damascene and quoted by Zonaras (*c.* A.D.

1120), we find mentioned: "... in his discourse *To the Greeks* (ἐν δὲ τῷ πρὸς Ἕλληνας) which bears the title (ἐπιγέγραπται) *Against Plato* (κατὰ Πλάτωνος) *On the Cause of the Universe* (περὶ τῆς τοῦ παντὸς αἰτίας)." (*Annal.* 6, 4) Thus the περὶ τοῦ παντός can be admitted to the *corpus* of the three or four bearing Gaius' or some other name.

We do of course have the Statue. But it is only because of this fact that we can now try to extend the *corpus* of three or four further. *Bibliotheca* 48 also showed that the work περὶ τῆς τοῦ παντός αἰτίας was also entitled simply περὶ τοῦ παντὸς, in some manuscripts, and this is equivalent to part of the title of the work on the Statue, namely, πρὸς Ἕλληνας καὶ πρὸς Πλάτωνα ἢ καὶ περὶ τοῦ παντός. An extract from this work was cited by John Philoponus in his own work of that title, as we shall see in the next chapter (4B 2 5 B 1.1). Pseudo-John Damascene also corroborated the later part of this title. But we would only be entitled, having found the Statue, to attribute the other works found there in addition to this title to the *corpus* of three or four if and only if the Statue could be so interpreted as a testimony to the fact that every title on the plinth was by the same author. We have argued in Chapter 2 that once it is conceded that Ligorio's reconstruction was false and that the original figure seated on the chair was allegorical, then indeed it does not necessarily follow that every work listed there must be of the same author.

The move in the argument for the reconstruction of the *corpus* necessitated by the concept of the Statue as a personal monument was that every title on the plinth of the Statue now be added to the *corpus* of three or four that we have so far established without reference to the Statue. And it was precisely at this point that the claim of Hippolytus to be author of that *corpus* too could now be pressed. The series of related collections of canons and Church Orders of which the anonymous *Egyptian Church Order* was a part were all attributed to St. Hippolytus.

Richard unfortunately had pointed out from the *ms. Ochrid* 86 that the *Egyptian Church Order* would have had to have been read with the title δια–τάξεις τῶν ἁγίων ἀποστολῶν and not as ἀποστολικὴ παράδοσις. But nevertheless, *if* the Statue had been a personal monument, then the general association of Hippolytus' name with that associated literature might have been sufficient to warrant his identification as the personal author of that work and therefore of all other works on the plinth. We have, however, shown grounds in Part 3D why it should not therefore follow that Hippolytus was its personal author given the literary *genre* involved. Given the original allegorical figure was symbolic of a school, it is quite consistent that the *corpus* of three or four thus established should have had their own individual author who was an acknowledged member of the Hippolytan community.

One example more difficult to deal with was the τὰ ὑπὲρ τοῦ κατὰ Ἰωάννην εὐαγγελίου καὶ ἀποκαλύψεως. We have argued that this was not equivalent to the Hippolytus/Gaius dialogue in Barsalîbî, nor indeed either with the ἀπολογία or the κεφάλαια of Ebed-Jesu. We regarded what we considered to be these two works to be part of the Hippolytan pseudepigrapha (3C 6-10). As such, since Hippolytus was not their real author, they could not have been present on the Statue as τὰ ὑπὲρ τοῦ κατὰ Ἰωάννην κ.τ.λ and thus constitute evidence that Hippolytus was the writer of all the works listed, on the assumption that it was a personal monument.

But even if my argument for the pseudepigraphic character of the latter works identified with this title were to have failed, nevertheless I have argued that the Statue was not a monument to a person but to a community. Thus even a genuine work of Hippolytus could, in principle, occur on the Statue along with works by another author. In the light of the general thesis of Chapter 2, the Statue can no longer be used as the centre of a web of literary relations that bind every work on the Statue to a single author that will be Hippolytus if those works connect with any of his genuine works, or will be instead a single author of a quite different identity, if they fail to connect.

The fact that neither John Damascene nor Photius nor John Philoponus will identify περὶ τοῦ παντός as Hippolytus' was one of the foundations of Nautin's argument that a certain Josephus (though not the Jewish writer) had been the author of the titles on the Statue and that indeed there were therefore two authors of the commonly received Hippolytan *corpus*. But even here the force of Ligorio's reconstruction was to continue to be felt, and to create very great problems. If this work were to be that of Josephus, then all other works on the Statue must be his as well. The seated doctor of the Church demanded an all-or-nothing recognition of his inscribed works. If περὶ τοῦ παντός was Josephus' then so was *De Psalmis* (εἰς τοὺς ψαλμούς), *De Psaul et Pythonissa* ([εἰς τὴν ἐγ]γαστρίμυθον), *De Apocalypsi*. (ὑπὲρ τοῦ κατα Ἰωάννην etc.), and the *De Pascha* (ἀπόδειξις χρόνων). But if this were the case, then it would fly in the face of the evidence of Jerome and Eusebius that mention these as works of Hippolytus. Let us look at the evidence of the Eusebius/Jerome lists to see to what extent they identify genuine Hippolytan works listed on the Statue.

3E 2. *The Statue and the Eusebian/Jerome Catalogues*

In 3E 1 we considered works that could not be ascribed to Hippolytus independently of the Statue, and on the questionable assumption that the Statue was a personal monument to the Church Father of that name. We moreover included the ἀποστολικὴ παράδοσις with the τὰ ὑπὲρ τοῦ κατὰ Ἰωάννην κ.τ.λ. in this category. Such evidence was the dubious evidence for the Hippolytan authorship of certain works that in turn becomes dubious evidence for authorship of the works on the Statue. We are now going to consider works that can be ascribed to Hippolytus independently of the Statue, and which, if they in fact are the equivalent of titles cited on the Statue, become evidence for the Statue as Hippolytus' personal monument. Thus the Statue will cease to be evidence for the Hippolytan *corpus* and instead the *corpus* or parts of it become evidence for the Statue, if connections can in fact be validly drawn.

In this category we find (in 3E 2.1) references common both to Eusebius and Jerome, and in (3E 2.2) titles which Jerome appears to share with the Statue alone.

3E 2.1. *Titles apparently common to Eusebius and Jerome*
If we look at Jerome's list of nineteen works for which Hippolytus is claimed as the author, we find two titles (Περὶ τοῦ Πάσχα/De Pascha and the Πρὸς Μαρκίωνα/Contra Marcionem), common to both, that might be regarded as shared also with the Statue.[232] Indeed, many other of the titles are common to both Jerome and Eusebius, but we confine ourselves here to the two which both writers can be claimed to share with what is inscribed on the Statue. The *ratio paschae et temporum canon*, linked by Jerome too with Caesar Alexander, may be identical with the ἀπόδειξις χρόνων on the *pinax* of the Statue though we shall examine a serious objection in 5A 2.1-2.2. If so, then the *De Pascha*, like Eusebius' Περὶ τοῦ Πάσχα, can be associated with the table on the Statue if and only if the grounds for the identification with Eusebius' reference are valid.

The evidence, therefore, for Jerome's dependence on Eusebius regarding the Περὶ τοῦ Πάσχα/De Pascha is far stronger than the evidence for the connection of either of them with the Statue, which neither of them mention. A similar point holds also for the second work on the lists of Jerome and Eusebius where the identity of the title that they share is more certain than the identity of their joint titles with a work listed on the Statue. Jerome's *Contra Marcionem* and Eusebius' Πρὸς Μαρκίωνα *may* be identical with περὶ τἀγαθοῦ καὶ πόθεν τὸ κακόν. But such titles as *De Pascha* (Melito) and *contra Marcionem* (Tertullian) were very common, and a philosophical treatise on the origin of evil does not necessarily have to be aimed at Marcion's two gods.

---

232 Eusebius, *H.E.* VI, 22: ... Ἱππόλυτος... τὸ περὶ τοῦ πάσχα πεποίηται σύγγραμμα... τῶν δὲ λοιπῶν αὐτοῦ συγγραμμάτων τὰ εἰς ἡμᾶς ἐλθόντα ἐστὶ τάδε· εἰς τὴν ἐξαήμερον, εἰς τὰ μετὰ τὴν ἐξαήμερον, πρὸς Μαρκίωνα, εἰς τὸ ᾆσμα, εἰς μέρη τοῦ Ἰεζεκιήλ, περὶ τοῦ πάσχα, πρὸς ἁπάσας τὰς αἱρέσεις. Jerome, *De Vir. Ill.* 61: "Hippolytus... in ratione paschae et temporum canone scripsit... Scripsit nonnullos in scripturas commentarios, e quibus haec repperi: *In Hexaemeron, In Exodum, In Canticum Canticorum, In Genesim, In Zachariam, De Psalmis, In Esaiam, De Daniele, De Apocalypsi, De Proverbiis, De Ecclesiaste, De Saul et Pythonissa, De Antichristo, De Resurrectione, Contra Marcionem, De Pascha, Adversus Omnes Haereses,* et προσομιλίαν *de Laude Domini Salvatoris*...

3E 2.2. *Titles common to the Statue and Jerome alone*

There are three additional titles which Jerome shares, or may share, with the Statue, but which are not on Eusebius' list. (i) *De Psalmis* may appear to correspond with εἰς τοὺς ψαλμούς, and (ii) *De Psaul et Pythonissa* with εἰς τὴν ἐγγαστρίμυθον. (iii)*De Apocalypsi* has been considered identical with τὰ ὑπὲρ τοῦ κατὰ Ἰωάννην εὐαγγελίου καὶ ἀποκαλύψεως, even though it seems strange that Jerome did not include the gospel in his title if it were the same work. But we have argued in 3C 6 that this identity does not hold, and if so, Jerome's title does not correspond to any work on the Statue any more than did Ebed-Jesu's titles or Barsalîbî's dialogue (3C 5).

If we thus fail to establish the equivalence of (iii) with a title on the Statue, the evidence for the equivalence of (i) and (ii) is correspondingly diminished. (i) and (ii) are titles for scriptural commentaries in general, that are quite frequently shared by multiple authors of different works. Such an argument is quite frequently used by advocates of the two-author hypothesis to show that the author of the works on the Statue is quite different from that of the lists of Eusebius and Jerome.[233]

But having challenged the necessity of a single writer whether Hippolytus or someone else as the author of all the titles on the plinth, that two-author will now have to support itself with reference to internal literary criteria that can establish internal homogeneity between those titles and their differences with Hippolytus' general works. The Statue as an artefact in itself cannot make that case. In the final analysis, the only certain equivalent between the Statue and the Eusebius/Jerome list is the Περὶ τοῦ Πάσχα. But our problem cannot be resolved with reference to this one title alone since even in this case there are problems which we shall deal in 5A 2.1-2.2 when we consider the internal evidence for a single or diverse authorship for the Hippolytan *corpus*.

3E 2.3. *In conclusion*

Supposing that we had, not the Statue whether in its original or restored Ligorian form, but simply the list of works inscribed upon it in some other form, say on a *stele* or on a piece of parchment. From the fact that the works were listed together it would not necessarily follow that the titles were from a single author. They may, particularly if found on a *stele*, be a library catalogue. Scriptural commentaries with titles indicating that they were about the Passover, the Psalms, or the *Apocalypse* would not of themselves equate them with the works of an author of similar titles, named Hippolytus, mentioned by Jerome and Eusebius.

Regarding the philosophical discourses, we have already seen that, on the evidence of Photius and Theodoret, there would be as much evidence for

---

[233] E.g. Nautin (1947) p. 84 and (1949) p. 226-230.

Origen, Gaius, and Josephus as for Hippolytus for the authorship of the περὶ τοῦ παντός. If περὶ τἀγαθοῦ καὶ πόθεν τὸ κακόν was to be identified with any treatise against Marcion, then it would be identical with that to which the Gaius (or Josephus or whoever) of the *Elenchos* makes a highly ambiguous reference (*El.* VII, 30 and 31). Apart from such veiled allusions, there would be no reason for identifying the treatise on the origin of good and evil with any tract against Marcion, and indeed it is surprising that the author of the *Elenchos* was not more specific about it when dealing with Marcion in view of his ready claim to the authorship of other works.

Regarding the title περὶ θεοῦ καὶ σαρκὸς ἀναστάσεως, if we associated it with the Syriac fragment in which a title of this name is associated with Julia Mamaea, then we could not with any security definitely attribute it to Hippolytus. It would still be possible for us to claim that Origen was the author of that title, on grounds of Eusebius *H.E.* VI, 21,3. In view of the records of Hippolytus' personal relationship with Origen, it would not be impossible to find a work by him listed in the library of Hippolytus' school. At all events, we could assign to Hippolytus the προτρεπτικὸς πρὸς Σεβηρεῖναν and claim that this was Hippolytus' πρὸς βασιλίδα τινὰ ἐπιστόλη mentioned under his name in Theodoret *Dialogus* 2. If the list was a catalogue of titles, with no named Statue of an owner seated above them, each title could be assigned the same or different authors according to the literary citations and other evidence.

It is now that we must turn to Nautin's thesis, as it has been criticized and adapted by Simonetti and others. We shall once again see that the fundamental problem with which that thesis has to grapple is the assumption that the Statue is a monument to an individual author, with the result that some titles which appear to be by Hippolytus are belied by other titles which seem clearly not. In consequence, regarding the internal evidence now as well, we shall demonstrate our thesis that the Statue and its list of works is a monument to a school and that the titles on its plinth are the works of three or more authors.

CHAPTER FOUR

THE STATUE AND THE TWO AUTHORS THEORY (I)

The Catalogue on the Statue and works related to the Elenchos

The consensus of nineteenth and early twentieth century scholarship adopted the position of Bunsen, Döllinger, Harnack and others discussed in 3B 1. The Statue had been that of Hippolytus, its character was dedicatory or commemorative, the list of works on the plinth were his, and all that remained was to identify such as could be with the Eusebius/Jerome catalogues and otherwise add hitherto unknown titles to the Hippolytan *corpus*. We saw that Cruice, Armellini, Newman and others denied the authorship of *El.* to Hippolytus on the confessional grounds that no saint and martyr of the Church could possibly have been an anti-pope. But their objection to Hippolytan authorship did not extend to the Statue but simply to *El.*, which the Statue had never mentioned. Gaius or Origen, or even Novatian,[1] despite the chronological problem, seemed better to fit the bill.

But no attention had been given to internal literary criticism in terms of which the Hippolytan authorship or otherwise of *El.* might be established. So far the discussion had focused on the congruence of one acknowledged as a Saint and Martyr of the Church having prefigured in the events of *El.* IX, 10-13 involving opposition to one whom the Liberian List was to recognise as the reigning pope. Da Bra was the first writer on grounds of literary criteria alone to deny that Hippolytus could have written *El.*[2] Nautin however was to go further than simply appealing to internal literary criteria in order to deny that Hippolytus was the author of *El.* His argument falls into five parts, namely:

(i) On literary grounds it can be established that *El.* and *C.N.* had different authors,

(ii) It can be established that the author of *El.* was responsible for one block of works in the Hippolytan *corpus* on grounds of literary, stylistic, and theo-

---

[1] J. Hergenröther, Hippolytus oder Novatian? in *Österreichische Vierteljahresschrift für Katholische Theologie* 2 (1863), p. 289-340. We have already examined (1B 2.3.3.1) such claims by De Rossi and others, and criticised Gieseler (3B 2.1 footnote 86), and will pursue the alleged Novatian connection further in Chapter 6. For a review of literature, see J. Barbel, Zu patrologischen Neuerscheinungen aus den Jahren- 1949-1954 Die Hippolytfrage, in *TheoRev* 51 (1955), p. 101-108.

[2] G. da Bra, *I Filosofumeni sono di Ippolito?* (Rome: 1942); ——, *Studio su S. Ippolito dottore.* (Rome: 1944).

logical similarities that those works share with *El.*, and that *these include the works on the Statue*.

(iii) It can be established similarly that the author of *C.N.*, whom Nautin accepts as the real Hippolytus, wrote another block in the *corpus*, identified similarly by the literary criteria which link its works with *C.N., and these works do not appear on the Statue*.

(iv) The internal literary criteria help us to construct distinct cultural and literary profiles for the two authors.

(v) The Statue originally was dedicated to Josephus, the author of *El.* and the works listed on the plinth, and named by Photius, John Philoponus, and Pseudo-Damascene.

Nautin's project was thus far more ambitious than Da Bra's. But it should be noted that positions (i)-(v) can stand independently of each other though each must be true to make Nautin's full case. *El.* and *C.N.* might be proven in terms of internal literary criteria to be by different authors ((i)), and yet fail to relate specifically and definitively to the other works with which they are claimed to form two different blocks ((ii)) and (iii)). The Statue may not support the uniform authorship of all works listed on its plinth if indeed it is, as we have argued, a monument to, or an icon of, the ethos of a school rather than an individual. The *corpus* would not then be seen to exhibit two distinct literary profiles. It will in that case be the internal literary criteria that establish the grounds for distinct cultural and literary profiles for the two authors ((iv)), and not the Statue *per se*. Josephus, as opposed to Gaius or a second Hippolytus with the same name might not be the author, who might have to remain therefore anonymous ((v)).

We shall see that, in relation to literary criteria, the assumption that the Statue is a monument to an individual provides the same distorting influence on the two-authors argument as it did on the reconstruction of the Hippolytan *corpus* itself (Chapter 3). Furthermore, even though we might concede that the other arguments succeed, we might still wish to argue that the two distinct literary biographies of the two authors fail to be coherently or convincingly constructed in terms of Nautin's discussion of them ((iv)).

In this chapter and the next we shall consider these points in greater detail. In this chapter we shall consider (i) (4A) and (ii) (4B) in order to study specifically the relation between what is known of the works listed on the Statue, and works which we shall establish to be related to *El.* rather than *C.N.* We shall discover that it is not possible to insulate the two authors from each other's work by means of the Statue. We shall detect the hand of the later as editor of some of the works of the earlier, cited in the inscription, notably as editor of the Συναγωγή–Χρονικῶν (4B 2.2.2), the ἀπόδειξις χρόνων (4B 2.2.2.2), and in certain additions to the Liberian *Catalogus* (4B 2.2.3.3-B 2.2.4). In the next chapter we shall consider (iii) (5A), (iv) (5B) and (v) (5C) arguing there that some of the works listed on the Statue, notably the ἀποστολικὴ παραδόσις (5A 1–1.2), and the ἀπόδειξις χρόνων (5A 2-2.2), are partly written by Hippolytus, and that the περὶ τἀγαθοῦ καὶ πόθεν τὸ κακόν (5A 3), the περὶ θεοῦ καὶ σαρκὸς ἀναστάσεως (5A 4) and the προτρεπτικὸς πρὸς Σεβηρεῖναν (5A 5) must be considered wholly his on the basis of their citation as such by Eusebius, Jerome, and Theodoret.

We shall begin with an analysis of arguments for a difference of authorship between the two major works of the Hippolytan *corpus* neither of which paradoxically is found on the Statue, but on the critical differences between them on which hangs the whole thesis of two distinct authors.

PART A. AUTHORSHIP OF THE *ELENCHOS* AND THE *CONTRA NOETUM*

Nautin claimed a distinction between the authors of these two works on theological, stylistic, and heresiological, grounds. On such grounds he pressed further the case for a cultural and educational formation that separated the two authors.[3] We shall argue the case here for a difference of authorship for these two works firstly and chiefly on theological grounds, focusing on the specific question of the relationship between *El.* and *C.N.* We shall omit stylistic considerations, since we admit a similarity of style which is consistent either with a single author or with two different authors within the same school.[4]

The appeal to a difference of method of refuting heretics is similarly inconsequential since the fact that *El.* refutes heresy by appeal to its alleged roots in Greek philosophy, and *C.N.* by appeal to Scripture is compatible either with two different authors or one author addressing different audiences.[5] We believe, in other words, that it is the theological differences that are fundamental. We wish furthermore to keep separate from the question of the re-

---

[3] P. Nautin, Hippolyte et Josipe: Contribution à l'histoire de la littérature chrétienne du troisième siècle, in *Etudes et Textes pour l'histoire du dogme de la Trinité*, (Paris: Éditions du Cerf 1947), Chapt. 3.

[4] Nautin (1947) p. 51 introduces the issue of stylistic differences, which were extensively reviewed by Da Bra (1942) p.18-39, who concluded on this basis a difference of authorship. His literary analysis was criticised by G. Oggioni, La questione di Ippolito, in *ScuCat* 78 (1950), p. 133-135 and footnote 47 on the grounds that he had relied on the authenticity of what Migne had published as the original texts. *In Sancta Theophania, Adversus Ioudaeos*, and *Contra Beronem*, for example are all cited as genuine works and made a basis for the comparison. On the other hand, B. Capelle, Hippolyte de Rome, in *RThAM* 17 (1950) discusses (A) general common traits in defence of single authorship (p. 156-159); (B) the prologues of *De Antichristo* and *Chronicon* (p. 159-161), (C) common doctrinal themes (p. 161-166), and (D) notable verbal correspondences (p. 166-170). His account is vitiated by his decision (later reversed (see footnote 47)) to regard *C.N.* as heavily interpolated. Deny *C.N.* as genuine evidence and of course the case for little difference can be made, see 4 A 3.1.

[5] Nautin (1947) p. 53. Such a view was advocated by Frickel as we shall see, references for and grounds against which I give in 4A 2.1.1. For another supporter of the two-audiences solution, see J. Daniélou, Review of Nautin's Hippolyte et Josipe, in *RecScRel.* 35 (1948), p. 597 ("Ces remarques, qui sont exactes, avaient déjà été faites. Une raison en avait été donnée: la différence des publics auxquels les ouvrages sont adressés.").

lationship between *El.* and *C.N.* the further question of which other works in the Hippolytan *corpus* might be by one or other of the two authors, without allowing the Statue necessarily to create two distinct blocks on the arguably tenuous grounds that connect it with the single author of the works inscribed on its plinth.

Since cultural differences are best considered in the light of a consideration of such links between groups of works within the *corpus* as a whole, we shall leave the question of a difference of cultural and educational formation of the two authors till later, restricting our initial argument to the theological distinctions between *El.* and *C.N.* alone. As both Frickel and Richard acknowledged, the distinctions, whether alleged or real, between these two works were of fundamental significance for the question the unity of the *corpus*, besides which the chronological differences between *Dan.* and the *Chronicon Paschale* were comparatively insignificant.[6] Let us now examine these differences.

Mainly following Nautin, whose insights we shall be seeking to develop, we may characterize the theological differences as (1) the justification of binitarianism, (2) the incarnation, (3) place of the Holy Spirit. We shall ignore the other differences that Nautin detected, since these rested on an argument from silence on the part of one work in comparison with the other.[7]

---

6 J. Frickel, *Das Dunkel um Hippolyt von Rom: Ein Lösungsversuch: die Schriften Elenchos und Contra Noëtum.* (Grazer Theologische Studien: Bauer 1988), p. 123: "Tatsächlich sind diese zwei Schriften von fundamentaler Bedeutung für die Frage, ob das bisher unter dem Namen Hippolyts bekannte Schrifttum von zwei verschiedenen Verfassern oder von ein und demselben Schriftsteller stammt. Gewiss wurden auch andere Unterschiede, zum Beispiel zwischen *Danielkommentar* und *Chronik*, für die Unterscheidung von zwei verschiedenen Autoren ins Feld geführt. Aber diese Abweichungen sind, wie besonders Richard gezeigt hat, zweitrangig im Vergleich zur Frage nach dem Verhältnis von El und CN." ——, Hippolyt von Rom: Refutatio, Buch X, in Paschke, F. (Ed.) Überlieferungsgeschichtliche Untersuchungen, in *TU* 125) (Berlin: 1981), p. 217-244. For a summary of his argument in defence of a single author see ——, Ippolito di Roma, scrittore e martire, in *StEphAug* 30 (1989), p. 36-41. Originally Frickel had defended the separate authorship of *El.* and *C.N.*, see ——, Contraddizioni nelle opere e nella persona di Ippolito di Roma, in *StEphAug.* 13 (1977), p. 137-149. More recently he has conceded that *El.* and *C.N.* must be by different authors, see ——, Hippolyts Schrift Contra Noetum: ein Pseudo-Hippolyt, in *Logos. Festschrift für Luise Abramowski*, (Berlin & New York: Walter de Gruyter 1993), p. 87-123. See also L. Abramowski, Drei christologische Untersuchungen, in *Beiheft zur ZNW* 45, (Berlin: De Gruyter 1981); R.M. Hübner, Die Hauptquelle des Epiphanius (Panarion, haer. 65) über Paulus von Samosata: Ps. Athanasius, Contra Sabellianos, in *ZKTh* 90 (1979), p. 203; ——, Die antignostische Glaubensregel des Noet von Smyrna, in *MuThZ* 40 (1989), p. 279-311; ——, Die Schrift des Apolinarius von Laodicea gegen Photin (Ps. Athanasius Contra Sabellios) und Basilius von Caesarea, (Berlin & New York 1989); ——, Melito von Sardes und Noet von Smyrna, in *Oecumenica et Patristica. Festschrift für Wilhelm Schneemelcher*, (Chambésy-Genf 1989), p. 220-223.

7 Nautin (1947) p. 49-51 would require us to add: (4) the conception of salvation, (5) the portrayal of the life hereafter, and (6) the humanity of Christ. He argues that : (4) (i) *El.* X, 33,7 (εἰ δὲ θέλεις καὶ θεὸς γενέσθαι, ὑπάκουε τῷ πεποιηκότι), and (ii) 34, 4-5 (γέγονας γὰρ θεός· ὅσα μὲν γὰρ ὑπέμεινας πάθη ἄνθρωπος ὤν, ταῦτα ἐδίδου σοι θεός, ὅτι ἄνθρωπος εἶς· ὅσα δὲ παρακολουθεῖ θεῷ, ταῦτα παρέχειν σοι ἐπήγγελται θεὸς ὅταν θεοποιηθῇς, ἀθάνατος γενηθείς... καὶ σὲ θεὸν ποιήσει...), indicate salvation as divinization, which is absent from *C.N.* Likewise for (5) he points out to the view of the afterlife, unmentioned in *C.N.*, described in *El.* X, 34, 2, which we discuss later (4B 2.1.4). In the case of (6) he cites the

4A 1. *The Trinity in* C.N. *and the binitarianism of* El.

El. is binitarian in its theology whereas *C.N.* is distinctly trinitarian and affirms the pre-existence of the Holy Spirit alongside that of the Son. It is important however to stress precisely how this comparison holds. In one respect it could be argued that in neither work does the writer give the Holy Spirit a distinct role in the creation, but in *C.N.* the Holy Spirit is introduced as a distinct though somewhat redundant person. However, as we shall now see, the way in which both associate νοῦς with λόγος is quite different, irrespective of the role of the Holy Spirit or its absence in both accounts.

In the ἀπόδειξις ἀληθείας (*El.* X, 33,1-2) the λόγος is both conceived in God's mind as a mental concept (μόνος... θεὸς λόγον πρῶτον ἐννοηθεὶς) and then begotten (ἀπογεννᾷ). He was alone begotten from what was in existence (μόνον ἐξ ὄντων ἐγέννα) and in this sense was uncreated, since what was in existence was the Father alone from whose existence he was begotten (τὸ γὰρ ὂν αὐτὸς ὁ πατὴρ ἦν, ἐξ οὗ τὸ γεννηθέν). The λόγος is therefore the begotten first principle of creation (αἴτιον τοῖς γινομένοις), and not the four ἀρχαί or first principles of the philosophers, earth, air, fire, and water which are real but created (*El.* X, 32,4-5; 33, 3-7). We shall now see how these components of Stoicism and Platonism, taken over in a raw form by the author of *El.*, are radically refashioned by the author of *C.N.* with an eirenic ecclesiastical purpose.

4A 1.1. C.N. *10 and* El. *X, 33,1-2: a refashioned metaphysics*
It is at this point that we should also note the famous philosophical formation of the author of *El.* in the way that he employs both Stoic and Platonic concepts in his understanding of the λόγος. The λόγος is begotten not as the mere voice (οὐ δὲ λόγον ὡς φωνήν) but rather like the Stoic "immanent reason" of the world soul (ἀλλ᾽ ἐνδιάθετον τοῦ παντὸς λογισμόν). As the Father's "firstborn (πρωτότοκος)," "he bore in himself the will of the one who begat him (ἐν ἑαυτῷ φέρων τὸ θέλειν τοῦ γεγεννηκότος)," and thus had "experience of the thought of the Father (οὐκ ἄπειρος ... τῆς τοῦ πατρὸς ἐννοίας)." The real comparison with a human voice was the way in which the λόγος "contained in himself like a voice the Ideas conceived in the Father's mind (ὡς φωνὴν εἶχεν ἐν ἑαυτῷ τὰς ἐν τῷ πατρικῷ νῷ ἐννοηθείσας ἰδέας)." It was from these Ideas supplied by the Father's mind that the λόγος

---

insistence throughout *C.N.* (4, 7 and 13; 6, 1; 8, 1; 17, 45; 18, 1 and 10) as showing and emphasis on the equality of the human and divine in Jesus absent from *El.* I have not discussed these points of comparison in the text because they are consistent with either one or two authors quite apart from resting on an argument from silence. The theme of divinization (4) or the afterlife (5), particularly in view of the salvation through knowledge indicated by δι᾽ ἧς ἐπιγνώσεως ἐκφεύξεσθε...κ.τ.λ. (*El.* X, 33,2), would be quite compatible with the thesis that *El.* was addressed to a pagan audience and *C.N.* to conflicting groups within the Church, but equally compatible with the thesis that there were two authors. For the theory of two audiences see footnote 4 above and my grounds for rejection Frickel's version of it in 4A 2.1.1.

"completed each particular thing (τὸ κατὰ ἓν λόγος ἀπετέλει)" in the world
"that was pleasing to God (τὸ ἀρέσκον θεῷ)."[8]

At first glance there might appear to be a significant agreement between
the ἀπόδειξις ἀληθείας in *El.* and *C.N.* God begets the λόγος as his counsellor and fellow-workman (σύμβουλον καὶ ἐργάτην ἐγέννα λόγον), and as
the originator of what is coming into being (τῶν δὲ γινομένων ἀρχηγὸν), and
conceives the world (ὃν κόσμον ἐννοηθεὶς) before he makes it (10, 1 and 4).
There seems to that extent to be a certain parallelism of expression between
the two texts regarding λόγον πρῶτον ἐννοηθεὶς/ ὃν κόσμον ἐννοηθεὶς, τελεῖ/
ἀπετέλει, αἴτιον τοῖς γινομένοις/ τῶν δὲ γινομένων ἀρχηγὸν, ἀπογεννᾷ/
ἐγέννα and so on.

However further examination establishes some quite radical differences.
In *C.N.* 11, 2, as earlier mentioned (2A 3.1), the author is quite ready to call
the λόγος by the highly gnostic term νοῦς (οὗτος δὲ νοῦς), and to use the
notion foreign to the λόγος-Christology of the Fourth Gospel reminiscent of
aeon speculation. In *C.N.* 11, 1 the νοῦς-λόγος, as we saw, was conceived as
a single power that comes from the Father (δύναμις γὰρ μία ἡ ἐκ τοῦ παντός·
τὸ δὲ πᾶν Πατήρ, ἐξ οὗ δύναμις λόγος) since God, according to *C.N.* 10, 2,
though one, was indeed manifold (αὐτὸς δὲ μόνος ὢν πολὺς ἦν). Indeed, so
conscious was the author himself of his indebtedness to his adversaries for
this way of conceiving things that in *C.N.* 11, 3 he appealed to them as albeit
perversely supporting his fundamental assumption (see also 5B 3.1.2).

Now it is this way of conceiving the λόγος as νοῦς that is quite alien, I
submit, to the author of *El.* and would establish him as a different identity to
the author of *C.N.* quite apart from the addition of the Holy Spirit, not
wholly redundantly, by the latter. The λόγος-νοῦς is more depersonalized in
C.N. 11, 2 before the incarnation, and is only revealed (ἐδείκνυτο) as παῖς
θεοῦ when he "proceeds into the world (ὃς προβὰς ἐν κόσμῳ)," as we shall
emphasize further in the next section (4B). In *C.N.* 10,4 the λόγος-νοῦς is
"sent forth (προῆκεν)" by God to the creation as God's own sovereign (τῇ
κτίσει κύριον) previously visible to himself alone as his own mind (τὸν ἴδιον
νοῦν αὐτῷ μόνῳ πρότερον ὁρατὸν ὑπάρχοντα).

But as we saw, in *El.* X, 33,1-2 the pre-existent λόγος was a far more independent entity. His will is separate from the Father who begat him which
he nevertheless bears in agreement as the πρωτότοκος who is can be
described as ἐν ἑαυτῷ φέρων τὸ θέλειν τοῦ γεγεννηκότος. The personhood of

---

8 *El.* X, 33,1-2: οὗτος οὖν ὁ μόνος καὶ κατὰ πάντων θεὸς λόγον πρῶτον ἐννοηθεὶς
ἀπογεννᾷ· οὐ δὲ λόγον ὡς φωνήν, ἀλλ' ἐνδιάθετον τοῦ παντὸς λογισμόν. τοῦτον οὖν
μόνον ἐξ ὄντων ἐγέννα· τὸ γὰρ ὂν αὐτὸς ὁ πατὴρ ἦν, ἐξ οὗ τὸ γεννηθέν. καὶ αἴτιον τοῖς
γινομένοις λόγος ἦν, ἐν ἑαυτῷ φέρων τὸ θέλειν τοῦ γεγεννηκότος, οὐκ ἄπειρος τε ὢν
τῆς τοῦ πατρὸς ἐννοίας. ἅμα γὰρ τῷ ἐκ τοῦ γεννήσαντος προελθεῖν, πρωτότοκος
τούτου γενόμενος, ὡς φωνὴν εἶχεν ἐν ἑαυτῷ τὰς ἐν τῷ πατρικῷ νῷ ἐννοηθείσας ἰδέας·
ὅθεν κελεύοντος πατρὸς γίνεσθαι τὸν κόσμον, τὸ κατὰ ἓν λόγος ἀπετέλει τὸ ἀρέσκον
θεῷ.

the Stoic λογισμὸς ἐνδιάθετος, who contains the Platonic τὰς ἐν τῷ πατρικῷ νῷ ἐννοηθείσας ἰδέας, is guaranteed by the fact that the λόγος is not in fact the νοῦς of the Father but a person who can experience and know nevertheless the Father's mind completely as οὐκ ἄπειρος... τῆς τοῦ πατρὸς ἐννοίας. He cannot be simply the Father's voice and therefore as such inseparable from him. The Father's voice is that of another person he has within himself and is therefore quite separate from himself (λόγον ὡς φωνὴν εἶχεν ἐν ἑαυτῷ).

The author of C.N. 10,4 is to the contrary quite prepared to acknowledge the relationship between the pre-incarnate λόγος and the Father as an uttered voice (πρότεραν φωνὴν φθεγγόμενος καὶ φῶς ἐκ φωτὸς γεννῶν, προῆκεν τῇ κτίσει κύριον τὸν ἴδιον νοῦν), inseparable in such a form from himself. We see here that the λόγος is far more an instrument of the Father's will than separate in his own right, though congruent in will, as represented in El. X, 33,2. The νοῦς is described as ἴδιος and is clearly under his direct control.[9] Although both works are self-conscious about the charge of ditheism, in depersonalising the λόγος, and reducing its will from that of an agent to an instrument, it is arguable that C.N. 10,4 and 11, 1 has gone further in accommodating Monarchian objections than El., as we shall now see.

4A 1.2. C.N.'s accommodation of El. with the Monarchians

Zephyrinus' original charge against the author in El. IX, 11,3 had been: "ἐγὼ οἶδα ἕνα θεὸν Χριστὸν Ἰησοῦν, καὶ πλὴν αὐτοῦ ἕτερον οὐδένα γεννητὸν καὶ παθητόν," but insisted in a way that the writer thought to be contradictory that: "οὐχ ὁ πατὴρ ἀπέθανεν, ἀλλὰ ὁ υἱός." When the author denied the latter, Zephyrinus replied by calling him and his circle "ditheists" (διθέους). Callistus himself, after Zephyrinus' death, re-expressed the doctrine as:

> The λόγος was himself the Son (τὸν λόγον αὐτὸν εἶναι υἱόν), himself also the Father (αὐτὸν καὶ πατέρα), being called by name "Son and Father" (ὀνόματι μὲν υἱὸν καὶ πατέρα καλούμενον), but they are one thing (ἓν δὲ ὄντα), the indivisible Spirit (τὸ πνεῦμα τὸ ἀδιαίρετον). For the Father is not one thing (οὐ γὰρ ἄλλο μὲν εἶναι πατέρα), and the Son another thing (ἄλλο δὲ υἱόν), but they subsist as one and the same Spirit (ἓν δὲ καὶ τὸ αὐτὸ πνεῦμα ὑπάρχειν)... and that which was enfleshed in the Virgin (καὶ εἶναι τὸ ἐν τῇ παρθένῳ σαρκωθὲν) was not a different Spirit alongside the Father (πνεῦμα οὐχ ἕτερον παρὰ τὸν πατέρα),[10] but one and the same thing (ἀλλὰ ἓν καὶ τὸ αὐτό). And this was what was said: "Do you not believe that I am in the Father and the Father in me." For that which is seen (τὸ μὲν γὰρ βλεπόμενον), because it is human (ὅπερ ἐστὶν ἄνθρωπος), this is the Son (τοῦτο εἶναι τὸν υἱόν), but that Spirit which is

---

[9] C.N. 10, 3-4: ὅτε ἠθέλησαν, καθὼς ἠθέλησεν, ἔδειξεν τὸν λόγον... δι᾽ οὗ τὰ πάντα ἐποίησεν. ὅτε μὲν θέλει, ποιεῖ...πάντα γὰρ τὰ γενόμενα διὰ λόγου καὶ σοφίας τεχνάζεται.. ἐποίησεν οὖν ὡς ἠθέλησεν· θεὸς γὰρ ἦν.

[10] I have resisted the temptation to translate πνεῦμα with τὸ ἐν τῇ παρθένῳ σαρκωθεν and the following οὐχ ἕτερον as masculine accusative so as to be translated: "...the Spirit which was enfleshed was not a different person etc." though this is possible and would further substantiate my interpretation here.

contained in the Son (τὸ δὲ ἐν τῷ υἱῷ χωρηθὲν πνεῦμα), this is the Father (τοῦτο εἶναι τὸν πατέρα). For I will not call them, he says, two Gods, Father and Son (δύο θεούς, πατέρα καὶ υἱὸν), but one (ἀλλ᾽ ἕνα). For the Father existing of himself (ὁ γὰρ ἐξ ἑαυτοῦ γενόμενος πατήρ), took in addition human flesh (προσλαβόμενος τὴν σάρκα) and made it divine (ἐθεοποίησεν), and uniting it with himself (αὐτὴν ἑνώσας ἑαυτῷ) he made it one (καὶ ἐποίησεν ἕν), so that the Father and the Son are called one God (ὡς καλεῖσθαι πατέρα καὶ υἱὸν ἕνα θεόν). And this, being one person (καὶ τοῦτο ἕν ὂν πρόσωπον), cannot be two (μὴ δύνασθαι εἶναι δύο), and in this way the Father suffered with the Son (καὶ οὕτως τὸν πατέρα συμπεπονθέναι τῷ υἱῷ)

El. IX, 12,16-19[11]

Thus we see that Callistus, like the author of *C.N.*, cannot attribute a separate will to the Son, since the Son is simply the Father after the incarnation (προσλαβόμενος τὴν σάρκα, αὐτὴν ἑνώσας ἑαυτῷ καὶ ἐποίησεν ἕν). He is the Spirit of the Father made visible (τὸ μὲν γὰρ βλεπόμενον), so that he can only be one person (καὶ τοῦτο ἕν ὂν πρόσωπον). Such a view of the incarnation the writer of *El.* clearly rejects in his view that the λόγος before the incarnation was a full person, not simply, as we have already seen, because he is described as ἐν ἑαυτῷ φέρων τὸ θέλειν τοῦ γεγεννηκότος with personal experience of the divine mind (οὐκ ἄπειρος...τῆς τοῦ πατρὸς ἐννοίας), but because as πρωτότοκος he possessed full personality before the incarnation.

It is however precisely this full personality that *C.N.* 11, 1-2 denies. Not only is the λόγος simply the Father's νοῦς or δύναμις and not a separate person with knowledge of that mind, but he is not revealed (ἐδείκνυτο) as παῖς θεοῦ before his procession into the world (ὃς προβὰς ἐν κόσμῳ). It is for this reason—quite different from *El.* who simply regards the charge of ditheism as self-evidently false—that *C.N.* claims he cannot therefore be charged with believing in two Gods. The λόγος ἄσαρκος as we have seen was a power and not a complete person, and asserted as such specifically in the context of the refutation of ditheism.[12]

In this respect *C.N.* appears closer to the view of Callistus who believed that before the incarnation the Son was simply the Father's Spirit, and could only become Son when able to be seen (τὸ μὲν γὰρ βλεπόμενον). In respect of the ἕν... πρόσωπον, *C.N.* 14, 2-3 (4A 3.2.2) he thus clearly differs from Callistus in asserting δύο or even τρία πρόσωπα. Thus the theology of *C.N.* is not so much an agreement with that of Callistus' monarchianism but a *rapprochement* with it. The unique theological solution of the author of *C.N.*

---

[11] Callistus' doctrine is summarized in identical terms in *El.* X, 27,3-4. See 7C 2.3.1 for a further discussion of these passages in connection with the Christology of Tertullian.

[12] *C.N.* 11, 1: καὶ οὕτως αὐτῷ παρίστατο ἕτερος. ἕτερον δὲ λέγων οὐ δύο θεοὺς λέγω, ἀλλ᾽ ὡς φῶς ἐκ φωτὸς... ἢ ὡς ἀκτῖνα ἀπὸ ἡλίου. δύναμις γὰρ μία ἡ ἐκ τοῦ παντός· τὸ δὲ πᾶν Πατήρ, ἐξ οὗ δύναμις λόγος.

to the problems of ditheism laid at the door of the author of *El.* can best be seen in the unique use of the concept of οἰκονομία in *C.N.*

4A 1.3. οἰκονομία *in C.N. as the mystery of the Trinity*

The use of οἰκονομία is mentioned as a heretical concept in connection with the Marcosans in *El.* VI, 47,1 and 3; 51,1 and 4-5; 52,9. It is not however used in any orthodox sense in the ἀπόδειξις ἀληθείας in X, 32-34, and is particularly absent there from the discussion of the godhead (X, 33, 10-17). Thus the use of the term marks a fundamental contrast in the theologies of the two works, since clearly it has no importance to *El.* save as an exposed heretical concept, but is central to orthodoxy as *C.N.* understands matters.

In *C.N.* οἰκονομία emerges as a central theme in Hippolytus' theology, uniquely reformulated in response to the author's own apologetic requirements.[13] It represents the mystery of the godhead by means of which the oneness of God is not denied by affirming two or three persons. In other words the term is central to Hippolytus' reconciliation with the theology of the school of Callistus in *C.N.* (4A 1.2), and in the following passages:

(i) *C.N.* 3,4: τίς γὰρ οὐκ ἐρεῖ ἕνα θεὸν εἶναι; ἀλλ' οὐ τὴν οἰκονομίαν ἀναιρήσει; Here Noetus is charged with destroying the mystery of the godhead and thus failing to see that God can be one and yet two or three.

(ii) *C.N.* 4,5: ἐν τίνι δὲ ὁ θεὸς ἀλλ' ἢ ἐν Χριστῷ 'Ιησοῦ τῷ πατρῴῳ λόγῳ καὶ τῷ μυστηρίῳ τῆς οἰκονομίας; Christ therefore remains in mystery separate but one in the paternal λόγος. The λόγος was thus πατρῷος both for Callistus in *El.* IX, 12,16-19 (4A 1.2) and for Hippolytus in *C.N.* 4,5 and 10.

(iii) *C.N.* 4, 7 where the Father in the Son is the μυστήριον οἰκονομίας in which both remain different but one through the incarnation (σεσαρκωμένου τοῦ λόγου καὶ ἐνανθρωπήσαντος), as in 4,8 (μυστήριον οἰκονομίας ἐκ πνεύματος ἁγίου ἦν οὗτος ὁ λόγος καὶ παρθένου ἕνα υἱὸν θεῷ ἀπεργασάμενος). We find in this assertion of what Callistus affirmed according to *El.* X, 27,4 (τοῦτον οὖν τὸν λόγον ὃν ἕνα εἶναι θεὸν ὀνομάζει, καὶ σεσαρκῶσθαι λέγει).[14]

(iv) *C.N.* 8,2 (κατὰ οἰκονομίαν ἡ ἐπίδειξις) uses the term once more applied to a nascent trinitarian definition, as also in 14,2 (πρόσωπα δύο, οἰκονομίαν τε τρίτην) and 14,4, (οἰκονομία συμφωνίας συνάγεται εἰς ἕνα θεόν).

(v) *C.N.* 16,3 replies to an objection of incomprehension (ἀλλ' ἐρεῖς μοι, πῶς γεγέννηται) regarding *Jn.* 16,27 and Hippolytus' commentary in which, in 16,2, τὸ ἐξῆλθον= λόγος= πνεῦμα... ἐξ αὐτοῦ γεννηθὲν. His reply is in terms of "mysterious plan" (τὴν περὶ τοῦτον οἰκονομίαν ἀκριβῶς ἐξειπεῖν οὐ δύνασαι). The author of *El.* had reflected the explanation of unity in the godhead in terms of πνεῦμα γεννηθὲν in his attack on the Callistian notion of τὸ πνεῦμα τὸ ἀδιαίρετον in *El.* IX, 12,16 (4A 1.2).

---

[13] M. Simonetti, Aggiornamento su Ippolito, in *StEphAug* 30 (1989), p. 91: "questo termine rappresentava una notevole innovazione terminologica di *C.N.*, in quanto questa parola, già in uso in accezione cristologica, viene qui adoperata a significare l'articolazione trinitaria della divinità in senso antimonarchiano."

[14] For a discussion of this passage in connection with Tertullian's theology, see 7 C 2.3.1

Thus particularly from (ii) (iii) and (v) we begin to see that Noetus is not regarded as speaking for Callistus, but the extreme Monarchians. We have in each case a *rapprochement* with the theology of Callistus attacked in *El.* (4A 1.2).

Consequently the very real differences between *C.N.* and *El.* extends further than the addition, or putative addition, of often redundant additions of the Holy Spirit to a binitarian pair on the part of the former. That addition is accompanied by a reconceptualizing of the problem of ditheism in terms of a new technical use of the term οἰκονομία, in a form that Callistus could have acknowledged as partly his own. The differences affect the pre-incarnate, ontological status of the λόγος ἄσαρκος himself or itself. We shall now show that the relationship between the binitarian differences and those regarding the incarnate and pre-incarnate λόγος–παῖς is not purely contingent. The characterization of the latter logically follows from the assumptions regarding the status of the pre-incarnate λόγος ἄσαρκος. Let us now explore these λόγος–παῖς Christologies in greater detail.

4A 2. παῖς θεοῦ *and the incarnation*

To be Son required, according to Callistus, being human at the same time (ὅπερ ἐστὶν ἄνθρωπος τοῦτο εἶναι τὸν υἱὸν) so that before the incarnation the λόγος was still the Spirit of the Father (τὸ δὲ ἐν τῷ υἱῷ χωρηθὲν πνεῦμα, τοῦτο εἶναι τὸν πατέρα). *El.* X, 33,11 directly contradicts any such lack of personality to the pre-existent λόγος when the author speaks of ὁ λόγος τοῦ θεοῦ, ὁ πρωτόγονος πατρὸς παῖς, ἡ πρὸ ἑωσφόρου φωσφόρος φωνή. The author of *C.N.* in contrast with *El.* is making therefore a fundamental *rapprochement* with the theology of Callistus when he claims:

(i) Christ was only "Son" in any complete sense (τέλειος υἱός) by the action of the Spirit on the Virgin, since as λόγος ἄσαρκος he lacked that completeness. He is therefore called υἱὸς ἀνθρώπου, (*Dan.* 7,13) not because of what he was in any pre-existent state, but because of what he was in the future to become.[15] Were this not the case, then the flesh of the pre-existent Son of Man would have to have been in heaven (*C.N.* 4,11), and this would make nonsense of the incarnation.[16] The language of *Ps.* 109,3, found in *El.* X, 33,11, is repeated in *C.N.* 16, 7 (ἐκ γαστρὸς πρὸ ἑωσφόρου ἐξεγέννησά σε) but its pre-incarnational significance is denied. It is a prophecy only for the future and does not describe a reality present before the incarnation.[17] The λόγος could only become complete Son therefore through the

---

15 *C.N.* 4, 10-13: μήτι ἐρεῖ ὅτι ἐν οὐρανῷ σὰρξ ἦν; ἔστιν μὲν οὖν σὰρξ ἡ ὑπὸ τοῦ λόγου τοῦ πατρῴου προσενεχθεῖσα δῶρον, ἡ ἐκ πνεύματος καὶ παρθένου τέλειος Υἱὸς θεοῦ ἀποδεδειγμένος. πρόδηλον οὖν ὅτι αὐτὸς ἑαυτὸν προσέφερεν τῷ Πατρί. πρὸ δὲ τούτου ἐν οὐρανῷ σὰρξ οὐκ ἦν. τίς οὖν ἦν ἐν οὐρανῷ ἀλλ' ἢ λόγος ἄσαρκος... ὃς τὸ κοινὸν ὄνομα καὶ παρὰ ἀνθρώποις χωρητὸν ἀνελάμβανεν εἰς ἑαυτόν, τοῦτο καλούμενος ἀπ' ἀρχῆς, υἱὸς ἀνθρώπου, διὰ τὸ μέλλον, καίτοι μήπω ὢν ἄνθρωπος.

16 For attempts to read *C.N.* 4,11 in the light of later Apollinariansim, which ignore the significance of such an issue in the early third century debate between Callistus and the author of *El.*, see the discussion in 4 A 3.1.3.2.

17 *C.N.* 16, 7: καθὼς διὰ τοῦ προφήτου τὴν τοῦ λόγου γέννησιν σημαίνων ὅτι γεγέννηται, τὸ δὲ πῶς φυλάσσει καιρῷ ὡρισμένῳ παρ' αὐτῷ μέλλων ἀποκαλύπτειν.

taking of flesh.[18] Indeed, *Ant.* 3 makes this point clear beyond one would have thought any controversy when it speaks of ὁ τοῦ θεοῦ παῖς, ὁ πάλαι μὲν λόγος ὤν, νυνὶ δὲ καὶ ἄνθρωπος δι᾽ ὑμᾶς φανερωθείς.

(ii) The reference of *Bar.* 3,36 to Jacob as παῖς and ἠγαπημένος, as revealed by *Mt.* 17,5, is a type of Christ only in so far as "the perfect Israel (ὁ τέλειος ᾿Ισραήλ) and the true Jacob (ὁ ἀληθινὸς Ἰακώβ) afterwards (μετὰ ταῦτα) was seen on earth (ἐπὶ τῆς γῆς ὤφθη) and conversed amongst men (καὶ τοῖς ἀνθρώποις συνανεστράφη)." "Israel" means "man seeing God," and this can refer only to "the servant and perfect man (μόνος ὁ παῖς καὶ τέλειος ἄνθρωπος) and the one who declared the will of the Father," in accordance with *Jn.* 1, 18 (*C.N.* 5, 2-5).

(iii) To regard the λόγος as υἱός τοῦ ἀνθρώπου or παῖς before the incarnation would imply that these terms could be applied simply figuratively or metaphorically (κατὰ τροπήν) to the λόγος. If this were possible before the incarnation, then it might be possible that the incarnation too could be regarded as an appearance (κατὰ φαντασίαν) and not a reality (ἀληθῶς γενόμενος ἄνθρωπος).[19] This would clearly leave open the gate to a docetic Christology that the author of *C.N.* 18 wishes clearly to close, since in that long concluding section he stresses every scene of Christ's physical humanity in the Gospels. By contrast, *El.* points briefly to Christ's human experiences in order to demonstrate the ability of fallen humanity to imitate Christ's teaching since Christ bore that humanity.[20]

We must therefore emphasize that, irrespective of whether references to the Holy Spirit are interpolations or afterthoughts or whatever, which we are still to consider, and even if in consequence both *C.N.* and *El.* are binitarian, the character of that binitarianism is radically different between the two works. The crux is the extent to which they differ over the nature of a pre-existent Christ before the incarnation, and in consequence, over the character of the incarnation itself. For the former the pre-existent λόγος is a complete person, with his own will that nevertheless knows and concords with that of the Father. For the latter the refutation of what Callistus had described as ditheism rests on the denial of complete personality before the incarnation to what is but the πατρῷος λόγος (*C.N.* 4, 5 and 10; 14, 7; 17, 4) or πατρῴα δύναμις, ὅ ἐστιν λόγος (11, 4; 16, 1).

It is furthermore important to point out that between *El.* and *C.N.* this affirmation or denial of complete personality to the pre-existent λόγος marks a

---

[18] Ibid. 15, 6- 16, 2: ποῖον οὖν Ὑιὸν ἑαυτοῦ ὁ θεὸς διὰ τῆς σαρκὸς κατέπεμψεν ἀλλ᾽ ἢ τὸν λόγον, ὃν Ὑιὸν προσηγόρευε διὰ τὸ μέλλειν αὐτὸν γενέσθαι; ... οὔτε γὰρ ἄσαρκος καὶ καθ᾽ ἑαυτὸν ὁ λόγος τέλειός ἦν Ὑιός, καίτοι τέλειος, λόγος ὤν, μονογενής· οὐθ᾽ ἡ σὰρξ καθ᾽ ἑαυτὴν δίχα τοῦ λόγου ὑποστῆναι ἠδύνατο διὰ τὸ ἐν λόγῳ τὴν σύστασιν ἔχειν. οὕτως οὖν εἰς Ὑιὸς τέλειος θεοῦ ἐφανερώθη... ἡ δύναμις ἡ πατρῴα, ὅ ἐστιν λόγος, ἀπ᾽ οὐρανοῦ κατῆλθεν καὶ οὐκ αὐτὸς ὁ Πατήρ.

[19] *C.N.* 17, 5: οὗτος προελθὼν εἰς κόσμον θεὸς ἐνσώματος ἐφανερώθη, ἄνθρωπος τέλειος προελθών· οὐ γὰρ κατὰ φαντασίαν ἢ τροπὴν ἀλλὰ ἀληθῶς γενόμενος ἄνθρωπος.

[20] *El.* X, 33,16-17: τοῦτον ἄνθρωπον ἴσμεν ἐκ τοῦ καθ᾽ ἡμᾶς φυράματος γεγονότα· εἰ γὰρ μὴ ἐκ τοῦ αὐτοῦ ἡμῖν φυράματος ὑπῆρξε, μάτην νομοθετεῖ μιμεῖσθαι τὸν διδάσκαλον. εἰ γὰρ ἐκεῖνος ὁ ἄνθρωπος ἑτέρας ἐτύγχανεν οὐσίας, τί τὰ ὅμοια κελεύει ἐμοί, τῷ ἀσθενεῖ πεφυκότι, καὶ πῶς οὗτος ἀγαθὸς καὶ δίκαιος; ἀλλ᾽ ἵνα δὴ μὴ ἕτερος παρ᾽ ἡμᾶς νομισθῇ, καὶ κάματον ὑπέμεινε, καὶ πεινῆν ἠθέλησε, καὶ διψῆν οὐκ ἠρνήσατο, καὶ ὕπνῳ ἠρέμησε, καὶ πάθει οὐκ ἀντεῖπε, καὶ θανάτῳ ὑπήκουσε, καὶ ἀνάστασιν ἐφανέρωσεν...

parting of the ways in terms of the patristic tradition that preceded these two works, as we must now examine in detail.

4A 2.1. *Pre-existence in Justin, Theophilus and Irenaeus*

Justin Martyr attributes full personality to the λόγος before the incarnation who is described in *Dial.* 45,4 as τὸν Χριστὸν τοῦτον τοῦ θεοῦ υἱόν ὃς καὶ πρὸ ἑωσφόρου καὶ σελήνης ἦν. In Theophilus of Antioch we find the writer amongst his predecessors closest to the theology of *El.* in his use of term λόγος ἐνδιάθετος. Although, in a way reminiscent of *C.N.* 10,3 and 16,4, the λόγος is thus called ἀρχή, σοφία, and δύναμις by Theophilus nevertheless he shows by contrast with the latter the non-instrumental sense in which he uses these terms when he speaks of God as "holding the immanent λόγος in his own bowels (ἔχων οὖν ὁ θεὸς τὸν ἑαυτου λόγον ἐνδιάθετον ἐν τοῖς ἰδίοις σπλάγχοις)" and claims that "he begat him... before the universe (ἐγέννησεν αὐτὸν... πρὸ τῶν ὅλων)."[21] Thus the personalized ἐν τοῖς ἰδίοις σπλάγχοις shows Theophilus' personalized conception of the pre-existent λόγος, in conformity with the imagery derived from *Psalm* 109,3-4, in which according to Justin the begetting of the λόγος from the paternal womb (ἐκ γαστρὸς γεννηθήσεσθαι) took place before creation (πρὸ ἡλίου καὶ σελήνης = πρὸ ἑωσφόρου), in contrast with that from the Virgin's womb in time.[22]

The *El.*-block has therefore the support of the earlier Fathers such as Justin Martyr in claiming complete personhood for the λόγος. For Justin generally the pre-existent λόγος had a quasi-human "form" (μορφή) or "image" (εἰκών) as the "angel of the Lord" that as such was humanly comprehensible, and in which he appeared (ἐφάνη) to Moses and the prophets. The παῖς and υἱός have a complete pre-existence and are more than δύναμις or πνεῦμα. Justin's λόγος appears (φανέντα) to Joshua as the "captain of the Lord's host" in human form (ἀνθρώπου μορφῇ).[23]

---

[21] In Theophilus of Antioch, *Aut.* 1, 7 we find σοφία used instrumentally and not personally (ὁ θεὸς διὰ τοῦ λόγου αὐτοῦ καὶ τῆς σοφίας ἐποίησε τὰ πάντα... «ὁ θεὸς τῇ σοφίᾳ ἐθεμελίωσε τὴν γῆν.» as also in 2, 18 («ποίησωμεν ἄνθρωπον κατ᾽ εἰκόνα καὶ καθ᾽ ὁμοίωσιν.» οὐκ ἄλλῳ δέ τινι εἴρηκε ποιήσωμεν, ἀλλ᾽ ἢ τῷ ἑαυτοῦ λόγῳ καὶ τῇ ἑαυτοῦ σοφίᾳ). But the λόγος is clearly personified in 2, 10: ἔχων οὖν ὁ θεὸς τὸν ἑαυτου λόγον ἐνδιάθετον ἐν τοῖς ἰδίοις σπλάγχοις, ἐγέννησεν αὐτὸν μετὰ τῆς ἑαυτοῦ σοφίας ἐξερευξάμενος πρὸ τῶν ὅλων. τοῦτον τὸν λόγον ἔσχεν ὑπουργὸν τῶν ὑπ᾽ αὐτοῦ γεγενημένων, καὶ δι᾽ αὐτοῦ τὰ πάντα πεποίηκεν. οὗτος λέγεται ἀρχή ὅτι ἄρχει καὶ κυριεύει πάντων τῶν δι᾽ αὐτοῦ δεδημιουργημένων. οὗτος οὖν, ὢν πνεῦμα θεοῦ, καὶ ἀρχὴ καὶ σοφία, καὶ δύναμις ὑψίστου κατήρχετο εἰς τοὺς προφήτας...

[22] Justin, *Dial.* 63,3: καὶ τὰ ὑπὸ Δαβὶδ εἰρημένα· «ἐν ταῖς λαμπρότησι τῶν ἁγίων σου ἐκ γαστρὸς πρὸ ἑωσφόρου ἐγέννησά σε.»(=Ps. 109, 3-4) which is almost wholly repeated in 83,4. Cf. also 76,7: καὶ Δαβὶδ δὲ πρὸ ἡλίου καὶ σελήνης ἐκ γαστρὸς γεννηθήσεσθαι αὐτὸν κατὰ τὴν τοῦ Πατρὸς βουλὴν ἐκήρυξε. Cf. also Meletius, *Hom. Pasc.* 82.

[23] Ibid. 61: μαρτύριον δὲ καὶ ἄλλο ὑμῖν... δώσω, ὅτι ἀρχὴν πρὸ πάντων τῶν κτισμάτων ὁ θεὸς γεγέννηκε δύναμίν τινα ἐξ᾽ ἑαυτοῦ λογικήν, ἥτις καὶ δόξα κυρίου ὑπὸ τοῦ πνεύματος τοῦ ἁγίου καλεῖται, ποτὲ δὲ υἱός, ποτὲ δὲ σοφία, ποτὲ δὲ ἄγγελος, ποτὲ δὲ θεός, ποτὲ δὲ κύριος καὶ λόγος· ποτὲ δὲ ἀρχιστράτηγον ἑαυτὸν λέγει, ἐν ἀνθρώπου μορφῇ φανέντα τῷ τοῦ Ναυῆ Ἰησοῦ. See also 62.

Moreover, in Justin *Dialog.* 1,63 we read that the Son is λόγος πρωτότοκος ὢν τοῦ θεοῦ... πρότερον διὰ τῆς τοῦ πυρὸς μορφῆς καὶ εἰκόνος
ἀσωμάτου τῷ Μωϋσεῖ καὶ τοῖς ἑτέροις προφήταις ἐφάνη. Though prophets
speak under the influence of the pre-existent λόγος in the *C.N.* block, the
pre-existent λόγος is never described as appearing to them in this way. To
Jeremiah, he was the shadowy ἐμφανὴς ὁ λόγος ἐσόμενος. (*C.N.* 13, 2)

It is not only in Theophilus and Justin but also in Irenaeus that we find the
fragmentary images from which *El.* has constructed his personalized picture
of the pre-existent λόγος which forms so marked a contrast with what, before
the incarnation, is the instrumental λόγος–σοφία–νοῦς in *C.N.* As with the
former two writers, so in places Irenaeus treats the *Verbum* and *Sapientia* in
a purely instrumental fashion[24] But he goes beyond pure instrumentality
when he equates, as *C.N.* never does, the pre-existent λόγος as *Filius*, who,
as both his "offspring" (*sua progenies*) and his "likeness" (*figuratio sua*),
"spoke in human form (*in figura locutus est humana*) to Abraham and to
Moses." The *Verbum* and *Sapientia* thus personified are inseparable from
Filius, and Irenaeus equates *Sapientia* with *Spiritus* and *Verbum* with Son in
such phrases as *Filius, qui est Verbum Dei, id est Filius et Spiritus Sanctus,
Verbum et Sapientia* to whom as *ministerium* in creation (*ministerio ad
fabricationem*) were subject all the angels (*quibus serviunt et subjecti sunt
omnes angeli*).[25] We shall return to the place of the Holy Spirit in pre-
Hippolytan patristic theology in 4A 3. For the moment we simply note that
C.N. has self-consciously turned away from the development of the non-
instrumental and personal conception of the λόγος thus represented in the
works of Justin, Theophilus, and Irenaeus, no less than in *El.*[26]

Thus the description of the pre-existent λόγος "administering all these
things (ταῦτα δὲ πάντα διῴκει)" before the incarnation as ὁ πρωτόγονος
πατρὸς παῖς, ἡ πρὸ ἑωσφόρου φωσφόρος φωνή, is no mere rhetorical flourish.
Rather it is a deep-seated part of the texture and pattern of the author's

---

[24] Irenaeus, *Adv. Haer.*, III, 24,2: "... plasmavit et insufflationem vitae insufflavit in eis et
per conditionem nutrit nos, Verbo suo confirmans, et Sapientia compingens omnia." See also
IV, 24,1: "esse autem huius Verbum eius, per quem constituit omnia."

[25] Ibid. IV, 7,4: "Propter hoc Judaei excesserunt a Deo, Verbum eius non recipientes, sed
putantes per seipsum Patrem sine Verbo, id est sine Filio, posse cognoscere. Deum nescientes
eum qui in figura locutus est humana ad Abraham, et iterum ad Moysem [Exod. 3, 7-8]... Haec
enim Filius, qui est Verbum Dei, ab initio praestruebat, non indigente Patre angelis... neque
rursus indigente ministerio ad fabricationem eorum... sed habente copiosum et inenarrabile
ministerium. Ministrat enim ei ad omnia sua progenies et figuratio sua, id est Filius et Spiritus
sanctus, Verbum et Sapientia, quibus serviunt et subjecti sunt omnes angeli." cf also IV, 20,1.
See also IV, 20,3 (cited by P. Nautin, *Hippolyte, Contra les hérésies, fragment. Étude et édition
critique*, (Paris: Les Éditions du Cerf 1949) as IV, 34,3 in note 1 p. 160): "Et quoniam Verbum,
id est Filius, semper cum Patre erat, per multa demonstravimus. Quoniam autem et Sapientia,
quae est Spiritus, erat apud eum ante omnem constitutionem, per Salomonem ait, "Deus
sapientia fundavit terram, paravit autem caelum prudentia. (*Prov.* 3,19)"

[26] It will be clear that I must therefore dissent from Nautin's judgement that in *C.N.* 10, 2-4
that "Hippolyte se réclamait expressément de l'évêque de Lyon, elle a certainement ici le même
sense que dans l'*Adversus haereses*, où nous lisons... [IV,34,3]." (Nautin (1949) p. 159-169 ff.

Christology, shared with Justin, Theophilus, and Irenaeus, that clearly differs from *C.N.* The writer of the latter has clearly negated the development of λόγος, πνεῦμα, and σοφία from an instrumental function to a personalized role. The two writers belong to the same school, and therefore it is no wonder that certain surface similarities will hold between them, which must not be allowed to mask these deep-seated differences.

Frickel originally argued for two writers, but then, in what may be described as his second position argued on the basis of such similarities for a common authorship. Most recently he has admitted that the claim that *El.* and *C.N.* are by the same author is quite impossible. In consequence, he has produced, as his third position, the thesis that *C.N.* is not simply a work with occasional interpolations, but is rather a pseudonymous work produced by means of quite radical interpolations into a small, genuinely Hippolytan core, which reflected the controversy between the followers of Apollinaris of Laodicaea and those of Marcellus of Ancyra.[27] We shall for the moment consider (4A 2.1.1) Frickel's earlier argument that (1) the differences can be overcome by postulating a difference of audience for the two works, and (2) the λόγος–παῖς theologies of the two works can be so reconciled as to make them part of the mind of a single author. We shall reserve the consideration of his more recent argument for a later section (4A 3.1.3.2).

4A 2.1.1. *Frickel and the two audiences*

It is impossible to claim that the differences in the binitarianism of the two works, or indeed additionally the trinitarianism of *C.N.*, is explicable, as Frickel's argument requires, on grounds that *El.* is addressed to a pagan, philosophical audience but *C.N.* to a Monarchian group within the Church.[28] Firstly, the *Logostheologie* of *C.N.*, which we argued (2A 3.1-3.2) and shall argue further (5B 3.1.2), was a fundamental part of the common Stoic/Platonic intellectual backcloth of both paganism and Christianity. Furthermore, it represented, in the form that it appears in *C.N.*, a far more radical a *rapprochement* with that paganism than that in which it appears in *El.* The doctrine of the λόγος, therefore, whether in *El.* or in *C.N.*, was equally of relevance to an inner-Church as well as to a pagan audience. Its relation with the supreme God, whether as one or as many aeons or emanations, was of interest and concern equally within the Church as without. It was Callistus in an inner-Church context that called the author of *El.* IX, 11,3 διθέους and not τριθέους which would have been the case if the former had any developed view of the role of the Holy Spirit in a Trinity.

---

27 Frickel (1993) p. 120-121.
28 Frickel (1988) p. 201: "Er tritt [*C.N.* VII, 1] also als Lehrer unter seinen Mitbrüdern auf, bei denen er für seine Logostheologie wirbt. Aber... wendet sich Hippolyt dabei zugleich *gegen eine innerkirchliche modalistische Theologie*, die Vater und Sohn nicht als zwei verschiedene Personen unterscheidet und sich dafür unter anderem auf Joh 10,30 beruft."

Secondly I have showed in my exposition that the arguments of Callistus' oponents within the Church (*El.* IX, 12,16-19) reveal a λόγος–παῖς Christology, reflected in *El.* X, 33,11, that equally with that of *C.N.* 10 is directed *gegen eine innerkirchliche modalistische Theologie*. Frickel may have convincingly shown against Nautin that the apologetic focus of *El.* X, 31-32 must indicate a work directed at a pagan audience.[29] The Chaldeans, Egyptians, and Greeks—"... these nations who investigate the nature of wisdom (ταῦτα τὰ περὶ σοφίαν ἠσχολημένα ἔθνη)"—"came after those who worshipped the truly existing God (μεταγενέστερα ὄντα τῶν θεὸν σεβασάντων)."[30] Thus the true wisdom of the Greeks must have come from the far older race.

Such was a very common apologetic argument for commending Christianity to paganism. But those versed in the true wisdom of the Greeks found their interest and their understanding converging with those within the Church when the inner-Church controversy was over the relationship between the λόγος–παῖς to the Father within the unity of the godhead. The very language and philosophy of the conflict was set in the forms of late Hellenistic religious speculation which was in a high state of development in becoming the common culture of both paganism and Christianity.

Frickel has laboured therefore to no purpose in endeavouring to show that *El.* is poorly and haphazardly constructed, but that Books I-IX are addressed to the internal concerns of the Christian community whereas Book X changes focus to direct its attention to a pagan audience.[31] I have shown that the λόγος–παῖς theology of the ἀπόδειξις ἀληθείας (*El.* X, 33,1-2) is consistent against *C.N.* with the defence of binitarianism in Book IX, and that

---

[29] Frickel (1988) p. 134-146.

[30] *El.* X, 30,6-31,1: ... Νῶε. ἐφ᾽ οὗ ὁ κατὰ πάντα τὸν κόσμον γίνεται κατακλυσμός, οὗ οὔτε Αἰγύπτιοι οὔτε Χαλδαῖοι οὔτε ῞Ελληνες μέμνηνται— ὧν κατὰ τόπους ὅ τε ἐπὶ τοῦ ᾽Ωρύγου καὶ ὁ ἐπὶ τοῦ Δευκαλίωνος γεγένηνται κατακλυσμοὶ—...ἐνιδεῖν οὖν ἔστι τοῖς φιλοπόνως ἱστορεῖν βουλομένοις, ὡς φανερῶς ἐπιδέδεικται τὸ τῶν θεοσεβῶν γένος ἀρχαιότερον ὂν πάντων Χαλδαίων, Αἰγυπτίων, ῾Ελλήνων... ἀλλ᾽ ἐπεὶ οὐκ ἄλογον ἐδόκει ἐπιδεῖξαι ταῦτα τὰ περὶ σοφίαν ἠσχολημένα ἔθνη μεταγενέστερα ὄντα τῶν θεὸν σεβασάντων, εὔλογον κρίνομεν νῦν εἰπεῖν καὶ πόθεν τὸ γένος αὐτοῖς...

[31] Frickel (1988) p. 125-134 claims that the dispute with Callistus concludes Books I-IX as a work directed to those within the Church, since the emphasis is to show that heresy derives from Greek Philosophy and ultimately from the Naasenes, and not from the Apostolic Succession. But in X, 9-29 this method of refutation by derivation is no longer deployed, but the Greek philosophers are instead simply regarded as ignorant, and the apologetic focus to which I have drawn attention is adopted instead. Although the disorganised character of *El.* raises its own problems, I do not believe that they are resolvable in terms of a clear-cut distinction between the presentation of the λόγος–παῖς within the community, and that externally. Certainly my argument that *C.N.* represents a *rapprochement* with the position of Callistus in *El.* IX, 12,16-19, demonstrates that *C.N.* is a work written after the time of *El.* with the consequence that *El.* cannot be regarded, as Frickel wishes, as the last work of Hippolytus, left in an incomplete and disarranged form, by his arrest and deportation to Sardinia, see p. 126-127: "Die tatsächliche Anordnung von Buch X... in dieser Form ursprünglich kaum konzeptiert geworden ist. Diese offensichtliche Diskrepanz ist schon früher aufgefallen und hat zu der Vermutung Anlass gegeben, der Elenchos sei überhaupt unvollendet geblieben oder stelle eine posthume Edition von ungeordneten Material dar. Man hat sich gefragt, ob der Abschluss des Werkes durch die Deportation Hippolyts nach Sardinien unterbrochen worden sei."

C.N. presupposes that particular binitarianism for the mediating position that it takes. Let us now consider how Frickel proposed specifically to deal with this particular theological issue in his second position, when he defended the thesis of a single author.

4A 2.1.2. *Frickel on the* λόγος–παῖς *theology*

Frickel pointed correctly to the origin of the ambivalence between the affirmation of the λόγος, not as φωνή and then as φωνή, as reconcilable in terms of the Stoic conception of the λόγος ἐνδιάθετος and the λόγος προφορικός. The λόγος, as "the immanent reason of the universe (ἐνδιάθετος τοῦ παντὸς λογισμός)," cannot be God's spoken voice immediately before the creation as its "firstborn" (πρωτότοκος γενόμενος φωνή), which he must rather be as προφορικός. (*El.* X, 33,1) Frickel then argues that this distinction is maintained in *C.N.* 10,4 where the λόγος as φωνή is previously unseen (ἔχων ἐν ἑαυτῷ ἀόρατόν τε ὄντα) when first uttered (προτέραν φωνὴν φθεγγόμενος), but is made visible (τῷ κτιζομένῳ κόσμῳ ὁρατὸν ποιεῖ) when sent forth to the creation as the creator's own mind (προῆκεν τῷ κτίσει κύριον τὸν ἴδιον νοῦν).

Undoubtedly, as Frickel admits, the Christological use of these Stoic categories is not shared by *C.N.* and *El.* alone using these categories. As we have seen, Theophilus of Antioch in particular was at home apologetically in describing Christology in such categories (4A 2.1). It cannot therefore be on grounds of an exclusive sharing of what is after all a common Christian and apologetic heritage that the authors of *C.N.* and *El.* can be declared to be identical. Furthermore, Frickel consistently misses the central point of what I have brought out in my previous exposition, namely the radical distinction between the λόγος become προφορικός as the firstborn of creation according to *El.* (and the tradition represented by Justin, Theophilus, and Irenaeus), and the λόγος become προφορικός at the incarnation according to *C.N.* This represents a quite radical difference in use of the admittedly shared, Stoic distinction. The λόγος was not, according to the passages we cited from *C.N.*, τέλειος υἱός before he became ἔνσαρκος.

Of fundamental importance in this connection are the differences which can in consequence be readily explained in the light of this distinction. *El.* never uses the concept of τέλειος for his own Christological statements, though he shows that such a concept was familiar and even characteristic of the theology of the heretics. We have seen that *C.N.* uses νοῦς to describe the depersonalized pre-incarnational λόγος (4A 1), of which likewise *El.* makes no Christological use, and confines entirely to statements of the heretics.[32] In

---

[32] E.g. The Naasenes speak of the τέλειος ἄνθρωπος (*El.* V, 7,7; 8,20; 8,37; 9,18. Amongst the Sethians (i) the νοῦν μεμορφωμένον ἐν τοῖς διαφόροις εἴδεσιν is called τέλειος θεός, and when νοῦς is released (ἀπολυθείη ὁ νοῦς) from the father of the lower world (ἀπὸ τοῦ πατρὸς τοῦ κάτω), he begats νοῦς as his τέλειος υἱός (γεννήσας νοῦν τέλειον υἱὸν ἑαυτῷ) (*El.* V, 19,15-16); and (ii) The ὁ ἄνωθεν τοῦ φωτὸς τέλειος λόγος is made like the

this respect, as we shall trace in further detail in 5B 3.1.2-3.2, the Christology of *C.N.* is far closer to Hellenistic syncretism than *El.*, despite the surface distinction of the biblical exegete versus the educated philosopher.

Frickel is undoubtedly correct that the use of παῖς θεοῦ as a description of the λόγος in creation is unknown before the Hippolytan *corpus*.[33] But if the connection between *El.* and *C.N.* is to be established as that of an identical author as opposed to two members of the same school, then they require a far greater agreement between them than a common exposition of *Isaiah* 42-43. He needs to show that *C.N.*, to be directly comparable in this respect to *El.*, uses this term of the pre-creational λόγος, and is not simply following Clement of Rome and the *Didache* in using this term of the Son after the incarnation.[34] Partly for reasons that we have already given, this would be difficult to establish, but let us pursue nevertheless this critical point with particular reference to Frickel's exegesis of *C.N.*

4A 2.1.3. *Scripture and the* λόγος–παῖς *in C.N.*

Frickel ignores the fact that *C.N.* does not use the expression πρωτότοκος or πρωτόγονος of the pre-existent λόγος—in fact he does not use these terms at all—as does *El.* X, 33,1 and 11.[35] In this respect *El.* is continuous with Melito even though Clement may appear at one point capable of an interpretation that would support *C.N.*[36] That he should not do so is fully consistent with my explanation of a second and latter writer attempting to soften the alleged ditheism of *El.* by depersonalising the not yet τέλειος υἱός before the incarnation and thus achieving a *rapprochement* with the community of Callistus' successor. Frickel has therefore to re-examine *C.N.* 5,3-5 and claims that, contrary to my exposition above, ὁ παῖς καὶ τέλειος ἄνθρωπος must be considered here to be the Israel as ἄνθρωπος ὁρῶν τὸν θεόν because *Jn.* 1,18 and 3, 13 and 32 is clearly pre-incarnational.[37] But it is

---

snake (ὁμοιωθεὶς... τῷ θηρίῳ, τῷ ὄφει) "in order that he might release (ἵνα λύσῃ) the bonds that enclose the perfect νοῦς (τὰ δεσμὰ τὰ περικείμενα τῷ τελείῳ νοΐ) (*El.* V, 19,19-21)."

[33] *Did.* 9, 2-3; 10,2 uses παῖς in the phrase ἐγνώρισας διὰ 'Ιησοῦ τοῦ παιδὸς σου but this refers to Christ post-incarnation.

[34] Frickel (1988) p. 221: "Wie im Neuen Testament [*Mat.* 12,18; *Acts* 3, 13 and 26; 4, 27 and 30], bezeichnet dieser auf Isaias 42-43 zurückgehende messianische Titel auch in der frühchristlichen Theologie immer den menschgewordenen Gottessohn [Clement, *Cor.* 59,4 and *Did.* 9, 2-3; 10,2], so dass die aus dem Wahrheitserweis des *El* bereits zitierte Stelle ὁ πρωτόγονος πατρὸς παῖς, ἡ πρὸ ἑωσφόρου φωσφόρος φωνή eine Neuheit darstellt und diese Anwendung des messianischen Titels παῖς auf den vorweltlichen Logos daher als eine charakteristische Eigenart der Theologie Hippolyts von Rom anzusehen ist."

[35] Simonetti (1989) p. 83-88 cogently criticizes Frickel (1988) p. 125-175) and (1989) p. 37-41 for claiming that *El.* X is addressed to a different public from I-IX.

[36] Melito, *Hom. Pas.* 82: ... ὅτι οὗτος ἐστιν ὁ πρωτότοκος τοῦ θεοῦ, ὁ πρὸ ἑωσφόρου γεννηθείς, cf. Clement, *Cor.* 59,4: ἐλπίζειν ἐπὶ τὸ ἀρχέγονον πάσης κτίσεως ὄνομά σου which is susceptible to a Rabbinic interpretation in which ontological personal pre-existence is not in view.

[37] Ibid. p. 223: "Nun ist es fraglos der eingeborene Sohn Gottes in seiner vorweltlichen Existenz, der Gott (den Vater) sieht und dessen Willen kennt. Dem Menschen Jesus aber

methodologically unsound to base an interpretation of *C.N.* on one interpretation of these Scripture citations which it is disputed that the former shared.

Yet Frickel admits that it is on the basis of his assumption of the way in which *C.N.* would have understood these citations that his claim for the preincarnational usage of παῖς depends.[38] As I pointed out in 2A 3.1, it is by no means obvious that late-second-century readers of the Fourth Gospel would have read *Jn.* 1,18 as pre-incarnational, but rather the reverse. This verse occurs after 1,14 and not before. The μονογενής θεός (or υἱός) can only declare (ἐκεῖνος ἐξηγήσατο) the unseen God (θεὸν οὐδεὶς ἑώρακεν πώποτε) after the incarnation which makes him visible. Although the μονογενὴς is ὁ ὢν εἰς τὸν κόλπον τοῦ πατρός, he is such not before the creation but as part of the mystery of the incarnate life in which his communion with God is continuous if unseen (*Jn.* 14, 9-10 etc.).

The author of the prologue (*Jn.* 1,1-18) self-consciously eschews all speculation about the relationship of the λόγος with the Father in terms of emanation or begetting. This was why the Monarchians used the Fourth Gospel as a quarry for proof texts which *C.N.* clearly takes a great deal of time and effort to interpret in a binitarian fashion. In such an ecclesiological context, it would not be surprising therefore if *C.N.* had interpreted *Jn.* 3, 13 and 32, in the absence of any such speculation about the ontological relationship of Father to Son prior to the incarnation, in terms of what I have shown (4A 1) to be his depersonalization of the pre-incarnational λόγος as a second God.

Frickel appreciates that νοῦς is used in *C.N.* alone but attributes this to the change of audience from pagans to the Monarchians within the Church. But he has failed consistently to grasp that the εἰς νοῦς πατρός of *C.N.* 7,3 ff., does not function in the argument only to maintain the unity of God but to deny that the λόγος ἄσαρκος is completely a person before it is sent into the world (προβὰς ἐν κόσμῳ) and is revealed (ἐδείκνυτο) as παῖς θεοῦ.[39] In this context it is quite wrong to appeal to the personal form of ἀρχηγός, σύμβουλος, and ἐργάτης (*C.N.* 10,4) whose use appears metaphorical in view of the pre-incarnational relationship of λόγος–πατήρ. That relationship is one of thought to person rather than person to person, as can be seen in 10,2 (οὔτε γὰρ ἄλογος οὔτε ἄσοφος οὔτε ἀδύνατος οὔτε ἀβούλευτὸς ἦν).[40] It

---

kommen Schau und Erkenntnis des Vaters deshalb zu weil er das menschgewordene Wort Gottes ist."

[38] Ibid. 224: "Wir fragen uns auf Grund der oben zitierten Schrifworte, ob nicht auch der Titel παῖς, ähnlich wie Israel, eine vorweltliche Bedeutung haben könnte?"

[39] See further 4A 1.1- 1.2 above with which cf. Frickel (1988) p. 224-242.

[40] Frickel (1988) p. 228: "Aber nicht nur an die Weltschöpfung von Gen. 1 denkt Hippolyt; er hat, wie die Rolle des Logos als Ratgeber (σύμβουλος) des Vaters zeigt... der als Gottes eigener Nus der Schöpfung als Herr vorgesetzt ist (προῆκεν τῇ κτίσει κύριον τὸν ἴδιον νοῦν)." I have shown in 4 A 1.1 above the depersonalization involved in the adoption of the last quoted phrase. Cf. also p. 230: "Diese ewige Kraft Gottes ist ja, wie Hippolyt im nächsten Abschnitt eigens hervorhebt, der Logos-Nus selbst. Er hat als Oberhaupt (ἀρχηγός) und

is very difficult to see how the author of *El.*, had he lived to see the treatment
of his work by *C.N.*, would have concluded anything other than a betrayal of
his original position by conceding too much to his original Monarchian
opponents. But there is an additional feature of Frickel's critique to which
attention must be drawn, and that is to the absence of πρωτότοκος and
πρωτόγονος from *C.N.*

4A 2.1.4. πρωτότοκος *and* πρωτόγονος *in* El. X. 33,2 *and 11*

Indeed, as Frickel is well aware,[41] both πρωτότοκος and πρωτόγονος are
common descriptions of the pre-existent Son, based as they are on *Ps.*
109,3 and *Col.* 1,15, in the second century Fathers, as we have seen in Clement and
Melito (4A 2.1.3). *C.N.* is clearly departing from a common tradition in not
using this term, by contrast with *El.* Moreover, Frickel, in his reply to
Nautin, notes the clear purpose of the author of *C.N.* to describe the pre-existent λόγος in strictly subordinationist terms in order to counter the charge of
ditheism.[42] It is for this reason he claims that in an anti-Monarchian work the
distinction between the Son and the Father needs to be maintained, whereas
in the ἀπόδειξις addressed to the pagans there is not the same imperative.

Thus the differences noted by Nautin between the two works can be resolved in a way that establishes, he believes, a common author. Yet we have
shown that the anti-Monarchian passage in *El.* which Frickel argues is addressed to those within the Church such as Callistus and Zephyrinus before
the alleged change of audience occurs in the disjointed and badly organized
text, also describes the pre-existent λόγος and in quite different terms to the
νοῦς of *C.N.* Here there was no subordinationism before the worlds offered
to Monarchian critics of the author but a clear independence combined with
congruence of wills that would have seemed to both Callistus and the author
of *C.N.* as warranting the charge of ditheism.

---

ausführender Arbeiter (ἐργάτης) der Welt überall in der Welt seine Spuren hinterlassen..."
Frickel himself acknowledges the depersonalization in his phrase "diese ewige kraft Gottes" but
I have shown 4A 1.2 above that the notion of the pre-incarnate λόγος as πατρῴα δύναμις was
quite foreign to the personalized binitarianism characterised as detheism of *El.*

[41] Ibid. p. 165-166.

[42] Frickel (1988) p. 237-238: "Es gibt jedoch, wenn ich richtig sehe, einen Weg, das
Dilemma um den Gebrauch des Titels παῖς bei Hippolyt aufzulösen: die Beachtung des *kos-
molischen* Kontexts und der Augmentation Hippolyts in C.N. 10-11. Wie bereits gezeigt, geht
es Hippolyt darum, die Einheit Gottes zu wahren, aber zugleich den Logos als zweite göttliche
Person neben dem Vater zu erweisen. Als Kraft Gottes oder Nus des Vaters ist der Logos immer
mit dem Vater eins. Als liebender Sohn ist er dem Vater untergeordnet, immer bereit, den
Willen des Vaters auszuführen." My argument is that *El.* differs from every point in what is
Frickel's correct exegesis of *C.N.* 10-11 as summarised by this quotation. Where in both the
context is "*kosmolischen*," only in *C.N.* is "die Einheit Gottes" guaranteed by reducing the
cosmological λόγος to the "Kraft Gottes oder Nus des Vaters," and thus depersonalizing the
λόγος so as to make him "dem Vater untergeordnet, immer bereit, den Willen des Vaters
auszuführen." Only by that subordination is *C.N.* able to "zugleich den Logos als zweite göttliche Person neben dem Vater zu erweisen" without involving himself in the ditheism of which
he is perhaps in half-conscious agreement that *El.* was justly accused.

We mentioned that the claim has been made that the numerous references in *C.N.* to the Holy Spirit were in fact later additions in order to service and to exemplify the "heresy" attacked by the anti-Chalcedonian collector of the *florilegium* in which *C.N.* is preserved in the one *ms.* tradition of *Vat. Graec.* 1431. Although we shall now give grounds against such a view, we have clearly demonstrated in this section (4A 1) that the case for two authors would remain almost unaffected by its adoption. Even if references to the Holy Spirit, albeit ambiguously, as a third person in the Trinity were able to be deleted, the radically different characterisation and justification of the binitarianism that would remain would nevertheless furnish a very strong case for different authors. Let us however consider now in greater detail the addition of the Holy Spirit to the theology of *C.N.* in comparison with *El.*

4A 3. *The alleged Chalcedonianism and the place of the Holy Spirit in* C.N.

Nautin was well aware of the earlier criticism that regarded the integrity of *C.N.* as suspect. Not only does this text have a one manuscript tradition, but the place that it occupied in that *ms.* (*Vat. Graec.* 1431 f. 360r 2-367r1) exemplified one of a number of Chalcedonian opinions which the Monophysite patriarch of Alexandria, Timothy Aelurus, considered heretical. Bunsen,[43] Volkmar,[44] Lipsius,[45] Dräske,[46] and Richard[47] all argued some version of an interpolation thesis. They differed however as to the extent of those interpolations. Perhaps Richard, in response to Nautin, was the most radical of

---

[43] C.C.J. Bunsen, *Hippolytus and his Age; or the Doctrine and Practice of the Church of Rome under Commodus and Alexander Severus*, (London: Longman, Brown, Green, and Longmans 1852), Vol. 1, p. 184-186.

[44] G. Volkmar, *Die Quellen der Ketzergeschichte bis zum Nicäum.* I, Hippolytus und die römischen Zeitgenossen. (Zürich: 1855), p. 136.

[45] R.A. Lipsius, *Die Quellen der ältesten Ketzergeschichte. Neue untersuchungen*, (Leipzig: Barth 1875), p. 134-137.

[46] J. Dräseke, Zum Syntagma des Hippolytos, in *ZWTh* 46 (1903), p. 67-69 was perhaps the most cautious of these critics. Though he agreed that the transmission was "not unchallenged" ("Dass der Schlussabschnitt, der Erweis der Wahrheit, mit seinen vielen bekenntnismässig gehaltenen Sätzen, nicht unangefochten in der Überlieferung blieb."), he criticized Bunsen, Lipsius and especially Volkmar for too large a claim for such interpolations. Of the latter he said: "Von den fünf Beobachtungen, die er (S. 136, A.1) verzeichnet, sind aber mindestens drei unzutreffend; sie erklären sich genugsam aus Hippolytos' Schreibweise und Darstellung; nur die vierte... ist zutreffend... [*C.N.* 17,2] λαβὼν δὲ καὶ ψυχὴν ἀνθρωπίνην [λογικὴν δὲ λέγω], wo die eingeklammerten Worte eine apollinaristischer Zusatz sind."

[47] M. Richard, Saint Hippolyte, «Hippolyte e Josipe»: Bulletin de Patrologie, in *MSR* 5 (1948), p. 294-308; ——, Hippolyte de Rome, in *Dictionnaire de spiritualité* VII (1969), p.533. Richard appeared to be supported by H. de Riedmatten, Review of Nautin's Hippolyte et Josipe, in *DomSt* 1 (1948), p. 169 and 171-172 and by Capelle (1950), p. 148 ff. ("une étude prolongée du cas d'Hippolyte m'a forcé à soulever des doutes sur la valeur du texte de l'Antinoët, tel qu'il nous est parvenu.") who in turn was criticized by P. Nautin, La controverse sur l'auteur de l'Elenchos, in *RevHE* 47 (1952), p. 36-39. But in B. Capelle, A propos d'Hippolyte de Rome, in *RThAM* 19 (1952), p. 193-202 he clarified his viewpoint and regarded *C.N.* as genuine but by the same author as *El.*, claiming the influence of the former work on Origen particularly in his Commentary on the Psalms (p. 201-202). See also M. Richard, Dernières remarques sur S. Hippolyte et le soi-disant Josipe, in *RecSciRel* 43 (1955), p. 392-394. See also C. Martin, Le Contra Noetum de saint Hippolite, in *RevHE* 38 (1941), p. 5-23.

them all in proposing that *C.N.* was primarily a homiletic composition from the Byzantine epoch constructed in a maladroit fashion from extracts from a few of Hippolytus' genuine writings.[48]

Clearly if *C.N.* was a work of the character that Richard had suggested, there would be no sense in asking whether the Holy Spirit passages in themselves were to be understood as later interpolations. Thus the case for a difference of authorship between *C.N.* and *El.*, if it rested solely on this one criterion as we have shown that it does not, would be significantly diminished. We shall begin therefore by defending the general integrity of *C.N.* before considering the Holy Spirit passages as a possible special case.

4A 3.1. *The integrity of* C.N. *and the age of Chalcedon*
In his commentary on *C.N.* Nautin took pains to defend the integrity of the text of *Vat. Graec.* 1431.[49] He pointed out that the quotations from *C.N.* 18, 1-9 in the fourth and fifth centuries both by Theodoret and by Gelasius attribute this passage to Hippolytus.[50] Although Richard might regard Theodoret's citation of this ἐκ τῆς ἑρμηνείας τοῦ β′ ψαλμοῦ as supporting his account, we saw in Chapter 3, particularly in view of Gelasius' location of this text *in memoria haeresium*, that the error is on the side of Theodoret (3A 2). Indeed Nautin was to derive considerable pleasure from Richard and Capelle's argument against the authenticity of *C.N.*, since that argument recognized the incompatibility of *El.* with *C.N.* as matters stood.[51] Frickel, following Hübner, has more recently renounced his earlier views and now believes (as his third position), on the basis of his argument for the authenticity of Theodoret's version, that *C.N.* is a document from the age of Chalcedon and heavily interpolated.[52]

Nautin proceeded in two separate ways to establish the authenticity of *C.N.* First he compared it with *Dan.*, *Ant.* and *Ben. Jac.* in order to show that, particularly in the kind of narrative passage that would have been the re-

---

[48] Although something like this had also been the view of Bunsen (1852) p. 136 cf. Richard (1948) p. 297-299; M. Richard, Encore le problème d'Hippolyte, in *MSR* 10 (1953), p. 177-180. Cf. P. Nautin, L'auteur du Comput Pascal de 222 et de la Chronique anonyme de 235, in *JThS* 42 (1954), p. 27-30.

[49] Nautin (1949) Chapters 2-3.

[50] Ibid. p. 82; Nautin (1947) Chapter 2.

[51] Nautin (1952) p. 38: "M. Richard et D. Capelle en font d'alleurs l'aveu implicite, ni l'un ni l'autre n'a cru pouvoir soutenir la thèse intrégrale acceptée jusqu'ici... *Pour introduire l'Elenchos dans l'oeuvre d'Hippolyte, ils se sont vus obligés d'écarter, par des voies différentes mais toujours* a priori, *le «fragment contre Noët», reconnaissant ainsi d'une manière concrète l'incompatibilité des deux oeuvrages.*" (His italics) Cf. G. Oggioni, Ancora sulla questione di Ippolito, in *ScuCat* 80 (1952), p. 524: "... Nell'ipotesi quindi che il *Frammento* sia autentico ed integro gli avversari di Nautin sentono tutta la gravità del suo argomento, ed è proprio su questo punto che molto abilmente egli riconduce i suoi oppositori... per mostrare come essi non hanno eliminato il suo argomento fondamentale..." Similarly de Riedmatten (1948) p. 171 pointed to alleged "Apollinarist corrections and falsifications" in *C.N.* 17-18 in order to explain the theological differences with *El.*, citing in support Capelle's (1950) original argument which he modified (1952), see footnote 47.

[52] Hübner (1989) p. 221-223; Frickel (1993) p. 101-119.

sponsibility of an anti-Chalcedonian forger, the similarity of style and expression show *C.N.* to be authentic and uncontaminated.[53] Secondly he compared *C.N.* 17,5-18,7 with its citation in Theodoret, *Eranistes*, 2, and, by comparing these with the aforementioned works, established the Chalcedonian alterations to rest with Theodoret. Let us now summarize these two kinds of argument in greater detail.

4A 3.1.1 C.N. *authenticated by* Ant., Dan. and Ben. Jac.
The descriptions of Noetus as φυσιωθεὶς εἰς ἔπαρμα or the ἔπαρμα καρδίας καὶ φυσίωμα πνεύματος ἀλλότριου is paralleled by Nebuchadnessar (φυσιωθεὶς... καὶ τῇ καρδίᾳ ἐπαρθείς) and the Antichrist (ἐπαρθεὶς τῇ καρδίᾳ).[54] Likewise with theological expressions that might seem to have the connotation of the age of Chalcedon, Nautin also points again to parallels with *Dan.* and *Ant.* which presumably cannot be held also to have experienced post-Chalcedonian contamination. In *C.N.* 4,7 we read of the μυστήριον οἰκονομίας· ὅτι σεσαρκωμένου τοῦ λόγου καὶ ἐνανθρωπήσαντος. But the second century currency of such Christological terms is guaranteed by (i) μυστήριον οἰκονομίας εἰς Χριστὸν προτυπούμενον in *Ben. Jac.* 8 and μυστήριον τὸ οἰκονομούμενον in *Dan.* II, 19,1, and (ii) by σαρκωθεὶς in *Ben Jac.* 8 and *Dan.* IV, 39,4, and ἐνανθρώπησιν in *Dan.* IV, 39,4.

Simply because the text of *C.N.* contains such expressions as τὴν οἰκονομίαν ἀναιρήσει (3,4), τῷ πατρῴῳ λογῷ καὶ τῷ μυστηρίῳ οἰκονομίας (4,5), μυστήριον οἰκονομίας (4,7 and 8), κατὰ τὴν οἰκονομίαν τριχῆς ἡ ἐπίδειξις (8,2), οἰκονομίαν τὲ τρίτην (14,1,2), οἰκονομίᾳ συμφωνίας (14,4),[55] it does not therefore follow that these terms are used as though they were contemporary with Chalcedonian controversies. Quite apart from parallels in Hippolytus' other works that we cited in the last paragraph, there are clear parallels to the Trinitarian use of this term both in Tertullian, in passages that we shall examine in detail later (7C 2.3.2), and in other second-century writers. We have shown moreover in detail how such passages in which these allegedly Chalcedonian terms preponderate are in fact a response to Callistus' theology and its conflict with *El.*'s ditheism (4A 1.2-1.3; 4A 2). Frickel in his most recent work strives in vain therefore to evidence fourth-century parallels for such usages, as if this of itself proves anything. He quoted with this aim from Gelasius' *De Duabus Naturis*, and the use made in the Monophysite debate of Hippolytus' theology, to try to make this point. But the term συναμφότερον is Gelasius' own, not Hippolytus', and used in connection with a term (τὴν ἔνσαρκον οἰκονομίαν) which had its own

---

53 See Nautin (1949) p. 42-49 for a full list of such comparisons the most pertinent of which I cite here.
54 *C.N.* 1,2 cf. *Ant.* 47; *Dan.* II, 15,2; III, 4,1,7; IV, 2,5; 12,5; 43,4; 49,5; *Ben. Jac.* 13 8.
55 See also *C.N.* 14,7 and 16,2.

meaning in second-century theology that is corroborated from other sources than *C.N.* alone.[56]

What Frickel must do is to show how the controversy over the two φύσεις that centred around Apollinarianism is somehow involved in such examples. But those that I have just quoted give no such parallels. The οἰκονομία in each case refer to the πρόσωπα of the Trinity, not to the mystery of the two natures in the incarnation (4A 2). Frickel passes now too readily from these passages to *C.N.* 17,5-18,1 where alone there is reference to Christ's φύσις, but where such terms as οἰκονομία or μυστήριον are not to be found at all, let alone to any οἰκονομίᾳ συμφωνίας of the two natures in the incarnation that might parallel the κατὰ τὴν οἰκονομίαν τριχῆς ἡ ἐπίδειξις that characterizes every occurence of this term in *C.N.* that we have cited in full detail.

Let us now examine this passage in greater detail.

4 A 3.1.2. *Theodoret,* Eranistes, *II and* C.N. *17,5- 18,7*

Nautin now turns to Theodoret and asks whether his version of *C.N.* 17,5-18,7 can possibly be the original version of that passage.[57] It might at first sight seem that Theodoret's οὗτος ὁ προελθὼν εἰς τὸν κόσμον θεὸς καὶ ἄνθρωπος ἐφανερώθη seems more original and that the οὗτος... θεὸς ἐνσώματος ἐφανερώθη, ἄνθρωπος τέλειος προελθών of *C.N.* 17,5. We could, after all, attribute the addition of ἐνσώματος and τέλειος to a Chalcedonian interpolation to the effect that the two natures of Christ, human and divine, were involved in the incarnation.

One problem here would be that these words could be interpreted as either pro-Chalcedonian, as I have just done, or indeed as anti-Chalcedonian, as implying that the one divine nature was completely human when incarnate. The only reason why one would prefer the first interpretation would be that otherwise *C.N.* would not have been found in the *florilegium* of the Monophysite Timothy Aelurus amongst the works of heretics as it does in *Vat. Graec.* 1431. We shall shortly need to pursue this point in greater detail in view of Frickel's most recent denial that *C.N.* was originally part of that *florilegium* (4A3.1.3.1),—a denial clearly needed in order to negate the force of such an objection. But if the theological statement is so imprecise as to produce, as we shall show, possible identifications with both Chalcedonian orthodoxy or the theology of Apollinaris (4A 3.1.3.2) or that of Marcellus of Ancyra (4A 3.1.3.3), it is difficult to see what advantage a fifth century interpolator or interpolators would have gained by so clearly ambiguous additions.

---

[56] Frickel (1993) p. 108-109. With τὴν οἰκονομίαν ἀναιρήσει (*C.N.* 3,4) cf. Tatian, *Orat. ad Graec.* 5,2: "what is partitioned takes on a distinctive function (τὸ δὲ μερισθὲν οἰκονομίας τὴν διαίρεσιν προσλαβὸν) cf. also Tertullian, *Adv. Prax.* 2,4.

[57] For an exhaustive examination of the differences see Nautin (1949) p. 49-56.

However, (i) ἐνσώματος is paralleled in *Dan.* III, 14,6 where the λόγος at the end of time will become corporeal (σωμαποιεῖσθαι) and (ii) ἄνθρωπος τέλειος is paralleled in *Dan.* IV, 36,5 where the human figure of the vision before the incarnation is οὔπω τελείως ἄνθρωπος and similarly in IV, 39,5 where we read οὔπω τότε τέλειος υἱὸς ἀνθρώπου ὤν. We see here therefore that neither ἄνθρωπος τέλειος nor ἐνσώματος can be a garbled reference to the disputes about the combination without confusion of the two natures in the incarnation that raged around the Chalcedonian definitions. Rather they form part of the theology of *C.N.* to which I have already drawn attention, namely the claim that the λόγος was not τελείος υἱός before the incarnation.

Undoubtedly the author of that theology, which is found in *Dan.* also, believed in *C.N.* that it had furnished him with the perfect anti-Docetic weapon. The human form of Jesus could not exist as the form of the Son of Man in Daniel's vision had existed on the level of mere appearance. His theology enabled him to articulate sharply the distinction between the vision of the λόγος in human form as it appeared before the incarnation and after the incarnation, as is made clear by the distinction between ἄσαρκος (*C.N.* 4,11 and 15,1) and ἔνσαρκος or ἐνσώματος (12,5; 15,7 and 17,5). But the theology that furnished such an instrument with which to refute Docetism was itself found faulty in terms of latter Nicene orthodoxy which could never admit that the πρόσωπα of Father and Son were only real after the incarnation and not eternally in existence.[58]

As such we can see why Theodoret should have excluded it from his citations. His purpose was to establish a strict distinction between the humanity and the divinity of Christ.[59] Such a purpose would not be well-served by a Christology that would have excluded Christ's full, divine personhood before the incarnation and that was otherwise quite ambiguous regarding the concerns of the age of Chalcedon. Theodoret likewise omits other passages that could not by themselves have serviced the Chalcedonian disputes so that there would have been no point for a later writer to have invented and inserted these, such as Christ's authority to lay down his life and take it again or his acknowledgment by John the Baptist (*C.N.* 18,4 and 6).

---

[58] *C.N.* 14: 2-3: εἰ δὲ οὖν ὁ λόγος πρὸς τὸν θεὸν θεὸς ὤν, τί οὖν φήσειεν ἄν τις δύο λέγειν θεούς; δύο μὲν οὐκ ἐρῶ θεούς, ἀλλ᾽ ἢ ἕνα· πρόσωπα δὲ δύο... Πατὴρ μὲν γὰρ εἷς, πρόσωπα δὲ δύο, ὅτι καὶ ὁ υἱός. Although R. Butterworth, Hippolytus of Rome, Contra Noetum: Text introduced, edited, translated, in *Heythrop Monographs* 2 (1977), p. 74 translates πρόσωπα in the later, Nicene, technical sense of "persons," I wonder whether "faces" would not here be more appropriate in view of my discussion about the pre-incarnational depersonalizing of the λόγος to which I have drawn attention.

[59] Nautin (1949) p. 55 "... il souligne en particulier que le Christ est *vu* par les bergers, qu'il est *désigné du doigt* par Jean, qu'il est *de Nazareth* et que le miracle de l'eau changée en vin eut lieu à *Cana*. Cette orientation antidocète convient parfaitement à Hippolyte, puisque le docétisme inquiétait tant les écrivains chrétiens de son temps, un Irénée—son maître en théologie—, un Tertullien ou un Origène." (His italics)

Nautin saw the use of the adjective θεϊκός as opposed to Hippolytus' θεῖος as indicative of the fact that Theodoret is the re-arranger of the text of *C.N.* rather than *vice-versa*. He adds in place of the quotation from *Isaiah* 53,4 in *C.N.* 18,5: τὸ δὲ θεϊκὸν αὐτοῦ πάλιν φανερῶς ἔστιν ἰδεῖν. Nautin interpreted this sentence, correctly I believe, as the counterpoise to the other insertion by Theodoret at 17,5- 18,1, namely: καὶ τὸν μὲν ἄνθρωπον αὐτοῦ εὐκόλως ἔστι νοεῖν in place of the rigorously anti-Docetic original.[60] The two statements represent a Chalcedonian theme, namely that of the strict division between the two natures in Jesus, both human and divine. "The human is easy to conceive" (the relation between the two natures etc.) whilst "the divine is plain to see." They refashion Hippolytus' text so as to introduce two distinct sections of Gospel scenes, one containing examples of Jesus' humanity, and the other of his divine powers.

In vain does Frickel endeavour to argue the authenticity of Theodoret's version by arguing that νοεῖν can mean "recognise" and not "conceive."[61] The additional problem, dealt with by Frickel in a footnote, is the unusual and Chalcedonian θεϊκόν that establish the secondary character of this text.[62] Thus the real Chalcedonian additions and alterations to Hippolytus' text are those found in Theodoret's citation and not *vice versa*. It was thus necessary for Theodoret, or perhaps the author of the *florilegium* from which he derives his quotations,[63] to soften the anti-Docetic polemic, not simply for negative reasons, namely a Christology on other grounds questionable, but for the way in which an anti-docetic emphasis of *C.N.* on the truly human mixed both the divine nature and human of him who was according to Chalcedon ἀσύγχυτος.[64]

---

[60] *C.N.* 17,5-18,1: ἄνθρωπος τέλειος προελθών· οὐ γὰρ κατὰ φαντασίαν ἢ τροπήν ἀλλὰ ἀληθῶς γενόμενος ἄνθρωπος. Οὕτως οὖν καὶ τὰ ἀνθρώπινα ἑαυτοῦ οὐκ ἀπαναίνεται ἐνδεικνύμενος θεὸς ὤν.

[61] Frickel (1993) p. 113-114: "Aber hier ist daran zu erinnern, dass νοεῖν nich nur denken, sondern auch wahrnehmen und erkennen (wie γιγνώσκειν) bedeutet."

[62] Ibid. p. 113, footnote 120 where he shows that, quite contrary to what he seeks to prove, that τὸ θεῖον in *El.* X, 30,5; 31,6; 34,1 "immer die Gottheit meint und mehr als unpersönliches Synonym für ὁ θεός steht..." But even if so, it is clear by the symmetry of the μὲν and δὲ that these two lines are artificially separated by the text placed between them, and that as they stand they are concerned with the Chalcedonian distinction between *Menschlikeit* and *Gottsein.*

[63] G.H. Ettlinger, *Theodoret of Cyrus: Eranistes. Critical Text and Prolegomena*, (Oxford: Clarendon 1975), p. 23-31, cf. L. Saltet, Les sources de l'Eranistes de Théodoret, in *RevHE* 6 (1905), p. 513-536; 741-754.

[64] Nautin (1949) p. 55-56: "... la citation de Théodoret... ne cherche plus directement à combattre le docétisme, mais à établir une distinction stricte entre l'humanité et la divinité du Christ... La première partie retient les traits humains de la première liste du fragment, en excluant tous les traits divins; et la seconde partie reproduit les traits divins qui composent la seconde liste du fragment, en sautant le passage qui insistait encore sur la réalité de l'humanité... Traits divins et traits humains sont ainsi nettement séparés... la partie de son *Eranistes* où il fait cette citation d'Hippolyte est précisément consacrée à défendre l'ἀσύγχυτος." Cf also Nautin (1952) p. 27-30.

It should also be noted that Origen, Hippolytus' contemporary, makes a distinction between the two natures of Christ in way that parallels in particular *C.N.* 18,2. In the *Hom. in Jerem.* 14,6 (*Jer.* 15, 10-19) he says:

God the Saviour does not thereby say (οὐχὶ ἧ θεὸς ὁ σωτὴρ λέγει) the expression "O my mother" (τὸ οἴμοι ἐγώ, μῆτερ) but thereby the Man (ἀλλ' ἧ ἄνθρωπος)... But the soul was human (ἡ δὲ ψυχή ἀνθρωπίνη ἦν), and for this reason it was troubled (διὰ τοῦτο καὶ τετάρακται), and for this reason it was exceedingly sorrowful (διὰ τοῦτο καὶ περίλυπος ἦν). But the Word who was in the beginning with God (ὁ δὲ λόγος ὁ ἐν ἀρχῇ πρὸς τὸν θεὸν ἦν) was not troubled (οὐ τετάρακται), the latter would not use (ἐκεῖνος οὐκ ἂν λέγοι) the expression "O my." (τὸ «οἴμοι») Nor did the Word undergo death (οὐδὲ γὰρ ὁ λόγος ἐπιδέχεται θάνατον), but the human is that which underwent this (ἀλλὰ τὸ ἀνθρώπινόν ἐστι τὸ τοῦτο ἐπιδεξάμενον), as we have often expounded (ὡς πολλάκις παρεστήσαμεν).

There is clearly an embryonic two natures theology in process of developing here in the early third century.

But Frickel has one other basic arguments against the authenticity of *C.N.* 17,5-18,10, namely the use of φύσις and of τροπή in this passage, which we shall now discuss.

4.A 3.1.2.1. C.N. *17,2 and 5 and 18,1 and Origen* Contra Cels. *4,18*

Frickel's first argument for the genuineness of Theodoret's version rests on the occurence of ἄυπνον ἔχων τὴν φύσιν ὡς θεός (18,1), and its alleged appropriateness only to the age of Chalcedon. But is certainly wrong to believe that φύσις was not used in the second and early third century to speak about both divine and human natures and their relationship. Not only do we have the θείας κοινωνοὶ φύσεως of 2 *Pet.* 1,4 but also Origen *Frag.* 71, 2 (*Lk.* 15,16). Here commenting on the meaning of the younger brother' desire, in the Parable of the Prodigal Son, to eat swines' food, Origen explains: ἡ λογικὴ φύσις ἐν ἀλογίᾳ γενομένη ἐπιθυμεῖ.[65]

Furthermore, in *Contra Cels.* 4,18, Origen addresses his opponents criticism of the incarnation. Now Celsus criticism reflects the very concerns of this passage in which the incarnation is οὐ κατὰ φαντασίαν ἢ τροπήν (*C.N.* 17,5) and Origen's reply reflects too an early third century response in terms of the human and divine natures of Christ. The former claims:

... either it is true (ἤτοι ὡς ἀληθῶς), as they claim, that God actually changes into a mortal body (μεταβάλλει ὁ θεός, ὥσπερ οὗτοι φασιν, εἰς σῶμα θνητὸν), and it has been admitted (καὶ προείρηται) that he cannot (ὅτι ἀδυνατεῖ), or he himself does not change (ἢ αὐτὸς μὲν οὐ μεταβάλλει) but makes those who look on think so (ποιεῖ δὲ τοὺς ὁρῶντας δοκεῖν) and so deceives and lies (καὶ πλανᾷ καὶ ψεύδεται).

And Origen replies:

---

65 M. Rauer, Origene Werke: Bd. 9: Die Homilien zu Lukas in der Übersetzung des Hieronymus und die griechischen Reste der Homilien und des Lukas-Kommentars, in *GCS* (Berlin: Akademie Verlag 1959), p. 321.

One might answer this objection (καὶ πρὸς τοῦτο λέγοιτ᾽ ἄν) partly with respect
to the nature of the divine Word (πῇ μὲν περὶ τῆς τοῦ θείου λόγου φύσεως),
since he is God (ὄντος θεοῦ), and partly with respect to the soul of Jesus (πῇ δε
περὶ τῆς Ἰησοῦ ψυχῆς)... But if one takes the change in reference to the soul of
Jesus (εἰ δ᾽ ἐπὶ τῆς Ἰησοῦ ψυχῆς λαμβάνει τις τὴν μεταβολήν), when it enters
his body (αὐτῆς εἰς σῶμα ἐλθούσης), we will ask what is the sense of "change"
(πευσόμεθα πῶς λέγει «μεταβολήν»)? For if it refers to the essence (εἰ μὲν γὰρ
τῆς οὐσίας), it refers not only to the latter (οὐ δίδοται οὐ μόνον ἐπ᾽ ἐκείνης) but
concerns any other rational human soul (ἀλλ᾽ οὐδὲ περὶ ἄλλου λογικῆς ψυχῆς).

Frickel's most recent argument that *C.N.* is heavily interpolated thus begins on the basis of the claim that, in comparison with Theodoret's allegedly
original version, it is clearly demonstrable that *C.N.* 17,5-18,1 is the interpolated version because of its focus upon the human soul of Jesus. But we
can now see, equally from the outset, that the theme of Christ's human
φύσις, and the problem of τροπή in connection with it, is already present
early in the third century with Origen. The latter, in reply to Celsus, has
spoken of τῆς τοῦ θείου λόγου φύσεως, in a sense comparable with that of
the ἄυπνον φύσιν of *C.N.* 18,1. He has also spoken of μεταβολή in
connection with λογικὴ ψυχή which enables the use of τροπή in 17,5 to be
associated with the ψυχὴν τὴν ἀνθρωπείαν, λογικὴν δὲ λέγω of 17,2.

Thus from the outset the claim that *C.N.*, in its present form, is the
product of the Apollinarist controversy of the later quarter of the fourth century, is, *prima facie*, questionable. But let us now examine further whether in
fact *C.N.* is pseudonymous and can be historically relocated to such a later,
Apollinarist situation, or whether indeed the differences with *El.* are, as I am
arguing, the differences between the leader of his group and his immediate
historical successor. Only in the light of Frickel's establishment of this
broader Chalcedonian context can his success in locating the allegedly interpolated assertions about φύσις or τροπή in this passage to such a context be
further evaluated.[66]

4A 3.1.3. C.N. *as an Apollinarist* pseudepigraphon

As we have seen (3A 1), the thrust of Richard's argument regarding *Vat.
Graec.* 1431 as interpolated in a pro-Chalcedonian direction was that it was
found in the section containing works considered heretical by the
Monophysite compiler (πρὸς εἴδησιν τῆς ἐν αὐτοῖς κακοπιστίας).
Butterworth is the most recent writer to have argued that both *C.N.* and *Adv.
Jud.* were an original part of that section.[67] Frickel argues both from the evi-

---

[66] Frickel (1993) p. 105. Frickel also adds (i) the term Ναζωραῖος (*C.N.* 18,7) and (ii) the
expression οὗτος ὁ θεὸς ἄνθρωπος δι᾽ ἡμᾶς γεγονώς (18,10) as evidence for a post-Nicene
date (p. 111-112). But (i) is a reference to *Acts* 2,22 and, although it is used in Pseudo-
Athanasius (Apollinaris) *Contra Arian.* 4,35, it does not follow that the latter was the first time
in Christian history that this text was used. Furthermore, there are pre-Nicene examples of (ii)
such as Hippolytus, *Ant.* 3: ἄνθρωπος δι᾽ ὑμᾶς ἐν κόσμῳ φανερωθείς.

[67] Butterworth (1977) p. 4-5. For further bibliography see 3A 1, footnote 1.

dence of the transmission and copying of this *ms.* itself, together with the surrounding circumstances, and then from the character of the theology represented. We shall therefore consider these two parts of his argument in detail.

4A 3.1.3.1. Was C.N. added to the florilegium by the copyists of Vat. Graec. 1431?

In order to create, *prima facie*, the conditions for regarding the contents of *C.N.* in its present form as primarily Apollinarian, Frickel has to be able to detach this and the work that follows it from any original position in Timothy Aelurus' *florilegium.* If it appealed to contemporary readers as an Apollinarian work, it could not have been listed as an heretical work, from Timothy's point of view, along with Leo's letters to Flavian of Const-antinople or to the Emperor Leo, or the decree of Chalcedon. As Frickel con-cedes, any possibility that an anti-Chalcedonic perversity had lead to the grouping of two works that supported Apollinarianism with Chalcedonian "heresy" is excluded by the fact that the compiler of *Vat. Graec.* 1431 was not only a Monophysite but a member of the party of Peter Mongus. The latter used Monophysitism to conceal his Apollinarianism as can be seen from his use of Apollinaris' *pseudepigrapha* (attributed to Athanasius) as did Timothy in his *florilegium.*[68]

In consequence, Frickel must now argue that, in order to be Apollinarian, originally *C.N.* and *Adv. Jud.* were not part of the original section to which the compiler of *Vat. Graec.* 1431 was hostile. Since that compiler is a crypto-Apollinarian himself, he could hardly have included an Apollinarian work amongst the heretical works since it would have supported his own cherished position. Frickel now gives as his reason firstly the change of scribal hand that marks the end of the Letter of Leo to the Emperor Leo and the beginning of *C.N.* (f.353r2-360r1), and secondly the incongruity of the title of *C.N.* with it original inclusion in a section comprized of heretical writings.

---

[68] Frickel (1993) p. 96: "Er is aber nicht nur Parteigänger des Petrus Mongus, sondern vertritt auch jenen getarnten Apollinarismus, der unter dem Deckmantel monophysitischer Theologie den schon von Timotheus Äluros (= 477) geführten Kampf gegen Chalcedon und das Dogma der zwei Naturen fortführte. Sein Apollinarismus zeigte sich schon darin, dass er das ganze Arsenal der apollinaristischen Pseudepigrapha, die schon Timotheus in seine Florilegien hineingemischt hatte, vollständig seiner Sammlung einverleibt hat." Frickel quotes in support E. Schwartz, Codex Vaticanus Graecus 1431: Eine antichalkedonische Sammlung aus der Zeit Kaiser Zenos, in *ABAW*, Phil. und hist. Kl., 32, 6 (1927), p. 146-150 and E. Mühlenberg, Apollinaris von Laodicea, in *Forschungen zur Kirchen- und Dogmengeschichte*, 23 (Göttingen: Vandenhoeck und Ruprecht 1969) p. 98. It is a moot point, however, whether Timothy and Peter Mongus did not believe in fact that the Apollinarian material was in fact by Athanasius and for this reason could not be regarded as heretical regardless of their specific contents.

4A 3.1.3.1.1. *The scribal conventions of* Vat. Graec. *1431*

The first of these objections have already been well-worked. As Butterworth pointed out against Schwartz, the different scribal hand that copied fol. *C.N.* and *Adv. Jud.* (fol.360r2) is the same scribal hand that copied 1r1-f.309v1.[69] Thus the second hand represents simply the resumption of the early work of this scribe, who with his colleague together copied the whole *ms.* that lay before them. It cannot be therefore that the second hand by itself can be held to represent a latter addition of extraneous material to an original work complete at *fol.* 360r, contrary to what Schwartz indicated in his text.[70]

Frickel repeats at this point Lietzmann's contention that the original conclusion of the *ms.* at *fol.* 360r1 is further marked by the original scribe who takes up the copying from his colleague at this point with a decorated line separating the two putatively pseudo-Hippolytan works from the original *florilegium*.[71] While this is true, what the point neglects is that a similar decorated line also marks the transition from the first scribe to the second at the conclusion of *fol.* 310r (Plate 22). Indeed the line itself can be seen in Lietzmann's own photograph of the text at this point![72] Thus the decorated line is the usual means of indicating a transition from the first copyist to the second and back again, and no inference can be made on such a basis regarding the addition of different material to an existing text. Even were one to concur with Nautin's view that the same scribe adopted two different styles of handwriting, the existence of such an embroidered line at two points would not give any significance to that mark at one point that it did not also have at the other.[73]

4A 3.1.3.1.2. *Inferences from the title given to* fol. *360r1*

Frickel's second move is to challenge the compatibility of Hippolytus' title (ὁμιλία ʻ Ἱππολύτου ἀρχιεπισκόπου ʻ Ρώμης καὶ μάρτυρος) with the original presence of the ὁμιλία in a catholic work considered heretical by the monophysite compiler of the *florilegium*. Both the title ἀρχιεπίσκοπος and μάρτυρ were, Frickel argues, names of honour not given to heretics.[74] Thus

---

[69] Butterworth (1977) p. 3.

[70] Schwartz (1927) p. 9: "f. 360r, Columne a: Schluss dieses Stückes und der ganzen Sammlung."

[71] Frickel (1993) p. 97: "Nach Leos Brief an Kaiser Leo ist (fol 360r col. 1) ein Schluss markiert mittels eines Unterbrechungszeichens, das der Kopist A gesezt hat, um dann mit der Überschrift von CN neu zu beginnen. Dadurch hat er die zwei folgenden Schriften CN und AJ deutlich von den drei voranstehenden abgehoben."

[72] P. Franchi de' Cavalieri, and J. Leitzmann, *Specimina Codicum Graecorum Vaticanorum*, (Marcus and Weber: Bonn 1910), para 33: "altera (fol. 310r) ab alio scriba eiusdem aetatis... continet excerpta s. Cyrilli." See also plate 33 where there is an embroidered line with petals following, commencing in the second scribal hand the heading: χρήσεις ἁγίων πρων συμφώνως διδάσκουσαι ἡμᾶς διαφορὰν εἰδέναι φύσεως σώματός τε καὶ θεότητος...

[73] Nautin (1949) p. 74.

[74] Frickel (1993) p. 97-98: "...ist es ganz unglaubhaft, dass eine Schrift desselben H. im Codex V [sc. *Vat. Graec.* 1431] zusammen mit dem Tomus Leonis als Irrlehre eingestuft werden sollte. Schliesslich spricht auch der Titel von CN im Codex V gegen eine solche Deklassierung... Er enthält einen doppelten Ehrennamen: Erzbischof und Märtyrer."

both titles had to originate from the scribe in the Patir monastery in South Italy who, around 1105, copied the *florilegium* and then added two works of an unknown provenance.[75] Let us take these two titles separately.

4A 3.1.3.1.2.1. ὁμιλία᾿ Ἱππολύτου... μάρτυρος

Undoubtedly Frickel concentrates on the title of μάρτυς which is strongest in making his case. Would the author of one of a number of works thought by the monophysite compiler to be heretical be described by such a title of honour? It must however remembered that, though the title of μάρτυρ might not so easily be conceded to heretics in the first four centuries, yet by the fifth and later "real" martyrdom could no longer be used to distinguish the later orthodox from the heretics since neither side in the Monophysite or Apollinarian controversies could make the supreme sacrifice before a pagan authority that no longer existed.

Furthermore, if the charge of heresy was to be associated with an author in this case, it was with an author who had lived in ancient times, and who was commemorated in the Liberian *Depositio* long before. In terms of the Christological debate of the fourth and fifth century, his text was considered heretical by one side or other in that debate. His commemoration in Damasus' inscription and in the Liberian *Depositio* would have secured the title which may have seemed warranted because at all events it was based on the legend of the recantation of Hippolytus when facing death (1B 2.3.3.1 and 2.3.3.5).

Frickel's further contention was that the desciption of Hippolytus as martyr would have been more convincing on the part of a pro-papalist scribe in South Italy around 1107 than in the fifth century. But as we have been at pains to point out, the association of Hippolytus the writer with a shrine and a martyrology distinct from Hippolytus the soldier and guard of St. Laurence is very difficult substantiate in Rome at the turn of the second millennium (1B 2.3.2). Let us therefore look at whether the use of the archiepiscopal title will allow us to exempt a work bearing Hippolytus name from the original monophysite category of heretical works.

4A 3.1.3.1.2.2. ὁμιλία᾿ Ἱππολύτου ἀρχιεπισκόπου᾿ Ρώμης

᾿Αρχιεπίσκοπος may be a term of greater honour or praise but if ἐπίσκοπος is used instead, it cannot be because the former are always orthodox but that the latter can be heterodox. Thus the ascription of ἀρχιεπίσκοπος t o Hippolytus but only ἐπίσκοπος to Leo of Rome (*fol.* 342 and 353: ἐπιστολὴ Λέοντος ἐπισκόπου ᾿ Ρώμης πρὸς Φλαυιανὸν... Λέοντα) cannot lead us of itself to conclude that the letters of Leo were in the original concluding "heretical" section, but *C.N.* was added to the *florilegium* later by a twelfth century scribe who found it perfectly orthodox.

---

75 Ibid. p. 92-94, 96-97.

The collector of the various pieces of the monophysite *florilegium* may indeed have favoured Cyril and Athanasius with frequent references to them as ἀρχιεπίσκοπος and μακάριος (e.g. *fol.* 23v, 24r, 165v, 259v, 297v etc.).[76] But this is not invariably his practice and often his headings refer to both Cyril and Athanasius, like Julius of Rome, as ἐπίσκοπος, with or without the epithet μακάριος (250r, 253v, 277v, 165v, 227v, 247v etc.). Sometimes indeed the name of Cyril as of Julius stands alone (258v, 206r, 230r etc.). The titles themselves may have held no particular differentiating significance to the compiler of the *florilegium* who may simple have taken them over from other collections, or from the name and title on the scroll or codex that he was using. Thus no significance can be attributed to the title ἀρχιεπίσκοπος alone regarding whether *C.N.* was or was not originally in the "heretical" conclusion of the anti-chalcedonian collection.

It would moreover be a mistake to regard ἀρχιεπίσκοπος as the kind of title a twelfth-century scribe in Southern Italy, pro-papalist, but with Constantinopolitan and other eastern connections, would use. At all events, as I have already pointed out (3A 2), the title itself, expressing the patriarchal as opposed to the papal status of the bishop of Rome, is indicative of an eastern rather than a western, pro-papalist perspective. By this time, as we have also seen, Hippolytus, whose name did not appear in the Roman, episcopal succession lists, had in Rome been assigned the quite fictitious See of Portus (1B 2.3.3.3-4). We should note that, from the time of the *Chronicon Paschale* (A.D. 630), Hippolytus was described as μάρτυς and ἐπίσκοπος... τοῦ... Πόρτου, and this title was used also by Anastasius Apocrisarius (665), George Syncellus (792), Nicephorus (828), and Nicephorus Callistus (1300).[77] We have seen that it was with this See that Ligorio's Roman contemporaries were quick to assciate him (1A 2, and 1B 2.3.2). Zonaras (1120), moreover, writing some fifteen years after the time of the transcription of *Vat. Graec.* 1431, was well aware that there was no space for Hippolytus as bishop of Rome proper in the succession list, with the result that he tried to associate Hippolytus as bishop of Portus with the pontificate of Urban.[78]

---

[76] For these and other references see Schwartz (1927) p. 5-9, cf. Frickel (1993) p. 98.

[77] *Chronicon Pascale*, p. 12: Ἱππόλυτος τοίνυν ὁ τῆς εὐσεβίας μάρτυς, ἐπίσκοπος γεγονὼς τοῦ καλουμένου Πόρτου; Anastasius Apocrisarius, *Ep. Ad Theodos. Gangren.*: "... ex dictis sancti Hippolyti episcopi Portus Romani ac martyris... τοῦ ἀγίου Ἱππολύτου ἐπισκόπου Πόρτου... καὶ μάρτυρος; George Syncellus, *Chronographia* p. 674: ἱερὸς φιλόσοφος ἐπίσκοπος Πόρτου; Nicephorus, *Antirrhetica* 2,13: τοῦ ἀγίου Ἱππολύτου ἐπισκόπου Πόρτου καὶ μάρτυρος; Nicephorus Callistus, *Eccles. Hist.* 4,31: Ἱππόλυτος ὁ Πόρτου τῆς Ῥώμης ἐπίσκοπος. For these and other references see J.B. Lightfoot, *The Apostolic Fathers*. (London: MacMillan 1890), 1,2, p. 328-351.

[78] Zonaras, *Annal.* 12,15: τότε Οὐρβανοῦ τῆς ἐπισκοπῆς τῆς Ῥωμαίων πόλεως προεστῶτος καὶ Ἱππόλυτος ἤνθει ἀνὴρ ἱερώτατος καὶ σοφώτατος ἐπίσκοπος τοῦ κατὰ Ῥώμην Πόρτου...

It was perhaps not accidental that the first ascription of Portus as Hippolytus' See, not counting the *Chronicon Paschale*, was that of Rome's official ambassador at the court of Constantinople, the *apocrisarius* named Anastasius. It was from such a source that the name of Hippolytus' See as that of Portus arose, since to call Hippolytus bishop of Rome was most embarassing to the See of Rome itself who had no note of such a name in its succession list. There was no such compunction felt by many Eastern Fathers who unflinchingly described Hippolytus' See, unknown to Eusebius and Jerome, as that of Rome itself. Such Eastern Fathers as Eustratius of Constantinople (A.D. 578), Leontius of Byzantium (620), Anastasius Sinaita (680), Pseudo-John Damascene (700), and finally Oecumenius (900) refer to Hippolytus as ἐπίσκοπος or προέδρως of Rome.[79] By A.D. 900 however, such a title is no longer used as Portus becomes the name of Hippolytus' See.

Thus I submit that, at the time of the copying of *Vat. Graec.* 1431, the title of ἀρχιέπισκοπος τῆς Ῥώμης, would have been most unlikely applied to Hippolytus had not that title already been present in the *ms.* before the pro-papalist copyist. Had the title been composed by such a copyist around 1105, then he would have given Hippolytus' See as Portus. If he had been unaware that this was the See consistently attributed to Hippolytus since Anastasius, and had he been unaware that the See could not be that of Rome without conflicting with the succession lists, then he would have called Hippolytus πάππα and not ἀρχιεπίσκοπος. The concept of an archbishop of Rome was resonant of "schismatic Byzantium." Indeed, as a title it fits far better with the age of Chalcedon, and the Eastern desire to create five or more autonomous patriarchs rather than to acknowledge one universal head of Christendom.

Frickel therefore fails to establish the first part of his case for separating *C.N.* from the *florilegium*, based upon an examination of the fabric of *Vat. Graec.* 1431 and the historical circumstances of its copying. Let us now examine the second part of that case based upon the internal evidence of the theology represented by the text itself and its historical genesis.

4A 3.1.3.2. *Is* C.N. *largely an Apollinarian text?*

Hübner had originally argued that *C.N.* was an interpolated text, on the same grounds as those of Richard and Frickel, namely that Theodoret had given the original version of *C.N.* 17,5- 18,10 (4A 3.1.2). He further agreed that the interpolations were explicable only against the background of the age of Chalcedon. However he insisted that the interpolator was a single person

---

[79] Eustratius of Constantinople, *Adv. Psych.* 19; Leontinus of Byzantium, *De Sect. Act.* 3,1; Anastasius Sinaita, *Hodegus* 23; K. Holl, Fragmenta vornicänischer Kirchenväter aus den Sacra parallela, in *TU* 5,2, (1899), p. 128 (343); Oecomenius, *In Apoc.* praesc.

with a single design, which was to defend Chalcedonian orthodoxy against Apollinarianism.[80]

The critical passages for Hübner, as for Frickel in the light of his work, were:

1. *C.N.* 4,8-11: ... οὗτος ὁ λόγος καὶ παρθένου ἕνα υἱὸν θεῷ ἀπεργασάμενος... μήτι ἐρεῖ ὅτι ἐν οὐρανῷ σὰρξ ἦν;... πρὸ δὲ τούτου ἐν οὐρανῷ σὰρξ οὐκ ἦν, and,

2. *C.N.* 17,2: λαβὼν δὲ καὶ ψυχήν τὴν ἀνθρωπείαν, λογικὴν δὲ λέγω...

The rejection of the notion that Christ's flesh was in heaven before the incarnation, and the implicit rejection of two sons by the affirmation ἕνα υἱόν in the first passage, was a rejection of Apollinarianism.[81]

Frickel, as we shall see, acknowledged that, apart perhaps from these assertions, the rest of the Christology of of *C.N.* could hardly be equated with Chalcedonian orthodoxy. He therefore proposed to go beyond Nautin's acceptance of only the second passage (17,2) as a Chalcedonian interpolation, which the latter had accordingly bracketed in his text,[82] to include also 17,5. Frickel sees rather *C.N.* 4,8-11 as an adaption of Apollinarianism that formed part of the text as originally interpollated by someone of that school.[83] We have already sought to show that the denial of pre-existent flesh was born of the depersonalization of the λόγος–παῖς, the denial that when pre-existent he could be τελείος υἱός, and the desire to make Daniel's Son of Man a prophecy of what was to come rather than a meeting with a pre-existent, personal λόγος (4A 2). We have also sought to exemplify the use of both λογικὴ ψυχή, and φύσις in connection with the problem of τροπή and the incarnation from Hippolytus' contemporary, Origen (4A 3.1.2.1). Let us now examine in closer detail whether these passages only or even properly belong in either an Apollinarian or a Chalcedonian context.

4A 3.1.3.2.1. *C.N.* 4,8: οὗτος ὁ λόγος... ἀπεργασάμενος

In this passage we observe that the being who fashions (ἀπεργασάμενος) the one Son for God from the Virgin is the λόγος. Furthermore, as we have shown throughout *C.N.*, the λόγος ἄσαρκος is never called υἱός but always παῖς as a hypostasis that lacks full personhood (4A 2). In the Chalcedonian literature, whether orthodox or Apollinarian, I submit that the pre-incarnate λόγος is never given that function, nor is full Sonship denied before the incarnation.

---

[80] Hübner (1989) p. 220-222.

[81] Ibid. p. 221: "Zwei Aussagen sind es, die apollinareische Problematik anzeigen: erstens dass der Inkarnierte *ein einziger Sohn* ist (vgl. auch C.Noet. 15,7); zweitens, dass das Fleisch des Inkarnierten vor der Menschenwerdung *nicht in Himmel* war." (his italics)

[82] Nautin (1949) p. 261, line 25-26 cf. Hübner (1989) p. 220: "Die antiapollinarischen Korrekturen in CN 17,5 und 17,2 dürften demnach spätere Interpolationen sein."

[83] Frickel (1993) p. 121.

In Apollinaris' ἡ κατὰ μέρος πίστις, 5, the pre-existent second person of the Trinity is described as εἰς υἱὸς ὁ λόγος.[84] In 32 the fully personal, pre-existent Son takes as an independent agent flesh of the Virgin (τοῦ υἱοῦ τοῦ θεοῦ σάρκα λαβόντος τὴν ἐκ παρθένου) and is not fashioned as Son by the λόγος.[85] As an agent the λόγος "himself pre-existing as Son (αὐτὸς ὁ προϋπάρχων υἱός), joined and established in flesh from Mary (ἐνωθεὶς σαρκὶ ἐκ Μαρίας κατέστη), consituted *himself* perfect man (τέλειον... ἄνθρωπον συνιστὰς ἑαυτόν)." (36)[86]

The λόγος is clearly distinguished from the πνεῦμα in *De Unione* 13, unlike in the afterthought of *C.N.* 14,2 regarding the pre-existent godhead,[87] where in interpreting *Luke* 1,35 Apollinaris writes: "it is from the descent of the Spirit (ἐκ δὲ πνεύματος ἐφόδου) and the overshadowing power (καὶ δυνάμεως ἐπισκιασμοῦ) that the holy infant is composed from the Virgin (τὸ ἅγιον ἐκ τῆς παρθένου συνίσταται βρέφος)."[88] Thus the λόγος does not have any instrumental function in the incarnation in Apollinaris, nor is the pre-existent Son ever called by the preferred, second-century description of παῖς.

Furthermore, the instrumental action of the λόγος in the incarnation is further discussed outside *C.N.* In *Ant.* 4, whose Hippolytan authorship is unquestioned, we read:

> For since the Word of God (ἐπειδὴ γὰρ ὁ λόγος ὁ τοῦ θεοῦ), being fleshless (ἄσαρκος ὤν), put on the holy flesh from the holy virgin (ἐνεδύσατο τὴν ἁγίαν σάρκα ἐκ τῆς ἁγίας παρθένου) as a bridegroom a garment (ὡς νυμφίος ἱμάτιον), having woven it for himself in the sufferings of the cross (ἐξυφήνας ἑαυτῷ ἐν τῷ σταυρικῷ πάθει), so that having mixed our mortal body with his own power (ὅπως συνκεράσας τὸ θνητὸν ἡμῶν σῶμα τῇ ἑαυτοῦ δυνάμει), and having mingled the corruptible into the incorruptible (καὶ μίξας τὸ φθαρτὸν τῷ ἀφθάρτῳ), and the weak with the strong (καὶ τὸ ἀσθενὲς τῷ ἰσχυρῷ), he might save the Man that is lost (σώσῃ τὸν ἀπολλύμενον ἄνθρωπον).
>
> *Ant.* 4

But in the words that follow the action of the λόγος is likened to the shuttle of a loom moving through the mouths of the prophets who weave the perfect robe of Christ.[89] In this passage, moreover, we have anticipations of the later speculation about the two natures but in an early third century form. Words such as συνκεράσας, ἐξυφήνας, and μίξας abound, and though the latter

---

84 H. Lietzmann, Apollinaris von Laodicea und seine Schule, in *Texte und Untersuchungen von Hans Lietzmann*, (Tübingen: J.B. Mohr 1904), p. 169,11.

85 Ibid. p. 180,7-8.

86 Ibid. p. 181,11-12.

87 In *C.N.* 12,5 the distinction between the three persons is only made subsequent to the incarnation, thus: οὐκοῦν **ἔνσαρκον** λόγον θεωροῦμεν πατέρα δι' αὐτοῦ νοοῦμεν, υἱῷ δὲ πιστεύομεν, πνεύματι ἁγίῳ προσκυνοῦμεν.

88 Lietzmann (1904) p. 191,7-9.

89 *Ant.* 4: ...κερκὶς δὲ ὁ λόγος, οἱ δὲ ἐργαζόμενοι πατριάρχαι τε καὶ προφῆται οἱ τὸν καλὸν ποδήρη καὶ τέλειον χιτῶνα ὑφαίνοντες Χριστοῦ, δι' ὧν ὁ λόγος διικνούμενος κερκίδος δίκην ἐξυφαίνει...

work φύσις is not found, certainly the typical second century antitheses of
φθαρτόν–ἄφθαρτόν, ἀσθενές–ἰσχυρόν are. It would be fair therefore to say
that in such unambiguous, early third century literature we have speculations
regarding the incarnation that clearly anticipate the later vocabulary of
Chalcedon. However since the emphasis on "one Son" in this context has
been considered anti-Apollinarian both by Hübner and Frickel, we shall now
give this phrase further consideration.

4A 3.1.3.2.2. C.N. 4,8: παρθένου ἕνα υἱὸν θεῷ and 15,7: εἷς υἱὸς τέλειος
θεοῦ
Frickel sought to connect these two passages, and to regard what they asserted as consistent with the later development of speculation on the process
of incarnation inspired by Apollinaris. The statement:

> Nor could the flesh have existence by itself disjoined from the Word (οὔθ᾽ ἡ
> σὰρξ καθ᾽ ἑαυτὴν δίχα τοῦ λόγου ὑποστῆναι) on account of its having its
> subsistence in the Word (διὰ τὸ ἐν λόγῳ τὴν σύστασιν ἔχειν). Thus therefore
> one perfect Son of God was made manifest (οὕτως οὖν εἷς υἱὸς τέλειος θεοῦ
> ἐφανερώθη).
>
> C.N. 15,7b

was held therefore to be inspired by an Apollinarian reflection on the two
natures of Christ only perfectly made one in unity because of the lack of a
human νοῦς, but otherwise posessing the two heavenly natures of Son of
God and Son of Man. According to Hübner the affirmation of "one Son"
denies that Apollinarianism,[90] but according to Frickel it somehow affirms it
in such terms as these.[91] But once again both read too much of the fourth
century into these earlier christological expressions.

What immediately precedes these words is a reiteration of the claim, denied by Apollinaris, that the λόγος ἄσαρκος was not τέλειος υἱός. As we
have seen, Apollinaris always claimed that both Son of God and Son of Man
were pre-existent, which was what gave rise to the claim both that there were

---

[90] Hübner (1989) p. 221-222.
[91] Frickel (1993) p. 119: "Im Kontext von CN 15,5-7 geht es, wie Hübner richtig gesehen
hat, um das zentrale Anliegen des Apollinaris, in Christus nicht zwei Söhne, sondern einzigen
Sohn zu verkünden. Dabei versucht der Autor hier nicht, dem Vorwurf des Apollinaris (zwei
Söhne zu lehren) zu entgehen, sondern vertritt selbst, wie Kap. 15 zeigt, die Lehre des
Apollinaris." I find Frickel at this point very confusing, especially when he then describes as
"the Word... sent from the Father (15,1), incapable of suffering because of the flesh (15,3-4)",
with reference to *Rom.* 8, 3-4 (15,5) as "Schärfer kann man die apollinarischen Lehren kaum
formulieren."

two sons, both τέλειοι,[92] and that the flesh had pre-existed in heaven.[93] But here, immediately preceding, we find:

> What kind of Son of himself (ποῖον οὖν υἱὸν ἑαυτοῦ) has God sent through the flesh (ὁ θεὸς διὰ τῆς σαρκὸς κατέπεμψεν) but the Word (ἀλλ᾽ ἢ τὸν λόγον), whom he addresses as "Son" (ὃν υἱὸν προσηγόρευε) because he would become so in the future (διὰ τὸ μέλλειν αὐτὸν γενέσθαι)? And the common name for affection amongst men (καὶ τὸ κοινὸν ὄνομα τῆς εἰς ἀνθρώπους φιλοστοργίας) he assumes when called "Son." (ἀναλαμβάνει υἱὸς καλούμενος) For neither fleshless (οὔτε γὰρ ἄσαρκος) nor by himself (καὶ καθ᾽ ἑαυτὸν) was the Word complete Son (ὁ λόγος τέλειος ἦν υἱός), even though he was complete (καίτοι τέλειος), being the Word (λόγος ὤν), as only begotten (μονογενής).
>
> C.N. 15, 6-7a

Here once again the depersonalized status of the pre-existent λόγος separates this description from Apollinaris' pre-existent Son. When Apollinaris affirms one Son of God (as opposed to the other Son of Man), it is clearly, as in the De Fide et Incarn.6, υἱὸν θεοῦ καὶ ἀληθινὸν τὸν πρὸ αἰῶνος.[94] But in this passage the λόγος is only provisionally υἱὸς... διὰ τὸ μέλλειν αὐτὸν γενέσθαι. He is not, in Apollinaris' words to which we have already referred, pre-existent as εἷς υἱὸς ὁ λόγος. As we shall shortly see, in order to obviate this serious difficulty, Frickel had further to modify his position. He had now to claim that the Apollinarist had modified his Apollinarianism in order to be able to refute Marcellus of Ancyra.[95] We shall return to the implications of such a thesis in a moment.

For the present, let us seek to answer to what end the writer of C.N. 4,8 and 15,7 can describe the λόγος ἔνσαρκος as εἷς τέλειος υἱὸς given early third century Christological assumptions about the σάρξ... ἐν λόγῳ τὴν σύστασιν ἔχειν.

4A 3.1.3.2.2.1. C.N. 4,8: ἕνα υἱὸν θεῷ and 15,7: εἷς υἱὸς τέλειος

The insistence on the one Son cannot, at all events, be the Chalcedonian unity of the two natures, as Hübner asserts, since as we have seen the pre-existent λόγος is not complete (τέλειος) without the incarnation. The notion of εἷς υἱὸς is purchased at the cost of the completeness of the pre-incarnate nature in C.N. This was precisely why οὔθ᾽ ἡ σὰρξ καθ᾽ ἑαυτὴν δίχα τοῦ

---

92 Ad. Dionys. 172: ... ἀλλὰ τὸ μὲν καταβεβηκὸς ἐξ οὐρανοῦ ἐκαλεῖτο ἂν υἱὸς θεοῦ καὶ οὐχ υἱὸς ἀνθρώπου, τὸ δὲ γεννηθὲν ἐκ γυναικὸς ἐκαλεῖτο ἂν υἱὸς ἀνθρώπου καὶ οὐχ υἱὸς θεοῦ (Lietzmann (1904) p. 258, 7-10). Cf. also his follower, Vitalis, περὶ πίστεως 172: υἱὸς γὰρ ὢν ἀληθῶς θεοῦ κατὰ τὴν ἀίδιον ἐκ θεοῦ γέννησιν γέγονε καὶ υἱὸς ἀνθρώπου κατὰ τὴν ἐκ παρθένου γέννησιν... εἷς καὶ ὁ αὐτὸς τέλειος θεός... καὶ τέλειος ἄνθρωπος (p. 273, 9-14).
93 Ep. Ad Dionysius A 7 (Lietzmann (1904) 259,5-7): βλασφημῶσιν ἡμᾶς ὡς τὴν σάρκα λέγοντας ἐξ οὐρανοῦ, ὅταν ἀναγινώσκωμεν τὰς θείας γραφὰς υἱὸν ἀνθρώπου λεγούσας τὸν ἐξ οὐρανοῦ.
94 Lietzmann 197,17-18.
95 Frickel (1993) p. 120: "Auch der folgende Passus (CN 15, 6-7) inspiriert sich an Apollinaris, wenn er eine vermittelnde Position zwischen diesen und Markell zu finden..."

λόγου ὑποστῆναι διὰ τὸ ἐν λόγῳ τὴν σύστασιν ἔχειν, but it was the complete reversal of Apollinarianism. For Apollinaris it was the incomplete σάρξ without a rational soul that was completed by the fully pre-existent τέλειος υἱός.

The third century context in which the insistence on the εἷς υἱός most properly fits is, as I have argued, the context of *rapprochement* between Hippolytus as the successor to the author of *El.*, and the successors of Callistus (4A 1.2). In *El.* IX, 12,16-19, we saw that the charge of ditheism was made by Callistus against the author, and that the latter's claim had been τὸ ἐν τῇ παρθένῳ σαρκωθὲν πνεῦμα οὐχ ἕτερον παρὰ τὸν πατέρα ἀλλὰ ἓν καὶ τὸ αὐτό. In consequence Father and Son were not two gods (δύο θεούς, πατέρα καὶ υἱόν), but one (ἀλλ᾽ ἕνα). This remained the case after the incarnation (ὁ... πατήρ, προσλαβόμενος τὴν σάρκα... ἐποίησεν ἕν). In consequence both Father and the Son are called one God (πατέρα καὶ υἱὸν ἕνα θεόν). But if this is the case, we can speak of either ἕνα πατέρα or ἕνα υἱόν. Hippolytus, as we have also argued (*C.N.* 11,1; 14,2), is sensitive to the charge of ditheism, and resolves the issue by only making the Son τέλειος at the incarnation so that there is no pre-existent, second God the Son. It is his *rapprochement* with Monarchianism that therefore explains the εἷς υἱός of *C.N.*

4A 3.1.3.2.2.2. σάρξ... ἐν λόγῳ τὴν σύστασιν ἔχειν

Speculation about the flesh sustained by the λόγος was also characteristic, in a certain form, of Christology by the early third century, where τέλειος also is frequently found. In the Naasene Psalm we read:

> ... the great Man from above (ὁ μέγας ἄνθρωπος ἄνωθεν)... is given a soul (ἐδόθη αὐτῷ καὶ ψυχή) in order that through the soul he might suffer (ἵνα διὰ τῆς ψυχῆς πάσχῃ) and the enslaved matter of...the perfect Man might be punished (καὶ κολάζεται καταδουλούμενον τὸ πλάσμα τοῦ... τελείου ἀνθρώπου).
>
> *El.* V, 7,7

There then follows speculation regarding the nature (φύσις) of this ψυχή (τίς ἐστιν ἡ ψυχὴ καὶ πόθεν καὶ ποταπὴ τὴν φύσιν). It never stays in the same shape or form (οὐ γὰρ μένει ἐπὶ σχήματος οὐδὲ μορφῆς τῆς αὐτῆς πάντοτε), and its changes are described in the Gospel of the Egyptians (τὰς δὲ ἐξαλλαγὰς ταύτας τὰς ποικίλας ἐν τῷ ἐπιγραφομένῳ κατ᾽ Αἰγυπτίους). As to its φύσις, the Naasenes "are perplexed (ἀποροῦσιν) whether it is from pre-existent matter (πότερόν ποτε ἐκ τοῦ προόντος), or whether it was self-generated (ἢ ἐκ τοῦ αὐτογενοῦς) or from the poured forth chaos (ἢ ἐκ τοῦ ἐκκεχυμένου χάους) (*El.* V, 7,8-9)."

We have already argued that the author of *C.N.* was seeking to expound the theology of λόγος and σάρξ in the Fourth Gospel in such a way as to deliver it from its use as a source of proof texts for the extreme Monarchians

(2A 2.4). In such a *milieu,* Hippolytus was prepared to use quite daringly, we argued, speculations that originally belonged to aeon speculation in Gnosticism (2A 3.1-2; 4A 1.1) in order to save the λόγος of the Fourth Gospel from a completely monarchical identity with the Father. We shall have more to say regarding the deceptive literary façade of the conservative biblical scholar who was quite prepared to use some quite radical, Hellenistic religious notions in his exegesis (5A 8 .4 and 5B 3.1.1-2.). In such a *milieu* it can now be seen that *C.N.* 17, 15-18 makes sense as an anti-Docetism that finds it quite appropriate to deny that the σάρξ of the incarnate λόγος the Fourth Gospel, in relation to the ἄνθρωπος ἄνωθεν of *Jn.* 3,13.

If one asks of whom he says μήτι ἐρεῖ ὅτι ἐν οὐρανῷ σάρξ ἦν or πρὸ δὲ τούτου ἐν οὐρανῷ σάρξ οὐκ ἦν (*C.N.* 4,10-11), we may answer in terms of the Christology of the early third century that it was directed against such sects as the Naasenes and their speculation on the composition of the σῶμα and ψυχή of the τέλειος ἄνθρωπος ἄνωθεν. For the σάρξ of *Jn.* 1,1-18 to be worn by the ὁ ἄνωθεν (*Jn.* 3, 12-13, 31), incarnation, in a specific human form, οὐ... κατὰ φαντασίαν ἢ τροπήν, was necessary (*C.N.* 17,5). There was no ψυχή composed ἐκ τοῦ προόντος and exhibiting ἐξαλλαγὰς ταύτας τὰς ποικίλας and clothing the πλάσμα τοῦ τελείου ἀνθρώπου.

If it be objected that ψυχή is not here indicative of flesh, it is to be emphasized that the ψυχή in question was to be found in the πλάσμα τοῦ τελείου ἀνθρώπου. Furthermore, as a commentary on the Valentinian hymn in *El.* VI, 37,7-8, we read: "flesh is matter according to them (σάρξ ἐστι ἡ ὕλη κατ᾿ αὐτούς) which hangs from the soul of the Demiurge (ἥτις κρέμαται ἐκ τῆς ψυχῆς, τουτέστι τοῦ δημιουργοῦ)." There is a quite easy transition between πλάσμα, ὕλη and σάρξ, containing ψυχή in Hellenistic religion, and the heavenly body (ἐκ τοῦ προόντος) of the ἄνθρωπος τέλειος, to whom a ψυχή is given.

4A 3.1.3.2.2.3. C.N. *4,8 and Apelles in* El. *VII, 36,2-3*
Furthermore Apelles shows us specifically how this speculation about the ψυχή–πλάσμα of the τέλειος ἄνθρωπος was discussed in terms of σάρξ. His belief is thus recorded:

> Christ descended from the higher power (τὸν δὲ Χριστὸν ἐκ τῆς ὕπερθεν δυνάμεως κατεληλυθέναι), that is from the good God (τουτέστι τοῦ ἀγαθοῦ θεοῦ), and he was the latter's Son (κἀκείνου αὐτὸν εἶναι υἱόν). But he was not born of the Virgin (τοῦτον δὲ οὐκ ἐκ παρθένου γεγενῆσθαι), nor was he he fleshless when he appeared in flesh, he says, (οὐδ᾿ αὖ ἄσαρκον εἶναι τὸν ἐν σαρκὶ φανέντα λέγει), but from the substance of the universe he took (ἀλλ᾿ ἐκ τῆς τοῦ παντὸς οὐσίας μεταλαβόντα) and fashioned a body of parts (μερῶν σῶμα πεποιηκέναι), that is to say of the hot and the cold, and the moist and the dry (τουτέστι θερμοῦ καὶ ψυχροῦ, καὶ ὑγροῦ καὶ ξηροῦ)...
>
> *El.* VII, 36,2-3

Here therefore we have a μερῶν σῶμα which is also acknowledged as σάρξ that is pre-existent in that it is οὐδ᾽ ἄσαρκον on the one hand but that it was also οὐκ ἐκ παρθένου γεγενῆσθαι on the other. Apelles might agree therefore with *C.N.* 4, 10-11 that ἐν οὐρανῷ σάρξ οὐκ ἦν but insist to the contrary that it was composed instead of the pre-existent primal elements, in other words ἐκ τῆς τοῦ παντὸς οὐσίας μεταλαβόντα, κτλ... As such he would agree with those Naasenes who asserted that the πλάσμα of the ἄνθρωπος τέλειος was ἐκ τοῦ ἐκκεχυμένου χάους and not ἐκ τοῦ προόντος. But in terms of the Hellenistic background of the early third century it was therefore quite possible for someone to assert that Apelles' pre-existent and unborn Χριστός ἐνσάρκος had a σάρξ that was ἐν οὐρανῷ. It would be more true of such an interpreter of Apelles in the second century than of Apollinaris in the fourth therefore to say of the author of *C.N.*, in the words of Hübner: *Seine Gegner hielten ihm deshalb vor, er sage, Christi Fleisch stamme aus dem Himmel und nicht aus Maria.*[96]

If this is the case, we would do well to inquire whether reference in *C.N.* 17,2 to the ψυχὴ λογική is the interpollation that both Nautin and Frickel, each for their own reasons, had to claim, particularly in view of the anticipation of a two-natures theology that we have witnessed as early as Origen (4A 3.1.2.1).

4A 3.1.3.2.2.4. C.N. *17,2:* ψυχὴν τὴν ἀνθρωπείαν, λογικήν

Origen, writing in the course of the first half of the third century, with whom, according to Jerome, Hippolytus had met (*De Vir. Ill.* 61),[97] makes reference in his *Hom. in Luc.* 22 to the ψυχὴν λογικὴν ἀνθρωπίνην.[98]As such he was continuing the theme already witnessed in *Contra Cels.* 4,18 (4A 3.1.2.1). In this passage the reference is to the Gentiles replacing their hearts of stone, but this is not as such unlike the ψυχή given to Adamas who previously lies ἄπνουν, ἀκίνητον, ἀσάλευτον ὡς ἀνδριάντα (*El.* V, 7,6) and who is describes as ὁ λίθος ἀκρογωνιαῖος (V, 7,35). Certainly therefore reference to the ψυχὴ ἀνθρωπεία taken to save τὸν πεπτωκότα ᾽Αδάμ is consistent with Hippolytus' daring, 'orthodox' appropriation of the Adamas imagery of the Naasene Psalm, as we shall argue in detail later (5B 3.2.2). But we noted also that in the Psalm (*El.* V, 7,7) a ψυχή was given to Adamas (= τέλειος ἄνθρωπος) and that speculation was rife as to the substance of this soul. It may therefore be the case that Nautin's admission of a Chalcedonian interpolation here was unnecessary. As Origen's reference shows, such an

---

[96] Hübner (1989) p. 222.
[97] Quoted 5A 8.3 and footnote 116.
[98] This phrase does not simply come from Jerome's translation ("Haud dubium quin postquam illi transierint, gentes lapidae esse cessabunt et pro duro corde recipient humanam in Christo rationabilemque naturam") but is represented in the Greek remains, see Rauer (1939), p. 139. See also *frag.* 10,7 on *Lk.* 8,16 (Ibid. p. 237): οὐ δεῖ τοίνυν τὸν ἅψαντα λύχνον ἐν ψυχῇ λογικὸν κρύπτειν.

idea was not alien to early-third-century, writers. We have already argued that the equation of λόγος with νοῦς had its single daring antecedent in Athenagoras, though there were traces of some kind of emanation theory in Tatian (2A 3.1).

Now Tatian is quite prepared to speak of the the pre-existent λόγος as λογικὴ δύναμις when he says in *Orat. ad Graec.* 5,1: θεὸς... τὰ πάντα σὺν αὐτῷ διὰ λογικῆς δυνάμεως αὐτὸς καὶ ὁ λόγος ὃς ἦν ἐν αὐτῷ ὑπέστησεν. Furthermore, men are distinguished in Athenagoras by the possession of both ψυχή and λογικὴ κρίσις.[99] For λογική to be used in proximity to language about ψυχή is not foreign therefore to second-century writers, whether it is about the human ψυχή or the λογικὴ δύναμις of the pre-existent λόγος.

It may well be therefore that we should accept λαβὼν δὲ καὶ ψυχὴν τὴν ἀνθρωπείαν, λογικὴν δὲ λέγω, etc. (*C.N.* 17,2) as part of the original text, and cease to read these words through the spectacles afforded by later controversies. The ψυχή was given to Adamas in order, it might be said, in the words of 17,2 ἵνα... σώσῃ τὸν πεπτωκότα 'Αδὰμ (= *El.* V,, 7,7: καταδουλούμενον τὸ πλάσμα τοῦ... τελείου ἀνθρώπου). λογική would thus simply record the fact that the ψυχή given in the incarnation was the λόγος ἔνσαρκος. We shall argue further that Hippolytus' exposition in *Ben Jac.* 119β and in *On the Great Ode* reflect the Adamas' *motif* of this passage marked in particular by the phrase τὸν πεπτωκότα 'Αδὰμ (5B 3.2.2). Athenagoras did after all argue that man must be composed both of soul and body in order to be able to continue eternally, and this could not happen without being raised (ἀδύνατον μὴ ἀνιστάμενον).[100]

Furthermore, we note in Irenaeus *Adv. Haer.* I, 6,1 that the Valentinians claimed that Christ possessed a spiritual body from Achamoth (ἀπὸ μὲν τῆς 'Αχαμὼθ τὸ πνευματικόν) but an animal or psychic body from the Demiurge (ἀπὸ δὲ τοῦ Δημιουργοῦ ἐνδεδύσασθαι τὸν ψυχικὸν Χριστόν), "in consequence of the divine arrangement of being invested with a body that possessed psychic substance" (ἀπὸ δὲ τῆς οἰκονομίας περιτεθεῖσθαι σῶμα, ψυχικὴν ἔχον οὐσίαν). In second century Christology there is a close connection between λόγος and πνεῦμα (and clearly οἰκονομία too) and Tatian, who has already given us the expression λογικὴ δύναμις (*Orat. ad Graec.* 5,1), continues in 13,1 to describe the salvation of the human ψυχή in terms of the λόγος in *Jn.* 1,5:

> For the soul did not itself preserve the spirit (ψυχὴ γὰρ οὐκ αὐτὴ τὸ πνεῦμα ἔσωσεν), but was preserved by it (ἐσώθη ὑπ' αὐτοῦ); and the light overwhelmed the darkness (καὶ δὲ τὸ φῶς τὴν σκοτίαν κατέλαβεν), by which [is meant] the

---

99 Athenagoras, *De Resurrect.*, 24,4: ἀνθρώπων ψυχῇ καὶ λογικῇ κρίσει χρωμένων.

100 *De Resurrectione* 15,6: ὁ δὲ καὶ νοῦν καὶ λόγον δεξάμενός ἐστιν ἄνθρωπος, οὐ ψυχὴ καθ' ἑαυτην· ἄνθρωπον ἄρα δεῖ τὸν ἐξ' ἀμφοτέρων ὄντα διαμένειν εἰς ἀεί, τοῦτον δὲ διαμένειν ἀδύνατον μὴ ἀνιστάμενον.

light of God is the Word (ἣ λόγος μέν ἐστι τὸ τοῦ θεοῦ φῶς), but the ignorant soul is darkness (σκότος δὲ ἡ ἀνεπιστήμων ψυχή).

If σκότος describes the ἀνεπιστήμων ψυχή by what adjective in such a context might the enlightened soul be described? By what adjective moreover would the soul of the Heavenly Man be described? Πνευματική ψυχή would sound too much like a category error in the ears of Hellenistic religious culture. The soul enlightened by the λόγος would surely be λογικὴ ψυχή? Thus the phrase would, shorn of Chalcedonian preconceptions, reflect well the *Zeitgeist* of second and early third century Christianity at the interface with Gnosticism.

Let us however now ask whether νοῦς is used in an Apollinarian sense in *C.N.*, as Frickel wishes to claim, and which, were it so, would clearly take us beyond the early-third-century to the late fourth.

4A 3.1.3.2.2.5. C.N. *10,4; 11,3:* νοῦς προβάς
Frickel insists that *C.N.* 11,2, when it states οὗτος δὲ νοῦς, ὃς προβὰς ἐν κόσμῳ ἐδείκνυτο παῖς θεοῦ, is making direct reference to *die Lehre des Apollinaris von dem fleischgewordenen Gott, von dem* νοῦς ἔνσαρκος.[101] We have already stressed that παῖς is never used of the pre-incarnate λόγος in Apollinaris, who would have said υἱός. Furthermore νοῦς is here not used of the incarnate Son but of an alternative description of the λόγος ἄσαρκος, who is always for that reason described as παῖς. At the creation, the order of the world, conceived in God's mind as νοῦς, was made visible in the λόγος–παῖς (10,4: προῆκεν τῇ κτίσει κύριον τὸν ἴδιον νοῦν). Hippolytus is concerned here therefore with the νοῦς as an alternative description for the pre-existent ἄσαρκος λόγος–παῖς and not with the υἱὸς ἔνσαρκος.

In the use of this term, we must therefore make a careful distinction between the νοῦς as an equivalent term for the λόγος ἄσαρκος as a separate hypostasis, however depersonalized, and νοῦς as the higher rational faculty of the soul which is displaced by the divine in the flesh given by the Virgin. Our argument is that νοῦς is always used in the former sense throughout *C.N.* but never found in that sense in Apollinaris, who always uses it in the latter sense. We have seen (2A 3.1; 4A 1.1) the bold adoption on the part of Hippolytus in *C.N.* of an almost emanationist explanation (προῆκεν, προβάς) of the λόγος as νοῦς (*C.N.* 10,4; 11,2), which he uses whilst protesting too much that he rejects the φλυαρία of the Valentinians and others (11,3). We shall pursue this question further when we shall see that there was to exist in the fourth century, at the Council of Philopolis in 347, a folk-memory of Hippolytus, not as an Apollinarian, but as a Valentinian, arguably on the basis of contemporary reaction at the time to what was to be found in *C.N.* (5B 3.2). But with Apollinaris νοῦς is always associated with what was

---

[101] Frickel (1993) p. 121.

lacking in the flesh given by the Virgin, and not with the pre-existent λόγος, as we can see from the following examples:

1. *Frag.* 69 (Lietzmann p. 220): οὐ γὰρ ἂν (φησιν) ἐν ὁμοιώματι ἀνθρώπου γεγονώς εἴη, εἰ μὴ τυγχάνοι καθάπερ ἄνθρωπος νοῦς ἔνσαρκος ὤν. Clearly here the phrase νοῦς ἔνσαρκος is a description of any human being (καθάπερ ἄνθρωπος), and was therefore implied in Christ's human likeness (ἐν ὁμοιώματι ἀνθρώπου), although in his case the νοῦς was divine and not human. Cf. also *frag.* 72 (p. 221): διὰ τοῦτο καὶ ἄνθρωπος ἦν· ἄνθρωπος γὰρ νοῦς ἐν σαρκὶ κατὰ τὸν Παῦλον.

2. *Frag.* 71 (p. 221): εἰ μὴ νοῦς ἔνσαρκος γέγονεν ὁ λόγος, ἀλλὰ σοφία ἦν ἐν τῷ νῷ, οὐ κατέβη ὁ κύριος οὐδὲ ἐκένωσεν ἑαυτόν. Here there is drawn a very close connection between the λόγος replacing the human νοῦς ἔνσαρκος otherwise, in accordance with *Jn.* 1,9-10, the λόγος would have remained the φῶς... ὃ φωτίζει πάντα ἄνθρωπον that is to say the σοφία... φωτίζουσα νοῦν ἀνθρώπου, and the incarnation would have been in no way unique. Cf. also *frag.* 70 (p. 220).

Thus in both cases νοῦς is not used like σοφία as a less than personal but independent instrumental hypostasis, but is used psychologically and anthropologically. In 2 we find a specific denial of the sense of the pre-existent νοῦς of *C.N.* 11,2, since in such a form it would simply have been the light which lightens everyone, and not specifically what was born of the Virgin.

Moreover there is no greater contrast than between Apollinaris' use of νοῦς and σοφία and that of *C.N.* 10, 2-3. There, as we have argued, the point of claiming that the God who was πολύς , whilst being μόνος , was nevertheless οὔτε ἄλογος and οὔτε ἄσοφος, was to show how the λόγος or σοφία or finally νοῦς (10,4) could proceed from God like gnostic emanations but without thereby becoming two or more gods (4A 1.1). In Apollinaris, as 1 indicates, νοῦς was part of the divine λόγος that described the anthropology of the incarnation.

We saw moreover that, though Athenagoras and Tatian anticipated in some respects such speculation, Hippolytus on his part in *C.N.* goes further than they are prepared to do (2A 3.1). Yet that speculation remained firmly within the context of the late second and early third century where its starting premises were firmly based. νοῦς was not a component of λόγος, as it became for Apollinaris, but a separate hypostasis, originally personal but to some extent depersonalized in terms of *C.N.*'s anti-ditheithistic concerns which temporized with Monarchianism. For Athenagoras νοῦς remained a fully personal, alternative description of the pre-existent Son, even though the term was not used as in *C.N.* to suggest procession but rather the reverse.[102]

Frickel had always been correct in rejecting the orthodoxy of the Christology of *C.N.*, judged by the standards of Chalcedon. Hübner was certainly wrong to have claimed the work in its entireity for Chalcedonian or-

---

102 *Legat.*, 10,2: ὄντος δὲ τοῦ υἱοῦ ἐν πατρὶ καὶ πατρὸς ἐν υἱῷ ἑνότητι καὶ δυνάμει πνεύματος, νοῦς καὶ λόγος τοῦ πατρὸς ὁ υἱὸς τοῦ θεοῦ.

thodoxy on the basis of 4,11 and 17, 2 alone. If they were testimonies (as we have argued that they were not) to Chalcedonian orthodoxy, and if we were permitted to read them only in the context of fourth-and fifth-century debates (as we have argued that we are not), then in the light of their incongruity thus read with the rest of the heterodox texts, we would have to follow Frickel, and, in the case of 17,2, Nautin, and regard them as interpolations. But even if we were prepared to do this, we could not now follow Frickel in indentifying the remaining heterodox text with Apollinarianism. Let us therefore consider briefly and finally the remaining fourth century contender for that theology, without the alleged interpolations, in the person of Marcellus of Ancyra.

4A 3.1.3.3. C.N. *10 as influenced by the theology of Marcellus of Ancyra*

Frickel's problem was always that the theology of *C.N.* had been in many respects a reversal of Apollinarianism. The former had denied full personality to the hypostatized λόγος before the incarnation, and withheld the description τέλειος until the incarnation. But for the latter the λόγος is perfect Son before the incarnation. As Apollinaris claims:

> ... for the Son is Wisdom (σοφία γὰρ ἐστιν ὁ υἱός), through which all things were created (δι᾽ ἧς τὰ πάντα ἔκτισται), And created things communicate wisdom (τὰ δὲ κτίσματα μηνύει τὴν σοφίαν) and God makes our acquaintence in wisdom (καὶ ὁ θεὸς ἐν τῇ σοφίᾳ γιγνώσκεται); but the Wisdom of God is not like that which a man has (οὐ τοιαύτη δὲ ἡ τοῦ θεοῦ σοφία οἵαν ἄνθρωπος ἔχει) but perfect, proceeding from perfect God (ἀλλὰ τελεία ἐκ τελείου τοῦ θεοῦ προελθοῦσα)... on account of this it is not only Wisdom, but also God (διὰ τοῦτο οὐ μόνον ἐστὶ σοφία, ἄλλὰ καὶ θεός), not only Logos but also Son (οὐδὲ μόνον λόγος, ἀλλὰ καὶ υἱός)...
>
> ἡ κατὰ μέρος πίστις: 4-8[103]

It is here that we find what looks suspiciously like a direct refutation of *C.N.* 10. In order to deny ditheism (11,1), the latter had argued anthropomorphically that, before the incarnation θεὸς μονός and πολύς was οὔτε... ἄλογος οὔτε ἄσοφος so that πάντα... διὰ λόγου καὶ σοφίας τεχνάζεται, λόγῳ μὲν κτίζων, σοφίᾳ δὲ κοσμῶν. But in this passage this line of argument against full (τέλειος) sonship is closed by attacking its literalism and correponding failure to proceed analogically (οὐ τοιαυτὴ δὲ ἡ τοῦ θεοῦ σοφία οἵαν ἄνθρωπος ἔχει). Although God "begat the λόγος (ἐγέννα λόγον)" it remained an instrument of his own will as τὸν **ἴδιον** νοῦν, and therefore the ἄσαρκος λόγος–παῖς was not τέλειος υἱός (15,7). Only after the incarnation is it possible to speak of two or even three πρόσωπα or persons (7,1; 14,2-3) (See also 4A 3.2.2). But for Apollinaris full personality in the light of analogous use of language (διὰ τοῦτο οὐ μόνον ἐστὶ σοφία, ἄλλὰ καὶ θεός) can be maintained and so σοφία like λόγος is both "perfect" (τελεία ἐκ τελείου τοῦ

---

[103] Lietzmann (1904) p. 168,23- 169,4.

θεοῦ προελθοῦσα) and is pre-existent as Son (οὐδὲ μόνον λόγος, ἀλλὰ καὶ υἱός). Thus each feature of the Christology of *C.N.* is denied by Apollinaris. For the latter it was the pre-existent perfect Son that supplied the νοῦς that perfected the flesh of the Virgin, not the flesh of the virgin that made perfect the λόγος ἄσαρκος who thereby became ἔνσαρκος as in *C.N.* Undoubtedly we find echoes of this reversal of Apollinaris' position in Marcellus of Ancyra, in language that once again appears to both reflect and, unlike Apollinaris, affirm the Christology of *C.N.* 10, 2-4.

Marcellus similarly against the Arian Asterius will deny personality to the pre-existing λόγος, as he says:

> For before the world was (πρὸ γὰρ τοῦ τὸν κόσμον εἶναι) the Word was in the Father (ἦν ὁ λόγος ἐν τῷ πατρί). But when the almighty God (ὅτε δὲ ὁ παντοκράτωρ θεὸς) designed to make everything in heaven and upon earth (πάντα τὰ ἐν οὐρανοῖς καὶ ἐπὶ γῆς ποιῆσαι προέθετο), the birth of the world required crafting energy (ἐνεργείας ἡ τοῦ κόσμου γένεσις ἐδεῖτο δραστικῆς); and for this reason (καὶ διὰ τοῦτο), when there was no-one other than God (μηδενὸς ὄντος ἑτέρου πλὴν θεοῦ)... then the Word proceeded (τότε ὁ λόγος προελθὼν) and became the maker of the world (ἐγίνετο τοῦ κόσμου ποιητής), he also previously having prepared him mentally within himself (ὁ καὶ πρότερον ἔνδον νοητῶς ἑτοιμάζων αὐτόν), as the prophet Solomon teaches us, (ὡς διδάσκει ἡμᾶς ὁ προφήτης Σολομὼν)... [*Prov.* 8,27-30]... For the Father naturally rejoiced (ἔχαιρεν γὰρ εἰκότως ὁ πατὴρ) making all things with wisdom and power through the Word (μετὰ σοφίας καὶ δυνάμεως διὰ τοῦ λόγου πάντα ποιῶν).
>
> *Frag.* 60[104]

We have here the λόγος being at God's side, as in *Prov.* 8,30, (συμπαρήμην αὐτῷ) just as in *C.N.* 11,1, in allusion to the same text: "Another took his stand beside him" (καὶ οὕτως αὐτῷ παρίστατο ἔτερος). But the λόγος is ἐνεργεία δραστική. Although God is one (μηδενὸς ὄντος ἑτέρου πλὴν θεου), the Word can exist within him mentally (ἔνδον νοητῶς ἑτοιμάζων) and as such does exist (ἦν ὁ λόγος ἐν τῷ πατρί). In a similar way, in *C.N.* 10, 2, the one God can still be "manifold (πολύς)" in the sense that he is not ἄλογος, so that the λόγος exists in him mentally.

Just as the birth of the λόγος, to whom *Ps.* 109,3 is addressed (πρό ἑωσ–φόρου ἐξεγέννησά σε), is in Marcellus made to refer to the birth of Jesus and the star followed by the wise men, so also, as we have seen (4A 2), contrary to *El.* X, 33,11, *C.N.* 16,7 makes this verse prophetic of Christ's birth (τὴν τοῦ λόγου γέννησιν σημαίνων).[105] Indeed both works, directed against

---

104 E. Klostermann and G.C. Hansen, Eusebius' Werke, 4: Gegen Marcell: Über die kirchliche Theologie: Die Fragmente Marcells, in *GCS*, (Berlin: Akamie Verlag 1906), p. 196,3-12.

105 Frag. 31 (Klosterman (1906) p. 190,1-4: οὗτος γὰρ ἦν ὁ τηνικαῦτα φανεὶς ἀστήρ, ὁ φέρων τε καὶ δηλῶν τὴν ἡμέραν τοῖς μάγοις. πρόδηλον οὖν τὸ «πρὸ ἑωσφόρου ἐγέννησα σε» ὑπὸ τοῦ παντοκράτορος εἰρῆσθαι δεσπότου περὶ τοῦ διὰ τῆς παρθένου γεννηθέντος σὺν τῇ ἀνθρωπίνῃ σαρκὶ λόγου... See also *frag.* 30 (p. 189, 25-27).

ditheism, can be accused of Monarchianism, as Marcellus most certainly was. But can *C.N.* be convincingly read as a fourth-century as opposed to a second-century *rapprochement* with Monarchianism, and be dated subsequent to Marcellus of Ancyra?

Against this it must be said that the Marcellus fragments show a theology far more developed in terms of a thoroughgoing consistency. Marcellus will not describe the procession of the pre-existent Word, his ὁ λόγος προελθών, as due to the action of a God who begets. πρωτότοκος is always used as referring to Christ as firstborn from the dead, and Asterius' application of it to the pre-existent λόγος is always denied.[106] While neither πρωτόγονος nor πρωτότοκος, both found in *El.* mainly in heretical contexts,[107] are completely absent from *C.N.*, nevertheless the latter was prepared to say of the Father at the creation, as opposed to the incarnation (16,7): ἐργάτην ἐγέννα λόγον (10,4).

As we have seen in *frag.* 60, the λόγος προελθὼν ἐγίνετο τοῦ κόσμου ποιητής. But Marcellus is not prepared to say that the Word was begotten as ποιητής. The λόγος is not ποιητής as a separate person but only so as God's ἐνεργεία δραστική. In *frag.* 61 the unity of θεός and λόγος is explained from a "humble example (ταπεινοῦ... παραδείγματος)." He continues:

> For neither is it possible to separate reason from manhood potentially and substantially (οὐδὲ γὰρ τὸν τοῦ ἀνθρώπου λόγον δυνάμει καὶ ὑποστάσει χωρίσαι τινὶ δυνατόν); for reason is one and the same thing as man (ἓν γάρ ἐστιν καὶ ταὐτὸν τῷ ἀνθρώπῳ ὁ λόγος), since it is separated in no other sense (καὶ οὐδενὶ χωριζόμενος ἑτέρῳ) than that in which the power [to act] alone is from the act (ἢ μόνῃ τῇ τῆς πράξεως ἐνεργείᾳ).

Thus Marcellus goes further than *C.N.* in a *rapprochement* with Monarchianism of which he was accused. It is not simply that he will join *C.N.* in refusing the title of πρωτότοκος to the λόγος before the incarnation—except in the latter's case by anticipation—but he will also have no truck with the concept of a τέλειος λόγος—and even a παῖς who is not a τέλειος υἱός—before the incarnation. The depersonalized λόγος still retained too much of personhood to provide a satisfactory weapon against Asterius' δεύτερος θεός, and the assertion of two or three πρόσωπα (4A3.2.2) certainly ran counter to Marcellus' doctrine of the one πρόσωπον.[108]

---

[106] *Frag.* 2 (Klostermann (1906) p. 185, 24-27): οὐ μόνον τοίνυν τῆς «καινῆς κτίσεως» πρωτότοκον αὐτὸν ὁ ἀπόστολος εἶναι φησίν, ἀλλὰ καὶ πρωτότοκον «ἐκ νεκρῶν» δι᾽ οὐδὲν ἕτερον, ἐμοὶ δοκεῖν, ἀλλ᾽ ἵνα διὰ τοῦ πρωτοτόκου «τῶν νεκρῶν», ὅπως καὶ «πτωτότοκος ἁπάσης κτίσεως» εἴρηται, γνωσθῆναι δυνηθῇ. Cf. *frags* 3-6 (p. 186,4-23) and *frag.* 96 (p. 205,24-206,4).

[107] πρωτόγονος: *El.* V 7,5; 19,13; X, 11,7; 19,19; ; πρωτότοκος: V, 9,2; 19,20. Both terms are used of the λόγος–παῖς X, 33,11 and 33,2.

[108] M. Simonetti, L' unità di Dio: L'oriente dopo Origene, in *Rivista di storia e letteratura religiosa*, 25 (1989), p. 193-233 reprinted in Studi sulla cristologia del II e III secolo, in *StEphAug* 44 (1993), p. 335.

Thus *C.N.* emerges as a second century work firstly, but not entirely because of a παῖς–λόγος theology, that is a daring adaption of second-century Christology in the light of a refashioning of certain concepts derived from Hellenistic religion that Hippolytus predecessor had rejected in *El.* It is shown to be pre-Marcellan by a not wholly consistent Christology that, though it appeared in the early third century to have satisfied the objections of a predominant Monarchian theology regarding the support of a λόγος Christology for two gods, by the fourth century it clearly had given too much to an Arian such as Asterius. It needed the more rigorous reformulation that Marcellus sought to give it, in order to service a full-blooded, fourth century, Monarchiansim.

As we shall now see, both the pneumatology and the teaching on the δύο πρόσωπα are consistent with an early third century date, particularly in view of the testimony of Tertullian to a doctrine of both in opposition to Monarchianism. In the course of our discussion we shall see that we have in *C.N.* represented a variety of concepts such as ἄσαρκος, ἐνσαρκος, πρόσωπα, τέλειος λόγος, πατρῷος λόγος, σύστασις, φύσις, οἰκονομία, νοῦς etc. which are mixed together in an somewhat ill-formed *rapprochement* with second century Monarchianism. These were to be taken up and more sharply formalized and harmonized by various sides, Apollinarian, Monophysite, Arian, and Chalcedonian, in various different ways. By constantly trying to read these concepts in a fourth century perspective, both Richard, Frickel, and Hübner, have been compelled to produce quite opposite theses about the true nature of the Christology in question. Frickel in particular has had to save the phenomena in his theorizing with reference to interpolationist hypotheses. I believe that my second century solution is far more satisfactory than the confusion that clearly a fourth century date has produced.

Let us now examine the Holy Spirit passages, and the claim about the δύο or τρία πρόσωπα to which they give rise. If these can be shown to be integral to the theology of *C.N.* and not later interpolations, we shall thus further support our position against those who would close the distinctions between *C.N.* and *El.* on which the case for two authors in the Hippolytan *corpus* rests by claiming that the latter has been radically changed as a result of interpolations.

4A 3.2. *The Holy Spirit passages*
Nautin's general critical method for defending the integrity of *C.N.* was fundamentally to show that a questioned theological concept or formulation was by no means anachronistic but paralleled both from elsewhere in the Hippolytan *corpus* and by contemporary patristic writers. Accordingly he sought to deploy this method specifically to the Holy Spirit passages. There is however a problem with this methodology when applied globally to these passages, since they fall into two distinct groups.

The first group (1) we might regard as normal trinitarian formulations based on the baptismal formulary and running parallel unproblematically with statements by other writers. The second group (2) consist of statements where the inclusion of the Holy Spirit appears redundant against the Christology, however much there may be contemporary patristic parallels. If the redundancy in (2) is not to constitute evidence for the hand of an interpolator, then we shall have to seek a better explanation of it, which we shall do in terms of our previous account of the pre-incarnational, instrumental theology of *C.N.* as a *rapprochement* with the school of Callistus. In so doing we shall in part be critical of Nautin's too ready assumption of an equivalence of view between that of *C.N.* and his contemporaries, such as Irenaeus and Tertullian.[109] We shall argue that it was in fact the depersonalization of the λόγος before the incarnation that lead to a redundancy for the Holy Spirit, whose presence he nevertheless retained from the tradition from which to some extent he was departing.

4A 3.2.1. C.N. *9,2 , 12,5:, and 14,6 Scriptures and the creed*

In the first of these two passages (*C.N.* 9 ,2) we read the author asserts on the basis of Scripture (ὅσα τοίνυν κηρύσσουσιν αἱ θεῖαι γραφαί... κ.τ.λ.) the foundations of faith (ὡς θέλει Πατὴρ πιστεύεσθαι πιστεύσωμεν), worship (ὡς θέλει Ὑίον δοξάζεσθαι δοξάσωμεν), and baptism (ὡς θέλει πνεῦμα ἅγιον δωρεῖσθαι λάβωμεν), in Father, Son, and Holy Spirit respectively. I take the last to be a reference to baptism as "enlightenment", and to the claim therefore that only the baptized community, and not the philosophical schools, can interpret the true nature of the godhead in the light of Scripture. The Scripture in question would appear to be *Matt.* 28,19-20.[110]

In *C.N.* 12,5 we find the bare statement that, subsequent to the incarnation (οὐκοῦν ἔνσαρκον λόγον θεωροῦμεν;) the Father is grasped conceptually through him (πατέρα δι' αὐτοῦ νοῦμεν), but the Father is believed by means of the Son (υἱῷ δὲ πιστεύομεν) and worshipped by means of the Holy Spirit (πνεύματι ἁγίῳ προσκυνοῦμεν). At this point, as with *C.N.* 9,2, it might be possible to regard these passages as later trinitarian additions. But with *C.N.* 14, 5-6 we find a passage which cannot·be explained as an interpolation in any such straightforward way.

---

[109] Nautin (1947) p. 44: "Les mentions du Saint-Esprit dans le fragment [11,1] contre Noët sont donc parfaitement conformes à la tradition ecclésiastique du temps, et apparaissent même comme un emprunt caractéristique d'Hippolyte à la théologie de son maître, saint Irénée."
[110] Nautin (1947) p. 41: "Et cela ne serait pas encore suffisant, car ces deux formules sont enclavées entre deux références à l'Écriture (ὅσα τοίνυν κηρύσσουσιν αἱ θεῖαι γραφαί, ἴδωμεν– ὃν τρόπον αὐτὸς ἐβουλήθη διὰ τῶν ἁγίων γραφῶν δεῖξαι, οὕτως ἴδωμεν [C.N. 9,2]), dans lesquelles nous devons reconnaître une allusion au texte trinitaire de saint Matthieu. Le passage depuis ὅσα τοίνυν jusqu'à οὕτως ἴδωμεν forme un bloc qui doit subir un sort unique."

In this passage we find another example of what Nautin would regard as a symmetrical arrangement of ideas, but which indeed is more than this, and which belies as such the notion of an interpolator:

> For God is one.
> For the Father commands (κελεύων), The Son obeys, (ὑπακούων) and the Holy Spirit gives understanding (τὸ δὲ συνετίζον ἅγιον πνεῦμα),
> He who is Father is over all (ἐπὶ πάντων), He who is Son is through all (διά πάντων), That which is Holy Spirit is in all (ἐν πᾶσιν).
> Else we could not conceive (νοῆσαι) the one God, if we did not truly believe in the Father, the Son, and the Holy Spirit.
> For the Jews glorified (ἐδόξασαν) the Father but they gave no thanks (οὐκ ηὐχαρίστησαν); for they did not recognize (ἐπέγνωσαν) the Son.
> The disciples recognized (ἐπέγνωσαν) the Son, but not in the Holy Spirit (ἐν πνεύματι ἁγίῳ); therefore they also denied him (ἠρνήσαντο).[111]

It is important furthermore to note that even the hypothesis that an interpolator imposed a symmetry where there had not been one in the original must fail in the light of this passage.

In the last two lines there is a transition required by the form of an assertion followed by a denial because of a shortcoming. For the disciples there must be a counterpart to the Jews regarding what they did and what they failed to do, and the reason why they so failed. The Son must be recognized by the disciples since the Jews had failed to do so, but just as the Jews had failed to give thanks because of their ignorance, the disciples must have denied Christ because they lacked the Holy Spirit that showed the fulfilment of prophecy in the Passion. The phrase οὐκ ἐν πνεύματι ἁγίῳ in μαθηταὶ ἐπέγνωσαν Υἱόν, ἀλλ' οὐκ ἐν πνεύματι ἁγίῳ· διὸ καὶ ἠρνήσαντο cannot therefore be detached as the work of an interpolator without destroying the structure of the passage which goes in this case far more deeply that mere symmetry.[112]

Frickel sought to defend his most recent, Apollinarian thesis with reference to such symmetrical arrangement. He also applied his analysis to C.N. 17,5-18,10 in defence of the view that we have already rejected, namely that Theodoret's version of this passage is the original (4A 3.1.2).[113] But we have argued that the theology of C.N. is nearer Marcellus than Apollinaris as one

---

111 *C.N.* 14, 5-6: εἰς γὰρ ἐστιν ὁ θεός. ὁ γὰρ κελεύων Πατήρ, ὁ δὲ ὑπακούων Υἱός, τὸ δὲ συνετίζον ἅγιον πνεῦμα. ὁ ὢν Πατὴρ ἐπὶ πάντων, ὁ δὲ Υἱὸς διὰ πάντων, τὸ δὲ ἅγιον πνεῦμα ἐν πᾶσιν. ἄλλως τε ἕνα θεὸν νοῆσαι οὐ δυνάμεθα, ἐὰν μὴ ὄντως Πατρὶ καὶ Υἱῷ καὶ ἁγίῳ πνεύματι πιστεύσωμεν. Ἰουδαῖοι μὲν γὰρ ἐδόξασαν Πατέρα, ἀλλ' οὐκ ηὐχαρίστησαν· Υἱὸν γὰρ οὐκ ἐπέγνωσαν. μαθηταὶ ἐπέγνωσαν Υἱόν, ἀλλ' οὐκ ἐν πνεύματι ἁγίῳ· διὸ καὶ ἠρνήσαντο.
112 Nautin (1947) p. 40: "Les deux propositions... sont inséparables. Le parallélisme très strict qu'elles présentent et la progression que la seconde marque sur la première montrent qu'elles ont été construites l'une pour l'autre. On ne peut supprimer l'une sans supprimer l'autre."
113 Frickel (1993) p. 99-109. He points in this respect to Pseudo-Julius, *De Unione* 4-6 (Lietzmann (1904) p. 186,14-188,4) and *Quod Unus sit Christus* 9 (Ibid. p. 300,18-20).

would expect in an early third century *rapprochement* with Monarchianism (4A 3.1.3.3). It should be noted that both Ignatius and Theophilus of Antioch use such paradoxical symmetry in the second century. Indeed Simonetti has strongly argued that the regnant "orthodox" (i.e. non-Gnostic) Christology of the second century was proto-Monarchian.[114] Indeed Hübner was to use the antitheses attributed to Zephyrinus and Callistus in *El.* IX, 10, 10-12 as reflecting Noetus' antitheses to be found also in Melito *frag.* 13.[115] His reasons for excepting *C.N.* we have already discussed and found wanting (4A 3.1.3.2), so that the antithetical or paradoxical literary form, as much at home in the second as in the fourth century, is no reason of itself for postulating the later rather than the earlier date.

But there are another group of passages in which the trinitarian formulas appear as an afterthought to an original binitarianism with which it appears to jar, and to these we now turn.

4A 3.2.2. C.N. *8, 1-2; 14, 2-3, 7-8:* τρίας and πρόσωπα δύο

In the first passage we seem to have almost a reference to a binitarian baptismal Creed:

> It is necessary therefore (ἀνάγκην οὖν ἔχει), even though one does not wish it (καὶ μὴ θέλων) to confess (ὁμολογεῖν) God the Father almighty (Πατέρα θεὸν παντοκράτορα) and Christ Jesus, Son of God, God having become man (καὶ Χριστὸν Ἰησοῦν Υἱὸν θεοῦ θεὸν ἄνθρωπον γενόμενον). To whom the Father subjected all things (ᾧ πάντα Πατὴρ ὑπέταξε), except himself and the Holy Spirit (παρεκτὸς ἑαυτοῦ καὶ πνεύματος ἁγίου). And these are really three (καὶ ταῦτ᾿ εἶναι ὄντως τρία).
>
> *C.N.* 8, 1

Although Nautin tried to soften the binitarianism of this passage by the amendment καὶ πνεῦμα ἅγιον for the *ms.* reading καὶ πνεύματος ἁγίου, the sense of the passage is quite clear without it. It is the Father and the Son who are the subject of the confession (ὁμολογεῖν), with the Holy Spirit hardly distinguished from the Father but grouped together (παρεκτὸς ἑαυτοῦ καὶ πνεύματος ἁγίου) with him. As such καὶ ταῦτ᾿ εἶναι ὄντως τρία appears almost as an inconsequential afterthought.

But it would be a mistake to read *C.N.* in this connection as a garbled and undeveloped formulation of an essential binitarianism struggling to express itself as a trinitarianism, and to be completed as such by a later interpolator. We have clear examples amongst both the author's predecessors and contemporaries of a clear trinitarianism that he could have unambiguously adopted had he wished. We have already noted and discussed Irenaeus *Adv.*

---

[114] Hübner (1989) p. 230-231. Cf. M. Simonetti, Il problema dell' unità di Dio da Giustino a Ireneo, in *Rivista di storia e letteratura religiosa*, 22 (1986), p. 201-239 reprinted in Studi sulla cristologia del II e III secolo, in *StEphAug* 44 (1993), p. 71-107.
[115] Ibid. p. 225-232.

Haer. III, 24,2; IV, 7,4, and 34,3 in which we saw that the Holy Spirit as *Sapientia* was used in a personal and not in an instrumental sense (4A 2.1).

The reason why the author of *C.N.* expresses himself ambiguously in the way that he does is, I believe, for the reason that I have already stated (4A 1). In the light of his *rapprochement* with the theology of Callistus, he broke self-consciously with the theology of both Irenaeus and *El.* in that the increasing personal understanding of, in the former case three, and in the latter two, eternal persons in the godhead was effectively depersonalized and instrumentalized. This is why, without recourse to a Chalcedonian interpolator, we can understand how he can take the threefold baptismal formula and endeavour to reduce the confession to two persons, the one eternally so (Πατέρα θεὸν παντοκράτορα), but the other only fully personal after the incarnation (καὶ Χριστὸν Ἰησοῦν Υἱὸν θεοῦ θεὸν ἄνθρωπον γενόμενον).

To have followed Irenaeus would therefore have run counter to the development of *C.N.*'s own theological *rapprochement* with the Monarchians. The more the λόγος before the incarnation is depersonalized and instrumentalized, the more the Holy Spirit as *Sapientia* ceases to be able to be distinguished from the λόγος, let alone acknowledged as a separate person. Yet the author is desperate to remain within the Irenaean tradition, however much an ever decreasing space could be left for the Holy Spirit as a distinct person whilst the pre-existent λόγος was ceasing to be so. Consequently he asserts almost in desperation καὶ ταῦτ᾽ εἶναι **ὄντως** τρία, even though hardly three persons.

The dilemma of his pre-incarnational, theological depersonalisation, becomes clear in *C.N.* 8,2. With what I have argued to be his retreat from the theology of *El.* in the light of Monarchian criticism, he begins tentatively by upholding the unity of God (εἰ δὲ βούλεται μαθεῖν πῶς εἷς θεὸς ἀποδείκνυται). His response is that: "Of the one God there is a single power (γινωσκέτω ὅτι μία δύναμις τούτου)." He then continues: "As far as concerns the power (ὅσον μὲν κατὰ τὴν δύναμιν), God is one (εἷς ἐστιν θεός). But as far as concerns the economy (ὅσον δὲ κατὰ τὴν οἰκονομίαν), the demonstration is triple (τριχὴς ἡ ἐπίδειξις)..."

We emphasized above (4A 1.1) the important distinction between *El.* X, 33,1-2 and *C.N.* 10,4. In the former, the λόγος clearly possesses an independent will from the Father, though one that is in perfect harmony with his own. In the latter, however, the depersonalized λόγος has become the power of the Father—the ἡ δύναμις ἡ πατρῴα of *C.N.* 14,1 or the ὁ πατρῷος λόγος of 14,7. It is thus the development of his Monarchian *rapprochement*, which we saw to be the cause of the departure of *C.N.* from the developing trinitarian theology which *El.* shared with Irenaeus, Justin, and Theophilus of Antioch, that accounts also specifically for his garbled references to the Holy Spirit.

If we now turn specifically to comparisons with the use of τρίας by *C.N.* and his contemporaries, we shall find that a similar explanation also applies. In *C.N.* 14,2-3 the author will once again contemplate the possibility of only two persons or πρόσωπα, which will correspond to the charge which he regards as false, namely that of two gods levelled also by Zephyrinus and Callistus at the author of *El.* IX, 12,16-19. Yet the Holy Spirit is included once again, without evidently being regarded as a third πρόσωπον:

> I will not say there are two gods (δύο μὲν οὐκ ἐρῶ θεούς) but one (ἀλλ᾽ ἢ ἕνα); and two faces (πρόσωπα δὲ δύο), and the third revelation the grace of the Holy Spirit (οἰκονομίαν τε τρίτην τὴν χάριν τοῦ ἁγίου πνεύματος). For one is the Father (Πατὴρ μὲν γὰρ εἷς), but the faces two (πρόσωπα δὲ δύο), including the Son (ὅτι καὶ ὁ Ὑιός) and the third also, the Holy Spirit (τὸ δὲ τρίτον καὶ ἅγιον πνεῦμα).

In view of what I have argued regarding *C.N.* 4, 10-13; 15,6- 16,2 and 17, 5 etc. in 4A 1.2, it seems proper to translate πρόσωπον as "face" and not person here, since before the incarnation there is neither complete personality nor independence of wills. By the same token I translate οἰκονομία as "revelation" though it means more something like "third stage in the plan." For the author of *C.N.* the Son is more like "that which is sent" rather than "he whom is sent." In this respect we see once again that the Holy Spirit at this point cannot be given the independent personhood that it had in the Irenaean tradition. It is the *rapprochement* with Monarchianism that is once more the source of the redundancy of the Holy Spirit, which *C.N.* took over from the tradition, but for which no real place could be found.

C.N. 14, 8 uses the word τρίας in an apparently trinitarian sense. Following, significantly, the baptismal commission of *Matt.* 28,19, which is quoted in full (14,7), and showing the foundations of trinitarian doctrine in the baptismal formula, the author says: διὰ γὰρ τῆς τριάδος ταύτης, Πατὴρ δοξάζεται. Πατὴρ γὰρ ἠθέλησεν, Ὑιὸς ἐποίησεν, πνεῦμα ἐφανέρωσεν. Once again will is ascribed to the Father alone, which the Son performs and the Holy Spirit reveals, in contrast with the personalized and relatively independent characterisation of the activity of the pre-incarnate λόγος in *El.* X, 33,2 (4A 1.1). In Theophilus of Antioch we have the three day-stars regarded as "types of the Trinity" (τύποι εἰσὶν τῆς τριάδος)—a Trinity which consists "of God and of his Word, and of his Wisdom (τοῦ θεοῦ, καὶ τοῦ λόγου αὐτοῦ, καὶ τῆς σοφίας αὐτου)."[116]

We saw that Irenaeus was able to equate σοφία, the third entity in Theophilus' Trinity, with *Sapientia quae est Spiritus* in *Adv. Haer.* IV, 20,3, because the *Verbum* was fully personal as *Filius* before the incarnation. Once

---

[116] Theophilus, *Autol.*, 2,15: ὁ θεὸς τέλειος διαμένει, πλήρης ὢν πάσης δυνάμεως καὶ συνέσεως καὶ σοφίας... ὡσαύτως καὶ αἱ τρεῖς ἡμέραι τῶν φωστήρων γεγονυῖαι τύποι εἰσὶν τῆς τριάδος τοῦ θεοῦ, καὶ τοῦ λόγου αὐτοῦ, καὶ τῆς σοφίας αὐτοῦ...

Filius is associated with the pre-existent *Verbum,* then *Sapientia* can be equated with the Spirit, and thus an embryonic doctrine of a Trinity of persons can begin to develop.

But once deny the equation of *Verbum* and *Filius* in any real as opposed to anticipatory sense, with the support indeed of the Fourth Gospel, which does not make this precise equation in its *Prologue,* then *Sapientia* cannot be then equated with the Holy Spirit as an independent person. This is the real reason why σοφία is completely instrumentalized in *C.N.* 10,3 (σοφίζεται... διὰ λόγου καὶ σοφίας τεχνάζεται, λόγῳ μὲν κτίζων, σοφίᾳ δὲ κοσμῶν). If the depersonalized λόγος is an instrument, then σοφία can only be equated with it and not with a third person as the Holy Spirit, as Irenaeus had done (4A 1.2.1). Nautin, therefore, despite his otherwise valuable and critical analysis of the literary problem, was fundamentally in error with his claim that *C.N.* "parfaitement conformes à la tradition ecclésiastique du temps" and in conformity with "la théologie de son maître, saint Irénée."[117]

If we now turn to Tertullian's use of *trinitas,* we shall observe a similar theological distinction from *C.N.* in texts which otherwise accord with his ambivalent binitarianism. In *Adversus Praxeam* 13 we read:

> ... duos quidem definimus, Patrem et Filium, et iam tres cum Spiritu Sancto, secundum rationem oiconomiae... Duos tamen Deos et duos dominos nunquam ex ore nostro proferimus: non quasi non et Pater Deus et Filius Deus et Spiritus Deus.

Nautin quotes this passage in fuller form, and correctly notes the concerns about the charge of ditheism that reveal Tertullian's concerns to have that near identity that in 7C 1-2 we shall argue to reveal an actual historical relationship between his group and the opponents of Callistus in Rome.[118]

Clearly, as Nautin demonstrates, the passage itself confirms in its parallelism with *C.N.* that the latter's references to the Holy Spirit cannot be interpolations.[119] The ambivalent description of *duos... Patrem et Filium et iam tres* clearly parallel the δύο πρόσωπα of *C.N.* 14,2-3 to which the Holy Spirit is added as οἰκονομίαν τρίτην in a way that closely parallels Tertullian's *secundum rationem oiconomiae.* But here the assertion *Pater Deus, Filius Deus et Spiritus Deus* establishes a connection with Irenaeus that we have seen that the pre-incarnational theology of *C.N.* sought expressly to deny. Full personality could only be attributed in that case to the Son provisionally, imperfectly, and with a view to the future, with a correspondent redundancy in personal terms for the Holy Spirit.

---

117 Quoted above footnote 26.
118 Nautin (1947) p. 46.
119 Ibid. p. 46-47: "Cependant personne n'a proposé d'amender le texte de Tertullien, car il nomme souvent les trois personnes divines ailleurs, et l'on voit facilement la raison qui lui a fait introduire ici le chiffre deux: c'est que la distinction du Père et du Saint-Esprit n'était pas en cause; le débat portait seulement sur la distinction du Père et du Fils." See also *Adv. Prax.* 27.

We shall be returning to a re-examination of the historical evidence for more general relationships between Tertullian and the community of *El.* in 7C 1-2. Indeed, I shall later argue in 7C 2 that it is *C.N.* that is dependent upon the argument of the *Adv. Prax.* here rather than *vice versa*, as Simonetti has argued.[120] We shall see that *C.N.* is deliberately denying the argument of Tertullian that because λόγος can be equated with υἱός, therefore the latter has full personality before the incarnation. *C.N.* will modify Tertullian's argument in *Adv. Prax.* in order to depersonalize the former's fully personally, pre-existing Son, just as he did in the case of *El.*, in order to find a *rapprochement* with the Monarchians that Tertullian's position would also have denied him. Suffice it to record here that we have established that Tertullian is also a witness to the integrity of the Holy Spirit passages in *C.N.*, since he shows that the concerns reflected in the latter writer's theology are part and parcel of the theological discussion within the Churches of Rome and North Africa at the beginning of the third century.

Let us therefore summarize what we have at this point so far established regarding the separate authors of *El.* and *C.N.*, and draw some provisional conclusions from the implications of those particular differences that we have so far noted.

4A 3.2.3. *Hippolytus and Pontianus:* C.N.'s *rapprochement*

We have traced the Christological *rapprochement* between *C.N.* and the community of Callistus, in contrast with the absolute antagonism of *El.*, regarding both the λόγος–παῖς Christology (4A 3.1) and the place of the Holy Spirit (4A 3.2). That theological *rapprochement*, prescinding for a moment the question of Tertullian's historical role in the debate, is of a piece with the indications of a general historical *rapprochement* between the two groups.[121] We shall deal with the historical clues in full detail in Chapter 5. But for the moment let us recall the position that we established in Chapter 1 regarding the link between the name of Hippolytus and the cult-shrine on the via Tiburtina against recent criticism that argued that the centre had no historical contact with Hippolytus the writer of Eusebius and Jerome, as opposed to the legend of the soldier-companion of St. Laurence (1B 1.3.1.4, 1B 1.3.3.3 and B 2.1-2.6).

---

[120] M. Simonetti, Due note su Ippolito, in *StEphAug* 13 (1977), p. 126-136.

[121] Frickel's first position on the dependence of *C.N.* upon *El.*, when he believed in two different authors, would seem to me to be therefore preferable. In Frickel (1977) p. 139-141, he points both to the introduction of the Holy Spirit in *C.N.* into the binitarianism of *El.* as a clear development ("una dottrina trinitaria assai sviluppata," p. 140) and his defence of the charge of ditheism mentioned in *El.* ("Il *C. Noetum*, pur correggendo l'atteggiamento filosofante dell'autore dell'*Elenchos*, difende perciò quest'ultimo contro il rimprovero di diteismo," p. 140) In consequence he concludes: "Non posso certo approfondire tale problema in questa mia relazione; penso però che i diversi indizi sopra indicati giustifichino la tesi sul *C. Noetum* di un documento postippolitiano, basato su di un trattato di Ippolito contro i Noeziani." But it is not simply that *C.N. defends El.* against ditheism, but rather that he *modifies* the ditheism of the former in a way designed to make it more acceptable to its critics.

We argued to the contrary (1B 2.3.3.3-3.3.5 and 2C) that the Chrono-grapher of 354 (Liberian *Catalogus*) had:

(i) in the *Catalogus Episcoporum* mentioned one single *Hippolytus presbyter* along with *Pontianus episcopus*, in a Roman community that clearly had so many in the ranks of that former office, and

(ii) in the *Depositio Martyrum* listed both (*Ypoliti in Tiburtina and Pontiani in Calisti*) as laid to rest on the same day, the 13th August (*Idus Aug.*).

From the identity of names, from the singling out of one presbyter amongst many (i), from the significance of 13th August as the festival of Diana that celebrated the incorporation of the Italian city-states into the *imperium Romanum* (ii) we were able to conclude that these entries were ciphers which concealed a division—perhaps a schism though not without the qualific-ations that we shall needs make in Chapter 5—which had now been healed.

We can as a result of our discussion in this Chapter now trace in terms of doctrine the course of that division that was healed. Hippolytus was indeed the name of the presbyter—and perfectly prepared to accept that he was a presbyter and not a bishop—by contrast with his predecessor as head of the community of *El.* IX, 11-12, though we argue in Chapter 6 that in that earlier generation the distinction between presbyter and bishop in the house/church/schools of the fractionalized Roman community was not then so clearly drawn. Unlike the author of *El.*, he was to introduce from the Irenaean tradition references to the Holy Spirit, which were absent from his predecessor's work. He was however to instrumentalize the Holy Spirit and to depersonalize the pre-existent λόγος. Thus he could make peace with Pontianus, successor to the Callistus, who had claimed that the λόγος was both Father and Son (αὐτὸν εἶναι υἱὸν καὶ πατέρα), united by virtue of an indivisible Spirit (ἓν δὲ ὄντα, τὸ πνεῦμα ἀδιαίρετον) (*El.* IX, 12,16). The entries in the Liberian List testify to a reconciliation between communities previously in conflict on the basis of the theological *rapprochement* rep-resented by *C.N.*, which we have outlined here.

It must be emphasized that so far the Statue has played no role in our dis-cussion, since neither *El.* nor *C.N.* are mentioned in the list on the plinth. So far our analysis of the theological character of the two works in combination with our interpretation of the cryptographic entry in the *Catalogus* and *Depositio* of the Chronographer of 354, and the events recorded in *El.* IX, have by themselves supported the historical and literary reconstruction with which we have concluded this section. We have not used the Statue as part of our argument for the two authors, though we established (3C and 3D) that neither the title τὰ ὑπὲρ κατὰ Ἰωάννην κ.τ.λ..., nor the ἀποστολικὴ παράδοσις necessarily correspond to any work clearly identifiable with that of Hippolytus and therefore of the *C.N.*

Thus we have chosen to follow Nautin's wise injunction that *C'est
...l'étude des textes qui peut nous guider le plus sûrement dans l'attribution
de la statue* and not *vice versa*.[122] But Nautin's argument additionally proceeds to claim all the works of the Statue, along with *El.*, as the work of a
writer other than Hippolytus. At this point the Statue is repeatedly cited as
conclusive evidence against the thesis of two authors, as we shall now see.

PART B. *ELENCHOS* AND RELATED WORKS CONNECTED TO THE STATUE

Nautin wanted to connect every work mentioned on the Statue with *El.*,
though it was unmentioned there, and to associate works mentioned in the
Eusebius/Jerome catalogues with the *C.N.* of which for their part they also
made no mention. We shall now have to examine this stronger thesis that
claims to show that the different theologies of *El.* and of *C.N.* are reflected in
these two blocks of works and which make them different. But in view of the
special use of the Statue to deny this possibility, let us begin by examining
this specific use.

Throughout the objections to Nautin's thesis, the fact of (i) the Statue and
the list of works inscribed upon it, together with (ii) the lists of Eusebius and
Jerome, established the unity of the *corpus*. Daniélou based his objections on
the implausibility of Nautin's thesis specifically on the two facts that he
found incontestable, namely (i) the statue on the via Tiburtina had to be a
representation of Hippolytus, and (ii) the secure Hippolytan authorship of
Ap. Trad. and the ἀπόδειξις χρόνων of Eusebius *H.E.* VI, 22.[123] Curiously he
did not add the τὰ ὑπὲρ τοῦ κατὰ 'Ιωάννην κ.τ.λ... generally—though I have
argued wrongly—regarded as the κεφάλαια believed to have been cited by
Barsalîbî (3C 1).

Capelle, whilst admitting that the via Tiburtina may not have been its
original location, believed that this would make no difference to the identification of the seated figure with Hippolytus as the author of the works on the
plinth. He therefore agreed with Daniélou on (i) and (ii), and added as (iii):
comparative analysis to form what he called a *funiculus triplex* , curiously, I
would have thought, in view of the association of the Statue with Hippolytus,
independent of literary indications, having been dependent on its discovery

---

[122] Nautin (1952) p. 33: "Il ne faut pas donc partir d l'attribution de la statue, établie sur
d'autres indices que les oeuvres de l'écrivain représenté, et conclure à l'attribution des textes,
ainsi qu'on a toujours fait. C'est au contraire l'étude des textes qui peut nous guider le plus
sûrement dans l'attribution de la statue."

[123] Daniélou (1948) p. 597: "En outre, pour établir sa thèse, M. Nautin doit contester que la
statue de la voie Tiburtine représente Hippolyte. Elle contient en effet des titres d'ouvrages qui
sont certainement du même auteur que l'*Elenchos*... Mais il reste que la statue porte l'indication
de deux ouvrages dont l'attribution à Hippolyte est difficile à contester... le comput pascal... et...
la *Tradition apostolique*."

in the vicinity of Hippolytus' cult-shrine.[124] Oggioni followed these writers in claiming that the works on the plinth indicated conclusively the identity of the seated figure.[125] Let us examine the texture of the three strands of this *funiculus triplex*, in order to see whether they are strong or frail.

4B 1. *The Statue does not imply a single Hippolytan* corpus

We have seen that at least one strand of the *funiculus triplex* (i) is challenge-able on every point that was cited as its strength. We saw in Chapter 2 that (a) the Statue was not a representation of an actual person (2A 1-2), but, in accordance with the conventions of early Christian art, iconographic and symbolic (2B 2.2.1.1-2.2.3.2.2), (b) in consequence it cannot be necessarily assumed that necessarily the list of works are those of a single author (2B and C), and (c) it is open to challenge that the Statue was originally located on the via Tiburtina (1B 2 and 2B). Significantly Guarducci, assisted by oth-ers, raised these questions in the context of a purely archaeological inquiry about the true character of the Statue (2A 1). Guarducci herself accepted the unity of the *corpus* and that the Statue was of Hippolytus without recognis-ing how her thesis challenged one member of the *funiculus triplex* on which that unity has clearly been argued.[126] Nautin's defence of his two-author the-sis, in pointing to the ambiguous character of both the Statue and its location, is thus seen to be remarkably perspicacious in the light of Guarducci's later archaeological analysis not conducted with any intention of defending his particular thesis.[127]

---

[124] Capelle (1950) p. 149-150 and 174: "... la statue fut découverte en 1551 sur la voie Tiburtine... Rien cependant ne nous garantit encore que la statue n'avait pas été transportée là d'ailleurs. Il faut, pour nous en assurer, étudier soigneusement quel est cet Hippolyte dont le souvenir se conservait au cimetière de la voie Tiburtine... Elle [démonstration] me paraît val-able, à cause de la conjonction de trois sources d'information concordantes... ce qui concerne la statue, la notice d'Eusèbe... l'analyse comparative... *Funiculus triplex difficile rumpitur.*" Cf. Capelle (1952) p. 194: "C'est sur cet emplacement même qu'a été decouverte la fameuse statue du musée du Latran, représentant assis un écrivain, auteur de l'*Elenchos contre les héresies*," and Oggioni (1952) p. 514: "La statua scoperta nel 1551 a Roma fu scolpita... Questo personaggio è autore dell'*Elenchos* perchè tale libro cita come opera dello stesso autore un *De Universo*, il cui titolo è iscritto tra i libri composti dalla persona rappresentata dalla statua. Quindi tutto ciò che l'autore dell'*Elenchos* dice di se stesso deve essere detto del personaggio della statua..." p. 522.

[125] Oggioni (1950) p. 128 and 130: "... descritto da una parte un ciclo pasquale... dall'altra un catalogo di opere. Evidentemente l'uno e l'altro hanno il loro autore nel personaggio rappre-sentato... Per tutti questi motivi non si può dubitare che l'*Elenchos* appartenga ad Ippolito. La sua figura si arricchisce quindi di tutte le abbondanti notizie autobiografiche di cui l'*Elenchos* è pieno..."

[126] M. Guarducci, La Statua di «Sant'Ippolito», in *StEphAug* 13 1977, p. 28: "Ciò conferma la convinzione che uno solo sia l'autore di tutti quegli scritti. Egli poi dovrà essere identificato col martire Ippolito..." Also after a considerable change of opinion on other matters, M. Guarducci, "La Statua di «Sant'Ippolito» e la sua Provenienza," in *StEphAug* 30 1989, p. 73: "Si è generalmente ritenuto, ed io stessa ho condiviso quest'opinione, che tutte quelle opere fossero da attribuirsi ad Ippolito."

[127] Nautin (1952) p. 33: Il s'agit en définitive d'identifier un homme. Or, par quoi un homme trahit-il le mieux sa personalité? Par le lieu, au reste mal connu, où sa statue a été dé-couverte? Par ce que nous disent des gens postérieurs d'un siècle et plus? Ou par ce qui vient de

We have argued against (c) that the discovery and location of the Statue was where Ligorio claims to have found it (1B 2 and 2B). But that admission on our part did not lead to the necessary conclusion that Hippolytus was the author of all works listed on the Statue since we rejected the case for the Statue being an artefact commemorating a particular individual as opposed to the icon of the inner life of the community (2A 2-3 and 2B 1). Indeed, we have seen in this Chapter that the association of the Statue with the cult centre of Hippolytus *presbyter*, the martyr reconciled with Pontianus *episcopus* in 235, was fully consistent with an earlier and different leader and writer of that same community having some if not all of his works listed on the community's artefact. The principal function of that artefact within his particular Church-group was to allow the computation of the customary date of Easter for such a group (2A 2.3-2.4). Some changes in theological direction would be required, consistent with the aim of reconciling two groups, bitterly opposed some twenty years before, and indeed consistent with the changes in *C.N.* to the theology of *El.* of the kind that we have described (4A).

In our analysis of the role of the Statue in the debate, we may therefore safely claim to have cut through the first strand (i) in the *funiculus triplex*. But we have not done so completely to Nautin's satisfaction in that we have not conceded that therefore every work listed there must be that of a single alternative author. We gave our reasons in the context of a discussion of the external evidence for the *corpus* (3E 1). The second strand was that of (ii) the relationship between works on the Statue and the Eusebius/Jerome catalogues and other works. We likewise have discussed this strand in terms of external evidence (3E 2), but it is to the internal implications for this evidence that we must now turn. It is to an examination of this strand that we now turn.

4B 2. *The Statue's inscriptions and Eusebius /Jerome catalogues*

Undoubtedly certain works on the Statue must have been written by the author of *El.* who expressly claims those titles as his own work, namely:

1. The περὶ τοῦ παντός οὐσίας,[128] identifiable with the πρὸς "Ελληνας καὶ πρὸς Πλάτωνα ἢ καὶ περὶ τοῦ παντός of the Statue, and attributed to Josephus by Photius, John Philoponus, and Pseudo John Damascene.[129]

---

lui-même et porte son empreinte personnelle, je veux dire par ses oeuvres?... et alors on aura vraiment le droit de soutenir, si on en a encore l'idée, que la statue est celle d'Hippolyte." Footnote 1 p. 33: C'est pourquoi la question de l'identification de la statue n'est pas de la compétence des archéologues comme tels... Car la question qui se pose en définitive n'est pas: Quelle est cette pierre? mais: Qui est cet homme? Et que peuvent dire de la pierre elle-même les archéologues, dans l'ignorance où ils sont de son emplacement exact?
[128] *El.* X, 32,4: ... εἰ φιλομαθήσουσι καὶ τὰς τούτων οὐσίας καὶ τὰς αἰτίας τῆς κατὰ τὸ πᾶν δημιουργίας ἐπιζητήσουσιν, εἴσονται ἐντυχόντες ἡμῶν τῇ βίβλῳ περιεχούσῃ περὶ τῆς τοῦ παντὸς οὐσίας...
[129] For a further discussion and references see 3E 1.

2. οβ' ἔθνη... ἐν ἑτέραις βίβλοις[130] identifiable with the Χρονικῶν (=βίβλοι) of the Statue and therefore with the συναγωγὴ χρόνων καὶ ἐτῶν ἀπὸ κτίσεως κόσμου ἕως τῆς ἐνεστώσης ἡμέρας.[131]

These, and these only two works can *prima facie* and directly, without further links, connect the Statue with *El.* Let us therefore look more closely at what can be established about the contents of each.

4 B 2.1. περὶ τοῦ παντός

El. X, 32,4 laid claim to the authorship of a work entitled περὶ τῆς τοῦ παντός οὐσίας. Photius knew this work under, as we have seen (3A 7), the name of Josephus (ἀνεγνώσθη 'Ιωσήπου), almost exactly as περὶ τῆς τοῦ παντὸς οὐσίας as well as περὶ τῆς τοῦ παντός αἰτίας, and also as partially the title of the Statue, namely as περὶ τοῦ παντός.[132] The work was in two volumes (ἐν δυσί λογιδίοις) which not only showed that Plato was inherently contradictory (δείκνυσι δὲ ἐν αὐτοῖς πρὸς ἑαυτὸν στασιάζοντα Πλάτωνα) but specifically attacked the Albinian theory of Forms ('Αλκίνουν ἀλόγως τε καὶ ψευδῶς εἰπόντα).[133]

In the Pseudo-Damascene *Sacra Parallela*, moreover, we find a work περὶ τοῦ παντός also combined with an attack on Plato as that read by Photius and indicated by the title on the Statue.[134] As the introduction to the fragment cited in this work we find, in the *ms.* tradition, variants of: 'Ιωσίππου ἐκ τοῦ λόγου ἐπιγεγραμμένου κατὰ Πλάτωνος περὶ τῆς τοῦ παντός αἰτίας καὶ κατὰ 'Ελλήνων, as found in *frag.* 353.[135] Thus we have evidence of a title of the work cited by Photius as a variant of the alternative title given by the Statue (ἢ καὶ περὶ τοῦ παντός). Pseudo-Damascene also confirms in the title that which Photius confirms in its contents, and which corresponds to the Statue's other alternative: πρὸς "Ελληνας καὶ πρὸς Πλάτωνα.

But in this case we have more than simply a hypothesis about the content of a work based upon a title. Holl's editing of the fragments of this work

---

[130] *El.* X, 30, 1 and 5: περὶ ἧς ['Ιουδαία] καὶ κατὰ τοῦτο τὸ μέρος τὸν λόγον οὐκ ἀμελῶς παρεδώκαμεν ἐν ἑτέραις βίβλοις... ἦσαν δὲ οὗτοι οβ', ἐξ' ὧν καὶ οβ' ἔθνη· ὧν καὶ ὀνόματα ἐκτεθείμεθα ἐν ἑτέραις βίβλοις...

[131] For the text see A. Bauer, Die Chronik des Hippolytos in Matritensis graecus 121, in *TU* 29,1 (1905).

[132] For my views on the Josephan authorship, see 5B 1.1, where the attribution of John Philoponus, *De Opificio Mundi*, also to 'Ιώσηπος ὁ 'Εβραῖος is also discussed.

[133] Photius, *Bibliotheca* 48: ἀνεγνώσθη 'Ιωσήπου περὶ τοῦ παντός, ὃ ἐν ἄλλοις ἀνέγνων ἐπιγραφόμενον περὶ τῆς τοῦ παντός αἰτίας, ἐν ἄλλοις δὲ περὶ τῆς τοῦ παντός οὐσίας. ἔστι δὲ ἐν δυσί λογιδίοις. δείκνυσι δὲ ἐν αὐτοῖς πρὸς ἑαυτὸν στασιάζοντα Πλάτωνα, ἐλέγχει δὲ καὶ περὶ ψυχῆς καὶ ὕλης καὶ ἀναστάσεως 'Αλκίνουν ἀλόγως τε καὶ ψευδῶς εἰπόντα, ἀντεισάγει δὲ τὰς οἰκείας περὶ τούτων τῶν ὑποθέσεων δόξας, δείκνυσί τε πρεσβύτερον 'Ελλήνων πολλῷ τὸ 'Ιουδαίων γένος.

[134] K. Holl, Fragmenta vornicänischer Kirchenväter aus den Sacra parallela, in *TU* 20 (N.F. 5), (1899), p. 137-143 with which cf. W.J. Malley, Four unedited fragments of the De universo of the pseudo-Josephus found in the Chronicon of George Hamartolus (Coislin 305), in *JThS* n.s. 16 1965, p. 13-25.

[135] For details see 5B 1.1 and footnote 135.

preserved in Pseudo-Damascene, and Malley's editing of the four fragments cited in *ms. Coislin* 305 of the *Chronicon* of George Hamartolus, has enabled us to reconstruct part of the text. Let us now see how these fragments compare both with Photius' description of the contents and with *El.*

4 B 2.1.1. The origin of Plato's philosophy in the Timaeus

We have firstly Coislin 305 *frag.* III published by Malley.[136] Here the *Timaeus* is cited as evidence that Plato's reputation amongst the Greeks was undeserved.[137] According to the *Timaeus*, he had learned his philosophy from an Egyptian priest, as the dialogue between the latter and Solon shows.[138] In *El.* VI, 22,1 we have a similar reference to this dialogue.[139] The dialogue is called a ὑπόθεσις in both works (*El.* τὴν ὅλην ὑπόθεσιν περὶ τῆς τοῦ κόσμου γενέσεως/ *frag.* κατὰ τὴν... τοῦ Πλάτωνος ὑπόθεσιν). Furthermore Plato is accused in *frag.* III of being wrong in not seeking the most ancient source "from where the Egyptian priest had received the teaching which he passed on to Solon the philosopher (οὐκ ἐπιζητήσας πόθεν παραλαβὼν ὁ Αἰγύπτιος ἱερεὺς ἀπήγγειλε Σολώνι τῷ φιλοσόφῳ)." Likewise in *El.* VI, 22,1 the Greeks whom Solon teaches are "young children (παῖδας νέους ὄντας) and have not grasped any older learning (καὶ πρεσβύτερον ἐπισταμένους μάθημα) involving theological speculation" (θεολογούμενον οὐδέν)."

It is at first sight puzzling why a work which Photius claims to be a refutation of Plato's doctrine (δείκνυσι δὲ ἐν αὐτοῖς πρὸς ἑαυτὸν στασιάζοντα Πλάτωνα) should make such play at its beginning[140] regarding the alleged, real origins, Egyptian and cultic, of Plato's thought. But this should not surprise us when we look at the method of refutation deployed by *El.* By contrast with *C.N.*'s refutation of Noetus' by means of Scriptural exegesis, *El.* adopts the historiographical method exemplified in Diogenes Laertius' διαδοχαὶ τῶν φιλόσοφων. Let us firstly therefore consider the significance of the citation of Solon in the *Timaeus* in this fragment.

---

136 Malley (1966) p. 15-16, cf. Plato, Timaeus 19 e 8-22 b 4.
137 Ibid. *frag.* III, 12-13: πρὸς τοῦτον ἡμῖν ἡ ἅμιλλα γινέσθω τῶν λόγων, τὸν καὶ πάντων νομιζόμενον παρ᾽ Ἕλλησι θεοσεβέστατόν τε καὶ ἀληθέστερον.
138 Ibid. *frag.* III, 21-24; 28-29: ὃς ὑπὸ τῆς ἀληθείας βιασθεὶς παρ᾽ οὗ ταῦτα ἦν ἀκηκοὼς ἱερέως ἐν Αἰγύπτῳ ἀπήγγειλε τοῖς ἰδίοις ἐπανήξας εἰς τὴν λάλον᾽ Ἑλλάδα ὡς ἴδια, οὐκ ἐπιζητήσας πόθεν παραλαβὼν ὁ Αἰγύπτιος ἱερεὺς ἀπήγγειλε Σολώνι τῷ φιλοσόφῳ, καθὼς ἐν τῷ Τιμαίῳ διαμέμνηται... ὁ Σόλων ὡς μεγάλα καὶ θαυμάσια κατὰ πᾶσαν τὴν Ἑλλάδα κηρύσσει κατὰ τὴν τοῦ ἱερέως καὶ τοῦ Πλάτωνος ὑπόθεσιν.
139 *El.* VI, 22,1: ἡ μὲν οὖν ἀρχὴ τῆς ὑποθέσεώς ἐστιν ἐν τῷ Τιμαίῳ τῷ Πλάτωνι σοφία Αἰγυπτίων· ἐκεῖθεν γὰρ ὁ Σόλων τὴν ὅλην ὑπόθεσιν περὶ τῆς τοῦ κόσμου γενέσεως καὶ φθορᾶς παλαιῷ τινι λόγῳ καὶ προφητικῷ, ὥς φησιν ὁ Πλάτων, τοὺς Ἕλληνας ἐδίδαξε, παῖδας νέους ὄντας καὶ πρεσβύτερον ἐπισταμένους μάθημα θεολογούμενον οὐδέν.
140 I follow here the most able reconstruction of Malley (1966) p. 20-21, using the plan of Theophilus *Ad Autolycum* as a parallel model, of the plan of the περὶ τοῦ παντὸς οὐσίας. I also note in support "He is the one we must refute (πρὸς τοῦτον ἡμῖν ἡ ἅμιλλα γινέσθω τῶν λόγων)" as implying the introductory nature of the passage to a refutation that will come later.

4B 2.1.1.1. *Solon and the* σοφοί, διαδοχή *and* ἀρχή

As I have discussed in greater detail elsewhere,[141] Laertius shared a methodology with such writers as Sotion, Sosicrates of Rhodes, and Lembus, that
consisted in tracing the various philosophical schools in terms of a number
of διαδοχαί that terminated in two ἀρχαί, the work of Thales and
Pherekydes, in the *Urzeit* of Greek civilisation. In that *Urzeit*, the eleven or
twelve σοφοί communicate with these two of their number by means of letters which thus serve to unite the two different διαδοχαί of which they are
the ἀρχαί into a common Hellenic civilization. Thus the σοφοί are brought
into a common relationship with their devotees, the φιλοσοφοί, through their
epistolary unity with Thales and Pherekydes.[142]

Laertius thus used the concept of διαδοχαί to demonstrate the cultural
purity of true philosophy as a phenomenon whose total origin or ἀρχή was in
Hellenic civilisation. No Latin writer such as Lucretius deserves mention
from him. Likewise in terms of origin philosophy does not derive from
Orphic religion which was not only non-Greek (Orpheus was a Thracian),
but also was what we might consider too theological to rank as philosophy.
As Laertius claims of Orpheus that he is wrong "to attribute (προστρῖψαι) to
the gods every human condition (πᾶν τὸ ἀνθρώπειον πάθος)."[143]

We can now see how *El.* VI, 22,1 and *frag.* III are seen to be part of the
general perspective of *El.* on how heresy is to be refuted. The heretics are
shown to owe their διαδοχή to Greek philosophy, and not to the apostles,
with the result that they have no part in the real Christianity of the apostolic
Urzeit.[144] The ἀρχή of the heretics is therefore in Greek philosophy.[145] But it
is from more than Greek philosophy; for where does that philosophy itself
derive its ἀρχή?

Contrary to what Laertius had denied about the origins of philosophy in
Orphism, the heretics found their ἀρχή in mystery religion too (τὴν ἀρχὴν
μὲν ἐκ δογμάτων φιλοσοφουμένων καὶ μυστηρίων ἐπικεχειρημένων). Indeed
philosophy was not a separate source for heresy from Hellenistic religion but
both were ἐκ τῆς Ἑλλήνων σοφίας. *El.* will later emphasize that philosophy's
real origin was in Hellenistic religion. In *El.* V, 6,3 the source of the error of
philosophy is the Serpent, the αἴτιος τῆς πλάνης ὄφις, the Νάας behind every

---

[141] A. Brent, Diogenes Laertius and the Apostolic Succession, in *JEH* 44,3 (1993), p. 367-
389.
[142] Ibid. p. 377-378 ff.
[143] Ibid. p. 374 where Diogenes Laertius, *Succ.* I. 5 is quoted.
[144] Ibid. p. 376-377. Cf. *El.* I prooem. 8: ἀθέους αὐτοὺς ἐπιδείξωμεν... ὅθεν τε τὰ
ἐπιχειρήματα αὐτοῖς γεγένηται, καὶ ὅτι μηθὲν ἐξ ἁγίων γραφῶν λαβόντες ταῦτα
ἐπεχείρησαν, ἢ τινος ἁγίου διαδοχὴν φυλάξαντες ἐπὶ ταῦτα ὥρμησαν... cf. also prooem.
9: ὁ πρωτοστατήσας τῆς αἱρέσεως ἐπλεονέκτησε λαβόμενος τὰς ἀρχὰς καὶ ἐκ τούτων
ἐπὶ τὰ χείρονα ὁρμηθεὶς τὸ δόγμα συνεστήσατο.
[145] Ibid. proem. 8:...ἀλλ᾽ ἔστιν αὐτοῖς τὰ δοξαζόμενα τὴν ἀρχὴν μὲν ἐκ τῆς
Ἑλλήνων σοφίας λαβόντα, ἐκ δογμάτων φιλοσοφουμένων καὶ μυστηρίων
ἐπικεχειρημένων καὶ ἀστρολόγων ῥεμβομένων.

apparently different ναός where apparently different pagan divinities were worshipped. Thus *El.*, though sharing a concept of διαδοχή with Irenaeus and Hegesippus, diverges markedly from them in that for the former the διαδοχαί of the heretics went back to Simon Magus the opponent of the apostles. Rather they go back *via* Greek philosophy to the worship of the Naasenes.[146]

We can in consequence now draw some very clear parallels between *El.* and *frag.* III on the use of the figure of Solon in the *Timaeus*.

4 B 2.1.1.2. Frag. *III and* El. *VI, 22,1:* διαδοχή and ἀρχή

In his reflections on the ἀρχή and διαδοχή of heresy, *El.* mirrors similar reflections of Laertius on the ἀρχή and διαδοχή of Greek philosophy. If not direct borrowing of the latter by the former, they appear clearly to share as a common backcloth the historiography of the Greek philosophical schools. One of the σόφοι, which *El.* I prooem. 1 regards as seven in number, was Solon.

We can now see why it is Solon's role in the *Timaeus* that attracts the attention of *frag.* III,23-24, since he declares only what he has learned from an Egyptian priest. Thus the διαδοχή of Greek philosophers goes back to an ἀρχή in Hellenistic religion such as *El.* affirmed and Laertius had denied. In the words of *El.*, Plato's fundamental error was not to have sought the true ἀρχή of this διαδοχή, or in the words of *frag.* III, 23-24: οὐκ ἐπιζητήσας πόθεν παραλαβὼν ὁ Αἰγύπτιος ἱερεὺς ἀπήγγειλε Σόλωνι τῷ φιλοσόφῳ.

El. VI, 22,1 focused also particularly on Solon in the *Timaeus*, and here too the emphasis was on the fact that ἡ ἀρχή τῆς ὑποθέσεώς ἐστιν... σοφία Αἰγυπτίων and that was the true ἀρχή of Plato's teaching, and not in Greek philosophy as such. The author of *frag.* III, though he may not use the terms ἀρχὴ and διαδοχή expressly in what accidentally survives, thus shows that he is the author of *El.* too by sharing the concern, unique and individual to *El.*, to ground the διαδοχὴ τῶν φιλοσόφων in Hellenistic religion that was older than the σοφοί mentioned by Laertius and other writers, and involved the theologizing that the latter had expressly denied them.

Laertius, in his assertion that philosophy was a Greek phenomenon, had eschewed early theological accounts. Not only did he expressly exclude Orpheus, but implicitly Homer and Hesiod, by never mentioning these writ-

---

[146] *El.* V, 9,12: τιμῶσι δὲ οὐκ ἄλλο τι ἢ τὸν νάας οὗτοι, Νααασηνοὶ καλούμενοι. νάας δὲ ἐστιν ὁ ὄφις· ἀφ᾽ οὗ φασι πάντας εἶναι τοὺς ὑπὸ τὸν οὐρανὸν προσαγορευομένους ναοὺς ἀπὸ τοῦ νάας, κἀκείνῳ μόνῳ τῷ νάας ἀνακεῖσθαι πᾶν ἱερὸν καὶ πᾶσαν τελετὴν καὶ πᾶν μυστήριον... See also G. Vallée, A Study in Anti-Gnostic Polemics: Irenaeus, Hippolytus, and Epiphanius, in *Studies in Early Christianity and Judaism* 1, (Canada: William Laurier University Press 1981) (Canadian Corporation for Studies in Religion); M. Marcovich, The Naasene Psalm in Hippolytus (Haer. 5.10. 2), in *The Rediscovery of Gnosticism. II: Sethian Gnosticism,* (Ed.) Bentley Layton Lugduni Batav., (Leiden: E.J. Brill 1981); J. Frickel, Hellenistische Erlösung in christlicher Deutung: die gnostische Naasenerschrift., in *Nag Hamadi Studies* 19, (Leiden: Brill 1984).

ers as founders of philosophy that was entirely a Greek phenomenon.[147] After all, they too attributed to the gods πᾶν τὸ ἀνθρώπειον πάθος. Laertius, from *El.*'s point of view, had thus never grasped the πρεσβύτερον...μάθημα θεολογούμενον, and so had never understood the true Naasene origin of Greek philosophy. The use by both *El.* and *frag.* III of Solon in the ὑποθέσις of the *Timaeus* specifically in such a context is too close and idiosyncratic to be accidental. Furthermore, in *frag.* I the point is again emphasized that the self acclaimed Greek philosophers (οἱ καθ᾽ "Ελληνας φιλόσοφοι ἐπαγγελλόμενοι) in vain dissociate themselves from Homer and Hesiod (τὴν 'Ησιόδου καὶ 'Ομήρου ματαιολογίαν) when they show agreement with (συνήραντο) their mythology (τὰ ὑπ᾽ αὐτῶν μεμυθευμένα) by their religious observance (διὰ τοῦ σέβειν).[148]

Having established the author of *El.* as the author of *frag.* III in respect of the use of Solon in the *Timaeus*, we can now look at the evidence of Photius' *Bibliotheca* 48 for the identity between *frag.* III and the περὶ τοῦ παντός of the Statue, and the discussion of the Albinian theory of the Forms in *El.* I, 19. We shall include in our discussion the Pseudo-Damascene fragment (Holl, 353), which will also take us beyond the mere equivalence between the title on the Statue and that cited in that work, and give us further internal evidence for their identity.

4B 2.1.2. *Albinus' Platonism in* περὶ τοῦ παντός *and in* El.

As is well known, Plato's successors developed the theory of Forms in two different directions. Speusippus, almost as if an Aristotelian, interpreted the theory in terms of Aristotle's criticism. The Forms, as uncreated and eternal essences, were in themselves self-sufficient and independent entities in the overall structure of reality and appearance. For Albinus, however, the un-created and eternal Forms were only such by virtue of their being ideas in the mind of God.[149]

In *Bibliotheca* 48 Photius tells us that the author of περὶ τοῦ παντός, on which he had found Josephus' name written, criticized a specifically Albinian version of Plato's Forms (ἐλέγχει δὲ... 'Αλκίνουν ἀλόγως τε καὶ ψευδῶς εἰπόντα). *El.* I, 18-19, 3 closely resembles an *Epitome* of Plato produced by Albinus.[150] We are informed that Plato taught that the universe

---

147 Diogenes Laertius, *Succ.* 1. prooem. 1 mentions the claims of the Egyptians to be the originators of philosophy but in 3 the authors who so attribute are argued to be mistaken. Hesiod is only mention in passing in 7,25 and 10,2.

148 Malley (1966) p. 15 *frag.* I, 2-7: οὐ συγχωρητέον... κατά γε τὴν 'Ησιόδου Θεογονίαν καὶ 'Ομήρου ματαιολογίαν· οἷς, εἰ μὴ θέλοιεν δοκεῖν πείθεσθαι οἱ καθ' "Ελληνας φιλόσοφοι ἐπαγγελλόμενοι, ἀλλά γε διὰ τοῦ σέβειν τὰ ὑπ᾽ αὐτῶν μεμυθευμένα συνήραντο.

149 For a detailed and classical discussion of the various versions of Plato's amongst the Fathers, see H.A. Wolfson, *The Philosophy of the Church Fathers: Faith, Trinity, and Incarnation*, (Cambridge Massachusetts: Harvard U.P. 1976), chapter 13.

150 Cited by M. Marcovich, Hippolyts Refutatio Omnium Häresium, in *Patristische Texte und Studien* Bd 25, (Berlin: De Gruyter 1986), p. 76 as Albinos, *Epit.* 8,2; 9, 1-2; 12, 1-2 ed.

consisted of θεός, ὕλη and παράδειγμα, and that the latter was in fact the "mind" or "intellect" of God (τὸ δὲ παράδειγμα τὴν διάνοιαν τοῦ θεοῦ εἶναι).[151] Παράδειγμα ("model," "outline") was of course a common description for Form in a Platonic sense, as is made clear (ὃ καὶ ἰδέαν καλεῖ). But, just as Albinus had asserted, there was for παράδειγμα/ιδέα no independent, concrete existence, since it was like the image (οἷον εἰκόνισμά τι) which God attached to the soul (προσέχων ἐν τῇ ψυχῇ) as a reflection of his own mind.[152]

Thus *El.* reflects the concern noted by Photius as that which the author of the περὶ τοῦ παντός believed he must refute, περὶ ψυχῆς καὶ ὕλης of Plato's doctrine. Likewise *frag.* III reflects in its case all three of the concerns represented in the Albinian *Epitome* cited by *El.* I, 19,1-2 when it begins with: Πλάτων... ὃς καὶ περὶ θεοῦ [θεός] καὶ ψυχῆς [παράδειγμα/ εἰκόνισμα/ ψυχή] καὶ κτίσεως [ὕλη] ἐπεχείρησε λέγειν. But Photius had added καὶ ἀναστάσεως to περὶ ψυχῆς καὶ ὕλης. It is at this point that Photius' description enables us to draw into our discussion Holl's *frag.* 353, claimed in the *ms.* tradition as from this work.[153]

4B 2.1.3. *Hades and* πρὸς "Ελληνας καὶ πρὸς Πλάτωνα

This protracted *frag.* 353 reveals in line 1 that it is about demons (ὁ περὶ δαιμόνων λόγος) and Hades (περὶ δὲ ᾅδου). Nevertheless, as we have seen (4B 2.1 and footnote 133), it bears, like Photius' *ms.*, Josephus' name, and Photius' titles, one of which is found on the Statue, and these titles variously bear Plato's name and that of the Greeks. Furthermore, as its contents show, it is directed against Plato's view of the soul in the light of the resurrection of the body.

The Greeks are to cease their unbelief (μάθετε μὴ ἀπιστεῖν).[154] God will raise bodies (αὐτὰ τὰ σώματα ἀνιστῶν), and not simply the souls of those at one time or another variously embodied (οὐ ψυχὰς μετενσωματῶν). Greek unbelief (ἀπιστεῖτε "Ελληνες) is based upon the fact that bodies are always seen to be broken up (ἃ ἀεὶ λελυμένα ὁρῶντες). The soul indeed is born (τὴν

---

[151] *El.* I, 19, 1-2: ... ἀρχὰς εἶναι τοῦ παντός θεὸν καὶ ὕλην καὶ παράδειγμα· θεὸν μὲν τὸν ποιητὴν καὶ διακοσμήσαντα τόδε τὸ πᾶν καὶ προνοούμενον αὐτοῦ... τὸ δὲ παράδειγμα τὴν διάνοιαν τοῦ θεοῦ εἶναι· ὃ καὶ ἰδέαν καλεῖ, οἷον εἰκόνισμά τι, ᾧ προσέχων ἐν τῇ ψυχῇ ὁ θεὸς τὰ πάντα ἐδημιούργει.

[152] In the light of my discussion, it will be seen that I find quite extraordinary the comment in C.E. Hill, Hades of Hippolytus or Tartarus of Tertullian? in *VCh* 43 (1989), p. 120: "Hippolytus in the *Refutation* shows himself a capable critic of Plato but neither in this work nor in any other does he ever mention Albinus, the second-century a.d. proponent of Middle Platonism." I show here that *El.* I, 19, 1-2 clearly describes Albinian Platonism and concludes it to be the source of heresy sufficiently to justify Photius' description.

[153] Holl (1899) p. 137.

[154] Holl *frag.* 353, 45-50: ... ἄχρι καιροῦ, ὃν ὁ θεὸς ὥρισεν ἀνάστασιν τότε πάντων ποιησάμενος, οὐ ψυχὰς μετενσωματῶν ἀλλ᾽ αὐτὰ τὰ σώματα ἀνιστῶν ἃ ἀεὶ λελυμένα ὁρῶντες ἀπιστεῖτε "Ελληνες. μάθετε μὴ ἀπιστεῖν. τὴν γὰρ ψυχὴν γενητὴν καὶ ἀθάνατον ὑπὸ θεοῦ γεγονέναι πιστεύσαντες κατὰ τὸν Πλάτωνος λόγον χρόνῳ μὴ ἀπιστήσητε καὶ τὸ σῶμα ἐκ τῶν αὐτῶν στοιχείων σύνθετον γενόμενον δυνατὸς ὁ θεὸς ἀναβιώσας ἀθάνατον ποιεῖν. Cf. also Malley (1966) *frag.* II, p. 15.

γὰρ ψυχὴν γενητὴν) and becomes immortal, according to Plato's argument (κατὰ τὸν Πλάτωνος λόγον), by God's act (ἀθάνατον ὑπὸ θεοῦ γεγονέναι). But God can bring back to life and make immortal even the body composed from the physical elements (καὶ τὸ σῶμα ἐκ τῶν αὐτῶν στοιχείων σύνθετον). Indeed, by an argument that Tertullian will echo, it is necessary for the unjust to rise too on Judgement Day in order that they may be capable of feeling the pain of their punishment.[155]

As we mentioned earlier (4A and footnote 7), Hades was also described by the author of *El.* and it is to a comparison of his description with that of *frag. 353* that we now turn.

4 B 2.1.4. *Hades in* frag. *353 and* El. *X, 34,2*

El. makes it clear that the fire of judgement is yet to come, and that it is a threat (ἐπερχομένην πυρὸς κρίσεως ἀπειλήν).[156] The fragment (353, 35-37) likewise speaks of "the angels set over" (οἷς οἱ ἐφεστῶτες ἄγγελοι) the unjust souls (οἱ ἄδικοι) in Hades "threatening (ἐπαπειλοῦντες)" them. Furthermore, the angels are "angels of punishment" (ἀγγέλων κολαστῶν), each with "fearful eye," in both *El.* and the fragment (353, 37), in an almost identical phrase (φοβερὸν ὄμμα ἀεὶ μένον ἐν ἀπειλῇ φοβερῷ ὄμματι ἐπαπειλοῦντες). In both works the judgment remains future in and through the resurrection of the body necessary for the fulfilment of that punishment. *Frag. 353, 43* declares that there is already there potentially an expection of this future event (τῇ προσδοκίᾳ τῆς μελλούσης κρίσεως ἤδη δυνάμει κολαζόμενοι).

Likewise *El.* claims that the "the worm (σκώληκα), the excrement of the body (σώματος ἀπουσίαν), ceaselessly curls around (ἀπαύστως ἐπιστρεφόμενον) the body that spawned it (ἐπὶ τὸ ἐκβράσαν σῶμα) as to its nourishment (ὡς ἐπιστροφήν)." Even the souls of the unrighteous yearn somewhat perversely to be restored to the body in which they will be eternally punished. The language here too is reflected in *frag. 353, 90* where, speaking now of the Last Judgment, we read: "And a certain fiery worm (σκώληξ δὲ τις ἔμπυρος), which neither dies (μὴ τελευτῶν) nor destroys the body (μηδὲ σῶμα διαφθείρων) continues bursting forth endless pain from the body without ceasing (ἀπαύστως ὀδύνην ἐκ σώματος ἐκβράσσων παραμένει)."

In consequence of the full punishment being "not yet," the description of Tartarus (Ταρτάρου ζοφεροῦ ὄμμα) in *El.* or of Hades or Gehenna (*frag. 353, 4 and 38*) has to construct the geography appropriately. The "lake of

---

[155] Ibid. 70: οἱ δὲ ἄδικοι οὐκ ἀλλοιωθέντα τὰ σώματα οὐδὲ πάθους ἢ νόσου μεταστάντα οὐδὲ ἐνδοξασθέντα ἀπολήψονται ἀλλ᾿ ἐν οἷς νοσήμασιν ἐτελεύτων καὶ ὁποῖα ἦν τοιαῦτα ἀναβιώσαντα ἐπενδύσονται καὶ ὁποῖοι ἐν ἀπιστίᾳ γεγένηνται τοιοῦτοι πιστῶς κριθήσονται. Cf. also Malley (1966) fragment IV, p. 16.

[156] *El.* X, 34, 2: δι᾿ ἧς ἐπιγνώσεως ἐκφεύξεσθε ἐπερχομένην πυρὸς κρίσεως ἀπειλήν, καὶ Ταρτάρου ζοφεροῦ ὄμμα ἀφώτιστον, ὑπὸ λόγου φωνῆς μὴ καταλαμφθέν, καὶ βρασμὸν ἀεννάου λίμνης γεννητρίας φλογός, καὶ ταρταρούχων ἀγγέλων κολαστῶν φοβερὸν ὄμμα ἀεὶ μένον ἐν ἀπειλῇ καὶ σκώληκα, σώματος ἀπουσίαν, ἀπαύστως ἐπιστρεφόμενον ἐπὶ τὸ ἐκβράσαν σῶμα ὡς ἐπιστροφήν.

unquenchable fire" is a "place set aside (τόπος ἀφώρισταί τις λίμνης πυρὸς
ἀβέστου)," and contains as yet no risen bodies of the damned (ἐν ᾧ μὲν
οὐδέπω τινὰ καταρερίφθαι ὑπερλήφαμεν). Rather it is "prepared for the day
appointed by God (ἐσκευάσθαι δὲ εἰς τὴν προωρισμένον ἡμέραν παρὰ τοῦ
θεοῦ)."[157]

The souls of the unjust, however, are driven by the near Gehenna
(πλησίον τῆς γεέννης, ἧς ἐγγίονες ὄντες) or the lake of fire, where they can
hear its continuous raging (τοῦ μὲν βρασμοῦ ἀδιαλείπτως ἐπακούουσιν), and
can both share in the smoking heat (τοῦ τῆς θέρμης ἀτμοῦ οὐκ ἀμοιροῦσιν)
as well as see the yellow flames (αὐτῆς δὲ τῆς ἐγγίονος ὄψεως τὴν φόβερὰν
καὶ ὑπερβαλλόντως ξανθὴν θέαν τοῦ πυρὸς (42) ὁρῶντες).[158] Likewise in El.
there is the similar sights and sounds described in similar vocabulary of the
"tumult of the ever flowing lake (βρασμὸν ἀεννάου λίμνης), which produces
the flame (γεννητρίας φλογός)."

Apart from the threatening sight and fury of the lake of fire, Hades is a
dark place.[159] Similarly for El. there is the "sight of gloomy Tartarus, unlit
(Ταρτάρου ζοφεροῦ ὄμμα ἀφώτιστον) and not illuminated by the voice of the
Logos (ὑπὸ λόγου φωνῆς μὴ καταλαμφθέν)." The strange allusion to not
being illuminated by a voice is presumably to be explained by the close
association of λόγος, φωνή, and πρὸ ἑωσφόρου φωσφόρος (El. X, 33,11, see
also 4A 2), which is characteristic of works associated with El., and foreign
to those associated with C.N.

Furthermore, not only do what we have seen to be the common features
of the description of the underworld in both El. and περὶ τοῦ παντός assist in
identifying a common author, but also they enable a distinct contrast to be
drawn with the Hippolytus' genuine works. In those latter works the souls of
the redeemed have already been released and are in the presence of God. But
in the former they are assigned to a place in the underworld (χωρίον
φωτεινὸν), awaiting the eternal rest to be afterwards enjoyed in heaven (τὴν
μετὰ τοῦτο τὸ χωρίον ἀνάπαυσιν... ἐν οὐρανῷ).[160] They are released as the

---

[157] Frag. 353, 7–13: ...ἄγγελοι φρουροὶ, πρὸς τὰς ἑκάστου πράξεις διανέμοντες τὰς
τῶν τόπων προσκαίρους κολάσεις. ἐν τούτῳ δὲ τῷ χωρίῳ τόπος ἀφώρισταί τις λίμνης
πυρὸς ἀσβέστου ἐν ᾧ μὲν οὐδέπω τινὰ καταρερίφθαι ὑπειλήφαμεν, ἐσκευάσθαι δὲ εἰς
τὴν προωρισμένην ἡμέραν παρὰ τοῦ θεοῦ.
[158] Ibid. 33–44 : οἱ δὲ ἄδικοι ἀριστερὰ ἕλκονται ὑπὸ ἀγγέλων κολαστῶν οὐκέτι
ἑκουσίως πορευόμενοι ἀλλὰ μετὰ βίας ὡς δέσμιοι ἑλκόμενοι, οἷς οἱ ἐφεστῶτες ἄγγελοι
ἐπιγελῶντες διαπέμπονται ἐπονειδίζοντες καὶ φοβερῷ ὄμματι ἐπαπειλοῦντες καὶ εἰς τὰ
κατώτερα μέρη ὠθοῦντες, οὓς ἀγομένους ἕλκουσιν οἱ ἐφεστῶτες ἕως πλησίον τῆς
γεέννης, ἧς ἐγγίονες ὄντες τοῦ μὲν βρασμοῦ ἀδιαλείπτως ἐπακούουσι καὶ τοῦ τῆς
θέρμης ἀτμοῦ οὐκ ἀμοιροῦσιν, αὐτῆς δὲ τῆς ἐγγίονος ὄψεως τὴν φόβερὰν καὶ
ὑπερβαλλόντως ξανθὴν θέαν τοῦ πυρὸς ὁρῶντες καταπεπλήγασι, τῇ προσδοκίᾳ τῆς
μελλούσης κρίσεως ἤδη δυνάμει κολαζόμενοι..
[159] Ibid. 4: ὁ ᾅδης τόπος ἐστὶν ἐν τῇ κτίσει ἀκατασκεύαστος, χωρίον ὑπόγειον, ἐν ᾧ
φῶς κόσμου οὐκ ἐπιλάμπει, φωτὸς τοίνυν ἐν τούτῳ τῷ χωρίῳ μὴ καταλάμποντος
ἀνάγκη σκότος διηνεκῶς τυγχάνειν.
[160] Ibid. 20-30: ...οἱ μὲν δίκαιοι εἰς δεξιὰ φωταγωγούμενοι... ἄγονται εἰς χωρίον
φωτεινὸν, ἐν ᾧ οἱ ἀπ᾽ ἀρχῆς δίκαιοι πολιτεύονται... οἷς ὁ τόπος οὐ καματηφόρος

immediate consequence of Christ's death, descent into the underworld, and resurrection. It is the ὁ τῶν νεκρῶν εὐαγγελιστής of I *Pet.* 3, 19-20 who is described as "drawing from lowest Hades (ἐξ ᾅδου κατωτάτου ἑλκύσας) ...humanity bound in the bonds of death (ἐν δεσμοῖς θανάτου κρατούμενον)."[161] Humanity is set free when Christ himself is loosed from the bonds of death.[162] We shall return later to this distinction when we examine Loi's attempt to assign Pseudo-John Chrysostom's *Paschal Homilies* I-VI to the author of *El.* (4C 2.2.2.1.4)

At this point we reach the end of our comparisons between the fragments of Holl (1899) and Malley (1966) and *El.* Photius does however give us a further item of information regarding the περὶ τοῦ παντός

4 B 2.1.5. περὶ τοῦ παντός *and the antiquity of Judaism*
Photius specifically draws attention to the author's argument that Judaism is older than Hellenism (δείκνυσί τε πρεσβύτερον Ἑλλήνων πολλῷ τὸ Ἰουδαίων γένος), which we have seen to be the theme of *El.* X, 30,6- 31,1.[163] Although such an argument was commonplace in early apologetic (4A 2.1.1), it nevertheless in conjunction with Photius' other remarks provides good cumulative evidence that it was the same writer that both produced the περὶ τοῦ παντός and *El.*

Let us therefore briefly summarize where our discussion and analysis of the literary testimony to the περὶ τοῦ παντός, on the basis of internal literary criteria, has led us.

4B 2.1. 6. περὶ τοῦ παντός, El. *and Photius: in conclusion*
Both the fragments of Holl (1899) and of Malley (1966) have taken us beyond a mere identification of a title on the Statue with titles mentioned in Photius' *Bibliotheca* 48. Photius' allusions to the contents of that work have enabled us to identify it firstly with *El.* as author, in terms of similarities of content rather than merely similarity of title. Secondly, the connection thus

---

γίνεται... ἀλλ' ἡ τῶν πατέρων δικαίων τε ὁρωμένη ὄψις πάντοτε μειδιᾷ ἀναμενόντων τὴν μετὰ τοῦτο τὸ χωρίον ἀνάπαυσιν καὶ αἰωνίαν βίωσιν ἐν οὐρανῷ...

[161] *Great Ode* I (Bonwetsch and Achelis (1897) p. 83, 3-6; Nautin (1953) p. 20): ὁ τὸν ἀπολωλότα ἐκ γῆς πρωτόπλαστον ἄνθρωπον καὶ ἐν δεσμοῖς θανάτου κρατούμενον ἐξ ᾅδου κατωτάτου ἑλκύσας, ὁ ἄνωθεν κατελθὼν καὶ τὸν κάτω εἰς τὰ ἄνω ἀνενέγκας· ὁ τῶν νεκρῶν εὐαγγελιστὴς καὶ τῶν ψυχῶν λυτρωτής.... Cf. also *De David et Goliath*, 11 in Garitte G. Traités d'Hippolyte sur David et Goliath, sur le Cantique des cantiques et sur l'Antichrist, in *CSCO*, 263-264 (Louvain: 1965).

[162] *Dan.* IV, 33,4: ὅσους οὖν ὁ σατανᾶς ἔδησεν βροχίσας, τούτους ἐλθὼν ὁ κύριος ἔλυσεν ἐκ τῶν τοῦ θανάτου δεσμῶν, αὐτὸν μὲν τὸν καθ' ἡμῶν «ἰσχυρὸν» δήσας, τὴν δὲ ἀνθρωπότητα ἐλευθερώσας... For other passages see Hill (1989) p. 105-115 where he defends against Richard (1969) col. 533-566 ff. the thesis that περὶ τοῦ παντός could not have been written by the author of *Dan.* etc. In consequence of his denying that *El.* could have had an identical author περὶ τοῦ παντός, he proceeds to assign the latter to Tertullian. (p. 115-122) It will be clear that I reject the grounds for his denial not merely because Tertullian is a Latin Father and Photius clearly commented upon a Greek work, since the former wrote in Greek works now lost. Cf. also Simonetti (1989) p. 129-130.

[163] Quoted in footnote 133.

established between *El.* and Photius' author has enabled us to employ both in identifying, again in terms of subject matter, the fragments in Holl (1899) (from the *Sacra Parallela* of Pseudo- John Damascene), and in Malley (1966) (from the *Chronicon* of George Hamartolus), as clearly parts of the same lost work. But, thirdly, both Photius, Pseudo-Damascene, and Hamartolus all give us the name of an author other than Hippolytus.

Whether in the Holl or the Malley fragments, we see that Josephus is the name attached to the περὶ τοῦ παντός, even though, in the case of both Photius and Pseudo-John Damascene, the pseudonymous writer knows of other works written by Hippolytus. To these three we may add as a fourth the fragment from John Philoponus, the brevity of which gives us evidence merely of the title and author, but not of the contents.[164] We saw something similar in the case of Theodoret's citations (3A 5-6) which clearly identify Hippolytus as the author of some works. It is the fact of these four quite different testimonies to Josephus as the name read as the title on many *mss.* that was the foundation of Nautin's attempt to identify this writer as the author of all the works on the Statue, as we shall consider further in 4D.

Let us now turn to the second title of the two works—and, it should be note, the only two—that unambiguously connect the author of *El.* with a title on the Statue, namely the Χρονικῶν.

4B 2.2. Χρονικῶν-συναγωγὴ χρόνων

The περὶ τοῦ παντός was identified with several different names such as Gaius, Josephus, etc., though never with Hippolytus himself. But the συναγωγὴ χρόνων, the contents of which closely resembles those of *El.* X, 30-31, is similarly anonymous. Indeed, in *El.* itself we do not find this title. Thus the identification of the contents with a work called the Χρονικῶν would be highly speculative without a further document. There was great interest in Chronographies, as Julius Africanus shows on the Christian side, and indeed on the pagan the whole *genre* of diadochic literature, of which Diogenes Laertius is the sole survivor, indicates that a work with such a title would be by no means unique.

The known contents of *El.*, and the unknown contents of the Χρονικῶν of the Statue, combined with the perceived allusion to a plural χρόνοι in the βίβλοι of the ἐν ἑτέραις βίβλοις (*El.* X, 30,1 and 5), would of themselves have therefore been unable to establish that identity. At that point we should have been dependent on the argument that every work on the Statue must be by one and the same author, which we have been reluctant to assume *a priori*, as has been done so far universally, with the exception of Simonetti. Only by accepting such an *a priori* could we be secure in our opinion that the contents of *El.* X, 30-31 were indicative of what would have been found written in the Χρονικῶν of the Statue, if we had no further evidence. If the works on the Statue had represented the library of a school, just because one of them was written by the writer of *El.* and named as Josephus by several late writers, it would not necessarily imply that the work entitled Χρονικῶν was also written by the same author.

But in this case we do have, as with the fragments of the περὶ τοῦ παντός, an independent corroboration of the contents of the Χρονικῶν, and therefore warrant independent of its appearance as a mere title in the list on the Statue. We have the anonymous work συναγωγὴ χρόνων καὶ ἐτῶν ἀπὸ κτίσεως κόσμου ἕως τῆς ἐνεστώσης ἡμέρας with whose contents we are able to compare *El.* X, 30-31. Indeed the anonymity of the work needs to be emphasised in view of the too quick assumption, which we have seen to be all too common for the health of this discussion, that it must have been by Hippolytus since the Statue must both have been his, and he himself the author of every work on the list.[165]

Before we examine the possible relationship between the Statue itself and the Συναγωγή, let us establish first at the internal characteristics indicative of a literary relationship between the Συναγωγή and *El.* In this way we shall be able to establish that the Συναγωγή is written by the same author (who was not Hippolytus) as *El.* and belongs therefore with the περὶ τοῦ παντός in a block of works on the Statue that may not prove to be co-extensive with every title on its plinth.

4B 2.2.1. Συναγωγή-Χρονικῶν *and El. X, 30-31*

In *El.* X, 30, 4-5 we read that the "names of which we have set out in other books (ὧν καὶ τὰ ὀνόματα ἐκτεθείμεθα ἐν ἑτέραις βίβλοις)" were those of the 72 nations (ἦσαν δὲ οὗτοι οβ΄... ἔθνη) who were the descendants of Noah scattered (διεσπάρησαν οἱ ἔκγονοι τοῦ Νῶε) in the time of Phalek (ἐπὶ δὲ τοῦ Φάλεκ). We find those 72 nations arising similarly in the συναγωγή. According to the Greek text preserved in *Matritensis Graec.* 121, we read: τῆς γῆς ὁ διαμερισμὸς τοῖς τρισὶν υἱοῖς τοῦ Νῶε μετὰ τὸν κατακλυσμόν. Thus the terms διεσπάρησαν/ διεμερίσθησαν of both works can be applied to the 72 nations, since the Συναγωγή will go on to speak of μετὰ τὸν κατακλυσμὸν... αἱ συγχυθεῖσαι γλῶσσαι οβ΄.[166]

---

[165] Bauer (1905) p. 140-141: "Unter den erhaltenen Büchertiteln liest man Z.12 Χρονικῶν, wozu βίβλος zu denken ist. Damit ist in authentischester Weise geglaubigt, dass Hippolytos neben der ἀπόδειξις χρόνων τοῦ Πάσχα und dem zum Zwecke der Osterberechnung auf der Kathedra der Statue aufgezeichneten πίναξ ein als Χρονικά   oder χρονικῶν   βίβλος bezeichnetes Werk verfasst hat." He then proceeds to claim *El.* as connected to the works on the Statue and therefore of Hippolytan authorship. See also Marcovich (1986) p. 12-15.

[166] Bauer (1905) p. 46-50: 45. τῆς γῆς ὁ διαμερισμὸς τοῖς τρισὶν υἱοῖς τοῦ Νῶε μετὰ τὸν κατακλυσμὸν ἐγένετο οὕτως τῷ Σήμ, τῷ Χὰμ καὶ τῷ Ἰάφεθ. 46. τῶν τριῶν ἀδελφῶν αἱ φυλαὶ διεμερίσθησαν...53. συνεχύθησαν δὲ αἱ γλῶσσαι μετὰ τὸν κατακλυσμὸν ἐπὶ τῆς γῆς· ἦσαν οὖν αἱ συγχυθεῖσαι γλῶσσαι οβ ΄...

272 CHAPTER FOUR

Furthermore, the "confusion of tongues" at Babel was a divine judgment for apostasy, and the 72 tongues after the flood are associated with that fact. When they divided (διεμερίσθησαν) at Babel "the confused tongues (αἱ συγχυθεῖσαι γλῶσσαι)" became 70 nations (oʹ), but when they did so, described in the same terms, at the Flood, they became 72 (oβʹ).[167] The equation of (δια)μερισμός with apostasy is also made in the introduction to the Jewish αἱρετισταί in *El.* IX, 18,1-2. Here under Moses as the one teacher (εἷς... παρὰ θεοῦ διδάσκαλος) they had "one custom (ἓν ἔθος)" and "one desert country (μία δὲ ἔρημος χώρα) and one mountain, Sinai (καὶ ἓν ὄρος τὸ Σινᾶ)." But when they crossed the Jordan, "they tore apart (διέσπασαν) by their disagreements (διαφόρως) the law of God... and so they discovered the opinions of heresies (δόξας αἱρέσεων ἐφευρόντες) and departed into division (εἰς μερισμὸν ἐχώρησαν)."[168]

It should be noted that, underlying *El.* IX, 18,1-2, there is the notion that not only is one people split into two by heresy, but geographical divisions also result. The εἷς διδάσκαλος produces not simply the εἷς ὁ διά τούτου δοθεὶς νόμος and the ἓν ἔθος, but also the μία ἔρημος χώρα καὶ ἓν ὄρος. The Συναγωγή reflects too the view that the division is geographical as well as linguistic and moral. The division after Noah was τῆς γῆς ὁ διαμερισμός. Thus when the author of the latter has fulfilled the promise of *El.* X, 30,5 to enumerate the 72 nations ἐν ἑτέραις βίβλοις,[169] he proceeds to delimit the geographical domains of the descendants of the three sons of Noah for the rest of the extant treatise.

It is in this context that explains universal history as part of the Jewish record of creation and the Fall that the concern of the table of contents in both *ms. Matritensis Graec.* and *Liber Generationis* I and II is to be understood. The author's task is to answer not only who were the nations that came from the three sons of Noah (τίνες ἐκ τίνων γεγένηνται) but also the kinds of cities and places each inherited (καὶ ποίας ἕκαστος αὐτῶν πόλεις καὶ χώρας κεκλήρωνται) and how many significant islands (πόσαι νῆσοι ἐπίσημοι).[170] *El.* X, 30, 1 again reflects that geographical interest when he

---

[167] Ibid. p. 50 (53) continues:...οἱ δὲ τὸν πύργον οἰκοδομήσαντες ἦσαν ἔθνη οʹ, οἱ καὶ ἐν γλώσσαις αὐτῶν ἐπὶ προσώπου τῆς γῆς διεμερίσθησαν.

[168] *El.* IX, 18,1-2: ᾽Ιουδαίων μὲν ἀρχῆθεν ἓν ἦν ἔθος· εἷς γὰρ ὁ τούτοις δοθεὶς παρὰ θεοῦ διδάσκαλος Μωϋσῆς καὶ εἷς ὁ διὰ τούτου δοθεὶς νόμος, μία δὲ ἔρημος χώρα καὶ ἓν ὄρος τὸ Σινᾶ· εἷς γὰρ ὁ τούτοις νομοθετήσας θεός. αὖθις δὲ, διαβάντες τὸν ᾽Ιορδάνην ποταμὸν καὶ τὴν δορύκτητον γῆν κληρονομήσαντες, διαφόρως τὸν τοῦ θεοῦ νόμον διέσπασαν, ἄλλος ἄλλως ἐπινοῶν τὰ εἰρημένα, καὶ οὕτως διδασκάλους ἑαυτοῖς ἐπεγείραντες, καὶ δόξας αἱρέσεων ἐφευρόντες εἰς μερισμὸν ἐχώρησαν.

[169] Bauer (1905) p. 50: 55. τὰ δὲ ὀνόματα τῶν ἑβδομήκοντα ἐστὶ ταῦτα. *Matritensis Graec.* reads 70 instead of the 72 given previously in 53, supported by the *Chron. Alex.* but corrected by *Liber Generationis* I. (p. 51). Bauer explained this discrepancy as a corruption in the former texts because two names had fallen out of the lists. (p. 138-139). Cf. A. Bauer and R. Helm, Hippolytus Werke, Bd. 4 Die Chronik, in *GCS* (46(36) (Berlin: Akademie Verlag 1955), p. 11: 53. Συνεχύθησαν δὲ αἱ γλῶσσαι μετὰ τὸν κατακλυσμὸν ἐπὶ τῆς γῆς· ἦσαν οὖν αἱ συγχυθεῖσαι γλῶσσαι οβʹ ... cf. 55. τὰ δὲ ὀνόματα τῶν ἑβδομήκοντά ἐστι ταῦτα.

[170] Ibid. p. 28-29 (2.).

assures us that what he has more carefully set out ἐν ἑτέραις βίβλοις is that "what is now Palestine and Judaea was once called Canaan."[171] Despite the Christian-apologetic use of such lists of kings, peoples, and places that the common stock of such Chronographies provided in a pagan context for purposes of schoolbook information, the secular origin of such material remains in that it is offered τοῖς φιλομαθέσιν by both *El.* and the Συναγωγή.[172]

On internal grounds, therefore, there is a strong case for identifying the Χρονικῶν of the Statue with the anonymous Συναγωγή, since *El.* X, 30-31 provides a clear statement of some of the contents and indeed the general interests of such a work the authorship of which the writer also claims. Having established the clear connection between two works on the Statue (the περὶ τοῦ παντός and the Χρονικῶν) with each other on the basis of *El.*, let us now consider how the connection of all three of these works with the authorship of the genuine Hippolytan *corpus* can now be broken by pointing to the discrepancies between the Συναγωγή-Χρονικῶν and the commentary *Dan.*

4B 2.2.2. Συναγωγή-χρονικῶν, ἀπόδειξις χρόνων and *Dan.*

Undoubtedly, and perhaps unfortunately, it was on the differences and similarities between these two works that Nautin's debate with Richard revolved. *Dan.* was not mentioned on the Statue but mentioned securely as the work of Hippolytus by Jerome. If this work could be shown to be by the same author as the Συναγωγή-Χρονικῶν mentioned both on the Statue with a text that survives that was also consistent with the ἀπόδειξις χρόνων τοῦ πάσχα which matches, on its own admission (κατὰ τὰ ἐν τῷ πίνακι), the Statue's inscriptions, then indeed the Statue commemorated the work of Hippolytus and all the works were his. This all-or-none-at-all-argument, based upon a misinterpretation of the Statue as commemorative of an individual, will have therefore its distorting effect on the debate in this particular instance.

Nautin mentioned five significant differences between the Συναγωγή and the ἀπόδειξις χρόνων of the Statue on the one hand, and *Dan.* on the other, with which Richard and others were to disagree.[173] We shall focus here on

---

171 *El.* X, 30,1: ... εἰς τὴν νῦν μὲν Παλαιστίνην καὶ Ἰουδαίαν προσαγορευομένην χώραν, τότε δὲ Χαναανῖτιν περὶ ἧς καὶ κατὰ τοῦτο τὸ μέρος τὸν λόγον οὐκ ἀμελῶς παρεδώκαμεν ἐν ἑτέραις βίβλοις.
172 *El.* X, 30,5: ὧν καὶ τὰ ὀνόματα ἐκτεθείμεθα ἐν ἑτέραις βίβλοις, μηδὲ τοῦτο παραλιπόντες, κατὰ τὸν ἡμέτερον τρόπον βουλόμενοι τοῖς φιλομαθέσιν ἐπιδεικνύναι ἣν ἔχομεν στοργὴν περὶ τὸ θεῖον τήν τε ἀδίστακτον γνῶσιν, ἣν ἐν πόνοις κεκτήμεθα, περὶ τὴν ἀλήθειαν. Cf. Bauer (1905) p. 34: 19 ... ἀναγκαῖον ἡγησάμην... ἐν συντόμῳ ποιήσασθαι λόγους ἐκ τῶν ἁγίων γραφῶν πρὸς καταρτισμόν σοι φιλομαθίας... 20. ἡμεῖς δὲ φιλομαθῶς ἱστορεῖν βουλόμενοι ἐπιγνωσόμεθα κατὰ ἀκρίβειαν τῶν τε ἐθνῶν τὸν διαμερισμόν...
173 The remaining differences were (3) the date of the Passion, (4) the Persian kings and (5) the ancestors of Christ.
Regarding (3) Nautin (1949) p. 217 originally pointed to *Dan.* IV, 23,3, according to which Christ suffered at the age of thirty-three, whilst the Συναγωγή gave Christ's age as 30. M. Richard, Comput et chronographie chez Saint Hippolyte, in *MSR* 8 (1951), p. 19-23 ff. had no

two of them, namely (1) the date of the Nativity, and (2) the list of the Passovers. We believe that these two differences in themselves are sufficient both to establish difference of authorship and, properly understood, to contribute to our interpretation of the Statue as essentially a cultural product with significance for the inner life of the community of Hippolytus and his predecessor(s).

4B 2.2.2.1. *The date of the Nativity*

The Συναγωγή agrees with the ἀπόδειξις of the Statue that the birth of Christ took place in the year 5502 of the creation of the world. According to the former, there are 4842 years from creation to the exile, and 660 years from the exile to the birth of Christ.[174] In consequence the birth took place in 5502 (=4842+660). With the year 5502 the Statue is in agreement.[175] Ogg's

problem in disposing of this claim since the figure was lacking in *Vaticanus Chisianus gr.* 36 and inconsistent with the other chronological data, and therefore a later, Eusebian interpolation. Nautin (1952) p. 19-21 was to accept this criticism, p. 20: "La phrase contient, en effet, des données contradictoires. Il y est dit d'une part que le Christ a souffert à 33 ans et en l'an XVIII de Tibère, qui correspond à l'an 32 de notre ère, et d'autre part que c'était le vendredi VIII des Calendes d'avril et sous le consulat de Rufus et de Rubellion, double indication qui correspond à l'an 29."). Nevertheless the adoption of a common date did not of itself imply an identity of author. The issue between them then revolved around whether Richard was correct that the use of a consular date indicated that Hippolytus must be Western and Roman rather than Eastern since the East had no interest in a date in terms of a month an a day before the fourth century, and as such must be unique and peculiar to a single author rather than two. See M. Richard, Comput et chronographie chez Saint Hippolyte, in *MSR* 7 (1950), p. 19-42; Nautin (1952) p. 21-26; Richard (1953) p. 145-163; Richard (1957), p. 379-394. M. Richard, Notes sur le comput de cent-couce ans, in *RevEtByz* 24 (1966), p. 257-277.

Regarding (4), the argument centred on the succession of the Persian kings, Nautin (1949) p. 217 had pointed out that according to Συναγωγή their succession had been Cyrus, Cambyses, Darius, Xerxes, and Artaxerxes. There were moreover six further kings before Darius III, whereas *Dan.* IV, 41,4 knows only five kings and makes Artaxerxes the predecessor of Xerxes. Richard (1950) p. 262 claimed that the fulfilment of *Dan.* IV, 11,2 required only four kings after Cyrus. In order to achieve this aim Richard supposed that the common author of these two works had manipulated his sources in order to procure their agreement. He found "Cyrus, Darius, and Artaxerxes" in the LXX for I Esdras VII, 4, but no Xerxes so that "ne trouvant pas dans les livres saints le troisième roi dont il avait besoin, se soit décidé à jeter un petit coup d'oeil sur une liste des rois perses." (p. 263) But the Xerxes in question had therefore to be Xerxes II. But as Nautin (1952) p. 16 was to point out, it was impossible that he should mention the latter king who had reigned for only two months without naming Xerxes himself. The characterization by Richard of a single author in terms of the precise peculiarity of mind ("se soit décidé à jeter un petit coup d'oeil sur une liste des rois perses") required to obviate the inconsistencies that clearly otherwise point to separate authors I criticize in 4B 2.2.2.1-2. See also Richard (1953) p. 173-177; Nautin (1954) p. 253-254.

Regarding (5), the Συναγωγή (686-687) computed 51 generations from Adam to the exile, and 14 from there until the birth of Christ, namely 65 in all, but *Dan.* II, 27,7 gives only 60. Richard (1950) p. 257-261 pointed to the list of patriarchs in Συναγωγή 11 consisting only of 60 names, which was therefore consistant with *Dan.* Nautin (1952) p. 16 was to point out that Richard's case rested on explaining as glosses in what he had argued to be the better witness, namely *Liber Generationis* I, in which the number is given as 65 by the inclusion of three ancestors of Christ not normally regarded as patriarchs, and by two others inserted between Josiah and Jechoniah. If that were the true reading of the original text, then indeed Συναγωγή and *Dan.* were at variance. The issue with Richard now revolved around this issue, see Richard (1948) p. 304-308; Richard (1953) p. 166-173; Nautin (1954) p. 243-252; Richard (1955) p. 379-394.

[174] Bauer and Helm (1955) p. 113-115, (686-688).

[175] Nautin (1952) p. 8 footnote 2: "Dans les deux passages, l'auteur indique expressément 5738 ans d'Adam à l'an XIII d'Alexandre Sévère, mais 30 ans de la Nativité à la Passion et 206

interpretation of the chronological method in the columns of tables of the ἀπόδειξις (*Canon*) lead him to the conclusion also that the Statue also computes the birth of Christ 5502 years after the creation.[176] Nautin also had come to this conclusion from the list of Passovers that we shall be separately examining.[177] Thus the Statue (ἀπόδειξις) once again shows a clear affinity with the Συναγωγή and hence with the περὶ τοῦ παντός and *El*.

In consequence, Nautin was able to point to a fundamental difference with *Dan*. IV, 23,3, which gives the year of Christ's birth 5500 *a mundo* (ἀπὸ δὲ᾽ Ἀδὰμ πεντακισχιοστῷ καὶ πεντακισχιοστῷ ἔτει).[178] That number moreover must be textually original, since Hippolytus gives the grounds for his calculation, for the reason that Ogg points out. *Dan*. IV, 9,2 dates year of the birth of Christ in the 42nd year of the reign of Augustus (ἐν τῷ τεσσαρακοστῷ δευτέρῳ ἔτει ἐπὶ Αὐγούστου Καίσαρος γεγέννηται ὁ Κύριος) from which, given his other data, the conclusion follows that it was 5500 years after the creation.[179]

There may furthermore be a difference between this work and both the Συναγωγή and the Statue (ἀπόδειξις) regarding the month and day of Christ's birth, though the state of the *ms.* tradition makes the precise difference difficult to specify. The ἀπόδειξις places the γένεσις χριστοῦ on 4 Nones April in the second year of the first cycle. It is a proper inference that the Συναγωγή would have agreed with this date in view of its agreement on the 5502 years, given the belief also that Jesus was born on the day of the Passover which would have fallen on that date in that year.[180] But according to the reading of the majority of *mss.* the text of *Dan*. IV, 23,3 gives the date as the 25th December (πρὸ ὀκτὼ καλανδῶν ἰανουαρίων) and not the 2nd April (4 Nones), as we shall now see.[181]

---

ans de la Passion à l'an XIII d'Alexandre Sévère. En soustrayant 236 (30+206) de 5738, on obtient 5502."

[176] G. Ogg, Hippolytus and the Introduction to the Christian Era, in *VCh* 16 (1962), p. 6: "In the *Canon* Hippolytus inserted a series of notes. In determining the place of each of these he had regard to what he had already written in his *Chronicle* as to its years from Adam or as to the interval between it and the last noted preceding event. From the point answering to Thursday 29th March (the meeting place of the fifth line and the seventh column) to the point where the note γενεσις χ ι is entered, is a period of (n x 112+13) years, n being an integer. When n=49, this is 5501, and the date of the Lord's birth is according to the *Canon* also is 5502 a.m." But Ogg begs here the question of whether Hippolytus was the author of either of these two works.

[177] Nautin (1952) p. 10 footnote 1: "L'*Apodeixis* comprenait elle-même une liste des grandes Pâques historiques qui totalisait 5502 ans de la Création à la Nativité..."

[178] Ibid. p. 8.

[179] Ogg (1962) p. 4 and 8.

[180] Ogg (1962) p. 6-7. Cf. G. Salmon, The Chronology of Hippolytus, in *Hermath* 1 (1873), p. 94 who tries to equate the term γένεσις on the Statue with the annunciation so as to preserve the 25th December date in the received text of *Dan*. IV, 23,3.

[181] *Dan*. IV, 23,3: ἡ γὰρ πρώτη παρουσία τοῦ κυρίου ἡμῶν ἡ ἔνσαρκος ἐν ᾗ γεγέννηται ἐν Βηθλεὲμ [πρὸ τεσσάρων ἀπριλίων], ἐγένετο πρὸ ὀκτὼ καλανδῶν ἰανουαρίων, ἡμέρᾳ τετράδι, βασιλεύοντος Αὐγούστου τεσσαρακοστὸν καὶ δεύτερον ἔτος, ἀπὸ δὲ᾽ Ἀδὰμ πεντακισχιοστῷ καὶ πεντακοσιοστῷ ἔτει. Ogg (1962) p. 8 cites *Reg. Par. gr.* 159 (P), the Greek text underlying the Old Slavonic (S), and the Chalki and Watopedi *mss.* (B and A) as supporting this reading. He includes the *Watopedi ms.* (A) because he insists,

4B 2.2.2.1.1. *Discrepancies on the day and month*

Ogg argued that the 25th December (πρὸ ὀκτὼ καλανδῶν ἰανουαρίων) was a latter interpolation, as it may well be. But at this point the *ms.* tradition gives us two alternatives. The first is the reading of the Chigi *ms.* (J) which simply states: ἡ γὰρ πρώτη παρουσία τοῦ κυρίου ἡμῶν ἡ ἔνσαρκος ἐν Βηθλεὲμ ἐπὶ Αὐγούστου γεγένηται πεντακισχιλιοστῷ καὶ πεντακοσιοστῷ ἔτει.[182]

The second is the *Watopedi ms.* (A) which inserts πρὸ τεσσάρων ἀπριλίων after ἐν Βηθλεέμ. Thus this reading, if original, would bring the text of *Dan.* into conformity with the Συναγωγή and the Statue once we have amended its nonsense to πρὸ τεσσάρων νωνῶν ἀπριλίων. But as Ogg concedes, this date would not be consistent with a Passover in 5500 but in 5502. This would mean that, given that both writers believe that nativity to be on the day of the Passover, its introduction into the text of *Dan.* is clearly an interpolation from the Συναγωγή or the Paschal Table itself.[183]

Such an interpolation is not problematic for Ogg since he assumes an identity of authorship between these works. We shall shortly see that it was nevertheless problematic for Richard since it would imply a date for *Dan.* after the compilation of the ἀπόδειξις and therefore after 222. But whatever the origin of the nonsensical interpolation in the second reading from A, it would seem that nevertheless the first from J is better supported. As Ogg himself mentions, Georgius, bishop of Horta, in his letter of 714, quotes from this passage of Hippolytus' *Dan.* in the form that it appears in J with only the year 5500 and without a date in months and days.[184] Thus we are presented with a clear distinction between *Dan.* and the Συναγωγή and Pascal Table of the Statue in that not only does the former date the nativity in 5500 and not 5502, but that it either gives no specification of a month and a day, or if it does it gives 25th December and not 2nd April as that specification.

In consequence, I believe that Nautin was too ready to accept that in terms of a date in terms of a day and a month that the 4 Nones April was shared by the original text of *Dan.* with the Συναγωγή and the ἀπόδειξις, but that the author of the former had learned the date from the author of the latter. We must now examine the implications of such a position.

4B 2.2.2.1.2. *The priority of the Συναγωγή and ἀπόδειξις*

Nautin rightly supported the priority of the Συναγωγή and ἀπόδειξις to *Dan.* but partly, I will now argue, for the wrong reasons. He had to so argue

---

following Bonwetsch, somewhat misleadingly as placing also in brackets [πρὸ τεσσάρων ἀπριλίων] after ἐν Βηθλεέμ where it is found alone and without πρὸ ὀκτὼ καλανδῶν ἰανουαρίων.

[182] Ogg (1962) p. 8.

[183] Ibid. p. 9: "The words πρὸ τεσσάρων ἀπριλίων are apparently the debris of an interpolation made from the *Canon.*"

[184] Ibid. p. 8.

against Richard who had asserted that the addition of this date was in a second redaction of *Dan.* after 222, in which Hippolytus had thus simply changed his earlier view. His reason was that 4 Nones April, on Wednesday (ἡμέρᾳ τετράδι) presupposed the particular calculation included in the ἀπόδειξις.[185] Richard's redaction-thesis Nautin rejected as *une ces hypothèses complaisantes* devised in order to *concilier l'inconciliable.*[186] There was, we have argued, no need for such a redaction-thesis since the weekday and day of the month did not form part of the original *ms.* tradition of *Dan.* and thus the writer whom we accept to have written subsequent to the ἀπόδειξις made no correction in the light of what he read there. It was not therefore for that reason that *Dan.* could be argued to be written subsequently to the Συναγωγή and the ἀπόδειξις.

But Richard was himself by no means on secure ground in assuming that *Dan.* was earlier than the ἀπόδειξις, given that Nautin had already given his opinion regarding the two authors of the *corpus.* The date of 202 for *Dan.* was, at all events, founded upon a number of questionable assumptions, amongst which was the unity the *corpus* that gave these works that place in the chronology of a single author. Richard needed such a date to support one explanation of the discrepancy of 5500 in comparison with 5502 since one of his explanations was that the single author had in course of time developed and refined his chronology. Since *Dan.* appeared written from an eastern perspective, it must have been written before Hippolytus came to Rome and before the conflict with Callistus recorded in *El.* The persecution to which *Dan.* I, 25 seemed to refer had therefore been that of Septimius Severus in consequence of his law against conversion. But this generally accepted view rests on slender foundations.

4B 2.2.2.1.3. Dan. *and Septimius Severus*

It is however a dangerous position to assume that cultural difference is the equivalent to geographical distance. Certainly there appears to have been Quartodeciman congregations in Rome, Asiatic in practice, alongside Western and Roman ones. A group whose culture was Alexandrian in practice could nevertheless still be located in Rome in the late second century, for reasons that I have already given (2A 2.4).

At this point emerges a further assumption that needs to be made on the single-author view, namely that neither persecutions occurred, nor the threat of them was felt, throughout the remaining Severan monarchs, and that Severus Alexander and the Empress Mamaea had a philo-Christian policy.

---

[185] Nautin (1954) p. 235: "... cette date, *mercredi IV des Nones d'avril*, est la conséquence du calcul particulier qui préside au comput de 222, et suppose ce comput déja établi. La conclusion que chacun en tire, c'est que le Commentaire sur Daniel, qui contient cette date, est postérieur au comput de 222."

[186] Nautin (1952) p. 9 note 1: "C'est là une de ces "hypothèses complaisantes" auxqelles il faut bien avoir recours quand on veut concilier l'inconciliable."

We have already given our grounds for questioning such a naive reading of events, particularly with the questionable and late support of the *Scriptores Historiae Augustae* (2B 2.2.3 -2B 2.2.4).

The *Liber Pontificalis* 17 cannot be trusted, particularly in the clear additions it makes to the Liberian *Catalogus*, but the addition that it makes regarding Callistus, namely *...sepultus in cimiterio Calepodii, via Aurelia, miliario tercio ab urbe...* has been verified archaeologically.[187] Furthermore, the entry for Zephyrinus (*in cimiterio suo iuxta cimiterium Calixti*) also has an archaeological basis,[188] in clear contrast with the entries for, for example, Eleutherus or Victor both of whom are described in *Liber Pontificalis* 14 and 15 as *sepultus... iuxta corpus beati Petri in Vaticano*, which the Vatican excavations clearly have not corroborated and are at best based upon a pious wish. Though clearly fabulous, the later *Acta S. Callisti* 8 may contain a shadow of the truth when it describes his death as *per fenestram domus praecipitari, ligatoque ad collum eius saxo, in puteum demergi et in eo rudera cumulari.*[189] In the Rome of the second year of Severus Alexander (223), which was also the Rome of Ulpian, even without a general edict of persecution or a general policy a Christian leader might still be the victim of a mob attack incited perhaps by an individual prosecution.

Indeed the existence of a general persecution, even restricted to converts as was that of Septimius Severus, would seem to be ruled out by *Dan.* IV, 17 which is at pains to point out that the end has not yet come. Even though *Dan.* IV, 18 uses a doctrine of the delay of the *parousia* in association with an attack upon Montanism, nevertheless in a general persecution the disassociation of that persecution from the final tribulation would have been unthinkable. Thus the location of the writing of *Dan.* in the Decian persecution is also ruled out. There is therefore no reason to challenge the date of the martyrdom of its author, Hippolytus, in 235 according to the Liberian *Catalogus*, to the implications of which we shall return in 4B 2.2.2.2.

We can still understand the reality of a fear of persecution expressed in *Dan.* I, 25 written after 223 but before the author's martyrdom with Pontianus in 235. At all events, the reference to persecution in *Dan.* I, 25,2 is an allegorical interpretation of the Jewish elders command to search for Susanna, whom they wish to kill (*C'est ce qui arrive de nos jours. Quand on*

---

[187] At all events legend would surely have placed him *in Callisto*, in the cemetery that bears his name, see P. Lampe, Die stadtrömischen Christen in den ersten beiden Jahrhunderten, in *WUNT* 2,18 (1989), p. 22-29. For the excavations of the cemetery of Calepodius, see A. Nestori, La Catacomba di Calepodio al III miglio dell'Aurelia vetus e i sepolcri dei papi Callisto e Giulio I, in *RivArC*, 44 (1968) p. 161-172; 47 (1971) p. 169-278, 48; (1972) p. 193-233; 51 (1975) p. 135 ff.

[188] *Liber Pontificalis* 16: "Qui etiam sepultus est in cimiterio suo iuxta cimiterium Calixti, via Appia, VII Kl. decemb." See also Lampe (1989) p. 14-17.

[189] *P.G.* X 108-120.

arrête les saints et qu'on les traîne au tribunal, toute la foule afflue pour voir ce qui va arriver). Such an interpretation is consistent with privately motivated accusations against individual Christians rather than a general, systematic persecution such as Ulpian shows were legally possible (2B 2.1.3.2).

It is of course one thing to establish that *Dan.* need not be an early work of Hippolytus, but another to establish that it was so. Nevertheless one argument of Nautin we believe to have failed, since the date in terms of a month and a day was never present in any form of the original text of *Dan.* But there are further, notwithstanding, more cogent reasons for the lateness of *Dan.*, to which we now turn.

4B 2.2.2.1.4. *5500 and 5502: Allegorism and Astronomy*

In view of our previous discussion, we do not need in the original text of *Dan.* IV, 23,3 the presence of the reading πρὸ τεσσάρων ἀπρίλων—that "debris of an interpolation"—in order to establish that *Dan.* was composed after the ἀπόδειξις. In 4A 3.2.3 we argued that the author of *C.N.* was indeed the author of *Dan.* and that he had been responsible for both an institutional and a theological *rapprochement* between the community of the author of *El.* and the community of Callistus. My argument has therefore established on quite separate grounds that *Dan.* was written subsequent to the works on the Statue, including the ἀπόδειξις, quite independently of the presence or absence of Wednesday 4 Nones April in its original text.

The existence of the "debris of an interpolation" from the same author always was problematic in view of another feature to which Nautin pointed, namely *Dan.* does not change 5500 because for him Scripture and not scientific calculation had guaranteed it. But if he refused to change the one, would he not also have refused to change the other? The more likely explanation of the reading is that a member of the reconciled group subsequent to 235 added the interpolation without grasping that 5500 would also need amending to 5502 as well.

It was this act therefore that contaminated the *ms.* tradition represented by the Watopedi *ms.* (A). Indeed the real evidence that the author of the ἀπόδειξις and the Συναγωγή could not be the same as the author of *Dan.* remains the discrepancy between the 5500 and 5502 as the year after creation. Even if he had revised his chronology after writing *Dan.*, then he would have amended *Dan.* If however *Dan.* IV, 24 was written after the ἀπόδειξις, clearly the scriptural argument from the dimensions in the ark of Noah clearly prevailed over the purely rational calculations of the ἀπόδειξις and Συναγωγή. In either case it is most unlikely that the author was the same since it would have involved a complete change of methodology from rational calculation to belief in the sole efficacy of the mystical interpretation of Scripture.[190]

The polemical tone of *Dan.* IV, 24,1 must therefore be noted in this connection. These words suggest that the writer is not correcting a mistake but rather is controverting a calculation with which he profoundly disagrees despite its rational persuasiveness. A challenge is implied (ἀλλὰ πάντως ἐρεῖ τις· πῶς μοι ἀποδείξεις;) over what it will not be easy to convince (εὐκόλως διδάχθητι, ὦ ἄνθρωπε).[191] We see here, therefore, one writer standing by a date arrived at by allegorical and scriptural exegesis, and because his conclusion comes from such a source, regretting the calculation of another.[192] His use of the verb ἀποδείξεις in a chronological argument is indicative of his consciousness that his own ἀπόδειξις χρόνων is a controverted alternative.

Corroborating evidence for the author of *Dan.* dissenting from the author of the ἀπόδειξις can also seen in the dual chronology inscribed on one section of the Statue giving an alternative chronology κατὰ Δανιήλ.[193] In consequence, we do not need the presence of the dubious πρὸ τεσσάρων ἀπριλίων to make the case for two authors. This additional inscription may show a desire to qualify as opposed to amend the earlier ἀπόδειξις in the light of *Dan.* rather than *vice-versa,* as Richard had supposed, though we must concede that inscriptions on marble are not as easy to amend or delete as those on paper. We shall now consider further the significance of the double chronology in the next section.

4B 2.2.2.2. *The list of the Passovers*
The Συναγωγή calculates a distance of 563 years between the Passover of Esdras and the Nativity.[194] But *Dan.* IV, 31,2 gives instead 434 years from the return under Esdras (μετὰ γὰρ τὸ ἐπιστρέψαι τὸν λαὸν Βαβυλῶνος ἡγουμένου... Ἔσδρα τοῦ γραμματέως) to the coming of Christ (ἕως

---

[190] Nautin (1952) p. 9-10: "Mais si l'on doit admettre que le *Commentaire sur Daniel* est postérieur au comput de 222, il devient vraiment impossible de les attribuer au même auteur... comment cet homme qui savait l'impossibilité mathématique de 5500... pourrait-il être celui qui écrit dans le *Commentaire sur Daniel* que «*la parousie de Notre-Seigneur a eu lieu en l'an 5500.*»" Cf. Richard (1953) p. 15-20; Richard (1955) p. 387-389.

[191] *Dan.* IV, 24,1: ... ἀλλὰ πάντως ἐρεῖ τις· πῶς μοι ἀποδείξεις, εἰ πεντακισχιλιοστῷ καὶ πεντακοσιοστῷ ἔτει ἐγεννήθη ὁ Σωτήρ; εὐκόλως διδάχθητι, ὦ ἄνθρωπε... He then continues to point to the dimensions of the Tabernacle amongst other references in evidence for this number.

[192] Nautin (1954) "L'auteur..." p. 242-243: "En adoptant 5502 au lieu de 5500, l'auteur du comput et de la Chronique... accorde plus de crédit, en fait de précision, à son système astronomique... qui permettait seulement l'an 5502. Hippolyte a l'attitude exactement inverse, quand il affirme catégoriquement 5500, alors qu'il connaît... le comput qui exige 5502: il accorde une valeur totale et inconditionnée au sens spirituel de la Parole de Dieu, et lui sacrifie tous les calculs des hommes." Cf. Richard (1950) p. 239-247 and (1953) p. 17-18 and p. 164-165 who refuses to consider this point (p. 18: "Les anciens n'avaient pas notre besoin de synthèse...") and tries to close the gap by one year. Cf. Nautin (1954) "L'auteur..." p. 242.

[193] For drawings and a transcription of the ἀπόδειξις see *P.G.* X 875-885. See also Richard (1950) p. 242-243.

[194] Bauer and Helm (1955) p. 117 (697).

παρουσίας Χριστοῦ). But rather than, on this occasion, the ἀπόδειξις according to the Statue supporting one work or the other, it succeeds in supporting both.

We have in column II, for the Passover on the 13th April, 238 for the number of the year, and in the margin Ἔσδρας κατὰ Δανιήλ καὶ ἐν ἐρήμῳ. Clearly the Passover in the year of Ezra's act was, according to Daniel, in 238, as was the beginning of the wilderness wandering two years after the Exodus. The latter event is noted as ἔξοδος κατὰ Δανιήλ for the year 236 (in column I) in which Passover occurred on 5th April. But the ἔξοδος, unqualified by κατὰ Δανιήλ, is recorded also for 327 (in column VII) for a 2nd April Passover, and the (equally unqualified) ἐν ἐρήμῳ for 329 (in column VII) for a 29th March Passover. Also in column VII for the year 332, an unqualified Ἔσδρας is noted in the margin, when Passover falls on 5th April.

For 243 (column III) a 29th March Passover is noted as Ἐζεκιάς κατὰ Δανιήλ καὶ Ἰωσείας, but Hezekiah alone is given for 224 (column I) for the 21st March. Furthermore the latter is disassociated from Josiah by one year and assigned to 225, also in column I, on a 9th April Passover. The date Ἰησοῦς κατὰ Δανιήλ is 276 (column IV) with Passover on 5th April, but Joshua alone is assigned to 256 (column III) for the 21st March. [195]

We clearly therefore have two separate chronologies inscribed on the Statue, one which accords with Hippolytus *Dan.*, and the other with the Συναγωγή. Furthermore, we can detect once again the faithfulness of *Dan.* to the literal text of Scripture, whereas the ἀπόδειξις adheres to the exigencies of the chronographic material. If we subtract the date κατὰ Δανιήλ for the Exodus from the date for Joshua we have 276-236=40 years. If we subtract the date of the Συναγωγή for these two events we have 327-256=71 years. How are we therefore to interpret the presence of this dual chronology constructed on quite different principles in the inscribed ἀπόδειξις of the Statue?

According to Richard the purpose of the dual chronology is not to be interpreted as a conflict between two writers. Rather it is an attempt to fit the Scriptural account into a chronology whose original purpose was solely to fix the Passover dates, which Scripture does not give at least according to a solar calendar.[196] The only fixed period is the interval between the Creation

---

[195] We are indebted here to Richard (1950) p. 242 for his Table I, reproduced as Nautin says (1952) p. 11 footnote 2 from *DACL* VI, 2423.

[196] Richard (1950) p. 248: "Les livres saints ne nous renseignent évidemment pas sur le jour de la semaine, ni à plus forte raison sur la date du calendrier solaire de ces Pâques. Le comput ne fournissait donc aucune indication nouvelle permettant de fixer l'année de ces événements. Il permettait seulement, une fois cette année fixée par les méthodes de la chronologie historique en usage à cette époque, de déterminer à quel jour de la semaine tombait le 14 Nisan correspondent."

and the Passion, reduced to the interval between the former and the Nativity.[197]

His treatment of the conflicting dates, according to Richard, proved very elastic and resulted by intentional manipulation finally to the difference between 5500 and 5502. He was finally prepared, after all his efforts, to leave these two figures unresolved, rather than either to revise the allegorical interpretations of *Dan.* or to manipulate further the figures of the contemporary chronologists on which his ἀπόδειξις had been based. It was a curious solution in modern terms, with our modern *besoin de synthèse*.[198]

It is clearly on this point that the case between Richard and Nautin rests. We must frankly ask whether *la solution,* which Richard admits was *extrêmement curieuse,*[199] is a credible explanation of how the same author could have been responsible for these two inconsistent chronologies. Richard's discussion follows the general tendency that I have criticized in regarding the Statue as personal monument. If indeed it were *bien évident* that *ces deux calculs... sur le socle de la statue* were in fact there *pour honorer celui que représentait ce monument* then in placing the two chronologies side-by-side something other than a correction of difference must be implied.[200]

But I have argued in Chapters 1-3 that such a view grossly misrepresents the character of this artefact which, with its Table for calculating Easter, is a monument with cultural significance for a Christian community in which the works inscribed on the plinth were honoured also. This being the case, the insertion of the dates κατὰ Δανιήλ is an event in the life of a community and not the act of an individual commemorated by the Statue who is wrestling with the conflict between Scripture and computational science. It is an act similar to the writer of *C.N.* and his reconstruction of the Christology of *El.* in order to provide a basis for reconciliation with the moderate Monarchians, as we have seen (4A). It is, furthermore, an act similar to the insertion into the Liberian *Catalogus* the references to *Pontianus episcopus et Yppolitus presbyter* and the hidden message concealed there of a divided community now reconciled (1B 2.3.3.5). We shall shortly examine further and separately the composition and relationship of the Liberian *Catalogus* to the work of

---

[197] Ibid. p. 248: "Par conséquent, les listes des Pâques établies par nos computistes supposent une chronologie biblique calculée antérieurement et qu'il s'agissait de faire cadrer avec la seule donnée fixe du comput, c'est-à-dire avec l'intervalle entre la Création et la Nativité, donc en fin de compte avec l'ère chrétienne adoptée."

[198] Quoted footnote 128. For the more detailed account of the alleged manipulations of a single author see Richard (1950) p. 248-257; (1953) p. 39-52.

[199] Ibid. p. 249: "La solution qu'il a adoptée est extrêmement curieuse."

[200] Richard (1950) p. 256: "En tout cas il est bien évident— et c'est tout ce dont nous avons besoin pour réfuter l'argument de M. Nautin, que ces deux calculs ont été gravés sur le socle de la statue pour honorer celui que représentait ce monument et non pour prouver malignement que sa chronologie contredisait celle des Livres saints." See also Richard (1953) p. 41-42; Richard (1955) p. 389-392.

the two writers, and the events within their community to which such works implicitly testify.

I find it frankly impossible to believe that the insertion of the alternative chronology is anything but the insertion of the alternative view of a different author. The texture of mind that could operate in holding the two lists as both true, with no *besoin de synthèse*, might be comprehensible in an Averroes but I find completely incomprehensible in terms of a Father of the third century. It is furthermore particularly incomprehensible in this instance. We have already noted in connection with the assertion of 5500 as the date of creation according to *Dan.* the polemical terms in which that statement is expressed as though directed against a specific alternative, rationalistic method of computation that did not accord with the author's mystic and allegorical scriptural exegesis (4B 2.2.2.1.4). Furthermore *Dan.* itself stresses the coherence of the prophet's visions as establishing their authencity.[201] He shows there a clear *besoin de synthèse* which is quite inconsistent with Richard's characterisation of *la solution* which he admits that, as a way of proceeding, was *extrêmement curieuse* for one and the same author.

Richard claims that we need to accept the priority of *Dan.* but the only grounds that he gives (other than what appears generally accepted) is that without that priority the two chronologies inscribed on the Statue cannot be explained.[202] Indeed he charges Nautin with having no positive explanation himself for this phenomenon.[203] But we have shown that there is such an explanation in terms of the Statue as the icon of the inner life of a community in process of a reconciliation in which it still remembers what it earlier valued but is prepared to abandon it as indifferent or mistaken, whether it is chronology, Christology, or the headship of a community. It is in such a community-context that the corrections κατὰ Δανιήλ have their place as part of the pattern of reconciliation.

But at this point in our discussion we must note that Hippolytus, the martyr of the via Tiburtina, has made his appearance on the Statue. In the addition of his chronology from *Dan.*, added by either himself or more probably by his successors, we already find the acknowledgment of a second author of the Hippolytan *corpus*. So far we have acknowledged three works from the list on the plinth of the Statue to be that of the opponent of Callistus, namely Συναγωγὴ-Χρονικῶν the ἀπόδειξις and περὶ τοῦ παντός, through the relations that we have established between those works and *El.*

---

[201] *Dan.* III, 12,1: ...ὡς καὶ ὁ Δανιὴλ ἐν τοῖς αὐτοῦ ὁράμασιν ὄντως ταῦτα γενόμενα διηγήσατο, περὶ ὧν ἐὰν ἐπιβησώμεθα ἐπὶ τὸν τόπον ἀμφότερα συγκρίναντες ὅμοια καὶ ἀληθῆ ταῦτα εἶναι ἐπιδείξομεν.

[202] Richard (1953): p. 40 "L'anomalie que constitue la présence de deux chronologies différentes sur la Table pascale est inexplicable si l'on n'admet pas que l'auteur de l'*Apodeixis* a composé le *Commentaire* avant de calculer son comput."

[203] Ibid. p. 44: "Nous n'avons pas pu découvrir comment notre contradicteur expliquait la présence de la chronologie selon Daniel sur la Table pascale du socle de la statue."

which is unmentioned on the Statue. But we are not obliged by our interpretation of the Statue as a monument of a community rather than an individual to concede that all the works on the Statue must be by the same author.

We will be arguing that some of them may in fact be by the martyr of the via Tiburtina, the successor to the opponent of Callistus and corrector of both his theology and his chronology. But we have a further document which, like *El.*, though not mentioned on the Statue, connects with the chronological concerns of the works that we have so far considered. The Liberian *Catalogus* itself is connected also with these works, and which mentions too the martyr of the via Tiburtina. It will be therefore convenient for us to consider this work here.

4B 2.2.3. The Συναγωγή–Χρονικῶν *and the Liberian* Catalogus

Lightfoot followed Mommsen in maintaining that the first part of the so-called Liberian *Catalogus*, the Chronographer of 354, was in fact the work of Hippolytus himself up until the year 235. The principal reason for assigning this to Hippolytus was however that the date of the Passion, with which section 8 of this work begins, was that given on the Statue, namely what we should call A.D. 29, and that the Statue was the personal monument of Hippolytus.[204] We have seen that any difference between this work and *Dan.* on the date of the Crucifixion and the length of Jesus' life is explicable in terms of later interpolations into some of the *mss*. The death of Christ took place on 25th March, in accordance with the Liberian *Catalogus*, in the consulship of the *duobus geminis* who were the Rufus and Rubellius mentioned in *Dan.* IV, 23,3.[205]

Both Lightfoot and Mommsen did not of course admit any difference between the writer of *El.* and the titles he claims as his own, one of which is the Χρονικῶν, and the writer of *Dan.* We have argued, partly following Nautin, that they were by different authors. But here a problem arises. It is not simply occasioned by the fact that the *Catalogus* shares a common date for the Passion with *Dan.*, since we have conceded that this is the case between the latter and the Συναγωγή–Χρονικῶν too. At all events, that similarity does not imply individual authorship since dates can be common to two or more authors who are members of the same school. Certainly the use

---

[204] Th. Mommsen, Über den Chronographien vom Jahre 354, in *Abhandlungen der phil.-hist. Classe der Königlichen Sächs. Gesellschaft der Wissenschaften* I (1850), p. 549 ff.; Lightfoot (1890) Part I S. Clement of Rome vol. I, p. 253-258. On p. 253 the list begins: IMPERANTE TIBERIO CAESARE PASSUS EST DOMINUS NOSTER IESUS CHRISTUS DUOBUS GEMINIS CONS. [A.D. 29] VIII KL. APR., ET POST ASCENSUM EIUS BEATISSIMUS PETRUS EPISCOPATUM SUSCEPIT. EX QUO TEMPORE PER SUCCESSIONEM DISPOSITUM, QUIS EPISCOPUS, QUOT ANNIS PREFUIT, VEL QUO IMPERANTE.

[205] Tertullian, *Adversus Judaeos*, 8,6: "Quae passio Christi intra tempora LXX ebdomadarum perfecta est sub Tiberio Caesare, consulibus Rubellio Gemino et et Fufio Gemino, mense Martio, temporibus Paschae, die octava Kalendarum Aprilium, die prima azymorum, qua agnum occiderunt ad vesperam, sicut Moyse fuerat praeceptum."

of that date by Tertullian *Adv. Jud.* 8,16 implies no monopoly over it by any one author. The problem is rather occasioned by the fact that the *Catalogus* mentions the martyrdom only of Hippolytus, yet the manuscript tradition of the Χρονικῶν in *Liber Generationis* I implied that the *Catalogus* used that work. Does not the *Catalogus* therefore betray the authorship of the Συναγωγή–Χρονικῶν as linked both with the Statue and with *Dan.*, and provide an argument after all for a single author of the Hippolytan *corpus*?

One resolution would be to follow Bauer and Helm in claiming that the Χρονικῶν had no episcopal succession list as part of its original text. Were such an argument to prevail, then we could sever any connection between the *Catalogus* and the Hippolytan *corpus*, since there would otherwise be no other reference to any literary activity on the part of the martyr of the via Tiburtina. Let us now examine in further detail this question.

4B 2.2.3.1. Liber Generationis *I and the* Catalogus

Ms. Matriensis graec. 121, fragmentary though it is, is the one surviving Greek manuscript and it has no such list. Furthermore it is possible to argue that this could not be due to the fragmentary character of this *ms.*, since in the table of contents with which it begins there is no mention of an episcopal list. But as Caspar pointed out, the problem with this particular *ms.* was not merely is fragmentary character, but rather the disorganisation of its material, seen particularly in the list of 72 peoples in which the order of *Liber Generationis* I is clearly the more original.[206]

Caspar furthermore examined the text from a form-critical perspective and argued that the *Liber Generationis* I was dependent upon a Greek original. The very phrase in its table of contents: *nomina episcoporum Romae* was not very idiomatic Latin. Were these words the product of the author of the Latin *ms.* then we should have expected instead *episcopi Romani* or *episcopi ecclesiae Romanae*. Fredegar's *Chronicle*, reconstructed principally from *ms. Parisinus* 10910 and *ms. Brit. Mus. cod. Harleianus* 5251, introduces its own papal list with the introduction *De episcopis Romanis*. Clearly the writer of the former was translating very unidiomatically a Greek original reading ὀνόματα τῶν ἐν῾ Ρώμῃ ἐπίσκοπων.

Furthermore, Caspar argued that the heading ὀνόματα in the original indicated that there was a list that contained no numbers for the years. The list employed by the scribe of *Liber Generationis* I would have already contained those added numbers as the result of assimilation with the regnal lists. We can see this process already at work in *ms. Matr. Graec.* 121.[207]

---

206 E. Caspar, Die älteste römische Bischofsliste, in *Schriften der Königberger Gelehrten Gesellschaft*, Geisteswissentschafliche Klasse 2,4, (Berlin: 1926), p. 384-385. Cf. Bauer (1905) p. 156-157. See also Bauer and Helm (1955), p. 139 footnotes 757-778.
207 Bauer (1905) p. 30-33 where we have titles for unnumbered lists of names in 11. ὀνόματα πατριαρχῶν ἀπὸ γενέσεως, 12. ὀνόματα προφητῶν, 14. βασιλέων ῾Εβραίων ὀνόματα and 16 ἀρχειρέων ὀνόματα, but numbered lists for kings, namely 9. Βασιλεῖς

There is furthermore evidence of such unnumbered ὀνόματα lists in the group of catalogues collated by Duchesne and Mommsen.[208] Five of these catalogues begin *incipiunt nomina/* and continue *apostolicorum/, episcoporum qui in urbe Roma fuerunt/, sacerdotum/, sanctorum episcoporum qui sede beati Petri sedere meruerunt.*[209] These not only lack the regnal year which was added to the archetypal list incorporated into *Liber Generationis* I, but also the further addition, found in the Liberian *Catalogus*, of months and days also.

We therefore have preserved in *Liber Generationis* I the contaminated archetype of the Liberian *Catalogus* both of which as such were later developments of a list of names of bishops without years, months, or days. The absence of such a list in the remaining *ms.* tradition of the Συναγωγή Caspar rightly therefore attributes to the fact that the latter scribes of *ms. Matr. Graec.*, the *Barbarinus ms.* or *Liber Generationis* II believed they had better and more sophisticated succession lists in their own time.[210] In consequence it is possible to see in the original, uncontaminated archetype the model that antedates the Liberian *Catalogus* itself.

What the author of that *Catalogus* did was to add the dates both after 234 and before. In doing so he was to betray himself in that he had accurate consular dates from the death of Pontianus onwards, but from before this point in time every bishop appears to die at the end of one consulship and his successor to be consecrated at the beginning of another. Antheros, for example, dies (*dormit*) on 3 *Non. Jan.* when Maximus and Africanus are consuls (*Maximo et Africano cons.=* A.D. 236). Fabius succeed him *a cons. Maximini et Africani* in the course of the same year, 236 until Decius and Gratus (*usque Decio ii et Grato*), namely in 250. But Pontianus immediate predecessor Urbanus succeeds Callistus *a cons. Maximi and Eliani* in 223 at the very point at which their predecessors for 222 leave office since Callistus reigns usque *Antonino iii et Alexandro*. This identical fabricated pattern is repeated respectively for all bishops before the death of Pontianus. Clearly the

---

Περσῶν ἀπὸ Κύρου καὶ τίς πόσα ἔτη ἐβασίλευσε, 15. βασιλεῖς οἱ ἐν Σαμαρείᾳ βασιλεύσαντες τῶν δέκα φυλῶν τίς ὁπόσα ἔτη ἐβασίλευσεν, 17. βασιλεῖς Μακεδόνων ἀπὸ Ἀλεξάνδρου καὶ τίς πόσα ἔτη ἐβασίλευσεν, and 18 βασιλεῖς Ῥωμαίων ἀπὸ Αὐγούστου, τίς πόσα ἔτη ἐβασίλευσεν. Clearly these regnal lists have not yet been used to give an artificial chronology to patriarchs, prophets and high priests, nor to the list of bishops to the presence of which *Liber Generationis* I testifies. A similar as yet unintegrated chronology is that for the Olympiads mentioned as 10. χρόνος ὀλυμπιάδων ἀπὸ Ἰφίτου ἕως τῆς ἐνεστώσης ὀλυμπιάδος.

[208] Duchesne, *Liber Pontificalis,* I p. 14; Th. Mommsen, *Gesta Pontificium Romanorum,* I p. 33 ff. For references see Caspar (1926) p. 390 footnotes 2 and 3.

[209] Ibid. p. 390.

[210] Ibid. p. 390-391: "Ihr Fehlen diente BAUER als Argument um die Existenz der hippolytischen Liste römischer Bischöfe zu bestreiten: die Übersetzer hätten ein so wichtiges Element nicht übergehen können, wenn sie es im Text gelesen hätten. In Wahrheit fehlt sie, weil die späteren Bearbeiter sie fortgelassen haben: sie glaubten etwas Besseres, nämlich eine „genauere", mit Daten versehene Liste—woran es ja in ihrer Zeit nicht mehr gebrach—an die Stelle der blossen Namenreihe setzen zu können."

consular *fasti* have been imposed upon a list consisting of names alone before Pontianus in order to give an appearance of accurate chronology which
does not survive careful scrutiny.

That ὀνόματα list without dates clearly lasted to 235 and thus to the
Sardinian exile and probable martyrdom of Hippolytus. For that martyrdom
we have already discussed the Liberian *Catalogus* and *Depositio* as
evidence, rejecting analyses of these documents that would disassociate
Hippolytus the martyr from the via Tiburtina (1B 2.3.3.5). But now two
further problems arise for the relationship between the *Catalogus* and the
Hippolytan *corpus*.

The first is the date of *El.* itself, since the events of IX, 11-13,1 are set
around 218. How is this compatible with the authorship of the Συναγωγή–
Χρονικῶν, which ends in 235 and thus must therefore have been written after
this time? The second is that *presbyter Hippolytus* is mentioned as exiled to
Sardinia and also probably martyred. What support does this give to the
assumption that Hippolytus therefore was the author of the first part of the
Catalogus and therefore of the Συναγωγή, if that indeed can be connected
with the latter? We shall now consider these problems in further detail.

4B 2.2.3.2. Συναγωγή–Χρονικῶν *and its conclusion in 235*

The question of compatibility of *El.* both with the Συναγωγή and with the
Catalogus must therefore arise if the former is mentioned in X, 30,1 (ἐν
ἑτέραις βίβλοις). The *Catalogus*, as we have seen, contained an ὀνόματα list
that clearly extended to Pontianus, who was the last miraculously to succeed
to the episcopate at the precise date that the consuls changed, namely 231
when Agricola and Clementus were succeeded by Pompeianus and
Peligianus. But if the Συναγωγή was written before 218 when *El.* records his
dispute with Callistus, then the text as it comes down to us has clearly been
completed and amended subsequently.

Thus the *Catalogus* terminated with Pontianus' death on 28th September
(*iiii Kal. Oct.*) 235 (*Severo et Quintiano cons.*). The imperial list of *Liber
Generationis* I terminates with the last year of Alexander Severus, March
234-March 235.[211] Thus though there is no problem with the author of the
ὀνόματα list being identical with the author of the Συναγωγή, there remains a
chronological problem for both being the work of the author of *El.*,
notwithstanding what we have said in favour of this identification (4B 2.2
-2.1).

One solution to the chronological problem is associated with Gieseler's
work, who sought to identify the Hippolytan events with those of

---

[211] Bauer (1905) p. 142-145. Bauer and Helm (1955), p. 140: (*Liber Generationis* I, 778
(398)), "Alexander ann. XIII d. VIIII."

Novatian.[212] But we shall now see that this produced the reverse problem, namely why the list was not extended from 235 until 251 or 258. Gieseler had in consequence to date *El.* after 251, and to claim that the account of the dispute with Callistus had taken place long after the events that it described. The one piece of direct evidence cited is the latter *Martyrologium Romanum,* which gives 13th August as the day of his martyrdom under Valerian in 258, which we have seen was also dubiously deployed by Cecchelli (1B 2.3.3.4-3.3.5). Whether indeed such accounts refer to Valerian or to Decius (253), the date of the Liberian *Catalogus* (13th August) has been transferred to that later time in order to associate Hippolytus with the cycle of legends around St. Laurence, Concordia, etc. whose martyrdom occurred at this later date.[213]

What therefore remains of Gieseler's argument is far more conjectural. He found it impossible that the author of *El.* should have been able to have written as stridently as he did about Zephyrinus and Callistus before he had finally broken with them. And apparently he believed, in a way characteristic, as we shall see, of nineteenth-century critics, that the only kind of schism possible would be one like Novatian only in evidence in the middle of the third century.[214] We shall return to a more detailed consideration of this question in Chapter 6. Suffice it to say here that the identification by Damasus and Prudentius with a Novatian presbyter we shall argue to be symptomatic of latter inability to conceptualize the Hippolytan events in any other terms of a later schism, with the result that a gross anachronism arose.[215]

It is however extremely difficult to read the events of *El.* IX, 11-15,1 as a reflection written some thirty to forty years after what is described. It is precarious to argue that the refutation of Callistus' status as a martyr in IX, 12, 10-13 implies that he has died by the time of writing, since μάρτυρες clearly means "confessors" in 12,10. Had Callistus' death itself occurred, then indeed we should have expected mention of it in the polemic sufficiently

---

[212] J.C.L. Gieseler, Über Hippolytus, die ersten Monarchianer und die römische Kirche in der ersten Hälfte des dritten Jahrhunderts, in *Theologische Studien und Kritiken*, (Hamburg: F. Perthes) IV (1853), p. 762-764.

[213] Ibid. p. 764. For Hippolytus' martyrdom "Id. Aug. tempore Decii," in an account already dependent on Prudentius' assimilation with the son of Theseus, see Florus Beda (870) or Ado of Vienne (874) ("sub Decio imperatore, Valeriano praefecto"), in Lightfoot (1890) 1, II p. 537 and 538. See also ibid. p. 363.

[214] Gieseler (1853) p. 761: "Aber das ist undenkbar, dass derselbe, der schon unter den Bischöfen Zephyrinus und Callistus Presbyter war und, wenn auch im Prestbytercollegium zur Opposition war und, wenn auch im Presbytercollegium zur Opposition gehörig, doch mit beiden Bischöfen in Kirchengemeinschaft stand, sogleich nach dem Tode des Callistus eine so schmachvolle Schilderung von dessen Character und Sitten haben veröffentlichen."

[215] Ibid. p. 764: "Während er bei allen anderen Sectenhäuptern einige Notizen über ihr Herkunft und ihr Zeitalter gibt, führt er den Sabellius... ohne alle Angaben über seine persönlichen Verhältnisse ein. Das konnte er nur, wenn Sabellius damals, als er schrieb, ein allgemein gennante und bekannter Mann war; das war derselbe aber noch nicht 222, wo noch Kleomenes an der Spitze der Partei stand, sondern wurde es erst später, seit 250, als er in Ptolemais als Sectenhaupt auftrat und von da durch seine Lehre den ganzen Orient in Bewegung brachte."

vicious in tone and intent to warrant disparagement of any hagiographically contrived death-bed scene, whether of natural causes or following the kind of popular riot, as I have suggested may have been the case.

Gieseler could not therefore solve the problem with the identification of the author of the Συναγωγή–Χρονικῶν with that of *El.* by postulating the lateness of the latter. His argument still cannot cope with the fact that the former work ends with the death of Severus Alexander in 235. But even granted that this would imply, *per impossibile* as we have argued, both the writing of *El.* during the episcopate of Urban after the death of Callistus and indeed the Hippolytan authorship of that work, this would still mean that Hippolytus' writing career had ended in 235 otherwise he would have extended the Συναγωγή up to 251 or 258.

We need therefore, as we shall now argue, a different explanation. We shall argue that, since *El.* was completed before the death of Callistus in 222, another hand updated the Συναγωγή as it had amended the ἀπόδειξις with the genuinely Hippolytan, κατὰ Δανιήλ additions, and given the latter its curiously dual chronology. In consequence and *a fortiori* the death of the author of *El.* will be presupposed before 235 because that is the date of the death of Hippolytus his emendator and successor.

It is thus that we come to our second problem, namely given that we admit that Hippolytus, the martyr of the via Tiburtina, has amended both the Συναγωγή–Χρονικῶν and the *Catalogus*, why is such a position superior to simply regarding him as the author of both and therefore also of *El.*?

4B 2.2.3.3. *Citation of* Yppolytus presbyter *in the* Catalogus

Since the commemoration of the name of Hippolytus *presbyter* appears with that of Pontianus *episcopus*, as those of the two Sardinian martyrs, does not this suggest that he was the original author of the ὀνόματα list and therefore also the Συναγωγή? If the author of *El.* himself continued this his original work in a second edition sometime before 215 to. 235, why, if he is other than Hippolytus, is he not commemorated himself rather than Hippolytus by the continuator of that work after their death in the *Catalogus*?

Clearly if the author of *El.* had been that of the Liberian *Catalogus*, he would certainly would not have included Callistus but himself on the succession list. That the episcopal list of the Συναγωγὴ–Χρονικῶν (as represented by *Liber Generationis* I) and the *Catalogus* end at the date of the death of the Hippolytus who was the martyr of the via Tiburtina indicates that he was the editor who completed the earlier work of the author of *El.* The ἕως τῆς ἐνεστώσης ἡμέρας mentioned in the full title of the συναγωγή χρόνων appears to be A.D. 234. The reason for this is to be found in the text of the *Liber Generationis* which is clearly an alternative Latin translation from the

same Greek original used by the Chronographer of 354.[216] This text terminates with the 13th year of Severus Alexander which is mentioned more than
once e.g. *a passione usque ad hunc annum, qui est xiii imperii Alexandri an-
nus.* The Catalogue of emperors ends *Alexander annis xiii, diebus ix.*[217] Thus
these texts mark both the extent of Hippolytus' literary activity and indeed of
his life.

From our argument so far, the work of Hippolytus the martyr as the editor
and emender of the work of *El.* should strike as neither as surprising nor
undocumented. In 4A 1-2 we established that the theology of *C.N.* had been
constructed in self-conscious opposition and correction to the theology of
El., and with the direct purpose of a *rapprochement* with a semi-
Monarchianism of the form propounded by Zephyrinus and Callistus. In 4A
3.1.1-2, moreover, we established a clear connection between the Christology of *C.N.* and *Dan.* which confirmed both the authorship of the former,
and the difference of authorship between these works and those by the author
of *El.* We then saw the hand of this self-same author of *Dan.* in the κατὰ
Δανιήλ inscriptions on the Statue (4B 2.2.2.2), added to correct the existing
chronological table originally inscribed there.

My thesis becomes therefore highly plausible that it was Hippolytus'
hand, that of the author of *Dan.*, that brought the ὀνόματα list of the author
of *El.* and the Συναγωγή–Χρονικῶν from the time of Zephyrinus down to the
accession of Pontianus in 231. The latter work did, after all, originally
predate *El.* written before the death of Callistus in 222. The hand of the conciliator who synthesized the theology of Callistus with that of *El.* is the same
hand that gave the succession to Pontianus through Callistus and Urban and
not the unnamed writer of *El.* It was he as the successor of *El.* who made
both theological and ecclesial peace, and who accepted the title of *presbyter*
and not *episcopus*. There is no need to construct a legend regarding
Pontianus and Hippolytus reconciled in the hour of their trial and
martyrdom. The reconciliation took place before that event and is witnessed
in the pages of *C.N.* and *Dan.*, and on the Statue's corrected inscriptions, and
also, as we now see, in the Liberian *Catalogus*.

The work of Hippolytus the reconciler was mentioned by a successor who
continued the *Catalogus* after his recorded martyrdom *in Sardinia, in insula
nociva.* The brief description of that martyrdom and the accompany date in
the *Depositio* was not without cryptic and discrete significance. The numbers
of the presbyters of the Roman Church were, according to the letter of
bishop Cornelius to Fabius bishop of Antioch (251), forty-six.[218] If there

---

[216] Lightfoot (1890) p. 258-259.
[217] Ibid. p. 259.
[218] Attacking Novatian and quoted in Eusebius *H.E.* VI, 43, 11: ὁ ἐκδικητὴς οὖν τοῦ
εὐαγγελίου οὐκ ἠπίστατο ἕνα ἐπίσκοπον δεῖν εἶναι ἐν καθολικῇ ἐκκλησίᾳ, ἐν ᾗ οὐκ
ἠγνόει, πῶς γάρ; πρεσβυτέρους εἶναι τεσσαράκοντα ἕξ, διακόνους ἑπτά,

were many presbyters martyred in the persecution of Maximus, the question remains why only is the one presbyter, Hippolytus honoured along with bishop Pontianus. On the other hand if he were the only one, it would be indicative that he as well as Pontianus was regarded by the imperial government as a leader of the Church, and was singled out as a particular leader. Eusebius makes it clear that Maximus' persecution was not general, but focused on leaders of the Church.[219]

In either case, whether the persecution were general or only of Church leaders, the note of their martyrdom in the *Catalogus* makes it clear that Hippolytus is regarded as an unusual and prominent presbyter.[220] Such a prominence would be fully consistent with his conciliatory leadership of a group that had engaged in *rapprochement* with a larger Roman community from which it had become estranged. The date of the commemoration for both Hippolytus and Pontianus on the 13th August was also the festival of Diana commemorating the incorporation of the Italian allied cities into the Roman Federation. Thus the date itself was evocative of the theme and emotions associated with unification after bitter strife.

The record of the martyrdom of Pontianus and Hippolytus together had clearly more than ordinary martyrological implications since theirs are the only martyrdoms given special mention in the Liberian *Catalogus*. The continuator of the *Catalogus* after Urban not only very crudely added, as we have noted, the dates from the consular lists to the ὀνόματα list of both the author of *El.* and its post-Zephyrinan completion by Hippolytus. He also added some brief, seemingly biographical, notes against two other entries, indicative of a similar eirenic purpose, which we shall now consider.

4B 2.2.3.3.1. *The biographical note on Hermas and Pius*
The first is against the name of Pius, indicating the writing of Hermas by his brother.[221] Clearly the group centred around the writing of *El.* had been a rigorist group, as the charges against Callistus of moral laxity testify. The writer had implied that for carnal sins (πρὸς τὰς ἡδονὰς) absolution was

ὑποδιακόνους ἑπτά, ἀκολούθους δύο καὶ τεσσαράκοντα, ἐξορκιστὰς δὲ καὶ ἀναγνώστας ἅμα πυλωροῖς δύο καὶ πεντήκοντα, χήρας σὺν θλιβομένοις ὑπὲρ τὰς χιλίας πεντακοσίας, οὓς πάντας ἡ τοῦ δεσπότου χάρις καὶ φιλανθρωπία διατρέφει.
[219] Eusebius *H.E.* VI, 28: ... Μαξιμῖνος Καῖσαρ διαδέχεται· ὃς δὴ κατὰ κότον τὸν πρὸς τὸν Ἀλεξάνδρου οἶκον, ἐκ πλειόνων πιστῶν συνεστῶτα, διωγμὸν ἐγείρας, τοὺς τῶν ἐκκλησιῶν ἄρχοντας μόνους ὡς αἰτίους τῆς κατὰ τὸ εὐαγγέλιον διδασκαλίας ἀναιρεῖσθαι προστάττει.
[220] P. Testini, Di alcune testimonianze relative a Ippolito, in *StEphAug* 13 (1977), p. 51-52: "E' da notare ad ogni modo che nel Catalogo non è questo il primo caso in cui un presbitero viene ricordato insieme al papa; e tuttavia una condanna all'esilio resta sicuramente un fatto eccezionale, talchè al solo Ippolito di essere esiliato con il capo della comunità romana." See also V. Saxer, La questione di Ippolito Romano: a proposito di un libro recente, in *StEphAug* 30 (1989), p. 58-59.
[221] Lightfoot (1890) 1, I, p. 254: "Pius, ann. xx, m. iiii, d. xxi. Fuit temporibus Antonini Pii, a cons. Clari et Severi [A.D. 146] usque duobus Augustis [A.D. 161]. Sub huius episcopatu frater eius Ermes librum scripsit, in quo mandatum continetur, quod ei praecipit angelus, cum venit ad illum in habitu pastoris."

granted by Callistus (ὑπ᾽ αὐτῷ ἀφίεσθαι τὰς ἁμαρτίας) (IX, 12,20). One such carnal sin (πρὸς θάνατον), adultery, was a mortal sin. He implies that the clergy have committed this mortal sin in being twice or thrice married (δίγαμοι καὶ τρίγαμοι) and that they were ordained (καθίστασθαι εἰς κλήρ-ους) by Callistus as such.[222] In blessing the unions of patrician ladies with slaves and freedmen with the result that they were using abortion-inducing drugs to escape capital punishment under the civil law Callistus had also been responsible for encouraging murder. Murder and adultery were therefore the two mortal sins for which he was granting absolution.[223] Now in making these charges he shows similar rigorist concerns to those of Tertullian after his adoption of Montanism (Chapter 7C).

The accusations of *El.* against Callistus may indeed be contrived. Rather than general laxity, Callistus may have been allowing widowed clergy to re-marry once or even twice and so, contrary to τὰ ἔθη καὶ τὴν παράδοσιν (*El.* IX, 12,26) found presumably in 1 *Tim.* 3,2; 12; *Tit.* 1,5, rather than allowing adultery in general. Nevertheless, *El.* clearly focuses upon the principle of absolution for the mortal sin of adultery and murder, however distorted may be the examples of how ἔθη and παράδοσις have been violated, and denies the correctness of such absolution. Though we shall discuss the relationship between Hippolytus and Tertullian in greater detail later, suffice it to be said here that Tertullian too is concerned about clerical absolution for mortal sin, and focuses too on carnal sin.

Tertullian singled out specifically *Hermas* in this context, as the work of "the adulterous shepherd," which he did not shrink from equating with idola-trous images on breakable glass cups (*cui ille si forte patrocinabitur pastor, quem in calce depingis*). Tertullian preferred to drink from the unbreakable words of the Shepherd of Scripture (*At ego eius pastoris scripturam haurio qui non potest frangi*).[224] *Hermas* had granted the possibility of a second re-pentance for mortal sin, and Tertullian accordingly attacks the *ovem secundae poenitentiae* under the symbol of the inebriated adulterer's chalice (*prostitutorem et ipsum Christiani sacramenti, merito et ebrietatis idolum, et moechiae asylum post calicem subsecuturae*). Thus the claim to second re-pentance identified *Hermas* with laxity in ecclesiastical discipline in the eyes

---

[222] *El.* IX, 12, 22: οὗτος ἐδογμάτισεν ὅπως, εἰ ἐπίσκοπος ἁμάρτοι τι, εἰ καὶ πρὸς θάνατον, μὴ δέῃ κατατίθεσθαι. ἐπὶ τούτου οὖν ἤρξαντο ἐπίσκοποι καὶ πρεσβύτεροι καὶ διάκονοι δίγαμοι καὶ τρίγαμοι καθίστασθαι εἰς κλήρους. εἰ δὲ καί τις ἐν κλήρῳ ὢν γαμοίη, μένειν δεῖν ἔφη τὸν τοιοῦτον ἐν τῷ κλήρῳ ὡς μὴ ἡμαρτηκότα...
[223] *El.* IX, 12,25: ὁρᾶτε εἰς ὅσην ἀσέβειαν ἐχώρησεν ὁ ἄνομος, μοιχείαν καὶ φόνον ἐν τῷ αὐτῷ διδάσκων.
[224] Tertullian *De Pudic.* 10,12-13: "Sed cederem tibi, si scriptura "Pastoris," quae sola moechos amat, divino instrumento meruisset incidi, si non ab omni concilio ecclesiarum etiam vestrarum inter apocrypha et falsa judicaretur, adultera et ipsa, et inde patrona sociorum; a qua et alias initiaris, cui ille si forte patrocinabitur pastor, quem in calce depingis, prostitutorem et ipsum Christiani sacramenti, merito et ebrietatis idolum, et moechiae asylum post calicem subsecuturae, de quo nihil libentius bibas, quam ovem paenitentiae secundae. At ego eius pastoris scripturam haurio qui non potest frangi..."

of the rigorists.[225] It is impossible to doubt in consequence that *Hermas*, a document, after all, of the Church of Rome, would also have been regarded with disdain by the community of *El.* whilst used as a justification for a more compassionate discipline by the community of Callistus.

It is furthermore important to observe that Tertullian finds it necessary to assail the scriptural status that *Hermas* had for such more liberal groups. He expressly questions with the protasis of his conditionals its scriptural status (*si scriptura "Pastoris," quae sola moechos amat, divino instrumento meruisset incidi*), but makes the extraordinary claim that its was "rejected amongst the apocryphal and false (*inter apocrypha et falsa judicaretur*)," "by every council of the Churches," (*si non ab omni concilio Ecclesiarum*) even the non-Montanist, catholic ones (*etiam vestrarum*).

We shall argue in Chapter 7 Part C) that Tertullian cannot here be referring, in the opening years of the third century, to Councils of bishops meeting in various places to determine issues as we shall see that there is proper documentary evidence that they did only from the time of Cyprian. It is significant that he use the plural *ecclesiarum* here and not the single *ecclesiae*. *Concilium* can of course have a sense other than of a formal Council, in the English sense. It can mean an informal assembly, or a collection of individuals meeting in local churches and making *ad hoc* decisions.

But Tertullian thus goes too far in the impression that he seeks to give. Eusebius makes it clear that it was generally received, and with justice he seems to think because Hermas (Ἑρμῆς) is greeted among others in *Rom.* 16, 13. However, since it is "spoken against by some" (πρὸς...τινων ἀντιλέλεκται), for this reason alone it "cannot be placed among accepted books" (δι οὓς οὐκ ἂν ἐν ὁμολογουμένοις τεθείη), but it is used "for elementary instruction (οἷς μάλιστα δεῖ στοιχειώσεως εἰσαγωγικῆς)."[226] Eusebius does not however rank it amongst the heretical, even though he regards it, in a second passage, as ἐν νόθοις, but in this category was also placed *Barnabas*, the *Didache*, and the Johannine *Apocalypse*.[227] Irenaeus had accepted the work.[228] To be judged *inter apocrypha* was not necessarily, as it suited Tertullian pretend, to be judged also as *inter falsa*.

We should however note here a parallel with the accusations of laxity regarding mortal sin in *El.* In IX 11,1 Zephyrinus is described as

---

225 Hermas, *Mand.* 3, 5-6: ὁ Κύριος... ἔθηκεν τὴν μετάνοιαν ταύτην, καὶ ἐμοὶ, ἡ ἐξουσία τῆς μετανοίας ταύτης ἐδόθη.... ἐάν τις ἐκπειρασθεὶς ὑπὸ τοῦ διαβόλου ἁμαρτήσῃ, μίαν μετάνοιαν ἔχει.

226 Eusebius *H.E.* III, 3,6: ... ἐπεὶ δ ὁ αὐτὸς ἀπόστολος ἐν ταῖς ἐπὶ τέλει προσρήσεσιν τῆς πρὸς Ῥωμαίους μνήμην πεποίηται μετὰ τῶν ἄλλων καὶ Ἑρμᾶ, οὗ φασιν ὑπάρχειν τὸ τοῦ Ποιμένος βιβλίον, ἰστέον ὡς καὶ τοῦτο πρὸς μέν τινων ἀντιλέλεκται δι οὓς οὐκ ἂν ἐν ὁμολογουμένοις τεθείη, ὑφ᾽ ἑτέρων δὲ ἀναγκαιότατον οἷς μάλιστα δεῖ στοιχειώσεως εἰσαγωγικῆς, κέκριται.

227 Ibid. 25, 4: ἐν τοῖς νόθοις κατατετάχθω καὶ τῶν Παύλου Πράξεων ἡ γραφὴ ὅ τε λεγόμενος Ποιμήν...κ.τ.λ.

228 Ibid. V, 8, 7 and Irenaeus *Adv. Haer.* 4,38, 3 quoting Hermas *Mand.* 1.

"inexperienced in the principles or canons of the Church (ἄπειρον τῶν ἐκκλησιαστικῶν ὅρων)," in a context that clearly refers to his Sabellianism. But ὅρος is further used in connection with the penitential discipline. The principle that anyone excommunicated by the author from his community can be absolved by Callistus is described as "the principle that gave pleasure to many whose conscience was frozen (οὗ τῷ ὅρῳ ἀρεσκόμενοι πολλοὶ τὴν συνείδησιν πεπηγότες) (IX, 12,20)." Finally, in *El.* X, 5,1, it is used in the form ὁ τῆς ἀληθείας ὅρος in the sense of *regula fidei*.

It is clear therefore that the author of *El.* would have shared with Tertullian the view that the penitential discipline and its non-applicability to mortal sin after baptism was an *articulus stantis vel cadentis Ecclesiae*. It is equally clear therefore that the author of *El.* would have shared Tertullian's opinion both of the "adulterous shepherd" and of its exclusion from the canon of Scripture as part of the rule or ὅρος of faith and morals. That the successor of Hippolytus who continues the Liberian List should therefore have written an addition that associates eirenically, but non-committedly, Hermas with the apostolic succession by making him the brother of Pius is not surprising. We shall return to the question of the relationship between the community of Tertullian and that of the author of *El.* and his conciliatory successor in 7C 1-7 C 2.

Though Hippolytus was one successor to the author of *El.*, he was a successor seeking reconciliation for himself and his community with that of Callistus. The continuator of the Liberian List at this point had already cryptically acknowledged that reconciliation in his note on the Pontian/Hippolytus martyrdom. Now in the note on Pius the continuator acknowledges the possibility of the absolution of mortal sin after baptism and thus departs from the extreme rigorism of *El.* The insertion of the comment on the authorship of *Hermas* is therefore part of the conciliatory pattern of the work of the continuator, and expresses here critically a theological *rapprochement* between the two formerly separated communities. We shall now observe in his third addition, on the Novatian martyrs, a similar conciliatory concern on the part of the continuator.

4B 2.2.3.3.2. *The biographical note on the Novatian martyrs*

We find our third and final additions by the continuator, which he has included in his entry for Fabius, Cornelius, and Lucius. We have pointed to the unusual character of these biographical additions to a lists of names, to which we have also argued that the continuator added the dates, after his recording of Hippolytus' death. We have detected the continuator's hand as beginning in 236 with Antheros when he made these unusual biographical additions as well as the haphazardly applied dates to the list of names of his predecessor, and the accurate dates for his successors. We may now locate the end of this particular continuator's work with Lucius (252-255), where biographical additions that have the common theme of reconciliation cease. Indeed any biographical additions to the names and dates ceases until the celebration of the building activity of Julius (337-352).[229]

We see finally in the Novatian martyrs the theme and purpose of the continuator, to reinforce the *rapprochement* of the community of Callistus and that of Hippolytus and his predecessors, the author of *El*. The first addition is to the entry for Fabius (236-250). Indeed, this entry records also the final completion of the development of the monarchical episcopate at Rome, which began in Victor's time, but was only ended, as we shall argue further in Chapter 6, with the building of special places of worship, owned by the community, and separate from the house-Churches, which could now be firmly under the control of a central bishop. The continuator marks the ideological development in support of this process as he emphasizes and seals the reconciliation in both theology and discipline between two opposing groups.

The continuator of 235, as we can now call him, now records the division of the Roman Church into regions under the (seven) deacons, and building works for the cemeteries as ordered (*fieri iussit*) by Fabius.[230] We see in this note a monarchical bishop controlling and organising church property which is now securely under community ownership. We shall follow Lampe who in the light of the archaeological evidence regards Callistus' earlier diaconal administration of Zephyrinus' cemetry as an inner-community arrangement which in the eyes of the external world was simply a case of a servant administering property that legally was owned privately by his master.[231] Here we have the final phase, as we have said, of the monarchical development.

But not all sections of the Roman community were, without protest, to follow this development of the continuator and his predecessor, Hippolytus' mediating theology. On Fabius' death, Novatus came from Africa and separated Novatian, secretary of the Roman presbyterate, from the Church. The confessors, presbyter Maximus, and deacon Nicostratus in prison supported this action against, as we are arguing, the final twist of events to an episcopal monarchy founded on a comprehensivism that rigorism found intolerable. They were the "certain confessors (*quosdam confessores*)" whom Novatus separated from the Church (*separavit de ecclesia*) along with Novatian after

---

229 Lightfoot (1890) 1, I, p. 256: "LUCIUS... Hic exul fuit, et postea nutu Dei incolumis ad ecclesiam reversus est." Thus Lucius as *exul* is united in a common theme with *Pontianus episcopus and Yppolitus presbyter exoles* as part of the cryptographic message of reconciliation. This observation incidentally also counts against the view that the note on Hippolytus might imply his survival of the Sardinian exile as Cecchelli and others argued (1 B 1.3.1.4). Were this the case we should have expected for Hippolytus the record *incolumis ad ecclesiam reversus*.

230 Ibid. p. 255: "FABIUS... Hic regiones divisit diaconibus et multas fabricas per cimiteria fieri iussit."

231 Lampe (1989) p. 15-22 and Chapter 6.

the death of one of their number, the presbyter Moyses (*postquam Moyses in carcere defunctus est*).[232]

But indeed there is here an ambiguity still precisely in what Novatus' original act of "separation" in 250 consisted. In the course of the short episcopate of Cornelius, that lasted from 251 to 252, Novatus ordained Novatian for Rome and Nicostratus for Africa *extra ecclesiam*.[233] That phrase itself was resonant with the new and original conceptualization of a theology of Church Order articulated by Cyprian bishop of Carthage. In the light of that theology, Cyprian, by means of his extant correspondence, ruthlessly intervened in the Roman situation, declaring eventually in favour of Cornelius, and claiming the consent by letter of the majority of bishops throughout the world to that decision.

Cyprian did so in the light of a theology that asserted that there was one episcopal monarch per given territory. Furthermore, not simply the unity, but the sacramental unity, of the Church was guaranteed by such a mutual recognition and acceptance of the bishops into each others' communion, and hence the mutual communion with each other through them of the people joined to each bishop. Outside the Church (*extra ecclesiam*) thus constituted sacramentally and mysteriously there was no salvation. As a good patrician from Romanized Carthage in North Africa, in order to license change he needed a collection of *mores maiorum*, the appeal to those time hallowed-traditions of ancestors that Cicero once claimed could be devised only yesterday. In purporting to describe the reality of the Church as it is and has always been, Cyprian was indeed creating a new conceptualization of Church Order that set the seal on the monarchical episcopate.

When Novatus in North Africa and Novatian in Rome created rival groups, it may not have been in order, as is generally supposed, to create an alternative rival Church in Cyprian's sense, each with its own true bishops in each place uniting the faithful in communion with them to the communion of each other. Novatian, secretary of the Roman presbyterate, came from a community that had a long memory of independent πρεσβύτεροι–ἐπίσκοποι presiding over the house-Churches of a fractionalized community, as we shall see in greater detail later (7A and B). Likewise Novatus' community in North Africa had memories of Tertullian as a Montanist whose group nevertheless arguably still met with their fellow Catholics for the Eucharist, and only discussed their more pneumatic experiences after the service. The "schism" of Tertullian, like that of the author of *El.*, was between groups

---

[232] Lightfoot (1890) 1, I p. 255: "Post passionem eius [Fabii] Moyses et Maximus presbyteri et Nicostratus diaconus comprehensi sunt et in carcerem sunt missi. Eo tempore supervenit Novatus ex Africa et separavit de ecclesia Novatianum et quosdam confessores, postquam Moyses in carcere defunctus est, qui fuit ibi m. xi, d. xi."

[233] Ibid.: "CORNELIUS... Sub episcopatu eius Novatus extra ecclesiam ordinavit Novatianum in urbe Roma et Nicostratum in Africa."

who could separate and break communion with each other on theological grounds, but not on grounds of the validity of each other's Orders (7C).

Cornelius in his letter (Eusebius *H.E.* VI, 43, 11) never spoke therefore a truer word when he said of Novatian οὐκ ἠπίστατο ἕνα ἐπίσκοπον δεῖν εἶναι ἐν καθολικῇ ἐκκλησίᾳ. Novatian would not have accepted the Cyprianic conceptualization of Order as Cornelius eagerly did as the beneficiary of its justification of his monarchical power. The Novatian martyrs however were also persuaded in the hour of the Church's trial in the fires of the Decian persecution of that theory of unity's validity. It was in consequence, not of "separation" itself, which they clearly did not understand in Cyprian's sense, but in terms of an act of ordination itself that they clearly did (*Novatus extra ecclesiam ordinavit Novatianum*), that they were reconciled with the community of Cornelius.[234]

The continuator clearly sympathized with this acceptance of the finally developed concept of monarchical episcopacy by the Novatian martyrs, and its triumph with Cornelius over a less monolithic view of the Church better able to tolerate some degree of fractionalism in which rigorism need not necessarily lead to any final and irreversible breach. It was the martyr Hippolytus that with Pontianus had exemplified the acceptance of such a view of Order in process of development, even at the cost of a *rapprochement* with Monarchianism and the acceptance of the lax *Hermas* in repudiation thereby both of the theology and the rigorism of the author of *El.* The Novatian martyrs had shown themselves to be of the same conciliating spirit as that of the community of Hippolytus, subsequent to the demise of the author of *El.*, whose works they nevertheless, in a spirit of true conciliation, honoured with reservation and appropriate emendment.

Let us summarize where our discussion of the Συναγωγή–Χρονικῶν and its relationship with *El.* and the Liberian *Catalogus* has now taken us.

4B 2.2.4. *Conclusion: Hippolytus in the* corpus *of* El.

We have thus traced the links in terms of authorship between *El.* and the Συναγωγή–Χρονικῶν, and between the latter and the Liberian *Catalogus*. But in each case we needed a second hand in order to explain problems with the literary data. We needed a hand that would bring the Συναγωγή down to 235 when the date of *El.* in which it was cited as already written was around 218. We saw too that the original version of this work, in *Liber Generationis* I, had contained a succession list that, in the form purely of an ὀνόματα list, without dates, had corresponded to the first part of the Liberian *Catalogus*. Thus the author of *El.* and the Συναγωγή must also be the author of the original list from which the *Catalogus* was later elaborated.

---

[234] Ibid. p. 255-256: "Hoc facto confessores, qui se separaverunt a Cornelio, cum Maximo presbytero, qui cum Moyse fuit, ad ecclesiam sunt reversi."

But this being the case, we needed a further hand to correct that list and to bring it down also to 235 where the corresponding regnal list had also ended, granted that the author of *El.* fades from the scene around the death of Callistus in 225. The hand of the corrector on this occasion moreover could certainly not have been that of the author of *El.*, since the list acknowledges Callistus as the successor of Zephyrinus and the predecessor of Urban and Pontian. Since the presbyter Hippolytus mentioned alongside bishop Pontianus was clearly an icon of reconciliation, it was reasonable to conclude that the hand of the corrector and up-dater of both these works was this Hippolytus. Such a conclusion was rendered cogent and taken beyond the realm of pure hypothesis by two further conclusions that we established, namely, that:

(i) the author of *C.N.* who was also that of *Dan.* reconciled the theology of *El.* with that of the semi-monarchianism represented by Callistus, and,

(ii) the ἀπόδειξις inscribed on the Statue had been corrected by the Hippolytan chronology of *Dan.*

In the light of the identifiable hand of Hippolytus correcting and amending the work of the author of *El.* in these two contexts it was reasonable to conclude that his was the hand that updated and amended both the Συναγωγή and the *Catalogus*.

The further hand that substituted Callistus and perhaps Urban for the author of *El.* and his successor in the latter also, as we have argued, added dates to the list which were accurately recorded from Pontianus onwards, but merely approximated for the previous names. The continuator of the first section of the *Catalogus* down to 255 thus both acknowledges the development after 235 of the concept of the bishop's office as similar to the reign of a monarch with its fixed dates, and also approves of the *rapprochement* of the community of Hippolytus, author of *C.N.*, with Pontianus, successor of the semi-Monarchians previously attacked by the work of the author of *El.* which Hippolytus accordingly emends.

We have further indicated that in our view there is no need to locate the writing of *Dan.* in the persecution of Decius if it cannot be located in that of Septimius Severus (4B 2). We believe in other words that *Dan.* was written by the martyr of 235 commemorated on the via Tiburtina, contrary to Cecchelli, whose views on this matter we criticized earlier (1B 1.3.1.4, 1B 1.3.3.3 and 1B 2.1-2.6). The author of the group of works, the chronology of two of which, the Συναγωγή and ἀπόδειξις, by this time would have died, as had Callistus his rival, perhaps in the same local riot as each other in an intervention by the civil power prompted by the very rivalry attested by *El.* IX etc. That the deaths of either are not commemorated and a low profile maintained is not remarkable in view of the process of reconciliation focused on *Pontianus episcopus et Yppolytus presbyter*.

But at this point we find that the presence of the hand of Hippolytus is already to be witnessed in the works listed on the Statue, whether in the Συναγωγή in the continuation of the ὀνόματα list, or in the ἀπόδειξις with the emendations κατὰ Δανιήλ. There is in the light of that presence no reason to rule out *a priori* that some of the works listed on the plinth of the Statue were written by Hippolytus however much others, clearly associated with *El.* as we have seen, were by a different author. The grounds upon which such an *a priori* claim was made was on the assumption that I have argued to be false, that the Statue was a personal monument and not a cultic and community object enabling a given community to calculate the date of Easter given their particular assumptions about the nature of that celebration, etc. Thus our literary analysis of the inscribed works corroborates independently our interpretation of the Statue as a community artefact.

We may therefore now examine on their merits the claim of the further works listed to be by Hippolytus or by the author of *El.*, without reference to a false unity imposed upon the list of works by a false interpretation of the nature of the Statue itself. We must keep before us the fact of pseudo-nymity as the common literary device by which the teaching of an individual became the teaching of a school. Successors to the founding teacher considered themselves, not so much as individuals making their own personal contribution, but rather expressing and continuing the corporate spirit of the school, whose collective personality took on the individual colouring of their founder. Pseudo Justin Martyr, Pseudo Clement, Pseudo Tertullian, and Pseudo Cyprian bear eloquent testimony to such a literary device. In this context, our 'school' interpretation of the Hippolytan *corpus* becomes but an unusual expression of a quite general rule.

We have in this chapter limited ourselves to those works that can be securely differentiated from Hippolytus, the author of *C.N., Dan.* and associated works, and allocated clearly to the author of *El.* But though *El.* may be uncontaminated along with περὶ τοῦ παντός (4B 2.1-6), we have seen with the other works that we examined, namely the ἀπόδειξις χρόνων and the Liberian *Catalogus* (4B 2.2.3.2) that there was another hand at work which we identified with the author of *C.N.* and corrector in that work of the theology of *El.* (4A 3.2.3) and the same hand that completed the Συναγωγή (4B 2.2.3.2). We must now examine the remaining titles inscribed on the Statue's plinth in order to ask whether indeed those titles may not indeed be the work of Hippolytus as author, whose hand appeared on those already examined as editor.

CHAPTER FIVE

THE STATUE AND THE TWO AUTHORS THEORY (II)

The Statue and works related to the Contra Noetum

We now come to those works listed on the plinth of the Statue which proved such an embarrassment to proponents of the two-authors thesis. The reason for this embarrassment was that although *El.*, περὶ τοῦ παντός, and the Συναγωγή were either anonymous or given names of other authors (Gaius, Josephus) by Photius, John Philoponus, or Pseudo-Damascene, the works ἀποστολικὴ παραδόσις, ἀπόδειξις χρόνων, περὶ τἀγαθοῦ καὶ πόθεν τὸ κακόν, περὶ θεοῦ καὶ σαρκὸς ἀναστάσεως, προτρεπτικὸς πρὸς Σεβηρεῖναν, εἰς ἐγγαστρίμυθον, and τὰ ὑπὲρ τοῦ κατὰ᾽Ιωάννην κτλ. seemed so very like titles attributed to Hippolytus in the Church Order literature, in the Eusebius/Jerome Catalogues, by Theodoret, and by Barsalîbî.

We may dismiss the latter as an individual exception, for reasons that I have already advanced (3C). But the list as a whole comes from different sources, citing names of numerous works that seem generally to be too similar for their association to be based on mere coincidence of name. Nautin, as we shall see, explained the similarities as coincidental titles on which various Christian writers composed works. Simonetti and Loi, alternatively, advanced the thesis that there were two Hippolyti with the same name. What our conclusion regarding the corporate and community character of the Statue and its list of works has now enabled us to do is to separate the two-authors thesis from any dependence on the Statue itself. We must frankly admit that the works inscribed are by two authors at least.[1]

In consequence we do not need to "save the appearances" of the two authors thesis by postulating either two authors with the same name, or different works by differently named authors with the same titles. We can consider seriously such theses quite independently of the Statue itself, rejecting

---

[1] A. Amore, La personalità di Ippolito, *Antonianum* 36 (1961), p. 3-28. M. Simonetti, Aggiornamento su Ippolito, in in *StEphAug* 30 (1989) still argues for two distinct authors to the *corpus*. However he notes the importance of the Statue for arguing a single author ("nell'elaborata costruzione che ha portato all'affermazione dell'unico Ippolito... la statua riveste funzione essenziale," (p. 117)), but then admits that if the figure depicted is not that of Hippolytus, then all the works listed do not have to be by a single author ("vanificata l'effigie di Ippolito... niente autorizza a supporre che i titoli incisi pertengano tutti a un sole autore ." (p. 121) He nevertheless does not go on to claim that the works thus listed can be assigned amongst two. But if the Statue is the symbol of a community rather than an individual, we need not limit necessarily the number of authors to only two but consider each case on its merits.

them if our analysis requires because we are thereby left free to claim some of the works listed are by the author of *Dan.* on the basis of their citation as such by Eusebius, Jerome, and Theodoret.

PART A. THE STATUE AND THE *C.N.* BLOCK

The delimitation of the *C.N.* block of works by means of the definition "those works none of which are listed on the Statue" we concluded to have failed (4B 1). It does not follow, as we saw that Nautin and others originally claimed, that because some of the works are clearly not by Hippolytus, in the light of the identification afforded by the nexus between those works and *El.* in comparison with *C.N.* and *Dan.*, then none of the works can be.[2] Our conclusion will, nevertheless, in a new form, be a vindication of the two-authors thesis. Indeed it will be seen to remove the need of the support of a *petitio principii* in arguments that whenever a name of a work appears on the list on the Statue, it must be an alternative work by a different author of the same name as that attributed to Hippolytus in the Eusebius/ Jerome catalogues.

Let us begin with the ἀποστολικὴ παραδόσις.

5A 1. ἀποστολικὴ παραδόσις *and the Hippolytan tradition*

In 3D 1.1 we examined Botte's attempt ito identify, on external evidence, the ἀποστολικὴ παραδόσις and περὶ χαρισμάτων (considered as a single work), with the *Egyptian Church Order,* and found severe problems for reasons that Richard had pointed out. The combination of two separate titles on the Statue as if they were one work could only be justified by reference to a chain of *ms.* evidence that was at certain critical points highly tenuous. The evidence of *Ochrid ms.* 86 had suggested that the original title of the *Egyptian Church Order* had been διατάξις διά ʿ Ἱππολύτου. But the inclusion of περὶ χαρισμάτων in that title was nor original but arose in *Ap. Con.* VIII from a heading inserted in one section alone of the *Epitome* (3D 1.2).

It would be possible, therefore, on one interpretation of the evidence, to dissociate the *Egyptian Church Order* from the ἀποστολικὴ παραδόσις of the Statue and be left with a mere title the contents of which we have no knowledge, and that interpretation may well be the correct one, in view of the argument that I presented. But let us assume for the sake of argument that nevertheless the two works were identical and that the περὶ χαρισμάτων ἀποστολικὴ παραδόσις, without any intervening ἤ was in fact one and the

---

2 See e.g. P. Nautin, Hippolyte et Josipe: Contribution à l'histoire de la littérature chrétienne du troisième siècle, in *Études et Textes pour l'histoire du dogme de la Trinité,* 2, (Paris: Les Éditions du Cerf 1947), p. 79-85; ——, *Hippolyte, Contra les hérésies, fragment. Étude et édition critique,* (Paris: Les Éditions du Cerf 1949), p. 228-230.

same work and identical with the *Egyptian Church Order*. The consequences of such an assumption would nevertheless be illuminating now to
trace in the light of our particular contribution to the argument about the title.

We pointed to the use of διὰ ʿΙππολύτου as a pseudonymous device
which in some manuscripts of the *Ap. Cons.* appeared as the pseudonymous
counterpart of διὰ Κλήμεντος (3D 2). We concluded that we had no need
therefore, in the world of the literary *genre* that attributed the *Clementines* to
Clement, to claim a particular author but rather an ecclesiastical tradition
(3D 4). Thus διὰ ʿΙππολύτου gave us no indication of a title of a work that
was real evidence for the name of its actual author.

Richard's original argument was therefore in one way of great service to
Nautin's case. If the two titles on the Statue could be kept separate as two
different works, and if they were not associated with Hippolytus' name, then
another fact could be established in the thesis that all works on the Statue
were by the author of *El.* and not by Hippolytus. Furthermore, in the light of
my further argument that διὰ ʿΙππολύτου stood for a pseudonymous *genre*
and not an individual, it can be seen that Hippolytus was not necessarily the
personal author of that work.

That his name is associated with the tradition of *Ap. Trad.* should, in the
light of my preceding account, cause no surprise. The original conciliator of
the theology of *El.* and the emender of the chronology of the Statue would
be the personality that adhered to the school of the author of *El.*, cemented
as that adherence was by the more than martyrological note of his reconcil-
iatory significance by the (after himself) second continuator of the Liberian
Catalogus. But that would make *Ap. Trad.* very much the document of a
school rather than of an individual.

Whether or not therefore the *Egyptian Church Order* was precisely the
ἀποστολικὴ παραδόσις of the Statue, that work must nevertheless be a document of the school of Hippolytus and the at least two figures within it that
have begun to emerge. We can establish this by two quite separate observations. First its connection with the author of *El.* and second the composite
nature of the work which contains two quite separate images of the relation
between the presbyterate and the episcopate.

5A 1.1. El. *and the alleged work* ἀποστολικὴ παραδόσις
In *Ap. Trad.* 3 we find the use of ἀρχιερατεύειν and its derivatives to describe the bishop's office. This represents the earliest usage of such sacral
and hierarchical terminology in Christian literature and is absolutely unique
both to *El.* and *Ap. Trad.* We shall consider the implications of this in
greater detail later, when we consider the character of Hippolytus' community, in view of the importance of the uniqueness of usage in challenging
Ehrhardt's thesis that such sacral imagery came from the Jacobean succes-

sion and generally conditioned episcopacy wherever it emerged.[3] But for the moment we note in *Ap. Trad.* 3 the expressions ἄρχοντάς τε καὶ ἱερεῖς καταστήσας, ἀρχιερατεύειν σοι ἀμέμπτως, and τῷ πνεύματι τῷ ἀρχιερατικῷ

In *El.* proem. 6 we have the idea of apostolic succession described in characteristically Irenaean terms, but with a significant addition to the Irenaean tradition.[4] As in Irenaeus before him it is the τὸ ἐν ἐκκλησίᾳ παραδοθὲν ἅγιον πνεῦμα οὗ τυχόντες πρότεροι οἱ ἀπόστολοι μετέδοσαν τοῖς ὀρθῶς πεπιστευκόσιν. It is of this charism of teaching that the ministerial successors of the apostles receive. But to this charism is now added also the ἀρχιερατεία which is also handed on and received (ὧν ἡμεῖς διάδοχοι τυγχάνοντες, τῆς τε αὐτῆς χάριτος μετέχοντες ἀρχιερατείας τε καὶ διδασκαλίας). It cannot be accidental that this unique usage unites *El.* with one section of *Ap. Trad.*, namely the prayer of consecration for a bishop in chapter 3.

Furthermore, we find also in *Ap. Trad.* 3 the use of ὅρος in the sense of "canonical boundary" or "limit," or perhaps just plainly "canons" or "ordinances." God is addressed as σὺ ὁ δοὺς ὅρους ἐκκλησίας διὰ λόγου χάριτός σου. Likewise in *El.* IX, 11,1 Zephyrinus is described as ἄπειρον τῶν ἐκκλησιαστικῶν ὅρων. Recipients of Callistus' absolution of mortal sin after baptism are described, in IX, 12,21, as οὗ τῷ ὅρῳ ἀρεσκόμενοι πολλοί. The same word is used as equivalent to the *regula fidei* in X, 5,1 in the expression ὁ τῆς ἀληθείας ὅρος which in the same sense is called τὸν τῆς ἀληθείας κανόνα in 5,2. In view of the uniqueness of this term used in the sense of general rule that goes farther than the more specific "canon" of later usage, it is clear that there is a link of authorship between *El.* and *Ap. Trad.* 3 at this point.

But as we shall argue, now briefly, and later in greater detail, *Ap. Trad.* in its present form is clearly a composite document. ὅρος is not found in this sense outside *Ap. Trad.* 3. It is significant in this connection that Botte had to correct Dix's attempt to find such a sense in *Ap. Trad.* 4 where, in the Eucharistic liturgy just before the words of institution, the purpose of the Passion is, according to the Verona Latin, *ut mortem soluat et vincula diaboli dirumpat, et infernum calcet et iustos inluminet, et terminum figat, et resurrectionem manifestet.* Here clearly the illumination of the just souls that precedes shows that the *terminus*, or ὅρος does not mean here "ordinance" or "custom" but the "limit" or "boundary" of hell established by

---

[3] See also A. Brent, Diogenes Laertiou and the Apostolic Succession, in *JEH*, 44, 3 (1993), p. 367-389, cf. Blum G.G., Apostolische Tradition und Sukzession bei Hippolyt, in *ZNW* 55 (1964), p. 95-110. See also M. Metzger, Nouvelles perspectives pour la prétendue Tradition apostolique, in *Ecclesia Orans* 5 (1988), p. 241-259.

[4] I explain in greater detail in 7B 2 why Irenaeus *Adv. Haer.* IV, 8,3 is not a reference to the ministerial priesthood but an expository rebuff to Marcion's use of *Mt.* 12,3-5. In IV,17,5-18,1, the words of consecration refer to the "pure sacrifice" about which *Mal.* 1,10-11 prophesied, but is regarded as the offering of the whole Church and not the succession of teachers.

Christ's descent there.[5] ὅρος in the sense of "ordinance" or "custom" therefore remains unique to *Ap. Trad.* 3.

There are certain similarities between *El.* and *Ap. Trad.* outside of chapter 3, but these do not possess so unique a character, nor are they so unambiguous, particularly if we concede that Hippolytus and his community knew the work of *El.* The reading of ἐπὶ τὸ κορυφαιότατον τῆς ἐκκλησιαστικῆς διατυπώσεως of *Ap. Con.* 3,2 reflects well the original Greek of the Verona Latin and the Ethiopian version's *ad verticem traditionis* for *Ap. Trad.* 1. In turn this expression is found in *El.* VI, 21,2 but not precisely in the same sense. Here the writer proposes to record in summary (δι' ἐπιτομῆς) the principle points (τὰ κορυφαιότατα τῶν αὐτοῖς ἀρεσκομένων) of Valentinian opinions in order to reveal their origin in Egyptian and Greek philosophy.[6] ἐπὶ τὸ κορυφαιότατον τῆς ἐκκλησιαστικῆς διατυπώσεως clearly means "to the summit (or heights) of the ecclesiastical tradition" and not to a summary of it. In IX, 31,2 moreover κορυφή is used once again but in the sense of a "summary of the whole" (κορυφὴν τοῦ παντὸς) of books I-IX in a single book X (ἐν μιᾷ βίβλῳ τῇ δεκάτῃ περιγράψαι).[7] The sense is again quite different from *ad verticem traditionis* and its Greek original.

Other comparisons with *El.* specifically, outside *Ap. Trad.* 3, are neither sufficiently direct nor sufficiently idiosyncratic to establish anything more than the common usage of what is emerging from our other analysis of the literary data as that of a distinct school with more than one writer. The comparison, for example, between the use of ἡδονή and προϊστάναι (of presidency of a school) in *Ap. Trad.* 43 with *El.* IX, 12,20 (συνεστήσατο διδασκαλεῖον... τὰς ἡδονὰς) is securely in this category in view of the Irenaean parallels.[8] The definitely individual links between *El.* and *Ap. Trad.* are therefore confined to chapter 3 of the latter document.

[5] B. Botte, La Tradition apostolique de saint Hippolyte. Essai de reconstitution, in *Liturgiewissenschaftliche Quellen und Forschungen*, 39 (1963) (Aschendorffsche Verlagsbuchhandlung: Munster: 1963), p. 15 note 4: "Dix traduit l'éthiopien par «ordinance». Il n'y pas de variante réelle dans E... Le grec avait donc sûrement ὅρος... Mais si le texte est certain, le sens demeure obscur. On pourrait se demander si, dans le contexte, il ne serait préférable de comprendre: fixer la limite (de l'enfer)."

[6] *El.* VI, 21,1-2: ... διὸ δοκεῖ ὀλίγα τῆς Πυθαγορείου καὶ Πλατωνικῆς ὑπομνησθέντας ὑποθέσεως ἄρξασθαι καὶ τὰ Οὐαλεντίνου λέγειν... ἀλλὰ γε καὶ νῦν οὐκ ἀλόγως ὑπομνησθήσομαι δι ' ἐπιτομῆς τὰ κορυφαιότατα τῶν αὐτοῖς ἀρεσκομένων, πρὸς τὸ εὐεπίγνωστα γενέσθαι τὰ Οὐαλεντίνῳ δόξαντα.

[7] Ibid. IX, 31,2: ... διὰ πάντων οὖν τούτων διαδραμόντες καὶ μετὰ πολλοῦ πόνου ἐν ταῖς ἐννέα βίβλοις τὰ πάντα δόγματα ἐξειπόντες... εὔλογον ἡγούμεθα ὥσπερ κορυφὴν τοῦ παντὸς ἐλέγχου τὸν περὶ ἀληθείας λόγον ἐπενέγκαι καὶ τοῦτον ἐν μιᾷ βίβλῳ τῇ δεκάτῃ περιγράψαι...

[8] Irenaeus, *Adv. Haer.* I, 27,2: διαδεξάμενος δὲ αὐτὸν Μαρκίων ὁ Ποντικός αὔξησε τὸ διδασκαλεῖον; I, 11,1 ὁ μὲν γὰρ πρῶτος ἀπὸ τῆς λεγομένης Γνωστικῆς αἱρέσεως τὰς ἀρχὰς εἰς ἴδιον χαραχτῆρα διδασκαλείου μεθαρμόσας Οὐαλεντῖνος οὕτως ὡρίσατο. For the concern of heretics with their own ἡδοναί, see V, 8, 2: "Qui ergo pignus Spiritus habent et non concupiscentiis carnis serviunt, sed subiiciunt semetipsos Spiritui... Eos autem qui abiiciunt quidem Spiritus consilium, carnis autem voluptatibus serviunt...etc." For these and other comparisons between *El.* and *Ap. Trad.* see V. Loi, L'identità letteraria di Ippolito di Roma, *StEphAug*, 13 1977, p. 79-82.

We shall discuss later and more generally the implications of the composite character of *Ap. Trad.* for the Hippolytan community. But let us here briefly emphasise what we shall later develop more fully by pointing to the two quite separate images of the relation between the presbyterate and the episcopate in *Ap. Trad.* 3 and 7.

5A 1.2. Ap. Trad. *3 and 7: Separate images of Church Order*

In *Ap. Trad.* 3 the imagery of the bishop's office is sacerdotal (ἀρχιερατεία). To "serve You as high priest (ἀρχιερατεύειν σοι ἀμέμπτως)" is "to offer to you the gifts (προσφέρειν σοι τὰ δῶρα)" and "to have authority to forgive sins (ἔχειν ἐξουσίαν ἀφιέναι ἁμαρτίας)." The action of the bishop is propitiatory (ἱλάσκεσθαι τῷ προσώπῳ σου), in a sacred place (ἀγίασμά) which God does not wish to be left unattended by an official ministry (ἀλειτούργητον). Abraham rather than Aaron is mentioned because presumably Abraham performed both sacrificial and leadership functions so that he as a model acted both παρά σου δύναμιν τοῦ ἡγεμονικοῦ πνεύματος and also τῷ πνεύματι τῷ ἀρχιερατικῷ.

By contrast *Ap. Trad.* 7 is Mosaic rather than sacerdotal or Aaronic. Indeed we may see in the adoption of Abraham rather than Aaron as the sacerdotal figure in chapter 3 a self-conscious shift of sacerdotal image from a priest who was subject to a non-priest, Moses, to one who was both supreme ruler as well as high-priest of his people. In no way can both *Ap. Trad.* 3 and 7 be part of an original single rite of the Roman community. The originally extraneous and non-integral character of chapter 7 is revealed by the claim that the same prayer is to be used to ordain a presbyter as that used to ordain a bishop (Verona Latin: *dicat secundum ea quae praedicta sunt, sicut praedixmus super episcopum*/ Sahidic, Aethiopic, Arabic: *oret super eum secundum modum quem praediximus super episcopum*). But the text of the prayer that then follows is totally different from that in chapter 3, which would have been in chapter 7 *ea quae praedicta*/ *secundum modum quem praediximus* regarding the bishop.

The bishop according to chapter 7 is a lay teaching figure comparable to Moses and not a sacerdotal figure like Abraham/Aaron. The presbyter is united to the bishop like the presbyters of the Old Testament were united to Moses in *Num.* 11, 17-25. They received a portion of Moses' spirit and prophesied like him (Verona Latin (Ethiopic) *praecepisti Moysi ut eligeret praesbyteros quos replevisti de spiritu tuo quod (quem) tu donasti famulo tuo (servo tuo Moysi)*). In the Greek of *Ap. Cons.* VIII, 16,4 the expressions πνεῦμα χάριτος καὶ συμβουλίας (Verona Latin: *spiritum gratiae et consilii praesbyteris*, Ethiopic: *spiritum gratiae et consilium praesbyterii*) and κυβερνᾶν (Verona Latin/ Ethiopic: *gubernet plebem tuam*) are pastoral and teaching terms rather than sacerdotal ones.

We shall consider these two ordination prayers in greater detail later, in the context of an anatomy of the Hippolytan community and the groups in which it originated. But for now we may connect these two prayers, the former with *El.* and the latter with *C.N.*, following the principal argument of this chapter. Following the clear connection between chapter 3 and *El.* I proem. 6 (μετέχοντες ἀρχιερατείας) that we have established, we can see that the rigorist tradition of the author's community was consistent with a sacral view of purity and the ability to absolve. It may be that the community of Callistus retained a view of binding and loosing in terms of determining the interpretation of Scripture by teaching authority, as we shall see is reflected in the *Clementines*, so that for them ritual purity was not the point at issue.

Certainly the atmosphere of *C.N.* 1,4 and 6-7 is highly presbyteral, since, quite extraordinarily in view of the emergence of the monepiscopate in Smyrna with Polycarp, Noetus is described as condemned twice at a hearing before the "blessed presbyters (οἱ μακάριοι πρεσβύτεροι)." We may find here a reassertion of the presbyteral tradition of *Ap. Trad.* 7, which recognised the common Spirit shared by the bishop with the presbyterate with which his ministerial acts formed a unity rather than a separation. Furthermore the statement that Noetus claimed that he was Moses and his brother Aaron perhaps reflected *El.*'s earlier polemics in the school of Hippolytus, in which he denied subservience of the sacral to the governmental by making the episcopal model sacral and Aaronic and not Mosaic. Such. will constitute some of the broader issues that we will consider in greater detail later.

We see therefore our argument that Hippolytus' hand may appear here on the Statue too, if indeed the composite *Egyptian Church Order* is the ἀποστολικὴ παραδόσις of the Statue, and chapter 7, reflected in *CN.* I, 4, has been eirenically included by this time. Yet the problem here is that a composite work of this liturgical and communal character is too fluid in its development and compilation to be able to fix at any one point of time an individual author. Yet one may perhaps well ask, more fluid that the Συναγωγή and the *Catalogus* begun by the author of *El.* and completed by Hippolytus before further addition to the latter by the continuator of 235?

But let us now pass on to the other titles on the Statue to which we see no longer any cause to deny in principle Hippolytan authorship as part author of the library of a community. We begin with one that seems to show *prima facie* some correspondence with certain surviving remains of a similar work, but under closer analysis fails the test of genuineness.

5A 2. *The* ἀπόδειξις χρόνων, περὶ τοῦ πάσχα, and *De Pascha*

In connection with our discussion of the Χρονικῶν as the work of the author of *El.*, we have already made reference to the ἀπόδειξις χρόνων τοῦ Πάσχα as an inscription on the Statue, corrected by Hippolytus, the author himself of *Dan.* in the additions κατὰ Δανιήλ (4B 2.2.2.2). But the catalogue of works on the plinth also appears to mention a written version of this title of which the inscribed Paschal Table itself may be the whole or indeed a summary, since it adds to this title κατὰ ἐν τῷ πίνακι. The κατὰ which follows this title may therefore mean a written work "according to" or "corresponding to" or "answering to the description of" what is inscribed "in the table (ἐν τῷ πινακὶ)," on the side of the chair.

The question that we must now seek to answer is on what grounds can this work be claimed to be either identical with or different from the περὶ του Πάσχα/*De Pascha* of the Eusebius/Jerome catalogues? If it can be then, unless we are prepared to accept the Loi-Simonetti thesis of two writers of the same name producing a confused series of identically entitled works, serious objections to the two-authors hypothesis can be raised in terms of such external evidence. A further question will then be whether that work can be identified with one or more of six fragments usually found amongst the spurious works of St. John Chrysostom.

5A 2.1. *Eusebius* H.E. *VI,22*

In *H.E.* VI, 22 we seem to have reference to two works which Eusebius seems to separate from each other. The list is at all events clearly a selection of his known works since Eusebius begins: Ἱππόλυτος συντάττων μετὰ πλείστων ἄλλων ὑπομνημάτων καί... The first work immediately then mentioned and described more fully than the rest is entitled or described as τὸ περὶ τοῦ πάσχα σύγγραμμα. But amongst the remaining other works, each of which is also described as a σύγγραμμα (τῶν δὲ λοιπῶν αὐτοῦ συγγραμμάτων τὰ εἰς ἡμᾶς ἐλθόντα ἐστὶ τάδε·...), he mentions again a περὶ τοῦ πάσχα. Are these two separate works, or, if not, has Eusebius simply slipped and mentioned the same work twice?

Eusebius chooses to describe the first περὶ τοῦ πάσχα σύγγραμμα in details that go beyond a bare reference. He informs us that Hippolytus "sets out a register of the times (τῶν χρόνων ἀναγραφὴν ἐκθέμενος) of the Passover, and adds a table of 16 years (καὶ τινα κανόνα ἑκκαιδεκαετηρίδος) regarding the Passover (περὶ τοῦ πάσχα)." Although Eusebius makes no mention of the σύγγραμμα as inscribed on the Statue, nevertheless at first sight this work appears to be a copy on parchment of what we find there in stone. The Statue presented on the right hand side of the chair a cycle of 16 years (222-333) which arguably corresponds to the τινα κανόνα ἑκκαιδεκαετηρίδος. Furthermore Eusebius refers to "the first year of the emperor Alexander (τὸ πρῶτον ἔτος Ἀλεξάνδρου αὐτοκράτορος), " which seems to correspond with ἔτους α΄ βασιλείας ᾽Αλεξάνδρου αὐτοκράτορος of the Paschal Table of the Statue.[9]

Since Eusebius would thus be identifying a work on the Statue with Hippolytus, this passage was accordingly embarrassing to those who believed that the individual monument to the author of *El.* must at all cost be dissociated from the works of Hippolytus. Accordingly, Eusebius' words were interpreted as indicating a different ἀναγραφή ("register") and κανών ("list") from that of the Statue. ἐπὶ τὸ πρῶτον ἔτος αὐτοκράτορος ᾽Αλεξάν-δρος τοὺς χρόνους περιγράφει was interpreted as indicating that Eusebius' work ended rather than began with Severus Alexander's first year. As the example of Julius Africanus shows, such computations were commonplaces of the early years of the third century and connected with the eschatological frenzy represented by Montanism.

One attempt to lessen the force of this objection was Cappelle's suggestion that τοὺς χρόνους περιγράφει means "determines the chronological indications," and ἐπὶ τὸ πρῶτον ἔτος means "at the time" of Alexander, and thus was consistent with a table of later dates then being given.[10] Marcovich rejected this translation of περιγράφει, on the grounds that in each of the references cited by Capelle it meant not "determine" but "finish." However he supported the translation of ἐπι with the accusative meaning "at" and not "up until" and the possibility thus of translating it so in *H.E.* VI, 22.[11].

It is however difficult to square this interpretation with Jerome's translation in *De Vir. Ill.* 61 which in fact is *ad primum annum Alexandri imperatoris*. Jerome may have mistranslated Eusebius, which might imply also that he had no direct access to these two works. But on the other hand he might have had such access. The existence of such a register up until Alexander's first year available to a continuator would be quite plausible in view of the fact that the calculation of the Jewish Passovers on the Statue obviously involved events before Alexander's time. But such a register, before the work of the author of *El.* mentioned on the Statue, could not have been written by Hippolytus who, as we have argued, was not the predecessor of the author of the Συναγωγή nor of the Paschal Table of the Statue, but rather his successor and corrector of the former's work.[12]

---

[9] Cf. R. Cantalamessa, L' omelia «in S. Pascha» dello Pseudo-Ippolito di Roma, in *Scienze Filologiche e Letteratura* 16 (1967), p. 31-33.

[10] B. Capelle, A propos d'Hippolyte de Rome, in *RThAM* 19 (1952), p. 197-178 where he quotes Eusebius *H.E.* VI,6 (Clement of Alexandria εἰς τὴν Κομόδου τελευτὴν περιγράφει); II, 22,6; In *Ps.* XXX, 22 (*PG* 23, 237 B); *Dem. Evang.* VIII, 2,88; Diodorus Sicilius II,31, Xenephon *Mem.* I, 4,12 and *Hell.* VII, 5,13.

[11] M. Marcovich, Note on Hippolytus' Refutatio, in *JThS* n.s. 15 (1964), p. 71-72 where he adds *Acts* 4,5 (ἐπὶ τὴν αὔριον) and 3,1 (ἐπὶ τὴν τὴν ὥραν τῆς προσευχῆς τὴν ἐννάτην).

[12] M. Da Leonessa, *S. Ippolito di via Tiburtina*, (Poliglotta Vaticana: Rome 1935) worked out in detail this difference, whilst maintaining, fallaciously, as we have argued, "Vi è un catalogo di opere, le quali saranno certamente quelle scritte dal raffigurato." (p. 12)

But as Marcovich also points out,[13] it is clear from some of the twelve marginal inscriptions, which also include the corrections κατὰ Δανιήλ, that the *Computio* (ἀπόδειξις) was used to determine past Easter dates as well as future ones. If Hippolytus was the author of all twelve additions, then he will have used the Paschal Table to indicate the (past) date of the Passion by placing ΠΑΘΟΣ ΧΥ in the margin against *viii Kl. Apr*, that is to say the 25th March, the common day of the crucifixion that he held with the author of the Συναγωγή.[14] That purpose is clearly indicated on the Paschal Table where it is stated, after giving the Passover date for 13 April (Emb.) on Alexander's first year (222), that:

> The following years shall fall (ἔσται δὲ τοῖς ἑξῆς ἔτεσιν) according to what is laid out in the Table (καθὼς ὑποτέτακται ἐν τῷ πίνακι). And [Passover] took place (ἐγένετο δὲ ἐν τοῖς παρῳχηκόσιν) in the previous years on the dates cited (καθὼς σεσημείωται).

Eusebius could therefore have been referring to a parchment account of this Table and still described it as one that "determines the times (τοὺς χρόνους περιγράφει) up until the first year of Alexander (ἐπὶ τὸ πρῶτον ἔτος αὐτοκράτορος 'Αλεξάνδρος)." If Hippolytus was, as we have suggested, the author of the corrections κατὰ Δανιήλ, and if these appeared in his parchment version of the Table, then it would not be surprising if Eusebius had read on the document Hippolytus' name as the editor and corrector and cited this as the author's. This would additionally not be surprising if the history of the author of *El.* and Callistus had been suppressed by their reconciled successors, as we have suggested that the Liberian *Catalogus* and *Depositio* indicated in more than one way.

Thus we do not require the Loi-Simonetti hypothesis of two authors of the same name in order to reconcile our two-authors interpretation of the discrepant data of the *corpus*. Hippolytus corrected the ἀπόδειξις document and the inscriptions derived from it with the chronology κατὰ Δανιήλ as well as bringing up to his own time the Συναγωγή–Χρονικῶν of the author of *El.* Eusebius thus identifies the editor with the author (4B 2.2.3.2). Though this may be unusual in ancient literature where such identifications are usually the reverse, in this case it is by no means strange. A calendar, like a liturgy, is very much a community production, where the particular individual author is unimportant.

Eusebius remembers the Hippolytus commemorated by the Liberian *Catalogus* for the very reason that we have argued that the latter is commemorated there (4B 2.2.3.3). The martyrdom of Hippolytus is commemorated with that of Pontianus because he was the force that reconciled the estranged community of *El.* with that of Callistus' successor. The final end of

---

13 Ibid. p. 72.
14 See 4B 2.2.2.2 footnote 204.

the author of *El.*, along with any specifics about that of Callistus, is deliberately lacking there because the reconcilers wish only to remember who or what has reconciled them. Eusebius thus finds only Hippolytus in his sources.

Eusebius, as we have said, appears to mention two works each of which would admit of the title περὶ τοῦ πάσχα σύγγραμμα. Since there is a disputed Pascal homily attributed to Hippolytus which we are next to consider, we might well ask here whether Eusebius' second work could not correspond with the contents of that homily in the way that clearly a text version of the inscription of the ἀπόδειξις χρόνων, with its sixteen-year cycle, clearly would not?

A comparison with Jerome, *De Vir. Ill.* 61 would support the existence of two distinct works.

5A 2.2. *Jerome* De Vir. Ill. *61*

Jerome's catalogue is clearly dependent on Eusebius who is cited as an authority for his reference to these works.[15] However, his description is far more distinctive of two works, and he may have had direct access to both of them, as we have indicated, despite his translation, though neither he nor Eusebius makes reference to the inscription on the Statue itself beyond an account on parchment of what we read there. Jerome's description of the first work (σύγγραμμα) corresponds to a written version of the inscription of the ἀπόδειξις of the Statue (*in ratione paschae et temporum canone*). But the second σύγγραμμα of Eusebius is described, not as a *ratio* (ἀναγραφή) or a canon (κανών) but as one of a number of Scripture commentaries (*nonnullos in scripturas commentarios*), with the (in Jerome) quite different title of *De Pascha*. Jerome clearly knows titles of Hippolytus' works other than those given by Eusebius, which underlies the strong possibility that he had direct access both to the titles that he cites as well as those of Eusebius.[16]

I believe therefore that Cantalamessa was quite wrong in arguing that there was only one work on the Passover written by Hippolytus, the ἀπόδειξις χρόνων, and that Eusebius had carelessly mentioned the same work twice. Although Rufinus, in his translation of Eusebius, omits the second from the summary list, this was more likely to have been the former's own confusion due to a similarity of title which the latter suggests but which

---

[15] Jerome, *De Vir. Ill.* 61: Hippolytus, cuiusdam ecclesiae episcopus—nomen quippe urbis scire non potui—in ratione paschae et temporum canone scripsit et usque ad primum annum Alexandri imperatoris sedecim annorum circulum, quem Graeci ἑκκαιδεκαετηρίδα vocant, repperit, et Eusebio, qui super eodem pascha decem et novem annorum circulum, id est, ἐν-νεακαιδεκαετηρίδα composuit, occasionem dedit.

[16] It is unfortunate that the evidence of Jerome is suppressed in the form of footnote 19 whilst the ommission in a second work, Rufinus' translation, is emphasised in Cantalamessa (1967) p. 31.

Jerome denies.[17] In the light of the way in which Jerome cites a second work on the Passover, it is idle for Cantalamessa to appeal to Eusebius' citation of a single work of Theophilus of Antioch as though there were two.

The *ms.* tradition for Eusebius *H.E.* IV, 26,2 is extremely corrupt in one of the readings for the first περὶ ψυχῆς καὶ σώματος of two works of that title attributed to Melito of Sardis. If the alternative reading is original, then Eusebius has cited two quite different titles and no careless tendency of Eusebius in this regard can be derived from this example. Furthermore this very citation undermines his case in another way in that it mentions that Melito himself wrote two books περὶ τοῦ πάσχα (Μελίτονος, τὰ περὶ τοῦ πάσχα δύο), so that it is by no means impossible that Hippolytus may have done likewise.[18] Furthermore, it does not follow that because Eusebius made one error in Theophilus' case he necessarily made an identical one in that of Hippolytus.

Granted therefore that a separate *commentarius*, not mentioned on the Statue, as opposed to κανών that is, may have existed under the authorship of Hippolytus, can this be equated with any surviving fragment? We shall argue that, in the last analysis, it cannot, and that the second work of Hippolytus has been lost, apparently irretrievably.

5A 2.3. *Reconstruction of the alleged* περὶ τοῦ πάσχα

Martin admitted that there were two distinct works, but acknowledged the great difficulty in reconstructing the second which is not mentioned on the Statue.[19] There are six or seven homilies, usually published amongst the *Spuria* of St. John Chrysostom, and found in four *mss.* so attributed the ear-

---

17 Nicephorus Callistus, *Eccles. Hist.* 4,31 is clearly dependent on Eusebius *H.E.* VI, 22, but he would support Jerome against Rufinus in that clearly the writer, who adds titles to the Eusebian and Jerome lists, sees no incongruity in Eusebius' two works. I cannot see that, what is a clear citation of τὸ περὶ τοῦ πάσχα σύγγραμμα which contrasts with the second περὶ τοῦ πάσχα merits in any way the description "Niceforo... ripete tale e quale la notizia di Eusebio, ma è più reticente sull'esistenza di due Peri Pascha" in Cantalamessa (1967) p. 31 footnote 19. However, it is late evidence, dating from the beginning of the fourteenth century. "Il fatto che Girolamo (nella traduzione della *Storia ecclesiastica* di Eusebio) come pure taluni manoscritti omettono la seconda volta di riperterlo," (p. 32) depends on the objective assessment of the evidential value of those *mss.* themselves. As I have argued, Jerome's list is no mere "traduzione." The latter scribes themselves may accidentally or arbitrarily reduced two works to one.
18 Cf. Cantalamessa (1967) p. 32: "Un fatto assolutamente identico si ripete a proposito di Melitone e ciò potrebbe indicare che a Eusebio sia occorsa più d'una volta la svista di ripetere due volte il titolo d'una stessa opera. Nella lista degli scritti di Melitone... si legge due volte il titolo: περὶ ψυχῆς καὶ σώματος. Ma è molto improbabile che il vescovo di Sardi abbia scritto due opere con questo identico titolo..." But as I point out, the τὰ περὶ τοῦ πάσχα δύο show that it is by no means "molto improbabile" quite apart from the possibility of corruption in the *ms* tradition indicating that the mistake is not "assolutamente identico."
19 Cantalamessa (1967) p. 13; Cf. C. Martin, Un περὶ τοῦ πάσχα de S. Hippolyte retrouvé? in *RecSciRel* 16 (1926), p. 148: "... Eusèbe, qui nous a conservé le catalogue des oeuvres d'Hippolyte de Rome, lui attribue au moins deux écrits sur la Pâque.. Le second... reste enveloppé de plus de mystère..." and C. Martin, Hippolyte de Rome et Proclus de Constantinople Εἰς τὸ ἅγιον πάσχα. À propos de l'originalité d'un homélie attribuée à Proclus de Constantinople, in *RevSR* 33 (1937), p. 275: "Eusèbe de Césarée dans son Histoire ecclésiatique attribuait déjà à saint Hippolyte un PP, distinct de ses travaux de chronologie pascale."

liest of which dates from the tenth century.[20] But *Hom.* VI has demonstrably a separate transmission. Notwithstanding that textual transmission, subsequently Martin argued,[21] with some reservations, that all six homilies could have come from the lost περὶ τοῦ πάσχα of Hippolytus. This position was wholeheartedly endorsed by Loi[22] but opposed by Connolly,[23] Cantalamessa,[24] and Nautin.[25]

Let us first list the external evidence that would link *Hom.* VI with Hippolytus. We shall subsequently examine the purely internal evidence for including one or more of *Hom.* I-V.

5A 2.3.1. *External Evidence for* Hom. *VI in relation to I-V*

In each of the following fragments of *Hom.* VI alone we find attributions to Hippolytus and not to St. John Chrysostom:

(i) One third of its text is found in the *Gottaferrata ms.* B.α.LV (8-9th cent.) But here it is not attributed to Chrysostom but has the title ΙΠΠΟΛΥΤΟΥ ΕΠΙΣΚ. ΡΩΜΗΣ ΚΑΙ ΜΑΡΤΥΡΟΣ ΕΙΣ ΤΟ ΑΓΙΟΝ ΠΑΣΧΑ.[26] There are moreover seven additional fragments reclaimed as part of its text found in:

(ii) Nicetas, *Caten. in Lc.* has three of these putative fragments, the first, corresponding to the beginning of *Hom.* VI, is cited simply as Ἱππολύτου.[27] However the second, and the third, attributed by Achelis, has been subsequently found to be the work of Eustathius of Antioch, and the third by an unknown writer since it is only identifiable with Hippolytus' work if the attribution of the second fragment had succeeded.[28]

(iii) Lateran Synod of A.D. 649, prefaced by: τοῦ ἁγίου Ἱππολύτου ἐπισκόπου καὶ μάρτυρος ἐκ τῆς εἰς τὸ Πάσχα ἐξηγήσεως, and with a short commentary on a version of *Mk.* 14, 36 (τὸ μὲν πνεῦμα πρόθυμον ἡ δὲ σάρξ ἀσθενης) and *Lk.* 22,42 (μὴ τὸ θέλη-μά μου ἀλλὰ τὸν σὸν γινέσθω),[29]

---

[20] *P.G.* 59 cols 723-755.

[21] Martin (1926) and (1937).

[22] V. Loi, L' omelia «In sanctum Pascha» di Ippolito di Roma, in *Aug.* 17 (1977), p. 461-484.

[23] R.H. Connolly, New Attributions to Hippolytus, in *JThS* 46 (1945) p. 92-200.

[24] Cantalamessa (1967).

[25] P. Nautin, Homélies Pascales, I, Une homélie inspirée du traité sur la Pâque d'Hippolyte, in *SC* 27, (Paris 1950), p. 38-46.

[26] For the full text see C. Martin, Fragments palimpsestes d'un discours sur la Pâque attribué à saint Hippolyte de Rome (Crypt. B.α.LV), in *Annuaire de l'Institut de Philologie et d'Histoire Orientales et Slaves,* IV (1936) p. 355-363. Cf. Martin (1937) p. 270; Nautin (1950) p. 13-16.

[27] Martin (1925) p. 149; Martin (1937); P. Nautin, *Le dossier d'Hippolyte et de Méliton dans les florilèges dogmatiques et chez les historiens modernes,* (Paris: Les Éditions du Cerf 1953), p. 75. For a full discussion of this Catena and its relationship to the Hippolytan corpus, see Nautin (1953), chapt. 6.

[28] H. Achelis, Hippolytus, in *GCS,* I, 2 (1897); ——, Hippolytstudien, in *T.U.* 16,4 (1897), p. 202-211; Cf. M. Spanneut, Hippolyte ou Eustathe? Autour de la Chaîne de Nicetas sur l'Evangile selon saint Luc, in *MSR* 9 (1952), p. 215-220. Cf. also Cantalamessa (1967) p. 26: "Questi due frammenti, che portano il lemma: «sul vangelo di Luca,» sono dall'Achelis attribuiti al *Peri Pascha* di Ippolito per la sola ragione che il frammento seguente, desunto anch'esso dalla catena di Niceta sul vangelo di Luca, coincide, in parte, con un frammento siriaco recante questa indicazione: «di Ippolito vescovo sulla pasqua.»"

[29] Martin (1926) p. 152-153. *Mt.* 26,39 (οὐχ ὡς ἐγὼ θέλω ἀλλ᾽ ὡς σύ) follows *Mk.* 14,36 (οὐ τί ἐγὼ θέλω ἀλλὰ τί σύ). See also Nautin (1950) p. 34-35.

(iv) Two fragments in the second appendix of the Syriac *Florilegium Edessenum anonymum* of 562. This is an abridgment of the *florilegium* of the Monophysite Timothy Aelurus. The first fragment (72) is headed "By Hippolytus bishop, on the Passover," and the second " By the same."[30]

Regarding *Hom.* I-V, these are found along with VI and a seventh[31] in the following *ms.* each with variants of the title τὰ σαλπίγγα τοῦ ἐν ἁγίοις πατρὸς ἡμῶν᾽Ιωάννου Χρυσοστόμου:[32]

(i) Monastery of Vlatées, Thessalonica *ms. cod.* 6, fol. 394[r]-405[r] (10th century),[33]
(ii) Bodleian, Oxford *cod. Barocc. graec.* 212 fol. 320[v]-327[r] (16th century),[34]
(iii)Vatican, *Ottobonianus graec.* 101 (17th century).[35]
(iii) Monastry of Vatopedi, Mount Athos *cod. graec.* 318 (17th century).[36]
(iv) Venice, Marcienne Library *Marcianus graec.* App. II 59 (16th century).[37]

Thus it is clear that we have only external evidence for attributing *Hom.* VI to Hippolytus where that work has survived in isolation from I-V and VII. For the latter, the only external attribution is to John Chysostom.

Attempts have been made to associate *Hom.* VI also with the extract cited in the *Chronicon Paschale* under the rubric: καὶ πάλιν ὁ αὐτὸς ἐν τῷ πρώτῳ λόγῳ τοῦ περὶ τοῦ πάσχα συγγράμματος.. The passage which follows affirms the Johannine date for the Passion on 14 Nisan, Passover Day before the Passover meal, as does the ἀπόδειξις χρόνων of the Statue. But there is no indication in the text of *Hom.* VI, which is the only externally attested of the six to Hippolytus, of the Johannine dating of the Crucifixion. *In Pasc.* 49 implies that the Last Supper was a Passover meal, and that Jesus desire to suffer as the Passover Lamb was fulfilled in type as he ate with the disciples.[38]

---

30 Martin (1937) p. 271-273; Nautin (1953) p. 75 and p. 79. These two fragments are found in *Brit. Mus. syr.* 729, *addit.* 12156 edited by I. Rucker, Florilegium Edessenum anonymum (syriace ante 562), in *SbMn* 5 (1933) p. 65 (fragments 72 and 73). See also W. Wright, *Catalogue of Syriac Manuscripts in the British Museum*, Part II, p. 639-648.
31 We have omitted discussion of the seventh as a fourth century addition, on the grounds of Martin (1937) p. 268-269: "Quant à la septième pièce, sa date est certainement postérieure. Le doute, ici, n'est plus possible. Cette pièce n'a rien à voir avec les précédentes, ni pour le fond ni pour la forme; elle n'a rien d'exégétique, et ne s'occupe en rien de l'interprétation du chapitre XII de l'Exode. L'attention de l'auteur porte avant tout sur la fixation chronologique de la fête... Ce n'est pas même une homélie destinée à la fête de Pâques, il faut plutôt la placer au début soit du carême soit du printemps."
32 Cited and described in greater detail in Martin (1937) p. 265-266, who mentions a further *ms.* used by Savile but unable to be found (p. 265).
33 S. Eustratiades, Κατάλογος τῶν ἐν μονῇ Βλατέων (Τσαοὺς–Μοναστῆρι) ἀποκειμένων κωδίκων, (Salonica 1918) p. 16-19; Nautin (1950) p. 16-18.
34 H. Coxe, *Catalogi codicum manuscriptorum bibliothecae Bodleianae*, pars prima, (Oxford: U. P. 1853) col. 369-372; Nautin (1950) p. 18-21
35 Nautin (1950) p. 26.
36 S. Eustratides, *Catalogue of the Greek Manuscripts in the Library of the Monastery of Vatopedi on Mount Athos*, (Cambridge Mass.: 1924); Nautin (1950) p. 26-27.
37 Nautin (1950) p. 21-23.
38 *In Pasc.* 49, 1-2: αὕτη ἡ σωτήριος ἐπιθυμία τοῦ᾽Ιησοῦ... δεῖξαι μὲν τοὺς τύπους ὡς τύπους, τὸ δὲ ἱερὸν σῶμα τοῖς μαθηταῖς αὐτοῦ ἀντιδοῦναι... διὰ τοῦτο οὐκ ἐπιθυμεῖ τοσοῦτον φαγεῖν ὅσον ἐπιθυμεῖ παθεῖν, ἵν᾽ ἡμᾶς τοῦ διὰ βρώσεως πάθους ἐλευθερώσῃ. All references to *In Pasc.* are to the Nautin (1950) edition.

Moreover, in view of the fact that we have defended the existence of two works in the Hippolytan *corpus* dealing with the Passover, we need not necessarily assign this σύγγραμμα to a lost section of *Hom.* VI. The words quoted could well have corresponded to a note defending the inscription of the ΠΑΘΟC ΧC against the 25th March 30 A.D. in the written account of the inscription, which we have argued to be a separate work from the *De Pascha*/περὶ τοῦ πάσχα of the Jerome/Eusebius lists (5A 2.1-5A 2.2).[39] In consequence the authorship of *Hom.* VI would be a quite separate issue from the authorship of the fragment found in the *Chronicon Paschale*.

If that issue is therefore a separate one, we must say firstly and once again that no problem arises for the two-authors thesis from the fact that a citation from the written work (σύγγραμμα), corresponding to the ἀπόδειξις χρόνων on the Statue, is here as in Eusebius attributed to Hippolytus. We need contrive no thesis about two authors with an identical name, since the fact in question has ceased to be embarrassing. In the light of our argument, there is no difficulty in admitting *prima facie* that there may be the works of two or more authors listed on the Statue.

Furthermore, there are two works listed by Eusebius of which Hippolytus may be the author of one (περὶ τοῦ πάσχα) and the final editor of the other (ἀπόδειξις χρόνων) giving his name to the final work. We can therefore deal with the issue of the authorship of *Hom.* VI separate from the fragment from the *Chronicon Paschale*. Indeed it would be theoretically possible to assign the original version of the ἀπόδειξις to the author of *El.* and *Hom.* VI to Hippolytus. There would be no need to combine the former with the latter so as to constitute one work, let alone combine it in addition with *Hom.* I-V for which there is no shred of external evidence.

What can be said, therefore, regarding internal evidence for that identification?

5A 2.3.2. *Internal Evidence for* Hom.*VI in relation to I-V*

The justification for publishing all six Homilies together under the name of Hippolytus—whether or not with the qualification of "Pseudo-"—was always made on internal grounds. Connolly's original examination of the issue reached two distinct conclusions, namely that, on stylistic grounds, (i) *Hom.* I-V are by the same author, and (ii) *Hom.* VI is by a different author but neither in the case of (i) nor of (ii) is the author Hippolytus.

In the case of (i) there is the clear contrast between I-V and VI in terms of ἅγιον πνεῦμα or τὸ πνεῦμα τὸ ἅγιον in the latter, and τὸ θεῖον πνεῦμα in the former.[40] παρουσία or ἡ προτέρα παρουσία (I, III, IV, and V) contrasts with ἐπιδημία as does πάσχα in the sense of ὑπέρβασις rather than πάθος

---

[39] M. Richard, Comput et chronographie chez saint Hippolyte, in *MSR* 7 1950, p. 242.
[40] *In Pasc.* 3,2; 6,2; 10,1; 15,2; 45,3; 47,2; 55,2-3.

(VI,5).[41] Furthermore, in the former sacred writers are mentioned by name or occupation, but in VI Scripture citations are in terms of πνεῦμα, τὸ θεῖον πνεῦμα or ἡ (θεία) γράφη. There are moreover important typological differences such as in *Hom.* I and V the five days (10-14th Nisan) are the five ages of the world, whereas in VI,3 they are the duration of Christ's custody with the High Priest.[42]

Regarding (ii), Connolly pointed out that (a) the style of VI hardly corresponds to the description of Photius, *Bibliotheca*, 121, (b) θεῖον πνεῦμα is never used in other works attributed to Hippolytus, (c) Scripture is never cited as described in the last paragraph, and (d) ἐπιδημία is never used for παρουσία. The ascription of *Hebrews* to Paul in VI is moreover non-Hippolytan.[43]

Accordingly Cantalamessa followed Connolly in rejecting Hippolytan authorship of both I-V and VI. But he sided with Martin in nevertheless accepting the possibility of a single author for both I-V and VI, despite the clear differences established by the latter which Martin had refused to accept. At very least in this regard Connolly's position was strong in view of the fact that external evidence, as we have seen, only connected VI with the name of Hippolytus. Cantalamessa's acceptance of I-V along with VI as part of a single work was too quick in view the high degree of tentativeness with which Martin had advocated that unity.[44]

Martin's argument was that I-V constituted *une unité organique* on the grounds that their subject matter was homogenous and centred around *Ex.* 12. III (καὶ ταῦτα ἡμῖν ἤδη προείρηται), and that IV (ὧν τὰ μὲν ἤδη τεθεώρηκας, τὰ δὲ ἐφεξῆς θεώρει κατὰ δύναμιν) contain references to the homily that precedes. But the only grounds on which VI was to be included in *unité organique* was that it was to be preached during the Saturday Vigil, and this placed it in the same context as I-V which were intended for the preceding days, probably Friday-Saturday.[45] But set against Connolly's account of the differences between VI and I-V such a point is far from conclusive. I therefore follow Nautin in his edition of regarding Homily VI as the only real contender as a work of Hippolytus.

Cantalamessa's further conclusion, against Richard, was that this single Homily was not the product of later Arianism but an example of second

---

41 Ibid. 7; 47,3; 56.
42 Ibid. 21, cf. Connolly (1945) p. 194-195.
43 Ibid. p. 196-198.
44 Martin (1937) p. 268: "Il est donc difficile de fournir une preuve, nette et décisive, péremptoire, que la sixième homélie ait été réellement rattachée *dès l'origine* aux cinq premières. Du moins, cette homélie, étonnamment apparentée aux précédentes, pour le fond, la méthode exégétique, le sens général donné, très probablement ... du même auteur, et à moins d'un hasard extraordinaire, a dû être jointe *très tôt* à la collection."
45 Ibid. p. 267: "Cette homélie fut certainement prononcée durant l'office nocturne du samedi de Pâques à l'aurore du jour. De ce point de vue elle fait suite d'une certaine manière aux précédentes homélies, qui manifestement n'étaient pas destinées à cet office nocturne du samedi au dimanche mais aux jours précédents, probablement le vendredi et le samedi."

century literary *genre* that was the Paschal Homily otherwise exemplified in
Melito of Sardis. But Loi more recently has advocated the thesis that the
problems for Hippolytan authorship can be removed, as well as the integrity
of a single composition can be defended, as a result of acknowledging a
double authorship of the Hippolytan *corpus*, and by attributing the alleged
single work, περὶ τοῦ πάσχα, to the author of *El.* and associated works.

It is to this thesis, that we shall find highly questionable, that we shall
now turn.

5A 2.4. *Loi, the author of* El., *and the* περὶ τοῦ πάσχα

Loi believes that the two-authors thesis gives support to Martin's argument
that, on internal evidence alone, all six of the Homilies attributed to St. John
Chrysostom are Hippolytus' and not simply *Hom.* VI for which there is the
external evidence that we have presented (5A 2.2.1). He apparently believes
that the differences noted by Connolly (5A 2.2.2) between Hippolytus'
works and both *Hom.* I-V and VI, considered separately and the former distinguished from the latter by internal criteria, can be obviated by relating the
contents to works associated with *El.* and the Statue, in contrast with works
unmentioned there and associated with *Dan.* and *Ant.*[46] Let us now list what
those allegedly common features are that supposedly united both I-V with
VI and both to *El.* and associated works.

5A 2.4.1. *The Johannine dating of the Crucifixion*

In *Pasc.* 49, in claiming that τοῦτο ἦν τὸ πάσχα ὃ ἐπεθύμησεν ὑπὲρ ἡμῶν ὁ
᾽Ιησοῦς παθεῖν, supports the exegesis of *Lk.* 22, 14-16 that combines nicely
the Johannine and the Synoptic dating by suggesting that the Last Supper
was both a Passover meal and in type Christ's sacrifice on the following
day. That dating and exegesis, as we have seen, was quite contrary to that
found in *Chronicon Paschale* (2A 2.4) and attributed to Hippolytus (τὸ δὲ
πάσχα οὐκ ἔφαγεν, ἀλλ᾽ ἔπαθεν). Furthermore, the Συναγωγή–Χρονικῶν
(Bauer and Helm (1955) 698) also reflects the latter but not the former exegesis when it states: *a generatione autem Christi post XXX annos cum
passus est dominus pascha celebratur, ipse enim erat iustum pascha.*[47]

Furthermore, once we reject the *ms.* tradition that gives us a different
length in Hippolytus *Dan.* for the life of Christ, as we have done (4B

---

[46] Loi, *Aug.* 17 (1977) p. 462: "Se si procede, infatti, a un confronto tra l'omelia *In sanctum Pascha* e il blocco delle opere catalogate sulla statua romana o ad esse direttamente ricol-
legabili per testimonianze esterne ed interne, quali l'*Elenchos*... e i frammenti del *Commento
alla Genesi*... balzano evidenti tante affinità e corrispondenze dottrinali e linguistiche, da im-
porre l'autenticità ippolitana dell'omelia, sicché i dati della critica interna confermano i dati
della tradizione testuale forniti dal codice di Grottaferrata, dal concilio Lateranense, e dai
frammenti siriaci del *Florilegium Edessenum anonymum*." I find however this statement confusing. As I point out in the text, the "dati della tradizione testuale" of these witnesses merely
confirm "l'autenticità ippolitana" of Homily VI " per testimonianze esterne". Homilies I-V
need therefore very strong internal corroboration to justify their inclusion in a single work περὶ
τοῦ πάσχα written by Hippolytus, which I argue to be lacking.
[47] Ibid. p. 463.

2.2.2.1-2.2.2), and once we recognise the hand of Hippolytus as correcting the inscription on the Statue and related works, the Johannine dating is no longer sufficient to distinguish Hippolytus as author of *Dan.* from works associated with the author of *El.* Furthermore, in view of our interpretation of the Statue as a community artefact (4B 1), it is impossible to use the Johannine dating to inviduate a particular author. Not only did Hippolytus, as we have argued, use and correct both the inscriptions and their written form in the ἀπόδειξις but he also updated the Συναγωγή–Χρονικῶν.

Furthermore, in view of the community character of these works, their chronological data cannot be used to individuate either Hippolytus or his predecessor. Melito of Sardis, amongst many others, also used in his paschal homily the Johannine dating. It was this fact amongst others that lead Cantalamessa to regard the περὶ τοῦ πάσχα as an anonymous work from second century Asia Minor with no necessary direct connection with Hippolytus of Rome.[48] Moreover, in view of the canonical status of the Fourth Gospel, it would not be surprising to find this theme made use of and the chronological conflict with the Synoptics ignored in a devotional text, without assuming here a feature that will distinguish necessarily individuals or communities. Loi clearly needs other more individual points of comparison which we must allow him now to present.

5A 2.4.2. *Passover and Creation:* In Pasc. *17,2*

The first point of comparison that we shall consider is the claim the creation of the world took place on the 14th Nisan with reference to a secret tradition of the Hebrews.[49] As Loi points out, on this idea is based also the further development of homiletic imagery in *In Pasc.* 3,3 where the paschal celebration is described as οὐρανοῦ καὶ γῆς ἱερὰ τελετὴ παλαιὰ καὶ καινὰ προφητεύουσα μυστήρια and in 39 as τὴν ἑβδοματικὴν ἐπὶ τοῦ κόσμου... περίοδον.[50]

But here Loi has failed to notice a fundamental difference between what is implied by the ἀπόδειξις inscription and such a claim. The Συναγωγή–Χρονικῶν, as we have seen, demanded 5502 years between Adam and the birth of Christ. This, as Ogg pointed out, implies that the first full-moon of the world, and thus the first Passover date would have been 29th March

---

[48] Melito, *In Pasc.* 80: καὶ σὺ μὲν ἦσθα εὐφραινόμενος, ἐκεῖνος δὲ λιμώττων· σὺ ἔπινες οἶνον καὶ ἄρτον ἤσθιες, ἐκεῖνος δὲ ὄξος καὶ χολήν. The "many others" include Apollinaris of Hierapolis and Clement of Alexandria, see Cantalamessa (1967) p. 67-81; and S.G. Hall, Melito of Sardis, in *OECD* (1979) p. xxiii-xxvii. It was no doubt Martin's tentativeness about Hippolytan authorship that made him consider one author instead of several second century authors for *Homilies* I-V and including VI. See also 2 A 2.3-4 for other groups such as the Quartodecimans and their relationship to the community of the Statue.

[49] *In Pasc.* 17,2: ...ὁ μὲν οὖν ἐν ἀπορρήτοις λεγόμενος Ἑβραίων λόγος τοῦτόν φησι τὸν καιρὸν εἶναι ἐν ᾧ ὁ τῶν ὅλων τεχνίτης καὶ δημιουργὸς θεὸς τότε ἐδημιούγησε τὸ πᾶν, καὶ τοῦτο εἶναι τῆς κτίσεως τὸ πρῶτον ἄνθος...

[50] Ibid. 39: ἐκεῖνοι μὲν οὖν ἄζυμα ἐσθιέτωσαν ἑπτὰ ἡμέρας, τὴν ἑβδοματικὴν ἐπὶ τοῦ κόσμου μελετῶντες περίοδον καὶ τὴν ἐπὶ γῆς ἔννομον ἐσθίοντες τροφήν...

against which would have been written, to use English rather than Greek let-
ters to indicate clearly the sequence, "E D C B A G F." That which was in-
scribed in fact began with 13th April appropriate for "G F E D C B A" was
solely due to the appropriateness of this to the first year of Alexander
Severus onwards, and subsequent Passovers against which the date of the
Christian Easter could be calculated according to what we have argued to be
Hippolytus' adaptation of the Asiatic and Quartodeciman practice to the
Roman one (2A 2.3-4).

But would the author of *El.* have therefore regarded the creation of the
world as taking place on 14th Nisan which was March 29th of the first year
of the eight year cycle? We possess a Pseudo-Cyprianic work *De Pascha
Computus* of the year 243 which argued on account of *Gen.* 1 that the world
would have already been in existence four days since the moon was only
created on the fourth day. The world was therefore created on 25th March. If
Pseudo-Cyprian was following in this detail the author of the ἀπόδειξις–inscription, as Ogg believes, then the latter clearly would not have held that
the creation of the world began with a Passover day.[51]

That he did not so believe is indicated by the fact that the belief in cre-
ation on Passover day is attributed to the heretic Monoimus in *El.* VIII, 14,6.
"The universe is (τὸ δὲ ὅλον ἐστί)... a new festival and one which grows not
old (καινή καὶ μὴ παλαιουμένη ἑορτή)... eternal (αἰώνιος)... observed as the
Passover of the Lord God (κυρίου τοῦ θεοῦ πάσχα, διατηρούμενον)."[52]
Furthermore he continues: "For the whole world (ὅλος γὰρ ὁ κόσμος), and
all the first principles of creation (καὶ πάντα τὰ τῆς κτίσεως στοιχεῖα), are a
Passover (πάσχα ἐστίν)." (*El.* VIII, 14,7) Thus this interpretation of the typology of *Ex.* 12, 18-19 services a particular heretical account of creation,
and would hardly have been endorsed subsequently as orthodoxy by the author of *El.* in another work.

The primeval chaos as unleavened. "Creation" (τὸ ὅλον) is "that which
consists as generally unleavened, in the one letter fragment that is the world
(τὴν ὑπάρχουσαν ἐν τῇ μιᾷ κεραίᾳ τοῦ κόσμου τὴν κτίσιν ἄζυμον οὖσαν ἐν
τοῖς ἅπασιν)." This "letter fragment... needs a certain substance (οὐσίας

---

[51] Ogg (1962) p. 5-6. Salmon (1873) p. 84-85 argued that Pseudo-Cyprian had read and
detected the inaccuracies of the ἀπόδειξις– inscription and had "been led, by a misunderstanding of the first chapter of Genesis, to place the moons originally on wrong days.
Accordingly, he pushes on each of Hippolytus' full moons three days, and having thus made
the table fairly represent the phenomena of his own time, he imagines that the sixteen years'
cycle so corrected will show all the full moons, past and future." But Pseudo-Cyprian would
not have read the 29th March on the first line but 13th April, so that such a correction would
have been by no means straightforward. Furthermore that the first day of the creation was a
Passover day was the view of a heretic according to *El.* as we note. It seems better therefore to
accept that the author of *El.* and of the Συναγωγή–Χρονικῶν was able to work out the
exegesis of *Genesis* for himself.
[52] *El.* VIII, 14,6: τὸ δὲ ὅλον ἐστί, φησί, τοῖς μὴ πεπηρωμένοις παντελῶς τὴν
διάνοιαν μυστήριον, καινή καὶ μὴ παλαιουμένη «ἑορτὴ νόμιμος» αἰώνιος εἰς τὰς
γενεὰς ἡμῶν, κυρίου τοῦ θεοῦ πάσχα, διατηρούμενον τοῖς δυναμένοις βλέπειν...

τινὸς) that is as it were with the leaven from outside (οἱονεὶ ζύμης ἔξωθεν)," and this is why ὅλος γὰρ ὁ κόσμος... πάσχα ἐστίν (*El.* VIII, 14,7-8) . In order to explain the enigmatic reference to the κεραία in this passage, we need to go back to the early explanation of the symbolism. The κεραία is taken to be a letter-stroke that is part of the ἰῶτα which symbolises the name of ᾿Ιησοῦς.[53] The First Man, Jesus, is therefore the ἰῶτα from whom comes his offspring the heavenly Son of Man, as the κεραία, who flows through and therefore "leavens" the created world.[54]

But it is quite foreign for the author of *El.* to adapt heretical views to his own Christology. In this respect we shall argue, in section 4D below, that this author is quite different from the Hippolytus of *C.N.* who is quite happy to do so, albeit as softened by his biblical exegesis. Loi himself finally has to concede that there is no direct relationship between the heretical exegesis of *El.* VIII,12 and *In Pasc.* 3,3, 17,2 and 39, but simply a common hermeneutical tradition.[55] Indeed, his admission was quite correct, since the typology of the leaven is quite different from that of the "leavening of creation" in Monoimus' cosmology in *El.* VIII, 14,6. In *In Pasc.* 39,1, to the contrary, τὴν ἑβδοματικὴν ἐπὶ τοῦ κόσμου περίοδον refers to the eating of unleavened bread as a type of "eating the legal nourishment from the ground (τὴν ἐπὶ γῆς ἔννομον ἐσθίοντες τροφήν)" before Christ's coming after which one can be nourished spiritually by the antitype that is Christ's sacrifice.[56]

A similar point might be made regarding another alleged parallel, namely the power of the Son of Man in *El.* VIII, 14,3 as typologically equivalent to Moses' rod with which he struck the water and changed it into blood, and the typological equivalence to the power of the λόγος in *In Pasc.* 35. In the former passage, Moses' rod is an allegory of the Son of Man as the κεραία or letter stroke of the phenomenal world from the transcendental world of the᾿I, which as we saw was the cosmic᾿Ιησοῦς. The Son of Man (ἡ ἰῶτα) is both "simple"(ἁπλῆ) but also "variegated"(ποικίλη) in that he contains within himself the residue of the forces of the transcendental world.[57]

---

53 *El.* X, 17,1-2: καὶ τὰ γενόμενα πάντα, καθὼς Μωσῆς λέγει, μὴ ἀπὸ τοῦ πρώτου ἀνθρώπου γεγονέναι, ἀλλ᾿ ἀπὸ τοῦ υἱοῦ τοῦ ἀνθρώπου, οὐχ ὅλου δέ, ἀλλ᾿ ἐκ μέρους τινὸς αὐτοῦ. εἶναι γὰρ τὸν υἱὸν τοῦ ἀνθρώπου ἰῶτα– ὅ ἐστι δεκάς, κύριος ἀριθμός...– τοῦτον δὴ οὕτως εἶναι ἰῶτα ἕν, καὶ κεραίαν μίαν, τέλειον ἐκ τελείου ῥυεῖσαν κεραία ἄνωθεν...

54 *El.* VIII, 12,2: Μονόϊμος... λέγει ἄνθρωπον εἶναι τὸν πρῶτον– ὅς ἐστιν ἡ ἀρχὴ τῶν ὅλων– ἀγέννητον, ἄφθαρτον, ἀΐδιον, καὶ υἱὸν ἀνθρώπου τοῦ προειρημένου γεννητὸν καὶ παθητόν.

55 Loi, *Aug.* 17 (1977) p. 464-465: "... questo non significa necessariamente che Ippolito, riconosciuto quale autore di *IP*, abbia dedotto l'esegesi proposta in *IP* direttamente da Monoimo; si potrebbe trattare di tematica comune alla tradizione gnostica e alla tradizione ortodossa analogamente a quegli altri casi che segnaleremo nel corso della nostra analisi..."

56 *In Pasc.* 39: «ἡμῶν δὲ τὸ πάσχα τέθυται Χριστὸς» καὶ τὸ νέον φύραμα τῆς ἱερᾶς αὐτοῦ συγκράσεως ἀπειλήφαμεν ὅλοι δυνάμει κρείττονι ἀναζυμωθέντες καὶ ἀναφυραθέντες αὐτοῦ τῷ πνεύματι.

57 *El.* VIII, 14,3: ὅταν οὖν, φησίν, ῥάβδον λέγῃ Μωϋσῆς στρεφομένην ποικίλως εἰς τὰ πάθη τὰ κατὰ τὴν Αἴγυπτον– ἅτινα, φησίν, ἐστὶ τῆς κτίσεως ἀλληγορούμενα σύμ-

In the latter passage, however, the reference is not to the powers of creation, but to the miracles of deliverance from Egypt, and to the ἑπτὰ πνεύματα τὰ ἅγια... τοῦ θεοῦ in *Is.* 11,2 displayed there.[58]

In the absence therefore of what Loi admits to be a lack of a direct literary relationship between the two works, where is the more general common tradition as evidence for equivalence of authorship? Arguments for a 'common tradition' are usually deployed to deny an equivalence of authorship. Such an argument does not take us therefore beyond Cantalamessa's conclusion of a second-century Asiatic author who may in fact be a collection of authors.

Let us however continue to consider Loi's principle further examples.

5A 2.4.3. ὁ πρὸ ἑωσφόρου *and the* περὶ τοῦ πάσχα

It is this Christological appellative and the radical departure from patristic developments of it by the author of *C.N.* that we saw to be the truly cogent features proving the case for two authors in the Hippolytan *corpus* (4A 2). But we saw also that, with reference both to Justin, Theophilus, and Irenaeus, exegetes of *Ps.* 109,3 had already proceeded to draw conclusions regarding the pre-incarnate λόγος which *C.N.* self-consciously attempted to change (4A 2.1). In consequence, there is a problem for Loi's argument in that the use of the common patristic exegesis in *El.* X, 33,11 constitute grounds for identifying *In Pasc.* with the author of *El.*, but not with Hippolytus. The case is clearly quite the reverse. Had *In Pasc.* shown parallels with *C.N.* then this would have constituted such evidence. But, as matters stand, *In Pasc.* is simply in a general patristic tradition of exegesis.

Moreover it is to be noted that, although ὁ πρὸ ἑωσφόρου may appear as an epithet in *In Pasc.* 1,1 (ὁ πρὸ ἑωσφόρου καὶ φωστήρων),[59] 3,2 (τὸν πρὸ

βολα–, οὐκ εἰς πλείονα πάθη τῶν δέκα σχηματίζει τὴν ῥάβδον, ἥτις ἐστίν, φησίν, ἡ τοῦ ἰῶτα μία κεραία, ἁπλῆ καὶ ποικίλη. Cf. Loi, *Aug.* 17 (1977) p. 464.

[58] *In Pasc.* 35: αἱ βακτηρίαι ὑμῶν ἐν ταῖς χερσὶν ὑμῶν, τῆς θείας δυνάμεως τὰ σημεῖα, τῆς λογικῆς ἰσχύος τὰ ἐρείσματα, ῥάβδος ἡ διὰ Μωϋσεως, ῥάβδος ἡ διὰ Ἀαρών, ῥάβδος ἡ καρυΐνη, ῥάβδος ἡ τεμοῦσα βάθη θαλάσσης, ῥάβδος ἡ γλυκάνασα πικρίαν πηγῶν, ῥάβδος ἐφ᾽ ἣν τὰ ἑπτὰ πνεύματα τὰ ἅγια ἀνεπαύσατο τοῦ θεοῦ [*Is.* 11,2].

[59] *In Pasc.* 1,1: ...ζωὴ τοῖς ὅλοις ἐφηπλώθη καὶ φωτὸς ἀπλήστου τὰ ὅλα γέμει, ἀνα–τολαὶ ἀνατολῶν ἐπέχουσι τὸ πᾶν καὶ ὁ πρὸ ἑωσφόρου καὶ φωστήρων, ἀθάνατος καὶ πολύς, ἐπανθεῖ μέγας Χριστὸς τοῖς ὅλοις ὑπὲρ ἥλιον. Here the present, cosmic Christ is welcomed in adoration, rather than his pre-existent status explored, and the reference, as in 3,2 (footnote 61 following), is to the resurrection at early dawn when ζωὴ and ὁ ἀθάνατος rises πρὸ ἑωσφόρου.

ἑωσφόρου ἀνατέλλοντα),[60] and 55,2 (τὸν πρὸ ἑωσφόρου),[61] the ascriptions are poetic and imprecise. The imagery is not developed into the theological concept of being begotten before the morning star. Furthermore, the references to πρὸ ἑωσφόρου in 1,1 and 3,2 are, in the context of the Easter Vigil, clearly to Christ arising with the dawn, "before the morning star," on the day of the resurrection. Though 55,2 is pre-resurrection, even here the title may be a reference to him who has already been greeted at the Easter dawn with this post-resurrection title.[62]

By contrast, in *In Pasc.* 17,3 the pre-existence of Christ is described in terms of τῶν πάντων νοητῶν τε καὶ ὁρατῶν πρωτόγονος ἐστι καὶ πρωτότοκος ἀπ᾽ ἀρχῆς.[63] But there is no connection drawn between the pre-incarnate state of Christ so described, and either λόγος or παῖς with πρὸ ἑωσφόρου from *El.* X, 33,11, or with γεννηθείς from *In Ps.* 16.[64] Indeed λόγος (as opposed to λογικὸς) is only found rarely in this sense and παῖς not at all.[65]

It is not therefore these terms in themselves that are unique to the author of *El.* and *In Ps.* but their conjunction. It is their conjunction in *El.* repeated in *In Ps.* that enables the latter to be grouped with works associated with *El.* as opposed to those associated with *CN.* (4A 2). πρωτόγονος is found in *In Pasc.* 17,3, but also in Justin 1 *Apol.* 58,3, so that the reference is not suffi-

---

60 Ibid. 3,2: ἑορταζέτωσαν καὶ οἱ τῶν ἀστέρων χοροὶ τὸν πρὸ ἑωσφόρου ἀνατέλλοντα μηνύοντες... Once again the reference is highly poetic, with its imagery of the stars "revealing him who rose before the morning star," but one should note that the image is ἀνατέλλοντα and not γεννηθέντα, and that the ἀνατέλλοντα is a reference to the risen Christ and not to the generation of the λόγος before creation. The writer ends 3,2 with the exhortation ἑορταζέτω καὶ πᾶσα ἀνθρωπίνη ψυχὴ εἰς τὴν παλιγγενεσίαν δι᾽ ἀναστάσεως ἀναψυχουμένη, thus making the context of early Easter dawn absolutely clear.

61 Ibid. 55,2: τότε οὐρανοὶ μὲν ἐσαλεύθησαν, ἀρχαὶ δὲ ἐκινήθησαν, ὑπερκόσμιοι θρόνοι καὶ νόμοι, τὸν ἀρχιστράτηγον τῆς μεγάλης δυνάμεως ὁρῶντες κρεμάμενον, μικροῦ δ᾽ ἂν ἐξέπεσον καὶ οἱ ἀστέρες τοῦ οὐρανοῦ, τὸν πρὸ ἑωσφόρου βλέποντες ἁπλούμενον... Once again τὸν πρὸ ἑωσφόρου enters a highly poetic passage from the reference to the heavenly powers being shaken and the stars falling at the sight of the cross of Christ. πρὸ ἑωσφόρου appears here alone as a pre-resurrection title, but hardly clearly to the pre-incarnate Christ. It arguably refers to what had happens to him who has already, post-resurrection, been greeted with this description. There is no theological intention, as with *El.* and *C.N.*, albeit a different intention in both cases.

62 Cf footnotes 59 and 60 with 61.

63 *In Pasc.* 17,3: ... νομίζω δὲ, ὃ καὶ μᾶλλον πεπίστευκα, διὰ τὴν τοῦ πάσχα πνευματικὴν ἑορτὴν ἀρχὴν καὶ κεφαλὴν καὶ πρώτην ἡγεμονίαν παντὸς τοῦ χρόνου καὶ αἰῶνος νενομίσθαι... ἵνα ὡς ὁ Κύριος τῶν παντῶν νοητῶν τε καὶ ἀοράτων πρωτόγονος ἐστι καὶ πρωτότοκος ἀπ᾽ ἀρχῆς, οὕτως καὶ ὅδε ὁ μὴν ὁ τὴν ἱερὰν τετιμημένος τελετὴν πρῶτος γεγένηται τοῦ ἐνιαυτοῦ καὶ παντὸς αἰῶνος ἀρχή.

64 *In Ps.* 16: καὶ ἐν ἑτέρῳ δὲ πάλιν «Ψαλμὸς τῷ ἀγαπητῷ» [*Ps.* 109]. τίς δ᾽ ἂν εἴη ὁ ἀγαπητὸς ἄλλος, ἀλλ᾽ ἢ ὁ παῖς τοῦ θεοῦ, λόγος ὁ «πρὸ ἑωσφόρου» γεννηθείς, δι᾽ οὗ τὰ πάντα ἐποίησεν ὁ πατήρ; All references to the Homily on the Psalms are cited as *In Ps.* from the text found in Nautin (1953) p. 161-188.

65 λόγος is found in *In Pasc.* 2,2 as the eucharistic words of Institution together with the chalice (καὶ ὁ κρατὴρ θείου γέμων αἵματός τε καὶ πνεύματος) that are the antitypes of the blood and the strip with which it is saturated. In 4, 1 the λόγος is not a pre-existent entity but the spiritual food of the Eucharist, and the events antitypical to the Passover that it represents (ἵνα δὲ καὶ κατὰ μέρος ἐστιαθῶμεν τοῦ λόγου). In 45,1 αὐτὸς ὁ λόγος is the title of Christ acting as redeemer (ὅλον τὸν ἀγῶνα τὸν ὑπὲρ ἡμῶν ἀνεδέξατο, πειθόμενος ταῖς πατρῴαις ἐντολαῖς), with the theme of pre-existence unexplored.

ciently unique of itself to constitute an argument for common authorship on the basis of its use alone.[66]

ὁ μονογενὴς υἱὸς τοῦ πατρός is found in *In Ps.* 20, in conjunction with ὁ παῖς τοῦ θεοῦ, ὁ λόγος, and with ἡ σοφία, but once again we find a contrast with *In Pasc.*[67] μονογενής is found in connection with πρωτότοκος alone in *In Pasc.* 46,1.[68] But unless in the latter μονογενής is not only linked with πρωτότοκος (πρωτόγονος) but also, and therefore decisively, with πρὸ ἑωσ‑φόρου, and then with παῖς, the connection is by no means conclusive. It is after all an allusion to *Jn.* 1,14 and 18, the use of which would not be re‑markable in the general literature of groups accepting the Johannine dating of the Passion. Once again Loi appeals to the use of μονογενὴς υἱός in *El.*,[69] but once again he is citing reports of Gnostic accounts to which the author did not subscribe, which is dubious evidence for the authorship of a text where such usage is the author's own.[70] It was indeed Hippolytus, as author of *C.N.* 15,7, who used μονογενής to refer, not to the pre‑existent λόγος as ἄσαρκος but to the post‑incarnational υἱὸς τέλειος.[71]

5A 2.4.4. *Descensus ad Infernos*

We have already demonstrated the common authorship of *El.* and the περὶ τοῦ παντός on the basis of a shared description of the geography of Hades (4B 2.1.3‑4). Moreover, this description was cited by Nautin as evidence of a difference of authorship between works associated with *El.* and those with *C.N.* But we did not see fit to stress this conception as in any way determin‑ing on its own a difference of authorship. That description served more to enable us to identify the author of περὶ τοῦ παντός with that of *El.* because of other and particular shared features, and in the light of external evidence that did not include the former in the Hippolytan *corpus* (4B 2.1).

---

[66] Loi, *Aug.* 17 (1977) p. 469 comments: "Tra gli Apologisti l'uso cristologico è testimo‑niato solo da Giustino..." but this amounts to an *argumentum e silentio* in view of Cantalamessa's case for paschal allusions referring to a largely lost *genre*.

[67] *In Ps.* 20: τῆς οὖν ἀποδείξεως ταύτης γεγενημένης, τηλαυγῶς ἐν ἀρχῇ ὁ παῖς τοῦ θεοῦ καταγγελλόμενος, ὁ λόγος, ἡ σοφία, ὁ μονογενὴς υἱὸς τοῦ πατρὸς διὰ τού‑των ἐσημαίνετο. Nautin (1953) p. 183, 7‑9. Cf. Loi, *Aug.* 17 (1977) p. 470.

[68] Commenting on *Ps.* 88, 27‑28 and 2,7‑8, *In Pasc.* 46,1: ὁρᾷς αὐτοῦ τὸν υἱὸν καὶ πρωτότοκον καὶ μονογενῆ, ὅρα καὶ τὸν θεόν.

[69] In *El.* VIII, 10,3 ὁ μονογενὴς υἱὸς ἐκεῖνος ὁ τῶν τριῶν αἰώνιων, τὰς ἄνωθεν ἰδέας βλέπων, and the τοῦ παιδὸς ἐκείνου τοῦ μονογενοῦς (9,3) or ὁ μονογενὴς παῖς ἄνωθεν (10,5) are references to Docetic doctrine. See also 10,9 and X, 16,6. Other references are from Valentinus (VI, 30,4; 31,4) or Ptolemaeus (38,6).

[70] Other examples cited are (i) συστολή or "contraction" to describe in explanation of the incarnation of the λόγος in *In Pasc.* 45, 1‑2: in comparison with Odes of Solomon 7, 3‑6 and the doctrine of the Docetists in *El.* VII, 10,3; (ii) marriage of Christ and the Church in *In Pasc.* 53,3: τὸ γὰρ ἔργον τῆς θηλείας λῦσαι θελήσας καὶ τὴν ἐκ πλευρᾶς πρότερον ῥεύ‑σασαν ἐπισχεῖν θανατηφόρον... ἐξ' ἧς τὸ ἱερὸν ἔρρευσεν αἷμα καὶ ὕδωρ, τὰ τέλεια τῶν πνευματικῶν γάμων τῶν μυστικῶν καὶ υἱοθεσίας καὶ παλιγγενεσίας τὰ σημεῖα. Cf. Gospel of the Egyptians and the Sethian doctrines of *El.* V, 19. Loi, *Aug.* 17 (1977) p. 471 and 468, cf. Cantalamessa (1967) p. 196‑199; 296‑298.

[71] *C.N.* 15,7: οὔτε γὰρ ἄσαρκος καὶ καθ' ἑαυτὸν ὁ λόγος τέλειος ἦν υἱός, καίτοι τέλειος, λόγος ὤν, μονογενής.

Amongst such features were *El.* X, 34,2, in comparison with Holl *frag.* 353, where Ταρτάρου ζοφεροῦ ὄμμα ἀφώτιστον ὑπὸ Λόγου φωνῆς μὴ κατα-λαμφθέν linked the description of Tartarus in both works via the concepts of λόγος, and φωνή, to the πρὸ ἑωσφόρου φωσφόρος of 33,11 (4B 2.1.4, see also 4A 2). But it was the latter concepts in particular, including the close details of the comparison, that established identity of authorship. We have seen that in the case of *In Pasc.* that comparison fails in the case of those concepts (5A 2.2.2.1).

In the light of these considerations, Loi's reference to a belief in the *descensus in infernos* cannot of itself establish a common authorship between *El.* and *In Pasc.* Moreover there are very few points of comparison other than the assertion of the belief between *El.* and associated works and *In Pasc.* 56-58. Here the emphasis is Christological, in contrast to the salvific context of X, 34,2 (and Holl *frag.* 353) involving the places for the punishment of the damned and the blessings of the redeemed in the geography of the under world. We have by contrast a Christological if not an anthropological explanation of where Christ was after death and in the Tomb before the Resurrection.[72] There follows no description of the geography of the underworld but the bare assertion in explanation that:

> The indivisible has been divided (μεμέρισται ὁ ἀμερής), in order that the universe might be saved (ἵνα τὰ πάντα σωθῇ), in order that neither the underworld (ἵνα μηδὲ ὁ κάτω τόπος) might remained unenlightened (ἀμύητος ᾖ) by the divine visitation (τῆς θείας ἐπιδημίας).
>
> *In Pasc.* 56

In this context too the appeal to *frag.* IV of the Commentary on Genesis does not assist in forging a connection with *In Pasc.* The former's geographical description of Paradise: ἔστι δὲ τόπος ἀνατολῆς καὶ χωρίον ἐκλογῆς certainly connects it correctly with περὶ τοῦ παντός (Holl *frag.* 353,24: χωρίον φωτεινόν) and hence with *El.* X, 34,2. But there is no direct reference in *In Pasc.* to such geography of Hades, nor is the *descensus* of Christ mentioned in connection with that geography.

In order to forge such a connection Loi once again has recourse to heretical exegesis.[73] In *In Pasc.* 61,2, *Ps.* 24,7-8 is used of Christ's ascension,[74] as in the Naasene psalm of *El.* V, 8,18 it is used of the ἄνοδος of

---

[72] Cf. also the fragment from the *Florilegium Edessenum*, published in Nautin (1953) p. 76: καὶ ἰδού ὁ μονογενὴς εἰσῆλθεν ὡς ψυχὴ μετὰ ψυχῶν, θεὸς λόγος ἔμψυχος· τὸ γὰρ σῶμα ἔκειτο ἐν μνημείῳ, οὐχὶ κενωθὲν τῆς θεότητος· ἀλλ᾽ ὥσπερ ἐν τῷ ἅδῃ ὢν τῇ οὐσίᾳ ἦν πρὸς τὸν πατέρα, οὕτως ἦν καὶ ἐν τῷ σώματι καὶ ἐν τῷ ἅδῃ ὢν· ἀχώρητος γὰρ ἐστι καὶ ὁ υἱὸς ὡς ὁ πατήρ, καὶ πάντα περιέχει· ἀλλὰ θέλων ἐχωρήθη ἐν σώματι ἐμψύχῳ, ἵνα μετὰ τῆς ἰδίας ψυχῆς πορευθῇ εἰς τὸν ἅδην καὶ μὴ γυμνῇ τῇ θεότητι.

[73] Loi, *Aug.* 17 (1977) p. 466.

[74] *In Pasc.* 61,2: βλέπουσαι δὲ αἱ δυνάμεις τὸ μέγα μυστήριον, συναναβαίνοντα ἤδη ἄνθρωπον ἐν θεῷ, ἐγκελευόμεναι ἐβόων μετὰ χαρᾶς ταῖς ἄνω στρατιαῖς· «ἄρατε πύλας, οἱ ἄρχοντες ὑμῶν, καὶ ἐπάρθητε, πύλαι αἰώνιοι, καὶ εἰσελεύσεται ὁ βασιλεὺς τῆς δόξης....»

Adamas in a sense in which I can observe no true parallel, since here the sense is cosmic and corporate and not individual (περὶ δὲ τῆς ἀνόδου αὐτοῦ– τουτέστι τῆς ἀναγεννήσεως).[75] A tenuous connection can only be forged by finding an aphorism from the *Gospel of the Egyptians* cited in *In Pasc.* 56.

Here, as we saw, we had a reference to ὁ κάτω τόπος τῆς θείας ἐπιδημίας ἀμύητος and thus to the *descensus ad infernos*. But all that connects this with the *Gospel of the Egyptians* is the aphorism (φωνὴν μὲν αὐτοῦ ἠκού- σαμεν, εἶδος δὲ αὐτοῦ οὐχ ἑωράκαμεν). Because this text is cited in con- nection with Christ's (Adamas') descent in *El.* V, 8, 14, it is claimed that we have a proof of common authorship between *El.* and *In Pasc.*[76] But the *de- scensus* according to *El.* (τὸ δὲ εἶδος τὸ κατελθὸν ἄνωθεν) once again is that of the universal, cosmic Adamas, to be found in all religions according to the Naasenes, and here the descent is from heaven to earth and not to the underworld. There is no tighter connection than the quite general and indi- rect links between writers sharing in the common, quite variegated paschal homiletic to which Cantalamessa pointed.[77]

The real references to the *descensus ad infernos* are found in *In Pasc.* 58,1 and 62,2.[78] But here the reference is to the just in the Old Testament and has as its background no direct connection with *El.* and περὶ τοῦ παντός but with a common background in terms of 1 *Pet.* 3,19. Indeed there is no reference to this text nor to Christ's *descensus* to the underworld in any of the descriptions of the geography of Hades in the former two works.[79] Rather *In Pasc.* in this respect reflects the view of *Dan.* and associated works in which the deliverance of the souls from Hades is effected by the death, *descensus*, and resurrection of Christ rather than at some future judgement day. We observed this contrast previously in our citations from *El.* in 4B 2.1.4. If there is any group of Hippolytan works to which these homilies could be putatively assigned it would be to the *C.N.* rather than the *El.* block, yet as Loi is aware, they do not on other grounds in the least fit there.

---

[75] *El.* V, 8,18: περὶ δὲ τῆς ἀνόδου αὐτοῦ– τουτέστι τῆς ἀναγεννήσεως–, ἵνα γέν- ηται πνευματικός, οὐ σαρκικός, λέγει, φησίν, ἡ γραφή·«ἄρατε πύλας, οἱ ἄρχοντες ὑμῶν, καὶ ἐπάρθητε, πύλαι αἰώνιοι, καὶ εἰσελεύσεται ὁ βασιλεὺς τῆς δόξης...»

[76] *El.* V, 8, 14: ... «φωνὴν μὲν αὐτοῦ ἠκούσαμεν, εἶδος δὲ αὐτοῦ οὐχ ἑωράκαμεν.» ἀποτεταγμένου γάρ, φησίν, αὐτοῦ καὶ κεχαρακτηρισμένου ἀκούεται φωνή, τὸ δὲ εἶδος τὸ κατελθὸν ἄνωθεν, ἀπὸ τοῦ ἀχαρακτηρίστου, ὁποῖόν ἐστιν, οἶδεν οὐδείς· ἔστι δὲ ἐν τῷ πλάσματι τῷ χοϊκῷ, γινώσκει δὲ αὐτὸ οὐδείς.

[77] Cf. Cantalamessa (1967) p. 253-259.

[78] *In Pasc.* 58,1: ὡς δὲ καὶ πολλοὶ τῶν δικαίων εὐαγγελιζόμενοι καὶ προφητεύοντες καὶ τὸν ἐν ἀναστάσει πρωτότοκον ἐκ τῶν νεκρῶν... ὁ δὲ καὶ τὴν τριήμερον ὑπὸ γῆν ὑπομονὴν ἐνέσχετο ἵνα ὅλον καὶ πᾶν σώσῃ τὸ ἀνθρώπων γένος, τὸ πρὸ νόμου, τὸ μετὰ νόμου, τὸ δι᾽ ἑαυτοῦ, and *In Pasc.* 62,2:᾽ διὰ ὃν ἐρράγησαν ᾅδου πύλαι καὶ κλεῖθρα ἐλύθησαν ἀδαμάντινα... καὶ ὁ μὲν κάτω δῆμος ἀνέστη τῶν νεκρῶν εὐαγγε- λιζόμενος, τοῖς δὲ ἄνω πληρώμασιν ἀπὸ γῆς ἀπεδόθη χορός.

[79] Cf. Loi, *Aug.* 17 (1977) p. 466 and Cantalamessa (1967) p. 245-253.

Indeed, the one reference to the *descensus* in literature associated with *El.* is *Ap. Trad.* 4,8 (*infernum calcet et iustos inluminet et terminum figat*) in a passage that we have already fully discussed (5A 1.1). Our conclusion there was that the present work, given the name ἀποστολικὴ παράδοσις from the title on the Statue, is composite, and that the passage in question comes from the Hippolytus who corrected many of the works associated with the author of *El.* In particular, the use of ὅρος (*terminum*) in *Ap. Trad.* 4,8 was at variance with the use of ὅρος (*canon*) in *El.* IX, 11,1; 12,21; X, 5,4. But if indeed this reference to the *descensus* comes from the second and later writer in the *corpus*, Loi cannot claim this feature in evidence that *In Pasc.* can be identified as the work of the author of *El.* nor that objections to Hippolytan authorship emanating from the *corpus* as a whole are somehow reduced when a comparison is made with *El.* and associated works alone.

Finally we come to the last feature to which we must draw attention, namely the concept of οἰκονομία which played a critical role in our distinguishing between the authorship of *El.* and *C. N.* (4A 1.3).

5A 2.5. οἰκονομία *in* In Pasc. *and* C.N.

The majority of references for οἰκονομία is to the general, patristic sense of the "allegorical meaning/mystery of Scripture." We find that this is the sense in which it is used in *In Pasc.* 5, 1 (ἡ περὶ τοῦ πάσχα οἰκονομία), 8 (τίς νόμου οἰκονομία), 43 (ἄκουε μετὰ τοὺς τύπους καὶ τὴν νομικὴν οἰκονομίαν). We saw (4A 1.3) that *C.N.* uses this term in the highly technical sense for the mystery of the relationship between the persons of the Trinity within the one Godhead. Indeed it is used very sparingly in this sense in the *C.N.* block generally, since despite frequent appeals to "mystical" reading of *O.T.* texts, it is never used in *Ant.* and only once in *Dan.* and in *Ben. Jac.*[80] It is almost as if Hippolytus avoids using the common term for allegorical Scripture interpretation so characteristic of his method of exegesis because of the precise and technical sense that he gives it in connection with his nascent doctrine of the Trinity.

Even in *In Pasc.* 52,2 (πληρῶσαι τὴν οἰκονομίαν βουλόμενος εἰς ἥν ἀπεστάλη), where the divine "plan" specifically of salvation comes clearly into view, the reference is not pre-incarnational, as with *C.N.*, but in fulfilment of the saving acts of the Cross and Resurrection. In other words, οἰκονομία is used there as in Ignatius *Ephes.* 18,2; 20,1 where it refers to the "mysterious plan" fulfilled in the saving events. The fact that it is not used

---

80 *Dan.* I, 14,1 where the Jews do not recognise without allegorical interpretation τὴν οἰκονομίαν τοῦ πατρός. In *Dan.* II, 19,1 (μυστήριον τὸ οἰκονομούμενον) the verb rather than the noun in used. But only in *Ben. Jac.* and never in *El.* do we find the noun, see C. Diobouniotis and N. Beïs, Hippolyts Schrift über die Segnungen Jakobs, in *T.U.* 38,13 Reihe 8, 8, only the second time in the *C.N.* block and never in *El.* we find ἥν τὸ γεγονὸς ὑπὸ τοῦ Ἰακὼβ μυστήριον οἰκονομίας εἰς χριστὸν προτυπούμενον. Cf. also Nautin (1949), p. 45.

of the Trinity itself corroborates further my case for excluding *In Pasc.* from
the earliest stages of the development of the Hippolytan *corpus*.

5A 2.6. *In conclusion: περὶ τοῦ πάσχα a composite work*

We see therefore that the views of both Nautin and Cantalamessa are confirmed, and that neither the author of *El.* nor of *C.N.* and their respective associated works can be either the author of Pseudo-Chrysostom's *Paschal
Homilies* I-V or of VI. We have seen that only the latter could be identified
with Hippolytus on external grounds (5A 2.2.1). This work possessed distinctive features that convince on internal grounds that it has no common
author with I-V, but that equally on internal grounds Hippolytus cannot be
its author (5A 2.2.2). At all events, the use of Hippolytus as an alternative to
John Chrysostom even for VI lacks credibility in so far as Hippolytus'
name, as we have seen, like that of Clement (3D 2), was used as a cipher for
a particular kind of historical tradition, in an era that had made Hippolytus
part of an idealized apostolic age, as references by Palladius (c. A.D. 421)
and Cyrillus of Scythopolis (c. A.D. 555) demonstrated (3C 9).

Indeed, if there was a clear, ongoing historical identification with
Hippolytus that predated the attribution to Chrysostom, we would do well to
ask how such an attribution was possible. Alternatively, if Hippolytus' name
had been clearly *ab initio* identified with VI, it is surely pertinent to ask why
(anonymous) *Hom.* I-V were not attributed to Hippolytus rather than
Chrysostom when the need was felt to assign this anonymous work to an author, and when I-V had become associated with VI. We have seen how Loi
admits that a single work would be required in order to resolve this difficulty (5A 2.4.1-2.4.4). Furthermore, in the light of his failure to establish
common authorship of the critical examples that I have cited, it was equally
contrived for Loi to endeavour to find equivalences to the idiosyncracies of
Hom. VI in the *El.* block, in reply to Connolly's case to the contrary.[81]

Our conclusion must therefore be that the second work (σύγγραμμα) *On
the Passover* (περὶ τοῦ πάσχα), mentioned in Eusebius *H.E.* VI, 22 (5A 2.1)
and Jerome *De Vir. Ill.* 61 (5A 2.2) has been apparently irretrievably lost. It

---

[81] See 4C 2.2.2 with which cf. Loi, *Aug.* 17 (1977) p. 478-483. Loi claims to begin with
"due premesse metodologicamente indispensabili," that (i) as a "panegirico pasquale" the style
would have been different from heresiology (*El.*), philosophy (περὶ τοῦ παντός), or exegesis
(*Com. in Gen.* or in *Pss.*), and (ii) a large part of the catalogue of the Statue has been lost. But
without a successful comparison with what we have, an appeal to what we allegedly have not
(ii) is not legitimate, and an appeal to a different *genre* (i) is plainly special pleading (p. 478).
The stylistic comparison of p. 480-482 I find insufficient to establish identity of author as opposed to *milieu*. The different use of ἐπιδημία for ἐπιφάνεια cannot be satisfactorily explained by the use of the former term for the advent of Elchasai (*El.* IX, proem. 4), nor can the
use of θεῖον πνεῦμα, without βοᾷ, (*El.* IV, 49; IX, 12)—or for that matter δύναμις θεῖα (X,
33)—relect a sufficiently unique correspondence that would ground securely any argument for
identity of authors. *Mutatis mutandis*, the use of βοᾷ with ὁ ψαλμός as its subject (*In Ps.* 16
17, and 19) but not τὸ θεῖον πνεῦμα must likewise fail (p. 483). These different ways of citation conceal a very different emotive response to the Scriptures cited.

can be identified neither with VI nor with I-V whether taken separately or together, amongst the *Spuria* of St. John Chrysostom (5A 2.2.1- 2.2).

Let us now turn to a more certain identification of a work on the Statue with one of Hippolytus, editor and corrector of the only surviving genuine witness to the ἀπόδειξις χρόνων, which is indeed that which is inscribed on the Statue, but written by another author, the author of *El.* In pursuing this more certain identification, we shall be once again assured of the wisdom of our premise which is that a common authorship is not necessarily implied for the works listed on the Statue's plinth.

5A 3. περὶ τἀγαθοῦ καὶ πόθεν τὸ κακόν/Contra Marcionem

Only at first sight περὶ τἀγαθοῦ καὶ πόθεν τὸ κακόν need not be regarded as equivalent to a work against Marcion and therefore equivalent to the *Contra Marcionem* listed in Jerome *De Vir. Ill.* 61 and the Πρὸς Μαρκίωνα in Eusebius *H.E.* VI, 22. The absence of that necessity might at first sight enable the title thus inscribed on the plinth of the chair of the Statue to be detached from Hippolytan authorship to which Eusebius and Jerome thus bear witness. But a comparison of the contents of Marcion's argument in Tertullian *Contra Marcionem* I with this title on the Statue shows that its lost contents must have approximated to a refutation of this particular heresy. Marcion's argument begins with *Matt.* 8,18, that is to say with the Parable of the Good and Bad Tree and its teaching that *neque bona malos neque mala bonos proferat fructus.* The parable is thus used to pose the *mali quaestionem, "unde malum?"* There can therefore be little doubt that the subject matter of the lost περὶ τἀγαθοῦ καὶ **πόθεν τὸ κακόν** was specifically a discussion of Marcion's heresy.

It is possible to appeal to the title of Tertullian's *Contra Marcionem* to show that books against Marcion were common, and that therefore the author of *El.* could have written one that was mentioned on the Statue, and that Hippolytus wrote another mentioned in the Eusebius/Jerome catalogues. Certainly the distinction between a work allegedly written by the author of *El.* could not be distinguished from one written by Hippolytus on the grounds of the more philosophical character of the title on the Statue in comparison with the hypothetically more biblically-based *Contra Marcionem.* As we have seen, any work whether 'biblical' or 'philosophical' against Marcion would have warranted such a title in view of the point from which Marcion's argument had begun (with *Matt.* 8,18). But such appeals are, in the light of our argument, now without purpose, since the Statue is not a monument to a single author with the result that the list of works inscribed need not be, and transparently are not, the work of a single writer represented by the seated figure.

5A 4. περὶ θεοῦ καὶ σαρκὸς ἀναστάσεως

This work is mentioned by Jerome, in his catalogue of Hippolytus' works in *De Vir. Ill.* 61, as *De Resurrectione*. Its text survives in a fragmentary form in Syriac *mss.* under this title with the addition of "(dedicated) to Queen Mamaea" and attributed to "Hippolytus bishop and martyr."[82] We have also two fragments in Theodoret whose contents correspond to this title. The first of these is on the theme of Thomas in *Jn.* 20, 24-29 but actually quoting a version of *Lk.* 24, 39.[83] Here we read, in Theodoret (Ettlinger (1975), *Eranistes*, III, 285, 5-6: ἀπαρχὴν τοῦτον εἰπὼν ἐπεμαρτύρησε τῷ ὑφ᾽ ἡμῶν εἰρημένῳ, ὡς ἐκ τοῦ αὐτοῦ φυράματος σάρκα λαβὼν ὁ σωτήρ ἔγειρε ταύτην, ἀπαρχὴν ποιούμενος τῆς τῶν δικαίων σαρκός, ἵν᾽ οἱ πάντες ἐπ᾽ ἐλπίδι τοῦ ἐγηγερμένου προσδόκιμον τὴν ἀνάστασιν ἔξομεν οἱ πιστεύσαντες εἰς αὐτόν. The second continues the theme of the body of the risen Christ being the first fruit (ἀπαρχή) and as such the risen bodies of the just will consist of the same substance (ἐκ τοῦ αὐτοῦ φυράματος) of the wheat (dough) that is that first fruit.[84] Both are cited as from a work τοῦ ἁγίου ᾽Ιππολύτου ἐπισκόπου καὶ μάρτυρος· ἐκ τῆς πρὸς βασιλίδα τινὰ ἐπιστολῆς.

We saw in 3A 5 that Theodoret was aware of the anonymous σμικρὸς λαβύρινθος, clearly the work of the author of *El.* and, therefore, of these works by him that we have identified on the Statue. He did not however associate that work with the name of Hippolytus, whose genuine works he cites clearly by name. Nautin was clearly unaware of the identification of the work of Hippolytus πρὸς βασιλίδα τινά with the περὶ θεοῦ καὶ σαρκὸς ἀναστάσεως of the Statue in the Syrian fragments through the conjunction of Mamaea's name. He proposed emending Theodoret's title to πρὸς βασιλίδην on the grounds both of its subject matter being allegedly directed against Basilides, and the hypothesis that though ἐκ τοῦ λόγου τοῦ εἰς τὴν τῶν ταλάντων διανομήν only mentions "Marcion, Valentinus, and the Gnostics," Basilides would surely have been nearby in that part of the fragment that is lost.[85]

The principle objection to Nautin's emendation is that the specifically docetic heresiarchs against which Hippolytus is recorded to be opposed by

---

[82] Achellis (1897) p. 249-253 citing (for Mamaea) *ms. Mus. Brit. syr.* 858, fol. 214ᵛ and 855 fol. 77ʳ (7th Cent.).

[83] Theodoret (Ettlinger (1975)), *Eranistes*, II, 172,10: ἀπαρχὴν οὖν τοῦτον λέγει τῶν κεκοιμημένων, ἅτε πρωτότοκον τῶν νεκρῶν. ὃς ἀναστὰς καὶ βουλόμενος ἐπιδεικνύναι ὅτι τοῦτο ἦν τὸ ἐγηγερμένον ὅπερ ἦν καὶ ἀποθνῇσκον, διστα ζόντων τῶν μαθητῶν, προσκαλεσάμενος τὸν Θωμᾶν ἔφη· δεῦρο ψηλάφησον καὶ ἴδε ὅτι πνεῦμα ὀστοῦν καὶ σάρκα οὐκ ἔχει καθὼς ὑμεῖς ἐμὲ θεωρεῖτε ἔχοντα.

[84] Theodoret, *Eranistes*, III, 285, 5-6: ἀπαρχὴν τοῦτον εἰπὼν ἐπεμαρτύρησε τῷ ὑφ᾽ ἡμῶν εἰρημένῳ, ὡς ἐκ τοῦ αὐτοῦ φυράματος σάρκα λαβὼν ὁ σωτὴρ ἔγειρε ταύτην, ἀπαρχὴν ποιούμενος τῆς τῶν δικαίων σαρκός, ἵν᾽ οἱ πάντες ἐπ᾽ ἐλπίδι τοῦ ἐγηγερμένου προσδόκιμον τὴν ἀνάστασιν ἔξομεν οἱ πιστεύσαντες εἰς αὐτόν.

[85] Nautin (1953), p. 26-27.

Theodoret[86] himself and Stephen Gobarus[87] are the Nicolaitans. Both these writers cite Hippolytus against the Nicolaitans as though this were a separate work. But once again the Syriac fragments make it clear that it is the Nicolaitans who deny the resurrection of the flesh against whom Hippolytus is writing, and it is to this work that Anastasius Sinaiticus refers when citing Ἱππολύτου ἐπισκόπου Ῥώμης ἐκ τοῦ περὶ ἀναστάσεως καὶ ἀφθαρσίας λόγου.[88]

In view of Jerome's clear identification of this work with Hippolytus, followed both by Theodoret, Anastasius Sinaiticus and the Syriac fragments, it seems idle to claim that this work is by the author of *El.* who was both different from that of the *C.N.* block but had the same name as him. Theodoret in that case too would have joined in Jerome's alleged confusion and named the author of the σμικρὸς λαβύρινθος as Hippolytus as well, even though he were a different Hippolytus.[89] The internal arguments are all that are left with which to identify this work with the author of *El.* and associated works on the Statue. Yet such arguments are inconclusive.

Syriac *frag.* 8 represents the φύραμα–ἀπαρχή image that unites, as we have already seen (in Theodoret *Eranistes* II, 172,10 and III, 285,5-6) the flesh of Christ as first-fruit (ἀπαρχή) of the wheat-harvest with the "dough (φύραμα)" of our mortal flesh. But the parallel with *El.* X, 33,16 is not sufficiently unique nor so specifically applied to carry conviction that the authors must be identical. The passage asserts: τοῦτον ἄνθρωπον ἴσμεν ἐκ τοῦ καθ᾽ ἡμᾶς φυράματος γεγονότα· εἰ γὰρ μὴ ἐκ τοῦ αὐτοῦ ἡμῖν φυράματος ὑπῆρξε, μάτην νομοθετεῖ μιμεῖσθαι τὸν διδάσκαλον. φύραμα is here of our human nature, our "dough" or "clay" which the teacher must possess if we can imitate him. The reference to the resurrection as ἀπαρχή is then picked up in *El.* X, 33, 17, as ἀπαρξάμενος ἐν πᾶσι τούτοις τὸν ἴδιον ἄνθρωπον ("having offered as first fruits in all these [saving] events his own humanity.")

The allusion to ἀπαρχή along with φύραμα was not here used originally for the first time. Already its originally Valentinian, exegetical (*Rom.* 11,16) presence in Irenaeus had made it available to both the author of *El.* and

86 Theodoret *Haer. Fab.* III, 1: κατὰ τούτων [τῶν Νικολαϊτῶν] καὶ ὁ προρρηθεὶς συνέγραψε Κλήμης καὶ Εἰρηναῖος καὶ Ὠριγένης καὶ Ἱππόλυτος ἐπίσκοπος καὶ μάρτυρ.
87 Photius, *Bibliotheca*, 232: ἔτι δὲ ποίας ὑπολήψεις ἔσχεν Ἱππόλυτος καὶ Ἐπιφάνιος περὶ Νικολάου τοῦ ἑνὸς τῶν ζ διακόνων καὶ ὅτι ἰσχυρῶς αὐτοῦ καταγινώσκουσιν...
88 For the text of this extract, see Nautin (1953) p. 84-85.
89 Loi, *StEphAug* (1977) p. 88: "Concludendo ci domandiamo se non sia legittimo affermare l'esistenza nella prima metà del III secolo di due scrittori ecclesiastici di nome Ippolito, l'uno presbitero a Roma, l'altro vescovo di una qualche sede dell' Oriente cristiano..."; M. Simonetti, Due note su Ippolito, in *StEphAug*13 (1977), p. 125; ——, Una ipotesi di lavoro, idem p. 153-154; ——, (1989) p. 114-115 ff.; V. Saxer, La questione di Ippolito Romano, in *St EphAug* 30 (1989), p. 53-54.

Hippolytus.⁹⁰ Furthermore, we have already argued that the work of *El.* was known to Hippolytus who corrected and reformulated it according to his conciliatory intentions. It would not therefore be surprising if imagery as striking as that of φύραμα–ἀπαρχή had been adopted from the former by the latter even if it had not already been available in the Irenaean tradition.

A similar point can be made regarding Anastasius Sinaiticus' citation of ἄφθαρτος οὐσία and angelic substance.⁹¹ As a parallel, we can cite *El.*'s speculation on οὐσία paralleled in περὶ τοῦ παντός.⁹² The former of these is a defence of a credal position as was indeed *El.* X, 33, 17. It is therefore the very kind of passage that we would expect to be represented by in the writings of the school that succeeded its author. Hippolytus used the work of his predecessor, the author of *El.* and cognate works. Even a defender of the thesis of two distinct authors with the same name, such as Simonetti, has to conclude that the later Hippolytus used the work of the alleged earlier one.⁹³

It will not do, finally, for Loi to argue that a treatise addressed to Queen Mamaea sets this work in the allegedly syncretistic tradition of *El.* in contrast with the allegedly anti-imperial polemic of Hippolytus, author of *Dan.* and *Ant.* We have already argued that *Dan.* has in view the kind of mob outbursts that lead magistrates to intervene of the kind that may have lead to the martyrdom of Callistus (4B 2.2.2.1.3). The alleged philo-Christian policy of the Severans has, at all events, been somewhat exaggerated (2B 2.2.4). Furthermore, the hostility of *Ant.* is considerably softened by the reflection that this work explains the delay of the *Parousia* and thus does not identify Antichrist with the Roman Empire (2B 2.1.3.2). We cannot therefore on such grounds detach περὶ θεοῦ καὶ σαρκὸς ἀναστάσεως from the works of Hippolytus whether from the group of them found on the Statue, or with the remainder of the *corpus* which are not, in the face of its clear identification by Jerome, Theodoret and Anastasius Sinaiticus.

5A 5. προτρεπτικὸς πρὸς Σεβηρεῖναν

Clearly this work cannot be identical with Theodoret's πρὸς βασιλίδα τινὰ since we have shown in 5A 4 that, from what he quotes, that work must be

---

⁹⁰ Irenaeus, *Adv. Haer.,* I, 8,3: ἀπαρχὴν μὲν τὸ πνευματικὸν εἰρῆσθαι διδάσκοντες, φύραμα δὲ ἡμᾶς, τουτέστιν τὴν ψυχικὴν Ἐκκλησίαν, ἧς τὸ φύραμα ἀνειληφέναι λέγ-ουσιν αὐτόν, καὶ ἐν αὐτῷ συνανεσταλκέναι, ἐπειδὴ ἦν αὐτὸς ζύμη.

⁹¹ Hippolytus ἐκ τοῦ περὶ ἀναστάσεως καὶ ἀφθαρσίας λόγου cited by Nautin (1953) p. 84: ἔσονται, φησίν, ἐν τῇ ἀναστάσει οἱ ἄνθρωποι ὡς οἱ ἄγγελοι τοῦ θεοῦ, ἐν ἀφθαρσίᾳ δηλονότι καὶ ἀθανασίᾳ· ἄφθαρτος γὰρ οὐσία οὐ γεννᾷ, οὐ γεννᾶται, οὐκ αὔξει... τοιαῦται οὐσίαι εἰσὶν ἥ τε ἀγγέλων ἥ τε τῶν ψυχῶν τῶν ἐκ σωμάτων ἀπηλλαγμένων, ἐπειδὴ καὶ ἀμφότεραι ἑτερογενεῖς εἰσι καὶ ἀλλότριαι τῆς ὁρωμένης καὶ φθειρομένης ταύτης τοῦ κόσμου κτίσεως.

⁹² *El.* X, 32,2: ... ἀρχὰς πρότερον ἐδημιούργει—πῦρ καὶ πνεῦμα, ὕδωρ καὶ γῆν—ἐξ ὧν διάφορον τὴν ἑαυτοῦ κτίσιν ἐποίει, καὶ τὰ μὲν μονοουσία, τὰ δὲ ἐκ δύο, τὰ δὲ ἐκ τριῶν, τὰ δὲ ἐκ τεσσάρων συνεδέσμει, and 33,4: καὶ γὰρ αἱ τούτων πρῶται οὐσίαι, αἱ ἐξ οὐκ ὄντων γενόμεναι—πῦρ καὶ πνεῦμα, ὕδωρ καὶ γῆ.

⁹³ For an alternative argument see Loi *StEphAug*13 (1977) p. 71-72.

identical with the περὶ θεοῦ καὶ σαρκὸς ἀναστάσεως mentioned by Anastasius Sinaiticus, who added the Syriac fragments as addressed to Mamaea. The latter clearly was a βασιλίς. Both its content and the person addressed are unknown, and therefore nothing further can be said regarding its authorship.

5A 6. εἰς ἐγγαστρίμυθον

This work can be identified with *De Saul et Pythonissa* in Jerome *De. Vir. Ill.* 61.[94] Clearly an ἐγγαστρίμυθος is a "ventriloquist" or "oracle", "Pythonissa" too is a word for the oracle or Pythian priestess, and so it is a commentary on the visit of Saul to the Witch of Endor to summon the shade of Samuel in 1 *Sam.* 28, 6-25.

Clearly the identification of this title on the Statue with a work cited by Jerome as that of Hippolytus was an embarrassment to Nautin's original version of the two-author thesis that insisted no work on the Statue could be by Hippolytus. Accordingly Nautin had to explain away the attribution of this work, along with a similar attribution by Jerome, to the περὶ θεοῦ καὶ σαρκὸς ἀναστάσεως (*De Resurrectione*) that we have already discussed (5A 4) and the works which follow (5A 7 and 8). He proposed doing so by using the argument that there was nothing exceptional about such titles and that they were used by various writers for their different works.[96]

Regarding the title that immediately follows (5A 7) I find it difficult to associate with the *De Apocalypsi* of Jerome, and I have already given grounds for not so associating it (3C). At all events, Jerome's title hardly includes the Gospel as well.

5A 7. τὰ ὑπὲρ τοῦ κατὰ' Ιωάννην εὐαγγελίου καὶ ἀποκαλύψεως

Were it possible to accept the genuineness of the Barsalîbîan fragments, then this would be yet another example of a work on the Statue attributed to Hippolytus. Such would of course be fatal to the thesis that the works on the plinth are by any other than Hippolytus, given the fallacious view that there was one individual that the Statue commemorated. We have argued however that the attribution by Barsalîbî is not authentic, on the grounds that he lifted

---

94 J.B. Lightfoot, *The Apostolic Fathers.* (London: MacMillan 1890), Part I, S. Clement of Rome, vol. II, p. 390; G. Bovini, Sant'Ippolito, dottore e martire del III secolo, in *Coll. amici delle catacombe* 15 (Città del Vaticano: Pontificio Istituto di Archeologia cristiana 1943), p. 56.

95 Lightfoot (1890) 1, II p. 390 cf. Achelis (1897) and Nautin (1953) p. 140 who nevertheless presents no argument for the assertion: "L'attribution à Hippolyte est une fantasie de Simon de Magristris."

96 Nautin (1947), p. 83-84: "A supposer que nous soyons pleinement rassurés sur la valeur de l'information de Jérôme sur Hippolyte, dont il n'avait même pas pu découvrir la ville, il resterait encore que ces quatre titres ne sont pas tellement caractéristiques qu'ils ne puissent se trouver reunis chez plusiers écrivains. Ainsi Origène a écrit à son tour un commentaire des Psaumes, un 'Υπὲρ τῆς ἐγγαστριμύθου, un commentaire de l'évangile selon Jean, et deux ouvrages sur la résurrection."

these passages from a *catena* anyway, and that 'Hippolytus' was a readily used author's name for pseudonymous works, particularly since he had become associated with an apostolic golden age (3C 7.2). With Nautin we argued that Ebed-Jesu had no independent source other than that of Barsalîbî, yet it was to the former that we owed this particular title which was not necessarily equivalent to the κεφάλαια κατὰ Γαΐου (3C).

We shall see later (5B 2) the problems raised by the Simonetti-Loi version of the two-authors thesis, arising from their claim, on internal literary grounds, that Barsalîbî's work belongs to the oriental, *C.N.* block whereas it is here listed on the Statue. Were this to be the case, it would fit better with my thesis that there are the works of both authors present on the Statue, though I remain doubtful about the genuineness of these late citations.

5A 8. εἰς τοὺς Ψαλμούς

A work of a similar title is attributed to Hippolytus by Jerome *De Vir. Ill.* 61 as *De Psalmis*. Once again Nautin was to appeal to the fact that this title is common to the different works of a number of early Christian writers in order to dissociate it with the title of the Statue and hence the latter from Hippolytus' name.[97] There is furthermore a work of this title attributed to Hippolytus represented by *ms. Brit. Mus. syr.* 860 (*add.* 12154), which contains an introduction to the Psalms to which alone the attribution was intended. This same introduction is found in various Greek *catenae*.[98]

Nautin produced a critical edition and a translation of this work, but, in view of the mention of Hippolytus' name, had in pursuance of his thesis to dissociate it from the title on the Statue whose contents therefore would remain completely unknown.[99] Our first question must therefore be the relation of this work and Jerome's catalogue and Theodoret's citations.

5A 8.1. *Jerome, Theodoret, and ms. Brit. Mus. syr. 860*
But was this introduction to the *Psalms,* and a commentary on Psalms 1 and 2, the remains of the work mentioned by Jerome if not the work engraved on the Statue? Nautin claimed that the author of the work was Hippolytus, on the grounds both of *ms. Brit. Mus. syr.* 860 and of parallels with *C.N.* and related works that I do not find sufficiently unique to be convincing.[100] Furthermore, it would seem probable that the work cited by Jerome is identical with that from which Theodoret quotes as that of Hippolytus.[101] That

---

[97] See quotation in footnote 96.
[98] *Vat. graec.* 754; *Ottobon. graec.* 398; *Laurent.* VI,3; *Parisinus graec.* 146.
[99] Nautin (1953) p. 166-183.
[100] Ibid. p. 103-105.
[101] Theodoret, *Eranistes*, (i) I, 88,22 (*Ps.* 23): τοῦ ἁγίου Ἰπολύτου ἐπισκόπου καὶ μάρτυρος, ἐκ τοῦ λόγου τοῦ εἰς τὸ Κύριος ποιμαίνει με...; (ii) II, 173,12 (*Ps.* 119): τοῦ αὐτοῦ ἐκ τοῦ λόγου τοῦ εἰς τὴν ᾠδὴν τὴν μεγάλην; (iii) II, 175,15 (*Ps* 2): τοῦ αὐτοῦ τῆς ἑρμηνείας τοῦ β΄ ψαλμοῦ (iv) II, 176,16 (*Ps.* 24): τοῦ αὐτοῦ ἐκ τοῦ λόγου εἰς τὸν κγ΄ ψαλμόν.

work, which included *Ps.* 2, was indeed a commentary proper. But the work presently being considered was rather an apologetic work against an unnamed person or persons who had there denied the Davidic authorship of *Psalms*.[102] His method of proof lay in defending the authenticity of the titles affixed to various psalms.[103]

Furthermore, it is improbable that this work, though mutilated, was originally the introduction of a longer work on all of the psalms, and which included Theodoret's citations. As Nautin pointed out, the work was in two parts the second of which was only ever intended to contain commentary on *Psalms* 1 and 2.[104] These two alone were to be further expounded, in an ending now lost, specifically because they were on the Lord's birth and passion, though lacking titles. Now, in the light of the introduction, we know the mystical meaning of David's titles (τὰς ἐπιγραφὰς ἐπέγνωμεν...ὧν καὶ τὰ μυστήρια ἐπέγνωμεν),[105] from which we can deduce the mystical subject matter of both these psalms from their first lines[106] as concerning the Birth and the Passion (ὁ μὲν πρῶτος γένεσιν αὐτοῦ, ὁ δὲ δεύτερος πάθος), the First and the Last (ἡ ἀρχὴ καὶ τὸ τέλος, καὶ τὸ Α καὶ τὸ Ω).[107] Are we then to regard this homily as quite distinct from the work cited by Theodoret, yet still attribute it to Hippolytus on the basis of *ms. Brit. Mus. syr.* 860?

Whilst not discussing the problem of the Theodoret citations requiring us to locate two different works on the Psalms, Nautin was adamant that the Syriac attribution was genuine, and that this work was not that listed on the Statue. Indeed, Nautin now tried to argue that defence of the Davidic authorship against an unnamed opponent(s) was made against the author of *El.*

---

102 *In Ps.* 1: ἀνάγκην ἔσχομεν, ἀγαπητοί, δεῖξαι τίς ἡ δύναμις τῶν ψαλμῶν, οὐχ ἑνὸς ψαλμοῦ κλωμένου πρὸς ἀπάτην ψυχῆς, οὐδὲ πλάνης αἱρέσεως καινῆς νομιζομένης.

103 Nautin (1953) p. 101: "On verra facilement que le but qu'il se propose chaque fois, c'est de montrer, d'une part, que ces titres ont un sens spirituel (ce que signifiait pour lui qu'ils sont inspirés), et, d'autre part, qu'ils se rattachent étroitement au contenu du psaume correspondant." Cf. ———, L'homélie d'Hippolyte sur le psautier et les oeuvres de Josipe, in *RevHisRel* 179 (1971), p. 137-179.

104 Nautin (1953) p. 102: "Il est possible que le texte original ait été amputé de sa fin... il manque la doxologie, qui était de règle... Mais ce que nous possédons encore, présente... une cohérence parfaite... Ce n'est pas un travail composé dans l'abstrait: c'est une œvre de polémique, où tout converge sur un adversaire déterminé."

105 *In Ps.* 18: ταύτης οὖν τῆς ἀποδείξεως γεγενημένης, περὶ πάντας τοὺς ψαλμούς, ὧν τὰς ἐπιγραφὰς ἐπέγνωμεν ἀναγκαίας καὶ διὰ πνεύατος ἁγίου κατηρτισμένας, ὧν καὶ τὰ μυστήρια ἐπέγνωμεν, ἀναδράμωμεν ἐπὶ τὴν ἀνάγνωσιν τὴν γεγενημένην. Δύο ἡμῖν ἀνεγνώσθησαν ψαλμοί, ὧν τὴν αἰτίαν διηγήσασθαι δεῖ πρώτων τυγχανόντων.

106 *In Ps.* 20: τῆς οὖν ἀποδείξεως ταύτης γεγενημένης, τηλαυγῶς ἐν ἀρχῇ ὁ παῖς τοῦ θεοῦ καταγγελλόμενος, ἡ σοφία, ὁ μονογενὴς υἱὸς τοῦ πατρὸς διὰ τούτων ἐσημαίνετο· φησὶ γὰρ οὕτως· «Μακάριος ἀνὴρ ὃς οὐκ ἐπορεύθη ἐν βουλῇ ἀσεβῶν» καὶ τὰ ἑξῆς, καὶ «ἵνα τί ἐφρύαξαν ἔθνη» καὶ τὰ ἑξῆς.

107 *In Ps.* 19: οὗτοι πρῶτοι ψαλμοὶ ἀνεπίγραφοί εἰσι, δηλοῦντες ὁ μὲν πρῶτος γένεσιν αὐτοῦ, ὁ δὲ δεύτερος πάθος. καὶ οὐκ ἦν ἀναγκαῖον ἐπιγράφειν αὐτούς, ὁπότε διὰ πάντων τῶν προφητῶν ὁ λόγος ἐκηρύχθη ἀρχὴ αὐτός· οὕτως γὰρ βοᾷ καὶ λέγει· Ἐγὼ εἰμι ἡ ἀρχὴ καὶ τὸ τέλος, καὶ τὸ Α καὶ τὸ Ω. Ὁπότε τοίνυν ὁ μακάριος Δαυὶδ πνεύματι διηγήσατο, οὐκ ἀνάγκην ἔσχεν ἐπιγραφὴν ποιήσασθαι.

His strongest argument rested upon the different literary profile that he claimed for the author of the *C.N.* block against that of *El.*

5A 8.2. *The Homily and the literary profile of the* C.N. *block*

A fundamental feature of that literary profile, which we shall show to be in some respects questionable (5B), was, according to Nautin, that the author of the *C.N.* block was a conservative biblical exegete in contrast with the secular philosophical formation of the *El.* block. Thus the mystical treatment of the titles of the psalms revealed the hand of the genuine Hippolytus, by contrast with the literalist use of Scripture in the Χρονικῶν to calculate world history, and the literalist setting of dates in the ἀπόδειξις χρόνων. The dates of both works were securely corrected by the mystical exegesis of the author of *Dan.*, as we have seen (4B 2.2.2).[108]

But apart from the questionable literary profile that we have yet to discuss, Nautin's argument is subject to the similar charges as those which he directed against Rondeau's criticism of his own thesis.[109] We have followed and developed Nautin's own observations regarding the use made by *C.N.* of *El.*, and the revisions made to the theology and chronology both of the latter and associated works by the former which it exhibits in turn in its own, associated block. We have established the character of the theology of that block as a *rapprochement* between the Monarchians and the community of *El.* In view of such a theology in *C.N.*, whose author is clearly Hippolytus, of *El.* and associated works, it seems almost impossible that the former should charge the latter, in "tearing away (κλωμένου)"[110] certain psalms "to

---

[108] Of the writer of *El.*, see Nautin (1953) p. 106: "C'était un homme soucieux de science et d'histoire exacte, qui cherchait dans l'Écriture, non pas des symboles comme Hippolyte, mais des données de fait pour une chronique générale de l'humanité." Cf. also ——, (1971) p. 162-163 and p. 175: "... c'est qu'il n'hésite pas à sacrifier certaines idées reçues chez les chrétiens ou même fournies par la Bible lorsqu'il les estime scientifiquement inexactes. C'est ainsi qu'il place la naissance du Christ en l'an 5502 de la création, et non en l'an 5500 généralement admis par les chrétiens, parce que cette date était incompatible avec le cycle lunaire qu'il utilisait."

[109] M-J. Rondeau, Les polémiques d'Hippolyte de Rome et de Filastre de Brescia concernant le psautier, in *RevHisRel* 171 (1967), p. 9-36 cf. Nautin (1971) p. 163-179.

[110] Rondeau (1967) p. 19-20 accepted the reading οὐχ ἑνὸς ψαλμοῦ κλονουμένου for κλωμένου, based upon the codex in the Moscow Historical Museum, *Bibl. Synodale* 194 (*Vladimir* 48) against *Mosquensis graec.* 358 and *Ambrosianus* B 106 sup. The reading itself is an emendation from ονουμένου. He was thus able to translate the phrase "since not even one psalm is refuted so so as to deceive the soul (πρὸς ἀπάτην ψυχῆς)." The "one psalm" only excluded by the αἵρεσις καινή is *Ps.* 115, 2 where the "ecstasy" was used by the Montanists as a proof text, as seen from Epiphanius, *Panar. Haer.* 48,7. Thus the heretic attacked is Caius for having denied this one psalm only because it supported Montanism, whereas Hippolytus supported a middle way between the latter and catholicism (p. 29-30). I find Rondeau's exegesis, based upon a dubious emendation highly questionable. It will be clear that neither Hippolytus nor the author of *El.* could have considered Caius a heretic, nor is there any evidence that he was so regarded in, e.g. the text of *El.* itself. I have already discussed this point in order to query the genuiness of the Barsalîbî fragments on the grounds of the anachronism involved (3C 7.1 and 3C 8.2), cf. p. 33-38. There is furthermore no citation or defence of *Ps.* 115, 2, and an argument for its original presence because the *ms.* is fragmentary is belied by the fact that the homily only originally extended to *Ps.* 1 and 2 (5A 8.1). Nautin (1971) p. 144-145 had no difficulty refuting the reading κλονουμένου ("Ce n'est pas conforme à la bonne

the deception of the soul (πρὸς ἀπάτην ψυχῆς)," and of "not thinking such error to be a new heresy (οὐδὲ πλάνης αἱρέσεως καινῆς νομιζομένης)."[111]

C.N., as we have seen, was prepared quite radically to alter the λόγος Christology of both Melito and Irenaeus to which *El.* was faithful, and in a way that was quite heretical in terms of later definitions of orthodoxy (4A 2.1.3). But there is no evidence that *C.N.* was prepared to regard the traditional view, shared by *El.* with these Fathers, as ἀπάτη or αἵρεσις, which he would surely have done so if he had regarded it as justifying the Monarchian charge of tritheism. Nor indeed is there any evidence of a kind of higher critical approach to Scripture in the *El.* block, let alone any specific denial of the David authorship of the *Psalms*. The kind of group attacked would rather be that in evidence in the *Clementines* in the passages about the so-called "false *pericopae*."[112] Furthermore, there seems grounds for identifying the homily with *El.* rather than *C.N.*

5A 8.3. *The Homily and the literary profile of the* El. *block*

Rondeau pointed to the fact that certain features of the homily resembled Χρονικῶν, and *El.* in the passages that we saw (4B 2 and 4B 2.2-4B 2.2.1) reflected the latter, rather than *C.N.*[113] The theme of the 72 nations arising from the division of languages (μερισμὸς ... γλωσσῶν) after the Flood, is, in particular, reflected in the homily. The selection of four singers, Asaph, Eman, Etham, and Idithum, with 288 accompanying singers, meant that to each of the former were assigned exactly 72 of the latter. This mystical significance (μυστήριον, σύμβολον τῆς ... οἰκονομίας) of this is that all nations will finally in unison praise God.[114] Rondeau correctly saw however the potentiality for confounding Nautin's two-authors thesis in this passage. The scientific, chronological information of the *El.* block now is treated allegorically and mystically after the contrasting, non-literal fashion of the *C.N.* block. Did not this fact show that the two authors were in fact one?[115]

---

méthode. Il falliat consulter d'abord le stemma des manuscrits. *Le Mosq. 194* ne pourrait nous avoir conservé seul une leçon primitive que s'il appartenait à une tradition indépendante des familles qui attestent κλωμένου.").

[111] See footnote 102.

[112] G. Strecker, Das Judenchristentum in den Pseudoclementinen, in *TU* 70, (1958), p. 166-184.

[113] Rondeau (1967) p. 11-13.

[114] *In Ps.* 3: ... Ἔστι δὲ καὶ πρὸς τοῦτο ἀπ᾽ ἀρχῆς τὸ προφητευθὲν θεωρῆσαι μυστήριον, ὅπερ ἐπὶ τῶν ᾠδῶν σημαινόμενον ἐπεδείκνυε τὸ πνεῦμα. Ἐκάστῳ γὰρ ἄρχοντι ἀπονέμονται οβ᾽· τὸ δὲ ἦν σύμβολον τῆς ἀρχῆθεν γενομένης οἰκονομίας ἐπὶ πᾶσαν ἀνθρωπότητα. Ἡνίκα γὰρ πύργος ᾠκοδόμητο ὑπὸ ἀπίστων ἀνδρῶν ὁμοφώνων οβ᾽ ἐθνῶν, ὀργῆς δικαίας ἐπ᾽ αὐτοὺς γενομένης, μερισμὸς ἐτελεῖτο γλωσσῶν· οἱ ἀσυμφωνίᾳ φωνῆς γενόμενοι εἰς διασπορὰν ἐχώρησαν, ὑπὸ τοῦ πνεύματος ἐλαυνόμενοι.

[115] Rondeau (1967) p. 14: "La manie de multiplier les transitions à caractère personel du type «cela ayant été fait, voyons ceci....» spécifique d'«Hippolyte» et à «Josipe,» comme l'a établi Dom Capelle." Cf. B. Capelle, Hippolyte de Rome, in *RThAM* 17 (1950), p. 145-174 and ——, (1952) p. 193-202.

Nautin's response was, essentially, that the allegorization of the 72 nations showed that it was Hippolytus using the work of *El.* but recasting it according to his allegorical exegetical style. Nevertheless, by using such an example, he was admitting the case of both Rondeau and Capelle regarding similarities of style and expression between the *El.* and *C.N.* blocks, and the serious problems raised for his two-authors thesis. But if indeed the author of *C.N.* was at home in the thought and style of *El.*, then this considerably lessened the force of a great deal of Nautin's claim that there were differences of this kind that established different authors.

We too have argued that not only did Hippolytus as the author of *C.N.* self-consciously refashion the theology of *El.* (4A 1-2), but that the selfsame Hippolytus brought the Χρονικῶν from 222 to 235 and was responsible for a middle, undated recension of the work completed by the Chronographer of 354 (4A 3.2.3 and 4B 2.2.3.2). Moreover we have argued that the corrections κατὰ Δανιήλ to the ἀπόδειξις χρόνων of the Statue are also an example of Hippolytus correcting the work of his predecessor (4B 2.2.2-4B 2.2.2.1.4.). There would not therefore be *prima facie* anything to object to in Nautin's claim for the Hippolytan authorship of the homily, particularly if it could be argued that its date was subsequent to what we have argued to be the likely death of the author of *El.* (4B 2.2.3.3).[116] But there are three specific obstacles to such a claim raised by the text of the homily.

5A 8.3.1. *The* λόγος-*Christology of* El. *in the Homily*

The first, mentioned surprisingly neither by Rondeau nor by Nautin, is the presence of the ascription ὁ παῖς τοῦ θεοῦ, λόγος ὁ πρὸ ἑωσφόρου γεννηθείς in the commentary on the Ψαλμὸς τῷ ἀγαπητῷ.[117] This conception of the pre-existent λόγος, characteristic of *El.* and related works, was, we argued, radically reformulated by the writer of *C.N.* despite its close conformity with

---

[116] Rondeau (1967) p. 16-18, following Jerome *De Vir.* Ill. 61 ("προσομιλίαν de Laude Domini Salvatoris, in qua praesente Origene se loqui in ecclesia significat"), claimed that Origen made use of this work in his own on the psalms. Since those works were published between 214 and 218, she concludes that the homily must have been a work of Hippolytus as a youthful writer around 212. (p. 17: "... la gaucherie du style, ponctué de tours rhétoriques mécaniquement répétés, trahit, à notre avis, la jeunesse d'un auteur qui évoluera ensuite vers plus d'aisance et de simplicité.") If indeed, as Rondeau will not admit, there were two authors in the *corpus*, the early date would point to the author of *El.*, rather than his editor and continuator, the author of *C.N.*

It would however be problematic so to argue since Nautin (1971) p. 138-139 contended in reply that Origen composed two commentaries, the one on psalms 1-15, composed around 220 at Alexandria, and a second which began with *Ps.* 1 but which "embraissait l'ensemble du Psautier." The latter was composed at Caesarea after 233. As such, this would support, *prima facie*, the homily as the work of Hippolytus the editor and continuator since we have argued that the autor of *El.* was dead by this time (4B 2.2.3.3). But Nautin goes on to argue (p. 140-143) by means of a comparison that Origen did not in fact use the homily, so that indeed there is no way of dating the homily, whether early or later, with reference to his work.

[117] *In Ps.* 16: καὶ ἐν ἑτέρῳ δὲ πάλιν «Ψαλμὸς τῷ ἀγαπητῷ» Τίς δ' ἂν εἴη ὁ ἀγαπητὸς ἄλλος, ἀλλ' ἢ ὁ παῖς τοῦ θεοῦ, λόγος ὁ πρὸ ἑωσφόρου γεννηθείς, δι' οὗ τὰ πάντα ἐποίησεν ὁ Πατήρ;

the tradition of Melito and Irenaeus. For *C.N.* the λόγος only became τέλειος as παῖς after the incarnation (4A 2.1.3-2.1.4 and 4A 3.1.2).

It is difficult therefore to see how Hippolytus as author of *C.N.* could have written such words as these, even though he read them in *El.*, without recasting them in terms of his own theology. We are dealing here with perhaps the most fundamental of the distinctions on which the two-authors hypothesis rests. If there are two authors, as Nautin insists against Rondeau, then the character of this comment on *Ps.* 44,1 would be indicative of the author of *El.* rather than of *C.N.*[118]

5A 8.3.2. *The use of* ὅρος *in the Homily*

In 5A 1.1 we saw that ὅρος in *El.* X, 5,1, as in the expression ὁ τῆς ἀληθείας ὅρος=ὁ τῆς ἀληθείας κανών in 5,2) meant a canon or ecclesiastical rule. Although ὅρος appeared in that sense in *Ap. Trad.* 3, we argued that this was a composite document, and might appear as such on the Statue substantially in the form in which we have it, or only there in a first draft. At all events, though the strand represented by chapter 3 represented the theology of Order in *El.*, chapter 4 used ὅρος in a completely different sense, and one that might be associated with the alternative ordination rites that represent the alternative ecclesiastical current associated with *C.N.* and therefore Hippolytus, whose name became later associated with the community of the Statue (5A 1.2). ὅρος did not in *Ap. Trad.* 4 mean "ordinance," but the "limit" or "boundary" of hell established by Christ's descent there.

In the homily, ὅρος is used in a sense very similar to which it is found in *El.* and the associated *Ap. Trad.* 3. His introduction has argued the Davidic authorship of the Psalms, and the failure of certain titles (τὰς ἐπιγραφὰς) to correspond with the chronology of David's life has been explained in terms of the previously mentioned mystery of allegory (διὰ πνεύματος ἁγίου ..τὰ μυστήρια) that enshrouds their application to Christ. At the end of this introduction, before embarking on *Ps.* 1 and 2 he concludes thus :

17. These principles properly enunciated (τούτων δὴ τῶν ὅρων δικαίως κεκηρυγμένων), and by this method doctrine being heard with faith (καὶ τῆς κατὰ τρόπον διδασκαλίας μετὰ πίστεως ἀκουομένης), we the hearers are constrained (ἀνάγκην ἔσχομεν, οἱ ἀκροαταὶ), moved with reverence towards God (φόβῳ φερόμενοι τῷ πρὸς τὸν θεόν), to receive them by faith (πίστει παραλαμβάνειν), and not to pay attention to deceitful arguments (μὴ προσέχειν

---

118 This similarities with *El.* were perceptively drawn by Loi, *StEphAug* 13 (1977) p. 74,- 76 where amongst other comparisons, he mentions also (i) *Chronicon* 19 ("Il numero e la divisione dei popoli nati dai figli di Noè... corresponde esattamente") (cf. 5A 8 .2), (ii) the αἵρεσις καινή of *El.* IX, 11,1; 12,16 and *In Ps.* 1: αἱρέσεως καινῆς νομιζομένης quoted footnote 102, (iii) *In Ps.* 14: οἵτινες κλῆροι, διάδοχοι τῶν πατέρων with *El.* I proem. 6, etc. The problem is that, although there is a greater degree of equivalence with *El.* than with *C.N.*, (iii) fore example, is in certain critical respects different. The διάδοχοι are mystical and symbolic, seen in the title of Ψαλμὸς τῶν ἀναβαθμῶν, and ecclesiastical Order and succession is never justified in such a way by *El.*

δὲ ἀπατηλοῖς λόγοις), but to follow the [spiritual] power of the Scriptures (ἀλλὰ δυνάμει γραφῶν ἀκολουθεῖν).

Here clearly ὅρος has the sense very akin to *El.* of a criterion for right doctrine. But it must be conceded that it is used in an exegetical context, involving mystery, allegory, and faith, which is strongly reminiscent of Hippolytus *Dan.* and associated works.

5A 8.3.3. *The use of* οἰκονομία *in* In Ps. *3*

We saw in 4A 1.3 that it was Hippolytus' particular reformulation of the term οἰκονομία in *C.N.* that was one of the marks that enabled us to distinguish Hippolytus from the author of *El.*, and to note a quite radical *rapprochement* with the school of Callistus. We note however that the homily uses this term quite differently both from *El.* who knew of it only as an heretical, Marcosan concept, and from *C.N.* (e.g. 14,4) who applied it to the mysterious unity, the οἰκονομία συμφωνίας between the persons (πρόσωπα) of the Godhead (14,8).

In Ps. 3 speaks of τὸ δὲ ἦν σύμβολον τῆς ἀρχῆθεν γενομένης οἰκονομίας ἐπὶ πᾶσαν ἀνθρωπότητα but with reference to the 72 nations after Babel. Thus the Homilist uses οἰκονομία as "providential plan" in the sense neither of *C.N.* nor any other related work. Thus we find that *In Ps.* does not fit the pattern of the two-authors thesis but raises additional problems for literary relations within the Hippolytan *corpus.*

We therefore find ourselves at the close of this section in a conundrum, finding in 5A 8.3.2 grounds for closing the gap between the two authors, but in 5A 8.3.1 strong grounds for maintaining this. Let us see how, in the light of our understanding of a two-authors thesis, this conundrum might be resolved.

5A 8.4. *The presence of a third writer in the school*

The argument for two authors is founded upon the difference between *El.* and *C.N.* over the pre-existent status of the λόγος–παῖς. But we have shown in addition to that fundamental distinction a variety of relations within the *corpus* that present cumulatively the case that there are at least two authors within the *corpus.* I believe that I have adequately demonstrated in both Chapter 4 and the present chapter that cumulatively the problems associated with the two-authors thesis are significantly less than the problems for claiming one author alone.

Our examination of the problems raised by the homily on the Psalms has demonstrated this point. The use of ὅρος with a meaning distinctive of *El.* is associated with a mystical exegetical method in this homily and thus of itself might have been sufficient to dissolve the distinguishing marks of two or more authors within the *corpus.* Of itself such a feature might be held to show that the literalist and scientific interest of Χρονικῶν and the ἀπόδειξις χρόνων, is compatible in the same author, writing in a different, homiletic *genre*, with a mystical and allegoric, exegetical method. As we have seen, not only in the case of the use of ὄρος but also the post-deluvian μερισμός of the 72 nations, such coldly scientific analysis can be synthesized without radical incoherence with a mystical and allegorical, spiritual reflection (5A 8.3).

Such a solution on its own is compatible with the operations of a single mind of a single author. But it is also compatible with a third writer who synthesises one approach with another. And my point, derivable from what 5A 8.3.1 has established, is that it is the second solution that we should adopt. An unreformed λόγος–παῖς theology would not have been acceptable to the Hippolytus who wrote *C.N.*, and would have been an affront to his *rapprochement* with the Monarchians (4A 2-4A 3.1.2).

I therefore suggest the hand of a third writer who synthesised the exegetical work of Hippolytus with the scientific work of *El.* but who remained in the latter's more conservative, Christological tradition. That his work should have been attributed to the name Hippolytus should not strike us as strange in view of what we have argued about the way in which his name as editor came to be associated with some texts, and the way in which his name generally was used corporately, like Clement's, to identify corporate writings, particularly Church Orders, in a certain tradition (3C 9 and 3D 2).

The limitation of the number of writers to two would, at all events, be arbitrary in view of what we have already argued regarding the character of the Statue as the icon of a community rather than of an individual. It was always the interpretation of the Statue as a monument to an individual that imposed an all-or-nothing character on the discussion. If all the works listed on the plinth were not by Hippolytus, then all must be the work of another individual author commemorated by the seated figure. We have shown that the Statue is to be interpreted otherwise (2A 2 -2A 3.1 and 3E), and that the hand of Hippolytus as well as the author of *El.* is to be seen as part of the community that had originally opposed Callistus but been reconciled with his successors (4B 2.2.2.1.4-4B 2.2..4). If it is possible on other grounds to detect more than two writers in the *corpus* connected with the titles on the plinth of the Statue, then there is nothing in principle about the character of the artefact in itself to rule out such a conclusion.

We have already had cause to draw parallels between the Hippolytan community, represented by the Statue but with a *corpus* of works by at least three authors, and the community of the Fourth Gospel and the Johannine literature (2A 1.2-2A 2.3). In one respect the history of literary criticism of the one is reflected in that of the other. In the case of the Johannine literature, first the similarity of style and diction was noted, and differences explained away in terms of an identical author writing in a different *genre*.[119] But the point was reached in which the connections between text and text, concept and concept, became too complex, and certain differences too fundamentally inconsistent for them to be held to be encompassable within a single mind of a single author.

In the context of the Johannine literature this was to surface in the fundamental difference between a fully realised eschatology where, for example, the Antichrist was fulfilled in Judas Iscariot, ὁ υἱὸς τῆς ἀπωλείας, ἵνα ἡ γραφὴ πληρωθῇ.(*Jn.* 17,12), whereas in 1 *Jn.* 2,18 and 22, and 2 *Jn.* 7 the Antichrist comes in the contemporary heretic or schismatic. For the Fourth Gospel, the "last hour" for the manifestation in "glory" and "exaltation" is the Cross.[120] In 1 *Jn.* 2,18 the ἐσχάτη ὥρα is taking place in contemporary events. Even in the context of a creative mind, evolving gradually over time, the transition from a literalist apocalyptic to one in which mysteriously the last things were being realised in the present, to a fully realised eschatology in the past saving events, was too great to be encompassed within a single mind. The differences and similarities were therefore to be explained in the context of the developing minds of different individuals within a common school.

There is a striking similarity between such Johannine similarities and those claimed in defence of a common authorship for the Hippolytan *corpus*. In this case it was not eschatology but Christology that finally shattered the hypothesis of a single mind whose creative development was to be observed in the conceptual and theological changes within the *corpus*. The λόγος–παῖς Christology, and the likely context for the development of those differences was simply too different.

In the case of *In Ps.*, it enabled us to show that this work was definitely not by the author of *C.N.*, whereas the mystical exegesis showed us that the author could not have been that of *El*. The problems of the Hippolytan literature, like those of the Johannine, will admit, in the final analysis, no satisfactory solution that has not at its background the history of a school that produces more than one writer and probably, in the case of Hippolytus, more than two. At all events, such an explanation does not require us to distort the literary evidence by denying the identity of the εἰς τοὺς Ψαλμούς

---

[119] One could point to (i) variants of the expression τηρεῖν τὸν λόγον μου in *Apoc.* 3, 8 and 10; 22, 9 in comparison with *Jn.* 8, 51-55; 14, 23-24; 15, 20; 17, 6; (ii) the use of λόγος as a title of Christ in *Apoc.* 19, 13 cf. *Jn.* 1, 1-14; (iii) ἀληθινός used of God and Christ, or to qualify their λόγοι in *Ap.* 3, 7 and 14; 6, 10; 19, 9 and 11; 21, 5; 22, 6 cf. *Jn.* 4, 37; 7, 28; 17, 3. On such a basis, one might argue identical authorship, urging that the writer was writing in a different literary *genre* in *Apoc.* One could then extend the same comparison to the epistles, citing 1 *Jn.* 1, 1-4 with *Jn.* 1, 1-14 so that these too could now be included in the nexus of a single author, with (i) exemplified in 1 *Jn.* 5, 20.

[120] *Jn.* 12,23 and 31-32: Ἐλήλυθεν ἡ ὥρα ἵνα δοξασθῇ ὁ υἱὸς τοῦ ἀνθρώπου... νῦν κρίσις ἐστὶν τοῦ κόσμου τούτου, νῦν ὁ ἄρχων τοῦ κόσμου τούτου ἐκβληθήσεται ἔξω, κἀγὼ ἐὰν ὑψωθῶ ἐκ τῆς γῆς, πάντας ἑλκύσω πρὸς ἐμαυτόν.

with the title on the Statue solely on terms of the witness to Hippolytan authorship of *ms. Brit. Mus. syr.* 860 (*add.* 12154).

The internal evidence for *In Ps.* shows, as we have argued, that this work has more in common with *El.* than *C.N.*, while in the final analysis that common ground falls short of identity of authors. There therefore were no good grounds for claiming that a work later associated with Hippolytus' name could not have occurred on the Statue along with works that decidedly were not so associated. The title of the Jerome catalogue, probably identical with that cited by Theodoret, may nevertheless be a different title and indeed that of the author of *C.N.*, and therefore genuinely Hippolytan as opposed to bearing what became the corporate title for the disparate works of a the tradition of the community of the Statue.

Let us look briefly now at the three remaining titles listed on the plinth of the Statue.

5A 9. ᾠδαὶ εἰς πάσας τὰς γραφάς

Lightfoot believed that this title referred to what has partly survived as the Muratorian Canon, which he both translated into Greek and reduced to hexameter verses. He then hypothesised that we have here the titles of two metrical compositions, one on the *O.T.* that has perished, but another on the *N.T.* which has thus survived. I find however his grounds tenuous.

The first ground is that the Muratorian Canon agrees with Hippolytus in accepting the *Apocalypse* but in rejecting *Hebrews*. Presumably this would rule out Gaius in Lightfoot's eyes since he believed that Gaius had rejected the *Apocalypse*. But we have already for our part registered our doubt regarding the latter on the grounds that Barsalîbî's quotations are pseudepigraphic and may themselves rest upon a misreading of Eusebius' quotations of his views (3B 2.1 -2.2). Furthermore Hippolytus or the writer of *El.* (whom Lightfoot believed to be one in the same) would not have been the only person(s) to have accepted the *Apocalypse* but rejected *Hebrews*. The Canon of Scripture in the late second century was still highly fluid, and only later generations would find rejection of either of these works at all remarkable.

Lightfoot secondly considered that "the language used of the Shepherd of *Hermas* is strongly in favour of its attribution to Hippolytus." He presumably did so on the grounds of his proposed Hippolytan authorship of Liberian *Catalogus*, and of the similar references to Hermas in both that and the Muratorian Canon. But having argued the distinction between Hippolytus and author of *El.*, it is only possible to assign the author of the *C.N.* block to the second stage in the development of the Liberian *Catalogus*, which, as I have already shown, contains the reference to Hermas and Pius (4B 2.2.3.3.1). Certainly it would be difficult to see how the rigorist author of *El.* IX, 12, 22-26 would have approved of the writing described by Tertullian as "the adulterous shepherd," if that author was responsible for this title on the Statue.[121]

But Hippolytus, we have argued, was responsible for the editorial additions to the ὀνόματα list that was incorporated from the author of *El.*'s original work, the Χρονικῶν (4B 2.2.3.1-3.3), one of which referred to Hermas and Pius. On the grounds of a similar reference to Hermas and Pius in the Muratorian Canon, then, this work too may be attributable to him. It is noteworthy that the Canon, like, we argued, the author of the second edition of the *Catalogus*, is conciliatory between rigorists who rejected Hermas outright, and those who used his work as Scripture.[122] Hermas ought not to be publicly read as Scripture, but only (*et ideo*) because it was written *superrime temporibus nostris in urbe Roma*, and not apparently for any reason to do with its moral laxity.[123]

If the Muratorian Canon can be accepted as a second century document despite the objections of Sundberg, then we may well connect it with the Liberian *Catalogus* and consequently as a work of Hippolytus, editor of the work of *El.*, and conciliator between his school and that of Callistus. But it must be frankly confessed that the grounds for identifying it as a work of Hippolytus are thus far stronger than the grounds for identifying it in turn with the title ᾠδαὶ εἰς πάσας τὰς γραφάς on the Statue, and thus making it yet another work of Hippolytus himself occurring there alongside those of the author of *El.* Perhaps too much hangs on the word ᾠδαὶ, the reconstruction of the Muratorian Canon as a poem in Greek hexameters, and the daring conclusion that it refers to a plural of two works only on the *O.T.* and *N.T.* of which, hypothetically, that Canon originally consisted.

One problem that Lightfoot frankly admitted was that ᾠδαὶ and εἰς πάσας τὰς γραφάς might refer to quite different works but had simply been squeezed together on the same line. But this happens no-where else, and clearly exegetical works have been listed separately as the three works in 5A 6-8 show. This would indicate that the title indicated a general work εἰς

---

[121] Tertullian, *De Pudic.* 10,12: "Sed cederem tibi, si scriptura "Pastoris" quae sola moechos amat, divino instrumento meruisset incidi, si non ab omni concilio ecclesiarum, etiam vestrarum, inter apocrypha et falsa iudicaretur, adultera et ipsa et inde patrona sociorum, a qua et alias initiaris, cui ille, si forte, patrocinabitur pastor, quem in calicem depingis..."

[122] Lightfoot (1890) 1,II p. 410: "pastorem vero nuperrime temporibus nostris in urbe Roma Herma conscripsit sedente cathedram urbis Romae ecclesiae Pio episcopo fratre eius et ideo legi eum quidem oportet se publicare vero in ecclesia populo neque inter prophetas completum numero neque inter apostolos in finem temporum potest."

[123] Lightfoot (1890) 1,II p. 412 begins his discussion: "To this view I am predisposed by the fact that there was no one else in Rome at this time, so far as we know, competent to produce it." There is small satisfaction in detecting the greatest Cambridge patrologist of the 19th century momentarily lapsing into one of the laxer scholastic strategies of his era. See also A.C. Sundberg, Canon Muratori: A Fourth Century List, in *HThR*, 66 (1973), p. 1-41, cf. G.M. Hahnemann, *The Muratorian Fragment and the Development of the Canon*, (Oxford: Clarendon 1992) and J.S. Jeffers, *Conflict at Rome: Social Order and Hierarchy in Early Christianity*, (Minneapolis: Augsburg Fortress 1991), p. 106-115.

πάσας τὰς γραφάς rather than a number of specific commentaries. Frickel was quite wrong, as Bammel points out, to regard this work as *generell exegetische Arbeiten... zu den Schriften des Alten Testaments*.[124] However she argues that there are indeed two tiles squeezed into one, and that the second, εἰς πάσας τὰς γραφάς, summarizes "the works not already listed." Lightfoot's argument against two titles presupposed a carefully drawn up list with a clarity and symmetry, whereas the inscriptions squeezed onto the limited space of the Statue's plinth belie that presupposition.[125]

That we may have in this particular title a work by Hippolytus listed on the Statue as opposed to the author of *El.* or someone else must therefore remain only a possibility. The argument for Hippolytus as the author of the Muratorian Canon, if it is genuinely a second century document, is far stronger. Had we any information about it contents, and were we to find that there was there an overlap with the commentaries listed in 5A 6-8, then that fact would lend some substance to a third writer in the list. A community will treasure commentaries by more than one writer on the same topic.

5A 10. [----------] ιους

This title is usually restored as πρὸς τοὺς Ἰουδαίους.[126] The grounds for doing so, originally adopted by Torrès and Possevino,[127] was the correspondence between such a reconstruction and the πρὸς Ἰουδαίους ἀποδεικτική which followed immediately after the text of *C.N.* in *Vat. graec.* 1431, and is therefore also represented by only a single *ms.* tradition (3A 1). But unlike *C.N.* this text is not attributed to Hippolytus but merely follows it in Timothy Aelurus' *florilegium*. There is no τοῦ αὐτοῦ corresponding to the ὁμιλία Ἱππολύτου ἀρχιεπισκόπου Ῥώμης καὶ μάρτυρος εἰς τὴν αἵρεσιν Νοητοῦ τινος which would serve to indicate that Timothy did not consider the authors to be the same. Thus Torrès gave Hippolytus as the author's name on highly tendentious grounds and was subsequently followed by other editors.[128]

---

124 J. Frickel, *Das Dunkel um Hippolyt von Rom: Ein Lösungsversuch: die Schriften Elenchos und Contra Nöetum.* (Grazer Theologische Studien: Bauer 1988) p. 84-85: "Denn es kann keinem Zweifel unterliegen, dass der etwas rätselhafte Titel ΩΔΑΙ C ΠΑCΑC ΤΑC ΓΡΑΦΑC, der bei Anbringung der Inschriften ursprünglich den Abschluss der Liste bildete... am besten mit „Oden zu allen Schriften" übersetzt dass also dieser Titel generell exegetische Arbeiten Hippolyts zu den Schriften des Alten Testaments bezeichnen soll."

125 C.P. Bammel, The State of Play with regard to Hippolytus and the *Contra Noetum*, in *Heythrop Journal*, 31 (1990) p. 196: "The list itself is not very expertly executed, squeezed into rather an unfortunate position on one of the back corners of the throne, the sides being occupied by the Easter table. The spacing of lines 5-8 may perhaps betray uncertainty about where one title ends and the next begins and in lines 14 and 18 letters have been forgotten and added."

126 Lightfoot (1890) 1,II p. 325.

127 F. Torrès and A. Possevino, *Apparatus Sacer*, (Cologne 1608) in this second edition inserted Hippolytus' name against the text set out in the Appendix under the title *S. Hippolyti Martyris Demonstratio adversus Judaeos.*

128 Nautin (1947) p. 351-357; Nautin (1953) p. 109-114.

In consequence, we must agree with Nautin that the reconstruction of the title is highly suspect. There are no other references in the literature, and nothing other than the misread testimony of *Vat. graec.* 1431 that Hippolytus ever wrote a work of this title. The original title of whatever work headed the Statue's list therefore remains permanently lost.[129]

5 A 11. [-------] νίας

This title is usually restores as περὶ οἰκονομίας. It is mentioned as such in Ebed-Jesu and attributed to Hippolytus.[130] Lightfoot argued somewhat speculatively that this in fact was the προσομιλία *de Laude Domini Salvatoris* mentioned in Jerome, *De Vir. Ill.* 61.[131] Although nothing is known of its contents, the title is characteristic of a work written by Hippolytus as author of the *C.N.* block rather than by the author of the *El.* block.

We saw in 4A 1.3 that οἰκονομία is a concept found only in the doctrine of the Marcosans (*El.* VI, 47,1 and 3; 51,1 and 4-5; 52,9). The complete absence as an orthodox concept in the ἀπόδειξις ἀληθείας in X, 32-34, particularly with reference to the Godhead (X, 33, 10-17), was extremely surprising in view of its use in defence of a nascent trinitarianism in *C.N.* Hippolytus' quite unique use of the concept in *C.N.* was thus part of his theological *rapprochement* with the theology of the school of Callistus. The author of *El.* would not, we argued (4A 1.3), have accepted this reformulation of the problem of ditheism and the unity of the godhead. We also saw that the different senses οἰκονομία in *In Ps.* 3 (5A 8.3.3) and in various places *In Pasc.* served to confirm our hypothesis that located these works outside the original collection of the Hippolytan *corpus* (5A 2.5).

It is extremely unlikely that anyone would have given a work the title περὶ οἰκονομίας if they only intended to write a work on how the *O.T.* could be interpreted allegorically. Methods, particularly in classical and patristic literature, are not so much expounded in second-order descriptions of them but rather displayed in first-order applications. It could have been the title of a work such as the author of *In Ps.* would have written. Furthermore, in the sense of the saving acts of the Cross and Resurrection, the term would have been more likely used as in *In Pasc.* 52,2 in a discourse on the Passover bearing a title relevant to that festival, or in a homily on the Gospels rather than in a quite contextless treatise.

---

[129] It was E. Bernard and T. Galée who added the letters before the IOΥϹ of the Statue, thus influenced by Torrès, and who were cited as such by J.A.S. Fabricius, *Hippolyti Opera non antea collecta.* (Hamburg: 1716), p. 79-81. Cf. Nautin (1947) p. 353-354; ——, (1953) p. 110-111.

[130] Ebed-Jesu, *Catalogus* 7, the relevant lines of which Lightfoot (1890) 1, II p. 350 translates: κύριος Ἱππόλυτος μάρτυς καὶ ἐπίσκοπος ἔγραψε βιβλίον περὶ οἰκονομίας...

[131] Ibid. p. 398 and 423.

Ebed-Jesu explicitly attests that a work of this name exists bearing the name of Hippolytus. It is more likely therefore that the Hippolytus who wrote the *C.N.* would have used this work as a title because he understood it in a sense unique at the time of his writing. It was this uniqueness that enabled it to entitle a distinctive work dealing with a distinctive theme as opposed to a general work dealing with a general theme. Furthermore, as the use of οἰκονομία in terms of the trinitarian mystery was a commonplace, and particularly an Eastern commonplace by Ebed-Jesu's time, there is some prospect that he may be citing one of the many Hippolytan pseudepigrapha that we have argued to have flourished at the time (3C 7.2).

I am not aware whether anyone has attempted to identify the title of this work as the original title of the *C.N.* in view of the latter's unique usage of οἰκονομία, along with Tertullian, to describe the mystery of the Trinity. If this were to be the case, then Hippolytus' principal work, that identifies the *C.N.* block, would appear on the Statue along with some works by the author of *El.* but not of course *El.* itself. But this would be too speculative, since we know nothing of its contents and so in what sense the word that constitutes its title was used.

5A 12. *In Conclusion*

Having in Chapter 4 considered those works on the Statue clearly written by the author of *El.*, we have now in this chapter considered the works listed that have been attributed to Hippolytus by name. We have considered both what is probably written by the author of *C.N.* (5A 3-5 A 7, and 5A 11), and what though by the author of *El.*, he has edited (ἀπόδειξις χρόνων/ *De Pascha* (5A 2). We have further considered what is by neither of these two, either because of a putative third hand (*In Ps.* (5A 8)), or because the works that survive cannot be identified, despite appearances, with those of the Statue. We considered these latter and pseudonymous additions to the *corpus* whilst within its general tradition (*Ap. Trad.* (5A 1); *In Pasc.* (5A 2.3),[132] and probably the Barsalîbîan dialogue (5A 7).

There are, we have concluded, at least three hands to be detected in works with literary remains that are probably identical with titles on the Statue. We must therefore now examine the implications of this conclusion for the thesis of two literary profiles that can be associated with two distinct authors, whether named Josephus and Hippolytus, or whether both have the same latter name.

---

[132] This work may be earlier than Hippolytus, but its attribution to his *corpus* is later.

PART B. THE LITERARY PROFILE AND THE TWO-AUTHORS THEORY

We have noted that the question of the Statue as a monument to an individual or the icon of a community affects both the question of two authors as
well as the question of two profiles. If the unity of authorship between the
works listed on the Statue breaks down, then clearly so does the coherence
of the extrapolated profile, whether of two or of a single author. Let us
therefore now turn firstly to the question of two authors, and next to the
question of the two literary profiles, to which the answer has given rise.

5B 1. *Nautin, Simonetti and Loi: Josephus or two Hippolyti*

Both Nautin on the one hand, and Simonetti on the other sought to attribute
all the works on the Statue to a single author. For the former his name was
Josephus, and for the latter, Hippolytus, although a different Hippolytus than
the author of *C.N.* and associated works. Theirs was an all-or-nothing argument in which either all the works on the Statue were written by the author
of *C.N.* or none of them were. If the latter were the case, as both of these
writers argued, then all the writings listed had to be by the same, different
writer, and a corresponding literary profile given to both, Thus yet again we
see the false interpretation of the Statue as a monument to an individual
reinforcing illegitimately a hypothesis about only two authors, and the literary profiles that they must wear.

5B 1.1. *Josephus and Nautin's thesis*
Nautin appealed to what he claimed were three separate and independent
attributions of the περὶ τοῦ παντός to Josephus, namely:

(i) Photius, *Bibliotheca*, 48 who acknowledges ἀνεγνώσθη᾽Ἰωσήπου περὶ τοῦ παντός.[133]

(ii) Pseudo John Damascene, *Sacra Parallela*, where the work is headed ᾽Ἰωσίππου
ἐκ τοῦ λόγου ἐπιγεγραμμένου κατὰ Πλάτωνος περὶ τῆς τοῦ παντός αἰτίας καὶ κατὰ
῾Ελλήνων, as found in Holl (1899) *frag.* 353.[134]

(iii) John Philoponus, *De Opificio Mundi*, whose brief quotation on the tripartite division of the waters at the creation is prefixed: ᾽Ἰώσηπος ὁ ᾽Εβραῖος ἐν τῷ περὶ τῆς
τοῦ παντὸς αἰτίας συγγράμματι.[135]

---

[133] For full quotation see 4B 2.1, footnote 133.

[134] K. Holl, Fragmenta vornicänischer Kirchenväter aus den Sacra parallela, in *TU* 20 (5),2
(1899), p. 137-143 where we find other *ms.* variants cited each of which nevertheless contains
κατὰ Πλάτωνος as (i) *ms. Marc.* 138 X-XI: ᾽Ἰωσίππου ἐκ τοῦ λόγου τοῦ ἐπιγεγραμμένου
Πλάτωνος περὶ τῆς τοῦ παντὸς αἰτίας καὶ κατὰ ῾Ελλήνων, (ii) *ms. Paris. reg.* 923 IX-X:
᾽Ἰωσίππου ἐκ τοῦ λόγου τοῦ ἐπιγεγραμμένου κατὰ Πλάτωνος περὶ τῆς τοῦ παντός
αἰτίας, (iii) *ms. Berolin.* 1450 s. XII-XIII: ᾽Ἰωσίππου ἐκ τοῦ λόγου τοῦ ἐπιγεγραμμένου
κατὰ Πλάτωνος (iv) *ms. Flor. Mon* 119 ᵉ⁻ᵛ:᾽Ἰωσίππου ἐκ τοῦ λόγου τοῦ ἐπιγεγραμμένου
κατὰ Πλάτωνος ἐκ τῆς τοῦ πάντων αἰτίας. See also W.J. Malley, Four unedited fragments
of the De universo of the pseudo-Josephus found in the Chronicon of George Hamartolus
(Coislin 305), in *JThS* n.s. 16 (1965), p. 23-24.

[135] Nautin (1947) p. 72-73.

An initial, *prima facie* case was thus established for the name of the author of περὶ τοῦ παντός, and by implication any other work such as *El.* that we have demonstrated to have been written by the same hand (4B 2-2.1). Clearly by the end of the 9th century this work was circulated under the name of Josephus.[136]

But this attribution was not without its problems. Photius had mentioned other names that he read ἐν παραγραφαῖς of the *ms.*, namely Caius, Justin, and Irenaeus.[137] In reply Nautin was able to claim that Josephus was not simply another name. It was rather the name that was read on the title page (ἀνεγνώσθη... ἐπιγραφόμενον). Furthermore, those other names written ἐν παραγραφαῖς were written there because the name Josephus was associated by him and others with the Jewish historian. Photius proceeded in terms of a literary analysis to demonstrate that the favoured author could not have in fact written the work, and thus opened the door for the alternative candidates, read ἐν παραγραφαῖς. As Photius says:

> Thus then he speaks these words (οὕτω μὲν οὖν... ταῦτα εἰπὼν) that do no justice to the anthropology of the Jews (ἀναξίως τῆς τε τῶν Ἰουδαίων περὶ ἀνθρώπου φυσιολογίας), nor their other practice in discussion (καὶ τῆς ἄλλης αὐτοῦ περὶ τοὺς λόγους ἀσκήσεως), and he even runs over (διέξεισι καὶ) the cosmogony (περὶ τῆς κοσμογονίας) in a summary fashion (κεφαλαιωδῶς). However, regarding Christ our true God (περὶ μέντοι Χριστοῦ τοῦ ἀληθινοῦ θεοῦ ἡμῶν) his theology is closest to our own (ὡς ἔγγιστα θεολογεῖ), even to using the same term for Christ (κλῆσιν τε αὐτὴν ἀναφθεγγόμενος Χριστοῦ), and writing without fault (ἀμέμπτως ἀναγράφων) the account of his ineffable begetting from the Father (καὶ τὴν ἐκ πατρὸς γέννησιν). This perhaps convinces some in their uncertainty (ὅ τινας ἴσως καὶ ἀμφιδοξεῖν... ἀναπείσειεν) that the composition is Josephus' (ὡς Ἰωσήπου εἴη τὸ συνταγμάτιον). But nothing of his turn of phrase (οὐδὲν δὲ τὸ τῆς φράσεως) fits the remaining works of Josephus (αὐτῷ πρὸς τὰ ὑπόλοιπα τοῦ ἀνδρὸς ἀποδεῖ).
>
> *Bibliotheca* 48

Thus Nautin is able to claim that a Christian writer named Josephus was confused with the Jewish historian, and for that reason a perfectly credible author's name was passed over in favour of others.

The situation was not however as straightforward as Nautin suggested when he commended Richard for his claim that *jusqu'au IXe siècle le traité «Sur l'Univers» a circulé dans les manuscrits sous le nom de Josipe-*

---

[136] Nautin (1949) p. 224 was able to quote his arch-adversary in his support when he quotes M. Richard, sainte Hippolyte, "Hippolyte e Josipe": Bulletin de Patrologie, in *MSR* 5 (1948), p. 296: "Nous n'avons donc pas affaire à trois lemmes douteux. Les témoignages de Jean Philopon, de saint Jean Damascène et de Photius nous révèlent des faits de libraire et nous avons le droit d'en conclure que jusqu'au IXe siècle le traité "Sur l'Univers" a circulé dans les manuscrits sous le nom de Josipe-Josèphe et seulement sous ce nom." Cf. G. Bardy, Le souvenir de Josèphe chez les Pères, in *RevHE* 43 (1948), p. 77-83.
[137] For full quotations see 3B 2 footnotes 75 and 76.

Josèphe et seulement sous ce nom.[138] Firstly, although Josephus was in many (perhaps even very many) manuscripts read "written on the title (ἐπιγραφόμενον)" and other candidates (Caius, Justin, and Irenaeus) only "in the margins (ἐν παραγραφαῖς)," nevertheless Photius makes it quite clear also in *Bibliotheca* 48 that some (perhaps many) *ms.* were untitled when he says:

> But when the discourse lacks a title (ἀνεπιγράφου δὲ καταλειφθέντος τοῦ λόγου), some say the author is Josephus (φασὶ τοὺς μὲν Ἰωσήπου ἐπιγράψαι), but others Justin Martyr (τοὺς τε Ἰουστίνου τοῦ μάρτυρος), and others Irenaeus (ἄλλους δὲ Εἰρηναίου), even as some attribute the Labyrinth to Origen (ὥσπερ καὶ τὸν Λαβύρινθόν τινες ἐπέγραψαν Ὠριγένους).

Thus in some cases *ms.* were untitled and Josephus' name was as hypothetical as the rest. Furthermore, the anonymity of all works of the *El.* block other than περὶ τοῦ παντός had serious implications for Nautin's identification that he refused to acknowledge.

5B 1.1.1. *Josephus Christian or Jew: alleged confusions*

If at least some *ms.* of περὶ τοῦ παντός were anonymous, certainly both Χρονικῶν and *El.* were either anonymous or attributed in the later case to Origen (3B). It seems therefore curious that Nautin should argue that the *mss.* of the *El.* block could not have been anonymous because they were the work of an antipope whose sect would exalt the name of their founder.[139] But we owe the survival of the Hippolytan *corpus*, not to the alleged *secte* of a *fondateur* but, like any other patristic *corpus*, to its acknowledgment by later orthodoxy.

As Bammel points out, Novatian provides us with a good counter example to schismatical works necessarily bearing the names of their authors. We shall consider further the alleged schismatical parallels with Hippolytus' group, in view of the comments of Damasus and Prudentius, in Chapter 6. Novatian was the author of many writings which may well have been lost had they not been preserved under the names of Tertullian and Cyprian.[140] If her parallel were to hold, this would tell against the survival in orthodox hands of the name of a Christian, schismatical writer named Josephus up un-

---

[138] Nautin (1949) p. 224. cf. M. Richard, saint Hippolyte, «Hippolyte e Josipe»: Bulletin de Patrologie, in *MSR* 5 (1948), p. 296-300 ff. where Richard does not really support the ascription of Josephus, but allows Nautin's case against Bardy in order to make everything depend on the thesis that the text of *C.N.* is corrupt and interpolated in consequence of which alone he claims to be able to demolish the two-authors thesis. See 4 A3-3.1.2

[139] Nautin (1947) p. 87: "Mais l'hypothèse de la publication anonyme des oevres de l'auteur à cause de la défaveur attachée à son nom depuis son schisme n'est pas croyable, car, même anonyme, l'*Elenchos* révèle clairement qu'il vient d'un antipape. Surtout il n'est pas dans les habitudes des sectes de tous ordres de rougir du nom et des travaux de leurs fondateurs ni d'éviter qu'on les distingue elles-mêmes de leurs adversaires."

[140] Bammel (1990) p. 195: "... it is instructive to compare the case of Novatian, whose schism (being fully publicized at the time of its inception and also long perpetuated) was familiar to later Greek historians, but whose writings (in Latin) were preserved under the names of Tertullian and Cyprian."

til its confusion with the Jewish writer of the same name. The name would have been suppressed and, since the schism is unrecorded by Eusebius, lost entirely as the price of the survival of the works in orthodox circles. We shall consider the problems of considering the events of *El.* IX, 11-13 in terms of the later concepts of "schism" and "antipope" as both Nautin and Bammel presume.

Furthermore, if the general attribution of Josephus to the works associated with *El.* has been suppressed due to its confusion by Photius with the Jewish writer, it is hard to explain why there is only evidence for that attribution in connection with περὶ τοῦ παντός alone, with the other works being anonymous. It is this fact that has considerable force against Nautin's argument that no-one would have invented the name Josephus for a Christian writer if he had not in fact had this name, since we are talking about only one work, the περὶ τοῦ παντός that has managed to acquire this name for its author. In this regard Nautin again calls to his aid some remarks of Richard in order to show that Josephus was *beaucoup trop connu pour qu'on ait pu lui attribuer intentionnellement un ouvrage philosophico-dogmatique chrétien.*[141]

But Bardy's argument remains, despite Nautin's rejection, that Josephus did enjoy a popularity in the ancient Church.[142]

5B 1.1.2. *The Christianized Josephus in the Church Fathers*
Josephus was extensively used by Eusebius in the *H.E.* Furthermore, Eusebius quoted him in connection with the famous *Testimonium Flavianum*, in which both Christ's miracles and resurrection after death are asserted (*H.E.* I, 11,7-9). The passage itself is often claimed to be a Christian interpolation into the text of *Antiquities* 18, 63-64.[143] But if so, we have in Eusebius a Christianized Josephus, such as might well have in Christian eyes have written a work περὶ τοῦ παντός and gone on to comment in passing on the doctrine of the Trinity. This did not deceive Photius, who first of all on grounds of textual criticism rejected Josephus's authorship. But it could have deceived the mass of readers by its appearance on some, perhaps the majority, of *ms.* as we have seen Photius' words to imply.

---

[141] Nautin (1949) p. 224-225. Cf. Richard (1948) p. 297.
[142] Despite Nautin's dismissive claim (1949) p. 224 , G. Bardy, L'enigme d'Hippolyte, in *MSR* 5 (1948), p. 182-191 assembled an impressive list of allusions to Josephus from Eusebius to Abelard. See also B. Botte, Note sur l'auteur du De universo, attribué à saint Hippolyte, in *RThAM* 18 (1951), p. 8-15, cf. P. Nautin, La controverse sur l'auteur de l'Elenchos, in *RevHE* 47 (1952), p. 39-43.
[143] S.C.F. Brandon, *Jesus and the Zealots*, (Manchester: University Press 1967), p. 28-32, 115-125 tries to extend the case for interpolation to the treatment of James in *B.J.* 2,166 (=*H.E.* II, 23,21-24). For further comments and bibliography, see A. Brent, *Cultural Episcopacy and Ecumenism*, (Leiden: E.J. Brill 1992), p. 135-136, and W. Schürer, *The History of the Jewish People in the Age of Jesus*, (Ed.) G. Vermes, F. Millar, and M. Black, (Edinburgh: T. and T. Clark 1979), p. 428-437.

Furthermore, as Botte pointed out, extracts in a *florilegium* that passed
from name to name, and which might include an extract from Josephus'
Contra Apionem, which treats in part on chronographic matters, could well
have associated its author with a following extract from an anonymous περὶ
τοῦ παντός.[144] But quite apart from such speculation, Josephus, in the
Antiquities, suggests that he intends to write such a work, and this fact could
well account for a tendency amongst Photius' contemporaries to assign such
an anonymous work to him.[145]

It is furthermore futile for Nautin to appeal to the fact that no-one would
have identified Josephus the Christian with Josephus the Jewish writer when
it was clear that he had written the Χρονικῶν ending 235 A.D., though our
own view was of course that Hippolytus continued the work of *El.* up until
this time (4B 2.2.3.2).[146] Josephus' name appears on no *ms* of that document
but only of the περὶ τοῦ παντός. But even if the common authorship of that
document with *El.* had made it permissible to associate his name with that
work too, there need be no immediately obvious inconsistency in the eyes of
writers and scribes of the patristic age.

One of the enigmas of the Statue is its failure to be mentioned and
therefore taken cognisance of by any writer in antiquity. Yet, like the
Χρονικῶν, that artefact through its inscriptions was one important way by
which the events of *El.* IX, 11-13 could be accurately dated. To some writers
it might have occurred to consult Eusebius' own *Chronicon*, though significantly Photius did not do so and thus found his rejection of Josephus on
such chronological grounds. If Josephus' name had, as Nautin's thesis
required, been found on a significant number of works of the *El.* block, we
might have expected Photius to have followed that trail, but not necessarily.
We have already seen how Hippolytus himself was assigned a place in the
apostolic age by Palladius, Cyrillus of Scythopolis, and others (3C 9). It is
not to be wondered at therefore if Josephus the Jewish writer could also
plausibly free-float in chronological terms.[147]

---

[144] Botte (1951) p. 9: "Il aurait suffi, par exemple, que le *De Universo* soit rapproché, dans
un manuscrit ou un florilège, du *Contra Apionem*, qui traite en partie le même sujet (l'antiquité
du peuple juif), pour que le nom de l'auteur passe de l'un à l'autre. Mais je n'insiste pas sur ce
point."

[145] Josephus, *Antiquit. Iud.* proem. 4,25: τοῖς μέντοι βουλομένοις καὶ τὰς αἰτίας
ἑκάστου σκοπεῖν, πολλὴ γένοιτ' ἂν ἡ θεωρία καὶ λίαν φιλόσοφος, ἣν ἐγὼ νῦν μὲν
ὑπερβάλλομαι, θεοῦ δὲ διδόντος ἡμῖν χρόνον, πειράσομαι μετὰ ταύτην γράψαι
πραγματείαν, and I, 1,1: τὴν δ' αἰτίαν ἱκανὸς μέν εἰμι ἀποδοῦναι καὶ νῦν· ἐπεὶ δ'
ὑπέσχημαι τὴν αἰτιολογίαν ἰδίᾳ συγγραψάμενος παραδώσειν, εἰς τότε καὶ τὴν περὶ
αὐτῆς ἑρμηνείαν ἀναβάλλομαι. For further discussion of both these passages see Botte
(1951) p. 11-16 where he rightly criticizes (p. 11) Nautin's dismissal of Eisler, cf. Nautin
(1947) p. 87.

[146] Nautin (1949) p. 225: "... ce nom parut une erreur grossière en tête d'une chronique
allant jusqu'à l'année 235 de notre ère ou en tête d'un catalogue des hérésies chrétiennes..."
Nautin says this of Eusebius but it might well apply to others.

[147] With Nautin (1947) p. 87: "Le nom de 'Ιώσηπος (ou ses équivalents phonétiques
mentionnés plus haut) n'a pas pu être introduit: il faut reconnaître qu'il était à l'origine du livre,
et qu'il désigne non l'historien des *Antiquités*, mais l'adversaire du pape Calliste." Cf. Bardy

5B 2. *The Simonetti-Loi thesis: two authors of the same name*

One of the real obstacles to the two-authors thesis, as traditionally argued, was the number of titles on the Statue to which it appeared that Hippolytus' name had been credited by Eusebius, Jerome, Theodoret and others. Indeed, in 5A 1-11 we have been concerned with those works thus identified with Hippolytus by name. Once what I have argued to have been the false move is made of regarding the Statue as a monument to an individual whose works are recorded on its plinth, then indeed that fact becomes a serious obstacle to two authors. Both Simonetti and Loi made that false move, and, being convinced, correctly, on grounds of literary analysis that there were two authors, had to find an alternative solution to Nautin's Josephus that could cope with the fact that the one name associated with the Statue, whether in terms of title of works or of the cult-centre on the via Tiburtina, was that of Hippolytus.

Simonetti had now to explain how the Hippolytan *corpus* had come to be attributed to one author when there had originally been two. His first suggestion therefore was that Jerome, whether in half conscious confusion or by deliberate design had alluded in *Ep.* 36,16 to a quotation from the *Benedictions of the Patriarchs* as *Hippolyti martyris verba ponamus,* and in *Com. in Matt. 1 praef.* to *Hippolyti quoque martyris.* Neither of these works is listed in *Vir. Ill.* 61, where, as we have seen, he lists and adds to the titles in Eusebius *H.E.* VI, 22.[148] Here Jerome clearly tried to find the city of Eusebius' unknown See, since his words are *nomen quippe urbis scire non potui.* Yet he makes no mention of trying to find the location of Hippolytus' martyrdom.[149]

Thus Simonetti is able to raise the possibility of two Hippolyti tacitly acknowledged by Jerome, namely Hippolytus the writer and bishop mentioned by Eusebius, and Hippolytus the martyr and presbyter commemorated by his patron Damasus' inscription. The presbyter is Roman, a martyr, and commemorated on the via Tiburtina and also by the Statue, but the bishop is of an unknown oriental See and responsible for the *C.N.* block. The problem with such a dichotomy between writers of the same name men-

---

RHE 43 (1948) p. 180 note 1: "Tout d'abord, nous sommes de mauvais juges en matière de possibilités ou d'impossibilités. Les anciens n'avaient pas les mêmes exigences critiques que nous, et il fallait beaucoup pour les étonner: qu'on se souvienne du nombre des pseudépigraphes aussi bien dans la littérature profane que dans la littérature chrétienne."

[148] Simonetti (1977) p. 155: "È ovvio che l'imbarazzo in proposito sia stato provocato in tempo molto antico dalla connessione del martire e scrittore Ippolito con Roma e dalla identificazione di questo Ippolito con quello orientale, che Eusebio conosceva come vescovo..."; Simonetti (1989) p. 81-82: "A me sembra... che Girolamo non identificasse i due autori o comunque avesse dubbi sulla loro identità... è più che ragionevole ritenere che egli identificasse l'Ippolito martire, autore dei due titoli da lui conosciuti, coll'omonimo martire romano, che, alla pari di Damaso, egli conosceva come presbitero e non come vescovo."

[149] Ibid. p. 79-80: "Ma quanto alla sede, ripete la generica annotazione eusebiana: *cuisdam ecclesiae episcopus,* e chiosa significativamente: nomen quippe urbis scire non potui. Neppure accenna al martirio."

tioned by Hippolytus and Jerome is that two writings listed by Eusebius
H.E. VI, 22 are found on the Statue, namely the τινα κανόνα
ἐκκαιδεκαετηρίδος and πρὸς Μαρκίωνα (5A 3). It is possible to construe
both as identical titles to different works by the two different Hippolyti, particularly in the case of the former, though we have argued to the contrary in
5A 2.1.

But his thesis even so did not avoid some fundamental problems regard-
ing the strict boundary that it sought to set between the *El.* and *C.N.* blocks.
Given the acceptance of the authenticity of τὰ ὑπὲρ τοῦ κατὰ ᾽Ιωάννην...
(5A 7) as part of the original Hippolytan *corpus*, there is a problem for
Simonetti for equating Barsalîbî's citations as from the work listed on the
Statue. Following Prinzivalli, Simonetti treated seriously objections to Loi's
thesis that Barsalîbî's work could be identical with the work on the
Statue.[150] Those citations seemed to them to reflect the "realistic" exegesis
of *Dan.* and *Ant.* as opposed to the allegorical exegesis of certain Arabic
fragments attributed to Hippolytus on *Mat.* 24,16 ff.[151] Thus Barsalîbî's
work is transferred from the Statue to the *C.N.* block.

But there are problems, as Simonetti frankly admits, in addition to those
which I have discussed, my solution to which may in fact support this case
(3C 5). We might dissociate the Barsalîbî citations from *El.* on the grounds
that Gaius was not cited as one of the heretics of that work. But on the other
hand the debate between Gaius and the Montanist Proclus took place in
Rome at the time of Zephyrinus.[152] But as I have already pointed out, the
Barsalîbî citations already reveal the anachronism of pseudonymity when
they regard Gaius as a heretic anyway, in terms of the late second century.
Furthermore, there were eastern as well as western congregation in Rome
divided over the date of Easter (2A 2.4). Cultural difference does not
necessarily equate with geographical distance in such a context. The case for
the alleged, geographically located oriental See of Hippolytus the bishop is
not therefore sustained by the eastern perspectives of *Dan.* or some of the
liturgical rites of *Ap. Trad.* Cultural difference does not thereby evidence
geographical difference. The existence of the eastern bishop is created by
the false assumption that the Statue represents a purely western artefact in
honour of a single author.

---

[150] E. Prinzivalli, Due passi escatologici del Peri pantos di Ippolito, in *Vetera
Christianorum* 16 (1979), p. 63; ——, Note sull'escatologia di Ippolito, in *Orpheus* 1 (1980), p.
305; ——, Gaio e gli Alogi, in *Studi storico-religiosi*, 5 (1981), p. 53.
[151] See also 3C 5.3 and cf. Simonetti (1989) p. 101: "... in *CD* [=*Dan.*] e *Ant* l'interpre-
tazione della catastrofe finale è tutta impostata su linea politica e in modo quanto mai realistico:
dell'Anticristo viene rilevata sopratutto la ricostituzione dell'impero e l'azione a favore del
popolo ebraico; nel testo arabo «siamo in presenza di un'esegesi allegorica che sistematica-
mente spiritualizza ogni tratto realistico»: l'Anticristo «piuttosto che un tiranno sanguinario è
un corruttore di anime» e «il pericolo che incombe sui santi è un pericolo di ordine spirituale.»"
The quotations were from Prinzivalli (1980) p. 130.
[152] Simonetti (1989) p. 101-102.

Such conclusions therefore rest in the last analysis on two premises, namely (i) that there is a problem with Hippolytus's name associated with some works on the Statue but not others, which require them therefore to be the works of a different 'Hippolytus,' and (ii) that Eusebius was confused about the See of Hippolytus the Eastern writer, knowing nothing about Hippolytus the Roman presbyter and martyr. Premise (i) we have denied in our thesis by the argument of this book so far, namely that the works on the Statue do not have to be by a single author. Premise (ii) requires us to hold that Eusebius genuinely knew neither Hippolytus' See, nor the Hippolytan events of *El.* IX, 11-13, and therefore did not seek to suppress both in order to remove the taint of schism from the writer.

We shall consider (ii) in detail in Chapter 6, where we argue that both Eusebius and Jerome were confused about the Hippolytan events rather than deliberately suppressing them. That confusion, however, was not occasioned by the existence of two Hippolyti but by the inability of both Eusebius and Jerome to understand and conceptualise pre-Cyprianic Church Order in the post-Cyprianic definition of ecclesiastical reality that they inhabited.

For the moment, however, let us note that Simonetti rested a large part of his case on the "eastern" as opposed to the western orientation of the *C.N.* block with its serious commitment to biblical exegesis, rather than simply listing the scriptural arguments of the heretics, as for example Irenaeus had done.[153] Undoubtedly his position was fortified by the work of Hanssens on *Ap. Trad.*, and the eastern liturgical tradition that he established,[154] notwithstanding the argument that this work was listed on the Statue, which we have sought to qualify in view of the obviously composite nature of that work (5A 1). But it must be remembered that cultural space is not the equivalent to geographical space.

A community with a Greek-speaking culture and eastern origin could well be found in the fractionalized, multi-cultural Roman community at the end of the second and beginning of the third century. There is no reason why therefore some works of that origin should not have appeared on the Statue, outside of a theory that we have discredited that the Statue is a personal monument. The Statue, as we argued in the last chapter, is the monument to at least two writers, one of which was named Hippolytus, and which represented disparate communities reconciled. It is in terms of that reconciled fractionalism that we shall examine the school of Hippolytus and his predecessor in Chapter 7.

---

[153] Ibid.. (1989) p. 112: "Rileviamo perciò un grande ritardo dell'Occidente rispetto all'Oriente quanto alla produzione letteraria di questo tipo..." and pl. 114: "Questa carenza va valutata sopratutto in confronto con la letteratura dello stesso genere: Ireneo prima di El, e sua fonte, ed Epifanio dopo sono soliti riportare la documentazione scritturistica prodotta dagli eretici che scrivono."

[154] J.-M. Hanssens, La liturgie d'Hippolyte: ses documents, son titulaire, ses origines et son caractère, in *OrChrA* 155, (1959).

But at this point we come to the question of two distinct literary profiles, whether or not their eastern or western orientation is geographically distant, or whether cultural and in geographical proximity. It is to this question that we can now turn.

5B 3. *The construction of literary profiles*

We have cast doubt on the use of the Statue to establish a block associated with *El.* distinct from that of *C.N.* We have furthermore suggested the presence of at least a third author in the *corpus* even at the stage of evolution represented by the list of works on the plinth. Nevertheless, since on literary grounds we have accepted that there are at least two authors, it will be well for us now to look at the literary profile afforded by those works definitely attributable to the author of *El.*, and those alternatively to the author of *C.N.*, and to analyse the literary profile claimed for both.

Nautin followed by Simonetti and Loi claimed that the distinction between the literary profiles were to be made in the following way. The author of *El.* has an encyclopaedic secular education, which he uses to expose heretical schools by tracing the διαδοχαί of their teachers back to allegedly pagan, philosophical roots.[155] The author of *C.N.* is, on the other hand, "a pastor of souls" disinterested in modern science, whose method of refutation rests purely on scriptural exegesis.[156]

We have already considered and rejected the thesis that the two groups of works are addressed to different audiences so that to those outside the church the author appears in the guise of the educated philosopher, but to those within he appears as the Scriptural exegete and pastor of souls (4A 2.1.1). But sometimes it is believed that the difference in literary and cultural physiognomy could be closed by postulating the development of a single writer from the more biblically based fundamentalism of for example

---

[155] Nautin (1947) p. 80: "La catalogue bibliographique et les tables gravées sur le siège de la statue nous font connaître quelqu'un qui a des prétentions dans toutes les sciences profanes: philosophie, histoire, calcul."; Loi *StEphAug* (1977) p. 67: "Possediamo, pertanto, un primo blocco di opere omogeneo dal punto di vista linguistico, stilistico, e culturale, il quale delinea per noi i tratti fondamentali necessari per ricostruire l'identità letteraria e culturale dell'autore delle opere indicate nella statua romana." For a discussion of *El.*'s reductionist methodology in refuting heresies, by contrast with Irenaeus, see G. Vallée, A Study in Anti-Gnostic Polemics: Irenaeus, Hippolytus, and Epiphanius, in *Studies in Early Christianity and Judaism* 1, (Canada: William Laurier University Press 1981) (Canadian Corporation for Studies in Religion). Cf. also K. Koschorke, Hippolyt's Ketzerbekämpfung und Polemik gegen die Gnostiker. Eine tendenzkritische Untersuchung seiner „Refutatio omnium häresium," in *Göttinger Orient-forschungen,* 6,4 (Wiesbaden: Harassowitz 1975). See also C. Osborne, *Rethinking Early Greek Philosophy: Hippolytus of Rome and the Presocratics.* (London: Duckworth 1987).

[156] Nautin (1947) p. 82: "un homme consacré avant tout à l'exégèse et s'attachant au sens typologique de l'Écriture."; Nautin (1949) p. 228: "*Une physionomie intellectuelle*, à savoir un érudit qui calcule un canon pascal, rédige un Chronique, un esprit qui a des préoccupations philosophiques, puisqu'il écrit sur la physique et qu'il consacre tout un livre à la question: D'où vient la mal?"

Dan. and *Ant.*, to the liberal maturity of *El.* and περὶ τοῦ παντός.[157] Such a view has however been encouraged by what I believe to be a false description of the two literary physiognomies which are nevertheless quite distinct. The falsity of the description in turn reflects a serious misunderstanding of the precise nature of the difference.

Though Hippolytus, author of the *C.N.* block, is a biblical exegete, the theology in terms of which he interprets Scripture is far more radical than that of the author of *C.N.* Furthermore, by the term "more radical" I must state at the outset that I mean "far more in accommodation with contemporary, Graeco-Roman paganism." I have emphasised more than once that the theology of *El.* represents a far greater coherence with the patristic tradition of Justin, Theophilus, Irenaeus and others than does the radical departure of *C.N.* from that tradition. Moreover, *El.* may have knowledge of systems of Greek philosophy, and of heretical thought, but these are held at arms length. His secular knowledge allows him mainly to detect the putative origins of what should not be believed rather than to illuminate what should be believed. *C.N.* on the other hand, in his doctrine of the λόγος and in his use of heretical texts, is far more prone to use such secular knowledge positively in order to unravel the meaning of the sacred text (4A 1.2-3.2.2).

As such it will become clear that any thesis of development between these two physiognomies in terms of a single mind over time will fail. The fundamental mind set in both cases begins as well as ends at quite different starting points. We shall now develop in further detail this totally incompatible character of two quite different mind-sets. We shall do so by firstly re-examining the λόγος Christology of *C.N.* that we have already discussed in connection with the reconciliation between parties within the Church (4A 1.2 and 4A 3.2.3), as also representing a *rapprochement* with the pagan, philosophical hinterground (5B 3.1). We shall then, secondly, show the relationship between works clearly identifiable with *C.N.* as well as *C.N.* itself, as reflecting, not the theology of *El.*, but partly the theology of the Naasene Psalm which *El.* IV, 6-10 records only to reject.

5B 3.1. *The* λόγος–παῖς *theology and Hellenistic religion*

El. did take over the λόγος ἐνδιάθετος τοῦ παντός who, as we saw, contained with in himself τὰς ἐν τῷ πατρικῷ νῷ ἐννοηθείσας ἰδέας (4A 1.1). Such

---

157 Capelle (1950) p. 173-174: "L'évolution n'est pas moins sensible—ni moins normale—dans son style, qui évite à la fin certains procédés de rhétorique fréquents dans ses premiers ouvrages... Les indices de mentalités différentes sont d'interpretation difficile. Ils preuvent signifier qu'on a affaire à deux auteurs, mais aussi bien que l'unique auteur a fort évolué," with which agreed G. Oggioni, Ancora sulla questione di Ippolito, in *ScuCat* 80 (1952), p. 518-519: "Anche perchè questa differenza può trovare varie spiegazioni: diversità di età nell'autore..." Cf. also ——, La questione di Ippolito, in *ScuCat* 78 (1950), p. 126-143 who on p. 141 quotes Bardy (1948) p. 82 and 87. See also S. Giet, Controverse sur Hippolyte, in *RevSR* 25 (1951), p. 83-5; H. de Riedmatten, Review of Nautin's Hippolyte et Josipe, in *DomSt* 1 (1948), p. 168-173.

concepts were taken over from a Stoic and Platonic synthesis. These philosophical concepts alone he was prepared to use in defence of revealed truth.
We have already seen that, in comparison with what we argued to be an
anonymous work, the *In Pasc.*, *El.* was not prepared to use heretical gospels
in defence of orthodox Christology (5A 2.4.2). But even *El.*'s restricted and
sparse use of a Platonic-Stoic synthesis was heavily controlled by the idea of
πρωτότοκος applied to the fully personal, pre-existent λόγος on the basis of
the use of *Ps.* 2,7; 44,1 and 109,3 by Justin, Athenagoras, and Theophilus
(4A 2.1; 4A 3.2.2; 5A 2.4.3).

We saw that, in the face of this tradition, *C.N.* asserted the doctrine that
the pre-existent λόγος was not τελείος or "complete" before the incarnation.
In *C.N.* νοῦς is related to λόγος in that νοῦς and παῖς occupy the extremes of
a pole the centre of which is occupied by the λόγος .[158] Thus νοῦς will
constitute the mind of God absolutely invisible and incomprehensible, but
which, by his own will or purpose, has generated or emanated (ἐγέννα,
προσῆκεν (10, 4) the λόγος as his agent in creation. But the λόγος, though
thus hypostatised, has no further form nor shape until his becoming flesh as
the τελείος υἱός (4, 10; 5, 2-3; 15, 7; 17, 5) or παῖς (*C.N.* 11, 3). There was
however a kind of emanationism in which what was emanated remained at
one with its source, like aeons in the *pleroma*, as the doctrine of a specialized οἰκονομία was to show.

5B 3.1.1. *The* οἰκονομία *of* C.N. *and Gnostic aeon speculation*
It is important not to misinterpret, as Frickel did (4A 2.1.2), the statement in
10, 4: προῆκεν τῇ κτίσει κύριον τὸν ἴδιον νοῦν αὐτῷ μόνῳ πρότερον ὁρατὸν
ὑπάρχοντα τῷ δὲ γινομένῳ κόσμῳ ὄντα ἀόρατον ποῖει, as though the focus
was on the νοῦς–λόγος seen and grasped in creation before the enfleshment.
Rather it is the that to which Hippolytus gave the word οἰκονομία as a
technical term (4A 1.3)—the total *oikonomia*— that is here in view, in
which the νοῦς proceeds to the hypostatised λόγος, which in turn proceeds
to the παῖς of the enfleshment, in a single, economical process. The passage,
after all, immediately continues ὅπως διὰ τοῦ φανῆναι ἰδὼν ὁ κόσμος
σωθῆναι δυνηθῇ, where "making manifest (φανῆναι)" "for the world's salvation (σωθῆναι)," is clearly subsequent to the enfleshment. The context
thus makes it clear that the "making visible (ὁρατὸν)" refers to the λόγος
after his taking of flesh, or perhaps together with the taking of flesh as part
of the *oikonomic* continuum.[159]

Thus *C.N.* had, in its concept of νοῦς προβάς, gone farther than the
poetic and figurative language of Justin and Theophilus, and had dared to

---

[158] A. Zani, La Cristologia di Ippolito, in *Richerche di Scienze teologiche* 22, (Brescia:
Morcelliana 1984) (Publicazioni del Pontifico seminaro lombardo in Roma), p. 116-119, 238.
See also P. Meloni, Ippolito e il cantico dei cantici, in *StEphAug* 13 (1977), p. 97-120.
[159] For interpretation of these passages discussed in the context of the theological differences with *El.* see Chapter 4 footnotes 9, 11, 12-23, 36, 58, 60, and accompanying text.

speculate further than Irenaeus on the process of generation of the λόγος from the Father in specific relation to the incarnation, and certainly further than the Fourth Gospel.[160] That speculation in itself was reminiscent of Gnostic speculation on emanation of aeons. The unashamed use of νοῦς along with σοφία and λόγος betrayed the character of that speculation as did the depersonalization of the λόγος ἄσαρκος.

Once metaphors and biblical and poetic imagery are judged insufficient in Christological debate, then the literal, metaphysical question is raised as to how the υἱός, πρωτότοκος before creation, can also be begotten again at the incarnation. *C.N.*'s answer was that the generation was incomplete before the creation, and only became complete at the incarnation. The added practical value of this literal, philosophical conclusion was the closing of the gap between the community of Hippolytus, the successor of *El.*, and the semi-Monarchian successors of Callistus' community. No longer could there be a second god begotten before the creation who was incarnate apart from the will of the Father (4A 1.2 -1.3), just as the *Propater* willed the aeons into existence from his own substance. The comparison would not have been far-fetched in the minds of Hippolytus' contemporaries, however strange it might appear to we who are conditioned to think of Hippolytus as a proponent of nascent orthodoxy, as we shall now see.

5B 3.1.2. *A folk-memory of Hippolytus the Valentinian*
We have already mentioned certain connections between Valentinian specu-lation and the Christology of *C.N.* 10 ,3-4 (2A 3.1). We also drew certain conclusions from those regarding the character of the Statue as an artefact, since Christ seems to have been depicted by the Carpocratian Gnostics as the female figure reminiscent of the statues of Serapis-σοφία (2A 3.2). Such a conclusion is, I submit, not to be regarded as far fetched in the light of the statement of the bishops of Philopolis, in the midst of the Arian controversy, in 347. Referring to events of more than a century before, they describe Callistus as expelling Hippolytus from the Church on the grounds that he was a Valentinian.[161] The details cannot be pressed, but as Döllinger pointed out, they contain a garbled folk-memory that nevertheless betray some impressions of how the *oikonomic* continuum of Hippolytus sounded to late second century ears.[162]

---

160 The writer before Hippolytus who attempted philosophical definition of the procession of the λόγος was Tatian, but for him it was the procession in creation and not in incarnation.
161 S. Hilarius, *ex oper. hist. frag.* II I ii 662; Socrates *H.E.* 2,15 cf. I. von Döllinger, *Hippolytus und Kallistus, oder Die römische Kirche in der ersten Hälfte des dritten Jahrhunderts,* (Regensburg: Manz 1853), p. 218. See also L. Prestige, Callistus, in *Fathers and Heretics,* (London: S.P.C.K. 1954).
162 Döllinger (1853) p. 220: "Wir besitzen noch in einem unten näher zu erwähnnen Römischen Denkmale einen Nachklang der Kämpfe... Hier wird Hippolyt als Valentinianer bezeichnet, als solcher soll er abgesetzt und verdammt worden sein... wohl mag Kallistus, als er ihn seiner Stelle entsetzte und aus der Kirchengemeinschaft ausschloss, die Bezeichnung, das seine Lehre theilweise Valentinisch sei, gebraucht haben."

Döllinger wrote before any discussion of a two-authors' hypothesis, and believed that what he said of the author of *C.N.* applied to *El.* But it is significant for our discussion that it was the former work on which he based his remarks on the shadow of Valentinianism, and its corresponding paganism. The universal Father, *Bythos* or *Monad,* was for innumerable ages alone with *Ennoia* or *Sige.* When he sought to break this silence he produced νοῦς as a substantial image of himself. Thus *C.N.* 10,1 reads, θεὸς μόνος ὑπάρχων καὶ μηδὲν ἔχων ἑαυτῷ σύγχρονον, ἐβουλήθη κόσμον κτίσαι. ὃν κόσμον ἐννοηθεὶς θελήσας τε καὶ φθεγξάμενος ἐποίησεν.[163] Indeed we might add that Hippolytus, in *C.N.* 11, 2, while speaking of the νοῦς ὃς προβὰς ἐν κόσμῳ ἐδείκνυτο παῖς θεοῦ, had immediately (in 11, 3) to defend himself against any Valentinian interpretation of what he was proposing. Thus he denied that he was speaking of πληθὺν θεῶν παραβαλλομένην κατὰ καιροὺς of the Valentinians by appealing to the instrumentality of the depersonalized λόγος, subject to God's will (αὐτοὶ μὴ θέλοντες τῇ ἀληθείᾳ ἕνα θεὸν λέγειν ποιήσαντα ὡς ἠθέλησεν), in direct contradiction to what *El.*'s alleged ditheism claimed.[164]

Indeed Döllinger at that point of his career was found supporting the supposed "papal" theology of Callistus against the author of *El.*, whom he mistakenly thought to be Hippolytus, author of *C.N.* and therefore in fact Callistus' opponent. Certainly his confusion was shared by the garbled folk-memories of the bishops at Philopolis. His grounds was of course that *C.N.*'s theology of the λόγος ἄσαρκος, who could only be the fully personal τέλειος υἱός after the incarnation, was quite heretical in terms of later orthodoxy. The problem was that, in some respects like Tertullian also, that theology presupposed that the Son was simply a part of the divine essence, and not a separate person, and proceeded from that essence, just like Minerva from the head of Jupiter. In consequence there could be a time when there was neither Father nor Son, in the words of Tertullian, or when in the words of Hippolytus θεὸς μόνος ὑπάρχων καὶ μηδὲν ἔχων ἑαυτῷ σύγχρονον.[165]

---

[163] Ibid. p. 202-204: "... Gott gleichfalls, nachdem er lange mit sich allein gewesen, den Beschluss sasst, seinen bisher schweigenden Nus aus sich zu entsenden, ihn zur Person zu lassen, womit dann die Hervorbringen einer Welt von Geistern und materiellen Geschöpfen ihren Anfang nimmt. Auch später hat man in der Kirche die Annahme, dass es erst eines Rathschlusses und Willensaktes des Vaters bedurft habe, um den Logos in's persönliche Dasein zu rufen, als die dem Valentinus eigenthümlich Lehre bezeichnet, wie diess Athanasius wiederholt that (Or. contr. Ar. III op. 1, 613)."

[164] Note the air of injured innocence in the rhetorical question of *C.N.* 11, 3: τίς τοίνυν ἀποφαίνεται πληθὺν θεῶν παραβαλλομένην κατὰ καιρούς; καὶ γὰρ πάντες ἀπεκλείσθησαν εἰς τοῦτο ἄκοντες εἰπεῖν ὅτι τὸ πᾶν εἰς ἕνα ἀνατρέχει. εἰ οὖν τὰ πάντα εἰς ἕνα ἀνατρέχει– καὶ κατὰ 'Οὐαλεντῖνον καὶ κατὰ Μαρκίωνα Κήρινθόν τε καὶ πᾶσαν τὴν ἐκείνων φλυαρίαν–καὶ ἄκοντες εἰς τοῦτο περίπεσαν ἵνα τὸν ἕνα ὁμολογήσωσιν αἴτιον τῶν πάντων, ἆρα συντρέχουσιν καὶ αὐτοὶ μὴ θέλοντες τῇ ἀληθείᾳ ἕνα θεὸν λέγειν ποιήσαντα ὡς ἠθέλησεν (See further 4A 1.1 and footnote 9).

[165] Ibid. p. 766: "Danach war auch Gott ein Körper, der in sich den Sohn– ebenfalls ein körperliches Wesen– geschaffen und gezeugt hatte. So war der Sohn ein Theil des ganzen göttlichen Wesens, in der Zeit von demselben hervorgebracht, so dass eine Zeit war, wo Gott noch nicht Vater war. Diese in der That heidnische Lehre– denn der Sohn ging nach derselben

We thus see that the Christology of the *C.N.* block is far more closely attuned than the *El.* block to late-Hellenistic, religious culture. The author of the latter's display of philosophical learning, and chronological and astronomical calculations has been successful in hiding that fact from modern critics. The author of *El.* never actually synthesised his vast though superficial philosophical learning with what he believed to be revealed truth. He held the former at arm's length and admitted only the apologetic minimum, using his secular knowledge chiefly to delineate what must be kept at arm's length. The ἀπόδειξις χρόνων of the Statue itself is witness to the superficiality of his understanding of astronomy (2A 2.4).

Perhaps even to his contemporaries the biblically-based, pastor of the *C.N. block* seemed like a conservative figure. Perhaps Hippolytus even believed this himself as he made peace with the semi-Monarchians who succeeded Callistus. But his Scriptural commentaries, as the later impressions of Valentinianism showed, could not hide the theological radicalism which might have concealed itself under such a literary form. The philosophical categories that he used were firmly entrenched within his secular culture and derived wholeheartedly from that source.

We shall see now a particular example of this in the way in which the concepts of the Naasene Psalm, held at arm's length by the author of *El.* and quoted only as part of his exposure of heresy, are incorporated in works associated with *C.N.* into the Christology of that block. Hippolytus will thus emerge, contrary to the usual assumption, as a far more radical theologian than the author of the *El.*-block.

5B 3.2. *The λόγος–παῖς theology in the Naasene Psalm*
We must now explore further, in the context of the writings of the Hippolytan school itself, from where the author of *C.N.* derived his conception λόγος ἄσαρκος as the hypostatised divine will, and indeed the expression of the divine δύναμις and πνεῦμα, but without form or shape that can be seen or apprehended before becoming τέλειος υἱός in the Virgin's womb? Certainly the author of *El.* X, 33,11, as we have seen, did not shrink from considering the λόγος as παῖς τοῦ θεοῦ before his coming into the world (4A 2).

C.N.'s commonly-described literary physiognomy, coinciding perhaps with his own self-image, is of a biblical scholar rejecting the wisdom of the world. But nowhere does his view of the λόγος ἄσαρκος as incomplete occur, as we have seen, in the hermeneutic tradition in which he wrote. And so why, we may ask, philosophically does he make this conceptual shift, quite apart from his political desire to reach a *rapprochement* with the Monarchians?

---

ebenso aus Gott hervor, wie Minerva aus dem Haupte des Jupiter, und war ein in der Zeit entstandener Untergott– musste in Rom eben so grossen Anstoss erregen..."

The reason is because, albeit perhaps subconsciously, the author of the *C.N.* block is influenced by the extra-biblical, Hellenistic background far more radically than appears as the case with the *El.*-block, despite the literary self-images of both. Let us look at the Naasene text, preserved in *El.* V, 6-10, in order to see the true character of *C.N.*'s 'biblical' doctrine. We shall find attested by the Naasene text certain aspects of the doctrine of the unformed pre-incarnate and incomplete λόγος, reflected later in *C.N.*, but insulated from orthodoxy by the author of *El.*, and confined strictly to the διαδοχαί of the heretics. Indeed, the fourth evangelist joined *El.* against *C.N.* in this respect, in that he never used νοῦς in connection with his λόγος Christology, in view of its Gnostic roots, as the *C.N.* unblushingly does.

5B 3.2.1. *The λόγος as mediator*

The λόγος, according to Frickel's reconstructed Naasene Text, is the mediating principle between the created and uncreated order.[166] The former is considered to undergo change: ἡ μεταβλητὴ γένεσις... μεταμορφουμένη κτίσις ἀποδείκνυται, through the agency of (ὑπὸ τοῦ) what is the "unutterable" (ἀρρήτου), "inconceivable" (ἀνεξεικονίστου), "incomprehensible" (ἀνεννοήτου)," and "formless (ἀμόρφου)" first principle (V, 7,23). The cause (αἰτία) of all birth, movement, and change is ἡ τοῦ πνεύματος οὐσία (V, 7,25), which, as the Attis Hymn and Commentary proceed,[167] is described as λόγος, and is personified by Hermes. In V, 7,29 we read: Ἑρμῆς ἐστι λόγος ὅς ἑρμηνεὺς ὢν καὶ δημιουγὸς τῶν γεγονότων ὁμοῦ καὶ γινομένων καὶ ἐσομένων. Thus what was described as "formless (ἀμόρφου)" in the Isis mysteries, now come to possess a "form" or "impress (χαρ-ακτῆρ)," since the *genitalia* of his statue, like that of Isis, "expresses in a certain form (τινὶ κεχαρακτηρισμένος σχήματι)" the desire to ascend from the lower to the higher world (V, 7,29).[168]

Not only in the syncretism of the Naasene text does the λόγος find expression in the statues of Isis and Hermes, but also in the Christ as Son of Man: οὗτος δὲ ἐστιν ὁ χριστός, ὁ ἐν πᾶσι τοῖς γενητοῖς υἱὸς ἀνθρώπου κεχαρακτηρισμένος ἀπὸ τοῦ ἀχαρακτηρίστου λόγος (V, 7,33). Thus we observe that whether the λόγος receives the character of Isis, Hermes, or the Son of Man, in each case the λόγος itself, apart from that impress or χαρακτῆρ, remains ἀχαρακτηρίστος, just as the οὐσία τοῦ πνεύματος of the

---

[166] J. Frickel, Hellenistische Erlösung in christlicher Deutung: die gnostische Naasenerschrift, in *Nag Hamadi Studies* 19, (Leiden: Brill 1984).

[167] For the reconstructed texts, see Frickel (1984) p. 42-69 and p. 82-89. For ease of reference I cite these with the notation in the text of *El.*

[168] *El.* V, 7, 23-29: "Ὀσιριν δὲ λέγουσι ὕδωρ· ἡ δὲ Ἴσις ἑπτάστολος, περὶ αὐτὴν ἔχουσα καὶ ἐστολισμένη ἑπτὰ στολὰς αἰθερίους... ἡ μεταβλητὴ γένεσις ἐστιν ἡ ὑπὸ τοῦ ἀρρήτου καὶ ἀνεξεικονίστου καὶ ἀνεννοήτου καὶ ἀμόρφου μεταμορφουμένη κτίσις ἀποδείκνυται... ὁ γὰρ Ἑρμῆς ἐστι λόγος ὅς ἑρμηνεὺς ὢν καὶ δημιουργὸς τῶν γεγονότων ὁμοῦ καὶ γινομένων καὶ ἐσομένων παρ᾽ αὐτοῖς τιμώμενος ἔστηκε τοιούτῳ τινὶ κεχαρακτηρισμένος σχήματι ὅπερ ἐστὶν αἰσχύνη ἀνθρώπου, ἀπὸ τῶν κάτω ἐπὶ τὰ ἄνω ὁρμὴν ἔχων.

Isis mysteries, with which it is equated, was "imageless (ἀνεξεικονίστος)
"and "formless (ἀμόρφος)." The pagan λόγος, like the λόγος ἄσαρκος of
C.N., was thus without image or form, without embodiment in a divine
being, which gave to it personality, such as Hermes or the Son of Man in the
case of the former, or the human Jesus begotten of the Virgin in the case of
the latter.

Within such a set of religious concepts drawn directly from Hellenistic
culture, any description in personal terms of the λόγος before the incarnation
would indeed therefore have implied δύο θεοὺς. This is why, in denying
this, Hippolytus described the pre-existent λόγος in strictly impersonal terms
as a δύναμις or a νοῦς before entering the world and being revealed in flesh
(C.N. 11, 1-2). Thus the successor to the author of El. was able to assure the
successors of Callistus that he was no ditheist. But the price thus paid for
that *rapprochement* was a far more radical and uncritical assimilation of
Hellenistic religious categories into the consensual theology of the reconciled communities. Thus we see the real, pagan and Hellenistic roots of the
refusal of the author of the C.N. block to acknowledge any form or personality to the λόγος before his enfleshment as παῖς, subsequent to which, and in
terms of which, the divine nature could be revealed and grasped.
Hippolytus' λόγος, like that of the Naasene Psalm, was ἀνεξεικονίστος
without the incarnation, as C.N. 7, 6 makes clear: διὰ γὰρ τῆς εἰκόνος
ὁμοίας τυγχανούσης εὔγνωστος ὁ πατὴρ γίνεται· εἰ δὲ τὴν εἰκόνα, ἥτις
ἐστιν ὁ υἱός...

We shall now see how Adamas as the redeemer figure of the Naasene
Psalm makes his appearance, albeit in a demythologized form, in the C.N.
block.

5B 3.2.2. *Adamas as redeemer by the λόγος in the* C.N. *block*
Whilst Hermes as a pagan deity cannot obviously represent the λόγος for
C.N., the latter is, nevertheless, elsewhere in the C.N. block, described as
ἑρμηνεύς or "interpreter," in Ben.Jac. 119β and 120α: αὐτὸς ὁ λόγος ἑαυτοῦ
ἑρμηνεὺς γένηται... ὁ λόγος ἐμηνεὺς τῶν ἑαυτοῦ μυστηρίων γινόμενος. The
λόγος as Hermes in the Naasene Text is furthermore brought into relationship with the redemption of the soul of Adamas (καλεῖται δὲ 'Αδάμας), the
Man from above who bears the Christian title "Son of Man" (ἡ πρώτη τῶν
ὅλων ἀρχὴ ἄνθρωπος ἐστι καὶ υἱὸς ἀνθρώπου) (El. V, 6,4), now enslaved in
matter (καταδουλούμενον τὸ πλάσμα τοῦ μεγάλου καὶ καλλίστου καὶ
τελείου ἀνθρώπου) (V, 7,7).

The "man of the earth" is Adamas' "image" (εἰκόνα ὑπάρχοντα ἐκείνου
τοῦ ἄνω, τοῦ ὑμνουμένου 'Αδάμαντος ἀνθρώπου).[169] We have similar

---

169 Following the list of the various names of the first man amongst various peoples, the
Psalm (El. V, 7, 6) continues: Χαλδαῖοι δὲ τὸν 'Αδάμ. καὶ τοῦτον εἶναι φάσκουσι τὸν
ἄνθρωπον, ὃν ἀνέδωκεν ἡ γῆ, σῶμα μόνον· κεῖσθαι δὲ αὐτὸν ἄπνουν, ἀκίνητον,

themes repeated in strikingly similar language in *On the Great Ode*, attributed to the *C.N.* block, and reconstructed by Nautin from Theodoret's *Eranistes*. The biblically-based, "pastor of souls" has applied the due process of *Entmythologizierung* to his doctrinal account, but in a demythologized form such fragments of Hellenism clearly remain.

Just as "the Man whom the earth produced (ὁ ἄνθρωπος, ὃν ἀνέδωκεν ἡ γῆ)" in the Psalm (V, 7,6) is infused with the soul of Adamas, so in *On the Great Ode* it is the "first-born Word (ὁ πρωτότοκος λόγος)" who "visits the first-fashioned Adam in the Virgin (τὸν πρωτόπλαστον ' Αδὰμ ἐν τῇ παρθένῳ ἐπισκεπτόμενος)". Just as the soul of Adamas is "enslaved (καταδουλούμενον)" and lead forth by Hermes-Logos, so here the Christ-Logos "draws from lowest Hades the lost Man first-fashioned from the earth mastered in the bonds of death (ὁ τὸν ἀπολωλότα ἐκ γῆς πρωτόπλαστον ἄνθρωπον καὶ ἐν δεσμοῖς θανάτου κρατούμενον ἐξ ᾅδου κατωτάτου ἑλκύσας)."[170] The Hermes-Logos of the Psalm is "leader and guide of souls (ψυχαγωγός... καὶ ψυχοπομπὸς)" who are lead (κατηνέχθησαν) from the blessed Man above... or Adamas (ἀπὸ τοῦ μακαρίου ἄνωθεν ἀνθρώπου... ἢ ' Αδάμαντος) into clay-like matter (εἰς πλάσμα τὸ πήλινον)." So the λόγος-ἑρμηνεύς of the *Blessings* becomes, in the *Ode*, the "redeemer of souls (τῶν ψυχῶν λυτρωτὴς)" who "descending from above brings to the realms above the (lost Adam) below (ὁ ἄνωθεν κατελθὼν καὶ τὸν κάτω εἰς τὰ ἄνω ἀνενέγκας)." The "spiritual Man" thus "seeks the Man of the earth in the womb (ὁ πνευματικὸς τὸν χοϊκὸν ἐν τῇ μήτρα ἐπιζητῶν)." Finally, he is the one "who has turned the man loosed on earth and who became the food of the serpent into adamant (hard metal) (ὁ τὸν εἰς γῆν λυόμενον ἄνθρωπον καὶ βρῶμα ὄφεως γεγενημένον εἰς ἀδάμαντα τρέψας)."

The biblically based pastor might appeal to 1 *Cor.* 15, 45-49 as the true source of his theology where ὁ πρῶτος ἄνθρωπος ' Αδάμ is described as ἐκ τῆς γῆς χοϊκὸς, and we are promised τὴν εἰκόνα τοῦ ἐπουρανίου having worn previously τὴν εἰκόνα τοῦ χοϊκοῦ. But although he might claim that "in Adam (ἐν τῷ ' Αδάμ) all die," Paul never equates the human condition with a metaphysically present fallen Man (τὸν ἀπολωλότα ἐκ γῆς πρωτόπλαστον ἄνθρωπον), nor is Christ "the redeemer of *souls*." Furthermore, not only is Hermes demythologized but yet firmly represented as the λόγος-ἑρμηνεύς, but so also is Adamas. The description of the process of redemp-

---

ἀσάλευτον, ὡς ἀνδριάντα, εἰκόνα ὑπάρχοντα ἐκείνου τοῦ ἄνω, τοῦ ὑμνουμένου ' Αδάμαντος ἀνθρώπου, γενόμενον ὑπὸ δυνάμεων τῶν πολλῶν...

[170] Theodoret, *Eranistes*, II, 173,12: ὁ τὸν ἀπολωλότα ἐκ γῆς πρωτόπλαστον ἄνθρωπον καὶ ἐν δεσμοῖς θανάτου κρατούμενον ἐξ ᾅδου κατωτάτου ἑλκύσας, ὁ ἄνωθεν κατελθὼν καὶ τὸν κάτω εἰς τὰ ἄνω ἀνενέγκας, ὁ τῶν νεκρῶν εὐαγγελιστὴς καὶ τῶν ψυχῶν λυτρωτὴς καὶ ἀνάστασις τῶν τεθαμμένων γινόμενος... ὁ πρωτότοκος λόγος τὸν πρωτόπλαστον ' Αδὰμ ἐν τῇ παρθένῳ ἐπισκεπτόμενος ὁ πνευματικὸς τὸν χοϊκὸν ἐν τῇ μήτρα ἐπιζητῶν... ὁ τὸν εἰς γῆν λυόμενον ἄνθρωπον καὶ βρῶμα ὄφεως γεγενημένον εἰς ἀδάμαντα τρέψας, καὶ τοῦτον ἐπὶ ξύλου κρεμασθέντα κύριον κατὰ τοῦ νενικηκότος ἀποδείξας. Cf. Nautin (1953) p. 20.

tion as "turning into adamant (εἰς ἀδάμαντα)" is, after all, an odd metaphor, were not the term for steel (adamant) also used in the writer's background of Hellenistic Gnosticism as the collective and personalized name of redeemed humanity (Ἀδάμας).

Furthermore, the Naasene text claims that the ascent of Adamas (περὶ τῆς ἀνόδου αὐτοῦ) is described in *Ps.* 23 (24) 7-10. (V, 8,18). In the citation of Theodoret (5A 8.1) from Hippolytus' genuine commentary on *Ps.* 23(24), the ascending Christ stops at the gates of heaven which are closed οὐδέπω γὰρ ἀναβέβηκεν εἰς οὐρανούς, πρῶτον νῦν φαίνεται ταῖς δυνάμεσι ταῖς οὐρανίαις σὰρξ ἀναβαίνουσα. The angels say these selfsame words to the heavenly powers in order to open the gates.[171]

That clearly the author of the *C.N.* block had, by contrast with the author of *El.*, radically integrated and synthesised Hellenistic philosophical and religious concepts with his scriptural exegesis has important consequences for attempts to deny the individuality of the literary profiles in discussion about the two-authors thesis.

5B 3.3. *Literary profiles in the debate about two authors*
We see therefore that the *El.* and *C.N.* blocks within the Hippolytan *corpus* can only superficially be distinguished in terms of the former as secular erudition supported philosophically, and the latter as the scriptural argument of a circle within the Church. The Christology of the *C.N.* block is too radically orientated towards the general culture of Hellenistic Gnosticism, in comparison with *El.*-block, to sustain such a simplistic thesis. But what implications are there in our redrawing of the literary profiles specifically for Frickel's second position, which we have rejected on other grounds (4A 2.1.1), namely that the differences are those of a single author addressing different audiences?

For Frickel's earlier solution to work, the more intra-ecclesiastical audience could not be addressed with Christological categories far closer to the heretics' use of them than the extra-ecclesiastical audience, as is precisely the case with the *C.N.* block. *C.N.* appears only superficially to reject Hellenistic religious culture for a biblical one. His view of being biblically-based is to take a fundamental part of the philosophy of Hellenistic and Gnostic syncretism as it stands, and simply to see how far it must be modified if one removes features required to support pagan cults and sacred stories in literature.

---

171 Theodoret, *Eranistes*, II, 176,16: ἔρχεται ἐπὶ τὰς ἐπουρανίους πύλας, ἄγγελοι αὐτῷ συνοδεύουσι, καὶ κεκλεισμέναι εἰσὶν αἱ πύλαι τῶν οὐρανῶν· οὐδέπω γὰρ ἀναβέβηκεν εἰς οὐρανούς, πρῶτον νῦν φαίνεται ταῖς δυνάμεσι ταῖς οὐρανίαις σὰρξ ἀναβαίνουσα. λέγεται οὖν ταῖς δυνάμεσιν ὑπὸ τῶν ἀγγέλων τῶν προτρεχόντων τὸν σωτῆρα καὶ κύριον «ἄρατε πύλας οἱ ἄρχοντες ὑμῶν καὶ ἐπάρθητε πύλαι αἰώνιοι, καὶ εἰσελεύσεται ὁ βασιλεὺς τῆς δόξης.» Cf. Nautin (1953) p. 28. See also L. Bertsch, *Die Botschaft von Christus und unserer Erlösung bei Hippolyt von Rom. Eine material-kerygmatische Untersuchung*, (Paulinus: Trier 1966).

Thus the author of the *C.N.* block proceeds in a biblically-based way in so far as he excludes such pagan authorities as the Attis or Homeric hymns, or Empedoklean verses, from his account, and leaves in place the Scripture quotations, used by the Naasenes and others, as part of their religious syncretism. In consequence, he cannot use, nor would wish to use, the crass genital symbolism introduced from the Isis-Hermes statues, on which the Gnostic interpretation is imposed in the Naasene text. But the Scripture quotations that are left, along with their reconciliation with Hellenistic religious philosophy, are allowed to remain without much radical alteration in that philosophy save omission of imagery and symbolism that the exclusion of Homeric and Attic images would necessitate.

In consequence his λόγος theology is more streamlined, with austere abbreviation and suppression of such pagan, cultic and literary elements, and, in consequence, economical. But it represents no less a radical intrusion into the original, Judaeo-Christian tradition of quite raw Hellenistic elements. Those elements are concealed to some extent by the fact that such Hellenistic religious images are depersonalized, not only when such images are in the form of the Isis-Hermes *genitalia*, but when the λόγος stands austerely as such alone, without the human feature of Hermes as messenger of the gods. But at an affective level one might well ask whether this was because such personal images affronted the author of *C.N.*, or whether it was because he needed, for inner-Church purposes, to depersonalise the λόγος ἄσαρκος in order to reach a *rapprochement* with the Callistian Monarchians, and to deny the charge of ditheism. The Statue itself, as we have seen (2A 1.2), has an affective message sympathetic to pagan iconography, and we have argued that it was the accomplishment of the community of Hippolytus, the successor of *El.* and the editor of many of his works.

In the final analysis, the one solution open to a defender of single authorship becomes therefore the developmental one suggested by Capelle and Oggioni.[172] But in that case, the *C.N.* block, in view particularly of the nascent trinitarianism that replaces the binitarianism (4A 1), would then be the product of the mature reflection of the originally raw ideas held by the same author when earlier he wrote the *El.*-block. But we would then have to suppose that, becoming converted to a more radical accommodation with Hellenistic philosophy, he was prepared to conceal that conversion under the new guise of a biblical expositor. One would better suppose that such a conversion of a mind set in the case of the author of *El.* would have resulted in a fuller acceptance of Valentinus or of the Naasenes. Rather we have completely different castes of mind between the two blocks and indicative of two different individual authors. Both come to the same kind of task within

---

[172] See footnote 157.

a common ecclesiastical school, but from completely different stand-points.[173]

The standpoint of *El.* is of someone who regards Scripture as literal and not allegorical, and as a quarry for chronographical research. Such research will establish the cultural purity of Judaism and its true successor, Christianity, and show that this common historical phenomenon to be far more ancient than its newer, philosophical corruptions by Hellenism. That methodology, exemplified in the Χρονικῶν before Hippolytus' editing, was the Christian counterpart to Diogenes Laertius' attack on a corrupting Roman civilisation in the interests of demonstrating both the antiquity and the purity of the cultural phenomenon of Greek philosophy. The theological sequel to the Χρονικῶν was *El.* which likewise studies Hellenistic philosophy in order to demonstrate that it had contaminated the purity of the διαδοχή ἀποστόλων in the heretical schools. The author of *El.* had no further interest in, nor apologetic use for, Hellenistic philosophy.

The author of *C.N.* on the other hand saw in Scripture not an antiquarian apologetic and a quarry for historical research, but rather a mystical allegory, not unlike the Hellenistic religious understanding of pagan mythology. The Scripture from which he started had therefore for him a completely different significance. Furthermore, as we have seen, Hellenistic philosophy took on for him a positive aspect, and enabled him to explain away the Monarchian proof-texts in the Fourth Gospel by means of a metaphysical doctrine of emanation which also won over the heirs of Callistus (2A 3.1). The mind of a single author would have had therefore to have changed radically its view of Scripture and its exegesis, and to have also changed the way it regarded pagan philosophy. Such differences would be too schizophrenic if explained in terms of the development of a single mind.

PART C. CONCLUSION: THE STATUE AND PAGAN PHILOSOPHY

At the conclusion of this section and of this chapter, therefore, we may remark how the Statue itself is a reflection of the problem of the Hippolytan *corpus* and *vice versa*. Our argument in Chapter 2 was that the Statue was a monument to a school and not an individual. In the course of Chapters 3-5 we have now argued that the literary *corpus* itself, when studied in relationship to the works listed on the plinth, and the Easter and Paschal inscriptions on its side, likewise reflect an ecclesial school with at least three writers, and

---

173 Thus one part of the conclusion stands in Loi (1977) p. 88: "Concludendo ci domand-iamo se non sia legittimo affermare l'esistenza nella prima metà del III secolo di due scrittori ecclesiastici... piuttosto che postulare una profonda evoluzione (che si potrebbe anche definire radicale trasformazione) psicologica e culturale di un unico personaggio."

indeed a composite liturgical text which continued for four centuries in a state of fluid and dynamic development, namely *Ap. Trad.*

We have traced within that *corpus* the movements of Christological conflict that involved a paradox. On the one hand there was a *rapprochement* with the conservative, Monarchian insistence on the unity of the Judaeo-Christian God in the school of Callistus. On the other hand that *rapprochement* itself involved a radical incorporation of the requirements of the emanation of the λόγος from the Godhead that had their origins in the metaphysical assumptions of Hellenistic paganism. The editor and corrector of the *El.*-block, Hippolytus, author of *C.N.*, therefore, paradoxically appeared as the conservative Scriptural commentator, condemning the φλυαρία of the Valentinians (*C.N.* 11,3) whilst accommodating fundamental parts of their theology.

That paradox too we saw to be reflected in the Statue. It appeared as the icon of an orthodox community, indeed the model community with now its unquestioned bishop-monarch from Pontian onwards and duly commemorated in the now properly and specifically dated *Catalogus Episcoporum* to be destined to be bought down to the time of Liberius by later editors (4A 3.2.3 and 4B 2.2.3.3-2.2.4). But its incongruencies suggested that all was not as it appeared with the Statue any more than with the allegedly conservative Scriptural exegete in the *C.N.* block, who so daringly appealed to disguised emanationist concepts drawn from the Naasene Psalm. As we have seen, the female features of λόγος–σοφία, created from the transformation of Themista, belied at an affective level the avowal of conservative orthodoxy (2A 3.1). To more sophisticated contemporaries, the seated figure must have seemed very like the Carpocratian depiction of Christ in the female form of σοφία (2B 2.2.1.2), reminiscent itself of the statues of Serapis (2A 3.2).

In this Chapter we have see how and in what way Nautin endeavoured to construct a thesis of two authors of the Hippolytan *corpus*. He carefully constructed, from evidence of style and content, a literary profile of one writer, Josephus, whose works are mentioned on the Statue, and whose titles include *El.* not mentioned on the Statue, but linked to the Statue by means of titles which the author cites as his own and which are also found there. He contrasted this writer with Hippolytus who wrote *C.N.*, the fragment of the lost σύνταγμα mentioned by Photius, whose quite different literary profile was associated with the works listed by Jerome. Simonetti rejected the identification with Josephus, yet argued that there were two writers of the same name, one of whom was a presbyter and martyr, the other a bishop and scholar.

But both then appeared to earn the rebuke of their critics by having to explain away the titles not only of the biblical commentaries mentioned as Hippolytus' by Jerome, Theodoret, and others, not only of Eusebius and Jerome's ἀπόδειξις χρόνων, but also of the περὶ χαρισμάτων and the ἀπο–

στολικὴ παράδοσις clearly associated with Hippolytus' name. At this point their opponents thought they heard the sounds of *petitio principii* when they had to reply that these titles were common to more than one author in antiquity, and that the works on the Statue by these names are quite different from those attributed to Hippolytus in the literature.

We have resolved the problem by dissolving the foundations which gave rise to it, namely the interpretation of the Statue as a monument to an individual. Because it is the icon of a community, we can study that community and the authors within it, and the currents of conflicting ideas within the parameters that give it identity as a community. We do not have to remove Hippolytus geographically from either his namesake at Rome or some other name there because we recognise that cultural differences do not equate with geographical differences in the multicultural Rome of the Severan dynasty. A Roman Statue is thus able to bear the inscription works of writers within the community that constructed it with both Eastern and Western backgrounds. We have shown that to be the probable account of the existence of Hippolytan and non-Hippolytan works on the Statue.

But we must now inquire into what we may gather, in addition to our resolution of the literary problem, about the general character of the school that was to bear the name of Hippolytus, successor to the author of *El.* and his associated works.

CHAPTER SIX

THE SCHOOL AND 'SCHISM' OF HIPPOLYTUS

The community of the Apostic Tradition *and the Novatian Presbyter*

In this chapter we shall consider (Part C) the kind of community to which the *Ap. Trad.*, in the form of Botte's reconstruction of that document (however unsatisfactorily) testifies. We have already argued the composite nature of that work in the light of which questions of individual authorship were irrelevant (5A 1-1.2), particularly in the light of Hippolytus' editing of such works of *El.* as the Χρονικῶν , and his responsibility for the κατὰ Δανιήλ addition to the ἀπόδειξις χρόνων (5A 2). It is *Ap. Trad.* therefore that will be our first crown witness to the kind of community that produced the Hippolytan *corpus* that we considered in the previous two chapters.

But before we look at such internal evidence, there is an external source as yet untapped from which we can also learn the character of the Hippolytan school, and that is the *carmina* of Prudentius and Damasus. We shall argue (Part A) that this evidence cannot be taken at its face value, and that indeed the description of the Novatian Presbyter is a legend. But behind the anachronism of the later legend we shall find illumination regarding the true character of what is falsely, and only in terms of a later conceptualization of Church Order, categorized as a 'schism' (Part B).

PART A. THE *CARMEN* OF PRUDENTIUS AND DAMASUS' EPIGRAM

We have already considered the possibility of identifying the Hippolytan events with the schism of Novatian and, on chronological grounds, found this wanting (3B 2.1 footnote 86). Such an identification would require that Hippolytus, as supposed author of *El.*, survived Sardinia in 235, and lived to be a Novatianic martyr around 251. This claim, made originally by De Rossi and defended recently by Cecchelli, would require, *inter alia*, that the entry in the Liberian *Catalogus* could be interpreted in such a way as to support such a survival. We examined the supporting arguments for this claim and found them wanting (1B 2.3.3.1-3.3.6).

But though the testimony of Damasus and Prudentius is not direct empirical evidence, legendary material can provide evidence of another kind in that it represents how a person such as Hippolytus was understood a century or more after his death. It enables us to see a historical personage as it were through the web of conceptual distortion wrought on the past by the interpretative discourse of the present. We saw that to be the case with the folklore in certain circles of Hippolytus the Valentinian (5B 3.1.2), and we shall now see how that is the case with Hippolytus the Novatianic martyr.

6A 1. *Prudentius'* carmen: *the alleged historical core*

Prudentius stood at the crossroads of martyrologies where history was rapidly being replaced with aetiological legends produced by the devotional needs of pilgrim sites. The form of execution of Saint Hippolytus, namely being torn apart between the wheels two chariots as in the case of his classical namesake, is clearly unhistorical. Similarly the scene of the execution at Portus is clearly aetiological involving the conflation of Hippolytus' martyrdom with that of Nonus in order to support the development of a cult-centre on that site.

But what the discovery of the fragments supporting the testimony of the epigram from *Corbeiensis* enabled De Rossi to accomplish was the establishment of a source, believed by him to be strictly historical, for the core details of the poem (1B 2.3.3.3). Thus De Rossi was to claim that we can find a historical core to Prudentius' *carmen* in Damasus' inscription. We must now assess this claim. Those details describe a presbyter of the Novatianic schism, who, on his way to execution, was suddenly overwhelmed by the grace of martyrdom, and exhorted his followers to return to the Catholic faith.[1] Thus Hippolytus had the orthodox mark of a true martyr, of whom Damasus could consequently say: *sic noster meruit confessus martyr ut esset.*

6A 2. *Damasus' inscription and historical evidence*

De Rossi's assessment of what he considered to be Damasus' historical core to Prudentius' *carmen* was to lead him to deny that Hippolytus could have been the author of the *Elenchos*.[2] The Novatianic schism began in 252 so that a Novatianic presbyter was unable to have been involved in the events of c. 217 between the author of the *Elenchos* and Zephyrinus and Callistus. De Rossi felt keenly the objection, quite frequently raised since, that Damasus' actual words hardly commend his own very great confidence in the historical accuracy of his account. His words are *Hypolitus fertur* (v. 1) and *Haec audita refert Damasus probat omnia Christus* (8). At first sight it would appear that Damasus is dependent upon an oral report in circulation

---

[1] See 1B 2.3.3.3 for fuller quotations from Prudentius. See also E. Schaeffer, *Die Bedeutung der Epigramme des Papstes Damasus für die Geschichte der Heiligenverehrung.* (Rome: 1932).
[2] G.B. De Rossi, Esame archeologico e critico della storia di s. Callisto narrata nel libro nono dei Filosofumeni, in*BArC* 4 (1866) ser.4, p. 1-99. See also A. Baruffa, Le Catacombe di San Callisto, in *Storia Archeologia e Fede*, (Leumann: Turin 1988).

(*haec audita*) to the details of which Damasus does not wish to commit himself. Damasus merely "passes on (*refert*)" what "is related" or "is passed on (*fertur*)" to himself. It is left to Christ to confirm (*probat*) the account.[3]

De Rossi sought to respond to this criticism by claiming that *fertur* and *refert* were formulaic expressions in Damasus' writings for referring to events before his birth or during his childhood, rather than to events which he intrinsically doubted. In his elegy on the martyrdom of Peter and Marcellinus, who were slain shortly before he was born, Damasus says: *percursor retulit Damaso mihi cum puer essem.* [4] Pope Marcellus died when Damasus was seven years old, and of his story he says: *haec breviter Damasus voluit comperta referre, Marcelli ut populus meritum cognoscere possit.*[5] When however Damasus refers to the distant past and a persecution at least before that of Diocletian, he uses the formula *fama refert*, as of an unnamed Greek martyr from an unknown time and place, or of the virgin Agnes of whom he says: *fama refert sanctos dudum retulisse parentes.*[6]

But the argument as it stands hardly yields a conclusion sufficiently precise to make De Rossi's case for an historically factual base for the story of Hippolytus as a Novatian Presbyter reconciled to the catholic church in the course of his martyrdom. Though the expression *fertur* and *retulit* may suggest a time closer than the unknown time and place of Agnes' *fama est* , what Damasus' has "*discovered* (*comperta*)" and "passed on" in Marcellus'· case is far nearer than what he has "*heard* and passed on (*haec audita refert*)" in that of Hippolytus.

De Rossi endeavoured to close the gap by appealing to Damasus' background. Damasus was born into a clerical family, as another of the Philokalian inscriptions from the cult-centre on the via Tiburtina makes clear.[7] As such he had been close to archival material. It was at this point that De Rossi claimed to have restored the true reading of *Carmen* XVIII (as *hinc puer exceptor, lector, levitas, sacerdos*) in consequence of which he could claim that in early youth Damasus had held the office of *exceptor* as well as reader.[8] Thus Damasus' holding of the post of *exceptor* (secretary or

---

[3] For full text of this epigram see 1 B 2.3.3.2 footnote 77.

[4] *Carmina* XII, cf. De Rossi (1881) p. 45; A. Ferrua, *Epigrammata Damasiana*. (Rome: Pontificio Istituto di Archeologia cristiana, Città del Vaticano 1943), 28,2.

[5] *Carmina* XXVI cf. De Rossi (1881) p. 45; Ferrua (1943) 40,7.

[6] *Carmina* II cf. De Rossi (1881) p. 46; Ferrua (1943) 37,1.

[7] Natus qui antistes sedis a[postolicae], see Lightfoot Vol II Part 1 p. 329; Ferrua (1943) 35,4.

[8] This reading is denied by Ferrua (1943) 57,1-8:
Hinc *pater* exceptor, lector, levita, sacerdos,
creverat hinc meritis quoniam meliorib. actis;
hinc mihi provecto Xps cui summa potestas,
sedis apostolicae voluit concedere honorem.
Archivis, fateor, volui nova condere tecta,
addere praeterea dextra laevaq. columnas,
quae Damasi teneant proprium per saecula nomen.

notary) under Pope Silvester is not simply the conflation of roles of father and son by later hagiographers, but indeed is shown to be historically true by means of a textual emendation. Thus De Rossi wished to argue that not only did Damasus the *exceptor* have access to archive material but, as a *puer exceptor* around 315, would have heard from the elderly *exceptores* their experiences of the Novatian schism, and the famous convert from it in 258.[9]

Unfortunately *puer* is not well attested and indeed has no coherence within the epigram itself. Damasus is not referring to himself even as *pater (puer) exceptor, lector, levita, sacerdotus* but to the various kinds of person he is benefitting by his building works for the archives (*Archivis... nova condere tecta*) at the Lateran. There was no *cursus honorum* in connection with Holy Orders at Rome at this time, and though a deacon (*levita*), Damasus himself never became a *sacerdos* (=*presbyter*) before becoming bishop of' Rome.[10] But to interpret the epigram on Hippolytus as the Novatianic Presbyter as if it was derived from such a factual, archival entry is to miss its real point.

The problem with such an account is that though it is correct that Damasus does have access to written archival material, it fails to come to terms with, and thus to explain the fact that he apparently chooses not to use such material. Damasus would have had access to written archive material if, doubtfully, he had been a *puer exceptor*. But he expressly denies, with the words *haec audita*, that his account of Hippolytus as a Novatian Presbyter is based upon anything written. We cannot therefore suppose that Damasus' purpose in this *carmen* was that of a disinterested researcher into archival material in order to preserve the events of Christian history. Recent studies in the philosophy of language have made us aware that, in using language, we operate with a variety of interpretative discourses that correspond to a variety of human purposes. Such interpretative discourses are termed "registers," and to select such a discourse related to one kind of purpose may be described as selecting a register. In the light of such a view, we may be, in the second half of the twentieth century, far more aware of what was the true purpose of Damasus' inscription than was possible in the culture of late nineteenth century historical positivism in which De Rossi wrote.

Damasus is not operating within the register of historical research based on documents, though we shall shortly see that such documents were available to him. When he speaks of what is heard and he passes on, without himself committing himself to the factual truth of what he says (*Hippolytus fertur* (v. 1) and *Haec audita refert Damasus probat omnia Christus.* (v. 8)), he is almost self-consciously constructing a legend set in the never-never time of *cum iussa tyranni premerent*, and *tempore quo gladius secuit pia*

---

[9] De Rossi (1881) op. cit. p. 48-49.
[10] *Collectio Avellana*, in *C.S.E.L.* XXXV, 1,2.

viscera matris. Such a register of legend construction serves Damasus with a number of human and political purposes, as we shall see.

One such purpose was Damasus' use of history, as indeed that of Eusebius, and for that matter of St. Luke before him in the Gospel and *Acts*, to construct an idealized version of the past to make sense of, and to order conceptually, contemporary events. In view of the particular conflict with Ursinus and his party over the succession, Damasus was not acting in his description of Hippolytus with the register of a disinterested scholar-pope. We shall see that the work of Testini and others at Portus reveals a cult-centre there shortly after Damasus' time, and arising from the conflation of various martyrologies. Damasus' (and, for that matter, Prudentius') decision to ignore that shrine in favour of the cult-centre on the via Tiburtina will require an explanation other than of Damasus as the disinterested antiquarian scholar.

We will turn first to one piece of evidence that might be thought to offer a thorough, empiricist explanation of Damasus' decision to regard Hippolytus as a Novatian martyr because of the presence of the tomb of Novatian in the vicinity of the cult-centre on the via Tiburtina (6A 2.1). We shall then analyse the evidence of the Liberian Chronographer, available, to Damasus as well as to us (6A 2.2), that contradicts his description of Hippolytus as a Novatian martyr. We shall thus (in 6A 2.3) be able to confirm our decision not to regard Damasus' epigram as the work of a disinterested scholar-pope, and to justify our seeking an understanding of Damasus' literary activity in terms of the construction of a legend that imposes meaning on the events of his own time. Those events we shall see to be the Luciferan connections of his rival Ursinus (6A 2.4), and the rival basilica at Portus, dedicated to Hippolytus, and which arguably fell within the sphere of Ursinian or Luciferan influence (6A 2.5).

6A 2.1. *Damasus and the aetiology of Novatian's tomb*

The alleged presence of Novatian's tomb in the vicinity of the cult-centre on the via Tiburtina can be argued to have lead Damasus to create an aetiological legend.[11] Such a view, which rests on the genuineness of the tomb in question, I will now argue to be essentially correct. But though the presence of such an artefact may be the necessary condition for the construction of such a legend, it is not sufficient. There will be additional motives, arising from contemporary preoccupations, that guide human minds in the weaving of such legends around geographically placed monuments.

The presence of the genuine tomb of Novatian the third-century schismatic in the vicinity of the cult-centre on the via Tiburtina may thus consti-

---

[11] G. Bovini, Sant'Ippolito, dottore e martire del III secolo, in *Coll. amici delle catacombe* 15 (Città del Vaticano: Pontificio Istituto di Archeologia cristiana 1943), p. 34 pointed to the closeness between the shrines of Hippolytus and of Novatian.

tute the factual core around which the legend arises as a solution for Damasus' contemporary concerns. But that Damasus connects the Novatian of one with Hippolytus the martyr of the other shows clearly that the martyr Hippolytus was connected in Damasus' mind with the cult-centre on the via Tiburtina which becomes a further reason against Cecchelli's conclusion that he could not have been located there (1B 2.3.3.1-3.3.6). Indeed, in questioning this scepticism and, more positively, arguing the case for the tomb as that of Novatian the schismatical bishop, we are furnished with evidence against the distinction between Hippolytus the presbyter and martyr and Hippolytus the writer of the *corpus*. But can we be sure that it is in fact the grave of the third-century schismatic?

Neither the *Itineraries* nor the *Liber Pontificalis* made mention of this grave of Novatian, which stands near the viale Regina Elena and was excavated in 1926 and 1929 by Fornari.[12] There was uncovered, on the second level, a grave with an inscription: NOVATIANO BEATISSIMO MARTYRI GAUDENTIUS DIAC[ONUS] FE[CIT].[13] The question was thus posed of whether this could be the Novatian martyred under Valerian in 257-258, or whether in fact the Novatian mentioned was a martyr of the reign of Diocletian. The gallery in which the tomb was found was originally believed to be well after 270, which made this questionable. In that event, Damasus could not have known the site of Novatian's tomb, and connected aetiologically that tomb with Hippolytus the martyr whom clearly he identified with the cult-centre on the via Tiburtina. But recent excavations have considerably modified this earlier scepticism.[14]

Quite clearly if Novatian's tomb was on the via Tiburtina, and that Hippolytus' neighbouring tomb suggested a connection between them that warranted a legendary aetiology, then this becomes evidence for the connection between the cult-centre on the via Tiburtina and Hippolytus the writer involved with a schism. Damasus' epigram will then be connected with the via Tiburtina and be evidence of the genuineness of De Rossi's attribution of the fragments from the Lateran pavement originally to Hippolytus' cult-centre there.

---

12 F. Fornari, Stagione degli scavi 1926-1927 in *RivAC* 4 (1927) p. 39-42; ——, Relazione circa una nuova regione cimiteriale a S. Lorenzo, in *RivAC* 6 (1929), p. 179-239; E. Josi, Cimitero alla sinistra della via Tiburtina al viale Regina Margherita, in *RivAC*, 10 (1933), p. 183-233.——, Cimitero alla sinistra della via Tiburtina al viale Regina Margherita, in *RivAC*, 11 (1934), p. 7-47, 203-246.

13 Josi (1933) p. 217 no. 43.

14 R. Giordani, «*Novatiano beatissimo martyri Gaudentius diaconus fecit*»— contributo all'identificazione del martire Novaziano della catacomba anonima sulla via Tiburtina, in *RivAC* 67,1-2 (1992), p. 233-258. F. Fornari, and S.-M. Scrinari, *Le catacombe di Novaziano e la necropoli romana*, (Rome 1973); P. Fasola, I cimiteri cristiani. Introduzione alla discussione, in *Atti del IX congresso internazionale di archeologia cristiana a 1975*, 32, 1 (Vatican 1978), p. 191-194.

Let us therefore consider in more detail the strength of the evidence for a cult-centre of Novatian on the via Tiburtina and its significance for Damasus' legend of the Novatian Presbyter.

6A 2.2. *The tomb of Novatian: evidence for its genuineness*

The cemetery, unknown in ancient topographical and liturgical documents, was abandoned in the course of the 5th century. The remains revealed two levels, the upper of which, in a high state of decay, collapsed in the course of the excavations. Its origins could however be accurately dated from no less than six inscriptions each with a consular date, four for 266 and two for 270. But the problem lay in the chronological relationship between the corner of gallery five through which the ancient entrance had come, and where these early inscriptions had been found, and the second level of the catacomb. It was on this level that was found the grave redecorated many times and developed on which deacon Gaudentius' epigraph had been found.[15] Mohlberg was to argue therefore that it was the tomb of a different Novatian.[16]

There had been a catholic martyr Novatian in Diocletian's time whose celebration the *Martyrologium Hieronymianum* had located between the 27th and 29th June.[17] Were this the identity of the occupant of this particular tomb, then indeed there would be no aetiological argument for the identification between the two martyrs in two neighbouring cemeteries on the via Tiburtina. Giordani had no problems of disposing of two of the arguments in favour of this obscure martyr. It followed neither from the absence of schismatical identity marks in the cemetery generally, nor from the absence of the title of *episcopus* on Gaudentius' inscription, that the mid-third-century schismatic was to be absolutely ruled out. The Novatians initially at least had no self-consciousness of being a separate group, particularly before the age of the Councils initiated by the Cyprianic definition of Church Order. Such distinguishing marks would be unprecedented from the artefact of any other heretical group.[18] Furthermore, the fact of the abandonment of the grave-shrine after the fifth-century itself corresponds to the clear allocation of the Novatians amongst the heretics only from that time.

The absence of an episcopal title in Gaudentius' inscription is far more problematic. But Ferrua demonstrated that the present inscription is not original but a copy. The original inscription would have been written on a mar-

---

[15] Giordani (1992) p. 234-237.

[16] L.C. Mohlberg, Osservazioni storico-critiche sull'iscrizione tombale di Novaziano, in *EphL* 51 (1937), p. 242. Cf. H. Koch, Martire Novaziano, in *Religio*, 14 (1938), p. 192-198. For the location of the tomb see Carta Archeologica di Roma, (Rome: Ministero dei Beni Culturali e Ambientali, Ufficio centrale per i beni ambientali 1987), Tavola III i no. 25.

[17] H. De la Haye, Contributions récents à l'hagiographie de Rome et d'Afrique, in *AnBol* 54 (1936) p. 265-268.

[18] Giordani (1992) p. 238: "... non sarà inutile riflettere come monumenti nati in contesti ben più propriamente e decisamente eretici quali, per es., il battistero degli ariani a Ravenna, o la chiesa di Sant' Agata dei Goti, a Roma, assolutamente nulla ci direbbero, di per sé stessi, di tale loro condizione eterodossa ove questa non ci fosse nota per altra via."

ble slab horizontally above the tomb and could have included the title of *episcopus*.[19] The copy dates from the middle of the fourth century.[20] Damasus also in composing epigrams for the martyrs Gennarus, Felicissimus, and Agapetus had omitted their titles as *diaconus*.

In consequence, it is the chronological relationship between the tomb of the second level, and the dates of the inscriptions by the angle of the entrance that become critical for the choice between Novatian the schismatic or Novatian the martyr under Diocletian. There can be no doubt that Novatian had died in exile as a martyr, as Cyprian himself seems to have acknowledged, during the persecution of Valerian (257-258).[21] Novatian died in 258, and his remains were deposited, *iusta sepultura*, during the peace of Gallienus in 260. How therefore can this series of events, reconstructed out of possibilities in order to meet the exigencies of the case to be answered, be consistent with a tomb whose evidence of earliest dates are the inscriptions of 266 and 270?

Ferrua considered that those inscriptions were not the first simply because they occupied a space in the square at the base of the entrance staircase. This would assume that the long parallel roads were filled first, beginning with the corner at the base of the stairs and proceeding lengthwise. Modern archaeology has established the development rather of a system of branches (*Zweigsystem*) in which the transverse roads are developed and filled before the main road as it were proceeds. Thus he was lead to conclude the commencement of the cemetery around 257-260.[22]

Giordani frankly admitted that these assumptions, on which Ferrua's contention rested, were possible.[23] Yet he was constrained by the case against it. The remains of Novatian, if laid to rest there *iusta sepultura*, would only finally be so at least six years after the peace of Gallienus, and

---

[19] Ibid. p. 239; A. Ferrua, Novatiano beatissimo martyri, in *CCa* 95 (1944), p. 232-239.

[20] Giordani (1992) p. 239-240: "La predetta iscrizione di Gaudenzio, invece, non è altro che un'iscrizione dedicatoria posta a ricordo di lavori di ornamento eseguiti intorno al sepolcro molti anni dopo la deposizione del martire (all'incirca nella seconda metà del IV secolo); e come tale poteva tranquillamente tralasciare la menzione della sua dignità episcopale."

[21] Pacianus, *Ep. 2 Ad Sympr.*: "praecessit me adversarius meus." Cf. Giordani (1992) p. 240-241.

[22] Giordani (1992) p. 242: "... egli [Ferrua (1944) p. 234-235] mostra come, a partire dalla galleria 1, alla quale immetteva direttamente la scala che discende dal sopratterra, si realizzò prima la grande trasversale 2, o almeno gran parte di essa, e più o meno contemporaneamente si incominciò anche a scavare, a ritmo ineguale, le otto gallerie che la tagliano pressoché ortogonalmente in direzione nord-est e sud-ovest. In questo quadro, e come dimostrano le testimonianze archeologiche costituite soprattutto dalle più volte menzionate epigrafi ancora in situ, intorno al 270 si erano già realizzati una ventina di metri della galleria 3, mentre lo scavo della galleria 4 sembra sia proceduto speditamente, tanto che intorno al 266 era arrivato già circa alla stessa altezza della precedente verso nord-est. Tutto questo... condurrebbe a riferire l'inizio dell'apertura di pressocché tutte le gallerie traversali intorno al 257-260, e di conseguenza in quella stessa epoca sarebbe avvenuto anche lo scavo del sepolcro del martire..."

[23] Ibid. 242: "... si fonda sul presupposto d'un rimpatrio precoce dei resti mortali di Novaziano dal luogo del suo esilio, e questo potrebbe costituire, forse, il lato meno solido della sia pur brillante ricostruzione."

eight years after his martyrdom. Such a translation from a place of exile on which the thesis rested was contrary to Justinian's *Digest*.[24] However, Giordani was able to list frequent examples of translations contrary to this law documented from the *Liber Pontificalis* such as Theodosius' permission in 381 to bring back to Constantinople the remains of the exiled bishop Paul, who died in 350, or in Ambrose's time (374) the restoration of the remains of Dionysius, bishop of Milan, who had died in 359.[25]

Thus the tomb of Novatian the martyr was arguably a centre of veneration for the followers of the founder of a schism in the time of Damasus. But Giordani also for our purpose demonstrates more. He shows that there was a clear relationship between the development of the cult of St. Laurence on one side of the via Tiburtina, and that of the martyred schismatical bishop Novatian, on the other. The Novatians, who assented to the symbol of Nicaea and who were well treated by that Council, enjoyed highly ambiguous relations with the catholic church during this period before their final condemnation and suppression under Innocent I (404-417) and Celestine (422-432).[26] But the agreements were agreements of self-interest, and therefore ephemeral. In such fluid circumstances, the official church constructed its legitimating ideology by developing the cult-centre around St. Laurence as a persuasive alternative to a more direct suppression of Novatian's cult.

Indeed the ideological development of the cult of St. Laurence the deacon was in opposition to the implications of the events within the Roman community after the martyrdom of Sixtus II whose successor as bishop, Dionysius, came from the presbyters and not the deacons, contrary to the Roman practice. Novatian himself was a presbyter and secretary to the Roman presbyterate during the interregnum following the martyrdom of Stephen. In the subsequent evolution of the ideology surrounding the two cult-centres, that of the via Tiburtina celebrated martyred deacons, by contrast with that of the cemetery of Callistus on the via Appia that celebrated Sixtus the martyred bishop with his four deacons and where indeed they had been buried.[27]

When the legend of Sixtus and his companions was associated with the legend of St. Laurence's shrine on the via Tiburtina, there is then, argued

---

[24] *Dig.* 48,24,2: "Si quis in insula deportatus vel relegatus fuerit, poena etiam post mortem manet, nec licet eum inde transferre alicubi et sepelire inconsulto principe."

[25] Giordani (1992) p. 243.

[26] Ibid. p. 255 where he quotes Socrates, *H.E.* V,10; VII,7 and 9 and *Codex Theodosius* XVI, 5,59.

[27] Giordani (1992) p. 251: "È forse... proprio per questa ragione che il culto di Lorenzo viene promosso e favorito... d'un chiaro indirizzo ideologico e programmatico, fors'anche ben oltre la statura reale del personaggio... il confronto polemico con Novaziano... una leggenda che si adopera con ogni mezzo— l'incontro, il dialogo, la predizione del martirio, l'affidamento dei tesori della Chiesa, l'atrocissimo martirio— a ricongiungere idealmente in ogni modo il primo diacono a Sisto II, solo vescovo legittimo..." Cf. L Reekmanns, L'implantation monumentale chrétienne dans la zone suburbaine de Rome du IVe siècle, in *RivAC* 44 (1968), p. 196-199.

Reekmans, a reconciliation between the two conflicting diaconal and presbyteral traditions of the Roman community, united under pressure of the Novatian cult-centre that stood over against them on the other side of the via Tiburtina, that represented the presbyteral strand. But clearly the legend awarded the prominence to the faithfulness in martyrdom of deacon Laurentius and not bishop Sixtus. Damasus, like his opponent Ursinus, had come from the seven deacons and not the presbyters, and his election therefore participated as it were in one of the two opposing currents. That diaconal current could now, as representative of the hierarchy of the Catholic Church, vaunt itself against Novatian the presbyter and illegitimate bishop.

Now given this ideological context convincingly established, as I have shown, by the labours of Gordiani and Reekmans, I would suggest that there is clearly more than antiquarian interest in Damasus' epigram which emphasizes Hippolytus' presbyteral though schismatic rank (*presbyter in scisma semper mansisse novati*). Clearly the cult shrine of Hippolytus, on the via Tiburtina but originally unconnected with San Lorenzo, would also have possessed such an ideological force, since this was a reconciled presbyter, not a deacon, who had lead his followers like a bishop. It is therefore in the ideological context serviced by developing aetiological legends that we must consider the interpretation of the purpose of Damasus' epigram.

But had there not been certain other events associated by Damasus with the name of Hippolytus the martyr, there would have been no cause for making such an aetiological connection. Damasus must have had therefore some other reason for constructing an aetiological legend than simply the proximity of Hippolytus' grave with that of a schismatic. That proximity was necessary but not sufficient for labelling Hippolytus as a schismatic. We need therefore to look at other features of the legend of the Novatianic presbyter to account for its construction in addition to the empirical fact of geographical proximity.

In order to consider further those features, let us now turn to other historical testimony.

6A 2.3. *Damasus' inscription and the Chronographer of 354*

We have two pieces of historical evidence which Damasus has not used and which, equally speculatively but with equal weight of probability, we could infer that the *exceptor* could have had access had he wished. Both are found in the work of the Chronographer of 354, completed at Rome under Damasus' predecessor, Liberius. This document contains a calendar recording the deposition of the remains of martyrs (*Depositio Martyrum*), and also a succession list of bishops with occasional biographical insertions (*Catalogus Episcoporum*).[28] Hippolytus is mentioned in both the *Depositio*

---

[28] Lightfoot Vol. II Part 1 p. 328 and Vol I p. 246-265 ff.

and the *Catalogus*, and we have argued against Cecchelli that the same person is intended (1 B 2.3.3.4).

In the *Catalogus* the places where the commemorations of the martyrs are held, if indeed it is not also their burial places, are recorded along with the dates of the commemorations. We have only three popes mentioned as follows:

viii Idus Aug.	Xysti in Calisti
Idus Aug.	Ypoliti in Tiburtina et Pontiani in Calisti
Pri. Idus Octob.	Calisti in via Aurelia, miliario iii.

De Rossi himself argued that where the mention of the cemetery in such instances was omitted, with the martyr's name in the genitive case, this was a shorthand form of *in eiusdem coemeterio*. Thus we should understand *Ypolitus, in eiusdem caemeterio* ("Hippolytus, in the cemetery of the same (name)"), by this shorthand form.[29] We have already cited the relevant entry in the *Catalogus* (1B 2.3.3.5). Pompeianus and Peligianus were consuls in 231, and Severus and Quintianus were consuls in 235. Thus both bishop Pontianus and presbyter Hippolytus were exiled during the reign of the emperor Maximinus the Thracian (235-238), who, on the death of Severus Alexander, in the words of Eusebius:

> He, through his hostility, of course, to the house of Alexander that consisted for the most part of Christians, stirred up a persecution and ordered the execution only of the leaders of the churches (τοὺς τῶν ἐκκλησιῶν ἄρχοντας) as those responsible for the teaching of the gospel (ὡς αἰτίους τῆς κατὰ τὸ εὐαγγέλιον διδασκαλίας).
>
> *H.E.* VI, 28,1-2

In order to make his case for the martyrdom of Hippolytus as a follower of Novatian some fifteen years after these events, it would be necessary to assume that only Pontianus actually died from their joint Sardinian experience. Presbyter Hippolytus would have thus survived to be martyred during the Decian persecution, having in the meantime joined the new Novatian schism and, having recanted that schism at the hour of his martyrdom, his remains could be deposited *in Tiburtina*. But this would not explain the silence of the Liberian Chronographer about this fact. Furthermore, it would run counter to Eusebius' clear dating of Hippolytus' literary activity in the time of Alexander bishop of Jerusalem, who in turn succeeds to the episcopate on the succession of Antoninus (Caracalla), son of Septimius Severus (211).[30]

If Hippolytus, as a confessor and presbyter, had been worthy of mention before his death and involvement in schism, surely he would have merited

---

[29] G.B. De Rossi, Il cimitero di S. Ippolito presso la via Tiburtina e la sua principale cripta storica ora dissepolta, in *BArC* 7 (1882) ser.4 anno 1, p. 14-15.
[30] Cf. *H.E.* VI ,8,7 with VI ,20,1-3.

such a mention on his death and return from schism? Furthermore, there is an implication that Sardinia had damaged the health of both of them (*in insula nociva*). Pontianus had actually died on the island (*In eadem insula distinctus*), but the death of Hippolytus too is implied not immediately but from what he too had suffered there not very long after, by a clear reference its injurious climate (*insula nociva*) and prisoner regime (1B 2.3.3.5).

We must look therefore for a different register in terms of which to explain Damasus' intentions in the *carmen* of his inscription than that of the register employed by a scholar engaged in disinterested historical research. We will now show that there is an encoded message in the description of the Liberian Chronographer. It was that code that Damasus' description of Hippolytus' ecclesiastical status partly picks up, but partly distorts, in terms of his different conceptual register.

6A 2.4. *Damasus' register and the Liberian Chronographer*

To discover the encoded message regarding Hippolytus' ecclesiastical office, we begin with Eusebius' references to major and minor Orders some fifteen years after the exile to Sardinia. Eusebius quotes Cornelius, bishop of Rome, against Novatus, that in the church of Rome there are "forty-six presbyters, seven deacons, seven sub-deacons, forty two acolytes, etc." (*H.E.* VI, 43,8) Thus some fifteen years earlier it was most unlikely that there would be only one presbyter to find martyrdom under Maximinus. As our previous quotation makes clear (*H.E.* VI,28,1-2), Maximinus' persecution was directed against church leaders.

Clearly Hippolytus is not simply one confessor/ presbyter amongst many but indeed a leading presbyter. He was considered, in Eusebius' words, as one "responsible for the teaching of the gospel." Such a description would normally fit a bishop in the western tradition, and the "leaders of the churches" would have been their bishops. But even if the entire presbyterate were regarded in such a light—all something reasonably less than forty-six of them as they were to be fifteen years later—it is curious that only one should singled out for mention.

To be mentioned along with Pontianus in the Liberian *Catalogus*, and to be honoured as few names are in that *Catalogus* with certain biographical details, is to have an ambiguous standing in the community, as a presbyter but indeed regarded as more than a mere presbyter. Hippolytus is a prominent or leading presbyter, sufficiently so to be honoured along with the acknowledged bishop of Rome himself. Indeed, though not identical with the author of *El.*, nevertheless, as the latter's successor, Hippolytus would have been considered by his group as an ἐπίσκοπος–διάδοχός before his work of conciliation had lead to the redefinition of his community's construction of ecclesiastical reality.

There is also a further encoded message in the *Depositio. Idus Aug.Ypoliti in Tiburtina et Pontiani in Calisti* records the deposition and therefore commemoration of both on the 13th August, the date also given in the Martyrology attributed to Jerome.[31] The 13th August was a patriotic feast to Diana as protectress of Rome, and also the festival commemorating the incorporation of the Italian allied cities into the Roman Federation. This date, with pagan, festive associations for the healing of division and the achievement of imperial unity and concord, had associations too for the healing of the ecclesiastical division between *Pontianus episcopus* and *Yppolytus presbyter.*

Indeed, Prudentius is a witness to the fact that the date of the *Depositio* was regarded as having such associations by Damasus' contemporaries. He identifies the Christian martyr with the Hippolytus of the classical legend who is a devotee of the Diana that had become the Roman protectress, and the spurner of Venus. The fate of the Christian martyr is prescribed to be that of his classical double when he is torn in two between wild horses. Thus the image of Novatian martyr reconciled along with his followers to the catholic faith is established as part of a register of related symbols invoking and commending peace and reconciliation to divided communities.[32]

Such a view of Hippolytus, regarded officially by the Roman community as a presbyter, but acknowledged as indeed as a leading presbyter by the very fact of particular mention in the persecution in the reign of Maximinus, is consistent with the events described in *El.*, and with a probable inference about the outcome of those events.

In *El.*. IX, 12,20 and 25 the author of *El.* records how his arch-rival Callistus, "founded a school (συνεστήσατο διδασκαλεῖον) having taught against the church (κατὰ τῆς ἐκκλησίας διδάξας)," whose members "presume (ἐπιχειροῦσι) to call themselves the Catholic Church (καθολικὴν ἐκκλησίαν ἀποκαλεῖν)." But Callistus, and not "presbyter" Hippolytus, whom we have argued to have been different from and the successor to the latter's opponent, the author of *El.*, was to appear later in the Liberian List as the bishop of Rome and successor of St. Peter, despite the latter's claim to apostolic succession.[33] This fact was indeed made more remarkable by Lightfoot's argument that Hippolytus, whom he believed to be the author of *El.*, himself was the author of the first part of the Liberian List. We have argued the existence of the hands of both writers in the composite development of that list. In the light of Hippolytus' irenic role regarding the stance of his

[31] P. Testini, Di alcune testimonianze relative ad Ippolito, in *StEphAug* 13 (1977), p. 51-51; 60-61 and tav. II p. 65.
[32] R. Reutterer, Legendenstudien um den heiligen Hippolytos, in *ZKTh* 95 1973, p. 286-310. See also J. Frickel, *Das Dunkel um Hippolyt von Rom: Ein Lösungsversuch: die Schriften Elenchos und Contra Nöetum.* (Grazer Theologische Studien: Bauer 1988), p.18-26
[33] J.B. Lightfoot, *The Apostolic Fathers*, Part I Clement of Rome, London 1890, p. 255.

predecessor, the absence of his inclusion of that predecessor in an episcopal list in which his community was only to claim for him the office of presbyter is not so remarkable (4B 2.2.4). But at all events, the claim of the author of *El.* and his circle to be themselves the catholic church, and the only true successors of the apostles, is not thereby corroborated in the light of subsequent history. But neither is the description of that group as either schismatical or heretical.

In consequence it is claimed that in both the references to Hippolytus in the Liberian *Depostitio* and *Catalogus* there is implied the reconciliation of both himself and his group with the catholic church of Pontianus' time.[34] But we see too that such a reconciliation has nothing historically to do with the later Novatian schism. Damasus has constructed a legend to express vividly and compellingly the obligation of orthodox schismatics to be reconciled with the communities from which they have divided.

We shall now consider Damasus' aims in redefining ecclesiastical reality, and the register that he selects in the *carmen* to achieve this redefinition. That conceptual register was constructed from the events of his own time, and the experiences of his personal biography.[35] We shall thus see that Damasus' struggle with the Luciferans, on whom Ursinus relied for support, is thus reflected in the legend of the Novatian Presbyter's return to the catholic faith. The legend of the Novatian Presbyter will therefore be seen to have a directive function for the Luciferans of Damasus' own time. To the details of these experiences we shall now turn.

6A 2.5. *Damasus' experience of the conflict with Ursinus*

We shall focus in this section on his relationship with the party of Ursinus and with the Luciferans, and the shadow cast by this relationship over the legend of the Novatian Presbyter. In section 2.6 we shall look at the excavations of the basilica at Portus and the cult of Hippolytus there at least nearly contemporary with Damasus' own time, and the possible connection between this cult and the Luciferan bishop Heraclida.

As is well known, in the days following the death of Liberius on 20th November A.D. 366 deacon Damasus became pope of Rome, amidst scenes of riots and bloodshed. The supporters of his rival, deacon Ursinus, had de-

---

[34] Frickel (1988), p. 1-36.

[35] We are fortunate in possessing *pro* and *anti* sources for the conflict between Damasus and Ursinus. In favour of the latter, in descending order of conviction we have (i) Faustinus and Marcellinus, *Liber Precum ad Imperatores Valentinianum, Theodosium, et Arcadium* (*P.L.* tom. XIII, p. 79-108), also in the *Collectio Avellana* (*C.S.E.L.* XXXV, Pt. 1 p. 58 ff.); (ii) *Gesta Liberii Papae* (*P.L.* VIII, col. 1387-1393); (iii) Ammianus Marcellinus XXVII, 3,12-13; 9,9). In favour of Damasus, (i) Jerome, *Chronicon* 366; (ii) Rufinus *H.E.* II,10; (iii) Socrates *H.E.*, IV,29; (iv) Sozomen, *H.E.*, VI,23. See also M. Simonetti, La Crisa Ariana nel IV Secolo, in *StEphAug* 11 (1975), p. 357, 388, 443-445, 525; M.R. Green, The Supporters of Anti-Pope Ursinus, in *JThS*, 22 (1971), p. 532-538; C. Pietri, *Roma Christiana: Recherches sur l'Eglise de Rome, son organisation, sa politique, son idéologie de Miltiade à Sixte III (311-440)*, (Rome: École Francais de Rome, Palais Farnèse 1976).

manded that the latter be ordained in the place of Liberius. They were
fellow-deacons Amantius and Lupus together with those who had remained
faithful to Liberius whilst in exile (*cum plebe sancta quae Liberio fidem
servaverat in exsilio constituto*). In the idiom of the sources, they "begun a
procession in the Julian basilica" (*coeperunt in basilica Juli procedere*), or,
as we should say, "held fellowship or communion," an idiom which was
well understood by Damasus (*Quaesisset populus ubinam procedere posset/
Catholicam dixisse fidem*). Ursinus was ordained (*benedicit*) by Paulus the
bishop of Tivoli (*Tiburtinus*).[36]

The violence which then followed Damasus' own consecration was un-
paralleled, involving charges that he had secured the exile of Ursinus, and
the deacons Amantius and Lupus, by bribing Viventius, the *praefectus urbis*
and Julianus, the *praefectus annonae*.[37] He then turned his attention on
Ursinus' congregation, who were unwilling to join his communion (or
"procession,"—*quae se nolebat procedere*), and endeavoured to subdue
them with violence. They took refuge in the *basilica Liberii*, the modern
Santa Maria Maggiore, together with their seven presbyters whom he had
tried to have arrested and expelled from the city.[38] Valentinian, in response
to the *Liber Precum* of the presbyters Faustinus and Marcellinus, rescinded
the exile of Ursinus (15th September) and his two deacons who were however again in exile on 22nd November.[39]

The Luciferans, far from being heretical, were vigorous supporters of
Athanasius and Nicaea. They objected to what they regarded as Damasus'
temporizing position for being prepared to accept the compromise of the
emperor Constantius and the Council of Ariminum on episcopal Orders. If
any bishop other than one of the Arian leaders were prepared to accept the
Creed of Ariminum and otherwise renounce his Arianism, then he would not
be degraded from his Orders before being allowed to return to the fold only
as a layman. Lucifer had objected to this in Constantius' time, and the
Ursinians, Faustinus and Marcellinus too will not admit the indelibility of
holy Orders in the case of lapses into heresy. Furthermore, they will not
communicate with any such bishop, however penitent, unless such a bishop
communicates with them only as a layman.[40]

---

[36] All quotations from the *Liber precum* are taken from, and cited from *Collectio Avellana*,
O. Günther, Epistulae imperatorum pontificum aliorum inde ab A. CCCLXVII usque ad A.
DLIII datae Avellana quae dicitur Collectio, in *CSEL* Vol. XXXV, Pt. 1, (Freytag: Leipzig
1895).

[37] Ibid. *Ep.* 1,6.

[38] Ibid. *Ep.* 1,4, cf. Ammianus Marcellinus XXVII, 3,12-13: "Damasus et Ursinus supra humanum modum ad rapiendam episcopi sedem ardentes, scissis studiis asperrime conflictaban-
tur... Ammianus also calls the *basilica Liberii* the *basilica Sicinii* "ubi ritus Christiani est con-
venticulum." (Ibid. 13)

[39] Ibid. *Ep.* 1,11: "Imperator nesciens quid Damasus perpetrasset, edictum prorogat, ut
Ursino exilio relegato, nulla ulterius populos contentio nefanda collideret."

[40] Ibid. *Ep.* 2,50: "..Has eorum impietates exsecrantes episcopi... per mutuas litteras apostolico vigore decernunt, nullo genere talibus episcopis posse communicari, qui fidem illo modo,

We can thus see the shadow of the Ursinians over the Novatian Presbyter as a legend connecting the example of Hippolytus with the events of Damasus' own time. The language of "procession" and "non-procession" is the language of "communion" and "excommunication" both in the *Collectio Avellana* and in Damasus' epigram. The Novatian Presbyter is asked *ubinam procedere posset.... fidem* in the latter, just as in the former the Ursinians are described, with reference to Damasus, as *Romanam plebem quae se nolebat procedere (Ep.* 1,6). The Luciferans are a rigorist sect, but wholly orthodox, like the Novatians, and indeed, like the Hippolytans, as would have appeared in the documents available to Damasus as *exceptor* regarding the conflict of Hippolytus' predecessor with Callistus. Writings under the name of Hippolytus had a λόγος Christology far closer to the faith of Nicaea than the semi-Sabellianism for which those writings castigate Callistus and Zephyrinus.[41]

Like the Novatians, the Ursinians had like-minded episcopal supporters, such as the consecrator of Ursinus himself, Paulus bishop of *Tiburtinus* or Tivoli *(Ep.* 1,5). Moreover, the violence of Damasus toward Ursinus' supporters, who were celebrating at the *stationes* of the martyrs without clergy, had lead to the refusal of a group of Italian bishops to condemn Ursinus.[42] Unlike the supporters of Novatian, these bishops had not broken off communion with Damasus. Likewise Macarius, a Roman presbyter, whose torture counted him as a confessor with the Ursinians,[43] was given refuge by Florentius, bishop of Ostia.

Florentius is described as having communion with Damasus *(communicans Damaso)*. He nevertheless held Macarius' death as like that of a martyr *(cum quadam veneratione)*, and buried him in honour in the basilica of the martyr Asterius, amongst his own presbyters *(ubi in loco presbyteri qui iuxta sepulturam habent) (Ep.* 2, 81-82) We shall latter explore my grounds for concluding that the similarity between the Hippolytans and the Luciferans, in terms of what Damasus could read about the former in the archives, was far closer than with the Novatians. The separation of the former, we shall argue was not formal, as the word 'schism' would imply,

---

quo supra retulimus, prodiderunt, nisi si laicam postulaverint communionem, dolentes suis impietatibus."

[41] Even if we deny that Damasus had never read *El.* IX, 12, 15-19 nor *C.N.* 4,7-12; 10,1-12,3 etc. because of the difficulty of identifying either of these titles with the *Adversus Omnes Hereses* on Jerome's list *(De Vir. Ill.* 61), we still have *Ant.* 3-4.

[42] *Collect. Avell. Ep.* 1,13: "Quod factum crudelissimum nimis episcopis Italiae displicebat. quos etiam cum ad natale suum sollemniter invitasset et nonnulli convenissent ex eis, precibus apud eos molitur et pretio, ut sententiam in sanctum Ursinum proferant. qui responderunt "nos ad natale convenimus, non ut inauditum damnemus."

[43] Ibid. *Ep.* 2,79-81: "...Macarius...ipsumque presbyterum comprehensum, non iam ducere dignantur sed per silices trahunt, ita ut in coxa eius perniciosum vulnus fieret, atque alio die sistunt eum ante iudicem, ut magni criminis reum. cui quidem iudex veluti sub imperiali rescripto et minis extorquere contendit, ut cum Damaso conveniat... praesentem iudicem non timens, reppulit perfidi communionem."

but Damasus could not understand from the standpoint of a latter ecclesiology why it was not.

Amongst the events of the struggle with the Luciferans, a name which emerges is that of Heracleida, bishop of Oxyrinchus. The Rescript of Valentinian, Theodosius and Arcadius, in reply to Faustinus and Marcellinus, also to be found in the *Collectio Avellana (Ep.* 2a, 5-6), orders that those in communion with Gregory of Spain and Heracleida of the East should be given freedom of worship without any attack (*oppugnatione*), molestation (*molestia*) or otherwise discrimination (*nullis insidiis circumventionibusque*). They were further described as "priests of the sacred law (*sacrae legis antistites*)" whom "we believe to be none other than Catholics (*non aliud nisi catholicos esse credamus*)."[44] Heracleida is a name with which we shall meet in connection with the excavations at Portus, which reveal an ambiguous relationship between Damasus and the basilica dedicated to Hippolytus that was to stand there.

We shall need to assess such archaeological evidence carefully since there is no mention in the documents of the *Collectio Avellana* of any connection between Heracleida and Portus. Heracleida's career centres on Egypt where, at Oxyrinchus, the majority of the citizens revolted against their bishop, Theodore, who had allowed himself to be re-ordained by the Arian George. They proceeded with their presbyters and deacons to get Heracleida ordained instead "by means of catholic bishops of that time (*per tunc temporis episcopos catholicos*)." Theodore retorted with action similar to that taken by Damasus. Heracleida and his community were harassed through the "civil power (*per publicas potentates*)" because they "exsecrated the impious company of the prevaricators (*exsecrantes nefariam praevaricatorum societatem*)." The basilica of Heracleida was attacked and destroyed, and the altar itself smashed with axes (*Ep.* 2, 95-96, 100-101). It is implied that Heracleida fled from the city into exile (*Ep.* 2, 97-98).

No indication is given of where Heracleida went. But in the Imperial Rescript which gave a brief peace before the renewal of the persecution, Heracleida is given a position of primacy with regard to the eastern Luciferans along with Gregory with regard to the West. The edict of toleration thus given is to those *communicates Gregorio Hispaniensi et Heraclidae Orientali. (Ep.* 2a,6). It is possible therefore that Heracleida's activity could have extended to communities such as those of Portus, neighbouring Ostia, and Paulus its bishop, sympathetic to the Ursinian cause, where he could have been responsible for the dedication of a basilica to

---

[44] Ibid. *Ep.* 2a,8: "...ita iubeat custodiri, ut Gregorium et Heraclidam sacrae legis antistites, ceterosque eorum consimiles sacerdotes, qui se parili observantiae dederunt, ab improborum hominum atque haereticorum tueatur et defendat iniuriis, sciantque cuncti id sedere animis nostris, ut cultores omnipotentis Dei non aliud nisi catholicos esse credamus." (*Rescriptum Theodosii pro Marcellino et Faustino presbyteris*)

Hippolytus. If so, we can see how pertinent was the deployment by Damasus' of the legend of Hippolytus the Novatian Presbyter to this particular situation. We have already seen, in the language of *communio* as *processio*, a similarity between the self-definition of the Ursinians and Damasus' characterisation of the question to the Novatian Presbyter in his epigram. The identification of Heracleida the Luciferan with the Heracleida-inscription at Portus could be further strengthened if we can find evidence of a concern in this respect on the part of Damasus in connection with the basilica at Portus.

We turn therefore to a consideration of the excavations at Portus and Damasus' involvement there.

6A 2.6. *Damasus' register and the excavations at Portus*

The excavations at Portus itself (Fiumicino) imply an involvement of Damasus in the development of a cult-centre there.[45] But if he were so involved, why does he confine his attention to the far smaller shrine associated with San Lorenzo on the via Tiburtina? Why, furthermore, should Prudentius have followed him in extolling the basilica on the via Tiburtina, but left that at Portus unmentioned, with which he knows Hippolytus to have become associated in legend? Let us now consider in detail those excavations at Portus, and the light that they may shed on Damasus' selection and use of his register.

We saw in 1A 2 how Baronius was convinced that Hippolytus' remains were to be found at Portus, and for that reason he initially found Ligorio's location of the Statue at the Castro Pretorio near the via Tiburtina unconvincing.[46] Whereas by now the designation of *mons Ippolyti* had been lost, though previously found in medieval maps on the left of the via Tiburtina, there were still visible the remains of the large sanctuary at Portus witnessed by Pius II on his visit to Isola Sacra (1463).[47] Recent excavations have uncovered the remains of a large, three-naved basilica whose open façades indicate an architectural style not later than the fifth century.

Inscriptions bearing Hippolytus' name are mainly late. There is a sarcophagus containing many relics which has received the late inscription +HIC REQUIESCIT BEATUS YPOLITUS MAR(*tyr*), the quality of whose lettering is indicative of a ninth century date. However, a fragmentary in-

---

[45] P. Testini, Damaso e s. Ippolito di Porto, in *Studi di Antichità cristiana* XXXIX (1986), Saecularia Damasiana, p. 293-303. ——, Sondaggi a s. Ippolito all'Isola Sacra. I depositi, reliquiari scoperti sotto l'altare, in *RPARA* 46 (1973-1974), p. 165-179. ——, Indagini nell'area di S. Ippolito all'Isola Sacra. L'iscrizione del vescovo Heraclida, in *RPARA*, 51-52 (1978/79-1979-1980); V. Saxer, Note di agiografia critica: Porto, l'Isola Sacra e Ippolito a proposito di studi recenti, in *Miscellanea A.P. Frutaz*, (Roma 1978), p. 110; M.L. Veloccia Rinaldi , and P. Testini, *Ricerche archeologiche nell'Isola Sacra*, (Rome 1975).

[46] P. Testini, Vetera et nova su Ippolito, in *StEphAug* 30 (1989), p.12.

[47] Ibid. p. 13 ("si era infatti ormai perduta la denominazione di *mons Ippolyti* data nelle carte medievali alla collina posta a sinistra della via Tiburtina") and p. 16ff., tav. I.

scription on a caposaldo for the foundations of the basilica has been restored
by Testini and reads: HERACLIDA EPISC(*opus*) SERVVS/ DEI
BASILICAM YPPOLITO/ [*beatissimo martyri/ fecit*]. Ferrua classifies the
letters as "semi-Philocalian" and therefore derive from the last years of
Damasus (384) or those of his successor Siricius (384-399). Thus the inscription links the basilica at Portus with either Damasus or his successor,
with the lettering used being consistent with the date suggested by the open
façade style of architecture.[48]

In the excavations of 1974, a hemicycle was uncovered at a level underground (dating from the age of Trajan to the third Century) beneath the later
basilica of Heracleida. This represents undoubtedly the existence of a
memorial which preceded the great basilica, which was erected between the
age of Constantine and the end of the fourth Century. Also in 1974 were uncovered two fragments of an inscription with the pure type of Philocalian letters, though Hippolytus' name is not there.[49] One cannot therefore definitely
conclude that the Damasian memorial was definitely dedicated to
Hippolytus. But it would be difficult to argue that Heracleida's basilica had
no connection with the memorial that preceded it.

Why if there was a connection of Hippolytus with Portus did Damasus
place his inscription over the cult-centre on the via Tiburtina? Why if he.
identified that cult-centre with Hippolytus' name in accordance with the
Liberian *Depositio*, did he ignore the account of the exile to Sardinia with
Pontianus and make Hippolytus a Novatian martyr some fifteen years after
the events recorded in the *Catalogus*?

In answer to both questions, it is necessary first to point to Saxer's conclusion that around 385 the inclusion of Hippolytus in the number of the
martyrs of Portus had already taken place, by identifying him with Nonus as
we find happening in the *Passio Censurini* (between 354-400).[50] Such a literary development might be said to have its own momentum, but such a development is hardly purely literary. The combined testimony of Damasus
and Prudentius on the one hand, and the excavations at Portus on the other,
show parallel developments of cult-centres in honour of Hippolytus each
claiming his relics. It is necessary therefore to ask why Damasus and, more
especially Prudentius, affirms one and ignores the other. Prudentius, after
all, clearly knew of the legendary associations with Portus, yet he is insistent
that the scattered relics are brought back to the shrine on the via Tiburtina.
What, then, is the character of the tensions and ecclesiastical currents con-
tributing to this rivalry that find their legendary resolution in the legend of
the Novatian Presbyter?

---

[48] Ibid. p. 15-16 and p. 16ff., tavole II-IV, VI-VII.
[49] Ibid. p. 16 and tav. X.
[50] Saxer (1978) p. 110; Testini (1989) p. 19.

Testini locates the answer to this question in the figure of bishop Heracleida himself. We cannot be certain that the Damasian shrine on which he built at Portus was dedicated to Hippolytus himself since the one fragmentary inscription in pure Philocalian letters does not give Hippolytus' name. Undoubtedly the basilica of Portus was a magnificent achievement, located as it was in the middle of a large naval and commercial centre spreading the influence of its cult by sea throughout the Mediterranean world. But the semi-Philocalian inscriber clearly thought that a bishop Heracleida had dedicated the *basilica* to Hippolytus (*Yppolito*). If we could identify this bishop with the bishop Heracleida who was involved in Damasus' personal biography, we might be able to show how the latter's reticence to be associated with this shrine was in turn related to his construction of the legend of the Novatian Presbyter.[51]

There is, as we have seen, no evidence for the direct identity of the Egyptian and the Portian Heracleida. Yet some kind of association between two similar groups at Portus and Oxyrinchus, or indeed between them both and Damasus' principal enemies at Rome would account for the self-conscious rivalry between the two shrines. It would fit into the pattern of evidence already established that links the Novatian Presbyter with the Ursinians in the process of Damasus' legend-construction. It would also account for the swift eclipse of the figure of Hippolytus of Portus in the martyrologies after 400 when the presbyter becomes simply a *senex* and then a bishop, then a martyr and soldier.[52] The eclipse in the martyrologies would correspond chronologically with the eclipse of the Luciferans themselves.

We could see, as a result, why Damasus, followed by Prudentius, should studiously ignore the claims of Portus to house Hippolytus' remains. Such a stance would be of a piece with Damasus' other claims, such as those regarding the *Aedicula* on the Vatican hillside and the *tropaea apostolorum*. But why in that case turn the presbyteral companion of bishop Pontianus into a returned Novatian schismatic? Why not simply commemorate with an inscription the martyr-presbyter Hippolytus, and parade his unsullied orthodoxy to the world as an example to the Luciferans who so wrongly claim him?

One reason that we have already suggested is that both the *Depositio* and *Catalogus* already contained encoded messages about a schismatical past. But if so, it would have suited one purpose of Damasus to leave the hidden message of the code unexpressed in order to establish the validity of the claim of the Roman cult of Hippolytus against that of Portus. As it is, he is left with an inscription that will convey a different message to the Luciferans, namely that as Hippolytus returned from the Novatian schism to

---

[51] Testini (1977) p. 53-54.
[52] Testini (1989) p. 17-21.

the catholic church, then so should the Luciferans, abandoning their cult of Hippolytus at Portus for the true cult-centre on the via Tiburtina. But why should he have invented specifically a Novatian schismatic and not simply appealed to Hippolytus own schism some twenty years before, if schism it was? We seem thus to be witnessing a struggle on Damasus' part to appeal to history, although forced to use, in explicating history in defence of his ec-clesiastical position, a conceptual register that was too anachronistic to ex-press the social and ecclesiastical reality of over a century before.

It is now that we reach a new issue in our discussion, and one that has not been broached before. So far we have explained Damasus' construction of the legend of the Novatian Presbyter in terms of his ordering of the events of his contemporary social and ecclesiastical reality. But our account so far has given no reason as to why he chose Novatian and not Hippolytus himself as the schismatic. I have already presented De Rossi's the case for Damasus' accessibility as an *exceptor* to written archives of the church of Rome. I have already discussed at length and to the contrary the fact that when he speaks of what is heard and he passes on, without himself committing himself to the factual truth of what he says, he is almost self-consciously choosing instead to construct a legend set in the never-never time of *cum iussa tyranni pre-merent*, and *tempore quo gladius secuit pia viscera matris* (6A 2).

I will now argue that such a register of legend construction did not simply serve Damasus as the means of ordering the events of contemporary ecclesiastical reality. Such a register in addition served Damasus as a means of making comprehensible what was incomprehensible in the written sources available to him of the one and one half centuries before his time. But the process of understanding the past in terms of the anachronistic categories of the present took place in an age which could not understand, nor take account of, as the example of Eusebius shows, the process of historical development. Inevitably the conceptualization of the Hippolytan events as 'schism' was, in such a context, a process of distortion, as we shall now show.

PART B. THE CONCEPTUALIZATION OF HIPPOLYTUS' SCHISM

Damasus thus, in the light of the social construction of the reality of ecclesi-astical Order pertaining at his time, reached his understanding of the troubles faced by the Roman community in the late second and early third century. Because that construction of reality was highly anachronistic, he found the information, available to him more fully than to us, very bewildering. He thus selected a historical example that he did understand, namely of Novatus a presbyter in schism, and applied this model of ecclesiastical reality to events of some twenty years previous that he found so incomprehensible.

This in itself implies of course a rapid development of episcopal government at Rome between the end of the second century and those of the Novatian schism in 258. We shall now see that such an account is supported by the complete silence on Hippolytus' reputation as a schismatic from Eusebius onwards.

6B 1. *'Schism' and the reputation of Hippolytus*

In justifying my claim, the first point that I must make is that Damasus, in holding up Hippolytus as an example of an early third century schismatic to the Luciferans, was making a quite unique claim about him, in comparison with other sources available to us. Epiphanius of Salamis does not include a reference to the "Hippolytans" amongst his list of heretics, and the "Hippolytans" do not arise like the "Origenists" as the subject of condemnation by provincial councils of bishops. But Epiphanius, though he acknowledges Hippolytus once in the same ranks as Irenaeus and Clement of Alexandria, heaps dignified epithets on the two latter whilst almost ignoring the former.[53] Filastrius of Brescia, Victorinus of Pettau, and Commodian of Gaza all use his works without naming him as a source as do Ambrose, Jerome, and Damasus.[54] Is this omission accidental, given his voluminous writings, or is it the silence of embarrassment of those who know his record as a reconciled schismatic?

If their silence is the silence of embarrassment, the embarrassment in turn is thus quite unique. We shall see examples of other reconciled schismatics such as Natalius, who were so described without embarrassment. Furthermore, Damasus is not embarrassed about reconciled schismatics since the Novatian Presbyter is clearly one. We must ask therefore whether his reaction is not one of *embarrassment* about Hippolytus' schism, which he clearly would not wish to conceal, but rather of *bewilderment* about the events in his sources and the extent to which the term "schism," comprehensible in the case of the Novatian schism some forty years later, could apply to what he read of Hippolytus' contemporary situation.

I propose now further exploring such a thesis by first examining, in particular detail, the question of the silence of Eusebius and Jerome on the location of Hippolytus' See. If we can show that both Eusebius and Jerome have, like Damasus, sources unavailable to us, and that like Damasus' they cannot conceptually cope with a situation that in anachronistic in terms of their own time, then we shall show that Damasus' strategy in creating the Novatian Presbyter is his own conceptual reaction to the general, fourth-century bewilderment about the character of the controversy of Hippolytus' predeces-

---

[53] Epiphanius *Pan.* XXXI,33,3 cf. Irenaeus is mentioned in XXXI,1,3; 33,1; 33,3; 35,4; XXXII,6,2 & 7, and Clement in XXXI,33,3 and XXXII,6,1.
[54] Frickel (1988) p. 36.

sor with Callistus. I will then examine the question of Eusebius' general historiography, a part of the pattern of which his treatment the subject of Hippolytus will be seen to form part.

6B 2. *Damasus' register and the silence of Eusebius and Jerome*

Eusebius and Jerome either cannot or intentionally will not state the name of Hippolytus' See. In recording some of the works of Hippolytus, Eusebius seems to claim that they are written by a bishop whose See he fails to identify in a reference that is studiously vague.[55] Eusebius thus regards Hippolytus as a "bishop" (or "president") of a See that he claimed not to know (ἑτέρας που καὶ αὐτὸς προεστὼς ἐκκλησίας).[56] Jerome likewise follows Eusebius, at least in Rufinus' version,[57] and makes Hippolytus a bishop of a See in Arabia the name of whose city he has been unable to discover (*nomen quippe urbis scire non potui*) (*De Vir. Ill. 61*). How are we to explain this silence?

Both Frickel[58] and Simonetti[59] give different accounts of that silence, the former that it is indeed embarrassment about the first anti-pope, and the latter that rather it is confusion over two distinct writers of the same name being confused with a Roman martyr, with the result that no clear See can be designated. We shall show to the contrary that the source of the confusion is rather the inability of their conceptual register, formed in the social and ecclesiastical matrix of the fourth century, to describe events that occurred in the much different matrix of over a century before. It is to this much-discussed question that we must therefore now turn.

Frickel has argued that Eusebius had access to Alexander's library at Jerusalem. He mentions Beryllus writing books and letters, and describes Hippolytus acting in a like manner (ὡσαύτως). If therefore Hippolytus wrote letters like Beryllus as well as books, Eusebius must have read in those letters information about the See of which he was a bishop, and of his problems in administering it.[60]

---

[55] Following a reference to the letters and treatises (συγγραμμάτων) of Beryllus of Bostra, he adds: ὡσαύτως δὲ καὶ Ἱππόλυτος, ἑτέρας που καὶ αὐτὸς προεστὼς ἐκκλησίας (*H.E.* VI,20,2 cf. 22,1).

[56] *H.E.* VI, 20,2: Of the "many learned churchmen" whose works were preserved at Aelia in bishop Alexander's library, Eusebius says: τούτων Βήρυλλος σὺν ἐπιστολαῖς καὶ συγγραμμάτων διαφόρους φιλοκαλίας καταλέλοιπεν, ἐπίσκοπος δ' οὗτος ἦν τῶν κατὰ Βόστραν Ἀράβων· ὡσαύτως δὲ καὶ Ἱππόλυτος, ἑτέρας που καὶ αὐτὸς προεστὼς ἐκκλησίας.

[57] Rufinus VI,16 translates VI, 20,2: Episcopus hic fuit apud Bostram Arabiae, urbem maximam. Erat nihilominus et Hippolytus, qui et ipse aliquanta scripta dereliquit, episcopus.

[58] Frickel (1988) op. cit. 1-36 ff and, ——, Ippolito di Roma, Scrittore e Martire, in *StEphAug* 30 (1989), p. 23-41. Cf. the change of position from J. Frickel, Contraddizioni nelle opere e nella persona di Ippolito Romano, in *StEphAug* 13 (1977), p. 137-149.

[59] M. Simonetti, Agiornamento su Ippolito, in *StEphAug* (1989), p. 75-130.

[60] Frickel (1988) p. 5-7.

Likewise Frickel argues that Jerome must have had more information than he is prepared to reveal. Writing in Bethlehem (*De Vir. Ill.* 61) in 392, he increased the list of titles beyond that which Eusebius gives, whilst mentioning his ignorance about his See. But previously he had written a letter to Damasus himself (*c.* 382), in which he calls Hippolytus a "martyr" but not a bishop (*Ep.* 36). What therefore was the situation in Hippolytus' letters and other documents that both Eusebius, Jerome, and Damasus found so bewildering? It is to the details of the problem that we must now turn.

Was this because Jerome, like Eusebius, knew of the claim that Hippolytus was bishop of Rome, in succession to the author of *El.*, whereas he read Callistus on his succession list instead, and that both choose to repress this fact? Was this why Jerome in particular will call Hippolytus *episcopus*, but not to Damasus as *episcopus Romae*? Frickel argues affirmatively that the silence is intentional and calculated. Eusebius has documentary evidence before him that Hippolytus was the schismatical bishop of Rome which he is too embarrassed to mention, in view of the fact that the schism had been healed.[61]

I believe and will further argue that both Eusebius and Jerome, rather than having a deliberate intention to conceal, were confused with what they saw in the literary material before them regarding Hippolytus' ecclesiastical status. Their confusion was due to the ambiguity of that status rather than a definite claim to be a rival bishop in the mid-third-century, post-Cyprianic definition of that office. Frickel goes too far with his charges against Eusebius of deliberate repression rather than honest confusion. For example, Frickel charges Eusebius with the suppression of the full list of Hippolytus' works in order to gloss over a prominence that he found embarrassing.[62] But Eusebius words are not evasive on this point regarding the identifiable works of Hippolytan authorship in the library at Aelia.

6B 2.1. *Eusebius' statement in* H.E. VI, 22, 1

Following a brief description of τὸ περὶ τοῦ πάσχα, Eusebius introduces his list of seven works with "Of the rest of his treatises (τῶν δὲ λοιπῶν αὐτοῦ συγγραμμάτων), the following are the ones that have come to us (τὰ εἰς ἡμᾶς ἐλθόντα ἐστὶν τάδε)." He concludes the list with the statement: "... you might find very many others preserved amongst many people (πλεῖστά τε ἄλλα καὶ παρὰ πολλοῖς εὕροις ἂν σῳζόμενα)." (*H.E.* VI,22,1) Thus Eusebius states quite definitely that he is recording those that were to hand, and that there might be others that were not before him. Furthermore it is not remarkable that if we are talking of books, he was unable to identify every work that Hippolytus had written, given the custom of not autographing, and given rows of works commenting on the Scriptures and bearing therefore

---

61 Ibid. p. 34-56ff. and (1989) p. 23-41.
62 Ibid. p. 7.

very similar titles. In this category we might place his failure to assign the
treatise against Artemon to Hippolytus.[63]

Had Eusebius actual letters of Hippolytus before him, then of course they
would have contained his title and the geographical location of his See.
Simonetti regards Eusebius' possession of such letters an unfortunate inference from the fact that he mentions Hippolytus after Beryllus and before
Gaius, and introduces the works of all three collectively as Βήρυλλος σύν
ἐπιστολαῖς καὶ συγγραμμάτων διαφόρους φιλοκαλίας καταλέλοιπεν (H.E.
VI, 26,2-3). The words "Hippolytus likewise (ὡσαύτως)" that follow can
indicate letters as well as books, as with Beryllus, but might well indicate
simply books, as with Gaius, and no letters.[64] Simonetti's first ground for
rejecting Frickel's new thesis is therefore that Eusebius (VI,20,2) mentions
Hippolytus between Beryllus who wrote both letters and treatises, and Gaius
who wrote only a treatise.[65] Therefore we can conclude that really only
Beryllus wrote letters. Without the availability of letters of Hippolytus with
details about the schism, his treatises, without personal references, would
merely lead to ignorance rather than concealment.

The problem however with Simonetti's reading of the text in this way is
that it supposes that Eusebius will later mention *letters* of Beryllus of Bostra.
It will be the reference to these latter letters in connection with Beryllus
alone that will confirm the reading of σύν ἐπιστολαῖς as evidencing the existence of his letters alone, and not any of Hippolytus or Gaius. But there are
no such letters of Beryllus mentioned later, since the ἔγγραφα attributed to
him will not bear that meaning.

6B 2.2. *The meaning of* ἔγγραφα *in* H.E. *VI, 33,3*

Eusebius' words are: "There are still extant at present (καὶ φέρεταί γε εἰς ἔτι
νῦν) documents (ἔγγραφα) both of Beryllus and of the Synod that was held
because of him (τοῦ τε Βηρύλλου καὶ τῆς δι' αὐτὸν γενομένης συνόδου)."
(H.E. VI, 33,3) ἔγγραφα as a neuter plural takes its general sense from the
adjective that means what is recorded in the sense of approved, and hence
what is recorded in Scripture, or the recorded non-biblical traditions of the
church.[66] Eusebius himself uses this adjective of confessions of faith, where
he describes "orthodoxy preserved in writing (ἡ τῆς πίστεως...ὀρθοδοξία)"
of Serapion of Antioch, Narcissus and others (H.E. V,22). Hippolytus' predecessor, the author of El., uses the neuter plural of the writings of the

---

[63] Simonetti (1989) p. 78.
[64] Ibid. p. 79: "«altrettanto» (ὡσαύτως) può indicare che di lui a Elia si conservano, oltre
che le lettere, anche alcuni scritti, come di Berillo; ma può anche indicare, come per Gaio,
soltanto gli scritti, senza le lettere, che non sono menzionate, a VI,22, dove Eusebio elenca gli
scritti di Ippolito che conosceva."
[65] Originally he had accepted the two-author hypothesis for the Hippolytan *corpus*, see
Frickel (1977) p. 137-149.
[66] For further references, see Lampe G.W. (Ed.), *A Patristic Greek Lexicon*, (Oxford:
Clarendon Press 1961), p. 397- 398.

Elkasatites (*El.* IX, 13,5; 14,3). Thus the expression never refers specifically to a letter. We cannot therefore deny the absence of letters of Hippolytus because these are not mentioned further by Eusebius in his text, since then we would have to deny the existence of Beryllus' letters too.

It should be added that, though Eusebius mentions many works of Origen by name, he mentions no letters specifically, though he alludes to information about the Decian persecution that he had got from Origen's letters (VI, 39,5). As we said, σύν ἐπιστολαῖς must equally be capable of applying likewise (ὡσαύτως) to both Hippolytus and Gaius, and the failure to name specific letters has no force in the present discussion. That Eusebius was precluded from having before him in the library at Aelia any letters by Hippolytus because he does not mention any in his list of works becomes therefore questionable.

Simonetti's claim that Eusebius is referring to Beryllus' letters since he does not mention those of Hippolytus' therefore fails. Simonetti is therefore wrong in his contention that the silence of Eusebius is due to the total lack of personal details in Hippolytus' treatises (but not letters) that alone he had to hand. He argues further that the silence of Jerome is further due to the confusion occasioned by the existence of two different authors of the same name, the first of whom was an oriental, and the second of whom was Roman, the latter having read some the works of the first shortly after their composition.[67]

Thus I believe that Simonetti's reading of *H.E.* VI, 20,2 does not undermine Frickel's claim about Eusebius' knowledge of written sources. Eusebius, in using ὡσαύτως ("likewise") clearly does associate Hippolytus with the letter- and treatise- writing activities of Beryllus rather than with the lone treatise of Gaius. The sentence moreover begins with τούτων, in which Beryllus is included with Hippolytus, in contrast with the following sentence that begins, referring to Gaius' dialogue, with ἦλθεν δὲ, which clearly separates it from the preceding sentence.

But if Eusebius had such information about Hippolytus in terms of letters that he had written, his failure to give us that information cannot have been a reluctance to mention a schismatic or heretical bishop. Simonetti, though wrong about the non-availability of letters, is however on far firmer ground when he cites the examples of both Beryllus and Narcissus in this connection, whose citations by Eusebius will now pay further discussion. If Eusebius wished to repress Hippolytus' schism because he found 'schism' so questionable in an ecclesiastical writer, why did he mention Beryllus and his works who was heretical, or indeed the martyrdom of Narcissus who was

---

67 M. Simonetti, A modo di conclusione: una ipotesi di lavoro, and, Due Note su Ippolito, both in *StEphAug* 13 (1977) p. 121-136, 151-156, and, ——, Aggiornamento su Ippolito, in *StEphAug* (1989), p. 75-130.

schismatical? We shall see that these two examples, albeit in a less straight-forward way than Simonetti claims, will nevertheless support his contention that schism was no reason for the repression of information in Eusebius.

6B 2.3. *Beryllus and Narcissus: defects of heresy and schism*
Beryllus is mentioned without ambiguity, and such details of his activities that are known are related, even though he was in serious error regarding the pre-existence of Christ. Simonetti therefore claims that there would in con-sequence equally be no grounds for embarrassment about activities such as those of Hippolytus that were merely schismatical, particularly since he was also to wash out every offence in his martyrdom. Beryllus of Bostra is both mentioned alongside Hippolytus in VI,20,2, and whose denial of Christ's pre-existence and the claim that Christ's divinity was purely derivative, is castigated in VI, 33,1. But his doctrinal error does not rule out the acknowl-edgment of Beryllus' See.

But the problem with this objection is that Beryllus' See is not disputed however much his doctrine may be. The example of Natalius may therefore serve Simonetti better, since here is an example of a schismatic bishop. The martyr Natalius lived slightly before Hippolytus' time, in the pontificate of Zephyrinus around A.D. 201. Eusebius mentions as his source the treatise "against the heresy of Artemon (ἔν τινος σπουδάσματι κατὰ τῆς αἱρέσεως Ἀρτέμωνος), which Paul of Samosata has tried to renew in our own time." (*H.E.* V, 28,1) The unknown author is orthodox, but among those whose "names are not given in their writings." (V, 27) The quotation is against the Monarchianism of Theodotus the Cobbler, excommunicated by Victor, and cites Justin, Miltiades, Tatian, and Clement "in all of which Christ is argued to be God (ἐν οἷς ἅπασιν θεολογεῖται ὁ Χριστὸς)." (V, 28,4) To these wit-nesses are added "all the psalms and hymns which were written by faithful Christians from the beginning reason Christ's divinity as the Logos of God (τὸν λόγον τοῦ θεοῦ τὸν Χριστὸν ὑμνοῦσιν θεολογοῦντες)." (V, 28,6)

It was to the successors of Theodotus the cobbler, namely Theodotus the banker and Asclepiodotus that Natalius the confessor was drawn in the time of Zephyrinus. He was persuaded "with a salary (ἐπὶ σαλαρίῳ) to be called bishop of this heresy (ἐπίσκοπος κληθῆναι ταύτης τῆς αἱρέσεως)." (V, 28,10) Having been warned in visions because "our merciful Lord Jesus Christ did not wish that someone go out of his Church who had been a wit-ness to his sufferings," he "was scourged all night by Holy angels." Finally he knelt before "Zephyrinus the bishop, rolling at the feet not only of the clergy but also of the laity, and was re-admitted into communion." (V, 28, 11-12)

The first point in qualification of Simonetti's use of the examples of Beryllus and Natalius against Frickel's case is therefore that they do not ex-actly fit that of Hippolytus in one important respect. Both are Monarchians, and regarded by Eusebius as precursors of Paul of Samosata. Beryllus is refuted by Origen, for whom Eusebius held the highest regard, and Natalius is refuted by an anonymous author who may have been Hippolytus himself. Both Origen and Hippolytus, like the author of the work against Artemon (if he were not Hippolytus), held a λόγος Christology that Eusebius, albeit in a semi-Arian form, held to be the true orthodoxy. The problem for him in what he read about what in the 19th and 20th century is regarded as the "Hippolytan schism" may have been that for Eusebius Hippolytus was not simply a schismatic but an *orthodox* schismatic opposing a heretical canonical bishop.

It may be that Eusebius could understand (i) a canonical bishop who erred in faith and was corrected by Origen, if indeed matters were as simply as he describes; or (ii) a schismatic bishop who also erred in doctrine and in discipline (acceptance of a salary). But he may have found completely incomprehensible a schismatic bishop who was orthodox and who had to be reconciled to a community in heresy, namely the community of Callistus in the time of his successor Pontianus. The Hippolytan community clearly won the Christological debate even if they did not win the place of their bishop (the *presbyter* of the Liberian List) on the succession list. But if this is the case, it is not ignorance, as Simonetti claims, but bewilderment that would account for the failure to mention his See.

6B 2.4. *Confusion not concealment as the source of the silence*
Simonetti's further explanation of the silence as due to genuine ignorance is that, like Natalius, Hippolytus had been a reconciled martyr. In Hippolytus' case, martyrdom, and returning to the true faith, would have washed out any such taint against both his writings and his ecclesiastical office.[68] But unfortunately Eusebius does not mention that Hippolytus was a martyr. The description of martyr we learn from combining Jerome *Vir. Ill.* 6 with *Ep.* 36,16 and the preface to the *Commentary on Matthew*. In *Vir. Ill.* 6 he translates Eusebius' words *cuiusdam ecclesiae episcopus, nomen quippe urbis scire non potui*, and adds many works to Eusebius' list, as well as adding to his account that their author was a martyr. Indeed Frickel appealed to Jerome's professed ignorance too in support of his thesis since he considered it impossible for so widely travelled a person to have been ignorant of Hippolytus' See. Undoubtedly the source for Jerome's information was his patron Damasus, whose inscription at the cult-centre on the via Tiburtina we have already considered. But if this is the case, a martyrdom of which Eusebius was ignorant could hardly have washed out all blame of schism in Eusebius' eyes.

---

[68] Ibid. p. 79.

The source of Jerome's information about Hippolytus' martyrdom was undoubtedly Damasus, to whom he addresses *Ep.* 36,16. In consequence our discussion has thus in one way come its full circle. Yet in another it has revealed a pattern that unites the Eusebius-Jerome references to Hippolytus and the Novatian Presbyter of Damasus' epigram. We have seen that both Damasus and Eusebius did have the archival resources for documentary research on the events of Hippolytus' career prior to his martyrdom. Both however did not so much conceal what they knew, but rather failed to make sense of what they read. Neither could fit those events into the ecclesiastical categories with which they were familiar, and without which there were powerless to understand them. The vagueness of Eusebius was due the failure of the conceptual framework in which Church Order was discussed in the fourth century to cope adequately with the state of affairs in the second, as revealed by the surviving literature examined by Jerome and Damasus. The silence of Eusebius was a silence of bewilderment. Damasus for his part overlays his bewilderment by the construction of the legend of the Novatian Presbyter.

Frickel was correct to describe both Eusebius' and Jerome's remarks as a response to what they read in the archives, but Simonetti was also right in claiming that the form of that response could not have been the charge of heresy or schism that equally apply to Beryllus and Natalius respectably, at least as Eusebius saw the latter. I believe that both Eusebius, Damasus, and Jerome were equally perplexed with their documentary evidence regarding Hippolytus' ecclesiastical status because that evidence reflected an earlier stage in the development of the threefold Order.

We must from the outset delineate two issues here that must not be confused. The first issue is the one with which I have so far been dealing, namely the mythopoeic use to which Damasus is giving his reconstruction of historical events, namely the ordering function of his encoded message regarding reconciliation within the church of his own day. But we must distinguish a quite different issue from the clear interest in encoded messages that his epigram shares with the entries of the Chronographer of 354. We will ask in section C how his reading of his sources allowed him to reconstruct them in this particular mythopoeic way rather than in some other. For the moment, by way of a conclusion for our present section, let us summarize in broad terms how the position established here has prepared us for that task.

6B 3. *The real events behind the conceptual confusion*

There are, I believe, important links between the description given by Damasus and the problem of the silence of the location of Hippolytus' See in Eusebius and Jerome. These three writers did not "know" the true identity of Hippolytus' See as bishop of Rome, contrary to what Frickel argues, in his belief about their silence about their "knowledge." But neither on the other hand were they in ignorance about that See as Simonetti claims. In order to "know" or "understand" one's sources, one requires a conceptual framework in terms of which those sources become comprehensible.[69]

The vagueness of Eusebius, like Damasus' anachronistic Novatian presbyter, will be seen to testify to the failure of the conceptual framework in which Church Order was discussed in the fourth century to describe adequately the state of affairs in the second. Like Damasus, Eusebius possessed documentary evidence, now lost, for the controversy between Hippolytus' predecessor and Callistus, but he lacked a conceptual framework for Church Order in early second century terms with which to understand that controversy. The silence of Eusebius will be shown, like Damasus' creation of the Novatian Presbyter, to be the response of bewilderment.

The silence of Eusebius and Jerome on the location of Hippolytus' See is neither the silence of evasion nor that of ignorance. Rather it is the silence of those who are perplexed about how to conceptualize, in terms of the historical discourse available to them, certain historical events of a time before which that discourse had been fully developed along with the social and ecclesiastical reality that it created. Damasus reflected the same perplexity in his anachronistic description of Hippolytus as a Novatian Presbyter, even though, like Eusebius, he had available the facts of the original situation, which he could not interpret adequately, and so self-consciously constructed an explanatory legend. As such all three writers share the kind of fault usually identified in Eusebius' anachronistic description of the activity of Victor, whom he interprets as behaving like a fourth-century Ambrose over the excommunication of the Quartodecimans.

What therefore was the situation in Hippolytus' letters and other documents that both Eusebius, Jerome, and Damasus found so bewildering? Can we clarify the pre-Cyprianic or pre-Novatianic situation in the Roman community which these writers conceptualise anachronistically in this way? We will need to reconstruct for ourselves the situation regarding Church Order in both the Roman and North African communities at the time of Hippolytus and Tertullian, bringing out the contrasts with the post-Cyprianic and post-Novatianic situation. It is to the details of the problem that we must now turn in our next section.

---

[69] My conclusions in this regard I believe derive support from the eminent Origen scholar, Caroline Bammel, who though not actively involved in the Hippolytan debate, remarks: "I would agree that much embarrassment *and probably also some confusion* is likely to lie behind the omissions in the testimonies..." (C.P. Bammel, The State of Play with regard to Hippolytus and the *Contra Noetum*, in *Heythrop Journal*, 31 (1990), p. 195).

PART C. HIPPOLYTUS' CONGREGATION IN THE ROMAN COMMUNITY

In Part B we traced the inability of Eusebius, Jerome, and Damasus to conceptualize the events of the Hippolytan schism without the gross anachronism implied by the construction of the legend of the Novatian Presbyter.
Behind that process of legend-construction, moreover, lay a conceptual register which was involved with dealing ideologically with contemporary
schisms such as those of the Luciferans, with whose rival cult-centre at
Portus that of Damasus and Prudentius on the via Tiburtina produced an aetiological variance. In this section we must look, with particular reference to
the fundamentally significant work of Lampe, at what can be arguably determined both archaeologically and from the written sources about the
character of the Roman Church at the close of the second century.[70]

In the light of such a general picture, we must examine the events described by the author of *El.* IX, 11-13 in order to ascertain the extent to
which the descriptions of Frickel and others of his position as that of a
"schismatic," "antipope," "illegal bishop," etc. will be seen to be as
anachronistic as Damasus' legend of the Novatian Presbyter. In consequence, we shall be in a position to reassess what it meant to be a *presbyter/
episcopus* in the fractionalized Roman community of the late second to early
third century. In the light of that picture, we will thus be able to substantiate
our claim that Eusebius' silence over Hippolytus' See was the silence of bewilderment rather than embarrassment about what he read in the archives at
Aelia. The true character of the "Hippolytus schism," begun allegedly by the
author of *El.*, was as difficult for him to conceptualize as it has been for us to
recover, even with the resources of critical scholarship.

Let us consider, therefore, the character of the Roman community at the
turn of the third century, in the context of which we can evaluate the witness
of the community of the author of *El.*, and of his successor Hippolytus, to
Church Order in the Age before Novatian.

6C 1. *From House-Churches to the Tituli parishes (55-217)*

Paul makes it clear (*Rom.* 16, 1-16) there were a number of distinct Christian
groups with separate leaders in Rome by A.D. 55. In *v.* 3 Priscilla and
Aquila are Paul's acknowledged "fellow-workers (τοὺς συνεργούς μου),"
with their house-church (τὴν κατ' οἶκον ἐκκλησίαν) included in the saluta-
tion (*v.* 4). Although many names that follow could be included in this single

---

[70] I am indebted for my general description of the Roman Church in the second century to
the seminal work of P. Lampe, Die stadtrömischen Christen in den ersten beiden Jahrhunderten,
in *WUNT* 2,18 (1989). See also Cf. also G.H. Luttenberger, The Priest as a Member of the
Ministerial College. The Development of the Church's Ministerial Structure from 96 to c. 300
A.D., in *RThAM* 43 (1976), p. 5-63.

house-church, references to distinct groups are nevertheless implied by the following phrases:

(i) "the brothers with them (οἱ σὺν αὐτοῖς ἀδελφοί) that follows references to Asynkritus, Phlegon, Hermes, Patrobas, and Hermas (v. 14),

(ii) "all the saints with them (οἱ σὺν αὐτοῖς πάντες ἅγιοι)" with reference to Philologus, Julia, Nereus and his sister Olympas (v.15),

(iii) "those of Aristobulus' house (οἱ ἐκ τῶν' Ἀριστοβούλου)", (v. 10) and

(iv) "those of Narcissus' house who are in the Lord (οἱ ἐκ τῶν Ναρκίσσου οἱ ὄντες ἐν κυρίῳ)," (v.11).

As Lampe points out, we look in vain in the literary evidence for any central organisation for these different circles.[71]

At the other end of the development, we have the *tituli* churches of Rome and their parishes. These are documented in the 5-6th century in *Liber Pontificalis* 1, 31,10 where each church is described as *quasi diocesis* with its own building, clergy, liturgy, and burial places.[72] There are 25 such *tituli*-parishes found listed in the proceedings of Roman Synods from 499-595.[73] It is important to ask what connection these *tituli* churches have with the house-communities described in *Rom.* 16.

Lampe argues that some twenty of these *tituli* churches are pre-Constantinian. Only the latest five of the twenty-five have any accounts of their foundation, showing that the remaining twenty are from time immemorial. Cornelius indeed, writing in 250 in the midst of the events of the Novatian schism which we shall be arguing was to mark the final, critical stage in the development of Church Order at Rome, mentions 46 presbyters, 7 deacons, 7 subdeacons, 42 acolytes, and 52 exorcists, readers, and door-keepers (Eusebius *H.E.* VI, 43,11). Cornelius finds it incongruous that Novatus (Novatian) should have failed to grasp that there was to be only one bishop in the catholic church, whilst he knew of the large numbers of these other ministers. But the incongruity seems on Cornelius' side. If there were a plurality of ministers, why should there only be one bishop?

If indeed there were only one bishop, how liturgically could he be served by 46 presbyters or 52 exorcists, readers, and door-keepers? As we shall mention in a moment, the building of cult and cemetery complexes onto private houses is concurrent with and a product of the events in which Cornelius participates and does not antedate them. These figures point to a

---

71 Ibid. p. 301-302: "Anzeichen für ein räumliches Zentrum der verschiedenen über die Stadt verstreuten Kreise bieten sich nirgends. Jeder Kreis dürfte je für sich in einer Wohnung Gottesdienst feiern, so dass er als Hausgemeinde anzusprechen ist."

72 T. Mommsen, Libri Pontificalis, in *MGH*, Gestorum Pontificium Romanorum 1, 31,10: "[Marcellus]... fecit cymiterium via Salaria et XXV titulos in urbe Romana constituit quasi diocesis..."

73 J.P. Kirsch, Die römischen Titelkirchen im Altertum, in *Studien zur Geschichte und Kultur des Altertums* (Paderborn: Schöning 1919), p. 6-7 and p. 127-129 and Lampe (1989) p. 302-304.

number of meeting places for worship, and if they were twenty in number corresponding to the earliest of the later *tituli*-parishes, this would account for the services of some two presbyters per *titulus*-parish, given that some six of them might have been too old to officiate. Certainly they would require only one door-keeper, and a plurality of doorkeepers would thus imply a plurality of meeting places. In such a context the claim of one monarchical bishop over all the congregations might itself seem the incongruity.[74]

Lampe does not consider this incongruity and thus reaches some arguably wrong conclusions about the date for the emergence of monepiscopacy at Rome (in the pontificate of Victor) in an unambiguous form, as we shall argue later in this chapter. For the moment, let us note that Cornelius' statement is evidence for a number of distinct communities meeting at Rome as the historic forebears of the later *tituli*-parishes, organized *quasi diocesis*. With such communities meeting in private houses the *tituli* themselves are consistent, standing as the names of the owners of the houses over their doors. *Titulus* in Roman law described the right of personal ownership, and not ownership by virtue of ecclesiastical office comparable with the latter term *beneficium*.[75]

The names of the *tituli* churches themselves are not those of people who were originally saints, despite some later hagiography. It was no wonder therefore that the names of the private individuals Tigrida, Byzas/Bizantius, and Equitius should have been replaced in the sixth century respectably by saints Balbina, John and Paul, and Silvester. Furthermore the names listed in the proceedings of the Roman Synod of 499 as *tituli Clementis, tituli Caeciliae* etc. by those of 595 have become listed as *sanctae Caeciliae, sancti Clementis* etc. The literary evidence corresponds with the proposition that the names of the *tituli* were originally the private owners of house-churches. *Acts of Nereus and Achilleus* 22 mentions that their house "was just as though a church (καὶ γέγονεν ὁ οἶκος... καθάπερ ἐκκλησία)."[76] In the *Acta Justini* we read of the meeting place of Justin's group "over the bath of Martin son of Timothy."[77] The Valentinian community at Rome, moreover, have left an inscription and a grave-stone associated with a Villa on the via Latina.[78]

Let us now examine in greater detail the significance for the early organisation of the Roman community of Lampe's work.

---

[74] Lampe (1989) p. 303-304.

[75] Ibid. p. 304.

[76] For other such references see ibid. p. 306.

[77] Ibid. p. 238-241 cf. *Acta Justina* III,3: When the prefect Rusticus asks him where he dwells, Justin replies: ἐγὼ ἐπάνω τινὸς Μαρτίνου τοῦ Τιμιοτίνου βαλανείου, καὶ... οὐ γινώσκω ἄλλην τινὰ συνέλευσιν εἰ μὴ τὴν ἐκείνου καὶ εἴ τις ἐβούλετο ἀφικεῖσθαι παρ᾽ ἐμοὶ, ἐκοινώνουν αὐτῷ τῆς ἀληθείας λόγων.

[78] Ibid. p. 257-264, p. 306.

6C 2. The relation of house community to philosophical school

Lampe, with the aid of a sophisticated use of archaeological sources which he can thus combine with literary ones, is the latest of a line of critics who have decisively refuted the myth of a church of Rome hierarchically governed from the first century, along with which, and more or less under the control of which, schools such as those of Justin, or, indeed, Valentinus, flourished before the latter broke away. Bardy argued the case for such a shadowy hierarchy in the background, even though he conceded otherwise that Roman Christianity would indeed have appeared from the standpoint of Graeco-Roman culture as a collection of different philosophical schools.[79] But Bardy's contention, that there existed a monarchical episcopate alongside the teachers in the schools, approving some teaching and judging other, and finally formalising everything in the pontificate of Victor, will not bear the weight of the evidence.

Ignatius *Romans*, whose author vigorously defended in Syria and Asia Minor an early form of the threefold hierarchy,[80] fails to mention any bishop at Rome. Whilst he fails to mention any presbyters and deacons too, his failure to mention the latter is corrected by Clement *Corinthians*, which otherwise fails to confirm the former. Clement uses the term ἐπισκόποι in the plural as a synonym for πρεσβύτεροι. In *Hermas*, moreover, a document dating from the mid second century, and even as late as in Irenaeus, these two terms are used interchangeably. Thus Lampe will conclude by analogy with the Jewish synagogue that there were a number of house-communities with councils of presbyters.

Furthermore, Justin's school was not simply a catechetical institution to provide converts for a quite different, sacerdotally and hierarchically governed church. From the *Acta Justini* III we can discover disciples' names, such as Evelpiste (born in Cappadocia, slave of Caesar), Hierax (born in Iconium in Phrygia), and a lady named Charito. When Rusticus the prefect asks whether Justin had made them Christians, Hierax replied that he was already and would continue to be so (ἤμην Χριστιανὸς καὶ ἔσομαι). When he asks Paian who had taught him, the latter replies that he had received "this good confession" from his parents (ἀπὸ τῶν γονέων παρειλήφαμεν τὴν καλὴν ταύτην ὁμολογίαν). Similarly Euelpistos replies: "I listened gladly to Justin's discourses, but my Christianity I received from my parents (Ἰουστίνου μὲν ἡδέως ἤκουον τῶν λόγων, παρὰ τῶν γονέων δὲ κἀγὼ

---

[79] G. Bardy, Les Écoles Romaines au Second Siècle, in *RevHE* 28,1 (1932), p. 501-532. See also G. La Piana, The Roman Church at the end of the second century, in *HThR* 18 (1925), p. 201-277.

[80] Ignatius however did not advocate monarchical episcopacy in the later sense of the *Didascalia Apostolorum*, see A. Brent, The Relations between Ignatius and the Didascalia, in *SecCent* 8,3 (1991), p. 129-156; G. Schöllgen, Monepiskopat und monarchischer Episkopat: Eine Bemerkung zur Terminologie, in *ZNW* 77 (1986), p. 146-157.

παρείληφα Χριστιανὸς εἶναι)." Thus the gathered community above the bath of Martin was an established Christian community, with members who were born into Christian families. They did not gather in such a place simply to be catechetized but to worship, as in *1 Apol.* I, 61-67.

In view of this picture of the school of Justin, it would, be clearly a mistake to over-emphasize the house-community as a model for the development of the Roman community.[81] The household image was only one of a number of images evoked about these communities in those who stood outside of them. Lampe is aware of other images such as a philosophical school (διδασκαλεῖον), or a cultic group (θίασος) can also apply. Moreover, he finds the concept of "house-community" barely adequate, since, for the second century, it requires qualifying with the presence of office holders called ἐπισκόποι–πρεσβύτεροι and διακόνοι. As such the definition would exclude first century communities without such an official ministry.[82] A further objection to the overemphasis on "house-community" as the definitive model would also be that such a conceptualization ignores the way in which the organisation of the Greek philosophical schools arose within the ambience of the Greek house. An organized house-community, meeting for common meals and with a common organisation, would not have appeared very different from a philosophical school to pagan contemporaries.[83]

We can illuminate this point further by examining the literary setting of debates within the Greek philosophical schools within the spatial context of the architecture of the Greek house.

6C 3. *The philosophical school as an extended* Hausgemeinde

Wycherley argued that a Greek philosophical school was essentially a specialized extension of the Hellenic household.[84] In Plato, *Protagoras* 314c-

---

[81] H.-J. Klauck, Hausgemeinde und Hauskirche im frühen Christentum, in *Stuttgarter Bibelstudien* 103, (Stuttgart: Verlag Katholisches Bibelwerk 1981). For a recent more qualified assessment of this question, see G. Schöllgen, Hausgemeinden Oikos-Ekklesiologie und monarchischer Episkopat. Überlegungen zu einer neuen Forschungsrichtung, in *JbAC* 31 (1988), p. 74-90.

[82] Lampe (1989) p. 320: "Für alle ist... der Begriff „Hausgemeinde" (= „gottesdienstliche Gemeinschaft in einem Hause") adäquat; es sei denn, wir definieren „Hausgemeinde" als eine Gruppe, die zugleich eine bestimmte Ämterordnung (mit Presbytern und Diakonen) aufweist. Dass das unmöglich ist, lehren die neutestamentlichen Gottesdienstversammlungen der ersten Generation, die dann nicht als „Hausgemeinden" zu bezeichnen wären.. Ich bin mir bewusst, lediglich die Tür auf einer „Rumpelkammer" von Problemen aufgestossen zu haben.

[83] For a judicious discussion of these and related problems, see R.L. Wilken, Collegia, Philosophical Schools, and Theology, in *The Catacombs and the Colosseum.* (Valley Forge: 1971), p. 268-291.

[84] R.E. Wycherley, Peripatos: The Ancient Philosophical Scene, in *Greece and Rome* 8 (1961) and 9 (1962), cf. M. Lechner, *Erziehung und Bildung in der griechisch-römischen Antike,* (München: Hüber 1938); A. Böhlig, Die griechische Schule und die Bibliothek von Nag Hammadi, in *Zum Hellenismus in den Schriften von Nag Hammadi* (Ed) A. Böhlig, F. Wisse *(Göttinger Orientforschungen* 6,2), (Wiesbaden: Harrassowitz 1957), p. 9-53; R. Scholl, Das Bildungsproblem in der alten Kirche, in *Zeitschrift für wissenschaftliche Pädagogik* 10 (1964), p. 24-43; G. Rubach, Das Eindringen des Christentums in die gebildete Welt, in

315e, we are confronted by the scene that follows the admission of Socrates and his unnamed friend into Kallias' house, having overcome the resistance of the slave-doorkeeper who had heard their animated discussion and thought they were merely sophists. They enter the typically Hellenistic house in which the men's room and women's room were approached through the αὐλή or courtyard. Along the sides of the latter, and thus almost surrounding it (apart from the opening vestibule), ran sleeping rooms opening into the αὐλή itself. Two colonnades enclosed the threshold and ran along the rooms on either side. In this instance, Protagoras walks up and down one colonnade in discussion with a deferential group of followers. In the opposite colonnade Hippias is installed on a professorial chair answering questions on astronomy from students seated on benches. Prodikus' voice carries from his bedroom where another group is listening to him. There was a cultic aspect to the Hellenistic house shared by the philosophical school. In *Rep.* 1, 328-331 Kephalos welcomes Socrates and his companions, who sit down with the guests already there around him. Kephalos was still wearing the garlands from his offering a sacrifice in the αὐλή, and it is to such activity that he returns, leaving philosophical discussion to his guests.[85]

Thus the *palaestra* (wrestling school) or gymnasium courtyard which we meet in *Lysis* 203a-204b is to be regarded as a magnification of a Greek house, like that of Kallias, and employed on a similar basis by Greek philosophical schools. Classrooms here would be the *exedrae*, which were the rooms situated around the central αὐλή, but in this case with one wall removed so as to open directly onto it. Some boys were busy with a sacrifice, whilst others indulged in a game of dice (206e).[86] There is little difference between the scene depicted here and that seen by the Roman Cicero on his visit to Athens in 79 B.C. In *De Fin.* V,1 Cicero and his friends walk after hearing a lecture by Antiochus of Gaza in the gymnasium called the Ptolemaion at Athens. They take an *ambulatio postmeridiana* (περίπατος δειλινός) and visit the κῆπος of Epicurus, the Academy of Plato, and the ἐξέδρα of Colonus, and are impressed by the various schools to which each belong.[87] Nor is there much difference between the setting of the scenes in the houses of Kallias or of Kephalos, or of that in the *palaestra*, and that "in the dwelling above the bath of Martin." Baths such as those of Caracalla gave access at the end of their spacious hall to enclosed *palaestra* with separate baths for athletes, and conformed to a general type of community centre such as that recorded in the *Lysis*.[88]

Kirchengeschichte als Missionsgeschichte, Vol.1 Die alte Kirche, (München: 1974), p. 293-310; G. Ruhbach. Klerusbildung in der alten Kirche, in *WuD* 15 (1979), p. 107-114.

[85] Ibid. p. 154-155.
[86] Ibid. p. 159.
[87] Ibid. p. 152.
[88] T. Fyfe, ART. Baths, in *The Oxford Classical Dictionary*, (Ed.) M. Cary etc., (Oxford: Clarendon Press 1968), p. 133.

Thus the character of a house-community resembling a Greek philosophical school is well represented by the community of Justin Martyr meeting "in the dwelling of a certain Martin, by the bath of Timothy." Justin Martyr's school, whether disputing with Trypho at Ephesus or teaching at Rome (*Dial.* 1,2; 3,1; 9,1), became the *locus* also for the liturgy the gathered church (I *Apol.* 65 and 66). There was no wider, central meeting place for this and other communities. This is the clear conclusion of the negative archaeological evidence where there are no examples of either separate church buildings, or indeed rooms in private houses, set aside exclusively for worship before the middle of the third century. The house on the Clivus Scauri was extended and modified at this time to form the church which survives today as St. John and St. Paul. Similar excavations under St. Clement and S. Martino ai Monti also date from this time.[89] Justin's house-community and school are the ἐκκλησία in the place of their gathering.

It is not insignificant in this context that Justin's famous description of the Eucharist calls the "president" by the term ὁ προεστώς, which is used most frequently in Diogenes for the head or founder of a philosophical school. Ἀκαδημαικῆς μὲν οὖν τῆς ἀρχαίας προέστη Πλάτων, τῆς μεσῆς Ἀρκεσίλαος, τῆς νέας Λακύδης ("Plato founded the Old Academy, Arcesilaus the Middle, and Lakudes the New"), and so on for the "founders" of other schools (*Succ.* proem. 19). Thus it is arguable that he who celebrates Justin's Eucharist is regarded more like the founder of a philosophical school, and derives his presidency from that fact rather than from a hierarchically-conceived authority.

It is of course important not to secularize the Graeco-Roman philosophical school. We have already mentioned that, as an extension of the Graeco-Roman house, sacrifice will be part of the furniture of philosophical discussion as the examples of Kallias and Kephalos have shown. Furthermore, cultic functions associated with the *paterfamilias* were also exercized by the προεστώς as head of the school. As the genuine account in Diogenes of Theophrastus' Will shows, there is a temple connected with Aristotle's school, in which Aristotle's statue is to be put back along with other consecrated objects (ἔπειτα τὴν Ἀριστοτέλους εἰκόνα τεθῆναι εἰς τὸ ἱερὸν καὶ τὰ λοιπὰ ἀναθήματα ὅσα πρότερον ὑπῆρχεν ἐν τῷ ἱερῷ) (*Succ.* 5, 51-52). The altar is to be repaired (ἐπισκευασθῆναι δὲ καὶ τὸν βωμόν). Furthermore, the property of the school is to be held "in joint possession, like a temple (ἀλλ' ὡς ἂν ἱερὸν κοινῇ κετημένοις)." (Ibid. 5,52-53) A Christian community organized on the pattern of a philosophical school, however perverse some of the analogies might be, could therefore have its cultic moments. The "president" or προεστώς of the school might offer the "pure sacrifice" of Malachi, as Justin (*Dial.* 117) describes the Eucharist, as part of the liturgy

---

[89] Lampe (1989) p. 307-310.

of the school, just as offering a cock to Aesclepius might be part of the ritual of a Socratic school, however loathe the early Fathers may have been to make verbally explicit such Eucharistic analogies with pagan cultic acts.

Furthermore, and consistent with Justin's apologetic purpose, it is significant, as Bammel has pointed out, that the concept of διαδοχή is in some instances linked with the ownership of the premises of either the place of cultus, or the place of the school. Ernst Bammel argues on the basis of an inscription published by Schubart in 1917 that the original significance of διαδοχή was sacerdotal and juridical, and the means by which pagan priests established the regularity and good order of their cult in the eyes of the Roman Emperor.

The inscription itself comes from the third century B.C. and concerns an ordinance of Ptolemy Philopator. Though διαδοχή itself is not a term that is used, each priest of the cult of Dionysius has to make a written, official declaration (ἀπογράφεσθαι) to Aristobulus at the registry in Alexandria (εἰς τὸ καταλογεῖον) stating who are their predecessors (παρὰ τίνων παρειλήφασιν τὰ ἱερά) for at least three generations (ἕως γενεῶν τριῶν), and to sign his name (ἐπιγράψαντα τὸ ὄνομα ἕκαστον τὸ αὑτοῦ ὄνομα) on a sealed and signed account of the doctrine (διδόναι τὸν ἱερὸν λόγον ἐσφραγισμένον) to which he adheres.[90] Thus there is a connection between validity of succession and legal title to the *temporalia* of the cultus. School and cultus are thus legally linked in terms of title to ownership of particular premises where their activities are housed. διαδοχή can moreover be understood to be a term indicative of that link, and thus reflect a Christian community understood in terms of, and even physically housed as, a philosophical school.[91]

Let us now see how such a description of the community as a philosophic school applies specifically to Hippolytus' community and the church of Rome in the second century. We begin with *Ap. Trad.* which we have already argued to have been a composite work and owned by the community rather than any particular of its two or three writers (5A 1-5A 1.2).

---

[90] W. Schubart, Ägyptische Abteilung (Papyrussammlung): Ptolemaeus Philopator und Dionysos, in *Amtliche Berichte aus den preussischen königlichen Kunstsammlungen (= Beiblatt zum Jahrbuch der preussischen königlichen Kunstsammlungen)* 38 (1916/1917) p. 190: Βασιλέως προστάξαντος τοὺς κατὰ τὴν χώραν τελοῦντας τῷ Διονύσῳ... ἀπογράφεσθαι πρὸς Ἀριστόβουλον εἰς τὸ καταλογεῖον...διασαφεῖν δὲ εὐθέως καὶ παρὰ τίνων παρειλήφασιν τὰ ἱερὰ ἕως γενεῶν τριῶν καὶ διδόναι τὸν ἱερὸν λόγον ἐσφραγισμένον ἐπιγράψαντα τὸ ὄνομα ἕκαστον τὸ αὑτοῦ ὄνομα.

[91] E. Bammel, Die Anfänge des Sukzessionsprinzips im Urchristentum, in La Tradizione: Forme e Modi, *StEphAug.* 31 (1990), 63-72. A cautionary note should however be registed in view of the absence of διαδοχή as such and also the argument of J. Gluckner, Antiochus and the Late Academy, in *Hypomnemata: Untersuchungen zur Antike und zu ihrem Nachleben* 56 (1978), 149-158 ff., who argues the essential distinction between διάδοχος as the heir to the teaching of a set of ideas and the possession of διάδοχα or the property of a school as such. The critical text here is the *Epistula Plotinae* in *IG* II and III Pars Prima, (Berlin 1913), 1099. See also J.H. Oliver, The Diadoché at Athens under the Humanistic Emperors, in *AmJPhil* 98 (1977), p.160-169.

6C 4. *Character of the Hippolytan community in the* Ap. Trad.

The church of Rome of the mid-to-late second century resembled a collection of philosophical schools, whilst no doubt emphasizing the religious and liturgical basis for the community's life more than normal for such schools. Many aspects of those schools could also represent images of house-communities, in view of the development of the ethos and organisation of such schools within the architectural parameters of Graeco-Roman private houses. Lampe quotes Hippolytus *Ap. Trad.* 28 (*si communiter vero omnibus oblatum fuerit quod dicitur graece* apoforetum *accipite ab eo*) which he seeks to illuminate with a reference to Petronius *Sat.* 56. The ἀποφόρητον clearly refers to the small gifts or mementos of the banquet given by a host such as Trimalchio in the course of conversations on such subjects as the virtues of Cicero and Publius.

In the context of *Ap. Trad.* 25-30 they refer to *agape* meals, with the usual injunctions to sobriety for such occasions. But meals where mementos are given by generous hosts, or indeed *agape* feasts where the mementos are food and clothing for the poor, were not only characteristic of social gatherings of friends. Such meals were characteristic too of philosophic schools such as those of Plato and Epicurus. Regular συμπόσια, which were banquets or drinking parties were held in the Academy, and they were held to be an essential element in education, with rules for their conduct and a regular calendar of responsibilities established.[92] In the school of Epicurus there was a banquet on the twentieth day of the month in honour of Epicurus and Metrodorus, and a special banquet in honour of the founder's birthday. Moreover, Epicurus' Will stipulated that contributions for such banquets be used for funeral offerings for members of his family.[93]

There is a clear connection, at the level of affective ethos, between the school of Epicurus and the church as the school of Jesus. Both schools were characterized by a devotion to the person of the founder-teacher unknown in the Academy, Lycaeum, or Stoa. Along with this personal veneration to which Lucretius so eloquently subscribed,[94] Cicero *De Fin.* II, 20 informs us that Epicurus' κυρίαι δοξαί were learnt by heart as producing happiness (*ad beatum vivendum*).[95] The Epicurean and Johannine literature both use φίλοι to indicate members of their respective schools. This title is particularly present in the Farewell Discourses in *Jn.* 14-16, which are reminiscent of Epicurus' death scene in Diogenes *Succ.* 10,16 (2A 2.2). We read the in-

---

[92] R.A. Culpepper, The Johannine School, in *Society for Biblical Literature* DS 26, (Missoula: 1975), p. 78. Aristotle continued this practice, see p. 93-94.

[93] Diogenes Laertius, *Succ.* X, 18: ...εἴς τε τὰ ἐναγίσματα τῷ τε πατρὶ καὶ τῇ μητρὶ καὶ τοῖς ἀδελφοῖς, καὶ ἡμῖν εἰς τὴν εἰθισμένην ἄγεσθαι γενέθλιον ἡμέραν ἑκάστου ἔτους τῇ προτέρᾳ δεκάτῃ τοῦ Γαμηλιῶνος, ὥσπερ καὶ εἰς τὴν γινομένην σύνοδον ἑκάστου μηνὸς ταῖς εἰκάσι τῶν συμφιλοσοφούντων...

[94] *De Rer. Nat.* 3,1 ff.

[95] Culpepper (1975) p. 108-109.

junctions χαίρετε (χαρήσεται), μέμνησθε τὰ δόγματα (μνημονεύετε τοῦ λόγ–
ου οὗ ἐγὼ εἶπον ὑμῖν), and laying down one's life for the φίλοι.[96] The
conversation at the banquet of the φίλοι, in honour and memory of the
teacher, is described, and the themes of ἀγάπη and ἀγαπητοί are celebrated
at the Christian *agape*-meal.[97]

We have seen that the celebrated Statue that prefigured with its Easter
Table as an important ecclesiastical artefact in the life of Hippolytus' community was originally that of a female Epicurean philosopher, Themista of
Lampsacus (2A 1-1.2). In Lucian *Alexander* 25,38 both Epicureans and
Christians are mentioned together. But Christianity and Epicureanism were
metaphysically so far apart at an epistemological level as to be mutually ab-
horrent.[98] But at an affective level, there was a fellow-feeling (2A 2.1) that
enabled the school of Hippolytus to take over Themista's Statue and to give
it an allegorical significance (2A 3). We should not therefore be too ready
with Lampe to assimilate completely the setting of *Ap. Trad.* 25-30 to a private dinner party of a house-community. When such a private dinner party
has become the formal meal of a community it has become, in Graeco-
Roman eyes, indistinguishable from that of a philosophical school.

Lampe may well emphasize the impression of the private dinner party
evoked by the injunction of the following passages:

> For every oblation (*oblationem*), let him who offers it be mindful of he who
> invited him (*memor sit qui offert eius qui eum vocavit*); for he himself has
> prayed earnestly (*depraecatus*) with a view that (*propterea*) he might come
> under his roof... If there is offered to all in comon the portion of the dish which
> in Greek is called an ἀποφόρητον, receive of it [or accept it from him]. If how-
> ever all are invited partake to their satisfaction (*ut omnes gustent sufficienter*),
> partake only so much so that there may be a remainder for the host to send to
> those whom he wishes as the remains of the holy things (*reliquiis sanctorum*).
>
> *Ap. Trad.* 27, 9-13 and 28, 7-15

The 'host' described here seems quite distinct from the bishop who clearly
presides at the meal and 'chairs' the conversation (28, 16-20). As Botte
comments, there appear to be two kinds of repast in view, one in which the
food is divided and packaged to be taken away, and the other in which the
course is partaken by the guests with the host sending the remains away for
others.[99] The reconstruction of the text is moreover difficult at this point

---

[96] *Jn.* 15, 14-15. Note also ποιῆτε ἃ ἐγὼ ἐντέλλομαι ὑμῖν quoted by Culpepper, and *Jn.*
15,3 with which cf. Diogenes *Succ.* 10, 120: καὶ ὑπὲρ φίλου ποτὲ τεθνήξεσθαι.

[97] Ibid. p.112-113, 119-121.

[98] A.D. Simpson, Epicureans, Christians, Atheists in the Second Century, in *Transactions of
the American Philological Association* 72 (1941), p. 372-381; R. Jungkuntz, Fathers, Heretics,
and Epicureans, in *JEH* 17,1 (1966), p. 10.

[99] B. Botte, La Tradition apostolique de saint Hipplyte. Essai de reconstitution, in *Liturgiewissenschaftliche Quellen und Forschungen*, 39 (1963) (AschendorffscheVerlagsbuch-
handlung: Munster: 1963), p. 71 (2), cf. E. Peterson, Meris, Hostien Partikel und Opfer-Anteil,
in *EphL* 61 (1947), p. 3-12.

since the Verona Latin has before *apoforetum* the words *oblatum fuerit quod dicitur graece*. Clearly these words were superfluous in the original Greek and marks the paraphrase of the translator. How far did his work of paraphrase extend? The Sahidic (with the agreement of A and E) omits any mention of this word and speaks only of *partes* or *partem* (μερίς). I have translated L's *reliquiis sanctorum* (*reliquias sanctorum* in S(AE)) as "remains of the holy things" since this phrase is common to both versions, and although it can refer to the remnants of a meal, the addition of *sanctorum* seems to require the unquestionably cultic sense of the "remains of a sacrifice."

But if this is the case, then *si communiter vero omnibus oblatum fuerit* will have also a cultic sense and the meaning of ἀποφόρητον at Trimalchio's banquet will have been transformed into a new, Christian meaning. Instead of a trinket given by the host it will become the community's sacred offering for the poor, to be divided and distributed uneaten, or to be partially eaten and partially distributed. I wonder, however, whether *apoforetum* was not a misinterpretation added by the scribe of L, who read *accipite ab eo* to mean "receive [something] from *him*" and supplied for the "something" an ἀπο−φόρητον, whereas clearly S(AE) read what was being received as a thing (*accipies partem tuam tantum*), as I translated *ab eo* in the quotation above. The host, after all, only appears after these lines in 28, 13 as *qui vocavit vos (te)* in both *ms.* traditions. If *partes/partem* (= μερίς) of S(AE) are more original, then those words themselves are more evocative of the cultic associations of the *reliquiae sanctorum*.

In either case, whether ἀποφόρητον represents a scribal misunderstanding of an original cultic reference, or whether the term is original and it has been reinterpreted in a new cultic way, we cannot accept Lampe's characterisation of Hippolytus' or any other Roman community as a *Hausgemeinde* in any straightforward way. Though the dependence of the community on a wealthy house-owner with premises sufficiently large for the community to assemble may distinguish it from that of Justin above the bath of Myrtinos, other features here also point to a philosophic community or school. The affective similarities with the school of Epicurus extend beyond Themista's Statue here too. We read, using the text of S(AE):

> 31. On the fruits which should be laid before the bishop.
> Let all be concerned (σπουδάζειν) to lay before (*offerre*) the bishop on every occasion the firstfruits (*primitias fructuum*/ ἀπαρχάς), the first seeds (*prima germina*/ γέννηματα) [*fructus natos primum quam incipiunt*= L]. Let the bishop receive them with a thankful gesture (*cum gratiarum actione*) and let him bless them (*benedicat eos*/ *qui autem offerit benedicat*, L) and let him name the name of him who has presented them to him.
>
> *Ap. Trad.* 31

The *ms. Barberini graec.* 336 then continues the bishop's prayer of blessing of the firstfruits:

We give you thanks (εὐχαριστοῦμεν), Lord God, and we offer the firstfruits (ἀπαρχὴν καρπῶν) which you have given us to share in bringing to perfection through your word (οὓς ἔδωκας ἡμῖν εἰς μετάληψιν τελεσφορῆσαι διὰ τοῦ λόγου σου).

Thus the Barberini *ms.* gives us confidence in the text of S(AE) since it describes, whilst following readings identical with L, what the bishop blesses as ἀπαρχὴν καρπῶν. Thus is confirmed *primitias fructuum/* ἀπαρχάς as the more technical reading of the original against L's *fructus natos primum quam incipiunt.*

The offering of the firstfruits to the bishop to be blessed with a prayer of thanksgiving on behalf of, and for the life of, the whole community is reminiscent of the fragment of the letter of Epicurus to Idomeus. Epicurus writes:

Send then firstfruits to us (ἀπαρχὰς ὑμῖν) for the nurture of the (my) sacred body (εἰς τὴν τοῦ ἱεροῦ σώματος θεραπείαν) both for its own sake (ὑπέρ τε αὐ-τοῦ) and for that of the children (καὶ τέκνων), for so I feel urged to express it (οὕτω γάρ μοι λέγειν ἐπέρχεται).[100]

As Culpepper points out, the meaning of this fragment is problematic. Though the words may refer to Idomeneus' own children in the care of Epicurus, this would not account for his closing apology for having expressed his thoughts analogously. Rather he would appear to be referring to his school as "the sacred body" and his disciples as his children, for whom he is receiving first fruits from such benefactors as Idomeus. As we have seen, the Hippolytan community, sharing in the affective ambience of Themista's Statue, likewise had their bishop receiving the firstfruits and giving thanks on behalf of the whole community for their sustenance.

Given, then, that the church of Rome consisted by the end of the second century of a number of house-schools—of which the group of Justin earlier, and that of the author of *El.* and of Hippolytus later, were typical examples—can we specify how such groups were governed, and how that government evolved into the hierarchy of the third century? It is to this question that we must now turn.

6A 5. *The House-Schools and the emergence of monepiscopacy*

Thus we have followed Lampe in his account of the church of Rome at the end of the second century as consisting of a number of house-communities. Against Lampe we have shown grounds for regarding these communities as philosophical schools in the natural setting and ambience of the Graeco-Roman house, rather than simply house-communities without further quali-

---

[100] Usener, *Epicurea*, fr. 130; Plutarch, *Moralia*, 1117E, quoted Culpepper (1975) p. 117.

fication. We must now see by what sort of organisation these house-schools
were run (later to survive as the *tituli* parishes) and the developments that
were to lead to monepiscopacy. We shall follow Lampe in the main in his
description of the organisation of the house-schools before the time of
Victor, but we shall take issue with him for the way in which he regards the
pontificate of Victor as decisive for establishing monepiscopacy. We shall
argue that the evidence of *El.* and *Ap.Trad.* show that many of the assumptions about Church Order that preceded Victor still held in the time of his
successors Zephyrinus and Callistus, and that the decisive development of
monarchical bishops took place as a result of those events in the period
leading up to Novatian. It was, we shall see, once again no accident that
Damasus was to conceptualize the events associated with Hippolytus and his
predecessor by means of the legend of the Novatian Presbyter.

Given that there existed a number of house-schools, to which the *tituli*
later bear silent witness, and given that there existed a plurality of πρεσβύτεροι–ἐπισκόποι to which Clement *Cor.* and Hermas bear witness, the
original organisation of such groups may be termed loosely "presbyterian."
But two further questions now emerge, namely (i) were each group independent, with their own presbyters, or was there any attempt at mutual recognition as a common ἐκκλησία? and (ii) was the term πρεσβύτερος completely
synonymous with ἐπίσκοπος or was it possible that they were two groups,
who membership possibly overlapped, with different functions?

In reply to the first question, Lampe points to the fact that although there
were many groups mentioned in *Rom.* 16, 1-20, they clearly were not sent
different letters, but a single letter that would be passed around the various
house-groups. Clement *Cor.*, the letter of Dionysius of Corinth to Soter c.
A.D. 170 (Eusebius *H.E.* IV, 23, 10), and Ignatius *Rom.* praes., all make it
clear that such letters could be sent to all the communities or, in the latter's
words, τῇ ἐκκλησίᾳ...ἥτις καὶ προκάθηται ἐν τόπῳ χωρίου ʽΡωμαίων...καὶ
προκαθημένη τῆς ἀγάπης. Indeed, we may add that Lampe's reconstruction
of the organisation of the early church of Rome helps us to explain this
enigmatic passage. τόπῳ χωρίου suggests a community either wide-spread or
difficult to locate spatially in any one place, hence the τόπῳ (location) requires extending with the addition in the genitive of χωρίου (of the district).
Lampe' characterization would suggest the difficulty of location of different
communities throughout Rome.[101]

But if the communities were difficult to locate, and were governed by
councils of presbyters, to whom would the letter be sent for circulation?
Lampe's particular answer to this question I myself arrived at independently

---

[101] Lampe (1989) p. 335.

in a paper which appeared in the same year as the first edition of his book.[102] We read the functions of someone who may indeed have been Clement of Rome himself in the following passage from *Hermas*:

> Then I saw a vision in my house. The elderly lady came and asked me if I had already given the book (βιβλίον) to the presbyters (τοῖς πρεσβυτέροις). I said that I had not given it. You have done well, she replied, for I have words to add. When I have completed all my words, through you they shall be made known to the elect. You will then write two books (βιβλαρίδια), and you will send one to Clement, and one to Grapte. Clement will then send one to the cities outside, for this has been committed to him (ἐκείνῳ γὰρ ἐπιτέτραπται); and Grapte shall advise the widows and orphans. But you shall read them to this city accompanied by the presbyters who preside over the church (μετὰ τῶν πρεσβυτέρων τῶν προϊσταμένων τῆς ἐκκλησίας).
>
> *Vis.* II, 4, 2-3

We see here a picture of presbyters who preside over different congregations (πρεσβυτέρων τῶν προϊσταμένων τῆς ἐκκλησίας) meeting to hear read out a book addressed to the church as a whole. We see also the figure of Clement who has the entrusted task or ministry (ἐκείνῳ γὰρ ἐπιτέτραπται) of writing to external churches on behalf of the Roman community.

In the light of this we can understand why Clement (or his namesake) could write anonymously in the name of the Church of Rome in such official terms as ἡ ἐκκλησία τοῦ θεοῦ ἡ παροικοῦσα Ῥώμην τῇ ἐκκλησίᾳ τοῦ θεοῦ τῇ παροικούσῃ Κόρινθον (*Corinthians* inscr.), though his identity was nevertheless generally known and cited by Eusebius on the authority of Dionysus' letter (*H.E.* IV, 22,,2; 23,11 cf. III, 38, 1-4). Eusebius indeed quotes from Irenaeus' extant works on his authorship (*H.E.* V, 6, cf. *Haer.* III, 3,3). We can furthermore understand how Eusebius, with the lack of any developmental perspective in his historiography, could read Dionysius of Corinth's letter to Soter (*H.E.* IV, 23,10), and have concluded that he was a monarchical bishop in a fourth century sense.

Lampe sees the role in collecting and administering poor relief to external cities as growing towards the end of the second century, and leading to what Brown had misnamed a 'mere' secretary becoming the monarchical bishop. Such relief administered externally, as Soter's case makes clear,[103] would have come to be associated with the function of ἐπισκοπή exercized by some presbyters (like the προεστώς of Justin *Apol.* 1,61) but not others. Thus a centralization of poor relief, necessitated by the internal growth of the

---

102 A. Brent, Pseudonymity and Charisma in the Ministry of the Early Church, in *Aug* 27,3 (1987), p. 347-376.

103 R.E. Brown and J.-P. Meier, *Antioch and Rome: New Testament Cradles of Catholic Christianity*, (New York: Paulist Press 1982), p. 164 cf. Brent (1987) p. 355. Dionysius wrote (Eusebius *H.E.* IV, 23, 10): ἐξ ἀρχῆς γὰρ ὑμῖν ἔθος ἐστὶν τοῦτο, πάντας μὲν ἀδελφοὺς ποικίλως εὐεργετεῖν ἐκκλησίαις τε πολλαῖς ταῖς κατὰ πᾶσαν πόλιν ἐφόδια πέμπειν, ὧδε μὲν τὴν τῶν δεομένων πενίαν ἀναψύχοντας, ἐν μετάλλοις δὲ ἀδελφοῖς ὑπάρχουσιν ἐπιχορηγοῦντας...

Roman community at the end of the second century, would have combined
external with internal episcopal functions and lead to monarchical episcopacy at Rome.[104]

My own account laid less stress on such economic factors and more on
the association of such 'secretarial' letter-writers with the apostolic, corporate personality of the community, as witnessed in those other unnamed
writers who were authors of the pseudonymous Pauline Pastoral Epistles.
Thus a link was forged with monepiscopacy as it emerged early in the second century in Syria and Asia Minor, at least in those communities recognized by Ignatius of Antioch, the clerical representatives of which Ignatius
always regards as mystically bearing the corporate personalities of their
communities.[105] We can in this way explain how, curiously, Clement can
write anonymously a letter with the title: "the Church of God which dwells
at Rome to the Church of God which dwells at Corinth," and yet be credited
with the pre-eminence which the later succession lists ascribe to him.

Lampe sees the pontificate of Victor as the catalyst for the emergence of
monarchical episcopacy. In dissenting from this view I will not be denying
his characterization of the situation before Victor as, "with two or three ex-
ceptions (Marcion, Cerdo; at all events the Carpocratians as well) a period of
ongoing tolerance (*eine Periode weitgehender Toleranz*)."[106] But I will argue
that the evidence of the Hippolytan community itself, and the characterisation of Hippolytus' office in the Hippolytan literature, show the emergence
of monarchical episcopacy to have been complete only in the time of
Novatian. But before I proceed with my argument, let us first examine the
events and character of the pontificate of Victor as it can be disentangled
from Eusebius' grossly anachronistic account of the Paschal Controversy.

6C 6. *Eusebius on Pope Victor: the Paschal Controversy*

Eusebius, in his brief description of the pontificate of Victor, describes him
as acting like a pope of the fourth century such as that other African,
Miltiades against the Donatists and under a Christian Emperor. The upshot
of the exchange of letters with Polycrates, who defended the Quartodecimans, he describes as follows:

> Upon this Victor, who presided at Rome (ὁ μὲν τῆς Ῥωμαίων προεστώς) at-
> tempted to cut off (ἀποτέμνειν) from the common unity (τῆς κοινῆς ἑνώσεως)
> the dioceses (παροικίας) of all Asia along with the adjacent churches on the
> grounds that they were committing heterodoxy (ὡς ἂν ἑτεροδοξούσας) and he

---

[104] Lampe (1989) p. 336-337.
[105] *Ephes.* 1,3; 2,1; 5,1; *Magnes.* 2; 6,1; *Tral.* 1,1; 2,2; *Smyrn.* 7,2. See Brent (1987) p. 252-
369; A. Brent, Ecumenical Reconciliation and Cultural Episcopates, in *AThR* 72,3 (1990), p.
255-279; ——, *Cultural Episcopacy and Ecumenism: Representative ministry in church history
from the Age of Ignatius of Antioch to the Reformation, with special reference to contemporary
ecumenism*, (E.J. Brill: Leiden 1992), p. 69-88, 118-126 ff.
[106] Lampe (1989) p. 330-334.

placarded the fact (στηλιτεύει) by means of letters and proclaimed that the brethren there were utterly excommunicate (ἀκοινωτήτους πάντας ἄρδην τοὺς ἐκεῖσε ἀνακηρύττων ἀδελφούς). But all the bishops were not pleased by these events.

H.E. V, 24, 9

However, far from Victor's attempt to act like a fourth-century pope having succeeded, Eusebius goes on to record its failure. Irenaeus as bishop of the Gallican community remonstrates with Victor on the grounds that a plurality of differing traditional practices over the length of the Easter fast licensed "personal preference (ἰδιωτισμὸν συνήθειαν)." He then mentions "the presbyters before Soter who presided over the church over which you are now leader (οἱ πρὸ Σωτῆρος πρεσβύτεροι οἱ προστάντες τῆς ἐκκλησίας ἧς σὺ νῦν ἀφηγῇ), namely Anicetus, Pius, Hyginus, Telesephorus, and Xystus." Polycarp had agreed to differ with Anicetus on this matter after the former's visit to him in Rome. Eusebius concludes with the description of Irenaeus as peacemaker (εἰρηνοποιός), which presumably means that he had in fact succeeded in mollifying Victor's demands (*H.E.* V, 24,10-16).

As McCue, following Jalland and Boulet, points out, Eusebius has once again been victim in this passage to his ideology which negates any idea of historical development, and assumes that the Church Order of the fourth century was unchanged since the time of the apostles. Eusebius admits that, in the written letter of Irenaeus that was his source, the discussion between Papias and Anicetus took place in Rome. The point about such a conversation was not to renew the broken bond of communion between geographically distant dioceses, as Eusebius assumes, but to reconcile to Victor a group with whom he was at variance within Rome itself.[107]

In this connection, it is important to note what was the due process of Victor's excommunication of Asiatic communities (or an Asiatic community) in Rome following the practice of Polycarp's Smyrna. No general council is held over which Victor presides, with resultant anathemas. Indeed Eusebius might insist that "many meetings and conferences were held (σύνοδοι δὴ καὶ συγκροτήσεις ἐπισκόπων)," but he has no joint synodical letter and merely hypothesizes such synods from the number of letters of various bishops (πάντες τε μιᾷ γνώμῃ δι' ἐπιστολῶν) expressing the conviction that the resurrection could only be celebrated on Sunday (*H.E.* V, 23,2). Unanimity of opinion between different episcopal letters in the archives at Aelia are sufficient for him to conclude that something like a fourth century episcopal Synod had taken place.

---

107 J.F. McCue, The Roman Primacy in the Second Century and the Problem of Development of Dogma in *ThS* 25 (1964), p. 161-196; T.G. Jalland, The Church and the Papacy, (London 1944), p. 115-222; N. Maurice-Denis Boulet, Titres urbains et communauté dans la Rome chrétienne, in *Maison Dieu* 36 (1953), p. 21. cf. Lampe (1989) p. 322-323 ff.

Similarly with Polycrates' letter which he quotes, Eusebius makes the author write as though he were speaking for a Synod of bishops:

> I could mention the bishops who are present (τῶν συμπαρόντων μνημονεῦσαι) whom you required me to summon (οὓς ὑμεῖς ἠξιώσατε μετακληθῆναι ὑπ᾽ ἐμοῦ καὶ μετεκαλεσάμην), and I did so. If I should write their names they would be many multitudes; and they knowing my feeble humanity, agreed with the letter, knowing that not in vain is my head grey, but that I have ever lived in Christ Jesus.
>
> *H.E.* V, 24,8

Eusebius here overreaches himself in his demand for our credibility. We are to believe that a second century bishop of Rome could require (ἠξιώσατε) a bishop in Asia Minor to summon a Synod of his fellow bishops consisting of "many multitudes of names." Furthermore, the function of such a Synod was not to issue their own encyclical letter, but simply to confirm Polycrates' personal reflections on the tradition followed by the seven members of his family who had been bishops, and his account of the luminaries who supported the Quartodeciman practice. Thus we may not unreasonably conclude that a similar distortion of the background of a second century individual episcopal letter into a fourth-century synodical form has also taken place elsewhere than in Eusebius' account of the Paschal Controversy.

In this category we might place the writings of Theophilus of Caesarea and Narcissus of Jerusalem along with those of Victor of Rome, Irenaeus, and Bacchylus of Corinth. Writings that express support for his position can readily be turned into Synodical decrees by Eusebius, particularly when he spares himself the responsibility of actually citing them. Bishops "expressing (ἐξενηνεγμένοι) one and the same opinion (μίαν καὶ τὴν αὐτὴν δόξαν)" in their writings can easily be regarded expressing "one and the same judgement (τε καὶ κρίσιν)," and then, by a further extension of meaning, be said to caste one and the same vote (τὴν αὐτὴν τέθεινται ψῆφον)." (*H.E.* V, 23,4)

At first sight therefore it would seem that part of Lampe's thesis regarding Victor is corroborated. The events recorded by Eusebius of Victor as between dioceses refer in fact to events within Rome itself and its factionalized communities. The Paschal Controversy could thus be represented as an attempt by Victor to act as a monarchical bishop over the various house-schools into which the Church of Rome was fractionalized at this time. Undoubtedly the form in which Victor's excommunication was expressed (ἀποτέμνειν τῆς κοινῆς ἑνώσεως) was in terms of not sending the *frumentum* to communities in Rome itself observing the Asiatic practice.

The tradition of the *frumentum* was continued in the case of the later *tituli*-parishes by the later genuinely monarchical bishops of Rome (Innocent, *Ep. Ad Decennium*, 5). Witness to the practice is found in Justin, *Apol.* 1, 65 and 67. Irenaeus in his letter to Victor says immediately preceding his record of the meeting of Polycarp with Anicetus in Rome:

> Never before were people excommunicated (ἀπεβλήθησαν) for this cause (διὰ τὸ εἶδος), but the presbyters before you (οἱ πρὸ σοῦ πρεσβύτεροι) who did not observe the practice used to send the Eucharist (ἔπεμπον εὐχαριστίαν) to those from other dioceses/parishes (τοῖς ἀπὸ τῶν παροικιῶν).
>
> *H.E.* V, 24,15

Clearly the Eucharist could not have been sent by Victor to the dioceses of Asia Minor, and the practice must refer to the various house-schools into which the Roman Church was fractionalized. Clearly παροικία, the normal term for a territorially distinct diocese, was associated later with the *tituli*, even though these were parishes. They were organized *quasi diocesis* (*Lib. Pont.* I, 31,10), as we have already mentioned. The term here thus refers to communities within Rome itself whom Victor had thus excommunicated.[108]

But as we have already argued, Eusebius account implies, with the intervention of Irenaeus, an attempt to assume monarchical powers that failed. We shall now show that attempt, only partially successful, to be reflected in *El.* IX, 12,15-26. We shall see in the course of our exposition that the same problems which confront us regarding the expression of Victor's allegedly monarchical powers also confront us with explicating the concept of schism in connection with the community at the time of the author of *El.* Thus we shall see once again the problem for Damasus' conceptualization of that schism, reflected in the creation of the legend of the Novatian Presbyter, presents us too with a similar problem of conceptualization that we must try to resolve in the light of a more scientific conception of history.

6C 7. *The schism of Hippolytus: A problem of conceptualization*

Eusebius' anachronistic portrait of Victor was indeed the picture of a monarchical bishop. But we must ask to what extent is our modified picture of Victor, as trying but only partly succeeding in imposing his own order on the fractionalized Roman communities, properly called "monarchical"? For example, a monarchical bishop, in the fourth century context, could, in a patriarchal See, summon other monarch/bishops to Synods in which rival bishops and their communities could be excommunicated. Because such bishops and their Sees were geographically distinct, the monarch bishop could, with other bishops, establish his own bishop and community in the geographical jurisdiction of his rival. He could also determine that any person or group that he excommunicated within his territory, if they moved to the territorial diocese of another, would also be excommunicated by the bishop with whom he enjoyed communion.

---

[108] Lampe (1989) p. 324-325.

But given Lampe's cogently-argued account that there was not that view of episcopacy prevailing in the second century (at least, according to his claim, before Victor), it is difficult to see what force the term "monarchical" could have. Granted Victor would be able to refuse to send the Eucharist to certain communities, such as those of the Quartodecimans, or the community of Blastus. But that action of itself would not disrupt the continuance of the internal life of their communities. They already occupied the same geographical territory as Victor in what Ignatius had called the τόπῳ χωρίου Ῥωμαίων (*Rom.* praes.) Thus there was no threat of an imposition of an alien bishop on their non-existent territory.

Now what is of relevance in these observations to our account of what was thought to be Hippolytus and his community is that similar problems are raised by the language of "schism" in connection with the question of how to interpret the literary and archaeological evidence discussed in our first two chapters. Frickel, in maintaining that the state of mind (at least of Eusebius and Jerome) was not one of bewilderment but deliberate though embarrassed concealment, sought support from the discussion of the secondary literature of the nineteenth century. Thus he used such words as *Gegenpapst* ("antipope"—from Döllinger), or his See as an *illegaler Bischofsitz* ("illegal See"—Bonwetsch). He sees Eusebius looking for agreement with his Roman Succession List and not finding it.[109] Indeed Hippolytus, undistinguished from the author of *El.*, was further for Bunsen one of the titular bishops of the city, like the later Cardinals, and for Wordsworth the precursor of the orthodox, Anglican bishop against the pretensions of the See of Rome.[110] Lightfoot alone endeavoured to locate Hippolytus in a developing Church Order, without separating him from the author of *El.*, and saw him as an Irenaean "elder," who was as such a geographically free "bishop to the nations."[111]

But as we have argued, we need to pause and ask ourselves what such terms as "illegal See," and "antipope" mean in late second and early third century terms, in order to grasp how anachronistic is not only the explanation of Damasus and Eusebius, but also Frickel, regarding Hippolytus' position.[112] We need to ask how anachronistic is the notion that indeed there was any juridical and canonical implication in Callistus appearing on the only surviving succession list for Rome at this time? What indeed would these terms mean at the turn of the third century?

---

[109] Frickel (1988) p. 7-9.

[110] C.C.J. Bunsen, *Hippolytus und seine Zeit.* (Leipzig: Brockhaus 1872); C. Wordsworth, *St. Hippolytus and the Roman Church in the Earlier Part of the Third Century.* (London: Rivington 1853).

[111] Lightfoot (1889-90) Part 1 Vol. II, p. 432-436.

[112] These questions have been asked more generally by Schöllgen (1988) p. 150-151 and in D.L. Powell, The Schism of Hippolytus, in *StudPat.* XII,1 (1975) p. 449-456.

They might imply the summoning of a council of bishops, the formal hearing and condemnation of a heretical bishop, his deposition and the due consecration by at least three other bishops of an orthodox successor. Conversely they might imply some bishops in one part of the world recognising one group that has separated on grounds of the laxity from an existing group, and other bishops recognising those from whom they have separated. But where in *El.* IX, 12, 15-26 do we find anything that fits with such definitions of "schism" or "legal bishop"? Indeed, in the light of our last two sections, we would find the absence of such definitions as part of the general, second-century historical background to these events as well.

6C 7.1. *The author of El.'s group and his relations with Callistus*

Let us begin with the charge of the author of *El.*, Hippolytus' predecessor, that Callistus founded a school, and the extent to which this implies a formal breach in mid-third century terms. *El.* states of Callistus that, having fallen into an ambivalent heterodoxy that was sometimes Sabellian and sometimes Theodotian:

> The wizard behaved so rashly and founded a school (συνεστήσατο διδα–σκαλεῖον) having thus taught against the catholic church (κατὰ τῆς ἐκκλησίας οὕτως διδάξας); and he was the first to plan to allow people to yield to their pleasures, claiming that they could all have their sins forgiven by him. For he who gathered with a different person (ὁ γὰρ παρ' ἑτέρῳ τινὶ συναγόμενος) and was called a Christian ([καὶ λεγόμενος] Χριστιανός), if he sinned, asserted Callistus, the sin would not be reckoned to him if he would flee to the school of Callistus. This rule (οὗ τῷ ὅρῳ) pleased many whose conscience had become hardened and at the same time, many who became excommunicated under the influence of many heresies (οἱ ὑπὸ πολλῶν αἱρέσεων ἀποβληθέντες), and some who had been expelled from the church by us (τινὲς δὲ καὶ ἔκβλητοι τῆς ἐκκλησίας ὑφ' ἡμῶν γενόμενοι) at an examination, (ἐπὶ καταγνώσει) attached themselves to him and swelled into his school (ἐπλήθυναν τὸ διδασκαλεῖον αὐτοῦ)... and in their vanity they attempted (ἐπιχειροῦσι) to call themselves the Catholic Church (καθολικὴν ἐκκλησίαν ἀποκαλεῖν). ·
>
> *El.* IX, 12,20-21 and 25

Callistus was to appear later in the Liberian List as the bishop of Rome and successor of St. Peter, and neither the author of *El.* nor his successor, "presbyter" Hippolytus, despite the former's claim to apostolic succession (*El.* I, prooem. 6). In consequence, this passage has often been read as though a single group had split into two, with the bishop of one excommunicating the bishop of the other and their followers.[113] Let us now examine whether this can possibly be the case.

To begin with, the situation here described is fully consistent with the organisation of the Church of Rome before the time of Victor, as we have re-

---

113 J.B. Lightfoot, *The Apostolic Fathers*, Part I,1 Clement of Rome, London 1890, p. 255. See also B. Kötting, Zur Frage der successio apostolica in frühkirchlicher Sicht, in *Catholica* 27 (1973), p. 234-247.

constructed it. The phrase ὁ γὰρ παρ' ἑτέρῳ τινὶ συναγόμενος clearly implies that in Callistus' time, two episcopal removes after Victor, there were still separated congregations at Rome meeting under separate presbyteral/ episcopal leadership. A member of such a group is recognized as a Christian ([καὶ λέγομενος] Χριστιανός), and not as a heretic who really followed Greek philosophers.

El.'s argument is not therefore that his group alone formed the true Church, and that anyone outside of his group was in schism. What he objects to is not that a member of his congregation ought not to join that of Callistus because the latter has no proper jurisdiction, but that the latter had admitted those convicted by him of heresy and other sins, and that others, not specified as being from his particular congregation, and moved by heresy and not orthodoxy (οἱ ὑπο πολλῶν αἰρέσεων ἀποβληθέντες), had taken the same route. Had Callistus remained orthodox, then there would have been no objection to his presidency of his own congregation.

There appear in this passage therefore two distinct group of adherents:

1. There is a general, large group (πολλοί... οἱ ὑπο πολλῶν αἰρέσεων ἀποβληθέντες). This phrase is consistently mistranslated as "excomunicated for many heresies" usually with the addition of "by us" though that addition does not occur in the text in connection with this phrase. Its sense is obscure but I suggest something like "driven out by the influence of many heresies." Of this wider group, who had joined Callistus' congregation that now has become a conventicle (διδασκαλεῖον), self-excommunication could therefore have been what *El.* is endeavouring to describe. Such self-excommunication, in which it is the heretic who takes the initiative in leaving, was characteristic of the Church of Rome also in the time before Victor and, we shall argue against Lampe, for the time after Victor until Pontianus too. The translation "become excommunicate under the influence of many heresies (πολλοί...οἱ ὑπο πολλῶν αἰρέσεων ἀποβληθέντες)" therefore either indicates:

(a) a process of such informal and self-driven excommunication which would seem justified by the contrast with the description of formal condemnation (ἐπὶ καταγνώσει) by the author of *El.* which now follows regarding a smaller and separate group (τινες), and which otherwise would be a redundant distinction, or otherwise:

(b) those excommunicated by, or leaving from, other congregations than those of that author himself who are in communion with each other and with his community through the exchange of the Eucharist (*frumentum*).

On either interpretation, this group testifies to the endurance of the pre-Victor situation in the post-Victor Church. But,

2. In addition to this larger group (πολλοί), there is mentioned a smaller group (τινες) who have been condemned and made excommunicated specifically by the author himself (ἐπὶ καταγνώσει ἔκβλητοι τῆς ἐκκλησίας ὑφ' ἡμῶν γενόμενοι). The Damasan interpretation of this passage, or the situation that it describes, like that of Frickel, supposes that there are only two groups involved, each claiming to be the true, "Catholic" Church, each describing the other as schismatical and its bishop accordingly invalid and even heretical. But if there are only two groups in question, one in a schismatical relation to the other, where did the larger group of excommunicants

(ἀποβληθέντες) come from? It would surely be unlikely that even that author of *El.* was being so egotistical here as to claim some special status for those (τίνες) condemned to excommunication by an ecclesiastical court (ἐπὶ καταγνώσει) of which he simply happened that day to be chairman? Clearly, in the background to his words here, there is more than one congregation with a πρεσβύτερος–ἐπίσκοπος exercising jurisdiction over its members that other πρεσβύτεροι–ἐπίσκοποι of other congregations are expected to respect.

It is this disciplinary convention of not communicating with those whom another has excommunicated that clearly constitutes the "customary boundary (οὗ τῷ ὅρῳ)" that Callistus is accused of overstepping in this passage. It would be anachronistic therefore to have translated ὅρος as "canon" in this context, but such a distortion is quite frequent in the literature. To quote one example, Preysing endeavoured quite inaccurately to find evidence for Callistus' alleged universal, papal edict from the use of the term ὅρος.[114] Only by defining this term in the sense of a canon or Church law could he refute Adam's obvious argument that there could be no edict of Callistus involved since the dispute was about what he taught (οὗτος ἐδογμάτισεν).[115]

If moreover these groups are centred on different house- or school-groups, it becomes quite comprehensible how the presbyter/episcopus of one such group can oppose the centrifugal forces that are in process of making a *presbyter/episcopus* of a larger group into a nascent monarchical bishop. We do not have here so much a schismatic presbyter seeking power and pre-eminence by means of a puritanical ideology. Rather we have in Callistus one bishop of one of several communities seeking spiritual power and jurisdiction over excommunicate members of others by a policy of deliberate laxity. If the dispute had been between two contenders to a single episcopal chair, as in the case of later antipopes, it is curious that the author of *El.* set out his account of the dispute in no such terms.

It is not simply that the author fails to acknowledge Callistus as bishop of Rome, but he nowhere claims that title for himself. All that he says enigmatically is that Callistus "thought that he had achieved what he desired (νόμιζων τετυχηκέναι οὗ ἐθηρᾶτο)," without further identifying this with Rome's sole episcopal chair, although earlier Callistus is described as "yearning for the throne of oversight (θηρώμενος τὸν τῆς ἐπισκοπῆς θρόνον)." (IX, 11,1 cf. 12,15) Zephyrinus is not described as occupying that seat before him, nor indeed is anyone else. His words are perfectly consistent with a refusal to acknowledge the presbyter of any one group occupying such a position. Thus in *El.* Callistus' full title is as nameless as Hippolytus' See in Eusebius *H.E,* VI, 20 and Jerome *De Vir. Ill.* 61.

---

114 K. von Preysing, Existenz und Inhalt des Bussediktes, in *ZKTh* 43 (1919), p. 358-362.
115 K. Adam, *Der Sogennante Bussedikt des Papstes Kallixtus,* (München: Letner 1917), p. 31.

But the passage also says of Callistus that he "founded a school," and it may at first sight seem that these words imply the separation of Callistus from the community of the author of *El*. We must now examine how such a phrase functions in the ideology and polemic of the Roman Church in the second half of the second century during the career of Hippolytus' predecessor, the author of *El*.

6C 7.2. σχολή, διδασκαλεῖον, and καθολικὴ ἐκκλησία in El.

What precisely does the passage mean when it says of Callistus that he συνεστήσατο διδασκαλεῖον? I shall now argue that this phrase does not indicate the physical separation of one group from another. Rather it is a term of value-judgement, in which the movement of thought is recorded on the part of the group so described from what is held to be apostolic Christianity to heresy as a thinly-disguised paganism.

The writer of *El*. follows Irenaeus in applying this description to a group that had become heretical. Irenaeus' community had every appearance of a school, as had the community of *El.*, even though he reserves the terms σχολαί or διδασκαλεῖα for heretical groups who had "left." Cerdon has his "school," in which the Marcion who "succeeded" him was a pupil.[116] Valentinus, who arrived under Hygenus and left under Anicetus, founded a school.[117] Thus we find in numerous passages the close association between such terms as διαδεξάμενος, αἱρέσεως τὰς ἀρχὰς, and διδασκαλεῖον. But it is to be emphasized that Valentinus at all events "left" of his own volition and was not excommunicated.

Furthermore, "left" may be a metaphorical way of expressing Valentinus' action in breaking with the Church in view of the fact that they were one group amongst many into which the communities were divided. We have the excavated house on the via Latina where the Valentinians met for the sacrament of the Bride-chamber. Valentinius' own presbyter, Florinus was accepted by Victor.[118]

Did leaving the church mean simply excluding psychics from that community, and amount to simply changing one's doctrinal stance finally and radically? Cerdo similarly and earlier was described by Irenaeus, *Adv. Haer.* III, 4,3, as "sometimes secretly teaching (...ποτὲ μὲν λαθροδιδασκαλῶν), but at others openly confessing (ποτὲ δὲ πάλιν ἐξομολογούμενος), and then refuted (ποτὲ δὲ ἐλεγχόμενος) for what he taught perversely (ἐφ' οἷς ἐδίδασκε κακῶς), and so departing from agreement with those of right faith (καὶ ἀφιστάμενος τῆς τῶν θεοσεβῶν συνοδίας)." There is here no monarchical

---

[116] *Adv. Haer.* 1,27,2: Διαδεξάμενος δὲ αὐτὸν Μαρκίων ὁ Ποντικὸς αὔξησε τὸ διδασκαλεῖον. cf. *El*. X,19.

[117] *Adv. Haer.* I, 11,1; *El*. VI,38,2; *Adv. Haer.* I,13,1: ὁ μὲν γὰρ πρῶτος ἀπὸ τῆς λεγομένης Γνωστικῆς αἱρέσεως τὰς ἀρχὰς εἰς ἴδιον χαρακτῆρα διδασχαλείου μεθαρμόσας Οὐαλεντῖνος οὕτως ὡρίσατο; *El*. VI,39,1; Tertullian *De Praesc.* 42.

[118] Lampe (1989) p. 326-327.

bishop presiding over a formal judicial process that excommunicates Cerdo, but, according to Rufinus' Latin translation, "he is refuted by certain persons (*ab aliquibus traductus in his quae docebat male*)." Lampe is surely right to see here Cerdo presiding over a house-school which, when criticized, itself by its own initiative refuses to continue to exchange the *frumentum*.[119]

Clearly, then, to found a school does not mean to be formally ex-communicated in the mid-third-century sense of that term. It does not mean action resulting from being expelled from, nor leaving of one's own volition, one community and self-consciously then founding another. Furthermore, from the standpoint of those outside the church, there would have appeared to be no formal difference between the communities of Victor, the Quartodecimans, or that of the author of *El.* There was no objective distinc-tion obvious to an external observer. All the Christian communities at Rome, as we have argued, would have appeared objectively as house-schools. The term διδασκαλεῖον had by the time of Irenaeus become the subjective and value-laden, pejorative term that it clearly was not in the writings of Justin Martyr, who regards his Eucharistic community precisely in terms of a philosophical school with a προεστώς who is both director of the school and president of the Eucharist.

The distinction between καθολικὴν ἐκκλησίαν ἀποκαλεῖν and συστήσ-ασθαι διδασκαλεῖον was the distinction between those who preserved the apostolic tradition, or changed it into a version of Greek philosophy, not the distinction between the new location and the old location of groups that had physically separated from each other. In the case of Callistus in this passage, we do not find him, any more than Cerdon, as physically moving to new premises. In this connection, we shall now do well to look at the concept of διαδοχή as used by the author of *El.,* in his own version of Irenaeus refer-ence to the apostolic succession, as specifically a succession of teaching. We shall be arguing later that the author of *El.*'s inclusion of the concept of ἀρχιερατεία (*El.* I, prooem. 6; *Ap. Trad.* 3) is quite foreign to Irenaeus and his predecessors, though this has been too frequently misunderstood.

In Irenaeus (*Adv. Haer.* III, 3,2) the primary focus is upon a succession of teachers. The Roman succession list is but an example of the διαδοχαί for all the churches (*omnium ecclesiarum... successiones*). That succession, more-over, is a teaching succession, for it is about "that tradition and faith which it has from the apostles and which is proclaimed to mankind and which reaches up to our time through the successions of bishops (*per successiones episcoporum*)." At Rome "the Tradition which is from the apostles" is pre-served. The point emphasized throughout Irenaeus' comments on the indi-vidual names in his list, such as that of Clement, is that the succession marks the reliability of what is taught. Clement "saw and consorted with the apos-

---

[119] Ibid. p. 331-332

tles" so that "the preaching of the apostles was ringing (*insonantem*) in his ears and the Tradition was before his eyes— not alone; since many then survived who had been taught by the apostles." At the conclusion with Eleutheros, it is emphasized that through "this order and succession (ταύτῃ τῇ τάξει καὶ διαδοχῇ ἥ τε ἀπὸ τῶν ἀποστόλων)" the tradition of the apostles in the church and the preaching of truth has come down to us." (*Adv. Haer.* III, 3,4)

Irenaeus sees the διαδοχαί of the heretics going back to Simon Magus, the opponent of St. Peter in *Acts* 8, 9-24 (*Adv. Haer.* I, 23,2-5). The connection however is a connection of ideas, not of any physical premises or continuing or separating group of individuals with a physically specifiable location. But the author of *El.* will not allow the heretical schools to be rooted in a founder such as Simon who was originally converted to Christianity but who, it is claimed, corrupted it. The author of *El.* would claim, rather, that all heresies are but thinly disguised versions of Greek philosophy whose final origin is in the snake worship of the Naasenes (*El.* V, 6,3).

Thus Marcion with his two gods, one good and the other evil, or at least one perfect and the other imperfect, is not a radical Paulinist wrestling with the theodicy implied by his master's teaching on law and grace, and arising within a Judaic and biblicist *milieu*. Rather the author of *El.* makes him a follower of Empedokles with the latter's two αἰτίαι of νεῖκος and φίλια. Thus most of *El.*'s account is valueless for the reconstruction of Marcion's history, however much it may contribute to the recovery of Empedokles' lost teaching (*El.* VII, 29-31). At the close of his account, however, he makes what is for our purpose a telling point. He says that Marcion: "having used Empedokles' discourses (τοῖς Ἐμπεδοκλέους λόγοις χρησάμενος) and adapting the philosophy devised by him to his own opinion (καὶ τὴν ὑπ' ἐκείνου ἐφηυρημένην φιλοσοφίαν ἰδίᾳ δόξῃ μετάγων) he composed a godless heresy (αἵρησιν ἄθεον συνεστήσατο)." (*El.* VII, 31,7)

A second example is *El.*'s description of Noetus himself, whose followers in reality he charges Callistus and Zephyrinus as being, and of whose διδασ–καλεῖον they are therefore members. Heracleitus speaks of "the universe as being (εἶναι τὸ πᾶν) divisible indivisable (διαιρετὸν ἀδιαίρετον), a begotten unbeggotten (γενητὸν ἀγένητον), a mortal immortal (θνητὸν ἀθάνατον), an eternal word (λόγον αἰῶνα), a father son (πατέρα υἱόν), a just God (θεὸν δίκαιον)." (*El.* IX, 9,1) The Sabellian claim, of which Zephyrinus under Callistus' influence, has produced an ambivalent version, also speaks of the indivisibility of the Father and the Son, of the one being the seen version of the other unseen. Thus the author of *El.* is able to claim that Callistus' concern is not in the Judaic tradition of maintaining the unity of the godhead, but rather is following Heracleitan paganism (*El.* IX, 8-10).

Thus both in the case of Marcion as well as Callistus to "compose a heresy (συστήσασθαι αἵρεσιν)," becomes equivalent to "establish a school (συστήσασθαι διδασκαλεῖον)." Its fundamental meaning is to reconstruct the apostolic tradition into something alien, and not necessarily to set up a new community in some new venue. In further confirmation of this point, we need only to look at the way in which Socrates and Plato are described in the following passage:

> Socrates then was the hearer of Archelaus the physicist, who put forward "know yourself," and having founded a great school (μεγάλην σχολὴν συστήσας), maintained that Plato was the worthiest of all of his disciples (ἔσχε πάντων τῶν μαθητῶν ἱκανώτατον τὸν Πλάτωνα), himself leaving no written treatise (μηδὲν σύγγραμμα καταλιπών). But Plato, re-composed[120] all of his wisdom (τὴν πᾶσαν αὐτοῦ σοφίαν), established the school (συνέστησε τὸ διδασκαλεῖον), having combined together physics, ethics and dialectic (μίξας ὁμοῦ φυσικὴν ἠθικὴν διαλεκτικήν).

El. I, 18,1-2

Since Socrates literally and physically set up the Academy and gathered his disciples that Plato inherited, only he in such a sense could be described as μεγάλην σχολὴν συστήσας. Plato can be described, as this passage shows, as in a metaphorical sense setting up a school by recomposing his master's wisdom. His μίξας ὁμοῦ φυσικὴν ἠθικὴν διαλεκτικήν amounts to founding a new school (συνέστησε τὸ διδασκαλεῖον), even though the community will remain housed on the same premises and remain approximately the same members. Plato did not establish a new school in the sense of physically separating with his disciples from those of Socrates and finding new premises.

Thus when *El.* claims (IX, 12,20) that Callistus συνεστήσατο διδασ–καλεῖον κατὰ τῆς ἐκκλησίας οὕτως διδάξας, his words should be taken to mean that it was Callistus own group, by their change of teaching, that had made themselves a school, with whom his own group would no longer associate. There are few objective facts to which appeal might be made in the light of which a community that is the Catholic Church could be distinguished from a heretical school. Such a description as συνεστήσατο διδασ–καλεῖον is not value-free, nor would the heretics or schismatics themselves have accepted it as a tribute to their Gnostic learning in comparison with the psychics. Rather διδασκαλεῖον and σχολή are prescriptive and pejorative, like σχίσμα and αἵρεσις, at least in the sense in which these terms are used by Christian writers though not by Diogenes Laertius. "School" and "church" are simply value-judgements applied to what in appearance are very similar institutions, having similar officials at their head making by this

---

120 ἀπομαξάμενος means literally "to wipe off or level corn."

time claim to stand in the apostolic teaching succession, and organized in very similar ways.[121]

Of course it could be argued that, although συστήσασθαι διδασκαλεῖον might be equivalent to συστήσασθαι αἵρεσιν/ δόξας/ δόγμα) in general,[122] in the case of Callistus and the author of *El.* συστήσασθαι διδασκαλεῖον could have involved the physical separation of two congregations originally meeting together whose doctrines came to diverge too greatly. This would mean that, though before Victor there were separate congregations under the presidency of presbyters, and exchanging the *frumentum*, after Victor any congregation other than that of him and his successors would be schismatical or heretical. Other congregations would now have become σχολαί, whilst his was the Catholic Church. It is to my answer to such an objection that I must now turn.

6C 7.3. *El. and Callistus: two house-schools in conflict*

In the last section I showed that there could not have been one single orthodox congregation at Rome recorded in the author of *El.*'s work because:

(i) with reference to Lampe's work itself, such an interpretation is inconsistent with the survival of the later *tituli*, each governed, as we have seen, *quasi diocesis*, and

(ii) it is also inconsistent with how the author of *El.* describes his relationship with the school of Callistus in *El.* IX, 12,20-21, 25). In this passage someone could still gather with someone else and be called a Christian (ὁ γὰρ παρ' ἑτέρῳ τινὶ συναγόμενος [καὶ λεγόμενος] Χριστιάνος), and from other such groups excommunicants are mentioned (οἱ ὑπὸ πολλῶν αἱρέσεων ἀποβληθέντες) as well as from *El.*'s own (τινὲς δὲ καὶ ἐπὶ καταγνώσει ἔκβλητοι τῆς ἐκκλησίας ὑφ' ἡμῶν γενόμενοι).

That such fragmentation was not itself the creation of Callistus' own activity can be further demonstrated from how the author of *El.* describes the situation whilst Zephyrinus is still alive. The passage describes how Noetus introduced what was really the philosophy of Heracleitus, how his deacon Epigonus came to Rome, and how Kleomenes became his disciple. The passage continues:

> Kleomenes, who was in life and conversation alienated from the church (βίῳ καὶ τρόπῳ ὢν ἀλλότριος τῆς ἐκκλησίας), adopted the teaching (ἐκράτυνε τὸ δόγμα) at the time when Zephyrinus thought that he was managing the Church (διέπειν νομίζοντος τὴν ἐκκλησίαν), being a common man and a money-grubber. Zephyrinus was persuaded by the pecuniary incentive offered him and communicated (σύνεχώρει) with those joining Kleomenes as his disciples (τοῖς προσιοῦσι τῷ Κλεομένει μαθητεύεσθαι), and he himself being in course of time

---

[121] See for an earlier version of such themes, A. Brent, Diogenes Laertius and the Apostolic Succession, in *JEH* 44,3 (1993), p. 367-389.

[122] For examples see *El.* I, prooem. 9; IV,47, 5; VI,21, 3 (Valentinus); 41, 20 (followers of Marcus); VIII, prooem. 4 (Tatian,Valentinus, Marcion); VII, prooem. 7 (Cerinthus).

dragged down, he was moved in the same direction since he had Callistus as counsellor and fellow protagonist in these evils.... The school of these men continued to be adopted (τούτων οὖν κατὰ διαδοχὴν διέμεινε τὸ διδασκαλεῖον κρατούμενον) and to increase due to the assistance of Zephyrinus and Callistus (ἐπαῦξον διὰ τὸ συναίρεσθαι αὐτοῖς τὸν Ζεφυρῖνον καὶ τὸν Κάλλιστον), even though we never communicated with them (καίτοι ἡμῶν μηδέποτε αὐτοῖς συγχωρησάντων), but we often opposed them and refuted them, compelling them reluctantly to confess the truth. They for a time showed shame, and drawn to conclusions (συναγόμενοι) by the truth, confessed it, but not long afterwards they were rolling themselves again in the same mire.

El. IX, 7,1-3

Here clearly even in Zephyrinus' time the author of *El.*'s community is spatially separate from that of the former, so that it cannot be the case that they separated only in Callistus' time. Both Zephyrinus and Callistus "communicate"—and he uses συνεχώρει, the technical term for being "in communion,"—with the διδασκαλεῖον of Kleomenes. But the author of *El.* or his group ("we") "never communicated with them (καίτοι ἡμῶν μηδέπ–οτε αὐτοῖς συγχωρησάντων)." If they had been members of the same liturgical group, they would have either communicated or not communicated with Kleomenes.

These words are therefore only consistent with two distinct groups, both of which are still in communion with each other (because they still exchange the *frumentum*?), one of which, that of the author of *El.*, will not communicate with a third group, whereas the other, that of Zephyrinus, will. Since *El.* only describes Callistus and never Zephyrinus with the phrase συνεστήσατο τὸ διδασκαλεῖον, we may conclude that the spiritual separation between the house-school of the author of *El.* and that of Zephyrinus never happened during the latter's lifetime. But they had always been physically separated communities, even before the pontificate of Victor.

Their intercommunion was indeed fragile in Zephyrinus' time. The author of *El.* had to bring pressure upon them and their constant readaptation of their ambiguous formularies. Zephyrinus and Callistus were considered to be following the Heracleitan and not the apostolic διαδοχή (τούτων οὖν κατὰ διαδοχὴν διέμεινε τὸ διδασκαλεῖον) in supporting Kleomenes and his predecessors (διὰ τὸ συναίρεσθαι αὐτοῖς τὸν Ζεφυρῖνον καὶ τὸν Κάλλιστον). Thus the successors to Victor acknowledged by the later Liberian succession list are not unambiguously acknowledged as such by their contemporaries.[123]

---

[123] One notes yet again an attempt to rehabilitate Zephyrinus on the assumption that later conditions of Church Order prevail in his time in B. Capelle, Le cas du pape Zéphyrin, in *RBen* 38 (1926), p. 321-330. Following a comparison of *El.* IX, 11,13 with the view of Noetus expressed before the "blessed presbyters" in *C.N.* 1 (p. 321-328) and finding their sentiments identical, he then challenges the validity of *El.*, p. 328 ("Le fait que le formule de Zéphyrin a-t-il pu s'exprimer ainsi? Le pape de Rome a-t-il pu s'approprier publiquement les termes d'une doctrine condamnée par un concile en communion avec lui?") Here we find intruding anachro-

We see however that the later principle did not appear to have been adopted at Rome at this time, namely that anyone who communicates with an excommunicated person are themselves excommunicated. Zephyrinus and Callistus, in communicating with those with whom the author of *El.* and his community will not communicate, do not themselves *ipso facto* break communion. Moreover there is no sentence of excommunication on whole communities rather than individuals (as in *El.* IX, 17, 21). The process of συστήσασθαι διδασκαλεῖον is a gradual one, with ambiguity in formularies as yet no reason for a decisive break. But if the two house-schools remain still in communion until they grow apart sufficiently in terms of doctrine, then indeed at that point schism is what is thus meant.

Frickel would dissent from such a conclusion, as we have seen. For him the documentary evidence before us must be interpreted in terms taken from 19th century historiography such as Hippolytus the *Gegenpapst*, or his See as an *illegaler Bischofsitz*. Thus he must show how other bishops of other Sees would have had to be involved in the excommunication of Callistus, if not through a synodical gathering, at least through the sending and receiving of formal episcopal letters.

The existence of such letters, after all, was necessary to Frickel's thesis regarding Eusebius' embarrassment, which we criticized in our last chapter, when we argued that the latter's reaction was rather one of perplexity and bewilderment. Frickel believed that Eusebius had such letters before him, and which accordingly lead to his embarrassment about naming Hippolytus' See. Hence he must regard *El.* IX, 12,15 as evidence that the author, supposedly Hippolytus, had written to other churches regarding his theological controversies with modalist Monarchians.[124] Thus we might have action resembling the correspondence between Cyprian and Cornelius, and culminating in Synods of bishops acknowledging their communion with one side in a disputed succession and declaring the other side schismatical. Hence we see once again that Damasus was not alone in finding the conceptual resources of the age of the Novatian Presbyter alone sufficient to comprehend the age of Hippolytus some thirty years earlier.

---

nistically the later notion of an ecclesiastical council passing judgement, rather than of a philosophical school analysing a doctrine and coming to some conclusion about its validity. I have argued here that the latter is the case in the late second century (6C 8.1-8.2). Such a reconstruction avoids the need to do violence to the patent evidence by simply arbitrarily ruling it out as in p. 329 ("Dans ces conditions, il paraît évident que Zéphyrin n'a pas prononcé la phrase qu'on lui prête. Non qu'Hippolyte ait menti. Le pape a dû formuler une déclaration blâmant les excès de la théologie de l'οἰκονομία—peut-être a-t-il rejeté le terme ἕτερος θεός.")

[124] Frickel (1988) p. 207-208: "Aber immerhin bezeugt der Passus, dass Hippolyt seine theologischen Auseinandersetzungen mit den modalisten Monarchianern den anderen Kirchen vorgetragen hat. Und seine Intervention lief darauf hinaus, die Lehre vom göttlichen Logos als einer eigenen göttlichen Person als rechtgläubig (ὀρθῶς) darzutun, die modalistische Lehre dagegen als irrgläubig oder fremdgläubig (ἀλλοτρίως) zu entlarven. Eine solche Intervention kann nur schriftlich erfolgt sein..."

But let us consider the relevant passage, and the issues that it raises, in further detail.

6C 7.4. *Ambiguous central authority* El. *IX, 12, 15-16*
The critical passage for Frickel's thesis is where, with reference to Callistus, the author of *El.* says:

> He, after Zephyrinus' decease, thinking that he had achieved what he desired (νομίζων τετυχηκέναι οὗ ἐθηρᾶτο), excluded (ἀπέωσεν) Sabellius for his unorthodox opinions (ὡς μὴ φρονοῦντα ὀρθῶς), because he had come to fear me (δεδοικὼς ἐμὲ) and thinking thus he would be able to subvert the charge against him to the churches (ἀποτρίψασθαι τὴν πρὸς τὰς ἐκκλησίας κατηγορίαν) on the grounds that his opinion was not alien; he was, then, a sorcerer and a rascal and for a time took in many. But having the poison residing in his heart, and simply thinking nothing whilst he was ashamed to tell the truth because in public he had insulted us (διὰ τὸ δημοσίᾳ ἡμῖν ὀνειδίζοντα) and said: "You are ditheists (δίθεοί ἐστε)," and other things as well because of Sabellius' constant accusation (διὰ τὸ ὑπὸ τοῦ Σαβελλίου συχνῶς κατηγορεῖσθαι) that he had transgressed the primitive faith (ὡς παραβάντα τὴν πρώτην πίστιν), he devised the following heresy. He said that the Logos himself was the Son and himself the Father, being called by name Son and Father, but being one, the indivisible Spirit.
>
> *El.* IX, 12, 15-16

Undoubtedly the phrase ἀποτρίψασθαι τὴν πρὸς τὰς ἐκκλησίας κατηγορίαν appears to refer to external churches. The various communities in Rome are never called by the plural ἐκκλησίαι. As we argued from Ignatius, *Rom.* praes., the congregations, spread throughout the various quarters of the city, are still collectively referred to in the singular as ἡ ἐκκλησία ... ἥτις καὶ προκάθηται ἐν τόπῳ χωρίου ῾Ρωμαίων. However, Marcovich's textual amendment excludes any application to foreign churches. Marcovich emends the reading in *Parisinus: suppl. graec.* 464: τὴν πρὸς τὰς ἐκκλησίας κατηγορίαν ("the charge made to the churches") to πρὸς τῆς ἐκκλησίας ("the charge arising from the church"). The congregation in question would therefore be the author of *El.*'s own, accusing the head of another local, congregation.[125]

In support of such an emendation, we should consider that what this phrase is held by Frickel to imply, namely the sending of letters by bishop Hippolytus (as he maintained) to other bishops to secure Callistus' condemnation, is denied by IX, 13,1. Here it is claimed that it was Callistus' teaching that was taken throughout the world (κατὰ πάντα τὸν κόσμον διηχηθείσης τῆς διδασκαλίας) and attracted Alcibiades and his Elkasite texts to Rome, not some general condemnation by a group of bishops recognizing the author's congregation. There is no evidence of such distant churches be-

---

125 M. Marcovich, Hippolyts Refutatio Omnium Häresium, in *Patristische Texte und Studien* Bd 25, (Berlin: De Gruyter 1986).

ing involved in any such controversy at Rome as happened some twenty years latter for the first time in connection with the Novatian schism. The later *tituli* churches and their archaeology, combined with the literary evidence, as we have seen, are clear indications that there never was simply one congregation at Rome in the second century.

We have already seen, in our analysis of *El.* IX, 12, 21, there appears to be more than one group with excommunicated members being received by Callistus. In the present passage (IX, 12,15-16) his language implies something less than absolute separation between the groups, since clearly Callistus must have considered him close enough to fear, if fear he did, when he excommunicated Sabellius (τὸν Σαβέλλιον ἀπέωσεν ὡς μὴ φρονοῦντα ὀρθῶς, δεδοικὼς ἐμέ). It would not have been the case, with two groups who presumably no longer exchanged the *frumentum*, that the leader of one could be described as fearing the other's charge of lack of orthodoxy. In such a situation, the person so accused would not fear to lose any status with his adherents from such charges. Such charges would rather be expected from someone who no longer had any *locus standi* with the particular group, and, in view of the final separation, treated with appropriate ridicule. These words are rather more compatible with two groups living in inter-communion with one another, but experiencing severe tensions in that relationship. They are also compatible with, if the author is to be close enough to fear, with two groups having access to a broader community judgment in the presence of the presbyters of each community in communion with each other.

Furthermore, the author of *El.* never claims to have excommunicated Callistus as the latter had Sabellius. As we have seen, Callistus group was conceived by him to have excommunicated itself when the former "composed his heresy" (συστήσασθαι αἵρεσιν), or, as *El.* likes to express this idea, "founded a school" (συστήσασθαι διδασκαλεῖον). Indeed it would appear that the right to jurisdiction claimed for the bishop of the "true church" was claimed in such terms by Callistus rather than Hippolytus. His congregation, and his alone, merited this title. Hippolytus does not respond with a counter claim in these terms. For Hippolytus, any community is lead by a successor of the apostles when that successor and his community exhibit a διαδοχή of teaching.

We shall need to discuss the concept of διαδοχή further, when we come to examine the character of Hippolytus' liturgy of ordination in Chapter 7. For the moment, let us record that it is Callistus who makes this claim for his group, without any counter claim from the author of *El.* for exclusivity of jurisdiction as opposed to rightness of doctrine and discipline. It is Callistus' group that "grew so proud of their outrageous deeds that they tried to call themselves the Catholic Church (καθολικὴν ἐκκλησίαν ἀποκαλεῖν) and some thought to benefit by associating with them." (*El.* IX, 12,25)

We are therefore seeing reflected in *El.* partly the situation that Lampe believed to exist pre-Victor, yet seeing also the beginnings of resisted monarchical claims. In consequence we must ask whether we can explain any further the relationship between the Roman communities modelled on a house-school, given their spatially different location, and their sending to one another the *frumentum*, unmentioned by the author of *El.* but the existence of which practice we have learned from Eusebius *H.E.* V, 24,15. We might further hypothesize that, as Anicetus "had yielded the celebration of the Eucharist (παρεχώρησεν) to Polycarp out of respect" (τὴν εὐχαριστίαν τῷ Πολυκάρπῳ, κατ᾽ ἐντροπὴν) as the representative of congregations within Rome itself, from time to time a similar "yielding" would have taken place between the leaders of various Roman house-schools between which a mutual recognition of orthodoxy existed (*H.E.* V, 24,17). But was there further any more general meeting amongst the presiding presbyters of the house-schools?

Our quotation from *El.* IX, 12,16 suggested a public occasion on which the house-schools, or their presbyteral leadership, could meet jointly. The insult of ditheism had been a public one (διὰ τὸ δημοσίᾳ ἡμῖν ὀνειδίζοντα εἰπεῖν· δίθεοί ἐστε).[126] Presumably the occasions for "Sabellius' constant accusation (διὰ τὸ ὑπὸ τοῦ Σαβελλίου συχνῶς κατηγορεῖσθαι), that he had transgressed the primitive faith (ὡς παραβάντα τὴν πρώτην πίστιν)," were equally public (δημοσίᾳ), outside the narrower house-school meeting. Lampe's reconstruction of the situation within the Roman Church before Victor is once again fully consistent with this post-Victor situation reflected in the dispute between the author of *El.* and Callistus.

The existence of a public meeting of Roman presbyters from the various house-school communities is reflected too not only by the account of Marcion's two condemnations by the presbyters at Rome but by that of Noetus. It does not of course matter that *C.N.* is quite fictional in speaking of Noetus condemned by the blessed presbyters at Smyrna. Polycarp, *Phillipians*, as well as Ignatius, *Smyrnaeans,* and *Polycarp* make it quite plain that Smyrna had been ruled by single bishops. But Hippolytus' fiction clearly reads upon the church of Smyrna the Roman situation that he assumes uncritically to have applied there too.

Lampe asks with regard to the apparent interchangeability of ἐπίσκοποι with πρεσβύτεροι, whether all presbyters are also bishops, or whether there

---

126 Note once again the persistent anachronism in the interpretation of this scene in Preysing (1918) p. 183: "Nun erwähnt H. zum zweiten Mal die Verwerfung seiner Lehre durch Kallist und bezeichnet sie als offizielle Amtshandlung (δημοσίᾳ εἰπεῖν); Kallist ist in seinen Augen in diesem Momente noch Bischof." See also K. Beyschlag, Kallist und Hippolyt, in *ThZ* 20 (1964), p. 103-124.

was a circle within the presbyterate called bishops.[127] In the former case, a "presbyter" would be called a "bishop" when his exercize of ἐπισκοπή was in focus, namely when his function as dispenser of material relief to the widows and poor was at issue. Lampe, though wishing to argue that the latter was the case, concedes that Justin *Apol.* 1,67 constitutes a possible counter-example. He need not however so concede. The προεστώς of this passage (and 1,65) is not called a πρεσβύτερος, and so might just as well be an ἐπίσκοπος. His function is described as collecting the offerings and distributing them to the poor the (ἕκαστος τὴν ἑαυτοῦ, ὃ βούλεται δίδωσι· καὶ τὸ συλλεγόμενον παρὰ τῷ προεστῶτι ἀποτίθεται, καὶ αὐτὸς ἐπικουρεῖ ὀρφανοῖς τε καὶ χήραις...). It is he who "gives aid to the widows and orphans."

If we refer again to the passage from Hermas *Vis.* II, 4,3 which I quoted earlier, the choice again confronts us of whether all presbyters were bishops in this sense, or only some of them. Clement, as we have argued, as so-called "secretary" of the Church of Rome, has the entrusted ministry of writing official communications in the name of all of the fractionalized communities to external churches, and to be the recipient of the incoming correspondence. In that passage, Hermas is instructed to send two books, one to Clement, for external transmission (πέμψει... εἰς τὰς ἔξω πόλεις), and one to Grapte for her to exhort the widows and orphans. But Hermas himself is to read it to the city itself (εἰς ταύτην τὴν πόλιν), in the company of the presbyters who preside over the Church (μετὰ τῶν πρεσβυτέρων τῶν προϊσταμένων τῆς ἐκκλησίας).

The question that we must try to answer is how this description fits Lampe's 'fractionalizing thesis,' which we have conceived in terms of separate congregations constituted as house-schools. In a given house school is there a plurality of such πρεσβύτεροι προϊστάμενοι, or indeed just one πρεσβύτερος προϊστάμενος? In Justin's house-school, as we have seen, there was mention of only one who was associated with the poor relief. It would, I believe, be wrong to interpret this expression as a description of a function that more than one person could perform at different times. As we shall see in greater detail in our next chapter, προεστώς is a term derived from Hellenistic philosophical schools who will only have one such president, as indeed Justin as a Christian teacher with his philosopher's gown clearly was himself.

Furthermore, at the close of the second century Natalius is described as an ἐπίσκοπος of the Theodotian monarchians, and as one who was "ensnared by the chief seat amongst them (δελεαζόμενος τῇ τε παρ᾽ αὐτοῖς πρωτοκαθεδρίᾳ)." (Eusebius *H.E.* V, 28,12) This example does not merely show that for every congregation within the city there was a single presbyter/

---

[127] Clement *Cor.* 42,4-5; 47,6; 54,2; 57,1 cf. Hermas *Vis.* III,5, 1.

bishop at the end of the second century.[128] It also illuminates Hermas' attack on "those who rule the Church (τοῖς προηγουμένοις τῆς ἐκκλησίας) and occupy the chief seats" (καὶ τοῖς πρωτοκαθεδρίταις) in the middle of the second century (*Vis.* III, 10,7). It shows us clearly that Hermas no more was describing here a plurality of πρωτοκαθεδριαί in the congregations of the house-schools, than he intended the πρεσβύτεροι προϊστάμενοι to refer to a plurality of presbyters in those same schools.

A further corroboration of a single πρωτοκαθεδρία and hence a single presbyter-bishop per congregation can, moreover, be found in Hermas, *Mand.* 11, 1 and 12. Here we read of the vision of a man "seated on a chair (καθήμενον ἐπὶ καθέδραν)" who is described as a "false prophet (ψευδο–προφήτης)." Afterwards he is described as wishing "to have the chief seat (θέλει πρωτοκαθεδρίαν ἔχειν)." Hermas never implies that there was anything wrong *per se* in the possession of the πρωτοκαθεδρία, but only in the qualities of those who were seated there at the time. Furthermore, clearly there is only one πρωτοκαθεδρία to desire as far as the individual congregation is concerned, and thus he corroborates one προεστώς per congregation also.

Consequently, the scene described in *Vis.* II, 4,3 may be the very situation that we need in order to explain how the public debate (δημοσίᾳ) between the congregations could take place, with Callistus' charge of ditheism, and Sabellius' further attack on Callistus for violating the primitive faith (*El.* IX, 12,16). Each individual προεστώς and each individual πρωτοκαθεδρίτης are called πρεσβύτεροι προϊστάμενοι and πρωτοκαθεδρίται because they are gathered from each individual community to hear and read out to the city itself the account of Hermas' vision. Hermas reads his βιβλαρίδιον εἰς ταύτην τὴν πόλιν, μετὰ τῶν πρεσβυτέρων τῶν προϊσταμένων τῆς ἐκκλησίας, in what Lampe rightly describes as "an dieser Stelle die Presbyter als Auditorium versammelt."[129] It would be in such a public forum that the various προϊστάμενοι of the various catholic congregations would have seemed to an external, pagan observer as so many Christian philosophical schools in debate, just like their pagan counterparts. To such and observer, of course, as we have seen, διδασκαλεῖα would not have had *El.*'s pejorative undertones.

In other words, each προεστώς of each community seem together to have formed a central, presbyteral council along with the minister entrusted with

---

[128] Of the example of Natalius quoted here, and of the Montanist Proclus/Proculus (Tertullian *Ad. Scap.* 4) Lampe (1989) p. 338 says: "Beide Beispiele vom Ende des Jahrhunderts illustrieren, was wenigstens bis zur Mitte des Jahrhunderts für jede Gruppe der Stadt galt: Jeder Einzelgemeinde stand ein eigener Presbyter-Episkopos vor." See also E. Hatch, *The Organisation of the Early Christian Churches*, (London: Rivington 1882); A.M. Javierre, Le Thème de la succession des apôtres dans la littérature chrétienne primitive, in *Unam Sanctam* 39 (1962), p. 171-221; E. Jay , From Presbyter-Bishops to Bishops and Presbyters, in *SecCent* 1 (1981), p. 125-162.
[129] Lampe (1989) p. 338.

what is really the function of a foreign minister rather than simply a secretary. Clement wrote on behalf of all the house-schools to foreign churches, and the holders of that office seem to have either possessed or gradually acquired also responsibility for administering poor relief to foreign churches, as the individual προεστώς did, as in the case of Justin, to his own community. It was before such a gathering of presbyters with their official letter writer that we may hypothesize the public arguments between Sabellius, Zephyrinus, and the author of *El.* took place, and for which Callistus received most of the blame from the latter.

The question that we must now ask is to what extent Zephyrinus and Callistus, as the immediate successors of Victor, can be said to represent a monarchical episcopate existing at Rome from the time of Victor?[130]

6C 7.5. El. *and* Victor's *supposed monarchical episcopacy*

As Lampe points out, Dionysius, in his letter to Soter, praises the beneficence of the Church of Rome:

> For from the beginning this has been your custom, to give benefactions in various ways to all brethren (πάντας μὲν ἀδελφοὺς ποικίλως εὐεργετεῖν) and to send maintenance to the many churches in every city (ἐκκλησίαις τε πολλαῖς ταῖς κατὰ πᾶσαν πόλιν ἐφόδια πέμπειν)... Your blessed bishop Soter has not only preserved this... ancestral custom (πατροπαράδοτον ἔθος) of the Romans, but has extended it (ηὔξηκεν), lavishing the abundance generally distributed (ἐπιχορηγῶν μὲν τὴν διαπεμπομένην δαψίλειαν) to the saints, and exhorting with blessed words, as a loving father to his children, the brethren who come to Rome.
>
> Eusebius *H.E.* IV, 23,9-10

Indeed this passage would imply that he who possesses Clement's ministry, in Hermas' terms specifically "entrusted" to him, of writing on behalf of the house-schools collectively to the external churches, seems also the person entrusted (ἐκείνῳ γὰρ ἐπιτέτραπται) with external poor-relief as well. He thus exercizes one form of ἐπισκοπή, though not the only form, since the προεστώς of each congregation is still charged with this responsibility internally. Such largesse might seem from the perspective of external observers like Dionysius to have been more the work of Soter than it actually was, though the "Romans" are praised equally in this passage.

But authority over external relief would not necessarily and in itself represent the development, in Soter's time, of a monarchical episcopate. The secretary/ foreign minister had always been associated with such external relief, presumably even from the time of Clement's *Cor.,* since he wrote the letters, and received the replies, establishing what was needed. In this respect such an arrangement was quite different from that of the self-govern-

---

[130] Such is Lampe's claim: "Erst ab der Mitte des 2. Jh. gewinnt dieser mit den auswärtigen Aufgaben betraute Presbyter immer mehr „Vorsprung" bis *spätens* mit *Victor* (ca. 189-199) ein machtvoller Monarchos entwickelt ist." Lampe (1989) p. 340.

ing Jewish synagogues. Though the fractionalism of the Christian Roman communities reflected a similar fractionalism of the Jewish synagogues, each of which were self-governing communities, in their case there is no evidence at all for a presbyteral council, a γερουσία, embracing them all.[131]

Indeed, as the congregations grew in size and, as Lampe argues persuasively and in detail, in social rank, and with it the largess to be distributed externally, the secretary/foreign minister's authority would have increased internally. The increase of that prestige vis a vis that of the προεστώς of an individual congregation would have been influenced by the increased external prestige such as exemplified by Dionysus' letter to Soter. We may arguably be at the beginning of the process that is to lead to monarchical episcopacy at Rome, and the inclusion of the early secretary/ foreign minister Clement on a succession list of individual monarchical bishops. The beginning of such a process is what we witness in the dispute between the author of El. and Callistus.

If our account, which has followed and sought to develop that of Lampe, is correct, then there would have been two sources of ἐπισκοπή. The one would have been exercized by each προεστώς of individual congregations who, as in Justin's case, would have administered a fractionalized poor-relief and thus each exercized ἐπισκοπή. But the external ἐπισκοπή was exercized by the secretary/ foreign minister. We might hypothesize that there would be tension between the two kinds of ἐπισκοπή as the equilibrium of prestige was upset by the increasing largesse exercised externally by the secretary/ foreign minister. Moreover, our proposal is more than mere hypothesis. It describes the very tension that we find between the author of El. and Zephyrinus, and afterwards Callistus.

We must recall that not only did an individual presbyter preside (προεστώς), as over Justin's congregation, but also as in Hermas, exercised ἐπισκοπή as administrator of the poor relief. Furthermore, such a προεστώς exercising ἐπισκοπή, was a πρωτοκαθεδρίτης and possessed a πρωτο – καθεδρία in terms of his individual congregation. There was neither a plurality of presbyters nor of πρωτοκαθεδρίαι in an individual congregation but only one, as with the πρωτοκαθεδρία of Natalius. Such was our argument as we developed Lampe's original account. Now in the dispute between the author of El. and Callistus the former accused the latter of "yearning for the throne of oversight" (θηρώμενος τὸν τῆς ἐπισκοπῆς θρόνον), but that finally he only "thought that he had achieved what he desired (νομίζων τετυχηκέναι οὗ ἐθηρᾶτο)." (El. IX, 11,1 cf. 12, 15)

El. cannot here be referring to the θρόνος or πρωτοκαθεδρία which Callistus possessed over his own congregation, since, as we have seen, El. did not object to Callistus' authority in that sphere so much as his attempts

---

131 For a list of these synagogues and this conclusion, see Lampe (1989) p. 367-368.

to apply his authority to absolving members of other congregations than his own. But if it is not the case, then the other form of ἐπισκοπή of which he only thinks (according to *El.*) that he has the θρόνος can only be that of the secretary/ foreign minister. Such would be consistent with his name occupying his place on the Liberian succession list, and not that of the author of *El.* instead. But *El.*'s νομίζων shows that far from the occupant of that position being acknowledge as the occupant of a throne above those of the presbyters presiding over the individual congregation, it is disputed.

Likewise Zephyrinus only thought that he was managing the Church (διέπειν νομίζοντος τὴν ἐκκλησίαν). As we have argued, Hippolytus never claims the sole θρόνον τῆς ἐπισκοπῆς for himself, however much he will not concede the position either to Zephyrinus or Callistus, Victor's immediate successors. Nor does he claim the title καθολικὴ ἐκκλησία for his group alone, however much he might deny its exclusive use by Callistus' group and indeed deny it use to any group, including that of Callistus, whose teaching does not succeed κατὰ διαδοχήν from the apostles but from Greek philosophers. It is not therefore the case that the author of *El.* acknowledges the position an occupant of the θρόνος τῆς ἐπισκοπῆς over all the house-schools, but claims that he himself should occupy it, as if he were a "schismatic" in the later sense of that word. It is the position itself that he finds questionable.

The author of *El.* will not deny the title ἐπίσκοπος to Victor. Indeed Victor, when asked for the names of the Sardinian martyrs by Marcia, is described as τὸν μακάριον Οὐίκτορα, ὄντα ἐπίσκοπον τῆς ἐκκλησίας κατ᾽ ἐκεινοῦ καιροῦ (*El.* IX, 12,10). But he never attributes to Victor even the putative possession of the θρόνος τῆς ἐπισκοπῆς as he does to Callistus. Indeed he never describes either Zephyrinus or Callistus as ἐπίσκοπος at all. But before we regard this fact as supporting the traditional understanding of the author of *El.* as leading a schism against Victor's lawful successors, we should ask ourselves in view of our previous discussion to what extent we are reading this description in terms of an almost Eusebian anachronism. ὄντα ἐπίσκοπον τῆς ἐκκλησίας κατ᾽ ἐκεῖνοῦ καιρου does not necessarily mean that Victor was the only bishop at Rome at this time. Certainly he is not described as desiring τὸν τῆς ἐπισκοπῆς θρόνον.

Furthermore, the only other point at which the title ἐπίσκοπος is used it appears in the plural. Of Callistus the author of *El.* says:

> This man taught as follows that if a bishop sinned (εἰ ἐπίσκοπος ἁμάρτοι), even if it was a sin unto death (εἰ καὶ πρὸς θάνατον), he need not be degraded (κατατίθεσθαι). At this time, then, bishops and priests, and deacons (ἐπίσκοποι καὶ πρεσβύτεροι καὶ διάκονοι) were ordained (καθίστασθαι εἰς κλήρους) having been married twice or three times (δίγαμοι καὶ τρίγαμοι).
>
> *El.* IX, 12,21-22

It would certainly be anachronistic to regard these other bishops as bishops of geographically locatable Sees outside of Rome, over whom Callistus is claiming universal jurisdiction such as to make the widowed or twice widowed (δίγαμοι καὶ τρίγαμοι) eligible for ordination or to remain in Holy Orders. The jurisdiction of the later papacy did not prevail in the late second-century, as we have argued earlier in the case of Eusebius' distortion of the role of Victor in the Quartodeciman controversy.

The plurality of bishops (ἐπίσκοποι), like the plurality of presbyters and deacons, must refer to bearers of these offices in Rome itself. They are indeed the πρεσβύτεροι προϊστάμενοι with whom we have already met, who are also πρωτοκαθεδρίται, each over their house-school congregation. We have already exposed as impossible the author of El. appealing to other bishops of other Sees against Callistus, and how Frickel's case to that effect was a result the corrupt reading of Parisinus ms. suppl graec. 464 at El. IX, 12, 15. His appeal was to his fellow πρεσβύτεροι προϊστάμενοι gathered for public (δημοσίᾳ) disputation.

Furthermore, if Victor was a monarchical bishop over all the Roman house-schools or tituli, and Zephyrinus and Callistus were the successors to that τὸν τῆς ἐπισκοπῆς θρόνον, it must be asked where the author of El. as schismatical bishop or anti-pope got the co-consecrators required in Ap. Trad. 2, 10-18 to make him a bishop. We shall discuss in the next chapter the claim of Ratcliff and Bradshaw that this passage has experienced textual corruption. The divergent readings of the various traditions of the text regarding the role of bishops and presbyters at an episcopal consecration conceal an original text in which the presbyters consecrated one of their own number without any neighbouring bishops.[132] But this in itself would reflect a Church Order at the turn of the third century at variance with later developments.

But as matters stand the hi qui praesentes fuerint episcopi.... inponant super eum manus can only be the πρεσβύτεροι προϊστάμενοι of other house-schools, who would in any case have already consecrated the author of El. as ἐπίσκοπος for his particular community in an act which was in no way at variance with Callistus being ἐπίσκοπος of his. Thus Victor as ὄντα ἐπίσκο-πον τῆς ἐκκλησίας κατ᾽ ἐκεῖνο καιροῦ is one bishop of one congregation at Rome. Though some might claim more for him, as for Zephyrinus and Callistus, namely τὸν τῆς ἐπισκοπῆς θρόνον, that claim is clearly controversial.

It is thus in claiming this title alone, together with being the sole καθο-λικὴ ἐκκλησία, that justifies for the author his constant accusation of vanity in application to Callistus. Callistus is "the most amazing (θαυμασιώτατος)"

---

132 P.F. Bradshaw, The participation of other bishops in the ordination of a bishop in the Apostolic Tradition of Hippolytus, in Stud. Pat. 18, 2, p. 335-338.

(*El.* IX, 12,26). His followers "pranced proudly around (γαυριώμενοι)" because the crowds were leaving the other congregations, including that of the author of *El.*, for Callistus' company and its indiscriminate absolution (12, 24). They were "beyond blushing (ἀπηρυθριασμένοι)" when they alone called themselves the Catholic Church (12, 26). For his alleged influence upon Alkibiades, *El.* says of Callistus that he "convicted this teaching as being the operation and design of a spurious spirit (πνευματος νόθου ἐνέργειαν καὶ ἐπίνοιαν) possessed by a heart inflated with pride (πεφυσιωμένης καρδίας)." (13, 5) Such an accusation is consistent with feelings toward a person and group making novel claims for their position previously unacknowledged.

Thus the Hippolytan events deny the emergence of monarchical episcopacy from Victor's pontificate, however much those events may mark the first controverted claims in that direction. Indeed the claim of Lampe that monarchical episcopacy begins with Victor would require the acceptance of some common conceptual assumptions with Frickel about "schism," "antipope," "illegal See," etc. We have argued that *El.* IX, 6-13 do not support the applicability of many of these assumptions even as late as the opening decades of the third century.

We shall now examine briefly three further of these assumptions.

6C 8. *Three conceptual requirements for the use of 'schism'*

There are three conceptual requirements for the description of a group as schismatic in the sense that this term has been used since Novatian's time. There is a conceptual connection between each of these assumptions and the meaning of what it is to be schismatic, namely (1) the connection between 'schism' and the corporate ownership of church property from which schismatics can be excluded, (2) the question of deposition of the schismatic episcopal communion by Synods in the late second and early third century, and (3) the significance of the episcopal succession lists as index of the presence and progress of monarchical bishops.

6C 8.1. *The corporate ownership of Church property*

The later conceptualization of "schism" requires the power of at least one monarchical bishop in the dispute to acquire the property of the congregation that he is excommunicating. Unless there is some connection between a congregation and its physical place of worship, then excommunication loses much of its force, since the excommunicated group simply denies the authority of the excommunicator, and continues in its privately owned house-school. When the excommunicator however actually controls through the corporate ownership of a wider community the actual physical place of worship, then indeed the threat of being declared schismatic has greater bite.

It is in that situation that the adjective "monarchical" can be said to apply to his power which has then become territorial.

Now Lampe would be assisted in his case if it could be shown that there existed in the time of Victor and his successors corporate ownership of property by the Church of Rome. But Lampe himself has to admit that this cannot be done by using the example of Callistus' charge over the cemetery that was subsequently to bear his name. As this example is pertinent to our general analysis of the Hippolytan events, I will now discuss the relevant passage, incorporating Lampe's interpretation of the evidence which I accept to the effect that this is not an example of corporate ownership by the Roman community.

The author of *El.*, having written his by all accounts scurrilous version of Callistus' earlier career, records how Marcia, Commodus' mistress, provided the presbyter Hyacinthus with a letter (τὴν ἀπολύσιμον ἐπιστολὴν) for the release of Christian martyrs in Sardinia, within whose ranks Callistus was included. Only Victor's compassion, claims the author, prevented him from objecting. Victor nevertheless took care to defend himself against possible attacks from those who remembered the earlier scandals, including Carpophorus. Consequently he kept Callistus at Antheium on a pension (*El.* IX, 12, 11-13).

It was after Victor's death that Zephyrinus recalled Callistus to Rome. Of Victor *El.* says:

> After his death (μεθ' οὗ κοίμησιν), Zephyrinus, wishing to have him as his co-operator (ὡς συναράμενον αὐτὸν θέλων ἔχειν) by ordination to the clergy (πρὸς κατάστασιν τοῦ κλήρου), he honoured him to his own harm, and to this end he brought him from Antheium to the cemetery (εἰς τὸ κοιμητήριον) and placed him in charge of it (κατέστησεν).
>
> *El.* IX, 12,14

Although *El.* has called Victor an ἐπίσκοπος, it is remarkable that he will never use this title in connection with Zephyrinus, nor will he call Callistus a διάκονος in his charge over the cemetery that was to bear his name. Instead he simply uses the general term "co-operator (συναράμενον)." Moreover, Zephyrinus, unlike Victor, as we have seen, is never called an ἐπίσκοπος.

Such a feature of *El.*'s description may seem, *prima facie*, to support the traditional account of Hippolytus leading a schism post-Victor, and claiming that he is the 'real' episcopal successor so that only his deacons are the 'real' deacons. However, the example of Epigonus, described as Noetus' deacon (*El.* IX, 7,1), shows that there was no reluctance in the patristic age to use such official titles of the ministers of sects that one considered heretical, as the Eusebian usage also shows. Such an argument for a traditional interpretation has therefore of itself no force, let alone in the face of the case that I have already made to the contrary regarding a plurality of ἐπίσκοποι and πρωτοκαθεδρίται at Rome, over a plurality of house-school congregations, in terms of which the author of *El.* could not be schismatical for simply refusing to accept the authority of one of them.

The real explanation of *El.*'s language would probably therefore lie in his political concerns expressed in the derogatory categories adopted to describe Zephyrinus and Callistus, even in comparison with his descriptions of others whom he considers heretical. He wishes in his polemic to depict the relationship between Zephyrinus and Callistus as purely individual, and as one of highly corrupt cronyism. Thus he will not describe their relationship in terms of the official titles of ἐπίσκοπος and διάκονος, with the formal ecclesiastical relations that are described by these terms. "Co-operator (συναράμενον)" goes far better as a crony term with descriptions of Zephyrinus as "an unlettered simpleton without experience of the rules of the Church (ἄνδρα ἰδιώτην καὶ ἀγράμματον καὶ ἄπειρον τῶν ἐκκλησιασ–τικῶν ὅρων)" and "susceptible to bribery (δωρολήπτην) and loving money (φιλάργυρον)." The term also fits better descriptions of his collusion with Callistus as "a man cunning in evil (ἀνὴρ ἐν κακίᾳ πανοῦργος), and deceitful in error (καὶ ποικίλος πρὸς πλάνην)." (*El.* IX, 11,1)

But what of Callistus' being ordained (πρὸς κατάστασιν τοῦ κλήρου) and placed in charge of the cemetery (εἰς τὸ κοιμητήριον κατέστησεν)? Does this not imply that Zephyrinus as bishop administered a corporately owned graveyard? Corporate ownership would mean that the immediate successors of Victor could behave as monarchical bishops in some respect, and 'schism' would derive some conceptual relevance since there would be common property of which to argue over the legal possession, and from which one group would endeavour to eject the other. But Lampe will concede that such a claim fails.

Callistus was not himself buried *in Callisto*, but rather in the cemetery of Calepodius where his grave has been discovered. Thus it was unlikely to have been the official burial place of the Roman community, or even of his particular house-school congregation at this time. The identification of the cemetery that bears his name as the crypt of the popes begins only at the time of Pontianus (died A.D. 235) and Anteros (died 236), at the beginning of an era when the real possibility of a meaningful schism was actualized in the events surrounding Novatian. The excavations of the so-called "crypt of the popes" (Plates 17-19) make it clear that the crypt itself was a new structure, with its own new entrance built on to a small existing cemetery. Great care was taken to respect the above-ground borders of the plot beyond which the diggers took care not to go. Above ground there exist the remains of a wall which marked the borders of the plot.

The initial inference that such an original structure was a private graveyard extended underground by private benefaction is strengthened when we look at the legal problems of regarding illegal Christian communities in the early third century at Rome as being able to hold corporate property. The usual argument to the contrary is based on corporate ownership of property being possible for an *arca communis* or funeral club, under cover of which Christian communities could have held corporate property. The problem is that under Roman law subscriptions to such a club for later burial were not regarded as contributions to a legal corporation with a separate legal personality, but were thought of simply as the sum total of the contributions of individual members. As such, they could not be left as inheritance in Wills and passed on.[133]

The literary evidence also supports the view that the burials under the above-ground tomb of Zephyrinus were the recipients of his private benefaction. We have literary records that Zephyrinus was buried *in cymiterio suo, iuxta cymiterium Callisti* (*Lib. Pont.* I, 16,14). Furthermore, according to the Salzburg Itinerary of the seventh century his memorial was above-ground, which corresponds with the earlier information of the epigraphical Catalogue of Sixtus III (c. 432-440) which records a list of bishops buried underground in which Zephyrinus' name does not appear.[134] The cemetery over which Callistus was put in charge was therefore Zephyrinus' private property, and the cemetery was quite literally his own (*in cymiterio suo*). But he provided burial places underground for the poorer members of his Christian community.

The cemetery of Zephyrinus and Callistus was not, despite *El.*'s definite article (τὸ κοιμητήριον), the only Christian cemetery in Rome. We have the remains of Christian frescoes from the first quarter of the third century, and therefore contemporary with these events in the Lucina Region. The grave of Callistus himself (A.D. 222) has been excavated in the catacomb of Calepodius. Either he wished for no pauper's grave for himself, or he was buried in the Trastevere region because this was where he lived, as *Lib. Pont.* I, 17,12-13 suggests.[135] Lampe's conclusion therefore that the cemetery was a private one seems inescapable, and this too would help explain why Hippolytus should not call Callistus a deacon in respect to his appointment over the cemetery. That this was his *diaconal* function after his ordination is something that is mere inference.

Such a conclusion, as Lampe shows, is of a piece with the other archaeological evidence for worship in private houses, the centres around which the later *tituli* parishes were built. As we have seen, there were no separate chapels until the mid-third century when complexes specifically designed for worship and for burial were built on. We can only date the passing of the

---

[133] Lampe (1989) p. 310.
[134] Ibid. p. 15. I have cited the *Lib. Pont.* from Mommsen's edition, see footnote 72.
[135] Ibid. p. 23.

Cemetery of Callistus into corporate ownership from 235 onwards, when the crypt of the popes is built as a separate structural addition, and Fabian buried Anteros and Pontian there where he was to be buried himself.[136]

It is I believe not accidental that we see once again here before us the period immediately before the events of Novatian. We have argued that the creation by Damasus of the legend of the Novatian Presbyter to explain the events in *El.* as 'schism' reflect the origins of the conceptual discourse which define "schism," "monarchical bishop" etc. in the mid-third century. In this section we have argued the connection between the corporate ownership of church property and the traditional conceptual apparatus in terms of which "schism" is defined and occurs. There is a conceptual connection between "schism," "monarchical bishop" and jurisdiction over property and territory. We have thus shown in this section that no such connection could pertain either in the so-called "pontificate" of Victor, or in the events recorded in *El.* that succeeded it. We have thus concluded that Victor was not a monarchical bishop, nor created monarchical episcopacy, and that the bewilderment of Damasus, Eusebius, and Jerome regarding Hippolytus' status, the successor to the author of *El.*, was once more a function of their anachronistic conceptual apparatus.

But we argued that "schism" was also conceptually associated with appeal to a wider community of episcopal judgement in recognition of a formal deposition of a cleric. "Schism" is not simply a term that arises from the possibility of a monarchical bishop, vested with jurisdiction over the corporate property of a community, excluding a rebel group and its leader from using hitherto common places of worship. Traditionally it also involves the monarchical bishop obtaining the formal support, by letters or through a Synod of other monarchical bishops like himself, territorially separated from him, recognising him as the rightful bishop and his followers as the true Church, and excommunicating the group of his rival if they should appear on any other episcopal territory.

Let us now look at the character of episcopal communications and Synods before such territorial monarchical power has been acquired, as revealed in Eusebius' description, contemporary with Hippolytus and his unmentioned predecessor, of the condemnation of Beryllus of Bostra.

6C 8.2. *Deposition of the schismatics Beryllus and Paul*
We saw earlier in this chapter, in Eusebius' account of the Quartodeciman controversy, a conceptualization of events in the later second century in terms of those of the fourth. The problems of Damasus and Eusebius with conceptualizing Hippolytus' true position in the church of Rome of the second century was therefore but one instance of a general problem of concep-

---

[136] Ibid. p. 310-313.

tualization. In corroboration of our analysis of *El.* IX, 6-13 as falsifying such an anachronistic conceptualization, it will repay us to look at another such general example from Eusebius, which is nevertheless related to the events of the controversy of the author of *El.* with Callistus. I am referring specifically to what his account of the Synod which met on the opinions of Beryllus of Bostra has specifically to tell us about the nature and type of episcopal authority in the second century.

We shall now see that no more than in the case of Victor does this example conform to the later construction of ecclesiastical reality in which a group of bishops intervene in a dispute by means of a formal Synodical declaration recognising one of the disputants, or declare a bishop heretical and proceed to consecrate an orthodox and canonical successor. That there was, before the age of Cyprian, no mechanism for summoning bishops and formally depriving one of their number for heresy or schism is supported by Eusebius himself in the account which he gives of Beryllus of Bostra. Indeed, the Council of Antioch (264) that deposed Paul of Samosata was the first council to behave in the way that Eusebius and Damasus found so bewilderingly absent in late second-century Rome. Thus we shall be confirmed in our conclusion that it is impossible to read *El.* IX, 12, 15-26 in such a later light.

Beryllus is identified as a bishop in *H.E.* VI, 20, 2, in contrast with Hippolytus, as we have seen. It is not surprising that he is so identifiable since Bostra is in Arabia, and thus in the region of Syria and Asia Minor where Ignatian episcopacy was of long antiquity, in contrast with Rome and Africa, by the late second century. Beryllus denied Christ's individual preexistence. But let us examine Eusebius' account of the Synod that examined those views and what transpired.

Eusebius records that Beryllus "tried to introduce things foreign to the faith (ξένα τινὰ τῆς πίστεως παρεισφέρειν ἐπειρᾶτο), perverting the Church's rule (τὸν ἐκκλησιαστικὸν παρεκτρέπων κανόνα)," and continues as follows:

> In consequence, after a great many bishops (πλείστων ἐπισκόπων) had conducted examinations (ζητήσεις) and discussions (διαλόγους) with this man, Origen was invited along with others and entered in the first instance into conversation (κάτεισι μὲν εἰς ὁμιλίαν) with the man, in order to test his opinion. But when he recognized what he was saying, and had corrected him for his lack of orthodoxy (εὐθύνας μὴ ὀρθοδοξοῦντα), and persuaded him with rational argument (λογισμῷ τε πείσας), he established him in the truth regarding his doctrine (τῇ περὶ τοῦ δόγματος ἐφίστησιν ἀληθείᾳ), and restored him to his former healthy opinion (ἐπί τε τὴν προτέραν ὑγιῆ δόξαν ἀποκαθίστησιν). There are still current written records (ἔγγραφα) of the Synod which took place on his account (τῆς δι' αὐτὸν γενομένης συνόδου), which include the inquiries addressed to him (πρὸς αὐτὸν ζητήσεις) by Origen and discussions that took

place in his own diocese (τὰς λεχθείσας ἐπὶ τῆς αὐτοῦ παροικίας διαλέξεις)and
each item of business.

H.E. VI, 33,2-3

We saw earlier in connection with the letter of Polycrates of Ephesus to
Victor the tendency of Eusebius to turn a letter from a single bishop citing
the authority of his community's tradition, and his personal biography, into a
synodical encyclical (*H.E.* V, 24,8 and 6C 6). We see a similar interest at
work in the account of the proceedings recorded against Beryllus. Eusebius
believes once again that the organisation of the Church has existed in a pristine form from the apostles time and without development. Thus an account
of discussion and debates involving Origen persuading Beryllus of his error
has been turned into a late-third to early-fourth-century full-blown, ecclesiastical Synod.

If a formal Synod had taken place, then we may be sure that Origen
would have been invited formally with the bishops, priests and deacons.
Origen appears to be summoned as an afterthought to the deliberation of
these πλείστων ἐπισκόπων whose names are suspiciously and unusually not
given. In this respect, as in others, we do well to read this passage alongside
Eusebius' description of the Synod of Antioch (265) that condemned Paul of
Samosata.

Here we are informed that, though Dionysius of Alexandria was too old
and infirm to respond to the invitation (παρακληθεὶς), "the remaining pas-
tors of the Churches (οἱ δὲ λοιποὶ τῶν ἐκκλησίων ποιμένες) from various
quarters (ἄλλος ἄλλοθεν)... all hastened to assemble at Antioch (συνήεσαν,
οἱ πάντες ἐπὶ Ἀντιόχειαν σπεύδοντες)." (*H.E.* VII, 27,2) Interestingly
enough we are not informed who summoned the Synod and sent out the
invitations. On the one hand we are told that Dionysius was invited
(παρακληθεὶς), but presumably this was not by the patriarch of Antioch,
Paul himself. On the other hand the description of the episcopal response to
Paul is described almost as spontaneous and self-initiated (συνήεσαν...
σπεύδοντες). Later the quotation from the resulting encyclical is to imply
that it was a local group of bishops jointly who decided on such action, perhaps the bishops named as attending.

Nevertheless in the case of the Synod of Antioch bishops who attend are
named as Firmilian (Caesarea), Gregory and Athenodore (Pontus), Helenus
(Tarsus), Nicomas (Iconium), Hymenaeus (Jerusalem), Theotechnus
(Caesarea), and Maximus (Bostra), together with presbyters and deacons.
(VII, 28,1) "General assemblies (πάντων οὖν... επὶ ταὐτὸν συνιόντων)" are
mentioned as taking place "on various occasions (κατὰ καιροὺς διαφόρως
καὶ πολλάκις)." Such sessions involve the arguments and discussions
(λόγοι/διαλόγοι) and inquiries (ζητήσεις) that we met with in the case of
Beryllus (VI, 33,2). But their object is not to persuade or convince of wrong

opinion, as was the case with the latter, but rather to serve the interest of one party to unmask the heterodoxy of the other trying to conceal it.[137]

A final Synod is held and "the originator of the Antiochene heresy (ὁ τῆς κατὰ Ἀντιόχειαν ἐκκλησίας ἀρχηγὸς), condemned for heterodoxy (καταγνωσθεὶς ἑτεροδοξίαν) by all, was excommunicated from the Catholic Church under heaven (τῆς ὑπὸ τὸν οὐρανὸν καθολικῆς ἐκκλησίας ἀποκηρύττεται)." Malchion, presbyter and "president of the school of rhetoric (παιδευτηρίων διατριβῆς προεστώς)," plays a leading role and arranges for his public examination (ζήτησιν) of Paul to be recorded by stenographers (ἐπισημειουμένων ταχυγράφων), which records are still extant in Eusebius' time (H.E. VII, 29, 1-2). The assembled bishops then send an encyclical letter addressed to Dionysius bishop of Rome and Maximus of Alexandria informing them of their unanimous decision, and outlining the nature of Paul's heresy and his manner of life. They begin with a list of their names, and mention that they are responsible for sending letters of invitation to other bishops (πολλοὺς καὶ τῶν μακρὰν ἐπισκόπων). (VII, 30,1-3)

Finally they depose him (ἕτερον ἀντ' αὐτοῦ τῇ καθολικῇ ἐκκλησίᾳ καταστῆσαι ἐπίσκοπον) and name his successor, Domnus, Demetrian's son. They ask also for letters of communion (κοινωνικὰ ... γράμματα) to be accepted from him by the other bishops, and for other bishops to write to him, reflecting the usual seal of recognition and intercommunion in the second half of the third century (VII, 30,17). Then they finally prevail upon Aurelian (270-275) to assign the church buildings ("house") that Paul refuses to vacate (μηδαμῶς ἐκστῆναι τοῦ Παύλου τοῦ τῆς ἐκκλησίας οἴκου θέλοντος) to those with whom the bishops of Rome and of Italy will communicate in writing (30, 18-19).

At first sight Malchion appear to play the same role in the Synod regarding Paul that Origen had done in that regarding Beryllus. Both conduct a ζήτησις of which there are written records, (ἔγγραφα / ἐπισημειουμένων ταχυγράφων) (VI, 33,3 cf. VII, 29,2). Both refute (διαλέξεις/ διήλεγξεν) (VI, 33,3 cf. VII, 29,2) and examine (εὐθύνας μὴ ὀρθοδοξοῦντα/ εὐθύνας) (VI,33, 2 cf. VII, 29,2). But such would be a superficial reading of their roles. The object of Origen' s ζήτησις, εὐθύνη, and διαλέξις is to persuade Beryllus with rational argument (λογισμῷ τε πείσας), to restore him to the right teaching (ἐπί τε τὴν προτέραν ὑγιῆ δόξαν ἀποκαθίστησιν), and to establish him in the truth regarding his doctrine (τῇ περὶ τοῦ δόγματος ἐφίστ–ησιν ἀληθείᾳ). (VI,33, 2) The object of Malchion's ζήτησις and εὐθύνη is that "having called him to account (αὐτὸν εὐθύνας), he refuted (διήλεγξεν) him for what he had concealed (ἐπικρυπτόμενον)." In other words, his object

---

[137] Eusebius H.E. VII, 28,2: τῶν μὲν ἀμφὶ τὸν Σαμοσατέα τὰ τῆς ἑτεροδοξίας ἐπι–κρύπτειν ἔτι καὶ παρακαλύπτεσθαι πειρωμένων, τῶν δὲ ἀπογυμνοῦν καὶ εἰς φανερὸν ἄγειν τὴν αἵρεσιν... διὰ σπουδῆς ποιουμένων.

is not to persuade but to uncover and unmask, and to this task his intellect is applied (VII, 29,2).

Malchion' function arises out of the function of the Synod which is to unmask and convict, and then to excommunicate, depose, and deprive of corporate property. His role in the passage is subordinate to the role of the named bishops, as part of the apparatus of whose power he operates. Origen's function was however quite different. He was the centre of the narrative, and his activity was that of a head of a philosophical school winning the philosophical argument, rather than that of the expert theological witness and advocate at an episcopal trial. Origen is described with the words κάτεισι μὲν εἰς ὁμιλίαν. Indeed, in comparison with the named bishops at Antioch, with their written encyclicals, the unnamed bishops involved with Origen in the refutation and correction of Beryllus of Bostra are very shadowy figures indeed. They are mere superfluous adjuncts to the events that take place.

We are told that there are records (ἔγγραφα), but are they records of a Synod of monarchical bishops capable of making a general and worldwide excommunication, if necessary, stick? Our suspicion is that, as in the case of Polycrates already discussed, Eusebius in *H.E.* VI, 33,2-3 has introduced the apparatus of a Synod of nameless bishops into his description of a debate whose terms are more like those of a meeting of a philosophical school. That such a Synod as that which condemned Paul could have met in the late second century would be an anachronism, as we have already argued.

Indeed, the events of Beryllus' discussion with Origen, read in such a light, appear very reminiscent of the proceedings as we have interpreted them between the author of *El.*, Callistus, and Zephyrinus. We saw that it was wrong to follow Frickel in believing that the documents that Eusebius had before him could possibly be letters to external churches attempting to convene a Synod (6 C 7.3). The τὴν πρὸς τῆς ἐκκλησίας κατ᾽ αὐτοῦ κατηγορίαν (*El.* IX, 12,15), that Callistus hoped to turn aside was an accusation in the presence of the representative πρεσβύτεροι προϊσταμενοι or πρωτοκαθεδρίται of the individual congregations or house-schools. What Eusebius had before him, and what caused him his bewilderment, would have been something like the ἔγγραφα of the debate between Origen and Beryllus, rather than a formal Synod in the late third-century sense, but which, in his usual fashion, he was determined to turn anachronistically into such an event.

There were no formal depositions or seizure of property in an age in which there was no sympathetic Aurelian to whom episcopal synods could appeal for a property judgement, and indeed no corporate property to seize, in the Roman house-schools of the second century, on behalf of the "valid" bishop. There was also no formal sentence of excommunication. Indeed, as we have seen, the process of excommunication was rather the demonstration philosophically of a διαδοχή with pagan philosophers which lead to the particular congregation in the particular house school being regarded as having excommunicated themselves.

The role of the "blessed presbyters" whom Hippolytus described, from his own, late second-century, Roman perspective, as excommunicating Noetus in the monepiscopate of Smyrna, was simply to acknowledge that the house-school no longer were to receive the exchange of the *frumentum* with the other orthodox communities, and no longer to play any role in the public (δημοσίᾳ) debates between the πρωτοκαθεδρίται/ προϊστάμενοι of the individual communities in the light of the failure to convince and persuade them of their error. Eusebius in his comment on the deposition of Paul of Samosata makes therefore a distinction which would have been quite impossible earlier when he says:

> When then Paul had fallen from the episcopate (τοῦ δὴ οὖν Παύλου... τῆς ἐπισκοπῆς ἀποπεπτωκότος), together with the orthodoxy of the faith (σὺν καὶ τῇ τῆς πίσεως ὀρθοδοξίᾳ), Domnus, as has been said, became the successor (διεδέξατο) to his ministry (τὴν λειτουργίαν) over the Church at Antioch.
>
> *H.E.* VII, 30,18

The late second century, that did not distinguish, as we have seen, between "compose a heresy (συστήσασθαι αἵρεσιν)" and, "establish a school (συστήσασθαι διδασκαλεῖον)." The distinction between τῆς ἐπισκοπῆς ἀποπεπτωκώς and τῆς ὀρθοδοξίας ἀποπεπτωκώς was not as clear in the late second century as it was in the late third. We have argued that it required a monarchical conception of episcopacy to enable that distinction to be clearly made, and that such a conception presupposed, amongst other things, corporate property ownership and the Synodical authority of other, geographically located, episcopal monarchs. And the archaeological artefacts have suggested that such a situation did not arise until the age of Cyprian, which saw the creation of the Church Order out of which the legend of Hippolytus as the Novatian Presbyter could be made.

But as Lampe regards the episcopal succession lists themselves as evidence for the emergence of monarchical episcopacy in the time of Victor, we shall now examine their claim to constitute such evidence. Lampe relies for his view that monepiscopacy emerges unambiguously with Victor on the concept of διαδοχή as a succession list with names, as such a concept emerges in Hegesippus and Irenaeus. Let us now therefore examine specifically whether the fact of succession lists at the time of Victor are indicative of the emergence of one monarchical bishop, as Lampe suggests.[138]

---

[138] Lampe (1989) p. 341-342.

6C 8.3. *Monarchical bishops and the succession lists*

Lampe sought to use the emergence of the Roman episcopal succession list in Irenaeus as an index for the establishment of monarchical episcopacy not later than the episcopate of Victor.[139] We shall be dealing with the concept of διαδοχή and episcopacy in greater detail in our next chapter, in connection with the self-awareness of the community of Hippolytus and his predecessor regarding the character of its Church Order. We shall keep specifically here to our account in this chapter of how Hippolytus' community, and that of the author of *El.*, appeared and functioned from a contemporary, external perspective, exhibited partly though fragmentary literary allusion, partly from archaeological artefacts, and partly by probing behind Eusebius and Jerome's anachronistic distortions to reconstruct what was their original data. We shall therefore content ourselves in this section with showing that the Roman, episcopal succession list of Irenaeus/ Hegesippus cannot constitute the kind of index that Lampe requires to identify the emergence of monarchical episcopacy with Victor. We shall see that it is rather an index of the organization of the Roman Church of the late second century in terms of house-schools where various communities are found under their individual πρεσβύτερος προϊστάμενος or πρωτοκαθεδρίτης.

If Irenaeus' succession list is an index of the establishement of monarchical bishops, then he must imply the essential character a personal chain of office holders to his concept of διαδοχή. Molland argued that this definitely was not the case, but rather for Irenaeus the succession of teachers was secondary to a succession of doctrine, the purity of which they guaranteed.[140] Let us examine his case in detail, citing his key passages and sometimes adding our own comments to Molland's own.

Hygenus "held the ninth place in the episcopal succession from the apostles downwards (ἔνατον κλῆρον τῆς ἐπισκοπῆς κατὰ διαδοχὴν ἀπὸ τῶν ἀποστόλων)." (*Adv. Haer.* I, 27,1) Since the school model is disputed by Ehrhardt, Telfer, and others who regard the Jewish, Maccabaean sacerdotal succession lists the true model, we shall have to address this issue in some detail in our next chapter. I would wish to argue in support of Molland that the proper home for the language of διαδοχή here is in the Greek philosophical schools, and in the conceptual orientation of that *genre* of literature, exemplified by Diogenes Laertius in his book *The Successions of the*

---

[139] Lampe (1989) p. 342-343. How does Lampe therefore reach the conclusion from what he himself describes as "zwölf-gliedrigen Namenskatalog von den Aposteln bis Eleutherus. Das Interesse der Liste ist, die gegenwärtige Lehre durch eine Sukzessions- Kette von Gewährsmännern bei den Aposteln zu verankern." (p. 342) to "... als Rom die Ausbildung des monarchischen Episkopats erlebt, wird eine zwölfgliedrige Namensliste bis zurück zu den Aposteln konstruiert. In Analogie zur Gegenwart des Eleutherus stellt man sich nun auch in der Vergangenheit je einem herausgehobenen Traditionsträger vor. Die Gegenwart eines monarchischen Traditionsträgers wird in die Vergangenheit zurückgespielt." (p. 343).

[140] E. Molland, Irenaeus of Lugdunum and the Apostolic Tradition, in *JEH* 1,1 (1950), p. 12-28.

Philosophers.[141] Thus in *Adv. Haer.* III, 3,3 the formulae for succession of the bishops mirrors that of thus successions of the philosophers.[142]

The purpose therefore of "enumerating (*annumerare*) those who were appointed bishops (*eos qui... instituti sunt episcopi*) over churches (*in ecclesiis*) by the apostles (*ab apostolis*)" is to make possible the discovery "in every church (*in omni ecclesia*)" of the "tradition of the apostles (*traditionem itaque apostolorum*) manifest in the whole world (*in toto mundo manifestam*)." Their successions (*successores eorum*) do not therefore establish the validity of their individual office and the jurisdiction pertaining to it, but rather the apostolic doctrine against the heretics (*Adv. Haer.* III, 3, 1). Clement's position in the list is not understood in terms of an indelible character given by an act of ordination that must be passed on for the Church to remain whole, but rather because he evidences the uncontaminated apostolic tradition. Thus Clement is described as "having seen the blessed apostles (ὁ καὶ ἑωρακὼς τοὺς ἀποστόλους)... and having the preaching of the apostles still in his ears (ἔτι ἔναυλον τὸ κήρυγμα τῶν ἀποστόλων), and their tradition before his eyes (καὶ τὴν παράδοσιν πρὸ ὀφθαλμῶν)." (*Adv. Haer.* III, 3, 3)

Molland was critical of Caspar for denying that the witness was tied to any episcopal office, but simply referred to whatever particular individuals seemed to know the tradition. He supported instead Lightfoot's account of the gradual development of a presidential presbyter into a monarchical bishop, that both Lampe and myself associated with a secretarial figure like Hermas' Clement. Furthermore Molland supported a date beginning with the episcopate of Anicetus for monarchical bishops, with which Lampe would be in agreement, erroneously, as we are arguing.[143]

I believe that on this point the argument is based upon a misconception on both sides created by modern assumptions about the historiography of the development of ideas. Perhaps the most extreme form of such a historiography would be the methods of contemporary analytic philosophers, who seem often to be trying to describe the relationship between systems of ideas in

---

[141] See also Brent (1993). p. 380-386.

[142] *Adv. Haer.* III, 3,4 (of Clement) διαδέχεται δὲ αὐτὸν Ἀνέγκλητος cf. (of Plato) διεδέξατο δ᾽ αὐτὸν Σπεύσιππος (*Succ.* 4,1); (Of Soter) διαδεξαμένου τὸν Ἀνίκετον Σωτῆρος; (of Socrates) τῶν δὲ διαδεξαμένων αὐτὸν (*Succ.* 2,47) etc. It is questionable whether parallels in Josephus to archieratic succession lists genuinely hold, since he is writing an apology to Rome and appears to be self-consciously assimilating Jewish institutions to Greek philosophical schools.

[143] Molland (1950) p. 24, note 2: Caspar thinks (p. 256) that the list was originally not a list of bishops, but a list of those men whom the local church considered as bearers of the apostolic tradition and guarantors of the genuineness of the tradition without necessarily being bishops... the difficulty is solved by Lightfoot's theory of a body of presbyter bishops... with a president..." Cf. E. Caspar, Die älteste römische Bischofsliste, in *Schriften der Königsberger Gelehrten Gesellschaft Geisteswissentschafliche Klasse*, 2,4, (Berlin: 1926), p. 222 ff. and p. 247 ff. See also H. Böhmer, Zur altrömischen Bischofsliste, in *ZNW* 7 (1906), p. 333-339. See also A. Lemaire, Les Ministères aux origines de l'Église: Naissance de la triple hiérarchie: évêques, presbytres, diacres, in *LeDiv* 68 (Paris: Éditions du Centurion 1974); ——, L'Église Apostolique et les ministères, in *RDroitCan* 23 (1973), p. 19-41.

themselves, prescinding from the particular prejudices, psychological, sociological or historical predispositions of the particular human bearers of them.
The *genre* of literature to which Diogenes Laertius bears witness will not
acknowledge that ideas develop independently of human bearers of them.
For consistency and development of ideas there must also correspond historically the succession of a διαδοχή of named bearers of those ideas, with an
accompanying account of their personal, human relations with one another.
We might ourselves lament, from a twentieth century point of view, that
Diogenes so poorly connects the ideas with the individual biography and
contemporary history of their human bearer, and descends to the level of
pure anecdote and gossip. Yet in making the attempt, he and his contemporaries remind us of the way in which quite falsely we try to conceive ideas
existing and developing in an ideational vacuum.

Caspar's position and Molland's criticism reflect, I believe, the assumptions of such a historiography made by many other participants in this particular discussion. The critical question for those who claim that διαδοχή
indicates doctrinal continuity, and those who claim that it indicates an authorized chain of successors, is how to translate Hegessipus' statement: διαδοχὴν ἐποιησάμην μέχρις ᾿Ανικήτου (Eusebius, *H.E.* IV, 22,2-3). Those for
διαδοχή as a chain of successors, such as Lightfoot, Turner, Caspar, and
Herzog, wished to translate these words as: "I composed a succession-list as
far as Anicetus." Thus they regarded Hegesippus as producing a list of
names as a model for Irenaeus' list which he was to complete down till the
time of Eleutheros.

Hyldahl, to the contrary, endeavoured to establish the meaning of διαδοχή
as doctrinal succession by denying that the term referred in Hegesippus to
any list of names. At Rome the latter did no more than at Corinth where he
observed that, until Primus' time (μέχρι Πρίμου), orthodox doctrine had prevailed (Eusebius *H.E.* IV, 22, 2). Thus his words are to be translated "I established a succession [of doctrinal orthodoxy] at Rome until Anicetus'
time." Thus he can conclude what his travels have show him. "In each succession (ἐν ἑκάστῃ διαδοχῇ) and in each city (ἐν ἑκάστῃ πόλει) it is the case
that the law is preached with the prophets and the Lord." (IV, 22,3)[144]

In the same way it would also be possible to understand Irenaeus' claim
that: "In this same order (τῇ αὐτῇ τάξει) and by the same succession (τῇ
αὐτῇ διαδοχῇ) the tradition from the apostles in the Church (ἥ ἀπὸ τῶν
ἀποστόλων ἐν τῇ ἐκκλησίᾳ παράδοσις), and the preaching of the truth (καὶ

---

[144] N. Hyldahl, Hegesipps Hypomnemata, in *StTh* XIV (1960), p. 100-103. See also H. von
Campenhausen, Lehrerreihen und Bischofsreihen im 2. Jahrhundert, in *In Memoriam Ernst
Lohmeyer*, Stuttgart 1953, p. 247: "Daher verzichtet sie auf die Datierung und überhaupt auf
jede historische Auswertung und zählt die Apostel nicht etwa selbst schon als das erste Glied
sondern nur den jeweiligen Abstand, in dem die späteren Bischofe als Erben ihrer Lehre in dem
Zusammenhang der διαδοχή erscheinen."

τὸ τῆς ἀληθείας κήρυγμα), have come down to us" (*Adv. Haer.* III, 3,3). Thus the transmission of Order (τῇ αὐτῇ τάξει) and the ἀπὸ τῶν ἀποσ– τόλων... παράδοσις and κήρυγμα can be equated with each other, and in that equation the meaning of τῇ αὐτῇ διαδοχῇ be explicated in terms of a succession of doctrine. Thus Irenaeus in this respect could be held to retain Hegesippus' τῇ ἑκάστῃ διαδοχῇ in a sense parallel with the continued preaching of "the Law, the prophets and the Lord in each city ἐν ἑκάστῃ πόλει."

In the light of the *genre* of literature on διαδοχή to which Diogenes bears witness, any interpretation such as that of Hyldahl, Campenhausen, or Molland that divorces the development of ideas or doctrines from the human bearers of them must be rejected. Hyldahl believed that he had been able to do justice to the objection of Harnack and Zahn that διαδοχή could not mean "list" or "catalogue," but avoided having to explain the word as a textual corruption for διατριβήν.[145] Neither Hegesippus nor Irenaeus would have found such an historiography comprehensible such as is required by Hyldahl's interpretation in which διαδοχή can have reference to disembodied doctrine alone.

Diogenes spoke of a διαδοχή in the singular of a work that describes named philosophers in a relation of succession with each other, in combination with epitomes of what they taught. Such a διαδοχή is not unlike the succession list which Irenaeus gives us, interlaced as the names of Clement and Linus are with incidents from their lives, with in Clement's case a credal synopsis of what he taught on the oneness of the Creator (*Adv. Haer.* III, 3,3 cf. *Succ.* proem. 1, 13-17; 4, 1.). There is an intimate connection in the Greek historiography of ideas between relations between doctrines, and the successions of individual heads of the philosophical schools, who are responsible, each as a as προϊστάμενος τῆς σχολῆς, for their transmission (Diogenes Laertius, *Succ.* 1 proem. 19). Thus a διαδοχή was never a list or catalogue of names *per se*, but as a literary *genre* would include such lists, as exemplified in the work of Diogenes and his predecessors.

We have seen, furthermore, that the emphasis of the author of *El.* on δια– δοχή as *doctrinal* succession is, if anything, more pronounced than that of Irenaeus, with his clear view that you can change your διαδοχή by changing Christian teaching into Greek philosophy in a concealed form, and that such a change, of itself, merits the description συστήσασθαι   διδασκαλεῖον. Nevertheless, *El.*'s community was one of several house-schools, which, like philosophical schools, had a προεστώς, and which, like a Jewish synagogue, also called him a πρεσβύτερος who occupied a πρωτοκαθεδρία. By virtue of his superintendence over the poor-relief, he was also called an ἐπίσκοπος. διαδοχή cannot therefore refer to a doctrinal succession existing in an

---

[145] Hyldahl (1960) p. 101.

ideational vacuum without any reference to human participants in that succession. διαδοχή has a quite specific meaning as a *genre* of literature in which the coherence of a systems of ideas is charted over time, and in which named lists of successors play a role in the description of that coherence. Such was furthermore their role in the house-schools of the author of *El.*, and of Callistus and Zephyrinus.

The author of *El.* does not therefore support by means of the concept of διαδοχή the concept also of monarchical episcopacy. But although the author of *El.* has been credited also with the authorship of the first part of the Liberian List, he does not take his stand upon any list of names which he calls a διαδοχή in his extant writings. Could not Irenaeus, by giving us a list of names, also be marking the development of monarchical bishops from Anicetus' time, as Molland claims, without, granted, claiming in addition that such bishops were in themselves sacramental links in the chain?

In the light of his inclusion of presbyters in Irenaeus' διαδοχή the answer to this question would be decidedly negative. We are "to obey (*obaudire*) those presbyters who are in the Church (*eis qui in ecclesia sunt presbyteris*) who have the succession from the apostles (*his qui successionem habent ab apostolis*)." Far from the guarantee being in the office of a single bishop ordained to the sacramental chain, there clearly can be a plurality of presbyteral as well as episcopal witnesses. In such a situation, one bishop will not need to be deposed and replaced by another if he lapses, since presbyters are part of the διαδοχή too.

Such presbyters "have received the secure charism of truth (*charisma veritatis certum*) together with the succession of the episcopate (*cum episcopatus successione*)." An Irenaean presbyter, like an Hippolytan one, as we have seen, can be concerned about the *episcopatus* or ἐπισκοπή which he possesses, and, we may suppose, be just as anxious to rebut the claims of a potential monarchical bishop like Zephyrinus or Callistus to possess the sole θρόνον ἐπισκοπῆς (*Adv. Haer.* IV, 26,2 cf. *El.* IX, 11,1). Such presbyters can "depart from the original succession (*absistunt a principali successione*)" just as Callistus had done who, as *El.* accordingly said, συνεσήστατο διδασκαλεῖον (*Adv. Haer.* IV, 26,2). But these were not then deposed by monarchical bishops on his named succession lists where they too might have appeared. Rather, "in whatever place they gather" (*quocumque loco colliguntur*), they are held in suspicion (*suspectos habere*), just as Zephyrinus and Callistus, in their house-school (*quocumque loco colliguntur*), were held in suspicion by the author of *El.* They excommunicate themselves, just as we have argued Callistus was regarded by the author of *El.* as having done when he composed his heresy (συστήσασθαι αἵρεσιν) like Marcion.

We thus find Irenaeus supporting our reconstruction of Church Order in the Rome of the late second century, to which *El.* bears witness. It is indeed a Church Order in a fluid state of development, where signs of movements such as those of Zephyrinus and Callistus towards a later monarchical episcopacy can be seen. But as yet there is no fully-fledged monarchical bishop, and no situation into which we can possibly follow Frickel by reading such associated terms as "illegal See" or "schismatic bishop." In consequence, we find the solution to the earlier problem of why a bewildered though not intentionally concealing Eusebius could not name Hippolytus' See.

Although Jerome translates προεστώς as *episcopus*, it is far less specific word than that used for either Beryllus (ἐπίσκοπος), in Eusebius' immediately preceding sentence, or Zephyrinus (ἐπίσκοπος) or Callistus (τὴν ἐπισκοπὴν ἐγχειρίζεται) in the immediate context (VI, 20,2 cf. 21,2). Indeed it is, for the Roman community at least, a far more archaic expression describing the function of Eucharistic presidency, such as the προεστώς of Justin Martyr (*Ap.* 1,65) or the πρεσβύτεροι προϊστάμενοι of Hermas (*Vis.* 2,4). The reference to Hermas is significant for our present discussion since it shows that in the mid-second century at Rome a presbyter could be said to "preside." Thus Eusebius' title for Hippolytus' position reflects a time before the unambiguous emergence of monarchical episcopacy at Rome, as would be the case with the same title for his predecessor, the author of *El.*

Thus at this stage in the development of Church Order at Rome we can follow neither Amore in claiming that Hippolytus must be regarded as a bishop because Eusebius (*H.E.* VI ,20,2) calls him a ἑτέρας που καὶ αὐτὸς προεστὼς ἐκκλησίας and presbyters cannot be said to preside.[146] Nor conversely can we follow Hanssens and claim that he was a presbyter. That office has not yet clearly separated out from that of bishop. πρεσβύτεροι do possess ἐπισκοπή in Irenaeus, Justin Martyr and Hermas, and also in the two latter cases also preside, in an age where, as in Clement *Cor.* the two terms can be used interchangeably. It was this situation that accounts for the bewilderment of Eusebius and Damasus, as we have argued. I appreciate nevertheless that the liturgies given in the *Ap. Trad.* do present problems for such a thesis with which I shall be dealing in my next chapter.

, In conclusion to this section, we shall do well to note that the Liberian List itself bears testimony, in the distinction in dating in its early and later parts, to the shift from the embryonic and developing situation that we have described in the late second century, and full blown monarchical episcopacy. We shall now see how the Liberian List itself provides evidence for a precise dating for the hardening of the concept of episcopal authority in the form that it was recognized by Eusebius and Damasus in the fourth century.

---

[146] A. Amore, La personalità di Ippolito, *Antonianum* 36 (1961), p. 3-28.

As is well established, the list of names in the Liberian List only have realistic dates subsequent to Pontianus (231-235), with whom, according to the
Liberian *Catalogus*, presbyter Hippolytus was to experience martyrdom in
Sardinia. Pontianus is the first name on the list for whom the days of the
commencement and termination of his episcopate is given. Previously each
bishop appears to either commence office or die exactly at the end of a consular year.[147] Now whereas a precisely dated list implies the notion of one
bishop per geographical See, as one bishop as it were must correspond to
one emperor, undated lists do not necessarily carry such an implication. The
period 235-250, issuing in the Novatian schism in Rome and North Africa,
was therefore critical for this development which is marked by this transition
from undated to dated episcopal reigns. This fact has increased significance
in the light of our earlier demonstration of Damasus' need to associate
Hippolytus anachronistically as a Novatian in order to make sense of what in
fact he was some thirty-five years earlier.

Before the lists of bishops were gradually collated with, and then assimilated to, the consular lists by the early-third-century chronographers such as
Julius Africanus, the undated lists, standing on their own, carried a quite different significance to that which they were to later possess. That significance
we have sought to bring out in our account of the concept of διαδοχή in
Hegesippus, Irenaeus, and *El.*, in the light of our reconstruction of the organisation of the Roman Church in the late second century. We have argued,
furthermore, that the community of the author of *El.*, to whose headship
Hippolytus succeeded, was reconciled both to the theology and the claims to
episcopal monarchy of the successors of Callistus (4B 2.2.3.3). The
reconciliation was particularly reflected in Hippolytus' contribution to one
earlier strand in the evolution of the Liberian List (4B 2.2.3.2), and by
further posthumous additions by his community, including the note on the
his death (4B 2.2.4). That note, along with the inclusion of dated episcopal
reigns, reflected the historical process within the Roman community by
means of which the community of the author of *El.* and then Hippolytus
became reconciled, despite the past history of the events recorded in *El.,*
with the Roman monarchical episcopate of the successors of Callistus.

We have argued that the early undated lists were concerned with witnesses to doctrine, in a teaching succession which required a teaching office,
but in which precise dates as such do not matter. It is this state of affairs,
with its assumptions, that is reflected in the first part of the Liberian List
where the names of successors are all that matter. But the desire of the second part of the List to mark the precise dates of each single bishop's episcopate indicates a new interest, namely an interest in the prerogatives of the
monarchical office itself, and not purely in the validity of a teaching succes-

---

[147] Lightfoot (1889-90) 1,I p. 253-258, and 260.

sion. And so our conclusion *prima facie* not to assume that the events of Hippolytus' time be read in the categories associated with the Novatian Presbyter of Damasus' epigram is shown once more to be justified.

The Liberian Chronographer moreover confirmed our argument that to read the Hippolytan events anachronistically in terms of "schism" and "illegal See" is also unjustified. In the Liberian *Catalogus* we read, in the entry for Cornelius, mention of reconciled, Novatian schismatics in the following words:

> In his episcopate Novatus ordained Novatian in the city of Rome, and Nicostratus in Africa, outside the church (*extra ecclesiam*). After this (*hoc facto*), the confessors who had separated from Cornelius (*se separaverunt a Cornelio*), with Maximus the presbyter, returned to the Church (*ad ecclesiam reversi*).

Thus in Cyprianic language (*extram ecclesiam, ad ecclesiam reversi, se separaverunt a Cornelio*) we have, during the episcopate of Cornelius (251-252), a conceptualizing of what it means to be 'schism.' The Chronographer also understood what it was for *confessores qui separaverunt a Cornelio* to be described as *ad ecclesiam reversi*.[148] But he did not choose to describe Hippolytus in Pontianus' entry, separated from Cornelius' only by that of Antheros and Fabius, in such a way. Hippolytus had been hardly the only presbyter at Rome to be exiled to Sardinia, and was thus so mentioned because his leadership rivalled that of Pontianus. That Hippolytus' schism is not so described shows that for the Liberian Chronographer, or his source, such categories that applied in Cornelius' time did not apply in that of Pontianus. It was still possible to have at that time ambiguous presbyters and ambiguous bishops.

Let us summarize, in conclusion, where this chapter has lead us.

PART D. CONCLUSION: ROMAN CHURCH ORDER BEFORE CYPRIAN

In this chapter we have utilized, in broad outline, Lampe's seminal analysis of the Church of Rome in the second century in order to (i) reconstruct the likely background both to the Hippolytan events recorded in *El* IX, 6-13 (Part B), and (ii) unravel the kind of Church Order which probably underlay the bewilderment of Eusebius and Damasus, which caused the former of them to fail to specify a See for Hippolytus' position as προεστώς, and the latter to construct the legend of the Novatian Presbyter (Part A).

We argued that passage of time, and the rapidity of developmental change had, in effect, deprived them of the original conceptualization of Order in the late second and early third century. The events surrounding Cyprian,

---

[148] Ibid. p. 255-256.

Novatian, and Paul of Samosata, which separated Eusebius and Damasus from Hippolytus in the century that lay inbetween, had produced a new phase in the development of Church Order. It was moreover the era in which the so called "Tomb of the Popes" made its appearance in the cemetry which bears Callistus' name, though he, before Pontianus and his successors, was buried *in Calepodio* (Plates 17-20). In a term deployed in the history of science by Thomas Kuhn, a "paradigm shift" had taken place, and an historical account of what it meant to live conceptually within the original, second-century paradigm had been lost (6C 8).

In this chapter we have seen evidence of that paradigm shift from a comparison of Eusebius' description of the Synod condemning Paul of Samosata with the dialogue of Origen and others with Beryllus of Bostra. Eusebius, true to his ideological historical perspective in which all development in Church Order was abolished, tried to turn that dialogue into Synodical proceedings, albeit with a less obvious slight of hand than that which he had used regarding the ghostly Synodical Fathers allegedly present whilst Polycrates of Ephesus wrote to Victor of Rome (6C 8.2). Thus the anachronism of Damasus in his inscription was confirmed, as forming part of a general pattern of later rewriting of history. The very form and expressions of his epigram of Hippolytus as a Novatian Presbyter returning to the catholic faith revealed, as we saw, that he is talking of a past for him barely recoverable (6A 2).

Damasus was taking a paradigm of schism, excommunication, and reconciliation from an age comprehensible to him, from the time after Novatian and Cyprian, and using these to interpret the remembered events and details of the generation before, partially represented in written form in the library at Aelia, that had perplexed Eusebius and Jerome as well. But, paradoxically, his very mistake is in itself a fundamental piece of evidence for the fact that a radical development had taken place in the conceptualization of the threefold Order between the time of Hippolytus and his predecessor, and that of Cyprian. That Damasus is compelled to measure the controversies of Hippolytus' time with the categories of Cyprian's shows that the development at this latter time had not occurred earlier (6B 2.4).

We have shown that we need to be more radical in our reconstruction of Eusebius' account of early Christian history than even that which scholars have so far felt necessary. Damasus' register of legend-construction served him as a means of making comprehensible what was incomprehensible in his written sources. It enabled him to understand the troubles facing the Roman community in the second century which, in view of the information available to him but not to us, he found very bewildering. He thus selected a historical example that he did understand, namely of Novatian, a presbyter in schism, and applied this model of ecclesiastical reality to events of some twenty years previous that he found so incomprehensible. That he had so to act in composing his epigram implies of course a rapid development of episcopal government at Rome between the end of the second century and those of the Novatian schism in 258. We have seen that paradigm shift to be also reflected in what counts as "schism" in the Liberian *Catalogus* itself (4B 2.2.3.2 and 6C 8.3).

We have sought therefore in this chapter to reconstruct the situation that both Eusebius and Damasus found so incomprehensible. We followed Lampe, with certain modifications, in regarding, in the light of literary and archaeological sources, the second century Roman Church as fractionalized into what he called house-churches, but which we gave our grounds for regarding rather as school-communities utilizing private houses. The nomenclature of the Graeco-Roman private house, following Wycherley, we saw also to characterize the philosophical school. Furthermore, the concepts of προεστώς and διαδοχή fitted the school rather than the house model of the community, particularly in the light of the evidence of Schubart, discussed by Bammel, that as a legal concept διαδοχή represented a bid for legal recognition and not a claim to own any particular corporate property (6C 3).

We argued in the light of Clement, *Corinthians*, 44, Hermas, *Vis.* III,9, 7, *Man.* 11, Justin, *1 Apology* I, 61-67. Irenaeus, *Adv. Haer.* IV, 26,2, and Eusebius, *H.E.* V, 28,12, read in the light of our reconstruction with the aid of archeological sources, that each fractionalized congregation of the Roman community was headed by one προεστώς possessing ἐπισκοπή, who as πρωτοκαθεδρίτης occupied a single πρωτοκαθεδρία over such a congregation. Although Eusebius' ideology that nihilated any conception of development made him unaware of the fact, the description of Hippolytus as προεστώς without a geographically defined See, but with a cultural or subcultural congregation, was thus the preservation of a genuine archaism garbled by an anachronistic historiography (6C 8).[149]

We used our reconstruction to interpret *El.* IX, 6-13. The author of *El.* and Callistus were each a προεστώς of two of such house-school congregations, of which the Roman Church was composed. Such congregations were bound loosely into a single community by the exchange of the *frumentum* (Eusebius, *H.E.* V, 24,16) (6C 6), and by a public meeting for general debate about doctrinal error and external poor-relief, in which the foreign secretary entrusted with writing external letters to other Churches on behalf of the community as a whole may have stood out as a figure of a cerain if ambiguous authority. In the claims of Callistus we appear to be at the beginning, perhaps on the basis of the foreign-secretarial office (Hermas, *Vis.* 4, 2-3) of one such πρεσβύτερος or ἐπίσκοπος, of a claim to a single, monarchical

---

149 For definitions of "cultural" and "subcultural" in connection with non-geographical concepts of episcopacy, see Brent (1992) chapters 2 and 3.

jurisdiction over all other congregations. It is the record of the resistance to some such movement that we find in *El.* IX, 6-13 (6C 7.4).

The two combatants seemed to be originally appellants to the same common presbyteral council, and seeking to avoid the same condemnation of that council (IX, 12, 15-16). But the inference that they formally separated in terms of the later understanding of "schism" was unwarranted. There was no report of one group separating from another following the condemnation of a given position. Rather the charges were that those excommunicated by one group are received by the other who are thus making themselves a διδασκαλεῖον as opposed to being made one by their being excommunicated as a group. Only individuals and not communities are the focus of excommunication (6C 7.1-7.2).

The author of *El.*'s quarrel with Callistus was not about his right to jurisdiction over Callistus' group, but rather over Callistus' admission to his jurisdiction of those excommunicated from his own. We saw with reference to the equivalence of συστήσασθαι διδακαλεῖον and συστήσασθαι αἵρεσιν, and with reference also to *El.*'s understanding of διαδοχή, that formal Synodical deposition would have been an anachronism in an age and situation in which excommunication was considered as self-initiated and self-inflicted (6C 7.3). Our comparison of the Beryllus-dialogue with the condemnation of Paul of Samosata reinforced this point. We thus argued the impossibility of regarding the events recorded by *El.* in the light of a situation where the later concepts of schism, involving physical separation and a juridicial, synodical act of assembled bishops, had no purchase. Accordingly we could not support Lampe's view on the emergence of monarchical episcopacy at Rome as early as the pontificate of Victor.

Indeed the true date for that emergence we claimed to have been indicated by the legend of the Novatian Presbyter, and to be therefore from 235 onwards. This was supported by the archaeological evidence in which the schools, located in private houses, became the *tituli* churches with their additional buildings, with burial places clearly set aside for exclusive community use, and no longer also used as purely private houses. It was also supported by the Liberian *Catalogus*. We argued that a key indication of the date of such a development is the appearance of reliable dates for the lengths of individual episcopates. We have seen that the occurrence of these in the Liberian *Catalogus* postdate the author of *El.*'s controversy with Callistus. The idea of apostolic succession in terms of personal possessors of geographically located Sees only hardened into a dogmatic postulate subsequently to Pontianus (231-235). The author of *El.*'s conflict with Callistus may indeed have contributed to the hardening of a conceptual development which in such a form did not antedate it (6C 8.3).

Thus we have seen the real explanation of the perplexity of Eusebius, Jerome, and Damasus about what they had read in their sources, which we discussed Part B. The fact that all three writers had to explain in terms of their own time earlier events that they could not fit into their universe of discourse without considerable perplexity enables us to reach one positive conclusion. If the later conceptualization had existed in and reflected an earlier historical reality, then they would have used it without distortion. That they had to distort the real character of those events shows that the earlier events themselves were unlike those of their own time. Their perplexity is, in other words, a powerful corroboration of the rapid development in Church Order that took place between Victor and Pontianus.

We have been able to corroborate that development by pursuing a variety of lines of inquiry, archaeological as well as literary. It was a development whose conclusion was marked by a proper and definite dating of episcopates only from Pontianus' time. The events of the dispute between the author of *El.* and Callistus are therefore part of a development of a Church Order in state of flux and not yet complete, to which the concepts of "schism," "legal bishop," "antipope" etc. cannot yet be intelligibly applied. The original forms of that flux, and its moving contours we have sought to delineate in Part C.

There is, however, an important objection to our thesis in this chapter. *Ap. Trad.* itself makes the office of bishop quite distinct from that of presbyter, and implies different theological assumptions for each respectively. This objection was perhaps the most cogent part of Lampe's argument that *El.* is in fact a witness to the emergence of monarchical episcopacy from Victor's time. We shall need in our next chapter, therefore, to assess both the evidence of that work for the role of Hippolytus and his congregation in the emerging pattern of Church Order in Rome, North Africa, Alexandria, and Syria in the first decades of the third century.

The picture that emerges will enable us to reassess in turn the relationship between the Roman community of Hippolytus and the North African community of Tertullian, particularly in the light of recent studies regarding whether the latter's Montanism implies schism, and the classical discussion of whether he in fact attacked Callistus. In the process we shall be lead to the question of the Hippolytan authorship of the first part of the Liberian List, and what Hippolytus' experience has to tell us about how concept of apostolic succession or διαδοχή should be understood.

CHAPTER SEVEN

HIPPOLYTUS AND CHURCH ORDER

The Apostolic Tradition, *and the development of monarchical episcopacy*

In the light of what we have established in Chapter 6, the evidence of the ordination liturgies in the *Ap. Trad.* 2-8 cannot in themselves be accepted at
their face value as supporting monarchical bishops in the threefold Order at
Rome in the time of Victor. We have at all events already indicated some of
our arguments regarding the composite character of this document (5A 1.1-
1.2). One question that we must always ask of such documents that emanate
from one congregation in conflict with another in such circumstances is to
what extent such literature reflects an existing social reality rather than creating a new one.

A cynic might observe that when a sectional interest claims adherence to
time-hallowed tradition that they allege their opponents to be flouting, what
in reality they are doing is asserting the new order to which their opponents
are offering resistance. Idealized and partial images of the past thus prove
powerful weapons with which to deconstruct the present. Alternatively a sectional interest, in claiming the support of the tradition, may take on the
claims of its opponents, which it refashions within its own perspectives, in
order to combat the encroachments upon what it believes to be its jurisdiction. We shall have, in the course of this chapter, some specific comments
on this phenomenon in application to the Hippolytan events.

We simply are not able to accept that the purpose of these ordination
liturgies was to reflect existing social reality rather than to create a new one.
Thus we cannot accept them unreservedly as evidence for monarchical
episcopacy at Rome from the time of Victor onwards. Not only is there the
problem of the corrupt state of the textual transmission of *Ap. Trad.* itself,
and the severe problem of resting any hypothesis on any fine and literal
analysis of any particular passage. The ordination liturgies, as we have
already claimed, themselves reveal a conflict of imagery (5A 1.2-1.3). We
shall now develop that claim by showing that conflict of imagery against the
far wider background of a series of developing versions of the composite *Ap.
Trad./ Didasc. Ap./ Ap.Con.*, integrating original extraneous elements
somewhat unsatisfactorily within the structure of their final recension. We
shall see that, from contrasts and parallels with the ordination rites preserved
in the contemporary *Clementines*, the *Ap. Trad.* forms part of the developing

construction and reconstruction of social reality rather than a reflection of a present and unambiguous social and ecclesiastical Order.

Let us begin with how Hippolytus' name, used as we have argued as a cipher for an ecclesiastical tradition (3C 9 and 3D 2-4), marks both in *pseudepigrapha* and *hagiographa* the development of that tradition.

PART A. 'HIPPOLYTUS' AND 'CLEMENT' AS CIPHERS FOR TRADITIONS

In 3D 2 we pointed to the use of διὰ Ἱππολύτου *and* διὰ Κλήμεντος in the *ms.* tradition of the fourth-century *Ap. Con.* to delineate various liturgical traditions. We pointed out there that there could not be any historical value in such attributions regarding the individual authors named, since they were clear additions to the *Didascalia Apostolorum* that did not originally contain the names of apostles, let alone the secondary 'Clement' and 'Hippolytus.' Additionally, the presence of Hippolytus' name itself showed the fabulous tendency witnessed by various later writers to associate Hippolytus quite anachronistically with the apostolic age. Palladius and Cyrillus of Scythopolis, for example, described him as γνωρίμος τῶν ἀποστόλων, and, significantly in view of the *ms.* tradition to which we have drawn attention (3C 9), Leontius of Byzantium grouped him with Clement as a bishop of Rome (Κλήμης καὶ Ἱππόλυτος ἐπίσκοποι Ῥώμης).

Let us now pursue further that comparison.

7A 1. Hippolytus "bishop of Rome" in the Eastern Fathers

Just as therefore the assertion of the role of Clement in both the *Clementines*, and in the work of the Constitutionalist on the *Didascalia* contains an encoded message about mutual recognition of conflicting church traditions in the writers' own times, so indeed we must conclude does the assertion of transmission under the name of Hippolytus. We are fortunate in the case of Clement to have the *Homilies* and the *Recognitions* as well as the *Ap. Con.*, and to have recovered the *Didascalia* incorporated into the latter. As a result we can deduce clearly and in far greater detail the encoded message behind διὰ Κλήμεντος than we can that behind διὰ Ἱππολύτου. But the method of encoding the literary and ecclesiological messages in the pseudonymous form of the one gives us adequate grounds for regarding the encoding process as the same in the case of the other, however much we may be lacking in specific details about the encoded message in this latter case.

At the back of this manuscript tradition of rivalry between the two names, there was a clearly documented attempt to locate Hippolytus in the apostolic age, and to make him a sign of apostolic witness, regardless of true historical chronology. Clement makes his appearance with Hippolytus alongside the apostolic fathers in this list of eastern writers only with Leontius, who is clearly in the *ms.* tradition that associates the two names, as we have seen was the case with *Vat. graec.* 827, *Vat. graec.* 1980, and *Vindobonensis hist. gr.* 7 (3C 10). Now the Eastern Church never acknowledged Hippolytus as anything other than bishop (or archbishop of Rome), as Leontius does in this passage, before the late legend of Portus as his See developed, beginning only with the *Chronicon Paschale* (c. A.D. 630). The failure to acknowledge his See is a Western failure, shrouded in Damasus' legend, which a few writers take up. Gregory of Tours (c. A.D. 577) does so obliquely when he places Hippolytus along with Laurence in the time of Sixtus II and Decius Trajan.[1] But Ado of Vienne (d. A.D. 874), however, records specifically the Damasan tradition.[2]

Thus we see however obscurely that Hippolytus' name at some time in the literary tradition of his works was self-consciously opposed to that of Clement. We have seen that association to prevail, not only over rival claims to be the transmitters of apostolic doctrine in insertions in the *ms.*, but also to reappear in claims about Hippolytus as a contemporary of the apostles. For a further more particular explanation we can only proceed hypothetically, however much we may have established firmly the general proposition that the ascriptions are part of the apparatus of pseudonymity employed by later editors of the *Constitutions*, the *Epitome*, and the *Canones* that bear Hippolytus' name.

We have further emphasized the bearing of the conclusion of Chapters 1-5 on this question, namely that the Statue of an allegorical figure cannot bear the evidential weight for the unity of the *corpus* in one author that was once and is still too often quite unreasonably supposed. Thus the over-hasty conclusion is not to be drawn that because the *Canones* and *Epitome* either bear, as in the former case, or contain, as in the latter, Hippolytus' name, he can be identified as the author of an anonymous work on which they depended. διὰ Ἱππολύτου, like διὰ Κλήμεντος, was inserted after the named apostles and some biographical details were also inserted as part of the device of pseudonymity. We argued in Chapters 1-2 that the Statue with its allegorical figure and Paschal Calendar were to be seen as the artefacts and symbols of a school rather than the personal commemoration of a named individual.

Furthermore, we saw in Chapter 6 clear evidence for characterizing Hippolytus' congregation, along with others in the diverse Roman community in the second century, as a congregation identifiable with a philosophical house-school. In consequence the inscribed Catalogue of works, and other

---

[1] Eustratius of Constantinople (c. A.D. 578), *Adv. Psychopannychitas* 19; Anastasius Sinaita (c. A.D. 680), *Hodegus* 23; John Damscene (c. A.D. 700), *Sacr. Parall.*; Germanus of Constantinople (c. A.D. 720) *Rerum Eccl. Contempl.*; George Hamartolus (c. A.D. 810), *Chron.* 3,134; Oecumenius (c. A.D. 990), *In Apoc. Praef.* all describe Hippolytus as ἐπίσκοπος τῆς Ῥώμης.

[2] "III KAL.FEBR. : Passio Sancti Hippolyti martyris qui Novati schismate aliquantulum deceptus, operante gratia Christi correctus ad charitatem ecclesiae rediit..." *Martyrologium.*

works associated with them, need not be the product of one or even two authors but rather of a school. In Chapter 5 we found that specific literary problems connected with the Hippolytan *corpus*, irresolvable on the hypothesis of either one or two authors, are best resolved by regarding them as community or school productions, by analogy, say, with the problems of the Johannine *corpus* in the New Testament.

For the moment, let us record how, like the name of Clement or John, the specific evidence considered in the chapter has lead us to the conclusion that Hippolytus' name must be regarded as standing as it were for the corporate personality of a school rather than the individual personality of an individual author. Just as διὰ Κλήμεντος served to bind his two letters, the second of which was pseudonymous, into a common *corpus* with the *Homilies* and the *Recognitions*, and the *Epitome* and *Ap. Con.*, so too διὰ 'Ιππολύτου is indicative of a similar process uniting disparate works that bear his name. Now the work of interpolation into the *Didascalia* that created the *Ap. Con.* took place, according to Funk, sometime after A.D. 380.[3] Let us consider in greater detail therefore these connections.

7A 1.1. Clement as Roman bishop: Clementines *and* Ap. Con.

Funk argued that the thread which bound the *Ap. Con.* to the *Clementines* was in fact an Apollinarianism which they shared with the longer recension of the Ignatian correspondence. Theodoret *H.E.* V, 3,38 mentions Apollinarians who returned to the Church, but sought surreptitiously to maintain their former tenets by attributing them to distinguished Church Fathers of the past. Rejecting the charge of Arianism for the author of the *Ap. Con.*, Funk focused upon the use of τάγμα, and the way in which this is used to imply a certain subordinationism of the Son to the Father, implied for example in the phrase τῶν ἄλλων ταγμάτων ποιητήν (*Ap. Con.* VI, 11,2).[4]

Although he does not quote this passage in this connection,[5] the most convincing indication of Apollinarianism would appear to be VI, 26,2: "Some of them are heretical in their impiety (ἑτέρως ἀσεβοῦσι), imagining the Lord to be a mere man (ψιλὸν ἄνθρωπον εἶναι φανταζόμενοι τὸν κύριον), thinking that he consists of soul and body (ἐκ ψυχῆς καὶ σώματος αὐτὸν εἶναι νομίζοντες)." The Chalcedonian argument clearly rejected the notion

---

[3] F.X. Funk, *Die Apostolischen Konstitutionen: Eine litterar- historische Untersuchung*, (Minerva GmbH., Frankfurt/Main 1970) (Rottenberg 1891); G. Strecker, Das Judenchristentum in den Pseudoclementinen, in*TU* 70 (1958 and 1981).

[4] Funk (1891/1970) p. 98-99 p. 105: "Wenn der Interpolator in der letzten der oben angeführten Stellen Gott als τῶν ἄλλων ταγμάτων ποιητὴν bezeichnet, so nimmt er wie auf der Seite der Kreatur so auch auf der göttlichen Seite oder innerhalb der Gottheit τάγματα an. Das war aber apollinaristische Theologie." Cf. also p. 354-355: "... wie ähnlich Apollinaris vormals selbst manche Glieder der Kirche für seiner Lehrer gewonnen hat, und Caspari hält es für das wahrscheinlichste dass diese kirchlichen Apollinaristen es waren, welche Schriften ihres Meisters unter dem Namen von angesehenen katholischen Vätern in Umlauf setzten."

[5] The passages that he discusses are *Ap. Con.* II,26, 6; V,7; VI,7; III,17; VI,18, 26; V,7; VII, 7; VI,11, cf. (1891/1970) p. 98-105 ff.

that the assertion that Christ consisted of a human soul and body (ἐκ ψυχῆς καὶ σώματος) was not necessarily the equivalent of describing him as a mere man (ψιλὸν ἄνθρωπον).[6]

The one work that bears Hippolytus' name in the title, the *Canones Hippolyti*, were probably composed in their present form about the the same time as Funk's dating of the *Ap. Con.* Botte considered that the occupations allowed to baptismal candidates (Canons 10-15), and the embryonic state of monastic organisation revealed in Canon 37, are indicative of a date between A.D. 313 and 400.[7] Bradshaw follows Coquin in further narrowing the date to between A.D. 336 and 340, with reference to the two types of pre-Athanasian fast mentioned in Canons 20 and 22, and the reference in Canon 1 to the "bad death" of "some heretics" i.e. Arius in A.D. 336.[8]

Bradshaw argues further that in the Canons "there is no trace of the doctrinal additions made at Constantinople," though the use of ὁμοούσιος in the original Greek of Canon 1 "would place the work between the councils of Nicaea (325) and Constantinople (381)."[9] But if the *Canones* are not after Constantinople, they appear certainly to oppose some of the Christological presuppositions of the *Ap. Con.* which, if they were Apollinarian, were condemned by that council. In Canon 19, as part of the credal interrogation, the baptizand is asked: "Do you believe in the Holy Spirit, the Paraclete flowing from the Father and the Son?" In *Ap. Con.* VI, 11,2 however, we read of "one God (ἕνα θεὸν), Father of the one Son (ἑνὸς υἱοῦ πατέρα), not more (οὐ πλειόνων), the maker of one Paraclete through Christ and of the other orders (ἑνὸς παρακλήτου διὰ Χριστοῦ, καὶ τῶν ἄλλων ταγμάτων ποιητήν)." The Paraclete clearly is described here as amongst the "other orders (ἄλλων ταγμάτων)" of creation, subordinate to the "one Son... not more (ἑνὸς υἱοῦ... οὐ πλειόνων)." Thus the Father is not in the same relation to the Paraclete as He is to the Son. Rather he is the maker of the Paraclete by means of the Son (ἑνὸς παρακλήτου διὰ Χριστου... ποιητήν).

Whether this passage makes the *Ap. Con.* an Arian, Macedonian, or, as Funk prefers, an Apollinarian work is not relevant to our purpose here. But what is relevant, and what we must now do, is to show that the apostolic tradition that he declares to be διὰ Κλήμεντος is clearly at variance with that which the *Canones* declare to be διὰ Ἱππολύτου.

---

[6] Funk (1891/1970) p. 95 does mention this passage in the context of his rejection of a later date, contemporary with Nestorius, and the marginal note against this passage in *Vindobonensis graec.* 73: κατὰ Νεστοριανῶν.
[7] B. Botte, L'origine des Canons d'Hippolyte, in *Mélanges en l'honneur de Mgr. Michel Andrieu*, (Strasbourg 1956), p. 54-60, cf. P. Bradshaw, The Canons of Hippolyte, in *Alcuin/Grove Liturgical Studies* 50 (1987), p. 6.
[8] R.-G. Coquin, Les Canons d'Hippolyte, in *PO* 31,2 (Paris 1966), p. 54-60, cf. Bradshaw (1987), p. 6-7.
[9] Bradshaw (1987) p. 6.

7A 1.2. *Variances in* Ap. Con. *and* Canones Hippoliti
The tradition of *Ap. Con.* διὰ Κλήμεντος clearly claims:

1. The deaconess, as type of the Holy Spirit, as the *Didascalia* says, must, adds the Constitutionalist, "do or say nothing apart from the deacon, as neither the Paraclete does nor says anything of himself, but glorifying Christ (δοξάζων τὸν Χριστὸν), awaits upon his will (περιμένει τὸ ἐκείνου θέλημα)." (*Ap. Con.* II, 26,6)

2. The Holy Spirit is the "Paraclete which is sent by Christ (τὸν ὑπὸ Χριστοῦ πεμπόμενον) and by him taught and preaching him (καὶ ὑπ ἐκείνου διδασκόμενον καὶ ἐκεῖνον κηρύττον)." (*Ap. Con.* III, 17,4)

3. God is not simply "the God and Father of Christ your only-begotten Son (ὁ θεὸς καὶ πατὴρ τοῦ Χριστοῦ σου καὶ μονογενοῦς υἱοῦ σου)," but "the God who is Lord of the Paraclete and of the universe (ὁ θεὸς τοῦ παρακλήτου καὶ τῶν ὅλων κύριος." (*Ap. Con.* VIII, 6,11)

In 2 we find again the tendency as with VI, 11, 2 to make the Holy Spirit part of the created order of things apart from the Father and the Son, of as it were a different τάγμα again even to that which exists between the Father and the Son. In 1 and 2 there is a subordination of the Paraclete to Christ, who not only is sent (πεμπόμενον) but also taught (διδασκόμενον) by him (2), just like the deaconess, subservient not to the bishop but to the deacon (1).

The tradition διὰ Κλήμεντος is thus clearly, in such tagmatic subordinationism, at variance with the tradition διὰ ʿΙππολύτου, which makes claims about "the Holy Spirit, the Paraclete flowing from the Father and the Son." (Canon 19) Furthermore, such subordinationism is contrary to the affirmation διὰ ʿΙππολύτου that the meaning of Christ's place in "the Trinity, equal and perfect in honour... equal in glory" is that "the Word, the Son of God... is also the creator of every creature." (Canon 1) Such a claim negates any view of Christ as a τάγμα comparable with other albeit lower ranks in a tagmatic order of existence.

Thus we see that conflicting traditions διὰ Κλήμεντος and διὰ ʿΙππολύτου are represented under these names around A.D. 380. Those traditions concern the very Christological issues to be debated at Constantinople and beyond, and were to experience a continued development in the light of the conflict around these issues. In these events, and in the device of apostolic pseudonymity, combined with the rival claims to sub-apostolic transmission, we see the historical setting for the origins of these *mss.* in later, pseudepigraphic patristic allusions to the figure of Hippolytus. The East is not impressed with the name of Clement, however much Clement's name and presence in the *Homilies* and *Recognitions* may have originally represented a confluence rather than a conflict of traditions, as we shall see from Photius' disparagement of that document as tainted with Arianism. The Eastern Fathers prefer the title of "bishop of Rome," which, as we have seen, only partially expresses his situation in the second century Roman Church, rather than the legend of the Novatian presbyter, which threatens to distort any historical account of that situation irrecoverably. Let us now see some post-Apollinarian appearances of the two traditions in conflict.

7A 1.3. *Post Apollinarian developments of the two traditions*

There is of course a logic of a kind in such a literary process of pseudonymous expression of ideas in conflict, though not one that would appeal to a more positivistic practitioner of a historical and critical approach to the study of the development of theological ideas. The Apollinarian denial of Christ as a mere man, a ψιλὸν ἄνθρωπον because he consisted of a human soul and body ἐκ ψυχῆς καὶ σώματος, and not the divine λόγος in a human, soulless body, may not have appealed finally to Clement's Church, in terms of the Tome of Leo. Certainly the work of Hippolytus "archbishop of Rome," the *Contra Noetum*, was to be found with such a primatial title, branded as heretical by the Monophysites who were responsible for the anti-Chalcedonian collection, *ms. Vat. Graec.* 1431.[10] But the device of pseudonymity is unsatisfactory to convey historical truth precisely because its very form encourages it to develop purely as a literary form quite apart from, and beyond the control of, the ideas that it was originally intended to convey.

The sixth century was at all events to see a pseudonymous work attributed to Hippolytus himself and directed against monothelete doctrines. The dossier of Theodosius of Gangra contained a purported text of Hippolytus, the *Contra Beronem*, transcribed by Anastasius Apocrisarius, on the *naturas, ita etiam et duas voluntates ac duas operationes*. Simonetti has argued for the spurious character of this work on the grounds that the alleged eight extracts from Hippolytus' work are too coherent to be extracts, and contain an allusion to the punishment of losing tongue and hand meted out to Anastasius Apocrisarius and Maximus Anastasius. His conclusion is that the purpose of the pseudepigraphy was to "introduce an illustrious doctor of the past to taunt the fictitious Berone with such confusion and altercations as a consequence of his identification of the divine and human operation in Christ."[11] Thus we see in a specifically Eastern context the ascription of Hippolytan authorship prefiguring in Christological debate about orthodoxy.

The monothelete controversy was not a specific East-West controversy, as is shown by pope Honorius' initial support of patriarch Sergius, and by the emperor Constans II's renunciation of his predecessor Heraclius. It was however Photius (died A.D. 891) who both emphasized divisions between East

---

[10] E. Schwartz, Codex Vaticanus Graecus 1431: Eine antichalkedonische Sammlung aus der Zeit Kaiser Zenos, in *ABAW* Philos. und hist. Klasse 32, 6 (München: 1927). See also 4A 3.1.3 ff.

[11] M. Simonetti, Un falso Ippolito nella polemica monotelita, in *Vetera Christianorum* 24, (1987), p. 113-146. His original words were "In questo senso l'atteggiamento di CB, che introduce un illustre dottore del passato a rinfacciare al fittizio Berone tale confusione e alterazione come conseguenza dell' identificare l'operazione divina e umana di Cristo..." p. 145.

and West, and who specifically mentions that the title of *Ap. Con.* was δια–
ταγαὶ τῶν ἀποστόλων διὰ Κλήμεντος but that what was delivered διὰ
Κλήμεντος had been corrupted with Arianism. Thus there appears in Photius
a distrust of that tradition. There was therefore a hidden polemical purpose,
however much obscured by the literary device of pseudonymity, that pro-
gresses under the influence of its own, provocatively imaginative, fabrications. We have seen that purpose in claims by various *mss.* that assign to
sections and whole works the title: διὰ ʽΙππολύτου in self-conscious opposition to διὰ Κλήμεντος and *vice versa.* We also see that polemical purpose
reflected in consequence in the separate uses of, and criticisms of, works
bearing their names independently of intentional contrasts, as in the case of
the *Contra Beronem,* and Photius' accusations of Arianism.

7A 1.4. *In conclusion:* Ap. Trad. *and dynamic development*

We have thus established that the text of the *Egyptian Church Order,* identified by Connolly and Schwartz with the ἀποστολικὴ παράδοσις and the περὶ
χαρισμάτων of the Statue, forms part of a pseudonymous *corpus* of literature
directly comparable in its continuous reworking and pseudonymous
development with the *Clementines.* Although it might be still possible to
argue with some plausibility that this identification is correct, it seems hardly
surprising, in view of the polemical interests of whatever kind that have
formed the further development of Church Order literature around
Hippolytus' name, that the *ms* tradition should be so corrupt, and that at the
end of the day we should be left with at best Botte's important *essai de
reconstitution,* with its parallels set out between the Latin, the Syriac, the
Aethiopic, the Arabic, and the Constitutionalist's Greek.[12] The original text
in the Hippolytan series, let us call it the *Ap. Trad.,* being a Church Order
document and not a letter like Clement, *Corinthians,* was itself as unlikely to
remain untouched and "unreformed," in the course of its transmission, any
more than the *Epitome,* the *Ap. Con.* and the *Canones* to which it gave rise.

Let us now look at some of the textual disturbances and reformations

7A 2. *The composite character of* Ap. Trad.

In connection with the claim that Hippolytus was what could later be called a
schismatic or even an anti-pope, we saw that the problem was raised of
where Hippolytus got his consecrators to enable him to set up as the
alternative bishop to Callistus. It led Frickel in particular to search the text of
El. IX, 12-13 1 for some allusion to letters to other Churches in search of
three co-consecrators. Dix, on the other hand, regarded the *Ap. Trad.* as
having been composed before the break in which presumably its provisions

---

12 B. Botte, La Tradition apostolique de saint Hipplyte. Essai de reconstitution, in
Liturgiewissenschaftliche Quellen und Forschungen, 39 (Aschendorffsche Verlagsbuchhandlung: Munster: 1963).

for co-consecrators were in some way relaxed. We have already given our reasons for regarding such problems as arising from an anachronistic misunderstanding of the state of development of the Roman community at the close of the second century. Let us now analyse in greater detail how the text of *Ap. Trad.* itself is evidence for our account of the Hippolytan events as we interpreted them in 6C 7.4-7.5.

7A 2.1. *The election of the bishop in* Ap. Trad. 2

In *Ap. Trad.* 2 we find that the bishop is elected by all the people (*electus ab omni populo* (L; S(AE)/ ὑπὸ παντὸς τοῦ λαοῦ ἐκλελεγμένον (*Epitome*)). The people assemble on Sunday, together with the presbyterate (συνελθὼν ὁ λαὸς ἅμα τῷ πρεσβυτερίῳ (*Epitome*, L)), or the presbyters and deacons (S(AE)). All consent (*consentientibus omnibus* (L)) or all the bishops consent (*episcopis omnibus consentientibus* (S(AE)), and place their hands over or on him (*inponant/ imposuerunt manus super eum* (L, S(AE)). Ratcliff argued with reference to parallel passages in the various versions of the *Canons* or *Statutes of the Apostles* that the choice of the bishop *ab omni populo* or ὑπὸ παντὸς τοῦ λαοῦ was in fact ἐκ τοῦ λαοῦ because of the Syriac word *men*, the Aethiopic *'em*, the Sahidic *ebol hem*, or the Arabic *min*. In consequence, Ratcliiff wished to argue that, in the original version of this ordination rite, the bishop was chosen from the people since presbyters and deacons were ordained to their respective offices for life and without any principle of progression.[13]

Ratcliff, more questionably in my view, for a further part of his discussion relied on the ability of *Epit.* III, 6[14] to represent some feature at least of the original rite. He rightly concludes from the words of the prayer in *Ap. Trad.* 3 *cordis cognitor* (L) or καρδιογνῶστα πάντων (*Epit.* IV, 4) and *dare sortes secundum praeceptum* (L) or διδόναι κλήρους κατὰ τὸ πρόσταγμά σου (*Epit.* IV, 4) a reference to *Acts* 1, 23-26. But it seems implausible to suggest that such an early form of *porrectio instrumentorum* such as the placing of the Gospel Codex on the head of a bishop being ordained (τῶν δὲ διακόνων τὰ θεῖα εὐαγγέλια ἐπὶ τῆς τοῦ χειροτονουμένου κεφαλῆς) has any reference to a situation pertaining in the second century.

This ceremony would appear to be later than even the consecration by three other bishops also mentioned (εἰς τῶν πρώτων ἐπισκόπων ἅμα καὶ

---

[13] E.C. Ratcliff, "Apostolic Tradition": Questions Concerning the Appointment of the Bishop, in *Liturgical Studies,* Ed. Couratin A.H. and Tripp D.H., (London: S.P.C.K. 1976), p. 156- 157, 159. See also J.V. Bartlet, The Ordination Prayers in the Ancient Church Orders, in *JThS* 17 (1916), p. 248-256; W.H. Frere, Early Ordination Services, in *JThS* 16 (1915), p. 323-369; P.M. Gy, La théolgie des prières anciennes pour l' ordination des évêques et des prêtres, in *RSPhTh* 58 (1974), p. 599-617; G. Kretschmar, Die Ordination im frühen Christentum, in *FZPhTh* 22 (1975), p. 35-69.

[14] The full text reads: καὶ σιωπῆς γενομένης εἰς τῶν πρώτων ἐπισκόπων ἅμα καὶ δυσὶν ἑτέροις πλησίον τοῦ θυσιαστηρίου ἐστώς, τῶν λοιπῶν ἐπισκόπων καὶ πρεσβυτέρων σιωπῇ προσευχομένων, τῶν δὲ διακόνων τὰ θεῖα εὐαγγέλια ἐπὶ τῆς τοῦ χειροτονουμένου κεφαλῆς ἀνεπτυγμένα κατεχόντων, λεγέτω πρὸς θεόν...

δυσὶν ἑτέροις), which itself reflects the compromize at Nicaea (A.D. 325) between the Donatist Numidian position of the requirement of twelve bishops in a province and their opponents.[15] Such features of the Epitomist's account at this point, along with the ecclesiastical furniture of a later age by which the consecrating bishop stands (πλησίον τοῦ θυσιαστηρίου ἑστώς), does not give much support to Ratcliff's thesis about an early rite of what he calls "evangeliomancy."[16]

But there is another feature of Ratcliff's account which may reflect a more ancient tradition, which we must now consider.

7A 2.1.1. *The imposition of hands in the bishop's ordination*

His original use of his claim to evangeliomancy was to show how, by analogy with the appointment of Matthias in *Acts* 1, 23-26 with lots, "the appointment of a bishop did not demand, as of necessity, the active assistance or even presence of other bishops." In consequence "the presbyters could conduct the proceedings."[17] Thus the election of the bishop as a layman directly out of the congregation could be turned into a consecration by their act of evangeliomancy alone, without imposition of hands. From Ratcliff's argument as it stands, however, it seems hard to see why only the presbyters could perform such an act of evangeliomancy. *Acts* 6, 6 after all, if read strictly grammatically, implies that the gathered Church, the πλῆθος, not only elected the deacons, on apostolic instructions, and "placed them in the presence of the apostles (οὓς ἔστησαν ἐνώπιον τῶν ἀποστόλων)," but also, the selfsame laity themselves, "having prayed (προσευξάμενοι), laid their hands upon them (ἐπέθηκαν αὐτοῖς τὰς χεῖρας)."

This last example perhaps shows us that the imposition of hands probably was simply omitted as an oversight of the Epitomist which he would have assumed anyway, rather than reflect a time when hands were only laid upon deacons, and bishops were ordained in self-conscious imitation of *Acts* 1, 23-26. The imposition of hands became so quickly universal that it seems difficult to suppose a period of time into which this rite could fit, between the emergence of single bishops on the one hand, and its adoption on the other. But undoubtedly the argument that the laity would perform this imposition of hands might have been argued to derive some support from the Verona Latin. In *Ap. Trad.* 2, after all, *Consententibus omnibus, inponant super eum manus* could refer not simply to the previously mentioned *qui praesentibus fuerint episcopi,* but also to the ***populus** una cum praesbyterio.* In consequence we

---

15 Cyprian, *Ep.* 67, 4. See also W.C.H. Frend, *The Donatist Church: A Movement of Protest in Roman North Africa*, (Clarendon Press: Oxford 1952/1985), p. 12.
16 Ratcliff (1976) p. 158.
17 Ibid. p. 159, cf. J. Coppens, L'imposition des mains et les rites connexes dans le Noveau Testament et dans l'Eglise ancienne, *Études de théologie positive*, (Paris: Wetteren 1925), cf. K. Küppers, Die literarisch-theologische Einheit von Eucharistiegebet und Bischofsweihegebet bei Hippolyt, in *ALw* 29 (1987), p. 19-30.

could argue that the text was originally, like that of *Acts* for the deacons, a record of ordination by imposition of hands of the *populus* or πλῆθος, with mention of bishops and presbytery only introduced later. Such would be the process which continues with the additions of S(AE) *episcopis omnibus consentientibus, **qui** imposuerunt manus* ... It should be remembered that *Didache* 15,1 cited the χειροτονία of ἐπίσκοποι and διάκονοι as the act of the people, where to translate χειροτονήσατε as "elect" would define an ambiguity equally as tightly and equally with lack of justification as to translate it "ordain."

Given therefore the presence of an explicit or at least an implicit imposition of hands in the text, let us now ask whether, despite *Acts* and the *Didache*, and by the time of one version of the dynamic development of the collection of parallel documents that we call the *Ap. Trad.*, this act would have become a clerical function of the presbyterate.

7A 2.1.2. The presbyterate and episcopal ordination

Bradshaw sought to develop Ratcliff's analysis in a way that avoids dependence on the *Epitome* in support of evangeliomancy, and which seeks to unravel a suppressed presbyteral rather than lay function in the layers of traditional material. For evidence he focuses on the silence of the presbyters, not only in the *Epitome*, but also in all versions of the *Ap. Trad.* In *Epit.* III, 6 the expression σιωπῆς γενομένης glosses favourably some strange textual variants over *Ap. Trad.* 2, where L reads *praesbyterium adstet quiescens*, and S(AE) simply *presbyteri stabunt.* The *Canones Hippolyti* have been shown to be composed between A.D. 336 and A.D. 340, in accordance with the arguments that I have reproduced above. Thus its version of the presbyteral silence will be important since it is earlier than the *Ap. Con.* and indeed the Verona Latin itself. Here in the parallel passage we read that the people "are to choose one of the bishops and presbyters..."[18]

Now Bradshaw argues that such variants reveal the transmission of the words regarding this presbyteral silence to be clearly corrupt, indicated by the extensive re-editing. Clearly the *Canones*, in speaking of both bishops and presbyters, reveal interpolation and re-editing the most clearly, since the consecrator could only have been from one group, and after the emergence of monarchical bishops or even single bishops no one would have inserted presbyters as a group from which a consecrator could be drawn. The obvious conclusion for Bradshaw is that the presbyterate originally were the group who consecrated the people's chosen candidate. Hence the *episcopis omnibus consentientibus qui imposuerunt manus* (S(AE))were not originally laymen, as we might conjecturally reconstruct from L, on the analogy with *Acts* 6,6, but indeed ordained presbyters, who had in addition to an originally purely

---

18 Bradshaw (1987) p. 12.

presbyteral rite to be ordered to remain silent in order to allow future monarchical bishops to exercize their new prerogatives.[19]

Such a reconstruction would undoubtedly also explain another critical textual alteration, namely the way in which *Ap. Trad.* 7 gives the following instruction to the bishop in the ordination of a presbyter: *dicat secundum ea q(uae) praedicta sunt* (L), (*oret super eum secundum modum quem* (S(AE)), *sicut praediximus super episcopum*. But when the actual prayer is then given, it is different from that used for a bishop. We can explain this, despite the somewhat contrived alternative of Turner and Dix, in terms of a presbyteral rite overlaying an episcopal one. Thus too we can explain a specifically historical as opposed to literary and textual problem, namely where Hippolytus found his consecrators.[20] As Bradshaw points out, "the first evidence we have for the participation of other bishops in their ordination comes from Cyprian in the third century."[21]

Thus we find that Ratcliff and Bradshaw have, in their literary and textual studies, illuminated the state of affairs that we argued in Chapter 6 to be reflected in *El.* and other literary and archaeological sources regarding the internal organisation of the Church of Rome at the end of the second century. Our discussion so far in this chapter establishes that the *Ap. Trad.* cannot be used as a counter-example to our thesis that monarchical episcopacy had not developed at Rome by the time of Victor. We see here that the very inability to fit the historical data presented by *El.* into a Cyprianic scheme of Church Order, with its concepts of schism and anti-popes recognized by due synodical process, whether within or between dioceses, also applies to the data presented by the *Ap. Trad.* and its various versions and forms. Bradshaw's correction of post-Cyprianic interpolations and interpretative recasting of the text in the light of the facts that the participation of bishops in consecrations is not witnessed before Cyprian confirms our account (Chapter 6 Part A) of why Damasus had to create the legend of Hippolytus as the Novatian presbyter.

But in the light of our specifically historical reconstruction of the Roman congregations with their προεστώς exercising ἐπισκοπή and occupying the πρωτοκαθεδρία of their individual congregation, we can give some historical substance and further definition to Ratcliff and Bradshaw's textual and literary reconstruction of the role of the Roman presbyterate. As we saw in

---

19 P.F. Bradshaw, The participation of other bishops in the ordination of a bishop in the *Apostolic Tradition* of Hippolytus," in *StudPatr* 18, 2: Critica, Classica, Ascetica, Liturgica, (Ed.) E. A. Livingstone, (Peeters Press: Leuven 1989), p. 335-338. See also ——, Ordination, in *Essays on Hippolytus*, (Ed. G.J. Cuming) Grove Liturgical Study 19, (Grove: Bramcote 1978), p. 34-36. Cf. J. Lécuyer, Episcopat et Presbyterat dans les écrits d' Hippolyte de Rome, in *RecSciRel* 41 (1953), p. 30-50 and K. Richter, Zum Ritus der Bischofsordination in der „Apostolischen Überlieferung" Hippolyts von Rom, in *ALw* 17 (1975), p. 7-51.
20 C.H. Turner, The Ordination Prayer for a Presbyter in the Church Order of Hippolytus, in *JThS* 16 1915, p. 542-547.
21 Bradshaw (1989) p. 337.

Chapter 6, in the light both of literary and archaeological evidence, there is no need to assume the existence of one large congregation as the focus of Hippolytus' rites of ordination. Thus there is no reason to regard the bishops present (*episcopis omnibus consentientibus, qui imposuerunt manus*) as presbyters in either a later or earlier sense.

Such πρεσβύτεροι–ἐπίσκοποι προϊστάμενοι do not come from distant dioceses but from other congregations with whom the congregation in question exchanges the *frumentum*. They form a body which meets in a way that we are not able to specify precisely other than that they had debates on questions of orthodoxy between themselves in some kind of forum that was otherwise concerned with the sending of charitable relief to external churches. That forum was, moreover, in some way connected with the "foreign secretary" who wrote, like Clement in *Hermas* (6A 5 6), to the heads of foreign churches in the name of all the congregations with a ministry "committed" to him (ἐκείνῳ γὰρ ἐπιτέτραπται). Lampe was uncertain whether all πρεβύτεροι at Rome exercized ἐπισκοπή, like Justin's προεστώς, and could preside or only some of them (6C 7.4).

Thus we witness also in the *Ap. Trad.* a fluid situation. Clearly πρεσβύτεροι who preside, who have a role in the consecration of other πρεσβύτεροι–προϊστάμενοι, and who exercize the poor-relief ministry of ἐπισκοπή are now being called *episcopi* in contrast to *presbyteri*. Only a presbyter presiding over a congregation could now ordain, albeit assisted by other presbyters. The two *different* prayers of consecration bear witness to the fact of this transition, just as the fact of the contradictory rubric commanding identical prayers establishes how new that precise distinction was. We saw that Irenaeus, similarly, bore witness to the interchangeability of the term ἐπίσκοπος and πρεσβύτερος and thus could be used in support of our reconstruction.

At all events, our reconstruction, in Chapter 6, in application to the fruits of literary analysis of the ordination rites of the *Ap. Trad.*, has taken us beyond the picture of a shadowy presbyterate with no really definable functions. To establish that an amorphous collection of presbyters could celebrate the Eucharist and ordain really tells us something about how in fact such a 'presbyterian' system functioned. Moreover, since, given some clearly observable facts of human nature, it would have been unworkable without some minimum norms of deference within the group that were to be maximized and defined in course of time, there must have emerged some such rules like those for the silence of the presbyters that we have described.

But let us now pursue further the different prayers in order that we can establish further the witness of *Ap. Trad.* to the development of Church Order which was to lead to, but not yet give us, the kind of episcopal monarchy of the age of Cyprian.

7A 2.2. *Presbyteral and episcopal Orders:* Ap. Trad. *7*

Segelberg endeavoured to analyse systematically the ordination prayers in order to determine the various layers of their development. His principle appears to have been a purely literary one. Direct biblical quotations are not very frequent in early liturgical texts, and, therefore, where they occur, they are indicative of the latest stratum. Words referring to the act of ordination itself are considered prior to comments upon the act by means of subordinate clauses which are in consequence considered to be later accretions. Texts with Old Testament allusions become indicative of the earliest stratum, those with direct quotations from the New Testament of the later.[22]

I am unhappy with the purely literary and *a-priori* character of such criteria, which are left unrooted in any historical situation identified by means of any strictly historical examination. I therefore propose, in this section, to examine the conflicting images used in the episcopal and presbyteral prayer, and then, in the following section, to endeavour to locate these images in genuinely historical situations of conflict. Let us begin with the prayer for the ordination of a presbyter which is directed to be as for the bishop but which curiously is not so.

7A 2.2.1. *Episcopal ordination in* Ap. Trad. *7*

In *Ap. Trad.* 7 the prayer for the presbyter to be ordained is that God is:

... to impart to him (*inpartire* (L), *impertire ei* (E), ἔμπλησον αὐτὸν (*Epit.*)) the Spirit of grace and council of the presbyterate/ of a presbyter (*spiritum gratiae et consilium praesbyterii* (E)/ *praesbyteris* (L), πνεῦμα χάριτος καὶ συμβουλίας (*Epit.*)) that he might assist (*adiubet* (L), *sustineat* (E), τοῦ ἀντιλαμβάνεσθαι (*Epit.*)) your people with a pure heart, just as you regarded the people of your choice and you commanded Moses that he should choose presbyters (*ut elegeret praesbyteros,* αἱρήσασθαι πρεσβυτέρους *(Epit.)*) whom you fill/ filled (*replesti* (L)/ *replevisti* (E), οὓς ἐνέπλησας (*Epit.*)) with your Spirit which you gave to your slave and servant Moses.

Now this is not a direct quotation from the Old Testament but an allusion to an Old Testatment passage, which is one criterion, according to Segelberg, of its being a very early stratum of the rite. The Old Testament passage in question is *Numbers* 11,14-17. According to this passage, Moses cannot cope with his role as ruler over Israel with all their demands. So, following the LXX version, God instructs Moses:

Gather together for me (συνάγαγέ μοι) seventy men from the elders (ἀπὸ τῶν πρεσβυτέρων) of Israel, whom you see (οὓς αὐτός σοι εἶδες) that these are (ὅτι οὗτοι εἰσιν) elders of the people and their scribes (πρεσβύτεροι τοῦ λαοῦ καὶ γραμματεῖς αὐτῶν). And you will lead them to the Tent of Witness, and they will stand (στήσονται) there with you. And I will descend and speak there with

---

22 E. Segelberg, The Ordination Prayers in Hippolytus, in *StudPatr* 13 (1975), p. 397-408. Cf. Richter (1975) p. 11-29 and Lécuyer (1953) p. 31-45. Cf, also E. Lohse, *Die Ordination im Spätjudentum und im Neuen Testament.* (Göttingen: Vandenhoeck & Ruprecht 1951).

you, and I will take (ἀφελῶ) from the Spirit that is on you (ἀπὸ τοῦ πνεύματος τοῦ ἐπὶ σοὶ) and I will place it upon them (ἐπιθήσω ἐπ' αὐτῶν). And they shall give aid (συναντιλήψονται) with you against the rush of the people and you shall not bear them alone.

Thus the elders (πρεσβύτεροι τοῦ λαοῦ) are a body, in the Old Testament case, a good symbolic seventy in number, selected from other elders or elder men (ἀπὸ τῶν πρεσβυτέρων). They are, in the words of the Aethiopic version of the *Ap. Trad.*, a presbyterate (*presbyterium*), bound together not so much by the Holy Spirit, as by τὸ πνεῦμα χάριτος καὶ συμβουλίας which God gave to Moses. That Spirit was divisible (ἀφελῶ ἀπὸ τοῦ πνεύματος τοῦ ἐπὶ σοὶ), and a portion given to each presbyter in order "to give aid" (τοῦ ἀντιλαμβάνεσθαι/ συναντιλήψονται). The presbyters "will stand" (στήσονται) with Moses just as the deacons "were stood (ἔστησαν)" before the apostles in *Acts* 6,6, and God "places the Spirit (ἐπιθήσω)" upon them just like the bishop "places his hands (*inponat manum*)" on the ordinands in *Ap. Trad.* 7.

There is a problem with regarding this prayer as developed later in order accommodate the emergence of the presbyterate as distinct from the episcopate, as otherwise the instruction to use the same prayer as for the bishop apparently lead Segelberg to believe.[23] The prayer itself, with a small shift of interpretation, and no verbal modification, could have provided a suitable form of consecration for a bishop, and thus itself have been the original prayer intended to be used both for presbyters and for bishops. The imagery is far better suited to the justification of a dependent presbyterate rather than one which is independent.

The presbytery has a head who is the antitype of Moses, whose Spirit is indeed the Spirit of Moses divided amongst individual participants in the presbyteral college who are only therefore individual presbyters by virtue of their participation in a whole whose unity is guaranteed by an anti-type of Moses. Moses' Spirit needed only be given to a bishop whole, while to a presbyter only in part, and the prayer in all versions is consistent with either kind of ordination. If a bishop is being ordained, then he receives the whole *spiritum gratiae et consilii* which is nevertheless the same *spiritum gratiae et consilium presbyteri* of which a presbyter receives only a part. If he is a bishop, like Moses, the Spirit will enable him *ut elegeret praesbyteros quos reples de spiritu tuo*. If he is a presbyter, he will be reminded of, and declared to be, a recipient of the act of Moses' antitype.

As we adumbrated in 5A 1.2, there is a fundamental conflict between the presbyteral and Mosaic imagery of *Ap. Trad.* 7 and the sacerdotal and Aaronic imagery of *Ap. Trad.* 3. It is to a more precise and detailed delineation of that conflict that we can now turn.

---

[23] Ibid. p. 402-404.

7A 2.2.2. *Episcopal ordination in* Ap. Trad. *3*

The major conflict of imagery between this and the prayer for the ordination of a bishop in *Ap. Trad.* 3 is that the bishop has become, not the antitype of Moses, but the antitype of Aaron. The theme of leadership such as would also be applicable to Moses, is continued in this prayer, and reveals the priority of the presbyteral prayer by that continuance. The Spirit that is on the bishop, like that of Moses, was a "Spirit of leadership" (*principalis spiritus* (L), δύναμιν τοῦ ἡγεμονικοῦ πνεύματος (*Epit.*)) which God is asked to "pour forth" (*effunde* (L), ἐπίχεε (*Epit.*)). But the principle image of the bishop's office is sacerdotal as can be seen in the following clauses:

1. God is he who "predestined from the beginning (ὁ προορίσας τε ἀπ' ἀρχῆς) from Abraham a just race (γένος δίκαιον), appointing rulers and priests (ἄρχοντας τε καὶ ἱερεῖς καταστήσας)."

2. "Not having left (τὸ τε ἁγίασμα σου μὴ καταλιπῶν ἀλειτούργητον) your sanctuary without a minister..."

3. "To exercize the high-priestly office for you (ἀρχιερατεύειν σοι) blamelessly (ἀμέμπτως), ministering night and day (λειτουργοῦντα νυκτὸς καὶ ἡμέρας)."

4. "Incessantly to propitiate your face (ἀδιαλείπτως τε ἱλάσκεσθαι τῷ προσώπῳ σου) and to offer to you the gifts of your holy Church (καὶ προσφέρειν σοι τὰ δῶρα τῆς ἁγίας σου ἐκκλησίας)."

5. "By the high priestly Spirit (τῷ πνεύματι τῷ ἀρχιερατικῷ) to have authority to forgive sins (ἔχειν ἐξουσίαν ἀφιέναι ἁμαρτίας) according to your command (κατὰ τὴν ἐντολήν σου)."

Clearly this prayer was not, like the allegedly 'presbyteral' one, able to be said for a presbyter as well as a bishop, and so was not the prayer to which the instructions *sicut praediximus super episcopum* referred. Thus, contrary to Segelberg's assignment of it to the earliest strata of the rites, it clearly is a secondary development of that "presbyteral" prayer, and thus we have falsified his criterion of an Old Testament allusion as determining the earliest strata.[24] The theme of Moses as the ἄρχων, implicit in the 'presbyteral' prayer and explicit in *Exodus* 2,16 ("Who appointed (κατέστησεν) you ruler and judge (ἄρχοντα καὶ δικαστὴν) over us?") is maintained in 1. But the

---

[24] Ibid. p. 400. See also A. Rose, La prière de consécration pour l' ordination épiscopale, in *Au service de la parole de Dieu. Mélanges offerts à Msgr. A.-M. Charue*, (Gembloux 1969), p. 129-145; W.L. Rordorf, L' Ordination de l' évêque selon la Tradition apostolique d' Hippolyte de Rome, in *QLP* 55 (1974), p. 137-150; C.-J.P. Oliveira, Signification sacerdotale du Ministère de l' Evêque dans la Tradition Apostolique d' Hippolyte de Rome, in *FZPhTh* 25 (1978), p. 398-427; A. Jilek, Bischof und Presbyterium. Zur Beziehung zwischen Episkopat und Presbyterat im Lichte der Traditio Apostolica Hippolyts, in *ZKTh* 106 (1984), p. 321-326; J.E. Stam., *Episcopacy in the Apostolic Tradition of Hippolytus*, Basel 1969 (ThDuss 3); ——, Charismatic Theology in the "Apostolic Tradition" of Hippolytus, in *Current Issues in Biblical and Patristic Interpretation. Studies in honour of Merill C. Tenney presented by his former students,* Ed. G.F. Hawthorn, (Grand Rapids 1975), p. 267-276; R. Zollitsche, Amt und Funktion des Priesters: Eine Untersuchung zum Ursprung und zur Gestalt des Presbyterats in den ersten zwei Jahrhunderten, in *F.ThSt* 96, (Freiburg-Basel- Wein: 1974).

addition of ἱερεῖς in the expression τε καὶ ἱερεῖς καταστήσας introduces the new and overlaying sacerdotal element.

In 2 the sanctuary which must have priestly ministry is introduced, and in 3 the perpetual office of high priest. In 4 we have propitiation, and the offering of the gifts of the Church, which is to be continued in the Eucharistic liturgy of *Ap. Trad.* 5, before coming to ordination to Orders of presbyter and deacon. Finally in 5 we have mention of the bishop/high priest functioning by means of τῷ πνεύματι τῷ ἀρχιερατικῷ We have no Old Testament allusions to the inspiration of Aaron in this way. The phrase is a pure development of the enabling presbyteral Spirit given to Moses and divided amongst the presbyters whom he appointed. It is only by analogy with that original prayer that we can understand the idiom in which the bishop's enabling for high-priestly office is here expressed.

There is however a third theme with a third set of images that has been interwoven into this rite. There is no necessary connection between priesthood and absolution. The phrase in 5 ἔχειν ἐξουσίαν ἀφιέναι ἁμαρτίας κατὰ τὴν ἐντολήν σου is a reference to the commandment of the risen Christ in *John* 20, 22b-23: λάβετε πνεῦμα ἅγιον· ἄν τινων ἀφῆτε τὰς ἁμαρτίας ἀφέωνται αὐτοῖς ... Schweizer has interpreted the inbreathing of this passage to the whole community, whereas, as I have argued previously, it applies to the Twelve (Eleven) as representatives of the New Israel. There is however no image of office in the apostolic succession of the Twelve in *John*, let alone any sacerdotal understanding of their ministry.[25] The addition of the phrase τῷ ἀρχιερατικῷ to τῷ πνεύματι as the means to the power of forgiving sins is therefore a redefinition of the Johannine tradition in the interests of the sacerdotal image that the author of this particular segment is imposing on that tradition.

The function of absolution is thus brought into connection with priesthood presumably by virtue of the episcopal right now asserted. In the rite that follows, it is the bishop's prerogative to be the normal minister of the Eucharistic sacrifice. Both the power to absolve and to sacrifice are thus brought into connection with the apostolic foundation of the Church. *John* 20,22, as I have said, makes no reference to images of apostles in ordered succession, in a gospel where the Twelve are never called by that term. But in *Ap. Trad.* 3 the δύναμιν τοῦ ἡγεμονικοῦ—though not the ἀρχιερατικοῦ πνεύματος—which clearly therefore by contrast belongs to the earlier, "presbyteral" strata, is described as "that which you gave (δεδώρησαι) through your beloved Son (διὰ τοῦ ἠγαπημένου σου παιδὸς) Jesus Christ to your holy apostles (τοῖς ἁγίοις σου ἀποστόλοις) who founded the Church (οἳ

---

[25] E. Schweizer, Der Johanneische Kirchenbegriff, in *TU* 73 (1959), p. 263-268. Cf. A. Brent, Cultural Episcopacy and Ecumenism: Representative ministry in church history from the Age of Ignatius of Antioch to the Reformation, with special reference to contemporary ecumenism, in *Studies in Christian Mission* 6, (E.J. Brill: Leiden 1992), p. 76-80.

καθίδρυσαν τὴν ἐκκλησίαν) in individual places (κατὰ τόπον)." The allusion is clearly to the Johannine Pentecost, but the connection with sacerdotal imagery is rather to the final stage of a development which first connected the scene with the apostolic office through the 'leadership' image of the earlier, 'presbyteral' rite of *Ap. Trad.* 7.

In this section we have therefore examined the conflicting images used in the episcopal and presbyteral prayers in *Ap. Trad.* 3 and 7 as a means of isolating various strata involved in the development of these rites. However, our criticism of Segelberg's methodology for *a-priorism* lead us to demand further the corroboration of our purely literary hypothesis by locating these conflicting images in genuinely historical situations of conflict. It is to this task that we must now turn.

PART B. ΔΙΑΔΟΧΗ AND APXIEPATEIA: THE CLEMENTINE DIMENSION

The image of the Johannine Pentecost, redefined first in apostolic and then in archieratic terms in the evolution of the rites in the *Ap. Trad.,* produced the perceptive comment from Ratcliff:

> If the author of *Apostolic Tradition* thought about apostolic succession, he did not think of it as a "sacramental succession" or in terms of a chain or series. He thought of the bishop as succeeding, by an immediate appointment of the Lord, to an apostolic vacancy, and so to an immediate apostolic relationship with the Lord, as Matthias had done.[26]

Now such an understanding of Church Order seems clearly different from the concept of the philosophical house-school with which we met in Chapter 6, and with which we argued the Hippolytan events to be consistent. Here the fundamental concept validating Order was the term διαδοχή which prefigures too in Irenaeus' succession list, and whose home we argued to be that of the Greek philosophical schools. The notion of the giving of the Spirit as "an immediate appointment of the Lord" to the apostolic council through which the Church was founded (τοῖς ἁγίοις σου ἀποστόλοις οἳ καθίδρυσαν τὴν ἐκκλησίαν) would have seemed potentially Gnostic to an Irenaeus whom, as we have seen, located the test for valid succession in the identity of doctrine between the διάδοχος and his predecessor.

This point is of fundamental importance, given the claims of single or dual authorship for the Hippolytan *corpus*, that in Chapter 1 we showed to be more dependent on our estimate of the precise character the Statue before the Ligorian reconstruction than has been previously supposed. In the light of our argument that the list of works of inscribed in the catalogue on the back of the chair may be better understood as the product of a school rather than

---

[26] Couratin (1976) p. 159.

of a single author, we may now begin with a re-assessment of the relationship between the *Ap. Trad.* and *El.* regarding the understanding of Order in these two works.

7B 1. διαδοχή and El. *I prooem. 6 and* Ap. Trad. *3 and 7*

The critical passage reads:

> These doctrines no other refutes (ἐλέγξει) than the Holy Spirit handed on in the Church (τὸ ἐν ἐκκλησίᾳ παραδοθὲν ἅγιον πνεῦμα) in which those who were previously the apostles (οὖ τυχόντες πρότεροι οἱ ἀπόστολοι) delivered to those whose faith was orthodox (μετέδοσαν τοῖς ὀρθῶς πεπιστευκόσιν). We have become their successors (ὧν ἡμεῖς διάδοχοι τυγχάνοντες), and we participate in the same grace of both high priesthood and teaching, (τῆς τε αὐτῆς χάριτος μετέχοντες ἀρχιερατείας τε καὶ διδασκαλίας), and, being reckoned as guardians of the Church (καὶ φρουροὶ τῆς ἐκκλησίας λελογισμένοι), we neither let our eye slumber (οὐκ ὀφθαλμῷ νυστάζομεν), nor do we keep silence about orthodox discourse (οὐδὲ λόγον ὀρθὸν σιωπῶμεν), but, labouring with all of our soul and body we do not grow weary, endevouring to make worthy repayment worthily to God our benefactor (ἄξια ἀξίως θεῷ τῷ εὐεργέτῃ ἀνταποδιδόναι).
>
> *El.* I, prooem. 6

In so far as presbyter/bishops[27] are said to τῆς τε αὐτῆς χάριτος μετέχοντες ἀρχιερατείας τε καὶ διδασκαλίας, it has been thought that here we have the link that binds together the bishop as high-priest as well as, in virtue of the διδασκαλία, being also one of the apostolic successors (οἱ ἀπόστολοι... ὧν ἡμεῖς διάδοχοι). Furthermore, the image of the presbyter given a portion of Moses' Spirit may seem to be recalled by their description as μετέχοντες. The deaconing prayer in *Ap. Trad.* 8 denies that the deacons are ordained to participate in the common spirit of the presbyter (*non accipiens communem praesbyteri spiritum eum cuius participes praesbyteri sunt* (L), *spiritum magnitudinis cuius presbyteri participantur* (S(AE))). Thus there would appear at first sight to be a close fit here between *El.* I, prooem. 6 and *Ap. Trad.* 3 and 7.

Such a comparison would however be too superficial. As we have already said, the concept of διαδοχή is not present in these prayers, and its appearance in *El.* is a quite different understanding of Order. Furthermore, the Spirit that is given is the Holy Spirit, τὸ ἐν ἐκκλησίᾳ παραδοθὲν ἅγιον πνεῦμα, that acts as guarantor of the succession of teachers, just as in the case of Irenaeus' *charisma veritatis* (*Adv. Haer.* IV, 26,2). But in the *Ap. Trad.* we are not dealing with "the Holy Spirit given in the Church." We are dealing with a more Old Testament view of Spirit, in which it is the antitype of Moses' spirit of leadership and governance, his *spiritum gratiae et*

---

[27] I cease to ask the question whether these lines could be said by a presbyter or a bishop, since I have argued sufficiently the character of Hippolytus' presidency as πρωτοκαθεδρίτης or προεστώς over one of the several congregations into which the Roman Church was divided and which can only anachronistically be describes as either one or the other, see Chapter 6.

consilii, which became, we have argued, first the bishop's δύναμιν τοῦ ἡγεμονικοῦ πνεύματος, and then the antitype of Aaron's spirit by analogy with Moses', τῷ πνεύματι τῷ ἀρχιερατικῷ ἔχειν ἐξουσίαν. ἀρχιερατεία, moreover, is not related to a spirit antitypical to the Aaronic in *El.* I, prooem. 6. We are dealing therefore with the ideas of a school in which different members and different groups place different nuances and emphases on shared images rather than the unity and interrelationship of ideas within a the mind of a single author, or, for that matter, between two related authors.

There is however one way in which we could harmonize the disparate character of the two prayers of *Ap. Trad.* 3 and 7, and the ἀρχιερατεία of *El.* I, prooem. 6. We could deny that διαδοχή is generally used by Christian writers as a didactic and philosophical concept and so not to be located in our reconstruction of the house-school situation in Chapter 6. Instead we could follow Ehrhardt in claiming that, far from διαδοχή having its origin in the kind of historiography of Diogenes Laertius' *Successions of the Philosophers*, the model for the episcopal succession lists rather was that of those for Jewish high priests. If indeed the term διαδοχή in Irenaeus, and διάδοχοι in *El.* carried already in his usage sacerdotal implications, then indeed what we have argued to be the disparate images of the school of Hippolytus would indeed become integrated into the mind of an individual author. Let us now consider Ehrhardt's thesis.

7B 2. *Erhardt on* διαδοχή *as* ἀρχιερατεία

Ehrhardt pointed to the apocalyptic concerns of the late second century as leading Eusebius to model his succession lists on the lists of priest-kings represented by the Maccabees in Josephus' writings.[28] Thus he believed that Hippolytus' sacerdotalism in the *Ap. Trad.* 3 was of a piece with the διάδοχοι of *El.* I, prooem. 6, because to be mentioned on a διαδοχή was equivalent to being both ruler and high-priest. Eusebius moreover confirmed the sacerdotal character of the succession lists when he placed the figure of James at the head of all episcopal successions.[29]

Julius Africanus, like Hippolytus, was well disposed towards the Severans. Indeed the catalogue on the Statue records a lost work dedicated to Severina. Julius, as we have seen, was architect of the pantheon, and the person to whose influence Alexander Severus' wish to have a statue of Christ in his chapel has been attributed (2B 2.1.3.1-2). In *Ad Arist.* IV, Julius was anxious to show the priestly and royal lines of the Maccabees continued in Christ, and in the light of this to explain the conflicting genealogies of

---

[28] *Ant.* XIII,11,301 cf. 20,10. Cf. A. Ehrhardt, *The Apostolic Succession in the First Two Centuries of the Church,* (London: Lutterworth Press 1953), p. 44-61, cf. W. Telfer, *The Office of a Bishop,* (London: Darton, Longman and Todd 1962), chpt. 4.

[29] Ehrhardt (1953) p. 63-65 ff. with which cf. L. Mariès , Le Messie issu de Lévi chez Hippolyte de Rome, in *RecSciRel* 40 (1952), p. 381-96.

Matthew and *Luke*. Like Hippolytus, he was the author of a Chronicle of world history against an eschatological background. The sacerdotalism of the author of the *Ap. Trad.* 3 and of *El.* no doubt was influenced by such hierocratic notions in their different kinds of sacerdotalism. But to what extent did that sacerdotalism predate the author of *El.* and his successor Hippolytus?

Ehrhardt argues that in both Irenaeus, Hegesippus, and Clement, διαδοχή was used in such a sacerdotal sense, which he whom he believed to be the author both of the *Ap. Trad.* and the *El.* I, prooem. 6 merely continued. He believed that one could trace a sacerdotally-understood line from the figure of James the Just in Jewish Christianity. According to Hegesippus, James was not simply first bishop of the Church of Jerusalem ordained by apostles, but was indeed so because of his natural blood-line with Jesus Christ, like the Maccabees, a priest-king. But as I have demonstrated in greater detail elsewhere, the case for an episcopal caliphate fails, and for basically the following reasons:

(a) James' rule as bishop of the church of Jerusalem never was legitimated in terms of a caliphate in the sense that a proven blood-line was the essential requirement for his office. According to Hegesippus he is succeeded as bishop of Jerusalem by "Symeon the son of his uncle Clopas." (Eusebius, *H.E.* IV, 22,4-5) But that the choice of Symeon was not merely because of his blood-line is corroborated by the fact that it is recorded that Thebouthis began the line of heretics out of disappointment that he had not been elected in succession to James. The former's candidature was not ruled out from the start because of his lack of blood-lineage. James' sacerdotal lineage was not therefore a requirement for his office, and there is therefore no notion of a sacerdotal διαδοχή linking him with his episcopal successors.[30]

(b) The historical witness of Josephus to James shows that he could not have been associated by his contemporaries with Maccabean priest-kings and their succession lines. Had there been such an association of blood relationship with a political Messiah, given his apologetic concerns in the Rome of the Flavians, Josephus could not have given the defence of James that he does. James would be too much identified with Judas of Galilee and the later Zealots.[31]

---

[30] Brent (1992) p. 132-134, 136-137 ff. One writer, influential in Roman Catholic circles, who insisted erroneously on this fact was J. Colson, *Les fonctions Ecclésiales aux deux premiers Siècles*, (Paris: Desclée de Brouwer 1956), p. 117-119: ".. ces juifs convertis de Jérusalem avaient choisi... celui qui était plus le proche par le sang du «Fils de David»... Ainsi s'était continuée la «dynastie macchabéenne.»... Sans doute «la chair et le sang» trouvent encore leur compte dans une telle mentalité." For a more recent defence of this position see E. Stauffer, Zum Kalifat des Jacobus, in *ZRGG* 4 (1952), p. 193-214, who replied to H. von Campenhausen, Die Nachfolge des Jacobus, in *ZKG* 63 (1950-52), p. 133-144. The most recent historical study assuming something like a caliphate view is M. Hengel, Jacobus der Herrenbruder– der erste Papst? in *Glaube und Eschatologie, Festschrift für W.G. Kümmel zum 80 Geburstag*, (Tübingen: J.C. Mohr 1985), p. 71-104. For the significance of σώτηριον γένος in Eusebius, *H.E.* 1,7,14, see Brent (1992) p. 134-135. See also J. Munk, Presbyters and Disciples of the Lord in Papias, in *HThR* 52 (1959), p. 232-243; U.H.J., Körtner, *Papias von Hierapolis*, (Göttingen: Vandenhoek and Ruprecht 1983).

[31] Brent (1992) p. 136-137.

(c) The references to the δεσπόσυνοι in Hegesippus (Eusebius *H.E.* 3,20) are primarily apologetic, and are not to be read in terms of claims to sacerdotal validity.[32]

(d) Hegesippus' description of James' sacerdotal position (Eusebius, *H.E.* II,23, 4-7) has been convincingly shown by Zuckschwerdt to be in fact an anti-sacerdotal description. James does not exercize a priestly role in the narrative, but rather that of one who has taken a life-long Nazirite vow. The whole tenor of the James' legend is to suggest in fact anti-sacerdotal conceptions of holiness which underlay the narrative.[33]

If the origins of *El.*'s ascription of ἀρχιερατεία to bishops cannot be located in any putative succession from James, *a fortiori* the texts from Hegesippus, Irenaeus, and Clement fail to reflect such putative origins. We may summarize our position, discussed more extensively in a previous article,[34] as follows:

(a) We have already argued in our last Chapter that in *Adv.Haer.* III,3,2 etc. the primary focus is to a διαδοχή of teachers in the Roman house-school communities. We did not however in the process commit the modern historiographical fallacy of assuming that ideas can be adequately described as developing from each other apart from any reference to their human bearers and their corresponding authority. But Telford, curiously, sought to understand *Adv. Haer.* IV, 8,3 as testifying to a hierocratic view of the apostolic succession, which thus witnessed such a fusion of ἀρχιερατεία and διαδοχή in a pre-Hippolytan form. Telford introduced into this text the view that "all the apostles of the Lord are priests."[35] But the passage is a commentary on *Matt.* 12,3-5, and is about "disciples" and not "apostles" as they are to be interpreted in the text. Irenaeus calls the disciples "priests" so that he can show that they did not really break the Mosaic Law and thus refute Marcion.

(b) In Irenaeus *Adv. Haer.* IV, 17,4-18,1 the words of consecration at the Last Supper are given as the fulfilment of the "pure sacrifice" about which *Mal.* 1,10-11 prophesied. But the sacrifice has no priesthood separate from the community to offer it. It is the offering of the Church, as the words *confessus est et novi Testamenti novam docuit oblationem; quam Ecclesia ab Apostolis accipiens in universo mundo offert Deo* make clear. The statement that it is the Church's offering (not the bishop's)

---

[32] Ibid. p. 136-137 ff.; Stauffer (1952), p. 193-214, cf. f. N. Hyldahl, Hegesipps Hypomnemata, in *StTh* 14 (1960) p. 87: "Die Fragen des Domitian an die Nachkommen Davids... sind Fragen die nur innerhalb einer ganz bestimmten Problemstellung einen Sinn hatten, nämlich bei der Frage nach dem Verhältnis der Christen und der Kaisermacht zu einander." For the apologetic character of Hegesippus' work, see, Hydahl (1960) p. 70-113. See also H.J. Lawler, *Eusebiana*, (London: Oxford University Press 1912), p. 18-35.

[33] E. Zuckschwerdt, Das Naziräat des Herrenbruders Jakobus nach Hegesippus, in *ZNW* 68 (1977), p. 276-287: "Die Tradition des lebenslangen Nazirtums.. wurde durch den Gegensatz zu dieser priesterlichen Konzeption und durch die sich heraus ergebenden, im Laufe der Zeit zunehmend verschärften Antithesen, die Wiederspiegelungen geschichtlicher Spannungen und hieraus erwachsender Gegensätze zum priesterlich bestimmen." Cf. also H. von Campenhausen, Der urchristliche Apostelbegriff, in *StTh* 1 Fasc. I-II (1947), p. 96-120 and, Die Nachfolge des Jakobs, in *ZKG* 63 (1952-3), p. 133-144.

[34] A. Brent, Diogenes Laertius and the Apostolic Succession, in *JEH* 44,3 (1993), p. 367-389.

[35] Telfer (1962) p. 114-115, cf. ——, Was Hegesippus a Jew? in *HThR* 53,2 (1960), p. 143-153. It is nevertheless strange therefore that Telfer (1962) should still insist : "It is thus the sacerdotal character of the bishop which Irenaeus sees as passing from the order of the apostles to the order of bishops." (p. 115)

is repeated two further times. (Irenaeus, *Adv. Haer.* IV, 2,2; 6,2.4; 8,1; 17, 6; 18, 1). There is no connection drawn here, therefore, between High Priesthood and the office of bishop as apostolic successor as occurs later in *El.*

(c) Since we have shown there to have been no caliphate of James, we cannot claim that his use of διαδοχή, taken over by Irenaeus, was understood sacerdotally by him. Hegesippus, as Telfer argued, was not the early writer so often assumed. A comparison of *H.E.* II,23,3 and IV,22,4,3 show that his date was after the time of Eleutheros (*A.D.* 175-189). Far from him being of Palestinian extraction, as putatively evidenced from his allusions being of direct contact with Palestine, he is using a written source whose knowledge of the Old Testament came from the LXX. Certainly his references to the Rechabites at James' stoning reveal a misreading of *Jeremiah* 35 rather than direct experience of first century Jerusalem.[36]

(d) Clement *Cor.* 44, 2-6, regards the bishops as succeeding (διαδέξωνται) to a liturgy (λειτουργίαν). Is this λειτουργία that of eucharistic presidency? In 44, 4 ἐπισκοπή is after all associated with προσενεγκόντας τὰ δῶρα. In 40, 5 and 41, 1-2 high priests, priests, and levites are mentioned with their ἴδιαι λειτουργίαι. But there is no type/ antitype correspondence drawn with bishops, priests, and deacons. Rather the comparison is simply one of several analogies drawn from nature and society as well as the Old Testament to show that God ordains order. No group whether in nature or society is to go beyond "the appointed rule of its ministry (τὸν ὡρισμένον τῆς λειτουργίας αὐτοῦ κανόνα)," but must remain "in its own rank (ἐν τῷ ἰδίῳ τάγματι)." Moreover, Clement's use of ἐλλόγιμοι ἄνδρες locates his διαδέξωνται in the characteristic conceptualization of the philosophical schools as found in Diogenes Laertius who describes eminent philosophers who head schools by this term (*Succ.* 8, 50,91; 9, 1; 10, 21,25). Josephus, who is Ehrhardt's principle alleged source for archierocratic succession lists, whilst he uses διαδοχή in the required sense (*Ant.* XX,16, 103, 197, 213, 229, 235, etc.), only uses ἐλλόγιμος of cities and temples in two places in one passage (*Ant.* XV, 297-298).

Thus we see the attempt to explain *El.*'s episcopal ἀρχιερατεία in terms of a sacerdotal and opposed to a scholastic and philosophical, teaching διαδοχή fails. The figure of James, whether in Josephus or the Hegesippan fragments, does not correspond to the heir of a Maccabean priest-king for whom such claims could be intelligibly made. Thus the Aaronic and archierocratic ordination prayer in *Ap. Trad.* 2 cannot be synthesized with the presbyteral and Mosaic imagery of *Ap. Trad.* 7.[37] The proposed link in the chain of resemblance, namely *El.* I prooem. 6, cannot be expounded to yield such explanation.

We must examine shortly where *El.*'s concept of episcopal ἀρχιερατεία came from if plainly not from the kind of διαδοχή to which Irenaeus and

---

[36] Telfer (1962) p. 143-156.
[37] I find it difficult in this connection to see how Ehrhardt (1953) p. 73 can possibly argue: "It seems that the position of St. James was exalted above the other Apostles because he was seen as Christ's successor in His priestly ministry... We find in Homilies 3.70 (Lag, 55.19ff.) the command to respect "the throne of Christ" as much as the "cathedra of Moses", and it is obvious that the analogy between Moses and Christ would give rise to a similar one between Aaron "the brother of Moses" and St. James "the brother of Christ." In everything that I argue here the relationship between priestly and Aaronic models and the Mosaic reveal a distinction between Moses and the sacerdotal and not an equivalence.

Hegesippus bear witness. We have argued Clement's analogies to be irrelevant here as he does not speak about types and antitypes in the Christian cultus as such. But before we do so, we will examine further *Ap. Trad.* 7 in order to explore the coherence of its imagery both with the pseudonymous letters with which the *Clementine Homilies* begin, and the coherence of both with Diogenes' historiography of philosophical schools.

7B 3. Ap. Trad. *7 and the Clementine tradition*

As we have argued, in 7A 2.2.1, *Ap. Trad.* 7 is the prayer both for an episcopal and presbyteral ordination. For a bishop the image of Moses is emphasized who is given the Spirit of counsel (συμβουλίας/*consilii*) for assistance (ἀντιλαμβάνεσθαι/*adiubet*) and guidance (κυβερνᾶν/*gubernet*). The concept of διαδοχή is unmentioned here, as indeed in *Ap. Trad.* 3. It is not the Irenaean *charisma veritatis* that they receive, but the *communem praesbyterii spiritum* in which they participate (μετέχειν/*participantur*). The chain of diachronological historical witnesses seems distant here. The timeless spirit possessed by Moses in type and received by the bishop as antitype and given partially to the presbyters is what validates his authority. It will be interesting now to compare these images with what we find in the *Clementine Homilies*.[38]

One would expect that it would be vain to look for the concept of διαδοχή in such documents, since their pseudonymous form requires the fiction that they are in the immediate apostolic and post-apostolic age. Peter writes to James in the ἐπιστολὴ Πέτρου πρὸς Ἰακώβον, and James' actions following that letter, though without written response, is recorded in the διαμαρτυρία περὶ τῶν τοῦ βιβλίου λαμβάνοντων. There follows the ἐπιστολὴ Κλήμεντος πρὸς Ἰακώβον. Due to the closeness of his death, Peter in this letter instructs Clement to inform James of his consecration at Peter's hands, as bishop of Rome (*Ep. Clem.* 2,1).

That pseudonymous literary exchange would appear to be itself the product of several recensions. However, the theme of Moses and the seventy elders, with which we meet in *Ap. Trad.* 7, occurs here too. Rather than share in the Spirit given to Moses, however, these presbyters are said to have received the chair as a symbol of teaching, and not (at least in *Ep. Petr. ad Iac.*) of συμβουλία or κυβέρνησις or ἀντίληψις He who receives the chair is first examined (δοκιμασθείς) and found worthy (ἄξιος εὑρεθῇ). Then he has passed on to him the books of Peter's preaching "by means of the educational method (τότε αὐτῷ κατὰ τὴν ἀγωγὴν παραδοῦναι) which Moses delivered to the Seventy (καθ' ἣν καὶ τοῖς Ἑβδομήκοντα ὁ Μωυσῆς

---

[38] For a detailed summary of research on the *Clementines*, see F. Stanley Jones, The Pseudo-Clementines: A History of Research, in *SecCent* 2 (1982) Part I, p. 1-33, Part II, p. 63-96. See also Strecker (1958,1981).

παρέδωκε), to those who received his Chair (τοῖς τὴν καθέδραν αὐτοῦ παρειληφόσιν)." (*Ep. Petr. ad Iac.* 1,2) It is by means of this ἀγωγή, which I have translated "teaching method," that they are able to harmonize discrepant Old Testament passages, "by reason of the rule delivered to them (κατὰ γὰρ τὸν παραδοθέντα αὐτοῖς κανόνα)." (*Ep. Petr. ad Iac.* 1,3-4) Moreover, the authority of the bishop over such elders is a teaching authority. They will only examine others and entrust them with the books of Peter's preaching, in accordance with the "mind of the bishop (ταῦτα ἐπὶ τῇ τοῦ ἐπισκόπου μου γνώμῃ ποιησάμενος)." (*Ep. Petr. ad Iac.* 2,2)

In the letter of Clement to James we find that the theme of the succession of the teaching presbyterate is continued, and also without any priestly or high-priestly imagery. Clement writes to James the record of his consecration, and records Peter as declaring his ordination (Κλήμεντα τοῦτον ἐπίσκοπον ὑμῖν χειροτονῶ). That ordination is however to a teaching chair, "the chair of my discourses (ᾧ τὴν ἐμὴν τῶν λόγων πιστεύω καθέδραν), (*Ep. Clem. ad Iac.* 2, 2) or indeed simply the "chair of the one who teaches (τὴν τοῦ διδάσκοντος... καθέδραν)," and who "is not ignorant of lifegiving discourses (ζωοποιοὺς λόγους ἀγνοῶν) and the rule of the Church (ἐκκλησίας κανόνα)." (19,4) A bishop is described as προκαθεζόμενος, a term common to an Ignatian bishop earlier and a Didascalian one later.[39] But unlike the Didascalian bishop, this term is not used in the epistle with τῆς ἐκκλησίας as its object. Clement is describes as τὸν ἀληθείας προκαθεζόμενον (2,5; 17, 1), where προκαθεζόμενος is to be translated "pre-eminent in truth," for reasons similar to those which I have pointed out elsewhere in connection with Ignatius.[40]

My interpretation of the reference of the phrase τὸν ἀληθείας προκαθεζόμενον with the communication of ζωοποιοὺς λόγους and further with "binding" and "loosing" is nowhere better confirmed than in the following passage:

> Preside (προκαθέσθητι) in order to provide in due season (πρὸς τὸ εὐκαίρως παρέχειν) the words that are able to save (τοὺς σῴζειν αὐτοὺς δυναμένους λόγους) and let them obey you (καὶ οὗτοι ἐπακουέτωσάν σου) because they know that (εἰδότες ὅτι) whatever the ambassador of truth binds on earth (ὁ τῆς ἀληθείας πρεσβευτὴς ὃ ἂν δήσῃ ἐπὶ γῆς) has also been bound in heaven (δέδεται καὶ ἐν οὐρανῷ), and whatever he looses has been loosed (ὃ δ᾽ ἂν λύσῃ, λέλυται). And you shall bind what needs to be bound (σὺ δὲ δήσεις ἃ δεῖ δεθῆναι) and loose what needs to be loosed (καὶ λύσεις ἃ δεῖ λυθῆναι). These

---

[39] For the clear differences of imagery between these two works, see A. Brent, The Relations between Ignatius of Antioch and the *Didascalia Apostolorum*, in *SecCent* 8,3 (1991) p. 129-156. See also P. Burke, The Monarchical Episcopate at the End of the First Century, in *JES* 7 (1970), p. 499-518.

[40] A. Brent, Ecumenical Reconciliation and Cultural Episcopates, in *AThR* 72 3 (1990), p. 255-279; ——, History and Eschatological Mysticism in Ignatius of Antioch, in *EThL*, 65 4 (1989), p. 309-329.

and things like them are the responsibility of he who is president (καὶ τὰ μὲν κατὰ σὲ τὸν προεστῶτα ταῦτά ἐστιν καὶ τὰ τούτοις ὅμοια).

Ep. Clem. ad Iac. 6, 1-4

Thus corresponding to this sense of "presidency" as "standing out" or "being pre-eminent," we find that "binding" and "loosing" has to do with ruling and interpreting, and not with the forgiveness of sins. In *Ap. Trad.* 3, as we have seen, binding and loosing was interpreted in the Johannine sense of forgiving sins (ἔχειν ἐξουσίαν ἀφιέναι ἁμαρτίας) according to the commandment (κατὰ τὴν ἐντολὴν) of *Jn.* 20,23. Moreover, unlike in *John, Ap. Trad.* 3 associates this ἐξουσία with the priestly office (προσφέρειν τὰ δῶρα... τῷ πνεύματι τῷ ἀρχιερατικῷ).[41] But in *Clement ad Iac.* the reference is, as in *Mat.* 16,19, to the Rabbinic binding and loosing of interpretations of Scriptual texts. We saw in *Petr. ad Iac.* 1, 2-3 that the function of the presbyter, in accordance with the mind of the bishop, was to harmonized discordant texts by means of a rule or κανών passed on to them. So too here with Clement. When Peter gives him "authority to bind and loose" (τὴν ἐξουσίαν τοῦ δεσμεύειν καὶ λύειν), he assures him that "whatever you ordain (χειροτονήσῃ) on earth will have been decreed (δεδογματισμένον) in heaven because you know the rule of the church (ὡς τὸν τῆς ἐκκλησίας εἰδὼς κανόνα)." (*Clement ad Iac.* 2,4)[42]

Thus the binding and loosing retains its rabbinic sense of harmonizing a body of doctrine. Clement as bishop is not high-priest but the elder in the succession of Mosaic teachers who "is pre-eminent in truth." [43] His ἐξουσία is a teaching ἐξουσία. To receive ἐξουσία is equivalent to receiving the teaching chair. The "honour of the chair (τὴν τῆς καθέδρας τιμὴν)" is also its "authority (τε καὶ ἐξουσίαν)". (*Clement ad Iac.* 3,1) There is, I believe, however, a development of imagery to be witnessed between *Petr. ad Iac.* and *Clement ad Iac.*, and the account in *Homilies* 3, 63 of the ordination of Zacchaeus. Such a development has been denied by Strecker in his thesis that both passages are part of the basic document around which the present, composite work has developed.[44]

Although the *Clementines,* in their final form, may be mid-third-century and subsequent to the author of *El.* and his successor Hippolytus, Waitz had

---

[41] Later, in *Ap. Con.* 2,25,9-13 what is done by means of a sacrifice in *Ap. Trad.* 3 is associated directly with the person of the high-priest/bishop who imitates Christ's sacrifice. See Brent (1991) p. 149-153.

[42] Cf. with this phrase Origen *De Principiis* 4,9: ἐχομένοις τοῦ κανόνος τῆς Ἰησοῦ Χριστοῦ κατὰ διαδοχὴν τῶν ἀποστόλων οὐρανίου Ἐκκλησίας.

[43] This teaching theme is further emphasised when Clement tries to refuse τὴν τῆς καθέδρας τιμήν τε καὶ ἐξουσίαν. Peter is pleased because the *cathedra* is not for anyone who desires the chair "but one whose conversation is pious and who is learned in argument (ἀλλ᾽ εὐλαβοῦς τὸν τρόπον καὶ πολυμαθοῦς τὸν λόγον)." (*Clement ad Iac.* 3,2) In 19,3 salvation, through the hearing of "lifegiving words," is related to ζωοποιοὺς λόγους, "the rule of the church (ἐκκλησίας κανόνα)" and the καθέδρα held in trust.

[44] Strecker (1958 and 1981).

argued that a common and early liturgy underlies both the report of Clement's consecration in *Ep. ad Iac.* and in *Hom.* 3, 62-71, with the latter's account as the more original.[45] Strecker argued that that liturgy had to date from around A.D. 200, in other words, from the time of *El.* and Hippolytus, principally on the grounds of the absence of mention of a specific order of widows evidenced later in *Ap. Con.* VIII, 12, 43; 13, 14 etc.[46] However, Strecker argued that Waitz was wrong in regarding *Clement ad Iac* as representing a later stage in development from *Hom.* 3, 62-71. Both passages, he wished to claim, were part of the *Grundschrift*, since the *Homilies'* passages are paralleled in the *Recognitions* 3,65-66.[47]

Waitz' real reason for regarding *Hom.* 3, 62-71 as the original rite from which *Clement ad Iac.* was derived was his wish to see in the latter reflections of the so-called *Indulgenzedikt* of Callistus. But he could only do so by grossly misinterpreting "binding" and "loosing," and the concepts of ἐξουσία and κανὼν τῆς ἐκκλησίας in the letter. These concepts in the letter itself are directly related to the authorative interpretation of scriptural passages, and "the life-giving discourses" of Peter. They do not relate directly to the foregiveness of mortal sins claimed by Callistus, according to the author of *El.* IX,12, 20-21, 24.[48]

In the light of the failure of this interpretation, it becomes impossible to connect either *Clement ad Iac.* 7, 4 or ἐπίσκοπος ἐπισκόπων (ibid. inscr.) specifically with an actual *Indulgenzedikt*, however much they might in the light of further discussion be held to reflect the misinterpreted events that lay behind the thesis postulating such an edict. In the former passage we read:

> For adultery is a great horror (πολὺ γὰρ δεινὸν μοιχεία), so much the more (τοσοῦτον ὅσον) is the second adultery punished (τὰ δευτερεῖα ἔχειν αὐτὴν τῆς κολάσεως) when the first is remitted to those in error (ἐπεὶ τὰ πρωτεῖα τοῖς ἐν πλάνῃ οὖσιν ἀποδίδοται) on condition that they live chastely (κἂν σωφρονῶσιν).

Second repentance was after all allowed for mortal sin, at least as early as the time of Hermas, *Mand.* 3, 1-2, so such a reference does not of itself identify the text with Callistus. Moreover, the administration of punishment for such a second offence is the duty of the presbyters and not of the bishop in this

---

[45] H. Waitz, Die pseudoklementinien, Homilien und Rekognitionen. Eine quellenkritische Untersuchung, in *T.U.* 25,4 (1904), p. 180 ff. and 245 ff. Cf. also C. Schmidt. Studien zu den Pseudo-Clementinen, in *TU* 46,1, (1929); B. Rehm, Zur Entstehung der pseudoclementinischen Schriften, in *ZNW* 37 (1938), p. 77-184.

[46] Strecker (1958, 1981) p. 112-116.

[47] Ibid. p. 101;

[48] Ibid. p.100-101. Indeed it will be observed that I believe that Strecker himself wrong when he says against Waitz: "Κανὼν τῆς ἐκκλησίας meint hier nicht mehr als den Brauch der Kirche, den Klemens auf seinen Wanderungen mit Petrus kennengelernt habe." Rather the phrase has reference to the "rule of interpretation," analogous to the ἀγαγωγή or "method of exposition," delivered by Moses to the Seventy (*Petr. ad Iac.* I).

passage, so that it is not directly applicable to Callistus' personal claims to additional powers.[49]

Strecker was nevertheless wrong in seeing no development in these texts, even though they are continuations of themes, as we shall see. We have yet to discuss the relations between Tertullian and *El.*, and the question whether his famous *pontifex maximus* and *episcopus episcoporum* was in fact Callistus or Agrippinus of Carthage. Certainly the description of James as ἐπίσκοπος ἐπισκόπων by Clement does not relate in any straightforward way to Callistus himself, though we shall argue it may refer to the perception of the way that he acted in absolving those excommunicated from other Roman congregations (7C 1.1.2.2). But quite apart from the specific question of the *El.*/Hippolytus/Tertullian relations, and prescinding from the results of that later discussion, I will now argue that:

(a) there is a development from *Petr. ad Iac.* through *Clement ad Iac.* to the Zacchaeus rite of *Hom.* III, 63-77 in which monarchical elements in Church Order are increasingly emphasized. Consequently, and quite the reverse of Waitz's thesis, it is the latter passage that represents the more developed form of Church Order (7B 3.1-3.2).

(b) there is a common tradition to which independent witness is born by the Mosaic 'presbyteral' *Ap. Trad.* 7, the Mosaic and Rabbinic *Clementine Homilies* on the one hand, and the Greek school concept of διαδοχή found in *El.* and Irenaeus and Hegesippus on the other (7B 5).

(c) the pseudonymous background, created by the introduction into the development of the ordination rites of the figures of Peter, Clement, and James, represents a stage in the development towards a monarch bishop at Rome which is also reflected in the dispute between the author of *El.* and Callistus. This relationship will hold irrespective of the existence or otherwise of an *Indulgenzedikt* which might form part of the references of passages in Tertullian (7 C).

7B 3.1. Petr. ad Iac., Clement. ad Iac. *and* Ap. Trad. *7*

In the presbyteral tradition represented by *Ap. Trad.* 7 the exercize of office by presbyters who possessed portions of the Spirit of Moses was characterized in terms of "guidance" (κυβερνᾶν/*gubernare*), or in terms of "help (ἀντιλαμβάνεσθαι/*adiubet*)." We argued that episcopal authority, following *Can. Hip.* 4 in this tradition, also applied to bishops. The first contrast with the tradition represented in the letters of Peter and Clement is that the role of

---

[49] Far from this passage constituting a development of *Hom.* 3,68, 2 where adultery is made the worst sin, Strecker considers it the correction of the Homilist to the *Grundschrift*: "Aber dieser Diskrepanz lässt sich nicht für die Waitzsche Hypothese dienstbar machen: Hom. 68,2c stammt ohne Zweifel vom Homilisten, denn es wird hier die gleiche Ansicht ausgesprochen, die sich in dem von H. verfassten Abschnitt H. XIII 14,2-21,2a (s.o. B XI S. 76ff.) findet: der Homilist korrigiert den Grundschriftautor, der der Auffassung ist, dass die ἐν πλάνῃ ὄντες dem ewigen Gericht unterworfen seien..." (Strecker (1958, 1981) p. 102). Cf. also W. Frankenberg, Recognitions, in *TU* 48,3 (1936).

Rabbinic interpreter according to an exegetical rule is absent from *Ap. Trad.,* even though the image of Moses and the Seventy continues (*Ap. Trad.* 7; 8; cf. *Petr. ad Iac.* 1; *Clement ad Iac.* 2 etc.). In other words in *Ap. Trad.* they have become judges who guide generally rather than judges whose authority is circumscribed by the authority of text and interpretative rule, as in the *Clementines.*

We see moreover a shift taking place in these letters themselves from a narrower scribal to a broader view of what it is to sit in judgement. *Petr. ad Iac.* 1 implies a presbyterate purely governed by the authority of the text and interpretative rule of the books committed to them. However in *Clement ad Iac.* the presbyters have responsibility for ecclesiastical discipline in matters of sex and marriage, and though it may be assumed that they act in the process as scribal interpreters too, the references that we have cited above are all to the bishop as possessing the *cathedra* of Moses (7-8 cf. *Hom.* 3, 67-68).

In *Clement ad Iac.* 3, moreover, there are several references to διοίκησις which at first sight seem to warrant more than the function of supreme scribal interpreter. In classical Greek the term refers to management of the treasury. Moreover, as we saw was the case in the house schools of *Ap. Trad.* 28-30, the bishop according to Clement's letter, superintends the poor-relief (πεινῶντας τρέφετε), and encourages common meals (πυκνότερον συνέστιοι ἀλλήλων) (9,2-3). As such he provides βοηθεία (3,6) and is the βοηθός "bearing the concerns (φορτισθεὶς φροντίδας) " of others. (16,2) As such, it is attractive to interpret διοίκησις in the sense of poor-relief administration, when Clement is said to "have learned the administration of the Church (τὴν διοίκησιν τῆς ἐκκλησίας ἐκμεμάθηκεν)" (3,3) or διοίκησιν ἐκκλησίας παρ' ἐμοῦ μεμαθηκώς (4,4), which is therefore a "just administration (δικαίαν διοίκησιν)." (16,5) Along with the role of scripture interpreter Clement has also acquired that of treasury adminstration, so that he is exhorted to abstain from worldy occupations "in order that you may have the care of the Church alone (ἵνα μόνης τῆς ἐκκλησίας τὴν φροντίδα ἔχῃς) both for administering her well (πρὸς τε τὸ διοικεῖν αὐτὴν καλῶς) and for providing the words of truth" (καὶ τὸ τοὺς τῆς ἀληθείας λόγους παρέχειν)." (5,6)

In such a development, we therefore witness a stage contemporaneous with the Hippolytan events. As in *Ap. Trad.* 7 there is no sacerdotal imagery, but the role, characterized there by the verbs κυβερνᾶν/*gubernare*), and ἀντιλαμβάνεσθαι/*adiubet*, is here characterized by the nouns βοηθεία or βοηθός, or the phrase φορτισθεὶς φροντίδας. But as the immediate context of the dispute of the author of *El.* with Callistus was the events which were to lead to the emergence of monarchical episcopacy, so too in the *Clementines* we find a radical shift in favour of monarchical concepts and images in the ordination rite of Zacchaeus in the text of the *Homilies* which follow the letters of Peter and Clement to James.

7B 3.2. *The Zacchaeus rite* (Hom. *III, 63-77*)

Zacchaeus is brought forcibly for ordination by Peter (ἐβιάζετο ἐπὶ τὴν αὐτοῦ καθεσθῆναι καθέδραν). The exercize of his office is clearly now more than βοήθεια or βοηθός, and those cognate ideas with which we have seen them to be related in either the Hippolytan school or the letters of Peter and Clement. The bishop is now conceived as a ruler.

When in *Hom.* III, 63,1 Zacchaeus is lead forcibly to the chair, he does not regard it as a teaching chair for the διοίκησις of τοὺς τῆς ἀληθείας λόγους. Rather the chair has become the chair of a ruler. He immediately pleads to be released from ruling (ὅπως τοῦ ἄρχειν αὐτὸν ἀπολύσῃ). He then promises that he will perform the work of a ruler (ὁπόσα ποτὲ χρὴ τὸν ἄρχοντα ποιεῖν), if only he will be allowed not to use the name (μόνον μοι τὸ ὄνομα τοῦτο μὴ ἔχειν χάρισαι). Indeed, he fears "to be endued with (ἐνδύσασθαι) the name of this rulership (τὸ τῆς ἀρχῆς...ὄνομα), for it abounds with bitter envy and danger (πικροῦ γὰρ φθόνου καὶ κινδύνου γέμει)." (63,2) This diffidence parallels a period in the Roman community when the monarch-bishop is a new and disputed institution, and when the τὸ τῆς ἀρχῆς ὄνομα will not be a name with which everyone is easy. It is however a change to monarchical episcopacy which is being handled with considerable ideological skill in the light of the clever blending in this section of older teaching and caring concepts with the new monarchical ones.

Peter assures Zacchaeus (III, 64,1) that he can be called "the one set over (καθεστὼς)" instead of "ruler (ἄρχων)." The ἐξουσία which we saw in *Clement ad Iac.* to be primarily authority to rule on scriptural interpretation has now become an ἐξουσίαν διοικήσεως, described also as as τοῦ προκαθεζομένου ἐξουσία, which clearly applies to more than a circum-scribed teaching focus (64,2). His authority is exercized ὑπὲρ τῆς ἀδελφῶν σωτηρίας, ὑπὲρ τῆς αὐτῶν οἰκονομίας καὶ σῆς ὠφελείας (64,4). Whilst σωτηρία can still be applied to the τοὺς σώζειν αὐτοὺς δυναμένους λόγους, (*Clement ad Iac.* 6,2) and ὠφελεία to the ideas of βοήθεια or βοηθός, οἰκο-νομία is a new term here in the *Clementines* and represents a far more exten-sive organisation of the poor-relief. οἰκονομία, or "adminstration," is the characteristic description of the more extended structure of poor relief within which the monarchical bishop of the *Didascalia* operates as opposed to its mystical and providential sense adopted by Ignatius.[50] This is why it is "wearisome as well as dangerous to administer the Church of Christ (κάματον καὶ κίνδυνον ἔχει τὸ τὴν Χριστοῦ Ἐκκλησίαν οἰκονομεῖν)"—de-scriptions which, like the word οἰκονομεῖν itself, are found in neither Peter's nor in Clement's letter, nor in the *Ap. Trad.* (*Hom.* III, 65,1).

As in the *Didascalia*, the presbyters now must obey their bishop as neither Ignatius, nor the *Ap. Trad.*, nor the letters of Peter and Clement ever com-

---

[50] *Didasc.* 2,25,2; 2,35,4; 6,19,2, cf. Brent (1991) p. 156.

manded them.[51] "Let the bishop as ruler (ὁ ἐπίσκοπος ὡς ἄρχων) be heard in what he says (περὶ ὧν λέγει ἀκουέσθω). Let the presbyters be anxious that what he orders takes place (οἱ πρεσβύτεροι τὰ κελευόμενα γίνεσθαι σπουδαζέτωσαν). (III, 67,1) Clearly the role of the bishop is no longer simply to confirm scriptural interpretations of the presbyters (ἐπὶ τῇ τοῦ ἐπισκόπου γνώμῃ ποιησάμενος). (Ep. Petr. ad Iac. 3,1) Zacchaeus must learn, as Clement did in the opening letter, the adminstration of the Church (διοίκησιν Ἐκκλησίας μεμάθηκας), but clearly this has become a far more extensive responsibility than previously (III, 65,4).

In consequence, the *cathedra* of Moses changes its status. Originally in *Petr. ad Iac.* 1-2 we saw that the church's Order was a teaching succession, though διαδοχή is never used in these documents, understood with reference to the typology of Moses and the Seventy. The presbyters who interpret κατὰ κανόνα were overseen in their work by a bishop (*Petr. ad Iac.* 2,2) so that the typology of the bishop as the antitype of Moses, and the presbyters as the antitypes of the elders was well preserved. In *Ap. Trad.* 7 and 8 a similar relationship between bishop and presbyters was preserved in terms of type and antitype, but one which included the notion of the apportionment of Moses' spirit. In *Clement ad Iac.* the *cathedra* is attributed to Clement as bishop alone, and never mentioned in connection with the presbyters. But in neither case is the *cathedra* attributed to the bishop because it is the *cathedra* of Christ the true Moses. In *Ap. Trad.* 7 and 8 the spirit given is not the Spirit of Christ and his gifts but that of Moses.

But in the Zacchaeus rite, that identification is now made between Moses and Christ, with a corresponding enlargement of the conception of episcopal power when the bishop is now equated with the Mosaic typology. The congregation are exhorted: "Honour therefore the throne of Christ (θρόνον οὖν Χριστοῦ τιμήσετε) because you are commended to honour the *cathedra* of Moses (ὅτι καὶ Μωϋσέως καθέδραν τιμᾶν ἐκελεύσθητε), even though those who presided were considered to be sinful (κἂν οἱ προκαθεζόμενοι ἁμαρτωλοὶ νομίζωνται)." (III, 70) With the equation of θρόνον οὖν Χριστοῦ/ Μωϋσέως καθέδραν, the conclusion can now be drawn that "he who presides (ὁ προκαθεζόμενος) is entrusted with the place of Christ (Χριστοῦ τόπον πεπίστευται). Therefore honour to or violence against the president (διὸ ἤτοι τιμὴ ἢ ὕβρις τοῦ προκαθεζομένου) is brought to Christ (εἰς Χριστὸν φέρεται) and from Christ it is conveyed to God (ἀπὸ δὲ Χριστοῦ εἰς θεὸν ἀναφέρεται)."

The monarchical development in the Zacchaeus rite is finally emphasized in the concluding passage where Peter lays hands on him and prays a prayer which contains the following words:

---

[51] Ibid. p. 130-134 ff.

For you are the ruler of rulers (σὺ γὰρ ἄρχων ἀρχόντων) and Lord of Lords, the master of kings (καὶ κύριος κυρίων, δεσπότης βασιλεών). Give authority to him who presides (σὺ δὸς ἐξουσίαν τῷ προκαθεζομένῳ), to loose what he needs to loose and to bind what he needs to bind (λύειν ἃ δεῖ λύειν, καὶ δεσμεῖν ἃ δεῖ δεσμεῖν). Make him wise (σὺ σόφισον). Guard through him as your instrument the Church of your Christ as a beautiful bride (συ ὡς δι' ὀργάνου δι' αὐτοῦ τὴν ἐκκλησίαν τοῦ Χριστοῦ σου ὡς καλὴν νύμφην διαφύλαξον).

Hom. III, 72,3-5

Here the bishop is no longer teacher but ruler, whose power is entrusted to him to guard the Church as the Bride of Christ. He is the instrument of God, the images of whom in this prayer are regal (ἄρχων ἀρχόντων... κύριος κυρίων, δεσπότης βασιλεών). Examples of binding and loosing are given, but from the images of this prayer the activity described would not involve the harmonizing of discrepant scriptural passages according to an interpretative rule. The ruler rather binds and looses in conquest and domination.

But unlike the later *Didascalia,* in which such monarchical episcopal images also preponderate, there is no use whatsoever here of images of priesthood or high-priesthood. Moreover, we saw in the differences between *Ap. Trad.* 3 and 7-8 that this text does employ ἀρχιερατεία in the case of the former, but not the latter, and seems therefore to represent two distinct traditions in which Church Order is conceived, a sacerdotal one, and a teaching, presbyteral one. Furthermore, one such strand did not so much follow by logical implication from the other but rather was antithetical to what it implied.

In making the bishop the antitype of Aaron, the tradition of *Ap. Trad.* 3 almost self-consciously refuses to develop concepts of episcopacy in terms of the office of Moses as ruler and judge. God is he "who dwells on high (ὁ ἐν ὑψηλοῖς κατοικῶν) and looks down upon the lowly (καὶ τὰ ταπεινὰ ἐφορῶν)." Ecclesiastical Order, rather than an every extending development of episcopal power, is rather the process by which "you set boundaries (or "rules" or "canons") for your Church (σὺ ὁ δοὺς ὅρους ἐκκλησίας) by the word of you grace (διὰ λόγου χάριτός σου)." The sacerdotal spirit is about forgiveness of sins, and shepherding the flock. It is not about bishops ruling or judging to the extent that the monarch-bishop of the Zacchaeus rite will rule and judge.

The author of this rite therefore reflects the conflicting currents leading to the gradual establishment of monarchical forms of Church government finally in the age of Cyprian. He reflects the very currents that were operative in the dispute between the author of *El.* and Callistus, and the *rapprochement* between the communities of Hippolytus and Pontianus. As the liturgical conceptualization of one position in opposition to another proceeds, however, in the concrete situation of a historically existent Church Order, there is an historical limit on the extent to which Church Order can be "moulded nearer to the heart's desire." In terms of the first decade of the third century, it would be idle to deny that the presiding presbyter-bishops of the house schools, in process of becoming the later *tituli* churches, did not in some sense 'rule.' Thus *Ap. Trad.* 3 will admit that God had "established from the beginning... both rulers and priests" (ἀπ᾽ ἀρχῆς... ἄρχοντας τε καὶ ἱερεῖς καταστήσας).

For the purpose of overseeing (ἐπισκοπεῖν) the poor relief in each congregation, each bishop had to possess δύναμιν τοῦ ἡγεμονικοῦ πνεύματος. But the author of this prayer did not wish for the foreign secretary of Hermas *Vis.* 2,4 to accumulate final control of all such relief so as to become, once the community began holding property corporatively, the sole monarch. This is why he eclipses regal power with sacerdotal power, and the images of ἁγίασμα, κατὰ τόπον ἁγιάσματος, ποιμαίνειν τὴν ποιμνήν, ἀρχιερατεύειν, ἱλάσκεσθαι, προσφέρειν σοι τὰ δῶρα, προσφέροντά σοι ὀσμὴν εὐωδίας etc. preponderate throughout.

The bishop as a high priest binds and looses sins not by a judicial act of will but by offering a sacrifice. It is of course one of the cruel paradoxes of history that rather than the Hippolytan sacerdotal imagery being negated by the triumphant ideolology of monarchial episcopacy, that ideology simply synthesized both regal thesis and sacerdotal antithesis into its conceptual scheme. The bishop of the Syrian *Didascalia* as well as of its North African contemporary, Cyprian of Carthage, were high priests as well as kings.

As part of our account of the development of episcopal imagery mentioned in the letters Peter and Clement, and their parallels in *Ap. Trad.* 7-8, we need now to consider in detail the common tradition (7B 4 and in 7B 5) represented by the pseudonymous background of these letters, and the interpretation that this background imposed on the rites themselves.

7B 4. Ap. Trad. *3 and 7-8 and* Petr. *and* Clement. ad Iac.

Basically *Ap. Trad.* 3 and 7-8 contain two traditions, the former Aaronic and the latter Mosaic. The archierocratic character of the former is ideologically antithetical to the latter, but we must register that we have yet to consider the further question as to whether the archierocratic strand is the invention of the Hippolytan community, or whether it itself has a history. For the moment we note simply that we have found in the letters of Peter and Clement parallels with the Mosaic but not with the Aaronic tradition.

Neither the *Ap. Trad.* nor the *Clementines* use the concept of διαδοχή itself. This in itself would indicate that the application of the ideology of the Greek philosophic school was the contribution of Irenaeus and the author of *El.*, each from a slightly different standpoint, in interpretation of a teaching succession that could be understood otherwise. Indeed in *Ap. Trad.* it is the possession of Moses' spirit by the bishop, or a fragment of it by the presbyters, rather than a chain of succession through secular history that constitutes validity of office. On the other hand, in *Petr.* and *Clement ad Iac.* we have seen that the teaching succession was understood in terms of a Mosaic *cathedra* handed down with scribal rules of interpretation. That Church Order in terms of teaching authority could be understood in terms of either a diadochal or scribal idiom is a cogent testimony to the antiquity of the conception of ecclesiastical Order in terms of teaching authority.

Undoubtedly the congregation that understood its common life in terms of the scribal and Mosaic imagery before the pseudonymous imposition of Jacobean and Petrine authorship, and before the monarchical claims of the Zacchaean rite, was quite distinct from that of Irenaeus and the author of *El.* The community of *Ap. Trad.* has after all developed the Mosaic typology in its own way. But we have seen from our development of Lampe's account that such distinctive congregations are what we should expect from archeological and literary evidence, albeit fragmentary, regarding the house-schools that antedated the *tituli* parishes.

Furthermore, there is a fundamental congruence in operational terms, between the kinds of ministry excersised by the community of *Petr. ad Iac.* and that of the *Ap. Trad.*, despite the differences in ideological conception of that ministry. Although *Petr. ad Iac.* might seem Jewish and Palestinian in its scope and even Syrian, it is important to remember that cultural space between communities was not a function of geographical distance, as Juvenal's remark about the Orontes contaminating the Tiber is one famous indication. At all events, the Rabbinic categories of παραδοῦναι, παραλαμβάνειν, and κανών etc. have been overlaid with Hellenistic concepts such as ἀγωγή, μεταρρυθμίζειν etc., so that the didadochal assimilation has clearly begun to take place.[52]

We know from the Quardodeciman controversy itself that there was present an Asiatic community in Rome, and Haansens has demonstrated Egyptian influence upon Hippolytus even if his credulity regarding the legend of the Novatian presbyter has lead him astray. The existence of such a Greek-speaking congregation behind the tradition of *Petr. ad Iac.*, whose rites and understanding of Church Order it inherited from a form of Palestinian Judaism that had migrated to Rome, would be quite consistent with what we know of the multi-culturalism of Rome at this time. But superimposed upon the tradition of this group has been the pseudonymous

---

[52] There is of course also the problem of possible Elchasite or Gnostic influence on the text of *Petr. ad Iac.* Strecker (1958, 1981), p. 139-145 denies this and endeavours to explain the text in general, and the Rabbinic and Mosaic features in particular, as a fictional attempt to deliberately archaize the text to make it appear ancient. In the light of my discussion here I remain unconvinced. The Mosaic imagery clearly was current in understanding Church Order as *Ap. Trad.* makes clear, and was not therefore part of an archaizing process. Furthermore, there remains the need to provide clear evidence that archaizing was deployed by ancient writers in the way in which it was used, say, in the nineteenth-century novels of a Walter Scott. See also O. Cullman, *Le problème littéraire et historique du roman pseudo- Clémentine,*(Paris: Éditions du Cerf 1930).

characters of Clement and Peter, and the two letters that each of them writes to James. We must now look at what messages are encoded in the pseudonymous form of this superimposition.

7B 5. Petr. *and* Clement ad Iac.: *the pseudonymous form*

With the imposition of the pseudonymous form, the substance of διαδοχή in the sense of the author of *El.*, though not the term itself, makes its appearance. In addition to the absence of the word, there are no succession lists in the *Clementines*. This may be due to their pseudonymous form, even though there also are no succession lists in *El.* We have argued nevertheless that he and Hippolytus his successor were authors of the first part of the Liberian List. The reason for the omission was undoubtedly that of Irenaeus, for whom the fundamental notion of succession was a coherence of teaching, though with reference to Diogenes Laertius, *The Successions of the Philosophers*, we argued that the names themselves were not merely legendary window-dressing for an abstraction. Greek historiography, unlike modern, could not cope with the idea of development of ideas in abstraction from the particular individual minds that developed them. The successions of named philosophers, like named bishops, were more than incidental to an account of the coherent development of systems of ideas.

The author of *El.* likewise would have found names as well as ideas part and parcel of the same succession. He does however focus on the succession of ideas rather than the names that he omits. We shall now see how both the author of the *Elenchos* and *Petr.* and *Clement ad Iac.* both draw in different ways upon the tradition of historiography of ideas of which Diogenes is the one surviving representative.[53] It is to be emphasized that the relationship between them is one of sharing in a common historiographic tradition about philosophical διαδοχαί rather than direct borrowing. Diogenes' wrote around c. A.D. 217, contemporaneous with the conflict between Callistus and the author of *El.*[54] We shall find that parallel no only in historiographical form shared by episcopal and philosophical succession lists, but also in the pseudonymous letters attributed to the founders of successions.

---

[53] Diogenes sources are Sotion (200-170 B.C.), Sosicrates of Rhodes, and Heraclides of Callatis or Alexandria, Antisthenes of Rhodes, Lembus (181-146 B.C.), and Alexander (8,24). Sotion's book was entitled *Successions of the Philosophers* (Διαδοχαὶ τῶν φιλοσόφων) and is regularly cited by Diogenes as ἐν Διαδοχαῖς. (*Succ.* 2,12.), as is Sosicrates' work (1,107; 6,80; 8,8), except on one occasion ("the Successors" (ἐν τρίτῃ Διαδοχῶν), (6,13)). Callatis is described as having written the Succession (Διαδοχὴν) (5.94).

[54] For a full discussion of the dating, see M. Trevissoi, Diogene Laerzio, L'età in cui visse, in *Rivista di Storia Antica* xii (1908), 482-505. See also R. Hope, *The Book of Diogene' Laertius: Its Spirit and Its Method*, (New York 1930), 6-7.

7B 5.1. διαδοχὴ φιλοσόφων *and* διαδοχὴ ἀποστόλων

Both Diogenes and the author of *El.* use the concept of διαδοχή in the service of a desire for cultural or doctrinal purity. *El.* does not share Irenaeus' interest in a list of named bishops as the successors of the apostles. Rather his interest is in the διαδοχαί of the heretics whom he wishes to show that they derived their origins from Greek philosophers and not from Judaeo-Christian culture. Simon Magus is not for him, as for Irenaeus, the founder of all heretical schools. Rather the heretical schools are the descendents of pagan philosophical schools in disguise, which in turn go back to the snake-worship of the Naasenes.[55]

Just as the author of *El.* uses the idea of διαδοχή to establish the doctrinal purity of what he believes to be orthodoxy, so too Diogenes use the same concept to demonstate the cultural purity of philosophy as solely derived from Hellenistic origins. What is to our purpose, however, in view of his likely dating, is that Diogenes ends his succession of the philosophers effectively with Epicurus (341-271 B.C.) and Chrysippus (282-206 B.C.). Any Greek writers that he mentions (Plutarch (*Succ.* 9,60) Epictetus (10,6), or Sextus Empiricus (9,87; 116), are thus treated as commentaries in footnotes to a phenomenon that has taken place but which is to all intents and purposes completed. Latin writers such as Lucretius, Cicero, and Seneca are completely ignored. Clearly he is a cultural purist who believed only Greek is cultural, and that the golden age is past.

Thus *El.*'s method of refutation of heresy parallels Diogenes' rejection of Latin or barbarian contributions to the Greek philosophical schools. Diogenes proposes to show that philosophy had its origin completely within Greek culture. He criticizes Sotion, as well as Aristotle in the *Magicus*, who had both begun their διαδοχαί of the philosophers with Persian or Babylonian and Assyrians magicians, with Indian gymnosophists, or with the Holy Ones of the Druids. Against them and other writers Diogenes asserts: "They ignore the achievements of the Greeks from whom not only philosophy but the human race itself begins, when they attribute them to the barbarians." (*Succ.* 1,3)[56]

But in order to exclude systematically all non-Hellenistic ideas and elements, Diogenes has to define his account of the διαδοχαί even more tightly.

---

55 In *El.* V,6,3 the claim αἴτιος τῆς πλάνης ὄφις indicates that, convinced by his new discovery of Gnostic texts, Justin 1 *Apol.* was wrong in ascribing to Simon Magus the origin of all heresy, as was Irenaeus *Adv. Haer.* I,22,2-23,1-4. M. Marcovich *Hippolytus' Refutatio Omnium haeresium,* (Berlin and New York 1986), p. 34-35.

56 For his further reasons for rejecting non-greek antecedents of Hellenistic philosophy see Brent (1993) p. 374 which finally grounds philosophy in Musaeus and Linos son of Eumolpus and Hermes and the Muse Ourania respectively, "so that both the human race and philosophy begin together with the Greeks, in the age when the gods consorted with humans." Thus it was no accident that φιλοσοφία was a Greek word incapable of translation into any barbarian language.

He cannot proceed purely descriptively but must prescribe for the various
διαδοχαί a common origin in either one of two ἀρχαί of philosophy. Thus he
can secure them through their putative origins solely within Greek culture
from contamination from barbarian culture. The "Ionic" ἀρχή which begins
with Anaximander ends with Cleitomachus and Chrysippus and
Theophrastus, and the "Italic" with Pythagoras ends with Epicurus." (proem.
14)

Such a prescriptive method, however, leads to an artificial and quite
forced classification, as when Anaximander, Anaximenes, and Archelaus are
associated as a single succession with Socrates and Plato (Ibid. 14). Indeed,
the Ionic succession has to be given three concluding philosophers,
Clitomachus on the one hand who descends from Plato through Speusippus
and Xenocrates, Chrysippus, who descends through Antisthenes, and
Theophrastus, who concludes the line of Aristotle's successors. Pherekydes,
by contrast, has a unilinear succession from Democritus to Epicurus. The
links in the chain of succession are weakly drawn (οὗ Δημόκριτος, οὗ πολλοί
μέν ἐπ᾽ ὀνόματος δὲ Ναυσιφάνης καὶ Ναυκύδης ὧν ᾽Επίκουρος). (Ibid. 15)
Thus emerge the four great schools of Diogenes' time, the Academic, Stoic,
Peripatetic, and Epicurean.[57]

The description of the relationships between members of the διαδοχαί do
not correspond precisely with the outline given in the prologue and are thus
not consistently drawn by Diogenes. Telauges, son of Pythagoras, in the prologue is described as the teacher of Xenophanes (*Succ.* 1,15), although in the
later's *Life* he is no-where mentioned in such a role (Ibid. 9,21). In the *Life of
Empedokles* (Ibid. 8,50) he does not appear as the subject's teacher, though
that is his description in the *Life of Pythagoras* (Ibid. 8,42). In 9,21
Parmenides is considered the pupil of the Pythagoreans, and not Xenophanes
as we would expect from 1,15.[58]

Undoubtedly these, along with other features of his account, indicate
Diogenes' work to be a "compilation very carelessly thrown together by a
collector... not only the materials of others, but also fragments of their out-
lines."[59] But Diogenes is not objectively describing the successions historically, as we have seen, but is prescribing the character of a Greek philosophy
that was the uncontaminated product of Greek culture. The "carelessness" is
thus explained. The precise details of its members of a διαδοχή and their
chronological relationship were relatively unimportant in the light of that objective, and therefore could be left in his text so haphazardly drawn.

Irenaeus (*Adv. Haer.* III,3,2-4) similarly, before *El.*, had used the historiographical method of establishing a διαδοχή between a series of teachers as a

[57] Hope op. cit. 133-134.
[58] For a full discussion of these see Hope, op. cit. 133-139.
[59] Ibid. 138.

guarantee of the coherence of a common Christian doctrine, untainted culturally by paganism. He drew up the episcopal succession list for the See of Rome, and claimed that it was typical of similar lists for other Sees. And he did so in a context in which christian communities, as we have seen, resembled conflicting philosophical schools. So too, as we have seen, did *El.* though his method was negative rather than positive: the heretics were not orthodox because their true ἀρχή was in Greek philosophy.

In this way we find Diogenes' historiography reflected in the methodology of the author of *El.* The schema of succession in critical parts is highly artificial, yet as a historiographical device its serves the author's purpose. Diogenes, writing in the mid-third century A.D., brought his διαδοχαί to an end in the mid-second century B.C. For him the philosophical possibilities are exhausted, and philosophy brought to its fully developed end, with Platonism, Stoicism, Aristotelianism, and Epicureanism. There is no further development, since as Plato claimed, change is an illusion, and as Aristotle held, development has a final end.

So too with *El.* Christian heresies are διαδοχαί from pagan philosophers. So the διαδοχή of Valentinus from Plato and Pythagoras, Justin from Herodotus, Marcion from Empedokles, Basilides from Aristotle, and Noetus from Heracleitus. The connections are highly tenuous. Empedokles' conception of the two first principles, Strife and Love, for example, are equated with Marcion's two Gods by a tortuous discussion intended to show that Marcion is a "stealer of [his] arguments (κλεψιλόγος)." (*El.* VIII,29-30) There are no new heresies and no new orthodoxy for the author of *El.*, no more than there are for Diogenes, and even though the latter may understand "heresy" in a less pejorative sense.[60] The diverse antecedents of heresy must be shown to emanate from a common ἀρχή in pagan culture.

In *El.* I prooem. 6 the author does not ground his orthodox succession in any named apostles who appointed bishops, as *Petr.* and *Clement ad Iac.* endeavour to do. Neither furthermore does the *Ap. Trad.*, in which neither διαδοχή nor named apostles appear. But Diogenes, as we shall now see, does endeavour to ground the origins of his ἀρχαί and διαδοχαί in pseudepigraphic letter-writing activity, which further circumscribes them within the culturally insulated boundaries of an uncontaminated Hellenistic *Urzeit.* We shall now demonstrate how, in so doing, Diogenes contains parallels with the *pseudepigrapha* of the *Clementines.*

---

60 Diogenes speaks of the ἀρχή of an αἵρεσις, used non-pejoratively, of a philosophical group following "a certain principle in their treatment of the visible" (τὴν λόγῳ τινὶ κατὰ τὸ φαινόμενον ἀκολουθοῦσαν) or "with a bias for coherent positive doctrines (πρόκλισιν δόγμασιν ἀκολουθίαν ἔχουσιν)." (*Succ.* 1,20)

7B 5.2. *Pseudonymous Letters of* ἀποστόλοι *and of the* σοφοί

Diogenes presented, not a historical argument, but a historical myth in terms of whose mythopoeic logic his purist thesis of culture is encoded. His thesis is that philosophy is a wholly Greek cultural phenomenon having reached its natural completion with Chrysippus, Theophrastus, and Epicurus. The legend of the seven sages or wise men of Greece is taken and reshaped in order to argue his point mythopoeically, rather in the way that we shall argue Peter and Clement are so used in the *Clementines*. Beginning with the usual seven Wise Men of Greek antiquity, Thales, Solon, Periander, Cleobulus, Chilon, Bias, Pittacus, he brings their number up to eleven or twelve by claiming that "with these are numbered (τούτοις προσαριθμοῦσιν) Anacharsis the Scythian, Myson of Chen, Pherecydes of Syros, Epimenides the Cretan; and by some even Pisistratus the tyrant." (*Succ.* 1,13)

These eleven or twelve Wise Men or σοφοί are kept quite distinct from the φιλοσόφοι. They exist for Diogenes, as it were, in the *Urzeit* of Greek civilization. Their unity in a common Greek civilization is not established by a comparison of the distinctiveness of the philosophical ideas which they shared together in contrast to the barbarians, any more than the relationship between the succession of philosophers was drawn as a succession of ideas rather than of persons. The wise men write letters to each other, and by means of this literary fiction, their unity, and thus the coherence of Greek civilization, is represented in the *Urzeit*. Thales writes to Pherecydes, and then to Solon, and Pherecydes replies (ibid. 1,43-4, and 1,122). Solon writes to Periander, then to Epimenides, then to Pisistratus and then to Croesus. Pisistratus also writes to Solon (ibid. 1,53, 64-7). And so on throughout the list runs a similar chain of epistolary interrelations.[61]

A direct parallel with such an historiography is to be found in the contemporary development of episcopal succession lists, witnessed by Irenaeus and *El.*, where the apostles are outside the succession itself in the Christian *Urzeit*. Both Pherekydes and Thales initiate their respective successions, though they are not its first member. These two Wise Men of Greece, like the apostles, stand outside the succession from which the two separate successions of Anaximander and Pythagoras, like Linus or Clement from Peter, begin.

Thus Thales communicates with Pherekydes and Pherekydes communicates with Thales. Anaximenes, "pupil of Anaximander (ἤκουσεν Ἀναξιμάνδρου)," (ibid. 2,3) who begins one philosophical succession, writes to Pythagoras who begins the other the succession (ibid. 2,4), and Anaximenes replies (ibid. 8,49). Thus the two rival successions maintain the unity of a

---

[61] Chilon to Periander (1,73); Pittacus to Croesus (1,81); Bias none; Cleobulus to Solon (1,93); Periander to the wise men and then to Procles, with a letter from Thrasybulus to him (1,99-100); Anacharsis to Croesus (1,105); Myson none; Epimenides to Solon (1,113-115).

common philosophical and Greek culture as philosophers, just as the Wise Men did in the *Urzeit*. Just as most of Wise Men of the *Urzeit* of Hellenistic culture have no other role than images of origin of cultural identity, so too neither do the majority of the apostles. Just as only Thales and Pherekydes, amongst the wise men, produced successions of philosophers through Anaximander and Pythagoras, so too only Peter and James amongst the apostles and their associates produce successions through Clement and the Roman list, and through the Jerusalem list.

The *Clementines* do not make direct reference to successions of bishops, like the successions of philosophers in Diogenes and his predecessors. Indeed such direct reference is excluded by the conditions of pseudonymity. The scene, depicted to give credence to the pseudonymic device, is in past time, where mention of successors will destroy the impression created that we are in the presence of the pristine ἀρχαί of the succession lists. In the *Urzeit* we view only the relationship of Peter and his immediate successor, Clement, and with James the Lord's brother.

Thus in such literature there is envisaged a Christian *Urzeit* which interestingly parallels Diogenes' *Urzeit* inhabited by the Wise Men, from whom the philosophers ultimately derived the wisdom of which they were the lovers. In the Christian *Urzeit*, the place of the "Wise Men," alternatively seven, eleven, or twelve in number, is taken by the twelve apostles. The philosophers' place is taken by the bishops, whose succession the former begin, but in whose number they are not included. Though the number and the names of the twelve Wise Men, like the twelve apostles, are important for the encoded message about a united and uncontaminated culture from which doctrine derives its ἀρχή, only two of the wise men (Pherekydes and Thales) and only one or perhaps two (Peter and perhaps James) actually initiate a teaching succession or successions.

True, though Thales and Pherekydes do not communicate by letter with those who begin the philosophic succession, Peter the apostle does communicate by letter with James, "Lord and bishop of the Holy Church." (*Pet. ad Iac.* 1,1) But James' position as ranking with the bishops or with the apostles was always ambiguous, as was Paul's, since before *Luke-Acts* the apostolic ministry of the church was not limited to the Twelve. Both James and Paul prefigure as apostles in the list of eyewitnesses in 1 *Cor.* 15,3-9. Clement, unambiguously a bishop, is instructed to write to James "Lord and bishop of bishops who rules the Holy Church of the Hebrews at Jerusalem, and the churches everywhere founded in the foreknowledge of God." (*Clem. ad Iac.* 1,1) But there is no pseudepigraphic attempt to produce a letter of James in reply to Clement. Furthermore, a pseudepigraphic reply in the form of a letter from Peter would be too incongruous. Clement, after all, is writing to James after Peter's death, which in itself is incongruous in view of the likely date of James' martyrdom before that of Peter.

James does not return Clement's letter, according to the conventions of Diogenes' *genre*, because Peter, and James, albeit ambiguously, are, like Thales and Pherekydes, inhabitants of the *Urzeit* outside of the two successions that they originate, but of which they cannot form part. Peter communicates by letter with James—like Pherekydes the ἀρχή of one succession does with Thales as ἀρχή of the other—regarding the preservation of the books of his teaching and its true interpretation (*Pet. ad Iac.* 2-3). But neither from the Christian *Urzeit* communicates directly by letter with Clement.

Granted Clement writes to James after Peter's death, on the latter's instruction, setting out the details of his consecration as bishop (*Clem. ad Iac.* 1,19), as indeed Pythagoras and Anaximander as φιλοσόφοι never did to Pherekydes and Thales as σοφοί. But as we have said, James' status as apostle, corresponding to σοφός, and bishop, corresponding to φιλοσόφος, always was ambiguous. Indeed there was a further and unrelated early catholic motive which had, as it were, a vested interest in such an ambiguity: James the brother of the Lord must be given apostolic status in recognition of the catholicity of a congregation with characteristics associated with the legendary character of James. Such an additional motive at work in second-century, Christian, reflection has therefore distorted the neatness of Diogenes' scheme in application to the christian διαδοχή.

But Clement's communication with James can be paralleled from Diogenes in another implication of the figure of James as bishop and not as apostle. Pythagoras, the first member of one succession whose ἀρχή was Pherekydes wrote to Anaximenes, second member of the other, and thus communicated directly with the alternative succession whose first member was Anaximander and whose ἀρχή was Thales (*Succ.* 2,3-4; 8,49). Likewise, Peter outside the succession does not communicate by letter directly with Clement, third bishop in the succession according to Irenaeus but first according to the Liberian *Catalogus*. Rather he instructs Clement to communicate with James, and thus the two successions here too are shown to be twin features of a common, early catholic orthodoxy. Thus the author of the two pseudepigraphic letters that stand at the head of the *Clementine Homilies*, whilst operating within the kind of historiographic perspective to which Diogenes bears witness, wished to make a somewhat different point from that of the unity of Greek culture in diversity.

We have argued that the Roman Church of the late second century represented a culturally diverse number of congregations acknowledging a union whose fragility was marked by the Quartodeciman controversy. They exchanged the *frumentum* and acknowledge a foreign secretary with a ministry of circulating incoming letters from other churches, and writing in the name of the Roman Church to those outside. We traced some further hints at the structure of that association in our discussion of *El* IX, 7-12 in Chapter 3. We have seen, moreover, in this chapter the conflicting currents of the development proceeding towards monarchical episcopacy represented in the various ordination rites represented in the *Clementines* themselves. The community of *Petr. ad Iac.* was far more 'presbyteral' than that of *Clement ad Iac.*, and the Zacchaeus rite was far more monarchical than the latter's bishop supreme in what was still essentially a teaching role.

The movement towards monarchical episcopacy was clearly demanding a far more homogeneous unity than that provided for Hellenistic civilization by Diogenes' two ἀρχαί. The community of "Clement," is probably the community of Callistus, in view of Strecker's dating, with its claims to supremacy over the rest, and its inabilty to recognize the "ecclesiastical limits (τῶν ἐκκλησιαστικῶν ὅρων)." (*El.* IX,11, 1 cf. *Ap. Trad.* 3) Through the device of pseudonymity Callistus' group, in the pseudonymous person of Clement, is acknowledging the Palestinian or Syrian group, which nevertheless speaks the Greek of the Roman communites, in the equally pseudonymous person of James. James is "Lord and bishop of the holy Church" (τῷ κυρίῳ καὶ ἐπισκόπῳ τῆς ἁγίας ἐκκλησίας). (*Petr. ad Iac.* 1,1) James is "the Lord and bishop of bishops (τῷ κυρίῳ καὶ ἐπισκόπων ἐπισκόπῳ), who administers the holy Church of the Hebrews in Jerusalem (διέποντι δὲ τὴν Ἰερουσαλὴμ, ἁγίαν Ἑβραίων ἐκκλησίαν), and churches well-founded everywhere by God's providence (καὶ τὰς πανταχῇ θεοῦ προνοίᾳ ἱδρυθείσας καλῶς)." (*Clement ad Iac.* 1,1) We need not see with Hengel in these words a reference to James as the first pope, presiding over a well-defined worldwide network of Jewish churches.[62] The pseudonymous writer is not referring to such a network, but speaks of καὶ τὰς πανταχῇ θεοῦ προνοίᾳ ἱδρυθείσας καλῶς in order to comprehend one such only, namely a congregation of such a cultural character in Rome itself, in intercommunion with his own.

The diplomatically expressed encoded message however is that, however honourable the traditions of this Jacobaean community might be, and however respectful 'Clement' must be to 'James' as τῷ κυρίῳ καὶ ἐπισκόπων ἐπισκόπῳ, Peter is the apostle, and needs only address James as τῷ κυρίῳ καὶ ἐπισκόπῳ τῆς ἁγίας ἐκκλησίας. 'Clement' has received his ordination from Peter, and so, like Callistus whom he represents, he can assume the supreme teaching authority over the other congregations, as he does in *El.* IX,12, 20-23, and disregard their presbyteral claims to the *cathedra* of Moses of this particular Roman congregation. Peter is "he who is on account of his true

---

[62] M. Hengel, Jakobus der Herrenbruder- der erste Papst? in *Glaube und Eschatologie, Festschrift für Werner George Kümmel zum 80 Geburtstag,* (Tübingen: J.B. Mohr 1985), p. 71-104.

faith (ὁ διὰ τὴν ἀληθῆ πίστιν) and the most sure premiss of his teaching (καὶ ἀσφαλεστάτην αὐτοῦ τῆς διδασκαλίας ὑπόθεσιν), the foundation of the Church" (τῆς ἐκκλησίας θεμέλιος), and described as "called, elect, (κλητός, ἐκλεκτός), the good and tried disciple (ὁ καλὸς καὶ δόκιμος μαθητής), the first of the apostles (ὁ τῶν ἀποστόλων πρῶτος)," etc. (*Clem. ad Iac.* 1,2-3) In the conflicting currents leading to monarchical episcopacy, Christianity, unlike Greek culture, cannot have two ἀρχαί but only one. The function of the pseudonymous imposition upon the ordination rites of Peter, James, and Clement in to reconstruct the social and ecclesiastical reality in the direction of the latter monarchical episcopacy of the Zacchaeus rite by an encoded argument for the presiding presbyter-bishop of one congregation to become the supreme teacher and occupant of one sole teaching chair.

We can now see the real reason why James represents a significant figure in the two pseudepigraphic epistles that begin the *Clementines*. The reason for this significance is the literary role of such a figure in a description of the Christian *Urzeit*. That he held this role because he was "the Lord's brother" is mentioned (ibid. *Ep. Clem. ad Iac.* 19,2), but never emphasized, let alone any putatively sacerdotal authority that may be derived from that relationship. Indeed, throughout the *Clementines*, the authority of the ministry is a teaching authority, and presidency at the Eucharist is unmentioned. In the *Clementines* we find a certain parallelism between the kind of historiography of the succession of philosophical schools represented later by Diogenes Laertius, who drew on his predecessors both substantively and formally in the literary *genre* in which he wrote.

7B 6. *Conclusion: relations between* Ap. Trad. *and* Clementines

We began this chapter by surveying the manuscript traditon and noting those features of it that encode an ideological and doctrinal message by means of the pseudepigraphic claims of sections of material claiming to be apostolic delivered διὰ Ἱππολύτου or διὰ Κλήμεντος. We noted that such claims were part of a tendency of Eastern fathers to make Hippolytus, like Clement, a contemporary of the sub-apostolic age, and to use both as an idealization of conflicting traditions. We connected the encoded literary message thus detected with a similar message to be found in Damasus' legend of the Novatian presbyter, which formed a principle part of our discussion in Chapter 6. Here it became clear that an encoded message was not confined to the Eastern tradition alone, but had its Western and Roman counterpart.

We analysed various and conflicting images, archieratic and scribal, Aaronic and Mosaic, in the different prayers of ordination in *Ap. Trad.* 2-3, 7-8 (7A 2.1-2.2.2), and connected these with three stages in the development of monarchical episcopacy evidenced in *Petr.* and *Clement ad Iac.* and *Hom.* III, 67-68 (7B 3.2). Once again we saw the pseudepigraphic literary form reflecting the various *pro* and *anti* currents within the Roman house-school communities of the late second and early third century, and expressing the dialectical movements of the shaping the ideology of nascent monarchical episcopacy.

Regarding the ideological function of the pseudonymous literary form, we drew comparisons between Irenaeus and *El.*, the *Clementines*, and the historiography of Diogenes Laertius, who also employed a similar literary pseudonymity to encode a cultural message. Recalling the concept of the Christian congregations at Rome as house-schools (Chapter 6), we established a clear connection between the διαδοχὴ τῶν ἀποστόλων and the διαδοχὴ φιλοσόφων. In both cases, moreover, tracing descent, however artificial, between schools of opinions seemed necessary for the demonstration of the truth or falsity of the enterprise, or at least its validity.

In the case of both apostolic and philosophic succession, the literary form expressed cultural identity by positing an *Urzeit*, whether populated by twelve apostles, or seven, eleven, or twelve wise men, and by the literary and legendary device that established an epistolatory network between them. The successions in both cases, moreover, being outside the *Urzeit*, are themselves fused into one. The correspondence between James and Peter in the *Clementines* establishes the succession but in this case, Clement as first on one succession list intervenes to combine the two lines of succession themselves into one, by writing to James at Peter's instruction. Likewise Anaximenes, pupil of Anaximander with first place in one succession list, writes to Pythagoras who has first place in the other and thus established the coherence of philosophical schools within a common Hellenistic culture.

Having therefore established a School of Hippolytus, centred on the Statue with its distinctive Easter Table and representative writings, we have now traced the emergence and integration of that School, behind a legendary and pseudepigraphic veil, into the common fabric of early Christian orthodoxy. We are now in a position to examine afresh a comparison between Hippolytus' community and that of Tertullian, in the context of church Order immediately prior to the age of Cyprian. As we argued in Chapter 6, monarchical episcopacy, in the final form of its development, was alone to be found in the age subsequent to Cyprian. Let us see, therefore, to what extent the Hippolytan events are mirrored in what we can infer regarding Tertullian's biography.

PART C. HIPPOLYTUS AND TERTULLIAN

Both in North Africa and in Alexandria the contemporary evidence for the emergence of single bishops is clear at this time. Cyprian twice mentions Agrippinus, a bishop of Carthage, whose date must be anything between 190 and 230 (*Ep.* 71,4 and 73,3).[63] Eusebius notoriously distorts early Christian history with his assumption that the Church Order of the fourth century had to be identical with that of the first, with the result that no development could have occurred. Eusebius bears garbled witness to the existence of single bishops in Alexandria in the famous event of Origen's life.

Demetrius is mentioned as the bishop who received a written request, along with the governor, delivered by "one of the military (τις τῶν στρατιωτικῶν)," from "the ruler of Arabia (παρὰ τοῦ τῆς Ἀραβίας ἡγουμένου), that Origen pay him a visit (VI, 19,15). Eusebius cannot be making anachronistic assumptions in this case regarding Demetrius' office since he cites the letter written to him as the appropriate authority by Alexander, bishop of Jerusalem, and Theoctistus bishop of Caesarea (VI, 19,17).

But although both Cyprian and Eusebius give evidence for the existence of single bishops, those bishops are hardly understood to be in full possession of their later prerogatives in terms of an ecclesiastical discourse in the context of which certain acts can be understood as 'schismatical' etc. We have argued that the Hippolytan events themselves, and indeed the character of his school as one member of a fractionalized Roman community in Lampe's sense, do not warrant conceptualization in terms of the later age of Cyprian (6C 7-7.1.3). As has often been argued, although Tertullian's Montanism leads to his relegation by later writers to the category of schismatic, his contemporaries did not regard him in such a light. Jerome in *De Viris Ill.* 53, reports the words of Cyprian's secretary that he read Tertullian every day and regarded him as his teacher (*magister meus*).

Both Tertullian and the far shadowy figure of Agrippinus, the predecessor of Cyprian in the See of Carthage, have been linked with the dispute between Callistus and the author of *El.*, their contemporaries. Callistus has been identified with the anonymous *pontifex maximus* and *episcopus episcoporum*, and has been credited with the *edictum preremptorium* of *De Pud.* 1,6. It will be of relevance, therefore, in conclusion, firstly to survey the earlier debate over the possibility of this link between the Hippolytan community and Tertullian (7C 1). Secondly we shall examine the related question of whether the Monarchian attacked in Tertullian's *Adversus Praxeam* was in fact Callistus himself, and, correspondingly, whether the nascent Trinitarianism of *C.N.* is not in fact reflected and developed in that treatise (7C 2). We shall find the different conclusions on both sides of that debate contrained by the kind of assumptions that we have witnessed in the case of Damasus and Eusebius, who failed to conceptualize other than anachronistically and therefore distortedly the earlier, fractionalized state of the development of monepiscopacy before Cyprian's time (Chapter 6 Part B).

---

[63] T.D. Barnes, *Tertullian: A Historical and Literary Study* (Oxford: Clarendon 1985), p. 71.

7C 1. *Tertullian and Callistus' alleged "edict"*

The discussion of the existence of this "edict" revolved around an argument which had two components frequently confused. The first component is an analysis that establishes a relation between *De Pudic.* and *El.* IX, 12 by comparing the charges made by Tertullian against an unnamed bishop and those of the author of *El.* against Callistus. The second component is then to conclude that Callistus must have behaved like a later pope and issued a general edict as binding on the bishop of Carthage as on all other bishops. The confusion of the two lead to the false conclusion that if there had been no possibility of a general edict, and no such power on the part of pope Callistus at that time, then there could be no relation between Tertullian and the author of *El.* Tertullian's remarks therefore would have a more local target such as the shadowy Agrippinus.

In the discussion which follows, we shall distinguish both components in various passages from Tertullian in comparion with *El.* IX, 12, showing that whilst there is a definite relation between the two writers, the context of ecclesiastical Order is not that which has been assumed.

7C 1.1. *The* De Pudic. *and* El. *IX, 12, 20-26*

Tertullian begins with the famous passage which reads as follows:

> I hear (*audio etiam*) that there has been published an edict (*edictum esse propositum*), and that a final edict (*et quidem peremptorium*). The Pontifex (mark you!) (*Pontifex scilicet*) Maximus (*maximus*), that is the bishop of bishops (*quod est episcopus episcoporum*), ordains (*edicit*): "I absolve (*dimitto*) both the sins of adultery and fornication (*et moechiae et fornicationis delicta*) when penance has been performed (*paenitentia functis*)." O edict to which there cannot be the appendage (*O edictum cui adscribi non poterit*): "A good well done! (*bonum factum*)" And where is that generosity published? (*Et ubi proponetur liberalitas ista*) In the same place (*Ibidem*), I conjecture (*opinor*), [as] on at the entrances of [houses of] lust (*in ipsis libidinum ianuis*), under the very arch that bears the title of those houses (*sub ipsis libidinum titulis*). There pentitence ought to have been declared (*Illic eiusmodi paenitentia promulganda est*) where the offence was committed (*ubi delinquentia ipsa versabitur*). There you shall read of your favour (*Illic legenda est venia*), where you enter in expectation of it (*quo cum spe eius intrabitur*). But this is read in the church (*Sed hoc in ecclesia legitur*), and in the church it is proclaimed (*et in ecclesia pronuntiatur*), and she is a virgin (*et virgo est*).
>
> De Pudic. 1, 6-8

This passage has given rise to three problems with disputed solutions, which may be summarised as follows:
1. How real was the "edict" to which Tertullian refers and to what extent was it the construction of his sarcastic and satirical representation of a bishop's policy?

2. What is the force of the terms *pontifex maximus* and *episcopus episcopo-rum*? Do they necessarily refer to the bishop only of Rome or can they be applied in Carthage or elsewhere?

3. To what extent can the events described in *El.* IX, 12,20-26 be understood to reflect the same situation as that to which Tertullian refers.

4. To what extent does the situation described in *El.* IX, 12,20-21 require the notion of an edict and thus reflects Tertullian's situation?

7C 1.1.1. *How literal did Tertullian intend his reference to the edict?*

Rolffs treated Tertullian's words (*dimitto et moechiae et fornicationis paeni-tentia functis*) as a direct quotation from an actual written decree, and made them central to his attempted reconstruction of the "edict."[64] But it must be noted that Tertullian claims only to have heared (*audio*) and not to have read himself the alleged "edict." Koch was to argue that his claim must be under-stood in terms of Tertullian's Montanist separation, which assumes that Montanist congregations gathered in quite separate churches out of catholic episcopal communion.[65] Such a view might, as we shall argue later, itself have been anachronistic. But such a view may well in any case fail to per-ceive the deep irony of Tertullian's position.

If indeed there had been that separation, that itself would make Tertullian's alleged quotation from the edict hearsay and garbled, and the existence of the edict to that extent nebulous. But I would suggest that it is the extremes of his satire that in fact require him to construct out of the articulation of a policy the quite false picture of an unmamed bishop producing an edict. His caustic wit needs for the parodying of his opponent the image of an actual decree more suitably pinned to the archway of a brothel (*sub ipsis libidinum titulis*) than that of a house-church. But it is an image born of satire.

Can we really imagine an edict pinned to the arch-door of a house-church whether by the bishop of Carthage or from the bishop of Rome? Why would such a document by pinned up by an early third-century—or a later one for that matter—when a bishop was the one president of one gathered flock rather than the absent head of a number of delegated presbyters? The bishop

---

[64] E. Rolffs, Das Indulgenzedikt des römischen Bischofs Kallist, kritisch untersucht und reconstruiert, in *T.U.* XI, 3 (1893), p. 114, 17.

[65] H. Koch, Kallist und Tertullian: Ein Beitrag zur Geschichte der altchristlichen Bussstreitigkeiten und des römischen Primat, in *SHAW* Philos.-hist. Klasse 22 (1919), comment-ing on Esser, p. 4: "...dass „audio"... so verstanden wurde, dass man „von katholischer Seite den Montanistischen Konventikeln das Edikt als ein solches vorgehalten hat, das jede Einrede ausschliesse," indem man „auf die Autorität des Urhebers hinwies." Similarly K. von Preysing, Der Leserkreis der Philosophoumena Hippolyts, in *ZKTh* 38 (1914), p. 444: "Eine lokale Schwierigkeit von Karthago [resp. Afrika] wird dadurch ohne Begründung auch auf Rom und Italien übertragen. In Wirklichkeit geht dem Tertullian die Nachricht von dem Edikt nur durch Hörensagen zu; der Inhalt desselben wendet sich nicht an ihn, sondern an die Kirche von Karthago." In both cases there is the assumption (i) that the Montanists are in separate com-munities and (ii) the event in causing the repercussions is in fact a written episcopal edict. Both these assumptions I question in my discussion.

would simply articulate his policy of penitence and absolution. Were however the policy to come from outside of Carthage, the form in which it would come in what we have established to be known, in the case of Beryllus of Bostra, regarding the early third century, would not have been in the form of an edict analogous to and imperial decree (6B 2.3 and 6C 8.2). Rather it would have been in terms of something more analogous to a philosophical discussion, in which the errant cleric was convinced rather than condemned in an age when heretics left the Church rather than were expelled (6C 7.2). Certainly the example of Clement of Rome a century earlier was not of a decree but an epistle exhorting and persuading towards a view of Church Order where allegedly "blameless" presbyters had been removed from their ministry.

But there remains nevertheless one set of conditions in which news of a change of policy within an external community could have occasioned Tertullian's satirical outburst. I have already argued that the character of Callistus' activities were not immediately those of a monarchical bishop claiming the adherence of his presbyters to a new, laxer discipline within the Roman community let alone issuing universal decress presupposing a claim to a universal jurisdiction. The charge of the author of *El.* IX,12, 20-21 against Callistus was not that he had been given episcopal directions that he could not follow and which invalidated in his eyes the authority of him who had so directed (6C 7.1). The charge of the author of *El.* was rather that Callistus had absolved and received those whom he had excommunicated from his group and thus indirectly undermined his authority over the kind of house-congregation presupposed by the *Ap. Trad.* (6C 4).

Callistus might protest that what he had done applied only to his own group. But his particular position as authorized secretary writing externally in the name of each congregration and collecting and distributing externally material aid for external churches meant that his action had further implications, diplomatically left unexpressed formally, that he could not, and may not have wished to deny (6A 5 and 6C 7.4). An act of absolution, like an act of ordination, given even the most rudimentary recognition of intercommunion such as the exchange of the *frumentum* between the Roman congregations, inevitably has implications for intercommunion (6C 6). But it is an act that Callistus needed no wider authority to perform than the authority that he possessed over a particular congregation. Once absolved, a member from another congregation that he admitted to his own became not his problem but the problem of other congregations who did not subscribe to the validity of the act.

The other congregations had either to accept such an act of absolution or to break communion over it. This was the means by which Callistus was furthering the revolution begun but not completed by Victor, in an age before

bishops became monarchs and had the precise years and months of their episcopal reigns duly chronicled (4B 2.2.3.2-3 and 6C 8.3). Having little power
beyond his immediate congregation, he discovered that what power he had,
when expressed in absolution, could change the Church. Not only were the
other fractionalized house-churches of the Roman community, each with
their presiding πρεσβύτερος–ἐπίσκοπος, required incidentally but necessarily
to take note of and assume a position on such an act, but it would also have
external repercussions particularly if Callistus had the function of a kind of
minister of foreign affairs in dealing with external churches.[66] As with Victor
and the Asiatic communities over the date of Easter (6C 6), other communities would associate themselves one way or another with the particular
Roman community with which they felt the closest cultural affinity.

Although there was as yet no centralized papacy nor any unambiguous
theory such as that of Cyprian as to what might hold orthodox communities
together above the local level, nevertheless there was at the close of the second century following Irenaeus a sense in which the unity of the Church was
perceived to be wider than the unity of a single local congregation based
upon a single city or region. Indeed in his earlier Catholic work Tertullian
had paid tribute to Rome's authority (*nobis auctoritas praesto est*) for
orthodox doctrine (*totam doctrinam*) on the grounds of the witness of both
Peter and Paul (*apostoli*) there.[67]

In the same work, a unity on the basis of the apostolic descent of the many
churches with a single tradition expresses itself (*probant*) in such practices as
reception of communicants (*communicatio pacis*), as the acknowledgement
of other congregations as "brotherhoods" (*appellatio fraternitatis*),
commitment to hospitality (*contesseratio hospitalitatis*) ruled by "the one
tradition of the same solemn obligation (*eiusdem sacramenti una traditio*)."[68]
It is impossible to read this passage (as Esser did) as an early reference to the
Roman primacy.[69] Clearly the unity of the church is ideal and created from
the unity of each expressed in the mutual recognition of bishops reinforced

---

[66] The Anglican communion experiences a similar crisis over ordination today in circumstances where the bishop of an individual diocese ordains women for that diocese with no jurisdiction over the rest, and yet through the presupposition of intercommunion succeeds in
changing for the most part the rest, since the consequences of a breakdown in intercommunion
are too hard to bear.

[67] Tertullian *De Praesc. Haer.* 36,2-3: "Si autem Italiae adjaces, habes Romam, unde nobis
auctoritas praesto est. Ista quam felix ecclesia, cui totam doctrinam apostoli cum sanguine suo
profuderunt."

[68] Ibid. 20,7-9: "Itaque tot ac tantae ecclesiae una est illa ab apostolis prima, ex qua omnes.
Sic omnes primae et omnes apostolicae, dum una omnes. Probant unitatem communicatio pacis
et appellatio fraternitatis et contesseratio hospitalitatis, quae iura non alia ratio regit quam
eiusdem sacramenti una traditio."

[69] G. Esser, *Der Adressat der Schrift Tertullians „De Pudicitia" und der Verfasser des
römischen Bussediktes.* (Bonn: Hanstein 1914), p. 6. Koch (1919) p. 70-71 describes such a
view of these passages as "eine Zeitwiedrigkeit derbster Art" and continues "So is jene erste
Kirche, aus der alle hervorgegangen sind, in allen den vielen und zahlreichen Kirchen, die aus
ihr hervorgegangen sind, wiederzufinden."

by apostolic foundations of every major See, and not by the primacy of one particular See (*omnes primae et omnes apostolicae*) that is clearly one in many (*dum una omnes*). In that respect one can well see why Cyprian should have described Tertullian as *magister meus*, to whose embryonic concept he was indebted for the development of his own concept of the Church. By Cyprian's time, councils of bishops could be added as the "glue" of mutual recognition, though significantly for our argument Tertullian does not mention such councils in his signs of external intercommunion.

But though Tertullian gives no support to an early Roman primacy, his concept of the Church clearly shows that the conditions of communion between one community and another could be affected by a disciplinary change. The degree of disturbance effected in this case could be considerably increased by the fact that Carthage and North Africa had a particular economic as well as geographic relationship with Rome in terms particularly of the corn supply. It could also be increased by the fact that Carthage had no record of apostolic foundation, so that its apostolicity might have been seen in its relationship with its close economic and geographic neighbour.[70] Furthermore, given a loose confederation between communities regarding themselves as orthodox throughout the Roman world, the issue of episcopal absolution would have been the very one to have created more than local repercussions at Rome itself. Absolution, like ordination, was the very kind of act which would impact on such signs of intercommunion as *communicatio pacis, appellatio fraternitatis,* or *contesseratio hospitalitatis.*[71]

The act of absolution, like that of ordination, therefore has a constraining effect upon others to recognize it far beyond the confines of the jurisdiction of the cleric who so acts. Both acts are irreversible. The denial of their legitimacy has little effect on the community where either had taken place, since there is not yet a central papacy, and no age of the Councils such as the post Cyprianic deposition of Paul of Samosata (6C 8.2). As we have argued, following Lampe, the buidings of the house/school Churches had yet to pass into corporate ownership with the powers of exclusion from premises that the bishop would thereby acquire (6C 8.1).

But the act itself compels other communities to acknowledge it or forfeit the tie of intercommunion. No wonder therefore that, in parodying this deve-

---

[70] See footnotes 74-77.

[71] It is interesting to note the use of *contesserare* ("to contract friendship by means of a certificate"), in *De Praes. Haer.* 36,3-4: in connection with doctrinal agreement with the apostle John, joined with Peter and Paul in Rome, but whose martyrdom there was miraculously curtailed (*posteaquam in oleum igneum demersus, nihil passus est*). "Let us see (*videamus*) that what he will have disseminated (*quid didicerit*), what he will have taught (*quid docuerit*), gives him a certificate of friendship even with the churches of Africa (*cum Africanis quoque ecclesiis contesseratis*)." The *quoque* expresses a feeling on Tertullian's part of a kind of apostolic distance concerning Africa. Certainly on veiling virgins the discipline of churches founded by apostles or apostlic men was a touchstone, see Tertullian, *De Virg. Veland.* 2,1 cf. C. Figini, Agrippino o Callisto? in *ScuCat* 1924 p. 204-211.

lopment, it should seem to Tertullian that a suitable ironic metaphor would be not simply the proclamation of an edict (*edictum esse propositum*), but a final, absolute and irreversible edict (*et quidem peremptorium*). Callistus' ostensible change of policy for his group had, beyond all his disingenuousness, the effect of being felt in that way by other congregations confronted by the implications of that change. It should be remembered that the pentitential discipline espoused by one Roman community in the past, that of *Hermas*, to which Callistus himself could appeal, was denigrated expressly by Tertullian in *De Pudic.* 10,12, in his comparison between the laxity that this extra-canonical work symbolized and the engraved drinking cups of debauchery.[72] Africa thus clearly took note of, and was not unaffected by, the penitential discipline of at least one Roman community.

But so far what we have said could be also consistent with a change of policy on the part of the bishop of Carthage himself with no or indeed tenuous connections with what transpired at Rome. Indeed, the belief in such tenuous connections was a kind of half-way-house erected between the two opposing views by Esser who believed that the edict had been Carthaginian but

---

[72] For a discussion of this text and its connection with the Muratorian Canon and the inscription on the Statue, ᾠδαὶ εἰς πάσας τὰς γραφάς, see 5A 9. The appropriate context of Hermas' community as one group in a fractionalized community has been recently expounded in J.S. Jeffers, *Conflict at Rome: Social Order and Hierarchy in Early Christianity*, (Minneapolis: Augsburg Fortress 1991), p. 3-33, 115-120 ff. It should be noted in the light of this argument and of my own how the earlier discussion of the relation between Callistus, Hippolytus, and Tertullian was distorted by anachronism. If one believed that these three along with Hermas, Clement, and Justin earlier were representatives of a monolithic community with a single episcopal monarch, then indeed the problem posed was simply whether it was Callistus who was the innovator or indeed Hippolytus or Tertullian. Hermas could be used to show that he was not, or reinterpeted to show that he was, the innovator. See A. d'Alès, *L'Édit de Calliste: Étude sur les origines de la pénitence chrétienne*, (Paris: Beauchesne 1914), e.g. p. 14: "L'Église hiérarchique, groupée autour de son évêque, est la dispensatrice normale de ce pardon, et l'offre de la réconciliation ecclésiastique, est la traduction concrète de l'offre du pardon divin. Cela résulte des témoignages tout à fait formels de saint Clément de Rome, de saint Ignace d'Antioche, d'Hermas, se saint Denys de Corinthe..." Cf. B. Poschmann, Paenitentia Secunda: Die kirchliche Busse im ältesten Christentum bis Cyprian und Origenes: Eine dogmengeschichtliche Untersuchung, in *Theoph* 1 (1940), p. 283-367. G. Bardy, L' édit d' Agrippinus, in.*RevSR* 4 (1924), argued from Cyprian *Ep.* 55, 20-21 that the rigorists were the innovators . But why then does Cyprian still recognise Tertullian though according to the Cyprianic theory he is cut off from the Catholic Church? Bardy continued, p. 8-9: "Les évêques, ou tout au moins plusieurs d'entre eux, se relâchèrent de leur excessive sévérité. L'un d'eux, et, pour autant qu'il paraît celui de Carthage, tout en refusant la communion ecclésiastique aux idolâtres et aux homicides, promulga un édit par lequel il déclarait remettre leurs fautes aux adultères et aux fornicateurs.. Loraque parut l'édit, Tertullian était déjà passé au Montanisme..." But this presupposes that Hermas' indulgence of the "adultères" and "fornicateurs" had previously been generally accepted so as to permit them "se relâchèrent de leur excessive sévérité." Koch (1919) p. 4-46 examined the thesis that Tertullian was as a Montanist strengthening his position against normal and traditional catholic laxity but was able to show the coherence of *De Pudic.* with his earlier catholic works such as *Apol.*, *De Paen.*, and *De Corona* . His conclusion was p. 57: "Zu verstehen ist Hippolyt's Standpunkt und Anklage nur, wenn er den alten Kirchenbegriff und die alte Strenge vertritt, Kallists grundsätzliche Nachsicht aber etwas Neues war. Somit war auch in der römischen Kirche die Strenge, nicht wie Adam will, die Milde, herkömmlich und damit fällt ein Hauptgrund Adams gegen die Herkunft des Erlasses aus Rom dahin," cf. *Adv. Prax.* 1. where the *psychici* were also Roman. See also footnote 136.

influenced by Callistus in Rome.[73] All that we have so far established is that events within a community at Rome could have had in Africa the repercussions that Tertullian describes. Such repercussions were not ruled out *ab initio* by the stage of development reached in Church Order by the early third century, as Bardy and others claimed.[74] But equally Tertullian could have been reacting to purely local events. Let us now examine whether we can specify more precisely which of these two alternatives can be better adopted with reference to the titles given by Tertullian to the anonymous bishop.

7C 1.1.2. pontifex maximus *and* episcopus episcoporum
Both the title *pontifex maximus*, referring to a bishop by analogy with the title of Emperor as head of the pagan cultus, and *episcopus episcoporum* at first sight appear to be describing a figure other than a local bishop of Carthage. Furthermore, the titles have been connected with the Petrine claims apparently mentioned by Tertullian in the following passage:

> I challenge now your judgement (*de tua nunc sententia quaero*), in consequence of which (*unde*) you ursurp this right of the Church (*hoc ius ecclesiae usurpes*). Since if the Lord will have said to Peter... [*Mat.* 16,18]... for that reason (idcirco) do you presume (*praesumis*) that you also have derived (*et ad te derivasse*) the power of binding and loosing (*solvendi et alligandi potestatem*), that is [given to] every church related to Peter (*id est ad omnem ecclesiam Petri propinquam*)? Who are you to (*Qualis es*) overturn and change (*evertens atque commutans*) the clear intention of the Lord (*manifestam Domini intentionem*) which confers this personally on Peter (*personaliter hoc Petro conferentem*)? He says: "I will build my Church on *you* (*Super te inquit aedificabo ecclesiam meam*) and: "and whatever *you* will have loosed or *you* have bound (*quaecumque solveris vel alligaveris*)," not what *they* will have loosed or *they* will have bound (*non quae solverint vel alligaverint*).
>
> *De Pudic.* 21, 9-10

---

73 A. d'Alès, Zephyrin, Calliste or Agrippinus? in *RecSciRel* 10 (1920), p. 255: "M. Esser compte non pas un adversaire mais deux: l'évêque de Rome, auteur de la décision incriminée; et l'évêque de Carthage, coupable d'appliquer cette décision."
74 It is this wider sense of unity present in the late second century but without any central papal or, for that matter, dispersed conciliar authority that was consistenty missed by Bardy (1924) p. 10-11: "Qu'importe ce qui se passe à Rome et dans les pays transmarins? Mais en Afrique à Carthage, il porte, et presque seul, le fardeau de toute l'Église montaniste à laquelle appartient toute son âme. Les adversaires, qu'il combat dans le *De Pudicitia,* ne sont donc pas les psychiques de tous les pays, mais ceux qu'il ne cesse de recontrer dans chacun des engagements auxquels il doit prendre part... Un édit, promulgué seulement à Rome, suffirait-il à exciter ainsi sa verve, et le *De Pudicitia* serait-il assuré de produire tout son effet s'il était destiné à l'Église transmarine?... Nous sommes plutôt tentés de chercher à Carthage même l'auteur de l'édit, et que nous ne nous tournerions vers Rome que si nous y étions en quelque sorte contraints." I have argued that (i) there was no formal *édit*, but that (ii) what developed in a given Roman community "suffirait-il à exciter ainsi sa verve." Though the remarks may not have been directed at "les psychiques de tous les pays", at all events Tertullian was sufficiently interested in the psychics of the Roman Hermas, see footnote 72. See also Koch (1919) p. 60: "Allein der schlagfertige Verteidiger der Kirche gegen Heidentum und Ketzerei, ein Schriftsteller von der Eigenart... war sicher weit über die Grenzen der karthagischen und afrikanischen Kirche hinaus bekannt und sein Bruch mit der Kirche hat nicht allein in Karthago und in Africa Aufsehen und Bedauern hervorgerufen."

It is often argued that the unnamed adversary in making this claim (*tua nunc sententia*) must be more than a local bishop. He must therefore be not simply a *pontifex* but a *pontifex maximus,* and not simply an *episcopus* but an *episcopus episcoporum.* Of course Tertullian, from a Montanist perspective, is denying this claim. But not, it should be noted, on grounds that the *potestas* in question was that of the spirit-filled community and not of an episcopal hierarch. Rather he claims that the binding and loosing is given to Peter personally, as any other *potestas* to heal or destroy is given as God's gift in an individual circumstance which is a once for all situation. What is given to the community, however is a *disciplina* which is not individual and once for all but collective and ongoing.[75]

Now we must initially concede that there is no claim by Rome at this time to universal jurisdiction based upon the text of *Mat.* 16,18.[76] The force of the power claimed to derive *ad omnem ecclesiam Petri propinquam,* is a power that the Montanist Tertullian will deny to any individual bishop. However, as we saw (7C 1.1.1), any church will be *propinqua* ("related") to the apostles, even if not founded by one of them or their associates, if there is a *consanguinitas* with them regarding doctrine (*in eadem fide conspirantes non minus apostolicae deputantur pro consanguinitate doctrinae*).[77] The Catholic

---

[75] D'Alès (1920) p. 256: "...le poids supérieur des raisons fait décidément pencher la balance du côté de Rome, en présence surtout des allusions pressantes à la chaire de Pierre, qu'on rencontre, Pud. xxi." Cf. Bardy (1924) p. 17-18 who argues that Peter is a personification of the episcopate as a whole, p. 19: "... «Petri propinqua.» Cette expression ne s'appliquerait pas à proprement parler à l'Église romaine qui est celle même de Pierre; mais elle vaut pour les chrétientés établies sur la pierre de l'épiscopat, puisque l'autorité de l'évêque est l'héritage transmis par Pierre à tous ses successeurs dans la catholicité." As such he supported K. Adam, *Der sogenannte Bussedikt des Papstes Kallixtus* (München: Letner 1917) p. 12-22. W. Köhler, Omnis ecclesia Petri propinqua, in *ZNW* 31 (1932), p. 60-67 rejected Harnack's emendation of "Romanam" for "omnem ecclesiam," (Harnack A. von, Ecclesia Petri propinqua. Zur Geschichte der Anfänge des Primats des römischen Bischofs, in *SPAW,* Phil. hist. Kl. (1927), p. 139) and agreed that the phrase must refer to any church in the apostolic succession (p. 61-63), but in consequence claimed it as Tertullian' own objection to Callistus' claim ("Dann kommt *ecclesia numerus episcoporum* auch auf sein [sc. Tertullian's] Konto und nicht auf das des Kalixt. Natürlich will er damit seinen Gegner schlagen, aber es fragt sich, ob er es mit gerechter Waffe tut und nicht dem Gegner etwas unterschiebt."). H. Koch, Zu Tertullian „De Pudicitia" 21,9 in *ZNW* 31 (1932), p. 68-72 replied that *derivare* showed that it was in fact Callistus's own expression, with whom thus Cyprian later would have sided against the Montanist Tertullian (p. 72: "Die Vielheit der Bischöfe ist ihm [sc. für Cyprian], um den trinitarischen Ausdruck Tertullians zu gebrauchen, eine die Einheit nicht aufhebende, sondern sie in liebevoller Verbundenheit wahrende *derivatio* des *Mt.* 16,18 ff. gegründeten unus episcopatus.") H. Koch, Nochmals zu Tertulian „De Pudicitia" 21,9 in *ZNW* 33 (1934), p. 317-318 continued his earlier argument. B. Altaner, Omnis ecclesia Petri propinqua, in *Theologische Revue,* 38 (1939), p. 129 reprinted in Kleine patristische Schriften (*T.U.* 83) (1967), p. 540-553 vigorously defended the connection of Peter with the Roman succession and therefore with Callistus on account of the martyrdom of Peter and Paul, and the use by Gaius of the *memoria Apostolorum in Vaticano* to defend Rome's episcopal succession against the Montanists.

[76] Indeed the use of this text in a specifically jurisdictional context was Gregorian, as the work of Congar has demonstrated, see Brent (1992), p. 180-187.

[77] It should be remembered that the test for apostolicity was not simply direct foundation by and apostle (*primus ille episcopus aliquem ex apostolis*), or being founded by one of their companions (*vel apostolicis viris*), but also "family similarity of doctrine (*pro consanguitate doctrinae*)," see *De Praes. Haer.* 32,1: "... edant ergo origines ecclesiarum suarum, evolvant ordinem episcoporum suorum, ita per successionem ab initio decurrentem, ut primus ille epis-

Tertullian of the *De Praesc.* mentions any number of apostles as the foundation of the Church, and Peter is mentioned here only because it was the promise given to him that was in dispute. Tertullian is not attempting to explain why this promise did not devolve upon the Roman bishop but why, on his earlier, catholic principle of doctrinal *propinquitas* and *consanguinitas*, it could not in this instance devolve on any or every church.

Having however granted this point, we are still left with the alternative of a change in discipline regarding clerical absolution either at Carthage or at Rome causing mutual repercussions. We reiterate our point that the conditions of the early third century would have allowed those repercussions without any claim to universal jurisdiction by a Roman bishop. We must therefore ask whether there were any distinctive features of the Roman community at this time that might be reflected in Tertullian's language that would not apply to Africa. And it is here the titles *pontifex maximus* and *episcopus episcoporum* become critical.

Callistus, whom we regarded as the representative of the Mosaic and therefore monarchical strand in the tradition (7B 3.2 and 7B 4), would not of course have accepted initially the negation of his power in terms of the sacerdotalism of *El.* as an alternative image. But as an image which the dialectical process of the controversy enabled to be synthesized with the monarchical, that image became even more valuable as a means of extending Callistus' claim to power, quite contrary to the intentions of those who had first adopted this image. Let us now examine Tertullian's parody of that image as Callistus and his party had now adopted it.

7C 1.1.2.1. pontifex maximus

The title *pontifex maximus* may be a cruel satire that compares a bishop with the emperor as pagan high priest.[78] But I submit that it is not simply that it is more applicable as a barbed reference to a Roman bishop that enables us through this allusion to regard Roman and not African events as the backcloth for Tertullian's protest. The allusion is sacerdotal, and the association of binding and loosing, with sacerdotal functions at this period was a distinctive Roman development.

The documents of the Hippolytan community itself points to the distinctiveness of the sacerdotal and Aaronic image of the bishop as *summus sacer-*

---

copus aliquem ex apostolis vel apostolicis viris, qui tamen cum apostolis perseveraverit..." He continues (32,6) that churches without such foundation "tamen in eadem fide conspirantes non minus apostolicae deputantur pro consanguinitate doctrinae." Thus no central authority is presupposed but nevertheless there is the notion of sufficient links to make what happens in one community impact upon another. Cf. Brent (1992) p. 155-160. Barnes (1985) p. 31: "The De Pudicitia attacks a bishop of Carthage, and the identification of Tertullian's opponent as Callistus can only be sustained by a tendentious emendation of the text" curiously believes that the sole case for Callistus as Tertullian's opponent was the illegitimate emendation of "omnem" for "Romanam." See also footnote 75.

[78] Tertullian uses the title in its pagan context for support for the practice of being married only once, see *De Exhort. Cast.* 13,2; *De Praes. Haer.* 40,5; *Ad Uxorem* I, 7,5; *De Mon.* 17,3.

dos. But we saw earlier that this was true only of one strand of the tradition of that community, represented by *Ap. Trad.* 3 (7A 2.2.2), with which we argued that the Mosaic image of the bishop in ordaining presbyters (*Ap. Trad.* 7) was at variance (7A 2.2.1). It was, we argued, a strand represented by *El.* I prooem. 6 by the writer who claims clearly that he and his fellow presbyters' presiding over the house-school churches share in the ἀρχιερατεία as well as in the διαδοχή (7B 1). It is in the context of Callistus claiming to override their right to bind or loose, to include or exclude, that his claim to sole ἀρχιερατεία can be understood, and hence Tertullian's parodying of him as *pontifex maximus.* He was thus appropriating and synthesising the rival sacerdotal model with the Mosaic and regnal that was his own.

We traced moreover within the *Clementines* the various *pro* and *anti* currents within the Roman house-school communities of the late second and early third century in the direction of monarchical episcopacy, even though the sacerdotal connotations remained absent. The Zacchaeus rite of *Hom.* III, 63-77 exhibited this tendency, and emphasizes *Mat.* 16,18 in a jurisdictional context (7B 3.2) that was quite absent from the rite to which *Petr.* and *Clement ad Iac.* attested. We witnessed there how authority to rule on scriptural interpretation in the latter became, in the Zacchaeus rite, an ἐξουσίαν διοικήσεως, exercized ὑπὲρ τῆς ἀδελφῶν σωτηρίας, ὑπὲρ αὐτῶν οἰκονομίας καὶ σῆς ὠφελείας. The οἰκονομία was now in the development represented by this rite taken to refer not simply to the poor relief administered by the authorized secretary of Hermas *Vis.* 2,4 (6A 5), but to the administration of the means of salvation. It was a combination of these monarchical developments with the general sacerdotalism to which the school of *El.* subscribed, and the particular and exclusive sacerdotal claim that Callistus' acts implied, that lead to Tertullian's taunt of *pontifex maximus* with its regal as well as sacerdotal overtones. It lead moreover to the conciliator Hippolytus (*C.N.* 1) to distract intentionally attention from Callistus himself by attributing to Noetus, in his legendary description, the combination of regal and sacerdotal power when he says that Noetus claimed to be Moses and his brother Aaron.

7C 1.1.2.2. episcopus episcoporum

If the *Clementines* reflect, as I have suggested, movements within the Roman community contemporary with Callistus, Hippolytus, and the author of *El.*, then the criticism of the *episcopus episcoporum* in *Pudic.* 1,6 becomes a strong argument that it is in fact Callistus whom Tertullian is attacking. Attempts have been made to find the use of this title, as of *pontifex maximus,* to refer to a bishop in Africa. But such attempts try to use later usage to explain Tertullian's earlier one. It is more likely that Cyprian's later usage is dependent upon Tertullian as his *magister*, and re-interprets his predecessor in application to the particular controversies of his time.[79]

The *Clementines* thus give a contemporary example of the use of *episcopus episcoporum* as a claim for primacy. It is the claim made by *Petr. ad Iac.* insc. which begins: Πέτρος ᾿Ιακώβῳ τῷ κυρίῳ καὶ ἐπισκόπῳ τῆς ἁγίας ἐκκλησίας, and this description of James was continued further in *Clem. ad Iac.* inscr. (7B 5.2). There can be no doubt that there is concealed in this pseudepigraphic device a message regarding currents within the Roman community, as the pivotal role of the Roman Clement shows. We also drew attention to the way in which the pseudepigraphic letters reflect the method of Diogenes Laertius in expressing the phenomenon of philosophy as purely Greek, and with its own coherence within the matrix of Hellenistic civilization (7B 5.1).

What was being expressed in the pseudepigraphic letters of the *Clementines* was the coalescing of two distinct traditions, that of Clement and that of James, in such a way that the prerogatives previously of James are now flowing into the common tradition and becoming the prerogatives of him who now claims to preside over that tradition. Clement succeeded Peter, who both recognized and was recognized by James, and both of whom recognized the authority of Clement as their successor. And, as the forerunner to the Liberian List showed, Callistus finally inherited their succession. It was a succession that Hippolytus, who continued and revised the episcopal list of the author of *El* that originally appeared in his Χρονικῶν, was finally along with his reconciled community, to acknowledge.

It should be remembered, moreover, that read in this light the Liberian *Catalogus* connects not only the Hippolytan reconciled community with that of Callistus. It also connects both Hippolytus and Callistus with the *Clementine* tradition, and particularly with the pseudonymous epistolary context presupposed by the exchange of letters in the preface to the *Homilies*. As Lightfoot originally pointed out, the Liberian *Catalogus* alters the succes-

---

79 Bardy (1924) p. 12 quotes Pontius, *Vita Cypriani* 9 and p. 13 Cyprian *Ep.* 66,3: "Quis autem nostrum longe est ab humilitate, utrumne ego qui cotidie fratribus servio... an tu qui te episcopum episcopi et iudicem iudicis ad tempus a Deo dati constituis," and to Council of 1.9.256: "neque enim quisquam nostrum episcopum se episcoporum constituit an tyrannico terrore ad obsequendi necessitatem collegas suos adigit." Cyprian however is arguing in an age characterized by a struggle with Rome a similar issue of the conditions of absolution, and the allusions in both quotations are claims to primacy. It is strange therefore that Bardy found difficulty with at least one application of this criticism to the pope on p. 14: "C'est une formule africaine, susceptible d'être appliquée à tout autre évêque que le pape." A. Donini, *Ippolito di Roma. Polemiche teologiche e controversie disciplinari nella chiesa di Roma agli inizi del III secolo.* (Roma: 1925), p. 181-186ff. had rejected the application to a Roman bishop. Cf. A.M. Vellico, "Episcopus Episcoporum" in Tertulliani libro De Pudicitia, in *Antonianum*, 5 (1930), commented, p. 36: "... A. Donini, spiritu etiam anticatholico motus, eamdem defendit opinionem, cum omnia, iuxta ipsum, in libro de Pudicitia adversarii proximitatem revelent, atque absurdum appareat romanos episcopos in pleno ethnicisimo titulum sibi vindicasse Romano Imperatori omnino proprium."

sion-list found in Irenaeus.[80] According to the latter Clement comes third in the succession, after Linus and Anacletus,[81] but according to the former he is consecrated second in succession to Peter.[82] The dates that he was thus able to be given (A.D. 68-76) made possible the chronology implied by the preface to the *Homilies*. The author realised that Peter needed to write to James shortly before his own death, without knowing the exact date either of the Neronian persecution or of the fact that the date of James' stoning was probably before that of Peter.

Furthermore, the former concentrates the ideology of succession more firmly on Peter himself legitimated by James, and not only Paul whom Irenaeus in the latter claims also to be conjoint founder of the Roman Church (ὑπὸ τῶν...δύο ἀποστόλων Πέτρου τε καὶ Παύλου ἐν ῾Ρώμῃ θεμελιωθείσης), without mentioning any Jacobean presence in the succession. The ideology of the *Clementines* and of the community of Callistus has thus been adopted by the reconciled Hippolytus in his eirenic editing of the Χρονικῶν (4B 2.2.3.2-3), in the succession list that we have followed Caspar in maintaining was orignally part of the latter work (4B 2.2.3.1). We should not therefore see James' jurisdiction as a historical fact emanating from an original Jerusalem caliphate in the middle years of the first century. Had it possessed that kind of historical facticity, then it would surely have been part of Irenaeus' account of the succession, particularly if Hegesippus had used the model of making succession lists on the basis of the alleged caliphate. For this reason too we were justified in our argument for rejecting Ehrhardt's too influential account of the Jewish-Christian origin of the concept of διαδοχή (7B 2).[83] The Jacobean legend is being refashioned in order to legitimate events in Rome in which the authority of Callistus as president of one community is in process of extension over many others, and fractionalized traditions are being harmonized into one.

The picture of James addressed as ἐπισκόπων ἐπισκόπῳ and διέποντι δὲ τὴν ῾Ιερουσαλὴμ ἁγίαν ῾Εβραίων ἐκκλησίαν, with its universal extension to other churches generally (καὶ τὰς πανταχῆ θεοῦ προνοίᾳ ἱδρυθείσας καλῶς),

---

[80] Lightfoot (1890) 1,I p. 156-157; 269-275 ff.

[81] Ibid. p. 253 where after the entries for Petrus and Linus we read: "Clemens, ann. ix, m. xi, dies xii. Fuit temporibus Galbae et Vespasiani, a cons. Tracali et Italici [A.D. 68] usque Vespasiano vi et Tito [A.D. 76]."

[82] Irenaeus, *Adv. Haer.* III, 3,2-3: ... ὑπὸ τῶν ἐνδοξοτάτων δύο ἀποστόλων Πέτρου τε καὶ Παύλου ἐν ῾Ρώμῃ θεμελιωθείσης... ἐκκλησίας τήν τε ἀπὸ ἀποστόλων παράδοσιν... κατὰ τὰς διαδοχὰς τῶν ἐπισκόπων κατηντηκυῖαν εἰς ἡμᾶς μηνύοντες, καταισχυνοῦμεν πάντας... θεμελιώσαντες οὖν καὶ οἰκοδομήσαντες οἱ μακάριοι ἀπόστολοι τὴν ἐκκλησίαν, Λίνῳ τὴν τῆς ἐπισκοπῆς λειτουργίαν ἐνεχείρισαν... Διαδέχεται δὲ αὐτὸν ῾Ανέγκλητος. Μετὰ τοῦτον δὲ τρίτῳ τόπῳ ἀπὸ τῶν ἀποστόλων τὴν ἐπισκοπὴν κληροῦται Κλήμης... Cf also Lightfoot (1890) 1,I p. 66-67.

[83] Ehrhardt (1953) p. 72-73 uses Tertullian as an indirect witness to the alleged Jacobean caliphate when he says: "On the other hand, it is equally significant that Tertullian used episcopus episcoporum, however sarcastically, for a description of the Roman Pope, Callistus. It seems that the position of James was exalted above the other Apostles, because he was seen as Christ's successor in his priestly ministry." See also footnotes 32, 33, 35 and 37.

is a literary and legendary picture. Our argument does not therefore create the problem of the anachronism of Callistus claiming universal jurisdiction throughout Christendom in succession to that of James. The focus of the impact of the legendary and literary construction is upon the fractionalized Roman community itself, just as, contrary to Eusebius' misunderstanding, Victor's judgement on the Quartodeciman practice was directed at Asiatic communities within Rome itself. The pro-Callistan message of the Clementine legend was towards Jewish-christian communities within the fractionalized Roman community, and it was through that community or group of communities that Callistus had begun to impose a new ecclesiastical Order through his policy of absolving those excommunicated by the presiding πρεσβύτεροι–ἐπίσκοποι of other congregations.

The ideology of those communities centred upon James and the Church of Jerusalem, which had long ceased to exist since A.D. 70. But his presidency over Jewish Christianity, with a number of Elders, was commemorated in *Acts* 15 and 21,17 (ʼIάκωβον, πάντες τε παρεγένοντο οἱ πρεσβύτεροι) as well as in the address of *Jam.* 1,1 (ταῖς δώκεκα φυλαῖς ταῖς ἐν τῇ διασπορᾷ χαίρειν). James' presence in *Acts* is described in accordance with Luke's deutero-Pauline purpose of conciliating Pauline and non-Pauline Churches in the late first or early second century. The inclusion of the pseudonymous epistle of James in the canon of the New Testament, whose pseudonymity expresses its testimony to one of the distinct cultural forms in which the Christianity of the first two century was expressed, itself indicates the use of the pseudepigraphic *genre* to express the harmonisation and integration of disparate forms of Christianity in the development of early catholicism.[84]

Paul's *Romans* itself reveals the presence of Christian communities in Rome as early as A.D. 57. There is clear evidence that many of the house-school-churches of the fractionalized Roman community arose out of Jewish Christianity, and indeed from the synagogues of Rome itself.[85] Frend has argued cogently that 1 *Clement*, with its almost exclusively Old Testament scripture quotations and allusions in exemplification of the need for Church Order, betrays a continuity between a certain Roman congregation or congregations and the Hellenistic synagogue. This was the real origin of the Hellenization of Jewish Christianity, and not Paul whose mission to the gentiles was more one of hope than fulfillment.[86]

---

[84] See A. Brent, Pseudonymity and Charisma in the Ministry of the Early Church, in *Aug.* 27,3 (1987), p. 347-376 for an account of how this later significance of pseudepigraphy was continous with the late first century where authorized letter-writers arguably were considered to be bearers of the corporate personality of individual apostolic communities.

[85] Jeffers (1991) p. 9-20.

[86] W.C.H. Frend, *Martyrdom and Persecution in the Early Church*, (Oxford: Blackwell 1965), p. 156-158 points to *Acts* 18, 6-8 where Paul, having declared to the Jews at Corinth: ἀπὸ τοῦ νῦν εἰς τὰ ἔθνη πορεύσομαι, then proceeds to go to the house of the god-fearer Titus Justus (καὶ μεταβὰς ἐκεῖθεν εἰς οἰκίαν τίνος ὀνόματι Τιτίου ʼΙούστου σεβομένου τὸν θεόν) which "bordered on the synagogue (Οὗ οἰκία ἦν συνομοροῦσα τῇ συναγωγῇ)." In

It is possible that writers such as Suetonius *Vit. Claud.* 25,4, and for that matter Dio Cassius, are silent about Roman Christianity because the form in which they met with it in Rome was indistinguishable in their eyes from a Jewish synagogue.[87] Certainly Callistus and his group, in maintaining what *El.* IX 11,1-3; 12,15-19 describes in terms of a modified Sabellianism, is reflecting a Jewish concern to defend the unity of the one God. The author of *El.* maintains that Callistus was proclaiming a doctrine with pagan roots, but no modern commentator has been deceived by his derivation of such a doctrine from Heracleitus ὁ σκοτεινός. Hippolytus himself has deceived many by the conservative appearance of his Scriptural exegesis in *C.N.* with which he conceals his radical use of Hellenistic concepts to reach a *rapprochement* with the successors of Callistus (4A 1.3).

Callistus was therefore more conservative even than the author of *El.*, and maintained the more judaistic ethos of his Roman community. It should be remembered that it was the community of the author of *El.*, and his successor Hippolytus, that called for the ἀπόδειξις χρόνων on the Statue as a distinctively Christian attempt to calculate astronomically the date of Easter, and to synthesize solar and lunar calendars. Callistus' congregation were presumably happy simply to follow Jewish calculations of Nisan 14 and celebrate on the following Sunday in accordance with the Western practice. It is feasible, therefore, that he should have made use of a Jacobean legend, created by *pseudepigrapha*, whose encoded message behind the claim to universality was about the cultural identity of a form of Christianity which spread to Rome and other centres of the mediterranean world. By this means he could reinforce his claim to jurisdiction over Roman communities other than his own by the surreptitious devise of incorporating his opponent's hierocratic model within his own, and then absolving those excommunicated by those communities. The claim to the title *episcopus episcoporum* through that Jacobean legend and the associated *epigrapha* would have been part of that strategy.

But just as Victor's treatment of the Quartodecimans within Rome would have had repercussions, however indirectly, upon the churches of Asia Minor, so too these events initiated by Callistus' action within the Roman community in like manner would have had repercussions upon North Africa.

---

consequence, Κρῖσπος δὲ ὁ ἀρχισυνάγωγος ἐπίστευσεν τῷ κυρίῳ σὺν ὅλῳ τῷ οἴκῳ αὐτοῦ. Clearly Paul in converting an ἀρχισυνάγωγος through his ministry in the house of a god-fearer, albeit with a Latin name, which Luke perhaps euphemistically describes as συνομοροῦσα τῇ συναγωγῇ in order not in fact to admit that it was a Hellenistic Jewish synagogue rather than a Hebrew one, is turning from a narrower to a broader form of Judaism within which to make his appeal. Any real mission to the Gentiles was to await the age of apologists such as Tatian or Justin Martyr.

[87] F. Millar, *A Study of Cassius Dio*, (Oxford: U.P. 1964), p. 179; E. dal Covolo, I Severi e il cristianesimo: Ricerche sull'ambiente storico-istituzionale delle origini cristiane tra il secondo e il terzo secolo, in *Biblioteca di Scienze Religiose*, 87 (Libreria Ateneo Salesiano: Rome 1989), p. 11-13.

Tertullian's strictures on Callistus as the *episcopus episcoporum* reflect those repercussions. It was in this way that Callistus' influence could be felt generally, even though his "primacy" at this point was limited to a subtle and surreptious claim to primacy in terms of the house-churches at Rome, rather than a the claim of one monarchical See to universal jurisdiction.[88]

Let us now turn to the question of the general similarities between what Tertullian criticises and what is found in *El.* IX, 12,20-26.

7C 1.1.3. *Tertullian's situation in* El. *IX, 12, 20-26*

The situation addressed by author of *El.* is not one in which he himself has failed to become a monarchical bishop whereas Callistus has. Rather he is protesting about the assumption of authority by Callistus as the presiding πρεσβύτερος–ἐπίσκοπος of another congregation to absolve members of his own congregation contrary to custom (6C 7.1). Our account thus explains Tertullian's counter-example to the interpretation of the parable of the lost sheep, where the grief rather than the joy of neighbouring congregations is recorded over someone who is excommunicated, in marked contrast to the joy of Callistus' congregation in absolving those excommunicated from another congregation. As Tertullian says:

> At that moment when it is public (*Simul apparuit*), as soon as a man is expelled from a church (*statim homo de ecclesia expellitur*), he neither remains there (*nec illic manet*) nor does he bring joy (*nec gaudium confert*) to the church that finds him (*repertrici ecclesiae*), but rather grief (*sed luctum*), and he does not have as his support the congratulation (*nec congratulationem advocat*) of the neighbouring (*vicinarum*) but the grief of the nearest fraternities (*sed contristationem proximarum fraternitatum*).
>
> De Pudic. 7,22

There is an allusion to Callistus as a bad shepherd, which might be read as counter to the argument of Tertullian's opponent here that he is the good shepherd, and thus provide some evidence for their identity.[89] But the parable of the Lost Sheep is but one of a number of examples examined by Tertullian in view of the role that such examples played in the argument of his opponent. Many of those examples, significantly in view of the background in Hellenistic Judaism of Callistus' *Clementine* congregation (7C 1.1.2.2), were from the *Old Testament*, and could only be refuted by Tertullian with reference to the greater severity of the New Covenant.

Nevertheless, the question that has then been raised is whether Tertullian must be criticizing a completely different opponent from the author of *El.* on two grounds:

---

[88] In this context alone is to be interpreted the phenomenon to which Koch (1919) p 69-98 draws attention.
[89] *El.* IX, 13,5: ... καὶ τοῦτον [sc. Ἀλκιβιάδην] λύκου δίκην ἐπεγηγερμένον εἶναι πλανωμένοις προβάτοις πολλοῖς, ἃ ἀποπλανῶν διεσκόρπισεν ὁ Κάλλιστος.

1. Tertullian is objecting to an existing practice of allowing "sins of the flesh" a second repentence whilst excluding idolatry and murder.[90] Tertullian therefore as a Montanist is the innovator. On the other hand, the author of *El.* was objecting to leniency regarding both adultery, second marriage of the clergy, and murder, and furthermore it was not him but his opponent who was the innovator regarding what was a new practice.

2. *El.* appears to distinguish fornication from adultery, whereas Tertullian's opponent is charged with confounding them.[91]

We will now therefore take *El.* IX, 12,21-25 in two sections, comparing the general claims presupposed by the specific examples which the author attacks with those of Tertullian. We shall show in both cases that Tertullian is challenging a similar set of proof texts as the author of *El.*, with similar basic principles and general argumentative form. Whether the charge is that the implications of the general principle specifically affect Church Order, or whether it leads to murder by abortion, in both cases the general form of the argument in *El.* is paralleled in Tertullian.

7C 1.1.3.1. *Clerical remarriage* El. *IX, 12,21-23*

The author of *El.* IX, 12,21-23 represented Callistus as allowing in his teaching clerical marriage,[92] and even the remarriage of those who were widowed once or even twice.[93] He condemns this apparently because it is a mortal sin,[94] presumably because he believes such a second or third marriage to be fornication. Certainly one text used cited by Tertullian from the defence of his adversary was the text of *Rom.* 14,14, used here in *El.*[95] to justify the practice, judged as mortal sin (πρὸς θάνατον), of the remarriage of clerical widowers. Tertullian attacks his adversary's general principal:

> Accordingly (*Itaque*) also the sons of God (*et filios Dei*) ought to be compassionate and peacemakers (*misericordes et pacificos esse oportebit*), giving in return (*donantes invicem*) just as Christ has given to us (*sicut et Christus*

---

[90] Bardy (1924) p. 4: "On conçoit fort bien, dans des circonstances particulières, un évêque qui ait pardonné certaines fautes charnelles, tout en refusant d'étendre le bienfait de la réconciliation ecclésiastique à d'autres péchés graves, tels que l'homicide et l'idolâtrie." See also Poschmann (1940) p. 351-356.

[91] *De Pudic.* 6,1: "Plane si ostendas de quibus patrociniis exemplorum praeceptorumque caelestium soli moechiae et in ea fornicationi quoque ianuam paenitentiae expandas." Cf. Bardy (1924) p. 2: "... la langue de l'auteur de l'édit est plus précise que celle de Tertullien; elle distingue clairement deux sortes de fautes que Tertullien confond." In *De exhort. cast.* 9 and in *De monogam.* 9, commenting on *Mat.* 5, 28 and 32, Tertullian translates πορνεία (*stuprum*) and μοιχεία (*adulterium*) as interchangeable words. But the author of the edict distinguishes both, for which Tertullian criticizes him.

[92] *El.* IX, 12,21-22: οὗτος ἐδογμάτισεν ὅπως... εἰ δὲ καὶ τις ἐν κλήρῳ ὢν γαμοίη, μένειν δεῖν ἔφη τὸν τοιοῦτον ἐν τῷ κλήρῳ ὡς μὴ ἡμαρτηκότα.

[93] Ibid. 12,22: ἐπὶ τούτου οὖν ἤρξαντο ἐπίσκοποι καὶ πρεσβύτεροι καὶ διάκονοι δίγαμοι καὶ τρίγαμοι καθίστασθαι εἰς κλήρους. I take it that these words refer to the δεῖ οὖν τὸν ἐπίσκοπον ἀνεπίλημπτον εἶναι, μιᾶς γυναικὸς ἄνδρα of 1 *Tim.* 3,2, which in turn I take to be a reference to not remarrying if widowed.

[94] Ibid. 12,21: ...εἰ ἐπίσκοπος ἁμάρτοι τι, εἰ καὶ πρὸς θάνατον, μὴ δέῃ κατατίθεσθαι.

[95] *El.* IX, 12,22: ἐπὶ τούτῳ φάσκων εἰρῆσθαι τὸ ὑπὸ τοῦ ἀποστόλου ῥηθέν· «σὺ τίς εἶ ὁ κρίνων ἀλλότριον οἰκέτην.»

donavit nobis), not judging that we be not judged (*non iudicantes, ne iudicemur*) [*Mat.* 7,1; *Lk.* 6,37]. For in his Lord (*Domino enim suo*) who stands and who falls (*stat quis vel cadit*): who are you that you should judge another's servant (*tu quis es ut servum iudices alienum*) [*Rom.* 14,14].

De Pudic. 2,2

We find however no reference to *Mat.* 7,1 and *Lk.* 6,37 ff. in *El.* Nor alternatively does the reference to the ark of Noah nor to the Parable of the Tares (*Mat.* 13,29-30) occur in Tertullian at this point.[96] But *El.* makes it clear, that these were only a selection from the proof-texts otherwise assembled by Callistus in defence of his position.[97] Furthermore, in *Adv. Prax.* 1,6 whose opponent we shall also identify with Callistus (7C 2), Tertullian does make an oblique reference to the Parable of the Tares in his development of the image of the *avenae Praxeanae* springing up and stifling Montanism.

As Rolffs pointed out, Tertullian, perhaps as a Montanist, may have intentionally omitted the reference to the Ark, which he had employed in a previous work where he had almost admitted Callistus' case. Though there may be unclean animals in the Ark, amongst which are the dog (*canis*/κύνες), wolf (*lupus*/λύκοι) and raven (*corvus*/κόρακες), and which may point as types to certain categories of persons, idolatry was not one of them.[98] Moreover, Tertullian seeks freqently to undermine his opponent's use of the Old Testament in defence of his view on absolution.[99]

Although Tertullian's point is a general one and the author of *El.* is attacking a specific practice, it is interesting to observe that Tertullian on another occasion adopts the same form of argument. The form of *El.*'s argument is that since mortal sins can be absolved, a cleric can still remain in office, and thus the ancient discipline of "married only once" fails. The general principle of absolving mortal sin has therefore these consequences for the or-

---

96 Ibid. 12,22-23: ἀλλὰ καὶ τὴν παραβολὴν τῶν ζιζανίων πρὸς τοῦτο ἔφη λελέχθαι·«ἄφετε τὰ ζιζάνια συναύξειν τῷ σίτῳ,» τουτέστιν μένειν ἐν τῇ ἐκκλησίᾳ τοὺς ἁμαρτάνοντας. ἀλλὰ καὶ τὴν κιβωτὸν τοῦ Νῶε εἰς ὁμοίωμα τῆς ἐκκλησίας ἔφη γεγονέναι, ἐν ᾗ ἦσαν καὶ κύνες καὶ λύκοι καὶ κόρακες καὶ πάντα τὰ καθαρὰ καὶ ἀκάθαρτα, οὕτω φάσκων δεῖν εἶναι καὶ ἐν τῇ ἐκκλησίᾳ.
97 Ibid. 12,23: ὁμοίως δὲ καὶ ὅσα πρὸς τοῦτο δυνατὸς ἦν συνάγειν, οὕτως ἡρμήνευσεν. The omission of the Parable of the Tares may not therefore be a serious problem. See also Rolffs (1893) p. 68 footnote 3.
98 Tertullian *De Idol.* 24,4: "Viderimus enim si secundum arcae typum et corvus et milvus et lupus et canis et serpens in ecclesia erit. Certe idolatres in arcae typo non habetur. Nullum animal in idololatren figuratum est. Quod in arca non fuit, in ecclesia non sit." Cf. Rolffs (1893) p. 68: "Früher in de idol. hatte Tert. jenes Bild für die Kirche unbedenklich acceptirt; es mochte ihm daher peinlich sein, eine früher von ihm vertretene Ansicht direct zu bekämpften; deshalb hat er es vermieden, sich in einer speciellen Auseinandersetzung auf diesen heiklen Punkt einzulassen..."
99 *De Pudic.* 6,5: "'Legem ergo evacuamus per fidem? Absit, sed legem sistimus [*Rom.* 3,31],' scilicet in his quae et nunc novo testamento interdicta etiam cumulatiore praecepto prohibentur," and 11,3: "Christiana enim disciplina a novatione testamenti et, ut praemisimus, a redemptione carnis id est Domini passione censetur." Cf. Rolffs (1893) p. 68: "... deshalb hat er es vermieden... es vorzogen, durch die prinzipielle Erörterung über das Verhältnis zwischen dem Alten und Neuen Testament dem von Kallist angewendeten Argument seine Beweiskraft zu nehmen..."

dained ministry. Tertullian exhibits the same form of argument in *De Monogamia* 11,4. He argues that since a cleric begins by being a layman, the whole Order of the Church must be affected if second marriage is allowed to laymen.[100]

7C 1.1.3.2. *Fornication and murder in* El. *IX, 12,24-25*

Following the attack on Callistus' practice of absolving "the pleasures which Christ did not allow (ἃς οὐ συνεχώρησεν ὁ Χριστός)" on account of which (διὰ τὰς ἡδονάς) those excommunicated elsewhere "flowed together into his school (τῷ διδασκαλείῳ συρρέουσιν ὄχλοι)," the author continues:

> For he even allowed women (καὶ γὰρ καὶ γυναιξὶν ἐπέτρεψεν), if they should be without husbands (εἰ ἄνανδροι εἶεν) and they burned due to their youthful age for a man (καὶ ἡλικίᾳ γε τε εἰς ἄνδρα ἐκκαίοιντο), they [being] of noble rank (αἱ ἐν ἀξίᾳ), if they were unwilling to degrade their rank (εἰ τὴν ἑαυτῶν ἀξίαν ἣν μὴ βούλοιντο καθαιρεῖν) through legal marriage (διὰ τοῦ νομίμως γαμηθῆναι), to take someone whom they should choose as a bedpartner (ἔχειν ἕνα, ὃν ἂν αἱρήσωνται, σύγκοιτον), whether household slave or free (εἴτε οἰκέτην εἴτε ἐλεύθερον), to treat this person (καὶ τοῦτον κρίνειν) as in place of a husband (ἀντὶ ἀνδρὸς) even though she was not married by law (τὴν μὴ νόμῳ γεγαμημένην). In consequence (ἔνθεν) women who were so called believers began to try (ἤρξαντο ἐπιχειρεῖν αἱ πισταὶ λεγόμεναι) even to bind themselves round with medicines against conception (ἀτοκίοις φαρμάκοις καὶ τῷ περιδεσμεῖσθαι) in order to abort what they had conceived (πρὸς τὸ τὰ συλλαμβανόμενα καταβάλλειν) because they were unwilling either to have a child from a slave (διὰ τὸ μήτε ἐκ δούλου βούλεσθαι ἔχειν τέκνον) or from one of lower class (μήτε ἐξ εὐτελοῦς), because of their noble and superior birth (διὰ τὴν αὐτῶν εὐγένειαν καὶ ὑπέρογκον οὐσίαν). You see to what enormous impiety the lawless fellow has descended (ὁρᾶτε εἰς ὅσην ἀσέβειαν ἐχώρησεν ὁ ἄνομος), teaching at the same time adultery and murder (μοιχείαν καὶ φόνον ἐν τῷ αὐτῷ διδάσκων).
>
> *El.* IX, 12,24-25

Thus beginning with the principle of generally absolving illegitimate pleasures (ἡδοναί), the author can argue that this will logically lead both to adultery and murder.

From this passage we can see that from the point of view of an adversary, Callistus could be regarded as confounding fornication with adultery in a way that would correpond with the position of Tertullian's adversary on which some critics rested their case for the denial of their identity (7C 1.1.3).

---

[100] *De Monog.* 11,4: "Si vult nos iterare coniugia, quomodo semen nostrum in Isaac semel marito auctore defendit? Quomodo totum ordinem ecclesiae de monogamis disponit, si non haec disciplina praecedit in laicis, ex quibus ecclesiae ordo proficit." Cf also the reference to the marriage of Peter in *De Monog.* 8,4: "Petrum solum invenio maritum, per socrum; monogamum praesumo per ecclesiam, qua super illum omnem gradum ordinis sui de monogamis erat collocaturus." See also *De Monog.* 12,3: "Quot enim et digami praesident apud vos!" and *De Exhort. Cast.* 11 In this respect these catholic writings were perfectly consistent with the Monatanist *Ad Uxor.* I,7,4: "Quantum detrahant fidei, quantum obstrepant sanctitati nuptiae secundae, disciplina ecclesiae et praescriptio apostoli declarat, cum digamos non sinit praesidere." See also the discussion of these passages in Koch (1919) p. 55-59.

The μοιχεία that Callistus taught may have arisen for the author from the remarriage of widowed clergy in the first passage previously discussed (7C 1.1.3.1), but this in turn arose not from his condoning only absolution from adultery, but was derived from his general absolution for sins of the flesh. The Church consisted of those who could become unclean generally through carnal sins, and not through adultery alone. The principle of adultery in a widowed cleric's remarriage was seen there specifically by the author of *El.* himself. For Callistus it mattered not whether such a sin was fornication or adultery, and Tertullian could therefore well have interpreted his teaching in reports that reached him as a confusion of the two sins.

In this second passage, we observe also confusion imposed on Callistus' teaching by the polemic of his opponent. He clearly considers the marriage of Roman noble women with either slaves (ἐκ δούλου) or with lower-class freedmen (ἐξ εὐτελοῦς) one of the sins of the flesh. As such, though the word is not used, his opponent could describe him as absolving from πορνεία. But indeed Callistus would have insisted that this was not πορνεία but Christian marriage. For the author of *El.* perhaps alternatively to be suggesting that this too might be somehow μοιχεία as a second sin in addition to the φονεία of their unborn children shows that the confusion his and not that of his opponent.

As has often been pointed out, the author of *El.* is taking a very patrician viewpoint in accepting the secular legal position that such marriages were illegal (διὰ τοῦ νομίμως γαμηθῆναι).[101] From the viewpoint of Callistus such marriages would not have been πορνεία but truly Christian, even though they were contrary to pagan Roman law. If the author of *El.* IX, 12, 25 is referring by the term μοιχεία not only to second clerical marriage but also to what he regards as illegal marriage, it is he and not Callistus that is confusing the terminology.

---

[101] I. von Döllinger, *Hippolytus und Kallistus, oder Die römische Kirche in der ersten Hälfte des dritten Jahrhunderts.* (Regensburg: Joseph Manz 1853), p. 254. See also Döllinger (1914) p. 425-429 who gives an illuminating reconstruction of the social class of the circle of the author of *El.* based upon the patrician sympathies of his criticism of μοιχεία and φονεία. He pointed to the fact that "es handelt sich an dieser Stelle um die Gestattung des Konkubinates (bezw. Contuberniums) für Senatorentöchter, denen mit Sklaven und Freigelassenen eine rechtsgültige Ehe unmöglich war und die durch eine gesetzliche Ehe mit einem Freigebornen niederen Standes ihre Ehrenrechte verloren hätten." According to the Digest it was a capital offence for the woman in question, and no wonder therefore the desperation to find the abortion-producing drugs. He cites e.g. Justinian, *Dig.* 23,2,42: "Modestinus, Bk 1 De ritu nuptiarum: Si senatoris filia neptis proneptis libertino vel qui artem ludicram exercuit cuiusue pater materue id fecerit nupserit, nuptiae non erunt," which clearly denies the validity of the marriage of αἱ ἐν ἀξία (= *senatoris filia*) to an ἐλεύθερος (= *libertinus*) or even a free εὐτελής (*vel qui artem ludicram*). In *Dig.* 1,9, 8, moreover, Ulpian, the contemporary of the author of *El.*, states that a *matrona* was subject to the death penalty for sexual relations with slaves. Preysing concludes with a description of the upper-class perspective of the *El.* group p. 434-442. For the social status of the later second century Roman community, see P. Lampe, Die stadtrömischen Christien in den ersten beiden Jahrhunderten, in *WUNT* 2,18 (1989), p. 94-99; 282-284. See also E. Jungklaus, Die Gemeinde Hippolyts dargestellt nach seiner Kirchenordnung, in *TU* 46 (1928).

Callistus would clearly not have regarded such marriages as either πορνεία or μοιχεία. Furthermore, Tertullian does not accuse his opponent so much of confusing these terms but of applying or withholding them in odd and unusual ways. He pointedly refuses to accept *occultae quoque coniunctiones, id est non prius apud ecclesiam professae*, and regards these instead as *iuxta moechiam et fornicationem* just like the author of *El.* in this passage.[102] There is therefore no evidence that he confused these terms but there is evidence clearly that Callistus' Roman critic confused them in his polemical misrepresentation of what he taught. It could therefore have been that misrepresentation that Tertullian attacked in his opponent.

Bardy's general objection therefore fails that the author of *El.* is fundamentally different from *un évêque qui ait pardonné certaines fautes charnelles,* as opposed to one who simply forgives sins indiscriminately. Like the author of *El.*, however much he may misrepresent the opponent which arguably they hold in common, Tertullian begins with the prohibition in the Ten Commandments against adultery, and argues that adultery like murder and idolatry are specific sins that rise out of fornication, that is to say the general sin of the flesh.[103] If Tertullian's opponent had been prepared to foregive idolatry and murder, then indeed his argument would have had no force that idolatry comes before and homicide after the commandment against adultery in the list of ten. You cannot therefore absolve one and not the other.

Furthermore it is Tertullian and not his adversary who must argue that fornication is the formally the same and must be included along with adultery as prohibited absolutely by the commandments even though not explicity mentioned.[104] It must be noted in this connection that it is not simply the juxtapostion in the text of the commandments on which Tertullian rests his case. It is his taxonomy of morals, in which the destruction of *Pudicitia* in general incontinence, beginning with fornication, necessarily leads to these

---

[102] *De Pudic.* 4,1-2; 4: "...Inprimis quod moechiam et fornicationem nominamus, usus expostulat. Habet et fides quorundam nominum familiaritatem. Ita in omni opusculo usum custodimus. Ceterum si adulterium et si stuprum dixero, unum erit contaminatae carnis elogium...Ita et ubicunque vel in quamcunque semetipsum adulterat et stuprat, qui aliter quam nuptiis utitur. Ideo penes nos occultae quoque coniunctiones, id est non prius apud ecclesiam professae, iuxta moechiam et fornicationem iudicari periclitantur, ne inde consertae obtentu matrimonii crimen eludant."

[103] I find impossible the conclusion of Poschmann (1940) p. 355 that in this passage: "ist nicht von Unzuchtsünden, sondern lediglich von der Heirat der Kleriker die Rede" which led to a general moral laxity without particular reference to the three mortal sins.

[104] *De Pudic.* 12,11: "... neque idololatriae neque sanguini pax ab ecclesiis redditur," cf. 5,15: "Quid agis, mollissima et humanissima disciplina?... Idolatren quidem et homicidam semel damnas, moechum vero de medio excipis? Idololatrae successorem homicidae antecessorem, utriusque collegam," and 22,11: "... quaecunque auctoritas, quaecunque ratio moecho et fornicatori pacem ecclesiasticam reddit, eadem debebit et homicidae et idololatrae paenitentibus subvenire...".

other sins to which it gives their common mortal character.[105] And this is precisely the form of argument of *El.* IX, 12,25.

Callistus is described as μοιχείαν καὶ φόνον ἐν τῷ αὐτῷ διδάσκων because, in the eyes of the author, although he apparently disapproves of both, his tolerance of carnal pleasure in allowing widowed clerics to marry and in blessing illegal unions across social class has lead, and necessarily will lead to such mortal sins with which they are inextricably connected. They are, in the words of *De Pudic.* 5,8, a *corpus cohaerentium* or a *nexus criminum*. It should be remembered that one example of *moechia* and not *fornicatio* or *stuprum* is marriage with a widow, so that Tertullian, once he focuses on clerical remarriage with the same speficity as the author of *El.* 12,22, might also therefore appear to fail to distinguish between the two terms.[106]

7C 1.1.4. El. *IX, 12,20-21*

We have already argued in 7C 1.1.1 that the irony of Tertullian's polemic had created a quite fictitious "edict." As such the objection collapses which claims that there is clearly no reference to an edict in *El.* and that therefore for that reason Tertullian's opponent cannot be found there. Preysing endeavoured quite inaccurately to found such an edict on the use of the term ὅρος.[107] Only by defining this term in the sense of a canon or Church law could he refute Adam's obvious argument that there could be no edict of Callistus involved since the dispute was about what he taught (οὗτος ἐδογμάτισεν).[108] It is significant, however, that in order to strengthen his point, he had to resort to a version of an *argumentum e silentio* in which he hypothesizes that the language of *El.* is such as it is in this passage because the author is seeking to conceal an alleged ecclesiastical process against himself.[109]

We have already discussed the use of this term in *El.* both in this passage and in others (5A 1.1). Here we argued that ὅρος in *El.* IX, 12,21 was used in the sense of "custom" in common with *Ap. Trad.* 3 but in contrast with *Ap. Trad.* 4, which was one of the arguments which established the composite character and authorship of that work. We have furthermore already

---

105 Ibid. 5,4; 8; 9; 12: "Itaque moechia adfinis idolatriae—nam et idolatria moechiae nomine et fornicationis saepe populo exprobata—etiam sorte coniungetur illi, sicut et serie; etiam damnatione cohaerebit illi, sicut et dispositione... Quis eam talibus lateribus inclusam, talibus costis circumfultam a cohaerentium corpore divellet, de vicinorum criminum nexu, de propinquorum scelerum complexu, ut solam eam secernat ad paenitentiae fructum? Nonne hinc idolatria, inde homicidium detinebunt et, si qua vox fuerit, reclamabunt: "... Etiam apud Christianos non est moechia sine nobis. Ibidem sunt idolatriae, ubi immundi spiritus res est; ibidem est et homicidium, ubi homo, cum inquinatur, occiditur...""
106 Ibid. 4,3: "Nec enim interest nuptam alienam an viduam quis incurset, dum non suam feminam; sicut nec de locis refert, in cubiculis an in triviis pudicitia trucidetur."
107 K. von Preysing, Existenz und Inhalt des Bussediktes, in *ZKTh* 43 (1919), p. 358-362.
108 Adam (1917) p. 31.
109 Preysing (1919) p. 359.

criticized the notion of the possibility before the age of Cyprian of the kind of judicial process that would give edge to the use of ὅρος strictly in the sense of νόμος (6C 8.2).

It is significant in this context that Preysing has to go to Ancyra and Nicaea in order to find ὅρος used strictly in the sense of νόμος or κάνων.[110] Preysing is quite wrong, therefore, to claim that in *El.* IX, 12,21 ὅρος has this sense. It does not follow from the fact that Zephyrinus is described as ἄπειρον τῶν ἐκκλησιαστικῶν ὅρων, that this means law as opposed to custom, or indeed philosophical discipline. The predominant meaning in *El.* is that of a philosophical definition,[111] *El.* I, 21,1; VII, 18,4-5.which in Greek philosophical schools had clear connection with discipline in view of the subservience of metaphysics to ethics.

The ὁ τῆς ἀληθείας ὅρος in *El.* X, 5,1 derives from the discourse of the philosophical school, which we argued to distinguish early Synodical examination of, e.g. Beryllus of Bostra, from later juridicial examples (6C 8.2). Far from such usage pointing to the fact that *unter* ὅρος *kann hier nur ein förmlicher Erlass verstanden werden*, the quite opposite is implied by the use of this term in the sense that it had in the philosophical schools.[112]

Clearly λέγων πᾶσιν ὑπ᾽ αὐτῷ ἀφίεσθαι τὰς ἁμαρτίας (IX, 12,20) does refer to an ὅρος in the sense of a customary practice involving words that are said rather than to a written decree. But this was precisely what we argued was really implied by Tertullian's invective in its production of the hyperbolic metaphor of an imperial decree (7C 1.1.1-1.1.2). Once we grasp however that there is no edict on either side, then this fact removes an obstacle to concluding that events at Rome were leaving their mark in Carthage, and inspiring a reaction from there too, and that it is reaction in each case to the same events. In the absence of a decree on any side alone, there is no reason to consider the Church of Carthage so insulated from the Church of Rome that revolutionary developments in Church Order in one place would not have direct repercussions on another. Callistus' activity inevitably had repercussions externally, even though there was as yet no possibility of the exercize of the powers of a monarchical bishop let alone a universal pope.[113]

---

[110] Ibid. p. 360.

[111] *El.* I, 21,1; VII, 18,4-5.

[112] Cf. Preysing (1919) p. 359-360: "Unter ὅρος kann hier nur ein förmlicher Erlass verstanden werden. Das Wort nun, das die Frage nach dem Vorliegen eines offiziellen Erlasses entcheidet, ist das Wort ὅρος. Unter ὅρος kann hier nur ein förmlicher Erlass verstanden werden. ὅρος heisst im wörtlichen Sinne Grenze; dem Äon das pleroma begrenzt wird Ὅρος als Eigenname beigelegt. Im übertragenen Sinne kann ὅρος (philosophische) Defenition bedeuten (El. VII,18-19). Hippolyt braucht es auch im Sinne von allgemeinem Gesetz, Naturgesetz (El. IX,30). Im kirchlichen Sprachgebrauch findet es sich, auch bei Hippolyt, im Sinne von Glaubensinhalt, summa (El. X,5). Die häufigste Bedeutung von ὅρος im kirlichen Sprachgebrauch is jedoch „Erlass, Dekret." cf. IX, 11."

[113] Bardy (1924) p. 23 laboured under the illusion that though there was a decree at Carthage, there was none at Rome recorded in *El.* IX, 12, 21 ("Selon Hippolyte Calliste se contente de se montrer miséricordieux pour les pécheurs, mais il ne formule pas sa volonté en un

So far we have considered the connection between Callistus and Tertullian from the point of view of the conditions for clerical absolution and inter-communion, in the light of our modified account of the development of Church Order. Let us now examine the doctrinal connections between Callistus as a semi-Monarchian and Tertullian's opponent in the *Adversus Praxeam*.

7C 2. *Tertullian's opponent in* Adversus Praxeam *1, 3-7*

It has often been pointed out that Praxeas is a very unusual name, indeed a somewhate comical name, whose employment would be consistent with a pseudonym. In consequence, in view of the anti-Monarchian content of this work, and in view of connections otherwise established regarding Tertullian's opposition to Callistus, it has been argued that "Praxeas" is in fact a pseudonym for the latter. The Greek word Πραξέας would presumably mean a "busybody."[114] There are two references in this passage, which would lead to a postive identification.

7C 2.1. *Callistus' martyrdom in* Adv. Prax. *1, 4?*

The possibility of a positive identification is afforded by the following pas-sage:

> For that man originally from Asia (*Nam iste primus ex Asia*) introduced onto the soil of Rome this kind of perversity (*hoc genus perversitatis intulit Romae humo*), a man in other respects disturbed (*homo et alias inquietus*), but above all swollen with boastful pride at his martyrdom (*insuper de iactatione martyrii inflatus*) on account of one only simple and brief nuisance of a prison-stay (*ob solum et simplex et breve carceris taedium*).
>
> *Adv. Prax.* 1,4

The *breve carceris taedium* can be read as a reference to the account of Callistus' life in which his martyrdom is denied.[115] Callistus was in Sardinia because of a criminal conviction, and only associated with true martyrs re-

---

texte de loi, et sa bonté n'a d'autre but que le recrutement de son école."). In consequence he denied the identity between the two events. But once we remove the problem of any edict, then his final conclusion works in favour of our position and not of his (p. 25: "Il n'est pas étonnant qu'à la même époque se soient manifestées à Rome et à Carthage des tendances analogues, que dans les deux Églises on ait pris des mesures de clémence en faveur de certaines catégories de pécheurs.").

114 Barnes (1985) p. 278-279 admits the possibility of the equivalence of Callistus and Praxeas but curiously denies that the adversary of *De Pudic.* can be anyone other than a bishop of Carthage, p. 31 and p. 247, where he is of the curious opinion that the sole grounds for identifying Callistus with Tertullian's opponent was a spurious emendation, namely "Romanam" for "omnem" in *De. Pudicit.* 21,10. See my discussion in 7C 1.1.2 to the effect that the unamended text, given other, cumulative evidence points to Callistus, see footnotes 72, 74, and 75. See also J. Jung, Zu Tertullians auswärtigen Beziehungen, in *Wiener Studien*, 13 (1891), p. 231.

115 *El.* IX, 11,4 makes it clear that the life story that follows (12, 1-14) is primarily intended as a refutation of a claim which it is implied was made by or on behalf of Callistus that he was a true martyr (οὗτος ἐμαρτύρησεν ἐπὶ Φουσκιανοῦ ἐπάρχου ὄντος τῆς ʿΡώμης, ὁ δὲ τρόπος τῆς αὐτοῦ μαρτυρίας τοιόσδε ἦν).

leased under (Commodus') Marcia's amnesty (τὴν ἀπολύσιμον ἐπιστολὴν) as the result of his beggar's tears (γονυπετῶν καὶ δακρύων ἱκέτευε καὶ αὐτὸς τυχεῖν ἀπολύσεως).[116] There is however in *El.* IX, 11,4- 12,1-14 no indication of Callistus' country of origin that would corroborate *nam iste primus ex Asia.* Perhaps at all events this detail need not be stressed. Asia was an extensive province, and perhaps Tertullian simply associated him generally with Smyrna, the birth-place of the reputed originator of the Monarchian heresy, Noetus, without having any more hard information than the author of *El.*

But there is a second reference that would render the identification problematic.

7C 2.2. *The Roman bishop in* Adv. Prax. *1, 5?*

In this passage we find Praxeas associated with a Roman bishop as follows:

> For this same man then compelled (*Nam idem tunc episcopum Romanum, agnoscentem iam prophetias Montani, Priscae, Maximillae... coegit*) the bishop of Rome who recognized the prophecies of Montanus, Prisca, and Maximilla, and by that recognition (*et ex ea agnitione*) brought peace to the Churches of Asia and Phrygia (*pacem ecclesiis Asiae et Phrygiae inferentem*) to revoke the letters of of peace that had been sent (*et litteras pacis revocare iam emissas*) by asserting strongly false things about the prophets themselves and their Churches (*falsa de ipsis prophetis et ecclesiis eorum adseverando*) and by defending the judgments of his predecessors (*et praecessorum eius auctoritates defendendo*) and to abandon his intention of receiving the spiritual gifts (*et a proposito recipiendorum charismatum concessare*).
>
> *Adv. Prax. 1,5*

I take it that the *pacem ecclesiis Asiae et Phrygiae* to which Tertullian refers are in fact congregations from Asia and Phrygia in Rome. Victor's letter would no more have affected Asia and Phrygia directly, any more than he could have excommunicated all of Asia Minor for its Quartodeciman practice, as though he were a fourth century pope, despite Eusebius *H.E.* V,24, 9, as we have seen (6C 6). It is significant that Tertullian immediately goes on to record the affect only upon Rome of the effects of Praxeas action in expelling prophecy and introducing heresy.[117]

But there is no reason to think that Irenaeus would have chided Victor on Montanism in the way in which he did regarding the latter's attack upon the Quartordecimans. Hall's attempt to identify Praxeas with Irenaeus was in-

---

[116] Ibid. 12, 11-13: τυχοῦσα οὖν τῆς ἀξιώσεως ἡ Μαρκία παρὰ τοῦ Κομόδου, δίδωσι τὴν ἀπολύσιμον ἐπιστολὴν ʽΥακίθῳ τινί, σπάδοντι ὄντι πρεσβυτέρῳ· ὃς λαβὼν διέπλευσεν εἰς τὴν Σαρδονίαν καὶ ἀποδοὺς τῷ κατ' ἐκεῖνο καιροῦ τῆς χώρας ἐπιτροπεύοντι ἀπέλυσε τοὺς μάρτυρας πλὴν τοῦ Καλλίστου. ὁ δὲ γονυπετῶν καὶ δακρύων ἱκέτευε καὶ αὐτὸς τυχεῖν ἀπολύσεως.

[117] *Adv. Prax.* 1,5: "... Ita duo negotia diaboli Praxeas *Romae procuravit*: prophetiam expulit et haeresin intulit. Paracletum fugavit et Patrem crucifixit."

dicative of the reverse, since Irenaeus was deeply opposed to Montanism.[118] The influence of Praxeas upon the Roman bishop is very reminiscent of Callistus' influence upon Zephyrinus. Callistus was the contemporary of Victor but had been held at arm's length by him, as the following passage, which describes his reaction to the latter's release, shows:

> When he arrived (οὐ παραγενομένου) Victor was extremely vexed at what had happened (ὁ Οὐίκτωρ πάνυ ἤχθετο ἐπὶ τῷ γεγονότι), but since he was compassionate (ἀλλ' ἐπεὶ εὔσπλαγχνος ἦν), he held his peace (ἡσύχαζε); but wary of the outrage felt by many (φυλασσόμενος δὲ τὸν ὑπὸ πολλῶν ὄνειδον)— for what had been outrageously done by him was not done at a distance (οὐ γὰρ ἦν μακρὰν τὰ ὑπ' αὐτοῦ τετολμημένα)—but with Carpophorus still resisting (ἔτι δὲ καὶ τοῦ Καρποφόρου ἀντιπίπτοντος), he sent him to reside in Antheion (πέμπει αὐτὸν καταμένειν ἐν 'Ανθείῳ), having allotted him a monthly sum for his keep (ὁρίσας αὐτῷ μηνιαῖον τι εἰς τροφάς).
>
> El. IX, 12,13

Taken at their face value, far from Callistus being a person in sufficient standing with Victor as to be able to persuade him to revoke letters of peace sent to Montanist congregations, Victor finds him an embarassment to be got out of the way and pensioned off in view of general scandal (φυλασσόμενος δὲ τὸν ὑπὸ πολλῶν ὄνειδον) and Carpophorus' grievances (τοῦ Καρποφόρου ἀντιπίπτοντος) against the slave who had swindled him.

There are two points to be made in this connection. The first is that the passage is highly polemical and clearly very prejudiced. The author of El. might have chosen to interpret the action of Victor in such a light, born out of the compassion (ἐπεὶ εὔσπλαγχνος ἦν) that one would not otherwise have associated with what we know of the person of Victor. In fact, behind the polemic, Carpophorus does not emerge in a very good light. Are we really to assume that he knew nothing of what his slave was doing in his banking business, and might it not be that he in reality left Callistus to take the blame for his own questionable dealings?

In such circumstances, Victor may have acted, not because of a sense of public scandal felt only by the author of El. and his association with patrician values, but because he wished to protect Callistus, whom he believed to have suffered enough, without antagonizing in turn a wealthy member of his community. The criticism of Callistus in El. IX, 12,24, in using the expression of the actions of αἱ ἐν ἀξίᾳ as τὴν ἑαυτῶν ἀξίαν...καθαιρεῖν διὰ τοῦ νομίμως γαμηθῆναι, reflected such social values.[119]

---

[118] S.G. Hall, Praxeas and Irenaeus, in StudPatr 14, T.U. 117 (1976) p. 147 argued that Πραξέας (a intriguer in crafty business deals) was used self-consciously by contrast with Εἰρηναῖος meaning "peaceable". But curiously he did not see this as a pun on the "litteras pacis" sent by Victor (7 C 2.2), but rather on Irenaeus himself whose theology Tertullian would have regarded as monarchian (p. 146-147). But the allusion to such business deals could well also be justified with reference to El. IX, 12, 1-14, and it would otherwise be a strange contrast.

[119] See also 7C 1.1.3.2 and footnote 101.

But even if Victor's attitude towards Callistus could be modified in this way, the latter would hardly be in a position, with his pension in exile at Antheium, to persuade Victor to withdraw the *litteras pacis* sent to Montanist congregations within Rome and its immediate neighbourhood. Furthermore, he did not yet possess any clerical rank, since, according to *El.* IX, 12,14, it was only on Victor's death (μεθ' οὗ κοίμησιν) that Zephyrinus ended his exile (μεταγαγὼν ἀπὸ τοῦ Ἀνθείου) and placed him in charge of the cemetary (εἰς τὸ κοιμητήριον κατέστησεν), having ordained him presumably as deacon (ὡς συναράμενον αὐτὸν θέλων ἔχειν πρὸς τὴν κατάστασιν τοῦ κλήρου).

However, it is important to note that Tertullian does not claim that his unnamed *episcopus Romanus* sent the *litterae pacis*. He simply claims that he revoked letters that had already been sent (*litteras pacis revocare iam emissas*). It may have been, therefore, that he is refering to Zephyrinus as the uncultivated and uneducated (ἄνδρα ἰδιώτην καὶ ἀγράμματον) bishop (*El.* IX, 11,1-3) whom Callistus (Praxeas) not only persuaded with gifts (ὃν πείθων δόμασι) but also lead into making publicly heretical statements (τὸν Ζεφυρῖνον παράγων ἔπειθε δημοσίᾳ ποτὲ μὲν λέγειν...κ.τ.λ.). In this case we would have Zephyrinus at Callistus' instigation reversing the *litteras pacis* sent by Victor immediately after the latter's death.

Certainly by his acts of absolution Callistus himself would have been no friend of Montanism. The circle of the writer of *El.* and Hippolytus were clearly themselves not the greatest admirers of this movement. It is however of great relevance to what will be my subsequent argument to note here that the author of *El.* was less of an opponent of Montanism than his successor Hippolytus. Tertullian will not give the author of *El.* the dignity of any mention, let alone a heroic mention, since clearly their groups are different in their theological assumptions yet united in their opposition to Callistus' group and to the revolution in Church Order that, we have argued, the latter is initiating within the fractionalized Roman community (7C 1.1.1), and indeed united in opposition Monarchianism.

Some grudging approval, however muted, therefore would have been given to the resistance by *El.* to the monarchical tendency as well as to the Monarchian Christology. It is for this reason perhaps that Tertullian leaves anonymous, or uses a pseudonym for, the main players in the conflicting currents on which he is commenting, and whose repercussions are being felt at Carthage. Yet he will not directly challenge those whose arguments on these subjects seem so sound, and whose censuring of Montanism is so mild by comparison. The author of *El.* X, 25,1 believes that they are orthodox on both creation and Christology.[120] Clearly in this respect the school of Montanus had more in common with the community of *El.* than did the

---

[120] *El.* X, 25,1: οὗτοι τὰ μὲν περὶ τῆς τοῦ παντὸς ἀρχῆς καὶ δημιουργίας ὀρθῶς λέγουσι, καὶ τὰ περὶ τὸν Χριστὸν οὐκ ἀλλοτρίως παρειλήφασιν...

school of Callistus. Their error was the new prophets whom they valued above the evangelists, and the new fasts contrary to tradition.[121]

But given this kind of relationship between the community of the author of *El.* and Hippolytus and Tertullian, the critical question that now arises is the relationship between the theology of *Adv. Prax.* and both *El.* and *C.N.* Curiously, *El.* X, 26,1 goes on as did the previous discussion in *El.* VIII, 19, 1-3 to identify certain Montanists with Noetus. Clearly, therefore, Tertullian as a Montanist would be looked closely at by the community of *El.*, and his attack on Praxeas would have been aimed at some of his Montanist confraternity as well as Callistus. Furthermore, it would indicate that the author of *El.* did not know of Tertullian nor his attack on the Praxeas, whose teaching he, as we shall now argue, would have identified with that of Callistus himself. Perhaps his failure to mention Noetus or Sabellius would indicate that he saw the error as Praxeas/Callistus had developed it as its most insidious form, typically held by the *psychici,* rather than the more moderate form maintained by some claiming to be Montanist *pneumatici.*

7C 2.3. *Theological relations between* Adv. Prax., El *and* C.N.
Simonetti examined the christology of *Adv. Prax.* with that of *El.* and *C.N.,* and argued that Tertullian was dependent on both of these works. His argument was that *C.N.* represented a less developed form of the theological argument of *Adv. Prax.,* and so for this reason Tertullian had used the argument of *C.N.* and not *vice versa.*[122] However, the theology of the latter is a unique Christological formulation that denied full personality to the λόγος ἄσαρκος before the incarnation in the womb of the Virgin when, and only when, the λόγος became τελείος υἱός (4A 1.1). Tertullian, to the contrary, continues mainstream Patristic Christology (4A 2.1). We shall argue therefore that though Tertullian is dependent upon the theology of *El.*, *C.N.* is in fact dependent upon Tertullian. We shall show that where Simonetti claims Tertullian develops, it is in fact *C.N.* which shortens and omits in order to depersonalize the pre-existent λόγος and thus forge a *rapprochement* with Monarchianism, which would have regarded a personal pre-existent λόγος as part of a ditheism or tritheism.

We shall accordingly focus upon features of Tertullian's argument which reveal, in contrast with *C.N.,* the assertion of a fully personal λόγος before the incarnation, which we have already shown *El.* to share, but *C.N.,* in contrast, to contradict (4A 1). We shall show:
1. Tertullian's adversary reflected the particular form of Monarchiansm of which Zephyrinus and Callistus were accused in *El.*, and,

---

[121] Ibid.: ... ἐν δὲ τοῖς προειρημένοις προφήταις σφάλλονται· ὧν τοῖς λόγοις ὑπὲρ τὰ εὐαγγέλια προσέχοντες πλανῶνται καὶ νηστείας καινὰς καὶ παρὰ τὰς παραδόσεις ὁρίζοντες. See also 2A 3.1 on *El.* VIII, 19, 1-3 cf. X, 26,1 where some of the Montanists are accused of siding with Noetus in christology.

[122] M. Simonetti, Due note su Ippolito, in *StEphAug.* 13 (1977), p. 126-136.

2. Whilst Tertullian accepts generally the tradition of Justin and Theophilus of Christ as τοῦ θεοῦ υἱόν ὃς καὶ πρὸ ἑωσφόρου (4A 2.1), he transfers the title σοφία from the Holy Spirit in Irenaeus to the Son, and thus emphasizes the personal character of the mental construct already personalized in the *Old Testament*. *C.N.* omits such *O.T.* personalizations in the interests of his language of instrumentality.

7C 2.3.1. El. *IX, 12-19; X, 27, 3-4 and* Adv Prax.
As we saw in *El.* IX, 12,15-19, which we quoted in full in 4A 1.2, Callistus held the view, summarized in X, 27,3-4, that Father and Son were one in nature (οὐσία δὲ ἓν ὄντα) so that the titles πατήρ and λόγος were separate names (λόγον ὀνόματι μὲν υἱὸν καὶ πατέρα... ὀνομαζόμενον) but of the substance (ἓν... πρόσωπον... ὀνόματι μὲν μεριζόμενον, οὐσίᾳ δὲ οὔ) of the one indivisible divine Spirit (τὸ πνεῦμα ἀδιαίρετον) that makes each identical. λόγος and πνεῦμα are thus equivalent to the πατήρ and δημιουργός.

Tertullian's attack is directed against such a Monarchian argument that insists that the distinction is a distinction in names and not in reality :

> That which itself (*Ipsum*) the Father and Son are said to be (*quod Pater et Filius dicuntur*), is not that one thing different from another (*nonne aliud ab alio est*)? For in any case (*Utique enim*) what all things are named, this they will be (*omnia quod vocantur, hoc erunt*), and what they will be this they will be named (*et quod erunt, hoc vocabuntur*); and the distinction between the words used does not make possible any confusion (*et permiscere se diversitas vocabulorum non potest omnino*) because there is none in the things which they designate (*quia nec rerum quarum erunt vocabula*).
>
> *Adv. Prax.* 9,4

Thus we find rebutted Callistus' distinction between οὐσίᾳ δὲ ἓν ὄντα and λόγον ὀνόματι...υἱὸν καὶ πατέρα... ὀνομαζόμενον.

The ἓν...πρόσωπον...ὀνόματι μὲν μεριζόμενον οὐσίᾳ δὲ οὔ Tertullian seeks to refute by insisting with Irenaeus on the distinctiveness of the Holy Spirit on which *El.* is notoriously mute. Significantly, the grounds on which he asserts the distinction of persons is by asserting the person of the Holy Spirit since it is by this means that the τὸ πνεῦμα ἀδιαίρετον can be deprived of its function in obliterating the distinctions of person between Father and Son. Tertullian had immediately previously insisted on the distinct personhood of the Spirit in the light of the Paraclete passages in *Jn.* 14,16:

> Happily the Lord, in using this word (*Bene quod et Dominus usus hoc verbo*) in the person of the Paraclete (*in persona Paracleti*) signifies not division but arrangement (*non divisionem significat sed dispositionem*): "I will ask the Father," he said, (*"Rogabo," inquit, "Patrem"*) "and he will send another advocate to you (*"et alium advocatum mittet vobis,"*), the Spirit of truth (*"Spiritum veritatis"*). Thus another person, a Paraclete other than himself (*Sic alium a se Paracletum*), he shows us as a third degree in the way in which (*quomodo*) [he showed us] another person apart from the Father as Son (*et nos*

a Patre alium Filium ut tertium gradum ostenderet in Paracleto), just as [he showed us] a second in the Son (*sicut nos secundum in Filio*) by means of the observation of the οἰκονομία (*propter oikonomiae observationem*).

Adv. Prax. 9,3

Tertullian appears to be attacking here something very like Callistus' argument that the πνεῦμα ἀδιαίρετον obliterated such distinctions and created the Father-Son of *El.* IX, 12,17 (4A 1.2). He is doing so by means of the personal term, *Paracletus/ Advocatus*, promised as the Spirit in *Jn.* 14, 15-31 ff., and by the personal, masculine adjective (*alius*) that thereby can be used to replace the Greek neuter.

Having reached this conclusion, it is no longer, as in the case of *El.*, a defence against ditheism that is required, but against tritheism. We have already drawn attention to the absence of a fully-developed role of the Spirit in *El.* (4A 2.1.1). Tertullian now introduces the term *trinitas,* in which he follows Irenaeus, with certain qualifications, and in which we shall argue that Hippolytus follows him in *C.N.*, after a modified and instrumental fashion.[123]

7C 2.3.2. σοφία, λόγος *and* πνεῦμα *in Irenaeus, Tertullian, and* C.N.

We can see in *Adversus Praxeam* 7 a clear distinction from the instrumental view of the pre-incarnate λόγος in *C.N.* (4A 1-1.1), and agreement with Irenaeus and the author of *El.* (4A 2-2.1). Tertullian is clearly aware that *sermo* can be given a purely instrumental sense. It can be simply the voice and sound from the mouth (*vox et sonus oris*), or simply something vacuous (*vacuum nescio quid*), empty (*inane*), and incorporeal (*incorporale*). (*Adv. Prax.* 7, 6) He continues:

> But I say that nothing can have come from God (*At ego nihil dico de Deo*) which is empty and vacuous (*inane et vacuum prodire potuisse*) because it would not have been produced from one who was vacuous and empty (*ut non de inani et vacuo prolatum*). [The Word] could not have been without substance (*carere substantia*) on account of the great substance (*quod de tanta substantia*) from which he proceeded (*processit*) and because he has made so great substances (*et tantas substantias fecit*). For even he himself has made those things which are made through him (*Fecit enim et ipse quae facta sunt per illum*). How can it be (*Quale est*) that he himself should be nothing without which nothing was made (*ut nihil sit ipse sine quo nihil factum est*)? ... Is the Word of God vacuous and empty matter (*Vacua et inanis res est sermo Dei*) who is called the Son (*qui Filius dictus est*), and who himself is surnamed (*Qui ipse Deus cognominatus est*) "God"? [*Jn.* 1,1; *Exod.* 20,7]... This one is certainly (*Hic certe est*) "he who was in the form of God (*qui in effigie Dei constitutus*), did not consider it robbery to be equal to God [*Philip.* 2,6] (*non rapinam existimavit esse se aequalem Deo*)." In what "form of God (*in qua effigie Dei*)?" Certainly (utique) in some form (*in aliqua*) but not in no form at

---

123 Cf. the use of τρίας in *C.N.* 14,8 (διὰ γὰρ τῆς τριάδος ταύτης Πατήρ δοξάζεται) with *Adv. Prax.* 3,1: "Numerum et dispositionem trinitatis divisionem praesumunt unitatis, quando unitas, ex semetipsa derivans trinitatem, non destruatur ab illa sed administretur." See also 4A 3.2.2

all (*non tamen in nulla*). For who will deny (*Quis enim negabit*) that God is body (*Deum corpus esse*) even if God is Spirit (*etsi Deus spiritus est*). For Spirit in its own form is a body of its own kind (*Spiritus enim corpus sui generis in sua effigie*). But even whatever things are invisible (*Sed et si invisibilia illa quaecumque sunt*) have in God's eyes (*habent apud Deum*) both their own body and shape (*et suum corpus et suam formam*), through which they are visible to God alone (*per quae soli Deo visibilia sunt*). What comes from the substance of [God] himself (*quod ex ipsius substantia missum est*) even more (*quanto magis*) [therefore] will not exist without substance (*sine substantia non erit*)! Whatever therefore was the substance of the Word (*Quaecumque ergo substantia sermonis fuit*), that I call a person (*illam dico personam*), and I claim (*vindico*) for him the name of Son (*illi nomen Filii*)..."

Adv. Prax. 7, 6-9

In *Adv. Prax.* 7, 2-3 Tertullian had already cited the proof texts of *El.* X, 33, 2 and 9 for the πρωτότοκος or *primogenitus*, and had associated, as Justin, Melito, and Theophilus had done, *Psalm* 2,7 with 109,3, and with *Col.* 1,15 (4A 2.1-2.3). Each of these he clearly interprets as referring to the pre-existent Son without the qualification of *C.N.* 16,7 that they are to be understood purely prospectively (τὴν τοῦ λόγου γέννησιν σημαίνων... καιρῷ ὡρισμένῳ παρ' αὐτῷ μέλλων ἀποκαλύπτειν). Each quotation is about he who is without qualification *Filius factus est... ante omnia genitus.* [124] It is therefore in such a pre-incarnational context, and in contrast with what we have argued to be the case in *C.N.*, that we are to understand Tertullian's discussion that remains within the tradition of Irenaeus and *El.*

In one respect however Tertullian might be thought to side with the interpretation of *C.N.* against Irenaeus in that *Sapientia* is equated with *Verbum/Sermo* and *Filius* and not with the *Spiritus Sanctus*. The proof text of *Prov.* 8, 22 is cited by Tertullian in support for the equation of *Sapientia* with *Sermo* just as in Irenaeus *Adv. Haer.* IV, 20,3 it is equated with the *Spiritus Sanctus*. [125] Why did Tertullian make this equation when otherwise he supported the Irenaean tradition, shared partly also by *El.* in repect of the binitarianism of that work, as revealed by common proof-texts?

---

[124] Tertullian, *Adv. Prax.* 7,1-2: "...exinde eum Patrem sibi faciens, de quo procedendo Filius factus est, *primogenitus* [*Col.* 1,15], ut ante omnia genitus et unigenitus ut solus ex Deo genitus, proprie de vulva cordis ipsius, secundum quod et Pater ipse testatur: *Eructavit cor meum sermonem optimum* [*Ps.* 44,1]. Ad quem deinceps gaudens proinde gaudentem in persona illius [*Ps.* 2,7]: *Filius meus es tu, ego hodie genui te*, et: *Ante luciferum genui te* [*Ps.* 109,3]." See also T. Verhoeven, *Studiën over Tertullianus' Adversus Praxean*: Voornamelijk Betrekking hebbend op Monarchia, Oikonomia, Probola in verband met de Triniteit, (Amsterdam: N.V. Noord-Hollandsche Uitgevers Maatschappij 1948); A. Quacquarelli, L'antimonarchisanesimo di Tertulliano, in *Rassegna di scienze filosophische*, 3 (1950), p. 31-63.
[125] Ibid. 6,1: "Haec vis et haec divini sensus dispositio, apud scripturas etiam in sophiae nomine ostenditur. Quid enim sapientius ratione Dei sive sermone? Itaque sophiam quoque exaudi, ut secundam personam conditam. *Primo Dominus creavit me .. etc.* [*Prov.* 8,22]..." Ibid. 7,11: "Tunc igitur etiam ipse sermo speciem et ornatum suum sumit, sonum et vocem cum dicit Deus: *Fiat lux* [*Gen.* 1,3]. Haec est nativitas perfecta sermonis, dum ex Deo procedit, conditus ab eo primum ad cogitatum in nomine sophiae: *Dominus condidit me initium viarum* [*Prov.* 8,22]."

At first sight this is curious because, as we have argued (7C 2.3.1), it was *El.*'s lack of a pneumatology that enabled πνεῦμα to obliterate distinctions between Father and Son in Callistus' theology. It would therefore have assisted his refutation of that obliteration if he could associate πνεῦμα with the personalized σοφία. I would suggest however that he was happy to give up this association because, in the use of the Johannine Paraclete, he had already, he believed, established beyond doubt the individual personality of the Spirit in texts carrying total conviction for a Montanist. He needed now σοφία, speaking with a personal and human voice, in *Prov.* 8,22, to buttress his argument for a fully personal pre-existent Son. It was that very proof text that Tertullian had so helpfully associated with the place of the pre-existent Christ in the godhead that *C.N.*, instrumentalising σοφία and hence λόγος, self-consciously ommitted. There was no room for a fully personal σοφία– λόγος from *Prov.* 8,22 in an account in which, in the words of *C.N.* 10,2-3, the God who was οὔτε ἄλογος οὔτε ἄσοφος...πάντα...τὰ γενόμενα διὰ λόγου καὶ σοφίας τεχνάζεται (4A 3.2.2).

Adv. Prax. 7 specifically seeks to attack the Monarchianism that *El.* attacks, and takes no note of the instrumentalist *rapprochement* of *C.N.* which is clearly later. Rather Tertullian's problem is the absence of a pneumatology in the tradition of *El.*, which he seeks to resolve by a modification of the Irenaean tradition from which *C.N.*'s *rapprochement* with Monarchianism would expressly and intentionally depart. It answers the problem of how the λόγος can be more than prospectively a person before the incarnation that makes it/him the τέλειος υἱός. Christ "in the form of God (*in effigie Dei*)" was in some form (*in aliqua*) than that of the incarnation of the Virgin but that does not mean he had not any form at all (*non tamen in nulla*). His existence was not, as *C.N.* was to suggest, purely or partially instrumental and less than completely personal.

The *sermo* must have the same substance as God from whom he proceeded (*quod ex ipsius substantia missum est*) and that substance must have a body of its own kind even though it is spiritual (*Spiritus enim corpus sui generis in sua effigie*). The substance of the *sermo*, being analogical to the *corpus* in its spiritual form, must therefore be a person and not an instrument which would only become completely personal through the incarnation. Therefore Tertullian can conclude: *Quaecumque ergo substantia Sermonis fuit illam dico personam et illi vindico nomen Filii.* Thus for Tertullian the pre-existent λόγος–παῖς was properly a person and therefore properly called υἱός/ *Filius* before the incarnation.[126]

---

[126] Cf. Nautin (1949) p. 162: "L'autre préoccupation d'Hippolyte est d'évoquer le Saint Esprit à côté du Fils en ajoutant la mention de la Sagesse à celle du Verbe... C'est à saint Irénée qu' Hippolyte emprunte non seulement la distinction du Verbe e de la Sagesse pour représenter le Fils et le Saint Esprit, mais aussi cette façon d'assigner le Verbe à la fabrication et la Sagesse à l'ornementation. [IV,34,2]." Nautin is quite wrong therefore to equate σοφία in *C.N.* 10,3 (...

Tertullian was not however acquainted with the theology of *C.N.* and its depersonalization and instrumentalization of the λόγος–παῖς before the incarnation. We have shown the theology of the former to be so radical a departure from the patristic tradition of the late second century, and so unique a theological contruction that it would scarcely have avoided Tertullian's express criticism if he had known and used it (4A 1.1). Furthermore, as the purpose of his reconstruction was a *rapprochement* with the heirs of Callistus' Monarchianism, he would scarcely have for that reason alone silently concurred with it (4A 1.2). The date of *Adv. Prax.*, moreover, is 210/211,[127] and we have argued *C.N.* and associated works to be those of Hippolytus, successor of the author of *El.*, subsequent to 225 (4B 2.2.2.1.3).[128]

It is true that *C.N.* 11,1 is anxious to rebut the charge of ditheism, and that concern is shared with Tertullian. But *El.* too was concerned with the charge of advocating a theology that creates only two Gods.[129] It does not follow that Tertullian, *Adv. Prax.* 8 therefore read and followed *C.N.* 11. It should be noted that Tertullian in *Adv. Prax.* 8,5 claims that the series of metaphors found in this exposition are from a Montanist vision (*quemadmodum etiam Paracletus*) and not from reading a text from a Roman community. Simonetti was too quick to identify Tertullian's description as a development of Hippolytus' metaphors and therefore dependent upon the latter.[130]

Both of Tertullian's apparent additions, the root and the shrub (*radix fruticem...*) are in fact explicable as deletions on the part of *C.N.* on the ground that the metaphor is too organic and insufficiently instrumental, given Hippolytus' revisionist purpose.[131] It is not, as Simonetti maintained, that

---

λόγῳ μὲν κτίζων, σοφᾳ δὲ κοσμῶν) with the Holy Spirit by contrast with Λόγος as παῖς. Tertullian clearly shows that *Sapientia* was not necessarily equated with *Spiritus* as it was for Irenaeus, and *C.N.* never equates σοφία with ἅγιον πνεῦμα, as I have shown. σοφία and λόγῳ in this passage simply refer to diferent aspects of the activity of the not-yet completely personal νοῦς. It may therefore be quite misleading in the case of the text of *C.N.* to spell λόγος with a capital Λ as Butterworth (1977) constantly does.

[127] Barnes (1985) p. 55.

[128] Simonetti (1977) p. 126 was to acknowledge this serious chronological objection to his thesis in limiting himself to a purely literary analysis ("... se si identifica l'autore del *Contra Noetum* con quello dell'*Elenchos*, operante a Roma intorno al 220-240, automaticamente il *Contra Noetum* risulta posteriore all'opera tertullianea, che viene collocata intorno al 213... io credo che non sia inutile mettere a confronto i nostri due testi senza partire da alcuna posizione preconcetta: è ovvio pertanto che il confronto sarà basato soltanto sui dati interni, deducibili dalle due opere, senza alcun riferimento, esplicito o implicito, a dati esterni." My problem is that far from the two-authors' hypothesis removing the problem of a single author *operante a Roma intorno al 220-240*, there are very convincing grounds for showing that Hippolytus is the reviser and reconciler of the work of the author of *El.* and therefore subsequent to him (4B 2.2.4).

[129] *Adv. Prax.* 13, 1 and 6: "Si tam durus es, puta interim tu; et adhuc amplius hoc putes, accipe et in psalmo duos deos dictos... Duos tamen deos et duos dominos nunquam ex ore nostro proferimus, non quasi non et Pater et Filius Deus et Spiritus Deus, et Deus unusquisque Deus..." cf. *El.* IX, 11,3: ἀπεκάλει ἡμᾶς διθέους and 12,16: δίθεοί ἐστε.

[130] Simonetti (1977) p. 132-133.

[131] *Adv. Prax.* 8,5: "Protulit enim Deus sermonem, quemadmodum etiam Paracletus docet, sicut radix fruticem et fons fluvium et sol radium. Nam et istae species προβολαὶ sunt earum substantiarum ex quibus prodeunt. Nec dubitaverim filium dicere et radicis fruticem et fontis

Tertullian must have this metaphor since Hippolytus could never have ommitted it if available to him since it was *perfettamente analoga, al fine di evitare l'accusa di diteismo*, but rather that it was quite inconsistent with his own refutation of ditheism in terms of a *rapprochement* with Callistan Monarchianism. The shrub is too different and developed an entity to be comparable with the λόγος ἄσαρκος not yet fully personal (4A 2.1.3).[132] Furthermore, neither can Hippolytus thus follow Tertullian in applying such personal terms to the Spirit since he is precluded by his temporizing theology from applying them to the pre-incarnate Son.

We therefore see that Tertullian would not have accepted the later *rapprochement* of *C.N.* with Monarchianism but would have held to, and developed the theology of the Holy Spirit in Irenaeus, and the pre-incarnational Christology of *El.* that accorded full personality to the Son before the world. We see reflected in these documents two groups at Rome and Carthage whose approach to theology and discipline are convergent, and both of whom are caught in the cross-currents of forces propelling dynamically the development towards a monarchical episcopacy (4B 2.2.3.3-2.2.4). It was a convergence for a time alone, since, as we have argued, the theological *rapprochement* of the community of Hippolytus with the Monarchians was also accompanied by a reconciliation with the larger group developing a monarchical episcopacy at Rome. The tactics of Callistus, whose approach to discipline and theology was so severely criticized in both *El.* and *De Pudic.* and *Adv. Prax.*, had finally succeeded with his successors.

Let us now conclude our argument in this monograph.

PART D. TERTULLIAN: PRE CYPRIANIC CHURCH ORDER

We saw, in connection with the Damasus legend, the phenomenon of earlier events in the development of Order reinterpreted in the light of a later situation. In the light of that analysis we were able to establish one more compo-

---

fluvium et solis radium, quia omnis origo parens est et omne quod ex origine profertur progenies est, multo magis sermo Dei qui etiam proprie nomen Filii accepit. Nec frutex tamen a radice nec fluvius a fonte nec radius a sole discernitur, sicut nec a Deo sermo." Cf. *C.N.* 11,1: ἕτερον δὲ λέγων οὐ δύο θεοὺς λέγω, ἀλλ' ὡς φῶς ἐκ φωτὸς ἢ ὡς ὕδωρ ἐκ πηγῆς ἢ ὡς ἀκτῖνα ἀπὸ ἡλίου. δύναμις γὰρ μία ἡ ἐκ τοῦ παντός· τὸ δὲ πᾶν πατήρ, ἐξ οὗ δύναμις λόγος. As Simonetti (1977) p. 133 indicates, φῶς ἐκ φωτὸς/ *sol radium* are already used from Justin, *Dialog.* 128 and Tatian, *Adv. Graec.* 5 and as such are unexpectional and establish nothing regarding the direction of dependence. However, both are inanimate metaphors and as such consistent with my thesis that Hippolytus deliberately selects instrumental descriptions from Tertullian who precedes him, whether directly or by report, (τὸ δὲ πᾶν πατήρ, ἐξ οὗ δύναμις λόγος) for the λόγος ἄσαρκος.

[132] Cf. Simonetti (1977) p. 133-134: "Se di contro facciamo dipendere Ippolito da Tertulliano, risulta difficile spiegare l'omissione dell'immagine della radice e del pollone, perfettamente analoga, al fine di evitare l'accusa di diteismo, alle imagini del sole e della fonte: l'unica spiegazione possibile è che Ippolito avrebbe considerato la terza immagine come superflua dopo le altre due."

nents in the Eusebian edifice of a static and unchanging Church Order from the first till the fourth century (6B). In the light of the critical development of monarchical episcopacy subsequent to the death of Hippolytus and in the age of Cyprian, and the subsequent inability to conceptualize previous historical conditions, we believe that we are justified in not using Cyprian's interpretation of past history in connection with the events in which Tertullian was involved.[133]

That interpretation was informed, like that of Damasus and Eusebius, by the conceptual universe of Church Order which Cyprian created whilst believing sincerely that he was simply reflecting it.[134] Instead, following Lampe's account of the fractionalized Roman community, and our own analysis of the ecclesiastical events represented by *El.* (6 C 7.1), we have sought to establish relations between the community of *El.* and of Tertullian against the back cloth of our reconstructed pre-Cyprianic Church Order (6C 1-7). In the light of that reconstruction, we saw that the relations between Tertullian and the author of *El.*, problematic if interpreted in the light of post-Cyprianic Church Order, become perfectly comprehensible (7C 1-7C 2).

Had Tertullian been, any more than the author of *El.*, a leader of a schism in the later sense, then Cyprian could never have described him as *magister meus*, as recorded in Jerome *De Viris Ill.* 53. Jerome continues that Tertullian, as a middle-aged priest, lapsed into Montanism because of the envy and insults of the Roman clergy.[135] But Jerome shows in this passage that the lapse into Montanism is his own conclusion from his reading of Tertullian's works. "Lapsed into Montanism" may not be equivalent in Tertullian's time with "leaving the church" as opposed to forming part of an *ecclesiola in ecclesiae* that still managed to remain part of the church.[136]

---

[133] See footnote 72.

[134] For a similar interpretation of the role of Ignatius in the development of the threefold Order in second century Asia Minor, see A. Brent, The Ignatian Epistles and the Threefold Ecclesiastical Order, in *JRH* 17,1 (1992), p. 18-32.

[135] Jerome, *De Vir. Ill.* 53,4: "Vidi ego quemdam Paulum Concordiae, quod oppidum Italiae est, senem, qui se beati Cypriani, iam grandis aetatis, notarium, cum ipse admodum esset adolescens, Romae vidisse diceret, referreque sibi solitum nunquam Cyrianum absque Tertulliani lectione unum diem praeterisse, ac sibi crebro dicere, Da magistrum: Tertullianum videlicet significans. Hic cum usque ad mediam aetatem presbyter ecclesiae permansisset, invidia postea et contumeliis clericorum Romanae Ecclesiae, ad Montani dogma delapsus, in multis libris Novae Prophetiae meminit...

[136] Tertullian *De An.* 9,4 is critical here. The natural reading of this passage seems to imply a private examination following a normal catholic service in which a charismatic intervention had taken place. But cf. U. Neymeyr, Die christlichen Lehrer im zweiten Jahrhundert: Ihr Lehrtätigkeit, ihr Selbsverständnis, und ihre Geschichte, in *Supplements to Vigiliae Christianae*, (Leiden: E.J. Brill 1989), p. 129-131: ".. Tertullian dies aus apologischen Absichten erwähnt, um zu zeigen, dass in den montanischen Gottesdiensten kein charismatisches Chaos herrsche, sondern alles seine Ordnung habe. Würde er von einem katholischen Gottesdienst berichten, brauchte er nicht auf diesen Usus hinzuweisen." See in reply D. Rankin, *Doctrines of Church and Ministry in Tertullian*, unpublished PhD thesis, (Melbourne College of Divinity 1991) and ——, *Tertullian and the Church,* (Cambridge: U.P. 1995).

However, although the mention of antagonism with the Roman clergy is not derivable from Tertullian's extant writings, it may be both historical and comprehensible in the light of our recontruction of the situation in the Roman community in the time of Hippolytus. It is historical evidence for a connection with Rome involving antagonism that we have argued to be the real basis for the dispute in both *De Pudic.* and *Adv. Prax.* (7C 1 and 7C 2). In the light of our own analysis of the Roman community as represented in *El.* (6C 7-8), it becomes clear why the dispute with Callistus and his associates with the community of *El.* could be with greater historical veracity seen as a dispute within a fractionalized community that fell well short of schism in the latter sense. A number of problems, irresolvable on the assumption that the dispute was with a monarchical bishop, could, in such a reformulated context, be resolved. We have sought to extend that reformulated context to Tertullian's North Africa, and to show how the factionalism at Rome had its approximate counterpart in North Africa.

Tertullian was involved in the fall-out from the disputes between the fractionalized house/school-churches, each with their own presiding πρεσβύτ-ερος-ἐπίσκοπος, and each reacting to the implicit claims of Callistus' liberal policy of absolution and reception of their excommunicated members, and the discrete implications for intercommunion and authority of such action (6A 5). It is no wonder that there should be a garbled memory of conflict between Tertullian and such Roman presbyters, before the time when an unambiguous episcopal monarchy had been established over such groups at Rome. Such a garbled memory pointed to an anachronistic conceptualization such as we have also established in the case of Damasus and Eusebius.

In North Africa, in Tertullian's time, therefore, we may conclude from *De Viris Ill.* 53, amongst other considerations, that the form of Church Order was far more fluid in comparison with what it was destined to become in course of the controversies of Cyprian's time, in particular the Novatian schism which left its mark upon the Roman community too.[137] A similar fluidity lies behind Eusebius' account of the life of Origen. Origen was not ordained a presbyter until 230 whilst travelling through Palestine by "the bishops,"—not it should be noted a single bishop—in Caesarea.[138] Before this time he had taught as a layman and preached regularly in church, at the

---

[137] W.C.H. Frend, The Seniores Laici and the Origins of the Church of North Africa, in *JThS* n.s. 122 (1961), p. 280-284 points to the constant recurrence of lay *seniores* in the North African Church in contexts which indicate a long history. Frend concludes p. 283: "it seems evident that many of the peculiar features of the organisation of the African Church may be explicable by reference to a distinctive primitive Christian tradition, indicating, perhaps, Judaeo-Christian influence." This example demonstrates for our purpose that a group of laymen forming a council that rivaled, and in some cases assumed, administrative authority usually associated with ordained presbyters exposes Cyprian's account as a construction of future social reality rather than a reflection of a present one.

[138] *H.E.* VI, 23,4: ...πρεσβείου χειροθεσίαν ἐν Καισαρείᾳ πρὸς τῶν τῇδε ἐπισκόπων ἀναλαμβάνει.

invitation of bishops such as Alexander and Theokistus (the "bishops" who had ordained him?), and Firmilian bishop of Caesarea in Cappadocia (*H.E.* VI, 27,1).

Demetrius had apparently protested about this on the ground that laymen should not preach in the presence of bishops. Eusebius quotes the reply of Alexander and Theoctistus who expressly deny that the practice is improper, and cite several bishops who alow the practice (*H.E.* VI, 19,17-18). Clearly Origen could function as a preacher and teacher of great renown, and the need to ordain him presbyter is only felt late in his career. The functions and prerogatives of the hierarchy are clearly not yet fixed everywhere unalterably, and although the later prerogatives are claimed, they are not as yet universally acknowledged.[139]

Origen's career therefore, in testifying to the fluidity of Church Order in Alexandria,[140] presents an interesting parallel with the 'Hippolytan' events and to what we have seen there too. Callistus's assumption of hierarchical powers over the pentitential discipline, denied by the author of *El.,* did not formally hold for any community other than Callistus's own. It has been interesting, in the light of our version of these events and their broader context in the fluid and dynamic state of Church Order of the Rome of the early third century, to have re-assessed an old debate regarding the identity of Callistus with Praxeas, and with the "edict" of the anonymous *pontifex maximus* that he so roundly condemned.

We have argued that there is a connection between the problem of Tertullian's Montanism, the problem of whether Hippolytus or his predecessor were in fact anti-popes, and the problem of Callistus' edict and its universality. Once we have made the conceptual readjustment that was beyond Damasus and Eusebius, and even Cyprian himself, to the pre-Cyprianic condition of Church Order, then we have found that the problems with such connections are sufficiently modified to make plausible what originally appeared unthinkable. We have in Tertullian's group a parallel example with that of

---

[139] Undoubtedly Eusebius tries to give Origen ecclesiastical status as head of a catechetical school that has an order and succession that goes back to Pantainos. That such a "succession" was Eusebius' own construction seems clear from his ambiguous description of whether it is a catechetical school or one of Christian higher learning (cf. *H.E.* V, 10,1 with 10,4 and 6,6).A comparison between *H.E.* V, 11,1 and 6,6 shows that the successor of the latter is the contemporary of the former. See Neymeyr (1989) p. 42-45.

[140] C. Gore, On the Ordination of the early bishops of Alexandria, in *JThS* 3 1902, p. 278-282, points to Jerome's statement that, until Heraclas, the Alexandrian presbyters appointed, in the sense of "ordained," their own bishop, and supports it with a letter of Severus, monophysite patriarch of Alexandria (518-538). He mentions the conclusion on p. 280: "Origen therefore, on this hypothesis, had intimate experience of a gradual change resulting in the clear differentiation in Alexandria of the episcopate from the presbyterate, and every reason for scanning with some jealousy the exaltation of the bishop." Though Gore did not wish to assent to this conclusion, he had to admit that the evidence for it had shaken his security regarding his formerly held traditional thesis regarding Church Order. See also K. Müller, Die älteste Bischofswahl und weihe in Rom und Alexandrien, in *ZNW* 28 (1929), p. 274-296; C.H. Roberts, Early Christianity in Egypt, in *JEgArch* 40 (1954), p. 92-96.

Hippolytus, with which it shared a similar rigorism, and similar trinitarian concerns.

Tertullian was a Montanist before being such required any absolute break with the wider Church. The revolution instigated by Irenaeus' undated succession list, and concluded by the dated Liberian List, took time to establish itself at Rome. Indeed the clarification and solidification of the implications of what Irenaeus begun was only complete when actual dates marked the assimilation of episcopal with consular lists in the work of the chronographers, which was in the time of Pontianus, after Callistus was dead, and with whom Hippolytus made his confession (4B 2.2.4). Both the examples of Tertullian as a catholic Montanist participating in after-service paraliturgies, and Origen as a lay catechetist, reveal a concept of less than absolute episcopal authority. Indeed without bishops as the supreme teaching authority, with a control over liturgy that Tertullian's example belies, it is difficult to use the term 'schism' with any precision.

When indeed in the post-Cyprianic age the conceptualization of Church Order took place that gave the term 'schism' its generally accepted meaning, then Tertullian became a Montanist heretic, separate from the church, with his own quite fictitious 'Tertullianist' following.[141] No such categorization was imposed upon the historical events of the group lead by the author of *El.* and subsequently Hippolytus, for reasons that we have seen. Hippolytus was reconciled with, and produced a revisionist theology that achieved a *rapprochement* with Pontianus, successor of Callistus. At that point the category of schism could not be applied by later writers to the development that had taken place, and so Hippolytus became the bishop, first of an unknown See, then archbishop of Rome, and then bishop of Portus.

But the name of Hippolytus, like that of Clement, became associated with community traditions of the fractionalized Roman community the validity of whose loose organization of house-or school-churches the post-Cyprianic age could not acknowledge nor indeed understand. They stood as ciphers of liturgical traditions within composite Church Orders, such as we have argued were not only the *Apostolic Constitutions* and the *Didascalia Apostolorum,* but also the so-called *Apostolic Tradition* itself. The sacralized view of ordination of the group around Callistus, as episcopal *pontifex maximus* and *episcopus episcoporum* (7C 1.1.2), assumed the character of διὰ Κλήμεντος in the *Clementines,* with which διὰ Ἱππολύτου was contrasted in *Ap. Con.* (3D 2; 7A 1). That sacralized tradition formed part of the liturgy of Hippolytus' group in the Aaronic *Ap. Trad.* 3 by contrast with the Mosaic *Ap. Trad.* 7, the presbyteral rite originally identical with the rite for ordaining

---

141 These are mentioned only first in Augustine *De Haer.* 1, 86 but the only detailed information comes from the anonymous "Praedestinatus" *Haer.* 1,86 where anachronistically Soter is the bishop who condemns them. Barnes (1985) rightly concludes p. 258: "A sceptic will be forgiven for concluding that the Tertullianistae need have no place in the study of Tertullian."

a bishop (*sicut praediximus super episcopum*). *Ap. Trad.* 3 was originally that of Callistus' group, although Callistus had commenced for his own purpose the synthesis with Aaronic and sacerdotal imagery that the author of *El.* accepted within limits. Both now stand incorporated incoherently into this composite record of the rites of the Hippolytan community with which that group was now reconciled in acceptance of the monarchical episcopate. That rite allowed the bishop to λύειν...πάντα σύνδεσμον, even the mortal sins which the author of *El.* has disallowed Callistus to remit.

And we have shown from the very beginning of our work that the Statue indeed always was a corporate icon of the distinctive community (Chapters 1-2) that had thus achieved a continuing influence under the continuing pseudonym of Hippolytus, and which contained at least two authors (Chapters 3-4).

BIBLIOGRAPHY

Abd el Mohsen el Khachab, ὁ καράκαλλος κοσμοκράτωρ, in *JEgArch* 47 (1961), p. 119-133.
Achelis H., *Die ältesten Quellen des orientalischen Kirchenrechtes.* 1. Die „Canones Hippolyti," in *TU* 6,4 (1891).
―――, Hippolytstudien, in *TU* 16,4 (1897).
―――, Hippolytus' Werke, Band 1,2: Kleinere Exegetische und Homiletische Schriften, in *GCS* (1897).
Adam A., Erwägen zur Herkunft der Didache, in *Sprache und Dogma: Untersuchungen zu Grundproblemen in der Kirchengeschichte*, (Ed.) G. Ruhbach, (Gütersloh: Mohn 1969), p. 24-70.
Adam K., *Der sogenannte Bussedikt des Papstes Kallixtus*, (München: Letner 1917).
Aland K. (and others), *The Greek New Testament*, United Bible Societies, (Stuttgart: Biblia Druck GmbH 1983).
Altaner B., Omnis ecclesia Petri propinqua, in *TheoRev*, 38 (1939) p. 129-141, reprinted in Kleine patristische Schriften (*T.U.* 83) (1967), p. 540-553.
Ambramowski L., Drei christologische Untersuchungen, in *Beiheft ZNW* 45, (Berlin: De Gruyter 1981).
Amelung W., *Die Sculpturen des Vaticanischen Museums*, (Berlin: Reimer 1908).
Amore A., Note su S. Ippolito martire, in *RivAC* 30 (1954), p. 63-97.
―――, La personalità di Ippolito, *Antonianum* 36 (1961), p. 3-28.
Armellini T., *De prisca refutatione haereseon Originis nomine ac philosophumenon titulo recens vulgata commentarius.* (Romae: Societas Jesu 1862).
Assemani J.S., *Bibliotheca Orientalis* III/1, (Romae: Vaticano 1725).

Bailey C., *The Greek Atomists and Epicurus*, (Oxford: Clarendon Press, 1928).
Bammel C.P., The State of Play with regard to Hippolytus and the *Contra Noetum*, in *HeyJn* 31 (1990), p. 195-199.
Bammel E., Die Anfänge des Sukzessionsprinzips im Urchristentum, in *StEphAug* 31 (1990), p. 63-72.
Barbel J., Zu patrologischen Neuerscheinungen aus den Jahren- 1949-1954 Die Hippolytfrage, in *TheoRev* 51 (1955), p. 101-108.
Bardenhewer O., *Des heiligen Hippolytus von Rom: Commentar zum Buche Daniel. Ein literargeschichtlicher Versuch*, (Freiburg im Breisgau: Herder 1877).
―――, *Geschichte der altkirchlichen Literatur*, Vol. 1 (Freiburg im Breisgau: Herder 1902).
Bardy G., L' édit d' Agrippinus, in *RevSR* 4 (1924), p. 1-25.
―――, Les écoles romaines au second siècle, in *RevHE* 28 (1932), p. 501-532.
―――, and Lefèvre M., Commentary on Daniel, in *SC* 14 (1947).
―――, L'enigme d'Hippolyte, in *MSR* 5 (1948), p. 63-88.
―――, La question des langues dans l'église ancienne, in *Études de Théologie Historique*, Tom. 1. (Paris: Beauchensne 1948).
―――, Le souvenir de Josèphe chez les Pères, in *MSR* 43 (1948), p. 179-191.
―――, Review of Nautin's Hippolyte et Josipe, in *MSR* 43 (1948), p. 197-200.
Barnard L.W., The Church of Rome in the first two centuries, in *NTS* 10 (1963-4), p. 251-260.

Barnes T.D., The Family and Career of Septimius Severus, in *Historia* 16 (1967), p. 87-107.
——, *Tertullian: A Historical and Literary Study,* (Oxford: Clarendon 1985).
Barrington Bayley J., Letarouilly on Renaissance Rome, in *The Classical America Series in Art and Architecture*, (New York: Architectural Book Publishing Co 1984).
Bartlet J.V., The Ordination Prayers in the Ancient Church Orders, in *JThS* 17 (1916), p. 248-256.
——, *Church Life and Church Order during the First Four Centuries,* (Oxford: Blackwell 1943).
Baruffa A., Le Catacombe di San Callisto, in *Storia Archeologia e Fede*, (Leumann: Turin 1988).
Batiffol P. *L'abbaye de Rossano: Contribution à l'histoire de la Vaticane*, (Variorum Reprint B 5), (Paris: Picard 1891).
——, *Anciennes littératures chrétiennes*. La littérature grecque, (Paris: Picard 1897).
Bauer A., and Helm R., Hippolytus Werke 4, Die Chronik, in *GCS* 46 (36), (1955).
——, Die Chronik des Hippolytos in Matritensis graecus 121, in *TU* 29,1 (1905).
Baur P.V.C., The Christian Chapel at Dura, in *AmJArch* 37 (1933), p. 377-380.
Baur V., Über die Philosophoumena Origenis, inbesondere ihren Verfasser, in *Theologisches Jahrbuch* (Tübingen: L.F. Fues) XII,1 (1853), p. 152-161.
——, Die Hippolytus-Hypothese des Herrn Ritter Bunsen, in *Theologische Jahrbuch*, (Tübingen: L.F. Fues) XII,3 (1853), p. 435-442.
Baynes N.H., The date and composition of the Historia Augusta, in *ClassRev,* 38, 7-8 (1924), p. 165-169.
——, *The* Historia Augusta, *Its Date and Purpose*, (Oxford: Clarendon 1926).
Beck E., Ephraim Cyrus: Against Julian, in *CSCO*, 174-175, Scriptores Syri 78-79 (1957).
Béranger J., Julien l'Apostat e l'hérédité du pouvoir impérial, in *Antiquit.* 4, 10 (1972), p. 75-93.
Bernulli J.J., *Griechische Ikonographie mit Ausschluss Alexanders und der Diadochen*, Erster Teil, (München: Bruckmann 1901).
Bertonière G., *The Cult Centre of the Martyr Hippolytus on the Via Tiburtina,* (B.A.R. International Series 260), (Oxford: 1985 5 Centermead, Osney Mead, Oxford OX2 OES).
Bertsch L., *Die Botschaft von Christus und unserer Erlösung bei Hippolyt von Rom. Eine materialkerygmatische Untersuchung,* (Paulinus: Trier 1966).
Bethe E., *Buch und Bild in Altertum*, E. Kirsten (Ed.), (Leipzig and Vienna: Harrassowitz 1945).
Beyschlag K., Kallist und Hippolyt, in *ThZ* 20 (1964), p. 103-124.
Bihlmeyer K., Die syrischen Kaiser Karacalla, Elagabal, Severus Alexander, und das Christentum, in *ThQ* 97 (1915), p. 71-91
——, *Die syrischen Kaiser zu Rom (211-235) und das Christentum,* (Rothenburg: Bader 1916).
Black M., The Account of the Essenes in Hippolytus and Josephus, in W.D. Davies and D. Daube (Ed.), *The Background to the New Testament and its Eschatology: Studies in honour of C.H. Dodd*, (Cambridge: U.P.), p. 172-175.
Blanc J., Lexique comparé des versions de la Tradition apostolique de saint Hippolyte, *Rechthéolancmédiév* 22 (1955), p. 173-192.
Blum G.G., Apostolische Tradition und Sukzession bei Hippolyt, in *ZNW* 55 (1964), p. 95-110.
Bodenmann R., Naissance d'une Exégèse Daniel dans l'Église ancienne des trois premiers siècles, in *Beiträge zur Geschichte der Biblischen Exegese* 28 (Tübingen: Mohr 1986).

Böhlig A., Die griechische Schule und die Bibliothek von Nag Hammadi, in *Zum Hellenismus in den Schriften von Nag Hammadi* (Ed) A. Böhlig, F. Wisse (*Göttinger Orientforschungen* 6,2), (Wiesbaden: Harrassowitz 1957), p. 9-53.

Böhmer H., Zur altrömischen Bischofsliste, in *ZNW* 7 (1906), p. 333-339.

Bonwetch G., and Achelis H., Hippolytus's Werke, Band 1,1 Exegetische und Homiletische Schriften, in *GCS* (Hinrich: Leipzig 1897).

Bonwetch G., Hippolyt's Kommentar zum Buche Daniel und die Fragmente des Kommentars zum Hohenliede, in *GCS* (Leipzig-Berlin: 1897).

———, Hippolytisches—Nachtrag dazu, in *Nachrichten von der königl. Gesellschaft der Wissenschaften zu Göttingen, Phil.-hist. Kl.* (1923), p. 27-32.

———, Studien zu den Kommentaren Hippolyts zum Buche Daniel und Hohen Lied, in *TU* 16, N.F. 1,2 (1897).

———, Hippolyts Erklärung von David und Goliath. Drei georgisch erhaltene Schriften von Hippolytus, in *TU* 26 N.F. 11, (1904).

Borgen P., The Early Church in the Hellenistic Synagogue, in *StTh* 37,1 (1983), p. 55-78.

Bosio A., *Roma Sotteranea, opera postuma compiuta, disposta et accresciuta dal M. R.P. Giovanni Severani*, (Roma: Faciotti 1632).

Botte B., L'épiclèse dans l'Anaphora d'Hippolyte, in *RThAM* 14 (1947), p. 249-251.

———, L' authenticité de la *Tradition apostolique* de saint Hippolyte, in *RThAM* 16 (1949), p. 177-185.

———, Note sur l'auteur du *De universo*, attribué à Saint Hippolyte, in *RThAM* 18 (1951), p. 5-18.

———, Note sur le symbole baptismal de saint Hippolyte, in *Mélanges J. de Ghellinck*, (Museum Lessianum—Section Historique), (Gembloux: Éditions J. Duculot, S.A. 1951), Tom. 1 Antiquité, p. 189-200.

———, Le texte de la Tradition apostolique, in *RThAM* 22 (1955), p. 161-172.

———, L'ordre d'après les prières d'ordination, in *Études sur le sacrement de l'ordre,* (Ed.) J. Guyot, in *Lex Orandi* 22, (Paris: Éditions du Cerf 1957), p. 13-41.

———, Charactère collégial du presbytérat et de l'épiscopat, in *Études sur le sacrement de l'ordre,* (Ed.) J. Guyot, in *Lex Orandi* 22, (Paris: Éditions du Cerf 1957), p. 97-124.

———, ΨΕΛΛΙΣΤΗΣ ΨΑΛΙΣΤΗΣ in *RevEtByz* 16 (1958), p. 162-165.

———, Les plus anciennes collections canoniques, in *OrSyr* 5 (1960), p. 331-349.

———, La Tradition apostolique de saint Hippolyte. Essai de reconstitution, in *Liturgiewissenschaftliche Quellen und Forschungen*, 39 (Münster: Aschendorffsche Verlagsbuchhandlung 1963).

———, Un passage difficile de la «Tradition apostolique» sur le signe de croix, in *RThAM* 27 (1960), p. 5-19.

———, Les heures de prière dans la «Tradition apostolique,» et les documents dérivés, in *La prière des heures*, Ed. B. Botte and C. Bezobrazov, in *Lex Orandi* 35, (Paris: Éditions du Cerf 1963), p. 101-115.

———, Tradition apostolique et Canon romain, in *MD* 87 (1966), p. 52-61.

———, A propos de la Tradition Apostolique, in *RThAM* 33 (1966), p. 177-186.

———, Hippolyte de Rome. La Tradition apostolique, in *SC* 11, (1968).

———, Extendit manus suas cum pateretur, *QLP* 49 (1968), p. 307 ff.

———, L' Ordination de l' évêque, in *MD* 98 (1969), p. 113-126.

———, L' Espirit Saint et l'Eglise dans la «Tradition Apostolique» de Saint Hippolyte, in *Didaskalia* 2 (1972), p. 221-133.

———, Le traité des charismes dans les «Contitutions apostoliques,» in *StudPatr* 12 (1975) (*TU* 93), p. 83-86.

———, Die Wendung „Adstare coram te et tibi ministrare" im Eucharistischen Hochgebet II, in *BiLit* 49 (1976), p. 101-104.

——, Le symbolisme de l' huile et de l' onction, in *QL* 62 (1981), p. 197-208.

Boulet N. Maurice-Denis, Titres urbains et communauté dans la Rome chrétienne, in *Maison Dieu* 36 (1953).

Bouyer L., *Eucharistie, théologie et spiritualité de la prière eucharistique*, (Paris: Tournai 1966).

——, The different Forms of Eucharistic Prayer and their Genealogy, in *St. Patr* 8,2 (1966) (*TU* 93), p. 156-170.

Bovini G., La Statua di S. Ippolito del Museo Lateranense, *Bollettino della commissione archeologica del governo di Roma*, (Rome: 1941).

——, Sant'Ippolito, dottore e martire del III secolo, in *Coll. amici delle catacombe* 15 (Città del Vaticano: Pontificio Istituto di Archeologia cristiana 1943).

Bowersock G.W., *Julian the Apostate*, (London: Duckworth 1978), p. 85-93.

Bradshaw P., The Canons of Hippolytus, in *Alcuin/Grove Liturgical Studies* 50 (1987).

——, *The Canons of Hippolytus*, (Liturgical Study 2), (Bramcote: Alcuin/Grove 1988).

——, The participation of other bishops in the ordination of a bishop, in the *Apostolic Tradition* of Hippolytus, in *StudPatr* 18, 2 (1989), p. 335-338.

——, Whittaker C. and Cuming G.J. *Essays on Hippolytus*. (Grove Liturgical Study 15) (Bramcote: Grove Books 1978).

Brandon S.C.F., *Jesus and the Zealots*, (Manchester: University Press 1967).

Brent A., Pseudonymity and Charisma in the Ministry of the Early Church, in *Aug* 27,3 (1987), p. 347-376.

——, Ecumenical Relations and Cultural Episcopates, in *AThR* 72,3 (1990), p. 255-279.

——, Hippolytus' See and Eusebius' Historiography, in *StudPatr* 24 (1991) p. 28-37.

——, Cultural Episcopacy and Ecumenism, Representative Ministry in Church History from the Age of Ignatius of Antioch to the Reformation, with special reference to contemporary ecumenism, *in Studies in Christian Mission* 6, (Leiden: E.J. Brill 1992).

——, The Ignatian Epistles and the Threefold Ecclesiastical Order, in *JRH* 17,1 (1992), p. 18-32.

——, Diogenes Laertius and the Apostolic Succession, in *JEH* 44,3 (1993), p. 367-389.

Brière M., Mariès L., and Mercier B., Sur les Bénédictions de Moïse. Versions Arménienne et géorgienne, in *PO* 27 (1954).

Brockhaus C., *Aurelius Prudentius Clemens in seiner Bedeutung für die Kirche seiner Zeit*, (Leipzig: Brockhaus 1872).

Brown R.E. and Meier J.-P., *Antioch and Rome: New Testament Cradles of Catholic Christianity*, (New York: Paulist Press 1982.

Bunsen C.C.J., *Hippolytus and his Age; or the beginnings and prospects for Christianity. Christianity and Mankind.* Vols I: Hippolytus and the Teachers of the Apostolical Age, (London: Longman, Brown, Green, and Longmans 1854).

——, *Hippolytus and his Age; or the Doctrine and Practice of the Church of Rome under Commodus and Alexander Severus and Ancient and Modern Christianity and Divinity Compared*, (London: Longman, Brown, Green, and Longmans 1852).

Burke P., The Monarchical Episcopate at the End of the First Century, in *JES* 7 (1970), p. 499-518.

Butterworth R., Hippolytus of Rome, Contra Noetum: Text introduced, edited, translated, in *Heythrop Monographs* 2 (1977).

Callmer C., Die ältesten christlichen Bibliotheken in Rom, *Eranos* 83 (1985), p. 48-60.

Campenhausen H. von, Der urchristliche Apostelbegriff, in *StTh* 1 Fasc. I-II (1947), p. 96-130.

——, Die Nachfolge des Jacobus, in *ZKG* 63 (1952-3), p. 133-144.

——, Kirchliches Amt und Geistliche Vollmacht in den ersten drei Jahrhunderten, in *BeitrHistTh* 14, (Tübingen: Mohr 1953).

——, Ostertermin oder Osterfasten? Zum Verständnis des Irenäusbriefs an Viktor (Euseb. Hist. Eccl. 5,24,12-17), in *VCh* 28 (1974), p. 114-138.

Cantalamessa R., L' omelia «in S. Pascha» dello Pseudo-Ippolito di Roma, in *Scienze Filologiche e Letteratura*, (Milan: Società Editriche vita e pensiero 1967).

Capelle B., Le cas du pape Zépherin, in *RBen* 38 (1926), p. 321-330.

——, L' introduction du catéchuménat à Rome, in *RThAM* 5 (1933), p. 129-154.

——, Le Logos, Fils de Dieu, dans la théologie d'Hippolyte, in *RThAM* 9 (1937), p. 109-124.

——, Hippolyte de Rome, in *RThAM* 17 (1950), p. 145-174.

——, A propos d'Hippolyte de Rome, in *RThAM* 19 (1952), p. 193-202.

Carta Archeologica di Roma, (Rome: Ministero dei Beni Culturali e Ambientali, Ufficio centrale per i beni ambientali 1987).

Cary E., Dio's Roman History, in *Loeb Classical Library*, (Cambridge Mass.: Harvard U.P. 1969).

Casel O., Älteste christliche Kunst und Christusmysterium, in *JJLiW* 12 (1934) p. 74.

——, Die Kirchenordnung Hippolyts von Rom, in *ArLiW* 2 (1952), p. 115-130.

Caspar E. Die älteste römische Bischofsliste: kritische Studien zum Formproblem des eusebianischen Kanons sowie zur Geschichte der ältesten Bischofslisten und ihrer Entstehung aus apostolischen Sukzessionreihen, in *SGK* Geisteswissentschaftliche 2,4, (1926).

Caspari C.P., Ungedruckte, unbeachtete und wenig beachtete Quellen zur Geschichte des Taufsymbols und der Glaubensregel, *Christiana* III, (Oslo: Malling 1875).

Cavalieri P., Franchi dé and Lietzmann J., *Specimina Codicum Graecorum Vaticanorum*, (Berlin-Leipzig: 1929).

Cecchelli C., *I Monumenti cristiano-eretici di Roma*, (Rome: Fratelli Palombi 1944).

Cecchelli M., Note Storico topgrafiche: Ancora su Ippolito, in *ArcCl* 34 (1982), p. 210-217.

Chadwick H., St. Peter and St. Paul in Rome: The problem of the Memoria Apostolorum ad Catacumbas, in *JThS*, n.s. 8,1 (1957), p. 31-52.

——, Prayer at midnight, in *Epektasis. Mélanges Patristiques offerts au Cardinal Jean Daniélou*, Ed. J. Fontaine and C. Kannengiesser, (Paris: Beauchesne 1972), p. 47-49.

Clarac Le Cte de M., *Description du Musée Royal Des Antiques du Louvre*, (Paris: Vinchon 1830).

Clark J.W., *The Care of Books: An Essay on the Development of Libraries and their Fittings, from the earliest times to the end of the XVIII century*, (Cambridge: U.P. 1902).

Clarke G.W., Two Christians in the Familia Caesaris, in *HThR*, 64 (1971), p. 121-124.

Clarke Lowther W.K., and Harris C., *Liturgy and Worship: A Companion to the Prayer books of the Anglican Communion*, (London: S.P.C.K. 1936).

Colson J., L'évêque dans les communautés primitives: Tradition paulienne et tradition johannique de l'épiscopat des origines à Saint Irénée, in *Unam Sanctam* 21, (Paris1951).

——, Les fonctions ecclésiales aux deux premiers siècles, in *Textes et études théologiques* (Paris: Desclée de Brouwer 1956).

——, *L'épiscopat Catholique. Collégialité et primauté dans les trois premiers siècles de l'église,* (Paris: Les Éditions du Cerf: 1963).

——, Ministre de Jesus Christ, ou Sacerdoce de l'Evangile; étude sur la condition sacerdotale des ministres chrétiens dans l'Eglise primitive, in *Théologie Historique* 4, (Paris: 1966).

Commelin J., *Rerum Britannicarum id est Angliae, Scotiae, vicinarumque insularum ac regionum; scriptores vetustiores ac praecipui,* (Heidelberg 1587).

Connolly R.H., The so-called Egyptian Church Order and derived documents, in *Texts and Studies* 8,4, (Cambridge: U.P. 1916).

——, The Ordination Prayers of Hippolytus, in *JThS* 18 (1917), p. 55-58.

——, An ancient prayer in the mediaeval euchologia, in *JThS* 19 (1918), p. 132-144.

——, The prologue of the Apostolic Tradition, in *JThS* 22 (1921), p. 356-361.

——, On the text of the baptismal creed of Hippolytus, in *JThS* 25 (1924), p. 131-139.

——, The Eucharistic Prayer of Hippolytus, in *JThS* 39 (1938), p. 350-369.

——, New Attributions to Hippolytus, in *JThS* 46 (1945), p. 192-200.

Coppens J., L'imposition des mains et les rites connexes dans le Noveau Testament et dans l'Eglise ancienne, *Études de théologie positive*, (Paris: Wetteren 1925).

——, Le sacerdoce chrétien, ses origines et son développement, in *AnLov* 5,4, (1970).

Coquin R.G., Les Canons d' Hippolyte, in *PO* 31,2 (1966).

Cotone M., The Apostolic Tradition of Hippolytus of Rome, in *ABenR* 19 (1968), p. 495-501.

Couratin A.H. and Tripp D.H. (Ed.), *Liturgical Studies,* (London: S.P.C.K. 1976).

Coxe H., *Catalogi codicum manuscriptorum bibliothecae Bodleianae*, pars prima, (Oxford: U. P. 1853) col. 369-372.

Coyle J.K., The exercize of teaching in the post-apostolic Church, in *EglTheo* 15 (1984), p. 23-43.

Cruice P., *Études sur de noveaux documents historiques empruntés à l'ouvrage récemment découvert des Philosophumena,* (Paris: Imperial Press 1855).

——, *Philosophoumena sive Haeresium Omnium Confutatio; Opus Origeni adscriptum*, (Paris: Imperial Press 1860).

——, Observations Nouvelles sur la première partie des Philosophumena, in *Journal Général de l'Instruction Publique*, 339, (Paris: Dupont 1859).

Cullman O., *Le problème littéraire et historique du roman pseudo- Clémentine,* (Paris: Éditions du Cerf 1930).

Culpepper R.A., The Johannine School: An evaluation of the Johannine-School hypothesis based on an investigation of the nature of ancient schools, in *Society for Biblical Literature* DS 26, (Missoula Montana: Scholars Press 1975).

Cuming G.J., Hippolytus: A Text for Students with Introduction, Translation, Commentary and Notes, 2nd Ed., in *Grove Liturgical Study* 8, (Nottingham 1979).

——, The Post-Baptismal Prayer in the Apostolic Tradition: Further Considerations, in *JThS*, 39 (1988), p. 117-119.

Cumont F. and Canet, L., Mithra ou Serapis ΚΟΣΜΟΚΡΑΤΩΡ, in *Comptes rendus de l' Académie des Inscriptions*, (Paris 1857-).

Curti C., Osservazioni su un passo dell'Ellenchos (I, praef. 1), in *StEphAug* 13 (1977), p. 89-95.

Cyril Alexandrinus, Contra Julianum, in *PG*. 76, 489-1058.

D'Alès A., *La Théologie de Saint Hippolyte*, (Paris: Beauchesne 1906).
——, *L'Édit de Calliste: Étude sur les origines de la pénitence chrétienne*, (Paris: Beauchesne 1914).
——, Zephyrin, Calliste or Agrippinus? in *RecSciRel* 10 (1920), p. 254-256.
Da Bra G., *I Filosofumeni sono di Ippolito?* (Rome: Vatican 1942).
——, *Studio su S. Ippolito dottore*, (Rome: Vatican 1944).
Dal Covolo E., Fonti epigrafiche del secondo-terzo secolo per uno studio dei rapporti tra gli imperatori Severi et il cristianesimo, in *StuPat* 35 (1988), p. 123-132.
——, I Severi e il cristianesimo: Ricerche sull'ambiente storico-istituzionale delle origini cristiane tra il secondo e il terzo secolo, in *Bibliotheca di Scienze Religiose*, 87 (Libreria Ateno Salesiano: Rome 1989).
——, Ancora sulla Statua di Sant'Ippolito per una «messa di punto» dei rapporti tra i Severi e il Cristianesimo, in *Aug* 32 (1992), p. 51-59.
Da Leonessa M., *S. Ippolito di via Tiburtina*, (Poliglotta Vaticana: Rome 1935).
Daniélou J., Review of Nautin's Hippolyte et Josipe, in *RecSciRel* 35 (1948), p. 596-598.
——, *La catéchèse aux premiers siècles*, (Paris: Fayard- Mame 1968).
Davis R. (trans.), The Book of the Pontifs (*Liber Pontificalis*), in *Texts for Historians*, Latin Series V, (Liverpool: U.P. 1989).
DelaHaye H., *Sanctus*, (Brüssel: Bureaux de la Société des Bollandistes 1912).
——, *Les origenes du culte des martyres*, (Brüssel: Bureaux de la Société des Bollandistes 1933).
——, Recherches sur le légenier romain, in *AnBoll* 51 (1933), p.34-98.
——, Contributions récentes à l'hagiographie de Rome e d'Afrique, in *AnBoll* 54 (1936), p. 265-315.
——, Contributions récents à l'hagiographie de Rome et d'Afrique, in *AnBoll* 54 (1936) p. 265-268.
De Riedmatten H., Review of Nautin's Hippolyte et Josipe, in *DomSt* 1 1948, p. 168-173.
De Rossi G.-B., Elogio Damasiano del celebre Ippolito martire sepolto presso la via Tiburtina, in *BArC.* 4, 6 (1881), p. 26-55.
——, La silloge epigrafica d'un codice già corbeiense ora nella Biblioteca imperiale di Pietroburgo, in *BArC* 6,3 (1881), p. 1-55.
——, Il cimitero di S. Ippolito presso la via Tiburtina e la sua principale cripta storica ora dissepolta, in *BArC* 7,4 (1882), p. 9-76.
——, Notizie: Continuazione delle scoperte nella cripta storica e nelle adiacenti gallerie del cimitero di s. Ippolito, in *BArC* (1882-1883), p. 176-177.
——, Esame archeologico e critico della storia di s. Callisto narrata nel libro nono dei Filosofumeni, in *BArC* 4,4 (1866), p. 1-99.
——, I monumenti cristiani di Porto, in *BArC* 4,3 (1866), p. 37-65.
——, *La Roma Sotteranea Cristiana*, Vols I-III, (Rome: Croma 1864-1867).
Desjardins M., The Sources for Valentinian Gnosticism, in *VCh* 40 (1986), p. 342-347.
Dessau H., Über Zeit und Persönlichkeit der Scriptores Historiae Augustae, in *Herm* 24 (1889), p. 337-392.
Devreesse R., Les premières années du monophysisme: une collection antichalcédonienne, in *RevScPhTh*, 19 (1930), p. 251-265.
——, *Introduction à l'étude des manuscrits grecs*, (Paris: Klincksieck 1954).
——, Les manuscrits grecs de l'Italie méridionale, in *Set* 183, (1955).
DeWitt N.W., Organisation and Procedure in Epicurean groups, in *ClPl* 31 (1936), p. 208-211
Dinkler E., Dura-Europas III, Bedeutung für die christliche Kunst, in *RGG* 2 (1958), cols. 290-292.
Diobouniotis C., Hippolyts Schrift über die Segnungen Jakobs, in *TU* 38,13 (1911).

Dionysius Barsalîbî, *In Apocalypsim Iohannis*, in J.-B.Chabot et. al., Scriptores Syri, 2a CI *in CSCO*, (Latin Translation I Sedlacek).

Dix G., *The Shape of the Liturgy*. (Westminster: Dacre 1945).

——, *The Apostolic Tradition*. (London: 1968).

Dobschütz E. von, Christbilder. Untersuchungen zur christlichen Legende, in *TU* 18, (1899).

Döllinger I von, *Hippolytus und Kallistus oder die römische Kirche in der ersten Hälfte des dritten Jahunderts, mit Rucksicht auf die Schriften und Abhandlungen der Herrn Bunsen, Wordsworth, Baur und Gieseler*, (Regensburg: Joseph Manz 1853).

——, *Hippolytus and Callistus, or the Church of Rome in the First Half of the Third Century, with Special Reference to the writings of Bunsen, etc.* (Trans.) A. Plummer, (Edinburgh: T. & T. Clarke 1876).

Domaszewski A. von, Die Personennamen bei den Scriptores historiae Augustae, in *SHAW*, Phil.-hist. Kl. 13 (1918).

Donini A., *Ippolito di Roma. Polemiche teologiche e controversie disciplinari nella chiesa di Romi agli inizi del III secolo*, (Roma: Vatican 1925).

D'Onofrio C., *Un Popolo di Statue Racconta: storie, fatti, leggende della città di Roma antica, medievale, moderna*, (Romana Società: Rome 1990).

Draguet R., Le florilège antichalcédonien du Vatic. Graec. 1431, in *RevHE* 24 (1928), p. 51-62.

Dräseke J., Zum Syntagma des Hippolytos, in *ZWTh* 46 (1903), p. 58-90.

Drijvers H.J.W., Edessa und das jüdische Christentum, in *VCh* 24 (1970), p. 4-33.

Ducati P., L'arte in Roma dalle origini al secolo VIII, in *Storia di Roma* 26, (Bologna: Istituto di Studi Romani 1939).

Duchesne L. and McLure M.L., *Christian Worship: Its Origin and Evolution*, (London: S.P.C.K. 1949), p. 342-383.

Dufourq A., Études sur les gesta martyrum romains, in *Bibliothèque des écoles françaises d'Athènes e de Rome*, 83, 1-3 (Paris: Ancienne Librarie Thorin et Fils: 1900-1907).

Dunbar D.G., The Delay of the Parousia in Hippolytus, in *VCh* 37 (1983), p. 313-317.

Duncker L., Besprechung von E. Miller's Erstausgabe der Refutatio (Elenchos), in *Göttingische gelehrte Anzeigen*, (1851) Band 3, p. 1530-1550.

Dünsig H., Der aethiopische Texte der Kirchenordnung des Hippolyt, nach 8 Handschriften herausgegeben und übersetzt, in *AAWG* Phil.-hist. Kl. 3,32 (1946).

Dziatzko K., Die Bibliotheksanlage von Pergamon, in *Beiträge zur Kenntnisse des Schrift, Buch, und Bibliothekswesens*, (Leipzig: Spirgatis 1896) 3,10, p. 37-47.

Easton B.S., *The Apostolic Tradition of Hippolytus translated into English with an Introduction and Notes*, (Cambridge: U.P. 1934).

Ehrhardt A., *The Apostolic Succession in the First Two Centuries of the Church*, (London: Lutterworth Press 1953).

——, Jewish and Christian Ordination, in *JEH* 5 (1954), p. 125-38.

Elfers H., *Die Kirchenordnung Hippolyts von Rom*, (Bonifacius: Paderborn: 1938).

——, Neue Untersuchungen über die Kirchenordnung Hippolyts von Rom, in *Abhandlungen über Theologie und Kirche, Fest. Karl Adam*, (Ed.) M. Reding, (Düsseldorf: Patmos 1952), p. 73-183.

Elliger W., Die Stellung der alten christen zu den Bildern in den ersten 4 Jahrhunderte, nach den Angaben der zeitgenössischen kirchlichen Shriftsteller, in *Studien über christlichen Denkmäler*, N.F. 20 (Leipzig: Dieter 1930).

Engberding H., Das angebliche Dokument römischer Liturgie aus dem Beginn des dritten Jahrhunderts, in *Miscellana Liturgica in honorem L.C. Mohlberg.* Band 1 (*Bibliotheca «Ephemerides Liturgicae»* 22), (Rome: Edizioni Liturgiche 1948), p. 47-71.

Esser G., *Die Bussschriften Tertullians De paenitentia und De pudicitia und das Indulgenzedikt des Papstes Kallistus,* (Bonner Universitätsprogramm 1905).

———, Tertullian de pudicitia c. 21 und der Primat des römischen Bischofs, in *Katholik* (1907), p. 184-204; 297-309; 1908 I, p.12-28; 93-113.

———, *Der Adressat der Schrift Tertullians „De Pudicitia" und der Verfasser des römischen Bussediktes,* (Bonn: Hanstein 1914).

Ettlinger G.H., The History of the Citations in the Eranistes of Theodoret of Cyrus in the fifth and sixth Centuries, in Paschke, F. (Ed.) Überlieferungsgeschichliche Untersuchungen, in *TU.* 125 (1981), p. 173-183.

———, *Theodoret of Cyrus: Eranistes. Critical Text and Prolegomena,* (Oxford: Clarendon 1975).

Eustratiades S., Κατάλογος τῶν ἐν μονῇ Βλατέων (Τσαοὺς–Μοναστῆρι) ἀποκειμένων κωδίδων, (Salonica : 1918), p. 16-19.

———, Catalogue of the Greek Manuscripts in the Library of the Monastry of Vatopedi on Mount Athos, in *Harvard Theological Studies* 11, (Cambridge Mass.: Harvard U.P. 1924).

Evans E., *Q. Septimii Florentis Tertulliani: Adversus Praxean Liber.,* (London: S.P.C.K. 1948).

Eynde B. van der, Les Normes de l'Enseignement Chrétien dans la littérature patristique, in *Universitas Catholica Lovaniensis* 2,25, (Gembloux-Paris: 1933).

Fabricius J.A.S., *Hippolyti, Episcopi et Martyris, quae superant opera* et fragmenta, (Hamburg: Christian Liebezeit 1716).

———, *Hippolyti Opera non antea collecta nunc primum e mss. in lucem edita,* (with contributions by F. Blanchini and J. Vignoli) (Hamburg: Christian Liebezeit 1716).

Faivre A., La documentation canonico-liturgique de l'Église ancienne, in *RevSR* 54 (1980), p. 285-297.

Fasola P., I cimiteri cristiani. Introduzione all discussione, in *Atti del IX cogresso internazionale di archeologia cristiana a 1975,* 32,1 (Rome: Pontificio Istituto di Archeologia Cristiana 1978), p. 191-194.

Fehrle R., *Das Bibliothhekswesen im alten Rom,* (Wiesbaden: Ludwig Reichert 1986).

Ferraro G., *Le preghiere di ordinazione al diaconato, al presbiterato, all' episcopato,* (Napoli 1977).

Ferrua A., Dura-Europo cristiana, in *CCa* 4 (1939), p. 334-337.

———, *Epigrammata Damasiana,* in Sussidi allo Studio delle Antichità Cristiane 2, (Rome: Pontificio Istituto di Archeologia Cristiana, Città del Vaticano 1943).

———, Novatiano beatissimo martyri, in *CCa* 95 (1944), p. 232-239.

———, Recensione [on Dal Covolo, *I Severi e il cristianesimo*] in *CCa* 141 (1990), p. 408-409.

———, Scritti vari di Epigrafia e Antichità Cristiana, (Edipuglia: Bari 1991).

Fessler J., Über den wahren Verfasser des unter den Titel: Philosophoumena Origenis, jüngste erschienenen Werkes, in *(Tübinger)ThQ* , (1852), p. 299-309.

Festiguère A.J., *Epicurus and his Gods,* (Oxford: B. Blackwell, 1955).

Fiala V.E., Die Handauflegung als Zeichnen der Geistmitteilung in den lateinischen Riten, in *Mélanges liturgiques offerts au R.P. Dom Botte O.S.B. de l' Abbaye du Mont César à l' occassion du 50 anniversaire de son ordination sacerdotale (4th June 1972),* (Louvain: Abbaye du mont César 1972), p. 121-138.

Figini C., Agrippino o Callisto? in *ScuCat* (1924), p. 204-211.
Fischel H.A., Rabbinic Literature and Graeco-Roman Philosophy, in *StPB* 21, (1973).
Fisher J.D.C., Confirmatìon then and Now, in *Alcuin Club Collections 60*, (London: Grove 1978).
Follieri E., Sant'Ippolito nell'agiografia e nella liturgia bizantina, in *StEphAug* 13 (1977), p. 31-43.
Forcella V., *Inscrizioni delle chiesa e d'altri edifici di Roma dal secolo XI fino ai giorni nostri,* (Roma: 1869).
Forchielli Ios. and Stickler A.M., Liber Pontificalis Glossato, in *Studia Gratiana* XXI-XXIII, (Roma: Collectanea Iuris Canonici 1978).
Fornari F., Relazione circa una nuova regione cimiteriale a S. Lorenzo, in *RivAC* VI (1929), p. 179-239.
——, Giornale di Scavo, in Archives of *Pontificia Commissione di archeologia cristiana*, (Rome 1925-1960), Vol 1-4.
——, and Scrinari S.-M., *Le catacombe di Novaziano e la necropoli romana*, (Rome: Pontificio Istituto di Archeologia Cristiana 1973).
Franchi de' Cavalieri P., and Leitzmann J., *Specimina Codicum Graecorum Vaticanorum*, (Marcus and Weber: Bonn 1910).
Frankenberg W., Recognitions, in *TU* 48,3 (1936).
Fraser P.M., *Ptolemais Alexandria*, Vols 1-2, (Oxford: Clarendon 1972).
Frend W.C.H., The Seniores Laici and the Origins of the Church of North Africa, in *JThS* n.s. 122 (1961), p. 280-284.
——, *Martyrdom and Persecution in the Early Church*, (Oxford: Blackwell 1965).
——, Open Questions concerning Christians and the Roman Empire in the Age of the Severi, in *JThS* n.s. 25 (1974), p. 333-351.
——, *The Rise of Christianity*, (London: Darton Longman and Todd 1984).
Frere W.H., Early Ordination Services, in *JThS* 16 (1915), p. 323-369.
Frickel J., Die apophasis Megale in Hippolyt's Refutatio (VI 9-18. Eine Paraphrase zur Apophasis Simons., in *OrChrA* 182, (1968).
——, Contraddizioni nelle opere e nella persona di Ippolito di Roma, in *StEphAug* 13 (1977), p. 137-149.
——, Hippolyt von Rom: Refutatio, Buch X, in Paschke, F. (Ed.) Überlieferungsgeschichtliche Untersuchungen, in *TU* 125 (1981), p. 217-244.
——, Hellenistische Erlösung in christlicher Deutung: die gnostische Naasenerschrift., in *Nag Hamadi Studies* 19, (Leiden: Brill 1984).
——, [Festschrift für J.B. Baür] Ein armenisch erhaltener Traktat Hippolyts über die Trinität? Anfänge der Theologie, *Charisteion* (Graz: 1987), p. 189-210.
——, *Das Dunkel um Hippolyt von Rom: Ein Lösungsversuch: die Schriften Elenchos und Contra Noëtum*. (Grazer Theologische Studien: Bauer 1988).
——, Ippolito di Roma, scrittore e martire, in *StEphAug* 30 (1989), p. 23-41.
——, Hippolyts Schrift Conra Noëtum: ein Pseudo-Hippolyt, in *Logos*. *Festschrift für Luise Abramowski*, (Berlin & New York: Walter de Gruyter 1993), p. 87-123.
Fries A., Spur einer Kenntnis von Hippolyts „Apostolische Überlieferung" im 13 Jahrhundert, in *FZPhTh* 18 (1971), p. 29-35.
Frobenius, *Beati Flacci Albini seu Alcuini Abbatis, Caroli Magni Regis ac Imperatoris, Magistri, Opera Omnia*, Tom. I-II, (Ratisbone: S. Emmeramus 1777).
Froidevaux L-M., Les questions e réponses sur la sainte Trinté, attribuée à Hippolyte, évêque de Bostra, in *RecSciRel* 50 (1962), p. 32-73.
Fulvio Andrea, *L'Antichità di Roma: Di nuovo con ogni diligenza corretta e ampliata, con gli adornamenti di disegni de gli edificii Antichi e Moderni*, (Francini: Venetia 1588).
Funk F.X., *Die Apostolischen Konstitutionen: Eine litterar- historische Untersuchung*, (Minerva GmbH., Frankfurt/Main 1970), (Rottenberg 1891).

———, *Didascalia et Constitutiones Apostolorum*, (Turin: Bottega d'Erasmo 1979).

Gallandi A., Bibliotheca Veterum Patrum antiquorumque scriptorum ecclesiasticorum. Tome II (Venice: Joannes Baptista Albritius1766).

Garitte G., Traités d'Hippolyte sur David et Goliath, sur le Cantique des cantiques et sur l'Antichrist, in *CSCO* (1965).

Gelston A., A Note on the Text of the Apostolic Tradition of Hippolytus, in *JThS* 39 (1988), p. 112-117.

Gelzer H., *Sextus Julius Africanus und die Byzantinische Chronologie*, 1 (Leipzig: Teubner 1880).

Gerkan A. von, Die frühchristliche Kirchenanlage von Dura, in *Römische Quartalschrift* 42 (1934), p. 219-232.

———, Zur Hauskirche von Dura-Europos, in *Mullus, Festschrift für Theodor Klausner. Reallexikon zur byzantinischen Kunst, Ergänzungsband* I (1964), p. 143-149.

Gieseler J.C.L., Über Hippolytus, die ersten Monarchianer und die römische Kirche in der ersten Hälfte des dritten Jahrhunderts, in *TheolStKrit* IV (1853), p. 759-789.

———, Über Hippolytus, die ersten Monarchianer und die römische Kirche in den ersten Hälfte des dritten Jahrhunderts,, in *Theologische Studien und Kritiken.* Heft 4 (1853), p. 759-787.

Giet S., Le texte du fragment contre Noët., in *RevSR* 24 (1950), p. 315-322.

———, Controverse sur Hippolyte, in *RevSR* 25 (1951), p. 83-85.

———, Le Texte des deux derniers chapitres du livre d'Hippolyte «Contre les Hérésies», in *RevSR* 25 (1951), p. 76-85.

Gilbert O., *Geschichte und Topographie der Stadt Rom in Altertum*, 3 vols, (Leipsig: Teubner 1883-1890).

Giordani R., «Novatiano beatissimo martyri Gaudentius diaconus fecit»— contributo all'identificazione del martire Novaziano della catacomba anonima sulla via Tiburtina, in *RivAC* 67,1-2 (1992), p. 233-258.

Giuliano A. et. al., *Villa Adriana*, (Roma: Silvana 1988).

Gluckner J., Antiochus and the Late Academy, in *Hypomnemata: Untersuchungen zur Antike und zu ihrem Nachleben*, Heft 56 (Vandenhoeck & Ruprecht: Göttingen 1978).

Gödecke M., Geschichter als Mythos: Eusebs „Kirchengeschichte", in *Europäische Hochschulschriften*, 23, 307 (Frankfurt am Main: Peter Lang 1987).

Goldin J., A philosophical session in a Tannaite Academy, in *Trivium* 21 (1965), p. 1-21.

Gore C., On the Ordination of the early bishops of Alexandria, in *JThS* 3 (1902), p. 278-82.

Gori F., *Della Porta e Basilica di S. Lorenzo*, (Rome: Vatican 1862).

Götze B., Antike Bibliotheken, in *JDAI* 203 (1937), p. 225-247.

Granger F., Julius Africanus and the Library of the Pantheon, in *JThS*, 34 (1933), p. 157-161.

Green M.R., The Supporters of Anti-Pope Ursinus, in *JThS*, 22 (1971), p. 532-538.

Grégoire H., Les Baptistères de Cuicul et de Doura, in *Byz*, (1938), p. 589-593.

Grenfell B.P. and Hunt A.S., *Oxyrinchus Papirus* III (412), (London: Egyptian Exploration Fund 1903).

Grimal P., Cicéron: Discours *In Pisonem*, in *Collection des universités de France*, XVI,! (Paris: Société d' édition Les Belles Lettres 1966).

Grisar H., Bedarf die Hippolytus-Frage einer Revision? in *ZKTh* 2 (1878), p. 505-533.

———, Bibel oder Bibliothek? in *ZKTh* 27 (1903), p. 131-138.

Grumel V., *Traité d' Études Byzantines, vol. 1 La Chronologie*, (Paris: 1958)
Guarducci M., Die Ausgrabungen unter St. Peter, in *Das frühere Christentum im Römischen Staat*, (Ed.) R. Klein) (Darmstadt: Wissenschaftliche Buchgesellschaft 1971).
——, La statua di «sant' Ippolyto» in Vaticano, in *RendPontAcc* (1974-5), p. 163-190.
——, La Statua di «Sant'Ippolito», in *StEphAug* 13 (1977), p. 17-30.
——, Epigrafi di Bibliotheche, in *Epigrafia Greca* II (Istituto Poligrafico dello Stato: Roma 1978), p. 574-579.
——, Le iscrizione della Statua di «sant'Ippolito,» in *Epigrafia Greca* IV (Istituto Poligrafico dello Stato: Roma 1978), p. 535-545.
——, Esempi di epigrammi sepolcrali, in *Epigrafia Greca* III (Istituto Poligrafico dello Stato: Roma 1978), p. 182-190.
——, La «Statua di Sant' Ippolito» e la sua provenienza, in *StEphAug* 30 (1989), p. 61-74.
——, *San Pietro e Sant'Ippolito: Storia di statue famose in Vaticano*, (Istituto Poligrafico dello Stato: Roma 1991).
Guidobaldi F., San Clemente, Gli edifici romani, la basilica paleocristiana, et le fasi altomedievali, in *San Clemente Miscellany* 4,1 (Rome: S. Clemens 1992).
Gwynn J., Hippolytus and his 'Heads against Gaius,' in *Hermath* 6 (1888), p. 397-418.
——, Hippolytus on St. Matthew XXIV. 15-22, in *Hermath* 7 (1890), p. 397-418.
Gy P.M., La théolgie des prières anciennes pour l' ordination des évêques et des prêtres, in *RSPhTh* 58 (1974), p. 599-617.

Haase F., *Altchristliche Kirchengeschichte nach orientalischen Quellen*, (Leipzig: Harrassowitz 1925).
Hahnemann G.M., *The Muratorian Fragment and the Development of the Canon*, (Oxford: Claredon 1992).
Hall S.G. (Ed.), Melito of Sardis: On Pascha and Fragments, in *OECT* (1972).
——, Praxeas and Irenaeus, in *StudPatr* 14, (*T.U.* 117), (1976), p. 145-147.
Hamel A., Kirche bei Hippolyt von Rom, in *Beiträge zur Förderung christliche Theologie*, 2,49, (Gütersloh: Bertelsmann 1951).
Haneberg B.D., *Canones S. Hippolyti Arabice e codicibus Romanis cum versione Latina et prolegomenis*, (Munich: Franz 1870).
Hanssens J.-M., La liturgie d'Hippolyte: ses documents, son titulaire, ses origines et son caractère, in *OrChrA* 155, (1959).
——, La liturgie d'Hippolyte. Assentiments et dissentiments, in *Greg* 42 (1961), p. 290-302.
——, La Liturgie d'Hippolyte: Documents et Études, (Rome: Universitas Gregoriana 1970).
Harnack A. von, *Zur Quellenkritik der Geschichte des Gnostizismus*, (Leipzig: Bidder 1873).
——, Zur Quellenkritik der Geschichte des Gnostizmus: Über das verlorengegangene Syntagma Hippolyt's, die Zeit seiner Abfassung und die Quellen, die ihm zu grunde liegen, in *Zeitschrift für die historische Theologie*, 44, 2 (1874), p. 141-226.
——, *Die Zeit des Ignatius und die Chronologie der Antiochenischen Bischöfe bis Tyrannus nach Julius Africanus und den späteren Historikern*, (Leipzig: Hinrich 1878)
——, Geschichte der altchristlichen Litteratur bis Eusebius. 2/II *Die Chronologie der Litteratur von Irenäus bis Eusebius*, (Leipzig: Hinrich 1904).
——, *Lehrbuch der Dogmengeschichte*, I (J.C.B. Mohr (Paul Siebeck: Tübingen 1909).

——, Über den Verfasser und den literarischen Charakter des Muratorischen Fragments, in *ZNW* 24 (1925), p. 1-16.

——, „Ecclesia Petri propinqua". Zur Geschichte der Anfänge des Primats des römischen Bischofs, in *SPAW* Phil.-hist. Kl. (1927).

Harris, Rendel J., *Hermas in Arcadia and other Essays*, (Cambridge: University Press 1896).

Hatch E., *The Organisation of the Early Christian Churches*, (London: Rivington 1882).

Hauler E., *Didascalia Apostolorum fragmenta Veronensia Latina. Accedunt Canonum qui dicuntur Apostolorum et Aegyptiorum reliquiae*, (Leipsig: Teubner 1900).

Hengel M., Jakobus der Herrenbruder- der erste Papst? in *Glaube und Eschatologie, Festschrift für Werner George Kümmel zum 80 Geburstag*. (Tübingen: J.B. Mohr 1985), p. 71-104.

Hennecke E., Hippolyt's Schrift „Apostolische Überlieferung," in *Harnack Ehrung*, (Leipzig 1921), p. 159-162.

——, Der Prolog zur „Apostolische Überlieferung," in *ZNW* 22 (1923), p. 144-146.

Hergenröther J., Hippolytus oder Novatian? in *Österreichische Vierteljahresschrift für Katholische Theologie* 2 (1863), p. 289-340.

Hicks R.D., Diogenes Laertius: Lives of Eminent Philosophers, in *Loeb Classical Library*, (Cambridge Massachusetts: Harvard U.P. 1929).

Hilgenfeld A., *Die Ketzergeschichte des Urchristentums, urkundlich dargestellt*, (Leipzig: Fues (Reisland) 1884).

Hill C.E., Hades of Hippolytus or Tartarus of Tertullian? in *VCh* 43 (1989), p. 105-126.

Hirzel R., *Der Dialog, ein literar- historischer Vesuch*, (Leipzig: Hirzel 1895).

Hohl E., Über den Ursprung der Historia Augusta, in *Herm* 55 (1920), p. 296.

Holl K., Die Sacra Parallela des Johannes Damascenus, in *TU* 16 N.F. 1, (1897).

——, Fragmenta vornicänischer Kirchenväter aus den Sacra parallela, in *TU* 5,2, (1899).

Holland D.L., The Baptismal Interrogation concerning the Holy Spirit in Hippolytus' Apostolic Tradition, in *StPatr* 10,1 (*TU* 107), (Berlin 1970), p. 360-365.

Holtzmann W., Die ältesten Urkunden des Klosters S. Maria del Patir, in *ByzZ* 26 (1926), p. 328-351.

Hope R., *The Book of Diogenes' Laertius: Its Spirit and Its Method*, (New York 1930).

Hopkins C., (B. Goldman (Ed.)), *The Discovery of Dura Europos*, (Newhaven: Yale U.P. 1979).

——, The Christian Chapel at Dura-Europos, in *Atti del III congresso internazionale di archeologia cristiana*, (Rome 1934), p. 483-492.

Horner G., *The Statutes of the Apostles or Canons Ecclesiastici: Edited with translation and collaction from Ethiopic and Arabic mss.*, (London: Williams and Norgate 1904).

Horsley G.H.R., *New Documents Illustrating Early Chrisitianity*, (Melbourne: Ancient History Documentary Research Centre).

Hübner R.M., Die Hauptquelle des Epiphanius (Panarion, haer. 65) über Paulus von Samosata: Ps. Athanasius, Contra Sabellianos, in *ZKTh* 90 (1979), p. 203.

——, Die antignostische Glaubensregel des Noet von Smyrna, in *MThZ* 40 (1989), p. 279-311.

——, Die Schrift des Apolinarius von Laodicea gegen Photin (Ps. Athenasius Contra Sabellios) und Basilius von Caesarea, in *Patristische Texte und Studien*, 30 (Berlin & New York: De Gruyter 1989).

——, Melito von Sardes und Noet von Smyrna, in *Oecumenica et Patristica.*
Festschrift für Wilhelm Schneemelcher, (Chambésy-Genf 1989), p. 220-223.
Hyldahl N., Hegesipps Hypomnemata, in *StTh* 14 (1960), p. 70-113.

Jacobi D., Ὠριγένους φιλοσοφούμενα ἢ κατὰ πασῶν αἱρέσεων ἔλεγχος. E
codice Parisino nunc primum edidit Emmanuel Miller. Oxonii 1851, in
Deutsche Zeitschrift für christliches Leben und christliche Wissenschaft
(Berlin: Wiegandt und Grieben) no. 26 June-July (1851), p. 203-206.
Jaeger W., *Early Christianity and Greek Paideia,* (Massachusetts: Harvard
University Press 1962).
——, Paedeia Christi, in Johann H.T. *Erziehung und Bildung in der heidnischen
und christlichen Antike,* (Darmstadt: 1976), p. 487-502.
Jalabert L. and Mouterde S.J., *Inscriptions Grecques et Latines de la Syrie,* Vols I-
VIII Institute Francais d' Archéologique de Beyrouth, in Bibliothéque
Archéologique et Historique Tome LI, (Paris: Libraire Orientaliste Paul
Geuthner, 1953).
——, Inscriptions grecques chrétiennes, in *DACL* VII (1926), p. 649.
Jalland T.G., *The Church and the Papacy,* (London 1944).
Jardé A., *Études critiques sur la vie et le règne de Sévère Alexandre* (Paris: Boccard
1925)
Jastrzebowska E., Untersuchungen zum christlichen Totenmahl der Monumente
des 3 und 4 Jahrhunderts unter der Basilika des Hl. Sebastian in Rom, in
Europäische Hochschulschriften 38,2 (Frankfurt/Bern/Lang: Cirencester
1981).
Javierre A.M., Le Thème de la succession des apôtres dans la littérature chrétienne
primitive, in *Unam Sanctam* 39 (1962), p. 171-221.
Jay E., From Presbyter-Bishops to Bishops and Presbyters, in *SecCent* 1 (1981),
p. 125-162.
Jeffers J.S., *Conflict at Rome: Social Order and Hierarchy in Early Christianity,*
(Minneapolis: Augsburg Fortress 1991).
Jilek A., Initionsfeier und Amt. Ein Beitrag zur Struktur und Theologie der Ämter
und des Taufgottesdienst in der frühen Kirche (Traditio Apostolica, Tertullian,
Cyprian), in *EHS.T* 130 (Frankfurt 1979).
——, Bischof und Presbyterium. Zur Beziehung zwischen Episkopat und
Presbyterat im Lichte der Traditio Apostolica Hippolyts, in *ZKTh* 106 (1984),
p. 321-326.
Jones A.H.M., Der Social Hintergrund zwischen Heidentum und Christentum, in
Das frühere Christentum im Römischen Staat, (Darmstadt: Wissenschaftliche
Buchengesellschaft 1971), p. 335-63.
——, Another Interpretation of the Constitutio Antoniana, in *JJRomS* 26,2
(1936), p. 223-225.
Jones Stanley F., The Pseudo Clementines: A History of Research, in *SecCent* 2
(1982) Part I, p. 1-33, Part II, p. 63-96.
Jonge M., The Pre-Mosaic Servants of God in the Testaments of the Twelve
Patriarchs and in the writings of Justin and Irenaeus, in *VCh* 39 (1985), p.
157-70.
Josi E., Cimitero alla sinistra della via Tiburtina al viale Regina Margherita, in
RivAC 10 (1933), p. 189-223.
——, Cimitero alla sinistra della via Tiburtina al viale Regina Margherita, in
RivAC 11 (1934), p. 7-47 and 203-247.
——, Quatro nuovi frammenti del carme di Damaso in onore di S. Ippolito, in
RivAC 13 (1936), p. 231-236.
——, Altre tre frammenti, in *RivAC* 16 (1939), p. 320-322.
Judge E.A., Christliche Gruppen in nicht christlicher Gesellschaft, in *Neue
Studienreihe* 4, (Wuppertal 1964).

——, The Early Christians as a Scholastic Community I, in *JRH* 1 (1960), p. 4-15.

——, *The Social Pattern of the Christian Groups in the First Century*, (London: Tyndale 1960).

——, The Early Christians as a Scholastic Community II, in *JRH* 2 (1961), p. 125-137.

——, The Social Identity of the First Christians. A question of Method in Religious History, in *JRH* 11 (1980), p. 210-217.

Jung J., Zu Tertullians auswärtigen Beziehungen, in *Wiener Studien*, 13 (1891).

Jungklaus E., Die Gemeinde Hippolyts dargestellt nach seiner Kirchenordnung, in *TU* 46 (1928).

Jungkuntz R., Fathers, Heretics, and Epicureans, in *JEH* 17,1 (1966), p. 3-10.

Jungman J.A., Beobachtungen zum Fortleben von Hippolyts „Apostolische Überlieferung," in *ZKTh* 53 (1929), p. 579-585.

——, Die Doxologien in der Kirchenordnung Hippolyts, in *ZKTh* 86 (1964), p. 321-326.

Kemler H., Heggesipps Römische Bischofsliste, in *VCh* 25 (1971), p. 182-196.

Kemp E.W., Criticism of Telfer on Alexandrian bishops, in *JEH* 6 (1955), p. 125-142.

Kenyon F.G., *Books and their Readers in Ancient Greece and Rome*, (Oxford: Clarendon 1932).

Kirsch J.P., Die römische Titelkirchen im Altertum, in *Studien zur Geschichte und Kultur des Altertums,* (Paderborn: Schöning 1919).

——, Der stadtrömische christliche Festkalender im Altertum, in *Liturgiegeschichtliche Quellen und Forschungen* 8,9, (Münster: Aschendorffsche Verlagsbuchhandlung 1924).

——, Die Entdeckung eines christliches Gotteshaus und einer jüdischen Synagoge mit Malereien aus der ersten Hälfte des 3. Jahrhunderts in Dura-Europos in Mesopotamien, in *OrChr* ser. 3,8 (1933), p. 201-204.

——, Die vorkonstantinischen Kultusgebäude im Lichte der neuesten Entdeckungen im Orient, in *Römische Quartalschrift* 41 (1933), p. 15-28.

——, La Domus Ecclesiae cristiana del III secolo a Doura-Europos in Mesopotamia, in *Studi dedicati alla memoria di Paolo Ubaldi,* (Milan 1937), p. 73-82.

——, La Basilica cristiana nell-antichità, in *Atti del IV congresso internazionale di archeologia cristiana* I, (Rome 1940), p. 113-126.

Kirsten E., Edessa, in *RAC* IV (1959), p. 588-593.

Klauck H.-J., Hausgemeinde und Hauskirche im frühen Christentum, in *Stuttgarter Bibelstudien* 103, (Stuttgart: Verlag Katholisches Bibelwerk 1981).

Kleinheyer B., Sakramentliche Feiern I. Die Feiern der Eingliederung in die Kirche, in *GdK Handbuch der Liturgiewissenschaften* 7,1, (Regensburg 1989).

Klostermann E., and Hansen G.C., Eusebius' Werke, 4Bd.: Gegen Marcell: Über die kirliche Theologie: Die Fragmente Marcells, in *GCS* (1972).

Koch H., Kallist und Tertullian: Ein Beitrag zur Geschichte der altchristlichen Bussstreitigkeiten und des römischen Primat, in *SHAW* Philos.-hist. Klasse 22 (1919).

——, Die altchristliche bilderfrage nach den literarischen Quellen, in *FRLANT* N.F. 10 (1917).

——, Zu Tertulian „De Pudicitia" 21,9 in *ZNW* 31 (1932), p. 68-72.

——, Zu Tertulian „De Pudicitia" 21,9 in *ZNW* 33 (1934), p. 317-318.

——, Martire Novaziano, in *Religio,* 14 (1938), p. 192-198.

Koch W., Comment l'empereur Julien tâcha de fonder une église païenne, in *Revue belge de philologie de d'histoire* 6 (1927), p. 123-146.

——, 7 (1928) p. 49-82.

——, 7 (1928) p. 511-550.

——, 7 (1928) p. 1363-1385.

Köhler W., Omnis ecclesia Petri propinqua, in *ZNW* 31 (1932), p. 60-67.

Konikoff A., *Sarcophagi from the Jewish Catacombs of Ancient Rome; A catalogue Raisonne*, (Steiner: Stuttgart 1990).

Körtner U.H.J., *Papias von Hierapolis*, (Göttingen: Vandenhoek and Ruprecht 1983).

Koschorke K., Hippolyt's Ketzerbekämpfung und Polemik gegen die Gnostiker. Eine tendenzkritische Untersuchung seiner „Refutatio omnium häresium," in *Göttinger Orientforschungen*, 6,4 (Wiesbaden: Harassowitz 1975).

——, Die Polemik der Gnostiker gegen das kirchliche Chistentum, in *Nag Hammadi Studies* XII, (Brill: Leiden 1978).

——, Eine neugefundene gnostische Gemeindeordnung, in *ZThK* 76 (1979), p. 30-60.

Kötting B., Amt und Verfassung in der Alten Kirche, in Zum Thema Priesteramt, (Ed.) Pesch, W., Kötting B. etc., (Stuttgart: 1970).

——, Zur Frage der successio apostolica in frühkirchlicher Sicht, in *Catholica* 27 (1973), p. 234-47.

Kraeling C. et. al., Narration in Ancient Art: A Symposium, in *AmJArch* 56 (1957), p. 44-91

Kraeling C.H., A Greek Fragment of Tatian's Diatessaron from Dura, in K. and S. Lake (eds) *Studies and Documents* (ed. K. and S. Lake) 3, (London: Christophers 1935).

Kraus F.X., *Roma Sotterranea. Die römischen Katakomben. Eine Darstellung der älteren und neueren Forschungen, besonders derjenigen De Rossi's*, (Freiburg im Bresgau: Herder 1879).

——, Hippolytus, *Real-Encyklopaedia der christlichen Altertümer*. Band 1 (Freiburg 1882), p. 660-664.

Kretschmar G., Die Ordination im frühen Christentum, in *FZPhTh* 22 (1975), p. 35-69.

Kroyman A. (Ed.), Pseudo-Tertullian: Adversus Omnes Haereses, in *C.S.E.L., Tertulliani Opera*, Pars III.

Kunze J., *De historiae gnosticismi fontibus novae questiones criticae*, (Leipzig 1894).

Küppers K., Die literarisch-theologische Einheit von Eucharistiegebet und Bischofsweihegebet bei Hippolyt, in *ALw* 29 (1987), p. 19-30.

La Piana G., *La Successione episcopale in Roma e gli albori del Primato*, (Roma: 1922).

——, *Il Problema della Chiesa Latina in Roma*, (Roma: 1922).

——, La primitiva communità cristiana di Roma e l'epistola ai Romani, in *Richerche Religiose* 1 (1925), p. 210-226, 305-326.

——, The Roman Church at the end of the second century, in *HThR* 18 (1925), p. 201-277.

Ladeuze P., Caius de Rome, le seul Aloge connu, in *Mélanges Godefroid Kurth*, Vol. 2 (Honoré Champion/Vaillant-Carmanne: Paris/Liége 1908).

Lagarde P.A. de, *Analecta Syriaca*, (Lipsius 1858).

——, *Hippolyti Romani, quae feruntur omnia graece et recognitione*, (London: Williams & Norgate 1858).

Lampe P., Review of Körtner's Papias of Hierapolis, in *JbAC* 29 (1986), p. 192-194.

——, Die stadtrömischen Christen in den ersten beiden Jahrhunderten, in *WUNT* 2,18 (1989).

Lanciani R., *Ancient Rome in the Light of Recent Discoveries*, (London: MacMillan 1888), p. 193-197.

——, *Pagan and Christian Rome*, (London: MacMillan 1892), p. 141-143.

————, *The Destruction of Ancient Rome: A Sketch of the History of the Monuments,* (London: MacMillan 1899), p. 18-99.

————, *Notes From Rome,* (Ed. A.L. Cubberly), (Rome: The British School 1988).

Lanne E., L' Eglise une dans la prière eucharistique, in *Irénikon* 50 (1977), p. 326-344.

Lawler H.J., *Eusebiana*: *Essays on the Ecclesiastical History of Eusebius of Caesarea,* (Oxford: U.P. 1912).

Le Nain L.S. de Tillemont, *Mémoires pour servir à l'histoire ecclésiastique des six premiers siècles justifiez par les citations des auteurs originaux,* III (Paris: 1695).

Le Bas P. and Waddington W.H., *Inscriptions greques et latines recueilles en Grèce et en Asie Mineure,* (Paris: Librairie Firmin Didot Frères: 1870).

Lebreton J., Le désaccord de la foi populaire et de la théologie savante dans l'Église chrétienne du III siècle, in *RevHE* (1923), p. 481-506.

Lechner M., *Erziehung und Bildung in der griechisch-römischen Antike,* (München: Hüber 1938).

LeClercq H., Hippolyte (Statue et Cimetière de Saint), in *DACL* 60,2 (1925), p. 2419-2483.

Lécuyer J., La grâce de la consécration épiscopale, in*RevScPhTh* 36 (1952), p. 389-417.

————, Episcopat et presbytérat dans les écrits d'Hippolyte, in *RecSciRel* 41 (1953), p. 30-50.

————, Mystère de la Pentecôte et apostolicité de la mission de l'église, in *Études sur le sacrement de l'ordre* (Ed.) (J. Guyot: Paris 1957), p. 168-170.

Lefèvre M., Commentair sur Daniel. Texte étabile et traduit par M. Lefèvre. Introduction de G. Bardy, in *SC* 14 (1947).

Legge F., Hippolytus Philosophumena, Vols I & II, in *Translations of Christian Literature,* (London: S.P.C.K. 1921).

Lemaire A., Les Ministères aux origines de l'Église: Naissance de la triple hiérarchie: évêques, presbytres, diacres, in *LeDiv* 68 (Paris: Éditions du Centurion 1974).

————, L'Église Apostolique et les ministères, in *RDroitCan* 23 (1973), p. 19-41.

Lengeling E.J., Hippolyt von Rom und die Wendung „extendit manus suas cum pateretur," in *QLP* 50 (1969), p. 141-144.

————, Ordnung und Freiheit in der Liturgie der frühen Kirche, in *Einheit in Vielfalt. Festgabe für H. Aufderbeck zum 65 Geburstag,* Ed. W. Ernst and K. Feiereis, in *EThSt* 32 (Leipzig 1974), p. 52-74.

Leon H.J., *The Jews of Ancient Rome,* (Morris Loeb Series), (Philadelphia: Jewish Publication Society of America 1960).

Lewis C.T., and Short C., *A Latin Dictionary,* (Oxford: Clarendon 1984)

Lietzmann H., Apollinaris von Laodicea und seine *Schule, in TU* von Hans Lietzmann), (Tübingen: J.B. Mohr 1904).

————, Die Drei Ältesten Martyrologien, in *Kleine Texte* 2, (Bonn: Marcus und Weber 1911).

————, Zur altchristlichen Verfassungsgeschichte, in *ZWTh* 55 (1913), p. 97-153.

Lightfoot J.B., *The Apostolic Fathers.* Part I S. Clement of Rome, vol. II (London: MacMillan 1890).

————, Gaius or Hippolytus? in *Journal of Philology* 1 (1868), p. 98-112.

Ligier L., L'anaphore de la «Tradition apostolique» dans le «Testamentum Domini,» in *The Sacrifice of Praise (Festschrift A.H. Couratin.* Ed. B.D. Spinks), (Rome 1981), p. 91-106.

Ligorio Pirro, *Libro delle Antichità di Roma,* (Venetia 1553).

Lipsius R.A., *Zur Quellenkritik des H. Epiphanios,* (Vienna: Braumüller 1865).

————, Die Papstverzeichnisse des Eusebios und der von ihm abhängigen Chronisten kritisch untersucht, (Kiel: Schwers 1868).

——, Chronologie der Römischen Bischöfe bis zur Mitte ders vierten
    Jahrhunderts, (Kiel: Schwers 1869).
——, Das Felicianische Papstbuch, in *Jahrbuch für Protestantische Theologie.
    Neue Studien zur Papstchronologie* (1879), p. 385.
——, Die ältesten Papstverzeichnisse, (vol. entitled: Neue Studien zur
    Papstchronolgie) in *Jahrbuch für Protestantische Theologie* 6 (1880), p. 78
——, Die Bischofslisten des Eusebius, (vol. entitled: Neue Studien zur
    Papstchronologie) in *Jahrbuch für Protestantische Theologie* (1880), p. 233.
——, *Die Quellen der ältesten Ketzergeschichte. Neu untersuchte,* (Leipzig: Barth
    1875).
Lohse E., *Die Ordination im Spätjudentum und im Neuen Testament.* (Göttingen:
    Vandenhoeck & Ruprecht 1951).
Loi V., Il 25 Marzo data pasquale e la cronologia giovannea della Passione in età
    patristica, in *EphL* 85,1 (1971), p. 48-69.
——, La problematica storico-letterara su Ippolito di Roma, in *StEphAug* 13
    (1977), p. 9-16.
——, L'identità letteraria di Ippolito di Roma, in *StEphAug* 13 (1977), p. 67-88.
——, L'omelia «In sanctum Pascha» di Ippolito di Roma, in *Aug* 17 (1977), p.
    461-484.
Long-Hasselman S., Un essai de théologie sur le sacerdoce catholique, in
    RecSciRel 25 (1951), p. 187-199, 270-304.
Lorentz R., *De Egyptische Kerkordening en Hippolytus van Rom,* (Leiden:
    1929).
Lowrie, W., *Art in the Early Church ,* (New York: Pantheon 1947).
Luttenberger G.H., The Priest as a Member of the Ministerial College. The
    Development of the Church's Ministerial Structure from 96 to c. 300 A.D., in
    RThAM 43 (1976), p. 5-63.

Maas P., *Textual Criticism,* (Oxford: Clarendon 1958).
Mabillon J., *Veterum Analectorum: Complectens Iter Germanicum Domini
    Johannis Mabillon et Domini Michaelis Germain è Congregatione Sancti
    Mauri, cum monumentis in eo repertis,* (Luteciae Parisiorum 1685).
MacMullen R., *Enemies of the Roman Order*, (Cambridge Mass.: Harvard U.P.
    1967).
Magie D., Scriptores Historiae Augustae, Vol. 2 in *Loeb Classical Library*,
    (Cambridge Mass.: Harvard U.P. 1967).
Magne J., La prétendue Tradition Apostolique d' Hippolyte de Rome s' appellait-
    elle ΑΙ ΔΙΑΤΑΞΕΙΣ ΤΩΝ ΑΠΟΣΤΟΛΩΝ- Les statuts des saints apôtres? in *OstkiSt*
    14 (1965), p. 35-67.
——, Tradition apostolique sur les charismes et Diataxeis des saints Apôtres:
    Identification des documents et analyse du rituel des ordinations, in *Origines
    Chrétiennes* 1 (Paris: 1975).
——, En finir avec la «Tradition» d' Hippolyte, in *BLE* 89 (1988), p. 5-22.
Mai A., *Scriptorum Veterum Nova Collectio e Vaticanis codicibus edita,* 6 Vols
    (Roma: Typis Vaticanis: 1825).
Malley W.J., Four unedited fragments of the De universo of the pseudo- Josephus
    found in the Chronicon of George Hamartolus (Coislin 305), in *JThS* n.s. 16
    (1965), p. 13-25.
Mandowsky E., Some Observations on Pyrrho Ligorio's drawings of Roman
    Monuments, in Cod. B XIII 7 at Naples, in *RendPontAcc* XXVII (1952-1954),
    p. 335-358.
——, and Mitchell C., *Pirro Ligorio's Roman Antiquities. The Drawings in ms.
    XIII. B.7 in the National Library in Naples.* (London: Warburg Institute 1963).
Marcovich M., Note on Hippolyts' Refutatio, in *JThS* n.s. 15 (1964), p. 68-74.
——, Hippolytus and Heraclitus, in *StudPatr* 7 (*TU* 92) (1966), p. 255-264.

——, Textual Criticism on Hippolytus' Refutatio, in *JThS* n.s. 19 (1968), p. 83-92.

——, Hippolytus, Refutatio X.33.9 Again, in *JThS* n.s. 24 (1973), p. 195.

——, Phanes, Phicola, and the Sethians, in *JThS* n.s. 25 (1974), p. 447-451.

——, The Naasene Psalm in Hippolytus (Haer. 5.10. 2), in *The Rediscovery of Gnosticism. II: Sethian Gnosticism,* (Ed.) Bentley Layton Lugduni Batav., (Leiden: E.J. Brill 1981), p. 770-778.

——, Hippolyts Refutatio Omnium Haeresium, in *Patristische Texte und Studien* 25, (Berlin: De Gruyter 1986).

Mariès L., Le Messie issu de Lévi chez Hippolyte de Rome, in *RecSciRel* 40 (1952), p. 381-96.

Martimort A.-G., Nouvel examen de la «Tradition Apostolique» in *BLitE* 88 (1987), p. 5-25.

——, La Tradition apostolique d' Hippolyte, in *ACan 23* (1979), p. 159-173.

Martin C., Un peri tou pascha de S. Hippolyte retrouvé? in *RecSciRel*, 16 (1926), p. 148-65.

——, Fragments palimpsestes d'un discours sur la Pâque attribué à saint Hippolyte de Rome (Crypt. B.α.LV), in *Annuaire de l'Institut de Philologie et d'Histoire Orientales et Slaves,* IV (1936) p. 321-363.

——, εἰς τὸ ἅγιον πάσχα, in *RevHE* 33 (1937), p. 255.

——, Le Contra Noetum de saint Hippolite, in *RevHE* 38 (1941), p. 5-23.

Maruchi O., *Le Catacombe Romane Secondo gli ultimi studi e le più recenti scoperte,* (Roma: Desclée Lefebure 1903).

Marx F. (Ed.), Sancti Filastri episcopi Brixiensis diversarum hereseon Liber, in *CSEL.* (1898).

Mazza E., Homelie pasquali e Birkat ha-mazon: fonti dell' anafora di Ippolito? in *EphL* 97 (1983), p. 409-481.

Mazzarino S., La Democratizzione della cultura nel basso Impero, in XIe *Congres International des Sciences historiques,* (Stockholm: 1960), Rapports ii, Antiquité.

McCue J.F., The Roman Primacy in the Second Century and the Problem of the Development of Dogma, in *ThS* 25 (1964), p. 161-96.

Meloni P., Ippolito e il cantico dei cantici, in *StEphAug* 13 (1977), p. 97-120.

Metzger M., Les deux prières eucharistiques des Constitutions Apostoliques, in *RevSR* 45 (1971), p. 52-77.

——, Nouvelles perspectives pour la prétendue Tradition apostolique, in *Ecclesia Orans* 5 (1988), p. 241-259.

Millar F., The Date of the *Constitutio Antoniana*, in *JEgArch,* 48 (1962), p. 124-131.

——, *A Study of Cassius Dio*, (Oxford: U.P. 1964).

Mohlberg L.C., Osservazioni storico-critiche sull'iscrizione tombale di Novaziano, in *EphL* 51 (1937), p. 242.

Molland E., Irenaeus of Lugdunum and the Apostolic Tradition, in *JEH* 1,1 (1950), p. 12-28.

——, Le dévelopment de l'idée de succession apostolique, in *RevHPhR* 34 (1954), p. 1-29.

Momigliano A., Severo Alessandro Archisynagogus. Una conferma alla Historia Augusta, in *Ath* n.s. 12 (1934), p. 151-153.

Mommsen T., and Krüger P. (Ed.), *The Digest of Justinian,* (trans. A. Watson), (Philadelphia: University of Pennsylvania Press 1985), vols 1-4.

Mommsen T., Über den Chronographien vom Jahre 354, in *Abhandlungen der philologische historische Classe der Königlichen Sächs. Gesellschaft der Wissenschaften* I (1850), p. 549-693.

——, Inschriften Büsten, in *Archeologische Zeitung* 38 (1880), p. 32-36.

——, Die älteste Handschrift der Chronik des Hieronymous, in *Herm* 24 (1889), 393-401.

——, Chronica minora I, in *MGH, Auctores Antiquissimi,* (1892).

——, Libri Pontificalis, in *MGH,* Gestorum Pontificium Romanorum 1, (1898).

Morin G., La liste épigraphique des travaux de Saint Hippolyte au Musée du Lateran, in *RBen* 17 (1900), p. 246-251.

Mortimer R.C., *The Celebrant and Ministers of the Eucharist,* (London: 1957).

Mosshammer A., Georgius Syncellus: Ecloga Chronographia, in *BSGT* (1984).

Muller C., *Fragmenta Historicorum Graecorum* IV (Zosimus), (Paris: 1851).

Mundle I., Dea caelestis in der religionspolitik des Septimius Severus und der Julia Domna, in *Historia* 10 (1961), p. 228-237.

Mühlenberg E., Apollinaris von Laodicea, in *Forschungen zur Kirchen- und Dogmengeschichte,* 23 (Göttingen: Vandenhoeck und Ruprecht 1969).

Müller K. Die Grundlagen des Ketzertaufstreits und die Stellung des Dionys von Alexandrien in ihm, in *ZNW* (1924), p. 235-247.

——, Kleine Beiträge zur Kirchengeschichte, in *ZNW* (1924), p. 231-234.

——, Die älteste Bischofswahl und weihe in Rom und Alexandrien, in *ZNW* 28 (1929), p. 274-296.

Munier C., *Autorité épiscopale et sollicitudine pastorale IIc- VIe siècles,* (Variorum/Gower 1991).

Munk J., Presbyters and Disciples of the Lord in Papias, in *HThR* 52 (1959), p. 232-243.

Naldini N., *Il cristianesimo in Egitto. Lettere private nei papiri dei secoli II-IV,* (Firenze: Le Mornier 1968).

Nauck A., *Euripidis Tragoediae,* (Lipsae: Teubner 1885).

Nautin P., In Sanctam Pascha. Homélies pascales I: Une homélie inspirée du traité Sur la Pasque d'Hippolyte, *SC* 27, (1950).

——, Notes sur le catalogue des oevres d'Hippolyte, in *RecSciRel* 34 (1947), p. 99-107, 347-359.

——, Hippolyte et Josipe: Contribution à l'histoire de la littérature chrétienne du troisième siècle, in *Etudes et Textes pour l'histoire du dogme de la Trinité),* (Paris: Les Éditions du Cerf 1947).

——, *Hippolyte, Contra les hérésies, fragment. Étude et édition critique,* (Paris: Les Éditions du Cerf 1949).

——, Le texte des deux derniers chapitres de livre d'Hippolyte contre les hérésies, in *RevSR* 25 (1951), p. 76-83.

——, La controverse sur l'auteur de l'Elenchos, in *RevHE* 47 (1952), p. 5-43.

——, Le dossier d'Hippolyte et de Méliton dans les florilèges dogmatiques et chez les historiens modernes. (Paris: Les Éditions du Cerf 1953).

——, Encore le problème d'Hippolyte, in*MSR* 11 (1954), p. 215-218.

——, L'auteur du Comput Pascal de 222 et de la Chronique anonymede 235, in *RecSciRel* 42 (1954), p. 226-257.

——, L'omélie d'Hippolyte sur le psautier et les oeuvres de Josipe, in *Revue de l'histoire des religions* 179 (1971), p. 137-179.

——, L'évolution des ministères au II e aux III siècle, in *RDroitCan* 23 (1973), p. 47-58.

Nestori A., La Catacomba di Calepodio al III miglio dell'Aurelia vetus e i sepolcri dei papi Callisto e Giulio I, in *RivAC* 44 (1968), p. 161-172.

——, La Catacomba di Calepodio al III miglio dell'Aurelia vetus e i sepolcri dei papi Callisto e Giulio I, in *RivAC* 47 (1971), p. 169-278.

——, La Catacomba di Calepodio al III miglio dell'Aurelia vetus e i sepolcri dei papi Callisto e Giulio I, in *RivAC* 48; (1972), p. 193-233.

——, La Catacomba di Calepodio al III miglio dell'Aurelia vetus e i sepolcri dei papi Callisto e Giulio I, in *RivAC* 51 (1975), p. 135-141.

Neuman K.J., *Hippolyt von Rom in seiner Stellung zu Staat und Welt: Neufunde und Forschungen zur Geschichte von Staat und Kirche in der römishen Kaiserzeit,* (Leipzig: Veit 1902).

Neymeyr U., Die christlichen Lehrer im zweiten Jahrhundert: Ihr Lehrtätigkeit, ihr Selbsverständnis, und ihre Geschichte, in *Supplements to VCh* 4, (Leiden: E.J. Brill 1989).

Nock A., Orphism or popular philosophy? in *HThR*, 33 (1940), p. 301-315.

Nogara B., *Guida ai Musei del Laterano*, (Vatican: Rome 1948).

Nohlac P. de, Notes sur Pirro Ligorio, in Mélanges Léon Renier, in *Bibliotèque de l'Éclole des Hautes Études* 73 (Paris: Vieweg 1887).

——, *La Bibliothèque de Fulvio Orsini*, (Paris: Honoré Champion 1976).

Nolan L., *The Basilica of San Clemente in Rome*, (Rome: Vatican 1934).

Nolte, Ein Excerpt aus dem zum grössten Theil noch ungedruckten Chronicon des Georgius Hamartolus, in *ThQ* (1862), p.467.

Norman A.F., Libanius: Orations, in *Loeb Classical Library,* (Cambridge Mass.: Harvard U.P. 1969).

Notopoulos J.A., Studies in the Chronology of Athens, in *Hesp.* 18 (1949), p. 26-27.

Ogg G., Hippolytus and the Introduction to the Christian Era, in *VCh* 16 (1962), p. 1-18.

Oggioni G., La questione di Ippolito, in *ScuCat* 78 (1950), p. 126-143; p. 315-322.

——, in *ScuCat* 43 (1951), p. 75-85.

——, Ancora sulla questione di Ippolito, in *ScuCat* 80 (1952), p. 513-525.

Oliveira C.-J.P., Signification sacerdotale du Ministère de l' Evêque dans la Tradition Apostolique d' Hippolyte de Rome, in *FZPhTh* 25 (1978), p. 398-427.

Oliver J.H., The Diadoché at Athens under the Humanistic Emperors, in *AmJPhil* 98 (1977), p.160-169.

Oltramre A., *Les origines de la diatribe romaine*, (Université de Genève, Faculté des Lettres Thesè no 47), (Geneva: 1926).

Omont H., Minide Mynas et ses missions en Orient (1840-1856), in *Memoires de l'Académie des Inscriptions et Belles-Lettres XL*, (Paris: 1916).

Osborne C., *Rethinking Early Greek Philosophy: Hippolytus of Rome and the Presocratics.* (London: Duckworth 1987).

Palachkovsky V., La Tradition hagiographique sur S. Hippolyte, in *StudPatr* 3*TU* 78 (Berlin: 1961), p. 97-107.

Parsons E.A., *The Alexandrian Library: Glory of the Hellenic World*, (London: Elsevier 1952).

Paulys-Wissowa A., *Real-encyclopädia der classischen Altertumswissenschaft,* 3 Band, (Metzler: Stuttgart 1899).

Pearson B.A., Gnosticism as Platonism with special reference to Marsanes (NHC 10,1), in *HThR* 77,1 (1984), p. 55-72.

Pekáry T., Statuen in der Historia Augusta, in *Antiquitas* 4,7 (1970), p. 151-172.

Périer J., Les 127 Canons des apôtres. Texte arabe en partie inédit publié et traduit d' après les manuscrits de Paris, de Rome et de Londres, in *PO* VIII,4, (1912).

Perkins A., *The Art of Dura-Europos*, (Oxford:Clarendon 1973).

Perler O., Melito de Sardis sur la Pâque et fragments, in *SC* 123, (1966).

Peterson E., La traitement de la rage par les Elkésaites d'après Hippolyte, in *RecSciRel* 34 (1947), p. 232-238.

Peterson E., Meris, Hostien Partikel und Opfer-Anteil, in *EphL* 61 (1947), p. 3-12.

Pietri C., *Roma Christiana: Recherches sur l'Eglise de Rome, son organisation, sa politique, son idéologie de Miltiade à Sixte III (311-440)*, (Rome: École Francais de Rome, Palais Farnèse 1976).

Pistolesi E., *Il Vaticano descritto e illustrato, III. Con disegni a contorni diretti dal pittore Camillo Guerra*, (Roma: Vaticano 1829).

Platner S.B. and Ashby T., *A Topograpical dictionary of Ancient Rome*, (Oxford: U.P. 1929).
Platthy J., *Sources of Earliest Greek Libraries*, (Amsterdam: Hakkert 1968).
Plecket H.W,. and Stroud R.S. et al. (Ed.), *Supplementum Epigraphicum Graecum* (Amsterdam: Gieben 1976-).
Plümacher E., Apostel/ Apostolat/ Apostolizität, in *Theologische Realenzyklopädia,* Band III (Berlin: Walter de Gryter 1978).
Poschmann B., Zur Bussfrage in der cyprianischen Zeit, *ZKTh* (1913), p. 25-54.
——, Paenitentia Secunda: Die kirchliche Busse im ältesten Christentum bis Cyprian und Origenes: Eine dogmengeschichtliche Untersuchung, in *Theoph* 1 (1940).
Powell D.L., Ordo presbyteri, in *JThS* 26 (1975), p. 290-328.
——, The Schism of Hippolytus, in *StudPatr* (*TU* 115) 12,1 1975, p. 449-456.
Prestige L., Callistus, in *Fathers and Heretics,* (London: S.P.C.K. 1954).
Preysing von K., Der Leserkreis der Philosophoumena Hippolyts, in *ZKTh* 38 (1914), p. 421-445.
——, Hippolyts Ausscheidung aus der Kirche, in *ZKTh* 42 (1918), p. 177-186.
——, Existenz und Inhalt des Bussediktes, in *ZKTh* 4 43 (1919), p. 358-362.
——, Des heiligen Hippolytus von Rom Widerlegung aller Häresien, in *Bibliothek der Kirchenväter* 40, (München: Kösel und Pustet 1922).
——, „δίθεοι ἐστε" (Hippolyt. Philos. IX. 12,16), in *ZKTh* 50 (1926), p. 604-608.
Prigent P., and Stehly R., Citations d'Hippolyte trouvées dans le ms. Bodl. Syr. 140, in *ThZ* 30,2 (1974), p. 82-85.
Prigent P., Hippolyte, commentateur de l'Apocalypse, in *ThZ* 28,6 (1972), p. 391-412.
——, Les fragments du De Apocalypsi d'Hippolyte, in *ThZ* 29,5 (1973), p. 313-333.
Prinzivalli E., Due passi escatologici del Peri pantos di Ippolito, in *Vetera Christianorum* 16 (1979), p. 63.
——, Note sull'escatologia di Ippolito, in *Orpheus* 1 (1980), p. 305.
——, Gaio e gli Alogi, in *Studi storico-religiosi*, 5 (Japadre Editore L'Aquila: Rome 1981), p. 53-68.
——, Ippolito (statua di), in *Dizionario Patristico e di Antichità Cristiane* 2, (Casale Monteferrato 1984), coll. 1798-1800.
Puchulu R., *Sur le Contre Noet d'Hippolyte- les attaches littéraires et doctrinales de la doxologie finale.* (Thèse de Doctorat presentée à la Faculté de Théologie de Lyon, Année académique 1959-1960).

Quacquarelli A., L'antimonarchisanesimo di Tertulliano, in *Rassegna di scienze filosophische*, 3 (1950), p. 31-63.

Rabe H., *Ioannes Philoponus: De Aeternitate Mundi Contra Proclum*, (Leipzig: Teubner 1899).
Rackham H., Cicero: De Finibus Bonorum et Malorum, in *Loeb Classical Library,* (Cambridge Massachusetts: Harvard University Press 1914).
——, Pliny: Natural History, in *Loeb Classical Library,* (Cambridge Massachusetts: Harvard University Press 1952).
Rahmani I.E., *Testamentum Domini nostri Iesu Christi nunc primum edidit, Latine reddidit et illustravit*, (Mayence:Kirchheim 1899).
Rankin D., *Doctrines of Church and Ministry in Tertullian*, unpublished PhD thesis, Melbourne College of Divinity 1991.
——, *Tertullian and the Church,* (Cambridge: U.P. 1995).
Ratcliff E.C., Justin Martyr and Confirmation, in *Liturgical Studies*. Edited by CouratinA.H., and Tripp D.H. (London: S.P.C.K. 1976), p. 110-117.

——, The Eucharistic Institution Narrative of Justin Martyr's "First Apology,". in *Liturgical Studies*. Edited by CouratinA.H., and Tripp D.H. (London: S.P.C.K. 1976), p. 41-48.

——, "Apostolic Tradition": Questions Concerning the Appointment of the Bishop. in *Liturgical Studies*. Edited by Couratin A.H. and Tripp D.H. (London: S.P.C.K. 1976), p. 156-60.

Raubitsche A.E., Greek inscriptions, in *Hesp.* 35 (1966), p. 241-251.

Rauer M., Origene Werke: Bd. 9: Die Homilien zu Lukas in der Übersetzung des Hieronymus und die griechischen Reste der Homilien und des Lukas-Kommentars, in *GCS* (1959).

Reekmanns L., L'implantation monumentale chrétienne dans la zone suburbaine de Rome du IVᵉ siècle, in *RivAC* 44 (1968), p. 196-199.

Rehm B., Zur Entstehung der pseudoclementinischen Schriften, in *ZNW* 37 (1938), p. 77-184.

Reichardt G. (Ed.), Filopono Giovanni, De opificio mundi, (Leipzig: Teubner 1897) text also in *PG*. X,296.

Reicke Bo., *Diakonie, Festfreude und Zelos in Verbingdung mit der altchristlichen Agapenfeier.* (Uppsala Univ. Arsskr.), (Uppsala: 1951).

Reutterer R., Legendenstudien um den heiligen Hippolytos, in *ZThK* 95 (1973), p. 286-310.

Réville J., *La religion à Rome sous les Sévères,* (Paris: Leroux 1886).

Richard M., Sainte Hippolyte, «Hippolyte e Josipe»: Bulletin de Patrologie, in *MSR* 5 (1948), p. 294-308.

——, Comput et chronographie chez Saint Hippolyte, in *MSR* 7 (1950), p. 237-268.

——, Comput et chronographie chez Saint Hippolyte, in *MSR* 8 (1951), p. 19-51.

——, Encore le problème d'Hippolyte, in *MSR* 10 (1953), p. 13-52, 145-180.

——, Dernières remarques sur S. Hippolyte et le soi-disant Josipe, in *RecSciRel* 43 (1955), p. 379-394.

——, Le Florilège Eucharistique du Codex Ochrid, Musée National 86, in Quelques nouveaux fragments des Pères Anténicéens et Nicéens, in *Symbolae Osloenses*, 38 (1963), p. 76-83, reprinted in ——, *Opera Minora*, (Turnhout/Leuven: Brepols/U.P.) 1,6.

——, Notes sur le comput de cent-couce ans, in *RevEtByz* 24 (1966), p. 257-277.

——, Hippolyte de Rome, in *Dictionnaire de spiritualité* VII (1969), p. 533.

——, Les difficultés d'une édition des oeuvres de S. Hippolyte, in *StudPatr* 12,1 (*TU* 115), (1975), p. 51-70.

Richardson C.C., A note on the epiclesis in Hippolytus and the Testamentum Domini, in *Rechthéolancmédiév* 15 (1948), p. 357-359.

Richter G.M.A., *The Portraits of the Greeks*, (London: Phaidon 1965).

Richter K., Zum Ritus der Bischofsordination in der „Apostolischen Überlieferung" Hippolyts von Rom, in *ALw* 17 (1975), p. 7-51.

Roberts C.H., Early Christianity in Egypt, in *JEgArch* 40 (1954), p. 92-96.

Rolfe J.C., Ammianus Marcellinus, Vol. 2 in *Loeb Classical Library*, (Cambridge Mass.: Harvard U.P. 1972).

Rolffs E., Das Indulgenzedikt des römischen Bischofs Kallist, kritisch untersucht und reconstruiert, in *TU* 11, 3 (1893).

——, Urkunden aus dem antimontanistischen Kämpfe des Abendlandes, in *TU* 12,4) (1895).

Rondeau M-J., Les polémiques d'Hippolyte de Rome et de Filastre de Brescia concernant le psautier, in *RevHisRel* 171 (1967), p. 1-51.

Rordorf W., L' Ordination de l' évêque selon la Tradition apostolique d' Hippolyte de Rome, in *QLP* 55 (1974), p. 137-150.

Rose A., La prère de consécration pour l' ordination épiscopale, in *Au service de la parole de Dieu. Mélanges offerts à Msgr. A.-M. Charue*, (Gembloux 1969), p. 129-145.

Rostovtzeff M.I., *Dura-Europos and Its Art*, (Oxford: Clarendon 1938).

——, *Social and Economic History of the Roman Empire*, (Oxford: Clarendon 1957)

Routh M.J., *Scriptorum Ecclesiasticorum Opuscula praecipua quaedam*, I (Oxford: U.P. 1832).

Rubach G., Das Eindringen des Christentums in die gebildete Welt, in *Kirchengeschichte als Missionsgeschichte*, Vol.1 Die alte Kirche, (München: 1974), p. 293-310.

Rucker I., Florilegium Edessenum anonymum (syriace ante 562), in *SbMn* 5 (1933).

Ruggieri, *De Portuensi S. Hippoyti sede. Dissertatio*, (Rome: 1771).

Ruhbach G., Klerusbildung in der alten Kirche, in *WuD* 15 (1979), p. 107-114.

Salmon G., The Chronology of Hippolytus, in *Hermath* 1 (1873), p. 82-128.

Saltet L., Les sources de l'Eranistes de Théodoret, in *RevHE* 6 (1905), p. 513-536; 741-754.

Salvatore P., Osservazioni sulla Struttura Letteraria del «De Christo e Antichristo» di Ippolito, in *Orpheus* 12 (1965), p. 133-155.

Sanders J.N., *The Fourth Gospel in the Early Church: Its Origin and Influence on Christian Theology up to Irenaeus*, (Cambidge: U.P. 1943).

Savile H., *Rerum Anglicarum Scriptores Post Bedam, praecipui, ex vetustissimis codicibus, manuscriptis nunc primum in lucem editi*, (Frankfurt: Wechelianis apud Claudium 1601).

Saxer V., Figura corporis et sanguinis Domini. Une formule eucharistique des premiers siècles chez Tertullien, Hippolyte, et Ambroise, in *RivAC* 47 (1971), p. 65-89.

——, Note di agiografia critica: Porto, l'Isola Sacra e Ippolito a proposito di studi recenti, in *Miscellanea A.P. Frutaz*, (Roma 1978), p. 110-121.

——, La questione de Ippolito Romano: a proposito de un libro recente, *StEphAug* 30 (1989), p. 43-59.

Schaeffer E., *Die Bedeutung der Epigramme des Papstes Damasus für die Geschichte der Heiligenverehrung*, (Rome: 1932).

Schermann Th., Eine neue Handschrift zur Apostolischen Kirchenordnung, in *OrChr* 2 (1902) p. 398-408.

——, Eine Elfapostelmoral oder die X-Recension der „beiden Wege," in *Veröffentlichungen aus dem Kirchenhistorischen Seminar München*, 2,2 (Lentner: München 1903).

——, *Die allgemeine Kirchenordnung, frühchristliche Liturgien und kirchliche Überlieferung*. 1. Die allgemeine Kirchenordnung des zweiten Jahrhunderts, (Studien zur Geschichte und Kultur des Altertums), (Paderborn: Schöningh 1914).

Schmid J., Studien zur Geschichte des griechischen Apocalypse-Textes, 1. Der Apocalypse-Kommentar des Andreas von Kaisareia, in *Münchener Theologische Studien*, (München: Karl Zink 1955).

Schmidt C., Studien zu den Pseudo-Clementinen, in *TU* 46,1, (1929).

Schoedel W.R., Theological Method in Irenaeus. (Adversus Haereses 2. 25-28, in *JThS* n.s. 35,1 (1984), p. 30-49.

——, Athenagoras, *Legatio* and *De Resurrectione*, in *OECT* (1972).

Scholl R., Das Bildungsproblem in der alten Kirche, in *Zeitschrift für wissenschaftliche Pädagogik* 10 (1964), p. 24-43.

Schöllgen G., Hausgemeinden Oikos-Ekklesiologie und monarchischer Episkopat. Überlegungen zu einer neuen Forschungsrichtung, in *JbAC* 31 (1988), p. 74-90.

——, Monepiskopat und monarchischer Episkopat: Eine Bemerkung zur Terminologie, in *ZNW* 77 (1986), p. 146-157.

Schubart W., Ägyptische Abteilung (Papyrussammlung): Ptolemaeus Philopator und Dionysos, in *Amtliche Berichte aus den preussischen königlichen Kunstsammlungen* (= *Beiblatt zum Jahrbuch der preussischen königlichen Kunstsammlungen*) 38 (1916/1917), p. 189-198.

——, *Das Buch bei den Griechen und Römern*, (Berlin: De Gruyter 1921), p. 36-75.

Schuhmacher W.N., Prudentius an der Via Tibertina, in *Spanische Forschungen der Görresgesellschaft*, 1 Reihe, (Gesammelte Aufsätze zur Kulturgeschichte Spaniens 16 Band), (Münster: 1960), p. 1-15.

Schürer W., *The History of the Jewish People in the Age of Jesus*, (Ed.) G. Vermes, F. Millar, and M. Black, (Edinburgh: T. and T. Clark 1979).

Schwartz E., Über den Tod der Söhne Zebedaei. Ein Beitrag zur Geschichte des Johannesevangeliums, in *AKWG* Phil.-Hist. Kl. N.F. 7,5, p. 29-30.

——, Über die pseudapostolischen Kirchenordnungen, in *Schriften wissensch. Gesellschaft im Strassburg*, 6, (Strasbourg: 1910).

——, Codex Vaticanus Graecus 1431: Eine antichalkedonische Sammlung aus der Zeit Kaiser Zenos., in *ABAW* Philos. und hist. Klasse 32, 6 (1927).

——, Publizistische Sammlungen zum accacianischen Schisma, in *ABAW* Phil. Hist. Abt. N.F., Heft 10, (1934).

——, Christliche und jüdische Ostertafeln, in *AKWG* Phil.-Hist. Kl., N.F. 8,6 (1905), p. 1-194.

Schweizer E., Der Johanneische Kirchenbegriff, in *TU* 73 (1959), p. 263-268.

Segal J.B., *Edessa "the Blessed City,"* (Oxford: Clarendon 1970).

Segelberg E., The Benedictio Olei in the Apostolic Tradition of Hippolytus, *OrChr* 48 (1964), p. 268-281.

——, The Ordination Prayers in Hippolytus, in *StudPatr* 13 (1975), p. 397-408.

Seni F.S., La Villa d' Este in Tivoli, in *Memorie Storiche tratte da documenti inediti*, (Roma: Tata Giovanni 1902).

Seston W., L'Église et le baptistère de Doura-Europos, in *Annales de l'école des hautes études de Grand*, (Paris: 1937), p. 161-177.

Settis S., Severo Alessandro e i suoi Lari. (SHA, 29, 2-3), in *Ath* 60 (1972), p. 237-251.

Simonetti M., *La letteratura cristiana antica greca e latina*, (Milano: 1969).

——, Note di cristologia pneumatica, in *Aug* 12 (1972), p. 201-231.

——, Due Note su Ippolito, in *StEphAug* 13 (1977), p. 121-136.

——, A modo di conclusione: una ipotesi di lavoro, in *StEphAug* 13 (1977), p. 151-156.

——, Prospettive Escatologiche della Cristologia di Ippolito, in *La Cristologia nei Padri della Chiesa*, (Accademia Cardinale Bessaronis: Rome 1979), p. 85-101.

——, Un falso Ippolito nella polemica monotelita, in *Vetera Christianorum* 24, (1987), p. 113-146.

——, Aggiornamento su Ippolito, in *StEphAug* 30 (1989), p. 75-130.

——, Il problema dell'unità di Dio da Giustino a Ireneo, in *Rivista di storia e letteratura religiosa*, 22 (1986), p. 201-239 reprinted in Simonetti (1993), p. 71-107.

——, Studi sulla cristologia del II e III secolo, in *StEphAug* 44 (1993).

Simpson A.D., Epicureans, Christians and Atheists in the Second Century, in *Transactions of the American Philological Association* 72 (1941), p. 372-381.

Smith M.A., The Anaphora of the Apostolic Tradition Reconsidered, in *StudPatr* 10,1 (TU 107), (1970), p. 426-430.

Smolak K., *Christentum und Römische Welt* (Orbis Latinus), (Hilder Pichler Tempsky: Wienna 1988).

Spanneut M., Hippolyte ou Euststathe? Autour de la Chaîne de Nicetas sur l'Evangile selon Saint Luc, in *MSR* 9 (1952), p. 215-220.
Stam J.E., *Episcopacy in the Apostolic Tradition of Hippolytus*, Basel 1969 (ThDuss 3).
———, Charismatic Theology in the "Apostolic Tradition" of Hippolytus, in *Current Issues in Biblical and Patristic Interpretation. Studies in honour of Merill C. Tenney presented by his former students*, Ed. G.F. Hawthorn, (Grand Rapids 1975), p. 267-276.
Stanton G.N., Aspects of Early Jewish Polemic and Apologetic, in *NTS* 31 (1985), p. 377-392.
Stauffer E., Zum Kaliphat des Jacobus, in *ZRGG* 4 (1952), p. 193-214.
Stead C., Review of Ricerche su Ippolito, in *JThS* n.s. 30,2 (1979), p. 549-551.
Stevenson J., *The Catacombs: Rediscovered monuments of early Christianity*. (London: Thames and Hudson 1978).
Straub J., Heidenische Geschichtsapologetik in der Spätantike. Untersuchungen über Zeit und Tendenz in der *Historia Augusta*, in *Antiquitas* 4,1 (1963).
Strecker G., Das Judenchristentum in den Pseudoclementinen, in*TU* 70 (1958 and 1981).
Strocka V.M., Römische Bibliotheken, *Gym* 88 (1981), p. 289-329.
Stroux J., Die Constitutio Antoniana, in *Phil* 88 (1933), p. 272-295.
Styger P., *Die Römischen Katakomben*, (Berlin: Verlag für Kunstswissenschaft 1933).
———, *Die Römischen Martyrgrüfte*, Vols I and II, (Berlin: Verlag für Kunstswissenschaft 1935).
Sundberg A., Canon Muratori: A Fourth Century List, in *HThR* 66 (1973), p. 1-41.
Swete H.B., *Essays on the Early History of the Church and Ministry,* (London: MacMillan 1918).
Syme R., *Historia Augusta* Papers, (Oxford: Clarendon 1983)

Taft R., The Dialogue before the Anaphora in the Byzantine Eucharistic Liturgy II: The Sursum Corda, in *OrChrP* 57 (1988), p. 47-77.
Tateo R. (Ed.), *Ippolito de Roma. Tradizione apostolica*, (Roma 1972).
Tattam H., *The Apostolical Constitutions or Canons of the Apostles in Coptic with an English translation*, (London: Oriental Translation Fund 1848).
Telfer W., Episcopal Succession in Egypt, in *JEH* 34 (1952), p. 1-13.
———, *The Office of a Bishop,* (London: Darton, Longman and Todd 1962).
———, Was Hegesippus a Jew? in *HThR* 53,2 (1960), p. 143-153.
Testini P., *Le catecombe e gli antichi cimiteri cristiani in Roma*, (Roma Cristiana 2), (Bologna: Capelli 1966).
———, Di alcune testimonianze relative ad Ippolito, in *StEphAug* 13 (1977), p. 45-65.
———, Sondaggi a s. Ippolito all'Isola Sacra. I depositi, reliquiari scoperti sotto l'altare, in *RendPontAcc* 46 (1973-1974), p. 165-179.
———, Indagini nell'area di S. Ippolito all'Isola Sacra. L'iscrizione del vescovo Heraclida, in *RendPontAcc* 51-52 (1978/79-1979-1980).
———, Vetera et nova su Ippolito, in *StEphAug* 30, (1989), p. 7-22.
———, Damaso e s. Ippolito di Porto, in *Studi di Antichità Cristiana* XXXIX, Saecularia Damasiana, p. 293-303.
Theissen, G., Die soziologische Auswertung religiöser Überlieferungen, *Kairos* 17 (1975), p. 284-299.
Till W., and Leipoldt J., Der koptische Text der Kirchenordnung Hippolyts herausgegeben und übersetzt, in *TU* 58,5 (1954).
Torrès F. and Possevino A., *Apparatus Sacer*, (Cologne 1608).
Toynbee J., and Ward Perkins, J. *The Shrine of St. Peter and the Vatican Excavations*, (London: Longmans Green 1956).

Treadgold W.T., The nature of the Bibliotheca of Photius, in *Dumbarton Oaks Studies*, XVIII (Washington: Harvard U.P. 1980).
Trevissoi M., Diogene Laerzio, L'età in cui visse, in *Rivista di Storia Antica* xii (1908), 482-505.
Troiano M.S., Alcuni aspetti della dottrina dello Spirito Santo in Ippolito, in *Aug* 20 (1980), p. 615-632.
Turner C.H., The Early Episcopal Lists, in *JThS* 1 (1899- 1900), p. 181-200, 529-553.
———, Tertullianea, in *JThS* 14 (1913), p. 556-564.
———, The Ordination Prayer for a Presbyter in the Church Order of Hippolytus, in *JThS* 16 (1915), p. 542-547.
———, The Early Episcopal Lists, in *JThS* 18 (1916-17), p. 103-34.
———, The "Blessed Presbyters" who condemned Noetus, in *JThS* 23 (1921), p. 28-35.
———, Cheirotonia, cheirothesia, epithesis cheiron, in *JThS* 24 (1923), p. 496-504.

Urlichs C.L., *Codex Urbis Romae Toptographicus*, (Wirceburgi: Ex Aedibus Steahelianis 1871).
Ursinus Fulvius, *Imagines et Elogia Virorum Illustrium,et Eruditorum ex Antiquis Lapidibus et Numismatibus expressae cum annotationibus*, (Lafrery-Formeis: Rome 1570).
Usener H., *Epicurea*, (Leipzig: B.J. Teubneri 1887).

Valentini R. and Zucchetti G., *Codice topografico della città di Roma*, Vol. 2, (Rome: Istituto Storico Italiano 1942).
Vallée G., A Study in Anti-Gnostic Polemics: Irenaeus, Hippolytus, and Epiphanius, in *Studies in Early Christianity and Judaism* 1, (Canada: William Laurier University Press 1981), (Canadian Corporation for Studies in Religion).
Vellico A.M., „Episcopus Episcoporum" in Tertulliani libro De Pudicitia, in *Antonianum* V (1930), p. 25-56.
Veloccia Rinaldi M.L., and Testini P., *Ricerche archeologiche nell'Isola Sacra*, (Rome 1975).
Verhoeven T., *Studiën over Tertullianus' Adversus Praxean*: Voornamelijk Betrekking hebbend op Monarchia, Oikonomia, Probola in verband met de Triniteit, (Amsterdam: N.V. Noord-Hollandsche Uitgevers Maatschappij 1948).
Viellefond J.-R., *Les "Cestes" de Julius Africanus: Étude sur l'ensemble des fragments avec édition, traduction, et commentaires*, (Firenze: Sansoni/ Paris: Didier 1970)
Villette J., Que représente la grande fresque de la maison chrétienne de Dura? in *Rbib* 60 (1953), p. 398-413.
Voicu S.J., Pseudoippolito in Sancta Theophania e Leonzio di Constantinopoli, in *StEphAug* 30 (1989), p. 137-146.
Volkmar G., *Die Quellen der Ketzergeschichte bis zum Nicäum. I, Hippolytus und die römischen Zeitgenossen*, (Zürich: 1855).
———, *Die Zeit der ältesten Haeresis und die Quellen ihrer Geschichte, mit besonderer Beziehung auf Lipsius' neue Untersuchung*, (Jena: Dufft 1875).
Vööbus A., The Synodicon in the West Syrian Tradition, in *CSCO* 367, Scriptores Syri Tom. 161.

Wagner G., Zur Herkunft der Apostolischen Konstitutionen, in *ZKG* 68 (1957), p. 1-47.
Waitz H., Pseudoclementines, in *TU* 25,4 (1904).

Walls A.F., A Note on the Apostolic Claim in the Church Order Literature, in *StudPatr* 2,2 (1957), p. 83-92.

———, The Latin Version of Hippolytus' Apostolic Tradition, in *StudPatr* 3 (1961), p. 155-162.

Watzinger C., Die Christen Duras, in *Theologische Blätter* 18 (1938), p. 117-119.

Wegman H., Généalogie hypothétique de la prière eucharistique, in *QL* 61 (1980), p. 263-278.

———, Une anaphore incomplète? Les Fragments sur Papyrus Strasbourg Gr 254, in *Studies in Gnosticism and Hellenistic Religions presented to Gilles Quispel on the Occassion of his 65th Birthday*, Ed. R. van den Broek and M.J. Vermaseren, (Leiden 1981), p. 432-450.

Wegner M., *Die antiken sarcophagsreliefs*, Vol. 5,3.

Wendel C., Versuch einer Deutung der Hippolyt-Statue, in *TheolStKrit*, 26 (1937-1938), p. 362-369.

Wendland P., Philo und die kynisch-storische Diatribe, in *Beiträge zur Geschichte der griechischen Philosophie und Religion*, (Ed.) P. Wendland und O. Kern, (Berlin: 1895).

———, Die hellenisch-römische Kultur in ihren Beziehungen zu Judentum und Christentum, in *Handbuch zum neuen Testament* 1,2, (Tübingen: 1912).

———, Hippolylus Werke: 3.: Refutatio Omnium Haeresium, in *GCS* (1916).

Whittaker M., Tatian: *Oratio ad Graecos* and Fragments, in *OECT* (1982).

Wiefel W., Die jüdische Gemeinschaft im antiken Rom und die Anfänge des römischen Christentums, in *Judaica* 26 (1970), p. 65-68.

Wilamowitz-Möllendorff U. von, Antigonos von Karystos, in *Philologische Untersuchungen,* (Ed.) A. Kiesing und U von Wilamowitz-Möllendorff, Heft 4 (Berlin: 1881).

Wilken R.L., Collegia, Philosophical Schools, and Theology, in *The Catacombs and the Colosseum,* (Valley Forge: 1971), p. 268-91.

———, Early Christian Chiliasm, Jewish Messianism, and the Idea of the Holy Land, in *HThR* 79 (1986), p. 298-307.

Williams M. Gilmore, Empress Julia Domna, in *Am. J. Arch.* 6 (1902), p. 259-305.

Wilpert G., *I sarcofagi cristiani antichi*, Vol. 1 (Rome 1929).

Wolf J.C., *Compendium historiae philosophae antiquae, h.e. Pseudorigenis Philosophumena, ex ipso M.S. Mediceo denuo collato et alio Taurinensi repetita vice emendata*, (Hamburgi: Christ. Liebzeit 1713).

Wolfson H.A., *The Philosophy of the Church Fathers: Faith, Trinity, and Incarnation*, (Cambridge Massachusetts: Harvard U.P. 1976).

Wordsworth C., *St. Hippolytus and the Roman Church in the Earlier Part of the Third Century, from the Newly Discovered Philosophumena*, (London: Rivington 1853).

Wright W.C., Vita Philosophorum, in *Loeb Classical Library*, (Cambridge Mass.: Harvard U.P. 1921).

———, Julian: Letters, in *Loeb Classical Library*, (Cambridge Mass.: Harvard U.P. 1969).

Wycherley R.E., Peripatos: The Ancient Philosophical Scene I, in *Greece and Rome* 8 (1961), p. 152-163.

———, Peripatos: The Ancient Philosophical Scene II, in *Greece and Rome* 9 (1962), p. 1-21.

Zani A., La Cristologia di Ippolito, in *Ricerche di Scienze teologiche* 22, (Brescia: Morcelliana 1984), (Publicazioni del Pontifico seminaro lombardo in Roma).

Zollitsche R., Amt und Funktion des Priesters: Eine Untersuchung zum Ursprung und zur Gestalt des Presbyterats in den ersten zwei Jahrhunderten, in *F.ThSt* 96, (Freiburg-Basel- Wein: 1974).

Zuchschwert E., Das Naziräat des Herrenbruders Jakobus nach Hegesippus, in *ZNW* 68 (1977), p. 176-87.

INDEX

1. Biblical Citations

2. Ancient Authors

3. Modern authors

4. Manuscripts and Inscriptions Cited

5. Greek Words and Phrases

21. HENNINGS, R. *Der Briefwechsel zwischen Augustinus und Hieronymus und ihr Streit um den Kanon des Alten Testaments und die Auslegung von Gal. 2,11-14.* 1994. ISBN 90 04 09840 2
22. BOEFT, J. DEN & HILHORST, A. (eds.). *Early Christian Poetry.* A Collection of Essays. 1993. ISBN 90 04 09939 5
23. McGUCKIN, J.A. *St. Cyril of Alexandria: The Christological Controversy.* Its History, Theology, and Texts. 1994. ISBN 90 04 09990 5
24. REYNOLDS, Ph.L. *Marriage in the Western Church.* The Christianization of Marriage during the Patristic and Early Medieval Periods. 1994. ISBN 90 04 10022 9
25. PETERSEN, W.L. *Tatian's Diatessaron.* Its Creation, Dissemination, Significance, and History in Scholarship. 1994. ISBN 90 04 09469 5
26. GRÜNBECK, E. *Christologische Schriftargumentation und Bildersprache.* Zum Konflikt zwischen Metapherninterpretation und dogmatischen Schriftbeweistraditionen in der patristischen Auslegung des 44. (45.) Psalms. 1994. ISBN 90 04 10021 0
27. HAYKIN, M.A.G. *The Spirit of God.* The Exegesis of 1 and 2 Corinthians in the Pneumatomachian Controversy of the Fourth Century. 1994. ISBN 90 04 09947 6
28. BENJAMINS, H.S. *Eingeordnete Freiheit.* Freiheit und Vorsehung bei Origenes. 1994. ISBN 90 04 10117 9
29. SMULDERS s.j., P. (tr. & comm.). *Hilary of Poitiers' Preface to his* Opus historicum. 1995. ISBN 90 04 10191 8
30. KEES, R.J. *Die Lehre von der* Oikonomia Gottes in der Oratio catechetica *Gregors von Nyssa.* 1995. ISBN 90 04 10200 0
31. BRENT, A. *Hippolytus and the Roman Church in the Third Century.* Communities in Tension before the Emergence of a Monarch-Bishop. 1995. ISBN 90 04 10245 0
32. RUNIA, D.T. *Philo and the Church Fathers.* A Collection of Papers. 1995. ISBN 90 04 10355 4